TUTORIAL: Software Testing & Validation Techniques

Second Edition

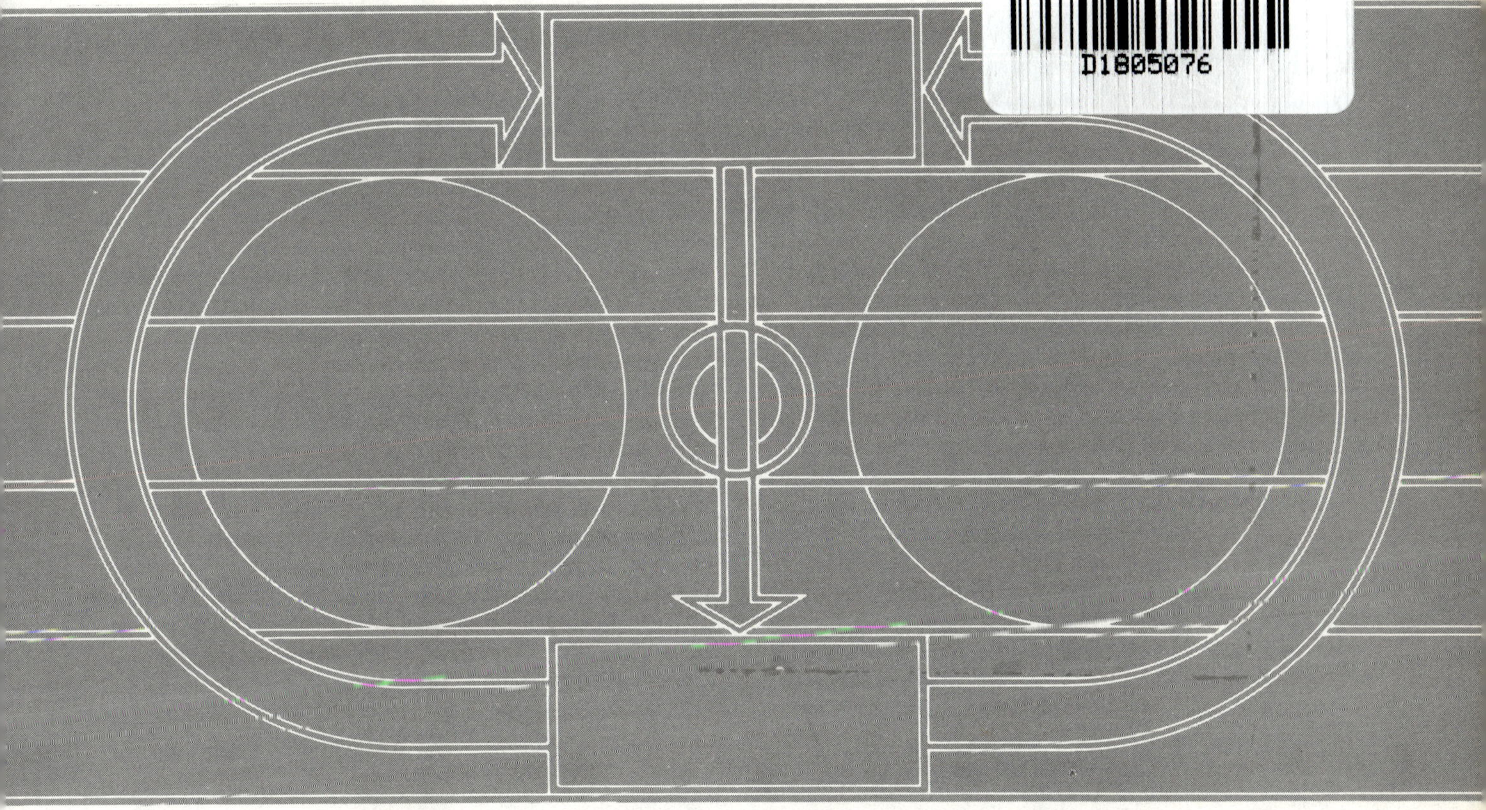

Edward Miller
Software Research Associates
San Francisco, California

William E. Howden
University of California, San Diego
San Diego, California

Additional copies available from:

IEEE Computer Society
10662 Los Vaqueros Circle
Los Alamitos, CA 90720

IEEE Service Center
445 Hoes Lane
Piscataway, NJ 08854

IEEE Catalog No. EHO 180-0
Library of Congress No. 81-81431
Order No. 365

Copyright © 1981 The Institute of Electrical and Electronics Engineers, Inc., New York, NY

   THE INSTITUTE OF ELECTRICAL AND ELECTRONICS ENGINEERS, INC.

Copyright and Reprint Permissions: Abstracting is permitted with credit to the source. Libraries are permitted to photocopy beyond the limits of US copyright law for private use of patrons those articles in this volume that carry a code at the bottom of the first page, provided the per-copy fee indicated in the code is paid through the Copyright Clearance Center, 21 Congress Street, Salem, MA 01970. Instructors are permitted to photocopy isolated articles for noncommercial classroom use without fee. For other copying, reprint, or republication permission, write to Director, Publishing Services, IEEE, 345 E. 47 St., New York, NY 10017. All rights reserved. Copyright © 1981 by The Institute of Electrical and Electronics Engineers, Inc.

Preface

This is the second edition of *Software Testing and Validation Techniques*. This edition updates and amends the set of papers included in the prior edition that was first organized in 1978.

Since that time, there have been several advances of significance in the software testing and validation field; a number of new papers have been published, and in many ways the field has become more mature and stable. In addition, the field has become deeper and richer, possibly as the result of increased emphasis on software quality and on quality assurance. Each year, the number of published papers of significance to software testing and validation has increased, as has the number of researchers actively involved in the field. All of this growth is reflected in the fact that this second edition contains 11 papers that did not appear in the prior edition. It is noted that five of the papers added were presented at the 1981 International Conference on Software Engineering, San Diego, California (March 1981). This can be taken as an indication of the excellence of that conference.

The papers we have added to this edition fall into the boundaries we have previously used to organize the book. Short descriptions of each new paper's place follow.

Theoretical Foundations

Some expansion of the original work by Goodenough and Gerhart ("Toward a Theory of Test Data Generation") has occurred in two directions. First, the paper by White and Cohen, ("A Domain Strategy for Computer Program Testing") proposes a refinement of the Goodenough and Gerhart ideas, and, second, some technical and conceptual extensions of the basic Goodenough and Gerhart results appear in the paper by Weyuker and Ostrand ("Theories of Program Testing and the Application of Revealing Subdomains"). The main thrust of these two papers is to deepen and sharpen the original Goodenough and Gerhart ideas, emphasizing practical applications and real programming problems.

In addition, Howden has completed some new work. The paper "Completeness Criteria for Testing Elementary Program Functions," first presented at the 1981 International Conference on Software Engineering, discusses the relationship between the completeness of sets of program tests and classes of program errors.

Static Analysis—Tools and Techniques

There have been new developments in the automatic static analysis of programs for data flow and concurrency anomalies (Taylor and Osterweil, "Anomaly Detection in Concurrent Software by Static Data Flow Analysis"). These results are important because they help identify some properties of systems that are highly important in regard to software system quality that can be "checked" automatically.

Dynamic Analysis—Tools and Techniques

In this area, three new areas of investigation are likely to be of importance in the coming years.

First, a paper by Richardson and Clarke ("A Partition Analysis Method to Increase Program Reliability," presented at the 1981 International Conference on Software Engineering) describes a method for dynamic analysis of program by symbolic evaluation methods that combines the ideas of path testing and symbolic evaluation.

Second, a paper by Howden ("Functional Testing and Design Abstractions") focuses on the issue of relating design-level specifications to actual functional testing of software.

Third, we have included a paper that describes the idea of mutation testing (DeMillo, Lipton, and Sayward, "Hints on Test Data Selection: Help for the Practicing Programmer"), an interesting new method in which large numbers of variants of a program are generated automatically and used to see how effective a set of tests is.

These three papers illustrate the growth direction for dynamic analysis, namely, in the domain of furthering the connection between formal specifications and the "objects" which they specify, computer programs.

Effectiveness Assessment

The fine work of Myers in his paper on analyzing structured walkthroughs and inspections forms a focal point for the additions in this section of the book. Myers' paper ("A Controlled Experiment in Program Testing and Code Walkthroughs/Inspections") tells about some unusual anomalies in the operation of a testing methodology. In addition, Myers describes how to conduct experiments and evaluate their results when the "object" is a methodology.

The paper by Andrews and Benson ("An Automated Program Testing Methodology and Its Implementation") shows how to build in a target function as the goal of a systematic methodology, and also provides some further insight into how such a goal function can assist in making testing more efficient.

Howden's paper ("Applicability of Software Validation Techniques to Scientific Programs") describes the application of static analysis, functional, and path-based testing methods to sets of scientific programs.

Finally, the paper by Woodward, Hedley, and Hennell ("Experience with Path Analysis and Testing of Programs") tells about practical experience with several straightforward testing techniques in a real-world setting.

Summary

Overall, we feel that these 11 new papers, when added to the papers that are carried over from the prior edition, portray the state of the art in software validation and testing technology.

Acknowledgments

Putting this book together the first time was a major piece of work, and making the revised second edition was similarly difficult. Neither edition would have happened without the fine counseling and excellent skills of Ms. Christina Taylor of the IEEE Computer Society's West Coast Office. To her we express our sincerest thanks. Furthermore, we owe a debt of thanks to Chip Stockton at the IEEE Computer Society's East Coast office for his skill in juggling schedules, reviewers, documents, text, and corrections.

The Computer Society support people are to be commented for their excellence.

Edward Miller
William E. Howden

TABLE OF CONTENTS

PREFACE iii

ACKNOWLEDGMENTS v

SECTION 1: INTRODUCTION

Introduction to Software Validation
William E. Howden 1

Introduction to Software Testing Technology
Edward Miller 4

SECTION 2: THEORETICAL FOUNDATIONS

Paper Summaries 17

Toward a Theory of Test Data Selection
John B. Goodenough and Susan L. Gerhart (IEEE Transactions on Software Engineering,
June 1975, pp. 156-173) 19

Reliability of the Path Analysis Testing Strategy
William E. Howden (IEEE Transactions on Software Engineering, September 1976,
pp. 208-215) 37

A Domain Strategy for Computer Program Testing
Lee J. White and Edward I. Cohen (IEEE Transactions on Software Engineering,
May 1980, pp. 247-257) 45

Theories of Program Testing and the Application of Revealing Subdomains
Elaine J. Weyuker and Thomas J. Ostrand (IEEE Transactions on Software Engineering,
May 1980, pp. 236-246) 56

Completeness Criteria for Testing Elementary Program Functions
William E. Howden (Proceedings, Fifth International Conference on Software
Engineering, 1981, pp. 235-243) 67

An Introduction to Proving the Correctness of Programs
Sidney L. Hantler and James C. King (ACM Computing Surveys, September 1976,
pp. 331-353) 76

SECTION 3: STATIC ANALYSIS—TOOLS AND TECHNIQUES

Paper Summaries 99

A Survey of Static Analysis Methods
William E. Howden 101

Independent Verification of Highly Reliable Programs
Marilyn S. Fujii (Proceedings, COMPSAC 77, pp. 38-44) 116

Design and Code Inspections to Reduce Errors in Program Development
M. E. Fagan (IBM Systems Journal, Vol. 15, No. 3, 1976, pp. 182-211) 123

DAVE—A Validation Error Detection and Documentation System for Fortran Programs
Leon J. Osterweil and Lloyd D. Fosdick (Software Practice and Experience, October-
December 1976, pp. 473-486) 153

Anomaly Detection in Concurrent Software by Static Data Flow Analysis
Richard N. Taylor and Leon J. Osterweil (IEEE Transactions on Software Engineering,
May 1980, pp. 265-278) 167

Testing Large Software with Automated Software Evaluation Systems
C. V. Ramamoorthy and Siu-Bun F. Ho (IEEE Transactions on Software Engineering,
March 1975, pp. 46-58) 181

Symbolic Testing and the DISSECT Symbolic Evaluation System
William E. Howden (IEEE Transactions on Software Engineering,
July 1977, pp. 266-278) 194

SECTION 4: DYNAMIC ANALYSIS—TOOLS AND TECHNIQUES

Paper Summaries...207

A Survey of Dynamic Analysis Methods
    William E. Howden..209

New Directions in Automated Tools for Improving Software Quality
    Leon G. Stucki (*Current Trends in Programming Methodology*, Vol. II: Program
    Validation, 1977, pp. 80-111)...232

Automated Generation of Testcase Datasets
    Edward Miller and R. A. Melton (*Proceedings, 1975 International Conference on
    Reliable Software*, pp. 51-58)...263

A Partition Analysis Method to Increase Program Reliability
    Debra J. Richardson and Lori A. Clarke (*Proceedings, Fifth International Conference
    on Software Engineering*, 1981, pp. 244-253)...............................271

Functional Testing and Design Abstractions
    William E. Howden (*The Journal of Systems and Software 1*, 1980, pp. 307-313)..........281

An Approach to Program Testing
    J. C. Huang (*ACM Computing Surveys*, September 1975, pp. 113-128).................288

Structural Techniques of Program Validation
    Edward Miller, Michael R. Paige, Jeoffrey P. Benson, and William R. Wisehart
    (*Digest of Papers, COMPCON Spring 74*, pp. 161-164)................................304

Automatic Software Test Drivers
    David J. Panzl (*Computer*, April 1978, pp. 44-50)..............................308

Testing a Multiprogramming System
    Per Brinch Hansen (*Software Practice and Experience*, April-June 1973, pp. 145-150).......315

Hints on Test Data Selection: Help for the Practicing Programmer
    Richard A. DeMillo, Richard J. Lipton, and Frederick G. Sayward (*Computer*,
    April 1978, pp. 34-41)..321

SECTION 5: EFFECTIVENESS ASSESSMENT

Paper Summaries...329

Some Experience with Automated Aids to the Design of Large-Scale Reliable Software
    Barry W. Boehm, Robert K. McClean, and D. B. Urfrig (*IEEE Transactions on
    Software Engineering*, March 1975, pp. 125-133)..........................331

A Controlled Experiment in Program Testing and Code Walkthroughs/Inspections
    Glenford J. Myers (*Communications of the ACM*, September 1978, pp. 760-768)............340

An Automated Program Testing Methodology and Its Implementation
    Dorothy M. Andrews and Jeoffrey P. Benson (*Proceedings, Fifth International
    Conference on Software Engineering*, 1981, (pp. 254-261))...................349

Applicability of Software Validation Techniques to Scientific Programs
    William E. Howden (*ACM Transactions on Programming Languages and Systems*,
    July 1980, pp. 307-320)..357

Quantitative Aspects of Software Validation
    Raymond J. Rubey, Joseph A. Dana, and Peter W. Biche (*IEEE Transactions on
    Software Engineering*, June 1975, pp. 150-155)............................371

Observations of Fallibility in Applications of Modern Programming Methodologies
    Susan L. Gerhart and Lawrence Yelowitz (*IEEE Transactions on Software Engineering*,
    September 1976, pp. 195-207)..377

Experience with Path Analysis and Testing of Programs
    Martin R. Woodward, David Hedley, and Michael A. Hennell (*IEEE Transactions
    on Software Engineering*, May 1980, pp. 278-286)..........................390

SECTION 6: MANAGEMENT AND PLANNING

Paper Summaries 399

Management of Software Development
  Edmund B. Daly (*IEEE Transactions on Software Engineering,* May 1977,
  pp. 229-242) 401

The Economics of Software Quality Assurance
  David S. Alberts (*1976 National Computer Conference Proceedings,* AFIPS Vol. 45,
  pp. 433-442) 415

A Service Concept for Software Auditing
  Edward Miller (*Proceedings of the NSF Software Auditing Workshop,* 1976, pp. 57-75) 425

The High Cost of Software
  Barry W. Boehm (*Practical Strategies for Developing Large Software Systems,*
  1975, pp. 3-14) 444

SECTION 7: RESEARCH AND DEVELOPMENT

Paper Summaries 457

Program Testing: Art Meets Theory
  Edward Miller (*Computer,* July 1977, pp. 42-51) 458

Program Testing Technology in the 1980's
  Edward Miller (*The Oregon Report: Proceedings of the Conference on Computing in
  the 1980's,* pp. 72-79) 467

GENERAL BIBLIOGRAPHY 475

GLOSSARY OF TERMS 497

Introduction to Software Validation

William E. Howden

Organization of Material

This book is organized into nine sections. Following this introductory section are six sections corresponding to each of the major topics that comprise software validation. Each of these six sections is briefly summarized below. The book concludes with a bibliography and glossary for guidance in further reading.

Theoretical Foundations (Section 2)

The goal of the theoretical work which has been carried out on program testing has been to provide a systematic formal approach to a technology which has in the past been ad hoc and intuitive. A number of interesting theoretical results have been proved which give insight into the testing process but which cannot be considered practical program testing tools. Reprints describing these results are included in Section 2. The section also includes reprints describing several more practical, but less general, theoretical results which can be used to test particular kinds of computational substructures.

The most widely studied formal validation method is the inductive assertion technique for proving the correctness of programs. This book emphasizes informal methods (the proofs of correctness paper contained in this section is included for completeness). The proofs of correctness approach to validation is not currently useful except for the validation of relatively small combinatorial algorithms. Accordingly, it is not emphasized here.

Static and Dynamic Analysis (Sections 3 and 4)

Integration of validation and development. Figure 1 contains a description of the traditional software development process in which validation is the last phase in a four-part process. The necessity of moving the validation phase to an earlier position in the development cycle has become increasingly apparent. In general, the later an error is discovered, the more expensive it is to fix. Figure 2 describes a software development process in which validation is part of each phase of the process and not carried out after everything else has been done. The diagram in Figure 2 is derived from a diagram which appears in a paper by M. S. Fujii.*

The types of validation methods that can be integrated into the development process and can be used during particular phases of the process are closely related to the types of system documents generated during the phase. This relationship can be used to classify validation methods as being requirements-, design-, or code-based.

Requirements-, design-, and program-based methods. Two types of validation activities can be carried out during each of the three phases of the software development process described in Figure 2: static and dynamic analysis. *Static analysis* involves an analysis of system

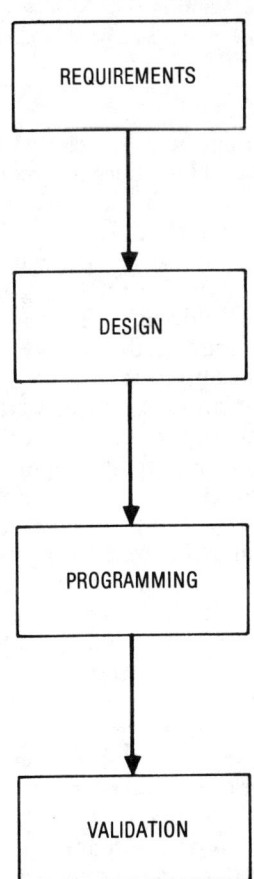

Figure 1. Traditional role of validation in the software development process.

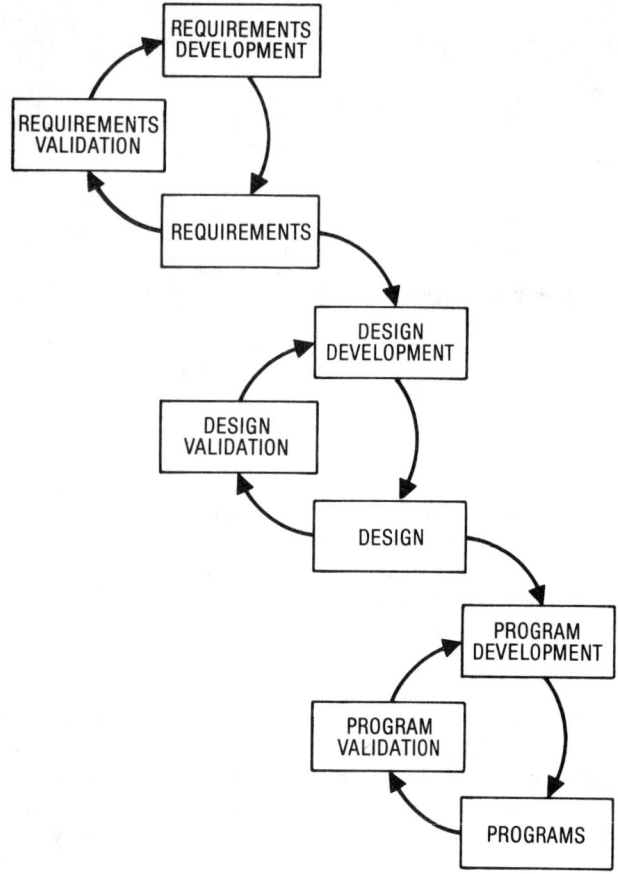

Figure 2. Integration of development and validation.

properties that can be derived directly from system documents and whose analysis does not require execution of the system. *Dynamic analysis* requires execution of a system. The most important dynamic analysis technique is program testing. The test data generation phase of program testing can be carried out during all phases of software development, although the actual running of tests requires completed code and can only be carried out in the program development phase.

Static analysis methods which rely on the requirements and design documents for a system involve an analysis of the documents for important properties such as consistency and completeness. Several automated systems have been built which can be used to partially automate the validation of machine-readable requirements and design specifications. Static analysis methods which rely on the source code involve a direct examination of the code. The examination may require the use of special features which are added to the language. Type and unit declarations can be added to FORTRAN, for example, to allow the use of a preprocessor for analyzing a program for units consistency in assignment statements.

Dynamic analysis methods which rely on requirements and design documents involve the construction of program test data based on information contained in these documents rather than on the source code. The requirements for a system, for example, should include a description of the allowable ranges and types for all input variables. Functional requirements testing will include the testing of a system over the boundaries of the ranges for these variables as well as over values lying in the middle of the ranges. Functional tests which are based on functional properties of design elements can also be constructed. Test data which is based entirely on the source code for a system can be both functional and structural. Structural test data is used to test particular computational constructs in the source code. A set of code-based tests, for example, might be constructed whose purpose is to test all the logical paths through a loop construct.

Sections 4 and 5 contain papers on static and dynamic analysis. Each section begins with a survey which organizes and classifies methods as requirements-, design-, or code-based. In addition to the surveys, papers are included which describe particular techniques or concepts.

Effectiveness (Section 5)

One of the most difficult problems facing the software engineer is the choice of validation method, and the uncertainty of its effectiveness in discovering the errors in his system. There is relatively little reliability data for both the newer and more traditional methods. It is difficult to measure the effectiveness of a method except through the use of expensive, controlled experiments.

The results of the studies reported in Section 5 are encouraging and indicate that there are patterns in the occurrences of errors and in their detection that can be used to guide the selection and development of validation methods.

Some of the material in Section 2, Theoretical Foundations, is closely related to the problems of effectiveness, and can be thought of as theoretical approaches to the problem. A mathematical characterization of a technique such as expression testing, for example, is a formal description of the situations in which the technique is completely effective.

Management and Planning (Section 6)

Even the use of the best design and requirements methods and of the best validation methods will not result in the construction of a cost-effective and usable system if the project is not properly managed. Section 6 contains a collection of reprints which describe the overall management of a system development project as well as the management of the project's validation phase. Reprints are also included which estimate the costs for validation. One of the papers estimates the life cycle cost increases that result from the failure to include a validation phase in a project. Another of the papers describes the structure of a software certification service that could be used to standardize the certification of a system.

Research and Development (Section 7)

The study of validation as a specialized topic of software engineering is a relatively recent phenomenon. Additional research groups are moving into this area and we can expect more material and new results to appear at an increasing rate. Section 7 contains papers which describe the current state of the art of the most widely studied validation method, program testing, and which predict what the future holds both for research and development.

*M. S. Fujii, "Independent Verification of Highly Reliable Programs," *Proceedings COMPSAC 77,* IEEE, 1977, pp. 38-44.

Introduction to Software Testing Technology

Edward Miller

Overview

Program testing is a rapidly maturing area within software engineering that is receiving increasing notice both by computer science theoreticians and practitioners. Its general aim is to affirm the quality of software systems by systematically exercising the software in carefully controlled circumstances.

Recent studies of past experience and important original theoretical work have produced results that serve to elevate program testing from an intuitive, *ad hoc* collection of methods into an integrated, systematic discipline. For example, techniques that were called merely "good testing practice" only a decade ago are now found as fully formalized and systematized techniques for which there is economic justification, effectiveness prediction, and a growing "user community."

As a result of the developments in the past five years it might be said that program testing has become possibly the only truly effective means to assure the quality of a software system of non-trivial complexity. Naturally, many of the techniques that are used need serious further development—both by theoreticians who would set things on a firm technical basis, and by technologists who would accumulate and codify experiences in practical applications.

The purpose of this book is to provide a cross-section of current program testing technology—ranging from philosophical issues to research and development concepts. To the extent that the known literature permits it, the aim has been to select papers that will make it simple and straightforward for a practitioner to apply the various sub-technologies of program testing in day-to day software quality assurance activities. A secondary objective is to provide a framework that could be used within the research and development community as the basis for continued work.

Program testing technology appears to divide itself into six primary areas, discussed below in more detail. The literature supports these areas with varying quality. For instance, there are several papers dealing with the theoretical foundations, but good quality material on management and control, or on measurement and evaluation, is more difficult to find. It is hoped the publication of this book will help fill this need.

Following the "natural" dividing lines of the technology, this book is arranged into the following six sections, each of which includes introductory remarks, comments on the papers, and of course the reprints themselves.

Summary. To help the reader obtain a perspective on this material it will be helpful to summarize each of the major sections before going on to the general introduction to the material.

Theoretical Foundations. These papers focus on key notions from the theory of graphs, from modern program proving technology, and from modern formal testing theory as they apply to a formal program testing discipline. This section reprints the now-famous Goodenough and Gerhart paper, which forms a cornerstone for modern program testing theory.

Static Analysis: Tools and Techniques. The papers included in this section focus on the range of methods that are used to determine or estimate program quality without reference to actual execution(s). It is important to appreciate that static and dynamic methods (the latter are discussed in the next major section) are sometimes inseparable, but can almost always be discussed separately. The technical material presented deals with the general subject of verification and validation, the use of code inspection techniques, the use of automated program analyzers of various kinds, and with the new method of symbolic/static analysis.

Dynamic Analysis: Tools and Techniques. The papers included in this section deal with specific methods for ascertaining and/or approximating program correctness through actual program executions; that is, with real data and under real (or nearly real) circumstances. This requires not only the instrumentation of the program (to tell what's going on inside it), but also the detailed examination of inputs and outputs. Naturally enough, this includes the synthesis of inputs, the use of structurally dictated testing procedures, and the automation of testing environment generation.

Effectiveness Assessment. It is well known that testing procedures have varying effectiveness, depending on the setting and depending on the intention (and application) of the results. The papers in this section summarize current technology that addresses the broad question of the ultimate effectiveness of any method of software quality assurance, and of program testing methods in particular. To the extent that it is possible, these assessments are made on a qualitative level of detail that should provide strong guidance for management decisions regarding choice of method and belief in the outcomes.

Management and Planning: Further assistance to management is provided in a set of papers that addresses—insofar as it is currently possible to do so—the question of the economics of program testing and allied software quality assurance disciplines. In addition, one paper provides a proposed framework for attacking the problem of organizing a software testing activity along reasonable lines. Finally, there is information relating to the high (and continually increasing) cost of software systems.

Research and Development. The two papers in this section address the modern view of an approach that appears to be effective in attacking program testing problems in general, and the problems that it now appears must be solved in order for program testing to "mature" before the mid-1980's timeframe.

The Philosophy of Testing. The underlying motivation of program testing is to affirm computer software quality with methods that can be economically and effectively applied to both large-scale and small-scale systems. Alternative methods of software quality enhancement (such as program proving) are deficient because they either are inapplicable to large-scale software systems, or are too weakly developed technically to be effective even for small-scale software systems.

The basic principle of program testing is controlled execution of a program with known inputs and outputs (both predicted and observed), combined with internal measurement of the behavior of the program. The notion of controlled execution forms the basis for a systematic methodology for carrying out the program testing process for a large-scale computer software system. A systematic methodology to accomplish the testing could be top-down, or bottom-up, or some other kind. Each step in the systematic methodology involves repeated applications of the basic testing principle.

Various organizational alternatives can be used to provide for program testing: in-line, and off-line groups within the main organization, or an independent verification and validation unit. Special procedures exist for certain kinds of military software, and are often stronger than their commercial counterparts.

The program testing activity should be considered as an integral part of the general software engineering process. In particular, it is sometimes important to consider adoptive software requirements, design, and implementation techniques which attempt to decrease the difficulty of testing.

Motivating Forces. The primary motivating force for program testing is cost. The cost factor can be interpreted in terms of either negative or positive costs. Negative costs include such items as:

- The cost of failure of the software system, which may include the subjective costs associated with loss of system image (product image).
- The cost of repair, which may include the costs to retrofit a "new" version of a software system in the field.
- The cost within the life cycle, which may decrease when effective program testing disciplines are employed.

Some of the positive costs would be:

- The cost for a software quality assurance program, including personnel, machine, and possibly automated tool costs.
- The costs in added machine time that would result from the existence of a formal program testing activity.
- The costs of installing new technology, both in terms of people's education cost and time, as well as in machine time during the learning stages.

The benefits of program testing include the reverse of all of these costs, plus the following:

- Better user acceptance, because the software system is more reliable.
- The opportunity for re-use of the software, a consequence of its demonstrated history of high-quality performance.
- An improvement in the "psychology" surrounding the software development activity resulting from confidence in the process of assuring quality and the resulting increased confidence (reduced anxiety) in the viability of the final product.

Testing Principles. The underlying principle of program testing is the following: a program is tested by providing known inputs to a copy of the program that is executed in a known environment so that the outputs the program generates can be examined for their appropriateness. It is important to collect some form of information about the interior control-flow behavior of the program as it executes the tests.

Typical test situations will involve a number of separate tests of individual software modules.* One of the objectives of testing is to construct tests that exercise a program's structure in a particular way (discussed later). It is also important to develop series of tests that affirm the actual content of the software system.

The testing activity is an affirmative one in the following sense: every action and outcome during the formal testing process contributes information that is useful to the process in some way. At the minimum, testing serves to demonstrate the presence of function. While it is known that program testing cannot assure program "correctness" except under very special situations (discussed later), it is important to recognize that program testing, if performed systematically, can serve to guarantee the absence of "bugs."

Traditional methods of program testing resemble debugging methods, particularly since they may involve the use of dumps or execution traces. More modern testing methods employ techniques of symbolic execution of programs (discussed later).

---

*A module is the smallest separately invokable piece of a software system, and corresponds to a SUBROUTINE or PROCEDURE, etc.

The most common application of program testing technology involves analyzing a fairly stable software system. This might occur when either individual programs or major parts of a larger system are "finished," i.e., past the essential program implementation state. In this environment the software is stable enough so that the majority of the simpler mistakes have already been found; note that the line between testing and debugging is generally taken as whether the mistakes that are found are "easy" or not.

Once an error is found it is assumed it will be removed immediately. While this may result in the need for a certain amount of retesting, it is better to fix mistakes immediately since doing so generally minimizes the impact they would have later in the testing process.

It is important that each testing action be oriented toward specific objectives. Some of the easiest goals to use involve attaining some measured level of testing coverage in terms of some structural basis. This kind of approach serves the need for a convenient metric, but it is important to recognize from the outset that the primary measurement of the effectiveness of testing is the level of comprehensiveness of system function that is attained by the testing activity.

Systematic testing methodologies (discussed in detail later) are important because they permit dividing the testing effort up into manageable pieces. Depending on the software development scheme used it may be appropriate to use bottom-up, or top-down, or alternative methodologies. The most important factor is to have a well-understood goal for the testing process. One of the advantages of using a systematic methodology is that it can (at least in principle) be automated to a great extent. Using automated techniques relieves the testing team of the necessity to keep detailed records and also (perhaps more importantly) minimizes the possibility that something would be missed during the testing process.

Overview of Methodology. A systematic methodology seeks to employ rational techniques to force sequences of actions that, in aggregate, accomplish some desired testing-oriented effect. The most common forms of testing involve *both* exterior and interior testing. "Exterior" testing attempts to demonstrate the presence of function by concentrating on the exterior specifications (requirements) of the software system; "interior" testing operates from knowledge of the source program. The basis for use of so-called white-box approaches is the following: any part of the software system is present for some specific reason and the testing process can be thought of as one involving relating each piece of a software system to the requirement it fulfills. In addition, if in the process it turns out that some part of the software system has no identifiable function, then its presence would certainly have to be considered a flaw of some kind.

Testing can be used both as a post-development Quality Assurance method and as a preventative technique. In the latter case, it is often important to recognize the possibility that the software system could be designed to make the testing process easier. In post-development testing the objective is to systematically determine, for each program part, either that the part is appropriate (i.e., functions properly) or is not (i.e., has some bug in it).

In a bottom-up testing methodology, the lowest level modules are examined first, and the focus of the testing activity moves upward through the software system's structural hierarchy until, finally, programs that reside at the topmost level are tested. This is a technique that corresponds to the maxim: "build with proven components." The top-down methodology is nearly the reverse, but begins with functional tests of the highest-level programs and ordinarily employs stubs to "simulate" the activity of lower-level modules relative to the actions of the modules under test.

Each software test involves inputs, outputs, and program responses. A wide variety of forms for input/output relationships, and perhaps an equally wide set of internal testing coverage measures are known. In many cases the program testing setup cannot be generalized: also, for certain classes of software it is important to take advantage of *a priori* knowledge about the form of tests for the system.

The most important factor is to have a controlled environment in which tests of a specific function can be run (and repeated). As a general rule, the testing process involves possibly quite a large number of repetitions of the following steps:

- Identify an object within the software system to be tested
- Choose data that "tests" that object
- Execute the object with the chosen test data
- Analyze the program outputs produced for appropriateness
- Examine the effect the test data had on the object
- Decide which "object" to treat next (after fixing errors)

Organizing for Testing. Because testing may involve a rather large number of instances of this sequence of basic steps, it is increasingly typical to assign the entire activity to a dedicated organizational unit. Even when the testing is done by the developing unit, the kinds of activities that go on during testing are sufficiently different from other activities that the testing process should be considered as a separate work function.

Some of the possible organizational schemes that could be used include the following:

- An in-line group, in which the responsibility for testing is specifically assigned as a separate function (either the developing group or an independent group)
- Client/customer function, performed in terms of an acceptance testing function.
- Independent contractor (independent verification and validation), who acts on behalf of the client/customer.

What tends to drive the testing function into an independent position, or at least a separated function, is the need to have a separate analysis. Psychological factors enter also, since it can be quite inefficient to have the developing unit also perform the testing role.

It may be important to consider partitioning the testing effort along the internal organization boundaries of the software system being analyzed. This would particularly be the case when the software system being treated is a large one, or when it involves major software subsystems that are fundamentally different in nature (e.g. a compiler plus a tactical data system written in a special-purpose language).

The procurement practices of the military services may require an independent verification and validation effort. Moreover, newly revised regulations may have a significant impact on the form and content of the so-called "test and evaluation" function.

Relation to Software Engineering. Contemporary thinking within the software engineering research and development community considers the software life cycle as composed of five distinct phases: requirements/specifications, software system design, implementation (programming), test and quality assurance, and maintenance.

The requirements/specifications phase involves developing clear statements about the intended function for a software system. Testing requirements can be handled during this phase by incorporating in the requirements/specifications documentation both: (a) rough indications of appropriate test data and (b) explicit requirements that the design meet clearly stated minimum standards of testability.

The software system design process, according to contemporary thinking, should involve the use of hierarchical decompositions of the "problem space" preparatory to completing the design process. The problems that might be encountered later during testing can, to a certain extent, be minimized by good design techniques. Generally speaking, the better structured a software system is the easier it is going to be to test.

While many of the "errors" that later must be found and removed arise from the requirements/specifications and software design process, the overwhelming majority of mistakes originate from coding errors. Programming is an opportunity to commit mistakes that has no parallel during the software life-cycle! The use of static analyzers, as well as enforcement of good programming standards, generally serves to minimize errors.

When finally in its intended use, a program must still be maintained. A recent study of very large-scale software systems (with lifetimes since inception of approximately 16 years) found that 50 percent of the total cost was associated in some way with maintenance. During maintenance, small changes are made to the software system and the parts affected are retested. In some cases new test data must be used, but very often the previously used test data suffices. One problem of testing after a modification to a software system is determining the extent of needed retesting.

Theoretical Foundations of Testing

Introduction. Program testing techniques are based in an amalgam of methods drawn from graph theory, programming languages, reliability assessment, and so-called reliable-testing theory.

Graph theory techniques are used to model the control and data flow in a program. Ordinarily the model used assigns arcs in a directed graph (digraph) to actions or segments in the program, and employs nodes in the digraph to represent "places" in a program. Data flow graphs are also used to examine the data relationships between various program actions.

Because program testing ordinarily operates from the source-language representations of a program, the techniques of syntactic and semantic analysis are quite important. The "meaning" of a program can be the basis for detailed analysis of the program's properties. Static analyses can be performed that exploit knowledge of the programming language semantics in series of tests (or allegation proofs) designed to identify common programming mistakes.

Reliability assessment methods can be used, although with some difficulty, in the process of developing predictive measures of in-place software system reliability.

Finally, program testing theory (a relatively recent development) addresses the issue of the impact of testing on the error-locating process. Current results suggest rather broad conditions under which carefully chosen tests are the effective equivalent of program proofs.

General Principles. The approach to program testing most often taken involves so-called "white box" testing, in which the source text as well as all associated program documentation is made available during the testing process. All of this information has some role to play since the important objective is to devise and run sets of tests that demonstrate the presence of wanted software function, and the absence of unwanted software function.

The objective of the graph theory approach to analyzing programs is to infer data about appropriate test forms directly from the control and/or data structure of the program. For example, the control flow can be modeled with a directed graph (digraph) in which edges correspond to program actions (also called segments), and nodes correspond to places where "control" could be during a program execution. In addition, this model allows relatively simple measurement of program testing coverage (discussed later).

Because one of the objectives of program testing is to eliminate program errors, it is important to understand the programming language characteristics quite thoroughly. Study of language characteristics can assist in identifying error-prone constructs which, in turn, can be "tested against."

For a software system which involves many modules it is crucially important to think in terms of quantifying the likelihood that the system will perform its intended function effectively. This is the task of reliability assessment. Various models have been proposed that accomplish this; at the present time only a few of these models have shown practical utility, however.

The digraph representations are also highly useful in analyzing the macroscopic structure of individual programs (or collections of programs), especially when developing test cases and associated test data. An example of this problem is constructing new test data to exercise a previously unexercised segment in a complex program.

The theory of reliable testing involves determining whether a test is sufficiently well designed, in terms of the properties of certain classes of program errors, to be effective in unambiguously determining the presence or absence of an error. This theory is important because it provides the theoretical basis (incomplete at the present time) for use of program testing in place of other techniques such as program proofs.

It is difficult to portray the "state of the art" in program testing in a few words; only in the recent years beginning approximately in 1971, has the field seen intensive development in either practice or theory. At the present time program testing experience suggests relatively high payoffs for systematic test activities in terms of error-rate reduction and resulting trouble-free performance. Current theory applies to practically important subsets of error classes; the expectation is that these error classes will be expanded and extended as research and development continues.

Graph Theory. The technology of program testing is strongly rooted in the notion of directed graphs. A directed graph consists of a set of nodes and edges (arcs) that are oriented to indicate flow (of something) from the originating node to the terminating node. The association between a program and a directed graph (digraph) is made in the following way: the nodes represent "places" within the program that the execution-point could pass, and the edges represent the actions the program takes in getting from one node to another.

The beginning of the program corresponds to the entry node in the diagraph, and the exit of the program (i.e., after its invocation is complete) is considered as the exit node of the program. The entry node has no incoming edges (inways); correspondingly, the exist node has no outgoing edges (outways). Any node that has more than one outway is called a decision node because it corresponds to a decision statement in the program. The normal succession rule (execute the next statement, and the next, and so on) creates nodes that have only one inway and one outway. When this happens the node and the two edges involved can be merged into a new edge that represents the action of the *pair* of statements. When a diagraph for a program has all instances of this kind of node removed it is said to be in reduced form.

When in this reduced form, the digraph effectively represents the decisions of the program, with each possible decision outcome assigned to an outgoing edge of a node. The program is effectively reduced from its original source-text form to a set of "decision to decision paths," or segments. A segment is, very simply, a set of program statements that are always executed together as the result of the outcome of some decision taken within the program.

This observation makes it possible to derive the control flow diagraph for a program simply by examining the decisional statements within the program. In Fortran, for example, these are the IF, GOTO (...), and DO statements, plus some others that involve statement labels and conditional transfers. In Cobol the decisional statements are the IF, the PERFORM, and several other statement types. The digraph model of the control structure of a program can be generated in a single pass through the program text.

Programs that have iteration are more interesting, and more complex, than programs that simply represent, say, a decision table without any iteration. (In fact, the utility of computer programs arises because of the use of iteration.) When a program iterates the digraph of the control structure will have cycles, that is, sequences of edges that repeat at least one node. A cycle is characterized by the number of entries and exits to/from the cycle. A single-entry, single-exit cycle is the kind that arises in a purely structured program though the use of the WHILE... END WHILE construct. In most programs, however, there will be many multiple-entry and/or multiple-exit cycles. This more complex cycle structure complicates the analysis of the program significantly.

All programs can be represented in purely structured form, using only the succession, alteration (IF...ELSE ...END IF) construction, and iteration (WHILE...END WHILE) construction. This representation may be possible (as is well known) only by the addition of variables and/or the repetition of edges. There are some important advantages for program testing by considering programs *as if* they were in purely structured format. This technique is discussed later, when hierarchical decompositions of programs are used as the basis for developing detailed test plans.

Analyzing the digraph for the control structure of a program may also involve the use of certain kinds of non-iterative (acyclic) sequences of edges (segments). For example, a reaching sequence is a set of edges that begins with the entry node and continues through the digraph until it "reaches" a particular edge or node in the program. Similarly, an unreaching sequence begins with some particular edge or node and continues without repeating an edge or node until the exit node is reached.

The use of these notions will become clear later, in discussions of techniques for generating test data for programs.

Another graph form that is useful is the data flow graph, which models the dependence between variables in the program on each other and on external variables that are used as the input and output for the program. In a data flow graph each node corresponds to a variable, and the edges indicate the dependence between variables. When the program computes the variable A from the content of the variable B, for example, there is an edge from the node A to the node B. Similarly, when the result of generating B is used in the final output of the program C, there would be an edge going from B to C.

The data flow graph makes it possible to determine some important properties such as the interdependence between segments (whether one segment is independent of another segment or not). Similarly, the data flow graph can be used to "prove" the allegation that all variables are set before they are used in the global, or multiple module, sense.

Program Behavior Modeling. The objective of program behavior modeling is to devise methods that make it possible to predict the effect of a program test, or to make it possible to devise tests that have a particular effect within a program. Most methods of the program behavior modeling focus on the control flow structure of the program, and in particular on the iterations within the program. A secondary reason for attempting to characterize program properties in a systematic way is to support automation of program analysis, particularly for large software modules or for large-scale software systems where the possibility of automation represents the difference between being able to do program testing effectively or not.

One scheme for modeling program structure involves identifying a set of "level-i paths," or sequences of segments in a program digraph that corresponds in an intuitive way with the "level of iteration" in the program. A level-0 path would correspond to one that involved *no* iteration. A level-1 path would involve one level of iteration. In general, a level-i path would involve a sequence of segments that forced iteration of some level-(i-1) path.

Once the set of level-i paths is constructed they can be organized in a tree-like format indicating their dependence on one another, and then used to plan a set of tests that exhaustively exercises the segments in the program.

Another method that has been considered is to attempt to partition the program's input space (the set of states that program inputs can take on) into independent regions, based on analysis of the internal decision structure of the program. If this can be done then appropriate tests would result by simply selecting data from each of the partitions within the program input space. Such tests would have predictable effects in terms of the run-time flow pattern they would induce within the program.

Still another method involves representing the program in terms of an equivalent but purely structured program. This can be done by decomposing the program step by step in terms of the basic structured programming primitives into a tree that relates segments with one another and with the program decisions that are the connections between them. This decomposition method can be a simple basis for identifying good sets of tests for the program, at least in the sense of providing minimum structural testing coverage.

What all these methods have in common is the attempt to build a set of relationships between the internal structure of a program (primarily the control structure rather than the data structure) and the set of tests that are effective in verifying that the intended software function of the program is present. It is important to recognize this area as one for which there is much current research. Methods that are known are sufficient as starting points for formal testing in practical terms and are under continual improvement.

Reliability Theory. There are two points of view for the application of reliability techniques to the program testing problem. One takes the macroscopic view and attempts to relate the kind of testing exercise given to a program to the overall system reliability that would be achieved by that software system when it is in actual use. The other view is more interior-oriented, and studies the theoretical properties of tests in relation to programs by attempting to determine if particular kinds of tests are successful in discovering certain classes of errors. Both of the approaches are classed under "reliability techniques" because they address the measure of testing's effectiveness in theoretical terms.

Applications of Statistics. Statistical approaches in assessing testing effectiveness rely on characterizing the degree of similarity in execution characteristics achieved in a controlled testing situation with that likely to occur in practice. This can be done using either path frequencies within individual programs or Markovian models of program decision transition sequences.

The objective of either method is to apply modern statistical methods to the problem of quantitatively predicting the likelihood of a program-originated failure at some time in the future. In effect, a confidence level of any value can be achieved doing enough testing of the software system. One of the problems, however, is that the number of tests required may be rather large.

Theory of reliability testing. "Reliable Test Theory" refers to a recently developed collection of results that address the conditions under which a test is the practical equivalent of a formal correctness proof. In pioneering work by Goodenough and Gerhart, and supported by subsequent work of Howden, it has been shown that it is possible to develop tests that have the same "strength" as program proofs under certain conditions on the types of errors that would be involved.

A reliable test is said to be one that unambiguously identifies program errors so long as the test is successful, and, if the test fails, will fail only because of a program error. Having a reliable test for a program part would then make it possible to "prove" that that program part did not contain any errors of the kind against which the test was already shown (in theory) to be reliable protection.

Although the theory is somewhat detailed, put simply, program faults (which cause a program with an error to differ from one that is "perfect") can be put into two categories: *case errors* and *action errors*. A case error exists when there is a fault in a program's decisional structure which causes it to differ from the correct program in a way that drastically changes the implied partitions of the input space, i.e., the so-called program "cases." An action error exists: (a) in the absence of a case error and (b) when a wrong output would be produced when the program is executed with valid test data for that case.

Current results show that reliable tests can be derived for the rather wide class of programs that contain no case errors. Also, programs that operate on the integers and with integer arrays and which contain at least one distinguishing statement within each program cycle can be tested with fully reliable tests. While there are a few negative results (ones that indicate program faults that cannot be tested against reliably), the general character of reliable testing theory seems to suggest the likelihood of extending the classes of program faults against which testing would be effective, although this may require the use of special programming devices in some cases.

Combinatorics. A final facet of the theoretical foundations for program testing involves the analysis of the combinatorics of program flow. This issue is important because practical application of program testing methods seems to be a kind of trade-off between the number of combinations of activities a program does and its size. For example, some programs are known to be composed of rather complicated but non-iterative internal logic, while others are known to be "complex" simply because of multiple-entry/multiple-exit iteration structures.

The combinatoric growth problem is much more severe when planning to test an entire software system, e.g., one composed of many hundreds, of perhaps thousands, of modules organized in a complex fashion. An example would be a modern operating system or sophisticated applications programming package. The notions that are important in looking at the combinatoric issue are also closely related to the measurement of complexity within computer programs, and the correlation of complexity with function and weight.

Tools and Techniques of Testing

Introduction. Given the motivation and sufficiently strong theoretical underpinnings, program testing can be applied in a practical way to problems of software unreliability. The character of programs to be tested tends to dictate the manner in which the theoretically sound methods are applied. It is also important to appreciate the wide spectrum of tools and techniques available, and that one of the critical factors in a program testing situation is the matter of choosing the particular tool and/or technique that applies to the software system being analyzed.

An important goal of program testing is to reduce the level of effort required to accomplish adequate testing, or to increase the effectiveness of a given level of effort. Very often this can be done by use of semiautomatic, (or so-called "automated,") methods. (There are many technical reasons why certain tools and techniques cannot be fully automated.) In use, any automated tool that is applied to the program testing process must be considered as a system that supports the objectives of the program tester. Many efforts fail because the personnel become more interested in the tool itself than in the process of using the tool.

There are two important categories of program analysis techniques: static and dynamic. In static analysis the program is analyzed without regard for its run-time behavior, while in dynamic analysis the program is executed under carefully controlled circumstances and its behavior is studied in many ways.

Static analysis tools can be applied to a software system immediately after the implementation process. In effect, a static analyzer is a program that "proves" an allegation about a program or a software system. When the allegation is false no instances of the feature the allegation is protecting against have been found. Automation is important here both to reduce the cost of this kind of testing, and to assure that the "proof" has been carried out comprehensively.

Dynamic testing involves a series of rather straightforward steps that lead from the initial identification of test data and test objectives, through the actual execution process, to the final stages in which the outcomes (results) of the test are analyzed and cataloged. There are several major categories of automated tools that help in the dynamic testing process. In addition, there are many tools of only secondary importance that can be quite useful also. Generally speaking, the role of the tools is secondary to that of the human tester, who ultimately must decide which steps should be taken next.

Even with automated assistance it is important to recognize that the testing process is one which will involve many repetitions of relatively simple actions. The utility of the process largely depends on accurately performing each and every step to the same standard of performance. This emphasis is recognized in the standardized systematic methodologies that can be used as general procedural guides during the program testing activity.

Two major categories of such methodologies are called bottom-up and top-down. In the bottom-up methodology the lowest elements in the software system hierarchy are tested first, followed by the next higher elements, until all of the system's modules have been tested. In the top-down methodology, the primary control functions (which reside at the top of the hierarchy) are tested first, and then in successive stages each next layer within the software system is tested comprehensively.

Throughout the process the test data generation problem dominates: how to find specific values of input data that cause a program under test to behave in a particular fashion. This problem can be handled with manual, semiautomated, and automated techniques; research and development activities in the program testing research community continue to increase the effective power of test data generators. At present, however, program testing teams have to be content with sophisticated test data generation advice and/or limited-function test data generators.

In the future symbolic testing methods will be increasingly important because they combine many of the benefits of rigorous and reliable testing with the methods of program proving. At present, symbolic testing systems are beginning to be introduced as an alternative to program provers.

General Principles. A program is well tested when the program tester has an adequately high level of confidence that there are no remaining "errors" that further testing would uncover. The way this is done, i.e., the specific methods chosen to reach that goal, have an important effect on the overall perception of software reliability. In addition, the particular methods used also determine the level and kind of quantification of software quality, if indeed such a quantification is actually sought.

Ordinarily the program testing process involves repetition of a few relatively simple procedures, a rather large number of times. It would not be uncommon for the total number of mental discriminations required during testing to approximate that originally required during the program implementation process. Naturally, current forms of testing fall far short of that. Thus, simply because budgets are limited and because the technology is also incomplete, it is important to optimally allocate available resources. Very often this is done by employing automated assistance in the form of testing support tools, intended to make the job easier to perform.

An effective testing setup would combine static and dynamic tests of the software. Static tests are applied to the program as if it were a document for which very high standards of quality are required. After the static testing phase is complete, and discovered errors are corrected, the testing activity moves into the dynamic testing phase. Now the program is run with "real" input data and the effects the test data has on the program both externally (what outputs it produces) and internally (what features of the program are exercised) are studied carefully.

During dynamic tests there are two kinds of outcomes: positive affirmations, in which required software functions are shown to be present (as intended); and negative indications, which suggest a deficiency either in the software or in the software testing process. In either case information is gained, and ultimately all of this kind of information will be of importance to the "quality assessment" that is made about the software system.

Because the testing process can become very intricate and complex, it is generally important to consider the use of automated techniques. There is a large and growing set of automated tools and techniques from which to choose.

Automated testing tools are program analyzers of one kind or another; a program analyzer typically operates on the source text of an entire software system (not just one module), and performs various kinds of analyses according to the user's commands. The outputs are either reports giving the answer to some "question" the user has asked about the properties of the software system, or the outputs may suggest (or generate) a specific system setup intended to make it possible to perform some kind of testing action. An example of the former is a static analysis check of the veracity of interprocedural communication; an example of the latter is the production of an instrumented version of a set of modules that are going to be monitored carefully during dynamic testing.

Static Testing. Static testing corresponds roughly to bench-testing of an electronic device without applying any power. The idea of a static analyzer is simple: attempt to demonstrate the truth of an allegation (a kind of weak theorem about the software system). If the allegation is true then the property that the allegation addresses is *not* present in the software system. Otherwise, there is something wrong with the program.

Allegations can be applied either at the single module level, or at the level of an entire software system. Most of the static analyzers operate at the single module level, but the stronger allegations are those that include single-module properties but which are "proved" globally, i.e., over all of the modules in the software system.

Allegations can be classified according to whether they address the structural, syntactic, semantic, interprocedural, or some other category of program feature. An example of a single-module structural allegation is to require that a program have no improperly nested iterations (e.g., Fortran DO loops) or that no improper transfers into the scope of an iteration are made. In both of these cases the allegation is a little stronger than what is typically considered an "error" by a compiler. (In a sense, static analysis can be thought of as an extension of the compilation process.)

A multiple-module interprocedural allegation, for example, is to require that all invocations to subroutines have actual parameter lists that correspond to the formal parameter list (given in the definition of the invoked module) in mode, type, number, and extent, etc. This is a kind of check that is rarely performed by a compiler since it normally has access only to one source module at a time.

Some very sophisticated static analyzers have been built and applied to software systems with good success. For example, the DAVE system (discussed later) performs a global set-before-use "proof" that implies, after processing, there will be no instances of variables that are uninitialized. This is important because a common source of software error is due to failure to initialize a variable under all possible circumstances of its use.

Once the allegations are understood and cataloged, it is possible (but not recommended) to "prove" them manually. The difficulty with this is that it can be rather a tedious process, and one as prone to error as the programming task was in the first place.

Dynamic Testing. Dynamic testing seeks to exercise a program in a controlled and systematic way to (a) demonstrate that required functions are present and (b) that unwanted functions are absent. To do this requires a rather close look at the actual content of a software system, and because a system can be very complex in many instances it is necessary to use automated methods. Besides the basic desire to demonstrate function there is a secondary objective of attaining a high value of some kind of testing coverage measure (discussed later). In practical situations it is unreasonable to expect to have "done everything possible;" hence there is emphasis on attempting to do the most important things that affect software quality as early as possible.

A dynamic testing situation has the following elements: Objectives, Data, Results, and Measurment. Objectives, are the goals associated with a specific test; in practice, the generic objective "show there's nothing wrong" often serves quite effectively. Data refers to the specific set of inputs that are going to be used during the test. In practice, when testing focuses on a part of a software system in the natural context it can be quite important to pay atention to the actual data that applies to the test; this data could be only a subset of a rather larger volume of data that is required simply to have the software execute realistically at all.

Results refers to the outcomes of the test, i.e., the values the program produces or the effects the program has. Measurement refers to the detailed internal knowledge about the software system collected during the testing process and used to measure progress.

In the ideal, the set of objectives, data, results, and measurements about each test would be achieved in some way as backup information; the same situation could be set up and run later if it were necessary to reaffirm the software system. The archiving process is particularly important because later in the system life-cycle, when doing program maintenance, it would only be necessary to re-run tests that affect the part of the program that was changed, rather than repeat the entire testing process.

Measurements. The measurement process in dynamic testing requires collecting information about the execution behavior of the program as it is running the "test." While it would be intuitively satisfying to record for potential use everything that the program does, this is generally impractical. Instead, because most of the testing coverage measures concentrate on observing the details of the program's control flow, it is only necessary to collect relatively limited information. The information is "limited" in comparison to the full data stream likely to be generated by a program.

One way of collecting information about control flow conveniently is to "instrument" the program in a way that preserves the logical structure and integrity but which makes collecting the control-flow data quite simple. This is done by inserting subroutine calls (or some equivalent) in a copy of the program so that data is emitted each time the program takes a decision. This is a relatively simple process for verifying the execution behavior of a program; the measurement effect can be accomplished in a variety of other ways besides modifying the program. Note that modifying the program would affect the execution time and execution space; when these features are critical ones then other means *must* be used.

Assuming that the program instrumentation and dynamic data collection methods are available, it then becomes important to study how to deal with the information that is collected, particularly when a substantial number of "software probes" are in use. The typical problem is "what to do with the mass of data?" Various presentation methods that allow a program tester to manage the critical testing coverage information, and not be confused by the superfluous data, are available (discussed later). The single notion that is most important to keep in mind is the method used to mark the beginning and end of each "test."

Testing the interface between modules (or between data structures, etc.) requires a somewhat different approach since it is the quality of data, rather than the sequence of control flow, that is critical. The techniques of interface testing include the use of stubs, the generation of special-purpose test beds, etc.

Automated Tools. Automated tools make it possible to achieve a level of thoroughness in the testing process that would be difficult, if not impossible, to accomplish manually. Automated assistance is motivated both technically and economically.

Automated tools can be put in several broad categories, usually based on whether the processing requires augmentation of the program, and whether the program is going to be executed as part of the process. The static analyzers already discussed require no program augmentation, and do not require execution. There is a range of automated tools that support processing of manually augmented programs (the augmentations would be removed prior to final delivery of the software). Finally, there are tools that assist in all the various stages of dynamic testing.

Static analyzers such as FACES, RXVP, and DAVE apply checks to FORTRAN software systems and report allegation violations to the users. Less sophisticated but still useful tools include programming standards enforcers and code auditors, both of which automatically search for certain forms that represent "bad programming practice."

Two major types of tools operate on augmented programs: self-metric instrumenters and dynamic assertion processors. A self-metric instrumentation system provides the capability to record virtually every aspect of the dynamic behavior of a program and reports the information collected to a user in a post-execution report. The PET system is an excellent example of a self-metric instrumentation system.

A dynamic assertion processor acts on user-inserted assertions about the expected behavior of the program. Ordinarily assertions are treated by the compiler as comments. When recognized by the processor the assertion is converted into an action template that is written into the program text, which is then compiled and executed in the normal fashion. During execution if the assertion is false a warning message is provided to the user; typically the message is placed with the normal computer program output.

The most critical testing tools are those supporting dynamic testing; among those tools the most often used is the execution verifier. During the testing activity a testing coverage standard (measure) would be defined; the execution verifier provides the tester specific information about the effect a test has on the internal control flow behavior of a program. This may be done with automatic instrumentation of the program text, or it could be accomplished through a number of other methods.

An execution verifier system includes a command interpreter, a run-time package, a post-execution processor, and a report generator. In operation the system follows instructions stated by the user in analyzing and instrumenting selected source programs; the instrumented versions are compiled and loaded, possibly with many other un-instrumented programs. During execution the instrumentation software (sometimes called the "software probes") emits data that is collected and recorded by the run-time package. After execution the post-processing system analyzes the information collected by the run-time package and produces coverage reports. The reports identify not only the level of testing (exercise) achieved, but also signal when a program component was *not* tested. A wide variety of methods for formatting and organizing the information can be used.

Two other tools also important during the dynamic testing activity are test data/file generators and output comparators. Test data generators are discussed later. A test file generator is a stand alone package that constructs input files (containing either dummy or systematically synthesized data) for use by the program being tested. An output comparator tool is used to compare two successive versions of a program's execution output to identify the differences.

Systematic Methodologies. Testing programs require both a rigorous planning method and the consistent application of it to all parts of a software system. A systematic methodology is essential if the testing is going to be *both* thorough and economical. Being systematic in the program testing process is tantamount to applying good engineering principles in the allocation of effort to produce desired results. In program testing technology a systematic methodology is a vehicle for thinking about the processes involved in the testing activity, and for expressing and using (or codifying) experience gained.

There are two major forms of systematic methodology: top-down and bottom-up. Deciding which of them to use would be based on knowledge of both the software system being tested, and the availability of support tools and techniques. Even at the present state of technology there are no hard and fast rules for selecting this fundamental approach.

A top-down methodology begins at the upper elements of a software system and continues to build increasingly detailed tests until all of the elements have been tested. The bottom-up methodology works the other way, beginning with comprehensive testing of the primitive elements of the system and continuing upward through the hierarchy until adequate tests of the whole system have been completed. Conceptually, bottom-up corresponds to "build with proven components," while top-down corresponds to the strict "hierarchical decomposition" technique that is gaining so much favor as an effective software design and implementation approach.

One advantage of the bottom-up methodology is that the already-tested modules can be used as the execution support environment when testing is focusing on the higher levels. On the other hand, present day thinking suggests that top-down designed tests are apt to be better functional representations of actual operating conditions. One alternative strategy is to test in a "sideways" fashion, choosing for testing focus what appears to be appropriate and possibly changing the strategy during the process as more and more information is gained.

Test Data Generation. The test data generation problem can be stated briefly as follows: given a part of a program (or part of a program set) that has not yet been tested, construct specific test data that will cause that part to be executed. Basically this involves first finding a path that can potentially lead from an invocation of the program (i.e., the program entry), and then determining whether there are test data that will cause the program to execute along that path. Note this visualizes the general case, in which the "part" of the program that needs to be executed is a segment somewhere in the "middle" of the program.

The path involved begins at the program entry (at the invocation point) and continues through a series of actions and decisions the last one of which arrives at the desired segment. The path here could be non-iterative (no segment is used more than once), or it could be iterative (some segments are repeated a finite number of times). For either type of path there will be a set of predicates that have particular value along the path. It is possible to "backtrack" along the path and develop a set of inequalities that represents the conditions that must be met on the input for the program to follow the particular path. These inequalities are called the "path constraints" because they represent constraints on the input to the program that, if satisfied, would make the program behave in the specifically desired way.

A path is called *feasible* if it could be executed by some set of program input data; otherwise, it is called infeasible. Although there are no guidelines, it would be a good estimate that the majority of the possible paths between the input and the "target segment" are infeasible, notwithstanding the fact that they are structurally legitimate connected segment sequences. This phenomena seems to be the consequence of the nature of programs: there is more decisional apparatus available in a program than is actually used (that is, than is actually employed in delivering the program's computational function).

A program analysis tool that assists in the test data generation problem would provide a capability to identify structurally feasible paths of interest and perform some of the computations needed in the analysis of that path to determine its potential as a possible actual test path. This is the kind of semi-automated assistance provided by the RXVP system, as well as several others. More sophisticated advice functions are based on analysis of the collections of paths that are "close" to the desired (or initially supplied) one(s). In such systems, the user is made aware of fairly general conditions that must be met in order for test data to be possible. For example, this is done in the NASA ATDG system. A different kind of advice is provided when the hierarchical decomposition of the program is portrayed for a user in terms of the program predicates and relations between them. Still another form of analysis that is useful is a system that tells when paths are logically infeasible.

Symbolic Testing. Symbolic testing systems are a rather recent innovation that combine that feature of path analysis and a limited form of program interpretation. Instead of dealing with actual input values, a symbolic testing system acts on the formulas that result from considering the tree of possible program flows that begin at the invocation point in a program. The tree is pruned as much as possible; that is, infeasible paths are removed as soon as they are discovered to be infeasible. In this way the growth of the tree is kept within reasonable limits and the system can handle practical-sized programs.

There is a close relationship between the operation of a symbolic testing system and a program prover: symbolic analyses simulate "execution" of a program path that has rather thoroughly-known properties. It is expected that symbolic testing techniques will grow in importance in future years, potentially to a point where they form the main tool supporting the program testing activity.

Planning and Management Issues

Introduction. Once the basic features of a program testing discipline are understood it is necessary to devise methods of planning and measurement that are appropriate to the specific testing methods chosen, and are technically sound and economically viable. The general objective of measurement techniques is to provide, for both management and technical personnel, essential information needed to monitor testing progress. The planning function is closely linked with the measurement process because good planning fully depends on knowledge of the current state of an activity.

The most important feature of a measure is its level of applicability. Good measures of testing indicate unambiguous quantities that reflect true testing accomplishment. It is possible to define a hierarchy of increasingly strong measures of testing coverage that can be applied, as appropriate, throughout the testing process. Planning during the testing process is equally important, both from the technical point of view (how well the tests are designed) and from the procedural point of view (how efficiently does the test strategy work). Apart from the systematic methodology chosen, it is still important to be able to plan tests that accomplish the stated objectives efficiently and effectively.

One technique of importance is the use of structured testing, a process by which tests are organized in a hierarchical fashion that follows the functional bounds implied by the requirements imposed on the software system.

Finally, it is important to be aware of the possible use of various kinds of complexity measures. Briefly, a complexity measure is intended to relate the "weight" of a software system's individual components in a way that makes it possible to assign the greater emphasis to the "heaviest" (i.e., most difficult to test) elements.

General Principles. Testing is a qualitative process that has quantitative attributes. A typical testing situation involves making tests on parts of a complex software system and then, based on the outcomes of that part of the task, choosing "next testing targets/goals" in a way that attempts to reach the end of the process as soon as possible (and as economically as possible).

The purpose of a testing coverage measure is to relate the execution-time activity within a program to the amount of activity that represents completion of the testing. The set of testing measures discussed below represents a range of practical measures of testing coverage. The underlying principle for measurement is to establish appropriate measures early in the testing process, and then abide by them (and their implications) throughout.

The testing coverage measure chosen can have an important effect on the test planning process: good knowledge of the current state of the activity and the cost to arrive at the state can make it much simpler to choose the "right" alternative. Because testing is a complex process, being able to make the right decision affects the cost and time the entire process is going to take.

Test structuring methods can be used to assist in organizing the test series. Basically, test structuring refers to a variety of methods that organize the tests made according to a hierarchical interpretation of the system requirements.

Coverage Measures. Current testing techniques are based primarily in various levels of structural analysis of programs, and it is natural that measures of testing coverage would arise from the relationship between tests and the structural elements of programs that the tests exercise. The most common measure is the C_1 measure, which requires that every segment in a program be exercised at least once. The C_1 measure corresponds with the notion that a program is not well tested unless every decisional outcome has been exercised at least once. A slightly stronger version is the C_1p measure, which requires, in addition to the C_1 level of coverage, that every predicate term be evaluated at least once to each possible truth value. For example, if the program predicate were A .AND. B the C_1p measure would require that *both* A and B be taken to the true and false outcomes (by comparison, C_1 requires only that the whole predicate A .AND. B be taken to the true and false outcomes).

At the next level of sophistication there is a class of coverage measures that relate to the checks made of the iterations within a program. The C_k measure requires that every iteration be exercised up to and including k repetitions of the loop; typically, k is set to 2. C_k implies C_1.

Another measure of practical interest is the C_d measure, which requires that each *dependent pair* of program segments be executed together in at least one test. This measure is stronger than C_1; provided that the means are available to find the dependent pairs, C_d can be quite an effective determinant of program quality.

There are several other testing measures which are important only for special testing circumstances. The ultimate measure of program testedness—to have executed a program for all possible different input circumstances—is of theoretical importance only since it is impossible to accomplish this in practice.

Presenting the current values of achieved testing coverage is ordinarily done by giving the individual values for modules in a tabular format that lists all the modules in the software system being tested. It is also important, when the measured coverages are close to 100 percent, to have the capability to show the parts of programs which are keeping the value from attaining the 100 percent maximum. This allows the program tester to concentrate on constructing tests that bring the coverage to 100 percent.

Test Structuring. A test of a program has a definite beginning and ending; during the test the program acts on the input data and produces the outputs (results) that it is designed to produce. A test may involve several modules at a time and each actual execution (run) may involve a series of tests. It is important to keep track of the boundaries of tests as part of the process of developing detailed relationships between tests and the programs being tested.

Test structuring is the process of organizing series of tests in a rational manner, so that the testing activity runs smoothly and efficiently. Tests can be organized in serial, inclusive, or mixed order. In a serial set of tests there is no overlap between functions tested; in inclusive tests part of the functional test of a sub-component is included in some larger test. Mixed tests involve combinations of these two. What determines the boundaries between tests is simply the method used to interpret the testing coverage information: this can be done either by controlling the execution trace (from an execution verifier tool) separately, or by incorporating special "test boundary" markers within the test sequence.

The notion of having a test include a subtest is important because it permits developing functional behavior information about the included test either independently or relative to the including test. For example, if a major function of a software system can be interpreted as a vector $A = (a_1, a_2, \ldots a_n)$ then a major test of A might involve a sequence of subtests of the a_i individually. Concentrating on organizations of test sequences that follow the hierarchical nature of the software system generally will result in less complex test data, and will provide more efficient testing (in the sense that a smaller number of actual tests will be required).

Tree-based techniques for test design are a mixed-mode type of test structuring. Decomposition relationships that describe the function of the software system are exploited directly in the design of tests that generally have excellent coverage properties. This notion is the basis of "structured testing."

Complexity Measures. Although generally acknowledged that it will never be possible to characterize the complexity of a software system in terms of its functional properties, because there are technical difficulties from the theory of effective computability, it is often quite valuable to have a means to assign relative "weights" to different parts of a software system. This would be useful, for example, when deciding between two alternative next steps in the overall testing strategy. It is intuitively clear that the greater testing effort should be mounted against the more complex parts of a software system; those are the places where design and/or programming errors are most likely to occur.

Measuring the complexity of individual modules is a topic that recently has gained significant interest. The work of Halstead (and others, notably Kolence) has suggested a strong relationship between such factors as error rates and execution time requirements and the general complexity of a program. These methods can be used directly to assess the relative complexity of individual programs, or of major components in complex software systems. The Halstead weight of a program is computed from a formula that involves the total number of operators and operands in the program. This weight is a static-based computation, since it does not take into account any of the possible effects of program iteration.

One method, developed by McCabe, computes the cyclomatic number of a control-flow graph as the basis for a complexity measure. The cyclomatic number is (number of edges)—(number of nodes) + 2* (number of separate components). McCabe has shown that the cyclomatic number is an accurate descriptor of, among other things, the degree to which a program is "well structured."

Another technique of complexity measurement assigns weights for individual segments that approximate the expected (relative) execution time for the segment, and then multiplys the segment weights by a value proportionate to the number of times the segment would be executed in an "average" program invocation. This leads to a module weighting that correlates complexity with running time. Still another method is to assign weights based on the use of variables in the context of the control-flow graph structure. This method emphasizes the data use patterns of the software system. Other complexity measures that have been tried include evaluation of the complexity of the hierarchical decomposition tree, possibly weighted by the segment complexity, and approximations inferred from data collected during the program executions.

Management Control of Testing. Management and control of the program testing process is vested in techniques of monitoring the current status of testing, of assessing the economics of various alternative testing, methodologies and strategies, and in minimizing future work by assuring that sufficient records are kept.

The economics of testing is a difficult subject to investigate, primarily because so very little is actually known about the separate costs of individual phases in the software life-cycle, but also because testing is so seldom performed in a rigorously controlled fashion. There is genuine reticence on the part of many organizations to release detailed data about software costs; this possibly is prompted by the unparalleled recent increase of software related costs.

Recent studies have indicated that for long lifetime software systems the costs of testing can be as much as 50 percent of the life-cycle total cost. By comparison, only about 2 percent or less is actually spent in the conceptual phase, during which the majority of design and specification decisions are made.

Management monitoring of the testing process should indicate clearly at the outset the importance of a wide spectrum of information that relates either directly or indirectly to testing progress. The simplest method is to ask testing personnel to share access to daily test progress reports—the same reports they would be using to plan next actions and to assess progress. There are other forms of documentation that are more important for the indications of progress they give than they are for their technical content; for example, monitoring the number of modules tested as a function of time may serve only as a very weak indicator of the effective progress (nearness to completion) of the testing activity.

Testing is a labor-intensive activity, and the choice of personnel can be of crucial importance. As studies begin to be reported, it is becoming increasingly clear that a somewhat different mix of talents contributes to success as a program tester than would make, say, a senior programmer. Thus the choice of a testing team can be an important ingredient in success.

Besides personnel costs, management can monitor testing progress indirectly by keeping close track on the computer resource devoted to testing activities. Studies have shown that there is a high correlation between turnaround time and the speed with which programs complete their testing phases; hence it is also a good idea to afford a reasonably high priority to the testing team in terms of access to machine resources.

Coverage measures and complexity measures are also effective tools for management, particularly at the level of assessing the level of testing that will be required or for determining the budget allocations needed to effectively complete a testing activity that is mid-way to completion. Current thinking in the applications community appears to suggest application of some relatively simple formulas that apportion the budget (for planning purposes) between conceptualization, design, implementation, and testing. Assuming that the design activity does not include any test design work, it is a good rule of thumb to allocate the same amount of effort for program testing as is applied to the combined design and implementation tasks. (Certainly, current budgets are quite short of this goal.)

Management must also be sensitive to the psychological interplay between program testers and program developers: in the simplest interpretation these two groups are at loggerheads all the time! It is ordinarily quite difficult for an accomplished software designer to accept the constructive criticism that an accomplished tester's normal activities would produce. Consideration should be given to having an independent test activity/function which is somewhat isolated from developing (and designing) teams. Besides providing a free kind of communication, the independent test and evaluation group has the possible advantage of economy of scale, particularly when program test tools must be either developed or procured from a vendor.

Archiving processes are poorly understood in contemporary program testing technology, but the principle that can be applied is a simple one: if it may be used again it is probably worth saving against that possibility. In many cases good tests are quite difficult (and therefore quite expensive) to develop, and the archiving costs are relatively small. Therefore, it is important to consider applying configuration management methods to the test process, to assure that information essential later during the program maintenance phase will be available.

Most maintenance activities involve relatively small changes to the software system, but very often these changes have rather broad implications and/or effect within the system. As much as possible it is a good technique to retest only those portions of a software system that are known to be affected by a change. It is possible that automated techniques would be used to assist in determining the span of effect for proposed changes. At the same time it would be possible to identify (possibly automatically also) the particular set of tests that would have to be re-executed.

Research and Development

Research and development activities in program testing can be divided into three areas: Methodology, Automated Tools, and Theory of Testing.

The goal of the theory of testing is to provide comprehensive technical investigations of the underlying principles of testing, and to indicate the way in which those principles can be applied to problems that arise during the testing process. Workable techniques follow closely on theoretical developments, which tend to simply point out the possibility that a particular kind of notion could be effective in particular kinds of situations.

Some of the currently known objectives for research and development in the theory of testing include the following:

- Further extension of the theory of reliable testing, possibly to include wider classes of programs and/or error classes that permit reliable tests.
- Detailed investigations into the methods that are most effective for structuring tests, and for understanding the processes involved in relating the effects of tests to one another.
- Methods for specifying the testing of system interfaces.
- Further development of automated test data generators, including the extension of known techniques to problems of the most widely known programming languages.
- Symbolic evaluation system development, particularly in the area of developing heuristic techniques that permit certain complex computations to proceed without human intervention.
- Techniques that can be applied to software that has special properties such as cooperating processes, real-time systems, etc.

Naturally it may also happen that theoretical developments which are not now considered even possible will become the cental avenues for future research and development.

To a large extent theoretical development precedes development of automated program testing support facilities. Most program testing tools that are currently considered are either already reduced to practice, or are implemented without technical risk using known techniques. The major areas of developments in automated tools would appear to be the following ones:

- Symbolic execution/evaluation systems, which process source text programs of arbitrary size and complexity and may form the basis for near-proof of programs.
- Assertion based systems, which support processing of ancillary information about expected program behavior stated as assertions about the program's state.
- Generalized program analyzers that are portable and extensible, and which would form the basis for general program testing facilities for wide varieties of programming languages and host environments.
- Automated production systems, which would permit rapid and accurate production of programs according to hierarchical and structured programming techniques.
- Test pattern processors which would make it possible to state the major features of good program tests within the source text and as part of the programming process, and which would simplify processing of tests during the formal testing stage.

These developments would be made in a context of utility in automated tool design that includes two additional important points: (1) there must be careful attention paid to the user interface (currently one of the weakest areas in automated tools), and (2) there must be highly automated archiving and record-keeping (record-making) facilities.

Given a sound theoretical basis and an adequate set of automated tools, research and development activities can then concentrate on methodologies that apply the known techniques in a rational and effective manner. This area would include the collection of experience on prior projects that has impact both on the design of effective methodologies and on the cost/benefit effectiveness of the overall program testing process.

It would seem that the methodological developments will focus on refinement of presently known methodologies, based on further research as well as codification of insights based on experience. As techniques are found to be effective it is important to incorporate them in the "standard" methodologies; it is equally important, of course, to eliminate techniques that have diminished effectiveness.

Section 2: Theoretical Foundations

Paper Summaries

J. B. Goodenough and S. L. Gerhart, "Toward a Theory of Test Data Selection," *IEEE Transactions on Software Engineering,* June 1975 (pp. 156-173).

This paper—the first published paper which attempted to provide a theoretical foundation for testing—contains what the authors call the "fundamental theorem of testing." The theorem characterizes the properties of a completely effective test selection strategy. A test selection strategy is completely effective if it is guaranteed to discover any error in a program.

In addition to the theoretical material, the paper contains two examples of programs containing errors. It summarizes the effectiveness of branch and path testing in discovering the error and proposes an alternative method involving the use of decision tables. The decision table method can be thought of as a mixture of requirements and design-based functional testing.

W. E. Howden, "Reliability of the Path Analysis Testing Strategy," *IEEE Transactions on Software Engineering,* September 1976 (pp. 208-215).

In the path testing approach to test selection, test data is selected so that each path through a program is traversed at least once. In practice, only a subset of the possibly infinite set of program paths can be tested. Studies of the reliability of path testing are interesting because they provide an upper bound on the reliability of strategies that call for the testing of a subset of a program's paths.

This paper begins by showing that it is not possible to construct a testing strategy that is guaranteed to discover all errors in a program. This is proved by using results from computability theory. It then goes on to characterize three commonly occurring classes of errors: computations, domain, and subcase. Properties that each of these classes of errors must have in order to guarantee that they will be discovered by path testing are defined. The definitions for the classes of errors and the reliability properties associated with the errors resulted from a study of the errors which are described in the "Common Blunders" section of Kernighan and Plauger's *The Elements of Programming Style.*

L. J. White and E. I. Cohen, "A Domain Strategy for Computer Program Testing," *IEEE Transactions on Software Engineering,"* May 1980 (pp. 247-257).

A *domain error* is one in which the subset of a program's input domain which causes a program path to be followed is incorrect; i.e., some of the input values in that subset should result in the execution of other paths. Domain errors can be caused by incorrect predicates in branching statements or by incorrect computations that affect variables in branch statement predicates.

White and Cohen's paper describes a set of constraints under which it is possible to reliably detect domain errors. Perhaps the strongest constraint is that no *coincidental correctness* should occur. This means that any two paths which have "adjacent domains" compute different output for different input.

The domain strategy involves the selection of test points that lie on and "just off" the boundaries of the subsets of the input domains associated with program paths. The paper develops the idea for linearly bounded domains. Linearly bounded domains are associated with program paths along which all branch predicates are linear in their variables.

The practical limitations of the approach are discussed, of which the most severe is that of generating and then developing test points for all boundary segments of all domains of all program paths. Several suggestions are included on possible ways to alleviate the path explosion problem. At the time of the paper's publication, a domain testing system was under construction.

The paper has been included in the theory section of the book because it provides useful insight into why testing succeeds or fails and indicates directions for continued research, both theoretical and engineering.

E. J. Weyuker and T. J. Ostrand, "Theories of Program Testing and the Application of Revealing Subdomains," *IEEE Transactions on Software Engineering,* May 1980 (pp. 236-246).

In their paper "Toward a Theory of Test Data Selection," Goodenough and Gerhart propose definitions for the reliability and validity of a test-selection criterion. Weyuker and Ostrand point out that the definitions provide insight into the testing process but do not indicate how a programmer is to find such test data. In addition, the authors discuss other problems with the definitions, such as their lack of independence (all test-selection criteria are either reliable or valid). They propose a notion of the reliability of a test-selection criterion that focuses on revealing subsets of the input domain which have the property that if a program works incorrectly for one element of the subset, it works incorrectly for all elements of the subset.

The approach to finding revealing subsets combines path testing, black box testing, and error analysis. The user starts by constructing path domains (subsets of the input domain that cause individual program paths to be followed). The intersection is taken of these subsets with domain subsets in the specifications over which the program is supposed to "do the same thing." Finally, the user takes each subset produced by this intersection and further refines it by considering the different classes of errors which could occur for that subset. The basic idea in this last step is to find subdomains that are revealing for particular errors, i.e., are guaranteed to reveal such errors if the errors exist. The strength of the paper lies in its emphasis on finding good testing subsets and on its discussion of the shortcomings of the Goodenough and Gerhart definitions.

Several possible areas in the suggested approach invite further research. The first is the familiar path-explosion problem. Most programs have too many paths to allow consideration of the domain for each path. There is no obvious systematic way of dealing with this problem except to group together paths which "intuitively" do the same thing. A second problem has to do with the selection of subdomains that are revealing for particular errors. No comprehensive systematic way for constructing tests that reveal well known classes of errors has been worked out. The paper gives several examples in which intuitively appealing subsets of the input domain are identified but no general procedure for finding the subsets is suggested. The overall strategy described in the paper is useful, but programmers should not expect a cookbook of revealing test selection formulae: programmers must ultimately depend on their informal understanding of the computational structure of their programs and the nature of the errors that could appear in such programs.

W. E. Howden, "Completeness Criteria for Testing Elementary Program Functions," *Proceedings, Fifth International Conference on Software Engineering,* March 1981 (pp. 235-243).

The functions implemented by a program range in complexity from the function implemented by the program as a whole to much simpler functions implemented by individual program statements. This paper describes a type of completeness which is stronger than branch testing and which is defined in terms of the types of errors that commonly occur in the elementary functions implemented by program statements.

A set of tests T is *reliable* for a function F implemented by a program or part of a program, if it can be used to distinguish F from other functions; i.e., $F = F'$ on T if and only if F and F' are identical functions. Reliability can be defined relative to a class of functions $\mathfrak{F}$: a test T is *reliable* for a function F in $\mathfrak{F}$, *relative to* $\mathfrak{F}$, if it can be used to distinguish F from other functions in $\mathfrak{F}$.

A set of tests T is *complete* for a program, relative to some testing criterion, if the set satisfies that criterion. Ideally the criterion would force the set to be reliable. In practice, this idea is difficult or impossible to achieve, and weaker kinds of completeness are used in program testing. A complete set of branch tests, for example, causes every branch in a program to be executed at least once.

Suppose that f is a function associated with a program statement s and that F is the set of all corresponding functions associated with statements s′ that differ from s by some programming error. For example, if s is a conditional branching statement and f is the function that computes the Boolean expression in s, then F may contain all functions which are computed by expressions that differ from the Boolean in s in a logical operator. It is easy to construct reliable test sets for classes F such as this. In the testing strategy proposed in the paper, a set of tests T for a program is complete if it results in the testing of elementary statement level functions over reliable sets of test data. The definition of completeness depends on the elementary functions that are identified as being implemented by program statements. It also depends on the classes F associated with each elementary statement level function.

The approach in the paper bears certain similarities to mutation testing. Classes of functions F are defined as they are in mutation testing: functions implemented by code which differs from the given code by a "mutation transformation." Unlike mutation testing, this approach requires the reliable testing of elementary functions rather than the reliable testing of the program function.

S. L. Hantler and J. C. King, "An Introduction to Proving the Correctness of Programs," *ACM Computing Surveys,* September 1976 (pp. 331-353).

This reprint was selected from various surveys of proof of correctness techniques because it is relatively recent and it fully explains the relationship between proofs of correctness and symbolic evaluation. It is included in the theoretical foundations section for two reasons: proofs of correctness are considered to be theoretical approaches to validation rather than empirical or pragmatic, and testing can be considered as the initial step in an inductive proof—the part of the proof where the first few cases are proved before the induction takes place. In this sense, testing is closely related to and built on the foundation of correctness proving. Proofs of correctness can be thought of as static analysis validation methods, so this paper could also have been included in the section on static analysis.

Toward a Theory of Test Data Selection

JOHN B. GOODENOUGH AND SUSAN L. GERHART

Abstract—This paper examines the theoretical and practical role of testing in software development. We prove a fundamental theorem showing that properly structured tests are capable of demonstrating the absence of errors in a program. The theorem's proof hinges on our definition of test reliability and validity, but its practical utility hinges on being able to show when a test is actually reliable. We explain what makes tests unreliable (for example, we show by example why testing all program statements, predicates, or paths is not usually sufficient to insure test reliability), and we outline a possible approach to developing reliable tests. We also show how the analysis required to define reliable tests can help in checking a program's design and specifications as well as in preventing and detecting implementation errors.

Index Terms—Proofs of correctness, testing.

I. INTRODUCTION

THE purpose of this paper is to survey the purpose and limitation of testing as presently conceived; to demonstrate a systematic procedure for developing valid and reliable test data; and to establish a view of the purposes and limitations of testing that will permit testing methods to be systematically improved. In the remainder of this Introduction we define some basic concepts relevant to software testing and lay the basis for a theory of test data selection. In Section II, we discuss two examples of programs published in the literature which contain errors. Our purpose there is to illustrate the problems a theory of testing must deal with. In Section III, we examine what others have said about the goals, methods, and difficulties of program testing before turning attention to our proposed method, which we present in Section IV. In Section V we apply our theoretical concepts to the results of Section IV.

The fundamental questions examined throughout this paper are: What are the possible sources of failure in a program? What test data should be selected to demonstrate that failures do not arise from these sources?

A. Fundamental Testing Concepts

The purpose of testing is to determine whether a program contains any errors. An *ideal* test, therefore, succeeds only when a program contains no errors. In this paper, one of our goals is to define the characteristics of an ideal test

in a way that gives insight into problems of testing. We begin with some basic definitions.

Consider a program F whose input domain is the set of data D. $F(d)$ denotes the result of executing F with input $d \in D$. $\text{OUT}(d,F(d))$ specifies the output requirement for F, i.e., $\text{OUT}(d,F(d))$ is true if and only if $F(d)$ is an acceptable result. We will write $\text{OK}(d)$ as an abbreviation for $\text{OUT}(d,F(d))$. Let T be a subset of D. T constitutes an ideal test if $\text{OK}(t)$ for all $t \in T$ implies $\text{OK}(d)$ for all $d \in D$, i.e., if from successful execution of a sample of the input domain we can conclude the program contains no errors, then the sample constitutes an ideal test. Clearly the validity of this conclusion depends on how "thoroughly" T exercises F. Most papers on testing (e.g., Poole [13], Stucki and Svegel [16]) equate a thorough test with one that is *exhaustive*, i.e., one for which $T = D$. But such a definition gives no insight into problems of test data selection. Instead, we define a "thorough" test, T, to be one satisfying COMPLETE(T,C), where COMPLETE is a predicate that defines, in effect, how some data selection criterion, C, is used in selecting a particular set of test data T. C defines what properties of a program must be exercised to constitute a "thorough" test, i.e., one whose successful execution implies no errors in a tested program. COMPLETE ensures that T satisfies all these properties. (We will discuss later, in Section V, the pragmatic reasons for using an incomplete test.)

The data selection criterion C must be defined so tests satisfying COMPLETE(T,C) produce consistent and meaningful results. We express this requirement by saying C must be *reliable* and *valid*. In general, reliability refers to the *consistency* with which results are produced, regardless of whether the results are meaningful. In particular, a data selection criterion is reliable if and only if every T satisfying COMPLETE(T,C) is processed successfully by F, or if every such T is unsuccessfully processed (see Fig. 1). In short, to be reliable C must insure selection of tests that are consistent in their ability to *reveal* errors, as opposed to necessarily being able to detect *all* errors. Note that if C is reliable, it is only necessary to test one complete set of test data—no further information will be derived from testing other complete sets of test data.

Validity, in contrast to reliability, customarily refers to the *ability* to produce meaningful results, regardless of how consistently such results are produced. Hence a test data selection criterion is valid to the extent it does not forbid selection of test data capable of revealing some error. C is valid if and only if for every error in a program there exists a complete set of test data capable of revealing the error (see Fig. 1 for a formal definition).

Manuscript received February 1, 1975. This work was supported in part by the U. S. Army, Frankford Arsenal, under Contract DAAA25-74-C0469.
J. B. Goodenough is with SofTech, Inc., Waltham, Mass. 02154.
S. L. Gerhart was with SofTech, Inc., Waltham, Mass. 02154. She is now with the Department of Computer Science, Duke University, Durham, N. C. 27706.

Given a program F, with domain D, output requirement OK(d) = OUT(d, F(d)) and test data selection criterion C:

(1) SUCCESSFUL(T) ≡ (∀t ∈ T) OK(t)
(2) RELIABLE(C) ≡ (∀T$_1$, T$_2$ ⊆ D)(COMPLETE(T$_1$, C) ∧ COMPLETE(T$_2$, C) ⊃ (SUCCESSFUL(T$_1$) ≡ SUCCESSFUL(T$_2$)))
(3) VALID(C) ≡ (∀d ∈ D)(¬OK(d) ⊃ (∃T ⊆ D)(COMPLETE(T, C) ∧ ¬SUCCESSFUL(T)))

<u>Fundamental Theorem</u>

(∃T ⊆ D)(∃C)(COMPLETE(T, C) ∧ RELIABLE(C) ∧ VALID(C) ∧ SUCCESSFUL(T)) ⊃ (∀d ∈ D) OK(d)

Fig. 1. Formal definitions and the fundamental theorem of testing.

But note: validity does not imply that every complete test is necessarily capable of detecting every error in a program. This is the case only if the data selection criterion is reliable as well as valid. Validity only implies it is possible to select data that will reveal an error; it does not guarantee that such data will be selected.

The formal definitions of RELIABLE and VALID given in Fig. 1 merely state precisely what we already have said informally about RELIABLE(C) and VALID(C). To show the utility of the definitions, we use them in stating and proving the fundamental theorem on which all testing is based (see Fig. 1). Its proof is simple:

Assume there exists some $d \in D$ for which F fails (i.e., ¬OK(d)). Then VALID(C) implies there exists a complete set of test data, T, that is not successful. RELIABLE(C) implies that if one complete test fails, all fail. But this contradicts the theorem's premise, i.e., that there exists a complete test that is successfully executed. Q.E.D.

The theorem is called "basic" not because it is deep—obviously we have constructed our definitions of RELIABLE, VALID, and COMPLETE to permit the theorem to be proven. Instead the theorem is basic because of the insight it gives into the concepts of test reliability and validity, and these concepts are basic to the construction of "thorough" tests. The theorem merely demonstrates that tests satisfying COMPLETE(T,C) where C satisfies RELIABLE and VALID are "thorough" in the appropriate sense. Note that proving a data selection criterion to be reliable and valid, and then finding and successfully executing a complete test satisfying this criterion is just a way of proving the correctness of the program. In effect, the theorem states that in some cases, a test *is* a proof of correctness.

The proof of a selection criterion's validity and reliability is easy in some cases. For example, if C is defined so the only complete test is an exhaustive one, i.e., if COMPLETE(T,C) ⊃ ($T = D$), then C obviously satisfies RELIABLE and VALID. Another interesting example is when C is unsatisfiable by any $d \in D$. Then T will be empty, i.e., no testing will be done. In this case, such a C clearly satisfies RELIABLE(C). Proof of C's validity, however, is more difficult. In fact, such a proof exists if and only if the program contains no errors. Hence in this case, proof of C's validity is equivalent to a direct proof of the program's correctness.

A proof of validity is trivial, however, if C does not exclude any member of D from some set of test data, i.e., if it can be shown that for all $d \in D$, there exists a T containing d and satisfying COMPLETE(T,C). In this case, some testing must be performed, and in general, the proof of C's reliability is not trivial. The remainder of this paper will concentrate on what must be known about programs to insure reliability in this case, and in Section V we will give some guidelines for finding nontrivial reliable test data selection criteria. Also in Section V, we will give a specific example of a type of data selection criterion and its corresponding definitions of COMPLETE, RELIABLE, and VALID. But to motivate this example, we first need to look at sources of errors in programs, both in general (Section I-B) and with reference to example programs (Section II).

B. Types of Program Errors

In general, software errors can be classed as performance errors (failure to produce results within specified or desired time and space limitations) and logic errors (production of incorrect results independent of the time and space required). It is useful to distinguish the following various types of logic errors:

construction errors (failure to satisfy a specification through error in an implementation);

specification errors (failure to write a specification that correctly represents a design);

design errors (failure to satisfy an understood requirement); and

requirements errors (failure to satisfy the real requirement).

Thorough tests must be able to detect errors arising for any of these reasons, and this means that test data selection criteria must reflect information derived from each stage of software development. Ultimately, however, each type of logic error is manifested as an improper effect produced by an implementation, and for this reason, it is useful to categorize sources of errors in implementation terms.

Missing Control Flow Paths: This type of error arises from failure to test a particular condition, and hence result in the execution (or nonexecution) of inappropriate actions. For example, failure to test for a zero divisor before executing a division may be a missing path error. Other examples will be given later. This type of error results from failing to see that some condition or combination of conditions requires a *unique* sequence of actions to be handled properly. When a program contains this type of error, it may be possible to execute *all* control flow paths through the program without detecting the error. This is why exercising all program paths does not constitute a reliable test.

Inappropriate Path Selection: This type of error occurs when a condition is expressed incorrectly, and therefore, an action is sometimes performed (or omitted) under inappropriate conditions. For example, writing IF A instead of IF A AND B means that when A is true and B false, an inappropriate action will be taken or omitted. When a program contains this type of error, it is quite possible to exercise all statements and all branch conditions without detecting the error. This error can also occur not merely through failure to test the right combination of conditions, but through failure to see that the method of test is not adequate, e.g., testing for the equality of three numbers by writing $(X + Y + Z)/3 = X$.

Inappropriate or Missing Action: Examples are calculating a value using a method that does not necessarily give the correct result (e.g., $W * W$ instead of $W + W$), or failing to assign a value to a variable, or calling a function or procedure with the wrong argument list. Some of these errors are revealed when the action is executed under any circumstances. Requiring all statements in a program to be executed will catch such errors. But sometimes, the action is incorrect only under certain combinations of conditions; in this case, merely exercising the action (or the part of the program where a missing action should appear) will not necessarily reveal the error. For example, this is the case if $W * W$ is written instead of $W + W$.

This classification of errors is useful because our goal is to detect errors by constructing appropriate tests. Other classifications are useful for other purposes, e.g., to understand the effect of a programming language on software reliability (Rubey *et al.* [14]), or to understand *why* errors occur (Boehm *et al.* [2]). But insight into test reliability is given by the proposed classification. For example, consider the test data selection criterion, "choose data to exercise all statements and branch conditions in an implementation." In evaluating the reliability of this criterion, we would ask, "Will all construction, specification, design, and requirements errors always be detected by exercising programs with data satisfying this criterion?" Clearly if a design error, for example, is manifested as a missing path in an implementation, then this criterion for test data selection will not be reliable. So our typology of implementation errors is useful to help understand factors impairing test reliability.

II. EXAMPLES OF PROGRAM ERRORS

In this section we will discuss errors in two programs that have appeared in the published literature to illustrate the kinds of problems testing must deal with and to lay the groundwork for our proposed testing methodology.

```
            bufpos := 0;
            outcharacter(LF);
            fill := 0;
    next character:
            incharacter(CW);
            if CW = BLANK ∨ CW = LF
            then begin
                if fill + 1 + bufpos ≤ MAXPOS
                then begin
                    outcharacter(BLANK);
                    fill := fill + 1  end
                else begin
                    outcharacter(LF);
                    fill := 0  end;
                for k := 1 step 1 until bufpos do
                    outcharacter(buffer [k]);
                fill := fill + bufpos;
                bufpos := 0;    end
            else
                if bufpos = MAXPOS
                then Alarm
                else begin
                    bufpos := bufpos + 1;
                    buffer [bufpos] := CW  end;
            go to next character;
```

Fig. 2. Naur's original program.

A. *Example 1: A Simple Text Reformatter*

In the article "Programming by Action Clusters," P. Naur [10] presents the following problem. "Given a text consisting of words separated by BLANKs or by NL (new line) characters, convert it to a line-by-line form in accordance with the following rules: 1) line breaks must be made only where the given text has BLANK or NL; 2) each line is filled as far as possible as long as 3) no line will contain more than MAXPOS characters." Naur's purpose is, in part, to justify an approach to algorithm construction "on the basis of General Snapshots needed to prove the algorithm." He does not intend to present a formal proof, but he does present "prescriptions" (assertions) and uses them to guide and justify the construction of action clusters in a top-down manner. So here we have a published article which attempts to use the top-down design method and the guidance of program proving, but the program (see Fig. 2) turns out to have at least seven problems.

N1) The program does not terminate when the end of the given text is reached, although Naur provides for termination (through the undefined language construct "Alarm") if a word containing more than MAXPOS characters (an *oversize* word) is seen. (Note that in this case the specification cannot be satisfied.) Nontermination on end of text will, of course, be discovered with any test data not containing an oversize word. The effect of processing an oversize word, however, would only be seen if test data contained such a word. A reliable test methodology will insure that oversize words are presented to the program (even though they are not mentioned in the specification), since such data are not excluded from the program's input domain and the program will not necessarily process oversize words correctly if it processes shorter words correctly.

N2) The last word in the text will not be output unless it is followed by a BLANK or NL.

N3) A blank will appear before the first word on the first line except when the first word is exactly MAXPOS characters long. This can cause a violation of constraint

2) for the first line. The reason for this error is clear. After creating action clusters for a word buffer, Naur makes the following assertion: "The input character preceding the one held in buffer [1] was a BLANK or NL. This has not been output" [10, p. 252]. This assertion is false for the first word and is never disproven. Thus a boundary type of case (first character, first word) causes a proof error. Of course this error will be found for any test data whose first word is less than MAXPOS characters long.

N4) When the first word is MAXPOS characters long, it will be preceded by two line breaks in the output, even though an empty line violates constraint 2).

N5) No provision is made for processing successive adjacent breaks (e.g., two blanks). This error arises because a word is defined as the characters (other than NL or BLANK) appearing between successive NL or BLANK characters, and words of zero length are simply not considered in any discussion of the program's assertions. Specification 2) requires as many words as possible on a line, and this specification makes no sense if zero-length words are permitted. So an important case has not been considered in either the program, the input description, or the program's informal proof. Naur's suggested test data for this program appear to maintain this implicit assumption about the form of the input (i.e., no consecutive BLANKS or NL characters) and so do not reveal the error. How can this sort of error be discovered through a systematic approach to testing?

N6) If the first word of the input text is preceded by a BL or NL, the output will contain either two blanks preceding the first word or a line containing just two blanks, violating constraint 2).

N7) The specifications use NL as the new line character but the program uses LF. This error probably arises from failure to proofread, but could also be traced to a failure to specify the character set of the problem. If LF and NL are distinct characters, then any input text containing an NL or LF character will reveal the problem.

What can we conclude from this example?

1) Top-down construction and very informal proofs do not always prevent program errors. Nor does the reading of the description of the program guarantee that errors will be caught. Presumably this paper went through some review process and was proofread, yet the errors persisted. The reviewer in *Computing Reviews* (Review 19 420) mentioned only the gratuitous blank preceding the first word (error N3). London [9] corrected errors N1, N3, N4, and N7 but not errors N2, N5, and N6, even though he "proves" his version of the program correct.

2) If this program had been coded and run on some test data, such as that used to illustrate the program output [10, p. 251], errors N1–N3, and N7 would have been detected. Errors N4–N6 would not have been revealed.

Since we wish to use this example to illustrate other types of possible errors and then again in Section IV to illustrate a general method for selecting test data, we will clean up the specifications and program.

Given an input text having the following properties:

I1) It is a stream of characters, where the characters are classified as break and nonbreak characters. A break character is a BL (blank), NL (new line indicator), or ET (end-of-text indicator).
I2) The final character in the text is ET.
I3) A *word* is a nonempty sequence of nonbreak characters.
I4) A *break* is a sequence of one or more break characters.

(Thus the input can be viewed as a sequence of words separated by breaks with possibly leading and trailing breaks, and ending with ET.)

The program's output should be the same sequence of words as in the input with the following properties.

O1) A new line should start only between words and at the beginning of the output text, if any.
O2) A break in the input is reduced to a single break character in the output.
O3) As many words as possible should be placed on each line (i.e., between successive NL characters).
O4) No line may contain more than MAXPOS characters (words and BL's).
O5) An oversize word (i.e., a word containing more than MAXPOS characters) should cause an error exit from the program (i.e., a variable Alarm should have the value TRUE).

The corrected version of Naur's program appears in Fig. 3. First let us look at the corrections for errors N1–N7.

N1), N2) The endless loop constructed with a GOTO in Naur's program has been replaced with a repeat-until having Alarm as a Boolean variable and ET as an end-of-text indicator.

N3) The condition fill ≠ 0 has been conjoined with the condition fill + bufpos < MAXPOS to prevent the output of a BL before the first word and to produce an NL instead. The condition fill ≠ 0 holds only for the first line, since every other line will contain at least one word. Equally well, we could have initialized fill to the value MAXPOS, insuring that fill + bufpos < MAXPOS would be false the first time.

N4) Line 2 of Naur's program, outcharacter (NL), is removed so that only one NL character will precede the first word of the output text.

N5), N6) An extra predicate, bufpos ≠ 0, prevents output when two consecutive breaks occur; the first break forces the word to be output and bufpos to be reset to zero. Note that breaks preceding the first word of the text will also be ignored.

N7) LF was systematically changed to NL throughout the program.

Note how sometimes several error symptoms are cor-

```
 1    Alarm := false;
 2    bufpos := 0;
 3    fill := 0;
 4    repeat
 5        incharacter(CW);
 6        if CW = BL ∨ CW = NL ∨ CW = ET
 7        then
 8            if bufpos ≠ 0
 9            then begin
10                if fill + bufpos < MAXPOS ∧ fill ≠ 0
11                then begin
12                    outcharacter(BL);
13                    fill := fill + 1; end
14                else begin
15                    outcharacter(NL);
16                    fill := 0   end;
17                for k := 1 step 1 until bufpos do
18                    outcharacter(buffer[k]);
19                fill := fill + bufpos;
20                bufpos := 0   end
21        else
22            if bufpos = MAXPOS
23            then Alarm := true;
24            else begin
25                bufpos := bufpos + 1;
26                buffer[bufpos] := CW   end
27    until Alarm ∨ CW = ET;
```

Fig. 3. Corrected version of Naur's program.

rected with a single program modification; it is often not clear whether the number of errors in a program should be measured by the number of corrections needed to produce a correct program, or by the number of symptoms discovered.

We will now use this program to show how testing based solely on knowledge of a program's internal structure cannot lead to reliable tests. To make our discussion more readily understandable and to lay the groundwork for further discussion in Section IV, we first cast the corrected program into the form of a limited-entry decision table (King [8], Pooch [12]) (see Table I). All predicates of the program are written in the condition stub and all assignment and input-output statements in the action stub. The relevant outcomes of the predicates are represented as Y, N, (Y), (N), or —, where (Y) means the outcome is necessarily true, (N) means the outcome is necessarily false, and — means the outcome can be either true or false. A rule is a single column in the table and specifies a sequence of actions to be performed for a particular condition combination, i.e., a particular set of outcomes of the predicates. For some rules, the outcomes of certain predicates imply that the outcomes of other predicates are either determined (and so of no interest) or are irrelevant. For example, when C4 is true, C6 is necessarily false, and so in rule 1, C6 need not be tested. Predicates whose outcomes are represented as (Y), (N), or — are not actually evaluated in the program represented by the decision table. For example, the table shows that when C1 is Y, conditions C2 and C6 are not evaluated (see King [8]).

The fact that the conditions specified in the condition stub are not all independent is represented by the *condition constraints* given at the right side of the table; it is there, for example, that the relation between the truth of C4 and the falsity of C6 is asserted. The predicates associated with the action stubs (e.g., $(C1 \lor C2) \land C3$) indicate under what conditions the associated action is to be performed. Specifying these conditions is not necessary, but provides useful redundancy in checking the correctness of a table.

The decision table format makes it easier to see how various sets of test data satisfy various test data selection criteria. Below the program are written four sets of test data. Each set assumes MAXPOS = 3 and meets some test data selection criterion based on the program's structure. D1 exercises all statements (by exercising rules 3, 5, 9, and 10). D2 all statements and composite predicates, and D3 all statements and individual predicates.[1] D3 also exercises all loop iteration paths, i.e., all paths through a loop that are possible on some iteration of the loop; by exercising all individual predicates as well, D3 ensures that all loop exiting conditions are also tested. D4 exercises all rules of the table. Note that exercising all rules is equivalent to exercising each statement under all condition combinations considered relevant by the writer of the program. Table II shows more clearly what combination of rules need to be exercised to satisfy the various test data selection criteria as well as how the data actually satisfy the criteria. For example, this table shows that the composite predicate C4 ∧ C5 (i.e., fill + bufpos < MAXPOS ∧ fill ≠ 0) is true for any data exercising rules 1 and 5 and false for any data exercising rules 2, 3, 6 or 7. For data exercising any other rule, the value of this composite predicate is irrelevant. The actual test data exercise rules 1 and 3.

We wish to show that none of these exercising criteria are completely reliable, i.e., it is possible to exercise a program containing an error using any of these criteria without necessarily discovering the error. This shows that tests based solely on a program's internal structure are unreliable; their success is poor evidence that a program contains no errors.

---

[1] An individual predicate is considered to be exercised when it is necessarily evaluated for some data and it takes on both true and false values. For example, data satisfying rules 1–4 are not considered to exercise C2 because C2 need not be evaluated. C2 is exercised by data satisfying one of rules 5–8 and either rule 9 or rule 10.

TABLE I
Decision Table Representation of Program and Test Data

		1	2	3	4	5	6	7	8	9	10	
C1:	CW = BL ∨ CW = NL	Y	Y	Y	Y	N	N	N	N	N	N	C1 ⊃ ¬C2
C2:	CW = ET	(N)	(N)	(N)	(N)	Y	Y	Y	Y	N	N	C2 ⊃ ¬C1
C3:	bufpos ≠ 0	Y	Y	Y	Y	Y	Y	N	(Y)	-	-	¬C3 ⊃ ¬C6
C4:	fill + bufpos < MAXPOS	Y	Y	N	-	Y	Y	N	-	(N)	-	C4 ⊃ ¬C6; ¬C4 ⊃ (C3 ∨ C5)
C5:	fill ≠ 0	Y	N	-	-	Y	N	-	-	-	-	¬C3 ∧ ¬C5 ⊃ ¬C4; ¬C5 ∧ C6 ⊃ ¬C4
C6:	bufpos = MAXPOS	(N)	(N)	-	(N)	(N)	(N)	-	(N)	Y	N	C6 ⊃ C3; C6 ⊃ ¬C4
A1 a:	outcharacter (BL)	X			X							(C1 ∨ C2) ∧ C3 ∧ C4 ∧ C5 ∧ ¬C6
b:	fill := fill + 1	X			X							
A2 a:	outcharacter (NL)		X	X		X	X					(C1 ∨ C2) ∧ C3 ∧ (¬C4 ∨ ¬C5)
b:	fill := 0		X	X		X	X					
A3 a:	for k := 1 until bufpos outcharacter (buffer [k])	X	X	X		X	X	X				(C1 ∨ C2) ∧ C3
b:	fill := fill + bufpos	X	X	X		X	X	X				
c:	bufpos := 0	X	X	X		X	X	X				
A4:	Alarm := TRUE									X		¬C1 ∧ ¬C2 ∧ C6
A5 a:	bufpos := bufpos + 1										X	¬C1 ∧ ¬C2 ∧ ¬C6
b:	buffer [bufpos] := CW										X	
A6 a:	incharacter (CW)	X	X	X	X					X		C1 ∨ (¬C1 ∧ ¬C2 ∧ C6)
b:	Repeat table	X	X	X	X					X		
A7:	Exit table					X	X	X	X	X		C2 ∨ (¬C1 ∧ C6)

Test Data		Rule Exercised	Rule Sequence Exercised
D1.1	A, A, A, A, ET	9, 10	10, 10, 10, 9
D1.2	A, A, A, BL, B, BL, C, ET	3, 5, 10	10, 10, 10, 3, 10, 3, 10, 5
D2.1	A, A, A, A, ET	9, 10	10, 10, 10, 9
D2.2	A, A, A, BL, B, BL, C, NL, ET	1 (NL), 3 (BL), 8, 10	10, 10, 10, 3, 10, 3, 10, 1, 8
D3.1	A, A, A, A, ET	9, 10	10, 10, 10, 9
D3.2	A, BL, B, NL, C, NL, ET	1 (NL), 2 (BL), 3 (NL), 8, 10	10, 2, 10, 1, 10, 3, 8
D4.1	A, A, A, A, ET	9, 10	10, 10, 10, 9
D4.2	A, BL, BL, B, BL, C, NL, ET	1 (BL), 2 (BL), 3 (NL), 4 (BL), 8, 10	10, 2, 4, 10, 1, 10, 3, 8
D4.3	A, ET	6, 10	10, 6
D4.4	A, BL, B, ET	2, 5, 10	10, 2, 10, 5
D4.5	A, BL, B, NL, C, BL, D, D, D, ET	1 (NL), 2 (BL), 3 (BL), 7, 10	10, 2, 10, 1, 10, 3, 10, 10, 10, 7

TABLE II
Rules Exercised to Satisfy Various Completeness Criteria

1. Composite Predicates

Composite Predicates	Rules To Be Exercised		Rules Exercised By D2		Rules Exercised By D1	
	TRUE	FALSE	TRUE	FALSE	TRUE	FALSE
C1 ∨ C2	(1-8)	(9, 10)	1, 3	9, 10	3	9, 10
Alarm ∨ C2	(5-9)	(1-4, 10)	8, 9	1, 3, 10	5, 9	10
C3	(1-3, 5-7)	(4, 8)	1, 3	8	3, 5	8
C4 ∧ C5	(1, 5)	(2, 3, 6, 7)	1	3	5	3
C6	(9)	(10)	9	10	9	10

2. Individual Predicates

Individual Predicates	Rules To Be Exercised		Rules Exercised By D3		Rules Exercised By D2	
	TRUE	FALSE	TRUE	FALSE	TRUE	FALSE
C1$_{BL}$	(1-4)	(1-10)	1, 2	3, 8, 9, 10	1	3, 8, 9, 10
C1$_{NL}$	(1-4)	(5-10)	3	8, 9, 10	3	8, 9, 10
C2	(5-8)	(9, 10)	8	9, 10	8	9, 10
C3	(1-3, 5-7)	(4, 8)	1, 2, 3	8	1, 3	8
C4	(1, 2, 5, 6)	(3, 7)	1, 2	3	1	3
C5	(1, 5)	(2, 6)	1	2	1	
C6	(9)	(10)	9	10	9	10
Alarm	(9)	(10)	9	10	9	10

3. Loop Iteration Paths

Distinct Paths	Rules Exercised By D3
(1, 5)	1
(2, 3, 6, 7)	2, 3
(4, 8)	8
(9)	9
(10)	10

TABLE III
EFFECT OF ERRORS

Error in Program	Error Type	Effect on Table
1. Change fill + bufpos < MAXPOS to fill + bufpos ≤ MAXPOS	inappropriate path selection	Condition C4 changed similarly.
2. Omit line 13 fill := fill + 1	missing action	No mark on Action A1b.
3. Omit bufpos ≠ 0 test (line 8) (This is Naur's error N5, 6.)	missing path	Condition C3 line will be removed and therefore rules 4 and 8 can be dropped.
4. Omit fill ≠ 0 from line 10 (This is Naur's error N3.)	inappropriate path selection	Condition C5 removed from table. Rules 2 and 6 are eliminated, being subsumed under rules 1 and 5.
5. Omit CW = ET from line 6	inappropriate path selection	Rules 5-8 eliminated and rule 9 is modified. See Table 4.

Five examples of errors are summarized in Table III. The errors can be characterized as follows.

1) *An incorrect predicate* (fill + bufpos ≤ MAXPOS instead of fill + bufpos < MAXPOS) causing rules 1 or 5 to be selected under circumstances where rules 3 or 7 should have been selected. This is an inappropriate path selection type of construction error. It will not be detected by any of the four test data sets. To show this error, the loop must be executed with fill + bufpos = MAXPOS *and* fill ≠ 0. This requires at least MAXPOS + 2 iterations of the loop and the word lengths must be just right. Although this is an "off-by-one" type of error, not just any data such that fill + bufpos = MAXPOS will reveal it, e.g., D1.2 and D2.2 do not do so.

2) *A missing action* (fill := fill + 1) yielding essentially the same effect as error 1 when there are only two words on a line. This error also will not be detected by any of the four test data sets.

3) *A missing predicate* (bufpos ≠ 0) yielding a missing path type of error that would not be detected with the D1 data set. (This is one of Naur's errors.) Although the other data sets would detect this error, different data sets can be constructed that will not detect the error and yet will satisfy the various exercising criteria for the erroneous program. For example, D1 as it stands would exercise all statements and composite predicates in the modified program (see Table II with C3 eliminated). Also, test D4.2 could then be eliminated and the other D4 data would then be sufficient to exercise all rules, interior loop paths, and individual predicates without revealing the error.

4) *A missing predicate* (fill ≠ 0) causing an inappropriate path selection. (This is also one of Naur's errors.) Alternatively, this error could be characterized as an inappropriate action (namely, fill := 0 in line 3 should be replaced with fill := MAXPOS). This error is easily detected by any data whose first word is less than MAXPOS characters long. Note that D1 and D2 do not detect this error precisely because the first word is exactly MAXPOS characters long. In fact, data set D2 exercises all individual predicates, interior-loop paths, and statements in the erroneous program without showing this error. It is also readily possible to devise data to exercise all rules in a decision table representation of the erroneous program without revealing the error.

5) *A missing predicate* (CW = ET in line 6) causing inappropriate path selection. This is essentially error N2. This error will not be found by D2 or D3. It also is not necessarily found by data exercising all rules in the decision table representing the altered program (see for example, Table IV; data D4.1 and D4.2 exercise all the rules in this table without revealing an error). This error shows that even when all conditions relevant to the correct operation of a program appear explicitly in the program, test data selection criteria based solely on a program's internal structure will not necessarily guarantee tests that will reveal the error.

This analysis of five possible errors shows the unreliability of test data selected merely to exercise all statements, composite predicates, individual predicates, loop iteration paths, or rules in a program's decision table representation. These examples of errors show the following.

1) To detect errors reliably, it is in general necessary to execute a *statement* under more than one combination of conditions to verify that its effect is appropriate under all circumstances. Exercising any statement just once is usually inadequate.

2) Equally well, the same *path* through a loop will usually have to be exercised more than once before the right combination of conditions is found to reveal a missing path or inappropriate path selection error. For example, error 5 (see Table III) requires exercising rule 8' of Table IV with bufpos ≠ 0 to show the error. This path should also be exercised with bufpos = 0 to guard against some other error, e.g., error 3, even though bufpos's value is not even tested when executing rule 8'.

In short, a reliable test is designed not so much to

TABLE IV
Decision Table Representation of Program Containing Error 5

		1	2	3	4	5	6	7	8'	9'	10	
C1:	CW = BL ∨ CW = NL	Y	Y	Y	Y				N	N	N	C1 ⊃ ¬C2
C2:	CW = ET	(N)	(N)	(N)	(N)				Y	–	N	C2 ⊃ ¬C1
C3:	bufpos ≠ 0	Y	Y	Y	N				–	(Y)	–	¬C3 ⊃ ¬C6
C4:	fill + bufpos < MAXPOS	Y	Y	N	–				–	(N)	–	C4 ⊃ ¬C6; ¬C4 ⊃ (C3 ∨ C5)
C5:	fill ≠ 0	Y	N	–	–				–	–	–	¬C3 ∧ ¬C5 ⊃ C4; C3 ⊃ C6 ⊃ ¬C4
C6:	bufpos = MAXPOS	(N)	(N)	(N)	–					Y	N	C6 ⊃ C3; C6 ⊃ ¬C4
A1 a:	outcharacter (BL)	X										C1 ∧ C3 ∧ C4 ∧ C5 ∧ ¬C6
b:	fill := fill + 1	X										
A2 a:	outcharacter (NL)		X	X								C1 ∧ C3 ∧ (¬C4 ∨ ¬C5)
b:	fill := 0		X	X								
A3 a:	for k := 1 until bufpos outcharacter (buffer [k])	X	X	X								C1 ∧ C3
b:	fill := fill + bufpos	X	X	X								
c:	bufpos := 0	X	X	X								
A4:	Alarm := TRUE								X			¬C1 ∧ C6
A5 a:	bufpos := bufpos + 1									X		¬C1 ∧ ¬C6
b:	buffer [bufpos] := CW									X		
A6 a:	incharacter (CW)	X	X	X	X					X		C1 ∨ (¬C6 ∧ ¬C2)
b:	Repeat table	X	X	X	X					X		
A7:	Exit table								X		X	C2 ∨ (¬C1 ∧ C6)

exercise program *paths* as to exercise *paths under circumstances such that an error is detectable if one exists.* Tests based *solely* on the internal structure of a program are likely to be unreliable.

To find data that reliably reveal errors like those illustrated here, all the conditions relevant to the correct operation of a program must be known and test data must be devised to exercise *all possible combinations of these conditions*, whether or not the program's internal structure indicates certain condition combinations cause different sequences of actions to be performed. For example, Tables I and IV actually represent 27 distinct rules if all DON'T CARE conditions are written out explicitly as different rules (see Table V). Test data required to exercise all 27 rules *will* detect error 5 because this error in effect combines rules 12, 13, 21, and 22 to form rule 9' and rules 10, 11, 14–18 to form rule 8'. If for errors 3 and 4, conditions C5 and C3 are retained in Table V even though they are not tested in the program, test data to detect these errors will necessarily be generated if all 27 condition combinations are exercised. Errors 1 and 2 will be found if the condition fill + bufpos = MAXPOS is added to the table. Data to exercise this condition in combination with all the others will necessarily reveal errors 1 and 2. (This condition adds only six rules to Table V because it is not independent of the other conditions.)

In short, the secret of reliable testing is to find all conditions relevant to a program's correct operation and to exercise all possible combinations of these conditions. In Section IV, we will illustrate how relevant conditions can be discovered.

B. Example 2: An Exam Scheduler

This program is presented by Hoare in Dahl *et al.* [4] as an example of the use of various abstract data structures and an informal proof of correctness.

The problem is to construct a timetable for university examinations such that the following apply.

1) The number of sessions is kept small, although no absolute minimum is stipulated.
2) Each exam is scheduled for one session.
3) No exam is scheduled for more than one session.
4) No session involves more than K exams.
5) No session involves more than h students.
6) No student takes more than one exam in a session.

The solution proposed by Hoare tries all combinations of unscheduled exams that satisfy 2)–6) and selects the combination that maximizes h.

The specifications and assertions, except 1), are precisely and formally stated such that a formal proof could be performed. However, an error creeps in related to 1). It is impossible to state 1) precisely since there is no way to predetermine the number of sessions, so it is assumed that the solution method will do the best it can. The error arises from a variable "remaining" which is to contain all those exams which do not appear in the table so far, i.e., unscheduled exams. The error is manifested in two ways.

1) *Performance:* Exactly 500 exams are always processed even if there are fewer than 500 exams to be scheduled. Since the program is recursive and searches all combinations of unscheduled exams, the performance will be degraded by processing "empty exams" (exams for which no student is registered).

2) *Violation of constraints:* Empty exams still have to be scheduled in some session, so it is possible that the limitation implicit in 1) could be violated unnecessarily. That is, the program as it stands may be unable to produce a solution where it should if empty exams were not processed.

This error is easy to correct by initializing "remaining" to include only those exams for which at least one student has registered.

This error is very different from those of Example 1 and is important for the following reasons.

1) This program would be very hard to understand

TABLE V
ALL FEASIBLE RULES IMPLIED BY TABLE I

		1	2	3	4	5	6	7	8	9	10	11	12	13	14	15	16	17	18	19	20	21	22	23	24	25	26	27	
C1:	CW = BL ∨ CW = NL	Y	Y	Y	Y	Y	Y	Y	Y	Y	Y	N	N	N	N	N	N	N	N	N	N	N	N	N	N	N	N	N	$C1 \supset \neg C2$
C2:	CW = ET	(N)	(N)	(N)	(N)	(N)	(N)	(N)	(N)	(N)	(N)	N	N	N	N	N	N	Y	Y	Y	Y	Y	(Y)	Y	Y	Y	Y	N	$C2 \supset \neg C1$
C3:	bufpos ≠ 0	Y	Y	(Y)	(Y)	Y	Y	(N)	(N)	N	Y	Y	(Y)	(Y)	Y	Y	N	Y	(Y)	N	Y	(Y)	(Y)	Y	Y	N	N	N	$\neg C3 \supset \neg C6$
C4:	fill + bufpos < MAXPOS	Y	(N)	(Y)	(N)	N	N	(Y)	(N)	N	Y	(Y)	(N)	(N)	N	N	N	(Y)	(Y)	N	Y	Y	(N)	N	N	N	N	(Y)	$C4 \supset \neg C6; \neg C4 \supset (C3 \lor C5)$
C5:	fill ≠ 0	Y	N	N	Y	Y	N	Y	(Y)	N	N	Y	(N)	(N)	Y	N	N	Y	N	Y	Y	N	(Y)	N	N	N	N	N	$\neg C3 \supset \neg C5; \neg C5 \supset C4; \neg C5 \land C6 \supset \neg C4$
C6:	bufpos = MAXPOS	(N)	(N)	(N)	(N)	N	Y	(N)	(Y)	(N)	(N)	(N)	(Y)	(N)	N	Y	N	(N)	(N)	N	N	Y	(N)	Y	Y	Y	(Y)	(N)	$C6 \supset C3; C6 \supset \neg C4$
	Table 1 Rule Numbers	1	2	3	3	3	3	4	4	4	5	6	7	7	7	7	8	8	8	10	10	9	9	10	10	10	10	10	
A1 a:	outcharacter (BL)	X									X																		$(C1 \lor C2) \land C3 \land C4 \land C5 \land \neg C6$
b:	fill := fill + 1	X									X																		
A2 a:	outcharacter (NL)			X	X	X	X					X	X	X	X	X													$(C1 \lor C2) \land C3 \land (\neg C4 \lor \neg C5)$
b:	fill := 0			X	X	X	X					X	X	X	X	X													
A3 a:	for k := 1 until bufpos outcharacter (buffer [k])			X	X	X	X	X	X	X		X	X	X	X	X													$(C1 \lor C2) \land C3$
b:	fill := fill + bufpos			X	X	X	X	X	X	X		X	X	X	X	X													
c:	bufpos := 0			X	X	X	X	X	X	X		X	X	X	X	X													
A4:	Alarm := TRUE																X	X	X	X	X			X	X	X	X		$\neg C1 \land \neg C2 \land C6$
A5 a:	bufpos := bufpos + 1																			X	X	X	X	X	X	X	X		$\neg C1 \land \neg C2 \land \neg C6$
b:	buffer [bufpos] := CW																			X	X	X	X	X	X	X	X		
A6 a:	incharacter (CW)	X	X	X	X	X	X	X	X		X	X	X	X	X	X	X	X	X	X	X	X		X	X	X	X		$\neg C2 \land (C1 \lor \neg C6)$
b:	Repeat table	X	X	X	X	X	X	X	X		X	X	X	X	X	X	X	X	X	X	X	X		X	X	X	X		
A7:	Exit table									X													X					X	$C2 \lor (\neg C1 \land C6)$

Rules Exercised

Test Data																													Rule Sequence Exercised
DX.1	A,A,A,A,ET																						X					X	27, 20, 20, 22
D1.2	A,A,A,BL,B,BL,C,ET				X	X	X				X										X		X			X		X	27, 20, 20, 5, 25, 6, 25, 10
D2.2	A,A,A,BL,B,BL,C,NL,ET			X	X	X	X				X										X		X		Y	X		X	27, 20, 20, 5, 25, 6, 25, 1, 17
D3.2	A,BL,B,NL,C,NL,ET	X					X	X									X	X								X		X	27, 2, 25, 1, 26, 6, 16
D4.2	A,BL,BL,B,BL,C,NL,ET	X	X				X	X				X					X									X	X	X	27, 2, 7, 25, 1, 26, 6, 16
D4.3	A,ET		X																									X	27, 11
D4.4	A,BL,B,ET	X	X										X													X	X	X	27, 2, 25, 10
D4.5	A,BL,B,NL,C,BL,D,D,D,ET	X	X				X					X							X						X	X	X	X	27, 2, 25, 1, 26, 6, 25, 19, 24, 12

and to test thoroughly without some sort of an informal proof to guarantee that all combinations are properly handled. But the proof only considers assertions 2)–6) and ignores 1) because it can not be formalized. The error then arises because 1) is not checked out informally even if it can not be formally stated and proven. Even formally specifiable necessary conditions for 1) to be satisfied are not proven, e.g., that no session schedules an empty exam. This error shows the danger of concentrating on the difficult parts of a program and the formalized specifications to the exclusion of the easier parts.

2) This program is similar to many other programs where the correct answer can not be formally characterized and where it would be difficult to even determine whether the produced timetable has the fewest number of sessions.

Assuming no proof existed or as confirmation of the proof, what type of test data should be selected? What criteria for test data can hope to yield a reliable test of this program? Our proposed approach is not yet sufficiently powerful to answer these questions. We cite this example to show the difficulties that must be resolved by a complete theory of test data selection as well as to show that these difficulties challenge even a proof of correctness approach to software reliability.

III. VIEWS ON TESTING

Having discussed some fundamental definitions in the testing area and examined examples of the problems to be solved by an approach to testing, we will now look at what others have said about the goals, methods, and difficulties of program testing before turning our attention to our proposed method.

A. "Exhaustive" Testing

"Software certification...ideally...means checking all possible logical paths through a program." (Boehm [1])

"Exhaustive testing, i.e., testing all possible (input)..." (Poole [13, p. 310])

Exhaustive testing, defined either in terms of program paths or a program's input domain (although these definitions are not equivalent),[2] is usually cited as the impractical means of achieving a reliable and valid test. The importance of the cited statements is in the questions which arise from them.

Is there a way to test a program which is equivalent to exhaustive testing (in the sense of being reliable and valid)?

Is there a practical approximation to exhaustive testing?

If so, how good is the approximation?

---

[2] Exhaustive testing of paths will not necessarily find all errors. For example, both paths in the following program can be tested without necessarily revealing the error:

```
IF (X + Y + Z)/3 = X.
   THEN PRINT ("X, Y, and Z are equal in value");
   ELSE PRINT ("X, Y, and Z are not equal in value").
```

It should be noted that exhaustive testing of a program's input domain is a process not necessarily guaranteed to terminate. There are some programs whose behavior (e.g., whether they stop) is impossible to verify by testing or any other means and some programs have infinite input domains, so exhaustive testing can never be completed.

Although some programs cannot be exhaustively tested, a basic hypothesis for the reliability and validity of testing is that the input domain of a program can be partitioned into a finite number of equivalence classes such that a test of a representative of each class will, by induction, test the entire class, and hence, the equivalent of exhaustive testing of the input domain can be performed. If such tests all terminate and if the partitioning is appropriate, a completely reliable test of the program will have been performed. This is not, of course, a novel idea. Hoare (in Buxton and Randell [3, p. 21]) has pointed out that the essence of testing is to establish the base proposition of an inductive proof (we pursue this idea further in Section V). This pinpoints the fundamental problem of testing— the inference from the success of one set of test data that others will also succeed, and that the success of one test data set is equivalent to successfully completing an exhaustive test of a program's input domain.

B. Is Proving Really Better Than Testing?

"Program testing can be used to show the presence of bugs, but never to show their absence!" (in Dahl et al. [4, p. 6])

"[When] you have given the proof of [a program's] correctness,...[you] can dispense with testing altogether." (in Naur and Randell [11, p. 51])

Just because testing is not a completely reliable means of demonstrating program correctness does not mean it is sensible to rely solely on proofs. Proofs are not completely reliable either. Proofs can only provide assurance of correctness if all the following are true.

1) There is a complete axiomatization of the entire running environment of the program—all language, operating system, and hardware processors.
2) The processors are proved consistent with the axiomatization.
3) The program is completely and formally implemented in such a way that a proof can be performed or checked mechanically.
4) The specifications are correct in that if every program in the system is correct with respect to its specifications, then the entire system performs as desired.

These requirements are far beyond the state of the art of program specification and mechanical theorem proving, and we must be satisfied in practice with informal specifications, axiomatizations, and proofs. Then problems arise when proofs have errors, specifications are incomplete, ambiguous, or unformalizable (as in Example 2), and systems are not axiomatizable. The two examples already discussed have clearly shown that an incomplete attempt at a program proof does not assure a program will not fail. These examples are very realistic in terms of the state of the art of program proving for real programs.

Despite the practical fallibility of proving, attempts at proof are nonetheless valuable. They can reveal errors and assist in their prevention. Furthermore, programs cannot be proven unless they can be understood. Facilitating provability sets a worthy standard for good languages, program structure, specifications, and documentation, and thereby assists in preventing errors.

In short, neither proofs nor tests can, in practice, provide complete assurance that programs will not fail. Even so, attempts to prove programs, like attempts to test them completely, are essential to the development of usable programs. Tests have the advantage of providing accurate information about a program's actual behavior in its actual environment; a proof is limited to conclusions about behavior in a postulated environment. Both have an essential role in program development, though each is a fallible technique. Testing and proving are *complementary* methods for decreasing the likelihood of program failure.

What testing lacks (and what this paper is attempting to provide a start towards) is a theoretically sound (but practical) definition of what constitutes an adequate test. When our understanding of what makes an adequate test is as good as our understanding of what makes an adequate proof, testing can assume its proper role in the theory and practice of software development.

C. The Effect of Testing Considerations on Program Development

"Testing must be planned for throughout the entire design and coding process." (Hetzel [6, p. 18])

Testing must not only be planned for, it is in fact performed in one way or another at every stage of the programming process, not just when a program has been completed. Specifications must be tested against examples to see if they are complete, consistent, and unambiguous; programs are desk checked by informally considering what will happen when certain kinds of data are processed; a proof must partition data into cases that affect the validity of assertions differently. Testing, in the sense of identifying distinguishable cases and evaluating their effect on the programming requirement, specifications, code, or a proof, occurs in every phase of programming. Moreover, the need to test affects the process of program construction in various ways.

1) Testing being inevitable, it is good practice to identify testing needs, e.g., weak or critical links in a system, early in program design (e.g., see Brinch Hansen [7]).

2) Programs should be structured so logical testing of various abstractions of the program can reduce actual testing of the final program.
3) Specifications must be precise enough to be testable.
4) The need to get special information just to verify the successful execution of a test run affects program design, (e.g., testing an operating system scheduler requires access to information not ordinarily available).

Improved understanding of the nature of testing will help in developing and performing tests at all stages in the program development process.

D. Conclusions

There is a general concept which unifies all the activities involved in demonstrating that a program does not fail. That concept is *case* analysis. Case analysis occurs in the following.

1) *Design and specification*, where it is necessary to exclude cases of data where the program is not expected to operate or to identify cases in the input or output which require special treatment. In Example 1, these would include successive break characters and termination characters, and in Example 2 the empty exam.

2) *Program construction*, where the solution to the problem dictates that certain cases require special treatment and other cases can be lumped together. These are illustrated in Example 1 where the predicates bufpos $\neq 0$ and fill $\neq 0$ form paths which treat successive break characters and the first word on the first line, respectively, and in Example 2 where the empty exam must be filtered out of the exams to be processed.

3) *Program proving*, where assertions must be made about special cases or generalized to cover several cases and where proofs break into cases. Example 1 shows an assertion which must have a case which covers the first word as well as the case that covers all nonfirst words, and Example 2 shows that the assertion which is not formalized must be checked out in a different manner from the more formalized assertions.

4) *Testing*, where it must be demonstrated that the total of all cases involved in program specification, design, construction, and proof have been correctly and completely handled. Ideally, the cases created during design specification, construction, and proof should be an adequate basis for test data selection, although the cases may need further analysis and combination in order to obtain a reasonably sized and still effective set of test data.

There is a great need for more examples to make vague testing concepts (e.g., "boundary" condition) at least more intuitively clear and for theories of test data selection which try to analyze the facts about testing in relation to each other for the purpose of guiding the selection of test data toward greater effectiveness. Section IV will illustrate a technique for selecting test data and Section

V will analyze this technique in terms of the theory sketched in Section I.

IV. DEVELOPING EFFECTIVE PROGRAM TESTS

Our goal is to define how to select test data for a particular program such that if the program processes all test data correctly, we can be reasonably confident the program will process *all* data correctly. For this to be possible, the test data must cover all errors in the program being tested, i.e., test data selection criteria must ensure that data revealing any errors will be selected.

Our approach to testing (and indeed, any approach) is based on assumptions about how program errors occur. Our approach assumes errors are primarily due to 1) inadequate understanding of all conditions a program must deal with, and 2) failure to realize that certain combinations of conditions require special treatment. We distinguish the following:

Test data, the actual values from a program's input domain that collectively satisfy some test data selection criterion.

Test predicates, a description of conditions and combinations of conditions relevant to the program's correct operation.

In short, test predicates describe what aspects of a program are to be tested; test data cause these aspects to be tested.

Our purpose in this section of the paper is 1) to illustrate the problems and issues faced in developing reliable and valid tests for a particular program so that later, in Section V, when we discuss formal criteria for reliability and validity, examples illustrating the formal criteria will be at hand; and 2) to show informally, what may, with further research, become a practical approach to defining reliable tests.

A. An Overview of the Method

There are several sources of information about the conditions and combinations of conditions relevant to a program's operation:

the general requirement a program is to satisfy;

the program's specification;

general characteristics of the implementation method used, including special conditions relevant to data structures and how data are represented; and the specific internal structure of an actual implementation.

None of these sources of information is by itself sufficient for generating a reliable test. Information from all these sources must be used to insure all combinations of conditions are identified.

Our technique for developing and describing test predicates is derived from decision table techniques, and will be called the *condition table* method. A condition table looks like the top half of a decision table. Each column in a condition table is a logically possible combination of conditions that can occur when executing the program being described. Each column is our representation of a test predicate. The basic idea is to identify conditions describing some aspect of the problem or program to be tested, and then build condition tables for groups of conditions. Sometimes separate condition tables are combined into a single table; when to combine tables and when to leave them separate is an important issue needing further study.

B. Deriving Test Cases from Specifications

A program's specifications are an important source of test predicates because data satisfying such predicates are able to detect missing path and inappropriate path selection construction errors. Such data can also detect design and specification errors, as we shall see. We will use Naur's specifications for Example 1 to illustrate test case development from specifications. Then, using knowledge of an actual implementation (either that shown in Fig. 2 or Fig. 3), we will show how to eliminate some test predicates without impairing test reliability. (It may also happen that some test predicates will have to be added when information about an actual implementation becomes available, but this does not occur here.)

The first part of Naur's specification states: 1) "Given a text, consisting of words separated by BLANK's or NL (new line) characters,..." This clause attempts to describe the program's input domain. We begin to develop a condition table by looking for conditions relevant to the input domain that are also relevant to the processing required by the specification, i.e., we try to extract conditions from the specification that we, as programmers, would consider relevant to deciding when it is appropriate to perform certain actions. For example, if we think in terms of scanning the input text character by character, then it is possible and reasonable to describe the input in terms of the character currently being scanned and the one immediately preceding it. This approach gives rise to the condition table shown in Table VI. The notation there shows that the values of PrevChar (condition C1) and CurChar (condition C2) constitute conditions relevant to the program's correct operation. In particular, the possible values for C1 and C2 are partitioned into three subsets, the value BL (for BLANK), the value NL, and all other character values, Ot. Any condition may, of course, be undefined (represented in the table by a question mark), and so there are four possibilities to be considered for each condition, yielding 16 predicates in all.

The next step is to check if all these predicates can be satisfied. Clearly the current or previous character may have an undefined value. C2 is undefined when the end of the text is found. C1 is undefined when the current character is the first character in the text. Predicate 16

TABLE VI
First Condition Table for Input Domain

	1	2	3	4	5	6	7	8	9	10	11	12	13	14	15	16
C1: PrevChar[BL, NL, Ot]	BL	BL	BL	BL	NL	NL	NL	NL	Ot	Ot	Ot	Ot	?	?	?	?
C2: CurChar[BL, NL, Ot]	BL	NL	Ot	?	BL	NL	Ot	?	BL	NL	Ot	?	BL	NL	Ot	?

TABLE VII
Revised Condition Table for Input Domain

	1	2	3	4	5	6	7	8	9	10	11	12	13	14	15	16	17	18	19	20	21	22	23	24	25	26	27	28	29	30	31	32
C1: PrevChar[BL, NL, Ot]	BL	BL	BL	BL	BL	BL	BL	BL	BL	BL	BL	BL	NL	NL	NL	NL	NL	NL	NL	NL	NL	NL	NL	NL	Ot	Ot	Ot	Ot	?	?	?	?
C2: CurChar[BL, NL, Ot, ET]	BL	BL	NL	NL	Ot	Ot	Ot	Ot	ET	ET	ET	ET	BL	BL	NL	NL	Ot	Ot	Ot	Ot	ET	ET	ET	ET	BL	NL	Ot	ET	BL	NL	Ot	ET
C3: First Word?	Y	N	Y	N	Y	Y	N	N	Y	Y	N	N	Y	N	Y	N	Y	Y	N	N	Y	Y	N	N	(Y)	(Y)	(Y)	(Y)	(N)	(N)	(N)	(N)
C4: Break length[1, >1]	?	?	?	?	1	>1	1	>1	1	>1	1	>1	?	?	?	?	1	>1	1	>1	1	>1	1	>1	?	?	?	?	?	?	?	?

Constraints between conditions
C2(BL) ∨ C2(NL) ⊃ C4(?)
C1(Ot) ⊃ C3
C1(?) ⊃ ¬C3

therefore is satisfied by an empty text. To make this interpretation of undefined values clearer, in later condition tables we will redefine the value set for CurChar to include the pseudo-character ET, designating end-of-text, and not permit C2 to be undefined.

Looking further at predicates 1 and 2, we immediately see an ambiguity in the specification. It is not clear whether words are separated by a *single* BLANK or NL character, or whether several such break characters are permitted. If only one is permitted, then predicates 1, 2, 5, and 6 are not satisfiable. Also, if breaks are not permitted after the last word in the text or before the first word, then predicates 4, 8, 13, and 14 can be eliminated as unsatisfiable. Permitting all these predicates to be satisfied seems the most reasonable approach since it provides more flexibility for dealing with various types of input media (e.g., cards or paper tape) and this interpretation subsumes the more restricted case of single break characters, so we adopt it. Of course, the ambiguity should be checked with the specification writer, since our reasoning for permitting data satisfying these predicates may not be valid in the context of the actual use of the program. It can be seen here how preparation of a condition table is a natural way to check a specification for completeness and lack of ambiguity, as well as for identifying characteristics of test data that should be presented to the program during the test phase.

Next we need to check the test predicates for reliability, i.e., if we select data to cover each predicate, will we be forced to select data capable of revealing all errors in an implementation? To answer this question, we must decide whether any conditions relevant to the correct operation of the program are missing from the table and whether value sets have been partitioned appropriately. We must also decide whether the test predicates are *independent*, i.e., whether the sequence in which test predicates are exercised when processing test data is potentially significant to the correctness of the program. For example, we can see that data chosen to exercise all the predicates in Table VI will have to include data where words are separated by at least two break characters, but all predicates can be exercised without necessarily having exactly one break character between any words.[3] Is the occurrence of a break of length one significant to the correct operation of a program? If a program correctly processes text containing breaks of length two or greater, will it necessarily correctly process text containing breaks of length one? What about breaks of length one and two preceding the first word in the text or following the last word? From experience, we know that errors involving all these sorts of conditions are quite possible, so we will add conditions to force selection of data that check these error possibilities.

To distinguish breaks before the first word, we add a condition "First Word?", which is false until one Ot character is seen and then true. To ensure that test data contain breaks of length 1, the condition "Break length" is added; its values refer to the length of a break preceding ET or Ot. Table VII results; note the conditions are not all independent. When C1 is undefined, C3 is false, etc. Constraints between conditions are indicated below the condition table.

Are the test predicates sufficiently independent now?

---
[3] For example, if predicate 9 is exercised followed by predicate 3, a break of length one has been processed, but if the sequence is 9,1,3, then the break is two characters long. So length of breaks is represented as a particular sequence of predicates being executed.

Do some sequences of test predicates execution correspond to special predicates that should be included? It can be seen that data consisting of at most one word would suffice to exercise all the test predicates. Equally well, all test data could consist of texts containing more than one word. It is highly unlikely that a program will process words correctly for texts several words long but not for texts one word long, or vice versa, although such a program could of course be specially written. We will be content, for now, with noting that the number of words in an input text might be a significant condition for some programs; later when an implementation is available we can decide whether the number of words in the text is a condition for which an error may exist; if so, the condition table can be modified to insure that this aspect of the program is thoroughly tested.

Test predicates can be eliminated (i.e., their exercising made unnecessary) if it can be shown that data satisfying the predicates are treated the same by the actual program and from the viewpoint of the specifications. For example, distinguishing between BL and NL in Table VII is unnecessary. Cursory examination of the programs in either Fig. 1 or Fig. 2 shows that every time CW is tested for equality with BL it is also tested for equality with NL; the specifications, moreover, do not require different effects depending on whether a BL or NL is the value of a break character. So we can safely partition the value set for CurChar into BL or NL, ET, and Ot and the value set for PrevChar into BL or NL, and Ot without reducing the reliability of this set of test predicates for these particular programs. This will reduce the number of test predicates in Table VII from 32 to 16 and the number of test runs required from ten (one for each ET condition) to six. This illustrates how the amount of testing can be safely reduced after a set of test predicates has been developed independently of program structure. Proofs of simple program properties can reduce the amount of testing required.

The next part of Naur's specification states: "...line breaks (in the output) must be made only where the (input) text has BLANK or NL..." This clause states a constraint on when the action of outputting an NL character is valid. Since we have already distinguished BLANK's and NL characters in Table VII, no new test conditions are suggested. Examining the clause with respect to Table VII, however, shows that a line break can never be made before the first word in the text unless the first word is preceded by one or more break characters. Naur's program itself violates this clause because it always puts out a line break at the beginning of the output. Undoubtedly, the intent of the clause was not to forbid an initializing line break in the output, but rather to say that a word in the input text must be contained completely on a single line in the output; here is another specification error (failure to correctly express the intent of the designer) readily detected by case analysis.

The remainder of the specification states that "each line is filled as far as possible as long as no line will contain more than MAXPOS characters." We will not construct a condition table for this part of the specification. Such a table would contain conditions describing the length of words, current and future lengths of lines, and possibly, the number of words on a line. The table will show how to exercise a program for all relevant combinations of boundary conditions. Arguments discussing what constitutes a proper set of test predicates for this part of the specification are complex and almost require a paper in itself. We only intend to sketch an approach to test predicate construction here.

C. Summary

There are two main features of the method of test data selection presented here—the use of test predicates and the use of a condition table.

Test predicates are the motivating force for data selection. A test predicate is found by identifying conditions and combinations of conditions relevant to the correct operation of a program. Conditions arise first and primarily from the specifications for a program. As implementations are considered, further conditions and predicates may be added. Conditions can arise from many sources, and as they come to mind, they are written down in the condition stub of a table. The columns of the table are then generated and checked. The checking process may suggest further conditions to be added. If the number of predicates becomes excessive, it is better to wait until information from an actual implementation is available to reduce the number of predicates so the impact of the reduction on test reliability can be explicitly assessed.

The major problem in our approach as illustrated so far is that conditions are considered as they spring to mind. This may mean wasting effort on conditions unlikely to be connected with errors in the actual implementation to be tested. Nonetheless, such conditions do test something about a program. The quality of the test predicates cannot be decided at the exact moment of their conception. Test predicate analysis must be carried out in its entirety and then checked for overall reliability before deleting individual test predicates.

The emphasis is on a systematic approach, and the condition table fulfills this purpose by recording conditions and their combinations in an orderly and mechanically checkable fashion. It forces attention toward specifications and what the program should do rather than an actual program structure and what a program seems to do. It avoids the flaws of testing methods that focus solely on the internal structure of a program, but is not necessarily divorced from a program's internal structure since all program predicates must ultimately be represented in the condition table if the table is to define a reliable set of test predicates.

The type of reasoning used in selecting test predicates is much like that used in creating assertions, and hence the approach focuses attention on the abstract properties of the program and its specifications. A test predicate analysis of a program may be a practical first step toward program proving with the advantage that both testing and proving could be performed sequentially or in parallel.

V. THE THEORY OF TESTING

The methodology illustrated in the preceding section constitutes an informal application of the theoretical concepts defined in Section I, i.e., Section IV demonstrates the use of COMPLETE(T,C) RELIABLE(C), and VALID(C), as a means of devising thorough tests when the test data selection criterion, C, consists of a set of test predicates. In this section, we will point out how our use of this sort of test data selection criterion satisfies these previously defined theoretical concepts.

Since a test predicate is a condition combination in a condition table, selecting data to *satisfy* a test predicate means selecting data to exercise the condition combination in the course of executing F. Notationally, if a datum $d \in D$ satisfies test predicate $c \in C$ in this sense, then $c(d)$ is said to be true. With this definition in mind, COMPLETE(T,C) is defined as follows:

if $T \subseteq D$, COMPLETE$(T,C) =$

$$(\forall c \in C)(\exists t \in T)c(t) \land (\forall t \in T)(\exists c \in C)c(t).$$

This definition states that every test predicate belonging to C must be satisfied by at least one $t \in T$, and every t must satisfy at least one test predicate. Both requirements are necessary, since proof of C's validity will require proving the correctness of a program for data that satisfy no test predicate, and hence, are included in no set of test data T.

The examples in Section II showed that it is readily possible to choose data that exercise test predicates in an overlapping manner (e.g., see Table V). This suggests a natural partitioning of the input domain into related equivalence classes, $E(C')$ defined as follows:

Let $C' \subseteq C$.

$E(C') = \{d \in D \mid (\forall c \in C')c(d) \land (\forall c \in C - C')\neg c(d)\}$,

i.e., $E(C')$ contains all $d \in D$ that satisfy all and only those test predicates belonging to C'. Note that data belonging to the equivalence class $E(\phi)$ satisfy no test predicate. The relation between these equivalence classes for a C containing three test predicates is shown schematically in Fig. 4. Note that data belonging to, for example, $E(C_{12})$ satisfy just test predicates c_1 and c_2, and that if test T contains data belonging to $E(C_{12})$, T need not also contain data belonging to $E(C_1)$ and $E(C_2)$ to satisfy COMPLETE. Note that a complete test, therefore, is equivalent to selecting one datum from a *subset* of the equivalence classes without selecting any data from $E(\phi)$.

Of course, not just any set of test predicates will constitute a reliable and valid test data selection criterion. The following relationship can be used, however, to show that C will satisfy the general definition of VALID given in Fig. 1.

$$(\forall d \in E(\phi)) \text{OK}(d) \supset \text{VALID}(C).$$

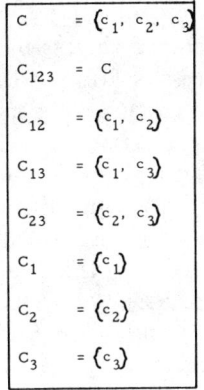
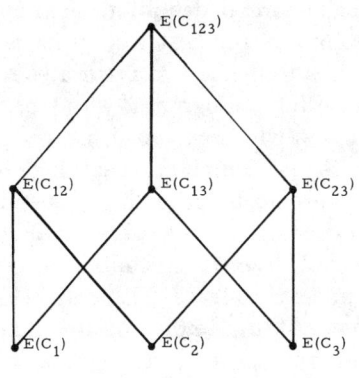

Fig. 4. Structure showing relationships between equivalence classes induced by a set of test predicates, C. If C is reliable, the correct processing of data drawn from one equivalence class (e.g., $E(C_{12})$) proves the correctness of the program for data drawn from certain other classes (e.g., $E(C_1)$ and $E(C_2)$), i.e., success propagates downwards in the lattice of equivalence classes. Similarly, failure propagates upward. For example, the incorrect processing of data from $E(C_3)$ implies data drawn from $E(C_{23})$, $E(C_{13})$, and $E(C_{123})$ will also be processed incorrectly.

This means C is valid if a program is correct for all data satisfying no test predicate. With respect to the condition table technique, this validity criterion requires that constraints among conditions be properly described; every condition combination excluded as impossible must actually be impossible. Moreover, the domain of values associated with some variable must be correctly described, e.g., CW in Section IV must at most take on the values BL, NL, ET, and Other. Although a nonempty $E(\phi)$ can be viewed as warning that a program can execute a reliable test successfully and still contain errors because it is invalid, it can also be viewed merely as indicating that the correctness of the program for such data is to be assessed by means other than the tests implied by C. Separate verification, for example, by proof, may be easier than verification by testing, or it may be that the data in $E(\phi)$ have already been verified by prior tests. It may be that a conscious decision has been made not to exercise certain test predicates because it is "obvious" the program will correctly process data satisfying them. This can reduce the total testing effort. In any event, the program's correctness for data belonging to $E(\phi)$ is not determined by the tests defined by C.

It may sometimes be impractical to conduct complete tests. In this case, if C is known to be valid because $E(\phi)$ is empty, then test data should be chosen just from equivalence classes that satisfy test predicates likely to be encountered in practice. While such a test will not necessarily be valid, it will still be reliable if C is reliable, and estimates of overall *program* reliability can be devised by estimating the frequency with which data satisfying unexercised test predicates will be encountered in actual use of the program. This sort of analysis can set a lower bound on the estimated frequency of failure in the program's actual operation, even when a program is tested only incompletely.

The formal definition of RELIABLE(C) implied by the use of test predicates is rather complex, but the essential idea is to define test predicates so success or failure when executing a program F with a particular datum d depends only on what *individual* test predicates d satisfies, not the particular combination satisfied. This is the sense in which test predicates must be independent. For example, using the definition of C given in Fig. 4, if $d_{12} \in E(C_{12})$ and OK(d_{12}), then the definition of COMPLETE says that there is no need to test F with data belonging to $E(C_1)$ or $E(C_2)$. Hence OK(d_{12}) implies OK(d_1) and OK(d_2), where $d_1 \in E(C_1)$ and $d_2 \in E(C_2)$ if C is reliable. Similarly, OK(d_1) and OK(d_2) implies OK(d_{12}), since one complete test could include d_{12} and another, both d_1 and d_2; regardless of which complete test is actually performed, the success of either complete test must imply the success of all others if C is reliable. Note also that the definition of COMPLETE implies that to be reliable, neither the sequence of test predicate execution nor the frequency of execution can be relevant to the successful processing of test data because data are said to satisfy a test predicate whether the data cause the predicate to be exercised one time or many times, and no matter what sequences of predicates are exercised before or after a particular one. If frequency or sequence of test predicate execution *is* potentially relevant to an error's existence, separate test predicates must be defined to cover all relevant sequencing or frequency possibilities. (This was the reason we added "Break length" and "First Word?" to the condition table created in Section IV.)

The formal definition of RELIABLE(C), when C is a set of test predicates, therefore is

$$\text{RELIABLE}(C) = (\forall C_1 \subseteq C)(\forall C_2 \subseteq C)((\exists t_1 \in E(C_1))$$
$$(\exists t_2 \in E(C_2))(\text{OK}(t_1) \land \text{OK}(t_2))$$
$$\supset (\forall C' \subseteq C_1 \cup C_2)(C' \neq \phi$$
$$\supset (\forall d' \in E(C')\text{OK}(d')))).$$

This means that if a program is correct for some datum, d, in equivalence classes other than $E(\phi)$, *then it is correct for any data satisfying a (nonempty) subset of the test predicates exercised by d*. Note that tests containing only data satisfying a large number of test predicates are more powerful in the sense that data selected from only a few equivalence classes suffices to demonstrate program correctness. Such tests are useful when the probability of finding an error is deemed low, as in regression testing (Elmendorf [5]). Tests using data satisfying only a few test predicates can fail for fewer reasons and so are useful in either localizing a failure or in attempting to identify as many different errors as possible in a set of test runs. Minimizing the cost of testing requires judgment in deciding which equivalence classes to choose from in satisfying COMPLETE(T,C).

We discussed earlier why proving validity need not be difficult. Proving reliability is harder. Such a proof suffers from the same problems as direct proofs of program correctness, insofar as insuring the correctness of the proof and axiomatization of the run-time environment is concerned. A proof of reliability may be somewhat easier than a direct proof of program correctness, however, since the proof can assume the program works correctly for some data. The principal problem in the proof is to show that data satisfying each test predicate are treated in sufficiently the same way that successfully exercising each test predicate *once* is sufficient to imply successful execution for all data satisfying the predicate. At a minimum, this requires understanding all conditions relevant to the successful processing of a test datum, but it does not require proving that the test datum *will* be successfully executed—that is proven by the success of a test run. This shows that proving test reliability is the induction step in an inductive proof of program correctness using the fundamental theorem; the test itself is, of course, the basis step.

Defects in a proof of reliability, aside from simple logical errors, are most likely to stem from failure to find all conditions relevant to the successful processing of data. For example, the set of test predicates described by a condition table will fail to be reliable if the domain of values associated with some variable is not correctly partitioned into relevant classes of values (e.g., the test predicates developed in Section IV would be unreliable if the only *relevant* values of CW were not BL, NL, ET, and Other, i.e., if these were not the only values relevant when certain actions are to be performed) or if some variable or condition were completely missing from the table (e.g., the predicate fill + bufpos = MAXPOS). Note the difference here between a reliability error and a validity error. Reliability requires partitioning the value set for CW correctly into sets of values "treated the same" by the program. Validity requires that the postulated value set for CW include all *possible* values for CW.

It is impossible to formulate general *necessary* conditions for reliability since reliability means that all errors in a program will be detected by a complete test. If a program in fact has no errors, *any* set of test predicates is reliable. For example, exercising all statements is not a necessary condition for reliability as long as unexercised statements are never responsible for an error. But suppose that test predicates are defined so data belonging to a particular equivalence class sometimes exercise a particular statement and sometimes do not. Then proving the reliability of these test predicates will be harder because it must be shown that the statements not exercised by some data in the equivalence class never cause an error. Otherwise, if an error is associated with the occasionally executed statement, some data in the class will execute successfully and some will not, and this contradicts RELIABLE(C). So, in general, we can only describe certain characteristics that if not satisfied either make a proof of reliability harder or make it more likely the test predicates are not reliable for the program to be tested. For example, it appears that a set of test predicates must at least satisfy the following conditions to have a reasonable chance of being reliable.

Condition 1: Every individual branching condition in the program must be represented by an equivalent[4] condition in the table.

Condition 2: Every potential termination condition in the program (Sites [15]), e.g., overflow, must be represented by a condition in the table.

Condition 3: Every variable mentioned in a condition must have been partitioned correctly into classes that are "treated the same" by the program.

Condition 4: Every condition relevant to the correct operation of the program that is implied by the specification, knowledge of the program's data structures, or knowledge of the general method being implemented by the program must be represented as a condition in the table.

Condition 5: The test predicates must be independent, e.g., all data satisfying a particular test predicate must exercise the same path in the program and test the same branch predicates.

Note that Conditions 1–3 are satisfied only with knowledge of the details of a program's implementation. Satisfying Condition 5 requires knowing something of the program's internal structure. Verifying Condition 4 may require both internal and external knowledge of a program. Undoubtedly, more constraints than these five need to be satisfied to insure reliability, but this is a subject for future work.

Clearly, satisfying all these conditions can lead to lots of test predicates requiring a large set of test data for a complete test. If an unreasonable amount of test data is required, a judicious combination of direct program proving and empirical judgment can reduce size of a complete test. As long as test predicates are eliminated only *after* all conditions potentially relevant to the correct operation of the program have been identified, any reductions in test validity are at least being made consciously rather than unwittingly.

VI. SUMMARY

In this paper, we have examined some fundamental questions and problems concerning program testing.

1) What is the proper role of testing in program development? How does testing compare to program proving as a means of improving software reliability?

2) What are the weaknesses of testing and to what extent can they be overcome?

3) What is a systematic method for selecting test data and how can the method be evaluated as to its reliability and validity?

4) Is there a theory of testing that can point the way to improved methods and principles of testing?

---

[4] This means verifying that the conditions represented in the condition table are being accurately tested inside the program; this check is needed to insure that a table predicate, e.g., "X, Y, and Z are all equal" is not actually evaluated in the program as $(X + Y + Z)/3 = X$.

In answering these questions we have shown the following.

1) The Role of Testing: Testing has an essential role in program development if for no other reason than the pervasiveness of case analysis in analyzing requirements, defining specifications, implementing programs, and proving program correctness. We have discussed how the practice of attempting formal or informal proofs of program correctness is useful for improving reliability, but suffers from the same types of errors as programming and testing, namely, failure to find and validate all special cases (i.e., combinations of conditions) relevant to a design, its specifications, the program, and its proof. Neither testing nor program proving can in practice provide complete assurance of program correctness, but the techniques complement each other and together provide greater assurance of correctness than either alone.

2) Test Weaknesses: The weakness of testing lies in concluding that from the successful execution of selected test data, a program is correct for all data. Criteria for test data selection based solely on internal program structure are clearly too weak to insure confidence in the results of a successful test, since such testing methods are too weak to necessarily reveal all design errors or many types of construction errors. Reliability is the key to meaningful testing and lack of reliability is the reason for the current weakness of testing as a method for insuring software correctness. Further work is needed to show when a test is reliable.

3) Test Methodology: We believe most software errors result from failing to see or deal correctly with all conditions and combinations of conditions relevant to the desired operation of a program. An effective methodology for reliable program development must focus on uncovering these conditions and their combinations. This is the motivation for our use of condition tables—it makes it easier to find and analyze condition combinations. Experimental use of condition tables and further study of the method is needed, however, before its full benefits can be realized in practice. In any event, a systematic approach to test data selection is clearly necessary to obtain effective test data with reasonable effort. Most systematic methods proposed to date have been based solely on knowledge of a program's internal structure, and yet such knowledge is insufficient by itself to yield adequately reliable tests.

4) Theory of Testing: We have made a start toward a theory of testing by defining some basic properties of thorough tests—reliability, validity, and completeness. We have also developed a specific version of the theory in which the test data selection criterion consists of sets of test predicates organized in a condition table. Other theoretical developments could proceed by defining other types of test data selection criteria.

The concept of proving test reliability, validity, and completeness and then testing a program (rather than attempting to prove the program correct directly or using a nonrigorous approach to testing) is important for software reliability. Presumably, every piece of software undergoes some type of testing, yet the fundamental techniques of test data selection have not previously been as carefully and critically analyzed as have some less widely used techniques such as proof of correctness. We know less about the theory of testing, which we do often, than about the theory of program proving, which we do seldom. This paper is a step toward redressing this imbalance.

REFERENCES

[1] B. Boehm, "Software and its impact: A quantitative assessment," *Datamation*, vol. 19, pp. 48–59, May 1973.
[2] B. W. Boehm et al., "Some experience with automated aids to the design of large-scale reliable software," in *Proc. Int. Conf. Reliable Software*, Los Angeles, Calif., Apr. 21–23, 1975.
[3] J. N. Buxton and B. Randell, *Software Engineering Techniques*. Brussels, Belgium: Scientific Affairs Div., NATO, Apr. 1970.
[4] O.-J. Dahl, E. W. Dijkstra, and C. A. R. Hoare, *Structured Programming*. New York: Academic, 1972.
[5] W. R. Elmendorf, "Controlling the functional testing of an operating system," *IEEE Trans. Syst., Sci., Cybern.*, vol. SSC-5, pp. 284–290, Oct. 1969.
[6] W. C. Hetzel, *Program Test Methods*. Englewood Cliffs, N. J.: Prentice-Hall, 1973.
[7] P. Brinch Hansen, "Testing multiprogramming systems," *Software Practice and Experience*, vol. 3, pp. 145–150, Apr.–June, 1973.
[8] P. J. H. King, "The interpretation of limited entry decision table format and relationships among conditions," *Comput. J.*, vol. 12, pp. 320–326, Nov. 1969.
[9] R. L. London, "Software reliability through proving programs correct," in *Proc. IEEE Int. Symp. Fault-Tolerant Computing*, Mar. 1971.
[10] P. Naur, "Programming by action clusters," *BIT*, vol. 9, no. 3, pp. 250–258, 1969.
[11] P. Naur and B. Randell, Eds., *Software Engineering*. Brussels, Belgium: Scientific Affairs Div., NATO, Jan. 1969.
[12] U. W. Pooch, "Translation of decision tables," *Comput. Surveys*, vol. 6, pp. 125–151, June 1974.
[13] P. C. Poole, "Debugging and testing," in *Advance Course on Software Engineering*, F. L. Bauer, Ed. New York: Springer-Verlag, 1973, pp. 278–318.
[14] R. J. Rubey, R. C. Wick, W. J. Stoner, and L. Bentley, "Comparative evaluation of PL/I," Rep. AD-669096, Apr. 1968.
[15] S. L. Sites, "Proving that computer programs terminate cleanly," Dep. Comput. Sci., Stanford Univ., Stanford, Calif., Rep. STAN-CS-74-418, May 1974.
[16] L. G. Stucki and N. P. Svegel, "Software automated verification system study," McDonnell Douglas Astronautics Corp., Huntington Beach, Calif., Rep. AD-784086, Jan. 1974.

John B. Goodenough received the B.A. degree in physics, and the A.M. and Ph.D. degrees in applied mathematics (computer science) from Harvard University, Cambridge, Mass., in 1961, 1962, and 1970, respectively.

He has been Director of Programming Technology at SofTech, Inc., Waltham, Mass., since 1972 and has been the principal technical participant in several language design studies and a research effort whose objective was to define current problems and the state of the art in language processing technology and modularity techniques. His current work focuses on the areas of software reliability and programming language development. His experience includes four years with an Air Force Psychology Laboratory as a Research Mathematician and System Programmer and five and one half years with the Air Force Command and Management Systems Deputate at its Electronic Systems Division as a Research Mathematician.

Dr. Goodenough is a member of the Association for Computing Machinery and Sigma Xi.

Susan L. Gerhart received the B.A. degree in mathematics from Ohio Wesleyan University, Delaware, in 1965, the M.S. degree in communication sciences from the University of Michigan, Ann Arbor, in 1967, and the Ph.D. degree in computer science from Carnegie-Mellon University, Pittsburgh, Pa., in 1972.

She was a Visiting Assistant Professor of Computer Science at the University of Toronto, Toronto, Ont., Canada, in 1972–1973 and since 1973 has been an Assistant Professor of Computer Science at Duke University, Durham, N. C. She has also been employed as a Senior Software Engineer at SofTech, Inc., Waltham, Mass., and a Visiting Scientist at ICASE, Hampton, Va., during the summers of 1974 and 1975, respectively. Her research interests are in the area of program verification, including testing, the theory and practice of proving correctness of programs, and programming methodologies which reduce the difficulties of verification.

Dr. Gerhart is a member of the Association for Computing Machinery and Sigma Xi.

Reliability of the Path Analysis Testing Strategy

WILLIAM E. HOWDEN

Abstract—A set of test data T for a program P is *reliable* if it reveals that P contains an error whenever P is incorrect. If a set of tests T is reliable and P produces the correct output for each element of T then P is a correct program. Test data generation strategies are procedures for generating sets of test data. A testing strategy is reliable for a program P if it produces a reliable set of test data for P. It is proved that an effective testing strategy which is reliable for all programs cannot be constructed. A description of the path analysis testing strategy is presented. In the path analysis strategy data are generated which cause different paths in a program to be executed. A method for analyzing the reliability of path testing is introduced. The method is used to characterize certain classes of programs and program errors for which the path analysis strategy is reliable. Examples of published incorrect programs are included.

Index Terms—Path analysis, program correctness, program testing, symbolic evaluation.

I. Introduction

OUR INTUITION tempts us into believing that when we test a program on a set of tests T we know more about the reliability of the program than its reliability over this set. When a program works correctly for a set of "well-chosen" tests we have the feeling that unless we have forgotten to test for some possible class of mistakes that the program is correct. This paper studies this phenomenon for a particular class of testing strategies.

II. Proving Correctness by Testing

Suppose that P is a program which is meant to compute a function F with domain D. Then the correctness of P can be determined by testing it on each element of D. If D is effectively infinite this approach is infeasible. In order to determine correctness by testing it is necessary to be able to generate a finite set $T \subset D$ which has the following two properties:

1) for each $x \in T$ there is a computable procedure for determining whether or not P terminates for x; and
2) $P(x) = F(x)$ for all $x \in T \Rightarrow P(x) = F(x)$ for all $x \in D$. The first condition is necessary so that a programmer will know when to stop a program which is caught in an infinite loop.

In practice, it is often possible to predict in advance an upper bound $b(x)$ such that if P fails to terminate for x within computation time $b(x)$, then P will not terminate. The correctness of programs having this property can be determined with test sets satisfying property 2) above. In this and the following sections we will assume that the programs P satisfy this property. The discussion could also be carried out without the assumption but at the cost of requiring that "reliable" test data satisfy both conditions 1) and 2) above, rather than just condition 2).

It is easy to prove that a test set T satisfying condition 2) exists for all programs P and functions F.

Theorem 1: Suppose that P is a program for computing a function F with domain D. There exists a finite subset T of D which can be used to determine the correctness of P, i.e., there exists a finite set $T \subseteq D$ such that

$$P(x) = F(x) \text{ for all } x \in T \Rightarrow P(x) = F(x) \text{ for all } x \in D.$$

Proof: Either P is correct or it is not. If P is correct choose $T = \{x\}$ for any $x \in D$. If P is not correct there exists some x such that $P(x) \neq F(x)$. Choose $T = \{x\}$. The set T satisfies the required conditions.

The proof of the above theorem is disappointing. If we knew whether or not P was correct it would not be necessary to test it. What is really required is a computable procedure, or test strategy, which can be used to generate a test set T for any program P. It can be proved that no such procedure exists.

Theorem 2: There exists no computable procedure H which, given an arbitrary program P and function F with domain D, can be used to generate a nonempty finite set $T \subset D$ such that:

$$P(x) = F(x) \text{ for all } x \in T \Rightarrow P(x) = F(x) \text{ for all } x \in D.$$

Proof: If such a procedure existed, it would be possible to use it to determine the equivalence of arbitrary primitive recursive functions. It is known that no such procedure exists [3]. The argument runs as follows. Let P_1 and P_2 be any two programs in a language for constructing programs which compute primitive recursive functions. Let F be the function computed by P_2. Since P_1 and P_2 are primitive recursive they terminate and H can be used for determining the correctness of P_1 for calculating F. This is equivalent to determining the equivalence of P_1 and P_2.

Theorem 2 tells us that the best that can be hoped for are test strategies which work for particular classes of programs $\mathcal{P}$. In the following sections we will examine the systematic testing strategy which is currently receiving the most attention. Classes of programs $\mathcal{P}$ are characterized for which the strategy is reliable. First the notion of reliability is considered.

III. Reliable Test Data

Any subset of a program's input domain can be considered a set of test data. A testing strategy is a procedure for choosing a set of test data.

Definition: Suppose P is a program for computing a function F whose domain is the set D. Let $T \subset D$. T is a *reliable test set* for P if:

$P(x) = F(x)$ for all $x \in T \Rightarrow P(x) = F(x)$ for all $x \in D$.

Another way of stating this is that T is reliable for P if T reveals that P is incorrect whenever P contains an error (i.e., $P(x) \neq F(x)$ for some $x \in T$).

The testing strategies we will consider are actually procedures for choosing a sequence $\{T_i\}_{i=1}^n$ of subsets of the input domain of a program. Each of the sets T_i is chosen to test some aspect of the program. In path analysis approaches to testing, each set T_i consists of the subset of the input domain which causes a path P_i in the program to be executed. We assume that the programmer constructs a test set T from the sequence $\{T_i\}_{i=1}^n$ by choosing one element from each T_i. This approach to testing strategies makes it possible to consider different levels of reliability.

Definition: Suppose P is a program and H is a testing strategy. Let $\{T_i\}_{i=1}^n$ be the subsets of the input domain of P generated by H. Suppose that any set T which can be constructed by choosing one element from each T_i is a reliable test set. Then H is a *reliable test strategy* for P.

Theorem 3: Suppose that P is a program for computing a function F and H is a testing strategy for P. Let $\{T_i\}_{i=1}^n$ be the sequence of input domain subsets generated by H. Then H is a reliable test strategy for P $\iff$ P is correct or there exists a set T_i such that $P(x) \neq F(x)$ for all $x \in T_i$.

In order to simplify our discussion we will assume in the following sections that input domain sets can be infinite and that variables are represented to arbitrarily precise accuracy. Some of the definitions, theorems, and examples are correct independently of this assumption. The others require occasionally awkward modifications.

In some cases a testing strategy H is "almost reliable" for a program P. Consider the program P in Example 1. The program is correct except for the missing initialization assignment SUM = X which should occur before the DO-loop. One possible strategy for testing P is to choose data which test all paths which cause less than n iterations of the loop in P. Suppose that the strategy H involves the generation of a sequence $\{T_i\}_{i=1}^n$ consisting of the subsets of the input domain which cause the loop in P to be executed i times, $1 \leq i \leq n$, and the selection of a set T containing one element chosen at random from each nonempty T_i. P gives incorrect answers for each element (X, E) of each T_i except for the pairs (Y, E) where Y is the default setting of the uninitialized variable SUM. Decompose each T_i into two sets T_i' and T_i'' where T_i' contains all (X, E) where $X \neq Y$ and T_i'' contains all (X, E) where $X = Y$. T_i, T_i', and T_i'' are all two-dimensional subsets of Euclidean 2-space. Since the two-dimensional area of T_i is nonzero and the two-dimensional area of T_i'' is zero, the chance of choosing an element at random from T_i which lies in T_i'' is negligible. It is almost certain that all of the elements of T will belong to the subsets T_i', and that the error in P will be revealed when P is tested on T. H is therefore "almost reliable."

Note that the phrase "almost reliable" is only meaningful for the strategy H in which elements of T_i are chosen at random. In practice, elements of T_i may not be chosen at random and

it will not be meaningful to describe the associated strategy as being almost reliable.

Example 1: The following program P is supposed to compute sine(x), using the Maclaurin series, for any real number x. It is missing an initialization assignment.

```
      DOUBLE PRECISION FUNCTION SIN (X, E)
C     THIS DECLARATION COMPUTES SIN(X) TO ACCURACY E
      DOUBLE PRECISION E, TERM, SUM
      REAL X
      TERM = X
      DO 20 I = 3, 100, 2
      TERM = TERM * X**2/(I*(I-1))
      SUM = SUM + ((-1)**(I/2)) * TERM
      IF ( DABS (TERM) .LT. E) GO TO 30
20    CONTINUE
30    SIN = SUM
      RETURN
      END
```

Definition: Suppose that P is a program for computing a function F whose domain D is a subset of Euclidean n-space and H is a testing strategy for P. Let $\{T_i\}_{i=1}^n$ be the sequence of input domain subsets generated by H. Suppose the T_i have subsets T_i' such that any set T' containing one element from each T_i' is a reliable test set for P. If $T_i' = T_i$ whenever the volume of T_i is zero, and T_i' contains all of T_i except a subset of zero volume whenever the volume of T_i is nonzero, then H is an *almost reliable test strategy* for P.

Theorem 4: Suppose that P is a program for computing a function F whose domain D is a subset of Euclidean n-space and that H is a testing strategy for P. Let $\{T_i\}_{i=1}^n$ be the sequence of input domain subsets generated by H. Then H is an almost reliable test strategy for P $\iff$ P is correct or there exists a set T_i such that:

1) the n-dimensional volume of T_i is zero and $P(x) \neq F(x)$ for all $x \in T_i$ or

2) the n-dimensional volume of T_i is nonzero and $P(x) \neq F(x)$ for all but a zero volume subset of T_i.

Theorems 3 and 4 indicate that we should attempt to choose test sets T_i so that if $P(x) \neq F(x)$ for some $x \in T_i$ then $P(x) \neq F(x)$ for (almost) all $x \in T_i$.

IV. Classes of Programs and Program Errors

The classes of programs $\mathcal{P}$ for which we will characterize the reliability of the path analysis testing strategy are associated with different kinds of errors in programs. We will be concerned with programs which are either correct or can be considered deviations from a hypothetical correct program P*. The "differences" between P and P* define the errors in P. Each class of programs $\mathcal{P}$ will consist of correct programs P* together with incorrect programs P which differ from P* by some type of error.

A *path* through a program corresponds to some possible flow of control. A path may be *infeasible* in the sense that there is no input data which will cause the path to be executed. Flows of control involving different numbers of iterations of loops are considered to be different paths. In general, a program containing loops will have an infinite number of paths. The errors in a program can be categorized in terms of their effects on the paths through the program.

Associated with each path through a program is the subset of the input domain which causes the path to be followed and a sequence of computations which is carried out by the path.

Definition: Suppose P_i is a path through a program P. Then the *path domain* $D_i = D(P_i)$ for P_i is the subset of the input domain which causes P_i to be executed. The *path computation* $C_i = C(P_i)$ for P_i is the function which is computed by the sequence of computations in P_i.

The domain of the functions C_i is considered to be the domain D of P. During execution of the program P, each computation $C(P_i)$ is only carried out over the path domain $D(P_i)$. In general C_i may not be defined over all of D or, since P may contain errors, even over all of D_i. In comparing two computations C_i and C_j, we say that C_i and C_j are equivalent ($C_i = C_j$) if C_i and C_j are defined for the same subset D' of D and $C_i(x) = C_j(x)$ for all $x \in D'$.

Symbolic evaluation of a path can be used to construct a system of predicates which describes the path domain of any finite path in terms of the path's input variables [2], [12], [14]. Symbolic evaluation can also be used to construct a set of expressions describing the path computation for any finite path in terms of input variables. In the symbolic evaluation process, symbols are used to stand for symbolic input values and variables in expressions are bound by substitution of the symbolic expressions representing their current symbolic values. Example 2 contains the path domains and path computations for two of the paths in the program in Example 1.

Example 2:

a) Path which exits from loop during first iteration. *Path domain:* All (x, E) such that $|x^3/(3*2)| < E$. *Path computation:* SUM $- x^3/(3*2)$.

b) Path which exits from loop during second iteration. *Path domain:* All (x, E) such that $|x^3/(3*2)| \geq E$ and $|x^5/(5*4*3*2)| < E$. *Path computation:* SUM $- x^3/(3*2) + x^5/(5*4*3*2)$.

The effects of program errors on the paths through a program can be described in terms of their effects on the path domains and path computations of the paths. Three simple classes of errors will be studied. If there is an isomorphism (one-to-one correspondence) between the paths P_i of P and the paths P_i^* of the correct version P^* of P such that $D(P_i) = D(P_i^*)$ and $C(P_i) = C(P_i^*)$ for all paths, then $P = P^*$ and P is correct. If P is not correct, no isomorphism having those properties can be constructed. Either the domains or the computations, or both, of P and P^* will be different.

Definition: Suppose P is an incorrect program for computing a function F and P^* is a correct program. Suppose there is an isomorphism between the paths P_i of P and the paths P_i^* of P^* such that for all pairs of paths (P_i, P_i^*), $D(P_i) = D(P_i^*)$ but that for some pair (P_k, P_k^*), $C(P_k) \neq C(P_k^*)$. Then P contains a *path computation* or *computation error*.

Definition: Suppose P is an incorrect program for computing a function F and P^* is a correct program. Suppose there is an isomorphism between the paths P_i of P and the paths P_i^* of P^* such that for all pairs of paths (P_i, P_i^*), $C(P_i) = C(P_i^*)$, but that for some pairs (P_k, P_k^*), $D(P_k) \neq D(P_k^*)$. Then P contains a *path domain* or *domain error*.

Definition: Suppose P is an incorrect program for computing a function F and P^* is a correct program. Suppose there is an isomorphism between the paths P_i of P and a subset of the paths P_i^* of P^* such that $C(P_i^*) = C(P_i)$ and $D(P_i^*) \subset D(P_i)$ for all paths P_i in P. Then P contains a *subcase error*.

Definition: $\mathcal{C}(P)$ is the set of all path computations for all paths in the program P. $\mathcal{D}(P)$ is the set of all path domains for all paths in P.

When a program contains a computation error we assume that the paths in P and P^* have been indexed so that $D(P_i) = D(P_i^*)$ for all paths. When it contains a domain or a subcase error we assume they have been indexed so that $C(P_i) = C(P_i^*)$ for all paths P_i in P.

Different relationships can be proved between classes of statement type errors and errors which are defined in terms of the domains and computations for a program.

Theorem 5: Suppose that P is an incorrect program and that the only difference between P and P^* is in some statement which does not affect the flow of control in P. Then P has a computation error.

Theorem 6: Suppose that P is an incorrect program and that the only difference between P and a correct program P^* is in some statement which affects the flow of control in P. Then P may have a computation, domain, or subcase error.

V. Path Analysis Testing Strategy

In the path analysis approach to testing a program, P is tested by generating test data which cause selected paths in P to be executed. Much of the current work in test data generation involves systems which automate parts of the path analysis testing strategy. In some of the systems the user selects program paths and the computer generates descriptions of the data which cause the paths to be followed. In other systems the program is automatically decomposed into classes of paths and one path is selected from each class. All of the systems result in the generation of a sequence of sets $\{T_i\}_{i=1}^n$ which correspond to path domains or to unions of path domains.

In practice, a program P may have an infinite number of paths. Any practical path analysis strategy will have to involve a procedure for selecting a subset of the total set of paths. In the analysis carried out in this section the potential reliability of path analysis strategies is examined by considering the degree of reliability that could be obtained if it were possible to test every path in a program. In this idealized situation the path analysis testing strategy results in the generation of a sequence of sets $\{T_i\}_{i=1}^n$ which corresponds to the complete set of path domains for a program. A (possibly infinite) set of test data T is constructed by choosing one element at random from each nonempty set T_i. This testing strategy will be referred to as *P-testing*.

Definition: Suppose P_i is a path in a program P. Then $P_i(x)$ is computed by carrying out the sequence of nontransfer statement computations in P_i, i.e., $P_i(x) = C_i(x)$ where $C_i = C(P_i)$.

Theorem 7: Suppose that $\mathcal{P}$ is a set of programs containing a correct program P^* for computing some function F. Then P-testing is reliable for testing the programs P in $\mathcal{P} \Leftrightarrow$ each

$P \in \mathcal{P}$ is either correct or has a feasible path P_i such that $P_i(x) \neq P^*(x)$ for all $x \in D(P_i)$.

In the following subsections the reliability of P-testing is characterized for different classes of programs $\mathcal{P}$.

A. Computation Errors

In this subsection we will assume that $\mathcal{P}$ is a set of programs for computing a function F and that the programs in $\mathcal{P}$ are either correct or contain computation errors. Recall that the type of error an incorrect program contains is defined with respect to a particular correct program. Each of the incorrect programs P in $\mathcal{P}$ are assumed to have computation errors relative to a particular correct program P^* which is also in $\mathcal{P}$. The paths in the incorrect programs P and the correct program P^* are indexed so that $D(P_i) = D(P_i^*)$ for all paths.

Theorem 8: P-testing is reliable for testing the programs in $\mathcal{P} \iff$ every program P in $\mathcal{P}$ is either correct or has a feasible path P_i such that $P_i(x) \neq P_i^*(x)$ for all $x \in D(P_i)$.

All of the examples in this section are taken from the "Common Blunders" section in *The Elements of Programming Style* [13]. Incorrect statements in the programs are italicized. Corrections are also italicized and are enclosed in angle brackets. The original incorrect programs are the programs without the statements in angle brackets. The corrected programs are the programs which contain the italicized statements in angle brackets but not the other italicized statements.

Example 3: The following program P is supposed to compute the number of class marks which fall within certain ranges. It contains an incorrect assignment statement which causes a computation error.

```
         DO 40 I=1, N
C        TEST IF DATA IS IN RANGE
         IF (MARKS(I) .LT. 1 .OR. MARKS(I) .GT. 100) GO TO 30
C        TRANSFORMATION TO DIRECTLY DETERMINE CLASS
C        INTERVAL MEMBERSHIP
         J = MARKS(I) – 1/10 + 1
         < J = (MARKS(I) – 1)/10 + 1 >
         NCLASS(J) = NCLASS(J) + 1
         GO TO 40
30       WRITE (3, 102) MARKS(I)
102      FORMAT (' ***MKS001 – DATA OUT OF RANGE ', 112)
40       CONTINUE
```

P-testing is reliable for testing P. (Let P_i be the path in P which causes the DO-loop to be traversed exactly once and which causes the incorrect statement to be executed during that iteration.)

Twelve of the eighteen errors in Kernighan and Plauger [13] are computation errors. P-testing is reliable or almost reliable for discovering nine of these errors. For one error it was not immediately obvious whether or not P-testing is reliable. In general, the P-testing reliability question is undecidable.

B. Domain Errors

In this subsection we will assume that $\mathcal{P}$ is a set of programs which are either correct or contain domain errors. The paths in the incorrect programs P and in the corresponding correct programs P^* are indexed so that $C(P_i) = C(P_i^*)$ for all paths in P.

The conditions for the reliability of P-testing for domain errors are simplified when a program's paths are "distinct."

Definition: Suppose P_1 and P_2 are two paths in a program P with domain D. P_1 and P_2 are *distinct* if $P_1(x) \neq P_2(x)$ for all $x \in D$. The paths in a program are distinct if any pair of paths in the program is distinct.

Theorem 9: Suppose that the paths in each correct program P^* in $\mathcal{P}$ are distinct. Then P-testing is reliable for testing the programs in $\mathcal{P} \iff$ every program P in $\mathcal{P}$ is either correct or has a feasible path P_i such that $D(P_i) \cap D(P_i^*) = \phi$.

Proof:

1) Suppose P-testing is reliable for each $P \in \mathcal{P}$. Let $P \in \mathcal{P}$ and suppose P is not correct. Theorem 7 implies there exists a feasible path P_i such that for all $x \in D(P_i)$, $P_i(x) \neq P^*(x)$. Suppose $D(P_i) \cap D(P_i^*) \neq \phi$. Choose $x \in D(P_i) \cap D(P_i^*)$. $C(P_i) = C(P_i^*) \Rightarrow P_i(x) = P_i^*(x)$. $x \in D(P_i^*) \Rightarrow P^*(x) = P_i^*(x) \Rightarrow P_i(x) = P^*(x)$ which is contradictory.

2) Suppose $P \in \mathcal{P}$ has a feasible path P_i such that $D(P_i) \cap D(P_i^*) = \phi$. Let $x \in D(P_i)$. $D(P_i) \cap D(P_i^*) = \phi \Rightarrow x \in D(P_j^*)$ for some $j \neq i$. $C(P_i) = C(P_i^*)$ and paths distinct $\Rightarrow P_i(x) \neq P_j^*(x)$. $P^*(x) = P_j^*(x) \Rightarrow P_i(x) \neq P^*(x)$. $\Rightarrow$ P-testing is reliable for P.

The necessary conditions for reliability in the above theorem do not depend on path distinctness. The following theorem is a special case of Theorem 9.

Theorem 10: If P-testing is reliable for testing the programs in $\mathcal{P}$ then every program $P \in \mathcal{P}$ is either correct or it has a feasible path P_i such that $D(P_i) \cap D(P_i^*) = \phi$.

Theorem 10 can be used to prove that P-testing is not reliable for the program P in the following example. For all paths P_i in P, $D(P_i) \cap D(P_i^*) \neq \phi$.

Example 4: The following program P is supposed to compute sine(x) using the Maclaurin series. It contains an incorrect transfer statement which causes a domain error.

```
         DOUBLE PRECISION FUNCTION SIN (X, E)
C        THIS DECLARATION COMPUTES SIN(X) TO ACCURACY E
         DOUBLE PRECISION E, TERM, SUM
         REAL X
         TERM = X
         SUM = X
         DO 20 I = 3, 100, 2
         TERM = TERM * X ** 2/(I*(I–1))
         SUM = SUM + ((–1)**(I/2))* TERM
         IF (TERM .LT. E) GO TO 30
         < IF (DABS (TERM) .LT. E) GO TO 30 >
20       CONTINUE
30       SIN = SUM
         RETURN
         END
```

The paths in the above program are not distinct. They are "almost distinct" in the sense that for any pair of paths P_i^* and P_j^* in P^*, $P_i^*(x) = P_j^*(x)$ for at most a zero area subset of the two-dimensional domain of P^*. A theorem similar to Theorem 9 can be proved which characterizes the conditions under which P-testing is almost reliable for programs containing almost distinct paths. P-testing is neither reliable nor almost reliable for this example.

Three of the eighteen errors in Kernighan and Plauger [13] are domain errors. P-testing is reliable or almost reliable for discovering only one of these three errors.

C. Subcase Errors

In this subsection we will assume that $\mathcal{P}$ is a set of programs which are either correct or contain subcase errors. The paths in the programs P and in the corresponding programs P* are indexed so that $C(P_i) = C(P_i^*)$ for all paths in P.

The domain error theorems in Section V-B depend only on the equivalence of path computations in P and P*. The same theorems can also be proved for subcase errors.

Theorem 11: Suppose that the paths in each correct program P* in $\mathcal{P}$ are distinct. Then P-testing is reliable for testing the programs in $\mathcal{P} \iff$ every program $P \in \mathcal{P}$ is either correct or has a feasible path P_i such that $D(P_i) \cap D(P_i^*) = \phi$.

Theorem 12: If P-testing is reliable for testing the programs in $\mathcal{P}$ then every program $P \in \mathcal{P}$ is either correct or it has a feasible path P_i such that $D(P_i) \cap D(P_i^*) = \phi$.

The paths in the correct version of the following program are distinct. Theorem 11 or Theorem 12 can be used to prove that P-testing is not reliable for P. For all paths P_i in P, $D(P_i) \cap D(P_i^*) \neq \phi$.

Example 5: The following program P is supposed to compute and print out a table of monthly mortgage payments. The program is missing a transfer statement. The omission causes a subcase error.

scribe a program having several incorrect statements as containing a single error while in other cases the program should be described as involving several errors. We will informally define an error E in a program P to be a set of "differences" between P and a correct program P*.

Two of the programs in the above examples are partially corrected versions of the programs in Kernighan and Plauger [13]. The original versions of these programs contained more than one error. In general, a program may contain several errors and it is important to consider the combinatorial effects of the errors on the reliability of the testing strategy. In this section we will characterize a set of conditions under which the reliability of P-testing for single errors is preserved when errors occur in combination.

Definition: Suppose $E = \{E_1, E_2, \cdots, E_k\}$ is a set of errors in a program P. Let P_{E_i} be the program which contains only the error E_i and not the other errors (i.e., E_i is the difference between P and a given correct program P*). Let $P_E = P$. An error E_i in E is *independent* in E if for all x in the domain of P,

$$P_{E_i}(x) \neq P^*(x) \Rightarrow P_E(x) \neq P^*(x).$$

An error E_i in a program is independent relative to a set of errors E if the introduction of the other errors into the program does not "correct" any of the incorrect output caused by the error E_i.

Theorem 13: Let $E = \{E_1, E_2, \cdots, E_n\}$ be a set of computation errors in a program P (i.e., P_{E_i} has a computation error

```
           DECLARE (A, R, M, B, C, P) FIXED DECIMAL (13, 4);
L10:       GET LIST (A, R, M);
           PUT SKIP EDIT ('THE AMOUNT IS', A) (A(13), F(10, 2))
                   ('THE INTEREST RATE IS', R) (A(23), F(6, 2))
                   ('THE MONTHLY PAYMENT IS', M) (A(25), F(8, 2));
           IF M < - A*R/1200 THEN GO TO L30,
           PUT SKIP(3) EDIT
           (' MONTH     BALANCE     CHARGE     PAID ON PRINCIPLE') (A);
           PUT SKIP;
           B = A;
           DO I = 1 TO 60;
              C = B*R/1200;
              IF B+C < M THEN GO TO L20;
              P = M-C; B = B-P;
              PUT SKIP EDIT (I, B, C, P) (F(13), 3 F(13, 2));
           END;
           C = B*R/1200;
 <L20:     IF B+C <.005 THEN GO TO L10>
   L20:    PUT SKIP(2) EDIT ('THERE WILL BE A LAST PAYMENT
                   OF:' , B+C) (A(35), F(8, 2));
           GO TO L10;
   L30:    PUT SKIP (2) EDIT ('UNACCEPTABLE MONTHLY PAYMENT') (A);
           GO TO L10;
```

Only one of the eighteen errors in Kernighan and Plauger [13] is a subcase error.

D. Combinations of Errors

Each of the programs in the above examples contains a single error. In each case the error is caused by a single incorrect statement. In some cases it is intuitively meaningful to de-

for each E_i). Suppose some error E_i is independent in E. Then if P-testing is reliable for P_{E_i} it is also reliable for P_E.

Proof: If P-testing is reliable for P_{E_i} then there exists a nonempty path domain D_j in $\mathfrak{D}(P_{E_i})$ such that $P_{E_i}(x) \neq P^*(x)$ for all $x \in D_j$. Since E contains computation errors, $\mathfrak{D}(P_E) = \mathfrak{D}(P_{E_i})$ which implies that $D_j \in \mathfrak{D}(P_E)$.

The conditions for the preservation of P-testing reliability are more complicated when other than computation errors are involved.

Theorem 14: Let $E = \{E_1, E_2, \cdots, E_n\}$ be a set of errors in a program P. Suppose E contains an independent error E_i and that P-testing is reliable for P_{E_i}. The reliability of P-testing for P_{E_i} implies the existence of a domain D_j in $\mathfrak{D}(P_{E_i})$ such that $P_{E_i}(x) \neq P^*(x)$ for all $x \in D_j$. If $D_j \in \mathfrak{D}(P_E)$ or $D_j \supset D$ for some $D \in \mathfrak{D}(P_E)$ then P-testing is reliable for P_E.

In practice, we will want each error E_i in a set E to satisfy the conditions of the above theorem relative to each subset $\overline{E}$ of E containing E_i. This will ensure that P-testing reliability is preserved as the errors in E are discovered and removed from the program.

The only simple example of error independence and testing reliability in Kernighan and Plauger [13] involves errors which are "almost independent" and for which P-testing is almost reliable. Suppose E_i is an error in a set of errors E and that P is a program whose domain is a subset of Euclidean n-space. Let X be the subset of the domain D of P for which $P_{E_i}(x) \neq F(x)$. Then E_i is almost independent in E if $P_E(x) \neq F(x)$ for all $x \in X$ if X has zero n-dimensional volume or for all but a zero volume subset of the elements of X if X has nonzero volume. Both Theorems 13 and 14 can be rewritten as theorems involving errors which are almost independent and strategies which are almost reliable.

Example 6: The program P in this example is another version of the sine program in Example 4. In its original form in Kernighan and Plauger [13] the program contains several errors, including the three in this example.

```
      DOUBLE PRECISION FUNCTION SIN(X, E)
C     THIS DECLARATION COMPUTES SIN(X) TO ACCURACY E
      DOUBLE PRECISION E, TERM, SUM
      REAL X
      TERM = X
      < SUM = X >
      DO 20 I = E, 100, 2
      TERM = TERM *X**2/(I*(I-1))
      SUM = SUM + (-1**(I/2))* TERM
      < SUM = SUM + ((-1)**(I/2))*TERM >
      IF (TERM .LT. E) GO TO 30
      < IF (DABS(TERM) .LT. E) GO TO 30 >
20    CONTINUE
30    SIN = SUM
      RETURN
      END
```

P_{E_1} is the program containing the missing assignment SUM = X. P_{E_2} contains the transfer statement with the missing DABS function and P_{E_3} the assignment with the missing parentheses. P_{E_2} is the program P in Example 4.

P-testing is almost reliable for P_{E_1} and P_{E_3} but not for P_{E_2}. E_1 and E_2 are almost independent relative to any subset of $E = \{E_1, E_2, E_3\}$. $\mathfrak{D}(P_{E_1})$ and $\mathfrak{D}(P_{E_2})$ both contain domains D_j which satisfy the special conditions of Theorem 14. This implies that P-testing is almost reliable for $P_{\overline{E}}$ where $\overline{E}$ is any subset of E containing either E_1 or E_3. Once E_1 and E_3 have been discovered and removed from P_E, P-testing will no longer be reliable for the remaining program P_{E_2}.

VI. Related Work

A number of different program testing tools have been developed which can be used to help automate the testing of programs. Earlier work in the area concentrated on the testing of program statements and branches rather than on program paths. The Algol W compiler [18] has an option which will cause a users program to be instrumented so that when the program is executed a table of statement execution counts is generated. The Fortran preprocessor PET [19] can be used to generate similar types of information for the statements and program branches in Fortran programs.

Several research groups have been involved in the design and construction of testing tools which concentrate on the testing of program paths. King [14] has built an interactive system in which the user directs the system to carry out a symbolic evaluation of selected paths. The system automatically constructs representations of the domains and computations for the paths. In the SELECT system [2] the user can either select a path or cause the system to select all paths which do not iterate a loop more than some given number of times. The system automatically constructs representations of the domains and computations for the paths. For simple cases it automatically generates test data. The basic elements of the path analysis testing strategy are described in [12]. A system implementing some of the features of the complete system plan outlined in [12] is described in [11]. The system automatically decomposes a program into a finite set of classes of paths and then generates descriptions of the computations and domains for each class. A logical notation in which groups of predicates can be asserted over the range of an expression is used to represent the domains for an infinite class of paths. The system was developed as part of the McDonnell Douglas Astronautics program in software reliability. The Program Validation Project at the General Research Corporation has constructed a commercially available system [15]. The system keeps track of untested program segments in a program and prints out descriptions of test data that will cause paths containing the modules to be executed. The TRW System [9] generates descriptions of a minimal set of paths through a program which tests all of the program's branches. Clarke [5] has constructed a path analysis testing system which interfaces with the DAVE Data Flow Analysis System [16]. The system is capable of generating temporary assertions which cause the generation of test data that test for common errors such as out of bounds array references and division by zero.

The path analysis testing strategy has features in common with and to some extent is derived from research on proofs of program correctness. Deutsch's interactive program verifier [6] uses a symbolic evaluation process to generate verification conditions. In [4] Burstall uses symbolic evaluation to construct inductive proofs of program correctness. The relationship between the use of symbolic evaluation in generating verification conditions to prove correctness and in generating a set of predicates for constructing test data is described in [10].

A number of papers have recently appeared in which the authors describe research into the classification and analysis of errors. Reference [7] contains a classification of the errors occurring in a release of an operating system and a discussion of the programming methods and constructs that would have prevented the errors from occurring. Shooman and Bolsky [17] describe the errors which were reported during the development of a 4K real time program. In their analysis of these errors, the authors discuss the nature of the changes required to correct the errors. The results of an analysis of a large system are reported in [1]. The authors describe a system for detecting classes of errors during the design phase of a software project. Their data are derived from a study reported in [20]. The study contains a comprehensive categorization of errors into both general and more specific categories. The frequency of the occurrence of the errors in several large projects is listed.

In general, the classifications and analysis of errors which have been carried out describe errors in terms of program constructs (e.g., incorrect loop condition, structural error, incorrect indexing, bit manipulation error, etc.). These classes of errors can be related to their effects on the computations and domains in a program but are not directly useful for characterizing the reliability of P-testing.

To the author's knowledge, the only other work which attempts to provide an underlying formal basis for the study of testing is described in a recent paper by Goodenough and Gerhart [8]. The use of the term "reliable" is derived from the work described in this paper.

The work described in this paper was influenced by the paper by Goodenough and Gerhart, and draws from the work on testing tools.

VII. Conclusions and Future Work

The path domain/path computation approach results in a relatively simple classification of commonly occurring errors. Sixteen of the eighteen errors in the Common Blunders section of [13] are either computation, domain, or subcase errors. The error classification can be refined to distinguish between other types of less commonly occurring errors.

The domain/computation approach provides a framework for the analysis and characterization of the reliability of path analysis testing strategies. The reliability of P-testing was analyzed for several classes of common errors.

P-testing was found to be reliable or almost reliable for about 65 percent of the program errors in the small survey of 11 programs in Kernighan and Plauger [13]. This means that if data for testing those programs are selected using the P-testing strategy, we will be "almost certain" of detecting 65 percent of the errors. This does not mean that the other errors would not be detected, only that we could not be certain of their detection.

The research described in this paper is only an introductory analysis of testing reliability. A complete analysis of reliability would involve a more extensive classification of errors. In our analysis we studied the potential reliability of path analysis testing strategies by assuming that we could test every path in a program. In any practical strategy the paths will have to be grouped into a finite set of classes of paths and one path from each class tested. The effects of different methods for grouping paths on the reliability of P-testing needs to be characterized. The continued study of P-testing reliability will have to deal with the problem of roundoff errors and data types. The programs in Kernighan and Plauger [13] contain two action errors for which P-testing is not reliable. The first involves the use of mixed mode expressions and the second results from roundoff of type REAL numbers.

The need for the development and analysis of testing strategies which are more powerful than the path analysis strategy is noted. How can the path testing method be supplemented to get closer to 100 percent reliability? A programmer has three sources of information for constructing test data: the program to be tested, its specifications, and his knowledge of commonly occurring programming errors. Path analysis testing strategies use only one of these sources. More complex strategies will involve the integration of several sources of information.

References

[1] B. W. Boehm, R. K. McClean, and D. B. Urfrig, "Some experience with automated aids to the design of large-scale reliable software," *IEEE Trans. Software Eng.*, vol. SE-1, pp. 125–133, Mar. 1975.

[2] R. S. Boyer, B. Elspas, and K. N. Levitt, "SELECT–A formal system for testing and debugging programs by symbolic execution," in *Proc. Int. Conf. Reliable Software*, Los Angeles, CA, Apr. 1975.

[3] W. S. Brainerd and L. H. Landweber, *Theory of Computation*. New York: Wiley, 1974.

[4] R. M. Burstall, "Proving correctness as hand simulation with a little induction," in *Proc. IFIPS 1974*. Amsterdam, The Netherlands: North-Holland, 1974.

[5] L. Clarke, "A system to generate test data and symbolically execute programs," Dep. Computer Sciences, Univ. of Colorado, Boulder, CO, Rep. CU-CS-060-75, Feb. 1975.

[6] L. P. Deutsch, "An interactive program verifier," Ph.D. dissertation, Univ. of California, Berkeley, May 1973.

[7] A. Endres, "An analysis of errors and their causes in system programs," in *Proc. Int. Conf. Reliable Software*, Los Angeles, CA, Apr. 1975.

[8] J. B. Goodenough and S. L. Gerhart, "Toward a theory of test data selection," in *Proc. Int. Conf. Reliable Software*, Los Angeles, CA, Apr. 1975.

[9] R. H. Hoffman, "NASA/Johnson Space Center approach to automated test data generation," in *Proc. Computer Science and Statistics: 8th Annu. Symp. on the Interface*, Los Angeles, CA, Feb. 1975.

[10] W. E. Howden, "Automatic generation of program test data and proofs of program correctness," Workshop on the Attainment of Reliable Software, Univ. of Toronto, Apr. 1974.

[11] W. E. Howden and J. Laub, "Automatic case analysis of programs," in *Proc. Computer Science and Statistics: 8th Annu. Symp. on the Interface*, Los Angeles, CA, Feb. 1975.

[12] W. E. Howden, "Methodology for the generation of program test data," *IEEE Trans. Computers*, vol. C-24, pp. 554–560, May 1975.

[13] B. W. Kernighan and P. J. Plauger, *The Elements of Programming Style*. New York: McGraw-Hill, 1974.

[14] J. C. King, "A new approach to program testing," in *Proc. Int. Conf. Reliable Software*, Los Angeles, CA, Apr. 1975.

[15] E. F. Miller, "RXVP: An automated verification system for FORTRAN," in *Proc. Computer Science and Statistics: 8th Annu. Symp. on the Interface*, Los Angeles, CA, Feb. 1975.

[16] L. J. Osterweil and L. D. Fosdick, "Data flow analysis as an aid in documentation, assertion generation, validation, and error detection," Dep. Computer Science, Univ. of Colorado, Boulder, CO, Rep. 15, Sept. 1975.

[17] M. L. Shooman and M. I. Bolsky, "Types, distribution, and test and correction times for programming errors," in *Proc. Int. Conf. Reliable Software*, Los Angeles, CA, Apr. 1975.

[18] R. L. Sites, *ALGOL W Reference Manual*, Stanford Univ., Stanford, CA, STAN-CS-71-230, 1971.

[19] L. G. Stucki, "Automatic generation of self-metric software," in

Proc. IEEE Symp. Computer Software Reliability, New York, NY, 1973.

[20] T. A. Thayer *et al.*, "Software reliability study," TRW Rep. 74-2260.1.9-29, June 1974.

William E. Howden was born in Vancouver, Canada, on December 8, 1940. He received the B.A. degree in mathematics from the University of California, Riverside, in 1963, the M.Sc. degree in mathematics from Rutgers University, New Brunswick, NJ, in 1965, the M.Sc. degree in computer science from Cambridge University, Cambridge, England, in 1970, and the Ph.D. degree in computer science from the University of California, Irvine, in 1973.

In 1965 and 1966 he was with Atomic Energy of Canada, Chalk River, Ont. From 1970 to 1974 he was a Lecturer in computer science at the University of California, Irvine. Since 1973 he has been a consultant to McDonnell Douglas, Huntington Beach, in software reliability. He is currently Assistant Professor of Information and Computer Science at the University of California, San Diego. His research interests are in software and system reliability and in interactive problem solving.

Dr. Howden is a member of the Association for Computing Machinery and the British Computing Society.

A Domain Strategy for Computer Program Testing

LEE J. WHITE, MEMBER, IEEE, AND EDWARD I. COHEN

Abstract—This paper presents a testing strategy designed to detect errors in the control flow of a computer program, and the conditions under which this strategy is reliable are given and characterized. The control flow statements in a computer program partition the input space into a set of mutually exclusive *domains*, each of which corresponds to a particular program path and consists of input data points which cause that path to be executed. The testing strategy generates test points to examine the boundaries of a domain to detect whether a domain error has occurred, as either one or more of these boundaries will have shifted or else the corresponding predicate relational operator has changed. If test points can be chosen within ϵ of each boundary, under the appropriate assumptions, the strategy is shown to be reliable in detecting domain errors of magnitude greater than ϵ. Moreover, the number of test points required to test each domain grows only linearly with both the dimensionality of the input space and the number of predicates along the path being tested.

Index Terms—Control structure, domain errors, path-oriented testing, software reliability, software testing, test data generation.

I. INTRODUCTION

THE purpose of this paper is to present a methodology for the automatic selection of test data for computer program testing. Computer programs contain two types of errors which have been identified as computation errors and domain errors by Howden [9]. A *domain error* occurs when a specific input follows the wrong path due to an error in the control flow of the program. A path contains a *computation error* when a specific input follows the correct path, but an error in some assignment statement causes the wrong function to be computed for one or more of the output variables. The proposed testing strategy has been designed to detect domain errors, and the conditions under which this strategy is reliable are given and characterized. A byproduct of this domain strategy is a partial ability to detect computation errors. This study and proposed methodology are described in greater detail in White *et al.* [12], [13] and in Cohen [3], [4].

There are limitations inherent in any path-oriented testing strategy, and these also constrain the proposed domain strategy. One such limitation might be termed *coincidental correctness*, which can occur when a specific test point follows an incorrect path, and yet the output variables coincidentally are the same as if that test point were to follow the correct path. This test point would then be of no assistance in the detection of the domain error which caused the control flow to change. Note that the problem of coincidental correctness also complicates testing for computation errors; no path-oriented test generation strategy can circumvent this problem.

Another inherent testing limitation has been previously identified by Howden [9] as a *missing path error*, in which a required predicate does not appear in the given program to be tested. Especially if this predicate were an equality, Howden has indicated that no path-oriented testing strategy could systematically determine that such a predicate should be present.

An important assumption in our work is that the user or an "oracle" is available who can decide unequivocally if the output is correct for the specific input processed. The oracle decides only if the output values are correct, and not whether they are computed correctly. If they are incorrect, the oracle does not provide any information about the error and does not give the correct output values.

In the next section, preliminary concepts are defined and discussed. Some assumptions must be made concerning the language in which the given computer program is written, and the ramifications of certain language constructs are explored. The important concepts of program path and path predicates, together with domains, are defined and characterized. The case of linear predicates is given particular emphasis since, in that situation, the domains assume the simple form of convex polyhedra in the input space.

II. PROGRAMMING LANGUAGE ASSUMPTIONS

In order to investigate domain errors, we need to consider the language in which programs will be written. The control structures should be simple and concise, and should resemble those available in most procedure-oriented languages; examples will be stated in an Algol- or Pascal-like language. For simplicity, we assume a single real-valued data type, and this is converted to integer values for use as DO-loop indices.

A number of programming language features are assumed not to occur in the programs we are to analyze for domain errors. The first feature is that of arrays; despite the fact that arrays commonly occur in programs, a predicate which refers to an element of an input array can cause major complications (Ramamoorthy [11]). A second class of language features which will be temporarily excluded in our analysis is that of subroutines and functions. Side effects and parameter passing can pose special problems for the computation of both control flow and environment. These two classes of language features are admittedly very important, and further research is needed to determine whether these features pose any fundamental limitations to the domain testing strategy.

Since input/output processing is so closely linked to a machine or compiler environment, we will assume that all I/O errors have previously been eliminated. Thus, only the most elementary I/O capabilities are provided; input is provided by a simple READ statement, and output is accomplished with a simple WRITE statement. The variables used in a program are divided into three classes. If a variable appears in a READ or WRITE statement, it is classified as an *input* or *output variable*, respectively; all other variables are called *program variables*.

The general predicate form used for control flow is a Boolean combination of arithmetic relational expressions. The logical operators OR and AND are used to form these Boolean combinations. Each arithmetic relational expression contains a relational operator from the set $(<, >, =, \leq, \geq, \neq)$. If a predicate consists of two or more relational expressions with Boolean operators, then it is a *compound predicate*. A *simple predicate* consists of just a single relational expression.

III. PREDICATE INTERPRETATIONS

Every branch point of a computer program is associated with a predicate which evaluates to true or false, and its value determines which outcome of the branch will be followed. The *path condition* is the compound condition which must be satisfied by the input data point in order that the control path be executed. It is the conjunction of the individual predicate conditions which are generated at each branch point along the control path. Not all the control paths that exist syntactically within the program are executable. If input data exist which satisfy the path condition, the control path is also an *execution path* and can be used in testing the program. If the path condition is not satisfied by any input value, the path is said to be *infeasible*, and it is of no interest in testing the program.

A simple predicate is said to be *linear* in variables $V_1, V_2, \cdots, V_n$ if it is of the form

$$A_1 V_1 + A_2 V_2 + \cdots + A_n V_n \text{ ROP } K$$

where K and the A_i are constants and ROP represents one of the relational operators $(<, >, =, \leq, \geq, \neq)$. A compound predicate is linear when each of its component simple predicates is linear.

In general, predicates can be expressed in terms of both program variables and input variables. However, in generating input data to satisfy the path condition, we must work with constraints in terms of only input variables. If we replace each program variable appearing in the predicate by its symbolic value in terms of input variables, we get an equivalent constraint which we call the *predicate interpretation*. A particular interpretation is equivalent to the original predicate in that input variable values satisfying the interpretation will lead to the computation of program variables which also satisfy the original predicate. A single predicate can appear on many different execution paths. Since each of these paths will, in general, consist of a different sequence of assignment statements, a single predicate can have many different interpretations. The following program segment provides example predicates and interpretations.

```
READ A, B;
IF A > B
   THEN C = B + 1;
   ELSE C = B - 1;
D = 2 * A + B;
IF C ≤ 0
   THEN E = 0;
   ELSE
       E = 0;
       DO I = 1, B;
           E = E + 2 * I;
       END;
IF D = 2
   THEN F = E + A;
   ELSE F = E - A;
WRITE F;
```

In the first predicate, $A > B$, both A and B are input variables, so there is only one interpretation. The second predicate, $C \leq 0$, will have two interpretations, depending on which branch was taken in the first IF construct. For paths on which the THEN $C = B + 1$ clause is executed, the interpretation is $B + 1 \leq 0$ or, equivalently, $B \leq -1$. When the ELSE $C = B - 1$ branch is taken, the interpretation is $B - 1 \leq 0$ or, equivalently, $B \leq 1$. Within the second IF-THEN-ELSE clause, a nested DO loop appears. The DO loop is executed:

no times if $B < 1$
    once if $1 \leq B < 2$
    twice if $2 \leq B < 3$
        etc.

Thus, the selection of a path will require a specification of the number of times that the DO loop is executed, and a corresponding predicate is applied which selects those input points which will follow that particular path. Even though the third predicate, $D = 2$, appears on multiple paths, it only has one interpretation, $2 * A + B = 2$, since D is assigned the value $2 * A + B$ in the same statement in each path.

IV. IMPORTANCE OF LINEAR PREDICATES

The domain testing strategy becomes particularly attractive from a practical point of view if the predicates are assumed to be linear in input variables. It might seem to be an undue limitation to require that predicate interpretations be linear for the proposed strategy. In fact, however, as the following discussion shows, this represents no real limitation for many important applications.

A number of authors have provided data to show that simple programming language constructs are used more often than complex constructs. Knuth [10] studied a random sample of Fortran programs and found that 86 percent of all assignment statements were of the forms

TABLE I
PREDICATE STATISTICS FOR 50 COBOL PROGRAMS

	Total	Avg.	Range
Total Lines	12 628	253	31-1287
Procedure Division Lines	8139	163	13-822
Total Predicates	1225	25	0-115
Linear Predicates	1070	21	0-104
Nonlinear Predicates	1	0.02	0-1
Input-Independent Predicates	154	3	0-28
Predicates with 1 Variable	945	19	0-97
Predicates with 2 Variables	125	2.5	0-20
Equality Predicates	779	15.5	0-76

$V_1 = V_2$,
$V_1 = V_2 + V_3$,

or

$V_1 = V_2 - V_3$.

Also, 70 percent of all DO loops in the programs contained fewer than four statements. Knuth also conducted extensive dynamic tests, and found that less than 4 percent of a program accounts for more than half its running time. Elshoff [5], [6] studied 120 production PL/I programs and showed similar results, including the fact that 97 percent of all arithmetic operators are + or -, and 98 percent of all expressions contain fewer than two operators.

An experiment of particular relevance to the present context is reported in Cohen [4] using typical data processing programs since program functions and programming practice tend to be reasonably uniform in this area. A random sample of 50 Cobol programs was taken directly from production data processing applications for this study. In this static analysis, each predicate is classified according to whether it is linear or nonlinear, and the number of input variables used in the predicate has also been recorded. It should be noted that linear predicates do not always correspond to linear predicate interpretations, for this depends upon the dynamic assignment of program variables used in these predicates; however, for these programs, the predicate interpretations were also linear in nearly every instance. The number of input-independent predicates were also tabulated since these predicates do not produce any input constraints. The number of equality predicates is also reported since these predicates are very beneficial in reducing the number of test points required for a domain. These data are summarized in Table I.

The most important result is that only one predicate out of the 1225 tabulated in the study is nonlinear. The predicates are also very simple since most of them refer to only one input variable, and no predicate in this sample uses more than two input variables.

In conclusion, while this study by no means represents an exhaustive survey, we believe the sample is large enough to indicate that nonlinear predicate interpretations are rarely encountered in data processing applications. It is clear that any testing strategy restricted to linear predicates is still viable in many areas of programming practice.

V. INPUT SPACE STRUCTURE

An *input space domain* is defined as a set of input data points satisfying a path condition, which consists of the conjunction of predicate interpretations along the path as defined in Section III. For simplicity in this discussion, each of these predicates is assumed to be simple. The input space is partitioned into a set of domains. Each domain corresponds to a particular execution path in the program and consists of the input data points which cause the path to be executed.

The boundary of each domain is determined by the predicate interpretations in the path condition and consists of *border segments*, where each border segment is the section of the boundary determined by a single simple predicate in the path condition. Each border segment can be open or closed, depending on the relational operator in the predicate. A *closed border segment* is actually part of the domain and is formed by predicates with $\leq$, $\geq$, or = operators. An *open border segment* forms part of the domain boundary, but does not constitute part of the domain, and is formed by $<$, $>$, and $\neq$ predicates.

The total number of predicates on the path is only an upper bound on the number of border segments in the domain boundary since certain predicates in the path condition may not actually produce border segments. An *input-independent predicate interpretation* is one which reduces to a relation between constants, and since it is either true or false regardless of the input values, it does not further constrain the domain. This case arises when a predicate is required for one or more paths, and yet lies along other paths for which it reduces to a tautology and is input-independent. A *redundant predicate interpretation* is one which is superceded by the other predicate interpretations, i.e., the domain can be defined by a strict subset of the predicate interpretations for that path. In general, the determination of which predicate interpretations are redundant is a difficult problem.

The general form of a simple linear predicate interpretation is

$$A_1 X_1 + A_2 X_2 + \cdots + A_N X_N \text{ ROP } K$$

where ROP is the relational operator, X_i are input variables, and A_i, K are constants. However, the border segment which any of these predicates defines is a section of the surface defined by the equality

$$A_1 X_1 + A_2 X_2 + \cdots + A_N X_N = K$$

since this is the limiting condition for the points satisfying the predicate. In an N-dimensional space, this linear equality defines a hyperplane which is the N-dimensional generalization of a plane.

Consider a path condition composed of a conjunction of simple predicates. These predicates can be of three basic types: equalities (=), inequalities ($<, >, \leq, \geq$), and nonequalities ($\neq$). The use of each of the three types results in a markedly different effect on the domain boundary. Each equality constrains the domain to lie in a particular hyperplane, thus reducing the dimensionality of the domain by one. The set of inequality constraints then defines a region

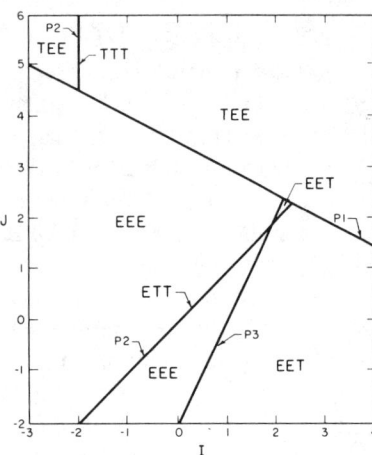

Fig. 1. Input space partitioning structure.

within the lower dimensional space defined by the equality predicates.

The nonequality linear constraints define hyperplanes which are not part of the domain, giving rise to open border segments as mentioned earlier. Observe that the constraint $A \neq B$ is equivalent to the compound predicate $(A < B)$ OR $(A > B)$. In this form, it is clear that the addition of a nonequality predicate to a set of inequalities can split the domain defined by those inequalities into two regions.

The following example should clarify the concepts discussed above.

```
        READ I, J;
        C = I + 2*J - 1;
(P1)    IF C > 6
            THEN D = C - I;
            ELSE D = C + I - J + 2;
(P2)    IF D = C + 2
            THEN E = I;
            ELSE E = 3;
(P3)    IF E ≤ D - 2*J
            THEN F = I;
            ELSE F = J;
        WRITE F;
```

Fig. 1 shows the corresponding input space partitioning structure for this program. The input space is in terms of inputs I and J, and is arbitrarily constrained by the following min-max conditions:

$$-3 \leq I \leq 4, \quad -2 \leq J \leq 6.$$

Each border in Fig. 1 is labeled with the corresponding predicate, and each domain is labeled with the corresponding path. The path notation is based upon which branch (THEN T or ELSE E) is taken in each of the three IF constructs, P1, P2, and P3. A three-character code then uniquely specifies the path, e.g., TEE.

The first predicate P1, $C > 6$, will be interpreted as $I + 2*J > 7$ since $C = I + 2*J - 1$. This single interpretation P1 is seen in Fig. 1 as a single continuous border segment across the entire input space. The second predicate P2 demonstrates the effects of both equality and nonequality predicates. Domains for paths through the THEN branch are constrained by the equality, and this reduction in dimensionality is seen in the fact that these domains consist of the points on the solid line segments ETT and TTT. Paths through the ELSE branch are specified by a nonequality predicate, and the corresponding domains consist of the two regions on either side of the solid line segments; in Fig. 1 these two regions are TEE and EEE, respectively, depending upon which branch is taken through predicate P1. Predicate P2 has two interpretations, depending upon the value assigned to D and produces two discontinuous border segments ETT and TTT.

The third predicate P3 might have four different interpretations, but only one border segment appears in the diagram. The other three interpretations do not produce borders since they are either redundant or correspond to infeasible paths. With three IF constructs, we have eight control paths, but the diagram contains only five domains since three of the paths are infeasible. Also, many of these domains have fewer than three border segments because of redundant and predicate interpretations. From this example, we can conclude that the input space partitioning structure of a program with many predicates and a larger dimensional input space can be extremely complicated.

The foregoing definitions and example allow us to characterize more precisely domains which correspond to simple linear predicate interpretations. For a formal statement of the characterization, we need the following definitions. A set is *convex* if for any two points in the set, the line segment joining these paths is also in the set. A *convex polyhedron* is the set produced by the intersection of the set of points satisfying a finite number of linear equalities and inequalities.

For an execution path with a set of simple linear equality or inequality predicate interpretations, the input space domain is a single convex polyhedron. If one or more simple linear nonequality predicate interpretations are added to this set, then the input space domain consists of the union of a set of disjoint convex polyhedra.

VI. Definitions of Types of Error

The basic ideas behind the classification of errors that we use are due to Howden [9], but our approach to defining them is somewhat more operational than that given in his paper.

From the previous sections, it is clear that a program can be viewed as

1) establishing an exhaustive partition of the input space into mutually exclusive domains, each of which corresponds to an execution path, and

2) specifying, for each domain, a set of assignment statements which constitute the domain computation.

Thus, we have a *canonical representation* of a program, which is a (possibly infinite) set of pairs $\{(D_1; f_1), (D_2; f_2), \cdots, (D_i; f_i), \cdots\}$ where D_i is the ith domain and f_i is the corresponding domain computation function.

Given an incorrect program P, let us consider the changes in its canonical representation as a result of modifications performed on P. It is assumed that these modifications are made using only permissible language constructs and results in a legal program.

Definition: A *domain boundary modification* occurs if the modification results in a change in the D_i component of some $(D_i; f_i)$ pair in the canonical representation.

Definition: A *domain computation modification* occurs if the modification results in a change in the f_i component of some $(D_i; f_i)$ pair in the canonical representation.

Definition: A *missing path modification* occurs if the modification results in the creation of a new $(D_i; f_i)$ pair such that D_i is a subset of D_j occurring in some pair $(D_j; f_j)$ in the canonical representation of P.

Notice that a particular modification (say a change of some assignment statement) can be a modification of more than one type. In particular, a missing path modification is also a domain boundary modification.

The errors that occur in a program can be classified on the basis of the modifications needed to obtain a correct program and consequent changes in the canonical representation. In general, there will be many correct programs and multiple ways to get a particular correct program. Hence, the error classification is not absolute, but relative to the particular correct program that would result from the series of modifications.

Definition: An incorrect program P can be viewed as having a *domain error* (*computational error*) (*missing path error*) if a correct program P* can be created by a sequence of modifications, at least one of which is a domain boundary modification (domain computation modification) (missing path modification).

Several remarks are in order. The operational consequence of the phrase "can be viewed as" in the above definition is that the error classification is relative not only to a particular correct program, but also to a particular sequence of modifications. For instance, consider an error in a predicate interpretation such that an incorrect relational operator is employed, e.g., use of > instead of <. This could be viewed as a domain error, leading to a modification of the predicate, or as a computation error, leading to a modification of the functions computed on the two branches. The fact that it might be more possible to change the relational operator rather than the function computations is a consequence of the language constructs, and it is not directly captured in the definitions of the types of error. In this paper, we would regard an error due to an incorrect relational operator as a domain error; it is a simpler modification to change the relational operator in the predicate than to interchange the set of assignment statements.

More specific characterizations of these errors can be made in the context of specific programming language constructs. In particular, the following informal description directly relates domain errors to the predicate constructs allowed in the language.

A path contains a domain error if an error in some predicate interpretation causes a border segment to be "shifted" from its correct position or to have an incorrect relational operator. A domain error can be caused by an incorrectly specified predicate or by an incorrect assignment statement which affects a variable used in the predicate. An incorrect predicate or assignment statement may affect many predicate interpretations, and consequently cause more than one border to be in error.

VII. The Domain Testing Strategy

The domain testing strategy is designed to detect domain errors and will be effective in detecting errors in any type of domain border under certain conditions. Test points are generated for each border segment which, if processed correctly, determine that both the relational operator and the position of the border are correct. An error in the border operator occurs when an incorrect relational operator is used in the corresponding predicate, and an error in the position of the border occurs when one or more incorrect coefficients are computed for the particular predicate interpretation. The strategy is based on a geometrical analysis of the domain boundary and takes advantage of the fact that points on or near the border are most sensitive to domain errors. A number of authors have made this observation, e.g., Boyer *et al.* [1] and Clarke [2].

It should be emphasized that the domain strategy does not require that the correct program be given for the selection of test points since only information obtained from the given program is needed. However, it will be convenient to be able to refer to a "correct border," although it will not be necessary to have any knowledge about this border. Define the *given border* as that corresponding to the predicate interpretation for the given program path being tested, and the corresponding *correct border* as that border which would be calculated in some correct program.

The domain testing strategy will be developed and validated under a set of simplifying assumptions:

1) Coincidental correctness does not occur for any test case.

2) A missing path error is not associated with the path being tested.

3) Each border is produced by a simple predicate.

4) The path corresponding to each adjacent domain computes a different function from the path being tested.

5) The given border is linear, and if it is incorrect, the correct border is also linear.

6) The input space is continuous rather than discrete.

Assumptions 1) and 2) have been shown to be inherent to the testing process, and cannot be entirely eliminated. However, recognition of these potential problems can lead to improved testing techniques. Assumptions 3) and 4) considerably simplify the testing strategy, for with them no more than one domain need be examined at one time in order to select test points, and as will be indicated shortly, a reduced number of test points will be required. As for the linearity assumption 5), the domain testing method has been shown to be applicable for nonlinear boundaries, but the number of required test points may become inordinate, and there are complex problems associated with processing nonlinear boundaries in higher dimensions. The continuous input space assumption 6) is not really a limitation of the proposed testing method, but allows points to be chosen arbitrarily close to the border to be tested. An error analysis has shown that pathological cases do exist in discrete spaces corresponding to integer data

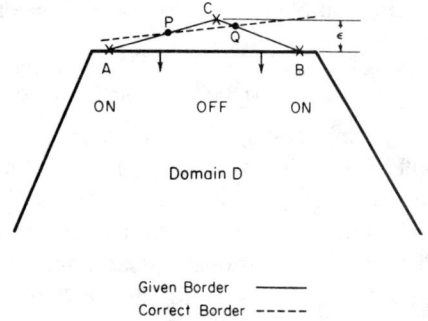

Fig. 2. Test points for a two-dimensional linear border.

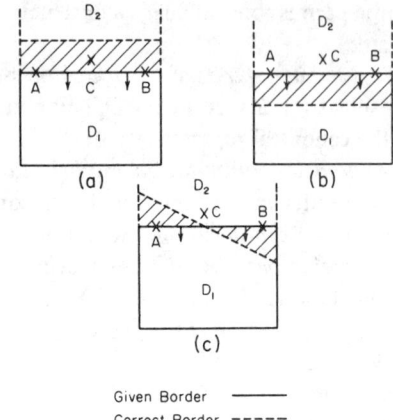

Fig. 3. The three types of border shifts.

types, but these occur only when domain size is on the order of the resolution of the discrete space itself; these results are available as [12].

VIII. Two-Dimensional Linear Inequalities

The test points selected will be of two types, defined by their position with respect to the given border. An *ON test point* lies on the given border, while an *OFF test point* is a small distance ϵ from, and lies on the open side of, the given border. Therefore, we observe that when testing a closed border, the ON test points are in the domain being tested, and each OFF test point is in some adjacent domain. Conversely, when testing an open border, each ON test point is in some adjacent domain, while the OFF test points are in the domain being tested.

Fig. 2 shows the selection of three test points A, B, and C for a closed inequality border segment. The three points must be selected in an ON-OFF-ON sequence. Specifically, if test point C is projected down on line AB, then the projected point must lie strictly between A and B on this line segment. Also, point C is selected a distance ϵ from the given border segment, and will be chosen so that it satisfies all the inequalities defining domain D except for the inequality being tested.

It must be shown that test points selected in this way will reliably detect domain errors due to boundary shifts. If any of the test points lead to an incorrect output, then clearly is an error. On the other hand, if the outputs of all these points are correct, then either the given border is correct, or if it is incorrect, Fig. 2 shows that the correct border must lie on or above points A and B, and must lie below point C, for by assumptions 1) and 4), each of these test points must lie in its assumed domain. So if the given border is incorrect, then the correct border can only belong to a class of line segments which intersect both closed line segments AC and BC.

Fig. 2 indicates a specific correct border from this class which intersects line segments AC and BC at P and Q, respectively. Define the *domain error magnitude* for this correct border to be the maximum of the distances from P and from Q to the given border. Then it is clear that the chosen test points have detected domain errors due to border shifts except for a class of domain errors of magnitude less than ϵ. In a continuous space, ϵ can be chosen arbitrarily small, and as ϵ approaches zero, the line segments AC and BC become arbitrarily close to the given border, and in the limit, we can conclude that the given border is identical to the correct border.

Fig. 3 shows the three general types of border shifts, and will allow us to see how the ON-OFF-ON sequence of test points works in each case. In Fig. 3(a), the border shift has effectively reduced domain D_1. Test points A and B yield correct outputs, for they remain in the correct domain D_1 despite the shifted border. However, the border has shifted past test point C, causing it to be in domain D_2 instead of domain D_1. Since the program will now follow the wrong path when executing input C, incorrect results will be produced. In Fig. 3(b), the domain D_1 has been enlarged due to the border shift. Here test point C will be processed correctly since it is still in domain D_2, but both A and B will detect the shift since they should also be in domain D_2. Finally, in Fig. 3(c), only test point B will be incorrect since the border shift causes it to be in D_1 instead of D_2. Therefore, the ON-OFF-ON sequence is effective since at least one of the three points must be in the wrong domain as long as the border shift is of a magnitude greater than ϵ.

Recall in Fig. 2 that we required the OFF point C to satisfy all the inequalities defining domain D except for the inequality being tested. The reason for this requirement is that some correct border segment may terminate on the extension of an adjacent border, rather than intersecting both line segments AC and BC as we have argued. In order to achieve this condition, C could always be chosen closer to the given border in order to satisfy the adjacent border inequalities.

We must also demonstrate the reliability of the method for domain errors in which the predicate operator is incorrect. If the direction of the inequality is wrong, e.g., $\leq$ is used instead of $\geq$, the domains on either side of the border are interchanged, and any point in either domain will detect the error. A more subtle error occurs when just the border itself is in the wrong domain, e.g., $\leq$ is used instead of $<$. In this case, the only points affected lie on the border, and since we always test ON points, this type of error will always be detected. If the correct predicate is an equality, the OFF point will detect the error.

The domain testing strategy requires at most $3*P$ test points for a domain where P, the number of border segments on this boundary, is bounded by the number of predicates encountered on the path. However, we can reduce this cost by sharing test points between adjacent borders of the domain. The requirement for sharing an ON point is that it is an extreme point for two adjacent borders which are both closed or both open. The number of ON points needed to test the entire domain boundary can be reduced by as much as one half, i.e., the number of test points TP required to test the complete domain boundary lies in the following range:

$$2*P \leqslant TP \leqslant 3*P.$$

Even more significant savings are possible by sharing the test points for a common border between two adjacent domains. If both domains are tested independently, the common border between them is tested twice, using a total of six test points. If this border has shifted, both domains must be affected, and the error will be detected by testing either domain.

IX. N-Dimensional Linear Inequalities

The domain testing strategy developed for the two-dimensional case can be extended to the general N-dimensional case in a straightforward manner. The central property used in the previous analysis was the fact that a line is uniquely determined by two points. We can easily generalize this property since an N-dimensional hyperplane is determined by N linearly independent points. So, whereas in the two-dimensional case we had to identify only two points on the correct border, in general we have to identify N points on the correct border and, in addition, these points must be guaranteed to be linearly independent. We might note that any N extreme points of the given border are automatically independent.

The validation of domain testing for the general linear case is based on the same geometric arguments used in the two-dimensional case. The key to the methodology is that the correct border must intersect every OFF-ON line segment, assuming that the test points are all correct. Since we must identify a total of N points on the correct border, N OFF-ON line segments are needed, and we can achieve this by testing N linearly independent ON test points on the given border and a single OFF test point whose projection on the given border is any convex combination of these N points. In addition, as in the two-dimensional case, the OFF point must also satisfy the inequality constraints corresponding to all adjacent borders.

Even though we do not know these specific points at which the correct border intersects the ON-OFF segments, we do know that these points must be linearly independent since the ON points are linearly independent. The OFF point is a distance ϵ from the given border, and in the limit as ϵ approaches zero, each OFF-ON line segment becomes arbitrarily close to the given border. However, as in the two-dimensional case, the ϵ-limitation means that only border shifts of magnitude greater than ϵ will be detected.

The domain testing strategy requires at most $(N + 1)*P$ test points per domain where N is the dimensionality of the input space in which the domain is defined and P is the number of border segments in the boundary of the specific domain. However, we again can reduce this testing cost by using extreme

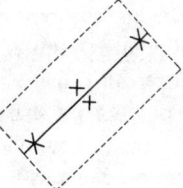

Fig. 4. Test points for an equality border.

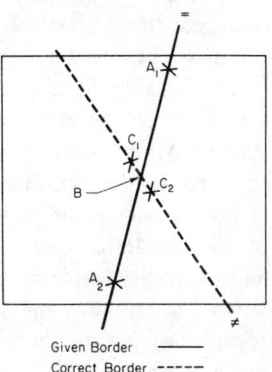

Fig. 5. A pathological case in domain testing for an equality predicate.

points as ON test points, and by sharing test points between adjacent domains.

X. Equality and Nonequality Predicates

Equality predicates constrain the domain to lie in a lower dimensional space. If we have an N-dimensional input space and the domain is constrained by L independent equalities, the remaining inequality and nonequality predicates then define the domain within the (N-L)-dimensional subspace defined by the set of equality predicates.

In Fig. 4, we see the equality border and the proposed set of test points. In a general N-dimensional domain, let us first consider a total of N ON points on the border and two OFF points, one on either side of the border. As before, the ON points must be independent, and the projection of each OFF point on the border must be a convex combination of the ON points.

Given an incorrect equality predicate, the error could be either in the relational operator or in the position of the border or both. The proposed set of test points can be shown to detect an operator or a position error by arguments analogous to those previously given. This set of points is also adequate for almost all combinations of operator and position errors, except for the following pathological possibility. Let us assume that the border has shifted and the correct predicate is a nonequality. If both OFF points happen to lie on the correct border while none of the ON points belongs to this border, the error would go undetected. This singular situation is diagrammed as the dashed border in Fig. 5 where A_1 and A_2 are the ON points and C_1 and C_2 are the OFF points. This problem can be solved by testing one additional point selected so that it lies both on the given border and the correct border for this case, i.e., at the intersection point of the given border with the line segment connecting the two OFF points. This additional point is denoted by B in the figure.

Each equality predicate can thus be completely tested using a total of (N + 3) test points. By sharing test points between all the equality predicates, this number can be considerably reduced, but the reduction depends upon values of N and L. In addition, since testing the equality predicates reduces the effective dimensionality to (N-L) for each of the inequality and nonequality borders, and the equality ON test points can be shared, even further reductions are possible.

For the case of a nonequality border, the testing strategy is identical to that of the equality border just discussed. The arguments for the validity of the strategy are analogous to those in previous cases. Again in this case, the pathological possibility discussed in connection with the equality predicate can occur, and can be handled in the same way. The major difference is that while test points can be extensively shared between equality and inequality borders, in general such sharing is not possible between nonequality and inequality borders.

The following proposition then summarizes the situation for testing linear borders in N-dimensions.

Proposition 1

Given assumptions 1)-6), with each OFF point chosen a distance ϵ from the corresponding border, the domain testing strategy is guaranteed to detect all domain errors of magnitude greater than ϵ using no more than $P*(N+3)$ test points per domain.

XI. AN EXAMPLE OF ERROR DETECTION USING THE DOMAIN STRATEGY

The domain testing strategy has been described and validated using somewhat complicated algebraic and geometric arguments. In this section, we hope to complement those discussions by demonstrating how a set of domain test points for a short sample program actually detects specific examples of different types of programming errors. In discussing each error, we will focus on a specific domain affected by the error, and a careful analysis of its effect on the domain will allow us to identify those domain test points which detect the error.

The short example program reads two values, I and J, and produces a single output value M. Therefore, the input space is two dimensional, and the following min-max constraints have been chosen so that the input space diagram would not be too large or complicated:

$$-8 \leq I \leq 8 \qquad -5 \leq J \leq 5.$$

Even though the input space is assumed to be continuous, the coordinates of each test point are specified to an accuracy of 0.2 in order to simplify the diagrams and discussions. Of course, in an actual implementation, each OFF point would be chosen much closer to the border.

The sample program is listed below and consists of three simple IF constructs, the first two of which are inequalities and the last of which is an equality. The input space structure is diagrammed in Fig. 6 where the solid diagonal border across the entire space is produced by the first predicate, the dashed

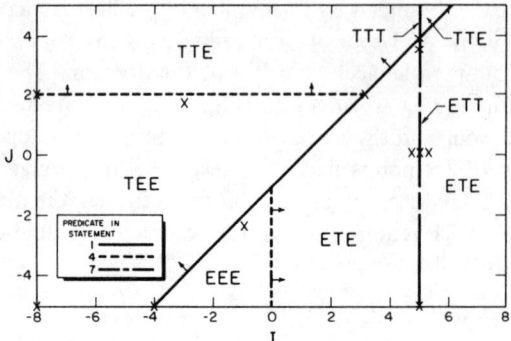

Fig. 6. Input space domain test points.

horizontal border and short vertical border at I = 0 are produced by the second predicate, and the vertical equality border at I = 5 corresponds to the third predicate. In addition, domain test points have been indicated for the two domains which we will discuss, viz. TTE and ETT.

Statement Number	READ I, J;
1	IF I $\leq$ J + 1
2	THEN K = I + J - 1;
3	ELSE K = 2 * I + 1;
4	IF K $\geq$ I + 1
5	THEN L = I + 1;
6	ELSE L = J - 1;
7	IF I = 5
8	THEN M = 2 * L + K;
9	ELSE M = L + 2 * K - 1;
	WRITE M;

Table II illustrates two types of errors we would like to consider. The first is an error in the inequality predicate in statement 4 of the above program (K $\geq$ I + 1) where it is assumed that the correct predicate should be (K $\geq$ I + 2). This corresponds to an inequality border shift, and the modified domain structure is shown in Fig. 7. Three points have been selected to test this border, and it can be seen in Table II that the two ON points detect this error where M and M' represent the output variables for the given program and for the assumed correct program, respectively. Note that as a result of this error, the vertical border at I = 0 in Fig. 6 has also shifted to I = 1 in Fig. 7 and, if tested, would also reveal this error.

Table II also shows the effect of an error in an equality predicate in statement 7 of the given program. It is assumed that the correct predicate should be (I = 5 - J) rather than the (I = 5) predicate which occurs in the given program. Fig. 8 shows the modified input space structure, and it can be seen that equality borders TTT and ETT have shifted. Table II shows the five points which test the ETT border, and note that two ON points both detect this shift.

XII. EXTENSIONS OF THE DOMAIN TESTING STRATEGY

Many assumptions were required in presenting the previous results, but to some extent, these assumptions were made to allow a simple exposition of the domain testing strategy. This section will discuss assumptions 3), 4), and 5) which deal with

TABLE II
DETECTION OF DOMAIN ERRORS FOR INEQUALITY AND
EQUALITY PREDICATES

Domain in Error	Given Statement in Error	Given Predicate Interpretation	Assumed Correct Statement	Correct Predicate Interpretation	Test Points for This Border		M	M'
TEE	4 IF $(K \geq I + 1)$ (Inequality Predicate) (See Fig. 7)	$J \geq 2$	IF $(K \geq I + 2)$	$J \geq 3$	ON	$(-8, 2)$	-22	14
					OFF	$(-3, 1.8)$	-4.6	-4.6
					ON	$(3, 2)$	11	8
ETT	7 IF $(I = 5)$ (Equality Predicate) (See Fig. 8)	$I = 5$	IF $(I = 5 - J)$	$I = 5 - J$	two ON points	$(5, -5)$	23	27
						$(5, 3.8)$	23	27
					two OFF points	$(4.8, 0)$	26	26
						$(5.2, 0)$	28	28
					extra ON point	$(5, 0)$	23	23

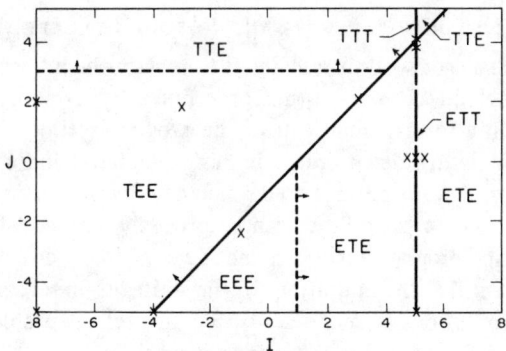

Fig. 7. Correct input space for a domain error.

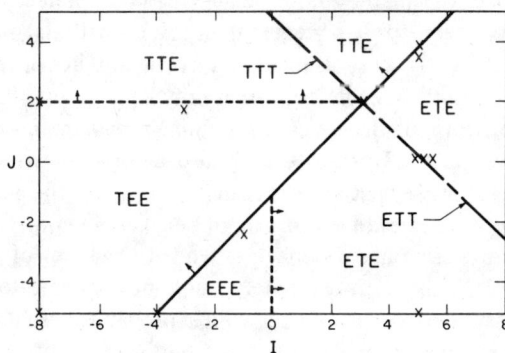

Fig. 8. Correct input space for an equality predicate error.

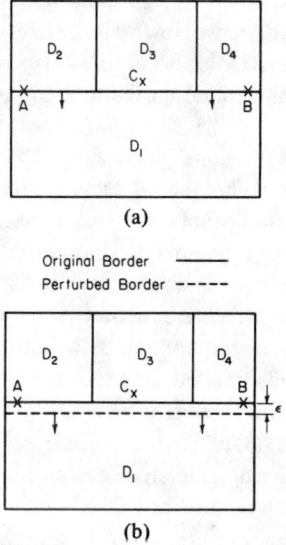

Fig. 9. The identification of adjacent domains.

compound predicates, adjacent domains which compute the same function, and nonlinear borders, respectively. The treatment of these cases will certainly require additional test points and, in some instances, will demand a considerable amount of extra processing. However, one of the main objectives of this section is to illustrate that none of the assumptions 3), 4), or 5) poses a theoretical limitation to the domain testing strategy which cannot be dealt with in some fashion.

First let us deal with the question of nonlinear predicates. A finite domain testing strategy cannot be effective for the universal class of nonlinear borders, but we must determine whether this is caused by some fundamental difference between linear and nonlinear functions. This question can be resolved by observing that if the nonlinear border can be limited to a restricted class specified by a finite set of parameters, then the domain strategy can be applied using a finite number of test points. This extension to nonlinear borders is examined in detail in [4] and [13]. Unfortunately, any but the simplest nonlinear predicates poses problems of extra processing which probably preclude testing except for restricted cases. For example, just finding intersection points of a set of linear and nonlinear borders can require an inordinate amount of computation.

If two adjacent domains compute the same function, any test point selected for their common border is ineffective since the same output values are computed for the test point regardless of the domain in which it lies. We will demonstrate how domain testing can be modified to deal with this problem.

In Fig. 9(a), assuming domain D_1 were being tested, we must compare the functions calculated in domains D_1 and D_2 for test point A, D_1 and D_4 for B, and D_1 and D_3 for C. One of the major problems to be solved is the identification of these adjacent domains. We assume that when testing domain D_1, the partitioning structure of the adjacent domains and the program paths associated with these domains is not known. It would be very complicated to have to generate the domains which are adjacent to the border being tested.

Fig. 9(b) illustrates an approach to this problem. The border being tested is shifted parallel by a small distance ϵ, so that test points A and B now belong to adjacent domains D_2 and D_4, respectively. The modified program is then retested using test points A and B which will, as a byproduct, identify the paths associated with these two adjacent domains. We can then compare the output for each test point before and after the shift. If it is different, then we can definitely conclude that the adjacent domain computes a different function, and this test point can safely be used. If the output is the same for that test point, then we can conclude that either assumption 1) or 4) is violated. However, there is no way to decide this, and the only resolution is to use further test points. If we know that coincidental correctness cannot occur, then we could conclude on the basis of a single point that the adjacent domain computes the same function.

In summary, a technique of testing each point twice will assure us that assumption 4) is valid, and this redundancy might be viewed as a reasonable price to pay to eliminate this restriction. However, if an instance is found where the assumption is not valid, a basic theoretical problem exists.

Assumption 3) stated that a path contained only simple predicates, and this implied that the set of input points could be characterized quite simply as a single domain. We must consider what complications can occur for compound predicates, and how the domain strategy can be generalized to test paths containing these predicates.

The set of inputs corresponding to a path is defined by the path condition, consisting of the conjunction of the predicates encountered along the path. If a compound predicate of the form [C(i) AND C(i + 1)] is encountered on the path, the path condition is still a single conjunction of simple predicates, and the only difference is that two of the simple predicates are produced as a single branch point on the path. No modifications of the domain testing strategy are required in this case.

However, compound predicates using the Boolean operator OR are more complicated. Consider a path containing the following predicates:

$$C_1, C_2, \cdots, [C_i \text{ OR } C_{i+1}], \cdots C_t.$$

The path condition in this case is the conjunction of these predicates, and in standard disjunctive normal form:

$$[C_1 \text{ AND } C_2 \text{ AND } \cdots \text{ AND } C_i \text{ AND } \cdots \text{ AND } C_t]$$
$$\text{OR } [C_1 \text{ AND } C_2 \text{ AND } \cdots \text{ AND } C_{i+1} \text{ AND } \cdots \text{ AND } C_t].$$

The set of input data points following this path consists of the union of two domains, each defined by the conjunction of simple predicates and, in general, any number of these domains is possible.

Assuming linear predicates, each of these domains is a convex polyhedron, but the domains may overlap in arbitrary ways. The major problem caused by these compound predicates is that the domains correspond to the same path, and the assumption that adjacent domains do not compute the same function is violated. We identify three cases of importance: domains which do not overlap, domains which partially overlap, and domains which totally overlap.

In the case where the domains do not overlap, the methodology can be applied to each domain separately. In the other two cases, more complicated procedures must be applied, and these details are discussed in [4] and [13].

In summary, compound predicates which utilize only the AND connective cause no special problems. However, when one or more OR connectives is used, a considerable amount of processing is required just to establish how adjacent domains overlap which correspond to this predicate. This additional processing probably precludes the domain strategy from constituting a viable approach for this case.

XIII. Conclusions and Future Research

The basic goal of this research is to replace the intuitive principles behind current testing procedures by a methodology based on a formal treatment of the program testing problem. By formulating the problem in basic geometric and algebraic terms, we have been able to develop an effective testing methodology whose capabilities can be precisely defined. In addition, since program testing cannot be completely effective, we have identified the limitations of the strategy. In several cases, these limitations have proven to be theoretical problems inherent to the general path testing approach.

The main contribution of this research is the development of the domain testing strategy. Under certain well-defined conditions, the methodology is guaranteed to detect domain errors in linear borders greater than some small magnitude ϵ. Furthermore, the cost, as measured by the number of required test points, is reasonable and grows only linearly with both the dimensionality of the input space domain and the number of path predicates. Domain testing also detects transformation errors and missing path errors in many cases, but the detection of these two classes of errors cannot be guaranteed.

Domain testing has also been extended to classes of nonlinear borders, but unfortunately, nonlinear predicates pose problems of extra processing which probably preclude testing except for restricted cases.

Coincidental correctness is a theoretical limitation inherent to the path testing process, and we have argued that it prevents any reasonable finite testing procedure from being completely reliable. In particular, the possibility of coincidental correctness means that an exhaustive test of all points in an input domain is theoretically required to preclude the existence of computation errors on a path. Within the class of all computable functions, there exist functions which coincide at an arbitrarily large number of points, but if there is sufficient resolution in the output space, further research is required to show that coincidental correctness is a rare occurrence for functions commonly encountered in data processing problems. The class of missing path errors, particularly those of reduced dimensionality, has proven to be another theoretical limitation to the reliability of any path testing strategy.

The domain testing strategy requires a reasonable number of test points for a single path, but the total cost may be unacceptable for a program containing a large number of paths. In particular, this may occur for programs with complicated control structures containing many iteration loops. Additional research is needed to substantially reduce the number of potential paths. One area being investigated is to obtain appropriate restrictions on control structures, especially iteration loops, so that a large number of paths can be tested as a single domain. If this approach is combined with the notion of module independence relative to domain errors, the combinatorial growth of the number of paths can be considerably reduced by domain testing small independent program modules separately. It remains to be shown that practical programs contain sufficient instances of such module independence to allow a reduction of the number of remaining paths to a practical figure.

We have assumed that an "oracle" exists which can always determine whether a specific test case has been computed correctly or not. In reality, the programmer himself must make this determination, and the time spent examining and analyzing these test cases is a major factor in the high cost of software development. One possible avenue for future research would be to automate this process by using some form of input-output specification. If the user provides a formal description of the expected results, the correctness of each test case can be decided automatically by determining whether the output specification is satisfied. This would reduce the cost of testing tremendously, and these new testing techniques would gain acceptance more quickly since the tedious task of verifying test data would be eliminated. In addition, any extra information supplied by the user might be useful in specifying special processing requirements which would indicate the existence of a possible missing path error.

The domain test strategy is currently being implemented, and it will be utilized as an experimental facility for subsequent research. Experiments should indicate what sort of programming errors are most difficult to detect, and should yield extensive dynamic testing data.

Acknowledgment

The authors would like to thank B. Chandrasekaran for his assistance in preparing this paper and, in particular, for his contribution concerning the definitions of domain and computation errors.

References

[1] R. S. Boyer, B. Elspas, and K. N. Levitt, "SELECT—A formal system for testing and debugging programs by symbolic execution," in *Proc. 1975 Int. Conf. Rel. Software*, Los Angeles, CA, Apr. 1975, pp. 234-245.

[2] L. A. Clarke, "A system to generate test data and symbolically execute programs," *IEEE Trans. Software Eng.*, vol. SE-2, pp. 215-222, Sept. 1976.

[3] E. I. Cohen and L. J. White, "A finite domain-testing strategy for computer program testing," Comput. Inform. Sci. Res. Cen., Ohio State Univ., Columbus, Tech. Rep. 77-13, Aug. 1977.

[4] E. I. Cohen, "A finite domain-testing strategy for computer program testing," Ph.D. dissertation, Ohio State Univ., Columbus, June 1978.

[5] J. L. Elshoff, "A numerical profile of commercial PL/I programs," Comput. Sci. Dep. General Motors Res. Lab., Warren, MI, Rep. GMR-1927, Sept. 1975.

[6] —, "An analysis of some commercial PL/I programs," *IEEE Trans. Software Eng.*, vol. SE-2, pp. 113-120, June 1976.

[7] J. B. Goodenough and S. L. Gerhart, "Toward a theory of test data selection," *IEEE Trans. Software Eng.*, vol. SE-1, pp. 156-173, June 1975.

[8] W. E. Howden, "Methodology for the generation of program test data," *IEEE Trans. Comput.*, vol. C-24, pp. 554-560, May 1975.

[9] —, "Reliability of the path analysis testing strategy," *IEEE Trans. Software Eng.*, vol. SE-2, pp. 208-215, Sept. 1976.

[10] D. E. Knuth, "An empirical study of FORTRAN programs," *Software—Practice and Experience*, vol. 1, pp. 105-133, Apr.-June 1971.

[11] C. V. Ramamoorthy, S. F. Ho, and W. T. Chen, "On the automated generation of program test data," *IEEE Trans. Software Eng.*, vol. SE-2, pp. 293-300, Dec. 1976.

[12] L. J. White, F. C. Teng, H. C. Kuo, and D. W. Coleman, "An error analysis of the domain testing strategy," Comput. Inform. Sci. Res. Cen., Ohio State Univ., Columbus, Tech. Rep. 78-2, Sept. 1978.

[13] L. J. White, E. I. Cohen, and B. Chandrasekaran, "A domain strategy for computer program testing," Comput. Inform. Sci. Res. Cen., Ohio State Univ., Columbus, Tech. Rep. 78-4, Aug. 1978.

Lee J. White (S'67-M'67) received the B.S.E.E. degree in electrical engineering from the University of Cincinnati, Cincinnati, OH, in 1962, and the Ph.D. degree in electrical engineering from the University of Michigan, Ann Arbor, in 1967.

He is currently a Professor and Chairman of the Department of Computer and Information Science, Ohio State University, Columbus, and holds a joint appointment in the Department of Electrical Engineering. His current research interests deal with the analysis of algorithms and software analysis and testing. He has published in the areas of pattern recognition, automatic document classification, combinatorial computing, and graph theory. He has served as a Consultant for the Monsanto Research Laboratory, Rockwell International Corporation, and a number of other industrial firms.

Dr. White is a member of the IEEE Computer Society, the Association for Computing Machinery, the Society for Industrial and Applied Mathematics, and Sigma Xi.

Edward I. Cohen was born in Boston, MA, in 1950. He received the B.S. degree in physics from Rensselaer Polytechnic Institute, Troy, NY, in 1972, and the M.S. and Ph.D. degrees, both in computer and information science, from Ohio State University, Columbus, in 1973 and 1978, respectively.

He was a Research and Teaching Associate in the Department of Computer and Information Science, Ohio State University, from 1972 to 1978. He worked as a Programmer for Neoterics, Inc., Columbus, in 1974 and as a Systems Analyst for the State Data Center, Columbus, in 1977. He is currently with the Poughkeepsie Programming Center, IBM Corporation, Poughkeepsie, NY. His current interests include program testing, software reliability, and high-performance multiprocessing system design.

Theories of Program Testing and the Application of Revealing Subdomains

ELAINE J. WEYUKER AND THOMAS J. OSTRAND

Abstract—The theory of test data selection proposed by Goodenough and Gerhart is examined. In order to extend and refine this theory, the concepts of a revealing test criterion and a revealing subdomain are proposed. These notions are then used to provide a basis for constructing program tests.

A subset of a program's input domain is revealing if the existence of one incorrectly processed input implies that all of the subset's elements are processed incorrectly. The intent of this notion is to partition the program's domain in such a way that all elements of an equivalence class are either processed correctly or incorrectly. A test set is then formed by choosing one element from each class. This process represents perfect program testing. For a practical testing strategy, the domain is partitioned into subdomains which are revealing for errors considered likely to occur.

Three programs which have previously appeared in the literature are discussed and tested using the notions developed in the paper.

Index Terms—Program testing, revealing subdomain, software error detection, software reliability, test data generation, theory of testing.

I. INTRODUCTION

THE primary goals of a theory of testing are to provide a basis for practical program testing methodologies, and to establish ways of determining the effectiveness of tests in detecting program errors. Ideally, one would like to construct tests which will detect all errors in a program.

In [5], Goodenough and Gerhart propose basic definitions for a theory of testing, and discuss criteria to be used in selecting test items from the domain of possible inputs to a program. They argue convincingly that test data selected solely on the basis of program structure will not in general be adequate for thorough testing. It is easy to construct simple incorrect programs in which every statement, every branch, or every path can be correctly exercised by appropriate test data.

This situation motivated the definition in [5] of an ideal test in terms of the input and output specifications of the program. An *ideal test* for a program F consists of a set of test data $T = \{t_i\}$ such that there is an input d in F's data domain for which an incorrect output is produced if and only if there is some $t_i \in T$ on which F is incorrect.

The successful execution of an ideal test constitutes a proof of correctness for the program. Given the difficulty of finding proofs of program correctness, we should not be surprised that ideal tests are difficult to discover.

In Sections II and III, we investigate the usefulness of the theory proposed in [5] for the purpose of constructing realistic program tests. Several problems are identified and possible remedies for them are suggested. In Section IV we examine a modification of the theory which would provide a basis for the testing of any program intended to meet a given set of specifications. This approach does not prove to be pragmatically fruitful.

In Section V we introduce the concepts of a revealing test selection criterion and a revealing subdomain in order to address some of the problems identified in earlier sections. In Section VI, three example programs are presented and tests are developed based on the notion of revealing subdomains. This notion represents a perspective on testing which is useful in guiding the selection of meaningful tests.

II. THE GOODENOUGH AND GERHART DEFINITIONS

We begin by examining the Goodenough and Gerhart definitions for test criteria properties. We use their notation: F is a program, D the input domain, and R the output domain for F. On input $d \in D$, F (if it terminates) produces output $F(d) \in R$. The output specification for F is given by $\text{OUT}(x, y)$, where $x \in D$ and $y \in R$. F is correct on input d (abbreviated $\text{OK}(d)$) if $F(d)$ exists and $\text{OUT}(d, F(d))$.

A *test* T for program F is simply a (finite) subset of D. A *test selection criterion* specifies conditions which must be fulfilled by a test. Any set of inputs which satisfies these conditions is said to be a *test selected by* the criterion C. For example, a criterion for a numerical program whose input domain is the integers might specify that each test contain one positive integer, one negative integer, and zero. $\{3, 0, -7\}$, $\{122, 0, -11\}$, and $\{1, 0, -1\}$ are three of the tests selected by this criterion. A test T is *successful* iff $(\forall t \in T)(\text{OK}(t))$. A test selection criterion C is *reliable* iff either every test selected by C is successful, or no test selected is successful. C is *valid* iff whenever program F is incorrect, C selects at least one test set T which is not successful for F. From these definitions, the fundamental theorem of [5] follows: If C is a reliable and valid criterion, then any test selected by C is an ideal test. We shall call a criterion which is both reliable and valid for a program F, an *ideal criterion*.

From the point of view of applying this theory, there are several serious difficulties. The first is that the concepts of

---

Manuscript received February 20, 1979; revised July 30, 1979 and October 9, 1979.

E. J. Weyuker is with the Courant Institute of Mathematical Sciences, New York University, New York, NY 10012.

T. J. Ostrand is with the Software Research Group, Sperry Univac, Blue Bell, PA 19424.

Reprinted from *IEEE Transactions on Software Engineering*, May 1980, pp. 236-246. Copyright © 1980 by The Institute of Electrical and Electronics Engineers, Inc.

reliability and validity are defined with respect to the entire input domain of a program. One does not in general know what errors are actually present in a program. Furthermore, for every element d in the domain, there is a program which processes every element other than d correctly, but is incorrect on d. Therefore, a criterion is *guaranteed* to be both reliable and valid if and only if it selects the entire domain as one test. Such exhaustive testing is clearly impractical. In Section V we discuss ways to divide the domain which reflect and discriminate among different potential errors.

The second difficulty comes about because all of the above definitions are relative to a single program. A criterion which is reliable or valid for F is not necessarily so for a slightly different program F'. The problems arising with tests based solely on the structure of a program are avoided in [5], but the tests are nevertheless based entirely on the behavior of the single program under consideration. This is clearly undesirable if reliability and validity are intended to reflect the quality of tests. A measure of a test's goodness should be independent of whether or not the program is correct, and if incorrect, should not depend on which errors actually appear in the program.

Furthermore, neither validity nor reliability is preserved throughout the debugging process. That is, a criterion which is valid at the start of debugging does not necessarily remain so for every intermediate program produced by successive corrections made on the way to an error-free program. Alternately, an invalid criterion may become valid as the program is transformed. The same is true for reliability.

Another problem is the lack of independence of the properties of validity and reliability. This problem will be discussed in Section III, where we show how it adversely affects the theory's practical applicability.

From the point of view of the programmer who has just designed a program or a person assigned the task of testing and debugging someone else's program, it is practically impossible to find test selection criteria which are both reliable and valid, since these properties depend on the nature of errors present in the program. The situation is illustrated with several simple examples.

First, if program F is correct, i.e., if $(\forall d \in D)(\text{OK}(d))$, then any test will be successful and every selection criterion C is reliable and valid. Of course, F is not known to be correct, and the programmer must use other means to show the reliability and validity of C. Such other means will be the equivalent of a proof of the program's correctness.

On the other hand, if F is not correct, there is in general no way of knowing whether a criterion is ideal without knowing the errors in F. The first example in [5] illustrates this point. The program F computes $d * d$, for d an integer, while the output specification is $F(d) = d + d$. Since F is correct for $d = 0$ and $d = 2$, and incorrect for all other inputs, a criterion which selects as tests only subsets of $\{0, 2\}$ is reliable but not valid, since it does not indicate the error in F. A criterion which selects subsets of $\{0, 1, 2, 3, 4\}$ exposes the error in F, and is therefore valid, but is not reliable since $T = \{0, 2\}$ is a successful test, while $T = \{0, 1\}$ is not successful.

A slight change in the program, while retaining the same output specification, completely changes the reliability and validity of these criteria. If F' computes $d + 2$, then $d = 2$ is the only input for which a correct answer is produced. Thus, choosing subsets of $\{0, 2\}$ becomes a valid, but not reliable criterion for F'. If F'' computes $d + 5$, the criterion which selects subsets of $\{0, 1, 2, 3, 4\}$ is now both reliable and valid.

A test designer using the theory of [5] is trying to find an ideal criterion. However, as the above examples show, there is in general no way to know if a criterion is ideal without already knowing the errors in the program, or at least knowing that any errors in the program are of certain specified types. In Sections V and VI we address this problem by introducing a property which is defined relative to specified errors. Successful test execution then enables one to conclude not that the program is correct, but rather that it does not contain these specified errors. The judicious selection of errors to be tested for can thus increase one's confidence that the program is correct, but does not assure correctness. This more modest goal is obviously easier to attain than correctness.

III. Practical Testing Considerations

We now examine the usefulness of an ideal test for the practical problems of program testing and debugging. Typically, a program goes through many different versions, steps of refinement, improvements, modifications, etc., as it is being written. It is desirable to verify the correctness of each stage in order to increase confidence in the correctness of the next one. An ideal test criterion for one version is not necessarily an ideal criterion for another. The debugging process constantly changes the program being worked on; errors are located and corrected, and sometimes new errors are inadvertently introduced.

Consider the following modification of the example presented earlier:

$$F(d) = (d * d) + 3$$

$$\text{OK}(d) \Longleftrightarrow [(d + d) + 6 = F(d)]$$

That is, F is supposed to double the integer d and add 6, but instead F squares d and adds 3.

Note that $\text{OK}(3)$ and $\text{OK}(-1)$, but for all other d, $\neg \text{OK}(d)$. Thus, $C(T) \Longleftrightarrow (T = \{t\}$ and $t \in \{0, 1, 2\})$ is a valid and reliable criterion. Now suppose that by running F on one of the input values of T, the error of adding the wrong constant is located. This error is corrected, and now $F(d) = (d * d) + 6$. At this point, $\text{OK}(0)$ and $\text{OK}(2)$, but for all other d, $\neg \text{OK}(d)$. Hence C is no longer a reliable criterion, since some tests satisfying C will detect the remaining error, and others will not.

Note that the reverse situation can also occur. Thus, for example, $C'(T) \Longleftrightarrow (T = \{t\}$ and $t \in \{-1, 1, 3\})$ is valid but not reliable for the original program containing two errors. For the partially corrected program, however, it is both valid and reliable.

Thus properties of criteria are not maintained throughout the debugging phase, nor are they even "monotonic" in the sense of being either always gained or preserved, or always lost or preserved.

Monotonicity of a test criterion's properties would be highly desirable as a means of simplifying debugging and to maintain the meanings of tests which satisfy the criterion. The existence of tests whose successful performance implies the lack of similar errors for all versions of a program is useful for regression testing, which is performed on improved versions of a program to assure that each new version at least achieves the quality of the previous ones.

In practice a criterion will specify characteristics which test data must include. It seems unlikely that a tester would want to *prohibit* testing on additional inputs. For that reason, any element in the domain would be permitted by a criterion and, as noted in [5], a criterion which excludes no input element is valid. For example, the criterion described in Section II which selects subsets of $\{0, 2\}$ is not valid precisely because it does not permit values other than 0 and 2 to be tested. Thus most practical criteria will in fact be valid. It is noted in [5] that it is even possible to explicitly exclude some domain elements from testing and still maintain validity.

A proof of reliability is in general the more formidable problem. The knowledge of a criterion's validity says nothing about its reliability or the program's correctness. Even assuming validity, to prove reliability one must be able to prove that if the program contains any errors, then every test selected by the criterion will fail. In general we have no reason to believe that this task will be easy to do.

Our first theorem points out an additional problem associated with the notions of reliability and validity: they are not independent. That is, at least one of the two properties must hold for any criterion.

Theorem 1: $(\forall C)(\text{Val}(C) \vee \text{Rel}(C))$.

This is true because an invalid test criterion exposes no errors, and therefore all of its tests are successful. In fact, if one could demonstrate that a criterion were invalid, then it would follow that:
1) there is an error in the program;
2) every test fulfilling the criterion will run successfully;
3) the criterion is reliable.

The second point says that, at least from the viewpoint of testing, there is nothing to be learned by running a test based on a criterion which is known to be invalid.

Thus, possession of either reliability or validity alone says little about the quality of a test selection criterion. In fact, a way to guarantee the validity or reliability of a criterion is to make sure that it does not possess the other property.

IV. Uniformly Valid and Reliable Test Criteria

We have seen that Goodenough and Gerhart's properties for ideal tests suffer from a fault similar to program structure-based tests, namely dependence on the program being tested. In particular, the reliability and validity of a criterion depend upon whether or not the program contains errors, and if errors are present, which ones. A possible remedy for the situation is to look for criteria whose validity and reliability are dependent only on the desired output specification. Such a criterion would be universal for any program written to satisfy the given specification. This is what is commonly known as black-box testing. Note that in the definitions of validity and reliability in [5] there is an implicit free variable F, referring to the particular program under consideration. The formal definitions of uniform validity and reliability given below bind this F with an outermost universal quantifier. Note that we have also modified the notation of [5] for succ and ok, by including the program F as an explicit parameter.

Given an input domain D and output specification $\text{OK}(F, d)$, criterion C is *uniformly valid* iff

$$(\forall F)[(\exists d \in D)(\neg \text{OK}(F, d)) \Rightarrow (\exists T \subseteq D)(C(T) \,\&\, \neg \text{SUCC}(F, T))].$$

Criterion C is *uniformly reliable* iff

$$(\forall F)(\forall T_1, \forall T_2 \subseteq D) [(C(T_1) \,\&\, C(T_2)) \Rightarrow (\text{SUCC}(F, T_1) \Longleftrightarrow \text{SUCC}(F, T_2))].$$

A *uniformly ideal* test selection criterion for a given output specification is both uniformly valid and uniformly reliable. Such a definition would solve all the program-dependent difficulties inherent in the definitions of [5]. Unfortunately, however, the concept of a uniformly ideal criterion also has serious flaws. Most important, for any significant program there can be no uniformly ideal criterion which is not in a sense trivial. To see this, let us call a criterion C *trivially valid* if the union of all tests selected by C is D. Obviously a trivially valid criterion is valid. However, a criterion C which is not trivially valid cannot be uniformly valid for a given output specification, since for any element d not included in any of C's tests, a program can be written which is incorrect for d, and correct for $D - \{d\}$. Thus we have:

Theorem 2: A criterion C is uniformly valid if and only if C is trivially valid.

A similar weakness holds for uniform reliability.

Theorem 3: A criterion C is uniformly reliable if and only if C selects a single test.

Proof: If C selects only one test it is clearly reliable for any program. Suppose C selects different tests T_1 and T_2, and that t is an input in T_1, but not in T_2. A program F exists which is correct on all the inputs in T_2, but incorrect on t. The two tests thus yield different results for F, and C is not reliable. □

As a consequence of Theorems 2 and 3 we have:

Corollary: A criterion C is uniformly valid and uniformly reliable if and only if C selects only the single test $T = D$.

Uniform validity and reliability, therefore, lead only to the impractical method of exhaustive testing. In contrast, there do exist valid and reliable criteria for any program which are satisfied by test sets other than the entire domain. But as discussed earlier, the only way to guarantee the reliability and validity of a criterion is to use exhaustive testing.

The next result reformulates the Corollary to say that no matter what criterion is used to select tests for a given specification, and no matter what test is chosen (if it is not all of D), there will always be a program which can defeat the test. This is another way of expressing the oft quoted statement that "testing can only reveal the presence of errors, never their absence" [3].

Theorem 4:

$$(\forall C)(\forall T)$$
$$[(C(T) \,\&\, T \neq D) \Rightarrow (\exists F)(\text{succ}(F, T) \,\&\, \neg\text{succ}(F, D))].$$

Proof: Since there is some input datum $t \notin T$, let F be a program which is correct on T and which does not halt on t. □

Other similar negative results have been proved. Weyuker [12], [13] has shown that there can be no algorithm which can decide whether or not a *given* statement, branch, or path of a program may ever be exercised, nor whether or not *every* such unit may be exercised. Thus, a testing methodology which requires the generation of data to do one or more of these things cannot be guaranteed to terminate.

Howden [7] showed that there is no procedure which, given an arbitrary program F and output specification, will produce a nonempty finite test set $T \subseteq D$ such that if F is correct on T then F is correct on all of D. The reason behind this result is that the nonexistent procedure is expected to work for all programs, and thus familiar noncomputability limitations are encountered. Howden's response is to look for subclasses of programs for which test-generating procedures can be successful.

Similarly, in practical terms, one does not have to design test criteria to deal with every possible incorrect program. As noted in [2], programmers "create programs that are close to being correct... [they] also have at their disposal a rough idea of the kinds of errors most likely to occur, [and] the ability and opportunity to examine their program in detail." A theory of testing should attempt to take advantage of classes of errors which are known to occur frequently, and should capture the essence of test selection criteria which can expose the presence of such errors or guarantee their absence.

V. Revealing Test Selection Criteria

The theory proposed in [5] shows that testing can establish the absence of errors in a program if the test selection criteria satisfy the right properties. For the reasons discussed in Sections II and III, we wish to modify and refine the Goodenough and Gerhart theory in order to make it more directly applicable to real program testing. Reliability and validity represent ideal abstract goals for test set selection. We now consider a revision of these goals. We begin by defining a notion which is pragmatically as unattainable as reliability and validity, and then revise this notion to make it more usable. In so doing we have lowered our sights from correctness to what might be called semicorrectness; i.e., exposing the presence of certain specified errors or demonstrating that these errors do not occur. We then outline an approach to, rather than a concrete methodology for, testing. Section VI demonstrates this approach for three sample programs.

We say a *test criterion C is revealing for a subset S* of the input domain if whenever S contains an input which is processed incorrectly then every test set which satisfies C is unsuccessful. Equivalently, if any test selected by C is successfully executed, then every input in S produces correct output. Formally, REVEALING(C, S) iff

$$(\exists d \in S)(\neg\text{ok}(d)) \Rightarrow (\forall T \subseteq S)(C(T) \Rightarrow \neg\text{succ}(T)).$$

Although the property of revealing may seem like a very strong requirement to put on a test selection criterion, the domain subset parameter provides enough precision to make the definition useful. Any test selected by a criterion which is revealing for subdomain S is an ideal test for S.

Two special cases of revealing criteria are important. The first is when the subdomain S is the entire input domain D of the program. In this case the property revealing is equivalent to the conjunction of validity and reliability, so long as vacuous criteria are excluded.

Theorem 5: A nonempty criterion C is revealing with respect to the domain D of a program if and only if C is both valid and reliable.

Proof: Suppose C is revealing. If there are any errors in D then every test meeting C must be unsuccessful. C is therefore reliable, and since it is nonempty, it is also valid. If C is both valid and reliable, then the presence of any error guarantees that every test meeting C will be unsuccessful. □

The second special case occurs when we eliminate the criterion from the definition, and allow any nonempty subset of S to be a test set. In this case we say that a *subdomain S is revealing* if the existence of an error on some element of S implies the failure of the program on any nonempty subset of S. In other words, one input in S is processed incorrectly if and only if all inputs in S are processed incorrectly. It is this notion of a revealing subdomain that forms the basis of our approach to testing, as illustrated in Section VI. Note that it eliminates the concept of a criterion entirely and intuitively says that a subdomain consists of elements which are all processed the same way and which, based on the specifications, should be treated the same. To make use of such a strong property requires that the problem's input domain be partitioned in an intelligent and meaningful way using both program-dependent and program-independent information. The approach we use combines the techniques of path domain testing [7], functional testing [9], and special values testing [6].

If S is a revealing subdomain, running successful tests from S only assures the correctness of the program on S. In fact, even this cannot in general be guaranteed. Showing that S is revealing requires a proof that *no* error, no matter how unlikely, can occur for the elements of S. Essentially this requires the equivalent of a proof of correctness for the subdomain (except of course if S is small and the program can be run on each of its elements). What can usually be guaranteed is not that S is revealing, but rather that it is revealing for certain specified errors.

Given a program F, an error E affects an input i if, when E is present in F, then $\neg\text{ok}(i)$. A *subdomain S is revealing for an error E* provided that if E is an error in F and E affects some element of S, then for every element d in S, $\neg\text{ok}(d)$. The correct execution of an element from such a subdomain then guarantees the absence of the specified error on that subdomain. The incorrect execution of an element does not necessarily assure the presence of such a specified error, although of course some error must be present. To detect a specific error E by testing, it is only necessary that one subdomain be revealing for E and produce incorrect output due to E. Testing of this sort is demonstrated for an exponentiation program (Example 2 of Section VI). For many of the errors in this example, some subdomains produce incorrect results, while other subdomains are unaffected and yield correct outputs.

Notice that a subdomain which is revealing for each of several different errors is not necessarily revealing for the simultaneous occurrence of two or more of the errors. This is because there may be inputs for which one error hides the effect of another.

The goal then is to partition the domain based both on the program-independent properties mentioned earlier and structural properties of the program, as well as potential errors which have been identified as likely. This last point is similar in a sense to the philosophy which underlies mutation testing [2]. In that approach, the authors have implicitly defined what they consider to be the class of most likely errors. By showing that they do not occur, they do not guarantee the absence of *all* errors, but rather that the program is not radically incorrect. It may be debated whether the authors of [2] have correctly identified what are in fact the most likely errors to occur, or whether such a class is definable abstractly without reference to the particular problem being considered. However, their ultimate goal of proving the absence of "likely" errors, while allowing for the possibility of "unlikely" errors, is appropriate. The classification into likely and unlikely errors requires problem-dependent judgment and is therefore not readily mechanizable.

In his study of symbolic testing and its effectiveness in detecting errors [8], Howden states that "both symbolic testing and actual data testing are unreliable for discovering most of the path-domain errors in the sample programs... Actual data testing can reveal the error if the programmer is lucky enough to choose a test which comes from the incorrect part of the domain."

The notion of a revealing subdomain is a partial solution to this problem. If a program's input domain can be successfully divided into revealing subdomains, then it is no longer necessary to rely on luck in choosing appropriate tests. Either every element of a subdomain produces the correct output, or none does.

VI. Constructing Revealing Subdomains

Test data should be developed from both program-dependent and program-independent sources which include the problem's specifications, the algorithm used, and the input/output data structures. In attempting to find revealing criteria or subdomains for a program, we start by considering the program separately from the program-independent sources.

The input domain is first partitioned into *path domains*. A path domain consists of a set of inputs which each follow the same path, or one of a family of related paths, through the program's flow graph. A second preliminary partition, the *problem partition*, is formed on the basis of common properties implied by the specifications, algorithm, and data structures. These two partitions are then intersected to form classes which are the basis for test selection. These classes can be characterized by the conjunction of the conditions which describe the classes of the path domain and problem partitions. This corresponds to the intuition described in the previous section. The partition induced by the path domains separates the domain into classes of inputs which *are* treated the same way by the program, while the problem partition separates the domain into classes which *should be* treated the same way by the program. Intersecting these classes yields subdomains with the desired property.

For example, a problem whose single input is an integer might have specifications which suggest a partition into the odd and even integers. Analysis of the program graph may show that all positive inputs follow one path, all negative inputs another, and zero is processed as a special case. Intersecting the problem partition with the path domain partition results in a set of five classes: odd positive, odd negative, even positive, even negative, and zero. If our understanding of the problem is good, these classes are likely to be revealing for many errors.

Usually the path domain partition does not differ as markedly from the problem partition as in the above example, since ultimately the program, data structures, and algorithm all derive from the original problem specifications. The differences which do exist are fruitful places to look for errors. This is the basic rationale behind our strategy for forming subdomains.

Informally, the process attempts to construct a partition of the input domain such that elements in an equivalence class are processed the same way by the program, and in addition are characterized the same way by the specifications and the algorithm. In constructing test data for the examples in this section we use the revealing subdomain concept. Since a revealing subdomain has the property that either each of its elements is processed correctly or each element is processed incorrectly, the actual selection of test data is reduced to choosing an arbitrary element from each subdomain.

We now give three examples of programs and revealing subdomain construction. The actual test data consists simply of an arbitrary element selected from each subdomain.

Example 1: This is a triangle classification problem which has been studied by several authors [2], [11]. The problem's specifications are

Input: Three positive integers A, B, C, with $A \geq B \geq C$.
Output: The program indicates which of the following descriptions is satisfied by $A, B,$ and C.
1) They do not represent the sides of a triangle.
2) They are the sides of an equilateral triangle.
3) They are the sides of an isosceles, but not equilateral, triangle.
4) They are the sides of a scalene right triangle.
5) They are the sides of a scalene obtuse triangle.
6) They are the sides of a scalene acute triangle.

Fig. 1 shows the program presented in [2] to meet these specifications. Throughout our discussion of this program, we use $A, B,$ and C to refer to the original input values. This

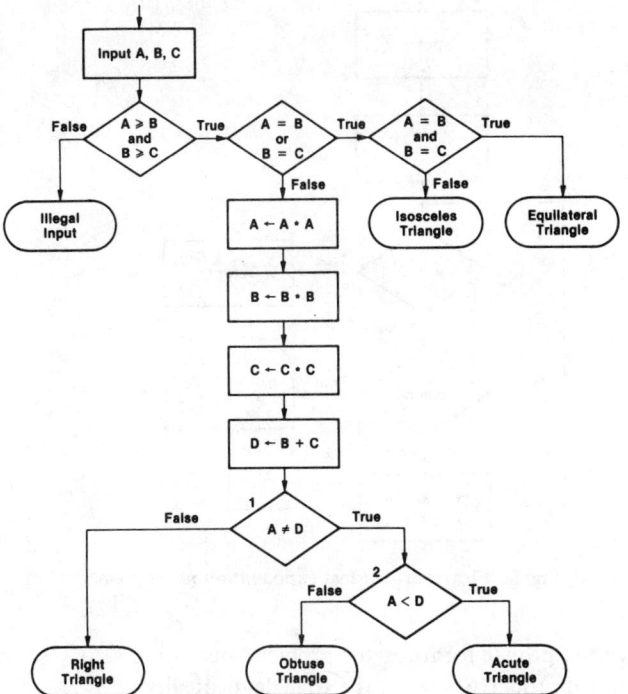

Fig. 1. Flowchart for triangle classification problem.

P_1: $\neg[(A \geq B) \& (B \geq C)]$, i.e., $(A < B) \vee (B < C)$
P_2: $(A > B > C) \& (A^2 = B^2 + C^2)$
P_3: $(A > B > C) \& (A^2 > B^2 + C^2)$
P_4: $(A > B > C) \& (A^2 < B^2 + C^2)$
P_5: $(A \geq B \geq C) \& [(A = B) \vee (B = C)] \& \neg[(A = B) \& (B = C)]$,
   i.e., $(A = B > C) \vee (A > B = C)$
P_6: $(A = B = C)$

Fig. 2. Path domain conditions for triangle classification program.

$D_1 = S_1 \cap P_1$: $(A < B) \vee (B < C)$
$D_2 = S_2 \cap P_3$: $(A \geq B + C) \& (A > B > C)$
$D_3 = S_2 \cap P_5$: $(A \geq B + C) \& (B = C)$
$D_4 = S_3 \cap P_6$: $(A = B = C)$
$D_5 = S_4 \cap P_5$: $(A = B > C)$
$D_6 = S_5 \cap P_5$: $(A > B = C) \& (A < B + C)$
$D_7 = S_6 \cap P_2$: $(A > B > C) \& (A^2 = B^2 + C^2)$
$D_8 = S_7 \cap P_4$: $(A > B > C) \& (A^2 < B^2 + C^2)$
$D_9 = S_8 \cap P_3$: $(A > B > C) \& (A^2 > B^2 + C^2) \& (A < B + C)$

Fig. 3. Subdomains formed by intersection of problem partition and path domain partition.

Domain	Test Data	Correct Output	Actual Output
D_1	(1, 2, 3)	illegal order	illegal order
D_2	(14, 6, 4)	not a triangle	obtuse
D_3	(2, 1, 1)	not a triangle	isosceles
D_4	(1, 1, 1)	equilateral	equilateral
D_5	(2, 2, 1)	isosceles	isosceles
D_6	(3, 2, 2)	isosceles	isosceles
D_7	(5, 4, 3)	right	right
D_8	(6, 5, 4)	acute	acute
D_9	(4, 3, 2)	obtuse	obtuse

Fig. 4. Test data and output for triangle classification program.

problem is especially suitable for the application of the revealing subdomain strategy. Since the very purpose of the program is to classify its input domain, there is an obvious specification-based partition. In addition, since there are no loops in the program, there are finitely many path domains. The resulting subdomains (constructed by intersecting the problem partition and the path domain partition) therefore separate all significant cases for this problem, and we can expect them to be revealing for many errors in classifying the triangles. They are not revealing for overflow in the arithmetic operations.

Each path domain for the triangle program is described simply by the conjunction of the predicate branches taken on the given path. Conditions describing the six path domains, P_1-P_6, appear in Fig. 2. We shall denote the path corresponding to domain P_i by $\mathcal{P}_i$, $i = 1, \cdots, 6$.

To form the specification-based partition, we first divide the universe of triples of positive integers into legal and illegal input forms. S_1 is all triples such that $\neg(A \geq B \geq C)$ or equivalently $(A < B) \vee (B < C)$; these are the illegal inputs. For the legal inputs we now distinguish two conditions. S_2 contains all triples such that $A \geq B \geq C$ and $A \geq B + C$; in this case the triangle inequality is not satisfied, and A, B, C cannot be the sides of a triangle ($B \geq A + C$ or $C \geq A + B$ cannot occur, since $A \geq B \geq C$). Inputs such that $A \geq B \geq C$ and $A < B + C$ are legally ordered and represent valid triangles. These triples are further divided into six subclasses:

S_3: $A = B = C$ (equilateral)
S_4: $A = B > C$ (isosceles)
S_5: $(A > B = C) \& (A < B + C)$ (isosceles)
S_6: $(A > B > C) \& (A^2 = B^2 + C^2)$ (right scalene)
S_7: $(A > B > C) \& (A^2 < B^2 + C^2)$ (acute scalene)
S_8: $(A > B > C) \& (A^2 > B^2 + C^2) \& (A < B + C)$ (obtuse scalene)

Intersecting the six path domains with the eight problem domains results in the nine nonempty subdomains D_1-D_9 shown in Fig. 3. The test data are chosen by arbitrarily selecting an element from each subdomain. Fig. 4 shows the test data, together with the program output and the correct output for each item. The program produces an incorrect result for subdomains D_2 and D_3. In both cases the program incorrectly reports that an invalid triple represents the sides of a valid triangle of a certain type. D_2 and D_3 are revealing for these errors; all of their elements will be processed incorrectly in the same way.

The subdomains in Fig. 3 are produced by intersecting the (program-independent) problem partition and the path partition for the program shown in Fig. 1. A different program with a different path partition would result in a different intersection partition.

Consider, for example, the error of writing the tests labeled 1 and 2 in the program (Fig. 1) as "$A \neq C$" and "$A < C$", respectively, i.e., comparing A^2 to C^2 instead of comparing A^2 to $B^2 + C^2$. Since the entire bottom section of the flowchart is accessible only to inputs such that $A > B > C$, this error will result in all such inputs taking path $\mathcal{P}_3$, and being

P_1': $(A < B) \vee (B < C)$
P_2': $\emptyset$
P_3': $(A > B > C)$
P_4': $\emptyset$
P_5': $(A = B > C) \vee (A > B = C)$
P_6': $(A = B = C)$

Fig. 5. Path domain conditions for incorrect triangle classification program.

classified as obtuse triangles. Paths $\mathcal{P}_2$ and $\mathcal{P}_4$ will be taken by no inputs. The path partition for this erroneous program is shown in Fig. 5. The subdomains of the intersection partition include $P_3' \cap S_6 = S_6$, $P_3' \cap S_7 = S_7$, and $P_3' \cap S_8 = S_8$. These are all revealing subdomains for this error; for elements of S_6 and S_7 the output is incorrect, while for elements of S_8 it is correct.

Although our primary concern is testing, i.e., exposing the presence of errors, knowledge of which subdomains lead to the incorrect outputs is obviously useful for debugging. In this case, all triples representing acute (S_7) and right (S_6) triangles are processed incorrectly, which implies a problem in the method of determining the type of scalene triangle. The debugger should be led to check the pertinent predicate and the calculation of values tested in that predicate.

The error just described provides a good illustration of the inherent defects of pure path testing methodologies. Note that the paths in the incorrect program which end at "Right Triangle" and "Acute Triangle" are both infeasible. That is, there is no data which will cause them to be executed. On the other hand, the feasible path ending at "Obtuse Triangle" can be traversed both by data which produce correct results and data which produce incorrect results. A path testing system which generates inputs to execute feasible paths might produce only an obtuse triangle to check the path, and thus not detect the error.

A symbolic execution system might detect the error by discovering that the "Right" and "Acute" paths are infeasible for positive inputs A, B, and C. To do so it is necessary to discover that the following path conditions are contradictory:

$A \geqslant B \; \& \; B \geqslant C \; \& \; A \neq B \; \& \; B \neq C \; \& \; A^2 = C^2$ for "Right Triangle"
$A \geqslant B \; \& \; B \geqslant C \; \& \; A \neq B \; \& \; B \neq C \; \& \; A^2 \neq C^2 \; \& \; A^2 < C^2$

for "Acute Triangle."

While our treatment of the triangle problem produces an effective set of test cases, it nevertheless fails to deal with a type of error which may be quite common in real programs. Note that the program in Fig. 1 will report that $(-3, -4, -5)$ are the sides of an acute triangle. However, this input and all other triples containing negative values are not included in any of the subdomains of Fig. 3. Naturally, we developed these subdomains on the assumption that the inputs would all be positive integers, but there is hardly more reason to make this assumption than to assume that the inputs will be in nondecreasing order. It is necessary to differentiate between two types of invalid input situations. In the first case the inputs simply are of the wrong form for the given problem, as with the negative triangle inputs. In the second case the inputs

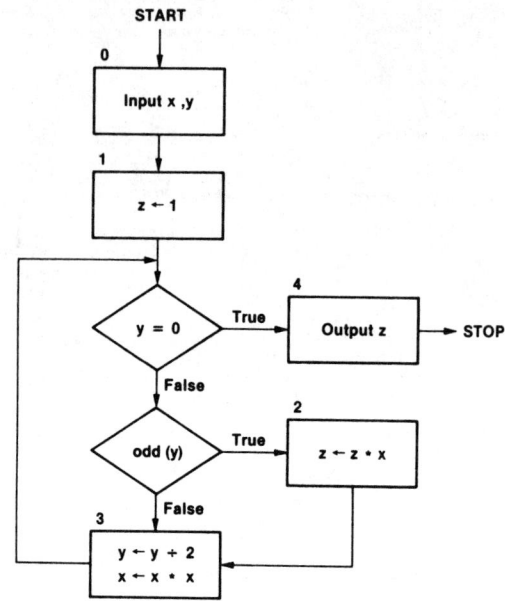

Fig. 6. Flowchart for fast exponentiation program.

have the proper form for the problem, but fail to satisfy some required property, such as the triangle inequality.

To expose the effects of a program's failure to respond properly to a wrong form type of input, a special subdomain can be established for all such inputs. The second type of invalid input should be treated similarly to valid inputs, since in general some processing beyond the input operations is needed to decide its invalidity.

Example 2: This program is simple enough to be proved correct, and many people have done so [1], [10]. The problem is to calculate x to the power y, where x is an integer and y is a nonnegative integer. The method used (Fig. 6) does the computation in time proportional to log y, by taking advantage of the binary representation of y.

As in Example 1, x and y refer to the program's initial inputs. Statements from the program are enclosed in quotation marks. The nontest boxes in the program's graph are numbered; the set of paths through the graph is a subset of the regular set $01(3 + 23)^*4$. The set of feasible paths for legal inputs consists of 014 for $y = 0$, and $01(3 + 23)^*234$ for the remaining cases, in which the most significant bit in the binary representation of y is 1. Note that the path taken for input (x, y) depends only on the value of y. In contrast to the previous example, this program has infinitely many feasible paths, and test data cannot be generated for each individual path domain. We choose several domains which are representative of different types of y values; the paths and their associated y values are shown in Fig. 7. The union of these path domains is the entire y input domain. P_4 represents odd inputs other than $2^n - 1$. Such inputs will take the TRUE exit from the "odd(y)" test on the first pass through the main loop, and on at least one pass will take the FALSE exit of that test. This latter requirement is to eliminate inputs of the form $2^n - 1$ which will always take the TRUE exit. P_5 is defined analogously.

We now examine the problem specifications and the algo-

Path Domain	Description of Paths	y Values Which Traverse Paths	Binary Representations of y Values
P_1	014	0	0
P_2	$013^n234, n \geq 1$	2^n	10^n
P_3	$01(23)^n4, n \geq 1$	$2^n - 1$	1^n
P_4	$0123(3+23)^a3(3+23)^b234$	odd, not $2^n - 1$	$1(0+1)^c0(0+1)^d1$
P_5	$013(3+23)^a23(3+23)^b234$	even, not 0 or 2^n	$1(0+1)^c1(0+1)^d0$

Fig. 7. Path domains chosen for exponentiation program.

X input classes
- X_1: $x < -1$
- X_2: $x = -1$
- X_3: $x = 0$
- X_4: $x = 1$
- X_5: $x > 1$

Y input classes
- Y_1: $y = 0$
- Y_2: $y = 2^n, n \geq 1$
- Y_3: $y = 2^n - 1, n > 1$
- Y_4: $y = 1$
- Y_5: y odd, not $2^n - 1$
- Y_6: y even, not 2^n or 0

Subdomains: $X_i \times Y_j$, $i = 1,...,5$; $j = 1,...,6$

Fig. 8. Subdomains for exponentiation program.

rithm to find natural ways of subdividing the x and y domains. An obvious partitioning for x is based on whether x is positive, negative, or zero. From positive x values we single out 1, since it is easy for the output to be correct if $x = 1$, but incorrect otherwise. We similarly single out $x = -1$. The x inputs are thus partitioned into the five classes:

X_1: $x < -1$
X_2: $x = -1$
X_3: $x = 0$
X_4: $x = 1$
X_5: $x > 1$.

From the specifications and algorithm we identify four special cases for the y values. When $y = 0$, the result should be 1. When $y = 1$ it is possible that the value of x^y is computed correctly even though the program might be incorrect for other values of y. When $y = 2^n$, the algorithm works by accumulating the entire power in x, and does not use z until the last loop iteration. Similarly, $y = 2^n - 1, n > 1$ is unusual, since the power is accumulated entirely in z. Note that two of these special cases for y were already identified as separate classes (P_1 and P_2) in the path domain analysis and the union of the other two classes was identified as class P_3 (see Fig. 7). The problem partition of the y inputs consists of the four special cases just identified, plus a fifth class containing all other positive y values.

Fig. 8 shows the classes of the intersection partitions for x and y, and the resulting subdomains from which test data will be drawn. Since the x input value has no influence on the path followed during program execution, the X input classes are the same as the classes of the X problem partition. Classes $Y_1, \cdots, Y_6$ are the result of intersecting the Y path and problem partitions.

We now examine some errors which could have been written into the code, and their effect on the program's output; our objective is to see for which errors the subdomains are revealing.

Error 1: z is initialized to 0 instead of to 1.

Effect: The program's output is always 0. This is incorrect for all inputs except $x = 0, y > 0$. Thus every input in the subdomains built from X_1, X_2, X_4, and X_5 will produce the wrong output; inputs in $X_3 \times (Y_2, Y_3, Y_4, Y_5, Y_6)$ produce correct output. The output is incorrect for the single member of $X_3 \times Y_1$. Every subdomain is revealing for Error 1.

Error 2: The "$y = 0$" test is written as "$y \neq 0$."

Effect: If $y = 0$, the program loops. If $y \neq 0$, the output is 1. This is incorrect except when $x = 1$, or $x = -1$ and y is even. All subdomains are revealing for this error.

Error 3: The test for "odd(y)" is written as a test for "even(y)."

Effect: Since this error effectively reverses the Yes and No exits of the test, the result will be to compute x^w, where w is the one's complement of the binary representation of y. The program's output will be $x^{(2^k-1-y)}$ where $k = \lfloor \log_2 y \rfloor + 1$, or the number of bits in y's binary representation. This is the wrong answer unless $y = 0$; all subdomains are revealing for this error.

Error 4: Failure to test for y odd; all loop iterations go through the $z \leftarrow z * x$ calculation. This error eliminates a test, and thus collapses the path domains $P_2, \cdots, P_5$ into the single domain whose paths have the form $01(23)^n4, n \geq 1$. Consideration of the algorithm, however, still leads to the classes $y = 0$, $y = 1$, $y = 2^n$, and $y = 2^n - 1$. The Y input classes from which the subdomains are formed thus include Y_1, Y_2, Y_3, and Y_4 from Fig. 8, and a class Y_7 which includes all values not in Y_1, Y_2, Y_3, or Y_4.

Effect: The result will be incorrect except when $y = 0$; $x = 0$; $x = 1$; $y = 2^n - 1$; or $x = -1$ and y is odd. The subdomains $(X_i \times Y_1)$, $(X_i \times Y_3)$, $(X_i \times Y_4)$, $i = 1, \cdots, 5$; $(X_3 \times Y_j)$, $(X_4 \times Y_j)$, $j = 1, 2, 3, 4, 7$, are all processed correctly. $X_1 \times Y_2$, $X_1 \times Y_7$, $X_2 \times Y_2$, $X_5 \times Y_2$, and $X_5 \times Y_7$ are processed incorrectly. $X_2 \times Y_7$ is not revealing, since for odd exponents in Y_7, the result will be the correct answer of -1, while for even values in Y_7, the result will be incorrect. Note that although this subdomain is not revealing, the error will be exposed by several of the other subdomains.

Two other errors for which every subdomain is revealing are

Error 5: Writing the "$z \leftarrow z * x$" statement as "$z \leftarrow z + x$", and

Error 6: Writing "$y \leftarrow y \div 2$" as "$y \leftarrow y - 2$."

The error of writing "$x \leftarrow x * x$" as "$x \leftarrow x + x$" is not exposed by each subdomain. For inputs $(0, y)$, $(x, 1)$ and for the pairs $(x, y) = (2, 2)$ and $(2, 3)$ the program would produce the correct result. Because of the last two cases, the subdomains $X_5 \times Y_2$ and $X_5 \times Y_3$ are not revealing. All other subdomains are revealing for the error, however, and in most of these the wrong answer is produced. The error will certainly be detected.

Example 3: The program in Fig. 9, taken from Geller [4], is supposed to find the number of days between two dates in the same calendar year. The input is two pairs (month1,day1) and (month2,day2), and a year. It is assumed that the first date precedes the second, and that the inputs will always be valid in all other respects.

```
procedure calendar (integer value day1, month1, day2, month2, year);
begin
    integer days;
    if month2 = month1 then days := day2 - day1
        comment if the dates are in the same month, we can compute
                the number of days between them immediately;
    else
        begin
            integer array daysin (1: 12);
            daysin(1) := 31; daysin(3) := 31; daysin(4) := 30;
            daysin(5) := 31; daysin(6) := 30; daysin(7) := 31;
            daysin(8) := 31; daysin(9) := 30; daysin(10) := 31;
            daysin(11) := 30; daysin(12) := 31;
            if ( (year rem 4) = 0) or
                ( (year rem 100) = 0 and (year rem 400) = 0)
                then daysin(2) := 28
                else daysin(2) := 29;
            comment set daysin(2) according to whether or not
                    year is a leap year;
            days := day2 + (daysin(month1) - day1);
            comment this gives (the correct number of days -
                    days in complete intervening months);
            for I := month1 + 1 until month2 - 1 do
                days := daysin(I) + days;
            comment add in the days in complete intervening months;
        end;
    write (days)
end;
```

Fig. 9. Calendar computation program.

The program as it appears in [4] has syntactic and logical errors which are presumably due to a proofreading oversight. We have corrected the syntactic errors but left the incorrect predicate in the second *if* statement (Fig. 9) to demonstrate the use of revealing subdomains. In deriving these subdomains we do not explicitly form the path domain and problem partitions.

The input domain divides very naturally, based on the structure of the input, on the expected output, and on observations about the program's treatment of inputs. The subdomains are as follows:

S_1: the set of date pairs such that month1 = month2.

Since the program explicitly tests for this condition, it is clear that there is significance to this subdomain.

For the remaining subdomains we must consider dates in different months; there are various ways to make the divisions, but consideration of whether or not a leap year calculation is involved will play a part in any partitioning.

S_2: month1 > 2 and month2 > month1 + 1

There is no leap year calculation and at least one intervening month.

S_3: month1 ≠ 2 and month2 = month1 + 1

Again there is no leap year calculation, but also no intervening months.

S_4: month1 = 1 and month2 > 2
S_5: month1 = 2 and month2 > 2

S_4 and S_5 contain inputs which require leap year calculations. To account for the different ways in which a year can be a leap year, we further divide S_4 and S_5 into four subclasses:

Y_1: year rem 4 = 0 and year rem 100 ≠ 0
Y_2: year rem 100 = 0 and year rem 400 ≠ 0
Y_3: year rem 400 = 0

Y_4: year rem 4 ≠ 0

The final set of subdomains is thus $S_1, S_2, S_3, S_4 \cap Y_i$, and $S_5 \cap Y_i$, $i = 1, 2, 3, 4$. The most obvious types of errors for the calendar program are "off-by-one" errors. We might expect the program's output to be the correct value ±1, or to be off by one month's worth of days.

Since the result is to be the difference between two dates, the correct result for elements in S_1 is of the form day2 - day1 + k, k an integer. Since these expressions define a set of parallel lines, the correct expression is completely determined by a single input pair together with its correct output.

Notice that we have not considered whether the subdomains are revealing if the proper expression were day1 - day2 + k rather than day2 - day1 + k. In fact S_1 is not revealing for this error since these expressions are no longer nonintersecting [when day1 = day2, (day1 - day2 + k) = (day2 - day1 + k)]. Thus if we feel that incorrect order of subtraction is a likely error, then S_1 must be further divided into the two subdomains:

S_1': month1 = month2 and day1 = day2
S_1'': month1 = month2 and day1 ≠ day2

The two new subdomains are revealing for each of these errors. S_1'', however, is not revealing if both errors occur in the program. For $k = 2$ and day1 = day2 - 1, the program succeeds, while if $k = 2$ and day1 = day2 - 2, the program fails.

Next we note that the table of daysin is initialized correctly for the months 1, 3, 4, ···, 12. This assures that the subdomains S_2 and S_3 are revealing. S_2 and S_3 were separated since the program does additional processing when intervening months occur. Typical errors for an S_2 input are to add one too many or one too few intervening months, and these errors would occur for every S_2 input. Similarly for S_3, if an intervening month's days were added in, this error would occur for all of S_3.

The subdomains formed out of S_4 and S_5 expose the errors existing in the original program. Any input from $S_4 \cap Y_i$ or

$S_5 \cap Y_i$, $i = 1, 3, 4$, produces an incorrect number of days for February, and will result in an incorrect output. The inputs in $S_4 \cap Y_2$ and $S_5 \cap Y_2$ all produce correct results.

Although the most likely off-by-one errors will be exposed by all of the subdomains constructed in the example, certain types of "double" off-by-one errors will not be exposed. Suppose that both indices on the *for* loop which adds in complete intervening months are one too high, i.e., the statement is

for I := month1 + 2 *until* month2 *do*

Then the proper number of months will be added to the sum of days, but they will be the wrong months. If the inputs are month1 = 4, month2 = 6 the error will be detected. Month1 = 4, month2 = 7, however, will produce the correct output for the wrong reason.

As usual, to guarantee detecting this error, a finer input partition is necessary. Because of the calendar's irregularity, a separate class is needed for each legal pair of input months. There are $\sum_{i=1}^{11}(12 - i) = 66$ such pairs.

A correct version of the program contains the following replacement for the *if* statement in Fig. 9.

if ((year *rem* 4) ≠ 0) *or*
(((year *rem* 100) = 0) *and* ((year *rem* 400) ≠ 0))
then daysin(2) := 28
else daysin(2) := 29;

The three examples in this section were chosen to show the applicability of revealing subdomains to a range of different types of programs. They have all appeared in the testing literature, and have had diverse testing methodologies applied to them.

Our approach seems most applicable to programs whose purpose is either a classification of their inputs, or a computation based on such a classification. However, it can also be effective for programs which process their entire domain in a uniform fashion.

Since the goal of the triangle problem is to classify its inputs, it is obviously well suited to an approach which requires a domain partition. The errors detected in this program indicate that one must also take into account the requirements of the problem.

The calendar computation, although not directly a partitioning of the inputs, is nonetheless based on a classification of dates. The intersection of the problem and path domain partitions which were derived for the calendar problem expresses this classification. The problem is just as well suited to the revealing subdomain approach as the triangle problem.

The exponentiation problem is the example to which the approach is the least obviously applicable; its computation does not make use of any significant partition of the input domain. However, a partition of the domain based on both the structure of the data and the program's treatment of inputs was sufficient to provide a set of test cases which would effectively detect many likely errors.

VII. Summary and Future Work

Although program testing has been a common practice since the first days of programming, until recently there had been no attempt to construct a theoretical basis for testing. The first efforts to construct such a theory showed the inadequacy of tests based solely on program structure, and gave conditions under which a successful test can demonstrate that a program is error-free.

In this paper we have examined the Goodenough and Gerhart theory of testing and identified problems which prohibit the ready application of this theory. In an attempt to rectify these pragmatic difficulties, we examined two modifications of their theory. The first attempt, introduced in Section IV, essentially amounted to a program-independent, or black-box testing version of the Goodenough and Gerhart theory. We demonstrated that these notions were also pragmatically unusable, since no realistic criterion can possess the necessary properties.

Our second modification recognized that if the theory was to become more than an unattainable ideal, we would have to be willing to accept a less ambitious goal than proving program correctness by testing. With this realization in mind, the notion of a revealing domain was introduced to remedy the dependence between validity and reliability, and to allow for the division of the domain into smaller, more manageable pieces. Defining good tests in terms of restricted subdomains allows us to concentrate on probable local errors, and increases the likelihood of finding good tests.

We also relativized the notion of revealing to errors and thereby revised our goal from showing program correctness to showing the absence of specified errors.

Much work remains to be done in making the concepts of a revealing criterion and subdomain applicable to a wide class of problems and programs. One of the most important tasks is to find more systematic or formal methods of constructing the problem partition. This will not be easy, since finding a good problem partition is quite similar to the task of creating the program itself. Since the latter is so difficult to formalize, we may expect the former to be difficult also.

Another point to be considered is the applicability of the revealing subdomain strategy to large programs. The effects of added program size and complexity will be felt primarily as increasing difficulty in accurately describing and forming the path domains. Thus the role of the problem domains in choosing test data will become increasingly important. This corresponds to current testing practice which commonly relies upon specification-based or black-box testing methods for defining test data for large programs. Of course, any refinement based on program structure is potentially useful, so the technique of intersecting the two types of subdomains to yield a finer domain partition is likely to yield better results than pure specification-based testing. As automated testing tools which determine path domains become more refined and usable for large programs, the revealing subdomain approach will become more applicable to such programs.

On the theoretical side, we may ask under what conditions a subdomain can be revealing for every possible error. Is this possible for any subdomain other than the trivial case of a singleton set? If we cannot achieve universally revealing, nontrivial subdomains, how close can we come? The problem is to combine realistically attainable characteristics of good tests with a reasonable level of confidence in the test results. The notion of a revealing subdomain brings us a little closer to this goal.

ACKNOWLEDGMENT

We are grateful to S. Gerhart, R. Hamlet, K.-C. Tai, P. Abrahams, and the referees for making many helpful comments.

REFERENCES

[1] R. M. Burstall, "Program proving as hand simulation with a little induction," in *Proc. IFIP Congr. 74.* Stockholm, Sweden: North-Holland, 1974, pp. 308-312.
[2] R. A. DeMillo, R. J. Lipton, and F. G. Sayward, "Hints on test data selection: Help for the practicing programmer," *Computer*, vol. 11, pp. 34-41, Apr. 1978.
[3] E. W. Dijkstra, "Notes on structured programming," in *Structured Programming*, O.-J. Dahl, E. W. Dijkstra, C. A. R. Hoare, Ed. New York: Academic, 1972, pp. 1-81.
[4] M. Geller, "Test data as an aid in proving program correctness," *Commun. Ass. Comput. Mach.*, vol. 21, pp. 368-375, May 1978.
[5] J. B. Goodenough and S. L. Gerhart, "Toward a theory of testing: Data selection criteria," in *Current Trends in Programming Methodology*, vol. 2, R. T. Yeh, Ed. Englewood Cliffs, NJ: Prentice-Hall, 1977, pp. 44-79.
[6] W. E. Howden, "An evaluation of the effectiveness of symbolic testing," *Software–Practice and Experience*, vol. 8, pp. 381-397, 1978.
[7] —, "Reliability of the path analysis testing strategy," *IEEE Trans. Software Eng.*, vol. SE-2, pp. 208-215, Sept. 1976.
[8] —, "Symbolic testing and the DISSECT symbolic evaluation system," *IEEE Trans. Software Eng.*, vol. SE-3, pp. 266-278, July 1977.
[9] R. E. Keirstead and D. B. Parker, "On the feasability of formal certification," in *Program Test Methods*, W. Hetzel, Ed. Englewood Cliffs, NJ: Prentice-Hall, 1973, pp. 291-301.
[10] Z. Manna, *Mathematical Theory of Computation*. New York: McGraw-Hill, 1974.
[11] C. V. Ramamoorthy, S. F. Ho, and W. T. Chen, "On the automated generation of program test data," *IEEE Trans. Software Eng.*, vol. SE-2, pp. 293-300, Dec. 1976.
[12] E. J. Weyuker, *Program Schemas with Semantic Restrictions*, Ph.D. dissertation, Dep. Comput. Sci., Rutgers Univ., New Brunswick, NJ, Tech. Rep. DCS-TR-60, June 1977.
[13] —, "The applicability of program schema results to programs," *Int. J. Comput. Inform. Sci.*, vol. 8, pp. 387-403, Oct. 1979.

Elaine J. Weyuker was born in New York City. She received the A.B. degree in mathematics from the State University of New York at Binghamton (Harpur College), the M.S.E. degree in computer and information sciences from the University of Pennsylvania, Philadelphia, and the Ph.D. degree in computer science from Rutgers University, New Brunswick, NJ.

She worked for IBM as a Systems Engineer from 1968 to 1969. From 1969 through 1975 she was a Lecturer of Computer Science at Richmond College, City University of New York. Since 1977 she has been an Assistant Professor of Computer Science in the Courant Institute of Mathematical Sciences, New York University, New York. She spent the summer of 1979 as a Visiting Senior Computer Scientist at the Sperry Univac Software Research Group, Blue Bell, PA. Her research interests include program testing and verification, program schemata, and the design and analysis of algorithms.

Dr. Weyuker is a member of the Association for Computing Machinery.

Thomas J. Ostrand received the S.B. degree in mathematics from the Massachusetts Institute of Technology, Cambridge, the M.S.E. degree from the Moore School of electrical engineering, University of Pennsylvania, Philadelphia, and the Ph.D. degree in computer and information sciences from the University of Pennsylvania.

He worked as a Systems Programmer for the RCA Computer Systems Division in 1970-1971. From 1971-1978 he was a faculty member of the Computer Science Department at Rutgers University, New Brunswick, NJ, where he taught a wide variety of graduate and undergraduate courses. His research areas included the theory of cellular automata, program verification, program transformations and equivalence, and parsing by finite state machines. Since September 1978 he has been a Senior Computer Scientist in the Software Research Group of Sperry Univac, Blue Bell, PA. His current interests include software verification and testing, design of reliable software, and analysis of algorithms.

COMPLETENESS CRITERIA FOR TESTING ELEMENTARY PROGRAM FUNCTIONS

William E. Howden

Department of Electrical Engineering
and Computer Sciences
University of California, San Diego
La Jolla, California

Abstract

Program testing metrics are based on criteria for measuring the completeness of a set of program tests. Branch testing measures the percentage of program branches that are traversed during a set of tests. Mutation testing measures the ability of a set of tests to distinguish a program from similar programs. A criterion for test completeness is introduced in this paper which measures the ability of a set of tests to distinguish between functions which are implemented by parts of programs. The criterion is applied to functions which are implemented by different kinds of programming language statements. It is more effective than branch testing and incorporates some of the advantages of mutation testing. Its effectiveness can be discussed formally and it can be described as part of an integrated approach to testing. A tool can be used to implement the method.

Keywords: Testing, error classes, reliability, completeness, branches, mutation analysis, equivalence.

Introduction

1. Completeness of a set of program tests.

A perfect criteria for the completeness of a set of program tests would have the property that the correctness of a program over a complete set of tests T would imply the correctness of the program over all data. It would be sufficient for a program to be correct over such a set of tests in order for it to be correct over all data. In practice it is impossible to define procedures for constructing finite complete sets of tests which can be used to prove program correctness [1] and weaker definitions of completeness have been accepted.

2. Branch testing.

The most widely used measure of test completeness is branch coverage [2]. A set of tests is considered complete if every program branch is traversed at least once during some test. A branch is a transfer of control from one program statement to the next, either through sequential execution of statements or through the execution of a go-to. Branch testing can be used to measure the degree to which a program has been tested by counting the percentage of branches that have been traversed during a set of tests. Complete branch testing is a necessary criteria for correctness in the sense that it is necessary to test all parts of a program in order to find all errors in the program. A significant advantage of branch testing is that a tool can be built which will keep track of the branches which have been traversed during a sequence of tests. The tool can be used to automatically record and report on the branch coverage completeness of a test set. Various generalizations of branch testing have been proposed but none have become widely used [3,4].

3. Mutation testing.

Empirical studies show that many errors may remain undetected in a program even when every program branch has been followed during at least one test [5-7]. They show that a significant number of these errors will be detected if different parts of a program are executed over data which takes into account the kinds of errors that can occur in that part of the program. Mutation testing is designed to construct test data of this type.

Mutation testing requires the definition of a class of mutation transformations which, when applied to a program statement, will introduce an "error" of a certain type into that statement. Typical mutation transformations interchange variables, alter labels in go-to's and add one to expressions in arithmetic relations. A set of tests T for a program P is complete if T distinguishes between P and any non-equivalent program P' which can be generated from P by the application of a mutation transformation; i.e., T is complete if P and P' give different output for some test in T [8-10].

One of the disadvantages of mutation testing is the large number of mutants P' which can be generated from a program P. It is estimated that there are on the order of n^2 mutants for an n-line program. This implies that if a proposed test set T contains t elements it is necessary to carry out on the order of n^2 to $n^2 t$ program executions to determine its completeness.

4. An elementary functional completeness metric.

This paper introduces a test completeness metric that is more refined than branch testing but not as powerful as mutation testing. It has the advantage that it requires substantially fewer program exectuions than mutation testing while retaining some of mutation testing's error revealing capabilities. It has the further advantage that its effectiveness can be discussed formally and that it can be described as an integral part of the general approach to testing known as functional testing [11]. It is closely related to and provides a systematic approach to what has been called "special values testing" [5].

The basic idea of the method can be explained with a simple example. Suppose that it is important to test for "wrong variable" errors in a program P. The approach followed in mutation testing is to create a mutation P' for each possible replacement of each occurrence of a variable in P with some other variable in P. A complete test set must contain a test that will distinguish each mutation P' from P. In the proposed method all that is required is that each occurrence of a variable in P take on a value that is different from the values of all other variables in P during at least one execution of the statement in P containing that occurrence of the variable. A complete test set must contain tests that will distinguish each occurrence of a variable in P from all possible replacements of that occurrence of the variable with some other variable in P.

In the proposed method a single program execution may be all that is required to test all possible wrong variable errors in a program (e.g. construct a test in which the values of all variables are distinct). This is a significant advantage over mutation testing which requires the separate execution of each mutation P' of P in which an occurrence of a variable has been replaced by some other variable. The disadvantage of the proposed method is that the effect of an error may be "cancelled out". Even though a wrong variable is guaranteed to act incorrectly on the specified test data the program may still give correct output due to some cancellation effect. Mutation testing enforces the use of tests which do not allow cancellation effects to hide errors.

The values of variables can be thought of as being retrieved by "data access functions". Each variable is associated with a different data access function. The type of test that is described above for the occurrence of a variable is "reliable" in the sense that if the wrong data access function has been implemented, it will evaluate to an incorrect value on at least one test. In the approach to testing which is described in this paper a set of tests is considered complete if it results in the evaluation of each function in a specified set of functions over a reliable set of tests for the function.

Functional Testing

There are two parts to functional testing: identification of functions and selection of functionally important test cases. Testing is carried out by executing the code which corresponds to the identified functions. Functional testing can be used to construct a unified life-cycle approach to program testing. Each phase of the life cycle involves the explicit and implicit definition of functions. Guidelines can be constructed for identifying the functions which appear in each phase and for constructing test data for those functions. The functions which are associated with life cycle documents vary from very general requirements functions which describe the overall functional capabilities of a system to very detailed specific functions which are implemented by language constructs. The details of function identification and test selection depend on the specification methods and programming languages which are used. Data flow requirements specifications, for example, include implicit and explicit references to functions which are performed by the processes in the data flow diagram. Structured design specifications include references to functions carried out by the modules in a top down design. If structured design is extended to include the design of individual programs, then each of the general and detailed design functions in a program's functional design structure can be identified for testing [12]. The functions which are implemented in programming language constructs differ for languages with different semantics of different kinds of statements.

Reliability of Functional Test Data

The reliability of a set of functional tests for a function f which is associated with part or all of a program is defined relative to a class of functions F_f. It is assumed that f and the functions in F_f are defined over the same domain and that $f \in F_f$.

<u>Definition</u>. A test set T is <u>reliable</u> relative to a class of functions F_f if for all functions f' in F_f, $f' = f$ over T implies that $f' = f$ over the entire domain for the functions in F.

The idea that a test set is reliable if it can be used to distinguish between the members of a class of functions or programs was introduced in [13] and is used in [14]. Alternative approaches include the concept of test set reliability used in [1] to study path testing, the definitions of reliability and validity of test data used by Goodenough and Gerhart in [7], and the idea of a revealing test set described by Weyuker and Ostrand in [15].

In order for functional test set reliability to be a useful concept it must be possible to define interesting classes of functions F_f and, at least in practice, possible to construct the associated test sets T. Suppose that a function f is implemented in or by a piece of program code p. The basic idea is to define F_f to contain all functions f' which can be implemented by pieces of program code p' which are "similar" to p.

Suppose that a programmer intended to write a piece of code p' to implement a function f' and instead incorrectly wrote code p which implements f. If the definition of similarity is sufficiently general and if programmers can be assumed to write code which is either correct or similar to the correct code then it can be concluded that f' is in F_f. This means that the error in the code p can be detected by executing p over a reliable test set T for F_f.

Two approaches to similarity have been used. In the first, general properties of the code p which implements a function f are identified and F_f is defined to contain all functions implemented by code which has those properties. Suppose for example, that f is implemented by a polynomial p of degree 3 in variables, x, y and z. Then F_f can be defined to contain all functions which can be implemented by polynomials in x, y, and z of degree 3 or less. A reliable set of tests T for F_f can be easily constructed [16]. If p (and hence) f is the wrong polynomial (i.e. gives "wrong" output for some input values) and if the correct intended polynomial p' computes some function f' in F_f, then testing p over T will reveal that it is incorrect. The use of this algebraic approach to test reliability was studied in depth in [13, 16] and continuing research is described in [17].

In the second approach to similarity, two functions f and f' are considered similar if the code p and p' implementing f and f' differs in such a way that p can be derived from p' by introducing a common "error" into p'. This is the approach that has been used in mutation testing and which is used in the method described in this paper. The classes F_f can be thought of as modelling classes of program errors.

Reliable Tests For Program Statement Functions

1. Simple program statement functions.

Each of the standard constructs which are found in a programming language implements one or more simple functions. Five simple functions that occur in three types of program statements will be considered. The statement types are: assignment statements, conditional statements and loop control statements. The five functions are: data access, data storage, arithmetic expression, arithmetic relation and boolean expression. Reliable test data sets T_f can be defined for each of those functions. The test sets T_f are reliable relative to classes of functions F_f which correspond to simple kinds of errors. The kinds of errors that are considered is not exhaustive and forms a minimal set that should be tested for. The discussion is limited to programs containing arithmetic and boolean operations but similar results can be proved for other programs containing other types of operations.

2. Data access functions.

The input to a data access function consists of variable state space for the program. An error that results in the accessing of the wrong variable corresponds to the use of the wrong data access function. Suppose that f is a data access function in a program for a variable or array element x. Let F_f be the class of all data access functions for the program. In order to catch wrong variable errors it is necessary to construct tests that will distinguish f from all other access functions in F_f. A test set T will be reliable for F_f if for each variable or array element y other than x there is at least one state space in T in which the value of x differs from the value of y.

3. Data storage functions.

The input to a data storage function consists of a variable state space and a value. The output is a (possibly) new state space. Errors that correspond to the use of the wrong storage function result in the storage of the value into the wrong variable. Suppose that f is a data storage function associated with some variable or array element x in a program. Let F_f be all of the data storage functions for the program. A reliable set of tests can be constructed for F_f which consists of a single test in which the value to be stored is different from the current value stored in x. A test of this type can be used to distinguish the data storage function f from any other data storage function in F_f.

4. Arithmetic expression evaluation functions.

The input to an expression evaluation function consists of a value for each variable in the arithmetic expression which evaluates the function. The ouput is a single value.

The types of errors which can occur in an expression are more complex than errors associated with data access and storage functions. Different classes F_f can be defined for different kinds of errors. Two very simple kinds of errors will be considered first, followed by a discussion of more general types of errors.

(a) Expression evaluation functions - simple additive errors. Suppose that an error results in the use of a rational form which is incorrect by an additive constant k. Let f be the expression evaluation function computed by that rational form and let F_f contain f and all functions computed by forms which differ by an additive constant from the form for f. Any test for f forms a reliable set of tests, it will distinguish f from all other non-equivalent functions in F_f.

(b) Arithmetic expression evaluation functions - simple multiplicative errors. Suppose an error

error results in the use of a rational form which is incorrect by a multiplicative constant k. Let f be the function for the form and F_f the functions for all forms which differ by a multiplicative constant. A single test which results in a non-zero value for f forms a reliable test set for F_f.

(c) Expression evaluation functions - general classes of errors. Suppose that f is computed by an expression M. More general classes F_f can be defined by allowing more general classes of errors in M. The approach which is investigated in [16] is to allow any error which does not alter the variables appearing in M and does not result in an increase in an upper bound on the exponents in M. Suppose for example that M is a multinomial in k variables over an integral domain and t is an upper bound on the exponents in M. Let M_M be the set of all multinomials in the same variables over the same integral domain as M and suppose that t is also an upper bound on the exponents in each multinomial in M_M. Let F_f be the functions computed by the multinomials in M_M. Then any cascade set of degree $t+1$ of k-tuples forms a reliable set of tests for F_f [16].

The reliability results for algebraic forms can be extended to cover rational forms over unique factorization domains, rational forms for which the singularities are known and even rational forms containing radicals. Unfortunately, the size of the reliable test sets for general classes of forms of this type becomes prohibitively large very quickly. Suppose, for example, that M is a rational form in the variables x, y and z, that the maximal exponent is 5 and the coefficients in M are integral. Let F_f contain functions which are computed by rational forms in the same variables as M and having largest exponent less than or equal to 5. Then a reliable set of tests for F_f of the type defined in [16] will contain 11^3 elements.

(d) Expression evaluation functions - probabilistic approach. An alternative approach for rational forms is to consider the use of "probably" reliable test sets. Suppose that M is a multinomial in k variables for computing a function f and that t is an upper bound on the exponents in M. Let M_M be the set of all polynomials in the same variable as M and having largest exponent less than or equal to t. Let $M' \neq M$ be chosen from M_M and let X be a randomly chosen k-tuple of values for the variables in M and M'. If $M' = M$ for X, then X is a root of $M' - M$. The roots of a multinomial of degree k form a subset of k-space of "measure" zero and the probability of choosing a root of $M' - M$ "at random" is arbitrarily small. This indicates random selection of a test point is probably sufficient to distinguish M from any other multinomial M' in M_M, so that any test is probably reliable for distinguishing f from the other functions in F_f where F_f contains the functions computed by M_M.

The probabilistic approach to the selection of reliable test data sets was suggested by De Millo et al in [18] for a simpler class of algebraic forms. To the authors' knowledge it has not been explored in general.

5. <u>Arithmetic relation functions.</u>

Arithmetic relation functions are computed by expressions of the form $E_1 \, r \, E_2$ where E_1 and E_2 are arithmetic expressions and r is one of the relational operators $<, >, \leq, \geq, =$ or $\neq$. Two simple but commonly occurring classes of errors will be considered. In the first, the wrong relational operator is used in the expression and in the second, one or both of the expressions is "off" by a constant.

(a) Arithmetic relation functions - illegal relation. Let f be the function computed by a relation $E_1 \, r \, E_2$ and let F_f contain f and all functions computed by expressions $E_1 \, r' \, E_2$ where r' is some other arithmetic relational operator. A reliable set of tests for F_f can be constructed by evaluating $E_1 \, r \, E_2$ over values for which $E_1 < E_2$, $E_1 = E_2$ and $E_1 > E_2$. The reliability of this set of tests can be seen by examining the table in Figure 1. For each possible pair of expressions, the outcome of the two expressions will differ on at least one test in this set.

$E_1 < E_2$	$E_1 = E_2$	$E_1 > E_2$	$E_1 \neq E_2$	$E_1 \leq E_2$	$E_1 \geq E_2$
T	F	F	T	T	F
F	T	F	F	T	T
F	F	T	T	F	T

Figure 1. Test outcomes for reliable test set.

For some programs it may not be possible to construct input data that will result in a reliable set of tests for an expression. It may not be possible for example, to test the expression $E_1 \, r \, E_2$ over data for which $E_1 < E_2$. It is sufficient to test the expression over as many as the three test cases as possible. The argument for the case where it is possible to construct data for $E_1 = E_2$ and $E_1 > E_2$ but not $E_1 < E_2$ will be considered. The other cases can be argued similarly. If no data can be constructed for which $E_1 < E_2$, then examination of Figure 1 indicates that it is not possible to distinguish between $E_1 > E_2$ and $E_1 \neq E_2$, and between $E_1 \leq E_2$ and $E_1 = E_2$. It is assumed that it is not necessary to distinguish $E_1 < E_2$ from the other expressions since this case cannot arise. Now if $E_1 < E_2$ can never occur, then $E_1 > E_2$ is equivalent to $E_1 \neq E_2$. Similarly, if $E_1 < E_2$ can never occur $E_1 \leq E_2$ is equivalent to $E_1 = E_2$. This implies that it is not necessary to distinguish between $E_1 > E_2$ and $E_1 \neq E_2$, and between $E_1 \leq E_2$ and $E_1 = E_2$ in a reliable set of test data because these are equivalent expressions (i.e. equivalent given that $E_1 < E_2$ can never occur).

(b) Arithmetic relation functions - off by a constant. To simplify the discussion, it is assumed that all arithmetic relations are of the form $E \, r \, 0$. Let f be the function computed by an expression of the form $E \, r \, 0$. Then F_f consists of f and all functions of the form $(E+k) \, r \, 0$ where k is any constant. In order to construct a reliable test set for F_f it is necessary to consider quantities such as "the largest number less than zero which can be taken on by E". This quantity is meaningful due to the finite representation of numbers. If E is an integer expression the quantity is at most -1. If E is real it is at most $-\varepsilon$ where ε is the smallest non-zero quantity which can be represented on the machine in use. In situations where it is impractical to require the generation of non-zero quantities ε which are as close to zero as possible it is still possible to construct reliable test data if there is a quantity ε which measures the smallest required degree of discrimination between numbers. Two numbers which differ by ε are considered to be effectively equal.

The definitions in Figure 2 are used to define the reliable test sets in Figure 3. Figure 3 defines the tests to be used on the basis of which relation r occurs in the expression for computing f.

a = maximum value of E which is less than zero

b = maximum value of E which is less than or equal to zero

c = minimum value of E which is greater than zero

d = minimum value of E which is greater than or equal to zero

e = zero

Figure 2. Constants used to define reliable test sets.

$r =$	choose tests where $E =$
$<$	a, d
$>$	c, b
$\leq$	c, b
$\geq$	a, d
$=$	e
$\neq$	e

Figure 3. Reliable test sets.

The reliability of the test sets in Figure 3 can be argued as follows. Suppose r is the relation "$<$". If $(E+k) < 0$ when $E = a$, $E+k$ is equivalent to E for all values for which E evaluates to a negative number. Otherwise, the test for which $E = a$ discriminates between E and $E+k$. If $E+k \geq 0$ when $E = d$, then $E+k$ is equivalent to E for all values for which E evaluates to a number greater than or equal to zero. If $E+k < 0$ when $E = d$ then the test for which $E = d$ discriminates between E and $E+k$. Hence either E and $E+k$ are equivalent or tests for which $E = a$ and $E = d$ distinguish between E and $E+k$.

The argument for the reliability of the tests for the other relations in Figure 3 are similar to that for the relation "$<$". If no values for the variables in E can be selected so that $E = 0$, then it will not be possible to test the expressions having relations "$=$" and "$\neq$". The impossibility of selecting these last values in itself points out the error.

The wrong relation and off-by-a constant results described above are derived from work described by Foster in "Error Sensitive Test Cases" [19]. In his paper Foster assumes that all variables are integer and that it is possible to construct tests which result in all possible relationships between the expressions E_1 and E_2 in an arithmetic relation $E_1 \, r \, E_2$. His paper contains an informal discussion of the test cases needed to detect wrong relation errors and off-by-a constant errors. The results are easily extensible to real valued relations and to generalized off-by-a constant errors. Foster also discusses a number of other, ad-hoc error based testing techniques for which there is no obvious formal argument of test reliability.

(c) Boolean expression functions. Boolean expression functions are computed by expressions of the form $L(E_1, E_2, ..., E_n)$ where E_i, $1 \leq i \leq n$, is a simple or some other compound boolean expression that evaluates to True or False. L is assumed to be a syntactically correct logical expression in the logical operators <u>or</u>, <u>and</u>, and <u>not</u>. Let f be the boolean function computed by L and let F_f contain both f and all other compound expressions in the subexpressions E_i, $1 \leq i \leq n$. The functions in F_f can be thought of as functions in n logical variables. A reliable test set T for F_f can be constructed by requiring that values for the variables in the E_i be selected in such a way that all possible combinations of True and False values for the E_i are generated. T is a reliable test set because it generates an exhaustive test of any function f in F_f. (Recall that f is treated as a function of the n expressions E_i and not of the variables that occur in the E_i). Note that T is still reliable if, due to dependence between the E_i, it is not possible to generate some combinations of True and False values.

Completeness of Program Test Data

The following definition of completeness depends on the specification of a set of functions P_f which are implemented in the code for a program. A set of tests is complete if it causes the "adequate testing" of the specified set of functions. A function f is considered to have been adequately tested if the code which implements it is executed over a set of tests T which is reliable relative to a class of functions F_f which models some class of possible errors.

<u>Definition</u>. Suppose that P_f is a set of functions which are computed by a program P, parts of P or as parts of statements in P. Suppose that each function f in P_f is associated with a class of functions F_f. Then T_p is a <u>complete test set</u> for P if the execution of P over T_p results in the evaluation of the code which implements each function f over a set of tests T_f that is reliable for f, relative to F_f.

The refinement of branch testing that is suggested in this paper requires that each instance of one of the five functions described earlier be tested over a reliable test set. This will result in a complete test set for a program, relative to that class of simple functions. The five functions occur in assignment, conditional and loop statements in the following ways.

(a) Assignment statements. The use of simple assignment statements in which the left hand side of the assignment contains a single variable or array element is assumed. All operators are assumed to be arithmetic. Each variable or array reference occurring on the right hand side of an assignment or in an indexing expression on the left hand side is associated with a data access function. A data storage function is associated with the variable on the left hand side. Indexing expressions and the expression on the right hand side of the statement are associated with expression evaluation functions.

(b) Conditional statements. The use of conditional statements of the form "IF BEXP THEN S" is assumed where S may be any kind of statement. Conditional statements are designed around the evaluation of a boolean expression function which is implemented by the expression BEXP. There is a data access function associated with each variable in BEXP, an arithmetic expression function associated with each arithmetic expression, an arithmetic relation function associated with each arithmetic relation, and a boolean expression function associated with the expression as a whole. The S part of the conditional statement either contains additional conditional statement functions (for nested conditional statements) or the functions associated with some other kind of statement.

(c) Loop statement. The use of loop statements of the form "FOR I = E_1 BY C TO E_2 DO:" and of the form "WHILE EXP DO:" is assumed.

FOR-loop statements can be thought of as implementing four sets of functions. The first contains the functions implemented by a loop entry relational expression $E_2 \geq E_1$ (for $C \geq 0$, or $E_1 \geq E_2$ for $C < 0$). The loop entry expression is used to determine if control should enter a loop. It implements an arithmetic relation function, data access functions for each variable contained in the expression and possibly one or two arithmetic expression functions, depending on the forms of E_1 and E_2. The second set of functions contains the functions implemented by a loop exit expression $I > E_2$. The expression is used at the end of each loop iteration to determine if control should leave the loop. The third set of functions are computed by the implicit assignment statement $I \leftarrow E_1$ which is used to initialize the loop index and the fourth by the implicit indexing assignment statement $I \leftarrow I + C$ which is used at the end of each loop iteration.

Two sets of functions are associated with WHILE-loops. The first contains the functions implemented by the loop entrance expression EXP. EXP is used to determine if control should enter a WHILE-loop. It is evaluated whenever control reaches the loop statement in which it appears. The second set of functions are associated with the loop exit expression which is also computed by EXP. It is used at the end of each loop iteration to determine if control should leave the loop.

The requirement that programs be tested over complete test data sets will result in the construction of tests which correspond to commonly occurring kinds of errors. Reliable test sets for arithmetic relation functions in conditional statements correspond to errors in conditional statements which only manifest themselves when the extremal conditions for a branch are tested. They also correspond to conditional statement errors that only reveal themselves when the "equal part" of a "less than or equal" relation is tested.

Reliable test data sets for the arithmetic relation functions that are used in loop statements to determine loop entry correspond to errors which only appear when a loop should just "barely" be entered (or not be entered) but is not entered (or entered). Reliable test data sets for relation functions that are used to determine loop exit correspond to off-by-one type errors where a loop is iterated for one to few or one to many iterations.

It is noted that there may be situations in which it is impossible to construct complete test data sets. It may not be possible, for example, to construct a set of program tests which results in the evaluation of a data access function over a reliable test set. The goal in this case is to construct as complete a test data set as possible. A software tool can be built that will report on the completeness of a set of program tests. The programmer is expected to analyze his program to see if he can increase the measure of completeness of the test set.

Reliable Test Data Sets For Requirements and Design Functions

The functional test set reliability results in this paper are limited to the simple functions that are implemented in single statements. It would be ideal if it were possible to define useful, reliable test sets T for the functions which are computed by a program as a whole or by functions which are computed by major design components of a program. Some work has been completed on functions like this but the results are very restricted. In "Algebraic Program Testing" [12] the author used results from algebra to prove the reliability of test data sets for classes of functions F_f which are implemented by "array manipulation programs". In "Theoretical and Empirical Studies on Using Program Mutations to Test the Functional Correctness of Programs" [14], Budd et al defined a reliable set of tests for classes of functions which are implemented by decision tables. The difficulty of deriving results for requirements and design functions indicates that perhaps some other approach is needed at this level.

Summary

An approach to defining the completeness of a set of test data has been described in which it is necessary for a set of tests to result in the evaluation of the functions which are implemented in program statements over reliable test data sets. The approach can be supported by a software tool, it can be described formally, it has a theoretical basis and it is an integral part of the general approach to testing called functional testing.

The completeness of a set of test data is defined relative to classes of functions F_f which model the kinds of errors for which the test data is effective. The types of errors for which the complete test data sets that are described in this paper are effective include: wrong variable errors, off-by-one conditional statement branch and loop control errors, wrong relation errors in arithmetic relations and wrong operator errors in boolean and arithmetic expressions. The approach can be used to test for additional kinds of errors through the identification of new kinds of program statement functions f and/or the definition of new error modelling classes of functions F_f.

The completeness of a set of program tests can be evaluated with a software tool that monitors statement usage and analyzes the reliability of the data over which functions in the statement are evaluated. Figure 4 summarizes the kinds of functions that were studied in the paper and the statement types which implement one or more of those functions. Figure 5 summarizes the characteristics of reliable test data sets for the statement functions in Figure 4. The monitoring of the reliability of test data sets for different statement functions is relatively straightforward for each of the five types of functions except for possibly data access functions. The expense of checking the reliability of the values over which access functions are evaluated may require a modified approach to testing for wrong variable errors.

Statement	Functions
1. Assignment	Data access, data storage, arithmetic expression
2. Conditionals	Data access, arithmetic expression, relational expression, boolean expression
3. Loops	Loop entry functions: data access, arithmetic expression, relational expression, boolean expression
	Loop exit functions: data access, arithmetic expression, relational expression, boolean expression
	Index initialization: data access, data storage, arithmetic expression
	Indexing: data access, data storage, arithmetic expression

Figure 4. Statement types and corresponding functions.

Functions	Reliable Test Data
1. Data access	Unique value for variable
2. Data storage	New value for variable
3. Arithmetic expression	Evaluates to non-zero quantity

4. Relational expressions (of the form $E_1 \, r \, E_2$)	Tests that evaluate E_1 and E_2 so that $E_1 < E_2$, $E_1 = E_2$ and $E_1 > E_2$; tests that evaluate E_1 and E_2 so that for
	 (i) $r = <, \geq$:
	   $E_2 - E_1$ is maximal and < 0
	   $E_2 - E_1$ is minimal and ≥ 0
	 (ii) $r = >, \leq$:
	   $E_2 - E_1$ is minimal and > 0
	   $E_2 - E_1$ is maximal and ≤ 0
	 (iii) $r = =, \neq$:
	   $E_2 - E_1 = 0$

5. Boolean expressions (of the form $B(E_1, E_2, \ldots, E_n)$)	Tests that evaluate E_i, $1 \leq i \leq n$, so that all possible combinations of True and False are generated

Figure 5. Reliable tests for simple errors in statement functions.

Acknowledgements

The author would like to thank Timothy Budd and Richard Hamlet for useful discussions of the nature of mutation testing.

References

[1] William E. Howden, Reliability of the path analysis testing strategy, IEEE Trans. on Soft. Eng., SE-2, 1976.

[2] Leon Stucki, New directions in automated tools for improving software quality, in Current Trends in Prog. Method., Vol. 2 ed. by R.T. Yeh, Prentice Hall, Englewood Cliffs, 1977.

[3] Simone Pinnont and J.C. Rault, A software reliability assessment based on a structural and behavioural analysis of programs, Proc. Second Internat. Conf. on Soft. Eng., IEEE 76CH1125-4 C, Long Beach, 1976.

[4] M.R. Woodward, M.A. Hennell and D. Heldey, Experience with Path Analysis and Testing of Programs, IEEE Trans. on Soft. Eng., SE-6, 1980.

[5] William E. Howden, An evaluation of the effectiveness of symbolic testing and of testing on actual data, Soft. Practice and Experience, 8, 1978.

[6] William E. Howden, Applicability of software validation techniques to scientific programs, ACM Trans. on Prog. Lang. and Systems, vol. 2, 1980.

[7] J. Goodenough and S.L. Gerhart, Toward a theory of test data selection, IEEE Trans. on Soft. Eng., SE-3, 1977.

[8] Timothy A. Budd, Richard J. Lipton, Richard A. De Millo, and Frederick G. Sayward, Mutation Analysis, Res. Rep. #155, Dept. of Comp. Sci., Yale Univ., April, 1979.

[9] R.J. Lipton and F.G. Sayward, The status of research on program mutation, Digest of Papers for Workshop on Soft. Testing and Test Documentation, Ft. Lauderdale, Dec. 1978.

[10] R.G. Hamlet, Testing programs with the aid of compiler, IEEE Trans. on Soft. Eng., SE-3, July, 1977.

[11] William E. Howden, Functional program testing, IEEE Trans. on Soft. Eng., SE-6, 1980.

[12] W.E. Howden, Functional testing and design abstractions, Jour. of Systems and Soft., (to appear)

[13] William E. Howden, Algebraic program testing, Acta Infor., 10, 1978.

[14] Timothy A. Budd, Richard A. De Millo, Richard J. Lipton, Frederick G. Sayward, Theoretical and empirical studies on using program mutation to test the functional correctness of programs, Pro. ACM Symp. on Principles of Programming Lang., Las Vegas, 1980.

[15] Elaine J. Weyuker and Thomas J. Ostrand, Theoreies of program testing and application of revealing subdomains, IEEE Trans. on Soft. Eng., SE-6, 1980.

[16] William E. Howden, Elementary algebraic program testing techniques, Univ. of Calif., San Diego, Dept. of EE&CS, report #12, 1976.

[17] John H. Rowland and Phillip J. Davis, On the selection of test data for recursive mathematical subroutines, Brown Univ., Div. of App. Math., May, 1979.

[18] Richard A. De Millo and Richard J. Lipton, A probabilistic remark on algebraic program testing, Infor. Proc. Letters, Vol. 7, June, 1978.

[19] K.A. Foster, Error sensitive test cases analysis (ESTCA), IEEE Trans. on Soft. Eng., SE-6, 1978.

An Introduction to Proving the Correctness of Programs

SIDNEY L. HANTLER

and

JAMES C. KING

Computer Sciences Department, IBM Thomas J. Watson Research Center, Yorktown Heights, New York 10598

This paper explains, in an introductory fashion, the method of specifying the correct behavior of a program by the use of input/output assertions and describes one method for showing that the program is correct with respect to those assertions. An initial assertion characterizes conditions expected to be true upon entry to the program and a final assertion characterizes conditions expected to be true upon exit from the program. When a program contains no branches, a technique known as symbolic execution can be used to show that the truth of the initial assertion upon entry guarantees the truth of the final assertion upon exit. More generally, for a program with branches one can define a symbolic execution tree. If there is an upper bound on the number of times each loop in such a program may be executed, a proof of correctness can be given by a simple traversal of the (finite) symbolic execution tree.

However, for most programs, no fixed bound on the number of times each loop is executed exists and the corresponding symbolic execution trees are infinite. In order to prove the correctness of such programs, a more general assertion structure must be provided. The symbolic execution tree of such programs must be traversed inductively rather than explicitly. This leads naturally to the use of additional assertions which are called "inductive assertions."

Keywords and Phrases: Program correctness, program proving, program verification, proving correctness of programs, symbolic execution, symbolic interpretation

CR Categories: 1.3, 4.13, 5.21, 5.24

INTRODUCTION

Interest in verifying that computer programs behave as they were intended to behave has existed since the advent of modern electronic computers. As the size and complexity of computer programs have increased, so has the importance of assuring that these programs behave reliably. Naturally, attention has been focused on the problem of specifying precisely what constitutes reliable behavior and on developing a thorough method for checking that a program will always meet those specifications.

It is the intent of this paper to give a tutorial presentation of one approach for showing that a program meets its specification. The basic approach of using "correctness assertions" and the particular form of induction used are due to Floyd

---

Copyright © 1976, Association for Computing Machinery, Inc. General permission to republish, but not for profit, all or part of this material is granted provided that ACM's copyright notice is given and that reference is made to the publication, to its date of issue, and to the fact that reprinting privileges were granted by permission of the Association for Computing Machinery.

Reprinted from *ACM Computing Surveys*, September 1976, pp. 331-353.
Copyright 1976, Association for Computing Machinery, Inc. Reprinted by permission.

CONTENTS

INTRODUCTION
1. PROGRAMMING LANGUAGE AND SEMANTICS
2. CORRECTNESS OF PROGRAMS
3. SYMBOLIC EXECUTION AND SYMBOLIC EXECUTION TREES
   Symbolic Execution
4. INFINITE SYMBOLIC EXECUTION TREES AND INDUCTION
5. PROCEDURES
6. PROBLEMS
SUMMARY
ACKNOWLEDGMENTS
REFERENCES

---

[7]. The strategy explained in this paper for composing a proof is similar to methods developed by Deutsch [5] and Topor [21]. The presentation is informal; no theorems are stated or proved. For the person who understands what it means to execute a program and who understands simple algebraic and mathematical concepts, the ideas presented here are quite straightforward. Rigorous presentations of similar material are available elsewhere [6, 13, 18].

We begin by defining a very simple programming language. Though simple, the language contains the important basic features of commonly used programming languages. All examples in the paper are written in this language, and in Section 2, the concept of correctness for programs written in the language is developed. The symbolic execution of programs is introduced in Section 3 as the basic tool for building correctness proofs. In Section 4 the proof method is further developed for programs with looping structures. In order to show the generality of the technique, it is extended to handle subroutines and functions in Section 5. Finally, in Section 6, there is a discussion of the state of the art of program verification and its computer automation, with an emphasis on research into problems that remain unsolved.

1. PROGRAMMING LANGUAGE AND SEMANTICS

In this section we describe a simple programming language of a PL/I style, suitable for introducing the notion of correctness. In order to facilitate the exposition and minimize the technical details, we choose a particularly simple language, with only basic statement types and simple arithmetic expressions.

Procedures are declared by statements of the form:

  name: **PROCEDURE** $(p_1, p_2, p_3, \ldots, p_n)$;
    ⟨statement-list⟩
  END;

where *name* is the procedure name and $p_1, p_2, p_3, \ldots, p_n$ are procedure parameters. As usual, the body of the procedure consists of a list of statements placed between the **PROCEDURE** and the corresponding **END**. There are two types of procedures: 1) functions, which are referenced from within arithmetic expressions; and 2) subroutines, which are invoked explicitly by a **CALL** statement. This distinction is discussed in more detail later.

Program variables are integer valued and are declared by the **DECLARE** statement. The statement

  DECLARE $variable_1, variable_2, \ldots, variable_n$ **INTEGER**;

creates integer valued variables named $variable_1, variable_2, \ldots, variable_n$. These variables are known only within the procedure in which they are declared and a "new" generation is created on each procedure call (cf., PL/I *automatic* variables). Arithmetic operations on the values of program variables yield new values. Values of program variables and integer constants may be added (+), multiplied (×), and subtracted (−). The basic assignment statement has the form:

variable ← ⟨expression⟩;

where *variable* is a declared program variable and ⟨expression⟩ is an arithmetic expression in declared variables, integer constants, and function names applied to the appropriate number of arguments.

A function name occurring in the right-hand side of an assignment statement causes the function procedure associated with that name to be invoked. Thus if *name* is a procedure with a single parameter which returns the value 7 when invoked with the argument 3, the result of executing

variable ← (2 × *name*(3)) + 4;

is that the value of *variable* becomes 18.

Statements may be grouped together into a compound statement by means of the **DO**; ⟨statement-list⟩ **END**; construct. When enclosed by the **DO-END** pair, the list of statements is treated as if it were a single statement.

Boolean primitives are constructed from Boolean constants *true* and *false* and arithmetic expressions (as on the right side of assignment statements) connected by the relational operators: less than (<), greater than (>), equal (=), and their complements ($\geq$, $\leq$, $\neq$). Boolean expressions (denoted by ⟨Boolean⟩ below) are constructed using the Boolean primitives connected by: and (&), or (|), implies (→), and not (¬). The value of a Boolean expression is either *true* or *false*.

The binary conditional is of the form:

IF ⟨Boolean⟩ **THEN** *statement*$_1$ **ELSE** *statement*$_2$

where *statement*$_1$ and *statement*$_2$ are statements or compound statements. As usual, either *statement*$_1$ or *statement*$_2$ is executed, depending on the truth value of the ⟨Boolean⟩.

The iterative statement is of the form:

DO WHILE ⟨Boolean⟩; ⟨statement-list⟩ **END**;

When control reaches the **DO WHILE** statement, if the value of the ⟨Boolean⟩ is *true*, the statement list is executed and control is returned to the **DO WHILE** statement. If the ⟨Boolean⟩ is *false*, control passes immediately to the statement following the **END** statement.

As mentioned above, function procedures are invoked by reference to the procedure name within an arithmetic expression. Parameters are passed exactly as described in the following discussion about subroutine procedures. In addition to the changes that may be effected through the parameters, function procedures return one special value to be used in the invoking expression evaluation. Subroutines are invoked and parameters are passed by means of the **CALL** statement. For example, the statement

CALL *name* ($a_1, a_2, a_3, \ldots, a_n$);

causes the subroutine named *name* to be invoked and the names of the formal parameters $p_1, \ldots, p_n$ to be associated with the names of the actual arguments $a_1, \ldots, a_n$, respectively. Parameter passing follows the PL/I "by reference" convention, i.e. references to the actual arguments are passed to the subroutine (or function). When an argument is an expression, its value is stored in a temporary storage location, a reference to which is passed to the subroutine.

For convenience in referring to the initial values of the parameters of a procedure from within correctness assertions, the initial values of the parameters are stored in special procedure variables which are denoted by primed symbols. For example, after execution of the **CALL** statement above, the values of $a_1, \ldots, a_n$ upon entry to *name* are preserved in the variables $p_1', \ldots, p_n'$, respectively.

Return from an invoked procedure is

```
1   ABSOLUTE:
      PROCEDURE(X);
3     DECLARE X, Y INTEGER;
4     IF X < 0
5       THEN Y ← -X;
6       ELSE Y ← X;
8     RETURN (Y);
9   END;
```

FIGURE 1. Function procedure *ABSOLUTE*.

achieved by means of the **RETURN** statement, which may appear at any place in a procedure. Each procedure has exactly one **RETURN** statement. A **RETURN** statement is of the form:

RETURN;

in a subroutine, and

RETURN (⟨expression⟩);

in a function. The latter statement returns the value of the ⟨expression⟩ as the value of the function.

2. CORRECTNESS OF PROGRAMS

Having defined a simple programming language in Section 1, we now discuss the meaning of "correctness" of procedures written in that language. We will provide a method for formalizing the intended behavior of a procedure. In particular, constraints on the inputs to a procedure and expected relations between inputs and outputs will be expressed as assertions over the program variables. An *input assertion* is a statement of the form:

ASSUME (⟨Boolean⟩);

and usually appears immediately after the **PROCEDURE** statement. For example, the input assertion

ASSUME ($p_1 > 0$);

asserts that the value of the parameter p_1 is assumed to be positive on procedure entry. An *output assertion* is a statement of the form:

PROVE (⟨Boolean⟩);

and usually appears immediately before the **RETURN** statement of a procedure. For example, the output assertion

PROVE (($X = Y'$) & ($Y = X'$));

indicates that the values of the variables X and Y have been interchanged. Note that this is the relationship between inputs and outputs which would be satisfied by a correct interchange procedure.

Naturally, the notion of "correctness" of a procedure should reflect this relation among the input assertion, output assertion, and procedure body. *A procedure is said to be correct (with respect to its input and output assertions) if the truth of its input assertion upon procedure entry insures the truth of its output assertion upon procedure exit.* Notice that the question of program termination is suppressed in this definition. Intuitively, a procedure is correct provided that it behaves as expected when it terminates. This is often called "partial correctness," with the term "correctness" or "total correctness" reserved for procedures that are partially correct and terminate for all inputs.

A simple procedure is shown in Figure 1. The function *ABSOLUTE* is intended to return the absolute value of its parameter. Inasmuch as no assumptions need be made about the input parameter to *ABSOLUTE*, the input assertion should be **ASSUME** (*true*). The output assertion must specify that, when the **RETURN** statement is executed, the value of the procedure variable Y is the absolute value of the initial value of the parameter X. Thus, an appropriate output assertion (among others), describing what this procedure does, is **PROVE** $((Y = X' \mid Y = -X')$ & $Y \geq 0)$. We will see later, that it is often important to specify what a procedure does not do, as well as what a procedure does. A more complete output assertion, specifying that the value of X is unchanged by the procedure *ABSOLUTE*, is **PROVE** $((Y = X' \mid Y = -X')$ & $Y \geq 0$ & $X = X')$.

The procedure, with correctness assertions, would then be as shown in Figure 2. In this simple example, it is quite clear that the procedure is correct. In the next section we discuss a formal method of proving that procedures (with input and output assertions) are correct.

3. SYMBOLIC EXECUTION AND SYMBOLIC EXECUTION TREES

A proof of correctness for a program is a proof over *all* program inputs. Certainly such a proof cannot, in general, be made using any finite (small) collection of specific inputs, but must be made with statements about *all inputs*. One can use a standard mathematical technique of inventing symbols to represent arbitrary program inputs, and then attempt a proof involving those symbols. If no special properties of the symbols, other than those expected to hold for all inputs, are necessary for the proof, then the proof is valid for *each* specific input. If special properties of the symbols must be assumed in order to construct a proof, then an exhaustive case analysis can be performed, providing a set of proofs, one for each case, which collectively give a complete proof.

Let us naively attempt to apply this strategy to devise a correctness proof for the simple program *ABSOLUTE* of Figure 2. A typical invocation of *ABSOLUTE* can be represented by using a symbolic argument, say α: *ABSOLUTE*(α). We proceed to execute the program using the symbol α as the input value of X. The **ASSUME** statement execution contributes nothing since its argument is *true*, which places no constraints on the input α. The execution of the **IF** statement is more interesting. Here one must determine if the value of X is negative; that is, if $\alpha < 0$. If α stands for the integer 3 the answer is no, but if α is -3 the answer is yes. To answer this question some assumption about the value of α must be made, and a case analysis is required:

Case 1: Assume $\alpha < 0$. In this case the **IF** test would produce *true* and execution would proceed into the **THEN** clause. Here Y becomes the negative of the value of X, (i.e., $-\alpha$). Arriving at the **PROVE** statement, one must show that, in this case, the present values satisfy $((Y = X' \mid Y = -X')$ & $Y \geq 0$ & $X = X')$. Since $Y = -\alpha$ and $X = X' = \alpha$, this becomes

$$(-\alpha = \alpha \mid -\alpha = -\alpha) \ \& \ -\alpha \geq 0 \ \& \ \alpha = \alpha$$

which simplifies to $-\alpha \geq 0$ or more simply

```
1   ABSOLUTE:
     PROCEDURE (X);
2      ASSUME (true);
3      DECLARE X, Y INTEGER;
4      IF X < 0
5        THEN Y ← -X;
6        ELSE Y ← X;
7      PROVE ((Y = X' | Y = -X') & Y ≥ 0 & X = X');
8      RETURN (Y);
9    END;
```

FIGURE 2. Procedure *ABSOLUTE* with correctness assertions.

$\alpha \leq 0$. Establishing the truth of the **PROVE** statement then reduces to showing $\alpha \leq 0$. But we have assumed $\alpha < 0$, so the proof is trivial. In the case $\alpha < 0$, the program is correct.

Case 2: Assume $\alpha \geq 0$. In this case the **IF** test would produce *false* and execution would proceed into the **ELSE** clause. Here Y becomes the value of X or α. Arriving at the **PROVE** statement, one must show that $((Y = X' \mid Y = -X') \& Y \geq 0 \& X = X')$ is *true*, when $Y = \alpha$, $X = X' = \alpha$. That is, to show that

$$(\alpha = \alpha \mid \alpha = -\alpha) \& \alpha \geq 0 \& \alpha = \alpha,$$

or simply $\alpha \geq 0$, is *true*. Again the proof is trivial since $\alpha \geq 0$ was assumed.

By the nature of the **IF** statement these two cases are exhaustive (either $\alpha < 0$ or $\alpha \geq 0$) and both yield correct results. Therefore the program is correct.

Several points about this example should be made. The assumptions used in the case analysis resulted from an unresolved execution of the **IF** statement. The assumptions were exactly the *evaluated* **IF** test and its negation and were Boolean valued expressions strictly over the input α. These assumptions were needed as hypotheses to establish the truth of the **PROVE** statement in each case.

Symbolic Execution

In this section we attempt to explain the basic "symbolic execution" technique used informally in the preceding example, more carefully and more completely. Within the scope of the programming language used here, consider the consequences of changing the underlying computation facilities of the language implementation (the program execution mechanism) from doing arithmetic operations over integers to doing algebraic operations over symbolic expressions. For example, suppose that the variables X and Y have the symbols α and β as their respective values. As a result of executing the statement $X \leftarrow Y + X$ the value of X becomes the formula $\alpha + \beta$. Executing $Y \leftarrow 3 \times X - Y$ next, would symbolically calculate the formula $3 \times \alpha + 2 \times \beta$ as the new value of Y.

Executing a program on a symbol manipulating machine one might hope to obtain algebraic formulas over the input symbols as the values of the output variables. Then, checking these results against the output assertion, one could establish the correctness, or incorrectness, of the program. As even the extremely elementary example, *ABSOLUTE*, shown above, demonstrates, this is not quite so simple. That example requires a case analysis, since Boolean expressions involving symbols often do not simplify to *true* or *false*. For example, the truth of $\alpha \geq 0$ is not determined without some information about α. However, symbolic execution does provide a complete way to establish program correctness when augmented by such case analyses and by a general inductive technique. Reconsider the definition of program execution given in Section 1, but assume that programs receive symbols or symbolic expressions as input and are executed on a machine capable of performing algebra. At procedure invocation (**CALL** or function reference), the transfer of control and the association of arguments to parameters work the same as before. Similarly the meaning of the **RETURN** statement is unchanged.

The first construct where something more interesting occurs is the assignment statement. The usual execution first replaces all variables in the right-side expression by their values, then performs the indicated arithmetic and assigns the resulting value as a new value of the left-side variable. The symbolic execution performs the algebraic equivalent. The variables in the right-side expression are replaced by their values (parenthesized to maintain the proper scope of operators). Since the values of variables are formulas, the indicated arithmetic operations cannot be done numerically but are simply represented symbolically, as in algebra. The resulting symbolic expression becomes the new value of the left-side variable.

When the arithmetic expression involves function calls the situation is more complex and is discussed in a later section dealing explicitly with procedure calls. There is also the issue of whether or not algebraic simplification should be performed on formulas resulting from the substitution of values for variables in the right-side expression. If no simplification is done, the formulas accurately characterize the exact computations that would have taken place had the inputs been numbers. In fact, those computations can be done later according to the formulas, getting the same results even with respect to overflow and other machine anomalies.

However, no simplification implies that the formulas may become quite unwieldy. As we will see shortly, theorem proving over these expressions is required, and the difficulty is increased if the formulas are very complex. Since the objective of this paper is to present the basic ideas of proving correctness of programs as simply as possible, this difficult question will not be addressed. When convenient in examples, the formulas will be simplified. In theory, the basic approach is valid whether or not the formulas are simplified. In the extreme, one must choose between very difficult theorem proving and specification writing (in the case of no simplification), and results that, when simplified, may not accurately apply in all cases to an actual computer execution.

The symbolic execution of conditional branching statements also parallels their normal execution but with additional complexity. Consider first the **IF** statement. Its symbolic execution begins by replacing all variables in its Boolean expression by their parenthesized values. The resulting expression may be equivalent to *true*, *false*, or some Boolean expression over the symbolic program inputs. The last situation may result in a case analysis as it did in the *ABSOLUTE* example. Whenever the Boolean result is neither *true* nor *false*, there is at least one numeric program input for which the result is *false* and at least one other for which it is *true*. The execution cannot proceed into either the **THEN** clause or the **ELSE** clause and be valid for all inputs. Thus, the case analysis is required.

Recall from the example that the assumptions which determine the cases are needed later to establish the truth of the **PROVE** predicate. The assumptions are also needed to avoid considering impossible subcases that may arise at subsequent conditional statement executions. For example, consider the execution of the two successive **IF** statements:

IF $X < 0$ **THEN** $Y \leftarrow 88$;
IF $X = 3$ **THEN** $Y \leftarrow 99$;

with the value of $X = \alpha$. There are four syntactic paths through these two statements, but only three are semantically possible. The impossible subcase can be detected if the conditions on α necessary to execute the choices of the first statement (i.e., $\alpha < 0$, $\alpha \geq 0$) are remembered and used to determine consistent choices on the second statement. These observations lead to the notion of a "path condition," abbreviated pc. It is a part of the symbolic execution-state and takes as its value the conditions over the program's symbolic inputs that determine each case, subcase, sub-subcase, etc. The pc is initialized to *true* at the beginning of a symbolic execution and is updated each time a new case is considered.

The complete description of the symbolic execution of an **IF** statement of the form:

IF ⟨Boolean⟩ **THEN** *statement*₁ **ELSE** *statement*₂

is as follows:

1) Evaluate the ⟨Boolean⟩ obtaining a value, B, over the symbolic inputs.

2) Now decide if subcases for B and $\neg B$ should be formed. If pc $\rightarrow B$, new subcases are unnecessary since enough assumptions

have already been made (recorded in the pc) to determine that *statement*₁ would always be executed next. The symbolic execution proceeds directly to *statement*₁. Similarly if pc → ¬B, the symbolic execution proceeds directly to *statement*₂. If neither (pc → B) nor (pc → ¬B), new subcases for B and ¬B are required as described in steps 3 and 4, respectively.

3) Establish a subcase assuming B. Update the pc with new conditions B by replacing it by (pc$_{old}$ & B), where pc$_{old}$ is the most recent value of the pc (i.e., do the assignment pc ← pc & B). In this case, the symbolic execution proceeds to *statement*₁ with the revised pc.

4) Establish a subcase assuming ¬B. Update the pc with new conditions ¬B by replacing it by (pc$_{old}$ & ¬B). In this case, the symbolic execution proceeds to *statement*₂ with this revised pc.

The case of an **IF** statement execution in which the evaluated Boolean reduces directly to *true* or *false* falls out at step 2. Since the pc is never allowed to be *false* (an impossible path), then (pc → *true*) is *true* and (pc → *false*) is *false* for any pc.

One can also define the symbolic execution of the **ASSUME** and **PROVE** statements which specify the program's correctness as follows:

ASSUME (⟨Boolean⟩):

1) Evaluate the ⟨Boolean⟩ by substituting parenthesized values for variables. Call the result B.

2) Update the pc to the value (pc$_{old}$ & B).

This has the effect of confining the subsequent symbolic execution to the case where the ⟨Boolean⟩ is *true*, which is the intention of the input assertion.

PROVE (⟨Boolean⟩):

1) Evaluate the ⟨Boolean⟩ by substituting parenthesized values for variables. Call the result B.

2) If (pc → B) print "verified" otherwise print "not verified."

This statement prints "verified" or "not verified" depending on whether or not the program variable's values satisfy the output assertions in this case. The conditions defining *this case* are given by the pc.

The complete symbolic execution of a program like *ABSOLUTE* of Figure 2 can be compactly represented by a "symbolic execution tree." The tree for that example is shown in Figure 3. It is similar to a program flowchart, with each statement execution being represented by a node, and a transfer of control between statement executions by an arc. The nodes are labeled with the program statement numbers, and the arcs leaving statements are labeled by the changes to the execution state, if any, caused by the execution of the preceding statement. Of course, a conditional statement execution node will have more than one arc leaving it when the choice of successor statement remains unresolved. Nodes for nonexecutable statements (e.g., **DECLARE**) are omitted from the trees shown here to conserve space. Since the tree of Figure 3 covers all possible executions of the program *ABSOLUTE*, in each case printing "verified," *ABSOLUTE* is correct.

We have yet to discuss the symbolic execution of **DO WHILE** statements. Without them in our language there is no means for program looping, and non-looping programs always have finite symbolic execution trees. As in the proof of the *ABSOLUTE* procedure, symbolic execution provides a convenient way to prove the correctness of procedures with finite symbolic execution trees. Such programs are correct provided that "verified" appears at each leaf of their symbolic execution trees.

However, infinite symbolic execution trees may occur when their corresponding procedures contain the iterative **DO WHILE** statement of the form

DO WHILE ⟨Boolean⟩; ⟨statement-list⟩
END;

Its symbolic execution follows naturally from the symbolic execution of the **IF** state-

An Introduction to Proving the Correctness of Programs

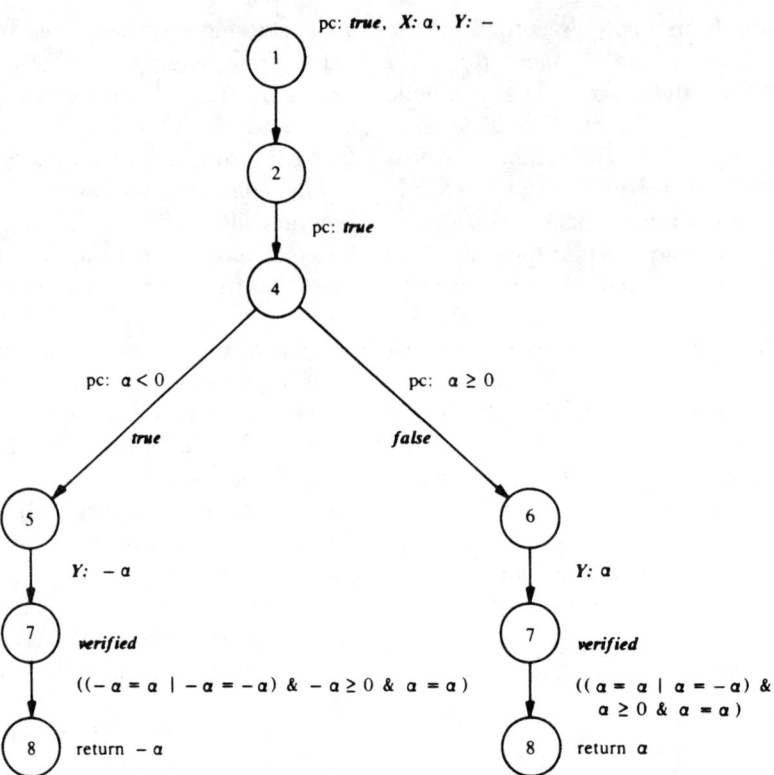

FIGURE 3. Symbolic execution tree for procedure *ABSOLUTE*.

```
1   GCD:
    PROCEDURE (M, N);
2      ASSUME (M > 0 & N > 0);
3      DECLARE M, N, A, B INTEGER;
4      A ← M;
5      B ← N;
6      DO WHILE (A ≠ B);
8        IF A > B
9          THEN A ← A − B;
10         ELSE B ← B − A;
11     END;
12     PROVE (A = (M, N));
13     RETURN (A);
14  END;
```

FIGURE 4. Procedure *GCD* with correctness assertions.

ment. The decision to execute the statement list, go on to the statement following the **END**, or develop those choices as alternative subcases is determined by examining the Boolean expression as was done for **IF** statements.

An example of an infinite symbolic execution tree is shown in Figure 5 for the procedure of Figure 4. The procedure of Figure 4 computes the greatest common divisor of its positive inputs *M* and *N*. The procedure's correctness is specified using the standard

84

mathematical notation where (M, N) stands for the greatest common divisor of M and N. For example, $(3, 12) = 3$, $(20, 15) = 5$, and $(4, 4) = 4$. Let a and b be integers. The greatest common divisor can be characterized by three axioms:

$(a, a) = a$ if $a > 0$,
$(a, b) = (b, a)$,
$(a, b) = (a + b, b)$.

Note that the infinite portion of the tree, as shown in Figure 5, is caused by the infinite sequence of unique conditions involving the symbolic inputs.

A program which has an infinite symbolic execution tree may have no particular input which causes an infinite program execution. The symbolic execution tree is infinite because there is always yet another, different, execution which requires more statement executions. Of course, a program which has a nonterminating execution has an infinite symbolic execution tree.

How can the method presented above be applied to programs which generate infinite symbolic execution trees? A general answer to this question is provided by using an inductive technique to "traverse" the infinite paths. This is discussed at length in Section 4. Otherwise one can reduce the problem to the one already discussed by restricting attention to finite subtrees of infinite symbolic execution trees. Recall that symbolic execution actually furnishes a proof of correctness for procedures with finite symbolic execution trees.

We illustrate this point by considering variants of the procedure GCD of Figure 4. Suppose, for instance, that we replace the initial **ASSUME** statement of that procedure by **ASSUME**(*false*). The resulting procedure not only has a finite symbolic execution tree (in fact, an empty tree), but it is also guaranteed to be correct. Naturally, the empty subtree of an infinite symbolic execution tree is an extreme and uninteresting subtree to study. A better choice of subtree results from a more subtle restriction of the initial assertion of the program.

Suppose that the initial **ASSUME** statement were modified to **ASSUME** $(M > 0$ & $N > 0$ & $M = C \times N$ & $C \leq 1000)$. We would then be restricting attention to that finite subtree of the GCD procedure corresponding to the case in which one of the variables is a small multiple of the other. Without inductive assistance of any kind, symbolic execution can provide a proof of correctness of this modified procedure.

Inasmuch as our principal interest is in the original GCD procedure rather than the modified procedure, it is perhaps better to think of the consideration of finite subtrees of an infinite symbolic execution tree as a form of testing. The finite subtrees represent the test cases of interest. Notice that testing using symbolic execution differs from more traditional testing techniques in at least two respects. First, ordinary testing covers at most a finite number of specific inputs, while testing by symbolic execution usually covers an infinite number of specific inputs. Second, when correctness assertions are supplied in procedures, symbolic testing provides a proof of correctness for the test cases being considered, rather than merely providing output values for each test case considered.

As a testing technique, symbolic execution appears to be an extremely promising new tool. It is the topic of a recent PhD thesis by Clarke [4], and Boyer et al. [1] have explored the generation of test cases using symbolic execution. The authors and their colleagues have developed a prototype symbolic execution system called EFFIGY [16] which includes features for program testing as well as for program proving.

4. INFINITE SYMBOLIC EXECUTION TREES AND INDUCTION

Programs contain a finite number of statements. Since the nodes on an infinite sym-

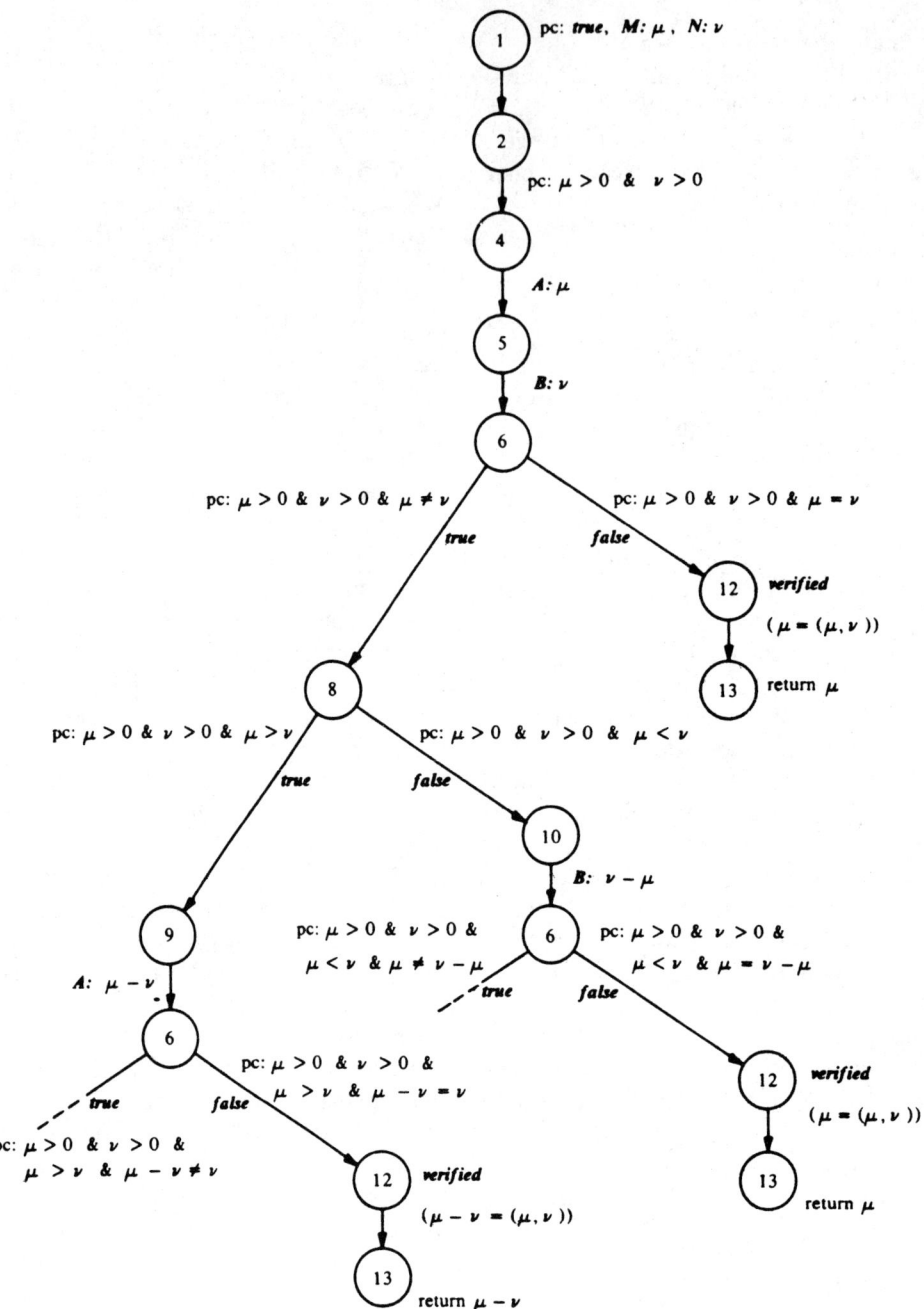

FIGURE 5. Symbolic execution tree for procedure *GCD*.

bolic execution tree are labeled by program statements, some statement labels must occur an infinite number of times. Thus, the infinite portions of the symbolic execution tree are generated by looping in the program. In the case of our programming language the sole loop construct is the **DO WHILE** statement.

Each loop traversal can be isolated by placing a "cut" (mark) at least once within every loop. The induction to be described is valid even if a loop is cut more than once, so it is trivially possible to cut all loops by placing a cut between every two program statements. Generally one cuts each loop just once. In our language, the cuts can be made by placing a mark between each **DO WHILE** and its statement body.

For simplicity in the subsequent discussion, consider that a cut has also been placed immediately after the **PROCEDURE** statement. Then imagine a symbolic execution of the program which begins at one of the cuts. Beginning at such an arbitrary point in a program, the "inputs" are, in fact, represented by the program state, so consider *all* program variables initialized to unique symbolic values, and the pc initialized to *true*. A symbolic execution, from this point on, is representative of all cases for which execution reaches the cut, independent of the values of the program variables; the new unique symbolic values represent all cases. The symbolic execution stops whenever any subsequent cut or the final program **RETURN** is encountered. Since each program loop has been cut, this symbolic execution will terminate in all cases and have a finite symbolic execution tree.

Call each such symbolic execution starting at a cut a *cut (symbolic) execution* and the corresponding tree a *cut (symbolic execution) tree*. If one were to place an **ASSUME** statement at a cut C and **PROVE** statements at each cut which terminates C's cut tree (the **RETURN** already has a **PROVE** just preceding it), the proof of correctness (with respect to those input/output assertions) for the cut execution of C can be discussed. Since the cut tree is finite, a proof as described in the previous section can always be attempted. If it succeeds, any execution which begins at the cut with values satisfying the cut input assertion is guaranteed to reach another cut and the program values at that point will satisfy the associated output assertion.

The proof of correctness of the entire procedure can be constructed from proofs of the cut executions. What is needed are the input/output assertions hypothesized for each cut tree and an explicit argument for the composition of the overall proof from the pieces. One appropriate assertion associated with each cut makes both possible. The word "appropriate" is used because these cut assertions (more commonly called "inductive assertions" or "inductive predicates") correspond to the inductive hypothesis in the usual proof by mathematical induction and are often quite difficult to discover.

```
 1         GCD:
               PROCEDURE (M, N);
 2  cut₂---    ASSUME (M > 0 & N > 0);
 3             DECLARE M, N, A, B INTEGER;
 4             A ← M;
 5             B ← N;
 6             DO WHILE (A ≠ B);
 7  cut₇---        ASSERT ((A, B) = (M, N) & A ≠ B);
 8                 IF A > B
 9                    THEN A ← A − B;
10                    ELSE B ← B − A;
11             END;
12             PROVE (A = (M, N));
13  return---  RETURN (A);
14         END;
```

FIGURE 6. Procedure *GCD* with inductive assertion

Suppose that by some "inductive genius" appropriate assertions are placed at each cut, except the first one, by use of a new statement of the form **ASSERT** (⟨Boolean⟩). Figure 6 shows the cuts and the inductive assertion for the *GCD* procedure of Figure 4. Two definitions for the symbolic execution of the **ASSERT** statement are supplied depending upon the context in which it is encountered. Refine the definition of cut execution such that the **ASSERT** statement is encountered as the first statement (just after the variables have all been set to unique symbols). (In this case, assume the actual cut-mark is placed just *above* the **ASSERT** statement.) When executing the **ASSERT** statement in this context, it is treated exactly as if it were an **ASSUME** statement; it supplies a cut execution input assertion. When each cut that terminates a cut execution is encountered, execute the associated **ASSERT** statement as if it were a **PROVE** statement. (In this context, assume the actual cut-mark is placed just *below* the **ASSERT** statement.) Note that one **ASSERT** statement can be treated as both an **ASSUME** statement and as a **PROVE** statement depending on the context.

Special cases at the beginning (**PROCEDURE**) and at the end (**RETURN**) of the program are obvious but must be mentioned. The initial cut after the **PROCEDURE** statement is never encountered as a terminating cut and is followed immediately by the **ASSUME** statement for the overall program, so no **ASSERT** statement is needed. The input cut assertion, for paths starting at the initial cut, is provided by executing the program's **ASSUME** statement. Whenever a cut execution is terminated by the program **RETURN** statement, the program's original **PROVE** statement will have just been executed; so here too no **ASSERT** statement is needed. The result of the program's **PROVE** serves as the result for the cut execution.

The following claim for this proof of correctness method is now easy to establish using an inductive argument. *If inductive assertions can be placed at each cut (except the first) by means of* **ASSERT** *statements such that the cut executions for all cuts are correct with respect to those assertions, then the program is correct. If such assertions do not exist, then the program is not correct.*

The proof of a cut execution establishes that for *any* set of values of the program variables that satisfy the cut input assertions (including those which result from an actual execution of the procedure to this point), the execution ultimately arrives at a subsequent cut and the associated output assertion is satisfied by the resulting values of the program variables. But since only *one* assertion has been associated with each cut, it is both the output assertion for all cut executions arriving at the cut and the input assertion for the cut execution leaving the cut. Any values which satisfy it as an output assertion also satisfy it as a subsequent input assertion.

For any particular program input which satisfies the program's input assertion, the values computed upon arrival at the next cut satisfy its associated cut assertion. But that, in turn, guarantees that the values computed upon arrival at the next cut satisfy its associated cut assertion. But the values computed upon arrival at the final program **RETURN** satisfy the program output assertion. Since a proof for *any* program input can be made from the cut proofs, the program is correct for all inputs. The program of Figure 6 has two cuts and therefore two cut executions. The cut trees for these two cut executions are shown in Figures 7 and 8. Since "verified" is printed at each leaf of these trees, the program is correct.

5. PROCEDURES

Any proof technique must be able to cope effectively with programs which call subroutines and functions. (We will denote the

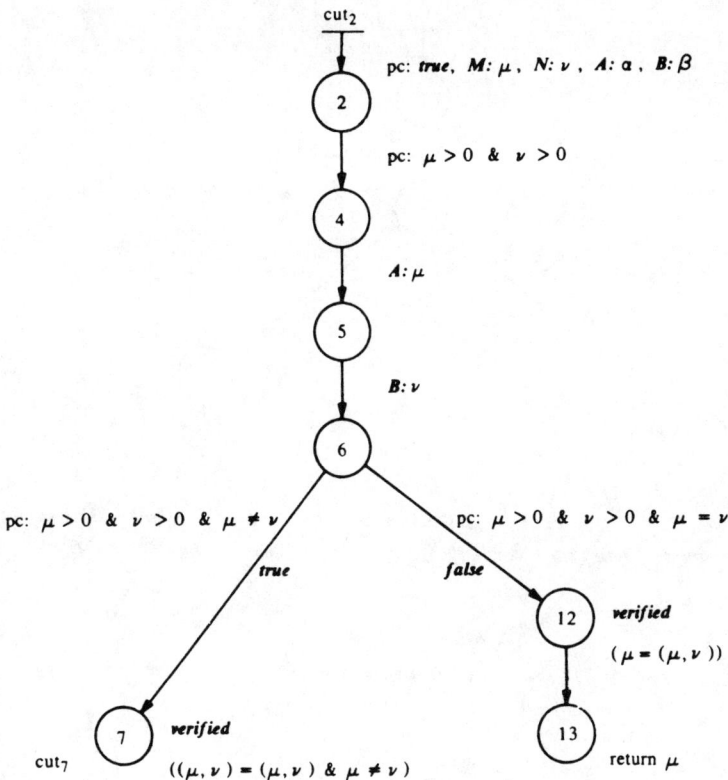

FIGURE 7. Cut tree for cut_2 of GCD.

subroutines and functions, subprocedures.) The notion of symbolic execution naturally extends to such calls, which involve transfer of control (with provision for return), some reassociation of variables and values and the creation/destruction of local procedure variables. All these operations remain conceptually the same whether the values of variables are symbolic formulas or numbers. A symbolic execution tree for a symbolic program execution including procedure calls is also conceivable, as is a proof of correctness as already presented. Consider the revised greatest common divisor procedure called $GCD2$ shown in Figure 9. It has been modified so as to call the $ABSOLUTE$ procedure of Figure 1. The cut execution for cut_2 is identical to that of Figure 7 for procedure GCD. The cut execution for cut_7 is shown in Figure 10. The symbolic execution "executes into" the procedure $ABSOLUTE$. The nodes in the tree resulting from executing statements in $ABSOLUTE$ are denoted by triangles to distinguish them from those of $GCD2$.

However, this method requires one to "start from scratch" with every proof, reproving properties of each subprocedure at each invocation. A method which allows one to prove a procedure is correct and then use this proof as a lemma in the proof for a calling procedure is needed. Such a method is described next.

Once a procedure (subprocedure) has been proved to be correct with respect to some input/output assertion pair, two consistent sources of information about that procedure's behavior exist: 1) The procedure itself as an executable algorithm (the procedure's codebody); and 2) properties proved correct as described in the input/output assertions.

There are two important points to note about the program characterization pro-

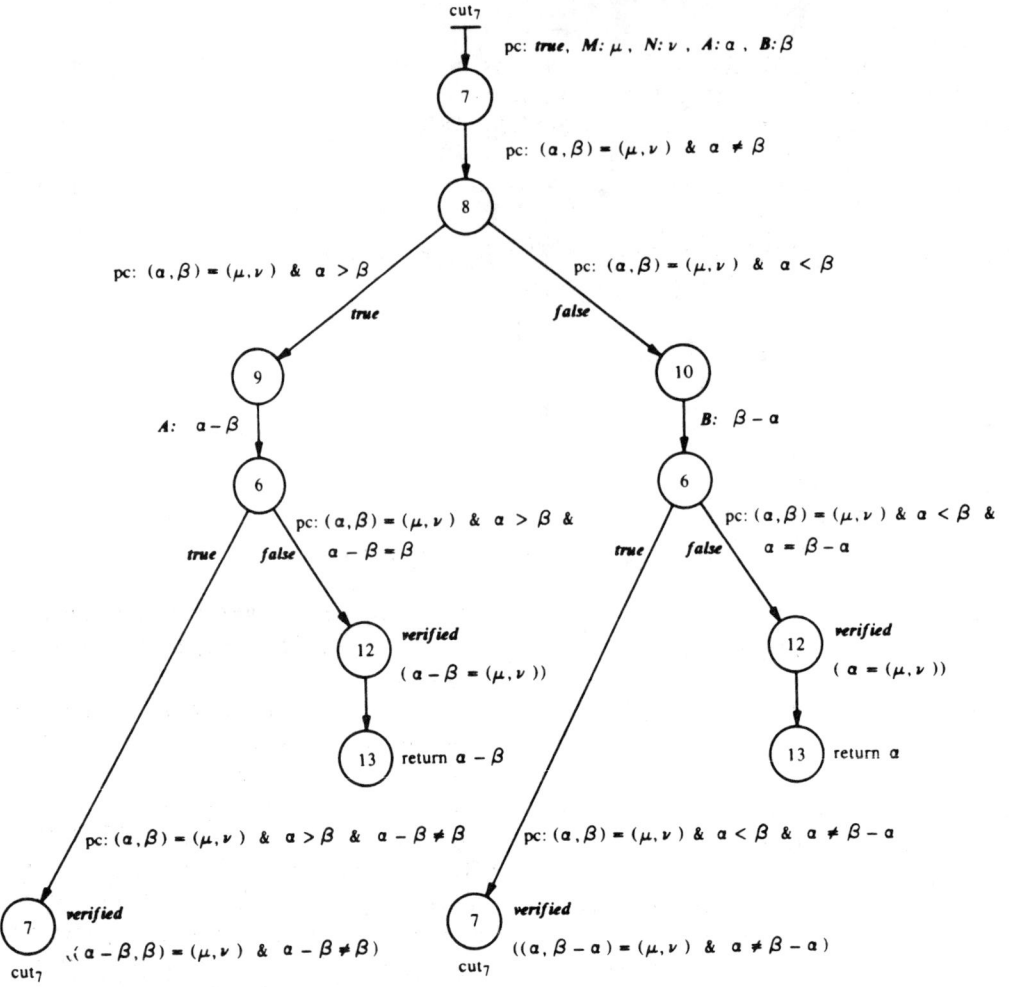

FIGURE 8. Cut tree for cut_7 of GCD.

vided by the input/output assertions:

1) They do not necessarily characterize everything the program does, but just some of the effects. Any program is correct with respect to the output assertion *true* which states nothing about the results. The output assertion is supplied by the programmer and includes only what he feels is important.

2) The information is not generally a description of how to compute the results, but rather a description of properties which the results satisfy. The output assertion on the program of Figure 2 $((Y = X' | Y = -X') \& Y \geq 0 \& X = X')$ does not describe how to calculate such a value for Y. The input/output assertions are more usable in a correctness proof for a calling procedure, than the subprocedure codebody since they do not involve the dynamics of how to calculate the procedure results but simply describe them.

The basic approach for dealing with subprocedures appeals to the same idea as does the main technique: use symbols to represent arbitrary values of program variables. The effect of executing a procedure is the alteration of some of the values of the calling procedure's variables and, in the case of a function call, the additional effect of returning a value for the function. New unique symbols are invented, one for each variable of the calling procedure which could have

```
1   GCD2:
        PROCEDURE (M, N);
2   cut₂---  ASSUME (M > 0 & N > 0);
3        DECLARE M, N, A, B, D INTEGER;
4        A ← M;
5        B ← N;
6        DO WHILE (A ≠ B);
7   cut₇---    ASSERT ((A, B) = (M, N) & A ≠ B);
8            D ← ABSOLUTE(A − B);
9            IF A > B
10             THEN A ← D;
11             ELSE B ← D;
12       END;
13       PROVE (A = (M, N));
14  return---RETURN (A);
15       END;
```

FIGURE 9. *GCD2* procedure which calls *ABSOLUTE*.

had its value altered by the procedure call. Instead of symbolically executing the procedure codebody, the values of the potentially affected calling program's variables are replaced by these new symbols. If the subprocedure has been proved correct, its output assertion holds for these new values and provides the information about these values needed for the proof.

The complete process can be explained precisely as the normal symbolic execution of an "abbreviated procedure" which is derived simply from the original subprocedure as follows:

1) Change the procedure's initial **ASSUME** statement to a **PROVE** statement, leaving its argument unchanged.

2) Change the procedure's final **PROVE** statement to an **ASSUME** statement, leaving its argument unchanged.

3) Replace the complete code body of the procedure by a sequence of assignment statements, one for each variable which can be altered by the procedure, of the form:

$$v_i \leftarrow \textbf{NEWSYMBOL};$$

The built-in function **NEWSYMBOL** is defined to return as its value a new symbolic value each time it is called.

The abbreviated procedure for the procedure *ABSOLUTE* of Figure 2 is shown in Figure 11.

Consider a program P which makes reference (either by **CALLs** or by function references) to procedures $Q_1, Q_2, \ldots, Q_n$. Assume that each procedure Q_i has been proved correct with respect to its **ASSUME/PROVE** statements. Replace each procedure Q_i by its abbreviated procedure. Suppose that P has **ASSUME/PROVE** statements and that each loop of P has been cut by an **ASSERT** statement. A proof of correctness of P, with respect to its input/output assertions, under the assumption of the correctness of the procedures Q_i, proceeds just as described before in Sections 3 and 4. The cut execution for cut_7 from *GCD2* of Figure 9, using the abbreviated procedure of Figure 11, is shown in Figure 12. The cut execution for cut_2 remains the same as before and is shown in Figure 7. These two cut executions establish the correctness of the procedure *GCD2*.

Whenever an invocation of a procedure occurs during the symbolic execution of paths of P, the abbreviated procedure is invoked. Suppose Q is such an abbreviated procedure. The proof of Q assures one that

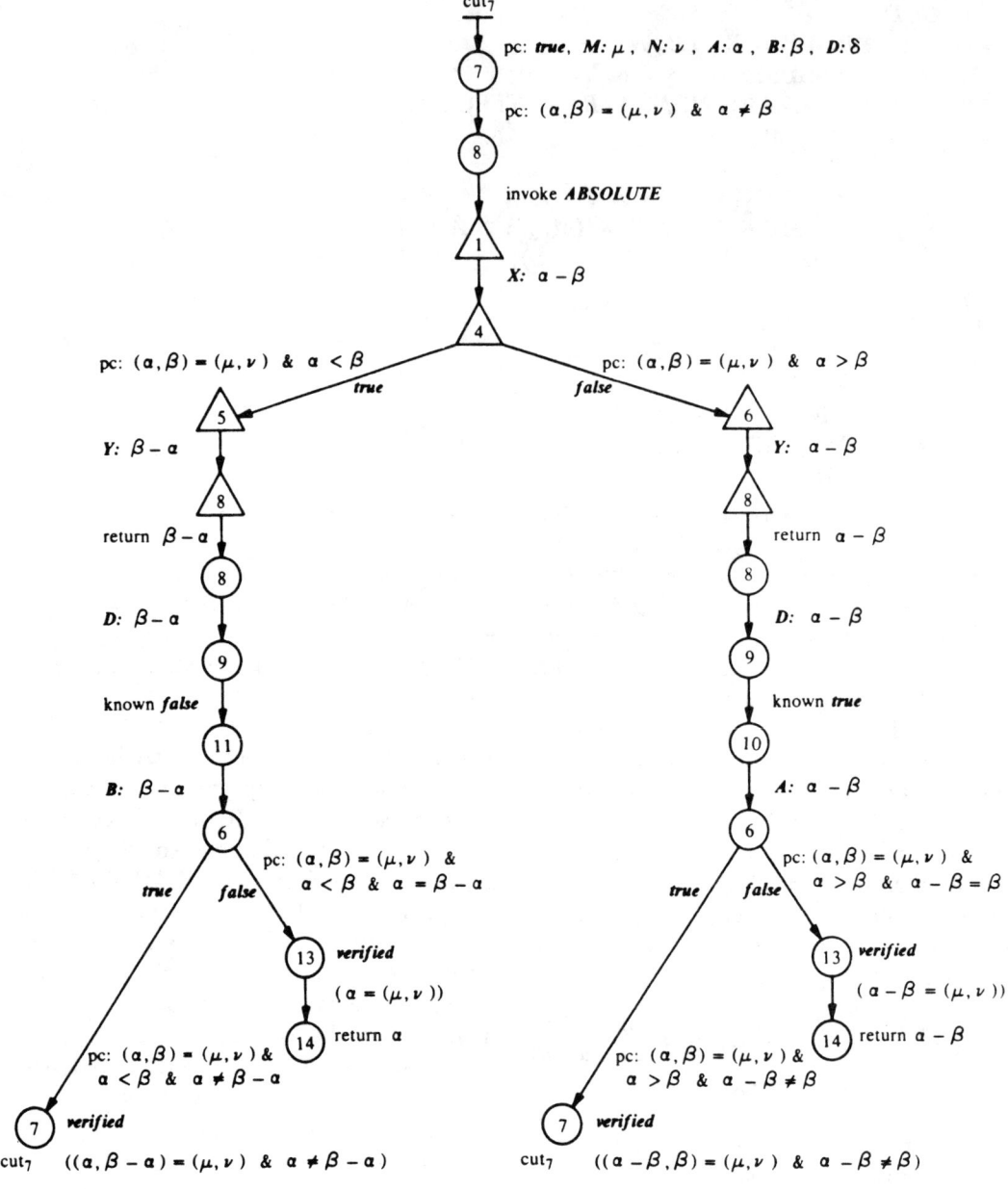

FIGURE 10. Cut tree for cut_7 of $GCD2$.

if the initial input assertion of Q is satisfied by the values of the variables at its invocation, the output assertion will be satisfied by the values at the **RETURN**. Therefore, one must now show that the values input to this invocation satisfy Q's original **ASSUME** statement. The first step in creating the abbreviated procedure (i.e., changing **ASSUME** to **PROVE**) provides the simple key to accomplishing this check. The symbolic execution into the abbreviated procedure up to and including the **PROVE** statement accomplishes the check in each case. A **PROVE** statement is defined to print "verified" or "not verified" depending upon whether or not its associated predi-

```
1   ABSOLUTE:
    PROCEDURE (X);
2       PROVE (true);
3       DECLARE X, Y INTEGER;
4       X ← NEWSYMBOL;
5       Y ← NEWSYMBOL;
6       ASSUME ((Y = X' | Y = −X') & Y ≥ 0 & X = X');
7       RETURN (Y);
8   END;
```

FIGURE 11. Abbreviated procedure *ABSOLUTE*.

cate is *true*. It should be noted that the pc (used by the **PROVE** statement) is considered as part of the underlying (symbolic) machine state, describing conditions over the symbolic constants. It does not relate to program variables and therefore is unaffected by the procedure invocation and has a global scope across the complete program execution.

If the execution of any **PROVE** statement results in "not verified," the proof of correctness fails. This includes the execution of the **PROVE** statement just discussed. If it does not hold, the output assertion of the procedure cannot be guaranteed to hold and its use would be invalid.

Next the symbolic execution of the abbreviated procedure Q would reset all variables accessible to Q to new unique symbols. These represent the new values the procedure Q would compute in an actual execution. In the case that Q is a function, one of these new symbols, being the value of the **RETURN** statement, would also subsequently be returned as the function's value. The abbreviated procedure next contains an **ASSUME** statement (the output condition of the original Q). The symbolic execution of this statement proceeds according to the previous definition. While the execution follows the same exact rules, one may need to generalize his understanding of the **ASSUME** statement and the pc. Changes to the pc previously were a refinement (constriction) of the case being considered. The execution of this **ASSUME** statement causes, rather, an elaboration. The abbreviated symbolic execution had just previously set all the variables, potentially receiving new values within the procedure, to new symbolic values. The execution of the **ASSUME** statement, in updating the pc, now constrains those new symbols to the case where they satisfy the output assertions of the subprocedure. That is, they now represent the subprocedure changes as characterized by its output assertions.

Control now returns to the calling procedure P. The new symbols invented within Q will become values for variables of P returned from Q and, in the case of function procedures, as *the* return value. The symbolic execution of P continues as before. Whenever "knowledge" of the properties of the new symbols is required as in the execution of subsequent **PROVE** statements, it is available in the pc.

Note that the primed variables occurring in the procedure's output assertions have as their values the *original* input values to the procedure. They are not affected by the assignments of new symbols. In general, after the symbolic execution of the abbreviated procedure, the pc contains expressions relating the procedure inputs (the symbolic expression values of the primed variables) to the procedure outputs (the newly invented symbols). Note also that the symbolic execution of the *abbreviated* procedure involves no loops and no cuts and can be considered as one basic step in the symbolic execution of the calling procedure. The symbolic execution of abbreviated procedures involves the new notions of:

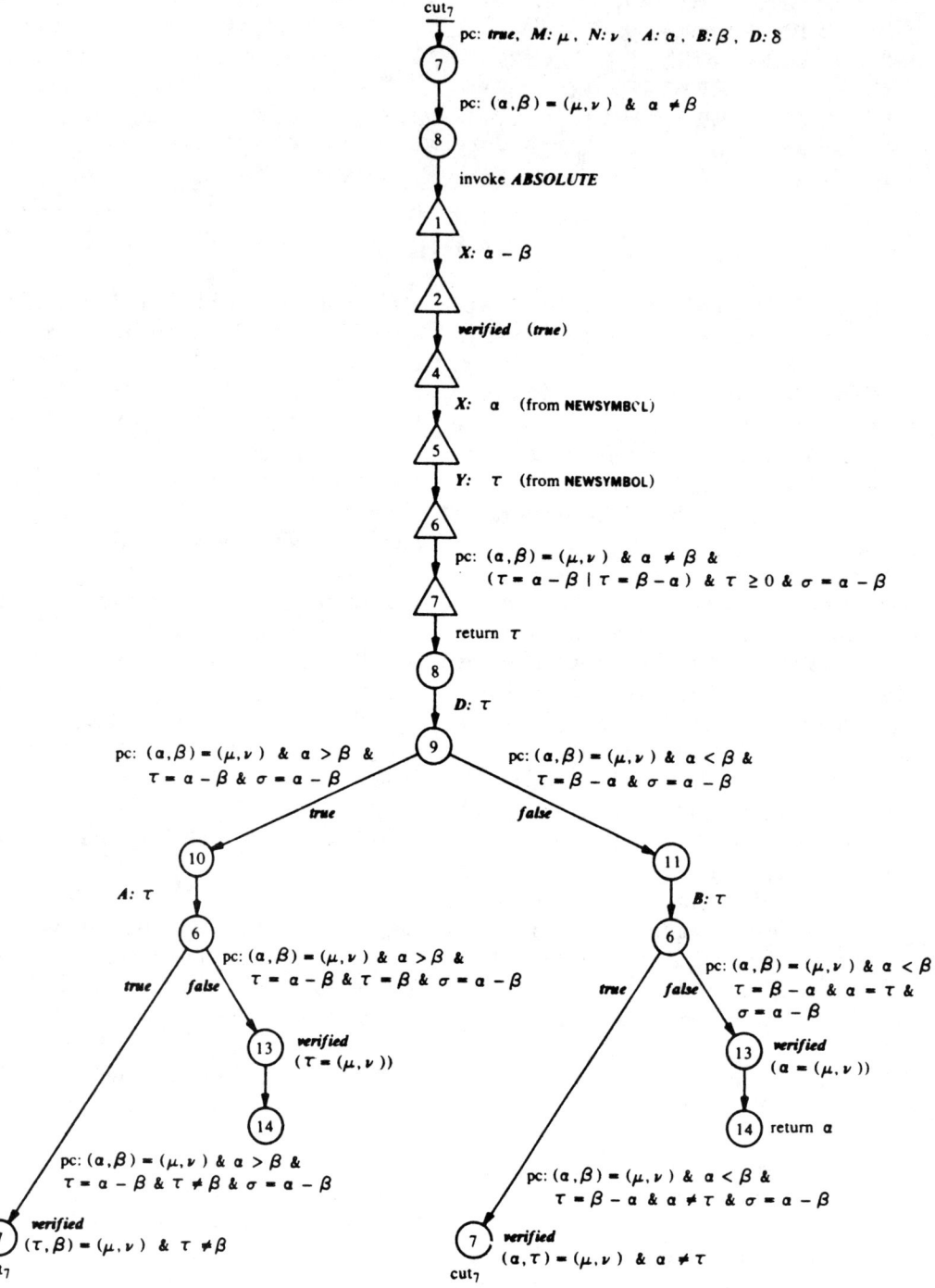

FIGURE 12. Cut tree for cut_7 of *GCD2* (using abbreviated *ABSOLUTE*).

1) The function **NEWSYMBOL** for generating unique new symbols;

2) The remark that the correctness of the program is contingent on *all* executions of the **PROVE** statement printing "verified," including the ones which check the procedure inputs. Those do not occur at a cut as do the others and could be overlooked.

Of course, one does not have to explicitly create an abbreviated procedure but can simply cause the equivalent effects to occur at the procedure invocation.

The definitions given here imply that the output assertions for the subprocedures must include statements of the form $X = X'$ for all variables X which the procedure could alter but, in fact, does not. Of course, such statements would be confirmed during the proof of the procedure itself and are therefore dependable. Thus, for procedures, the output assertions must not only include statements about what the procedure does but also statements about what it does not do (e.g., does not change X). If the programming language itself provides for, and guarantees, the "read-only" nature of some arguments, the statements, $X = X'$ are unnecessary for those parameter variables. In that case, one must also change the definition of abbreviated procedures at step 3 to avoid overwriting these variables with new symbols.

The presence of read-only arguments does eliminate one minor notational nuisance of the method as we describe it. The values of unchanged variables get renamed at each procedure invocation. For example, suppose X is an argument to a procedure and has the value α. Suppose that the subprocedure denotes that parameter by Y and includes $Y = Y'$ in its output assertion. Suppose further that the new symbol invented for Y during the abbreviated execution is β. Then the effect for the calling procedure over the subprocedure's execution is that X will change from α to β, but the pc will include $\alpha = \beta$. With known read-only variables built into the language, X would simply maintain the value α throughout and β would not even be generated.

One feature of the simple language defined and used here causes some problems in proofs involving subprocedures. Consider the procedure shown in Figure 13 which exchanges the values of its two arguments without use of a temporary variable. Its proof of correctness by the method described is quite straightforward. However, if it is called using the same argument for both formal parameters as in:

CALL *EXCHANGE*(Z, Z);

it has the same effect as:

$$Z \leftarrow Z - Z;$$
$$Z \leftarrow Z + Z;$$
$$Z \leftarrow Z - Z;$$

which results in setting Z to zero. (Remember that we have assumed a "call-by-reference" definition like that found in PL/I and FORTRAN.) In this case the output assertion is certainly not satisfied. But what about the alleged proof? At the beginning of each cut execution used in the proof, each

```
1  EXCHANGE:
     PROCEDURE (X, Y);
2    DECLARE X, Y INTEGER;
3    ASSUME (true);
4    X ← X - Y;
5    Y ← X + Y;
6    X ← Y - X;
7    PROVE (X = Y') & (Y = X'));
8    RETURN;
9  END:
```

FIGURE 13. Procedure *EXCHANGE*.

procedure variable is initialized to a unique symbolic value *independently and assuming they are distinct variables*. This results in a proof of correctness which only holds for procedure invocations involving distinct arguments.

There are two solutions to this problem. One is to disallow procedure invocations which use the same argument variable in more than one parameter position (at least those which are not read-only within the subprocedure). The other is to extend the proof method to handle such cases correctly. If one considers the form of the **CALL** while performing the proof of correctness, the method is easily extended. For the procedure *EXCHANGE* there are only two cases, represented by:

1) **CALL** *EXCHANGE*(Z, W);
2) **CALL** *EXCHANGE*(Z, Z);

For each case the symbolic executions need be faithful to the rules used in the regular executions. That is, case 2 would treat X and Y as the same variable. The proof of that case would then fail since the final value of Z would be zero. One would then know that this procedure has not been proved correct for calls of the second form, which must be disallowed. The more typical exchange program involving a temporary variable (e.g., with body $T \leftarrow X; X \leftarrow Y; Y \leftarrow T$) can be proved correct with respect to the given input/output assertions for both forms of calls.

For procedures with many parameters, the number of combinations in which two or more arguments may be coincident is quite large. So one might prove the program is correct for the favored case of no coincidence, and then prove only the forms of coincidence which are needed for the higher-level program proofs.

6. PROBLEMS

Much of the work in performing a proof of correctness of a program is tedious and error prone. Considerable research has been done in attempting to get the computer itself to construct or at least to assist in the construction of program proofs [2, 5, 8, 11, 14, 17, 20, 21]. In fact, the method of proof presented here was developed first by Deutsch [5] for his automated program verifier. In this section, a brief summary of the difficulties in constructing program proofs is given. Some of the problems become exaggerated when one tries to automate the process.

Some effort has gone into developing programming languages in which proofs of correctness are easier [9, 10]. In pursuing this goal one must realize the inherent limitations. A programming language is a medium in which to describe algorithms, perhaps algorithms of a certain type, or which operate on certain data. That medium can encourage obscure descriptions of algorithms and make formal analysis difficult or impossible by providing clumsy, overly general, and ill-defined features. However, the reason an algorithm performs a desired computation correctly is independent of the notation in which it is described. For example, the fact that the simplex algorithm can be used to optimize linear functions subject to a set of linear constraints is based on significant mathematical theory. Without that theory, or without rediscovering it, the most elegant simplex algorithm written in the perfect programming language cannot be proved correct.

The proof method based on symbolic execution is appealing because it is an extension of the notion of normal program execution. One can often devise the "proper" proof technique for a class of language constructs by considering their behavior under regular execution. The implementation of a program verifier on a computer, based on symbolic execution, closely follows that of an interpreter for the language.

Much recent work [3, 19, 23] has been concerned with programs that manipulate complex data structures (e.g., list structures). The difficulty with such programs appears to be the lack of an established notation, manipulative techniques, and known results concerning data structures. The simple mathematical model of variable and value is complicated by the introduction of, what corresponds to in one form or another, computer storage cells. Variables refer to storage which contains values, and the associations between these (variables, storage, values) are changed by the program execution.

Closely related to the data structure problem is the problem of developing a general, flexible, easy-to-read specification language. A program is proved correct with respect to its input/output assertions. The examples in this presentation were chosen for the ease with which their input/output assertions could be expressed.

A major area of concern in implementing program verifiers on a computer is providing the formula manipulation and theorem proving power required. The symbolic execution of programs requires an efficient and comprehensive formula manipulation system. Each execution of a **PROVE** statement requires establishing the truth of a formula of arbitrary complexity. Program proving has spurred work on efficient, domain-dependent computer theorem provers.

The last major problem area discussed is that of composing inductive assertions. The input/output assertions which a programmer must supply are often difficult to determine. However, the need for such input/output assertions does not seem artificial; a programmer must somehow express what the program was intended to do. The necessary inclusion of inductive assertions which cut the loops in the program does seem artificial. These are required not so much to specify the program properties but as an inductive assistance to the program proving method. One can pose the generation of the inductive assertions as a theorem proving problem by formulating one large theorem for the complete program of the form: show that there exist inductive assertions $P_1, P_2, \ldots, P_n$ such that all of the expressions resulting from **PROVE** statements are *true*. In general, this is a very difficult theorem to prove. For simple programs, inductive assertions can be generated automatically and some exploration into their automatic generation and/or enhancement for larger programs using heuristic methods is reported in [12, 22].

SUMMARY

This paper attempts to give a basic introduction to the fascinating world of proving that computer programs meet their specifications. One style of producing program specifications, in the form of input/output assertions, was introduced to allow a definition of a "correct program." Then the symbolic execution of programs was explained as one way of establishing the consistency between the program's code and its input/output assertions.

Note that, among all the program specification methods and program proof methods which have been proposed and developed, we have presented a very narrow glimpse of one. It is the most intuitive approach of which we know and, therefore, one of the most likely candidates for productive future development and use.

ACKNOWLEDGMENTS

Many of the ideas presented here were the outgrowth of our work with Jerry Archibald, Steve Chase, Ahmed Chibib, Claus Correll, and John Darringer on the EFFIGY system [15].

REFERENCES

[1] BOYER, R. S.; ELSPAS, B.; AND LEVITT, K. N. "SELECT—A formal system for testing and debugging programs by symbolic execution," *Internatl. Conf. on Reliable Software*, 1975, ACM, New York, 1975, pp. 234–245.

[2] BOYER, R. S.; AND MOORE, J. S. "Proving theorems about Lisp functions," *J. ACM* **22**, 1, (Jan. 1975), 48–59.

[3] BURSTALL, R. M. "Some techniques for proving correctness of programs which alter data structures," *Machine intelligence 7*, D. Michie (Ed.), American Elsevier, New York, 1972.

[4] CLARKE, LORI, *A system to generate test data and symbolically execute programs*, Report #CU-CS-060-75, Univ. of Colorado, 1975.
[5] DEUTSCH, L. P. "An interactive program verifier," PhD Dissertation, Dept. Computer Science, Univ. of Calif., Berkeley, 1973, Xerox PARC Report CSL-73-1, Palo Alto, Calif.
[6] ELSPAS, B. et al., "An assessment of techniques for proving program correctness," *Computing Surveys* **4**, 2 (June 1972), 97–147.
[7] FLOYD, R. W. "Assigning meanings to programs," in *Proc. Symposium Applied Math.*, Vol. 19, American Mathematical Society, Providence, R.I., 1967, pp. 19–32.
[8] GOOD, D. I.; LONDON, R. L.; AND BLEDSOE, W. W. "An interactive program verification system," *IEEE Trans. on Software Engineering* **1**, 1, (April 1975), 59–67.
[9] GOOD, D. I.; AND RAGLAND, L. C. "Nucleus—a language of provable programs," in *Program test methods*, W. Hetzel (Ed.), Prentice-Hall Inc., Englewood Cliffs, N.J., 1973, pp. 93–117.
[10] HOARE, C. A. R.; AND WIRTH, N. "An axiomatic definition of the programming language PASCAL," *Acta Informatica* **2**, (1973), 335–355.
[11] IGARASHI, S.; LONDON, R. L.; AND LUCKHAM, D. C. "Automatic program verification I: a logical basis and its implementation," *Acta Informatica* **4**, (1975), 145–182. Also in USC Information Sciences Institute Report ISI/RR-73-11, May 1973.
[12] KATZ, S. M.; AND MANNA, Z. "A heuristic approach to program verification," in *Proc. Third Internatl. Joint Conf. on Artificial Intelligence*, SRI Publications Dept. Stanford Calif., 1973, pp. 500–512.
[13] KING, J. C. "Proving programs to be correct," *IEEE Trans on Computers* **C-20**, 11, (Nov. 1971), 1331–1336.
[14] KING, J. C. "A program verifier," PhD Dissertation, Carnegie-Mellon Univ., Pittsburgh, Pa., 1969.
[15] KING, J. C. "A new approach to program testing," in *Internatl. Conf. on Reliable Software*, 1975, ACM, New York, 1975, pp. 228–233. Also appears in *Programming methodology, lecture notes in computer science*, **23**, Springer-Verlag Inc., New York, 1974, pp. 278–290.
[16] KING, J. C. "Symbolic execution and program testing," *Comm. ACM* **19**, 7, (July 1976), 385–394.
[17] LONDON, R. L. "The current state of proving programs correct," in *Proc. of ACM Annual Conf.*, 1972, ACM, New York, 1972, pp. 39–46.
[18] MANNA, Z. *Mathematical theory of computation*, McGraw-Hill Book Co., New York, 1974.
[19] OPPEN, D. C.; AND COOK, S. A. "Proving assertions about programs that manipulate data structures," in *Seventh Annual ACM Symposium on Theory of Computation*, 1975, ACM, New York, 1975, pp. 107–116.
[20] SUZUKI, N. "Automatic program verification II: verifying programs by algebraic and logical reduction," in *Internatl. Conf. on Reliable Software*, 1975, ACM, New York, 1975, pp. 473–481.
[21] TOPOR, R. W. "Interactive program verification using virtual programs," PhD Dissertation, Univ. of Edinburgh, Edinburgh, Scotland, 1975.
[22] WEGBREIT, B. "The synthesis of loop predicates," *Comm. ACM* **17**, 2, (Feb. 1974), 102–112.
[23] WEGBREIT, B.; AND SPITZEN, J. M. "Proving properties of complex data structures," *J. ACM* **23**, 2 (April 1976), 389–396.

Section 3: Static Analysis—Tools and Techniques

Paper Summaries

W. E. Howden, "A Survey of Static Analysis Methods." (Original paper.)

A method for classifying static analysis techniques is introduced in which each technique is classified as based on analysis of requirements, of design, or of code. Requirements- and design-based static analysis techniques involve analysis of the requirements and design documents. Design review is a design-based analysis technique. Code-based static analysis techniques require an analysis of the code but do not require its execution. The traditional static analyzers that analyze code for program anomalies such as uninitialized variables are code-based static analyzers. Each of these three different kinds of static analysis—requirements-, design-, and code-based—is surveyed.

M. S. Fujii, "Independent Verification of Highly Reliable Programs," *Proceedings, COMPSAC 77* (pp. 38-44).

The integration of development and validation, which is emphasized in this book, is closely related to the approach to validation described in this short reprint. The reprint also examines the role of the independent validation team in the development of a software system. The sections on informal analysis of requirements and design in Howden's survey paper, "A Survey of Static Analysis Methods," were derived from this reprint.

M. E. Fagan, "Design and Code Inspections to Reduce Errors in Program Development," *IBM Systems Journal,* Vol. 15, No. 3, 1976 (pp. 182-211).

One of the most commonly used practical methods for validation is simply that of re-reading design documents and source code. A number of procedures have been formalized which can be used to guide the software engineer during the reading process. This reprint describes a method involving error checklists. It is similar to, and may be compared with, structured walkthroughs.

L. J. Osterweil and L. D. Fosdick, "DAVE—A Validation Error Detection and Documentation System for Fortran Programs," *Software Practice and Experience,* October-December 1976 (pp. 473-486).

The DAVE system is a static analyzer developed at the University of Colorado. It performs an exhaustive search for data flow anomalies at a processing rate which is linearly proportional to the product of the number of edges in the control-flow graph and the total number of program variables. The algorithm used is classified as a "depth first search" because it attempts to operate at the lowest parts of the required search tree as early as possible.

DAVE is an exceptional static analyzer for its thoroughness. In addition to the "normal" data flow dependence associated with program paths, DAVE also is sensitive to implied equivalences through program COMMON declarations—a feature unique to DAVE.

R. N. Taylor and L. J. Osterweil, "Anomaly Detection in Concurrent Software by Static Data Flow Analysis," *IEEE Transactions on Software Engineering,* May 1980 (pp. 265-278)

This paper is a followup to the prior paper and extends some of the ideas expressed there to the analysis of concurrent communications properties of software systems.

The same principle as used in DAVE applies: static analysis of programs at the source code level makes it possible to detect certain kinds of defects. In the present case, the defects sought are those which cause problems with program intercommunication and control primitives. These defects are: (1) waiting for an unscheduled process, (2) waiting for a process guaranteed to have already terminated, and (3) scheduling a process in parallel with itself.

Other defects that can be detected are: (1) referencing a variable while defining it in a parallel (i.e., currently executing) process, (2) referencing a variable with indeterminate value, and (3) failing to use a variable at all.

Detailed algorithms for all of these defects are presented in the paper. The paper concludes with some comments on "unsolved" problems that may still need attention.

C. V. Ramamoorthy and S. F. Ho, "Testing Large Software with Automated Software Evaluation Systems,"

IEEE Transactions on Software Engineering, March 1975 (pp. 46-58).

This paper describes a static analysis tool, the FACES system—Fortran Automated Code Evaluation System. In addition, the paper presents a good taxonomy of automated tools of all kinds.

A primary motivation for the use of automated tools is to reduce the error content of a program or to increase the error discovery rate during the early stages of acceptance testing. Either will decrease the cost of a software system. Automated tools can be classified according to the operational mode, by the phase in the life-cycle where they are applied, or according to the function of the tool. Static analysis tools can be applied during acceptance testing (operationally). They can also be used immediately after or during the program development stage, or as an auxiliary tool during program testing.

The FACES system performs a number of structural and syntactic checks including the following:

- Error-prone construct identification, e.g., when an actual parameter is a constant and the corresponding formal parameter is modified.
- Interface checks, focusing on consistency of use in COMMON statements.
- Program structure checks, used to guarantee reachability properties.
- Coding standard checks, e.g., enforcement of ANSI Standards.
- Uninitialized variable checks.

The FACES system is currently in use in a number of installations.

W. E. Howden, "Symbolic Testing and the DISSECT Symbolic Evaluation System," *IEEE Transactions on Software Engineering,* July 1977 (pp. 266-278).

Several symbolic evaluation systems have been constructed which can be used to symbolically test programs. Some of the systems can also be used to generate test data from a system of symbolic predicates. The distinguishing feature of the DISSECT system is the DISSECT command language, which can be used to write procedures that, when executed by the DISSECT command language interpreter, will cause a set of symbolic analyses of a program to be carried out.

A SURVEY OF STATIC ANALYSIS METHODS

William E. Howden

University of Victoria

Victoria, Canada

Abstract - The term "static analysis" has traditionally been used to refer to program analysis methods that assist the user in verifying his program, but which do not require its execution. Static analysis includes techniques which produce general information about a program, such as cross-reference tables, as well as techniques which search for particular kinds of errors, such as uninitalized variables. This survey describes both traditional static analysis methods as well as other validation methods that do not require program execution. It includes techniques that involve the analysis of system documents other than the program code, such as requirements and design analysis. It also includes code analysis techniques such as symbolic evaluation.

A SURVEY OF STATIC ANALYSIS METHODS

1. INTRODUCTION TO STATIC ANALYSIS

Static analysis of a software system involves the use of validation methods that do not require the actual execution of the system. Static analysis often involves some form of simulated execution and may use techniques similar to those used in dynamic analysis. In general, the types of simulated executions that are involved in the analysis of requirements and design are more limited than those involved in the static analysis of source code.

Static analysis involves the examination of the documents produced by the requirements, design and programming phases of the software development process. The types of analysis that are carried out on requirements and design documents are usually less formal and not as easily automated as the analyses which are carried out on the code. The development of more formal, and more highly automated methods for the analysis of requirements and design depends on the successful development of formal languages for the specifications of requirements and design. The following sections contain a brief description of static analysis techniques for requirements and design followed by a more detailed discussion of static analysis of source code.

2. STATIC ANALYSIS OF REQUIREMENTS DOCUMENTS

2.1 <u>Requirements</u>. The requirements for a system are defined in terms of the <u>needs</u> of the customer. Performance requirements describe the efficiency with which a system must operate. Functional requirements describe the functions which it must implement. Functional requirements may be very general. For example, they may state that the system is to maintain a salary and work record data base for each employee and allow certain updating and report generation facilities. Alternatively, they may be very detailed. The requirements for a program in a mathematical subroutine library may involve the specification of a particular algorithm or mathematical formula. The borderline between requirements and design is often not well-defined.

2.2 <u>Informal requirements analysis</u>. The traditional method of requirements analysis involves the use of checklists. The checklists describe general properties of a set of requirements. Figure 1 contains a list of some of the general properties that requirements should have.

<u>Consistency</u>. Each requirement should be consistent with other requirements.

<u>Necessity</u>. Each requirement should be necessary in order to achieve the goals for the system.

<u>Sufficiency</u>. The requirements documents should be examined for missing or incomplete requirements.

<u>Feasibility</u>. Requirements should be analyzed to see that they are feasible using existing hardware and technology.

<u>Testability</u>. It should be possible to construct tests which will determine if a requirement has been satisfied.

Figure 1. Requirements Checklist.

In reference [1] Marilyn Fuji tests the following methods for checking requirements to see that they have properties such as those in Figure 1: comparison with existing systems or standard references, documentation analysis, mathematical analysis of timing requirements, simulation models and analytic models. Figure 2 tests several of the types of errors which are found during informal requirements analysis.

2.3 <u>Formal requirements analysis</u>. Several research projects have investigated the use of requirements documents that involve the use of a formal, machine readable requirements language. One of the most highly developed formal requirements systems is the PSL/PSA system developed by Professor D. Teichrow at the University of Michigan [2].

The PSL/PSA system consists of a language PSL (problem statement language) and an analyzer PSA (problem statement analyzer). The PSL language

Error type	Detection Method	Description of Error
Sufficiency	Comparison with existing system	Incomplete specification of performance requirements for a raw data preprocessor.
Feasibility	Timing analysis	Restart capability cannot be met with existing hardware.
Sufficiency	Documentation analysis	Incomplete specifications of range and data type for input data.

Figure 2. Requirements Errors.

allows the user to create a model of the system under construction. PSL models include objects, relationships between objects and object properties. The PSA system checks PSL statements for consistency during the building of the PSL data base. PSA can be used to generate reports that can be used by the programmer to check his requirements model for completeness. Two of the types objects which can be included in a PSA model, for example, are sets and processes. Sets are collections of information. In order for a PSL model to be complete, every set must be "used" or "updated" by at least one process. "Uses" and "updates" are PSL relations.

3. STATIC ANALYSIS OF DESIGN DOCUMENTS

3.1 <u>Design artifacts</u>. Different kinds of elements can occur in a design. They include mathematical equations, algorithms, module descriptions, module interfaces, data flow diagrams, logic flow diagrams, abstract data structures and abstract operators.

3.2 <u>Informal design analysis</u>. The elements of a software system design can be analyzed using informal checklists similar to those used for requirements analysis. Figure 3 describes some of the important properties that a design should have.

Different methods can be used to analyze each of the properties in Figure 3. Cross-referencing of design elements and requirements can be used to check both the necessity and sufficiency of the design elements. Comparison of common parts of different design elements can be used to analyze the consistency of interfaces. The control logic in a design can be checked by analyzing each of the different logical paths through the top levels of a top down design. Different logical paths should correspond to different classes of data.

<u>Consistency</u>: Module interfaces should be consistent. Consistency of data base formats with input data space formats should be checked.

<u>Necessity</u>: It should be possible to trace each design element back to a requirement.

<u>Sufficiency</u>: Each requirement should be implemented by one or more design elements.

<u>Correctness</u>: The correctness of mathematical equations and computational algorithms should be checked. The correctness of control logic in the design should be analyzed.

Figure 3. Design Checklist.

Modelling and simulation can be used to determine whether a design will meet performance requirements.

Computational algorithms can be verified by comparing them with independently derived algorithms, through modelling and simulation and through functional analysis. Functional analysis involves an examination of the actions taken for different classes of input data and is similar to functional testing. Mathematical equations can be verified by comparing them with independently derived equations and with standard references. Units analysis is also useful in verifying the correctness of equations.

One of the most commonly used informal methods of design validation involves the use of structured walkthroughs. The structured walkthrough method is simple, but has proved to be very effective. There are two basic ideas in structured walkthrough. The first is that of simulated execution. Typical classes of input are selected and then the actions of the system for that class of data are traced through the design, step by step. The second basic idea is that the programmer responsible for the design should carry out the structured walkthrough in front of other members of the software development group. Refinements on the technique have been developed to suit different types of system and organizational structures.

Design inspections are similar to but differ from structured walkthroughs in several respects [3]. The most significant is that the specific goal of a design inspection is to find errors. Design inspections involve the use of error frequency statistics and "how to find errors" checklists. Structured walkthroughs do not involve checklists and their goals are more general, including the education of the rest of the design team and the promotion of the discussion of design alternatives.

Figure 4 contains some examples of the types of errors that have been discovered using informal design analysis techniques.

3.3 **Formal design analysis**. The most widely studied formal design analysis tool is the inductive assertion method for proving the correctness of algorithms. The technique can also be used to analyze actual code, but due to a number of cost-effectiveness limitations, the technique has been applied primarily to descriptions of individual algorithms whose function can be easily identified, rather than to programs in general.

Recent work on the role of modules in the design process has resulted in the construction of tools which can be used to formally verify the consistency of module interfaces. Users of TRW's Design Analysis Consistency Checker are required to formally state properties of the input and output variables for system modules in the form of input and output assertions [4]. The assertions describe the names, type, units, coordinate systems and dimensions of individual variables or data structures. The DACC then checks the module connections for consistency of related input and output assertions. It also contains facilities for carrying out certain kinds of completeness checks.

Error type	Detection Method	Description of Error
Sufficiency	Cross-referencing of requirements and design	Missing abstract operator (module) for checking validity of operator console commands.
Correctness of Algorithms	Independent derivation and comparison of simulated results	Incorrect initalization of variables in a real-time estimation algorithm resulting in slow responses.
Correctness of control logic	Structured walkthrough	When current data contains errors it is not saved. Results in the misleading display of old data.

Figure 4. Design Errors.

4. STATIC ANALYSIS OF PROGRAMS

4.1 Introduction to static analysis of programs.

Most of the research that has been carried out on static analysis has been on static analysis of source code. Three kinds of source code static analysis methods can be identified. The first involves analyses which produce general computational information about a program and which are not designed to search for any particular kind of error in a program. This first class of analyses includes traditional programming tools such as symbol cross-referencers. The second kind of analysis includes techniques which are designed to detect specific classes of errors or anomalous constructs in a program. It includes techniques for analyzing the consistency of actual and formal parameters and techniques for detecting the use of uninitialized variables. This second class of techniques will be called static error analysis techniques. The third kind of static analysis is symbolic evaluation. The following discussion is limited to the second and third kinds of static analysis.

4.2 Static error analysis.

Static error analysis involves the analysis of a program to determine if certain kinds of errors or "dangerous" constructs are present in the program. In some cases it is possible to build a tool which will automatically carry out the analysis required to find a particular kind of error. In other cases the analysis must be carried out manually.

(a) Type and units analysis. Programming languages can be extended to include type specifications that allow a syntactic preprocessor to analyze a program for type usage errors. Two commonly used types which can be added to a language are subscript and counter. If a variable is declared to be of type subscript it can only be used as an array reference subscript. Similarly, counter variables can only be used as counting variables in loops with loop headers of the form "FOR I=1 BY 1 TO N". In this case I is the counter. The PASCAL programming language includes facilities for typing variables and the PASCAL compiler will check for type inconsistencies.

Units analysis is closely related to type specification. Programming languages can be extended to include two constructs that allow the automatic detection of units inconsistencies. The first is the <u>unitname</u> construct which allows the user to declare a type of unit. The second is the <u>units</u> construct which allows a user to declare that the value of a variable is always measured in a particular unit. Units analysis requires the use of a preprocessor which is capable of processing algebraic expressions and determining, through the use of the usual composition and cancellation rules, the units that the value of the expression is measured in. Reference [5] contains an example of a program in which an error involves the use of an incorrect variable. The program contains three array variables OLDSCORES, NEWSCORES and GRADE. All three arrays are used to store exam scores. It also contains an array ID which is used to store student identification numbers. The program contains the incorrect assignment;

OLDSCORES (I,EXAM) = ID(L)

instead of the correct assignment

OLDSCORES (I,EXAM)=GRADE(L).

This error could have been identified by a units analysis tool if the variables were classified using the following units analysis declarations.

<u>unitname</u>   GRADEUNIT, IDUNIT;

<u>units</u>   GRADEUNIT: GRADE( ), OLDSCORE( ), NEWSCORES ( ); IDUNIT ( ): ID( )

More complex examples involving algebraic expressions can be constructed for scientific calculation programs.

(b) Reference analysis. The most extensively studied kind of static error analysis involves techniques for detecting <u>reference</u> <u>anomalies</u>. A reference anomaly occurs when a variable is referenced along a program path before it is assigned a value along that path, or if a variable is assigned a value along a path but is not later referenced along the path. It is important to note that a reference anomaly is not necessarily an error. The output variables in a routine, for example, will be assigned values which are not later referenced in the routine. In addition, a reference anomaly may occur along a program path which is infeasible. (i.e., a path which is never traversed, one for which there exists no input data that will cause its execution).

The detection of reference anomalies requires the examination of each path through a program. The paths through a program can be examined by completing a modified depth-first traversal of the program's flow graph. A relatively simple reference anomaly detection tool can be built using modified depth-first traversal. The method requires the use of two lists, a <u>deflist</u> and an <u>unreflist</u>. Each list contains a list of variable names. The deflist contains the list of variables which have been "recently defined".

It contains the names of variables that have been assigned values since the last undefinition of the variable. A variable becomes undefined when its value is no longer valid. In FORTRAN programs, for example, the value of a DO-loop index becomes undefined when control leaves the loop. The unreflist contains the list of variables which have been assigned values which have not yet been referenced.

The reference anomaly detection algorithm assumes that the program's flowgraph is available and that it is possible to temporarily store copies of deflists and unreflists at the nodes of the graph during the depth-first traversal. When a node in the graph is reached which has outdegree > 1, depth-first traversal requires that the part of the graph which is reached by traversing the "leftmost" branch be explored before the traversal of the other branches. Before traversing the leftmost branch, the detection method stores the current contents of the deflist and unreflist at the flow graph node. When the part of the graph which is reached by traversing the leftmost branch has been explored, the depth-first traversal mechanism will return to the node, restore deflist and unreflist to the old copies of the lists stored there, and then traverse the second leftmost branch. This process continues until all branches from the node have been explored.

The detection method begins by initializing the deflist and unreflist to the empty list. The depth first traversal begins with the entrance node to the graph. Two classes of computations involving the deflist and unreflist are carried out, one resulting in the discovery of referenced but undefined values and the other in the discovery of defined but not referenced values.

Each time a node in the flowgraph is reached which corresponds to a statement in which a variable is referenced, a search is made of the deflist. If the variable does not appear in the deflist then the detection algorithm has discovered a reference anomaly in which a variable is referenced along a program path before it is defined on that path. Each time a node is reached which corresponds to a statement in which the value of a variable becomes undefined, then that variable is removed from the deflist. If a node is reached which corresponds to a statement in which a variable is assigned a value then that variable name is added to the deflist, if it is not already part of the list.

The unreflist is used to detect the second kind of reference anomaly, that in which a variable is assigned a value which is not later referenced. Each time a node is reached which corresponds to a statement in which a variable is referenced, the variable is removed from the unreflist, if it occurs in the list. There are three situations in which the second kind of reference anomaly can occur. The first is when a node is reached which corresponds to a statement in which a variable is assigned a value. If the variable is already in the unreflist then an anomaly has been discovered. If not, the variable is entered in the unreflist and processing continues. The second situation occurs when a node is reached which corresponds to a variable undefinition for some variable in the unreflist. After reporting the error, the error detection algorithm removes the variable from the unreflist and processing continues. The third situation occurs when a node corresponding to an exit or return statement is encountered. If the unreflist is not empty then a reference anomaly of the second type has been discovered.

Figure 5 contains a PL-360 sort routine from a paper by Wirth that has a missing assignment statement. The variable R3 should be reinitialized at the beginning of each iteration of the outermost loop in the routine. Figure 6 contains a picture of the program's flowgraph, complete with deflists and unreflists, at the point at which the reference anomaly is discovered. The arrow indicates the node in the graph which has been reached during the depth-first traversal when the anomaly is discovered. The error is discovered when the rightmost branch from statement 4 is traversed.

The reference anomaly algorithm which is sketched out above can be extended to distinguish between reference anomalies in which a variable is referenced in a program before it is assigned a value along <u>any</u> path leading to that reference and reference anomalies in which a variable is referenced before it is assigned a value along <u>some</u> path leading to the reference. A similar distinction can be made for errors in which a variable is assigned a value which is not later referenced. Reference [6] contains the description of a system which is capable of discovering reference anomalies as well as carrying out other types of static error analysis.

(c) Expression analysis. Certain classes of commonly occurring errors are associated with the

```
read a( ), N                          0
for R1=0 by 1 to N begin              1
    R0 ← a(R1)                        2
    for R2=R1+1 by 1 to N begin       3
        if A(R2) > R0 then begin      4
            R0 ← a(R2)                5
            R3 ← R2                   6
end                                   7
    R2 ← a(R1)                        8
    a(R1) ← R0                        9
    a(R3) ← R2                       10
end                                  11
                                     12
```

Figure 5. PL-360 sort routine.

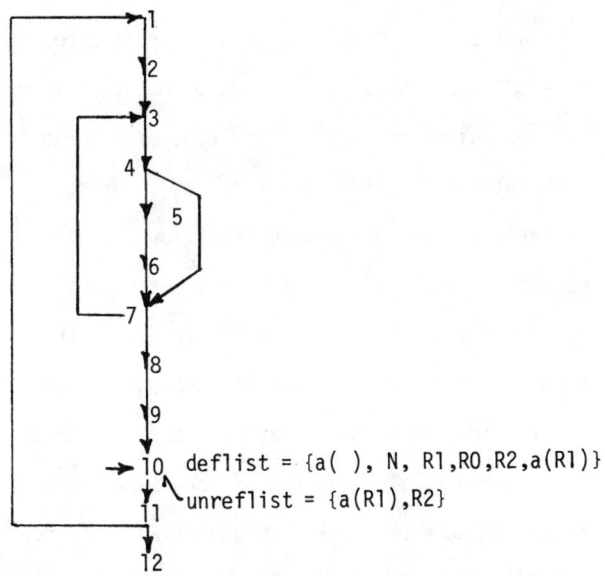

Figure 6. Sort routine flowgraph.

evaluation of expressions in a program and can be avoided if the expressions are subjected to analysis.

Errors in expressions are often due to incorrect or incomplete parenthesis. If a programming standard is adopted in which all expressions must be completely parenthesized, many of these errors can be avoided. Such a standard would, for example, prohibit the use of expressions like:

A*2.0/B*3.0.

A code auditor could be built which would automatically, amongst other things, check for conformance to the <u>complete parenthesis standards</u>.

Another well known error occurs when an array reference involves the calculation of an out of bounds array index. There are certain situations in which it is possible to detect <u>out of bounds array references</u> directly from the source code. If the dimensions of an array are constant and the index in the array reference is constant then the check for out of bounds references is straightforward. If the dimensions are constant and the reference index is a variable, it may still be possible to check for out of bounds or potential out of bounds references. It is common practice, for example, to access the elements of an array inside an indexed loop and to use the loop index as the array reference index. In situations like this out of bounds array references can be checked by analyzing the loop bounds for the indexed loop.

Algebraic expressions which contain divisions must be analyzed to verify that the expression is never evaluated with a zero divisor. This can be done by tracing the expression back to requirements that specify that the values of input variables which would result in zero divisors are not in the program's input space. Alternatively, the expression can be traced back to code which checks for values that would lead to a zero divisor and which prevents the expression from being evaluated in those cases. Symbolic evaluation is useful for tracing an expression back to, and rewriting an expression in terms of input variables.

The analysis of expressions for potential singularities like the square root of a negative number or the cotangent of π should also be carried out and is similar to zero divisor analysis.

The most complex kind of expression analysis deals with the problems of <u>finite representation arithmetic</u>. This is basically a subject for numerical analysis but there are general, problem independent situations which can be easily identified as potentially dangerous. One example is the use of floating point numbers in predicates involving the equality operator. Due to inexact binary representation of decimal fractions, such predicates may unexpectedly evaluate to false when expected to be true.

(d) Interface analysis. Consistency of interfaces is a topic for static error analysis of programs as well as a topic of design analysis. Design analysis of interface consistency is concerned with the consistency of interfaces between modules and between a module and an external data base. Source code analysis is concerned with interface consistency at the subroutine and function level. Formal and actual parameters should be checked for consistency of type, number, dimension and use. A similar analysis of consistency should be carried out when communication between routines is carried out using global variables and blocks of common variables.

4.3 Symbolic evaluation.

(a) Introduction to symbolic evaluation. The basic idea in symbolic evaluation is to allow numeric variables to take on "symbolic values" as well as numeric values. A symbolic value is either an elementary symbolic value or an expression in numbers, arithmetic operators and other symbolic values. An elementary symbolic value is any text string and is used by the programmer to stand for the value of a variable. Elementary symbolic values are often just variable names.

In order to symbolically execute a program, it is necessary to have a program execution system which is capable of symbolic evaluation of expressions. In addition, the system must have certain other special features. The most obvious is some mechanism for path selection. If a program is executed on actual data, predicates in branching statements can be evaluated to TRUE or FALSE and the appropriate branch chosen. If an evaluated predicate contains symbolic as well as actual values, then it may not be possible to determine whether it is TRUE or FALSE. When a programmer symbolically evaluates his program he must decide which paths he wants executed in addition to assigning values to input variables. There are a number of other less obvious problems which the execution system must also have facilities for dealing with.

The symbolic evaluation of a path is carried out by symbolically evaluating the sequence of assignment statements occurring in the path. Assignment statements are symbolically evaluated by symbolically evaluating the expression on the right hand side of the assignment. The resulting symbolic value becomes the new symbolic value of the variable on the left hand side. An arithmetic or logical expression is symbolically evaluated by substituting the symbolic values of the variables in the expression for the variables.

The branch conditions or branch predicates which occur in conditional branching statements can be symbolically evaluated to form symbolic predicates. The symbolic system of predicates for a path can be constructed by symbolically evaluating both assignment statements and branch predicates during the symbolic evaluation of the path. The symbolic system of predicates consists of the sequence of symbolic predicates that are generated by the evaluation of the branch predicates.

Figures 7 and 8 illustrate the two kinds of output that can be generated using symbolic evaluation. Figure 8 contains the final symbolic value of the variable x after the symbolic execution of a path in the program in Figure 7. Figure 8 also contains the symbolic system of predicates for the path.

```
read a,b
x ← a*b+2
if x > 100 then x ← 100-x
x ← x-50
if x < 0 then x ← 0
print x
```

Figure 7. Sample program.

symbolic input: "a", "b"

symbolic output for variable x
   for true/false path: x = 48-a*b

symbolic system of predicates
   for true/false path: a*b+2 > 100
                         48-a*b ≥ 0

Figure 8. Symbolic output for sample program.

Symbolic evaluation can be used to reconstruct the logic and computations used in a program. Figure 9 contains a program from the Common Blunders section of Kernighan and Plauger [7]. The program is supposed to compute SIN(X) = X-X**3/3!+X**5/5!-.... It contains four errors.

The errors are: SUM is not initialized to X, the last value of TERM is not added onto the final value of SIN, the -1**(I/2) in statement 9 should be (-1)**(I/2) and the predicate in statement 8 should be (DABS(TERM).LT.E). Figure 10 contains the symbolic output for SIN for a particular path

```
         DOUBLE PRECISION FUNCTION SIN(X,E)      1
      C  THIS COMPUTES SIN(X) TO ACCURACY E      2
         DOUBLE PRECISION E, TERM, SUM           3
         REAL X                                  4
         TERM = X                                5
         DO 20 I=3,100,2                         6
         TERM = TERM*X**2/(I*(I-1))              7
         IF (TERM.LT.E) GO TO 30                 8
         SUM = SUM + (-1**(I/2))*TERM            9
      20 CONTINUE                                10
      30 SIN = SUM                               11
         RETURN                                  12
         END                                     13
```

Figure 9. SIN program with errors.

through the program. The notation ?SUM indicates that the variable SUM was not initialized.

<u>symbolic input</u>: "X", "E"

<u>symbolic output</u> for variable SIN for path which loops 3 times:

SIN= ?SUM-(X**3/6)-(X**5/120)

<u>symbolic system</u> of predicates for path which loops 3 times

(X**3/6).GE.E

(X**5/120).GE.E

(X**7/5040).LT.E

Figure 10. Symbolic output for SIN program.

The symbolic system of predicates for a path can be used to assist the user in constructing test data. The symbolic system of predicates for a program path describes the subset of the input domain that causes that path to be executed. If the system of predicates for a path is unsolvable (i.e., inconsistent), then the path is <u>infeasible</u> and need not be tested. A path is infeasible if there is no test data that will cause it to be executed. If the system of predicates is solvable, then any solution to the system will be a test that causes the path to be executed. Several symbolic evaluation systems contain routines for solving simple (usually linear) system of predicates [9,10].

Symbolic systems of predicates can also be used to prove the correctness of programs. The <u>input variables</u> to a path or subpath are those variables which receive values through the execution of input statements, or which are referenced in the path before they are assigned values. Suppose that Φ is an assertion on the input variables to a path (or subpath) P and that Ψ describes properties of and relationships between final values of variables in P. Let π be the symbolic system of predicates for P and let $P(\Psi)$ be the expression which is obtained when the symbolic values computed by P are substituted for the variables in Ψ. Then if the assertion Φ and $\pi \rightarrow P(\Psi)$ is true, the path P is correct.

(c) Symbolic evaluation systems. Two approaches have been followed in the design of symbolic evaluation systems: interactive and batch. In the interactive approach the user chooses the path which is to be followed by interactively directing the symbolic evaluation system each time it comes to a conditional branching statement [8,9,10]. In the batch approach the user constructs descriptions of the paths to be tested before initiating the symbolic evaluation system [8,9,11,12,13]. The DISSECT system [11] contains sophisticated user facilities for batch usage of symbolic evaluation techniques. DISSECT can be used to analyze FORTRAN programs. The system includes a well developed language that allows the user to "program" the analyses he wants carried out. DISSECT allows the user to "dissect" his program, to divide it up into individual sets of paths and to examine the composition and computational effects of each path.

Figure 11 contains a typical sequence of DISSECT commands.

```
   25      ASSIGN A = "INITIAL A", (B(I) = 0,I = 1,10)
   50      LOOP 3
  100      SELECT ALL(TRUE,FALSE)
150,200    OUTPUT X,Y
```

Figure 11. DISSECT Commands.

The first command in Figure 11 is an input command. Each time the DISSECT evaluator executes the Fortran source program statement which has sequence number 25 it will also execute this input command. The command causes the assignment of the symbolic value "INITIAL A" to the variable A and the actual value zero to the elements of the array B. ASSIGN commands are usually used to assign initial values to variables at the beginning of the execution of a program.

The second and third commands in Figure 11 are path selection commands. The first path selection command is used for controlling the number of times a loop is iterated. It specifies that 3 complete iterations of the loop beginning at statement 50 should be carried out each time the loop is executed. The second path selection command is used to select branches to follow from a logical conditional branching statement. The construct ALL(...) is used to specify more than one branch. It causes the symbolic evaluator to traverse the paths associated with the first branch in the list and then to return and go down the paths associated with the second branch, and so on.

The fourth command in Figure 11 causes the DISSECT evaluator to print out the current symbolic values of variables X and Y each time statements 150 and 200 are executed.

ACKNOWLEDGEMENTS

The research which is described in this paper was supported by the National Bureau of Standards and was carried out under the supervision of Dr. Dennis Fife.

REFERENCES

[1] Marilyn S. Fuji , "Independent Verification of Highly Reliable Programs," Proceedings COMPSAC 77, IEEE, 1977 pp. 38-44.

[2] D. Teichroew and E.A. Hershey, III, "PSL/PSA: A Computer-Aided Technique for Structured Documentation and Analysis of Information Processing Systems," IEEE-Transactions on Software Engineering, SE-3, 1977 (41-48).

[3] M.E. Fagan, "Design and Code Inspections to Reduce Errors in Program Development," IBM Systems Journal, 15, 1976 (182-211).

[4] B.W. Boehm, R.K. McClean and D.B. Urfrig, "Some Experience with Automated Aids to the Design of Large-scale Reliable Software," IEEE Transactions on Software Engineering, SE-1, 1975 (125-133).

[5] W.C. Hetzel, "An Experimental Analysis of Program Verification Methods," University of North Carolina, Ph.D. Dissertation, 1976.

[6] L.J. Osterweil and L.D. Fosdick, "DAVE - A Validation, Error Detection and Documentation System for FORTRAN Programs," Software -- Practice and Experience, 6, 1976 (473-486).

[7] B.W. Kernighan, and P.J. Plauger, The Elements of Programming Style, McGraw-Hill, New York, 1974.

[8] R.S. Boyer, B. Elspas, and K.N. Levitt, "SELECT-A formal system for testing and debugging programs by symbolic execution, in Proc. 1975 Int. Conf. Reliable Software, 1975 pp. 234-245.

[9] L.A. Clarke, "A system to generate test data and symbolically execute programs," IEEE Transactions Software Engineering, SE-2, 1976 (215-222).

[10] J.C. King, "Symbolic execution and program testing," CACM, 19, 1976 (385-394).

[11] William E. Howden, "Symbolic Testing and the DISSECT Symbolic Evaluation System," IEEE Transactions on Software Engineering, SE-3, 1977 (266-278).

[12] E.F. Miller and R.A. Melton, "Automated generation of test-case data sets," in Proceedings 1975 International Conference on Reliable Software, 1975 pp. 51-58.

[13] J.C. Huang, "An approach to program testing," Computing Surveys, 7, 1975 (113-128).

INDEPENDENT VERIFICATION OF HIGHLY RELIABLE PROGRAMS

Marilyn S. Fujii
Head, Software Analysis Section
Digital Systems Department
Strategic and Information Systems Division
Logicon, Inc.
San Pedro, California 90733

Abstract

Verification is presented as a method of ensuring high reliability of software systems. Verification consists of an early analysis of program requirements and design specifications, followed by extensive program analysis and system/program execution testing. It is performed in parallel with software development by an organization independent of the development group, with the objective of detecting conceptual and implementation errors before program acceptance. Software analysis and testing aids for cost-effectively automating routine tasks are described. The results of several verification projects are discussed to illustrate common types of errors and techniques for their detection. Key aspects of verification planning are presented for projects that are required to achieve highly reliable software.

Introduction

As software has become an increasingly important part of systems performing complex and critical functions, the risks of having a software-caused failure have dramatically increased. Software personnel now generally agree on the need for methods of increasing software reliability by eliminating errors made during software development. Industry and academic institutions have responded to this need in two ways. The first is through use of improved (less error-prone) development methods, such as those embodied in current software engineering technology. The second is through use of a rigorous methodology employing systematic checks for detecting errors in the software during its development process. This second technique for achieving reliable software--verification--is the subject of this paper.

Verification emerged from the need for ultra-reliable software in launch vehicle and missile projects, where an error in the booster or targeting program would cause mission failure--loss of a vehicle and its payload--resulting in enormous time and financial setbacks. Verification began about 15 years ago, in certain of these high-risk environments, as a systematic analysis and testing process to increase software reliability. Verification is now widely applied to computer programs performing functions such as tracking, command and control, avionics, electronic warfare, mission planning, and communications. These programs are representative of the highly reliable software discussed in the remainder of this paper.

The primary goal of verification is to immediately detect and correct software development errors using the two evaluation criteria shown in Figure 1. The first criterion is that the software adequately and correctly performs all intended functions. The second, more subtle, criterion is that the software does not perform any intended functions that, either singly or in combination with others, can degrade the performance of the entire system.[1]

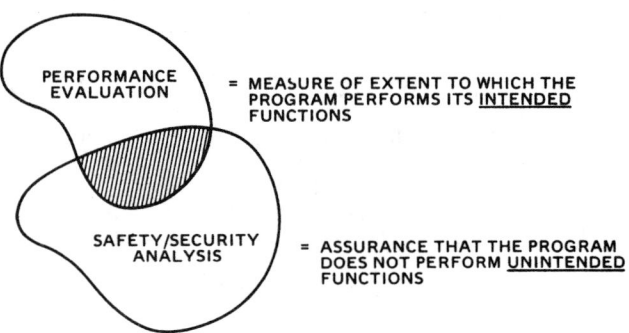

Figure 1. Evaluation Criteria for Independent Verification

Verification Concepts

Three key characteristics distinguish verification from other test and evaluation activities. The first, conceptual objectivity, mandates that the verification group be independent of the development group. Independence provides a fresh viewpoint in assessing the program and precludes politically motivated bias in critiquing the software development's products. The need for independent verification is widely recognized throughout the Department of Defense, which commonly employs separate contractors for development and verification.[2]

Verification's second characteristic is that it is performed in parallel with the software development in order that errors may be detected and corrected as soon as they are made. We now realize that it is more costly to correct an error late in the development cycle because of the need to correct the design and specifications in addition to correcting the malfunctioning portion of the coded computer program. Parallel verification has gained acceptance because it is less costly than after-the-fact verification performed after development is complete. Parallel verification determines the software's acceptability in time for the buy-off decision.

The third characteristic of verification is that it is a comprehensive set of analyses and tests to establish the adequacy of software, rather than a quick evaluation to assure the manager of a software development that everything looks normal. Verification is designed to uncover program flaws the developer normally does not see because of his natural motivation to demonstrate his product's acceptability. Adequate software appraisal requires a thorough scrutiny of the program using highly trained personnel, automated aids, and a rigorous methodology.

The Verification Process

The verification process is closely tied to the steps in software development. There are several different formal procedures for software development, such as those promulgated by military standards, regulations, and instructions. Disregarding differences in nomenclature and specialized adaptations, the basic steps illustrated by the lightly outlined rectangles in Figure 2 are common to most well-planned software development efforts.

The first development step, referred to as software requirements definition, defines the program requirements for all functions to be performed by computer program processing. Next, a computer program design is formulated; this design should satisfy the requirements defined in the previous step. During the third step, code development, the design is actually implemented ("coded") in a computer programming language. Finally, program checkout tests the computer program to ensure that it performs the intended functions correctly. (In practice, code development and checkout overlap as shown in the figure.) As the developer completes each of these steps, the customer reviews the results and, if the results are approved, authorizes proceeding to the next development step.

Verification methodology has evolved into a well-defined process that parallels each development step

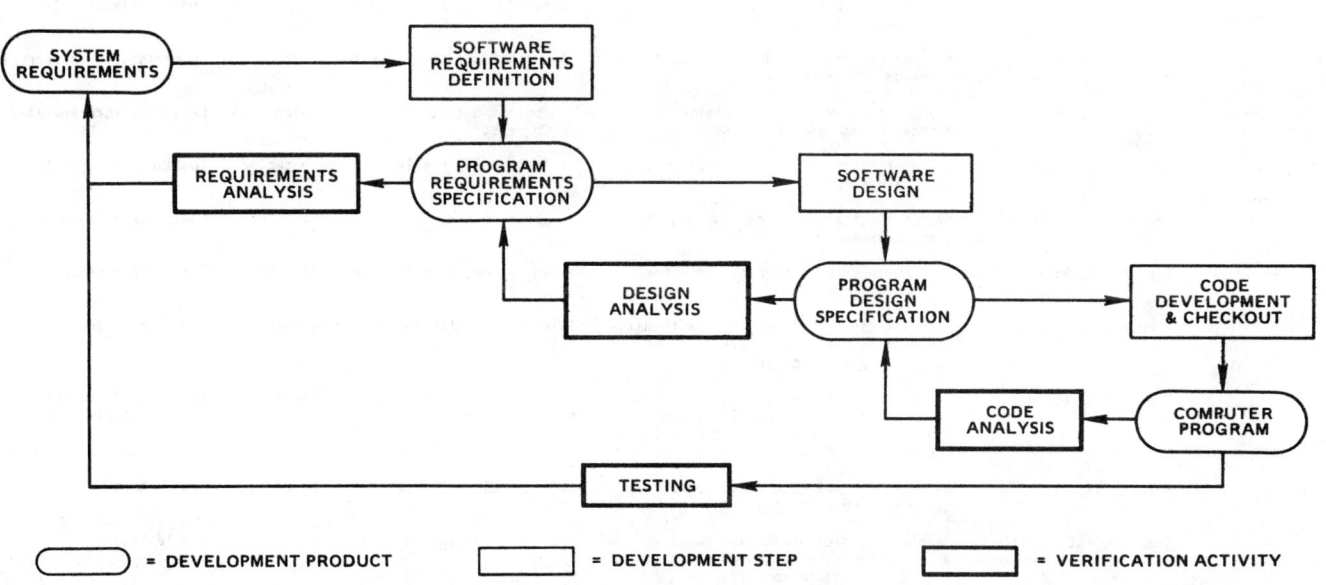

Figure 2. The Software Development and Verification Processes

with a corresponding verification activity, as also shown in Figure 2. Each verification activity applies techniques proven effective in detecting errors common to that step in the development process.[3] The four verification activities are described below. Specific examples of the types of errors detected by each, and the typical detection method, are given in Table 1.

Requirements Analysis

Requirements analysis is performed to ensure that the developer's software requirements are completely and correctly defined. As part of this activity, analysts check each software requirement for consistency with other requirements and, where possible, trace software requirements to their source in system requirements, interfaces, or user needs. Each requirement must be determined correct by independent derivation, by comparison to similar existing systems, or by consulting standard references. For those software requirements whose validity cannot be determined a posteriori, other specialized techniques such as modeling, timing, and sizing are used. Analysts evaluate requirement testability to ensure that measurable acceptance criteria are implied by each software requirement. Finally, the entire set of software requirements is evaluated for completeness and for proper allocation of requirements to software functions.

If errors remain undetected, program design and implementation will go awry. Program acceptance will be based on fuzzy criteria that do not match desired program capabilities. Requirements analysis is therefore one of the most crucial verification activities for highly reliable programs.

Table 1. Examples of Errors Detected by Each Verification Activity

Verification Activity	Error Type	Error Cause	Error Effect	Detection Method
Requirements analysis	Incomplete requirement	Partial specification of filter performance requirements	Unacceptable filter initialization/reinitialization	Comparison to existing system
	Missing requirement	Omitting error detection and recovery requirements	Insufficient program protection	Documentation analysis
	Incorrect requirement	Restart requirement cannot be met with existing hardware	Inadequate restart capability	Timing analysis
	Improper requirement allocation	Specifying accuracy for later processing within initialization requirements	Requirement overlooked during design	Independent derivation
	Untestable requirement	Requiring new program to meet or exceed accuracy of old program	Impractical to test: too many test cases; can't tell which is "better" if answers differ	Documentation analysis
Design analysis	Inefficient algorithm	Incorrect weighting factors for initializing real-time estimation algorithm	Output data remain "noisy" for twice as long as expected	Independent derivation/simulation
	Inadequate algorithm	Editing algorithm that detects only single-point failures	Biased data cause system failure	Independent derivation
	Incorrect algorithm	Incorrect criteria for selecting best data source	Poor-quality source selected, good source ignored	Logic analysis/simulation
	Logical error	Skipping logic to save data when current data contain errors	Misleading display of old data	Logic analysis
	Design oversight	No legality check of operator console commands before processing	Illegal command causes system crash	Comparison to references
Code analysis	Data accessing	Incorrect array index calculation for second, third, and fourth sensors	Meaningless output for second, third, and fourth sensors	Data structure analysis
	Sequencing error	Order of calculations inverted: using data before they are updated	Predicted value remains one cycle behind	Equation reconstruction
	Branching and iteration	Branch predicate required two contradictory conditions to be true	Unexecutable code	Logic reconstruction
	Interruptibility	Failure to save/restore two of three index registers	Meaningless results if higher priority interrupt occurs	Real-time conflict analysis
	Hardware interface	Overflow sets negative overflow to maximum positive value and sets positive overflow to maximum negative value	Misleading erratic jumps in real-time plots	Manual code analysis
Testing	Programming error	Negatively scaled constants converted to incorrect binary value; diagnostic routine made similar error in converting back to decimal	Inaccurate site constants that operator could not diagnose	Module test (dumped binary value)
	Missing capability	Hardware did not save data needed for power failure restart	Program could not recover from power failure	System test
	Insufficient accuracy	Double-precision divide and multiply accuracy could be as low as 6 digits (12 significant digits required)	Inaccurate program results	Module test
	Design oversight	Catastrophic restart destroyed time value	Loss of real-time velocity vs. time plot	System test

Design Analysis

Design analysis ensures that the computer program design is correct and that it satisfies the defined software requirements. The first step in design analysis is to check for design completeness by correlating design elements with their source requirements. This correlation produces a cross-reference between design and requirements that is later used when evaluating each element of the design. Different techniques are then applied to verify the various types of design elements: mathematical equations, algorithms, and control logic. Techniques for verifying mathematical elements include independent derivation, dimensional analysis (to check unit consistency), and comparison to references. To verify certain algorithms, such as those for estimation and automatic control, simulations and models are used to evaluate the algorithm's response to external stimuli. Control logic is more difficult to verify because analysts must search for conceptual flaws in the design that will cause program failure under certain conditions. Control logic is analyzed by determining the set of conditions for which the program must execute correctly, then manually analyzing the logic paths for each of these conditions.

The computer program design is the specification from which the programmers actually develop the computer program. Verification design analysis eliminates design errors that would otherwise be propagated into the coded computer program.

Code Analysis

Code analysis is performed to verify that the computer program, as coded, is a correct implementation of the specified design. Code analysts examine the computer program's source language and its compiled or assembled object code using a variety of techiques. The source language program's equations and logic are reconstructed, either manually or using automated aids, then compared to those specified in the design to identify errors made in translating the design into the programming language. Data structures are checked for conformance to their design, as are all addressing techniques used to reference data structures. Error-prone constructs due to specialized language or machine features (such as conditional assembly, partial-word addressing, special-purpose registers, reserved memory cells) are identified and analyzed for correctness. Real-time programs subject to interruptibility problems are examined for proper interrupt enabling and disabling and for potential conflicts in the use of machine or program resources. Any violations of programming standards are identified and, finally, the object program is verified to be a correct assembly or compilation of the source code.

In addition to programming errors, code analysis detects poor programming practices. These result from taking advantage of a system quirk, using an instruction for other than its intended purpose, and tricky programming. Even though these practices may not introduce current errors, they are error-prone in the long term because they make use of code that is difficult to understand and modify. Code analysis results in program code that is both reliable and maintainable.

Testing

Verification testing is performed to evaluate the developed computer program's execution in the operational environment. Testing begins with test planning, which formulates a set of tests that will establish whether the program satisfies all software and system requirements. A test procedure is written for each test, specifying the test steps and the expected program results at each step. All tests are completely specified in a test plan/procedures document before verification testing formally begins.[4] Testing begins with individual program modules and proceeds through program integration. Program modules are tested individually to determine if they satisfy their corresponding functional requirements. Next, groups of program modules are tested to verify proper interaction at hardware and software interfaces. Finally, system-level testing exercises the integrated program as a unit to determine the extent to which program performance requirements and system requirements are satisfied. For highly critical software, system-level testing may also entail executing the program for a particular mission, exercising both nominal and worst-case scenarios. This process results in certification that the program will perform reliably for that mission.

Testing can detect many types of errors, including incorrect requirements, design, or coding not detected by previous verification activities. If the preceding verification analysis has been effective, verification testing primarily confirms the existence of previously known errors and identifies relatively few significant new errors.

Use of Automated Tools

Verification tools are computerized aids that automate portions of the analysis and testing activities. Their capabilities range from the primitive, such as identifying all occurrences of a specified class of instructions, to the sophisticated, such as symbolically executing all logical paths through a computer program. Tools are used throughout the verification process to perform several important functions, such as identifying code sequences that need further analysis, generating test data, serving as the test controller and environment, and summarizing test results in a format easily understood by the analyst.[5] Table 2 lists several types of commonly used verification tools and summarizes their functions.

There has been much recent emphasis on developing and using improved verification tools. A positive benefit of the recent tool technology is increased effectiveness of program analysis and, especially, program testing. A somewhat negative side-effect also resulted: The attractiveness of using the latest tool has often obscured the fact that a tool is only a tool.[6] Especially in verification of highly reliable software, tools must be judiciously applied and their use must be coupled with adequate analysis of the results they provide.

Verification Planning

Verification planning encompasses five essential management activities:

- Program planning
- Control procedures definition
- Tool preparation
- Monitoring technical activities
- Final report generation

Program planning must be completed before beginning any other technical or management activity. The program plan schedules the entire verification effort so that it synchronizes with the development and provides results when needed at critical decision points such as design reviews. It identifies all deliverables and specifies their format and content. It also specifies which verification techniques will be applied and selects the appropriate verification tools.

In the second management activity, control procedures are defined for development materials, verification materials, and contact with the developer. A configuration control library is given responsibility for ensuring that all development materials (such as specifications, tapes/decks, and listings) are complete, current, and unaltered. Verification materials (such as verification tools, test data, and results) are similarly controlled by the configuration control library. Finally, under joint agreement with the developer, contact with the developer is limited, to minimize the possibility of bias or interference.

The tool preparation activity readies the tools needed for verification analysis and testing, then ensures that they perform reliably. New tools are developed and existing tools are modified to fit the needs of the current verification project. Documentation and user instructions are also prepared. Before using any tool, it must be qualified by a series of tests that evidence its error-detection capabilities.

Table 2. Common Types of Verification Tools

Verification Tool	Function
Source code comparator	Identify differences between two versions of source code
Flowcharter	Generate a flowchart from the source code
Syntax analyzer	Analyze the syntax of each program statement
Structure analyzer	Analyze the program's structural characteristics
Standards auditor	Check code for adherence to programming conventions
Code checker	Identify portions of the code requiring manual analysis
Cross-referencer	Generate a global cross-reference of all variables in a program
Branch analyzer	Determine what paths have been exercised and how often
Execution monitor	Alter variables, force execution, monitor results
Symbolic executor	Generate path analysis and execution conditions
Functional simulation	Evaluate alternative configurations, estimate system capacity
Analytical simulation	Evaluate algorithms or design alternatives
Interpretive simulation	Model computers, interfaces, environmental factors

Monitoring technical performance entails holding management reviews for all verification activities and reporting technical results in a timely manner. It may also involve coordinating and co-chairing technical interface meetings with the developer in order to discuss development problems or to clarify program anomalies (errors or discrepancies identified by the verification group).

When all verification activities are complete, a final report is prepared to present the conclusions and recommendations for the developed computer program. The final report summarizes the findings of the entire verification effort, giving the status of all anomalies as of the final program version. The impact of these anomalies on program performance is the basis for conclusive recommendations concerning operational use of the developed computer program.

Conclusions

At this point, we have discussed verification in some detail: what it is, why and how it is done, and what tools are used. At the close of this paper, the author would like to present some conclusions reached based on research and experience in performing verification for highly reliable programs.

Verification in Parallel With Development

The primary motivation for parallel verification is to detect errors early, thus allowing quick correction with minimal cost impact. Surveys of error incidence have shown that the single most frequent source of program errors (ignoring documentation errors) is improper sequencing and control.[7] This type of error originates in program requirements and design. Examining these errors more closely reveals that they are not only the most common, but also the most severe in terms of potential to cause program failure.[8] This result underscores the importance of parallel verification to detect requirement and design errors early in the development process.

Verification of Preliminary Products

The objective of verification is to eliminate errors in computer program products (specifications and code) prior to customer buy-off. One way to improve the reliability of final products is to use verification as a method of removing errors from preliminary versions. In one instance, this was done with such effectiveness that verification of the final program found no serious errors, causing the customer to question the value of the verification effort. The response to the customer's question is shown in Figure 3, which tabulates the officially reported errors in final materials plus the informally reported errors in preliminary versions. All high- and intermediate-severity errors identified in preliminary versions were corrected in the final products; the total number of errors in

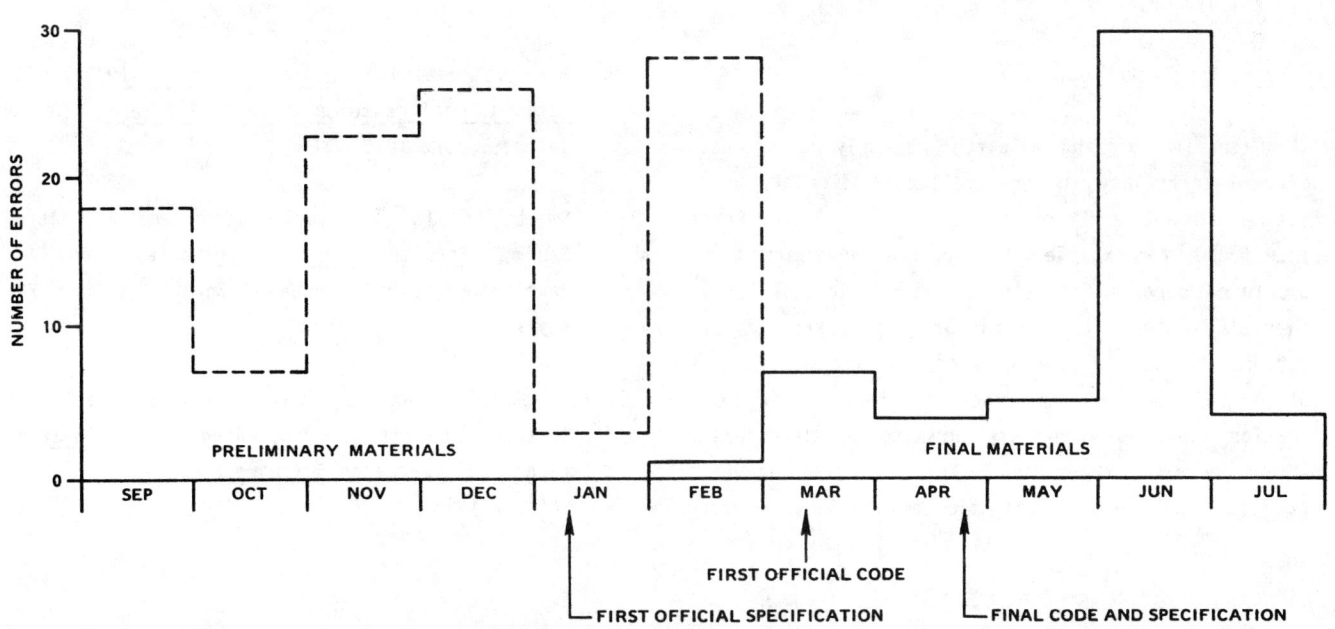

Figure 3. Error-Reporting Rate for Sample Project

the final program was significantly reduced by verifying preliminary products.

Balancing Analysis and Testing

Verification planning must establish the relative emphasis to be applied to each of the four verification activities. Traditionally, verification has heavily emphasized testing, even if it meant reducing the effort allocated to analysis. The risks of deemphasizing analysis are illustrated by statistics compiled from several verification projects shown in Figure 4, where the shaded areas show the observed variation in the percentage of errors detected by each verification activity. Even at the lowest error incidence, requirements analysis and design analysis detected nearly one-third of the total number of program errors. The effectiveness of code analysis is similarly high.

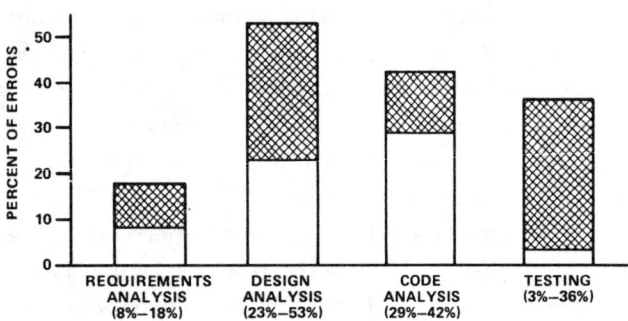

Figure 4. Errors Detected by Verification Activity for Sample Projects

Applying New Technology

Extensive ongoing research in applying advanced software technology in verification is directly benefitting current verification projects. An Air Force study found, for example, that top-down development and structured programming methods enhance verification.[9] Other studies have identified software quality factors that can be used in verification to better evaluate software.[10] In addition, research into many new verification tools is vigorously pursuing the development of more powerful techniques. This research has great potential to advance verification methodology if practitioners incorporate improved verification techniques in their current work.

References

1. Hartwick, R. Dean, Verification and Validation, Text for UCLA Short Course on Software Reliability, January 1974

2. Biché, P. W. et al., Independent Test and Evaluation Survey, Logicon Report DS-74018, 18 March 1974

3. Biché, P. W. et al., Independent Test and Evaluation Guidelines, Logicon Report DS-74036, 26 July 1974

4. Hartwick, R. Dean, "Test Planning," AFIPS Conference Proceedings, Vol. 46, 1977 National Computer Conference, 13-16 June 1977

5. Reifer, Donald J., and Stephen Trattner, "A Glossary of Software Tools and Techniques," Computer, July 1977

6. Brown, John R., "Why Tools?" Proceedings of Computer Science and Statistics: 8th Annual Symposium on the Interface, 13 and 14 February 1975

7. Boehm, Barry W., "Software and Its Impact: A Quantitative Assessment," Datamation, May 1973

8. Rubey, Raymond J., "Quantitative Aspects of Software Validation," Proceedings of the 1975 International Conference on Reliable Software, SIGPLAN Notices, June 1975

9. Smith, Ronald L., "Verification and Validation Study," Structured Programming Series, Rome Air Development Center, RADC-TR-74-300, Volumn XV, May 1975

10. Boehm, B. W. et al., "Quantitative Evaluation of Software Quality," Proceedings of 2nd International Conference on Software Engineering, 13-15 October 1976

Substantial net improvements in programming quality and productivity have been obtained through the use of formal inspections of design and of code. Improvements are made possible by a systematic and efficient design and code verification process, with well-defined roles for inspection participants. The manner in which inspection data is categorized and made suitable for process analysis is an important factor in attaining the improvements. It is shown that by using inspection results, a mechanism for initial error reduction followed by ever-improving error rates can be achieved.

Design and code inspections to reduce errors in program development

by M. E. Fagan

Successful management of any process requires planning, measurement, and control. In programming development, these requirements translate into defining the programming process in terms of a series of operations, each operation having its own exit criteria. Next there must be some means of measuring completeness of the product at any point of its development by inspections or testing. And finally, the measured data must be used for controlling the process. This approach is not only conceptually interesting, but has been applied successfully in several programming projects embracing systems and applications programming, both large and small. It has not been found to "get in the way" of programming, but has instead enabled higher predictability than other means, and the use of inspections has improved productivity and product quality. The purpose of this paper is to explain the planning, measurement, and control functions as they are affected by inspections in programming terms.

An ingredient that gives maximum play to the planning, measurement, and control elements is consistent and vigorous *discipline*. Variable rules and conventions are the usual indicators of a lack of discipline. An iron-clad discipline on all rules, which can stifle programming work, is not required but instead there should be a clear understanding of the flexibility (or nonflexibility) of each of the rules applied to various aspects of the project. An example of flexibility may be waiving the rule that all main paths will be tested for the case where repeated testing of a given path will logically do no more than add expense. An example of necessary inflexibility would be that *all* code must be

Figure 1 Programming process

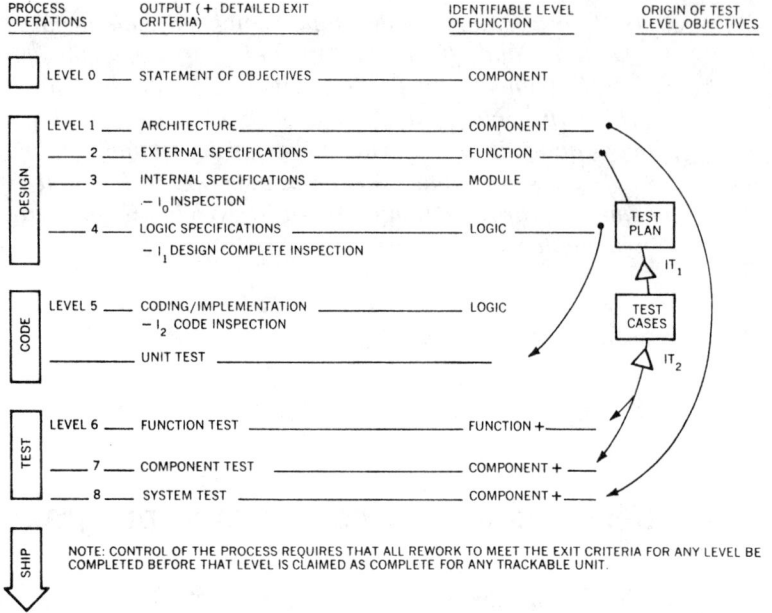

inspected. A clear statement of the project rules and changes to these rules along with faithful adherence to the rules go a long way toward practicing the required project discipline.

A prerequisite of process management is a clearly defined series of operations in the process (Figure 1). The miniprocess within each operation must also be clearly described for closer management. A clear statement of the criteria that must be satisfied to exit each operation is mandatory. This statement and accurate data collection, with the data clearly tied to trackable units of known size and collected from specific points in the process, are some essential constituents of the information required for process management.

In order to move the form of process management from qualitative to more quantitative, process terms must be more specific, data collected must be appropriate, and the limits of accuracy of the data must be known. The effect is to provide more precise information in the correct process context for decision making by the process manager.

In this paper, we first describe the programming process and places at which inspections are important. Then we discuss factors that affect productivity and the operations involved with inspections. Finally, we compare inspections and walk-throughs on process control.

The process

a manageable process

A process may be described as a set of operations occurring in a definite sequence that operates on a given input and converts it to some desired output. A general statement of this kind is sufficient to convey the notion of the process. In a practical application, however, it is necessary to describe the input, output, internal processing, and processing times of a process in very specific terms if the process is to be executed and practical output is to be obtained.

In the programming development process, explicit requirement statements are necessary as input. The series of processing operations that act on this input must be placed in the correct sequence with one another, the output of each operation satisfying the input needs of the next operation. The output of the final operation is, of course, the explicitly required output in the form of a verified program. Thus, the objective of each processing operation is to receive a defined input and to produce a definite output that satisfies a specific set of exit criteria. (It goes without saying that each operation can be considered as a miniprocess itself.) A well-formed process can be thought of as a continuum of processing during which sequential sets of exit criteria are satisfied, the last set in the entire series requiring a well-defined end product. Such a process is not amorphous. It can be measured and controlled.

exit criteria

Unambiguous, explicit, and universally accepted exit criteria would be perfect as process control checkpoints. It is frequently argued that universally agreed upon checkpoints are impossible in programming because all projects are different, etc. However, *all* projects do reach the point at which there is a project checkpoint. As it stands, any trackable unit of code achieving a clean compilation can be said to have satisfied a universal exit criterion or checkpoint in the process. Other checkpoints can also be selected, albeit on more arguable premises, but once the premises are agreed upon, the checkpoints become visible in most, if not all, projects. For example, there is a point at which the design of a program is considered complete. This point may be described as the level of detail to which a unit of design is reduced so that one design statement will materialize in an estimated three to 10 source code instructions (or, if desired, five to 20, for that matter). Whichever particular ratio is selected across a project, it provides a checkpoint for the process control of that project. In this way, suitable checkpoints may be selected throughout the development process and used in process management. (For more specific exit criteria see Reference 1.)

The cost of reworking errors in programs becomes higher the later they are reworked in the process, so every attempt should be made to find and fix errors as early in the process as possible. This cost has led to the use of the inspections described later and to the description of exit criteria which include assuring that all errors known at the end of the inspection of the new "clean-compilation" code, for example, have been correctly fixed. So, rework of all known errors up to a particular point must be complete before the associated checkpoint can be claimed to be met for any piece of code.

Where inspections are not used and errors are found during development or testing, the cost of rework as a fraction of overall development cost can be suprisingly high. For this reason, errors should be found and fixed as close to their place of origin as possible.

Production studies have validated the expected quality and productivity improvements and have provided estimates of standard productivity rates, percentage improvements due to inspections, and percentage improvements in error rates which are applicable in the context of large-scale operating system program production. (The data related to operating system development contained herein reflect results achieved by IBM in applying the subject processes and methods to representative samples. Since the results depend on many factors, they cannot be considered representative of every situation. They are furnished merely for the purpose of illustrating what has been achieved in sample testing.)

The purpose of the test plan inspection IT_1, shown in Figure 1, is to find voids in the functional variation coverage and other discrepancies in the test plan. IT_2, test case inspection of the test cases, which are based on the test plan, finds errors in the test cases. The total effects of IT_1 and IT_2 are to increase the integrity of testing and, hence, the quality of the completed product. And, because there are less errors in the test cases to be debugged during the testing phase, the overall project schedule is also improved.

A process of the kind depicted in Figure 1 installs all the intrinsic programming properties in the product as required in the statement of objectives (Level 0) by the time the coding operation (Level 5) has been completed—except for packaging and publications requirements. With these exceptions, all later work is of a verification nature. This verification of the product provides no contribution to the product during the essential development (Levels 1 to 5); it only adds error detection and elimination (frequently at one half of the development cost). I_0, I_1, and I_2 inspections were developed to measure and influence intrinsic

Figure 2 A study of coding productivity

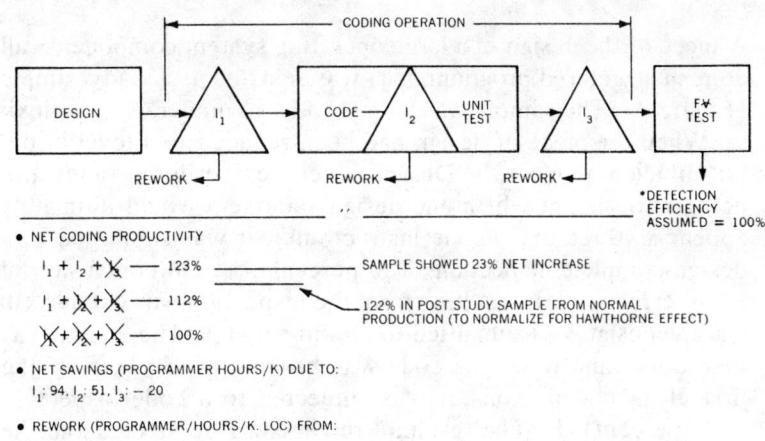

quality (error content) in the early levels, where error rework can be most economically accomplished. Naturally, the beneficial effect on quality is also felt in later operations of the development process and at the end user's site.

An improvement in productivity is the most immediate effect of purging errors from the product by the I_0, I_1, and I_2 inspections. This purging allows rework of these errors very near their origin, early in the process. Rework done at these levels is 10 to 100 times less expensive than if it is done in the last half of the process. Since rework detracts from productive effort, it reduces productivity in proportion to the time taken to accomplish the rework. It follows, then, that finding errors by inspection and reworking them earlier in the process reduces the overall rework time and increases productivity even within the early operations and even more over the total process. Since less errors ship with the product, the time taken for the user to install programs is less, and his productivity is also increased.

The quality of documentation that describes the program is of as much importance as the program itself for poor quality can mislead the user, causing him to make errors quite as important as errors in the program. For this reason, the quality of program documentation is verified by publications inspections (PI_0, PI_1, and PI_2). Through a reduction of user-encountered errors, these inspections also have the effect of improving user productivity by reducing his rework time.

A study of coding productivity

A piece of the design of a large operating system component (all done in structured programming) was selected as a study sample (Figure 2). The sample was judged to be of moderate complexity. When the piece of design had been reduced to a level of detail sufficient to meet the Design Level 4 exit criteria[2] (a level of detail of design at which one design statement would ultimately appear as three to 10 code instructions), it was submitted to a design-complete inspection (100 percent), I_1. On conclusion of I_1, all error rework resulting from the inspection was completed, and the design was submitted for coding in PL/S. The coding was then done, and when the code was brought to the level of the first clean compilation,[2] it was subjected to a code inspection (100 percent), I_2. The resultant rework was completed and the code was subjected to unit test. After unit test, a unit test inspection, I_3, was done to see that the unit test plan had been fully executed. Some rework was required and the necessary changes were made. This step completed the coding operation. The study sample was then passed on to later process operations consisting of building and testing.

inspection sample

The inspection sample was considered of sufficient size and nature to be representative for study purposes. Three programmers designed it, and it was coded by 13 programmers. The inspection sample was in modular form, was structured, and was judged to be of moderate complexity on average.

coding operation productivity

Because errors were identified and corrected in groups at I_1 and I_2, rather than found one-by-one during subsequent work and handled at the higher cost incumbent in later rework, the overall amount of error rework was minimized, even within the coding operation. Expressed differently, considering the inclusion of *all* I_1 time, I_2 time, and resulting error rework time (with the usual coding and unit test time in the total time to complete the operation), a *net* saving resulted when this figure was compared to the no-inspection case. This net saving translated into a 23 percent increase in the productivity of the coding operation alone. Productivity in later levels was also increased because there was less error rework in these levels due to the effect of inspections, but the increase was not measured directly.

An important aspect to consider in any production experiment involving human beings is the Hawthorne Effect.[3] If this effect is not adequately handled, it is never clear whether the effect observed is due to the human bias of the Hawthorne Effect or due to the newly implemented change in process. In this case a *control sample* was selected at random from many pieces of work *after the I_1 and I_2 inspections were accepted as commonplace*. (Previous experience without I_1 and I_2 approximated the net coding productivity rate of 100 percent datum in Figure 2.) The difference in coding productivity between the experimental sample (with I_1 and I_2 for the first time) and the control sample was 0.9 percent. This difference is not considered significant. Therefore, the measured increase in coding productivity of 23 percent is considered to validly accrue from the only change in the process: addition of I_1 and I_2 inspections.

control sample The control sample was also considered to be of representative size and was from the same operating system component as the study sample. It was designed by four programmers and was coded by seven programmers. And it was considered to be of moderate complexity on average.

net savings Within the coding operation only, the net savings (including inspection and rework time) in programmer hours per 1000 Non-Commentary Source Statements (K.NCSS)[1] were I_1: 94, I_2: 51, and I_3: −20. As a consequence, I_3 is no longer in effect.

If personal fatigue and downtime of 15 percent are allowed in addition to the 145 programmer hours per K.NCSS, the saving approaches one programmer month per K.NCSS (assuming that our sample was truly representative of the rest of the work in the operating system component considered).

error rework The error rework in programmer hours per K.NCSS found in this study due to I_1 was 78, and 36 for I_2 (24 hours for design errors and 12 for code errors). Time for error rework must be specifically scheduled. (For scheduling purposes it is best to develop rework hours per K.NCSS from history depending upon the particular project types and environments, but figures of 20 hours for I_1, and 16 hours for I_2 (*after the learning curve*) may be suitable to start with.)

quality The only comparative measure of quality obtained was a comparison of the inspection study sample with a fully comparable piece of the operating system component that was produced similarly, except that walk-throughs were used in place of the I_1 and I_2 inspections. (Walk-throughs[5] were the practice before implementation of I_1 and I_2 inspections.) The process span in which the quality comparison was made was seven months of testing beyond unit test after which it was judged that both samples had been equally exercised. The results showed the inspection sample to contain 38 percent less errors than the walk-through sample.

Note that up to inspection I_2, no machine time has been used for debugging, and so machine time savings were not mentioned. Although substantial machine time is saved overall since there are less errors to test for in inspected code in later stages of the process, no actual measures were obtained.

Table 1 Error detection efficiency

Process Operations	Errors Found per KNCSS	Percent of Total Errors Found
Design I₁ inspection ⎤ Coding I₂ inspection ⎦	38*	82
Unit test ⎤ Preparation for acceptance test ⎦	8	18
Acceptance test	0	
Actual usage (6 mo.)	0	
Total	46	100

*51% were logic errors, most of which were missing rather than due to incorrect design.

inspections in applications development

In the development of applications, inspections also make a significant impact. For example, an application program of eight modules was written in COBOL by Aetna Corporate Data Processing department, Aetna Life and Casualty, Hartford, Connecticut, in June 1975.[6] Two programmers developed the program. The number of inspection participants ranged between three and five. The only change introduced in the development process was the I_1 and I_2 inspections. The program size was 4,439 Non-Commentary Source Statements.

An automated estimating program, which is used to produce the normal program development time estimates for all the Corporate Data Processing department's projects, predicted that designing, coding, and unit testing this project would require 62 programmer days. In fact, the time actually taken was 46.5 programmer days including inspection meeting time. The resulting saving in programmer resources was 25 percent.

The inspections were obviously very thorough when judged by the inspection error detection efficiency of 82 percent and the later results during testing and usage as shown in Table 1.

The results achieved in Non-Commentary Source Statements per Elapsed Hour are shown in Table 2. These inspection rates are four to six times faster than for systems programming. If these rates are generally applicable, they would have the effect of making the inspection of applications programs much less expensive.

Table 2 Inspection rates in NCSS per hour

Operations	I_1	I_2
Preparation	898	709
Inspection	652	539

Inspections

Inspections are a *formal, efficient,* and *economical* method of finding errors in design and code. All instructions are addressed

Table 3. Inspection process and rate of progress

Process operations	Rate of progress* (loc/hr) Design I_1	Code I_2	Objectives of the operation
1. Overview	500	not necessary	Communication education
2. Preparation	100	125	Education
3. Inspection	130	150	*Find errors*
4. Rework	20 hrs/K.NCSS	16 hrs/K.NCSS	Rework and resolve errors found by inspection
5. Follow-up	–	–	See that all errors, problems, and concerns have been resolved

*These notes apply to systems programming and are conservative. Comparable rates for applications programming are much higher. Initial schedules may be started with these numbers and as project history that is keyed to unique environments evolves, the historical data may be used for future scheduling algorithms.

at least once in the conduct of inspections. Key aspects of inspections are exposed in the following text through describing the I_1 and I_2 inspection conduct and process. I_0, IT_1, IT_2, PI_0, PI_1, and PI_2 inspections retain the same essential properties as the I_1 and I_2 inspections but differ in materials inspected, number of participants, and some other minor points.

the people involved

The inspection team is best served when its members play their particular roles, assuming the particular vantage point of those roles. These roles are described below:

1. *Moderator* — The *key person* in a successful inspection. He must be a competent programmer but need *not* be a technical expert on the program being inspected. To preserve objectivity and to increase the integrity of the inspection, it is usually advantageous to use a moderator from an unrelated project. The moderator must manage the inspection team and offer leadership. Hence, he must use personal sensitivity, tact, and drive in balanced measure. His use of the strengths of team members should produce a synergistic effect larger than their number; in other words, *he is the coach*. The duties of moderator also include scheduling suitable meeting places, reporting inspection results within one day, and follow-up on rework. *For best results the moderator should be specially trained.* (This training is brief but very advantageous.)
2. *Designer* — The programmer responsible for producing the program design.
3. *Coder/Implementor* — The programmer responsible for translating the design into code.
4. *Tester* — The programmer responsible for writing and/or executing test cases or otherwise testing the product of the designer and coder.

If the coder of a piece of code also designed it, he will function in the designer role for the inspection process; a coder from some related or similar program will perform the role of the coder. If the same person designs, codes, and tests the product code, the coder role should be filled as described above, and another coder—preferably with testing experience—should fill the role of tester.

Four people constitute a good-sized inspection team, although circumstances may dictate otherwise. The team size should not be artificially increased over four, but if the subject code is involved in a number of interfaces, the programmers of code related to these interfaces may profitably be involved in inspection. Table 3 indicates the inspection process and rate of progress.

scheduling inspections and rework

The total time to complete the inspection process from overview through follow-up for I_1 or I_2 inspections with four people involved takes about 90 to 100 people-hours for systems programming. Again, these figures may be considered conservative but they will serve as a starting point. Comparable figures for applications programming tend to be much lower, implying lower cost per K.NCSS.

Because the error detection efficiency of most inspection teams tends to dwindle after two hours of inspection but then picks up after a period of different activity, it is advisable to schedule inspection sessions of no more than two hours at a time. Two two-hour sessions per day are acceptable.

The time to do inspections and resulting rework must be scheduled and managed with the same attention as other important project activities. (After all, as is noted later, for one case at least, it is possible to find approximately two thirds of the errors reported during an inspection.) If this is not done, the immediate work pressure has a tendency to push the inspections and/or rework into the background, postponing them or avoiding them altogether. The result of this short-term respite will obviously have a much more dramatic long-term negative effect since the finding and fixing of errors is delayed until later in the process (and after turnover to the user). Usually, the result of postponing early error detection is a lengthening of the overall schedule and increased product cost.

Scheduling inspection time for modified code may be based on the algorithms in Table 3 *and on judgment*.

I_1 inspection process

Keeping the objective of each operation in the forefront of team activity is of paramount importance. Here is presented an outline of the I_1 inspection process operations.

Figure 3 Summary of design inspections by error type

		\multicolumn{3}{c}{Inspection file}		
VP	Individual Name	Missing	Wrong	Extra	Errors	Error %
CD	CB Definition	16	2		18	3.5 ⎫ 10.4
CU	CB Usage	18	17	1	36	6.9 ⎭
FS	FPFS	1			1	.2
IC	Interconnect Calls	18	9		27	5.2
IR	Interconnect Reqts	4	5	2	11	2.1
LO	Logic	126	57	24	207	39.8 ←
L3	Higher Lvl Docu	1		1	2	.4
MA	Mod Attributes	1			1	.2
MD	More Detail	24	6	2	32	6.2
MN	Maintainability	8	5	3	16	3.1
OT	Other	15	10	10	35	6.7
PD	Pass Data Areas		1		1	.2
PE	Performance	1	2	3	6	1.2
PR	Prologue/Prose	44	38	7	89	17.1 ←
RM	Return Code/Msg	5	7	2	14	2.7
RU	Register Usage	1	2		3	.6
ST	Standards					
TB	Test & Branch	12	7	2	21	4.0
		295	168	57	520	100.0
		57%	32%	11%		

Figure 4 Summary of code inspections by error type

		\multicolumn{3}{c}{Inspection file}		
VP	Individual Name	Missing	Wrong	Extra	Errors	Error %
CC	Code Comments	5	17	1	23	6.6
CU	CB Usage	3	21	1	25	7.2
DE	Design Error	31	32	14	77	22.1 ←
F1			8		8	2.3
IR	Interconnect Calls	7	9	3	19	5.5
LO	Logic	33	49	10	92	26.4 ←
MN	Maintainability	5	7	2	14	4.0
OT	Other					
PE	Performance	3	2	5	10	2.9
PR	Prologue/Prose	25	24	3	52	14.9 ←
PU	PL/S or BAL Use	4	9	1	14	4.0
RU	Register Usage	4	2		6	1.7
SU	Storage Usage	1			1	.3
TB	Test & Branch	2	5		7	2.0
		123	185	40	348	100.0

1. *Overview* (whole team) — The designer first describes the overall area being addressed and then the specific area he has designed in detail — logic, paths, dependencies, etc. Documentation of design is distributed to all inspection participants on conclusion of the overview. (For an I_2 inspection, no overview is necessary, but the participants should remain the same. Preparation, inspection, and follow-up proceed as for I_1 but, of course, using code listings *and* design specifications

as inspection materials. Also, at I_2 the moderator should flag for special scrutiny those areas that were reworked since I_1 errors were found *and other design changes* made.)

2. *Preparation* (individual) — Participants, using the design documentation, literally do their homework to try to understand the design, its intent and logic. (Sometimes flagrant errors are found during this operation, but in general, the number of errors found is not nearly as high as in the inspection operation.) To increase their error detection in the inspection, the inspection team should first study the ranked distributions of error types found by recent inspections. This study will prompt them to concentrate on the most fruitful areas. (See examples in Figures 3 and 4.) Checklists of clues on finding these errors should also be studied. (See partial examples of these lists in Figures 5 and 6 and complete examples for I_0 in Reference 1 and for I_1 and I_2 in Reference 7.)

3. *Inspection* (whole team) — A "reader" chosen by the moderator (usually the coder) describes how he will implement the design. He is expected to paraphrase the design as expressed by the designer. Every piece of logic is covered at least once, and every branch is taken at least once. All higher-level documentation, high-level design specifications, logic specifications, etc., and macro and control block listings at I_2 must be available and present during the inspection.

Now that the design is understood, *the objective is to find errors*. (Note that an error is defined as any condition that causes malfunction or that precludes the attainment of expected or previously specified results. Thus, deviations from specifications are clearly termed errors.) The finding of errors is actually done during the implementor/coder's discourse. Questions raised are pursued only to the point at which an error is recognized. It is noted by the moderator; its type is classified; severity (major or minor) is identified, and the inspection is continued. Often the solution of a problem is obvious. If so, it is noted, but no specific solution hunting is to take place during inspection. (The inspection is *not* intended to redesign, evaluate alternate design solutions, or to find solutions to errors; it is intended just to find errors!) A team is most effective if it operates with only one objective at a time.

Within one day of conclusion of the inspection, the moderator should produce a written report of the inspection and its findings to ensure that all issues raised in the inspection will be addressed in the rework and follow-up operations. Examples of these reports are given as Figures 7A, 7B, and 7C.

Figure 5 Examples of what to examine when looking for errors at I_1

I_1 Logic
  Missing
  1. Are All Constants Defined?
  2. Are All Unique Values Explicitly Tested on Input Parameters?
  3. Are Values Stored after They Are Calculated?
  4. Are All Defaults Checked Explicitly Tested on Input Parameters?
  5. If Character Strings Are Created Are They Complete, Are All Delimiters Shown?
  6. If a Keyword Has Many Unique Values, Are They All Checked?
  7. If a Queue Is Being Manipulated, Can the Execution Be Interrupted; If So, Is Queue Protected by a Locking Structure; Can Queue Be Destroyed Over an Interrupt?
  8. Are Registers Being Restored on Exits?
  9. In Queuing/Dequeuing Should Any Value Be Decremented/Incremented?
  10. Are All Keywords Tested in Macro?
  11. Are All Keyword Related Parameters Tested in Service Routine?
  12. Are Queues Being Held in Isolation So That Subsequent Interrupting Requestors Are Receiving Spurious Returns Regarding the Held Queue?
  13. Should any Registers Be Saved on Entry?
  14. Are All Increment Counts Properly Initialized (0 or 1)?
  Wrong
  1. Are Absolutes Shown Where There Should Be Symbolics?
  2. On Comparison of Two Bytes, Should All Bits Be Compared?
  3. On Built Data Strings, Should They Be Character or Hex?
  4. Are Internal Variables Unique or Confusing If Concatenated?
  Extra
  1. Are All Blocks Shown in Design Necessary or Are They Extraneous?

4. *Rework* — All errors or problems noted in the inspection report are resolved by the designer or coder/implementor.

5. *Follow-Up* — It is imperative that every issue, concern, and error be entirely resolved at this level, or errors that result can be 10 to 100 times more expensive to fix if found later in the process (programmer time only, machine time not included). It is the responsibility of the moderator to see that all issues, problems, and concerns discovered in the inspection operation have been resolved by the designer in the case of I_1, or the coder/implementor for I_2 inspections. If more than five percent of the material has been reworked, the team should reconvene and carry out a 100 percent reinspection. Where less than five percent of the material has been reworked, the moderator at his discretion may verify the quality of the rework himself or reconvene the team to reinspect either the complete work or just the rework.

commencing inspections

In Operation 3 above, it is one thing to direct people to find errors in design or code. It is quite another problem for them to find errors. Numerous experiences have shown that people have to be taught or prompted to find errors effectively. Therefore, it

Figure 6 Examples of what to examine when looking for errors at I_2

INSPECTION SPECIFICATION

I_2 *Test Branch*
　Is Correct Condition Tested (If X = ON vs. IF X = OFF)?
　Is (Are) Correct Variable(s) Used for Test
　(If X = ON vs. If Y = ON)?
　Are Null THENs/ELSEs Included as Appropriate?
　Is Each Branch Target Correct?
　Is the Most Frequently Exercised Test Leg the THEN Clause?

I_2 *Interconnection (or Linkage) Calls*
　For Each Interconnection Call to Either a Macro, SVC or Another Module:
　Are All Required Parameters Passed Set Correctly?
　If Register Parameters Are Used, Is the Correct Register Number Specified?
　If Interconnection Is a Macro,
　Does the Inline Expansion Contain All Required Code?
　No Register or Storage Conflicts between Macro and Calling Module?
　If the Interconnection Returns, Do All Returned Parameters Get Processed Correctly?

is prudent to condition them to seek the high-occurrence, high-cost error types (see example in Figures 3 and 4), and then describe the clues that usually betray the presence of each error type (see examples in Figures 5 and 6).

One approach to getting started may be to make a preliminary inspection of a design or code that is felt to be representative of the program to be inspected. Obtain a suitable quantity of errors, and analyze them by type and origin, cause, and salient indicative clues. With this information, an inspection specification may be constructed. This specification can be amended and improved in light of new experience and serve as an on-going directive to focus the attention and conduct of inspection teams. The objective of an inspection specification is to help maximize and make more consistent the error detection efficiency of inspections where

Error detection efficiency

$$= \frac{\text{Errors found by an inspection}}{\text{Total errors in the product before inspection}} \times 100$$

The reporting forms and form completion instructions shown in the Appendix may be used for I_1 and I_2 inspections. Although these forms were constructed for use in systems programming development, they may be used for applications programming development with minor modification to suit particular environments.

reporting inspection results

The moderator will make hand-written notes recording errors found during inspection meetings. He will categorize the errors

Figure 7A Error list

1. PR/M/MIN   Line 3: the statement of the prologue in the REMARKS section needs expansion.
2. DA/W/MAJ   Line 123: ERR–RECORD–TYPE is out of sequence.
3. PU/W/MAJ   Line 147: the wrong bytes of an 8-byte field (current–data) are moved into the 2-byte field (this year).
4. LO/W/MAJ   Line 169: while counting the number of leading spaces in NAME, the wrong variable (I) is used to calculate "J".
5. LO/W/MAJ   Line 172: NAME–CHECK is PERFORMED one time too few.
6. PU/E/MIN   Line 175: In NAME–CHECK, the check for SPACE is redundant.
7. DE/W/MIN   Line 175: the design should allow for the occurrence of a period in a last name.

Figure 7B Example of module detail report

DATE_____

CODE INSPECTION REPORT
MODULE DETAIL

MOD/MAC: __CHECKER_____ SUBCOMPONENT/APPLICATION_____

SEE NOTE BELOW

PROBLEM TYPE:	MAJOR*			MINOR		
	M	W	E	M	W	E
LO: LOGIC		9			1	
TB: TEST AND BRANCH						
EL: EXTERNAL LINKAGES						
RU: REGISTER USAGE						
SU: STORAGE USAGE						
DA: DATA AREA USAGE		2				
PU: PROGRAM LANGUAGE		2				1
PE: PERFORMANCE						
MN: MAINTAINABILITY					1	
DE: DESIGN ERROR					1	
PR: PROLOGUE				1		
CC: CODE COMMENTS						
OT: OTHER						
TOTAL:		13			5	

REINSPECTION REQUIRED? __Y__

*A PROBLEM WHICH WOULD CAUSE THE PROGRAM TO MALFUNCTION: A BUG. M = MISSING, W = WRONG, E = EXTRA.
NOTE: FOR MODIFIED MODULES, PROBLEMS IN THE CHANGED PORTION VERSUS PROBLEMS IN THE BASE SHOULD BE SHOWN IN THIS MANNER 3(2), WHERE 3 IS THE NUMBER OF PROBLEMS IN THE CHANGED PORTION AND 2 IS THE NUMBER OF PROBLEMS IN THE BASE

and then transcribe counts of the errors, by type, to the module detail form. By maintaining cumulative totals of the counts by error type, and dividing by the number of projected executable source lines of code inspected to date, he will be able to establish installation averages within a short time.

Figures 7A, 7B, and 7C are an example of a set of code inspection reports. Figure 7A is a partial list of errors found in code inspection. Notice that errors are described in detail and are classified by error type, whether due to something being missing,

Figure 7C Example of code inspection summary report

						ELOC Added, Modified, Deleted									Inspection People-hours (X.X)				
Mod Mac Name	New or Mod	Full or Part Insp.	Programmer	Tester		Pre-insp			Est Post			Rework			Prep	Insp Meetg	Re-work	Follow-up	Sub-component
					A	M	D	A	M	D	A	M	D					
	N		McGINLEY	HALE	348				400			50			9.0	8.8	8.0	1.5	
				Totals															

CODE INSPECTION REPORT SUMMARY Date 11/20/-
To: Design Manager KRAUSS Development Manager GIOTTI
Subject: Inspection Report for CHECKER Inspection date 11/19/-
System Application _____ Release _____ Build _____
Component _____ Subcomponents(s) _____

Reinspection required? YES Length of inspection (clock hours and tenths) 2.2
Reinspection by (date) 11/25/- Additional modules/macros? NO
DCR ='s written C-2
Problem summary: Major 13 Minor 5 Total 18
Errors in changed code: Major ___ Minor ___ Errors in base code: Major ___ Minor ___
LARSON   McGINLEY   HALE
Initial Desr   Detailed Dr   Programmer   Team Leader   Other   Moderator's Signature

wrong, or extra as the cause, and according to major or minor severity. Figure 7B is a module level summary of the errors contained in the entire error list represented by Figure 7A. The code inspection summary report in Figure 7C is a summary of inspection results obtained on all modules inspected in a particular inspection session or in a subcomponent or application.

inspections and languages

Inspections have been successfully applied to designs that are specified in English prose, flowcharts, HIPO, (Hierarchy plus Input-Process-Output) and PIDGEON (an English prose-like meta language).

The first code inspections were conducted on PL/S and Assembler. Now, prompting checklists for inspections of Assembler, COBOL, FORTRAN, and PL/I code are available.[7]

personnel considerations

One of the most significant benefits of inspections is the detailed feedback of results on a relatively real-time basis. The programmer finds out what error types he is most prone to make and their quantity and how to find them. This feedback takes place within a few days of writing the program. Because he gets early indications from the first few units of his work inspected, he is able to show improvement, and usually does, on later work even during the same project. In this way, feedback of results from inspections must be counted for the programmer's use and benefit: *they should not under any circumstances be used for programmer performance appraisal.*

Skeptics may argue that once inspection results are obtained, they will or even must count in performance appraisals, or at

Figure 8 Example of most error-prone modules based on I_1 and I_2

Module name	Number of errors	Lines of code	Error density, Errors/K. Loc
Echo	4	128	31
Zulu	10	323	31
Foxtrot	3	71	28
Alpha	7	264	27 ←Average
Lima	2	106	19 Error
Delta	3	195	15 Rate
.	.	.	.
	67		

least cause strong bias in the appraisal process. The author can offer in response that inspections have been conducted over the past three years involving diverse projects and locations, hundreds of experienced programmers and tens of managers, and so far he has found no case in which inspection results have been used negatively against programmers. Evidently no manager has tried to "kill the goose that lays the golden eggs."

A preinspection opinion of some programmers is that they do not see the value of inspections because they have managed very well up to now, or because their projects are too small or somehow different. This opinion usually changes after a few inspections to a position of acceptance. The quality of acceptance is related to the success of the inspections they have experienced, the *conduct of the trained moderator*, and the *attitude demonstrated by management*. The acceptance of inspections by programmers and managers as a beneficial step in making programs is well-established amongst those who have tried them.

Process control using inspection and testing results

Obviously, the range of analysis possible using inspection results is enormous. Therefore, only a few aspects will be treated here, and they are elementary expositions.

most error-prone modules A listing of either I_1, I_2, or combined $I_1 + I_2$ data as in Figure 8 immediately highlights which modules contained the highest error density on inspection. If the error detection efficiency of each of the inspections was fairly constant, the ranking of error-prone modules holds. Thus if the error detection efficiency of inspection is 50 percent, and the inspection found 10 errors in a

Figure 9 Example of distribution of error types

	Number of errors	%	Normal/usual distribution, %
Logic	23	35	44
Interconnection/Linkage (Internal)	21	31 ?	18
Control Blocks	6	9	13
—	.	8	10
—	.	7	7
—	.	6	6
—	.	4	2
		100%	100%

module, then it can be estimated that there are 10 errors remaining in the module. This information can prompt many actions to control the process. For instance, in Figure 8, it may be decided to reinspect module "Echo" or to redesign and recode it entirely. Or, less drastically, it may be decided to test it "harder" than other modules and look especially for errors of the type found in the inspections.

If a ranked distribution of error types is obtained for a group of "error-prone modules" (Figure 9), which were produced from the same Process A, for example, it is a short step to comparing this distribution with a "Normal/Usual Percentage Distribution." Large disparities between the sample and "standard" will lead to questions on why Process A, say, yields nearly twice as many internal interconnection errors as the "standard" process. If this analysis is done promptly on the first five percent of production, it may be possible to remedy the problem (if it is a problem) on the remaining 95 percent of modules for a particular shipment. Provision can be made to test the first five percent of the modules to remove the unusually high incidence of internal interconnection problems.

distribution of error types

Analysis of the testing results, commencing as soon as testing errors are evident, is a vital step in controlling the process since future testing can be guided by early results.

inspecting error-prone code

Where testing reveals excessively error-prone code, it may be more economical and saving of schedule to select the most error-prone code and inspect it before continuing testing. (The business case will likely differ from project to project and case to case, but in many instances inspection will be indicated). The selection of the most error-prone code may be made with two considerations uppermost:

Table 4. Inspection and walk-through processes and objectives

Inspection		Walk-through	
Process Operations	Objectives	Process Operations	Objectives
1. Overview	Education (Group)	–	–
2. Preparation	Education (Individual)	1. Preparation	Education (Individual)
3. Inspection	Find errors! (Group)	2. Walk-through	Education (Group) Discuss design alternatives Find errors
4. Rework	Fix problems	–	
5. Follow-up	Ensure all fixes correctly installed	–	

Note the separation of objectives in the inspection process.

Table 5 Comparison of key properties of inspections and walk-throughs

Properties	Inspection	Walk-Through
1. Formal moderator training	Yes	No
2. Definite participant roles	Yes	No
3. Who "drives" the inspection or walk-through	Moderator	Owner of material (Designer or coder)
4. Use "How To Find Errors" checklists	Yes	No
5. Use distribution of error types to look for	Yes	No
6. Follow-up to reduce bad fixes	Yes	No
7. Less future errors because of detailed error feedback to individual programmer	Yes	Incidental
8. Improve Inspection efficiency from analysis of results	Yes	No
9. Analysis of data → process problems → improvements	Yes	No

1. Which modules head a ranked list when the modules are rated by test errors per K.NCSS?
2. In the parts of the program in which test coverage is low, which modules or parts of modules are most suspect based on $(I_1 + I_2)$ errors per K.NCSS and programmer judgment?

From a condensed table of ranked "most error-prone" modules, a selection of modules to be inspected (or reinspected) may be made. Knowledge of the error types already found in these modules will better prepare an inspection team.

The reinspection itself should conform with the I_2 process, except that an overview may be necessary if the original overview was held too long ago or if new project members are involved.

Inspections and walk-throughs

Walk-throughs (or walk-thrus) are practiced in many different ways in different places, with varying regularity and thoroughness. This inconsistency causes the results of walk-throughs to vary widely and to be nonrepeatable. Inspections, however, having an established process and a formal procedure, tend to vary less and produce more repeatable results. Because of the variation in walk-throughs, a comparison between them and inspections is not simple. However, from Reference 8 and the walk-through procedures witnessed by the author and described to him by walk-through participants, as well as the inspection process described previously and in References 1 and 9, the comparison in Tables 4 and 5 is drawn.

Figure 10A describes the process in which a walk-through is applied. Clearly, the purging of errors from the product as it passes through the walk-through between Operations 1 and 2 is very beneficial to the product. In Figure 10B, the inspection process (and its feedback, feed-forward, and self-improvement) replaces the walk-through. The notes on the figure are self-explanatory.

effects on development process

Inspections are also an excellent means of measuring completeness of work against the exit criteria which must be satisfied to complete project checkpoints. (Each checkpoint should have a clearly defined set of exit criteria. Without exit criteria, a checkpoint is too negotiable to be useful for process control).

Inspections and process management

The most marked effects of inspections on the development process is to change the old adage that, "design is not complete until testing is completed," to a position where a very great deal must be known about the design before even the coding is begun. Although great discretion is still required in code implementation, more predictability and improvements in schedule, cost, and quality accrue. The old adage still holds true if one regards inspection as much a means of verification as testing.

Observations in one case in systems programming show that approximately two thirds of all errors reported during development are found by I_1 and I_2 inspections prior to machine testing.

percent of errors found

Figure 10 (A) Walk-through process, (B) Inspection process

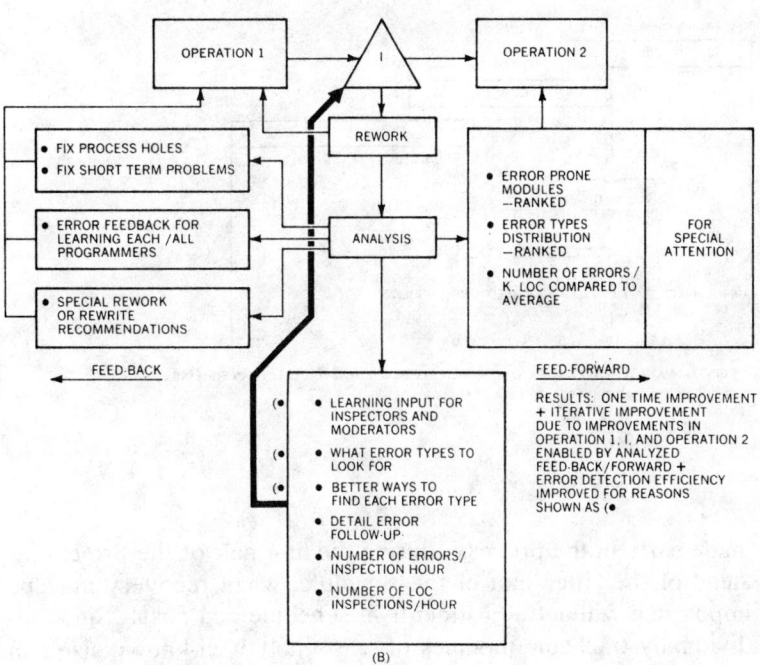

The error detection efficiencies of the I_1 and I_2 inspections separately are, of course, less than 66 percent. A similar observation of an application program development indicated an 82 percent find (Table 1). As more is learned and the error detection efficiency of inspection is increased, the burden of debugging on testing operations will be reduced, and testing will be more able to fulfill its prime objective of verifying quality.

effect on cost and schedule

Comparing the "old" and "new" (with inspections) approaches to process management in Figure 11, we can see clearly that with the use of inspection results, error rework (which is a very significant variable in product cost) tends to be managed more during the first half of the schedule. This results in much lower cost than in the "old" approach, where the cost of error rework was 10 to 100 times higher and was accomplished in large part during the last half of the schedule.

process tracking

Inserting the I_1 and I_2 checkpoints in the development process enables assessment of project completeness and quality to be

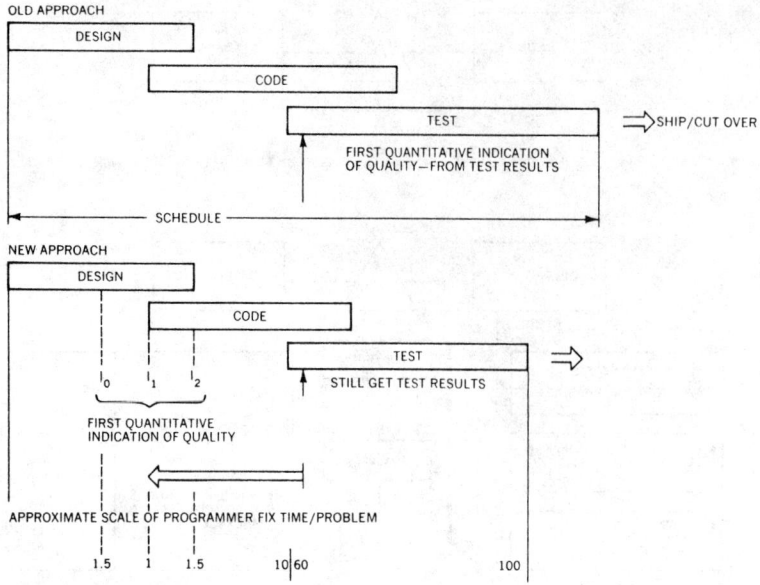

Figure 11 Effect of inspection on process management

made early in the process (during the first half of the project instead of the latter half of the schedule, when recovery may be impossible without adjustments in schedule and cost). Since individually trackable modules of reasonably well-known size can be counted as they pass through each of these checkpoints, the percentage completion of the project against schedule can be continuously and easily tracked.

The overview, preparation, and inspection sequence of the operations of the inspection process give the inspection participants a high degree of product knowledge in a very short time. This important side benefit results in the participants being able to handle later development and testing with more certainty and less false starts. Naturally, this also contributes to productivity improvement.

effect on product knowledge

An interesting sidelight is that because designers are asked at pre-I_1 inspection time for estimates of the number of lines of code (NCSS) that their designs will create, and they are present to count for themselves the actual lines of code at the I_2 inspection, the accuracy of design estimates has shown substantial improvement.

For this reason, an inspection is frequently a required event where responsibility for design or code is being transferred from one programmer to another. The complete inspection team is convened for such an inspection. (One-on-one reviews such as desk debugging are certainly worthwhile but do not approach the effectiveness of formal inspection.) Usually the side benefit of finding errors more than justifies the transfer inspection.

inspecting modified code

Code that is changed in, or inserted in, an existing module either in replacement of deleted code or simply inserted in the module is considered modified code. By this definition, a very large part of programming effort is devoted to modifying code. (The addition of entirely new modules to a system count as new, not modified, code.)

Some observations of errors per K.NCSS of modified code show its error rate to be considerably higher than is found in new code; (i.e., if 10.NCSS are replaced in a 100.NCSS module and errors against the 10.NCSS are counted, the error rate is described as number of errors per 10.NCSS, not number of errors per 100.NCSS). Obviously, if the number of errors in modified code are used to derive an error rate per K.NCSS for the whole module that was modified, this rate would be largely dependent upon the percentage of the module that is modified: this would provide a meaningless ratio. A useful measure is the number of errors per K.NCSS (modified) in which the higher error rates have been observed.

Since most modifications are small (e.g., 1 to 25 instructions), they are often erroneously regarded as trivially simple and are handled accordingly; the error rate goes up, and control is lost. In the author's experience, *all* modifications are well worth inspecting from an economic and a quality standpoint. A convenient method of handling changes is to group them to a module or set of modules and convene the inspection team to inspect as many changes as possible. But all changes must be inspected!

Inspections of modifications can range from inspecting the modified instructions and the surrounding instructions connecting it with its host module, to an inspection of the entire module. The choice of extent of inspection coverage is dependent upon the percentage of modification, pervasiveness of the modification, etc.

bad fixes

A very serious problem is the inclusion in the product of bad fixes. Human tendency is to consider the "fix," or correction, to a problem to be error-free itself. Unfortunately, this is all too frequently untrue in the case of fixes to errors found by inspections and by testing. The inspection process clearly has an operation called Follow-Up to try and minimize the bad-fix problem, but the fix process of testing errors very rarely requires scrutiny of fix quality before the fix is inserted. Then, if the fix is bad, the whole elaborate process of going from source fix to link edit, to test the fix, to regression test must be repeated at needlessly high cost. The number of bad fixes can be economically reduced by some simple inspection after clean compilation of the fix.

Summary

We can summarize the discussion of design and code inspections and process control in developing programs as follows:

1. Describe the program development process in terms of operations, and define exit criteria which must be satisfied for completion of each operation.
2. Separate the objectives of the inspection process operations to keep the inspection team focused on one objective at a time:

Operation	*Objective*
Overview	Communications/education
Preparation	Education
Inspection	Find errors
Rework	Fix errors
Follow-up	Ensure all fixes are applied correctly

3. Classify errors by type, and rank frequency of occurrence of types. Identify *which types* to spend most time looking for in the inspection.
4. Describe *how* to look for presence of error types.
5. Analyze inspection results and use for constant process improvement (until process averages are reached and then use for process control).

Some applications of inspections include function level inspections I_0, design-complete inspections I_1, code inspections I_2, test plan inspections IT_1, test case inspections IT_2, interconnections inspections IF, inspection of fixes/changes, inspection of publications, etc., and post testing inspection. Inspections can be applied to the development of system control programs, applications programs, and microcode in hardware.

We can conclude from experience that inspections increase productivity and improve final program quality. Furthermore, improvements in process control and project management are enabled by inspections.

ACKNOWLEDGMENTS
The author acknowledges, with thanks, the work of Mr. O. R. Kohli and Mr. R. A. Radice, who made considerable contributions in the development of inspection techniques applied to program design and code, and Mr. R. R. Larson, who adapted inspections to program testing.

Figure 12 Design inspection module detail form

```
                                                              DATE_____
                       DETAILED DESIGN INSPECTION REPORT
                                MODULE DETAIL
MOD/MAC:_____ SUBCOMPONENT/APPLICATION_____
                                             SEE NOTE BELOW
```

	MAJOR*			MINOR		
PROBLEM TYPE:	M	W	E	M	W	E
LO: LOGIC						
TB: TEST AND BRANCH						
DA: DATA AREA USAGE						
RM: RETURN CODES/MESSAGES						
RU: REGISTER USAGE						
MA: MODULE ATTRIBUTES						
EL: EXTERNAL LINKAGES						
MD: MORE DETAIL						
ST: STANDARDS						
PR: PROLOGUE OR PROSE						
HL: HIGHER LEVEL DESIGN DOC.						
US: USER SPEC.						
MN: MAINTAINABILITY						
PE: PERFORMANCE						
OT: OTHER						
TOTAL:						

REINSPECTION REQUIRED?_____

*A PROBLEM WHICH WOULD CAUSE THE PROGRAM TO MALFUNCTION: A BUG. M = MISSING, W = WRONG, E = EXTRA
NOTE: FOR MODIFIED MODULES, PROBLEMS IN THE CHANGED PORTION VERSUS PROBLEMS IN THE BASE SHOULD BE SHOWN IN THIS MANNER: 3(2), WHERE 3 IS THE NUMBER OF PROBLEMS IN THE CHANGED PORTION AND 2 IS THE NUMBER OF PROBLEMS IN THE BASE.

CITED REFERENCES AND FOOTNOTES

1. O. R. Kohli, *High-Level Design Inspection Specification*, Technical Report TR 21.601, IBM Corporation, Kingston, New York (July 21, 1975).
2. It should be noted that the exit criteria for I_1 (design complete where one design statement is estimated to represent 3 to 10 code instructions) and I_2 (first clean code compilations) are checkpoints in the development process through which every programming project must pass.
3. The Hawthorne Effect is a psychological phenomenon usually experienced in human-involved productivity studies. The effect is manifested by participants producing above normal because they know they are being studied.
4. NCSS (Non-Commentary Source Statements), also referred to as "Lines of Code," are the sum of executable code instructions and declaratives. Instructions that invoke macros are counted once only. Expanded macroinstructions are also counted only once. Comments are not included.
5. Basically in a walk-through, program design or code is reviewed by a group of people gathered together at a structured meeting in which errors/issues pertaining to the material and proposed by the participants may be discussed in an effort to find errors. The group may consist of various participants but always includes the originator of the material being reviewed who usually plans the meeting and is responsible for correcting the errors. How it differs from an inspection is pointed out in Tables 2 and 3.
6. *Marketing Newsletter*, Cross Application Systems Marketing, "Program inspections at Aetna," MS-76-006, S2, IBM Corporation, Data Processing Division, White Plains, New York (March 29, 1976).

7. J. Ascoly, M. J. Cafferty, S. J. Gruen, and O. R. Kohli, *Code Inspection Specification*, Technical Report TR 21.630, IBM Corporation, Kingston, New York (1976).
8. N. S. Waldstein, *The Walk-Thru—A Method of Specification, Design and Review*, Technical Report TR 00.2536, IBM Corporation, Poughkeepsie, New York (June 4, 1974).
9. Independent study programs: *IBM Structured Programming Textbook*, SR20-7149-1, *IBM Structured Programming Workbook*, SR20-7150-0, IBM Corporation, Data Processing Division, White Plains, New York.

GENERAL REFERENCES

1. J. D. Aron, *The Program Development Process: Part 1: The Individual Programmer*, Structured Programs, 137–141, Addison-Wesley Publishing Co., Reading, Massachusetts (1974).
2. M. E. Fagan, *Design and Code Inspections and Process Control in the Development of Programs*, Technical Report TR 00.2763, IBM Corporation, Poughkeepsie, New York (June 10, 1976). This report is a revision of the author's *Design and Code Inspections and Process Control in the Development of Programs*, Technical Report TR 21.572, IBM Corporation, Kingston, New York (December 17, 1974).
3. O. R. Kohli and R. A. Radice, *Low-Level Design Inspection Specification*, Technical Report TR 21.629, IBM Corporation, Kingston, New York (1976).
4. R. R. Larson, *Test Plan and Test Case Inspection Specifications*, Technical Report TR 21.586, IBM Corporation, Kingston, New York (April 4, 1975).

Appendix: Reporting forms and form completion instructions

Instructions for Completing Design Inspection Module Detail Form

This form (Figure 12) should be completed for each module/macro that has valid problems against it. The problem-type information gathered in this report is important because a history of problem-type experience points out high-occurrence types. This knowledge can then be conveyed to inspectors so that they can concentrate on seeking the higher-occurrence types of problems.

1. MOD/MAC: The module or macro name.
2. SUBCOMPONENT: The associated subcomponent.
3. PROBLEM TYPE: Summarize the number of problems by type (logic, etc.), severity (major/minor), and by category (missing, wrong, or extra). For modified modules, detail the number of problems in the changed design versus the number in the base design. (Problem types were developed in a systems programming environment. Appropriate changes, if desired, could be made for application development.)

Figure 13 Design inspection summary form

DESIGN INSPECTION REPORT
SUMMARY

Date ______

To: Design Manager ______ Development Manager ______
Subject: Inspection Report for ______ Inspection date ______
System Application ______ Release ______ Build ______
Component ______ Subcomponents(s) ______

Mod/Mac Name	New or Mod	Full or Part Insp.	Detailed Designer	Programmer	ELOC Added, Modified, Deleted									Inspection People-hours (X.X.)				Sub-component
					Est. Pre			Est. Post			Rework			Over-view & Prep.	Insp Meetg	Re-work	Follow-up	
					A	M	D	A	M	D	A	M	D					
				Totals														

Reinspection required? ______ Length of inspection (clock hours and tenths) ______
Reinspection by (date) ______ Additional modules/macros? ______
DCR #'s written ______
Problem summary: Major ______ Minor ______ Total ______
Errors in changed code: Major ______ Minor ______ Errors in base code: Major ______ Minor ______

Initial Desr ______ Detailed Dr ______ Programmer ______ Team Leader ______ Other ______ Moderator's Signature ______

4. REINSPECTION REQUIRED?: Indicate whether the module/macro requires a reinspection.

All valid problems found in the inspection should be listed and attached to the report. A brief description of each problem, its error type, and the rework time to fix it should be given (see Figure 7A, which describes errors in similar detail to that required but is at a coding level).

Instructions for Completing Design Inspection Summary Form

Following are detailed instructions for completing the form in Figure 13.

1. TO: The report is addressed to the respective design and development managers.
2. SUBJECT: The unit being inspected is identified.
3. MOD/MAC NAME: The name of each module and macro as it resides on the source library.
4. NEW OR MOD: "N" if the module is new; "M" if the module is modified.
5. FULL OR PART INSP: If the module/macro is "modified," indicate "F" if the module/macro was fully inspected or "P" if partially inspected.
6. DETAILED DESIGNER: and PROGRAMMER: Identification of originators.
7. PRE-INSP EST ELOC: The estimated executable source lines of code (added, modified, deleted). Estimate made prior to the inspection by the designer.

Figure 14 Code inspection module detail form

DATE_____

CODE INSPECTION REPORT

MODULE DETAIL

MOD/MAC:_____ SUBCOMPONENT/APPLICATION_____

SEE NOTE BELOW

PROBLEM TYPE:	MAJOR*			MINOR		
	M	W	E	M	W	E
LO: LOGIC						
TB: TEST AND BRANCH						
EL: EXTERNAL LINKAGES						
RU: REGISTER USAGE						
SU: STORAGE USAGE						
DA: DATA AREA USAGE						
PU: PROGRAM LANGUAGE						
PE: PERFORMANCE						
MN: MAINTAINABILITY						
DE: DESIGN ERROR						
PR: PROLOGUE						
CC: CODE COMMENTS						
OT: OTHER						
TOTAL:						

REINSPECTION REQUIRED?_____

*A PROBLEM WHICH WOULD CAUSE THE PROGRAM TO MALFUNCTION: A BUG. M = MISSING, W = WRONG, E = EXTRA.
NOTE: FOR MODIFIED MODULES, PROBLEMS IN THE CHANGED PORTION VERSUS PROBLEMS IN THE BASE SHOULD BE SHOWN IN THIS MANNER: 3(2), WHERE 3 IS THE NUMBER OF PROBLEMS IN THE CHANGED PORTION AND 2 IS THE NUMBER OF PROBLEMS IN THE BASE.

8. POST-INSP EST ELOC: The estimated executable source lines of code. Estimate made after the inspection.
9. REWORK ELOC: The estimated executable source lines of code in rework as a result of the inspection.
10. OVERVIEW AND PREP: The number of people-hours (in tenths of hours) spent in preparing for the overview, in the overview meeting itself, and in preparing for the inspection meeting.
11. INSPECTION MEETING: The number of people-hours spent on the inspection meeting.
12. REWORK: The estimated number of people-hours spent to fix the problems found during the inspection.
13. FOLLOW-UP: The estimated number of people-hours spent by the moderator (and others if necessary) in verifying the correctness of changes made by the author as a result of the inspection.
14. SUBCOMPONENT: The subcomponent of which the module/macro is a part.
15. REINSPECTION REQUIRED?: Yes or no.
16. LENGTH OF INSPECTION: Clock hours spent in the inspection meeting.
17. REINSPECTION BY (DATE): Latest acceptable date for reinspection.

Figure 15 Code inspection summary form

CODE INSPECTION REPORT
SUMMARY

Date________

To: Design Manager________ Development Manager________

Subject: Inspection Report for________ Inspection date________

System/Application________ Release________ Build________

Component________ Subcomponents(s)________

					ELOC Added, Modified, Deleted									Inspection People-hours (X.X)				
					Pre-insp			Est Post			Rework							
Mod/Mac Name	New or Mod	Full or Part Insp.	Programmer	Tester	A	M	D	A	M	D	A	M	D	Prep	Insp Meetg	Re-work	Follow-up	Sub-component
				Totals														

Reinspection required?________ Length of inspection (clock hours and tenths)________

Reinspection by (date)________ Additional modules/macros?________

DCR #'s written________

Problem summary: Major________ Minor________ Total________

Errors in changed code: Major____ Minor____ Errors in base code: Major____ Minor________

Initial Desr — Detailed Dr — Programmer — Team Leader — Other — Moderator's Signature

18. ADDITIONAL MODULES/MACROS?: For these subcomponents, are additional modules/macros yet to be inspected?
19. DCR #'S WRITTEN: The identification of Design Change Requests, DCR(s), written to cover problems in rework.
20. PROBLEM SUMMARY: Totals taken from Module Detail forms(s).
21. INITIAL DESIGNER, DETAILED DESIGNER, etc.: Identification of members of the inspection team.

Instructions for Completing Code Inspection Module Detail Form

This form (Figure 14) should be completed according to the instructions for completing the design inspection module detail form.

Instructions for Completing Code Inspection Summary Form

This form (Figure 15) should be completed according to the instructions for the design inspection summary form except for the following items.

1. PROGRAMMER AND TESTER: Identifications of original participants involved with code.
2. PRE-INSP. ELOC: The noncommentary source lines of code (added, modified, deleted). Count made prior to the inspection by the programmer.
3. POST-INSP EST ELOC: The estimated noncommentary source lines of code. Estimate made after the inspection.

4. REWORK ELOC: The estimated noncommentary source lines of code in rework as a result of the inspection.
5. PREP: The number of people hours (in tenths of hours) spent in preparing for the inspection meeting.

DAVE—A Validation Error Detection and Documentation System for Fortran Programs*

LEON J. OSTERWEIL AND LLOYD D. FOSDICK

Department of Computer Science, University of Colorado, Boulder, Colorado, U.S.A.

SUMMARY

This paper describes DAVE, a system for analysing Fortran programs. DAVE is capable of detecting the symptoms of a wide variety of errors in programs, as well as assuring the absence of these errors. In addition, DAVE exposes and documents subtle data relations and flows within programs. The central analytic procedure used is a depth first search. DAVE itself is written in Fortran. Its implementation at the University of Colorado and some early experience are described.

KEY WORDS   Program testing   Data flow analysis   Software validation   Automated documentation   Debugging

INTRODUCTION

This paper describes an operational system to improve software reliability. It is designed to examine a program and report the presence, possible presence or complete absence of a significant class of programming errors. We call it and other systems designed primarily for this purpose *software validation systems*. Other approaches to software reliability using the computer as a primary instrument are verification or proof of correctness,[1] debugging[2] and dynamic testing.[3] Falling in a different category are those approaches which deal with communication between humans and machines. Here are included language design,[4] top down systems design[5] and step-wise refinement.[6] Finally, there are those approaches which deal with the organization and management of the people who construct software.[7] Each of these approaches is important and most need much more development. Although significant problems remain in designing validation systems, the work described here shows that it is currently possible to build validation systems capable of aiding programmers engaged in actual software construction.

Data flow analysis is the primary methodology in our approach to software validation. We use it to reveal suspicious or erroneous use of data. Others have used data flow analysis to study machine design,[8] and for global optimization of computer programs,[9] but it has seen little use as a tool in software validation. Since it provides information about the use of variables in a program it is also an important tool in automatic program documentation.

Our system, called DAVE, is characterized by the following features.

1. It performs an exhaustive search for data flow anomalies in time which is linearly proportional to the product of the number of edges in the flow graph and the number of program variables.

---

* Supported in part by NSF Grants GJ-36461 and DCR-75-09972.

Received 2 July 1975
Revised 18 November 1975

© 1976 by John Wiley & Sons, Ltd.

2. It applies to programs written in ANSI Fortran, and can be modified to apply to other languages.
3. It employs a static analysis of the program; i.e. it avoids executing the program.
4. It classifies the usage of all local and global variables.
5. It applies to an entire program or to selected parts of a program.
6. It is written in Fortran, and is designed for ease of portability.

DEFINITIONS AND EXAMPLES OF DATA FLOW ANOMALIES

In data flow analysis attention is directed at the sequential pattern of definitions, references and undefinitions of values for variables. The actual values assigned or referenced are ignored, only the fact that an assignment, reference or undefinition was made is used. Two rules concerning the sequence of these events along each path from the start of a program to a stop are expected to be obeyed.

1. A reference must be preceded by an assignment, without an intervening undefinition.
2. A definition must be followed by a reference, before another definition or undefinition.

Violation of the first rule should cause an erroneous result during program execution; moreover, in the case of Fortran it is a violation of the ANSI Standard[10] (Section 10.3). Violation of the second rule should result in a waste of time, but not an erroneous result.

Many things can cause a violation of either or both rules. Forgetting to initialize a variable is the most obvious cause of a violation of the first rule. However, spelling errors, confusion of names, misplaced statements and faulty subprogram references also cause violations of this rule. The second rule may be violated when a programmer forgets that a variable is already defined or that it will not be used later. Many optimizing compilers remove this 'dead' variable assignment, assuming these to be the only causes. However, many common errors also cause violations of the second rule. We call violations of the two rules anomalies 'type 1' and 'type 2' respectively.

Figure 1 is a simple illustration of how anomalies can arise in a program segment. A linear scan of the program text will detect the type 1 anomaly and some compilers (e.g. MNF[11], WATFOR[12] and G. E. Time Sharing[13]) detect this condition by performing such a scan. Many compilers enable detection of this condition during execution by initializing each variable to some distinguished value. In more complex cases both approaches prove unsatisfactory. Consider the example in Figure 2. Here, as in Figure 1, a misspelling of PI (or P) is present, but now it is far less apparent. A simple linear scan stands no chance of detecting the anomaly, and any execution of DOLS for which the second argument is not equal to 2 will not cause it to be detected during execution.

```
          PI = 3.1416
          READ(5, 100) X
          AREA = P*X**2
          WRITE(6, 100) AREA
          STOP
100       FORMAT(E12.4)
          END
```

Figure 1. A program containing a type 1 anomaly (the variable P is referenced before definition) and a type 2 anomaly (the variable PI is defined but never referenced afterwards). The programmer probably intended P to be PI, or conversely

```
            SUBROUTINE DOLS(PSF, LCRT, D1, D2, COST)
            PI = 3.1416
            IF(LCRT.NE.1) GO TO 10
            COST = PSF*AREAR(D1, D2)
            RETURN
      10    IF(LCRT.NE.2) GO TO 20
            COST = PSF*AREAC(P, D1)
            RETURN
      20    COST = PSF*AREAT(D1, D2)
            RETURN
            END
            FUNCTION AREAR(X, Y)
            AREAR = X*Y
            RETURN
            END
            FUNCTION AREAC(PI, R)
            AREAC = PI*R**2
            RETURN
            END
            FUNCTION AREAT(B, H)
            AREAT = 0.5*B*H
            RETURN
            END
```

Figure 2. A more complicated example of a program having a type 1 anomaly and a type 2 anomaly. Notice that the function subprogram AREAC is executed without initialization of the first argument (dummy argument PI) and that there is no use of PI in the subroutine DOLS after it is assigned a value in the first statement; evidently PI should be P or vice versa

Our system, DAVE, is designed to locate anomalies in these and other far more complex situations. It prints a description of each anomaly located which is designed to simplify the difficult task of identifying the cause. For example, in the case of the program displayed in Figure 2 DAVE would report that in the program unit DOLS

> THE LOCAL VARIABLE NAMED P IS REFERENCED BEFORE BEING DEFINED ON SOME PATHS

and following this message one such path would be printed. DAVE would also report that in the program unit DOLS

> THE VARIABLE NAMED PI IS ASSIGNED A VALUE IN ITS LAST USAGE ON ALL PATHS

and following this message one such path would be printed. A complete list of messages produced by DAVE is available.[14]

THE DEPTH FIRST SEARCH PROCEDURE

The heart of the DAVE system is a depth first search procedure which determines the input and output usage of a variable, α, within a program unit.

A variable α is strict input to a statement if the statement cannot be executed successfully until the value of α is obtained. For example, α is a strict input to each of the following statements: $X = A+\alpha$; $ARRAY(\alpha+2) = 2.9$; $DO\ 10\ I = 1, \alpha, 3$.

A variable α is strict output from a statement if the value which α had before execution of the statement is replaced by a value generated during execution of the statement. For example, α is strict output from each of the following statements: $\alpha=0$; $DO\ 100\ \alpha=1, 10$; $READ\ (5, 25)\alpha$.

We extend these concepts to a leaf subprogram; i.e. a subprogram which does not reference another subprogram. Let S be a Fortran subprogram consisting of the statements $s_1, s_2, ..., s_n$.* Form G_S, the program flow graph of S, by taking the vertex set of G_S to be $\{s_1, ..., s_n\}$, where it is assumed that s_1 is the statement containing the unique entry point of S, and the edge set of G_S to be the set of all ordered pairs of vertices (s_x, s_y) for which it is possible to execute s_y immediately after s_x. Hence the vertices of G_S are the statements of S and the edges of G_S are the possible transfers of control between statements. For simplicity we have used s_x to stand for a statement in S and a vertex representing that statement in G_S; similarly in discussing the flow graphs we will use the terms 'statement' and 'vertex' interchangeably. For the definitions of other graph theoretic terms used in this paper, see Harary.[15]

A *path* through G_S is a sequence of vertices $s_{i_1}, s_{i_2}, ..., s_{i_x}$ where $(s_{i_j}, s_{i_{j+1}})$ is an edge of G_S for $j = 1, 2, ..., x-1$, $i_1 = 1$ and s_{i_x} is a STOP or RETURN statement. It is to be noted that a path is determined entirely by the incidence relations which define the graph and does not take into account any constraints that might be implied by execution of the statements s_{i_j}. Thus a path does not necessarily represent a sequence of statements that could actually be executed; the latter we call an *execution path*.

A minimum function, min(X), and a maximum function, max(X), on a finite set of integers, X, are defined as follows:

$$\min(X) = \begin{cases} \infty & \text{if } X = \phi, \\ \text{smallest integer in } X & \text{if } X \neq \phi \end{cases} \qquad \max(X) = \begin{cases} -\infty & \text{if } X = \phi, \\ \text{largest integer in } X & \text{if } X \neq \phi \end{cases}$$

Sets $I_{p,\alpha}$, $O_{p,\alpha}$ and $U_{p,\alpha}$ for a path, $p = s_{i_1}, s_{i_2}, ..., s_{i_x}$, in S are defined as follows:

$I_{p,\alpha} = \{j \mid \alpha \text{ is a strict input variable for } s_{i_j}\}$
$O_{p,\alpha} = \{j \mid \alpha \text{ is a strict output variable for } s_{i_j}\}$
$U_{p,\alpha} = \{j \mid \alpha \text{ becomes undefined after execution of } s_{i_j}\}$

If the condition

$$(\min(I_{p,\alpha}) \neq \infty \land \min(I_{p,\alpha}) \leq \min(O_{p,\alpha}) \land \min(I_{p,\alpha}) \leq \min(U_{p,\alpha}))$$

is true for no p in G_S, then α is a *non-input variable for S*, if it is true for some p in G_S then α is an *input variable for S*, if it is true for all p in G_S, then α is a *strict input variable for S*. If the condition

$$\max(U_{p,\alpha}) < \max(O_{p,\alpha})$$

is true for no p in G_S then α is a *non-output variable for S*, if it is true for some p in G_S then α is an *output variable for S*, if it is true for all p in G_S then α is a *strict output variable for S*.

Hence we recognize three input classes and three output classes for the variables of a subprogram.

Two algorithms, *inpvar* and *outpvar*, are presented below to illustrate the depth first search we employ to make the input/output classification of a variable in a subprogram represented as a directed graph. It is convenient to present them in Algol though their implementation in DAVE is in Fortran. Each of these algorithms operates on a subprogram S, where S must be a leaf subprogram. The first algorithm, *inpvar*, determines for a given

---

* In the following discussion it is convenient to think of a logical IF statement as being not one, but rather two separate consecutively numbered statements, the first consisting of the letters IF and the parenthesized logical expression which follows, and the second consisting of the subsequent executable statement.

variable *v* its input type: strict input, input or non-input. The second, *outpvar*, determines the output type for *v*.

Program notes for the procedure *inpvar*

Global quantities

Procedures.

  bboutpv (*a*, *b*)—Boolean procedure, with *bboutpv* assigned the value **true** if the variable *b* is a strict output variable for statement *a*; otherwise it is assigned the value **false**.

  bbinpv (*a*, *b*)—Boolean procedure, with *bbinpv* assigned the value **true** if the variable *b* is a strict input variable for statement *a*; otherwise it is assigned the value **false**.

  undef (*a*, *b*, *c*)—Boolean procedure, with *undef* assigned the value **true** if the variable *c* becomes undefined upon traversing the edge from statement *a* to statement *b*; otherwise it is assigned the value **false**.

Arrays.

  outdegree [*a*]—the outdegree of the statement *a*.

  head [*a*, *b*]—the statement at the head of the edge *b* from the statement *a*.

Variables.

  n—The number of statements, an integer.

Formal parameters

  v—integer identification of variable being classified.

  input—a Boolean variable which is assigned a value by *inpvar*: **true** if *v* is an input, or a strict input variable for S, **false** otherwise.

  strict—a Boolean variable which is assigned a value by *inpvar*: **true** if *v* is strict input, **false** otherwise.

Thus upon exit from *inpvar*:

  input = **false** implies *v* is non-input;

  strict = **false** $\wedge$ *input* = **true** implies *v* is input;

  strict = **true** $\wedge$ *input* = **true** implies *v* is strict input;

Numbering conventions

  Statements of a subprogram are assumed to be numbered 1, 2, ..., n where n is the number of statements in the subprogram. The unique entry vertex of the subprogram graph represents statement 1.

  The edges from a vertex are numbered 1, 2, ..., n_e where n_e is the outdegree of the vertex.

```
    procedure inpvar (v, input, strict);
      integer v; Boolean input, strict;
    begin
      Boolean array visited [1:n]; integer j;
      comment statements are numbered 1, 2, ..., n;
      procedure dfsrchi (statement);
        integer statement
      begin
        integer edge;
        visited [statement] := true;
        if bbinpv (statement, v) then input := true
```

```
            else
              if (outdegree [statement] = 0 ∨ bboutpv (statement, v))
                then strict := false
              else
                for edge := 1, edge+1 while
                    ((edge ⩽ outdegree [statement]) ∧ (strictly ∨ ¬input))
                do
                begin
                  if undef (statement, head [statement, edge], v)
                    then strict := false
                  else
                    if ¬visited [head [statement, edge]] then
                      dfsrchi (head [statement, edge]);
                end
        end dfsrchi;
          strict := true; input := false;
          for j := 1 step 1 until n do visited [j] := false;
          dfsrchi (1)
  end inpvar
```

Program notes for procedure *outpvar*

Global quantities

Procedures.

　bboutpv (*a*, *b*)—Boolean procedure, with *bboutpv* assigned the value **true** if the variable *b* is a strict output variable for statement *a*; otherwise it is assigned the value **false**.
　undef (*a*, *b*, *c*)—Boolean procedure, with *undef* assigned the value **true** if the variable *c* becomes undefined upon traversing the edge from statement *a* to statement *b*; otherwise it is assigned the value **false**.

Arrays.

　indegree [*a*]—the indegree of statement *a* in the subprogram graph.
　tail [*a*, *b*]—the statement at the tail of the edge *b* to statement *a*.
　leaf [*j*]—the statement which is the jth leaf (i.e. a vertex with outdegree $=0$) of the subprogram graph.

Variables.

　n—the number of statements in the subprogram graph.
　number of leaves—the number of leaves in the subprogram graph.

Formal parameters

　v—integer identification of variable being classified.
　output—a Boolean variable which is assigned a value by *outpvar*: **true** if *v* is an output or strict output variable for S, **false** otherwise.
　strict—a Boolean variable which is assigned a value by *outpvar*: **true** if *v* is strict output, **false** otherwise.
　Thus upon exit from *outpvar*:

　　output = **false** implies *v* is non-output
　　strict = **false** ∧ *output* = **true** implies *v* is output;

strict = **true** ∧ *output* = **true** implies *v* is strict output;
procedure *outpvar* (*v*, *output*, *strict*);
  integer *v*; **Boolean** *output*, *strict*;
  begin
    Boolean array *visited* [1:*n*]; **integer** *j*;
    comment statements are numbered 1, 2, ..., n;
    procedure dfsrcho (*statement*);
      integer *statement*;
    begin
      integer *edge*;
      visited [*statement*] := **true**;
      if *bboutpv* (*statement*, *v*) **then** *output* := **true**
      else
        if *indegree* [*statement*] = 0 **then** *strict* := **false**
        else
        for *edge* := 1, *edge* + 1 **while**
            ((*edge* ⩽ *indegree* [*statement*]) ∧ (*strict* ∨ ¬*output*))
        do
        begin
          if *undef* (*tail* [*statement*, *edge*], *statement*, *v*)
            then *strict* := **false**
            else
              if ¬*visited* [*tail* [*statement*, *edge*]]
                then *dfsrcho* (*tail* [*statement*, *edge*])
        end
    end *dfsrcho*;
    strict := **true**; *output* := **false**;
    for *j* := 1 **step** 1 **until** *n* **do** *visited* [*j*] := **false**;
    for *j* := 1 **step** 1 **until** *number of leaves* **do**
      dfsrcho (*leaf* [*j*])
  end *outpvar*

The execution time of both procedures for a given variable is linearly proportional to the number of edges in G_S, because the algorithms guarantee that no edge of G_S is examined more than once in either procedure. Moreover, because the procedures operate on G_S, and not a program source text, the two procedures could be applied to subprograms written in languages other than Fortran.

It should be noted that if there are vertices of G_S which cannot be reached from the start vertex *outpvar*'s analysis may be incorrect. Such source routines have an obvious flaw, detected by most compilers, which should be fixed before attempting the more complex analysis discussed here.

DAVE SYSTEM DESCRIPTION

The structure of DAVE is indicated in Figure 3. The subject program consisting of a main program and all subprograms referenced either directly or indirectly is assumed to have been found syntactically correct either by a compiler or a verifier such as PFORT.[16] DAVE begins by dividing the program into program units. These are then divided into statements and statement type determination is made. Next, the subject program is passed to a lexical analysis routine which creates a token list to represent each of the program's source statements.

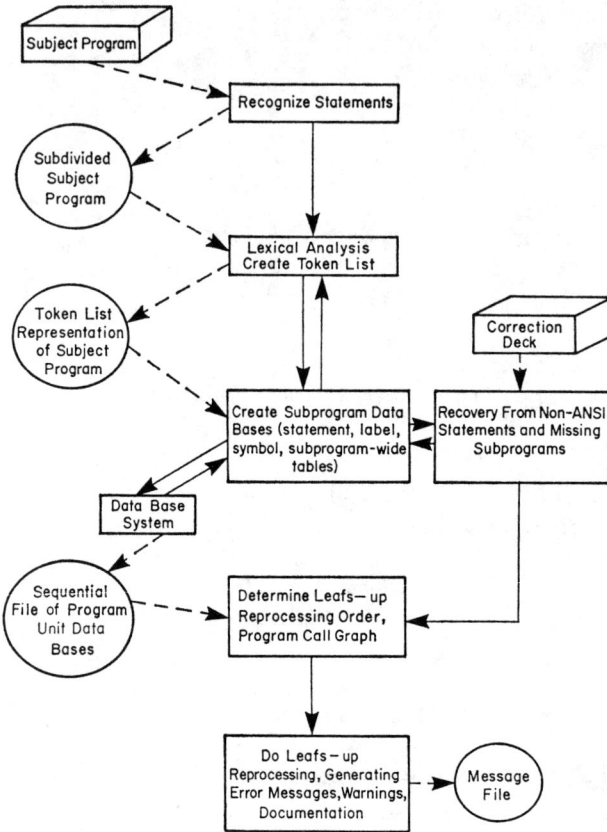

Figure 3. Structure of DAVE

As the token lists are created, comprehensive data bases for each of the program units are also created. Each of these data bases contains a symbol table, label table, statement table and table of subprogramwide data. The symbol and label tables contain the same kind of information found in most compiler symbol and label tables, listing symbol and label attributes as well as the locations of all references to the symbols and labels. The data bases are accessed using a data base creation and accessing package, designed to facilitate data base restructuring.[17]

During this lexical scan phase DAVE determines the input/output classifications of all variables used in each statement, except variables used as actual arguments in subprogram invocations, and loads this information into the statement table. DAVE contains the input/output classifications for all ANSI Fortran intrinsic functions and basic external functions. the input/output classes of variables used as actual arguments in these function invocations are also loaded into the statement table during this phase, otherwise blanks are placed in the statement table for the input/output classifications of variables used as actual arguments in subprogram invocations, and these will be filled in during a later phase of processing.

The table of subprogramwide data for a program unit contains an external reference list containing all subprograms referenced by the program unit, as well as representations of all non-local variable lists; i.e. the program unit's dummy argument list and COMMON block lists. Ultimately these lists will contain the information necessary to establish the input/output classification within the invoking program unit of all variables used as actual arguments in invocations of this program unit. The external reference lists are used to construct the program call graph, a structure that indicates which subprograms invoke which other subprograms.

DAVE is capable of pausing after this phase of processing and accepting a correction deck containing replacements for statements which are not syntactically defined under the ANSI Standard. DAVE also examines the external reference lists to determine whether all referenced subprograms have been submitted. If not, new symbolic decks may also be incorporated in the correction deck.

After all the program units of the subject program have been processed in this way, DAVE enters the main phase of *d*ocumentation, *a*nalysis, *v*alidation and *e*rror detection. The program call graph is examined, and a leaf subprogram is selected for processing. Because this subprogram is a leaf, the input/output search procedures described above are immediately usable.

The local variables of the subprogram are analysed first. An error message is generated for all local variables which are found to be strict input for the subprogram, since this situation implies a type 1 anomaly is certain. Correspondingly, local variables found to be of type input cause the generation of a warning message. The last usage of all local variables is also determined by means of an algorithm which is similar to the output category classification algorithm, but searches only as deeply as the last usage of the variable. If a local variable is used last as an output, a type 2 anomaly is present and a warning is issued.

The input/output classifications of the non-local variables of the subprogram are then determined. These classifications are printed, and also stored in the subprogramwide table of the subprogram under study. Warning messages are also printed for all dummy arguments which are found to be non-input and non-output. This table is then copied into a master data base, so that all invoking program units will be able to easily access the data needed to classify the input/output categories of variables used as actual arguments in invocations of this subprogram.

The system makes a special check of the usage of all DO-loop index variables following satisfaction of their DO's. If the first use of a DO index following DO satisfaction is input or strict input, a type 1 anomaly is indicated and a warning or error message is produced. These situations are detected by initiating an input category determination trace for the DO index where the trace is begun with the flow graph edge which represents the DO satisfaction branch.

The analysis of a non-leaf program unit is more complicated. Such a program unit will, of course, not be analysed until all subprograms which it calls have been analysed. Then DAVE can fill in all entries which had been left blank during the creation of the calling unit's statement table. Certain Fortran errors are detected as this proceeds. For example, mismatches between either the types or numbers of actual arguments in an invocation and the members of the corresponding dummy argument list are detected here. The use of an expression or function name as an argument to a subprogram whose corresponding dummy argument is either an output or strict output variable is also detected here.

Illegal side effects, as defined by the ANSI Standard[10] (Section 8), are also detected. It is easily seen that an illegal side effect is certain to occur if a single variable is used within a single statement, but not within the same function invocation, once as a strict input variable, and a second time as a strict output variable (other than on the left of an assignment statement). For example, in the statement $X = F1(A, B) + F2(A)$ an illegal side effect occurs if the first dummy argument of F1 is classified strict input, and the dummy argument of F2 is classified as strict output (or vice versa). DAVE prints an error message in such cases. A warning message is issued if either classification is non-strict.

DAVE also exposes concealed data flows through subprogram invocations. Concealed data flows result from the use of COMMON variables as inputs (or outputs) to (from) an invoked subprogram. Such situations are easily exposed by examination of the COMMON block variable lists in the subprogramwide table of the invoked subprogram. Because data flows through such COMMON variables just as surely as through explicitly referenced parameters, the statement table entry of such an invocation statement is augmented by the input/output classifications of such variables. This assures that the results of global input/output category determination within the invoking program unit will be correct for these variables. DAVE can also print the names (those by which they are referenced in the invoked subprogram) and usages of all the variables which are used as inputs or outputs for a statement but are not explicitly referenced. This information seems useful as a form of automated documentation. It also seems to be useful as a debugging aid in that it alerts a programmer to data flows which are hidden, perhaps forgotten, and hence more prone to error.

The omission of a COMMON block declaration in an invoking program unit presents a difficult problem. If the COMMON block is referenced in the invoked subprogram, then the variables named in the COMMON block may or may not become undefined upon return to the calling program unit. Undefinition will not occur provided that the COMMON block is defined in some program unit currently invoking the program unit which omits the COMMON declaration. In the absence of such a reference by a higher level program unit, errors are possible. In particular, variables in such a COMMON block which are strict output or output from the invoked subprogram will become undefined—a type 2 anomaly—and a warning is issued. Variables in such a COMMON block which are strict input or input can receive values only through BLOCK DATA subprograms. Hence a check of the subprogramwide tables of such subprograms is made. If no data initialization is found, a warning is issued.

If a COMMON block, B, is declared by a high level program unit which invokes a subprogram, S, in which the block is not declared, then the ANSI Standard[10] (Section 10.2.5) specifies that B must still be regarded as implicitly defined in S provided that some subprogram directly or indirectly invoked by S does declare B. Hence data referenced by the variables in B may flow freely through routines which do not even make reference to B. As already observed, such data flows are noted and monitored by DAVE. In addition, DAVE is capable of printing the names and descriptions of all COMMON blocks whose declarations are implicit in a given subprogram. This, too, seems to be useful program documentation. The algorithm for determining which blocks are implicitly defined in which routines involves a preliminary leafs-up pass through the program call graph and then a final root-to-leafs pass.

After all of the above described checking and insertion of input/output data into the statement table has been done, DAVE proceeds with the analysis of the variables, explicit and implicit, local and non-local, as described in the case of a leaf subprogram. The algorithms used here are generalizations of those described in the previous section. Allowance is made in these algorithms for the possibility that variables may be input (but not strict input) or output (but not strict output) to or from a statement.

Subprograms are processed in this way until the main program is reached. Processing of non-COMMON variables in the main program is the same as the processing of such variables in any non-leaf, but COMMON variables must be treated differently. Any COMMON variable which has an input or strict input classification for the main program must be initialized in a BLOCK DATA subprogram. If not, a warning message (if the classification is input) or an error message (if the classification is strict input) is issued. Similarly, if a COMMON variable's last use was as an output from a main program a warning message is issued.

As implied by the foregoing discussion the messages issued by DAVE are divided into three categories: error, warning and general information. An error message is issued whenever DAVE is certain that a type 1 anomaly is present on an execution path. A warning message is issued whenever a type 1 anomaly might be present on an execution path. In particular, if a variable is strict input for some statement and is not defined on all paths leading to the statement an error message is issued, but if there might be at least one path on which the variable is defined then a warning message is issued. A warning message is issued if a type 2 anomaly is detected, but error messages are never issued for type 2 anomalies. The most common type of general information message which is issued consists of an input/output classification of all variables in a program unit.

LIMITATIONS, EXPERIENCE AND FUTURE PLANS

DAVE is written in ANSI Fortran except for a small number of non-ANSI, or machine dependent subprograms. It contains approximately 25,000 source statements, and executes in four overlaid phases, the largest of which requires approximately 50,000 decimal words of central memory on the CDC 6400. Analysis of a program consisting of approximately 2,000 source statements can be expected to require several minutes of CPU time on the CDC 6400.

DAVE is designed to allow the analysis of programs consisting of large numbers of program units of modest size. After each program unit is processed during the data base creation phase of DAVE, both the source text and partially completed data base are written out to a mass storage file. A copy of the subprogram's subprogramwide table is retained in a master data base which remains central memory resident. In the next processing phase, the data bases are randomly accessed from mass storage in the leafs-up order dictated by this phase. The recalled data base and central memory master data base are all that are necessary for the final analysis of the recalled subprogram. After this analysis, the completed data base is again written out to mass storage. Thus no more than the master data base and one subprogram data base need be central memory resident at any time, enabling DAVE to process a program consisting of a large number of program units. This is because the master data base entry for a subprogram is usually small. On the other hand, DAVE is more limited in analysis of a single large program. With a 6,500 word data base area on the CDC 6400, subprograms consisting of up to approximately 200 source statements can be analysed. This maximum program unit size is determined by array sizes which are easily changed, and we have observed that the cost of running DAVE does not change noticeably as these are altered.

The current version of DAVE is an experimental prototype. Some inefficient structures and algorithms have been employed in order to gain flexibility. It is expected that a future version of DAVE, redesigned for efficiency, will be capable of analysing larger program units in a smaller data base area, and will execute faster. We now feel that we understand the kinds of data structures that are required so they can be frozen, losing flexibility but gaining speed and space. We also see a way[18] to use faster algorithms developed for global optimization.

We have characterized DAVE by calling it a validation system because it can determine the presence or absence of type 1 and 2 data flow anomalies. It might also be regarded as a debugging tool since it exposes bugs and as a documentation tool since it provides information about the input/output use of variables. We do not regard these matters of terminology as being important. Time and experience will determine the utility and appropriate characterization for such systems.

We have had some experience in using DAVE. One of the first programs analysed by DAVE was found to have a misspelling error despite the fact that the program had been in use for several months and was thought to be error free. DAVE detected that the misspelled variable was referenceable before definition along all paths, and that the correctly spelled variable was, on some paths, defined but not subsequently referenced (because the succeeding reference was misspelled). Another program comprising part of a Master's thesis in Computer Science was analysed by DAVE and found to contain a variety of errors. Most were ANSI Standard violations (e.g. mismatched actual argument and formal argument list lengths, use of exhausted DO indices and failure to reference COMMON blocks, either directly or indirectly, in program units which invoked subprograms attempting to share the COMMON variables) and did not prevent the program from running correctly on the permissive compiler used in developing the program. Such errors might be obstacles in transferring the program to another compiler. At least one such error, referencing an exhausted DO-loop index, is not to our knowledge infallibly detected by any other diagnostic system.

In the experience we have had using DAVE we find that interesting and useful messages are produced, but many uninteresting messages are also produced. We expect to focus future effort on the problem of reducing unwanted output or at least permitting the user to suppress or de-emphasize certain specifiable classes of diagnostic output.

Some of DAVE's current limitations are due to fundamental problems of decidability. In particular, the question of whether an arbitrarily selected path is executable is not decidable. Thus we can never be sure, in general, that anomalies detected by DAVE are significant in the sense that they lie on executable paths. However, one should not be too discouraged by this. We have already shown one situation where it can be determined that an anomaly is present on an executable path, and there are clearly others in the case of Fortran programs. Furthermore, recent results by Clarke[19] suggest a technique that may prove useful for dealing with this path separation problem. Closely related to this is the problem of proper identification of array elements when the subscript is a variable. Since it is not decidable whether an arbitrarily chosen variable has a particular value at an arbitrary point in the execution it follows that one cannot in general know which array element is being referenced or defined in a statement. Again, there are many situations in Fortran where one can resolve this identification problem with some effort. The present DAVE system treats all elements of the same array as a single variable. Slightly different are the problems which arise in attempting to analyse a large program by analysing its segments. The segmentation we use is natural for Fortran, our segments being the program units. The path information we pass across these boundaries is incomplete. The result is that we sometimes report that an anomaly is present only on some paths when in fact it is present on all paths.

Other limitations are not so fundamental. The restriction to ANSI Fortran can be easily overcome and a modification currently nearing completion will permit many non-ANSI constructions. The restriction to syntactically correct programs is not fundamental. It arose because of a desire to simplify the lexical analysis and it did not appear to us to be an important restriction considering the way in which we expected DAVE to be used. DAVE also cannot currently handle subprogram names passed as actual parameters. An algorithm for analysing such programs has been produced[20] but has not been incorporated into DAVE. Finally, DAVE does not detect all type 2 anomalies. When this project began we focused on type 1 anomalies and somewhat ignored the significance of type 2 anomalies. The present algorithms used in DAVE miss type 2 anomalies that arise on paths across subprogram boundaries. This will be corrected in later versions of DAVE.

While it is evident that the data flow analysis currently employed could be improved to provide sharper results, it is also evident that there are practical limits to improvements that depend only on more exhaustive analysis of the code. We believe that these practical limits as well as the theoretical limits mentioned earlier can be greatly relaxed by providing for the possibility of an interchange of allegations between the user and an analytic package such as DAVE. Others[21] have suggested interactive systems for proving programs correct, and of course interactive debugging systems are rather well-known.[22] The kind of interactive system we are suggesting here would lie somewhere in between; falling short of proof of correctness but being far more sophisticated than the usual debugging system. Moreover, such a system would provide a powerful documentation and testing tool.

We expect that the direction of our future work with DAVE will be moulded by continuing experience with the system, results of evaluation experiments currently in progress, as well as the growing literature on observed distributions of types of errors in programs.[23]

REFERENCES

1. B. Elspas, K. N. Levitt, R. J. Waldinger and A. Waksman, 'An assessment of techniques for proving program correctness', *ACM Computing Surveys*, **4**, 97–147 (1972).
2. R. Grishman, 'The debugging system AIDS', *AFIPS 1970 SJCC*, **36**, 59–64, AFIPS Press, Montvale, N.J.
3. R. E. Fairley, 'Introduction to the Interactive Semantic Modelling System', University of Colorado, Department of Computer Science, *No. CU–CS–038–74*.
4. J. D. Gannon and J. J. Horning, 'The impact of language design on the production of reliable software', *Proceedings of 1975 International Conference on Reliable Software*, IEEE Cat. No. 75CHO 940–7CSR, pp. 10–23, New York.
5. H. D. Mills, 'Top-down programming in large systems', in *Debugging Techniques in Large Systems* (Ed. R. Rustin), Prentice-Hall Inc., Englewood Cliffs, N.J., 1971, pp. 41–45.
6. N. Wirth, 'Program development by stepwise refinement', *CACM*, **14**, 221–227 (1974).
7. F. T. Baker, 'Chief programmer team management of production programming', *IBM Systems Journal*, **11**, 56–73 (1972).
8. D. J. Kuck *et al.*, 'Measurements of parallelism in ordinary FORTRAN programs', *Computer*, **11**, No. 1, 37–45 (1974).
9. F. E. Allen, 'A basis for program optimization', *Proceedings of IFIP Conference, 1971*, North Holland Publishing Company, Amsterdam, 1971, pp. 385–390.
10. American National Standards Institute, *FORTRAN*, ANSI X3.9 (1966).
11. *MNF Reference Manual for CDC 6000/7000/Cyber Series Computers* (Ed. M. Frisch and L. A. Liddiard), University of Minnesota Univ. Computer Center, Revision 3, November 1974, Minneapolis, Minn.
12. P. Cress, P. Dirksen and J. W. Graham, *Fortran IV with WATFOR and WATFIV*, Prentice-Hall Inc., Englewood Cliffs, N.J., (1970).

13. *Fortran IV Reference Manual 3102.01A, Mark III Foreground* (March 1973), General Electric, Information Services Business Division.
14. L. Osterweil and L. D. Fosdick, 'DAVE—A Validation, Error Detection and Documentation System for Fortran Programs', University of Colorado, Department of Computer Science, *TR No. CU–CS–071–75*.
15. F. Harary, *Graph Theory*, Addison-Wesley, Reading, Mass., 1969.
16. B. G. Ryder, 'The PFORT verifier', *Software–Practice and Experience*, **4**, 359–378 (1974).
17. L. Osterweil, L. Clarke and D. W. Smith, 'A Fortran System for Flexible Creation and Accessing of Data Bases', University of Colorado, Department of Computer Science, *TR No. CU–CS–057–74*.
18. L. D. Fosdick and L. Osterweil, 'Validation and global optimization of programs', *Fourth Texas Conference on Computing Systems (1975)*.
19. L. Clarke, 'A System to Generate Test Data and Symbolically Execute Programs', University of Colorado, Department of Computer Science, *TR No. CU–CS–060–75*.
20. V. Kallal, *An Algorithm for Constructing the Flowgraph of an Assembly Language Program*, Master's thesis, University of Colorado, Department of Computer Science (to appear).
21. D. I. Good, R. L. London and W. W. Bledsoe, 'An interactive program verification system', *Proceedings of 1975 International Conference on Reliable Software*, IEEE Cat. No. 75CHO 940–7CSR, pp. 482–492, New York.
22. R. M. Balzer, 'EXDAMS: extensible debugging and monitoring system', *AFIPS 1969 SJCC*, **34**, 567–580, AFIPS Press, Montvale, N.J.
23. R. Rubey, 'Quantitative aspects of software validation', *Proceedings of 1975 International Conference on Reliable Software*, IEEE Cat. No. 75CHO 940–7CSR, pp. 246–251, New York.

Anomaly Detection in Concurrent Software by Static Data Flow Analysis

RICHARD N. TAYLOR AND LEON J. OSTERWEIL

Abstract—Algorithms are presented for detecting errors and anomalies in programs which use synchronization constructs to implement concurrency. The algorithms employ data flow analysis techniques. First used in compiler object code optimization, the techniques have more recently been used in the detection of variable usage errors in single process programs. By adapting these existing algorithms, the same classes of variable usage errors can be detected in concurrent process programs. Important classes of errors unique to concurrent process programs are also described, and algorithms for their detection are presented.

Index Terms—Concurrent software, data flow analysis, error detection, HAL/S, process synchronization errors, uninitialized variables.

I. INTRODUCTION

DATA flow analysis has been shown to be a useful tool in demonstrating the presence or absence of certain significant classes of programming errors [1]. It is an important software verification technique, as it is inexpensive and dependably detects a well-defined and useful class of anomalies. Work to this point has been directed at the analysis of single-process programs. Investigation of the applicability of data flow analysis to concurrent programs is just beginning [8], [13], [15]. Concurrency causes difficulty in the detection of most errors which occur in single-process programs; it also creates the possibility of new classes of errors.

One of the simplest errors which can occur in both categories of programs is referencing an undefined variable. (The authors recognize that this error can be eliminated by requiring that all variables be declared and given initial values at the point of declaration. Most programming languages do not have this requirement, however. Moreover, the presentation and discussion of this error is useful for pedagogical purposes.)

Another programming *anomaly* which may occur in both categories is a dead variable definition. This occurs when a variable is defined twice without an intervening reference, or if a variable is defined, yet never subsequently referenced. (The notion of an anomaly is described in more detail in [1] and [7].)

In concurrent software, these types of anomalies and errors can occur in more subtle ways than in single-process programs. For example, within a system of concurrent processes, one process may reference a shared variable while a parallel process may be redefining it. It is clearly desirable that such errors and anomalies be analytically detected or shown to be absent from programs.

In this paper, the authors show that data flow analysis can reliably demonstrate the presence or absence of these and other programming anomalies for both single-process and concurrent programs. While the anomalies are of interest in themselves, they are particulalry important because experience has shown that consideration of why they arose in the program's construction often leads to the detection of significant design errors.

II. EXAMPLE AND BASIC DEFINITIONS

A. Programming Language Description

In order to clarify the types of errors being addressed, several examples are needed. The interest here is in designing analytic techniques which may be applied to a variety of languages supporting concurrent programming, such as Concurrent Pascal [2], Modula [3], and Jovial. The languages which are currently used for real-time, concurrent process programming display a variety of techniques to allow synchronization and communication. Some are more error-resistant than others (to say the least). Still more constructs and techniques are being proposed. For example, Ada [4], the new, proposed, common higher order language for embedded applications developed for the Department of Defense displays a number of new techniques. We have attempted to avoid language and methodology dependence in developing analytic techniques, so that they will remain as current as possible. Only the existence of a few constructs common to nearly all contemporary concurrent languages has been assumed, because tools are needed now for the languages which are already in use. It appears likely, however, that the techniques designed in creating these tools will not be made obsolete by new language designs or concurrency constructs.

The programming language which forms the basis for this presentation is derived from HAL/S, an algorithmic language designed for the production of real-time flight software [5].

Manuscript received February 25, 1979; revised July 20, 1979. This work was supported by the National Aeronautics and Space Administration under Contract NAS1-15253 and by the National Science Foundation under Grant MCS77-02194.

R. N. Taylor is with the Space and Military Applications Division, Boeing Computer Services Company, Seattle, WA 98124.

L. J. Osterweil is with the Department of Computer Science, University of Colorado, Boulder, CO 80309.

Reprinted from *IEEE Transactions on Software Engineering*, May 1980, pp. 265-278. Copyright © 1980 by The Institute of Electrical and Electronics Engineers, Inc.

HAL/S was developed for use on the Space Shuttle and is employed elsewhere within NASA for a variety of tasks [6]. The authors have extracted a simple yet powerful subset of this language and slightly altered the syntax and semantics of several of its constructs.

HAL/S bears many similarities to Algol 60 and PL/I. Hence, the syntax and semantics of these languages can generally be safely used in understanding the examples in this paper. Of particular interest, however, are the following language constructs which will be analyzed and with which the examples will be formed.

1) Assignment statement. This statement is of the form

variable = expression;

In executing this statement, the expression is evaluated and the result is then assigned to the variable.

2) Process declaration statements (**program**, **task**, and **close**). The declaration of each process begins with a declaration statement. The main program begins with a **program** declaration statement. Other processes begin with a **task** declaration statement. The end of a process declaration is marked with a **close** declaration statement.

3) Schedule statement. The execution of any process except for the main program is enabled through execution of a **schedule** statement. Execution of a **schedule** does not guarantee that the specified process will begin immediately; it merely indicates that the process is ready for execution. The actual time of initiation of a process is determined by the system scheduler. Any number of processes may be enabled for concurrent execution, but a process may not be scheduled to execute in parallel with itself. The schedule statement explicitly names the process or processes to be started; run-time determination of processes to be scheduled is not allowed.

4) Wait statement. This statement causes the executing process to wait for another process (or processes) to terminate before continuing with its own execution. A process has *terminated* when it has completed its execution and no longer resides in the system scheduler's "ready" queue. As with the **schedule** statement, the process(es) waited for is (are) named explicitly in the declaration; run-time determination is not allowed. The statement may be formulated two ways:

wait for process_name$_1$ **and** process_name$_2$ ...

or

wait for process_name$_1$ **or** process_name$_2$ ...

When the process names are joined through logical disjunction, the wait is interpreted as **wait**-for-any. As soon as one of the named processes has terminated, the waiting process may proceed. When the process names are joined by logical conjunction, *all* of the named processes must terminate before the waiting process may proceed. This is referred to as a **wait**-for-all statement.

5) Shared variables. Program variables have associated with them Algol-like scoping rules. This scoping exists at the program level, meaning that two processes may both access the same variable. We assume that no protection mechanism exists.

6) Transput. Input to a program is accomplished through a **read** statement. Values are output via a **write** statement.

B. Example

Using the above constructs, a sample program (Fig. 1) is presented which contains several anomalies.

A few of the anomalies are listed below.

1) An uninitialized variable (x) may be referenced at line 5, as task T1 may execute to completion before task T2 begins.
2) The definitions of y as found in task T2 (line 10) and the main program (line 20) may be "useless," since y may be redefined at line 22, before y is ever referenced.
3) y is defined by two processes which act in parallel—thus the reference at line 23 may be to an "indeterminate" value.
4) Variable x is assigned a value by task T2 (line 9) while simultaneously being referenced by the main program at line 19.
5) There is a possibility that task T1 will be scheduled in parallel with itself at line 25 since there is no guarantee that T1 terminated after its initial scheduling.
6) The **wait** at line 24 is unnecessary, as T2 was guaranteed to have terminated at line 21, and it has not subsequently been rescheduled.
7) The **wait** at line 6 will never be satisfied as T3 was never scheduled.

C. Event Expressions

Clearly, many of these error phenomena are interrelated. Hence, a more precise categorization and definition system is desirable. Some notions employed in [7] are modified here to gain this precision. In [7] errors were described in terms of anomalous or illegal sequences of events occurring along a path through a program.

For instance, the events "reference" (accessing a value from a variable), "define" (setting a value into a variable), and "undefine" (causing the value of a variable to become undefined, such as by satisfying the running index of a loop) are the significant ones in the detection of undefined variable references and dead variable definitions. Thus, in determining the presence or absence of these errors in a given program, the execution of the program is modeled as the set of all potential execution sequences of these three events happening to each of the program variables. In a single-process program, any path traceable through the program's flowgraph is taken to represent a potential execution.

Now denote the events "reference," "define," and "undefine" by r, d, and u, respectively. Then clearly an undefined variable reference can occur within a program if and only if there is a path subsequence of the form "ur" for some variable and some potential execution. Similarly, a dead variable definition is indicated by either a "dd" or "du" path subsequence.

In a concurrent program, it is more difficult to determine the potential executions and hence the potential sequences of events. Different processes may be executing simultaneously on different CPU's, or in some nondeterminable interleaved order on a single CPU. If these processes operate on shared data, then the sequence of events happening to that data cannot be predicted, even though the code for each process is known. All that can be safely assumed is that every interleaving of the statements of all processes which can act concurrently must be

```
 1   Main: program;
 2       declare integer x,y;
         /* x,y are global variables known
            throughout the main program and all tasks */
 3       declare boolean flag ;
 4       T1: task;
 5           write x ;
 6           wait for T3 ;
 7       close T1 ;
 8       T2: task;
 9           x = 5 ;
10           y = 6 ;
11       close T2 ;
12       T3: task;
13           read x ;
14       close T3 ;
         /* end of declarations */
15       schedule T1 ; /* first executable
                         statement of Main*/
16       schedule T2 ;
17       read flag ;
18       if flag then x = 8 ;
19       write x ;
20       y = 9 ;
21       wait for T2 ;
22       if flag then y = 10 ;
23       write y ;
24       wait for T2 ;
25       schedule T1 ;
26   close Main ;
```

Fig. 1. Sample program with several data flow and synchronization anomalies.

considered a potential execution. Hence, the set of *execution sequences* for a given concurrent program is the set of all possible sequence of events which could result from a potential execution of the program.

Thus, for example, in Fig. 1, noting that all variables are initially undefined and that a **write** is a reference, variable x may have the sequence "urd," "udr," "ud," "ur," or "u" by the time line 17 is reached. "urd" corresponds to task T1 acting first, then T2; "udr" corresponds to T2 actually executing before T1 (there is nothing in the program prohibiting this); "u" corresponds to tasks T1 and T2 both being ready to execute, but not actually having done so.

D. *Error Categorization and Definitions*

Using the notation developed above, definitions may now be formulated for the errors in which we are interested. The following are anomalies which we wish to detect in all programs. Their detection is more complicated in programs using concurrency constructs.

1) Referencing an uninitialized variable. An execution during which this error occurs will have an event sequence of the form "purp'" for some program variable, where p and p' are arbitrary event sequences.

2) A dead definition of a variable. An execution during which this anomaly occurs will have an event sequence the form "pddp" for some variable.

The following are errors and anomalies to be detected in concurrent code. In the following, the **schedule** event will be denoted by an "s," the **wait** by a "w." All processes will be assumed to be in state "u," unscheduled, when not scheduled.

3) Waiting for an unscheduled process. This anomaly is represented by the event expression "puwp'."

4) Scheduling a process in parallel with itself. This anomaly is represented by the event expression "pssp'."

5) Waiting for a process guaranteed to have previously terminated. The expression "pwwp'" is symptomatic of this condition.

6) Referencing a variable which is being defined by a parallel process. There exists a **schedule** s_0 such that for some variable both the event sequence "$ps_0 rdp'$" and the event sequence "$ps_0 drp'$" are possible.

7) Referencing a variable whose value is indeterminate. There exists a **wait** w_0 and two separate definition points for a given variable, d_1 and d_2, such that both the event expressions "$pd_1 d_2 w_0 r$" and "$pd_2 d_1 w_0 r$" are possible.

For each of the above anomalies, an interesting determination will be whether they exist in the event expression *at* a statement (i.e., the event expressions consisting of the preceding events concatenated with the current event), or in the event expression which represents the transformations undergone after *leaving* a statement. In addition, it will be important to distinguish between errors which are *guaranteed* to occur and those which *might* occur.

E. *Program Representation*

At the heart of data flow analysis are algorithms which operate on an annotated graphical representation of a program. Single process programs may be represented by a flowgraph [7]. As introduced in [8], communicating concurrent process programs may be represented by a *process augmented flowgraph*, or PAF. A PAF is formed by connecting the flowgraphs representing the individual processes with special edges indicating all synchronization constraints. In the sample languages given here, an edge must be created for each ordered

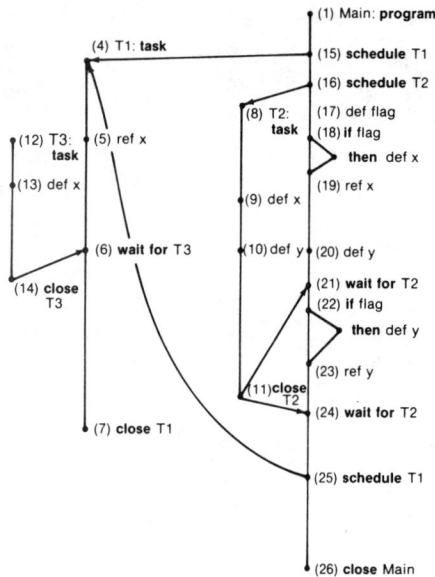

Fig. 2. Process-augmented flowgraph for the program of Fig. 1.

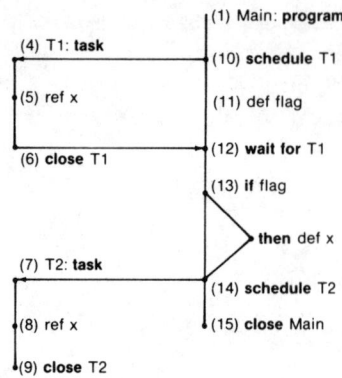

Fig. 3. PAF for program with two uninitialization anomalies.

pair of nodes of the type (**schedule** p_name, **task** p_name) and (**close** p_name, **wait for** p_name).

Fig. 2 is a PAF for the example program of Fig. 1. The creation of the PAF for programs in the sample language is quite straightforward. It is important to note, however, that most actual languages incorporate synchronization constructs which greatly complicate the construction of the PAF. In fact, it is impossible to create a fixed static procedure capable of constructing the PAF of any program written in a language which allows run-time determination of tasks to be scheduled and waited for. These issues will be discussed later in this paper.

F. Data Flow Analysis Algorithms

Data flow analysis algorithms arose out of research in global program optimization [9], [10]. The function of these algorithms, described in detail in [7] and [11], is to infer global program variable usage information from local program variable usage information. Our usage of them has a different objective from program optimization, however. The global usage information will be used to infer verification and error detection results.

The local variable usage is represented by attaching two sets of variables, *gen* and *kill*, to each program flowgraph node. The global data usage is represented by attaching two sets, *live* and *avail*, to each node. The algorithms presented in the references cited assure that when they terminate: 1) a variable v is in the *live* set for node n, if and only if there exists a path p from n to another node n′, such that v is in the *gen* set at n′, but that v is not in the *kill* set of any node along path p; 2) a variable v is in the *avail* set for node n if and only if for every path p leading up to n there exists a node n′ on p, such that v is in the *gen* set at n′, but v is not in the *kill* set for any node between n′ and n along p.

The implications and usage of these algorithms, and the modifications required as a result of concurrency considerations, will become apparent from considering some examples.

III. Detection of Uninitialization Errors

Before examining the extensive example given in Section II-B, consider the following one:

1 Main: **program**;

2   **declare integer** x;
3   **declare boolean** flag;

4   T1: **task**;
5   **write** x;
6   **close** T1;

7   T2: **task**;
8   **write** x;
9   **close** T2;

10   **schedule** T1;
11   **read** flag;
12   **wait for** T1;
13   **if** flag **then read** x;
14   **schedule** T2;

15 **close** Main;

The PAF for this program is given in Fig. 3. All the nodes are annotated corresponding to the program statements.

Now consider the uninitialization errors which are present and how they may be detected.

Two uninitialization errors are present in the program. When task T1 is executed, the write statement will reference uninitialized variable x. (It is not possible that x was initialized, even by the main program which operates in parallel with the task.) When task T2 is executed, there exists a *possibility* for referencing x as uninitialized. If "flag" has the value **true**, then x will be initialized and no error will occur. If, however, flag is **false**, x will still be uninitialized. Thus, there is an instance of an error which "must" occur and an instance of an error which "might" occur. In addition, each of these anomalies may be detected at two different places: the point of variable reference, or at the start node. Thus, there are four different subcategories of the uninitialized variable reference error.

The balance of this paper will be devoted to specifying algorithms for detecting the various subcategories of this error and a variety of other errors and phenomena of interest in the analysis of concurrent software. These algorithms will, in general, involve the use of the LIVE and AVAIL procedures described in Section II-F of this paper. It will be shown that a diversity of diagnostic algorithms can be fashioned by using a variety of criteria for marking the nodes of the program flow graph with *gen* and *kill* notations, and choosing suitable criteria for interpreting the output of the LIVE and AVAIL procedures.

For these reasons, it should be apparent that the algorithms presented here are much involved with placing *gen* and *kill* annotations of flowgraph nodes and interpreting *live* and *avail* annotations that subsequently appear on flowgraph nodes. This annotation information will be represented by means of bit vectors, denoted in the following way:

$$\text{AVAIL}(n) = \textbf{intersect} \ (\text{GEN}(n_i) \ \textbf{union} \ (\text{AVAIL}(n_i) \ \textbf{intersect not} \ \text{KILL}(n_i)))$$
all n_i, immediate predecessors of n

If an annotation criterion dictates that a particular variable, say x, is "*gen*'ed" at a node n, this will be indicated by setting the value of the function *gen*(n, x) to 1. Otherwise, the value of *gen*(n, x) is 0. The function *kill*(n, x) is defined similarly. (The difference between the two functions is that for a given application of the analysis algorithms, one annotation criterion will determine at which nodes each variable is *gen*'ed, while a different criterion will determine at which nodes each variable is *kill*ed. A sample criterion might be "Is variable x defined at this node?")

Assume that the program unit being analyzed has v variables, and that a one-to-one function f has been defined, mapping the variables of the program unit onto the integers $(1, \cdots, V)$. Hence, a bit vector is defined by the values $(gen(n, x_1), \cdots, gen(n, x_i), \cdots, gen(n, x_V))$, where x_i is used to denote the variable x for which $f(x) = i$. This bit vector is used as the definition of the function GEN(n). KILL(n) is defined similarly.

It will also be assumed that there exists algorithmic procedures, LIVE and AVAIL, which operate upon a flowgraph containing N + 2 nodes, and annotation functions GEN and KILL defined on the N + 2 nodes. It will always be assumed that node 0 represents an initialization action immediately preceding the first executable statement of a program unit. Node N + 1 represents a termination action immediately following all statements which end execution of the program unit (i.e.,

the **close** of the main program), or end execution of any process which is not **waited** for (i.e., all process **close** nodes which are not joined to any **wait** nodes). LIVE and AVAIL, when executed, compute annotation functions LIVE(n) and AVAIL(n), respectively, defined on the N + 2 nodes. The values of LIVE(n) and AVAIL(n) are V-bit vectors for n between 0 and N + 1. The bits of LIVE(n) and AVAIL(n) are defined by *live*(n, x_i) and *avail*(n, x_i), respectively, where x_i is the variable x for which $f(x) = i$.

As described in Section II-F of this paper, the AVAIL algorithm is devised to assure that at termination, a variable x will be *avail* at n if and only if for every possible execution of the program leading up to n, there is a previous *gen* of x without an intervening *kill* of x. For single process programs, AVAIL(n) is computed correctly at every flowgraph node n, provided that the following equality is achieved at termination of the AVAIL algorithm.

The LIVE algorithm is devised to assure that at termination, a variable x will be *live* at n if and only if there exists an execution sequence beginning at n, such that there is a *gen* of x before there is a *kill* of x. For single process programs, LIVE(n) is computed correctly at every flowgraph node n, provided that the following equality is achieved at termination of the LIVE algorithm.

$$\text{LIVE}(n) = \textbf{union} \ (\text{GEN}(n_i) \ \textbf{union} \ (\text{LIVE}(n_i) \ \textbf{intersect not} \ \text{KILL}(n_i)))$$
all n_i, immediate successors of n

If *live*(n, x) = 1, then "variable x is *live* at node n." If *avail*(n, x) = 1, then "variable x is *avail* at node n."

An algorithm for detecting all statements at which an uninitialized variable reference "must" occur appears in Fig. 3. This algorithm is designed to detect that the reference to x at statement 5 is a "must" uninitialized reference error. For this and subsequent algorithms, the functions REF(n) and DEF(n) must be defined on the nodes of the flowgraph. These functions will be used as annotation criteria in establishing the *gen* and *kill* notations for a particular application of the analysis algorithms. REF(n) is a V-bit vector whose i-th component is defined by *ref*(n, x_i). *ref*(n, x_i) is 1 if and only if the statement represented by node n involves a reference to the variable x which is mapped by f onto index value i. Otherwise, *ref*(n, x_i) is 0. DEF(n) is defined similarly. *def*(n, x_i) is 1 if and only if the statement represented by node n defines the variable x which is mapped by f onto the index value i. Otherwise, *def*(n, x_i) is 0. Also, **0** is defined as a V-bit vector, all of whose components are 0. **1** is a V-bit vector all of whose components are 1.

Algorithm 1:

```
/* initialize bit vectors */
for n := 1 to N + 1 do
    GEN(n) := 0;
    KILL(n) := DEF(n); /* DEF is the criterion employed
    in establishing the KILL sets */
od;
GEN(0) := 1; /* all variables are in the GEN set of the start node */
KILL(0) := 0; /* no variables are in the KILL set of the start node */
/* invoke analysis algorithm */
call AVAIL;
/* generate error messages */
for n := 1 to N do /* loop through program nodes */
    for i := 1 to V do /* check all variables at each node */
        if ref(n, i) = 1 and avail(n, i) = 1 /* the error condition */
            then print ("an uninitialized reference to", f⁻¹(i),
                "must occur at node", n);
        fi;
    od;
od;
```

It is important to observe that Algorithm 1 is designed to assure that the error message will only be generated when a particular variable cannot possibly be initialized by any execution sequence leading up to the reference at the node to which the message pertains. In particular, it is important for the reader to verify that this algorithm correctly analyzes the program, in Fig. 3. Fig. 4 shows the contents of each set (*gen, kill*, etc.) at each node upon termination of Algorithm 1. Note that variable x is in the *avail* set at the **write** node in task T1. Also note that x is not in the *avail* set at the **write** in task T2. Thus, an error message will definitely be produced for the reference to x at statement 5, but not for the reference at statement 8.

An algorithm is now presented for detecting "may" uninitialized variable reference errors at a node. This algorithm is designed to detect a variable reference occurring at a statement for which there exists an execution sequence that leads up to the statement and does not initialize the variable. Referring to Fig. 3 again, such an error clearly occurs at statement 5, but of more interest there is also such an error at statement 8. Algorithm 1 does not detect the error at statement 8, but Algorithm 2 will.

Before presenting Algorithm 2, a necessary modification to the AVAIL algorithm must be explained.

Suppose n_w is a flowgraph node which represents a **wait** statement. In the PAF G of the program containing n_w, n_w will be the head of some edges which are usual flow of control edges, and the head of at least one edge whose tail represents the termination activity for a concurrent task. Suppose now that the set of usual flow of control edges whose heads are n_w is given by $((f_1, n_w), (f_2, n_w), \cdots, (f_F, n_w))$, and that the set of concurrent task termination edges which have n_w as their heads is given by $((p_1, n_w), (p_2, n_w), \cdots, (p_P, n_w))$. Now, create a new graph node n'_w, delete the edges $((f_1, n_w), \cdots, (f_F, n_w))$ and replace them by the edges $((f_1, n'_w), \cdots, (f_F, n'_w), (n'_w, n_w))$. Suppose this is done for every **wait** node in

NODE	REF	DEF	GEN	KILL	AVAIL
0			x,flag		x,flag
1					x,flag
2	--	--	--	--	--
3	--	--	--	--	--
4					x,flag
5	x				x,flag
6					x,flag
7					
8	x				
9					
10					x,flag
11		flag		flag	x,flag
12					x
13	flag	x		x	x
14					
15					
16					

Fig. 4. Contents of the data flow analysis sets for the PAF of Fig. 3.

G. Denote the resulting graph by G'. Now compute AVAIL(n) as usual, except use the following equilibrium condition at the **wait**-for-any nodes of G' only.

$$(*) \text{AVAIL}(n_w) = \underset{(p_i)_{i=1}^P}{\text{intersect}} \text{AVAIL}(p_i) \text{ union AVAIL}(n'_w)$$

This condition allows a variable to be computed as *avail* at a **wait**-for-any only if it will be *avail* regardless of which task completes first (and thus satisfies the **wait**).

A different equilibrium condition is required at **wait**-for-all nodes.

$$(*) \text{AVAIL}(n_w) = \underset{(p_i)_{i=1}^P}{\text{union}} \text{AVAIL}(p_i) \text{ union AVAIL}(n'_w)$$

A variable will be *avail* here if it is *avail* on any one of the tasks which feed into the **wait** (as the **wait**-for-all guarantees that all the tasks will have executed before the **wait** is satisfied).

The resulting AVAIL(n) bit vectors will be quite useful here. Thus, denote the algorithm which employs the starred formulas as the equilibrium conditions for all of the wait nodes of G' as AVAIL*. In all the algorithms which follow, it is assumed that graph G' has been created and that the analysis takes place on that graph.

Algorithm 2:

```
/* initialize the bit vectors, but differently from 3.1 */
for n := 1 to N + 1 do
    KILL(n) := 0;
    GEN(n) := DEF(n);
od;
KILL(0) := 1;
GEN(0) := 0;
/* invoke the revised analysis algorithm */
call AVAIL*;
/* generate error messages as before */
for n := 1 to N do
    for i := 1 to V do
        if ref(n, i) = 1 and avail(n, i) = 0 /* note the
            revised error condition */
            then print ("an uninitialized reference to",
                f⁻¹(i), "may occur at node", n);
        fi;
    od;
od;
```

Using a different algorithm, the event sequence associated with this anomaly may be indicated to the programmer. Unfortunately, many such event sequences are unexecutable. This problem and partial remedies to it are discussed elsewhere [12]. In the example here, variable x is not in the *avail* set at either write statement in task T1 or T2. Thus, the potential for error is reported at both nodes. In this case, the associated event sequences are clearly executable.

An algorithm is now presented for detecting at the start node all the "must" uninitialization errors. In the example of Fig. 3, interest is again in detecting the error which occurs at the reference to x in statement 5, except in this case the point of detection (and error message generation) will be the start node of the program.

Analogous to the presentation of Algorithm 2, a necessary modification to the LIVE algorithm must be explained. For concurrent programs, it is useful to define a different equilibrium condition than that presented earlier. This revised condition is applied only at **schedule** nodes.

Since an error should be signaled only if a definition is encountered on both the scheduling process and all the scheduled processes, the intersection of the live sets on all successors of the **schedule** is taken.

The algorithm which creates the *live* sets, employing (*) at all **schedule** nodes of G, is denoted by LIVE*. (A graph G' is not required in this case, as a schedule node only has a single control flow edge leaving it. All others lead to a **task initialization** node.)

Algorithm 3:

```
/* initialize bit vectors */
for n := 0 to N do
    GEN(n) := DEF(n);
    KILL(n) := REF(n);
od;
GEN(N+1) := 1;
KILL(N+1) := 0;
/* invoke the revised analysis algorithm */
call LIVE*;
for i := 1 to V do /* now check all the variables
    at the start node */
    if live(0, i) = 0 /* the error condition */
        then print ("an uninitialized reference to", f⁻¹(i),
            "will occur");
    fi;
od;
```

In Fig. 3, variable x will be missing from the *live* set at the start, due to the *kill* present at line 5. (The *live* set at the **wait** node does contain x, however, as the error in task T2 is dependent on the execution sequence taken.)

The detection of *possible* errors is achieved through the following algorithm.

Algorithm 4:

```
/* initialize the bit vectors, same criteria at all nodes */
for n := 0 to N+1 do
    GEN(n) := REF(n);
    KILL(n) := DEF(n);
od;
/* use the standard analysis algorithm */
call LIVE;
for i := 1 to V do /* check for errors at the start node */
    if live(0, i) = 1 /* a different error condition from 3 */
        then print ("an uninitialized reference to", f⁻¹(i),
            "may occur");                                  )
    fi;
od;
```

In this example, variable x is in the *live* set at the start because of the references in both tasks. (Now note that the **wait** node has x in its *live* set, indicating that there is an execution

---

$$(*)\ \text{LIVE}(n) = \text{intersect}\ (\text{GEN}(n_i)\ \textbf{union}\ (\text{LIVE}(n_i)\ \textbf{intersect not}\ \text{KILL}(n_i)))$$
$$\text{all } n_i,$$
$$\text{immediate}$$
$$\text{successors}$$
$$\text{of } n$$

---

sequence following which encounters a reference before any initialization. An error in that execution sequence would depend on x not being initialized before the **wait**, which of course it is not.)

To summarize briefly, two basic algorithms are involved. One computes *live* sets; the other *avail* sets. With suitably created *gen* and *kill* sets attached to the PAF and special rules applied at **wait** nodes during the computation of *avail* and at **schedule** nodes during the computation of *live*, a comprehensive set of programming anomalies may be detected in concurrent process programs.

That is not the end of the problem, however.

IV. PARCELING OF ANALYSIS ACTIVITIES

Now return to the example of Section III and modify the program slightly. In that example, task T2 performed the same actions as task T1. There was no need to declare two tasks, except that it made the analysis simpler. The program shown below is written with only a single task declaration.

```
1  Main: program;

2      declare integer x;
3      declare boolean flag;

4      T1: task;
5          write x;
6      close T1;

7      schedule T1;
8      read flag;
9      wait for T1;
10     if flag then read x;
11     schedule T1;

12 close Main;
```

The PAF for this program is given in Fig. 5. As before, the nodes are numbered and annotated with the corresponding statements. Note that the PAF has been drawn with two edges entering the task's start node.

Suppose now that "must" uninitialization errors should be located and detected at the point of reference. The concern, therefore, is to compute the *avail* sets as described in Algorithm 1. Using this algorithm on the graph as shown will result in x not being in the *avail* set at the reference (at line 5). Thus it cannot be stated that whenever this node is executed an uninitialization error will result. Indeed, this is a correct statement when applied to the second time the task is scheduled: there is only the possibility for an error at this line. This is somewhat unsatisfactory, though, as it is clear that the first time T1 is scheduled an error will occur, regardless of the execution sequence.

The strength of the analysis may be improved in this regard by parceling the PAF and detecting the error not at the reference, but at the point where the task is scheduled. One disadvantage to doing this is that one will not be able to point directly to the statement in the task at which the error occurs.

The method for doing this is based on the technique presented by Fosdick and Osterweil for handling external procedures when performing data flow analysis on single-process programs [7]. Their technique abstracts the data flow in each procedure using the LIVE and AVAIL algorithms, and attaches this abstracted information to all invoking nodes for each procedure. Data flow analysis can then be performed on the invoking procedure. This technique is adapted here to the analysis of tasks for anomalous event sequences. The data usage patterns within each task are determined using LIVE and AVAIL. These abstractions are attached to all **schedule** and **wait** nodes referring to each task. Analysis of this remarked ("trimmed") graph then proceeds as described previously.

For the example of Fig. 5, the analysis will proceed roughly as follows. The algorithms 1–4 would be run for the local variables in task T1 first. (Since there are no local variables, this step is omitted.) Next, T1 is annotated as described in Algorithm 3 for global variables (in this case, x). The LIVE algorithm is run, giving the result that x is *live* at the **task** node, 4. Consequently, nodes 7 and 11 are labeled with $ref(n, x) = 1$, indicating that execution of node 7 or node 11 always results in a subsequent reference to x. Algorithms 1–4 can now be run for the variables local to Main. Algorithm 1 will show that x is *avail* at 7, indicating an uninitialized reference to x will always occur as a consequence of executing node 7. Ideally, the resulting error message will indicate that the error actually occurs "somewhere" in the scheduled task. Determination of the error's precise location would be relegated to a separate (depth-first) scan of the task.

Clearly, it is possible to continue passing up data usage abstractions through an arbitrary number of levels of task scheduling. The restriction that must be imposed on the program in order to adopt this technique is that the process invocation graph be acyclic. In the single-process program situation there is an analogous restriction that the subroutine call graph be acyclic; recursion is prohibited. This prohibition exists for multiprocess programs as well, but the process invocation graph is also required to be acyclic. This is a stronger restriction, as it is possible to have a cyclic process invocation graph which does not involve any recursion, either on the process or the subroutine level. For the moment we are satisfied that a significant class of programs is nevertheless being addressed, but further investigation is clearly called for here.

V. ADDITIONAL REFERENCE/DEFINITION ANOMALIES

A. *Referencing a Variable While Defining It in a Parallel Process*

Reconsider the example of Section II-B. At line 5, in task T1, there is a reference to variable x which, in the absence of a "fortunate" sequencing of events, will be uninitialized when the task is first scheduled. If Algorithm 1 is run on the PAF corresponding to this program (Fig. 2), an "always" uninitialization error will be detected at the reference. (It is assumed that the analysis is carried out in the parceled manner described in the preceding section, as the second time the task is scheduled the possibility exists that x is defined.)

Would it be proper to report this as an always error? What is termed a "fortunate" sequence really makes this an anomaly. It is conceivable that known operating environment conditions guarantee that the initialization performed by task T2 transpires before the reference in task T1. A "sometimes" er-

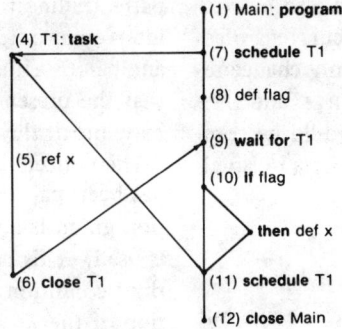

Fig. 5. PAF for program with two uninitialization errors, written with a single task.

ror message is unsatisfactory, though, as such "guarantees" are outside the domain of the program. This confusion is due to the referencing and defining of a variable by two processes which may be executing in parallel. This construction, besides impairing the other analyses in the manner described, seems inherently dangerous and should be reported as an anomaly in its own right.

This anomaly may be detected in a rather naive manner, given that it can be determined which sections of the program may be operating concurrently. Assume that the PAF is parceled into S subgraphs, G_i. Each section corresponds to a task or a portion of a task. Briefly, section boundary nodes are **program, task, close,** and **wait** nodes. (The notion of a section is roughly equivalent to that of a task which contains no **wait** statements.) Also, assume that a Boolean function, PARALLEL, is available which determines which sections can execute in parallel. That is, PARALLEL defines a function of two variables, i and j, such that PARALLEL(i, j) is **true** if and only if G_i and G_j represent sections which might execute in parallel. It is important to note that the algorithm for determining this is not trivial. Indications of how such an algorithm can be constructed may be found in [13] and [14]. Based on these assumptions, an algorithm can be presented for detecting the possibility of referencing and defining a variable from parallel tasks or sections.

Suppose the nodes of graph G_i are numbered from $n_{i,0}$, the logical predecessor to the sections start node, to $n_{i,1_i}$ the logical successor to the sections final node. For clarity, also assume as before that f maps all the variables of the program onto the integers 1-V.

Algorithm 5:

```
for i = 1 to S do /* loop through each section */
    for j = 1 to 1_i do /* annotate the start node within the
    section according to the actions at each node within
    the section */
        REF(n_{i,0}) := REF(n_{i,0}) union REF(n_{i,j});
        DEF(n_{i,0}) := DEF(n_{i,0}) union DEF(n_{i,j});
    od;
od;
for i := 1 to S do /* examine every possible section/section pair */
    for j := 1 to S do
        if i ≠ j
            then if PARALLEL(i, j)
                then if REF(n_{i,0}) intersect DEF(n_{j,0}) ≠ 0
                    then print ("the following may be referenced",
                    "and defined in parallel by sections", i, "and", j);
                    for v := 1 to V do /* check each variable */
                        if ref(n_{i,0}, v) = 1 and
                           def(n_{j,0}, v) = 1
                           then print (f^{-1}(v));
                    fi;
                    od;
                fi;
            fi;
        fi;
    od;
od;
```

This algorithm detects the possibility of references and definitions occurring in parallel. An algorithm can also be constructed that determines when this error must occur, regardless of the execution paths within the process. The only change required to Algorithm 5 is in the creation of the REF and DEF sets at the nodes $n_{i,0}$. The REF sets at $n_{i,0}$ would be computed by an algorithm similar to 3, and the DEF sets by an algorithm similar to 1.

B. Unused Variable Definitions

A programming anomaly that is not truly erroneous, but which often indicates the presence of a design error, is an unused variable definition. The example of Section II-B contains such an anomaly. Variable y is defined both by task T2 and by the main program (at line 20). Y is then possibly redefined at line 22, before ever being referenced. (The anomalous situation which occurs at the reference to y (line 23) will be examined in the next section.)

This anomaly may be detected by techniques very similar to those presented in Section III. Here, as with uninitialization errors, there are four cases to examine: detecting errors which always occur through examining all possible event sequences which follow a node, detecting the possibility of such errors, detecting errors which always occur through examining all event sequences preceding a node, and detecting possible errors by examining the preceding event sequences. The algorithm presented here is only for determining the anomalous situation where a variable v is defined at node n, yet on all paths leading to n, v has been previously defined without any intervening reference. Algorithms for the other three related anomalous situations should be derivable by analogy. Note that the presence of reference-definition in parallel anomalies may impair the quality of the analysis here, as it did before.

The procedure given here assumes that the program graph has been parceled into task subgraphs, that the process invocation graph is acyclic, and that the labeling used in Algorithm 5 is used. This particular error also requires that a new equilibrium condition be defined for application during the computation of the AVAIL sets at **wait** nodes. The new condition is as follows:

(**) AVAIL(n_w) =

intersect AVAIL(p_i) **union** AVAIL(n'_w) - **intersect** REFED(p_i)
$(p_i)_{i=1}^P$ $(p_i)_{i=1}^P$

This condition applies at **wait**-for-anys. At **wait**-for-alls:

(**) AVAIL(n_w) =

union AVAIL(p_i) **union** AVAIL(n'_w) - **union** REFED(p_i)
$(p_i)_{i=1}^P$ $(p_i)_{i=1}^P$

AVAIL ** will denote the algorithm which employs the double-starred formulas as the equilibrium conditions for all the **wait** nodes of G'. REFED(n) is a V-bit vector used during the computation of AVAIL **, which is used to save the value of some intermediate AVAIL sets.

Algorithm 6:

```
declare bit vector PROCESSED (1:S);
PROCESSED := 0; /* nothing has been processed yet */
while PROCESSED ≠ 1 do /* loop until all processes analyzed */
    for i := 1 to S do /* find an un-analyzed process */
        if processed_i = 0 and processed_t = 1 for all tasks, t,
            for which G_i waits /* ensure all the processes G_i
            waits for are analyzed */
        then
            processed_i := 1; /* mark this process as analyzed */
            for j = 1 to l_i do /* annotate the processes nodes*/
                GEN(n_{i,j}) := REF(n_{i,j});
                KILL(n_{i,j}) := 0;
            od;
            KILL(n_{i,0}) := 1; /* block off any references which
            occur before this section */
            call AVAIL*;
            /* a variable is now avail if it is referenced along paths */
            REFED(n_{i,1_i}) := AVAIL(n_{i,1_i}); /* save the avail sets */
            /* remark the graph */
            for j := 1 to l_i do
                GEN(n_{i,j}) := DEF(n_{i,j});
                KILL(n_{i,j}) := REF(n_{i,j});
            od;
            KILL(n_{i,0}) := 1; /* block any definitions which
            precede the start node of the section */
            call AVAIL**; /* this algorithm used the REFED vector */
            for j := 1 to l_i do /* generate the messages */
```

```
                if DEF(n_{i,j}) intersect AVAIL(n_{i,j}) ≠ 0
                then print ("the definition(s) at node", n_{i,j},
                    "is always immediately preceded by another",
                    "definition. The variable(s) is (are): ");
                    for k := 1 to V do
                        if def(n_{i,j},k) = 1 and avail(n_{i,j},k) = 1 then print (f^{-1}(k)); fi;
                    od;
                fi;
            od;
        fi;
    od;
od;
```

C. *Referencing a Variable of Indeterminate Value*

In the above presentation, the anomalous data flow situation existing at the reference to variable y, occurring at line 23 of the sample program in Section II-B was not discussed. Y is defined by task T2 at line 10, by the main program at line 20, possibly again in the main program at line 22. If, for the moment, the definition at line 22 is ignored, then it is indeterminate whether the definition from the task or from the main program is referenced at line 23. If the presence of the definition at line 22 is acknowledged, depending on the event sequence (namely, whether variable flag is true), the reference at line 23 may be to an indeterminate value.

The algorithm now presented is designed to detect indeterminate reference anomalies which will occur, regardless of execution sequence. The anomalies will be detected at the point of indeterminate reference.

Algorithm 7:

```
declare bit vector PROCESSED (1:S); /* will indicate which sections have been processed */
PROCESSED := 0;
while PROCESSED ≠ 1 do /* loop until all sections processed */
    for i := 1 to S do /* seek an unprocessed section */
        if processed_i = 0 and processed_t = 1 for all tasks, t,
            for which G_i waits /* the condition for processing */
        then
            processed_i := 1; /* mark this section as processed */
            for j := 1 to 1_i do
                GEN(n_{i,j}) := DEF(n_{i,j});
                KILL(n_{i,j}) := 0;
            od;
            KILL(n_{i,0}) := 1; /* block off the effects of definitions prior to execution of this section */
            call AVAIL*;
            /* if a variable is avail at section i's stop node, its value must have been set as the result of executing task i */
            DEFED(n_{i,1_i}) := AVAIL(n_{i,1_i}); /* this information is needed for processing other tasks which wait for this task */
            for j := 1 to 1_i do
                GEN(n_{i,j}) := 0; KILL(n_{i,j}) := DEF(n_{i,j});
                /* GEN will be reinitialized below. KILL is set to
                1 iff there is a definition local to this task which could supercede definitions in other tasks */
            od;
            for all w_{i,a}, wait nodes in G_i do
                COUNT := 0;
                for all predecessor nodes, p_{i,a,b}, of w_{i,a} do
                    COUNT := COUNT plus AVAIL(p_{i,a,b});
                od;
                /* COUNT now contains, for each variable, the number of different tasks which may set the value of the variable immediately before execution resumes at node w_{i,a} */
                GEN(w_{i,a}) := 0;
                for v := 1 to V do
                    if COUNT_v greater than 1
                    then GEN(w_{i,a},v) := 1; /* potential for error exists */
                    fi;
                od;
            od;
            call AVAIL;
            /* avail is 1 iff on no path will a necessarily multiple definition be screened by an unambiguous local (to this task) definition */
            for j := 1 to 1_i do
                if AVAIL(n_{i,j}) intersect REF(n_{i,j}) ≠ 1
                then print ("indeterminate reference at", n_{i,j});
                fi;
            od;
            AVAIL(n_{i,1_i}) := DEFED(n_{i,1_i}); /* label this task's stop node with reference information needed by tasks which wait for it */
        fi;
    od;
od;
```

VI. PROCESS SYNCHRONIZATION ANOMALIES

As an outgrowth of the author's investigation into the detection of data flow anomalies in concurrent process software, it became clear that some forms of synchronization errors could be detected in essentially the same manner. The nature of these errors was alluded to in the Introduction. They will now be considered in detail. Note that in form the synchronization anomalies are analogous to data flow anomalies. In addition, as with data flow, many of the anomalies are not strictly errors, but they are conditions which may be interpreted as erroneous in the sense of indicating deeper problems. At the very least, they represent conditions which should be clearly documented.

A. Waiting for an Unscheduled Process

This anomaly is perhaps the most apparent, and the closest in form to the data flow anomalies already discussed. The example of Section II-B contains such an error at line 6 in task T1. Task T3 is never scheduled, yet T1 waits for it. The analogous data flow anomaly is an uninitialized variable. As such, Algorithm 1 is rewritten to detect this anomaly. Thus, the interest here is in detecting anomalies which must occur, and the anomaly is to be detected at **wait** nodes. Our notation requires the introduction of functions SCH(n), WAIT_ALL(n), and WAIT_ANY(n). All function values are T-bit vectors. It will be assumed that the program unit being analyzed has T processes, and that a one-to-one function g has been defined, mapping the process names onto the integers $(1, \cdots, T)$. The i-th component of SCH(n) is defined by $sch(n, t_i)$. $sch(n, t_i)$ is 1 if and only if the statement represented by node n schedules the task t, which is mapped by the function g onto index value i. WAIT_ALL and WAIT_ANY are similarly defined for the two types of **wait** statements in this language.

Algorithm 8:

    for n := 1 to N+1 do
        GEN(n) := **0**;
        KILL(n) := SCH(n);
    od;
    GEN(0) := **1**;
    KILL(0) := **0**;
    call AVAIL;
    for n := 1 to N do
        for i := 1 to T do
            if (*wait all*(n,i) = 1 or *wait any*(n,i) = 1)
                and *avail*(n,i) = 1
                then print ("the reference to process", $g^{-1}(i)$,
                "at node", n, "is to a process which has
                not been scheduled.");
            fi;
        od;
    od;

In Fig. 2, task T3 will be in the *avail* set at the node corresponding to line 6. Thus the error will be detected.

As may be expected, there is also an analogue to the reference-definition in parallel condition here. The following program presents such a condition.

  1   Main: **program**;

  2   T1: **task**;
  3   **schedule** T2;
  4   **close** T1;

  5   T2: **task**;
  6   /* do something */
  7   **close** T2;

  8   **schedule** T1;
  9   /* do something */
10   **wait for** T2;

11 **close** Main;

In this program, there is the possibility that task T2 will be scheduled before the **wait** at line 10 is encountered. The analysis described above will cause an "always" message to be generated. Thus, a "schedule/wait in parallel" analysis must be performed to give a complete description of the situation. This would be performed in a manner analogous to that of reference/definition in parallel analysis.

B. Waiting for a Process Guaranteed to Have Already Terminated

The example of Section II-B still has errors that must be considered. At line 24, the main program waits for task T2 to complete. Yet, the task was already assured to have terminated at line 21. The second **wait** is therefore superfluous and possibly misleading. Since the language syntax used here enables specification of **wait**-for-all and **wait**-for-any, one must be careful to distinguish the errors which will be detected and the algorithms which apply in each case.

To indicate the nature of the technique, a single case will be considered: looking for constructs which, regardless of event sequence, assure us that at least one of the processes named in a **wait**-for-all has in fact already terminated at a previous **wait**.

Algorithm 9:

    for n := 1 to N+1 do
        KILL(n) := SCH(n);
        GEN(n) := WAIT_ALL(n);
        if the statement represented by node n is
            a **task** statement for t_i
                then *gen*(n, t_i) := 1;
        fi;
    od;
    GEN(0) := **1**;
    KILL(0) := **0**;
    call AVAIL;
    for n := 1 to N do
        for i := 1 to T do
            if *avail*(n,i) = 1 and *wait all*(n,i) = 1
                then print ("termination has already been
                ensured for task", $g^{-1}(i)$, "at node", n);
            fi;
        od;
    od;

In Fig. 2, task T2 is in the *avail* sets of all predecessor nodes of the node corresponding to the first **wait** (line 21), but is in only one of the *avail* sets of the predecessor nodes of the **wait** at line 24. Thus, the first **wait** is correct, while the second is anomalous.

The algorithm presented here may be easily modified to detect the possibility of anomalies. To detect anomalies occurring at **wait**-for-anys, new procedures must be developed to account for situations such as:

```
wait for T1 or T2;
    ⋮
wait for T1 or T2;
```

In the absence of other synchronization statements, the second **wait** is spurious; satisfaction of the first **wait** guarantees immediate satisfaction of the second.

C. Scheduling a Process in Parallel with Itself

The last synchronization anomaly which will be examined is that of scheduling a process to execute in parallel with an already active incarnation of the same process. In the example of Section II-B, there is an instance of this error at line 25, where task T1 is scheduled for the second time (the first being at line 15). At no point in any process, let alone before the second **schedule**, has T1 been guaranteed to have terminated.

An algorithm will be presented for detecting situations where, regardless of event sequence, termination has not been assured by the time a **schedule** is reached.

Algorithm 10:

```
for n := 1 to N + 1 do
    GEN(n) := SCH(n);
    KILL(n) := WAIT_ALL(n) union WAIT_ANY(n);
od;
KILL(0) := 1;
GEN(0) := 0;
call AVAIL *;
for n := 1 to N do
    for i := 1 to T do
        if sch(n,i) = 1 and avail(n,i) = 1
            then print ("termination of process", g⁻¹(i),
                "has never been ensured before the
                schedule at node", n);
        fi;
    od;
od;
```

If this algorithm is applied to the example, an error will be detected at line 25.

As may be expected, if a **schedule** may be performed in parallel with a **wait** (on the same process) the quality of this analysis is impaired. In particular, if such a condition exists, Algorithm 10 will detect a "for sure" error, where in fact there is an event sequence where termination takes place.

VII. Conclusion

A. Summary

In this paper we have presented several algorithms useful in the detection of data flow and synchronization anomalies in programs involving concurrent processes. Data flow is analyzed on an interprocess and interprocedural basis. The basis of the technique is analysis of a process augmented flowgraph, a graph representation of a system of communicating concurrent processes. The algorithms have excellent efficiency characteristics, and utilize basic algorithms which are present in many optimizing compilers. A procedure is outlined which allows analysis to proceed on "parcels" of the subject program. Only the most basic synchronization constructs have been considered, however.

B. Open Problems

Several matters discussed in this presentation clearly warrant further investigation. The most pressing need now is a consideration of additional synchronization and communication constructs. These will introduce new classes of errors and may require that changes be made to the algorithms presented here.

One issue not addressed here is the creation of correct process-augmented flowgraphs. In the sample language presented in this paper this was a relatively trivial task, but as additional (real) synchronization constructs are added significant problems are anticipated. It is not clear at this point if "correct" PAF's can always be generated. The analysis schemes may require alteration to accommodate such a situation.

Dynamic determination of synchronization paths has not been considered at all here, but work has been done in this area [15]. Likewise, recursive procedures and processes have been precluded. Work has been done in data flow analysis of recursive routines [16], but it appears inadequate for the analysis performed here.

References

[1] L. J. Osterweil and L. D. Fosdick, "DAVE–A validation, error detection, and documentation system for FORTRAN programs," *Software–Practice and Experience*, vol. 6, pp. 473–486, 1976.

[2] P. Brinch Hansen, "The programming language concurrent Pascal," *IEEE Trans. Software Eng.*, vol. SE-1, pp. 199–207, June 1975.

[3] N. Wirth, "Modula: A language for modular multiprogramming," *Software–Practice and Experience*, vol. 7, pp. 3–35, Jan. 1977.

[4] DoD Requirements for High Order Computer Programming Languages, STEELMAN, June 1978.

[5] F. H. Martin, "HAL/S–The avionics programming system for shuttle," in *Proc. AIAA Conf. Computers in Aerospace*, Los Angeles, CA, Nov. 1977, pp. 308–318.

[6] T. A. Straeter, et al., "Research flight software engineering and MUST–An integrated system of support tools," in *Proc. COMPSAC 77*, Chicago, IL, Nov. 1977, pp. 392–396.

[7] L. D. Fosdick and L. J. Osterweil, "Data flow analysis in software reliability," *Computing Surveys*, vol. 8, pp. 305–330, Sept. 1976.

[8] R. N. Taylor and L. J. Osterweil, "A facility for verification, testing, and documentation of concurrent process software," in *Proc. COMPSAC 78*, Chicago, IL, Nov. 1978, pp. 36–41.

[9] F. E. Allen, "Program optimization," *Annu. Rev. Automatic Programming*, New York, pp. 239–307, 1969.

[10] F. E. Allen and J. Cocke, "A program data flow analysis procedure," *Commun. Ass. Comput. Mach.*, vol. 19, pp. 137–147, Mar. 1976.

[11] M. S. Hecht and J. D. Ullman, "A simple algorithm for global data flow analysis problems," *SIAM J. Computing*, vol. 4, pp. 519–532, Dec. 1975.

[12] L. J. Osterweil, "The detection of unexecutable program paths through static data flow analysis," Dep. Comput. Sci., Univ. Colorado, Tech. Rep. #CU-CS-110-77, 1977.

[13] W. Riddle, G. Bristow, C. Drey, and B. Edwards, "Anomaly detection in concurrent programs," in *Proc. 4th Int. Conf. Software Eng.*, Munich, Germany, Sept. 1979.

[14] J. L. Peterson, "Petri nets," *Computing Surveys*, vol. 9, pp. 223–252, Sept. 1977.

[15] J. H. Reif, "Data flow analysis of communicating processes," in *Proc. 6th Annu. ACM Symp. Principles of Programming Languages*, Feb. 1979.

[16] J. M. Barth, "A practical interprocedural data-flow analysis algorithm," *Commun. Ass. Comput. Mach.*, vol. 21, pp. 724–736, Sept. 1978.

Richard N. Taylor was born in Denver, CO, in 1952. He received the B.S. degree in applied mathematics and the M.S. degree in computer science from the University of Colorado, Boulder, in 1974 and 1976, respectively.

From 1974-1976 he was a Systems Analyst with the U.S. Bureau of Reclamation, Engineering and Research Center. During 1976 he began further graduate studies in computer science at the University of British Columbia, Vancouver, B.C. He is now continuing these studies at the University of Colorado. Since the fall of 1977 he has been with the Boeing Computer Services Company, Seattle, WA, where he is presently a Senior Software Engineer within the Systems Engineering Technology organization. His research interests include systems and software engineering and, in particular, techniques for automated software verification and testing.

Mr. Taylor is a member of the IEEE Computer Society and the Association for Computing Machinery.

Leon J. Osterweil received the A.B. degree in mathematics from Princeton University, Princeton, NJ, in 1965 and the M.S. and Ph.D. degrees in mathematics from the University of Maryland, College Park, MD, in 1970 and 1971, respectively.

He was Vice-President of Language and Systems Development, Inc., Silver Spring, MD, from 1969 to 1971. Since 1971 he has been on the faculty of the Department of Computer Science, University of Colorado, Boulder, CO, where he is now an Associate Professor. From 1977 to 1978, while on leave of absence, he was a Technology Research and Development Manager in the Space and Military Applications Division of Boeing Computer Services Company, Seattle, WA. His research interests include program testing and verification, software engineering, graph theory, combinatorics, and enumeration. He is one of the designers of the DAVE static program analysis system.

Dr. Osterweil is a member of the Association for Computing Machinery.

Testing Large Software with Automated Software Evaluation Systems

C.V. RAMAMOORTHY, MEMBER, IEEE, AND SIU-BUN F. HO

Abstract—In the past few years, research has been actively carried out in an attempt to improve the quality and reliability of large-scale software systems. Although progress has been made on the formal proof of program correctness, proving large-scale software systems correct by formal proof is still many years away. Automated software tools have been found to be valuable in improving software reliability and attacking the high cost of software systems. This paper attempts to describe some main features of automated software tools and some software evaluation systems that are currently available.

Index Terms—Automated tools, correctness, performance, software evaluation systems, software reliability.

INTRODUCTION

THE MAJOR expense in computer systems at present and in the future is in the software. U.S. users spend over $10 billion for software every year. By 1985, computer software expenses will constitute about 90 percent of total system cost [1]. Although great efforts have been spent in recent years to study software, problems still persist in the development of large software systems.

Our experience with software development has been depressing. Most of the software development projects are unsuccessful in terms of specification, time, and cost. The final software product delivered often deviates significantly from the original specifications.

Delivery schedule slippage and cost overrun have been common in software development. O/S 360 was delayed more than a year. Delivery delay denies the user the availability of needed capability. Additional staffing is often ineffective for accelerating the process. The added manpower is eroded by increased communications and administration needs intrinsic in larger groups.

Some operational systems have little documentation. Others have incomplete or inaccurate documentation. There is usually a time lag between the implementation of changes and updating of documentation. Since documentation is usually the last thing to be completed in a project, the final set of changes may never be recorded resulting in an unmaintainable system.

Testing and debugging is the most tiring, expensive, and unpredictable phase of software development. Due to the size and complexity of large software systems, they are usually developed by a large number of programmers (possibly at different locations). The system developed may consist of a number of components with complicated interactions. For these reasons, operational software systems are not free from errors despite the high cost of testing (40–50 percent of total effort). Residual errors contribute an unexpected (and usually heavy) cost to the user beyond normal development and operating expenses. Errors in the missile defense system or air traffic control system may be disastrous. Software systems used for the Apollo manned spaceflight program are probably one of the most thoroughly tested programs in the world. Yet, software failures were detected in Apollos 8, 11, and 14.

The reliability problem is further complicated by executing these systems on complex, parallel machines. In order to improve hardware utilizations, the program and data must be restructured. For pipeline machines, like operations are clustered together to reduce the number of pipe reconfigurations. For Illiac IV [2], matrix elements are stored in a "skewed" fashion to facilitate row and column operations in parallel. Furthermore, errors may be introduced by the support software of the computer. For example, the compiler and the operating system may contain errors.

Formal proof of program correctness is currently infeasible for large systems. In this paper, automated tools and software evaluation systems are introduced as means to improve the reliability and reduce the cost of large software systems by automation. Automated tools can be defined as programs that check the presence of certain software attributes which can be program syntax correctness, proper program control structures, proper module interface, testing completeness, etc. By ascertaining the presence of these attributes, the implementation or construction of the program is assured to contain no major flaws.

A software evaluation system is a composite system consisting of a set of automated tools for the purposes of system design analysis, debugging, testing, and partial validation. Partial validation is the process of demonstrating the validity of a program to an acceptable degree of reliability and performance. Current software evaluation systems only partially fulfill this definition. They analyze the source code but the design and specifications are generally not validated.

Manuscript received October 1, 1974; revised January 24, 1975. This research was sponsored by the Office of Naval Research under Contract N00014-69-A-0200-1064.
The authors are with the Computer Science Division, Electronics Research Laboratory, Department of Electrical Engineering and Computer Sciences, University of California, Berkeley, Calif. 94720.

REQUIREMENTS FOR SOFTWARE SYSTEMS

There are two basic requirements for all software systems: correctness and performance. A system is correct if it meets the specification requirements and is free from design and implementation errors. A system performs satisfactorily if it meets the timing and storage requirements.

There are active and passive approaches to achieve program correctness. The active approach takes the form of program proofs. However, techniques for proving the program correct are still at the early stages of development. Proving large software systems correct by formal proofs is still many years away.

The passive approach takes the form of traditional testing and debugging. Testing can only show the presence of bugs, but not their absence. There are no means to estimate the number of errors remaining in the system and hence no absolute correctness measures. Organized system testing can improve the degree of correctness and the confidence level of the users. Degree of correctness can be qualitatively defined as the probability of obtaining correct results from the inputs.

Performance requirements are usually stated in terms of storage sizes and program execution time. Performance requirements are both application and machine dependent. An air traffic control system may have strict timing constraints due to its application needs and size requirements imposed by the machine on which the system is to be executed. The performance of a program is a function of the storage sizes and execution time actually measured when executed by a machine. The performance of a software system is machine dependent. A program is expected to run faster on a pipeline or parallel computer than on a conventional minicomputer. Performance can also be improved by choosing suitable algorithms that fit the hardware environment, e.g., parallel processable algorithms for a multiprocessor. Given the computer hardware resources and the performance requirements, validating the performance against the performance requirements analytically is very difficult because of possible complex interactions with the operating system and the external environment. However, performance can be estimated by running benchmark programs on the system or by simulation and then compared with the performance requirements.

SOFTWARE DEVELOPMENT

Software development usually undergoes the following phases:

1) Application Requirement Specifications
2) Software Requirement Specifications
3) Design and Analysis
4) Software Implementation
5) Module Testing
6) Software Defenses Instrumentation
7) System Integration and Validation
8) Documentation.

Current software development methodologies permit specification and design errors committed early in the development cycles to remain undetected until implementation and validation [3]. The cost of finding and correcting an error in the system increases as the process comes nearer to completion. Errors found during specification are relatively inexpensive to correct as against errors discovered during system integration. More people are involved and communications among different groups may become a problem.

In most cases, incorrect implementation is the result of incomplete or inconsistent specifications. Studies [1], [31] indicated that most software errors (up to two-thirds) are introduced during specification and design. There is an urgent need for specification languages in which system requirements can be unambiguously stated and validated. Updated documentation throughout the complete development phase together with detailed test plans prepared during design and analysis can improve system understanding both amongst the maintenance engineers and users. Test cases and documentation can be generated manually or with the aid of automated tools.

Top-down design [4] can greatly reduce the complexity of design and analysis. The goal of top-down design is to minimize logical errors and inconsistencies through structural simplification of the development process. System design consists of a sequence of refinement steps. In each step, a given task is broken up into a number of subtasks until the subtasks are simple enough to be coded into a module with high reliability. The final system design can be validated by simulations or formal proofs.

Implementation is the process of coding individual modules according to design specifications. At this stage, communications among programming teams can be improved by proper management techniques (e.g., the chief programmer team) [5]. Program reliability can be enhanced by using the structured programming approach, choosing a suitable high-level language for implementation and imposing programming standards. Programming standards not only discourage the programmers from using error-prone constructions, but also normalize differences in programming style among programmers.

Software defenses are a set of techniques used to protect the integrity of the system against unexpected or unauthorized modifications of the source code and provide fail-safe and fail-secure instrumentations to trap and contain the propagation of software errors. These techniques have been found valuable for real-time systems like the automated telephone system, process control systems and missile defense systems [3].

The correctness of a program can be assured by the following:

selective testing;
exhaustive testing;
formal proofs; and
partial validation using software evaluation systems.

Selective testing exercises the program by data prepared

by the programmers. Unavoidably, this set of test inputs is biased. The programmer may fail to observe some special cases and program correctness cannot be assured by selective testing.

Exhaustive testing requires that every executable path be exercised at least once. However, the concept of achieving total reliability in a software system by exhaustive testing is, in most cases, prohibited by cost and schedule; and for the most part unrealizable [6]. For example, there are only nine unique paths within the loop in Fig. 1. However, if the loop is allowed to execute 10 times, there are 9^{10} ($\approx 10^{10}$) possible execution sequences. Therefore, exhaustive testing is impractical.

Although some progress has been made on the proof of program correctness [7], e.g., by predicate calculus, inductive assertions, and interval arithmetic, this approach appears to be far from a practical reality. To begin with, these techniques are costly to implement for large systems. A 433 statement program in Algol required 46 pages of proofs [8]. Secondly, these techniques also have various constraints that severely restrict their use in programs that utilize special hardware facilities, e.g., programs that are parallel processable. Thirdly, the average programmer may not have adequate mathematical background to support it.

Software evaluation systems are valuable in attacking the high cost and low quality of software systems. Studies indicated that fully automated support of software development activity would result in a 20–25 percent reduction in cost. Retesting of the Houston Operations Predictor–Estimator (HOPE) program aided by automated tools reduces 30 percent of computer time and human effort with an increase in test thoroughness [9].

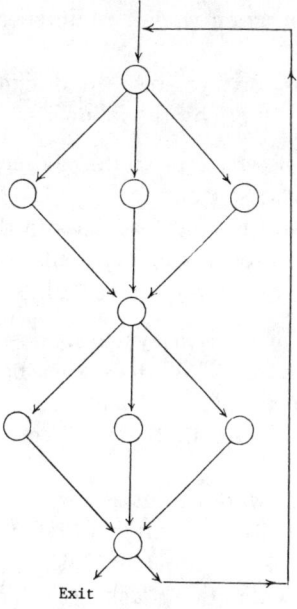

Fig. 1.

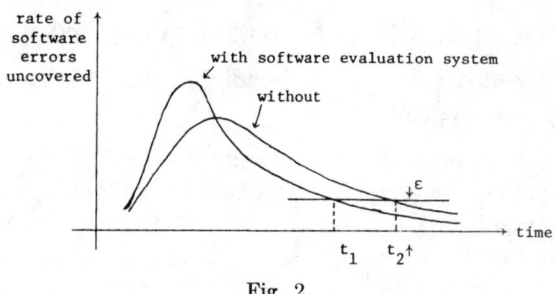

Fig. 2.

AUTOMATED SOFTWARE TOOLS AND SOFTWARE EVALUATION SYSTEM

Computers should be used not only to run programs, but can also be made to aid the programmers in system development. Automated software tools are tools designed to meet this demand. One major problem in dealing with large software systems is the size. Automated tools can scan a large volume of source code and indicate questionable features to the human programmer (e.g., unreliable programming constructs), and free the programmer from repetitive tasks.

As a debugging aid, automated tools can be used to remove simple coding errors, and allow the programmers to concentrate on advance system check out. As an optimization tool, automated tools can indicate code sections that merit detailed examination. Successful application of program correctness proofs to large software systems also depends on the automatic generation of assertions by automated tools or automatic theorem provers. In short, automated tools allow a small programming team to examine a large volume of code which is otherwise impossible.

Software evaluation systems can be defined as a composite system consisting of various automated tools for the purposes of system design analysis, debugging, testing and partial validation.

Fig. 2 shows how the use of software evaluation systems affects the software error discovery rate during the lifetime of a large software system [10]. Studies by Haney [11] on Xerox Universal Time Sharing System indicate similar results. A software system becomes "operational" when the rate of error detected is less than ϵ, which represents the level of tolerance of the user to software bugs. The number of bugs uncovered (i.e., the area under the curve) is the same for both cases. It is important to note that the number of errors detected and fixed after the system is operational seems to be almost constant. There are possibly two explanations. 1) Correcting an error may plant additional errors into the system. This is known as the ripple effect. A study by McGonagle [12] indicates that ripple effect constitutes 19 percent of software errors detected. 2) Since it is true for almost all software systems that a small portion of the code is exercised most of the time, a major portion of the code is minimally exercised. Errors in this portion are discovered much later in the life cycle of the program when certain special conditions are met.

Software evaluation systems are designed to reduce errors from these sources by the following:

predicting the effects of program modifications to contain ripple effects;
generating and evaluating test cases so that a program is tested more thoroughly and systematically; and
generating a data base for future maintenance.

With software evaluation systems, most bugs are uncovered during testing. Thus the system becomes "operational" much sooner (t_1 rather than t_2), and the possibility of bugs appearing later in the program is significantly reduced.

Examples of software evaluation systems are Product Assurance Confidence Evaluator (TRW) [9], Program Evaluator and Tester (McDonald Douglas) [13], Research Software Validation Package (General Research Corporation) [14], and Fortran Automated Code Evaluation System (University of California at Berkeley) [15]. Some features of these evaluation systems will be discussed in more detail in the following sections.

CLASSIFICATION OF AUTOMATED TOOLS

Automated tools can be broadly classified under three categories, namely:

based on the mode of operation;
based on the development phase in which the tool is applicable; and
based on the function of the tool.

A. Operational Mode Classification

Classification can be based on whether the code is analyzed during its execution or the analysis is done without its execution, i.e., static or dynamic analysis. For static analysis, program execution is not required and the source code is analyzed for program logic consistency and program structure well-formation. Structural characteristics are identified and questionable constructs are pinpointed for further manual inspections. Static analysis removes simple errors, sets up a running configuration of the system for further analysis, and generates a program data base for future maintenance.

Dynamic analysis requires the execution of the program to observe the behavior of a program and collect statistics. Supplemental codes (monitors) are inserted into the source code to record run time program behaviors. For example, frequency counters in the form of $\text{COUNT}(I) = \text{COUNT}(I) + 1$ are inserted into the program branches to record the frequency of path traversals. Due to the size of the programs, monitor insertions should be automated with minimum support from programmers. The inserted monitors may affect the storage requirement, execution time, and sometimes even the flow of control of the program. The loading and interference effects of the monitors should be predictable and should not affect the program performance. The loading effect of monitors should be justified for real-time systems.

Dynamic analysis which is used for studying the program behavior during execution is valuable in the following.

Debugging

Test Case Evaluation: The amount of code not exercised by the source code and revealed by the frequency counters indicates test ineffectiveness and hence the additional test cases required.

System Tune Up: Code sections which are most frequently executed are candidates for optimization.

B. Application Classification

Automated tools can be classified according to the development phases in which they are applicable.

1) Design and Analysis Tools: Design and analysis aim at the detection and removal of inconsistencies in the application requirement specifications and the module specifications.

2) Testing and Debugging Tools: Testing is the process of exercising the system by test cases to uncover errors while debugging is the process of error location and correction. Testing tools can aid the generation of test cases to exercise the program until some predefined criteria are met, e.g., every statement has been exercised at least once. Debugging tools, on the other hand, aid error location (e.g., by variable trace) once errors are discovered.

3) Maintenance Tools: Maintenance includes modification implementations to meet changing environment/user requirements and the diagnosis and correction of errors as they are discovered. These tools contain ripple effects due to program modifications by predicting the effect of changes and indicating test cases required for system retesting.

This classification of automated tools is not "disjoint" as the same tool can be used in more than one development phase. For example, debugging tools can be used in the testing and debugging phase as well as the maintenance phase.

C. Functional Classification

Automated tools can be classified according to the specific functions they perform. Under this classification, the major functions of automated tools and their operational complexities will be discussed. However, the set of tools presented is not complete. These tools only serve to indicate the general characteristics and the areas that their application may be profitable.

System Design Analysis
    A. Automated Design Tools
    B. Automated Simulation Tools
Source Program Static Analysis
    C. Tools for Code Analysis
    D. Tools for Program Structure Checks
    E. Tools for Proper Module Interface Checks
    F. Tools for Event Sequence Checks

Source Program Dynamic Analysis
    G. Tools for Monitoring Program Run-Time Behavior
    H. Tools for Automated Test Case Generation
    I. Tools for Checking Assertions
    J. Tools for Inserting Software Defenses
Maintenance
    K. Tools for Documentation Generation
    L. Tools for Validating Modifications
Performance Enhancement
    M. Tools for Program Restructuring
    N. Tools to Extract and Validate Parallel Operations
Software Quality Evaluation
    O. Tools for Software Quality Evaluation

SYSTEM DESIGN ANALYSIS

A. Automated Design Tools

These tools provide capability to assess the potential system design. This set of tools basically works from the specification language which is designed to provide understandable communication between man and machine. The user expresses the software system input, output, and processing characteristics using the specification language. These requirements are then analyzed and checked for inconsistencies and incompleteness. Automated design tools can also be used to inspect the input, output characteristics to determine missing data, redundant data, the minimum data base, and discrepancies in the use of data. Information System Design and Optimization System (ISDOS) [16], Time-Automated Grid System (TAG) [17] and LOGOS [18] are some systems that contain such automated design aids. With ISDOS, user specifies a problem description in Problem Statement Language (PSL) and this will be automatically analyzed by the Problem Statement Analyzer (PSA). PSL is designed to provide the system analyst with a better method of stating the requirements for an information processing system. TAG basically consists of a set of forms describing an entire application which are filled out by the user or system analyst. These forms are then machine analyzed for use by programmers and file designers. Note that these design tools are quite application dependent. For example, ISDOS is designed to aid primarily the development of business data processing systems.

B. Automated Simulation Tools

Simulation tools can be used throughout the development of software systems to verify that the design satisfies the specification and performance requirements. Simulation is a technique for modeling the system hardware/software to study its characteristics. During system design and analysis, simulation enables the designer to determine if the original system objectives are satisfied by the set of derived requirements and test out various proposed algorithms. During testing and evaluation, simulations can be used to provide the work load and program working environment which may not be yet available, e.g., the sky scenario for an air traffic control system. LOGOS and Autascript [19] are some systems that contain tools to aid simulations and provide mechanisms for inserting models into simulation runs.

SOURCE PROGRAM STATIC ANALYSIS

C. Tools for Code Analysis

This set of tools performs syntax analysis on the source code, extracts information which can be used later for checking relationships among modules, and looks for error prone constructions. Error prone constructions are syntactically correct, but logically suspicious constructs in the program. For example, Fortran computed GO TO statements are compiler dependent if the index variable is negative or larger than the length of the statement list.

Code analysis tools can be as complicated as a compiler if complete syntax analysis of source code is required. However, one can assume that source code submitted for investigation is at least compilable without errors. In this case, syntax analysis are limited to aid the extraction of "interesting" program constructs and will be much simpler than a compiler. Usually the source code is not scanned more than twice.

D. Tools for Program Structure Checks

The analysis of program structure is essential to the validation process. Structural analysis includes program graph generation, well formation checks and loop termination checks.

Program graph can be modeled as a directed graph with nodes representing statements and arcs representing program flow of control. This graph can be stored as a connectivity matrix requiring n^2 bytes where n is the number of statements. Since the flow control structure is simple for most programs, most of the entries in this matrix are empty. Other representations, e.g., using predecessor and successor tables may have lower storage requirements which are proportional to n. Fig. 3 shows the graph representations using these two schemes.

Well formation checks require processing the program graph to look for structural flaws within a program, e.g., improper loop nestings, unreferenced labels, unreachable statements and statements with no successors. The operational complexity of graph processing [20] is proportional to n^2, where n is the number of nodes.

Loop termination checks look for data-sensitive and data-insensitive loops. Termination of data-insensitive loops can be guaranteed by examining the source code. For example, in Pascal

    FOR I := 1 TO 10 DO

    BEGIN · · · END;

will terminate after ten iterations.

Data-sensitive loops are characterized by having the final (target) value of control variables changed during

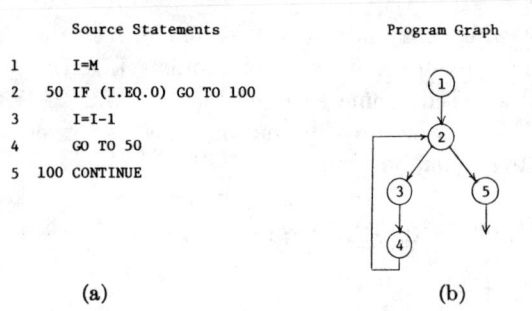

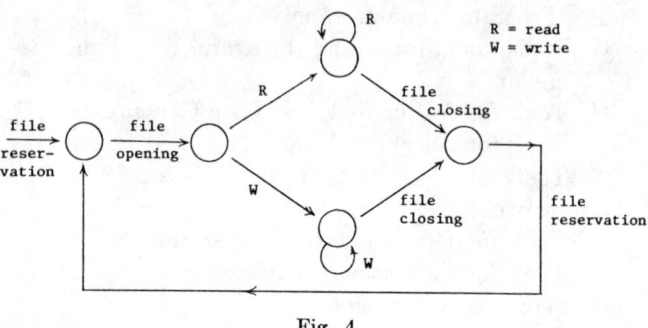

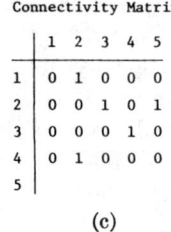

(c)

Connectivity Matrix

	1	2	3	4	5
1	0	1	0	0	0
2	0	0	1	0	1
3	0	0	0	1	0
4	0	1	0	0	0
5					

(d)

Fig. 3.

execution or the control variable increment (decrement) function dependent on other variables. For data-sensitive loops, terminations cannot be easily determined from source code. For example

$$\begin{array}{l} I = \text{MINUS} \\ \quad \vdots \\ \text{IF } (I.LT.0)\ I = N + 2 \\ M = MN * 2 + 1 \\ \quad \vdots \\ \text{IF } (I.GT.M)\ \text{GO TO } 1. \\ \quad \vdots \end{array}$$

Termination properties in these cases can be checked from algorithmic considerations such as proofs of convergence of certain numerical procedures.

Fig. 4.

E. Tools for Proper Module Interface Checks

Code analysis and program structure analysis are local tests, i.e., checks are limited to the module being analyzed. Module interface checks look for various semantic anomalies across module boundaries and are global checks. These tools detect inconsistencies in the declaration of data structures and improper linkages among modules. For example, the called and calling routine should have the same number of parameters and the corresponding parameters should have similar types.

F. Tools for Event Sequence Checking

Sequencing errors can be detected through automatic extraction from program code of certain specified events. The flow of paths defined by these sequences of events are then compared with the proper sequences. For example, in using a certain file system, the following sequence must be observed: 1) file reservation, 2) file opening, 3) a sequence of read or write, 4) file closing. This sequence of events can be modeled as a graph (Fig. 4).

File activities extracted from the program are compared with the graph above to search for discrepancies. Based on this approach, Howard and Alexander [21] have implemented TRACE to verify that the UT2 operating system used at the University of Texas Computation Center adheres to the correct protocols for accessing the Job Status Table. The complexity of event sequencing check is approximately the product of the length of the longest path in the graph obtained from the program and the number of paths.

SOURCE PROGRAM DYNAMIC ANALYSIS

G. Tools for Monitoring Program Run-Time Behavior

Monitor insertions are required to collect program run-time behavior. Due to the large volume of source code, the process of monitor insertions should be highly automated. Some general purpose dynamic monitors are the following.

1) Bounds Checking: Extract bounds or trace variables during execution.

2) Frequency Monitoring: Record frequency of traversal in code sections. For a graph with p arcs and n nodes, the minimum number of counters is $p - n + 2$ [22].

3) Execution Path Tracing: record paths exercised by particular test cases.

H. Tools for Automated Test Case Generation

As exhaustive testing is impossible, "complete" testing is defined in more relaxed terms. For example, a program is tested if all executable statements within the program have been executed at least once. An alternative definition requires that every executable statement and every possible outcome of each branch statement be exercised at least once. Automated tools can be constructed to aid programmers in generating test cases to satisfy these requirements.

In particular, an algorithm based on analyzing program graphs has been devised by Miller and Paige [14] to find a minimum set of test cases to satisfy the latter requirement. The algorithm detects statements and branches not exercised and indicates conditions necessary to traverse that path. The programmer then provides the necessary inputs. Extensive man-machine interactions are required.

I. Tools for Checking Assertions

Although formal program proof by assertions is not feasible for large programs, checking user embedded assertions during run time can improve software reliability. Assertion checks can be viewed as software redundancy to improve program reliability. The assertions may take the form of range checks, state checks, reasonableness checks, and inverse checks. A range check ensures that values of data are within the specified range during execution. A state check verifies that certain conditions hold among the program variables. A reasonableness check is applied to the input data to avoid system misbehavior due to abnormal input data. An inverse check is used to ensure the correct operation of the system. For example, in finding the solution to a set of simultaneous equations, the roots are substituted back into the equations to check for correctness.

Program Evaluator and Tester (PET) [13] automatically instruments source code to perform assertion checks during program execution. Assertion commands are inserted into the program as comments by the programmers. The preprocessor then instruments the source code according to the commands. The ability of checking assertions during run time offers a practical step towards the design and implementation of more reliable programs.

J. Tools for Inserting Software Defenses

These are tools for the insertion of security measures to protect the program against unexpected or unauthorized modifications of the program and the instrumentation of fail-safe and fail-secure procedures to trap and contain the propagation of software errors, e.g., rollback point insertions [23] and "relay runner" scheme [24]. Relay runner scheme provides protection against illegal execution of the code by an infiltrator as well as prohibiting illegal jumps and modifications due to software errors or hardware malfunctions. A program is partitioned into blocks separated by relay checkpoints. These checkpoints are conditional statements to test if the program carries the valid, up-to-date relay code. The relay codes are generated upon legal entry into the system. After the validity of a relay code is checked at a checkpoint, the current relay code is replaced by new generated code. The relay runner scheme has been implemented on a CDC 6400 system with COMPASS support. Fig. 5 shows the run-time overhead with various block sizes.

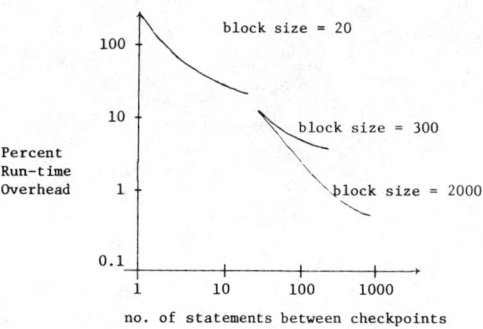

Fig. 5. Run-time overhead of relay runner scheme.

The integrity of a system is particularly important in large real-time systems since the program is controlling an ongoing process such as a nuclear reaction, air traffic control system or a national antiballistic missile defense system. Extensive integrity checks have been implemented on the Electronic Switching System (ESS) [25] developed by the Bell System to ensure correct program execution.

MAINTENANCE

K. Tools for Documentation Generation

Besides source listing, program documentation usually contains all the information that a user can find about the system. Most of the information extracted during code analysis and program structure analysis can be recorded as documentation. For instance, the structure of a program can be displayed in a flow-chart form. Various cross reference tables (like subroutine calling sequences and variable cross reference tables) can also be generated for documentation.

L. Tools for Validating Modifications

Maintenance tools aim at predicting the effect of proposed changes, locating potential error sources and minimizing the ripple effects. The success of maintenance tools depends heavily on the data base which provides a convenient means of storing test cases, error history and statistics, and cataloguing detailed program characteristics.

Program output can be expressed as a function of its input variables. Potential changes in the program have to be checked for validity against its input domain. Simi-

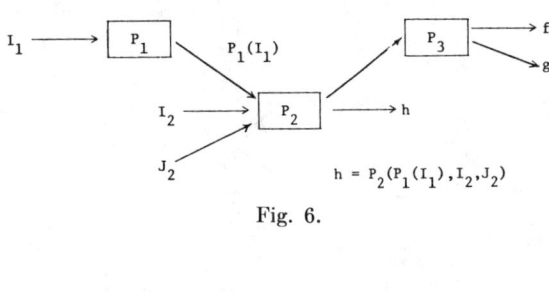

Fig. 6.

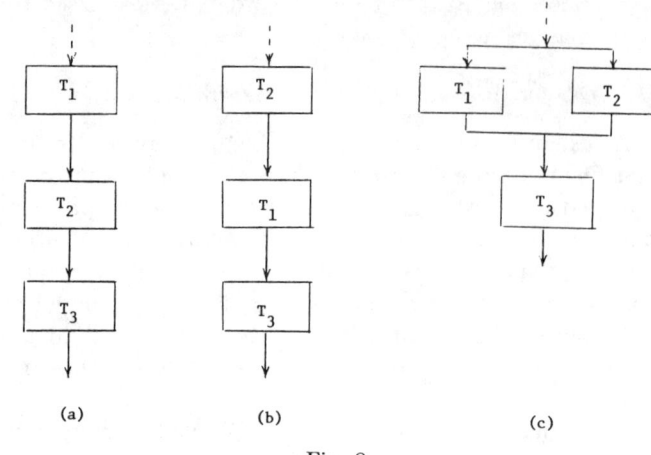

Fig. 8.

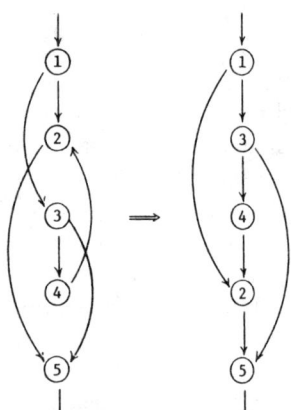

Fig. 7.

larly all other programs which use the output of this program directly or indirectly should also be checked.

In Fig. 6, changes in module P_1 may have an unexpected effect on the input range of P_2. Therefore, all interactions both at the input and output of P_1 should be checked before modifications are authorized. An organized data base would help in fast retrieval of program characteristics and selecting test cases for retesting. The Fortran Automatic Code Evaluation System (FACES) and the TEST program [a component of Product Assurance Confidence Evaluator (PACE)] are some systems that provide automated maintenance support.

PERFORMANCE

M. Tools for Program Restructuring

Programs are restructured for the following reasons: 1) to improve program understandability, ease debugging and maintenance and 2) to reduce run-time overhead and improve the utilization of specific hardware facilities.

GO TO statements are considered as harmful in some cases. In Fortran programs, unnecessary backward GO TO statements can be eliminated by rearranging blocks of statements. For an example see Fig. 7.

For efficient program execution on super-computers, the programs should be reorganized to reduce run-time overhead and improve the utilization of specific hardware facilities. For pipeline machines, clustering like operations together can greatly reduce the number of pipe reconfigurations. For example

$K = A * B$
$F = B/C$ require 4
$L = D + E$ reconfigu-
$P = F * C$ rations
$H = P + A$

$F = B/C$
$K = A * B$ require 2
$P = F * C$ reconfigu-
$L = D + E$ rations.
$H = P + A$

For parallel machines, operations are rearranged to increase the degree of parallelism. For Illiac IV, matrix elements are stored in a "skewed" fashion to facilitate row and column operations in parallel. For machines with virtual storage, program and data are reorganized according to the program and data reference pattern to minimize the number of page faults. The PLUM [26] compiler instruments source code to collect program transfer and data reference characteristics. The reference pattern obtained provides the programmer with information on how to regroup statements, subroutines and data blocks to reduce page faults.

Restructuring of programs by automated tools may require graph processing and the operational complexity may thus be proportional to the square of the number of statements in a module.

N. Tools to Extract and Validate Parallel Operations

For programming languages with no constructs to specify parallel operations, automated tools can be used to extract parallel processable tasks. A task can be a program module, a code section, a statement or even a microinstruction. Bernstein's [27] conditions can be applied to identify parallel processable tasks to aid parallel processing scheduling.

Consider several tasks, T_i, of a sequentially organized program illustrated by a flow chart as shown in Fig. 8. If the execution of task T_3 is independent of the order that tasks T_1 and T_2 are executed, then parallelism is said to exist between T_1 and T_2. However, "commutativity" is a necessary but not sufficient condition for parallel processing. There may exist, for instance, two processes which can be executed in either order but not in parallel. For example, the inverse of matrix A can be obtained in either of the two ways shown below.

1) Obtain transpose of A.
2) Obtain matrix of cofactors of the transposed matrix.
3) Divide result by determinant of A.

1) Obtain matrix of cofactors of A.
2) Transpose matrix of cofactors.
3) Divide result by determinant of A.

Thus obtaining the matrix of cofactors and transposition operation are two distinct processes which can be executed in alternate orders with the same result. They cannot, however, be executed in parallel because both processes access the same memory locations.

Automated tools can be used to extract parallel processable tasks and validate their cooperation on a mutual data base. A Fortran parallel task organizer was built into the Automatic Centran Evaluation System [10].

Not all programs are suitable for parallel processing. A program is considered suitable for parallel processing if either many parallel paths exist or, if the parallel paths are few, they must be long. Since the overhead of extracting parallel processable tasks increases as the square of the number of statements within a program, it is desirable to have a tool to determine the suitability of a program for parallel processing with little overhead. Such an automated tool has been built by Gonzalez and Ramamoorthy [28] with satisfactory results.

O. Tools to Evaluate Software Quality

The quality of a software system is always subject to human judgment. There is no formal definition for software quality. A system which is easy to maintain and understand with good documentation is considered to be of high quality.

Lacking an absolute quality rating, the figure of merit (FM) of a program is proposed to compare software quality on a relative basis, i.e., compare one program with similar programs, rank constituent modules in a system, or measure the improvement of an updated system relative to a previous version. The basic approach will be to identify a set of software characteristic attributes. This set of attributes should represent good and bad, reliable and unreliable programming practices. For each attribute, measures called metrics are formulated. For example, the DO loop metric may depend on the number of statements in a DO loop and the level of nesting. The FM of a program module is a weighted average of the attribute metrics. The FM of a software system is again a weighted average of the FM of each program module. The attached weights should be a function of the execution frequency, task criticality, and attribute or module importance to the whole system. TRW, Inc. has performed some preliminary studies in evaluating software quality using this approach [29].

CRITERIA FOR GOOD AUTOMATED TOOLS

In providing support tools for software, the needs, desires, and frustration of personnel should be considered. The support system should be constructed to provide the human investigator with valuable information and not simply inject more data into an already confused situation. For these reasons, more effort is required than simply representing the program in a "new format"; rather, the ability to extract "interesting details" from the bulk of the source code is required. Based on this, the resolution power is the major factor in evaluating automated tools. The result of analysis should be absolute rather than ambiguous. For example, finding an uninitialized variable is more valuable than finding a variable that may be uninitialized.

Generality should be considered in the design of automated tools. These tools should be applicable to different languages with minimal changes. This essentially requires transforming the program into an intermediate representation (e.g., a data base) which is language independent, and let the automated tools interrogate this data base. Automated tools should be designed to work at various levels of abstractions. For example, parallel processable operations can be identified at statement level, object code level and even microcode level. The parallel task recognizer should be able to extract and validate parallel operations at all these levels with minimum modifications.

Another criterion for evaluation is ease in use. Due to the large volume of code, human beings are slow, inefficient, and error prone. Automated tools should be highly automated requiring minimum support from the programmers.

Automated tools should be well structured, documented, and thoroughly tested. If the tool itself is not validated, how can it be used with confidence to validate other software systems or enforce standards?

Lastly, the automated tools should be machine independent and flexible to facilitate transferability among machines and meet the need of new environments. Word lengths and internal character representations are different among machines. Automated tools should be able to respond to different environments and maintain its effectiveness.

SOFTWARE EVALUATION SYSTEMS

A software evaluation system is a composite system containing various automated tools for the purpose of system design, debugging, testing, maintenance, and partial validation. The set of tools selected for implementation depends on the programming language, the design methodology and the capabilities already provided by the compiler and loader. Linear programming techniques can be applied to select an optimal set of test tools for implementation. The contribution of a test tool to a test attribute is a measure on how well a test attribute is tested by the tool. For example, the contribution of variable trace to debugging is 40 and the contribution of syntax checks to debugging is 5. Let

- m_{ij} be the contribution of tool j to test attribute i,
- t_j be the cost of executing tool j, and
- E_i be the testing effectiveness required for test attribute i.

Then the optimal set of test tools with minimum cost can be formulated as

$$\min \sum_j n_j t_j$$

subject to

$$\sum_j m_{ij} n_j \geq E_i$$

$$n_j = 0 \quad \text{or} \quad 1.$$

For example:

Tools

	T_1	T_2	T_3	T_4	E_i
R_1		10	30		20
R_2	15	5	15		20
R_3		20		30	20
R_4	30			40	30
t_j	20	15	30	10	

Test Attributes on the left.

Optimal Solution:

T_j	T_1	T_2	T_3	T_4
	0	1	1	1

cost = 55

One major drawback in applying linear programming techniques to tool selection is the linear programming assumption that contributions of the various tools are strictly nonoverlapping and additive. Some pairs of tools will discover the same error twice while other pairs can be used to discover errors that neither used singly can catch. Other obstacles are difficulties in identifying test attributes and assigning numerical values to contributions.

Software evaluation systems may be incorporated into the compiler or developed as a separate system. Compilers have made significant changes in recent years. The early compilers detect syntax errors and convert a source language program into object code. Semantic errors are usually not detected and produce unpredictable results during run time. Second generation compilers like PEBUG [30] provide extensive run-time checks, as well as trace and dump facilities. Modern compilers not only generate object code, but also determine the quality of the program, analyze program structures and instrument source code to record program characteristics during run time, e.g., PLUM [26]. With these additional tasks, the compiler may become less efficient. The user should have the option to use or not to use these development aids.

Since the compiler is already a complicated piece of software, another approach is building software evaluation system as a separate system. This has the advantages of simplifying the development of the language processor (no object code is generated) and leaves more room for extensions. A number of software evaluation systems have been built using this approach, for example, PACE (TRW), Research Software Validation Package (General Research Corporation) and FACES (University of California, Berkeley).

OPERATIONAL EXPERIENCE

There have been a number of reports on successes resulting from the utilization of automated software evaluation systems in the development and maintenance of various software systems. In this section, the operational experience of some systems is described.

A. FACES

The FACES system is a tool designed for assisting the development, testing, modification and maintenance of Fortran programs. FACES consists of two parts: the Fortran Front End and the Automatic Interrogation Routine (AIR). Fig. 9 gives an overall configuration of FACES. The Fortran Front End is essentially a language processor to transform the program source code to the appropriate tabular representation in the data base. The tabular representation is a transactional format of program operations which is relatively free of implicit language properties.

The data base generated consists of three main tables.

1) Symbol Table: Symbolic elements of the input source code such as variable names, statement labels, subprogram names, etc., are catalogued. The symbolic name given the element and the type of item (e.g., integer or real variable) are recorded.

2) Use Table: The Use Table indicates how and where in the source code the symbolic element is referenced, for example, where calls appear to subroutines and what variables are involved in assignment statements. Uses of the same symbol are linked by a linked list pointed to by the Symbol Table.

3) Node Table: The node Table records the program flow structure. The structure is modeled as a directed graph with each statement represented by a node. For each statement, all possible predecessors and successors are listed in the Predecessor and Successor Tables, respectively.

These tables are linked together by logical associations so that the movement from one table to another causes a logically related item to be addressed. For example, mov-

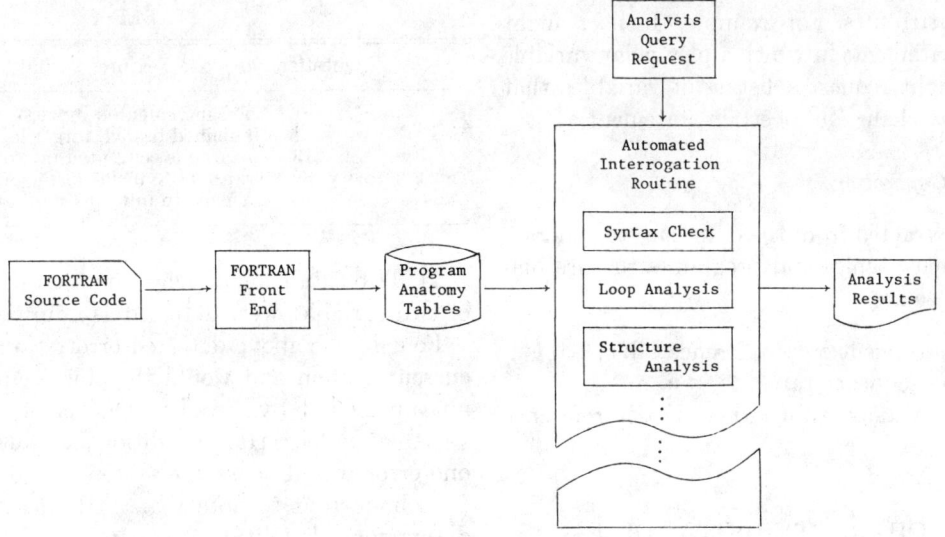

Fig. 9. Overall FACES configuration.

ing from the Symbol Table to the Use Table creates an access to a list of statements using the element. Similarly, movement from the Node Table to the Use Table evokes a list of symbolic elements referenced in that statement.

AUTOMATIC INTERROGATION ROUTINE (AIR)

The AIR interprets queries and automatically searches the data base for specified language constructs. The type of queries include 1) software quality checks, 2) specific user requests, and 3) documentation production.

A. Software Quality Inspection

This is a set of application independent queries used to improve the reliability and quality of software systems.

1) Error Prone Construct Identifications: Queries have been set up to identify syntactically correct but logically suspicious constructs in the program. For example, calls to subroutines which pass explicit constants as parameters are prone to errors. If the constant parameter is modified by the called subroutine, a subtle side effect may result. Consider the sequence,

$$\text{CALL SUB } (A,2,B) \qquad \text{SUBROUTINE SUB } (A,I,B).$$
$$Q = 2*B$$
$$I = I - 1$$

Most compiler implementations will cause the location containing constant 2 to be modified which may affect the computation of Q and subsequent calls to subroutine SUB.

2) Interface Checks: This set of queries confirms the consistent declaration of common descriptions, and type matching of formal subroutine parameters. COMMON block alignment check ensures that corresponding COMMON blocks have the same number of entries, type, dimension and (optionally) name.

For parameter alignment checks, the calling and called routine should agree in the number of parameters, type and (optionally) dimensions.

3) Program Structure Tests: Redundant and unreachable code are identified. Loops are examined for nesting and terminal properties. Data sensitive loops (number of iterations not fixed during compile time) are flagged for manual inspections.

4) Coding Standard Checks: Programming standards are set up for the purpose of maintainability, program transferability among machines and avoiding error prone constructions. For example, ANSI Standard Fortran and specified programming standards have to be observed. Queries are set up to see that these standards are not violated.

5) Uninitialized Variable Check: This query looks for variables which are used in a manner that might presume prior initialization. Checks are limited to local variables within a module. Variables that are interfaced with other modules, e.g., parameters and variables declared in COMMON blocks are assumed to be initialized. Mispunched variables, in most cases, will be uncovered as uninitialized variables. The ability to perform variable traces across program boundaries is currently being investigated.

B. Specific User Requests

AIR allows the user to specify queries and then automatically searches the data base for user-specified language constructs. The user may specify the area of search to be the entire software system or an individual routine. The user-specified language constructs can be variable names to lists of system attributes. For example, the user might wish to know all statements in which a particular variable is referenced or might request a listing of variables that can be affected by a change in a certain statement.

C. Documentation Generation

Information is extracted from the data base to generate various cross-reference tables and program structure diagrams. Some of these are

variable versus statement cross reference table,
subroutine calling sequence table,
common block versus subroutine cross reference table, and
program graph.

OPERATIONAL CHARACTERISTICS OF FACES

The FACES system is implemented in and analyzes ANSI Standard Fortran. The system consists of about 6000 cards for the Fortran Front End, and 2000 cards for the AIR. All routines written are completely documented.

Designed for transferability among machines (namely, IBM 360, UNIVAC 1108, and CDC 6000), table word lengths were restricted to 32 bits. Routines requiring machine dependent features (e.g., I/O facilities) are isolated in the system with detailed documentation. The conversion from UNIVAC 1108 (where the initial FACES version was developed) to CDC 6400 under the current contract activities was a very smooth process. Only file handling routines (which write and read tables from secondary mass storage) and bit manipulation routines were modified.

Limited by the table sizes, the current FACES system can analyze software systems with a maximum of 200 modules and less than 700 statements in each module. However, table sizes can be easily adjusted to handle larger systems. For the current configuration, execution requires 36 K words of memory and the processing rate is about 10 cards/s on the CDC 6400.

EXPERIENCE

FACES has been used not only to evaluate other software systems, but has also been used to analyze itself on subsequent developed versions. This not only provides integrity assurance, but also presents feedback to direct further FACES development.

While analyzing AIR by FACES, the following errors are discovered.

1) Three instances of misspelling of variables and one instance of transposition of variables in COMMON BLOCK declaration were detected by the COMMON BLOCK Alignment Check, e.g., the statement read

COMMON/BLOCK/···B,A,···

but should have been

COMMON/BLOCK/···A,B,···

TABLE I
Questionable Code Features Found by ACES

1	Loop incremented by zero
1	Undefined branch target label
13	Hazardous computed GO TO's
30	Transfers to inside of a loop
19	Loops with untested parameters

2) Two subtle keypunch errors that changed the names of two variables were detected as uninitialized variables.

Four of the above detected errors would not affect the current system and would therefore remain unnoticed if not uncovered by FACES. One error would cause the variable, under certain conditions, to contain garbage and one error would cause the system to go into oscillations. It is important to note that AIR was developed with a design for reliability and maintainability. Programs are written with care and cards are punched by a professional keypunch service. Yet, errors still occurred.

A. Automated Code Evaluation System (ACES) [10]

The ACES system contains features such as data base generation, thorough structural analysis, unreliable construct detection, profile generation, and critical variables monitoring. This system has been successfully used by the Safeguard System Evaluation Agency as a gross survey of substantial amounts of program code. For example one partial process—a small portion (unclassified) of the complete software system—which was analyzed by ACES consists of 90 routines and subroutines containing approximately 23 000 executable statements. Results (Table I) showed unreliable practices such as computed GO TO statements with untested jump parameters, DO-loops with untested initial and final values of the loop parameters, and transfers of control into the middle of DO-loops. These conditions were further investigated by the user and either resolved or reported to the developer for modification.

B. PACE, TRW, Inc. [9]

In testing and maintenance of the HOPE program, cost savings achieved by the use of the PACE system was $8000 per year. The PACE system disclosed that the existing test file consisting of 33 test cases covered only 85 percent of the programs and that one-half of this number were exercised by almost every test case. It required 4.5 h of computer time and 35–50 man-hours of test results evaluation. Consideration of these statistics initiated the subsequent analysis to produce a more effective test file. A file of six cases was generated. With this set of test cases, 93 percent of the subprograms were exercised and required less than 24 man-hours of test results examination.

FUTURE WORK

A brief review of current software evaluation systems indicates that the problems of developing large software systems are tackled in an ad hoc manner. Software evaluation systems are built independent of the development methodology and aim at solving problems at the code level (i.e., after implementation). Yet, most of the software errors are design errors.

Automated software evaluation systems should be designed as part of the development methodology. Systems should be designed with the goal of validation in mind. Well conceived design processes can increase the effectiveness of validation. Automated tools should verify the design decisions as they are made and simulate the complete system design to ensure that the application requirements are met.

There is an urgent need for a specification language for stating system requirements unambiguously. With such a specification language, the problem of verifying design decisions written in specification language will be the same as verifying programs written in a programming language. Fortunately, a partial solution already exists for the latter problem.

CONCLUSION

Partial validation with the aid of software evaluation systems appears to be the most cost effective approach to improve the reliability of large software systems. Although absolute correctness cannot be achieved by this approach, the degree of assurance obtained by these tools is acceptable in most practical situations.

The implementation and use of software evaluation systems are still in the early stages of development and experimentation. The authors hope that this paper has served to summarize the capabilities of automated tools and form a basis for further development.

REFERENCES

[1] B. W. Boehm, "Software and its impact: a quantitative assessment," *Datamation*, May 1973.
[2] D. E. McIntyre, "An introduction to the Illiac IV computer," *Datamation*, Apr. 1970.
[3] C. R. Vick, "Specification for reliable software," in *Proc. EASCON 74*.
[4] H. D. Mills, "Top down programming in large systems," in *Debugging Techniques in Large Systems*, R. Rustin, Ed. Englewood Cliffs, N.J.: Prentice-Hall, 1971.
[5] F. T. Baker, "Chief programmer team management of production programming," *IBM Syst. J.*, vol. 11, 1972.
[6] K. W. Krause, R. W. Smith, and M. A. Goodwin, "Optimal software test planning through automated network analysis," in *Rec. 1973 IEEE Symp. Computer Software Reliability*.
[7] B. Elpas et al., "An assessment of techniques for proving program correctness," *Comput. Surveys*, vol. 4, no. 2, June 1972.
[8] D. I. Good and R. L. London, "Computer interval arithmetic: definition and proof of correct implementation," *J. Ass. Comput. Mach.*, vol. 17, Oct. 1970.
[9] J. R. Brown et al., "Automated software quality assurance," in *Program Test Methods*, W. C. Hetzel, Ed. Englewood Cliffs, N.J.: Prentice-Hall, 1973.
[10] C. V. Ramamoorthy, R. E. Meeker, and J. Turner, "Design and construction of an automated software evaluation system," in *Rec. 1973 IEEE Symp. Software Reliability*.
[11] H. M. Haney, "Module connection analysis—a tool for scheduling software debugging activities," in *1972 Fall Joint Comput. Conf., AFIPS Conf. Proc.*, vol. 40. Montvale, N.J.: AFIPS Press, 1972.
[12] J. D. McGonagle, "A study of a software development project," James P. Anderson and Co., Sept. 1971.
[13] L. G. Stucki, "Automatic generation of self-metric software," in *Rec. 1973 IEEE Symp. Computer Software Reliability*.
[14] E. F. Miller et al., "Structurally based automatic program testing," in *Proc. EASCON 74*.
[15] C. V. Ramamoorthy and S. F. Ho, "FORTRAN automatic code evaluation system," Electron. Res. Lab., Univ. of Calif., Berkeley, Rep. M-466, Aug. 1974.
[16] D. Teichroew, "Problem statement language in MIS," in *System Analysis Techniques*, Couger and Knapp, Eds. New York: Wiley, 1974.
[17] *The Time Automated Grid System (TAG): Sales and Systems Guide*, IBM Corp., Yorktown Heights, N.Y., IBM C20-8075 (1961) and F20-8136 (1963).
[18] C. W. Rose, "LOGOS and the software engineer," in *1972 Fall Joint Comput. Conf., AFIPS Conf. Proc.*, vol. 40. Montvale, N.J.: AFIPS Press, 1972.
[19] R. T. Burger, "AUTASIM: a system for computerized assembly of simulation models," presented at the Winter Simulation Conference, SIGPLAN Notices, Jan. 1974.
[20] C. V. Ramamoorthy, "Analysis of graphs by connectivity considerations," *J. Ass. Comput. Mach.*, vol. 13, Apr. 1966.
[21] J. H. Howard and W. P. Alexander, "Analyzing sequences of operations performed by programs," in *Program Test Methods*, W. C. Hetzel, Ed. Englewood Cliffs, N.J.: Prentice-Hall, 1973.
[22] D. E. Knuth and F. R. Stevenson, "Optimal measurement points for program frequency counts," *BIT*, 1973.
[23] K. M. Chandy and C. V. Ramamoorthy, "Optimal rollback," *IEEE Trans. Compt.*, vol. C-21, pp. 546–556, June 1972.
[24] C. V. Ramamoorthy, R. C. Cheung, and K. H. Kim, "Reliability and integrity of large computer programs," Electron. Res. Lab., Univ. of Calif., Berkeley, Rep. M-430, Mar. 1974.
[25] J. R. Connet, E. J. Pasternak, and B. D. Wagner, "Software defenses in real time control systems," in *1972 Int. Symp. Fault-Tolerant Computing, Dig. Papers*, June 1972.
[26] M. V. Zelkowitz, "Compiler generated program analysis," to be published.
[27] A. J. Bernstein, "Analysis of programs for parallel processing," *IEEE Trans. Electron. Comput.*, vol. EC-15, pp. 757–763, Oct. 1966.
[28] M. J. Gonzalez and C. V. Ramamoorthy, "Program suitability for parallel processing," *IEEE Trans. Comput.*, vol. C-20, pp. 647–654, June 1971.
[29] B. W. Boehm et al., "Characteristics of software quality," TRW Systems Group, Rep. TRW-SS-73-09, Dec. 1973.
[30] J. Blair, "Extendable non-interactive debugging," in *Debugging Techniques in Large Systems*, R. Rustin, Ed. Englewood Cliffs, N.J.: Prentice-Hall, 1971.
[31] D. J. Reifer, "Automated aids for reliable systems," in *Proc. 1975 Int. Conf. Reliable Software*.

C. V. Ramamoorthy (M'57) received the undergraduate degrees in physics and technology from the University of Madras, India, the M.S. degree and the professional degree of Mechanical Engineer, both from the University of California, Berkeley, and the M.A. and Ph.D. degrees in applied mathematics and computer theory from Harvard University, Cambridge, Mass.

He was associated with Honeywell's Electronic Data Processing Division, Waltham, Mass., for over eleven years, most recently as Senior Staff Scientist. He was a Professor in the Departments of Computer Science and Electrical Engineering at the University of Texas, Austin. He is currently a Professor in the Department of Electrical Engineering and Computer Science at the University of California, Berkeley.

Siu-Bun F. Ho was born in Hong Kong, China on January 21, 1952. He received the B.S. degree in computer science from the University of California, Berkeley in 1974.

Currently he is doing graduate work at the University of California, Berkeley under the University Fellowship. He has been a research assistant in the Electronics Research Laboratory, University of California, Berkeley, since 1974.

Symbolic Testing and the DISSECT Symbolic Evaluation System

WILLIAM E. HOWDEN

Abstract—Symbolic testing and a symbolic evaluation system called DISSECT are described. The principle features of DISSECT are outlined. The results of two classes of experiments in the use of symbolic evaluation are summarized. Several classes of program errors are defined and the reliability of symbolic testing in finding bugs is related to the classes of errors. The relationship of symbolic evaluation systems like DISSECT to classes of program errors and to other kinds of program testing and program analysis tools is also discussed. Desirable improvements in DISSECT, whose importance was revealed by the experiments, are mentioned.

Index Terms—Automated aids, data flow analysis, program correctness, program specifications, program testing, software errors, software reliability, symbolic evaluation, test data generation.

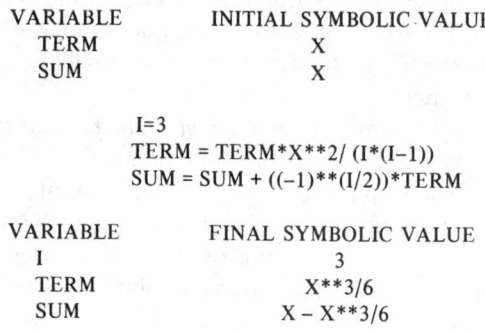

Fig. 1. Symbolic evaluation.

I. INTRODUCTION

IN THE conventional program testing situation, a program P is executed on a set of input values X and then the correctness of the output Y is examined. The program testing process assumes the existence of an external mechanism M which can be used to determine if a given test pair (X,Y) is correct. M may involve manual calculation of results, table lookup, or comparison of X and Y with input and output specifications.

In practice, programmers will use tests (X,Y) in which Y may contain information other than the output values of a special set of output variables. Y may contain traces of selected variables or may contain dummy output that is printed each time some statement is executed. In this case, the existence of a more general mechanism M, which can be used to check for correct program behavior, is assumed. In this paper, an approach to testing is discussed in which X may include "symbolic" as well as "actual" data and Y may include symbolic formulae and systems of predicates. The structure of a symbolic evaluation system called DISSECT is described and the results of a sequence of experiments which were designed to investigate the utility of symbolic evaluation and DISSECT are summarized. The paper includes a description of some of the classes of program errors which were not revealed by either actual or symbolic testing and some recommendations for dealing with these kinds of errors.

II. SYMBOLIC TESTING

Research in the use of symbolic evaluation for program analysis has been carried out by several research groups over the past three or four years [1]-[6]. The basic idea is to allow numeric variables to take on "symbolic values" as well as numeric values. A symbolic value is either an elementary symbolic value or an expression in numbers, arithmetic operators, and other symbolic values. An elementary symbolic value is any text string which the programmer uses to stand for the value of a variable. Elementary symbolic values are often just variable names.

When a program is executed using symbolic evaluation, variables are initially assigned either actual (i.e., numeric) or symbolic values. When an assignment statement is executed the values of the variables on the right-hand side are substituted into the right-hand side. The resulting expression is simplified and becomes the new symbolic value of the variable on the left-hand side. Fig. 1 contains the final symbolic values of several selected variables after the symbolic evaluation of the Fortran code in the figure.

In order to symbolically execute a program, it is necessary to have a program execution system which is capable of symbolic evaluation of expressions. In addition, the system must have certain other special features. The most obvious is some mechanism for path selection. If a program is executed on actual data, predicates in branching statements can be evaluated to TRUE or FALSE and the appropriate branch chosen. If an evaluated predicate contains symbolic as well as actual values, then it may not be possible to determine whether it is TRUE or FALSE. When a programmer symbolically evaluates his program he must decide which paths he wants executed in addition to assigning values to input variables. There are a number of other less obvious problems which the execution system must also have facilities for dealing with.

Different kinds of testing are appropriate for different programs. For some programs the most natural kind of testing is to trace the values of a particular variable. In this case it is assumed that the programmer independently knows what the correct sequence of values should be. There are many programs for which symbolic testing is as natural as testing on

```
      DOUBLE PRECISION FUNCTION SIN(X,E)        1
C     THIS COMPUTES SIN(X) TO ACCURACY E        2
      DOUBLE PRECISION E, TERM, SUM             3
      REAL X                                    4
      TERM = X                                  5
      SUM = X                                   6
      DO 20 I = 3,100,2                         7
      TERM = TERM*X**2/ (I*(I-1))               8
      SUM = SUM + ((-1)**(I/2))*TERM            9
      IF (DABS(TERM) .LT. E) GO TO 30          10
 20   CONTINUE                                 11
 30   SIN = SUM                                12
      RETURN                                   13
      END                                      14
```

Fig. 2. SIN program.

SUM = X - X**3/6
SUM = X - X**3/6 + X**5/120

Fig. 3. Symbolic output values for SIN.

DABS(X**3/6) .LT. E   DABS(X**3/6) .GE. E
                             DABS(X**5/120) .LT. E

    (a)   (b)

Fig. 4. Symbolically evaluated systems of predicates. (a) Symbolic path predicates for single iteration of loop. (b) Symbolic path predicates for two iterations of loop.

actual data and for which symbolic testing is more revealing. The code in Fig. 1 is taken from the program in Fig. 2. The program is supposed to compute SIN(X) using the Maclaurin series $x - x^{**}3/3! + x^{**}5/5! - \ldots$. If x is assigned the symbolic value X and the paths causing the loop in the program to be iterated 1 and 2 times are executed, SUM will take on the symbolic values in Fig. 3.

The output in Fig. 3 is more revealing than two numerical output values of SUM for two numerical input values. The formulae can be compared directly with the program specifications to certify that the program is correct for data that cause 1 or 2 executions of the loop.

In addition to generating symbolic values of variables, symbolic evaluation can be used to analyze the subsets of the input domain that cause particular program paths to be executed. Suppose that the paths in SIN that were used to generate the symbolic values in Fig. 3 are executed with variables X and E set to symbolic values X and E, respectively, and that the branch predicate in statement 10 is symbolically evaluated and printed out each time it is encountered. The two systems of predicates in Fig. 4 will be generated.

Symbolic systems of predicates can be used in different ways. The system in Fig. 4 could be solved and used to generate actual data for testing the associated program paths. This use of the predicates is emphasized in [1]-[4], [6]. The systems described in [2] and [4] contain facilities for solving symbolically evaluated systems of predicates. Techniques for solving predicate systems are discussed in [7]-[9]. The predicates

X**3/6 .LT. E   X**3/6 .GE. E
                           X**5/120 .LT. E
SUM = X   SUM = X - X**3/6
    (a)   (b)

Fig. 5. Symbolic output and predicates for incorrect program. (a) Symbolic path predicates and output for single iteration of loop. (b) Symbolic path predicates and output for two iterations of loop.

could also be printed out along with symbolic path output in order to check that the program has the correct formulae associated with the correct class of input data. The program in Fig. 2 is a corrected version of a program in Kernighan and Plauger [10]. The incorrect program has statements 9 and 10 interchanged and the DABS function is omitted. Fig. 5 contains the symbolic output and systems of predicates for the first two iterations of the incorrect program.

It is immediately obvious from the output in Fig. 5 that the program does not use the last term which it computes in the final value for SUM.

III. THE DISSECT SYMBOLIC TESTING SYSTEM

The DISSECT system is built on an earlier system [5] and is derived from research initially described in [1]. The current system was influenced by the EFFIGY [3] and SELECT [2] systems and the symbolic evaluation system described in [4]. DISSECT can be used to symbolically evaluate ANSI standard Fortran programs.

The input to the DISSECT system consists of two files. One file contains the program to be symbolically tested and the other contains one or more cases. Each case contains a list of commands that cause DISSECT to carry out a symbolic evaluation of the program.

The DISSECT commands fall into three categories: input, output, and path selection. Each of the commands can be executed before the evaluation of the program, after the evaluation terminates, or at intermediate points during program evaluation. Program statements are expected to have sequence numbers and the user specifies that a command is to be executed at some intermediate point during program evaluation by associating one or more sequence numbers with the command. Most commands can be executed conditionally based on several possible kinds of conditions.

A. Input Commands

The input commands allow actual (numeric) or symbolic (text strings) values to be assigned to variables at different points during the execution of a program. All variables which occur in Fortran input statements (e.g., READ statements or subroutine headers) are automatically assigned default symbolic values each time the statement is executed during program execution. Each time the statement is executed it will occur at some position in the program path being traversed. The position is known as its "path index." Default symbolic values are constructed from variable names and path indices. The statement READ 5, X, for example, will cause the assignment of symbolic values of the form X:k to X, where k is a path index. The use of the path index in a variable value makes it possible to distinguish between different occurrences

```
 5  FORMAT (I5)       1
10  READ 5,X          2
    PRINT 6,X         3
    IF X 10,20,20     4
20  CONTINUE          5
```

Fig. 6. Fortran program fragment.

```
Path Index
    :2    10   READ 5,X
    :3         X = X:2
    :5    10   READ 5,X
    :6         X = X:5
```

Fig. 7. Values of X at statement 3 as program loop is iterated twice.

```
    DIMENSION X(10)    1
 5  FORMAT I2          2
    DO 10 I = 1,10     3
10  X(I) = 0           4
    READ 5,I           5
    X(I) = 10          6
    Y = X(2)           7
```

Fig. 8. Program fragment with ambiguous array reference.

of a symbolic value resulting from different executions of the same input statement.

B. Output Commands and Variable Values

The output commands allow the values of individual variables to be printed as well as the evaluated systems of predicates associated with program paths. When a program is being evaluated, values of variables are substituted into conditional statement predicates and the predicates are then simplified. If all values are actual, then a predicate will simplify to T or F. If some values are symbolic, the predicate will be a Boolean expression in symbolic values. The evaluated system of predicates associated with a path or partial path can be printed out at any point during symbolic evaluation of the path. In addition to variable values and systems of path predicates, it is also possible to print out the sequence of statement sequence numbers for the program path which is traversed during a program execution, as well as the path itself.

When a program is executed using symbolic data, there are two kinds of situations in which the symbolic value of a variable which occurs in some statement cannot be described without reference to other program statements. The first kind of situation is illustrated by the program fragment in Fig. 6.

Suppose that the path which causes the loop to be iterated twice is symbolically executed and that the value of X is to be output each time statement 3 is executed. Assume that X is assigned the default symbolic values X:2 and X:5 the first and second times the READ statement is executed. (The two occurrences of the READ statement will be in the second and fifth positions of the traversed path.) The symbolic value X:k means "the value assigned to X when the READ statement in the kth position of the traversed path was executed." In order to print this information out in a meaningful way, when DISSECT prints out a symbolic value of a variable at some point in the execution of a program path, it also prints out all statements in the path which were used in forming that symbolic value. The statements and values are printed out in the order of their occurrence in the program path. Fig. 7 contains the output that will be printed out for the example in Fig. 6. In this particular example, the colon extensions of the symbolic values are redundant since the "source" of each symbolic value X is the immediately preceding READ statement. DIS-

SECT will, in fact, delete the colons in this case and print out symbolic values of the form X rather than X:k. There are examples in which the colons cannot be eliminated and they were included here to illustrate how DISSECT deals with the symbolic value problem in general.

The second kind of situation in which the definition of the value of a variable is complicated, occurs when an array reference is not well defined. Suppose, for example, that a program P contains a sequence of assignments to an array X, then an assignment to X(I), where I is an input variable, and then a reference to an array element X(i) where i is a constant. If P is being executed on symbolic data I will have a symbolic rather than an actual numeric value. It will not be clear whether the value of X(i) in the array reference is the value assigned to X(I) (i.e., I=i) or some earlier assignment to X(i) (i.e., I≠i). Fig. 8 contains a program fragment that illustrates this problem.

When statement 7 in the program in Fig. 8 is symbolically evaluated, it is not clear whether the value of X(2) is zero or ten, the value assigned to X(I) in statement 4 or the value assigned in statement 6.

In the colon extension method discussed above, the execution of an input statement results in the creation of symbolic values of the form X:k. k is the path index of the input statement that was the source of the symbolic value X. The colon extension ":k" is used to disambiguate multiple copies of a symbolic value which are generated by repetitions of the same input statement. DISSECT solves the problem of ambiguous array references by generalizing the use of the colon extension notation. DISSECT keeps an ordered list of the (symbolic) values that are assigned to variables during the symbolic evaluation of a path. Each element of this list contains an assigned value, the name of the variable or array element receiving the value, and the path index of the assignment. DISSECT evaluates references to a variable by calling on a value routine which searches backwards through the value list. Suppose that at some point DISSECT has to evaluate an array element reference X(I) where I can have either a symbolic or numeric value. There are three possible outcomes to the backwards search which is carried out by the value routine. The first is that the value of X(I) is ambiguous. The value of X(I) will be found to be ambiguous if a value for an array element X(J) is found for which it is not possible to determine if I=J, before a value for an array element X(M) is found for which M=I. If the value of X(I) is found to be ambiguous then the value routine returns a special symbolic value which it creates. The special symbolic value stands for the value of X(I) at that point in the execution of the program and it denotes the source of the ambiguity. Suppose that the value

```
:4    X(2) = 0            :4    X(2) = 0
:22   READ 5,I            :22   READ 5,I
:23   X(I:22) = 10        :23   X(I) = 10
      Y = X(2):23               Y = X(2).
         (a)                       (b)
```

Fig. 9. Final symbolic value of Y. (a) Output including colon extensions. (b) Output with colon extensions deleted.

of X(I) is found to be ambiguous due to the presence in the value list of a value for an array element X(J) for which it is not possible to determine if I=J. Suppose that k is the path index associated with this value for X(J). Then the value routine returns the symbolic value X(I):k. The notation "X(I):k" means that the value of X(I) is either the value assigned when the assignment with path index k was executed or it is the value assigned to an element of the array X in some earlier assignment.

The second of the three possible outcomes of the backwards search for the value of X(I) is that the value of X(I) is well-defined. This occurs when a value for an array element X(J) is found for which it can be determined that J=I, before a value for any array element X(M) is found for which it cannot be determined if M=I. The third possible outcome occurs when it can be determined that X(I) has not been assigned a value.

Suppose that it is required that DISSECT print out the symbolic value of a variable V at some point in the execution of a program path and that the value of V is a symbolic expression E containing a symbolic value of the form X(I):k. In order for the output for V to be meaningful it will be necessary to precede the printing of the expression E with a listing of all the possible values of X(I) which are denoted by the symbolic value X(I):k. The presence of the symbolic value X(I):k in E indicates that DISSECT encountered an ambiguous array reference and that the value for that reference is either the value in the value list that is associated with path index k, or some value which occurs earlier in the value list. DISSECT searches back through the value list, starting at the element of the list with path index k, and finds all possible values for X(I). These values will be printed as part of any output which contains expression E.

Fig. 9 contains the output that will be generated for the example in Fig. 8 if the final symbolic value of Y is requested. The output in Fig. 9(a) contains all of the colon extensions of the symbolic values. DISSECT will actually print the output in Fig. 9(b), deleting the colon extensions as unnecessary. They are unnecessary since the assignments referred to by the extensions occur immediately before the references. Fig. 9(a) contains both kinds of colon extensions. The extension :22 in the symbolic value I:22 is used to disambiguate between different possible occurrences of the symbolic value I which could result from different executions of the READ statement. The extension :23 in the symbolic value X(2):23 is used to denote that the value of X(2) is ambiguous. It is either ten, the value assigned to X(I) by the assignment with path index 23, or some earlier value assigned to an array element. In this example the only other possible value is zero, the value assigned to X(2) by the assignment with path index 4.

The ambiguous array reference problem can be significantly more complicated than in the simple example of Figs. 8 and 9. It is important to note that the use of the colon notation, both for ambiguous symbolic input values and for ambiguous array references, can be completely avoided by the user of DISSECT. The notation is included in DISSECT in order to make the system completely general. If the user overrides the default assignments of symbolic values to input variables with his own assignments and always assigns actual values to any input variable that can occur as an array index then neither of the two complicated variable value situations which require the use of the colon notation will arise.

An alternative approach to the problem of ambiguous array references is to use the pseudopath approach described in [2]. In the pseudopath approach, when an ambiguous array reference is encountered, a separate program path is set up and followed for each of the possibilities. DISSECT contains features for allowing a user to do this but the approach described above appears to be more satisfactory for generating symbolic variable values, although it will inhibit the generation of systems of predicates for automatic test data generation. One of the problems with the pseudopath approach is that it may not be possible to determine all of the possible values for an ambiguous array reference.

C. Path Selection Commands

The path selection commands are used to specify which paths are to be symbolically evaluated during the execution of a program. If more than one path is specified by a set of commands, then the output is divided into separate subcases, one for each path.

There are two basic path selection commands. The first is of the form n SELECT α, where n is a sequence number for some conditional branching statement and α specifies one of the branches. If n is an arithmetic IF, α specifies the particular branch to be taken by naming one of the relations .LT., .LE., .EQ., .NE., .GT., or .GE. If n is a logical IF statement, α will be T or F. If n is a computed GOTO, α is an integer, and if n is an assigned GOTO, α is a statement number. α can also be set to ALL or ANY to specify all the branches or a single arbitrary branch. Each time statement n is executed during the execution of the program, branch(es) α will be followed.

In the case where all the variables in a conditional statement predicate have actual values, the user can cause normal execution of the statement to take place by specifying SELECT ANY CONSISTENT. This means that the system is to select any branch which does not involve a false predicate. Suppose, for example, that X has the value -1 and the statement IF X A,B,C is to be executed. The branch to statement A (.LT.) is the only branch involving a branch predicate which is not false. The other branch predicates are -1=0 and -1>0. The CONSISTENT option can also be used with the other forms of the SELECT command (e.g., SELECT .LT. CONSISTENT). It causes each of the specified branches in the command to be examined to see if their predicates are true or false. Only those branches having true predicates are followed.

The word "CONSISTENT" was used for this feature of the language because it was originally planned that the CON-

SISTENCY routine would operate by adding the branch predicate for a selected branch to the system of branch predicates for the rest of the program path. The CONSISTENCY function would then carry out the much more difficult task of examining this system of predicates for consistency. This expensive level of sophistication is not included in the current system but may be incorporated if it appears to be useful enough.

The other basic path selection command is the n LOOP k command. This command can be used with a DO-loop to specify the number of times a loop is to be iterated. When a path enters a DO-loop, a counter is set up which is incremented each time an iteration of the loop is completed. If the DO-loop has an associated n LOOP k command, then the iteration terminates and the path exits from the loop if the count ever reaches k. If there are exits from the middle of the loop, SELECT commands can be used to cause the path to leave the loop before the loop counter has a chance to reach k.

The following forms of the LOOP command can also be used: n LOOP ANY $(k_1,k_2,\cdots,k_n)$ {CONSISTENT} and n LOOP ALL $(k_1,k_2,\cdots,k_n)$ {CONSISTENT}. The braces { } mean that the CONSISTENT specification is optional. The first command causes the program to be executed some number of times k_i, where i is selected arbitrarily such that $1 \leq i \leq n$. The second command causes a separate path to be set up for each of the elements in the looplist, $(k_1,k_2,\cdots,k_n)$. Each path will correspond to some number of iterations of the loop. The CONSISTENT option can be used to check the loop iteration predicate. Suppose the DO-loop header is DO N I = A,B,C and an entry k in a looplist specifies that a path is to be generated which iterates the loop k times. If the consistency option is specified, the path will be generated only if $I \leq B$ after k iterations have been carried out.

In addition to SELECT and LOOP, there are two other kinds of path selection commands. The SPLIT $((P_1,A_1),\cdots(P_n,A_n))$ command causes a path to split into n subpaths. It can be used to simulate the effect of an n-way branch occurring immediately following a statement in a program. The P_i are predicates that will be associated with each branch. The A_i are path attributes and are explained below. The n SKIP k will cause DISSECT to skip over the program from statement n to statement k. The n HALT command will cause DISSECT to terminate execution at statement n.

D. Conditional Execution of Commands

Most of the commands can be executed conditionally by embedding them in a conditional form "n IF condition THEN command 1 ELSE command 2." The conditions can be any legal Fortran Boolean expression in program variables and in the special variables LOOPCOUNT, LOOPCOUNT(m), and ATTRIBUTE. When statement n is encountered during the symbolic evaluation of a path through a program, DISSECT evaluates the condition to see if command 1 (or command 2) should be executed. The special variable LOOPCOUNT is equal to the number of times that the innermost loop containing statement n has been iterated. LOOPCOUNT(m) is the number of times loop m has been iterated. Loops are named by the sequence number of their first statement. LOOPCOUNT and LOOPCOUNT(m) refer to the number of iterations of a loop during the execution of the loop now taking place and not

```
      DOUBLE PRECISION FUNCTION SIN(X,E)        1
C     THIS COMPUTES SIN(X) TO ACCURACY E         2
      DOUBLE PRECISION E, TERM, SUM              3
      REAL X                                     4
      TERM = X                                   5
      DO 20 I=3,100,2                            6
      TERM = TERM*X**2/ (I*(I-1))                7
      IF (TERM .LT. E) GO TO 30                  8
      SUM = SUM + (-1**(I/2))*TERM               9
20    CONTINUE                                  10
30    SIN = SUM                                 11
      RETURN                                    12
      END                                       13
```

Fig. 10. SIN program with errors.

some previously completed execution. Statement n is expected to be contained inside loop m.

The user of DISSECT is allowed to attach "attributes" to paths. An attribute is any text string and is attached to a path when a particular branch is followed during the traversal of the path. Any number of attributes can be attached. Attributes are used for labeling paths, and can be referred to in conditional commands. Suppose, for example, that two conditional statements, m and n, occur at different points in a program and that the branch to be followed from statement n depends on which branch was followed when statement m was encountered. This dependency can be implemented by associating a unique attribute with each of the branches from statement m and then testing for the attribute when selecting the branch to be followed from statement n.

In addition to the above commands, DISSECT contains a number of other facilities, some of which are illustrated in the following example.

E. DISSECT Example

In the following example, DISSECT was used to test the program in Fig. 10. This program was taken from the Common Blunders Section of Kernighan and Plauger and contains four errors. The program appearing in Fig. 2 is a corrected version of this program. The program is supposed to compute $SIN(X) = X - X^{**}3/3! + X^{**}5/5! - \cdots$. The four errors are: SUM is not initialized to X, the last value of TERM is not added on to the final value of SIN, the $-1^{**}(I/2)$ in statement 9 should be $(-1)^{**}(I/2)$ and the predicate in statement 8 should be (DABS(TERM) .LT. E).

Three cases were prepared for testing SIN. Fig. 11 contains the list of commands for the three cases. The commands appear in two sections. The global commands apply to all cases. The case commands for each case apply only to that case.

The MAXPATHS and MAXLENGTH commands set upper limits on the number of paths and the path lengths that can be generated by each case. In case of errors in DISSECT commands or in the program to be analyzed, they prevent the system from going into infinite loops or processing unexpectedly long paths. PATH and PREDICATES cause the output of each path's sequence numbers and its predicates. 6 DEFAULT LOOP 10 specifies that unless some other loop command for loop 6 can be found, it should be iterated 10 times. 12 OUTPUT SIN specifies that the value of SIN should be output each

```
TITLE: ANALYSIS OF SIN PROGRAM FROM KERNIGHAN AND PLAUGER
GLOBAL COMMANDS:
MAXPATHS 10;
MAXLENGTH 30;
PATH; PREDICATES;
6   DEFAULT LOOP 10
12  OUTPUT SIN

CASE 1: LOOP ONCE              CASE 3: LOOP THREE TIMES
CASE COMMANDS:                 CASE COMMANDS:
8 SELECT T;                    8 SELECT F,F,T

CASE 2: LOOP TWICE
CASE COMMANDS:
8 SELECT F,T
```

Fig. 11. DISSECT commands for SIN program.

```
CASE 1: LOOP ONCE
CASE COMMANDS:
8 SELECT T;

PATH:        1-8 11-12
PREDICATES:
   :1   1    DOUBLE PRECISION FUNCTION SIN(X,E)
   :5   8    (X**3/6) .LT. E
OUTPUT:
   :6  11    NOTE: REFERENCE TO UNITIALIZED VARIABLE SUM
   :7  12    SIN = ?SUM?
```

Fig. 12. DISSECT output for case one.

```
CASE 2: LOOP TWICE
CASE COMMANDS:
8 SELECT F,T;

PATH: 1-10 6-8 11-12
PREDICATES:
   :1   1    DOUBLE PRECISION FUNCTION SIN(X,E)
   :5   8    (X**3/6) .GE. E
   :10  8    (X**5/120) .LT. E
OUTPUT:
   :1   1    DOUBLE PRECISION FUNCTION SIN(X,E)
   :6   9    NOTE: REFERENCE TO UNITIALIZED VARIABLE SUM
   :12 12    SIN = ?SUM? - (X**3/6)
```

Fig. 13. DISSECT output for case two.

time statement 12 is executed. The 8 SELECT F,T command in CASE 2 is shorthand notation for IF LOOPCOUNT=1 THEN SELECT F; IF LOOPCOUNT=2 THEN SELECT T. In this particular example, the exits from the middle of the loop are taken before the loop count for the loop reaches the value in the loop command.

Figs. 12-14 contain the output which DISSECT generates when it tests the SIN program using the commands in Fig. 11. The case commands for each case are repeated at the beginning of the output for each case. The two numbers preceding each line of output are path indices (of the form :k) and sequence numbers. They refer to the position in the path where the output was generated and the program statements associated with the commands causing the output. Lines of output associated with program statements having statement numbers (i.e., labels) are preceded by a third number, the program statement number.

Reference [11] contains a detailed description of the DISSECT system and the complete output for several different kinds of examples.

IV. Experiments with Incorrect Programs

DISSECT has been run on a number of different kinds of programs. Two classes of experiments with DISSECT are reported here. The first class of experiments was carried out on the 12 simple programs and program fragments in the

```
          CASE 3: LOOP THREE TIMES
          CASE COMMANDS:
          8 SELECT F,F,T;

          PATH: 1-10, 6-10, 6-8, 11-12
          PREDICATES:
            :1  1    DOUBLE PRECISION FUNCTION SIN(X,E)
            :5  8    (X**3/6) .GE. E
            :10 8    (X**5/120) .GE. E
            :15 8    (X**7/5040) .LT. E
          OUTPUT
            :1  1    DOUBLE PRECISION FUNCTION SIN(X,E)
            :6  9    REFERENCE TO UNITIALIZED VARIABLE SUM
            17 12    SIN = ?SUM? - (X**3/6) - (X**5/120)
```

Fig. 14. DISSECT output for case three.

Common Blunders Section of Kernighan and Plauger [10]. Some of those programs are in Fortran and the others in PL/1. The use of DISSECT for the PL/1 programs was simulated by hand.

The approach followed in the experiments was to analyze each program and to try to imagine which tests would be most useful in illustrating that the program was correct. Both symbolic and actual values were used in constructing the tests. Any of the different kinds of output that can be generated using DISSECT was allowed as test output. This includes intermediate values of variables or unevaluated listings of paths, as well as the final symbolic values of "output variables." The procedure for choosing the tests was essentially intuitive and not founded on any theory which could be used to demonstrate that the tests proved that the programs are correct. In general, each path (up to iteration of loops) was tested at least once. All loops were executed at least twice. A theory for selecting tests based on the concept of a "program model" is under development. The use of this approach was first described in [12].

After the tests had been selected, DISSECT was used to analyze the programs and to generate the desired test output. The output was then examined to see if the presence of the bugs in the programs was obvious from the output.

We assumed that when the programs were originally written, the programmers missed the bugs because they did not notice the presence of certain erroneous or missing constructs. When the output from the tests was examined, we assumed that the same types of erroneous constructs would not be noticed; i.e., we did not cheat by assuming that the programmer would notice an erroneous construct in test output that was the same as that which he had missed in the program. Two examples of this kind of error involved missing parentheses. A formula in a program which had missing parentheses appeared unaltered in the symbolic output for the program. Two other examples of this kind of error involved the use of type-real variables in predicates involving the equality operator. We assumed that since the programmer was not aware of the problems this can cause when he wrote his program, he would probably still not be aware of it when examining symbolic output.

A. Reliability of Symbolic Testing

The 12 programs that were examined contained 22 errors. Of these, 13 would almost certainly be discovered if symbolic testing was used to analyze the program. Even from this small sample, it was possible to come to several conclusions about the types of errors that would or would not be discovered using a symbolic testing system like DISSECT.

The different kinds of errors occurring in the programs can be conveniently classified using the following definitions. We assume that the programmer wrote a program P to compute some function F with domain D. Call P* the "correct version" of P. Each program P has one or more paths P_i. Each path is meant to carry out some *path function* F_i and is executed for all input in some *path domain* D_i. P and P* can be compared by comparing their paths, path domains, and path functions. Some errors in P result in missing paths: there are paths in P* that are not present in P. Some result in incorrect path domains: the paths in P and P* are the same but the domain D_i of some path P_i in P is different from the domain D_i^* for the corresponding path P_i^*. Other errors result in incorrect path functions: a path P_i computes the value of some function F_i which is not the same as the function F_i^* for P_i^*.

In some cases a program is incorrect because some computation or sequence of computations C is incorrect. If the computation affects the function computed by a path, it results in a *path-function error*. If it affects the predicate in a conditional statement, it results in a *path-domain* error. Path-domain errors can also be caused by the use of the wrong logical operators or wrong variables in a conditional statement predicate, or by putting a conditional statement in the wrong place in a program. The path/path-domain/path-function approach to error classification is studied in [13] and is similar to a classification of errors used by Goodenough and Gerhart in [14].

Of the 13 errors which are revealed by symbolic testing, 9 are path-function errors: the function which is supposed to be computed by some path is wrong. When the path is symbolically evaluated, a function is formed which is obviously incorrect. In three other examples the errors were due to faulty initialization of variables. These three other examples can also be considered path-function errors, since the existence of the errors was revealed during the construction of the symbolic representation of the path functions for the programs. The remaining error is a path-domain error. One of the nine path-function errors occurs along with a path-domain error. Both the path-domain component and the path-function component of this error are revealed by symbolic testing.

$$J = MARKS(I) - 1/10 + 1 \qquad J = (MARKS(I) - 1)/10 + 1$$
$$P \qquad\qquad\qquad\qquad P^*$$

Fig. 15. Parenthesis error.

$$J = MARKS(I) - \frac{1}{10} + 1$$

Fig. 16. Two-dimensional output.

The errors in the SIN program in Fig. 10 are typical of the sorts of errors that occur in the programs from Kernighan and Plauger. The missing initialization of SUM and the missing parentheses around the −1 in statement 9 cause path function errors and their presence is revealed in the symbolic tests in Figs. 12–14. The failure to add the first value of TERM to the output variable SIN is also obvious from the symbolic test output: the last value of TERM appears in the predicates for a path domain but not in the symbolic representation of the path function. This particular error is one of the few path-domain errors which occurred in the experiments which were revealed by symbolic testing. The last error, the omission of the DABS function from statement 8, causes a path-domain error that is no more apparent in the symbolic test output than it was in the original program. Symbolic testing is not "reliable" for discovering this error.

Of the 9 errors that would possibly not be revealed by symbolic testing, 3 are path-function errors, 4 are domain errors, and 2 are missing path errors. Two of the path-function errors are due to missing parentheses and the third to an incorrect format statement. One of the parentheses errors is illustrated in Fig. 15. Although it is not fair to assume that a user would notice a parenthesis error just because it is printed out as part of a symbolic formula, it may be fair to assume that he would notice it if it is printed in two-dimensional format as in Fig. 16. If a testing system that generates two-dimensional output is used, then the two parentheses errors will be discovered by symbolic testing.

The incorrect format statement error mentioned above results in the attempt to read a value using a floating point format into a type integer variable. This error is an example of the type of error which could be discovered by an appropriate static source program analysis system [15]. Systems like this have been built which check for different kinds of data flow anomalies and nonstandard program constructs. Ramamoorthy's FACES system [18], the DAVE data flow system of Osterweil and Fosdick [16], and TRW's ATDG [17] all contain facilities for static source analysis. Static source analysis would also find the three uninitialized variable errors. Both the format-statement error and the uninitialized variables could be detected by a compiler with type checking facilities and which kept a record of variable use and definition in its symbol table.

If the use of an integrated system of testing tools which contains both a symbolic evaluator with 2-d output and a static source analyzer is assumed, then the number of errors in the Kernighan and Plauger programs that will not be discovered can be reduced from 9 to 6.

The remaining six errors all have one interesting property in common. They involve paths which have correct path functions but which have path domains that contain both correct and incorrect elements; i.e., they involve paths P_i such that $F_i = F_i^*$ and $D_i \neq D_i^*$ but $D_i \cap D_i^* \neq 0$. In each case D_i differs from D_i^* in some way which did not come to the attention of the programmer who wrote the program. In some cases he forgot to refine a domain D into two subdomains and construct a new path function for one of the subdomains. In other cases, elements which should be included in one path domain are included in another through the use of a "slightly incorrect" branching predicate or a "slightly incorrect" computation for computing the value of a variable in a predicate. In all six cases the symbolic systems of predicates for the domains do not contain anything that is any more likely to catch the programmer's attention than the error in the original program.

In four of the six path-domain and missing path errors, the error seems to be due to the programmer having forgotten about certain possible classes of inputs, and may be specification and design errors rather than implementation errors. In one example a program is correct for positive input but the programmer appears to have failed to consider the possibility of negative input. In another, the input was assumed to consist of sequences of distinct elements of length at least two. One of the four errors is present not only in the "incorrect" program in Kernighan and Plauger but also in their corrected version of the program (the current program on p. 79). The program fails to work correctly for input which should cause a loop to be executed exactly once (SC=TC and CI=0).

The need for design and specification tools has been emphasized in different papers [18], [19]. In their paper on theory of testing [14], Goodenough and Gerhart suggest a method for program testing that concentrates on different important combinations of conditions in the input data that can be constructed from program specifications and from the properties of a proposed implementation. The user is expected to construct tables of conditions as part of the testing process. In [20], Henderson describes a program development technique in which the values of variables and data structures are decomposed into abstract classes. The classes can be thought of as abstract variable values and can be used to model a program at different levels of detail. Different combinations of abstract values correspond to different abstract program states. This approach, like the method of Goodenough and Gerhart, focuses the attention of the program developer on the important combinations of classes of input values and may be useful in avoiding path-domain errors.

One simple expedient that may help with the path-domain error problem would be to require the user of a symbolic testing system to provide a system of predicates that describes the domain D of a program. These predicates, together with the path-domain predicates may be enough to alert the user to possible error situations.

The remaining two of the six path-domain and missing path errors that would not be discovered by symbolic testing involve sequences of computations that can arrive at unexpected values, rather than computations that begin with unexpected classes of input. The first error involves the failure to test if an expression has become zero before executing an output statement that only makes sense when the expression is nonzero. This error might be more likely to be noticed if the user were required to provide predicates describing a program's output values and the intermediate values of key variables and expressions, as well as predicates describing program input.

DISSECT, SELECT, and EFFIGY all have facilities for asserting that certain conditions hold for the values of variables at arbitrary points in the program. A similar facility is available in elementary form in Algol W[21], in sophisticated form in Fairley's ISMS System [22], and is currently being studied by Stucki [23]. In Fairley's and Stucki's systems the assertions are evaluated at execution time to provide run-time statistics. In DISSECT, SELECT, and EFFIGY, the assertions are appended to the path-domain predicates and can be used in several ways.

The second of the two remaining path-domain errors that would not be discovered by symbolic testing results from the use of type-real variables in a predicate that tests on equality. This is another example of a data flow anomaly that could be detected by a source program static analyzer.

B. Actual versus Symbolic Testing

In the experiments described above, the programs were tested with combinations of actual and symbolic input data. The facilities required for carrying out symbolic evaluation impose extra overhead on the testing process and it is important to consider whether the extra overhead is justified by increased reliability in the testing process.

Each of the 12 programs from Kernighan and Plauger was tested first with actual data and then with symbolic data. In order to compare the two types of testing certain assumptions were made about strategies for choosing test data. For both types of testing, each path (up to iterations of loops) was tested at least once and each loop was iterated at least twice. When the programs were tested with actual data the test elements for exercising particular paths were chosen at random from the elements which cause the paths to be traversed. The effect of a "more intelligent," nonrandom choice of data was also considered. When the programs were tested with symbolic data, the test elements were constructed by assigning combinations of actual and symbolic values to input variables. Input values were selected that would cause the generation of symbolic output and symbolic systems of predicates that could be compared with specifications for the program.

Of the 22 errors in the programs, 13 would be discovered using symbolic testing and nine if the testing process were constrained to the use of actual data. If a symbolic testing system is used which produces two-dimensional output the number of errors that would be discovered by symbolic testing would be increased from 13 to 15. If a nonrandom strategy for selecting data for testing particular paths is used, the number of errors that would be discovered by testing with actual data would probably be increased from 9 to 11. The incorrect path functions for two errors give correct answers for only single inputs or correct answers for input whose choice would be unlikely if some strategy other than random selection were used.

The four errors for which symbolic testing is always reliable but for which it is unlikely that actual data testing will be reliable are different kinds of path-function errors. In two examples, the path functions give correct answers for large sets of input data even though it is clear from the symbolic representation of the path function that the function is incorrect. The remaining two of the four errors for which symbolic testing is reliable but for which actual data testing is not reliable involve the computation of formulae which, although they are incorrect, may give "correct-looking" answers. If we assume that the programmer uses a table with less accuracy than the program or simply looks to see if the answers "look OK," then he may miss the errors. The errors occur in approximation programs which add on one too many or one too few terms of an approximation series before terminating. The errors are obvious in the symbolic test output for the programs.

Both symbolic testing and actual data testing are unreliable for discovering most of the path-domain errors in the sample programs. In a certain sense, symbolic testing may be considered to be more unreliable than actual data testing for these errors. In each case the path domain is partially correct and partially incorrect (i.e., $D_i \neq D_i^*$ but $D_i \cap D_i^* \neq \emptyset$). Symbolic testing is unreliable because the error is not revealed by the symbolic output and symbolic systems of predicates for the paths. Actual data testing is not reliable because there is no reason for assuming that the programmer will test a path over the incorrect part of the path domains (i.e., $D_i \sim (D_i \cap D_i^*)$). But it is still possible for actual data testing to reveal the error if the programmer is lucky enough to choose a test which comes from the incorrect part of the domain. In general, it appears as though the path-domain errors for which symbolic testing is unreliable are those for which the path domains are only partially incorrect. Really gross errors where the domains are completely incorrect are detected by both symbolic and actual data testing.

In summary, symbolic testing was found to be somewhat more reliable than actual data testing for computational errors that affect a program's path functions. In the sample of 12 incorrect programs, a testing strategy which used actual data would have been reliable or probably reliable for discovering 11 of 22 errors and symbolic testing for 15 of the 22 errors. Symbolic testing was not reliable for path-domain errors or for certain kinds of data flow anomalies. It may be possible to increase the reliability of symbolic testing for path-domain errors by requiring that the user supply systems of predicates describing program input or a table showing all the different possible combinations of different kinds of input data that will affect the choice of path functions that must be used in the program.

V. Experiments with Correct Programs

The second class of experiments which are described in this paper were carried out for a diverse set of programs for which there were no known errors. The programs were taken from the CACM, the IBM Scientific Subroutine Package, and [24]. The experiments were carried out to evaluate the use of symbolic testing in analyzing programs and confirming that they agreed with their functional specifications.

```
              SUBROUTINE INTERP(X, Y, NPTS, NTERMS, XIN, YOUT)   #0
              DOUBLE PRECISION DELTAX, DELTA, A, PROD, SUM       #1
              DIMENSION X(1), Y(1)                               #2
              DIMENSION DELTA(10), A(10)                         #3
C                                                                #4
C             SEARCH FOR APPROPRIATE VALUE OF X(1)               #5
C                                                                #6
      11 DO 19 I=1, NPTS                                         #7
           IF (XIN - X(I)) 13, 17, 19                            #8
      13 I1 = I - NTERMS/2                                       #9
           IF (I1) 15, 15, 21                                    #10
      15 I1 = 1                                                  #11
           GO TO 21                                              #12
      17 YOUT = Y(I)                                             #13
      18 GO TO 61                                                #14
      19 CONTINUE                                                #15
           I1 = NPTS - NTERMS + 1                                #16
      21 I2 = I1 + NTERMS - 1                                    #18
           IF (NPTS - I2) 23, 31, 31                             #19
      23 I2 = NPTS                                               #20
           I1 = I2 - NTERMS + 1                                  #21
      25 IF (I1) 26, 26, 31                                      #22
      26 I1 = 1                                                  #23
      27 NTERMS = I2 - I1 + 1                                    #24
C                                                                
C             EVALUATE DEVIATIONS DELTA                          #26
C                                                                #27
      31 DENOM = X(I1+1) - X(I1)                                 #28
           DELTAX = (XIN - X(I1)) / DENOM                        #29
           DO 35 I=1, NTERMS                                     #30
           IX = I1 + I - 1                                       #31
           DELTA(I) = (X(IX) - X(I1)) / DENOM                    #32
      35 CONTINUE                                                #32.1
C                                                                #33
C             ACCUMULATE COEFFICIENTS A                          #34
C                                                                #35
      40 A(1) = Y(I1)                                            #36
      41 DO 50 K=2, NTERMS                                       #37
           PROD = 1.                                             #38
           SUM = 0.                                              #39
           IMAX = K - 1                                          #40
           IXMAX = I1 + IMAX                                     #41
           DO 49 I=1, IMAX                                       #42
           J = K - I                                             #43
           PROD = PROD * (DELTA(K) - DELTA(J))                   #44
      49 SUM = SUM - A(J)/PROD                                   #45
           A(K) = SUM + Y(IXMAX)/PROD                            #46
      50 CONTINUE                                                #47
C                                                                #48
C             ACCUMULATE SUM OF EXPANSION                        #49
C                                                                #50
      51 SUM = A(1)                                              #51
           DO 57 J=2, NTERMS                                     #52
           PROD = 1.                                             #53
           IMAX = J - 1                                          #54
           DO 56 I=1, IMAX                                       #55
      56 PROD = PROD * (DELTAX - DELTA(I))                       #56
      57 SUM = SUM + A(J)*PROD                                   #57
      60 YOUT = SUM                                              #58
      61 RETURN                                                  #59
           END                                                   #60
```

Fig. 17. Interpolation subroutine.

Fig. 17 contains one of the "correct" programs that was analyzed using DISSECT. The program can be used for doing polynomial interpolation and is taken from [24]. The input consists of two vectors X and Y which hold a set of NPTS pairs of values (x_i, y_i). The pairs are assumed to belong to some function f for which $y_i = f(x_i)$. The routine uses NTERMS of these pairs to define a polynomial which is used to compute the value of YOUT at the point XIN.

```
 8     XIN .LT. X(I)
 9 13  I1 = I - NTERMS/2
10     I1 .LE. 0
11 15  I1 = 1
18 21  I2 = I1 + NTERMS-1
19     NPTS .LT. I2
20 23  I2 = NPTS
21     I1 = I2 - NTERMS+1
22 25  I1 .LE. 0
23 26  I1 = 1
24 27  NTERMS = I2 - I1+1

 8     XIN .LT. X(I)
 9 13  I1 = I - NTERMS/2
10     I1 .LE. 0
11 15  I1 = 1
18 21  I2 = I1 + NTERMS-1
19     NPTS .LT. I2
20 23  I2 = NPTS
21     I1 = I2 - NTERMS+1
22 25  I1 .GT. 0

 8     XIN .LT. X(I)
 9 13  I1 = I - NTERMS/2
10     I1 .LE. 0
11 15  I1 = 1
18 21  I2 = I1 + NTERMS-1
19     NPTS .GE. I2
```

Fig. 18. Test output for first segment of INTERP program.

The documentation for the program describes it as consisting of four segments. The first segment finds the "most appropriate" set of NTERMS pairs for carrying out the interpolation. It does this by finding a set of NTERMS pairs which "straddle" XIN as evenly as possible. The set of pairs is selected by choosing values for I1 and I2. The set of pairs $(X(I1), Y(I1))$, $(X(I1+1), Y(I1+1)), \cdots, (X(I2), Y(I2))$ are the pairs that are used for the interpolation. NTERMS is defined to be $I2-I1+1$.

The first segment consists of a complicated mixture of simple computations and branching conditions. After several experiments, it appeared that the best test output for this segment would be unevaluated listings of the different paths through the segments. Not counting multiple iterations of loops, there are ten paths in the segment. Fig. 18 contains a reproduction of three of the paths. The path index numbers in both Figs. 18 and 20 have been deleted. The two columns of numbers preceding the output are sequence and statement numbers. The complete set of path listings (no multiple iterations of loops) indicates that the segment carries out the correct sequence of tests and assignments to I1 and I2. Symbolic evaluation did not appear to be useful for analyzing this segment.

The second, third, and fourth segments of the program compute the formulae in Fig. 19. The most useful kind of test output for all three segments proved to be symbolic representations of the path functions and path domains through the segments. Fig. 20 contains the test output for the third segment which is generated when the outer loop in the segment is executed three times. Symbolic evaluation was equally useful for analyzing each of the last three segments of the program.

$$DELTAX = \frac{XIN - X(I1)}{X(I1+1) - X(I1)} \qquad DELTA(I) = \frac{X(I1+I-1)-X(I1)}{X(I1+1) - X(I1)}$$

$$A(I) = \frac{Y(I1+I-1)}{\prod_{K=1}^{I-1} DELTA(I) - DELTA(K)} - \sum_{J=1}^{I-1} \frac{A(J)}{\prod_{K=1}^{I-1} DELTA(I) - DELTA(K)}$$

$$YOUT = A(1) + \sum_{J=2}^{NTERMS} A(J) \prod_{I=1}^{J-1} (DELTAX-DELTA(I))$$

Fig. 19. Formulae for INTERP program.

The output in Figs. 18 and 20 is typical of the kind of output that can be generated using DISSECT. The two classes of experiments that were carried out indicated that the kind of testing that could be carried out with DISSECT was more useful than conventional testing both for discovering bugs and for confirming that a program matches its specifications.

Informal validation of a program requires several, careful detailed readings of the program. Once the reader has a good understanding of the overall structure of the program and its relationship to the program's semantics, he can begin to relate collections of program paths and loop structures to particular computations and patterns of computations expected in the program. It is at this point that DISSECT becomes useful in helping to read the program by unravelling collections of paths and generating symbolic descriptions of path functions and path domains. In the first segment of the INTERP program, DISSECT was used to unravel a collection of nonlooping paths. In the third segment, it was used to unravel a collection of

```
OUTPUT:
    47 50 A(1) = Y(I1)
          A(2) = -A(1) / (DELTA(2) - DELTA(1))
                +Y(I1+1) / (DELTA(2) - DELTA(1))

          A(3) = -A(2) / (DELTA(3) - DELTA(2))
                -A(1) / ((DELTA(3) - DELTA(1)) (DELTA(3) - DELTA(2)))
                +Y(I1+2) / ((DELTA(3) - DELTA(1)) (DELTA(3) - DELTA(2)))

PREDICATES:
    45 49 T
    47 50 3 .LE. NTERMS
    45 49 T
    45 49 T
    47 50 4 .GT. NTERMS
```

Fig. 20. Test output for second segment.

paths constructed from a single path and a nested loop structure. It was used to select paths corresponding to several iterations of the loops and to generate symbolic representations of the computations carried out by the paths.

Most of the loop structures that were encountered in the programs in the experiments were for manipulating arrays or computing the terms of a series-type formula. Array manipulation loops are usually designed to carry out the same pattern of computations over arrays of different dimensions. The loop bounds correspond to the dimensions and a symbolic representation of the pattern of computations can be generated by selecting particular array dimensions. Series computation loops usually contain a fixed computational procedure for computing the "next" term in the series from the previous terms. The correctness of a series computation loop can be analyzed by generating the first term of the series and then as many other terms as are required to indicate that the term generation procedure is correct.

VI. Summary and Future Work

The experiments with DISSECT indicate that symbolic testing, and path analysis in general, has a part to play in software reliability analysis. Although they will not completely solve the software reliability problem, symbolic evaluation and the other types of program analysis techniques which are now available can be used to significantly reduce the number of bugs and to increase the level of confidence in a program. In the programs from Kernighan and Plauger, symbolic testing and source code static analysis can be used to raise the bug detection rate from 11 out of 22 for conventional testing to 17 out of 22. The remaining bugs are path-domain-type errors which may require the use of a design or specification tool or a method like that described by Goodenough and Gerhart in [14].

The experiments with classes of programs known to contain naturally occurring (i.e., not seeded) errors are continuing and will provide more conclusive data on the effectiveness of symbolic testing and other types of program analysis.

DISSECT was found to be quite easy to use and the idea of a program test language for describing symbolic tests to be carried out is very convenient. Experience with the system revealed several operational deficiencies which will be corrected in an improved version. One type of deficiency involves the use of sequence numbers for attaching DISSECT commands to program statements. In many situations it is more appropriate and useful to attach the commands to the flow edges "between" statements. Another deficiency involves the mixing together of path selection and input commands. They should be separated so that several sets of path input can be easily used for the same selected set of paths.

VII. Acknowledgment and Related Work

The DISSECT system evolved from an initial research project which was funded by the National Bureau of Standards at McDonnell Douglas in 1973. It appears that the use of symbolic evaluation for generating test data was independently proposed by the author and several others [1]-[4], [6] around that period of time. Since then the development of DISSECT and the research described above has been both directly and indirectly influenced by the work of several people. The closest contacts have been with the research on symbolic evaluation systems [2]-[4], test data generation systems [6], [17], [26], and theory of testing [14]. The work is related to other types of program analysis systems such as the FACES system [18], the DAVE data flow analysis system [16], and the program structure analysis capabilities of RXVP [25] and ATDG [17]. In its earliest stages the work was influenced by the description of EXDAMS appearing in [27]. The EXDAMS approach to testing is related to the ISMS system developed by R. E. Fairley [22]. Several of the people involved in those projects have made useful criticisms and suggestions.

In addition to the research in path analysis, DISSECT is also related to work on proofs of program correctness. Deutsch's program proof system [28] and Burstall's paper on proving correctness in [29] use symbolic evaluation to generate verification conditions.

The National Bureau of Standards Research Project at McDonnell Douglas was supervised by D. Fyfe and R. Stillman who contributed invaluable advice at different points throughout the project. L. Stucki and Z. Jelinski supervised the project at McDonnell Douglas and were involved in the evolution of DISSECT during the entire period of research and development. Mr. Stucki provided a broad perspective on the problem based on his experience with other types of testing tools such as PET [30] and his current work on dynamic assertions [23].

The predecessor of DISSECT was completed in 1974 and is described in [5]. J. Laub of the University of California, San Diego, implemented large portions of the system and designed a Fortran parser and program model builder that is still used in DISSECT. R. E. Hoffman of the University of California, San Diego, implemented parts of DISSECT and was responsible for much of the symbolic evaluator and output modules.

The algebraic simplifier used in the DISSECT symbolic evaluator is derived from the simplifier in the SRI program verifier [2].

The importance of the above, and possibly other forgotten sources for and contributions to the DISSECT system is gratefully acknowledged.

REFERENCES

[1] W. E. Howden, "Methodology for the generation of program test data," *IEEE Trans. Comput.*, vol. C-24, pp. 554-560, May 1975.
[2] R. S. Boyer, B. Elspas, and K. N. Levitt, "SELECT-A formal system for testing and debugging programs by symbolic execution," in *Proc. 1975 Int. Conf. Reliable Software*, 1975, pp. 234-245.
[3] J. C. King, "Symbolic execution and program testing," *Commun. Ass. Comput. Mach.*, vol. 19, pp. 385-394, July 1976.
[4] L. A. Clarke, "A system to generate test data and symbolically execute programs," *IEEE Trans. Software Eng.*, vol. SE-2, pp. 215-222, Sept. 1976.
[5] W. E. Howden and J. Laub, "Automatic case analysis of programs," in *Proc. Computer Science and Statistics: 8th Annu. Symp. on the Interface*, 1975, pp. 347-352.
[6] E. F. Miller and R. A. Melton, "Automated generation of test-case data sets," in *Proc. 1975 Int. Conf. Reliable Software*, 1975, pp. 51-58.
[7] J. C. Huang, "An approach to program testing," *Comput. Surveys*, vol. 7, pp. 113-128, Sept. 1975.
[8] W. E. Howden and L. G. Stucki, "A methodology for effective test case selection-Phase I," McDonnell Douglas Astronautics, Huntington Beach, CA, Tech. Rep. MDC G5301, Jan. 1974.
[9] B. Elspas, M. Green, A. Korsak, and P. Wong, "Solving nonlinear inequalities associated with computer program paths," Stanford Res. Inst., Stanford, CA, preliminary draft.
[10] B. W. Kernighan and P. J. Plauger, *The Elements of Programming Style*. New York: McGraw Hill, 1974.
[11] W. E. Howden and L. G. Stucki, "A methodology for effective test case selection-Phase III," McDonnell Douglas Astronautics, Huntington Park, CA, Tech. Rep. MDC G6211, Mar. 1976.
[12] W. E. Howden, "Models of correct programs and program testing," Dept. Appl. Phys. and Inf. Sci., Univ. California, San Diego, Comput. Sci. Tech. Rep. 10, Nov. 1974.
[13] —, "Reliability of the path analysis testing strategy," *IEEE Trans. Software Eng.*, vol. SE-2, pp. 208-214, Sept. 1976.
[14] J. B. Goodenough and S. L. Gerhart, "Toward a theory of test data selection," *IEEE Trans. Software Eng.*, vol. SE-1, pp. 156-173, June 1975.
[15] C. V. Ramamoorthy and S. F. Ho, "Testing large software with automated software evaluation systems," *IEEE Trans. Software Eng.*, vol. SE-1, pp. 46-58, Mar. 1975.
[16] L. J. Osterweil and L. D. Fosdick, "Data flow analysis as an aid in documentation, assertion generation, validation, and error detection," Dep. Comput. Sci., Univ. Colorado, CU-CS-055-74, Sept. 1975.
[17] R. H. Hoffman, "User information for the interactive automated test data generator," NASA, Johnson Space Center, JSC Internal Note 74-FM-88, Jan. 1976.
[18] C. V. Ramamoorthy and S. F. Ho, "FORTRAN automatic code evaluation system," Electron. Res. Lab., Univ. California, Berkeley, Rep. M-466, Aug. 1974.
[19] B. W. Boehm, R. K. McClean, and D. B. Urfig, "Some experience with automated aids to the design of large-scale reliable software," *IEEE Trans. Software Eng.*, vol. SE-1, pp. 125-133, Mar. 1975.
[20] P. Henderson, "Finite state modelling in program development," in *Proc. 1975 Int. Conf. Reliable Software*, 1975, pp. 221-227.
[21] R. L. Sites, "Algol-W reference manual," Dep. Comput. Sci., Stanford Univ., Rep. CS-230, Feb. 1972.
[22] R. E. Fairley, "An experimental program testing facility," *IEEE Trans. Software Eng.*, vol. SE-1, pp. 350-357, Dec. 1975.
[23] L. G. Stucki and G. L. Foshee, "New assertion concepts for self-metric software validation," in *Proc. 1975 Int. Conf. Reliable Software*, 1975, pp. 59-71.
[24] P. R. Benington, *Data Reduction and Error Analysis for the Physical Sciences*. New York: McGraw Hill, 1969.
[25] E. F. Miller, "RXVP: An automated verification system for FORTRAN," in *Proc. Computer Science and Statistics: 8th Annu. Symp. on the Interface*, 1975, p. 328.
[26] K. W. Krause, R. W. Smith, and M. A. Goodwin, "Optimal software test planning through automated network analysis," in *Proc. 1973 IEEE Symp. Comput. Software Reliability*, 1973, pp. 18-22.
[27] R. M. Balzer, "EXDAMS-Extendable debugging and monitoring system," in *1969 Spring Joint Comput. Conf., AFIPS Conf. Proc.*, vol. 34. Montvale, NJ: AFIPS Press, 1969, pp. 567-580.
[28] L. P. Deutsch, "An interactive program verifier," Ph.D. dissertation, Univ. California, Berkeley, May 1973.
[29] R. M. Burstall, "Proving correctness as hand simulation with a little induction," in *Proc. IFIPS 74*. Amsterdam, The Netherlands: North-Holland, 1974.
[30] L. G. Stucki, "Automatic generation of self-metric software," in *Proc. 1973 IEEE Symp. Comput. Software Reliability*, 1973, pp. 94-100.

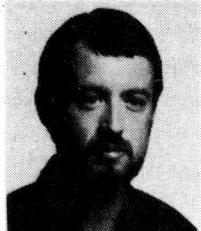

William E. Howden received the B.A. degree in mathematics from the University of California, Riverside, in 1963, the M.Sc. degree in mathematics from Rutgers University, New Brunswick, NJ, in 1965, the M.Sc. degree in computer science from Cambridge University, Cambridge, England, in 1970, and the Ph.D. degree in computer science from the University of California, Irvine, in 1973.

He is currently Assistant Professor of Information and Computer Science at the University of California, San Diego. He has previously held positions at Atomic Energy of Canada, the University of California at Irvine, and has been a consultant to McDonnell Douglas, Huntington Beach, in software reliability. His research interests are in software and system reliability and in interactive problem solving.

Dr. Howden is a member of the Association for Computing Machinery and the British Computing Society.

Section 4: Dynamic Analysis—Tools and Techniques

Paper Summaries

W. E. Howden, "A Survey of Dynamic Analysis Methods." (Original paper.)

This survey, like the survey of static analysis methods by Howden, classifies methods in terms of the software documents on which they are based. Requirements and design-based validation methods are based on the requirements and design documents. Code-based methods are based on the program itself. Requirements and design-dynamic analysis involves the generation of test data from the information contained in the requirements and design specifications. Code-based dynamic analysis involves the generation of test data that is related to computational structures contained in a program. Each of these three types of test data generation methods is surveyed.

L. G. Stucki, "New Directions in Automated Tools for Improving Software Quality," *Current Trends in Programming Methodology,* Vol. 2, 1977, R. Yeh, ed. (pp. 80-111).

This paper describes a series of extensions to the Program Tester and Evaluator System (a self-metric instrumentation system) that focus on the use of programmer supplied assertion techniques. Assertions are considered as either local or global, depending on their scope of application (as specified by the user). Complete command formats are given for a prototype system that processes both types of assertions.

E. F. Miller and R. A. Melton, "Automated Generation of Testcase Datasets," *Proceedings, 1975 International Conference on Reliable Software* (pp. 51-58).

This paper addresses the problem of automatically generating test data for a program. The technique used is to begin with a particular path within a set of closely equivalent paths that run from the entry of the program to the desired "testing target." This is done by using a form of subschema reduction that helps simplify the path analysis task.

Once a particular path is chosen, it is "backtracked" to produce a set of inequalities that describe the conditions necessary for the path to be logically feasible. An interesting technique is used during the formula generation process: values are written into the formula during the "reverse execution" process as soon as they are available and the current formula is evaluated. This approach tends to minimize the lengths of the formulas and also tends to eliminate paths that otherwise would have to be considered in much greater detail. The paper contains examples in which feasible and infeasible test case data are identified.

D. J. Richardson and L. A. Clarke, "A Partition Analysis Method to Increase Program Reliability," *Proc., Fifth International Conference on Software Engineering,* San Diego, March 1981 (pp. 244-253).

This paper discusses a method of software analysis and testing that combines some of the features of path testing, of symbolic analysis, and of consistency checking based on specification analysis. The method described, called the "partition analysis method," uses information both from the specification of the software and from its implementation.

The basis of the method is the use of symbolic evaluation methods to partition the "input space" of the candidate program into subdomains in a way that assures that on each such subdomain, individual data elements are processed uniformly by both the implementation and the specification. This in effect "divides" the input domain into more manageable parts than previously.

Consistency between the actual program and the formal specification is accomplished by choosing actual "test data" that either (a) attempts to reveal errors in the implementation, or (b) demonstrates confidence in the implementation's correctness for the entire input domain. Note that this is an idea closely related to the notion of a revealing subdomain in Weyuker and Ostrand's paper "Theories of Program Testing and the Application of Revealing Subdomains," reprinted elsewhere in this book.

The operational specifications of programs are in a mathematically precise but non-procedural form (i.e., not necessarily a program that can be executed). Enough information in the specification is required to assure that partitioning of the "input space" can go forward easily. (The paper presents some examples of how this is done.) Defects are found when there is some kind of disagreement in the processes used to establish the direct correspondences between a specification's subdomain and the implementation's subdomain.

W. E. Howden, "Functional Testing and Design Abstractions," *The Journal of Systems and Software,* Vol. 1, 1980 (pp. 307-313).

Functional testing involves the selection of program tests that test each of the functions implemented by a system or program. The usual practice is to identify functions from requirements specifications. This paper discusses the necessity of testing design as well as requirements functions. Design functions are functions invented during the design of a program. They often correspond to sections of code documented by comments which describe the effect of the function.

The paper indicates how systematic design methods, such as Structured Design and the Jackson design methodology, can be used to construct functional tests. Structured Design can be used to identify the design functions that must be tested in the code, and the Jackson method can be used to identify the types of data which should be used to construct tests for those functions. It is noted that design-based functional testing may require the use of test harnesses in order to allow parts of programs (those corresponding to design functions) to be individually tested.

J. C. Huang, "An Approach to Program Testing," *ACM Computing Surveys,* September 1975 (pp. 113-128).

This paper introduces the basic notions of dynamic testing based on detailed path analysis in which full knowledge of the contents of the source program being tested is used during the testing process.

A common test criteria is to have every statement in the program executed at least once. Huang suggests, and demonstrates with an example, that a better criteria is to require that every edge in the program digraph be exercised at least once. This translates into requiring each decision outcome in the program to be executed at least once.

Huang also discusses the process of instrumenting a program by inserting probes along each segment in the program. After a discussion of ways of measuring testing coverage, the paper provides a neat analysis of the program test data generation problem, expressed in terms of path predicates.

E. F. Miller, et al., "Structural Techniques of Program Validation," *Digest of Papers, COMPCON Spring 74* (pp. 161-164).

This paper describes an approach to analyzing programs with an automated testing support system that focuses on identification of a program's iteration structure as a way of developing effective tests. The system, called RXVP, processes Fortran programs. Within individual modules the program is decomposed into "decision to decision" paths, and then into a set of "level-i paths." The tree of level-i paths for a program is then used as the basis for developing tests for the program.

The primary emphasis of the paper is on the use of RXVP to present program paths in a format that makes it relatively simple to manually select data that exercises the part of the program selected.

D. J. Panzl, "Automatic Software Test Drivers," *Computer,* April 1978, (pp. 44-50).

Automatic test drivers can be used to automate the tedious procedure of executing a program over a sequence of tests and of checking test output against expected output. They can also be used to construct test beds for validation of individual modules and routines. The reprint describes several test drivers, including IBM's Automated Unit Test System and General Electric's Test Procedure Language. The paper concentrates more heavily on the TPL system, which was developed by Panzl at the GE Research Center.

P. Brinch Hansen, "Testing a Multiprogramming System," *Software Practice and Experience,* April-June 1973 (pp. 145-150).

This paper contains an example which illustrates the influence of testability considerations on the design of a message facility in a process-based operating system. The techniques used to test the synchronization of processes during message transmission are explained. The paper describes the influence of the necessity for testing a system on a system's design.

R. A. DeMillo, R. J. Lipton, and F. G. Sayward, "Hints on Test Data Selection: Help for the Practicing Programmer," *Computer,* April 1978 (pp. 34-41).

This paper provides a basic introduction to the idea of "mutation testing." Briefly, the idea of mutation testing is to systematically implant small defects in a program to find out if the existing tests discover them. When the tests do not find the "program mutations" (as they are called), then more tests are added. The effectiveness of testing can then be quantified, based on the proportion of mutants that are (and are not) detected.

The mutation technique is highly automatable and can actually be done with interpretation techniques (to avoid the costs of many recompilations).

The method involves the controversial "competent programmer hypothesis," which asserts that programmers are known to produce programs that are "close to" the correct ones. The argument made is that checking the correctness of a program with a large number of small changes is justified, since these changes "model" what the programmer might have done wrong. Not understood yet is what the relationship between mutation testing and errors really is.

A SURVEY OF DYNAMIC ANALYSIS METHODS

William E. Howden

University of Victoria
Victoria, Canada.

Abstract - A scheme for classifying program testing methods is introduced. Program testing methods are classified according to whether they involve the generation of test data which is based on the requirements specifications, the design specifications or the source code for a program. Detailed descriptions of functional requirements and functional design based testing are included. Source code methods which are described include branch testing, path testing, file testing and expression testing. Other dynamic analysis techniques, such as dynamic assertions and recovery control blocks are also described.

Acknowledgements

The research which is described in this paper was supported by the National Bureau of Standards and was carried out under the supervision of Dr. Dennis Fife.

A SURVEY OF DYNAMIC ANALYSIS METHODS

1. INTRODUCTION TO DYNAMIC ANALYSIS

The principal dynamic analysis technique is program testing. In addition, dynamic analysis includes several new techniques such as dynamic assertions and recovery control blocks.

Program testing involves the execution of a program over sample test data followed by analysis of the output. Different kinds of test output can be generated. It may consist of final values of program output variables or of intermediate value traces of selected variables. It may also consist of timing information, as in real time systems.

The use of testing requires the existence of an external mechanism which can be used to check test output for correctness. This mechanism is referred to as the test oracle. Test oracles can take on different forms. They can consist of tables, hand calculated values, simulated results, or informal design and requirements descriptions.

A program testing strategy is a method for selecting input test data. Program testing strategies can be divided into three classes: requirements, design and program based testing. In requirements based testing test data is generated by examination of system requirements. Design based testing involves the selection of test data which will test each of the elements of a design. Program based testing involves the selection of test data which will test different computational structures in the program and is based on an analysis of the source code. The sets of test data that are generated by the three different kinds of testing strategies are not necessarily disjoint. For some programs they could turn out to be identical. Each type of strategy involves an examination of the program from a different point of view. The use of each type of strategy is necessary to ensure that the test sets are comprehensive.

Current work in techniques for requirements and design specification will result in the development of better requirements and design based testing. Most of the current work in testing has been on program-based testing.

2. REQUIREMENTS-BASED TESTING

2.1 Functional Testing. The traditional requirements-based program testing method is functional testing. In functional testing a program or software system is viewed as a "black box" which accepts input from one of a number of different classes of input data and applies the relevant function to the input data and generates output belonging to one of a number of different possible classes of output data. Functional testing involves the testing of the system over each of the different possible classes of input, the testing of each function implemented by the system, and the generation of test output in each of the possible output classes [1]. Functional requirements-based testing results in the testing of a system over the input data classes, functions and output data classes that are described in the requirements documents for a system.

2.2 <u>Classes of input data</u>. Each input variable for a program is defined over a set of elements called its <u>variable domain</u>. The elements of a variable domain have properties which can be used to define classes of input data. Different kinds of variable domains will contain elements with different kinds of properties. The simplest kinds of elements have only one property, their <u>value</u>. In theory there is a distinction between the values of a variable (i.e., the elements of the variable domain) and the values of the elements in the variable domain. In practice, this distinction is not made and the value of a variable is simply the value of an element in the variable domain.

More complicated kinds of variable domains contain elements with more complicated kinds of properties. Two commonly occuring types of properties are <u>type</u> and <u>dimension</u>. Variable domains are often restricted to consist of elements of a single type (i.e., type string or type integer). If a variable domain contains data structures, then the elements can have different dimensions (i.e., the number of dimensions of an array, and the size of each dimension).

The properties of the elements in a variable domain can be used to define the domain. Consider for example, the set of all numbers of type integer. The properties of the elements can also be used to define subsets of the variable domain. If a variable domain contains elements with different types of properties, then each type may be used to define a subset of the domain. The properties of the elements of a variable domain are often numeric. (E.g., the values of type real elements are real numbers, the number of rows and columns of a two-dimensional matrix are integers). Variable domains, or a subset of a variable domain, can be defined by specifying the allowable range for the numeric properties of the elements of the domain or subset of the domain. Consider, for example, the domain of all elements of type real in the range $[0, 2^{24}]$ or the subset of all two dimensional arrays for which the number of rows is exactly two.

The <u>program domain</u> for a program consists of all possible combinations of values from the variable domains of its input variables. There are several ways of dividing a program domain into classes of input data. The simplest is in terms of the properties of the elements of variable domains of individual input variables. Suppose, for example, that a program is supposed to read in sales transactions and use the information to update an accounts file. Suppose that one of the fields in the input records is read into an input variable DISCOUNT-CODE and that the variable domain contains elements of type integer whose value property lies in the range [1, 10] and a single element of type blank to signify "no discount". The accounts update system should carry out two different kinds of actions, depending on whether the input element for DISCOUNT-CODE is a blank or of type integer. The type property for the elements of the variable domain of the variable DISCOUNT-CODE can be used to define two classes of input, each corresponding to a different kind of functional computation to be carried out by the accounts update program.

Program domains can be divided up into classes of input data which are defined in terms of relationships between the properties of elements in different variable domains as well as classes which are based on the properties of the elements of a single variable domain. Consider, for example, a search program that looks for an occurrence of an element x in a sorted table $T(1), T(2), \ldots, T(100)$. The requirements for the program will specify two kinds of actions, one for input data which satisfies the relationship $T(1) \leq x \leq T(100)$, and one for data which does not satisfy the relationship. In this case, a relationship between the value property of elements of the variable domain for x and the value property of elements of the variable domain for T is used to define two classes of input data.

2.3 *Extreme cases*. A complete set of functional tests includes both input data from "inside" each class of input data and input data from the edge or "boundary" of the class. The complete set of functional tests should also include input data that causes the generation of output which is "inside" each class of output data and output which is on the edge or boundary of each output class.

Suppose that a class of input or output data is defined in terms of an allowable range of values for one or more properties of the elements of an input variable domain. Then the data on the edge or boundary of the class corresponds to variable domain elements whose properties lie at the ends of the ranges. Suppose, for example, the input data for a program P includes input for a variable X, and that the variable domain for X consists of two-dimensional arrays. Suppose that arrays can range in size from one-by-one to twenty-by-twenty. The elements of the variable domain for X have the two properties "row-dimension" and "column-dimension". The properties are restricted to lie in the ranges [1,20] and [1,20]. Input data which contains input arrays for X which are of size one-by-one and twenty-by-twenty can be thought of as being on the edge or boundary of the program domain of P.

Classes of input or output data which are defined in terms of relationships between the properties of variable domain elements can also be thought of as having edges or boundaries. Consider, for example, input data classes in which the numeric properties of the elements in the domain of one variable are used to define the allowable range of a numeric property of the elements of some other variable domain. Data on the boundary of the class corresponds to variable domain elements for which the properties of the domain elements of the second variable fall at the ends of the ranges defined by the properties of the domain elements of the first variable. In the search program example described above, input data for which $x = T(1)$ or $x = T(100)$ can be thought of as being on the boundary of a class of input data.

An *extreme case* is a set of input data that lies on the edge or boundary of a class of input data or which generates output that lies on the boundary of a class of output data. Functional testing requires that programs be tested on extreme cases.

2.4 <u>Special values</u>. In addition to the testing of the functionally different input classes, functional testing often involves testing over certain other types of special classes of input data. These special classes are often related to commonly occurring errors and not to the functional properties of the program being tested.

Non-numeric programs, for example, often contain sequences of assignments whose only purpose is to "move" data from one variable or array element to another. No changes, or only very simple editing operations, are made to the data. Several rules have been proposed which can be used to check that in a sequence of movements of data the data is selected from the correct initial locations and ends up in the correct finishing locations. The basic idea in the rules is to use distinct data elements so that one data element can be readily distinguished from another. The program in Figure 1 is derived from a PL-360 sort routine in a paper by Wirth [2]. The program contains an error which is readily revealed if the input array contains distinct elements and if all paths are tested for arrays having one, two or three elements. The error is not necessarily revealed when the input data is not distinct, even if all paths are tested at least once. The error consists of a missing assignment to the variable R_3 at the beginning of the outermost loop. In the test example it is assumed that all variables are initialized to zero by the system before execution of a program begins. Figure 2 contains sample input and output for the program for a particular selection of distinct input elements.

```
for R1 = 0 by 1 to N begin
    R0 ← a(R1)
    for R2 = R1 + 1 by 1 to N begin
        if a(R2) > R0 then begin
            R0 ← a(R2)
            R3 ← R2
        end
    end
    R2 ← a(R1)
    a(R1) ← R0
    a(R3) ← R2
end
```

Figure 1. PL-360 sort routine.

$$a(0) = 3 \quad a(0) = 4$$
$$a(1) = 4 \quad a(1) = 2$$
$$a(2) = 2 \quad a(2) = 2$$

Figure 2. Distinct input.

2.5 <u>Classes of output data</u>. The techniques which are used for defining classes of input data can be used for defining classes of output data. For some programs the relevant classes of input and output data can be described independently of each other. In other cases, the output classes for a program are defined indirectly in terms of the input class. For example, an output class R_1 for program P might be defined to consist of the set of all output values when P is applied to data in an input class D_1. In some cases, it is possible to identify one or more classes of output data which are independently definable and for which there is no corresponding independently definable class of input data.

The Common Blunders Section of The Elements of Programming Style [3] contains several examples of errors which are revealed when test data is selected which generates output belonging to easily identifiable classes of output data for which there is no corresponding independently definable class of input data. In one example, the program generates reports on the line printer. The reports in the output space for the program have a number of different properties, two of which measure the size of the report. Each report consists of some number x of full pages plus a partial page consisting of y lines. The property y is restricted to lie in the range $0 \leq y \leq 45$. A complete set of functional tests should contain test data that generates the extreme output case in which the value of y is 0. Test data of this type clearly reveals the error in the program.

In general, it is important to consider output classes of invalid data as well as input classes of invalid data. The generation of tests which lie in invalid input classes tests the ability of the program to deal with unexpected input. Invalid output classes consist of data which should not be generated by the program. The attempt to construct data which generates invalid output may reveal undetected errors in a program. This is particularly true of extreme cases in which output lies on the boundary between a valid and an invalid class of output data. Reference [3] contains an example in which a program is supposed to compute a schedule of mortgage payments. One of the output variables for the program contains the value of the last monthly payment. The variable domain for this variable contains type real numbers. The value property of these elements is constrained to lie in the range $(0,\infty)$. The program is capable of generating output for which the value of the last monthly payment variable is zero. The execution of the program over test data which results in this invalid output value confirms the existence of the error in the program. In general, it may not be necessary to actually execute a program over test data which is alleged to cause invalid output in order to confirm the existence of an error.

3. DESIGN-BASED TESTING

3.1 Design elements. A system or program design is constructed from different kinds of design elements. Examples include mathematical formulae, algorithms, modules, module interfaces and abstract data structures. Design based testing involves the construction of test data which is based on the important properties of the design elements in a design. Different test data generation techniques are appropriate for different kinds of design elements.

One of the most widely studied approaches to design is the top down method in which a design consists of a hierarchy of abstract operators which act on abstract data structures.

The following sections describe an approach to design-based testing in which tests are constructed which are based on the abstract operators and data structures in a top down design.

3.2 _Functional testing of abstract operators_. The functional testing method can be used to construct design-based tests for systems or programs whose design involves abstract operators and abstract data structures. The abstract operators in a top down design are defined over input domains of abstract data structures and they generate abstract data structures in an output domain. Abstract data structures, like the elements of variable domains, have properties which can be used to divide sets of abstract data structures into classes and to identify extremal elements. Design-based tests can be constructed for a program by constructing tests that result in the functional testing of each of the abstract operators involved in the design of the program. A complete set of functional tests for an abstract operator includes extremal elements from the input domain of the operator and, in addition, tests which result in the generation of extremal abstract data structures in the output domain of the operator.

3.3 _Input and output data_. The abstract operators in a design can be directly implemented in a program using the subroutine or function construct in the programming language in which the program is written. Functional testing of an abstract operator can be carried out either by testing the abstract operator as a separate module or as part of an integrated system. If the operator is tested as part of an integrated system then it will be necessary to print out the input values to the abstract operator and the output values generated by the operator. It is necessary to assume the existence of a test oracle which can be used to check the correctness of output generated by abstract operators.

Ideally, an abstract operator would be tested by printing out the values of its input abstract data structures before the application of the operator and the values of its output abstract data structures after the application of the operator. In general, this is not possible since there is no way to define abstract data structures in most programming languages. Abstract data structures are usually simulated using elementary data structures and certain associated variables. Functional testing of an abstract operator will usually require the analysis of elementary input and output values and data structures. In order to analyze the operator in terms of abstract input and output data structures it is necessary to reconstruct the abstract data structures from the elementary data structures and variables that are used to simulate the abstract structures.

3.4 _Merge-sort example_. The following example illustrates the use of abstract operators and data structures in the design of a program. It illustrates the functional approach to the construction of designed-based test data.

Merge-sort is one of the standard sorting methods for sorting large amounts of data stored on tapes or discs. The basic design idea in merge-sort is to treat the list of items to be sorted as a list of sorted sublists. The sorted sublists are all the same length, except for possibly one shorter sublist. The method successively splits the list into two other lists, each of which contains "half" of the sublists from the original list. (One of the two lists will have an extra sublist if the original list contained an odd number of sublists). The two lists are then merged back together into a single list in such a way that the sorted sublists in the resulting list are twice as long as the sorted sublists in the original list (except for possibly one shorter sublist).

The design of a well-structured merge-sort program will be based on the following abstract operators and data structures.

(a) Lowest level of abstraction. At the lowest level of abstraction there is a single abstract data structure <u>sublist</u>. Each sublist is a sorted list of items from the original list. There is a single abstract operator <u>submerge</u>(s_1, s_2). submerge(s_1, s_2) merges two sublists s_1 and s_2 to form a sublist s_3. s_3 is a sorted list containing the elements from s_1 and s_2.

(b) Highest level of abstraction. At the highest level of abstraction there is a single abstract data structure <u>biglist</u>. biglist is a list of sublists. There are two abstract operators <u>bigmerge</u>(b_1, b_2) and bigsplit(b). bigmerge takes two biglists b_1 and b_2 and generates a new biglist b_3. The sublists in b_3 are formed by applying submerge to successive corresponding pairs of sublists in the biglists b_1 and b_2. If one of the biglists contains an extra sublist then that sublist is copied directly onto the biglist b_3 after the other sublists have been merged by submerge. bigsplit takes a biglist b and generates two biglists b_1 and b_2, each of which contains half of the sublists in b. If b has an odd number of sublists, b_1 will have one more sublist in it than b_2.

3.5 <u>Properties of merge-sort abstract data structures</u>.

(a) Lowest level of abstraction. Each sublist s has the property length(s) $\geq$ 0. <u>Length</u>(s) is equal to the number of elements in s. The length property can be used to identify extremal elements and to define certain relevant classes of sublists.

(b) Highest level of abstraction. Each biglist b has the property <u>biglength</u>(b). Biglength(b) is equal to the number of sublists in b. Biglength can be used to identify extremal elements. The abstract operation bigmerge is defined over pairs (b_1, b_2) of biglists. Classes of input to bigmerge can be defined in terms of relationships between the biglengths of biglists. Possible classes are those for which biglength(b_1) > biglength(b_2) or biglength(b_1) < biglength(b_2). The biglengths of b_1 and b_2 can also be used to define the extremal input class biglength(b_1) = biglength(b_2).

3.6 <u>Simulation of abstract data structures</u>. The biglist data structure can be simulated using a special variable <u>sublength</u>, together with an <u>end-of-list</u> marker. Each sublist in a biglist is represented by a consecutive sequence of sublength elements, except for possibly the last sublist which may have fewer elements. If the last sublist is shorter than the other sublists then the end of the sublist is signified by the end-of-list marker. The testing of the abstract operations in merge-sort will involve the testing of the mechanisms used to simulate the biglist data structures.

The correctness of abstract operators at lower levels of abstraction is assumed during the validation of abstract operators at high levels. This implies that the validation of merge-sort should begin with tests based on the functional properties of the abstract operator at the lowest level of abstraction, submerge. The correctness of submerge is assumed during the validation of bigmerge.

The bigmerge operator needs to keep track of the sublists in the two input biglists b_1 and b_2 and to apply submerge to the appropriate pairs of sublists to produce a new biglist b_3. It is necessary to examine b_3 to see that the sublists in the output from bigmerge were formed from the appropriate pairs of sublists in b_1 and b_2. The assumed correctness of submerge implies that the set of elements in the sublist generated by an application of submerge to two sublists s_1 and s_2 is the union of the elements in s_1 and s_2. If all elements are distinct, then it will be possible to determine from which sublists in b_1 and b_2 a sublist in b_3 was formed. The use of distinct input data, together with the values of sublength can be used to check the operation of bigmerge over the simulated biglist data structures.

3.7 Selection of test data. In order to apply the method of functional testing to the abstract operators in merge-sort it is necessary to print out samples of input and output data for each operator during the execution of the program. The following classes of tests can be used to validate the abstract operators in merge-sort.

(a) submerge(s_1, s_2). The length property of sublists can be used to define the following extremal tests of submerge: length(s_1) = length(s_2) = 0; length(s_1) = length(s_2) = 1; and length(s_1) = length(s_2) > 1. In addition, submerge should be tested over non-extremal data in the two classes of data for which length(s_1) > length(s_2) > 1 and length(s_2) > length(s_1) > 1.

(b) bigmerge(b_1, b_2). The biglength property of biglists can be used to define the following extremal tests of bigmerge: biglength(b_1) = biglength(b_2) = 0; biglength(b_1) = biglength(b_2) = 1; biglength(b_1) = 0 and biglength(b_2) = 1; biglength(b_1) = 1 and biglength(b_2) = 0; and biglength(b_1) = biglength(b_2) > 1. In addition, bigmerge should be tested over non-extremal data for which biglength(b_1) > biglength(b_2) > 1 and biglength(b_2) > biglength(b_1) > 1.

(c) bigsplit. Test data similar to that recommended for the testing of bigmerge can be selected to test bigsplit.

The biglist abstract data structures are represented using ordinary unstructured lists and the special variable sublength. The value of sublength must be printed along with the contents of the unstructured input and output lists for bigmerge and bigsplit to enable the reconstruction of the simulated input and output abstract data structures.

The functional testing of the abstract operators in merge-sort should include the testing of the mechanisms used to simulate the biglist abstract data structures. Let n be the number of elements in the list of elements to be sorted. The extremal case in the use of sublength to keep track of the ends of sublists (sublength = 1) will occur at least once during an execution of merge-sort for all choices of $n \geq 1$. The non-extremal case, that in which sublength is used to keep track of sublists whose length is greater than 1, will occur if n is a power of 2 and $n > 2$. The use of the end-of-list marker in keeping track of the ends of sublists in the input biglists b_1 and b_2 for bigmerge will occur for $n > 2$ and n not a power of 2. If n is of the form $m2^k - 2^{k-1}$ for some $m \geq 1$, $k \geq 1$, then the use of an end-of-list marker will occur for the sublists in the output biglist from bigmerge but not in the input biglists. The use of sublength and end-of-list in keeping track of the ends of sublists can be examined by including appropriate test output statements in the programs.

3.8 <u>Design and requirements based testing</u>. There are two important differences in the use of design-based rather than requirements-based testing for merge-sort. The first is in the type of output generated during the testing process. In requirements-based testing the only output that would be generated for merge-sort is the final value of the sorted list. Design-based testing requires the printout of the intermediate values of the lists in the program, together with the values of the variable used to simulate abstract data structures. The intermediate values are used to carry out functional testing of the abstract operators. Design-based testing involves an analysis of how a program works as well as what it does. Requirements-based testing is restricted to an analysis of what a program does.

The second important difference is in the choice of test data. Requirements-based testing of merge-sort will involve the selection of extremal case test data in which the input list contains 0 or 1 elements, and non-extremal test data in which the input list contains more than 2 elements, say at least 10 or 20. Design-based testing results in the generation of additional specific requirements on the test data. In order to test bigmerge and bigsplit, for example, it is necessary to test merge-sort over lists of distinct elements. The use of distinct elements is required to enable the identification of different sublists in a biglist. It is also necessary to test merge-sort over lists containing $n > 2$ elements where n is not a power of 2. This type of test is necessary to examine the use of end-of-list markers for denoting the ends of sublists in a biglist.

4. GRAPH-THEORETIC MODELS

4.1 <u>Control Structure and directed graphs</u>. Several program-based dynamic analysis methods involve the use of directed graphs. A short introduction to graph-theoretic terminology is included to facilitate the description of those methods. Directed graphs can be used to model the control structure of a program. Figure 3 contains a program together with its graph.

```
read x,y;
if (x<0 and y≥0)
  or (y<0 and x>0) then s ← -1;
x ← abs(x);
y ← abs(y);
z ← 0;
repeat while y > 0
  z ← z + x;
  y ← y -1;
end repeat;
print z*s;
```

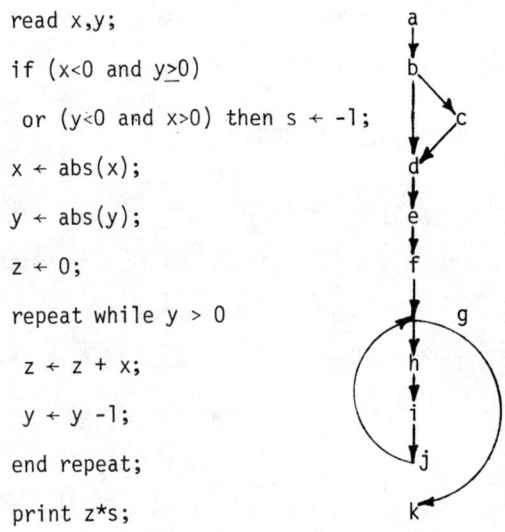

Figure 3. A program and its flowgraph.

A directed graph is a collection of <u>nodes</u> and <u>edges</u>. Edges join nodes together. Each node in the graph model of a program's control structure corresponds to a statement in the program. The edges correspond to possible flows of control from one statement to the next.

4.2 <u>Graph-theoretic terminology</u>. The following terminology is useful in defining and analyzing graph models of program control structure. The examples refer to the graph in Figure 3.

(a) <u>predecessors</u> and <u>successors</u>. n_i is a predecessor of node n_{i+1} if there is a directed edge e from n_i to n_{i+1}. n_{i+1} is a successor of n_i. b and c are predecessors of d. e is a successor of d.

(b) <u>indegree</u> and <u>outdegree</u>. The number of successors of a node n is its outdegree. The number of predecessors is its indegree. The indegree of d is 2. The outdegree of f is 1.

(c) <u>entrance</u> and <u>exit</u> nodes. n is an entrance node to a graph g if n has no predecessors. n is an exit node if it has no successors. a is an entrance node and k an exit node.

(d) <u>complete paths</u> and <u>subpaths</u>. Let $p = (n_i, n_{i+1}, \ldots n_{s-1}, n_s)$ be a sequence of nodes in a graph which has the property that n_{j+1} is a successor of n_j for $i \leq j \leq s-1$. If n_i is an entrance node to the graph and n_s an exit node then p is a complete path through the graph. Otherwise p is a subpath in the graph. The word path is used to denote both complete paths and subpaths. Suppose $p_1 = (n_1, n_2, \ldots, n_s)$ is a path in a graph and $p_2 = (n_j, \ldots, n_k)$ is a consecutive subsequence of the sequence of nodes in p_1. Then p_2 is a subpath of p_1. a b d e f g k is a complete path. d e f g is a subpath of the path.

(e) <u>segment</u>. A segment $s = (n_i, n_{i+1}, \ldots n_s)$ in a graph is a path with the following properties: (i) indegree (n_j) = outdegree (n_j) = 1 for all nodes n_j in s for which $i < j < s$; (ii) indegree $(n_i) > 1$ or outdegree $(n_i) > 1$; and (iii) indegree $(n_s) > 1$ or outdegree $(n_s) > 1$. It follows that no segment is a subpath of some other segment. d e f g and b c d are segments.

(f) <u>reachability</u>. A node n_k is reachable from a node n_1 if there is a path $= (n_1, \ldots n_k)$ from n_1 to n_k. j is reachable from g. b is not reachable from c.

(g) <u>reachability matrix</u>. Suppose a graph G has k nodes. Then the reachability matrix $R = (r_{i,j})$ $1 \leq i \leq k$, $1 \leq j \leq k$, for G is defined as follows: $r_{i,j} = 1$ if and only if n_j is reachable from n_i. Otherwise $r_{i,j} = 0$.

(h) <u>cycle</u>. A path $(n_1, n_2, \ldots, n_k)$ is a cycle if $n_1 = n_k$. g h i j g is a cycle.

(i) a graph is <u>acyclic</u> if it contains no cycles. The graph in Figure 1 is not acyclic.

(j) <u>bidirected graphs</u>. A bidirected graph is a graph in which the edges come in pairs (e, e'). For every pair of nodes (n_i, n_j) such that there is an edge e from n_i to n_j, there is an edge e' from n_j to n_i.

(k) <u>path traversing</u>. The traversal of a path involves the "examination" of each of its nodes in the order in which they occur in the path.

(l) <u>depth-first traversal</u>. The traversal of a graph involves the examination of each of its nodes in a special order. Suppose that the graph has a single entrance node e. In depth-first traversal first e is examined and then the leftmost branch from e is followed. A sequence of nodes and leftmost branches is examined until a node with outdegree 0 is reached or a node which has been visited before. When this happens the traversal process backs up to the most recently visited node which has outdegree > 1 and chooses the leftmost untraversed branch from the node to continue the traversal process. If there is no untraversed branch it backs up even further. The process stops when there are no untraversed branches. Variations on this procedure are used to carry out different kinds of path traversal processes.

(m) <u>tree</u>. A tree is a directed graph with a single entrance node in which each node except the entrance node has indegree = 1.

5. PROGRAM-BASED TESTING

5.1 <u>Program structures</u>. One of the weaknesses of requirements-testing is its failure to test computational features of a program which are related to the design and implementation of the program and which are not part of its requirements. Design-based testing results in the construction of tests which can be used to validate the more abstract computational properties of a program, some of which may not correspond to program properties described in the requirements. Program-based testing involves the selection of test data which tests specific computational structures in a program.

The most widely studied program-based testing methods are those that involve the selection of test data which causes the execution of specific statements, branches or paths in a program. These methods are defined in terms of the structure of a program and are referred to as <u>structured testing methods</u>. Other kinds of program-based testing methods include <u>expression testing</u> and <u>data-flow testing</u>. Each of these is described in the following sections.

5.2 <u>Branch testing</u>. Branch testing was the earliest form of structured testing to be studied and systematically applied to the testing of programs [4-9]. The technique requires that test data be constructed that causes each branch in a program to be traversed at least once. Each program branch corresponds to an edge in the program's flow graph. A more restricted kind of structured testing, called <u>statement testing</u>, requires that each statement in a program be executed at least once on some test.

The use of branch testing requires the availability of a program testing tool that can be used to keep track of which branches are traversed during a sequence of tests. A number of such tools have been constructed. The typical branch testing tool consists of a <u>preprocessor</u> for instrumenting the program to be tested and a <u>postprocessor</u> for processing the data generated by the preprocessor. The function of the preprocessor is to insert special pieces of code called <u>probes</u> into the program to be tested. The probes generate data during the execution of a program that are used by the postprocessor to construct branch execution statistics.

Different kinds of probes can be constructed. Some preprocessors insert direct inline code in a program. The code updates the contents of a special execution count array. Code for declaring the array must also be inserted in the program. Different programming languages may require different techniques for modifying the source text of a program to insert probes. In general, probes are inserted in a program at places where a path splits into two subpaths and at places where different paths flow together to form a single path. Paths split into separate subpaths at conditional branching statements. A subpath is associated with each branch from the statement. Separate paths flow back together to form a single path at loop leader statements (e.g., FORTRAN DO statements) or in general, at statements which have labels.

Figures 4 and 5 contain a FORTRAN program before and after instrumentation with direct inline code. The approach used in Figure 5 makes it easy to postprocess a program. The statement counts for each statement can be computed as follows. Set a variable COUNT to 1 and start reading the program from the beginning. Each time a probe of the form $SORT(k)= $SORT(k)+1 is encountered reset COUNT to $SORT(k). If a DO-loop header is encountered, reset COUNT to the value of the $SORT element which is incremented in the probe directly following the header before processing the header. The COUNT variable contains a count of the number of times that each source code statement which is encountered has been executed.

Branch-test program testing tools often contain sophisticated facilities for the generation of information about a program execution other than statement and branch counts. The PET System [4], for example, keeps track of the minimum and maximum values which are assigned to a variable by each assignment statement in a program. It records the minimum and maximum number of times each loop was traversed and relative timing statistics for each subroutine.

```
        SUBROUTINE SORT(A,N)           1
        DIMENSION A(N)                 2
        DO 100 I=2,N                   3
          DO 100 J=I,-1,2              4
            IF A(J).GE.A(J-1) GO TO 100  5
            T=A(J-1)                   6
            A(J-1)=A(J)                7
            A(J)=T                     8
100     CONTINUE                       9
        END                           10
```

Figure 4. FORTRAN sort program before instrumentation.

```
        SUBROUTINE SORT(A,N)
        DIMENSION A(N),$SORT(6)
        $SORT(1)=$SORT(1)+1
        DO 100 I=2,N
        $SORT(2)=$SORT(2)+1
          DO 100 J=I,-1,2
          $SORT(3)=$SORT(3)+1
            IF A(J).GE.A(J-1)  GO TO 10
            $SORT(4)=$SORT(4)+1
            T=A(J-1)
            A(J-1)=A(J)
            A(J)=T
10        $SORT(5)=$SORT(5)+1
100     CONTINUE
          $SORT(6)=$SORT(6)+1
        END
```

Figure 5. Program after instrumentation with in-line probes.

Figure 6 contains a sample of the types of output which can be generated by the PET system.

An alternative approach to the insertion of probes involves the use of calls to special statistics gathering subroutines rather than the direct insertion of in-line code. Reference [8] describes a method for counting the number of times that each DD-path in a program is executed during a test of the program. A DD-PATH is a program subpath that corresponds to a segment in the program's flow graph. The counting technique used in the method involves the insertion of subroutine calls to a probe subroutine. The reference describes the rules for the construction and insertion of the probes.

5.3 **Generation of test data for branch testing.**
Several program testing tools have been developed which can be used to assist the programmer in the generation of a complete set of branch tests. One of the earliest tools of this type accepts a program, together with a listing of already tested branches, as its input [9]. The tool carries out an analysis of the program's flow graph and generates a set of program paths which, if executed, result in the testing of the remaining untested program branches. The QTRAK tool accepts a program, together with the description of an untested program branch, as its input and generates a listing of the sequence of statements in the program that affect the decision variables

PROGRAM LISTING	COUNT	DETAILS
SUBROUTINE SORT(A,N)	1	N=30
DIMENSION A(N)		
DO 100 I=2,N	1	MIN 29 MAX 29
DO 100 J=I,-1,2	29	MIN 1 MAX 29
IF A(J).GE.A(J-1) GO TO 100	435	TRUE 320 FALSE 115
T=A(J-1)	115	MIN 0 MAX 999
A(J-1)=A(J)	115	MIN 0 MAX 999
A(J)=T	115	MIN 0 MAX 999
100 CONTINUE	435	
END	1	

Figure 6. Sample PET output.

associated with the branch [5]. The RXVP system contained one of the first uses of symbolic evaluation for generating test data [10]. RXVP will accept the description of an untested program branch as its input. It will then construct a path from the beginning of the program which reaches the untested branch. It symbolically evaluates the path to form a symbolic system of predicates that describes the set of input data causing that path to be followed. If the program is executed over test data which is generated by solving the system of predicates then the untested branch will be traversed.

The use of tools which count the number of times that each branch is traversed during an execution of a program has been widely accepted. The use of test data generation tools has not been as widely accepted. There are several reasons for this. The first is cost-effectiveness. The tools are very expensive to build, and in the case of symbolic evaluation, expensive to use. Branch count statistics provide valuable information about the testing of a program. This does not mean that branch testing should be an end in itself and the criteria for a good test is not simply that it causes the execution of a previously untested branch. Results of recent studies of the effectiveness of different testing methods indicate that branch testing is relatively ineffective when not supported and complemented by the use of other methods [11,12].

The other reasons for the lack of widespread use of test data generation tools involves certain technical problems in the approach. The most serious is the problem of infeasible paths. An <u>infeasible path</u> is a path through a program which is never executed; one for which there is no input data which will cause its execution. Any path that includes the traversal of a sequence of conditional statement branches that have mutually exclusive branch predicates is infeasible. Test data generation tools use graph-traversal algorithms for constructing program paths that include the branch(es) to be tested. The algorithms are not capable of <u>a priori</u> distinguishing between a feasible and an infeasible path. Situations occur in which the algorithms will result in the generation of an enormous number of infeasible paths before generating a feasible path which could have been easily constructed by hand, without the use of the tool.

5.4 <u>Path testing</u>. Several studies of the effectiveness of branch testing indicate that there are large numbers of errors whose existence is not necessarily revealed by the testing of all branches in a program [11,13]. Many of the errors are related to combinations of branches and are revealed only by a test that causes a program path to be followed that contains the combination. Different authors have suggested that every "logical path" through a program should be tested at least once (eg. [14]). The difficulty with this idea is that a program which contains loops will, in general, have an infinite number of possible paths. The program in Figure 4, for example, contains paths which cause the outer loop to be iterated exactly n times for all choices of $n \geq 1$. The solution to this difficulty has been to group the set of all paths through a program into a finite set of classes and then to require the testing of one path from each class. This approach to testing is referred to as <u>path testing</u> [15,16].

Several approaches to path testing have been proposed. In the <u>boundary-interior</u> method two paths are grouped together in the same class if the only difference between them is the subpath they follow through one or more loops during some traversal of the loop other than the first [16]. Figure 7 describes some of the paths from the program in Figure 4. Paths 1,2 and 3 belong to the same class as paths 4 and 5.

Even relatively small programs may contain a prohibitively large number of boundary-interior classes of paths. The path testing approach can only be successfully applied to programs that have been designed in a top down manner using structured programming. Path testing is then used to test each of the program modules separately including those at higher levels of abstraction.

One of Dijkstra's original arguments for top down design was that it resulted in modules that are simple enough that it is possible to test all logical paths (up to loop iterations) through each module [17].

Unlike branch testing, path testing has not been widely studied. Path testing is closely related to symbolic testing and there are a number of symbolic evaluation tools that can be used to help the programmer carry out a schedule of path tests.

5.5 <u>File structure testing</u>. COBOL and other business data processing programs typically have relatively simple logic and involve only simple arithmetic computations. They may have a large number of complicated data structures and files. It is important to test COBOL programs over each of the different kinds of input files that the program should be able to deal with.

COBOL file generation tools were the first type of test data generation system to be constructed and there are a number of such systems commercially available.

Path	
1	1 2 3 4 5 6 7 8 9 10
2	1 2 3 4 5 6 7 8 9 3 4 5 6 7 8 9 4 5 6 7 8 9 10
3	1 2 3 4 5 6 7 8 9 3 4 5 9 4 5 9 10
4	1 2 3 4 5 9 10
5	1 2 3 4 5 9 3 4 5 6 7 8 9 4 5 9 10

Figure 7. Program paths in FORTRAN sort program.

There are several advantages to the use of a file generation system. The manual construction of test files for data processing applications is a time consuming, error-prone, tedious process. File generators allow a user to quickly and accurately generate files having desired structure and contents. The use of "live" files (i.e., real input data) for testing is often inappropriate due to the size of the files involved. It may be necessary to run a program on a large number of large live files in order to test the different possible kinds of input records. In addition, the information on the live files may be private or secure and not available to a programming group.

There are several possible approaches to the construction of a file generation tool. In general a system must have three basic capabilities. The user must be able to specify the formats of the files and their contained records, the contents of individual fields in the records, and he must be able to select one or more different types of records using the file generation process. In some systems the DATA DIVISION from the program to be tested is used to specify the format of files and records [19,20].

The user of the TDG-II [18] system supplies a program's DATA DIVISION and one or more specification cards. The system constructs a COBOL program which can then be run to generate the desired files. The user of DATAMACS [19] inserts special commands in the ENVIRONMENT and DATA DIVISIONS of the program to be tested. The system generates the desired files directly from these modified divisions of the COBOL program.

Some systems do not use the DATA DIVISION of the COBOL program to be tested, but use separate file specification commands [20,21]. The command language has to be rich enough to specify both logical and physical file characteristics. Files can be fixed or variable length record, blocked or unblocked, labelled or unlabelled, odd or even parity, sequential or indexed, or single or multiple record format. In addition they can be stored on different types of tapes and discs.

5.6 <u>Expression testing</u>. Several techniques have been developed which can be used for testing the correctness of arithmetic expressions [22,23]. Arithmetic expressions occur in programs in a variety of different ways. Simple expressions may occur as indices in array references or as loop bounds in DO-loop branches. More complex expressions occur on the right hand side of assignment statements in numerically oriented programs. Arithmetic expressions may occur indirectly in a program. A value assigned to a variable in a program may be equal to the value of an expression which is not computed directly in the program but is computed by a sequence of assignment statements. The expression is equivalent to the cumulative effect of the sequence of assignments. An arithmetic expression may be closely associated with the operation of a program even though it does not directly or indirectly represent the value of a variable in the program. For example, the number of times that a loop in a program is iterated during each execution of the loop can often be written as a simple arithmetic expression in input variables. The expression may be closely related to, but in general, will be different from, the loop bound expressions in the loop header for the loop.

Expression testing techniques use results from algebra and can only be used in situations in which an upper bound is known on the algebraic complexity of the "correct version" of the expression. Suppose, for example, that a program contains a loop L and that it is known that the number of times that L should be iterated during each operation of the loop is a linear function of two input variables x and y. It is known that a linear function in two variables can be uniquely determined with four appropriately chosen points. Suppose that the program is tested over input data containing four such points and that the loop is iterated the correct number of times over each test. Then this implies that the loop will be iterated the correct number of times for all input data. Expression testing will often involve the print-out of intermediate values of variables and requires the availability of a test oracle that is capable of verifying the correctness of intermediate values.

Figure 8 contains the PDIV program from the IBM scientific subroutine package. The program divides the polynominal whose coefficients are stored in the vector x by the polynominal whose coefficients are stored in vector y. The coefficients of the quotient are returned in the vector w. The dimensions of x,y and w are idimx, idimy and idimw. The division process is carried out by subtracting successive multiples of the divisor from the dividend. It is assumed that idimx $\geq$ idimy > 0.

```
procedure pdiv(idimx,x,idimy,y);
array x(idimx), y(idimy), w(idimx-idimy+1);
idimw ← idimx - idimy + 1;
idimx ← idimy - 1;
repeat for i ← idimw by -1 to 1
    il ← i + idimx;
    w(i) ← x(il)/y(idimy);
    repeat for k ← 1 by 1 to idimy
        j ← k - 1 + i;
        x(j) ← x(j) - w(i)*y(k);
    end;
end
```

Figure 8. PDIV program.

The values of the indices in the vector references in PDIV are computed by sequences of simple but obscure arithmetic expressions. If it is assumed that the correct vector indices in PDIV should be linear functions of the input variables idimx and idimy and of the loop counters i and k in PDIV, then the following theorem can be used to prove the correctness of the vector indexing operations in PDIV.

Theorem Suppose that f and g are linear functions of the variables $x_1, x_2, \ldots, x_{s-1}$. Let $x_{i,j}$, $1 \leq i \leq s$, $1 \leq j \leq s-1$ be s sets of values for the variables x_j, $1 \leq j \leq s-1$, and let T be the matrix in Figure 9. Suppose that f = g over each test T_i, $1 \leq i \leq s$, where

$$T_i = (x_{i,1}, x_{i,2}, \ldots, x_{i,s-1}).$$

Then if T is non-singular, f and g are identical polynominals.

$$T = \begin{pmatrix} x_{1,1} & x_{1,2} & \cdots & x_{1,s-1} & 1 \\ x_{2,1} & x_{2,2} & \cdots & x_{2,s-1} & 1 \\ & & \vdots & & \\ x_{s,1} & x_{s,2} & \cdots & x_{s,s-1} & 1 \end{pmatrix}$$

Figure 9. Test values matrix.

Let I be one of the vector references in the innermost loop in PDIV. Analysis of PDIV reveals that I is a linear function f of idimx, idimy, i and k. Suppose it is known that I should be a linear function of those variables. Then the correct value of I is a linear function g of idimx, idimy, i and k. If I is observed to be correct over a sequence of tests in which the values of idimx, idimy, i and k can be used to form a non-singular matrix like that in Figure 9, then f and g are equivalent. This implies that the function f used to compute I is correct.

In order to check the validity of the array indexing computations in PDIV it is necessary to print out the values of idimx, idimy, i and k that are used to compute the indices as well as the indices themselves. It is not difficult to construct tests for which the values of idimx, idimy, i and k can be used to form the required non-singular matrix and it is not difficult to check the correctness of the vector indices that are computed during an execution of the program.

The above theorem is a special case of a more general theorem which can be used to prove the equivalence of non-linear functions [24]. It is possible to prove equivalence theorems for rational expressions and algebraic forms containing radicals as well as for polynomials [22]. The usefulness of expression testing is limited to algebraic expressions with a small number of variables and of low degree since the number of tests required to prove the equivalence of two expressions increases rapidly as the number of variables and the degree increases. If v is the number of variables in two polynomials and n is the largest exponent, the number of tests required to prove equivalence is proportional to v^{n+1}. Continued research on expression testing may make it possible to lower this number for special classes of functions.

5.7 <u>Self-validating programs</u>. In all of the program-based techniques described above, the program is executed over a sequence of input tests and then the output from the program is verified by the programmer. Self-validating software validates its own output in the sense that it includes code for checking the validity of the values which it computes. In general, self-checking software includes code for validating both final and intermediate variable values.

(a) Dynamic Assertions. Leon Stucki has built a PL-1 system that allows the user to embed assertions in his program which describe important properties of and relationships between program variables [25,26]. A preprocessor translates the assertions into code which is executed at run time. The assertions can be used to monitor variable ranges and to check that relationships between variable values remain invariant during program execution.

Figure 10 contains two examples of assertions. The first assertion is a global "assertion". It declares that the values of I and J should always lie in the range [1,100]. The second assertion is a local assertion. It causes a check on the values in the first row of the array A to be carried out each time the part of the program containing the assertion is encountered. It asserts that the elements of the first row in A should be positive.

```
ASSERT VALUES  (I,J)  (1:100)
              .
              .
              .
ASSERT LOCAL  (A(1,4)  .GT.0)
```

Figure 10. Dynamic Assertions.

(b) Recovery Control Blocks. The concept of a "recovery block" was first developed by a research group at the University of Newcastle [27]. Recovery blocks have two basic features. The first is a sequence of _alternatives_. Each alternative is a section of code. The second feature is an _acceptance test_. An acceptance test is a section of code that evaluates to true or false. When a recovery block is entered, the first alternative is evaluated followed by the evaluation of the acceptance test. If the test evaluates to false, the second alternative is evaluated, followed by an evaluation of the acceptance test, and so on. If the acceptance test evaluates to true, the block is exited. If all of the alternatives are exhausted without a true value having been returned from the acceptance test then an error condition is returned from the recovery block to the code surrounding the block.

5.8 _Other testing methods_. A number of program-based test selection rules can be found scattered through the literature and in different books on programming. Many of these, such as "construct tests which cause each loop to be executed at least once" are special cases of path testing. Others are not special cases of more general rules and are useful for particular kinds of programs.

Several research projects have recently been initiated which seek to refine and expand the effectiveness of the techniques described in this paper. A project in which the combined use of functional and structured testing is under investigation is currently being carried out by the author. An interesting variation of path testing called _finite-domain testing_ is being investigated by a research group at Ohio State [29].

The most unusual recently proposed testing technique is "mutation testing" [30]. Mutation testing involves the application of a set of mutation transformations to a user's program. Each transformation results in a mutant. A set of test data is considered complete if, for each mutant, there is at least one test for which the user's program and the mutant generate different output.

References

[1] E. Kearstead and B. Parker, "On the Feasibility of Formal Certification," in W. Hetzel, ed. *Program Test Methods*, Prentice Hall, New Jersey, 1973, pp. 291-301.

[2] N. Wirth, "PL-360, A Programming Language for the 360 Computer," *JACM*, Vol. 15, 1968.

[3] B.W. Kerringhan and P.J. Plauger, *The Elements of Programming Style*, McGraw-Hill, New York, 1974.

[4] L.G. Stucki, "Automatic Generation of Self-Metric Software," in *Proceedings 1973 IEEE Symposium on Computer Software Reliability*, IEEE, 1973, pp. 94-100.

[5] J.R. Brown et al., "Automated Software Quality Assurance," in *Program Test Methods*, W.C. Hetzel, ed., Prentice-Hall, Englewood Cliffs, N.J., 1973, pp. 181-204.

[6] E.F. Miller et al., "Structurally Based Automatic Program Testing," *Proceedings EASCON* 74, 1974.

[7] C.V. Ramamoorthy and S.F. Ho, "FORTRAN Automatic Code Evaluation System," Electronics Res. Lab., Univ. of Calif., Berkeley, Rep. M-466, August, 1974.

[8] M.R. Paige and J.P. Benson, "The Use of Software Probes in Testing FORTRAN Programs", *Computer*, 18-25 (1974).

[9] K.W. Krause, R.W. Smith and M.A. Goodwin, "Optimal Software Test Planning through Automated Network Analysis", *Proceedings IEEE Symposium on Computer Software Reliability*, IEEE, 1973, pp. 18-22.

[10] E. Miller and R.A. Melton, "Automated Generation of Test Case Data Sets," *Proceedings of International Conference on Reliable Software*, IEEE, 1975, pp. 51-58.

[11] W.E. Howden, "An Evaluation of the Effectiveness of Symbolic Testing and of Testing on Actual Data," *Software Practice and Experience* (to appear).

[12] W.C. Hetzel, "An Experimental Analysis of Program Verification Methods," Ph.D. Thesis, University of North Carolina, 1976.

[13] William E. Howden, "Symbolic Testing--Design Techniques, Costs and Effectiveness", U.S. National Bureau of Standards GCR77-89, National Technical Information Service. PB268517, Springfield, Virginia, 1977.

[14] R.W. Wolverton, "The Cost of Developing Large Scale Software," in *Practical Strategies for Developing Large Software Systems*, ed. Ellis Horowitz, Addison Wesley, Reading, Mass., 1975, pp. 73-100.

References Continued

[15] William E. Howden, "Reliability of the Path Analysis Testing Strategy," IEEE-Transactions on Software Engineering, SE-2, 208-214 (1976).

[16] William E. Howden, "Methodology for the Generation of Program Test Data," IEEE-Transactions on Computers, C-24,554-559 (1975).

[17] E. Dijkstra, "Structured Programming," in J.N. Buxton and B. Randell, eds. Software Engineering Techniques, NATO Science Committee, Brussels, 1969.

[18] COBOL-TDG-II. Information Management Incorporated, San Francisco, California.

[19] DATA-MPCS. Management and Computer Sciences, Inc., Valley Forge Pennsylvania.

[20] TESTCUBE. Computer Services Corporation. Southfield, Michigan.

[21] PRO/TEST Data Generator. Synergetics Corporation, Burlington, Mass.

[22] William E. Howden, "Elementary Algebraic Program Testing Techniques," University of California, San Diego, APIS Computer Science Technical Report 12, 1976.

[23] Mathew Geller, "Test Data as an Aid in Proving Program Correctness," Proceedings of Second Symposium on Principles of Programming Languages, 1976, pp. 209-218.

[24] William E. Howden and Peter Eichhorst, "Proving Properties of Programs for Traces," University of California, San Diego, APIS Computer Science Technical Report 18, 1977.

[25] L.G. Stucki, "New Directions in Automated Tools for Improving Software Quality," in R.T. Yeh, ed. Current Trends in Programming Methodology, Vol. 2, Prentice Hall, Englewood Cliffs, New Jersey.

[26] L.G. Stucki, "The Use of Dynamic Assertions to Improve Software Quality," McDonnell Douglas, G6588, November 1976.

[27] T. Anderson and R. Kerr, "Recovery Blocks in Action," Proceedings Second International Conference on Software Engineering, IEEE, 1976.

[28] R.L. Sites, Algol-W Reference Manual, Computer Science Report CS-230, Stanford University, 1972.

[29] E.I. Cohen and L.J. White, "A Finite Domain-Testing Strategy for Computer Program Testing," Ohio State Tech. Rep. OSU-CIRSC-TR-77-13), Columbus, 1977.

[30] T.A. Budd, R. DeMillo, R.J. Lipton, F. Sayward, "The Design of a Prototype Mutation System for Program Testing," Proceedings - 1978 National Computer Conference, Anaheim, Calif.

NEW DIRECTIONS IN AUTOMATED TOOLS FOR IMPROVING SOFTWARE QUALITY

LEON G. STUCKI
Space and Military Applications Division
Boeing Computer Services
Seattle, Washington

The Production of Quality Software Is a Problem

At the time Jules Verne was writing his fictional novel on a journey to the moon, no one took him seriously. But in the early 1960s as President John F. Kennedy issued his goal of reaching the moon within a decade, the task appeared to be much more reasonable. The major difference between the nineteenth and twentieth century attitude can be attributed to new tools such as the computer, which have greatly extended man's scope of feasible problem solving. As with any tool, however, one must utilize the computer with some degree of caution.

Programming has been described by Dijkstra [1972] as the most complex mental activity ever undertaken by mankind. Advances in computer hardware capabilities have brought previously unsolvable problems into the scope of solvability. Man's rapidly increasing reliance upon the correct behavior of complex software systems is of definite concern. As new systems realizing more complex hardware and software functions continue to evolve, accurate and efficient implementation of these systems become increasingly critical.

BACKGROUND AND SIGNIFICANCE

The concept of structured programming associated with Dahl-Dijkstra-Hoare [1972], Mills [1972], et al., was originally suggested as a vehicle for improving software quality through a disciplined development of programs. The use of a restricted set of control structures within programs was one part of that concept. Today common use of the term "structured programming" is associated with so many diverse activities that Dijkstra, the term's originator, now attempts with great vigor to avoid its use [Dijkstra, 1974].

Wirth presents another very interesting treatment of the processes for methodically and systematically designing algorithms. He goes beyond the notions of restricted flow of control and addresses issues of data representation and operations allowed on data in his development of Pascal [Wirth, 1973].

In an attempt to bring the benefits of structured programming into common use, many zealous prophets have arisen, each with his own new set of restricted control structures and associated bag of tools, usually a preprocessor, for allowing the use of these control structures with existing languages e.g., Fortran and Cobol) [Horowitz, 1975].

Another set of tools has also been introduced over the last few years to deal with control flow through programs [Estrin, 1967], [Russell, Estrin, 1969], [Ingnalls, 1971], [Joseph, 1972], [Brown, 1972], [Brown, Hoffman, 1972], [Stucki, 1972]. Software probes or instrumentation are automatically placed into a program for monitoring the dynamic execution behavior of an algorithm. Software probes in the form of source language statements are inserted into the source code to gather statistics during program execution. These probes can provide insight into many aspects of algorithmic behavior beyond a simple flow of control analysis. The notion of building self-metric (self-measuring) software has been introduced previously by this author [Stucki, 1973]; however, significant expansion of this concept is now being explored as a vehicle for improving software quality [Stucki, Svegel, January 1974], [Stucki, February 1975], [Stucki, Foshee, April 1975], [Stucki, May 1975], [Stucki, November 1975], [Boettcher, 1974], [Stucki, April 1975].

In order to illustrate the type of automated tool capabilities currently available and some of the new techniques now under consideration, the tool most familiar to the author will be described. It is hoped that this currently operational system will offer some insight into the concept of self-metric software and show a few of the measurement schemes available for dynamic program analysis.

AUTOMATED TOOLS

The Program Evaluator and Tester System— A Program for Generating Self-Metric Software

Several powerful tools have been and are currently being developed in the area of software validation. A Fortran implementation of the Program Evaluator and

Tester (PET) demonstrates the value of a self-metric testing approach for higher-level languages. Similar tools for other source languages are also being developed [Stucki, 1972], [Stucki, 1973], [Stucki, Howden, 1976].

These tools essentially instrument the software under test by inserting the software equivalent of sensors into the subject programs. This has the effect of making the programs self-measuring. Each time the software under test performs a significant event, the occurrence of this event is recorded, with the exact nature of the recording process depending on the measurements desired and the type of event performed.

Source Program Instrumentation

Figure 4.1 shows a sample Fortran program segment and its related flow diagram. Optional instrumentation points are identified for three sets of sensors applicable to this particular program segment. The execution-count sensors are shown at all points on the flow diagram where the internodal traversal frequency is not obvious.

These execution-count sensors can be most efficiently realized by associating a unique counting cell with each sensor and inserting these sensors only at those points where logical program breaks occur. The min/max/first/last sensors for assignment statements appear following nontrivial assignment statements. A trivial assignment statement, or one in which a constant or literal is assigned to a variable, causes no instrumentation to be generated. The min/max/first/last sensors for DO-loop control variables are inserted after the label or statement number, if present, and before the invocation of the loop if variable parameters are used in any of the three loop-controlling fields.

Two techniques have been experimentally used in implementing these and several other types of software sensors: (1) direct code insertion, and (2) invocation of runtime routines. The direct code insertion appears to be faster in most cases but the runtime routine is more flexible in that measurements can be more easily altered at execution time. The current PET system utilizes a hybrid scheme employing the selective use of both types of instrumentation.

As a result of running the instrumented program, a profile is produced containing part or all of the following measurements:

1. The number and percentage of all potential executable source statements which were executed one or more times.
2. The number and percentage of those program branches taken.
3. The number and percentage of those subroutine calls which were executed.
4. The number of times each subroutine was called, together with a list of those subroutines that were never entered.
5. Relative timing on the subroutine level.
6. Specific data associated with each executable source statement.
   a. Detailed execution counts

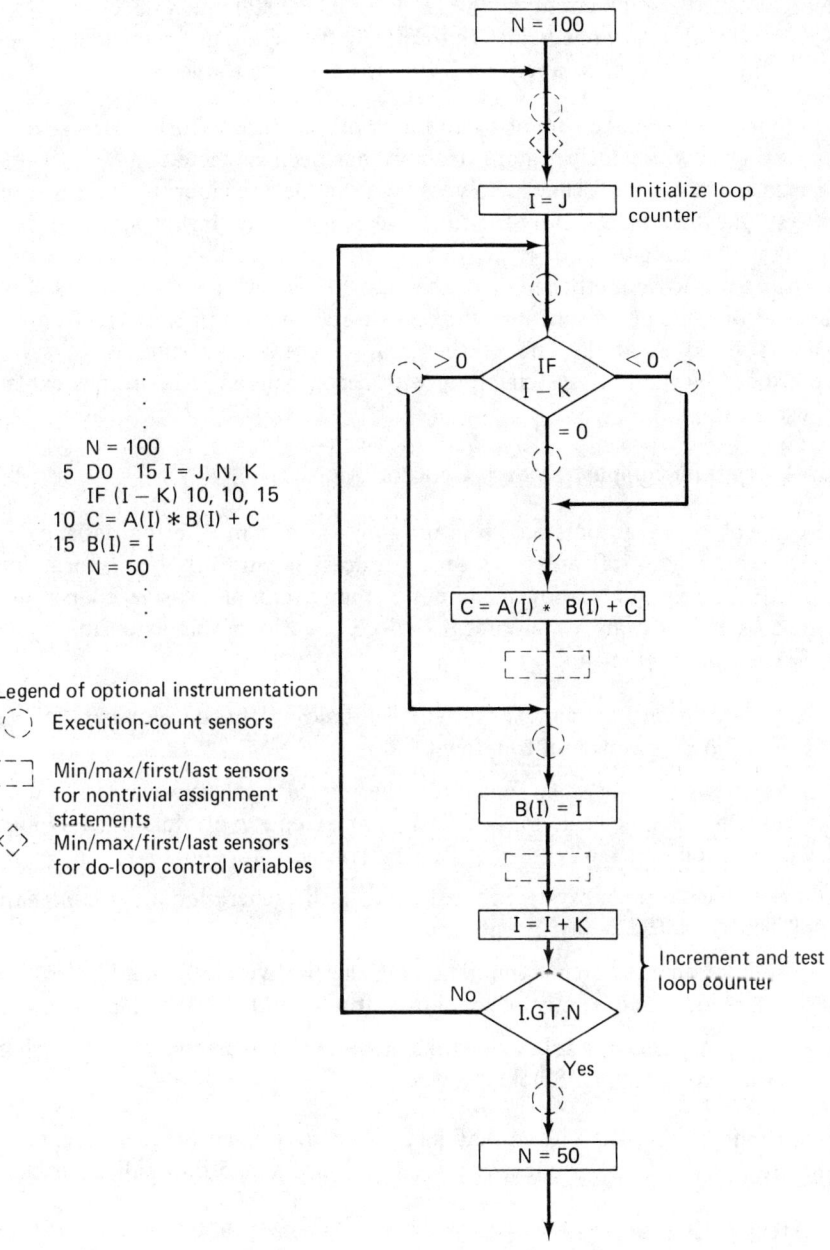

Figure 4.1. FORTRAN program segment showing optional instrumentation.

b. Detailed branch counts on all IF and GOTO statements
   c. Optional data range values (min/max/first/last) on assignment statements
   d. Optional min/max ranges on DO-loop control variables

These summaries and detailed reports can be employed to establish a figure for the degree of testing to which the program structure has been subjected.

The measurements performed allow us to examine the internal structure of a software system rather than merely treating it as if it were a "black box." While the testing process does not technically prove the correctness of the algorithms used, it does allow us to observe the behavior of the algorithms with actual test data. From these observations, the effectiveness of the software validation process can be greatly improved. Appendix A at the end of this chapter contains a number of sample reports produced by the PET system along with accompanying descriptions explaining their use.

Automated Program Support System Concept

The concept of an automated program support system offering assistance in several new areas of the software engineering process is currently being formulated to incorporate present tools and techniques within a comprehensive collection of automated aids for software development and certification. This extensible system contains five major components:

1. A program development subsystem for guiding the development of well structured programs in a top-down fashion;

2. A test statistics subsystem for both gathering static measurements and monitoring the dynamic behavior of software (an extension of McDonnell Douglas Corporation's currently existing PET system; see Appendix A);

3. A documentation subsystem for assisting in the generation and maintenance of detailed software documentation;

4. A simulation subsystem for monitoring the behavior of assembly language software and scaling real-time data used for validation testing; and

5. A test data generation subsystem for synthesizing and assessing tests of critical software components [Stucki, Howden, 1976].

Each component tool of this system may be applied to a given program separately, although the tools can be most effectively used in a disciplined rational sequence.

Current Areas of Research

The balance of this chapter will be restricted to describing new research currently underway on the test statistics subsystem referred to above.

There is currently a large gap between exhaustive testing of all potential program paths and the statement that all program branches or segments have been exercised a least once. Advance research efforts are being conducted in several areas in an attempt to help bridge this gap. One very promising area involves the incorporation of an assertion capability into existing languages.

Assertion and Monitor Capabilities for Existing Languages

A number of new languages are currently being investigated by researchers for possible use in proving the correctness or consistency of programs. Although the various proof techniques differ to some extent, one common requirement is the development of assertions describing the nature of the algorithms. The program provers are currently exploring techniques for checking the consistency of these assertions in a static logical sense for specialized languages.

The assertion concepts for programming languages which are now being developed constitute major extensions to our ability to carry out systematic programming. These new assertion concepts affect all phases of the software life cycle from initial requirements and design phases down through certification, and maintenance iterations. These assertion concepts are designed to encourage the development of algorithmic validation criteria as the implementation evolves from the initial algorithm requirements and specifications down to the final program code. The idea can be illustrated by Figures 4.2 and 4.3, which show how the point at which validation and/or other quality criteria can be attached directly to the software definitely affects the quality of the end software and the effort needed to validate and maintain that software.

ASSERTION CONCEPTS FOR IMPROVING SOFTWARE QUALITY

Generalized Local Assertion

A generalized local assertion may be embedded in a comment at any point within the executable code of a program where another executable statement may appear. The local assertion is designed to enhance the documentation of critical algorithms throughout the entire life cycle of the software. Dynamic execution time checks can be activated at selected times to ensure that the actual run-time environment is consistent with the logical state specified in the assertion. This dynamic assertion checking can be used to great benefit in debugging, validation, certification, and maintenance of complex systems.

The format of the generalized local assertion is:

```
ASSERT LOCAL(extended-logical-expression) [optional-qualifiers]
                                          [control-options]
```

The exact placement and treatment of the assertions will be tailored to the existing language facilities in currently defined languages. In these currently available languages

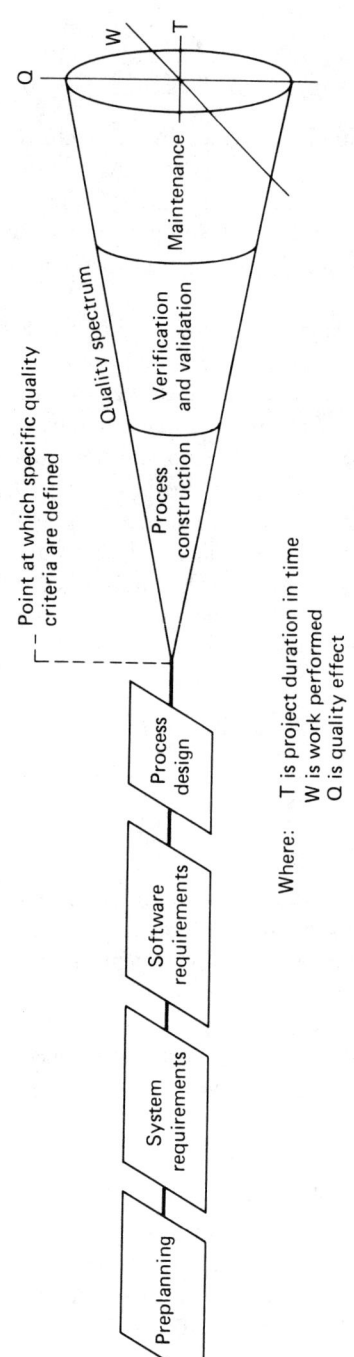

Where: T is project duration in time
W is work performed
Q is quality effect

Figure 4.2. Effect of delaying quality considerations.

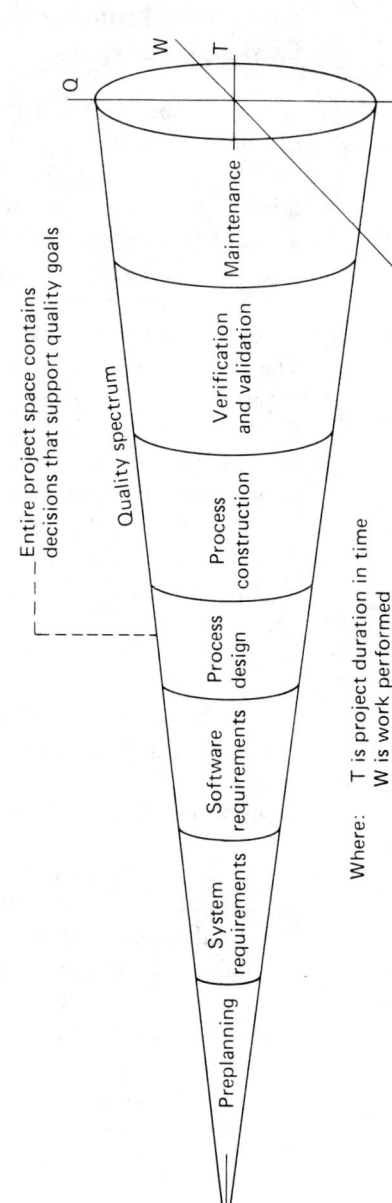

Where: T is project duration in time
W is work performed
Q is quality effect

Figure 4.3. Effect of continuous quality consideration.

the assertions will be implemented through specialized comments processed by a source code preprocessor. New language development and future compilers for existing languages may contain options for directly implementing the assertions.

Optional-Qualifiers

In order to provide an existential and universal qualifier notion to the generalized local assertion an optional looping capability is defined:

$$\ldots \text{FOR} \left[\left\{ \begin{matrix} \text{ALL} \\ \text{SOME} \end{matrix} \right\} \right] \begin{matrix} n \\ 1 \end{matrix} \;[(\text{variable-list}) \;(\text{set of ranges/values})]$$
$$\text{WHERE} \;(\text{qualifier-controlling-logical-expr})$$
$$\text{e.g.} \;/* \;\text{ASSERT} \;(X(I) \neg= X(J)) \;\text{FOR ALL} \;(I,J) \;(1:8) \;\text{WHERE} \;(I \neg= J)*/$$
$$\text{means:} \;[\forall I, J \;\text{such that} \;1 \leq I \leq 8 \wedge 1 \leq J \leq 8 \wedge I \neq J] \rightarrow X(I) \neq X(J)$$

Assertion Control Options

The total control alluded to above (i.e., ignoring all assertions by treating them as comments) offers the user a binary choice as to whether or not to apply dynamic assertions during program development; however, other levels of control are provided within the assertion language itself.

The assertion language itself contains three hierarchical levels of control:

1. *instrumentation control*—control of those sets of assertions which will be instrumented at a given level of testing,
2. *dynamic control*—run-time control of those instrumented assertions which are to be dynamically checked, and
3. *threshold control*—user control when assertion violations are observed.

Instrumentation control is provided by a LEVEL option. The syntax of this option is:

$$\ldots \underline{\text{LEVEL}} \;(\text{preprocessor-control-expression}) \ldots$$

The LEVEL option provides information to the preprocessor telling it which sets of assertions should be considered for dynamic analysis. This level of control provides a means for testing selected software features at various points within the software development cycle and fits in well with the top down approach to program development. This also allows a user to group sets of assertions together for various types of dynamic checks.

Dynamic control is provided by a CONDITION option. The syntax of this option is:

$$\ldots \text{CONDITION} \;(\text{dynamic-control-expression}) \ldots$$

The CONDITION option provides run-time control of the assertions which have been built into the program. This option affects only those assertions which have been actually instrumented, thus the CONDITION option is of lower priority than the LEVEL option. It should also be noted that the CONDITION option can be dynamically changed under program control to activate or deactivate the assertion as often as desired.

Threshold control is provided by a LIMIT option. The syntax of this option is:

$$\ldots \text{LIMIT } n[\text{VIOLATIONS}] \quad \left[\begin{Bmatrix}\text{HALT} \\ \text{EXIT } [\text{VIA}] \text{ proc-name}\end{Bmatrix}\right] \ldots$$

The LIMIT option provides user control in the event of n violations of the corresponding assertion. The user can specify that control be transferred to a wrap-up procedure proc-name if the EXIT phrase is specified. Otherwise, the HALT phrase will simply terminate execution and generate an assertion report automatically if n assertion violations are encountered. Motivated by a need to make assertions about arrays as well as scalars, the following notation has been adopted.

Array Notation for Assertions

Two areas of concern immediately arise when discussing data arrays, namely array indices and array values. Thus, if one is monitoring program behavior, it is not enough to monitor array values alone, since program logic is invariably concerned with where these values are stored within the array.

The approach is to generalize the assertion and monitor capabilities to include data arrays. Array notation is as follows:

>Assume an array of the form $A(I_1, I_2, I_3, \ldots, I_n)$. References to specific subsets of array values or array indices are indicated by $A(I'_1, I'_2, I'_3, \ldots, I'_n)$, where I'_i is a subrange of I_i. This notation is position dependent; i.e., if I'_2 is not referenced, its position must be indicated by an asterisk (∗), as in $A(I'_1, *, I'_3, \ldots, I'_n)$. The format of each I_i is $l: \mu$, where $l \leq \mu$. If $l = \mu$, then the pair $l: \mu$ may be replaced by the simple token μ, as $A(l_1: \mu_1, \mu_2, \ldots)$. Thus, for $A(10, 20)$ we might reference
>
>A(5,10:15)
>A(∗,3)
>A(2:5,∗)
>A(2:6,2:10)

Extended Logical Expressions

Two types of extended logical operations have initially been defined for the assertion language. An array to scalar logical operation will be allowed with its result being defined as true if and only if all component to scalar operations are found to be true. An array to array logical operation will be allowed for identically specified array cross sections with its result being defined to be true if and only if each pairwise component operation yields a result of true.

Local Assertion Examples

A simple local assertion example is shown below in a typical report format. The assertion simply indicates that at the point where it is inserted into the source code we expect the value of the variable MOVE to be less than 9. The report format indicates that this assertion was checked 9 times. Violations were noted on the sixth and seventh executions of the assertion. It is furthermore noted that MOVE actually contained the value 9 on those two instances. A snapshot is taken of all pertinent variable values associated with the violation when the trace mode is specified.

	EXECUTION COUNT	SPECIFIC EXECUTION DATA	
C ASSERT LOCAL (MOVE .LT. 9) LIMIT 10	9	ASSERTION VIOLATIONS	2
		EXEC NUMBER VARIABLE	VALUE
		6 MOVE	9
		7 MOVE	9

It is also worth noting that had we encountered ten violations we would have halted execution at this point in the program.

Examples of the use of array cross sections in extended logical expressions include the following (assume an array A(10, 20) has been defined):

(a) ASSERT LOCAL (A(*,3) .LT. 10)   LIMIT 6 VIOLATIONS
(b) ASSERT LOCAL (A(2:6,2:10)   .NE. 0)
(c) ASSERT LOCAL (A(*,*)   .GT. 0)

In (a), the value of each array element whose second subscript = 3 is checked and reported as a violation if its value is not less than 10. Ten array values will be checked in all. Any number of assertion violations within an array operation cause the operation to be counted as a single assertion violation. Thus, the HALT ON 6 parameter is concerned with only the number of invalid operations but not with the number of violations within the array.

In (b), only array values within the specified subscript ranges are checked for an assertion violation. In (c) all array values are checked for an assertion violation.

Specialized Local Assertions

A number of additional specialized local assertions are proposed to facilitate the expression of user validation criteria. This extensible attribute of the local assertion concept is illustrated by the following constructs:

```
ASSERT LOCAL VALUE[S] (variable-list) (set-of-legal-ranges-and/or-values) ...
ASSERT LOCAL VALUE[S] (variable-list) NOT (set-of-illegal-ranges-and/or-values) ...
ASSERT LOCAL VALUE[S] (variable-list) INVARIANT ...
ASSERT LOCAL SUBSCRIPT RANGE (list-of-array-specifications) ...
ASSERT LOCAL ORDER (array-cross-section)  [{ASCENDING / DESCENDING}] ...
```

All of these specialized local assertions could be replaced by one or more generalized local assertions, however, their existence facilitates the graceful transition from program requirements and their associated validation criteria to embedded program documentation in the evolving code.

These constructs cause instrumentation to be generated at the position where they occur or at the next executable statement. Forms three and four will monitor the execution of the following statement to ensure that it does not alter the value of an invariant variable (e.g., through side effects from subroutine or function calls) or use subscripts outside the specified ranges.

The ASSERT ORDER statement checks a sequence of array values as follows:

ASSERT LOCAL ORDER (A(*,3)) ASCENDING

For an array A(10,20), the following assertion violation summary illustrates the type of information traced for a violation:

EXECUTION COUNT	SPECIFIC EXECUTION DATA		
229	ASSERTION VIOLATIONS		1
	EXEC NUMBER	SEQUENCE SNAPSHOT	VALUE
	18	A(7,3)	6
		A(8,3)	100*
		A(9,3)	8

The ASSERT VALUES statement checks variable values against a specific set of ranges and/or values to assure that it lies within the desired range. Distinct ranges are specified by pairs "min-expr:max-expr." Each range pair or distinct value within a set of value specifications is separated by a comma. For example, the following assertion could be used to check the value of the variables X and Y.

/* ASSERT LOCAL VALUES (X,Y) (0,3,5:7,11:13,21)*/

In the example the current values of X and Y would be compared with the set:

(0,3,5,6,7,11,12,13,21)

Any discrepancies (i.e., any current values not in the set of specified legal values) would then constitute an assertion violation. The ASSERT SUBSCRIPT RANGE statement will check addressing on those arrays specified to ensure that only those portions of the array specifically selected are accessed. A subsequent example will illustrate the usefulness of this concept later in this chapter. All of these latter constructions will result in providing similar traces to those already presented for out of bound conditions.

A TRACE statement is available to allow the user to control the number of execution snapshots reported for local assertion violations. The format of the TRACE statement is:

TRACE [{FIRST / LAST / OFF}] n [VIOLATIONS]

If a TRACE statement is not coded in the source program, detailed traces for local assertion violations will not be reported. If TRACE statements are coded, the first TRACE statement encountered causes the first (or last) n violations of subsequent local assertions to include snapshot information. Any subsequent TRACE statements encountered reset the values specified by the previous TRACE statement. TRACE OFF halts the reporting of execution snapshots for local assertions until the next TRACE statement is encountered.

The Concept of a Global Assertion

Expanding our notion of assertions, we immediately identify the need to expand the scope of application for our asserted program properties. In an effort to avoid requiring several similar local assertions within a particular program region, the concept of a global assertion has been introduced. This is a novel approach which promises to have a significant impact on the way we design, implement, and test software.

Global assertions will allow us to extend our capacity to inspect certain behavioral patterns for entire program modules, selected regions of modules, or module interfaces (entries and/or exits). Global assertions appear in the declaration section of the program module. Formats include:

```
ASSERT  [ { GLOBAL
            REGIONAL (region name)
            ENTRY
            EXIT } ]                    (extended-logical-expression) ...

ASSERT  [ { GLOBAL
            REGIONAL (region-name)
            ENTRY
            EXIT } ]                    VALUES ...

ASSERT  [ { GLOBAL
            REGIONAL (region-name) } ]  SUBSCRIPT RANGE ...

ASSERT  [ { ENTRY
            EXIT } ]                    ORDER ...
```

These global assertions will have effect within the scope defined (i.e., globally at all pertinent points, regionally over the named region, collectively for all entries and/or all exits).

The VALUES statement inspects each specified variable as its value changes and reports when: (option 1) the new value is not one of the specified legal ranges and/or values, or (option 2) the new value assumes a specified illegal range and/or value, or (option 3) checks to make sure the values of the selected variables are preserved (i.e., no direct or externally caused changes are permitted).

The ASSERT SUBSCRIPT RANGE statement verifies that array subscripts fall within a specified range whenever the array is referenced during program execution. It should be noted that this statement provides a means for checking portions of arrays as well as normal upper and lower bounds. For this reason, it is more powerful than the PL/I type ON SUBSCRIPT RANGE check.

Instrumentation will be inserted into the source program by the preprocessor to accumulate the following statistics relative to assertion violations:

1. Identify the statement that caused the assertion violation. For that statement an execution count and violation execution counts identical to those obtained for local assertions are reported.
2. The actual value that caused the violation. This value is linked to the statistics identified in (1) above.

A GLOBAL TRACE statement will be available to allow the user to control the number of execution counts and associated data values reported for global assertion violations. The format of this statement is:

$$\text{GLOBAL TRACE} \left[\begin{Bmatrix} \text{FIRST} \\ \text{LAST} \\ \text{OFF} \end{Bmatrix} \right] \quad n \quad [\text{VIOLATIONS}]$$

Some Fortran examples follow:

```
             .
             .
             .
20           DIMENSION A(10,20)
21    C      GLOBAL TRACE 10 VIOLATIONS
22    C      ASSERT VALUES (I,J,K,L) (0:100)
23    C      ASSERT VALUES (II,LL) (-10:10)
24    C      ASSERT VALUES (KK,NN) (2,4,6,8,10)
25    C      ASSERT SUBSCRIPT RANGE (A(*,3))
26    C      ASSERT VALUES (X,Y,Z) INVARIANT
             .
             .
             .
102          K = K + 1
103          II = A(L,J) + LL
             .
             .
234.         K = A(J,K) + I*100
235          II = II + 2
236          NN = KK*(I-J)
             .
             .
300          CALL ROUTINEX(X,Y)
             .
             .
```

If assertion violations occurred in this example, the following statistics are indicative of what would be reported by the postprocessor:

Annotated Program Listing	Execution Count	Specific Execution Data	
. . .			
102 K = K + 1	511	ASSERTION VIOLATIONS	1
		ASSERT VALUE (K)	(0:100)
		EXEC NUMBER	VALUE
		10	101
103 II = A(L,J) + LL	511	ASSERTION VIOLATIONS	3
		ASSERT VALUE (II)	(−10:10)
		EXEC NUMBER	VALUE
.		22	20
.		ASSERT SUBSCRIPT RANGE	(A(∗,3))
.		EXEC NUMBER	VALUE
		5	A(12,3)
		105	A(1,4)
234 K = A(J,K) + I∗100	125	ASSERTION VIOLATIONS	4
		ASSERT VALUE (K)	(0:100)
		EXEC NUMBER	VALUE
		52	101
		53	102
		ASSERT SUBSCRIPT RANGE	(A(∗,3))
		EXEC NUMBER	VALUE
		52	A(5,4)
		53	A(6,4)
235 II = II + 2	125	ASSERTION VIOLATIONS	1
		ASSERT VALUE (II)	(−10:10)
		EXEC NUMBER	VALUE
		50	12
236 NN = KK∗(I−J)	38	ASSERTION VIOLATIONS	1
.		ASSERT VALUE (NN)	(2,4,6,8,10)
.		EXEC NUMBER	VALUE
.		20	7
300 CALL ROUTINEX(X,Y)	53	ASSERTION VIOLATIONS	1
		ASSERT VALUE (X)	INVARIANT
.		VALUE OF CALL PARM X	
.		EXEC NUMBER BEFORE CALL AFTER CALL	
.		30 −10 −20	

SUGGESTED USE OF ASSERTIONS

Basic Philosophy

Assertions should be developed and incorporated into a program during program design and not after the fact.

A Suggested Approach

1. Prior to generating any detailed code, write down a capsulized program specification containing as a minimum the following:
   a. a statement of the problem
   b. a short description of the solution techniques involved
   c. summarized input requirements
   d. summarized output requirements
   e. testing/validation requirements
   f. performance requirements
2. Following the design and declaration of each variable, array, and structure, include a comment defining its global by asserted attributes.

Example

    DCL I FIXED BIN (15,0);
    /*ASSERT VALUE (I) (0:8) */
    DCL A(1:100) FIXED BIN (15,0);
    /* ASSERT VALUE (A(1:8)) (0,1) */
    /* ASSERT SUBSCRIPTRANGE (A(1:8))*/

3. It is suggested that assertions be used to test entry and exit conditions for all internal procedures.
4. It is further recommended that they be applied at entry/exit to internal algorithms within individual procedures (e.g., before and after important loop structures or procedure calls).
5. Operations or key algorithmic logic subject to possible singularities should be proceeded by appropriate assertions (e.g. $A = B/Z$, where Z has been calculated previously should be preceded by an assertion checking for Z not equal to 0).
6. Use as desired for debugging and other testing.

A Sample Program

Specification

   Problem:
     Create a program to solve the 8-queens problem.
   Description:
     Given an 8×8 chessboard and 8 hostile queens. Find a position for each queen (or a total board configuration) where no queen may capture any other queen.
   Inputs:
   • None
   Output:
   • 8×8 chessboard configuration describing the placement of the 8 hostile queens

Test/Validation Criteria

- data integrity (ASSERT board size is 8 × 8, ASSERT # QUEENS is 8)
- every row, column contains 1 queen
- diagonals, contain at most 1 queen

Performance Criteria

- solution should be found in 20 cpu sec on an IBM 360/91.

Program Development

Stepwise generation of partial solutions using a top-down development scheme might produce the following version of a program:

```
QUEENS: PROC;
    DECLARE
        board,pointer,safe;
    data_integrity_assertions;  /* LEVEL (2) */
    consider_first_column;
    LOOP: DO UNTIL (last_column_done V regress_out_of_first_col);
        try-column;
        IF safe
          THEN
            DO;
                setqueen;
                consider_next_column;
            END;
          ELSE
            regress;
    END LOOP;
    algorithmic_validation_assertions;  /* LEVEL (4)    */
END QUEENS;
```

Although the final solution differs in many respects it basically follows N. Wirth's development of this program in his article "Program Development by Stepwise Refinement," *CACM*, Vol. 14, No. 4 (1971).

```
QUEENS: PROC;
    DECLARE I FIXED BIN (15,0);
      /* ASSERT VALUE (I) (0:8) LEVEL (2) */
    DECLARE J FIXED BIN (15,0);
      /* ASSERT VALUE (J) (0:9) LEVEL (2)         */
    DECLARE X(1:8) FIXED BIN (15,0);
      /* ASSERT VALUE (X(1:8)) (0:8) L(2)        */
    DECLARE (A(1:8),B(2:16),C(-7:7)) FIXED BIN (15,0)
        INIT((8)0,(15)0,(15)0);
      /* ASSERT VALUES (A(*),B(*),C(*))(0,1)L(2) */
    DECLARE SAFE FIXED BIN(15,0)
      /* ASSERT VALUES(SAFE) (0,3)L(2) */
```

```
              J=1;
              I=0;
              DO UNTIL (J>8|J<1);
                DO UNTIL (SAFE=0|I=8);
                  I=I+1;
                  SAFE=A(I)+B(I+J)+C(I-J);
                END;
                 IF SAFE=0
                   THEN
                     BEGIN;
                       /* ASSERT LOCAL VALUE (I,J)(1:8) LEVEL(5) */
                       /* ASSERT LOCAL VALUES(A(I),B(K+J),C(I-J)) (0) L(5) */
                       A(I)=A(I)+1;        /*                              */
                       B(I+J)=B(I+J)+1;    /* SET QUEEN                    */
                       C(I-J)=C(I-J)+1;    /*                              */
                       X(J)=I;
                       J=J+1;
                       I=0;
                     END;
                   ELSE
                     CALL REGRESS (I,J,A,B,C,X);
              END;
                /* ASSERT LOCAL VALUES X(*)) (1:8) LEVEL(4)          */
                /* ASSERT (X(II)¬=X(JJ)) FOR ALL (II,JJ) (1:8) WHERE
                    (II¬=JJ) L(4)                                    */
                /* ASSERT LOCAL VALUES A(*) (1) L(4)                 */
                /* ASSERT LOCAL VALUES (B(*),C(*)) (0,1) LEVEL (4)   */
                IF J>8
                  THEN
                    PUT DATA (X);
                  ELSE
                    PUT LIST ('FAILURE');
                STOP;
         END QUEENS;

         REGRESS: PROC(I,J,A,B,C,X);
              DECLARE(I,J) FIXED BIN (15,0);
              /* ASSERT VALUE (I) (0:8) LEVEL(3)       */
              /* ASSERT VALUE (J) (0:9) L(3)           */
              DECLARE (A(1:8),B(2:16),C(-7:7)) FIXED BIN (15,0);
              /* ASSERT VALUE (A(*),B(*),C(*)) (0,1) L(3) */
              BEGIN;
                J=J-1;  /*   RECONSIDER_PRIOR_COL        */
                IF¬(J<1) /* ~REGRESS_OUT_OF_FIRST-COL */
                  THEN
                    BEGIN;
                    /* ASSERT LOCAL VALUE (I,J) (1:8) LEVEL(6) */
                    /* ASSERT LOCAL VALUE (A(I),B(I+J),C(I-J)) (1) L(6) */
                    I=X(J);     /*
```

```
                A(I)=0;    /*              */
                B(I+J)=0;  /*REMOVE QUEEN */
                C(I-J)=0;  /*              */
                IF       I = 8
                  THEN
                    BEGIN;
                      J=J-1;  /* RECONSIDER_PRIOR_COL    */
                      IF¬(J<1) /*~REGRESS_OUT_OF_FIRST_COL */
                        THEN
                          DO;
                          /* ASSERT LOCAL VALUE (I,J)(1:8) LEVEL (6) */
                          /* ASSERT LOCAL VALUE (A(I),B(I+J),C(I-J)(1)L(6) */
                          I=X(J);    /*              */
                          A(I)=0;    /*              */
                          B(I+J)=0;  /* REMOVE QUEEN */
                          C(I-J)=0;  /*              */
                          END;
                    END;
                 END;
             END;
      END REGRESS;
```

APPENDIX A—SAMPLE PET OUTPUT

Overview

The Program Evaluator and Tester (PET) is a package of programs designed as an automated aid to assist in the debugging, testing, and documenting of computer programs. The preprocessor module of PET operates on a Fortran source deck, gathering information on source statement characteristics and inserting Fortran code for automatically gathering run-time statistics. It generates a modified Fortran program containing both the original source code and the inserted source code for later compilation and execution of an ordinary program case. Run-time statistics are retrieved at program termination or under user control by a run-time library. Reports are generated in a separate step by the PET postprocessor.

Run-time statistics that may be gathered include statement execution and branch counts, min/max and first/last values of assignment statements and DO-loop parameters, detailed branching counts and relative subroutine execution timing. All but execution and branch counts are optional. Source statement characteristics gathered include percentages of executable and nonexecutable statements, number of comment statements and number of statements with ANSI standard Fortran violations which would affect portability of the program to other Fortran systems.

PET accepts as input any Fortran deck running on the host machine. No program modifications are necessary. PET is currently available on the CDC 6000 and 7000 series, the IBM 360 and 370 OS systems, and the Univac 1100 series (ASCII Fortran compiler).

Sample PET Reports

The reports produced by the PET system present both detailed statement by statement statistics as well as program summary statistics.

a. Subroutine Listing and Execution Counts. This contains specific statement execution data as well as a profile of the subroutine. The execution and branch counts are matched back with the original source code and presented in the form of an annotated source listing.

First, the subroutine source is listed. An N is printed to the left of any statement that violates standard Fortran. To the right is the specific execution data: execution count for that statement, min/max and first/last values for assignment statements (if those options were indicated), and specific branching information for applicable statements. True/false counts are reported for logical IF statements and branch counts for arithmetic IF and assigned or computed GOTO statements.

Examples of the report for branching statements follow:

original statement	execution count	true count	false count
	100	TRUE 70	FALSE 30
IF (A . EQ. B) GOTO 100		# of transfers to 100	# of transfers to 200
GOTO (100, 200, 300), N	30	BRANCH1 5 BRANCH3 13	BRANCH2 12
		# of transfers to 300	

Figure 4.4 illustrates a subroutine listing and execution count page.

b. Subroutine Summaries. Following the listing is the subroutine profile. The syntactic profile gives the total number of statements of all kinds in the subroutine and then lists statements of various types, giving the number and percent of each in the subroutine.

The statement types and their PET definition are:

Executable source	All Fortran statements except comment and nonexecutable
Nonexecutable source	COMMON, DIMENSION, Type statements, DATA, EQUIVALENCE, OVERLAY Control Cards, STATEMENT FUNCTIONS, FORMAT
Comment	Statements with C in Column 1
Nonstandard	Statements that violate standard Fortran (Figure 1.4)
BRANCH	Total of all GOTO and IF branches

PET CASE 1 (MCDONNELL-DOUGLAS PROPRIETARY PROGRAM PRODUCT)	DATE 5/04/76	PAGE 76
PROGRAM LISTING (LEADING N INDICATES CONVERSION WARNINGS)	COUNT	SPECIFIC EXECUTION DATA

```
      SUBROUTINE INPUT                                            02107
C                                                                 02108
      REAL IFVD, MACHM, MACHT                                     02109
C                                                                 02110
      COMMON /GGG/ G(100)                                         02111
C                                                                 02112
      COMMON /ENT/ IENTRY                                         02113
      COMMON /CONST/ DATA(100)                                    02114
      EQUIVALENCE ( DATA(1) , DTR       )                         02115
C                                                                 02116
C                                                                 02117
      NAMELIST /IN/ THETA,PSI,PHI,VM,GAMMA,SIGMA,XG,YG,ZG,ENDTME, 02118
     * ENDSTG,PI1,PI2,PI3,PI4,PI5,PT1,PT2,PT3,PT4,PT5,VT,XT,YT,ZT,02119
     * TLON,YSTA,IFVD,PSIT,THETAT,AMODE,DT,AXT,AXT,AZT,           02120
     * PP, QQ, RR, MACHM, MACHT, R, GMA                            02121
N C                                                               02122
      GO TO (100, 200, 300, 400, 500, 600, 700), IENTRY           02123
```

```
  100 CONTINUE                                                    02124
      RETURN                                                      02125
  200 CONTINUE                                                    02126
N     READ(5, IN, END=800)                                        02127
N   1 PRINT 1                                                     02128
      FORMAT(1H1)                                                 02129
N     WRITE (6,IN)                                                02130
      G(1)=THETA                                                  02131
```

```
      G(2)= PSI                                                   02132

      G(3)= PHI                                                   02133

      IF ( VM .GT. 0. )   GO TO 210                               02135
      CALL ATMOS ( -ZG, PA, VS )                                  02136
      G(4) = VS * MACHM                                           02137
      GO TO 211                                                   02138
  210 CONTINUE                                                    02139
      G(4) = VM                                                   02140
  211 CONTINUE                                                    02141
      G(5)=GAMMA                                                  02142

      G(6)=SIGMA                                                  02143

      G(7)=XG                                                     02144

      G(8)=YG                                                     02145

      G(9)=ZG                                                     02146

      G(39)=ENDTME
```

	5	BRANCH 1 2 BRANCH 2 2
		BRANCH 3 0 BRANCH 4 0
		BRANCH 5 0 BRANCH 6 0
		BRANCH 7 1
		SPECIFIC BRANCHING INFORMATION
	2	MIN= 0.0 MAX= 0.0
	2	FIRST= 0.0 LAST= 0.0
	2	MIN= 0.0 MAX= 0.0
	2	FIRST= 0.0 LAST= 0.0
	2	MIN=-0.450000E 02 MAX=-0.450000E 02
	2	FIRST=-0.450000E 02 LAST=-0.450000E 02
	0	TRUE 1 FALSE
	0	LOGICAL IF BRANCHES
	1	MIN= 0.754200E 03 MAX= 0.754200E 03
	1	FIRST= 0.754200E 03 LAST= 0.754200E 03
	1	MIN= 0.0 MAX= 0.0
	1	FIRST= 0.0 LAST= 0.0
	1	MIN= 0.0 MAX= 0.0
	1	FIRST= 0.0 LAST= 0.0
	1	MIN= 0.0 MAX= 0.0
	1	FIRST= 0.0 LAST= 0.0
	1	MIN=-0.100000E 05 MAX=-0.100000E 05
	1	FIRST=-0.100000E 05 LAST=-0.100000E 05
	1	MIN= 0.300000E 02 MAX= 0.300000E 02
	1	FIRST= 0.300000E 02 LAST= 0.300000E 02

Annotations: NONSTANDARD FORTRAN (pointing to line 02127); STATEMENTS NOT EXECUTED (pointing to lines 02135–02138).

Figure 4.4. PET annotated source listing.

CALL	All subroutine CALL statements. Function subroutine references are not delineated.
UNFORMATTED I/O	All binary read and write statements
FORMATTED I/O	All read and write statements with a format

The operational profile gives the total execution count for the subroutine and then, by statement type, lists the number of statements that were executed and the percent that were executed. For branch (i.e., GOTO and IF statements), it gives the number of branches that were taken and the percentage of the possible branches that were taken. Figure 4.5 shows a typical summary report.

c. Program Summary. The information on this page has been compiled from the subroutine profile into a composite profile of the entire program. It includes a program syntactic profile and an operational profile in the format described in the previous section.

d. Subroutine Operational Summary. This section summarizes selected subroutine operational statistics. The information gives a picture of how well the case(s) that were executed actually exercised the program branches. It can be used by the analyst to design additional test cases to exercise other areas of code or to determine that some areas of the code can never be executed.

Figure 4.6 illustrates a subroutine operational summary. The following list explains the information on the report by column.

For each subroutine that was executed the following information is given.

Column	Information
A	Subroutine name
B	Number of executable statements that were actually executed.
C	Percent of the total executable statements that were actually executed. Refer to the subroutine summary page for the total number of executable statements.
D	Number of subroutine calls that were actually executed.
E	Percent of the subroutine calls that were executed. Refer to the subroutine summary page for the total number of call statements.
F	Number of branches that were actually taken.
G	Percent of the possible branches that were actually taken.

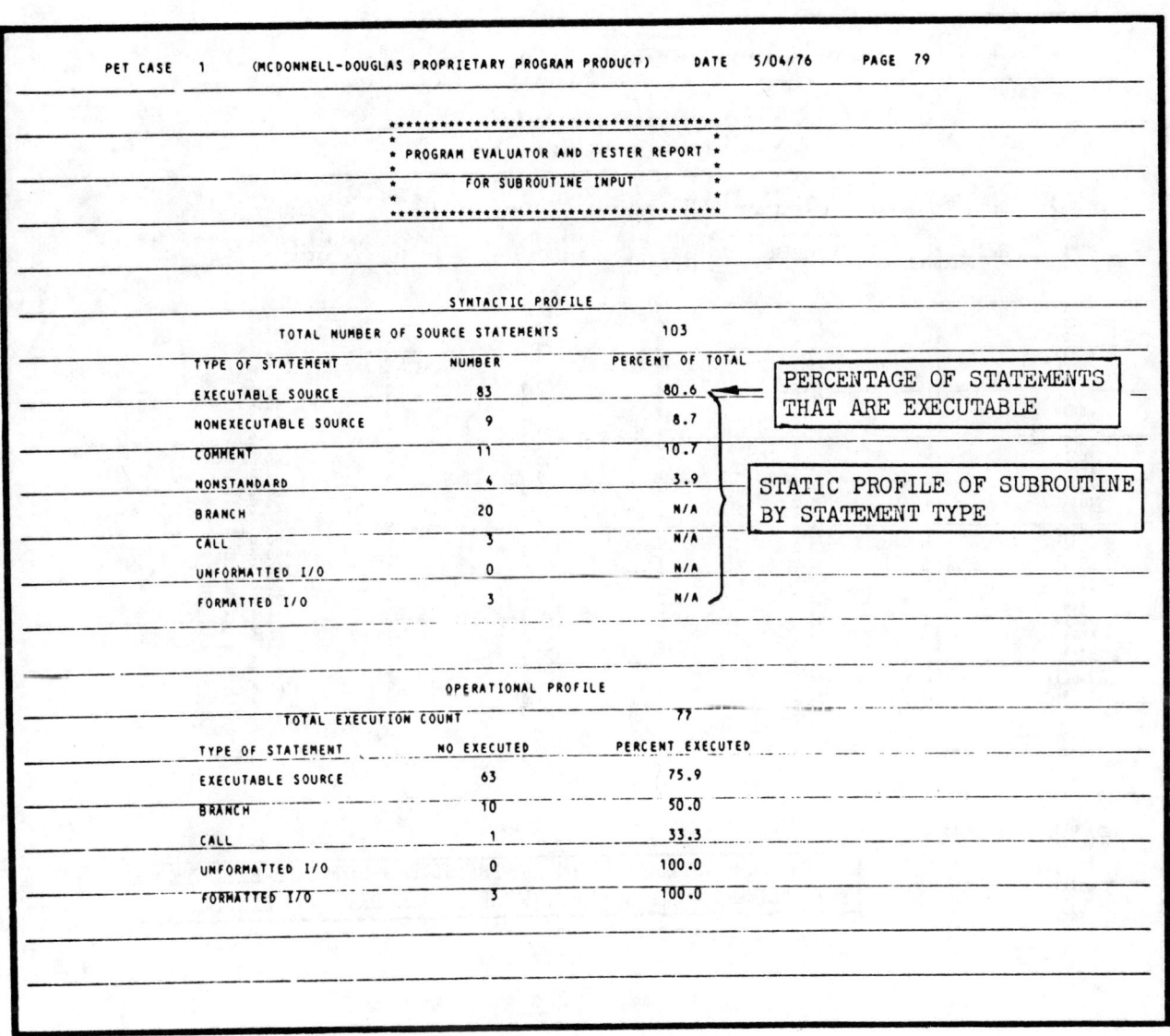

Figure 4.5. PET subroutine summary report.

```
PET CASE   1    (MCDONNELL-DOUGLAS PROPRIETARY PROGRAM PRODUCT)      DATE   5/04/76      PAGE 134

                       ******************************************
                       *                                        *
                       *  PROGRAM EVALUATOR AND TESTER REPORT   *
                       *                                        *
                       *       SUBROUTINE OPERATIONAL SUMMARY   *
   (A)         (B)         (C)  ******* (D) ******* (E) ******* (F)         (G)
SUBROUTINE   NO OF       PERCENT     NO OF       PERCENT      NO OF        PERCENT
  NAME      STATEMENTS   EXECUTED    CALLS       EXECUTED    BRANCHES      EXECUTED
            EXECUTED                 EXECUTED                EXECUTED
```

SUBROUTINE NAME	NO OF STATEMENTS EXECUTED	PERCENT EXECUTED	NO OF CALLS EXECUTED	PERCENT EXECUTED	NO OF BRANCHES EXECUTED	PERCENT EXECUTED
(MAIN)	39	100.0	13	100.0	5	55.6
AUTS	69	95.8	0	100.0	9	81.8
ARCRFT	21	84.0	0	100.0	5	71.4
ATMOS	21	70.0	0	100.0	8	42.1
CHECK	15	57.7	0	100.0	12	50.0
CLIP	2	100.0	0	100.0	0	100.0
CNTRL	115	60.8	7	35.0	39	50.6
DERIV	77	78.6	42	71.2	8	66.7
EQOM	35	89.7	0	100.0	5	71.4
EXPLT	1	100.0	0	100.0	0	100.0
PLOT1	1	100.0	0	100.0	0	100.0
FCC	70	83.3	1	100.0	6	30.0
GUIDE	119	96.7	4	100.0	31	93.9
INIAL	46	85.2	1	100.0	3	42.9
INPUT	63	75.9	1	33.3	10	50.0
INVR3	16	100.0	0	100.0	0	100.0
LOOK1	5	100.0	1	100.0	0	100.0
LOOK2	9	100.0	2	100.0	0	100.0
LOOK3	15	100.0	3	100.0	0	100.0
M3X1	6	100.0	0	100.0	0	100.0
PRINT	31	72.1	0	100.0	1	14.3
RELT	83	91.2	0	100.0	3	42.9
RKS4	125	85.0	8	80.0	32	45.7
SACS	112	96.6	10	100.0	40	90.9
TARGET	31	88.6	0	100.0	6	66.7
TMULT1	6	100.0	0	100.0	0	100.0
TFFS	20	83.3	1	100.0	8	72.7
VPCS	19	82.6	1	100.0	6	66.7
PROGRAM	1172	82.5	95	73.8	237	57.9

```
SUBROUTINES NOT EXECUTED
  BLKDAT.
  BLKDAT.                 ┌─────────────────────────────────────────────────────────┐
  BLKDAT.                 │ THESE SUBROUTINES WERE INSTRUMENTED BUT NOT EXECUTED.   │
  GRAFIX                  │ THE THREE NAMED BLKDAT. WERE BLOCK DATA ROUTINES.       │
  PLOT1                   └─────────────────────────────────────────────────────────┘
  STAGE
```

Figure 4.6. PET operational summary.

The above information is then totaled and combined with the syntactic statistics for the subroutines that were not executed to give the program operational summary (H).

Following the summary is a listing of the names of the subroutines that were instrumented but not executed (I).

e. Subroutine Execution Summary. This page summarizes the execution data for all the monitored subroutines. It gives a profile of the types of operations actually performed by the subroutine (i.e., is it mainly performing I/O or logic or calling other subroutines). The information on this page combined with the timing information described in the next section can help the analyst determine where a program is spending its time and how it could be improved. Figure 4.7 shows a subroutine execution summary. The information on the report is explained by the column below.

Column	Information
A	Subroutine name
B	Number of times the subroutine was called
C	Total execution count = sum of the execution counts for each statement
D	Total call count = sum of the execution counts for each call statement
E	The percent of the executions that were subroutine calls (i.e., total call count/total execution count)
F	Total branch count = sum of the execution counts for each branch statement
G	The percent of the executions that were branches (i.e., total branch count/total execution count)
H	Total input/output count = total execution count for formatted and unformatted read and write statements.
I	The percent of the executions that were I/O (i.e., total input-output count/total execution count).

f. Subroutine Timing Summary. The statistics for subroutine timing are gathered by accessing the system clock at all entries into and exits from a subroutine. The accumulation of timing statistics is turned off when a subroutine call is made and when a user-supplied function subroutine is referenced in the first term of an assignment statement. Note that timing is not turned off when a function subroutine is referenced in an IF statement, thus the time spent in the function will be included in the total time of the calling subroutine. In order to obtain the most accurate timing history, it is

PET CASE 1 (MCDONNELL-DOUGLAS PROPRIETARY PROGRAM PRODUCT) DATE 5/04/76 PAGE 135

PROGRAM EVALUATOR AND TESTER REPORT

SUBROUTINE EXECUTION SUMMARY

(A)	(B)	(C)	(D)	(E)	(F)	(G)	(H)	(I)
SUBROUTINE NAME	NUMBER TIMES ENTERED	TOTAL EXECUTION COUNT	TOTAL CALL COUNT	PERCENT OF TOTAL EXECUTIONS	TOTAL BRANCH COUNT	PERCENT OF TOTAL EXECUTIONS	TOTAL I/O COUNT	PERCENT OF TOTAL EXECUTIONS
(MAIN)	1	679	18	2.65	5	0.74	0	0.0
AUTS	970	50194	0	0.0	2860	5.70	21	0.04
ARCRFT	970	2940	0	0.0	970	32.99	21	0.71
ATMOS	946	17979	0	0.0	1893	10.53	0	0.0
CHECK	17955	90111	0	0.0	88	0.10	0	0.0
CLIP	15146	30292	0	0.0	0	0.0	0	0.0
CNTRL	106	9151	246	2.69	2949	32.23	102	1.11
DERIV	970	34293	9650	28.14	1915	5.58	0	0.0
EQOM	970	25590	0	0.0	970	3.79	0	0.0
EXPLT	1	1	0	0.0	0	0.0	0	0.0
PLOT1	102	102	0	0.0	0	0.0	0	0.0
FCC	1	70	1	1.43	6	8.57	11	15.71
GUIDE	970	47258	968	2.05	11580	24.50	63	0.13
INIAL	4	51	1	1.96	4	7.84	0	0.0
INPUT	5	77	1	1.30	12	15.58	6	7.79
INVR3	102	2652	0	0.0	0	0.0	0	0.0
LOOK1	2835	17010	2835	16.67	0	0.0	0	0.0
LOOK2	4725	56700	9450	16.67	0	0.0	0	0.0
LOOK3	1890	83160	5670	6.82	0	0.0	0	0.0
M3X1	1	18	0	0.0	0	0.0	0	0.0
PRINT	21	651	0	0.0	21	3.23	315	48.39
RELT	967	75764	0	0.0	967	1.28	21	0.03
RKS4	1	347186	1047	0.30	1943	0.56	0	0.0
SACS	970	80467	7560	9.40	15793	19.63	21	0.03
TARGET	970	9558	0	0.0	1915	20.04	21	0.22
TMULT1	945	17010	0	0.0	0	0.0	0	0.0
TFFS	970	10472	945	9.02	2860	27.31	0	0.0
VPCS	970	9527	945	9.92	1915	20.10	0	0.0

Figure 4.7. PET execution summary.

```
PET CASE   1    (MCDONNELL-DOUGLAS PROPRIETARY PROGRAM PRODUCT)    DATE   5/04/76    PAGE 136


                         ******************************************
                         *                                        *
                         *   PROGRAM EVALUATOR AND TESTER REPORT  *
                         *                                        *
                         *        SUBROUTINE TIMING SUMMARY       *
                         *                                        *
                         ******************************************


TOTAL EXECUTION TIME FOR THIS CASE      23.253 SEC
TOTAL TIME IN MONITORED ROUTINES        15.251 SEC   TOTAL TIME SPENT IN ROUTINES WHERE TIMING WAS
TOTAL TIME IN OTHER ROUTINES             8.002 SEC   TURNED ON VERSUS TIME SPENT IN ALL OTHER ROUTINES


                         DETAILED SUBROUTINE TIME MONITORING

SUBROUTINE      TIME RELATIVE TO MAXIMUM              ACTUAL TIME       PERCENT OF TOTAL
   NAME         SUBROUTINE EXECUTION TIME             IN SECONDS        MONITORED TIME
                (*  = TWO PERCENT)
(MAIN)                                                   0.010              0.07
AUTS            *****************************           1.201              7.87
ARCRFT          **                                       0.073              0.48
ATMOS           *******                                  0.283              1.85
CHECK           ******************************          1.224              8.03
CLIP            **********************************      1.397              9.16
CNTRL           ***                                      0.133              0.87
DERIV           ***********************                  0.882              5.78
EQOM            ********                                 0.329              2.16
PLOT1                                                    0.003              0.02
FCC             *                                        0.030              0.20
GUIDE           ********************                     0.812              5.32
INPUT           *                                        0.060              0.39
INVR3           *                                        0.043              0.28
LOOK1           ****************                         0.576              3.77
LOOK2           *******************************          1.281              8.40
LOOK3           *****************************            1.118              7.33
PRINT           *******                                  0.266              1.75
RELT            ***************************************  1.444              9.47
RKS4            ****************************************** 2.029           13.31
SACS            ************************************     1.327              8.70
TARGET          *******                                  0.273              1.79
TMULT1          ****                                     0.156              1.03
TFFS            ****                                     0.163              1.07
VPCS            ***                                      0.136              0.89


TOTAL TIME IN POSTPROCESSOR        3.771 SEC
```

Figure 4.8. PET timing summary.

recommended that function references be made in separate assignment statements. Note also that time spent in Fortran-supplied functions and in system routines will be accumulated in the calling routine.

The timing history obtained is distorted by the PET instrumentation. For this reason, it is recommended that when an accurate timing history is desired that the min/max and first/last option not be used. However, experience has shown that the relative time spent in subroutines is not significantly distorted by the PET instrumentation.

A function subroutine reference will be considered to be user supplied unless:

1. it is in a table of Fortran-supplied functions;
2. it is a Fortran intrinsic function, but was referenced in an external or type statement.

The various types of timing information output on the subroutine timing summary are enumerated below.

- The total execution time for the case is the elapsed time from entry into the main routine to exit from the instrumented programs.
- The total time in monitored routines is the total time spent in routines for which the timing option was turned on.
- The total time in other routines is the difference between the first two numbers.
- The histogram of subroutine timing is output for those subroutines for which the timing option is turned on and which accumulated sometime on the clock.
- The actual time and the percent of monitored time spent in each of the above subroutines is output to the right of the histogram.
- The elapsed time spent in the postprocessor is output.

If the timing option was not used, only the total execution time for the case and the total time in the postprocessor will be given.

Figure 4.8 shows a typical timing summary. Subroutine XUB accumulated the largest amount of time, so it was printed with 50 asterisks. The actual time spent in XUB was 31.926 sec and the percent of monitored time was $\frac{31}{71} = 35\%$. Subroutine PCUM accumulated 25.709 sec, so it has 40 asterisks = $25.705/31.926 \times 50$.

APPENDIX B—SAMPLES FROM A PROPOSED STRUCTURED FORTRAN ASSERTION SYSTEM

Sample Reports

	Original source code listing	*Execution count*	*Assertion information branch counts, truth values, data ranges*
	ANNOTATED PROGRAM LISTING	COUNT	SPECIFIC EXECUTION DATA

```
00001        PROGRAM TICTAC (INPUT,OUTPUT)
00002   C
00003   C    INTERACTIVE TIC-TAC-TOE PLAYER
00004   C
00005        INTEGER FIRST,GAMES,MOVE,PLAYER,TURNS,WINNER
00006        INTEGER HUMAN,MACHINE,NOBODY,QUIT,BOARD(9),NAME(10)
00007        COMMON CONST/HUMAN,MACHINE,NOBODY,QUIT,NAME
00008   C
00009   C    GLOBAL TRACE 10 VIOLATIONS
00010   C    ASSERT VALUES (TURNS) (0:5)
00011   C    MONITOR RANGE FIRST LAST (PLAYER,MACHINE,TURNS)
00012   C    MONITOR CHARACTER RANGE FIRST LAST (NAME(*))
00013   C
00014        DATA NOBODY/1/,MACHINE/2/,HUMAN/3/,QUIT/4/
00015        DATA NAME/2HTL,2HTC,2HTR,2HHL,2HHC,2HHR,2HBL,2HBC,2HBR
     X 2HMO/
00016        CALL PRINTRO                                              1
00017   C    PLAY SOME GAMES
00018        FIRST=HUMAN                                               1
00019        GAMES=0                                                   1
00020        LOST=0                                                    1
00021        MYSCORE=0                                                 1
00022        WINNER=NOBODY                                             1
00023        WHILE WINNER NE.QUIT DO                                   1
00024   C    PLAY 1 GAME
00025            GAMES=GAMES+1                                         3
00026            WINNER=NOBODY                                         3
00027            TURNS=0                                               3
00028            FOR I=1 STEP 1 UNTIL 9 DO                             3
```

	Original source code listing	Execution count	Assertion information branch counts, truth values, data ranges
	ANNOTATED PROGRAM LISTING	COUNT	SPECIFIC EXECUTION DATA
00029	BOARD(I)=NOBODY	27	
00030	ENDDO	27	
00031	IF FIRST.EQ.MACHINE THEN	3	TRUE 1 FALSE 2
00032	BOARD(5)=MACHINE	1	
00033	TURNS=1	1	
00034	PRINT 90005 NAME(5)	1	
00035 90005	FORMAT(*I HAVE SELECTED SQUARE*,A2)		
00036	ENDIF	3	
00037	WHILE WINNER.EQ.NOBODY .AND. TURNS.LT.9 DO	3	
00038	PLAYER=HUMAN	10	MIN= 3 MAX= 3
			FIRST= 3 LAST= 3
00039	CALL HUMNMOV (BOARD,MOVE)	10	
00040	IF MOVE.NE.10 THEN	10	TRUE 9 FALSE 1
00041	BOARD(MOVE)=HUMAN	9	
00042	TURNS=TURNS+1	9	MIN= 1 MAX= 9
			FIRST= 1 LAST= 3
			ASSERTION VIOLATIONS 4
			ASSERT VALUES(TURNS) (0:5)
			EXEC NUMBER VALUE
			3 6
			4 7
			5 8
			6 9
00043	CALL CHEKWIN (BOARD,MOVE,TURNS,PLAYER,WINNER)	9	
00044 C	TRACE 10 VIOLATIONS		ASSERTION VIOLATIONS
00045 C	ASSERT (MOVE.LT.9) HALT ON 10	9	EXEC NUMBER VARIABLE VALUE
			6 MOVE 9
			7 MOVE 9

	Original source code listing	*Execution count*	*Assertion information*
	ANNOTATED PROGRAM LISTING	COUNT	SPECIFIC EXECUTION DATA
00046 C	TRACE OFF		
00047	IF WINNER.EQ.NOBODY.AND.TURNS.LT.9 THEN	9	1 TRUE 8 FALSE
00048	PLAYER=MACHINE	9	2 MIN= 2 MAX=
			2 FIRST= 2 LAST=
00049	CALL MACHMOV (BOARD,TURNS,MOVE)	8	
00050	BOARD(MOVE)=MACHINE	8	
00051	TURNS=TURNS+1	8	MIN= 2 MAX= 8
			FIRST= 2 LAST= 4
			ASSERTION VIOLATIONS 3
			ASSERT VALUES (TURNS) (0:5)
			EXEC NUMBER VALUE
			3 6
			4 7
			5 8
00052	CALL CHEKWIN (BOARD,MOVE,TURNS,PLAYER,WINNER)	8	
00053	ENDIF	9	
00054	ELSE	1	
00055	WINNER=QUIT	10	
00056	ENDIF	10	
00057	ENDDO	3	
00058	CALL PRESULT (BOARD,WINNER,GAMES,MYSCORE,LOST)	3	
00059	IF FIRST.EQ.MACHINE THEN	3	2 TRUE 1 FALSE
00060	FIRST=HUMAN	1	
00061	ELSE	2	
00062	FIRST=MACHINE	2	
00063	ENDIF	3	
00064	ENDDO	3	
00065	END	1	

Sample Reports

> *Automated verification system*
> *operational profile*
> *subroutine tictac*

Type of statement	Number	Number executed	Percent executed
TRANSFER			
IF	4	4	100.0
TRUE CONDITIONS		4	100.0
FALSE CONDITIONS		4	100.0
CALL	6	6	100.0
GOTO	0	0	N/A
CASE	0	0	N/A
ALSO CONDITIONS	0	0	N/A
OTHERWISE CONDITIONS	0	0	N/A
DO	3	3	100.00
WHILE CONDITIONS	2	2	100.00
ASSIGNMENT	19	19	100.00
I/O			
READ	0	0	N/A
WRITE	1	1	100.00
OTHER EXECUTABLE SOURCE	9	9	100.00

Sample Reports

Instrumentation summary

Local assertions

STMT No.	Assertion	Exec count	Violations
00045	ASSERT (MOVE.LT.9) HALT ON 10	9	2

Global assertions

ASSERT VALUES (TURNS) (0:5)

Variable	Statements that change the value of variable	Statements that caused an assertion violation
TURNS	00027 00033 00042 00051	00042 00051

MONITOR RANGE FIRST LAST (PLAYER,MACHINE,TURNS)

Variable	Statements that change the value of variable	Values attained Min	Max
PALYER	00038 00048	2	3
MACHINE	00014	2	2
TURNS	00027 00033 00042 00051	0	9

MONITOR CHARACTER RANGE FIRST LAST (NAME(*))

Variable	Statements that change the value of variable	Values attained Min	Max
NAME(*)	00015	'BC '	'TR '

AUTOMATED GENERATION OF TESTCASE DATASETS

E. F. Miller, Jr., R. A. Melton
Program Validation Project
General Research Corporation
Santa Barbara, California

Key Words

    Testcase Generation
    Automated Verification Systems
    Software Quality
    Software Reliability

Abstract

Software quality enhancement can be achieved in the near term through use of a systematic program testing methodology. The methodology attempts to relate functional software testcases with formal software specifications as a means to achieve correspondence between the software and its specifications. To do this requires generation of appropriate testcase data.

Automatic testcase generation is based on a priori knowledge of two forms of internal structure information: a representation of the tree of subschema automatically identified from within each program text, and a representation of the iteration structure of each subschema. This partition of a large program allows for efficient and effective automatic testcase generation using straightforward backtracking techniques.

During backtracking a number of simplifying, consolidating, and consistency analyses are applied. The result is either (1) early recognition of the impossibility of a particular program flow, or (2) efficient generation of input variable specifications which cause the testcase to traverse each portion of the required program flow.

A number of machine output examples of the backtracking facility are given, and the general effectiveness of the entire process is discussed.

Introduction

The problem of software unreliability has become an important issue in the Computer Science Community. Software, as a component in a computer-oriented system, costs on the order of three times as much as the hardware. Yet software is often a pacing item in many system implementations. Worse yet, many systems fail (or are judged ineffective) because of problems with the software. The interest everyone expresses in finding better ways to design, implement, check out, test, install, and use computer software has refocused serious attention on a variety of ways to alleviate the "software reliability problem" before, during, and after

software system installation.

At least one research area, the theory of program proving, offers a long-term solution to providing arbitrarily good assurances of software quality. Unfortunately, the state-of-the-art of program proving makes it impossible to apply those techniques to any but the smallest (and not practically important) programs. Intermediate means for software quality enhancement must approximate the surety which would be obtained by program proofs if they could be completed.

Comprehensive testing (i.e., exercise) of completed software systems is one important route to achieving increased reliability. Provided that good measures for testing coverage can be defined-- measures which make sense both theoretically and practically--systematic exercise of software systems can lead to real improvements in the near term; if well designed, the methodology can be extended to merge nicely with program proof disciplines in the long term.

Generating testcase data which meets specific testing objectives for medium and large computer programs is a difficult problem, however. In typical large computer programs the total number of possible program flow patterns (not counting the number of loop traversals within each pattern) is in the range 10^5 to 10^7. A systematic automatable methodology for identifying testcase forms, finding appropriate testcase data, and verifying the effectiveness of the testcase data is a desirable tool to have available when imposing a uniform testedness measure on a large-scale software system.

Such a methodology has been identified, and a number of experiences in the use of the methodology have already been accumulated.[1-3] In this paper we deal primarily with a specific problem which arises as the result of application of the testing methodology: the identification of testcase data for non-iterative program sequences.

The Basis of Testing

Figure 1 shows a typical software development process.[4] The verification processes shown in the figure attempt to "reverse" the production process or subprocess they span; "verification" or "validation" generally means something like "making sure that everything is satisfactory". The most important checking step among those shown is the

Reprinted from *Proceedings, 1975 International Conference on Reliable Software*, pp. 51-58. Copyright © 1975 by The Institute of Electrical and Electronics Engineers, Inc.

Software Validation (Testing and Evaluation) Step. Figure 2 shows the details of this step in a way that indicates the route by which the process of "implementing" a software system can be "reversed" by orderly structure-based testing.[5] Providing software validation involves three distinct phases, described next.

1. _Testcase Identification_. In this phase, the software system as it was implemented is analyzed to identify the internal control structure. (How this is done is discussed in some detail below.) The internal structure information is used to identify a collection of testcase patterns which, according to some pre-specified measure, comprehensively exercise the program(s) in terms of that measure.

2. _Testcase Selection_. After the particular patterns of program flow are identified, values in the input space of the program are chosen which make the program execute in the manner intended. This process involves specific reference to the program text since it is necessary to have testcase data which is both "realistic" in terms of program computational behavior, and effective in the sense that it induces the appropriate program flow.

3. _Testcase Analysis_. After comprehensive sets of testcases for a program are identified, they can be compared with the set of System Functional Specifications (which state what the program is _supposed_ to do). There are three possibilities:

3a. If the functional testcase set corresponds 1:1 with the set of functional requirements, then the software has been "validated".

3b. If there is a functional testcase for which there is no corresponding functional requirement, then (because the testcase is based on analysis of the implemented specification) one knows that there is some code present which should not be.

3c. If there is some functional specification for which there is no functional testcase, then one knows that the software system is deficient in some way.

The aggregate of these three steps will, if performed with a sufficiently strong measure of program testedness, identify all differences between the "needs" stated in the requirement, and the "facts" of the implementation.

The relationship between this technique and a formal program proof is important to appreciate. If the measure of program testing against which testcases are developed represents "all possible patterns of program flow," then the testing process corresponds directly with a formal program proof.[6] Each testcase represents an instantiation by data of a formal program verification condition. As is well known, if the program can also be shown to halt, and if the instantiated data is effectively representative of the more abstract verification assertion, then the program has been proved correct. If the testing coverage measure is a weaker one, then the testcase set represents a kind of approximation to a formal program proof. The weakest possible coverage measure is to require a testcase set which exercises each predicate in the program at least once to each of its possible outcomes, but not necessarily in every possible combination.

Program Structures

Achieving this testing measure--or any other, more complex testing measure--for a very large program is complicated by problems of combinatorics within the program. Our basic approach to dealing with such issues is to partition each module (if it is large enough to require it) into a series of smaller internal modules each of which is dealt with separately. The partitioning process involves identifying a hierarchy of subschema within the program's digraph; each subschema has the property that it is single entry/single exit. After the internal modular structure of a program is identified, appropriate aggregations of modules are made and the iteration structure for each of these is identified. The ways these computations are performed are discussed in the next two sections.

Subschema Structure. The unique hierarchy of program subschema is found by automatically performing a series of reductions of the program digraph. (The program digraph consists of a set of arcs connecting assigned node numbers within the program, with one arc corresponding to each decision outcome within the program.) Three types of reductions are performed:[7,8]

1. Series reduction. A sequence of digraph arcs is merged into one "derived arc".

2. Parallel reduction. Two or more digraph edges which begin and end on the same node are merged into one arc.

3. Self-loop reduction. A self-loop arc (called the iteration arc) and the ensuing next digraph arc (called the exit arc) are merged into a simple arc.

The third form of reduction is specially flagged so that it can be employed later, when the full reduction process is analyzed to determine how to recombine the reductions for the greatest possible testcase generation benefit.

An example of this process is shown in Fig. 3a through 3c, in which a 10-arc digraph is shown before and after a total of eight reductions, which reach a tree height of 3. Only the reduction involving arcs 9, 10 is a self-loop reduction.

For medium sized programs, as well as for large programs, this reduction process leads to a rich tree structure. For example, one 80-statement FORTRAN program containing 55 predicate outcomes required 32 reduction applications of the primitive reduction forms described above. The maximum tree height in this case was 10, even though only two self-loop reductions were needed. For large programs the tree height increases correspondingly, and the tree remains very rich. The rates of increase are, very roughly, linear in the program's number of statements, although the rate of reduction is highly dependent on the internal features of individual programs.

Our main objective in deriving the subschema representation of the program structure is:

1. To identify the points at which iteration reduction (self-loop reduction) has to be

performed.*

2. To provide a basis for organizing the search for satisfactory testcase data so that the problems of combinatorial growth within the backtracking process are minimized.

This determination is made by observing that each sub-tree of the subschema tree represents a single entry/single exit sub-digraph, which possibly also represents a sub-digraph which contains iteration. Thus, the boundaries chosen in the backtracking process are (a) at the points when self-loop reduction has been performed, and (b) when a threshold on included total non-iterative program flow has been exceeded.

This reversal of the decomposition process results in a series of about-equal-sized submodules some of which contain iteration and some of which do not. All of the submodules are treated in the same manner, described next.

Iteration Structure. After the hierarchical subschema reductions are complete, and reaggregations of the reductions are assigned, the resulting program digraph can be considered as a new and separate problem, for which the iteration structure must be analyzed. The main objective of finding the iteration structure is to permit construction of individual reaching sequences of program digraph arcs (which may, at this point, represent whole submodules). These sequences are then analyzed by the automatic backtracking facility.

The iteration structure of a program consists of a collection of ith level sequences of digraph arcs. A sequence is at the 0th level if it involves no iteration of any kind; in general, a sequence at the ith level of this structure is one which forces repetition (iteration) or some sequence present at the $(i-1)$th level.

A three level example of an iteration structure is shown in Fig. 4. The sequence $A_1, \ldots, A_4$ is a representation of four predicate-outcomes in which no predicate is evaluated more than once. The sequence $B_1, \ldots, B_4$ and $C_1, \ldots, C_3$ represent sequences of predicate-outcomes which force repetition of predicate-outcomes at the 0th and 1th level of program flow, respectively.

The set of all such sequences forms a tree, where the links (branches) of the tree correspond to the ancestry dependence between each flow pattern, and the nodes (leaves) of the tree are the flow classes themselves. Figure 5 shows a tree of flow classes, $L_{i,j}$, where the root of the tree is L. The flow pattern which results from the three-class subtree of Fig. 4 is shown as the sequence $L: L_A: L_B: L_C$ in Fig. 5.

All possible program execution patterns are included in the iteration structure tree's power set,
that is, the set of all its subtrees. Logically impossible program flow patterns may appear in the tree as a result of the fact that the iteration structure is found by analyzing only the program control structure: the tree is constructed independently of any information about program semantics. Details of how this iteration structure is found are given in Ref. 7.

Testing Within the Iteration Structure

Structural patterns of program flow correspond to subtrees such as shown in Figs. 4 and 5. A pattern does not necessarily display full information about program flow, because the iteration counts are not known. From the testing standpoint, however, this information is not strictly necessary, as described next.

Testing oriented to achieving the weakest possible testing coverage (every immutably executable segment) can proceed in stages. Initial testcase executions will identify those segments (predicate outcomes) or a program which are not exercised; this data is obtained with conventional program instrumentation/data collection techniques. Achieving the testing goal requires that some untested segment have testcase data for it which does test it; if possible, additional testcases added in this way should seek to test a number of such untested segments. In effect, however, we must only address the following simpler problem: construct testcase data which causes at least one untested segment to be exercised.

The primary technique for doing this is to consider classes of non-iterative flow which include the untested segment. Suppose, for example, that the sets of testcase run thusfar on a program leave the segment C_3 untested (see Fig. 4). A likely non-iterative flow to examine is the sequence:

$$A_1 \rightarrow A_2 \rightarrow B_1 \rightarrow B_2 \rightarrow C_1 \rightarrow C_2 \rightarrow C_3$$

This is called a "reaching sequence" for segment C_3. The corresponding program text contains all of the information which may be sufficient to generate testcase data.

Backtracking

The process of analyzing a non-iterative flow for purposes of constructing input data which makes the flow occur in practice is called backtracking. An automated facility to perform this kind of analysis has been implemented in an Automated Verification System for FORTRAN.[8,9] This preliminary capability turns out to be highly effective in finding adequate program testcase data, as examples described later will show. First, however, we describe the processes by which the backtracker works.

The sequence of statement texts corresponding to a non-iterative reach sequence within the iteration structure will contain a number of program actions all of which potentially affect the value of the predicates within the reach sequence. A testcase dataset will have been found if values for all of the inputs to this statement sequence can be specified in a way that makes each decision statement in the sequence have the proper outcome. For the reach sequence above, for example, these input-space settings must provide for a particular outcome of the program predicate which corresponds

---
*Special techniques are employed when a program cycle has more than one entry and/or more than one exit.

to segment C_3. The backtracking operation begins with the statement of this predicate.

Each statement type encountered when traversing the statement sequence in reverse order affects the input-space settings needed to satisfy the demands of this predicate. Different backtracker actions are taken for each statement type; the rules for FORTRAN are as follows:

1. An assignment statement of the form $x = y$ causes all instances of the term x to be replaced with y in the current formula.

2. A data-input statement, such as READ..., causes all instances of the variables which receive value to be replaced with an artificial variable name. This name "stands for" the input value which must be supplied.

3. An iteration control statement, such as the statement at the end of a FORTRAN DO-loop, causes replacement of all instances of the iteration index to be replaced with the incremented value. This is an assignment statement of the form: <index> = <index> + <increment>.

4. An iteration initiation statement, such as a FORTRAN DO-statement, causes replacement of instances of the <index> with its <initial-value>.

5. When a decision statement is encountered, the appropriate value of that predicate is added as an .AND. term to the current formula.

6. A subroutine CALL causes introduction of artificial names for all symbols which appear in the argument list. In effect, this substitution assumes that the communication space resulting from a subroutine call is fully accessible in the test-case exercise environment.

7. A function call, which may occur in an assignment statement or in any other statement form, is assumed to have "read only" actual parameters, and no substitutions result.

8. A statement label assignment results in replacement of instances of the label-name with the actual label.

The general effect of this process (with or without the reductions described below) is to produce a set of simultaneous non-linear inequalities involving only program input-space variables and constants. The reach sequence works as a structural testcase if this set of inequalities can be satisfied. At present, only all-constant terms and certain other forms can be eliminated from this set of inequalities; generally, however, it is a relatively simple matter to demonstrate satisfiability or unsatisfiability manually.

Formula Reduction

During the backtracking process, which may involve a large number of decision statements and therefore may generate very long formulas, it is advantageous to identify certain kinds of inconsistencies as early as possible. These initial rules for intermediate processing have been implemented:

9. Whenever a term in the formula reduces to all-constants, then the value of that term is found by explicit simulation. (This is relatively easy because the formula's terms are all kept in Postfix notation.) If false, then the backtracking process for that particular reach sequence stops.

10. Whenever a term contains only constants and input-space artificial values, then all instantiations within that term cease.

11. Whenever identical forms between terms are found, differing only in the constants employed and in the sense of the relational operators, then the terms are combined. For example, if there are two terms of the form:

i. $A - B$ .GT. $5 + 17$
ii. $A - B$ .GT. $6 + 864$

then they combined into a single term of the form:

j. $A - B$ .GT. 870

The general effect of these reductions is to make the backtracking process relatively efficient at (a) locating inconsistent non-iterative flows, and (b) generating reasonably compact input-space specifications.

Examples

To illustrate the backtracking process, consider the two short program texts given in Fig. 5. In Fig. 5a, stage 3 of the backtracking process results from incorporating the effect of the assignment $I = 4$, which results in the transformation $B(I) = 6.5$ into $B(4) = 6.5$, and the replacement (according to rule (11)) into the first term. The final term, which is explicitly true, shows that the sequence is executable as it stands; that is, control will be transferred to "100".

The sequences shown in Fig. 6b show the use (and format for) input-space variables. If the remainder of the reach sequence requires immediate transfer to "200", then the requirement IFLAG::::1 .GT. 1 must be met.

Sample Output

Figure 7 shows a sample of the automated backtracker in action.* The program sequence shown is a reach sequence, as seen by noting that statement No. 20 occurs twice. Because there are four decisions in the reach sequence, there are four terms in the input space. The .TRUE. term results from the entry predicate of the program: it is necessary to invoke the program in order to obtain the indicated flow. The single resulting input condition specifies a relation on the formal parameters and variables in PROGRAM COMMON (not shown) which make the testcase flow legitimate.

Figure 8 shows a sample of a more complicated situation. In this case, the input conditions apply to the READ operation in statement No. 29 (for ITT:::::24, IDEG::::25 and JDEG::::28), and to the outcome of the function call ITS = IFEOF(5) in statement 12. The other variables READ by this sequence do not affect the legitimacy of this reach sequence.

Figures 9, 10 and 11 show examples where the backtracking process has led to some kind of contradiction. In all three cases the simulated reverse

---
*For clarity, the examples have been produced from programs small enough that the automatic sub-modularization process was not necessary.

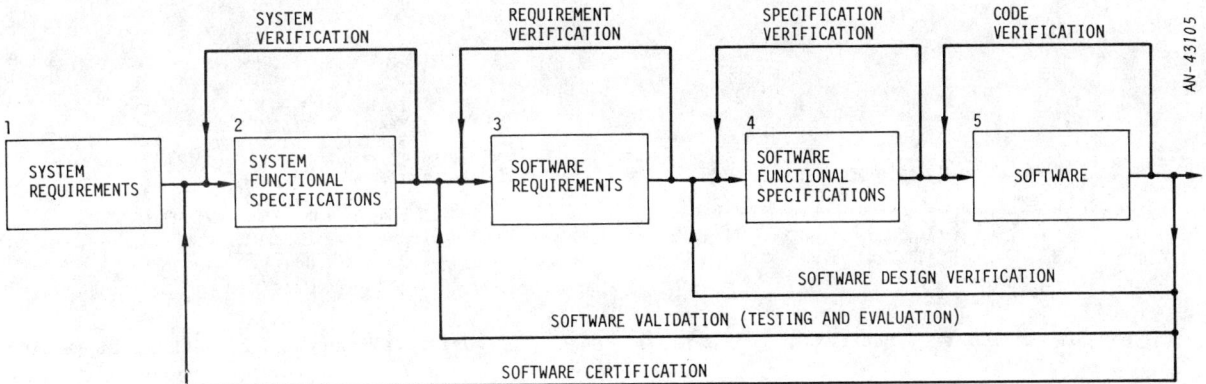

Figure 1. Overview of Software Development Processes, Showing Role of Various Verification Steps

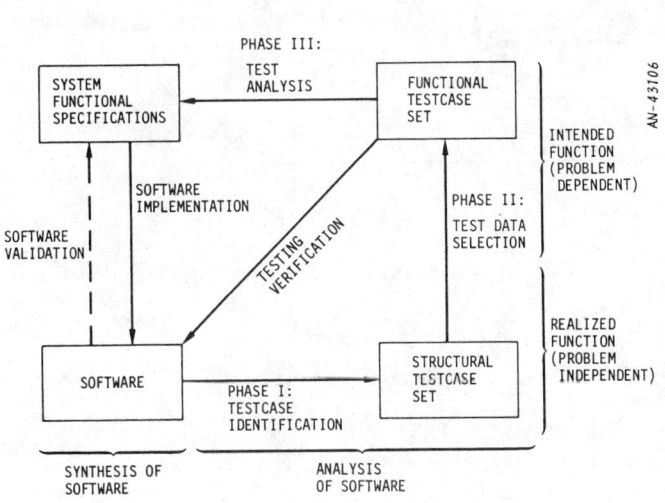

Figure 2. Detailed Description of Software Validation Process

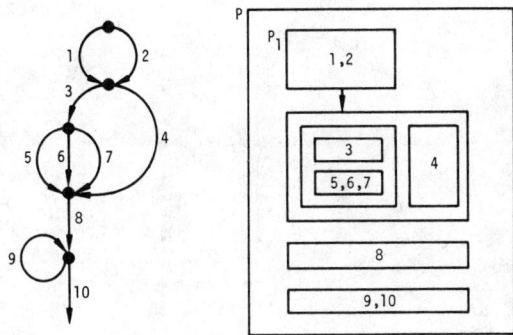

a. Simple Digraph P   b. Subschema Hierarchy

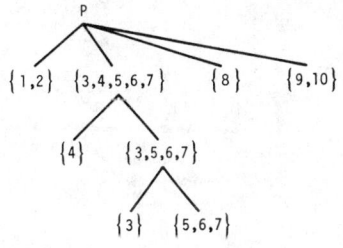

c. Tree Representation

Figure 3. Example of Hierarchical Subschema Reduction

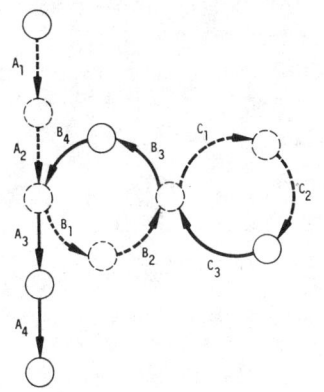

Figure 4. Typical Iteration Structure

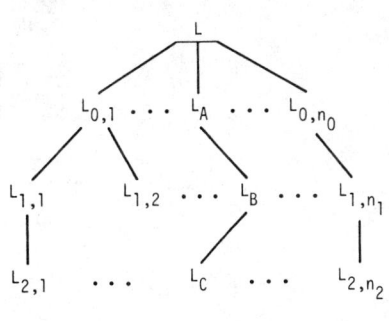

Figure 5. Iteration Structure Tree

PROGRAM TEXT SEQUENCE:

```
...
A = 18.4
I = 4
B(I) = 6.5
IF(A.GT.B(4)) GOTO 100
```

TERMS MAINTAINED DURING BACKTRACKING STAGES

STAGE	TERM
1	A .GT. B(4)
2	A .GT. B(4) .AND. B(I) = 6.5
3	A .GT. B(4) .AND. B(I) = 6.5 .AND. I = 4
3a	A .GT. 6.5
4	18.4 .GT. 6.5

Figure 6a. Examples of Backtracking Action

PROGRAM TEXT SEQUENCE:

```
...
    DO 100 J = I, L
    READ(...) IFLAG
    IF(IFLAG.GT.J) GOTO 200
100 CONTINUE
200 CONTINUE
```

TERMS MAINTAINED DURING BACKTRACKING STAGES

STAGE	TERM
1	IFLAG .GT. J
2	IFLAG::::1 .GT. J
3	IFLAG::::1 .GT. I

Figure 6b. Examples of Backtracking Action

```
RXVP-1.1 GRC PROPRIETARY PROGRAM PRODUCT.                                      02/06/75  PAGE NO.       10

     REACH  SEQUENCE       1   3   4  18
 ASSIGNED NODES  STMT.                                                             DD-PATH
      (P)   (S)   NO. LABEL  STATEMENT TEXT...                                     NUMBERS...
-----------------------------------------------------------------------------------------------
     [  1]          1        SUBROUTINE MACHMOV ( BOARD , TURNS , MOVE )           (  1)
                             *** *** ***
     [  2]          9        PTBLPTR = 1
     [  3]         10        WIN = 0
     [  4]         11        BLOCK = 0
     [  5]         12        FORK = 0
     [  6]         13        BETTER = 0
     [  7]         14        GOOD = 0
     [  8]         15        ANY = 0
     [  9, 10]     16        IF ( 1 .GT. 9 ) GOTO 90001                            (  2,  3)
     [ 11]         17        DO 90000 I = 1 , 9 , 1
     [ 12]         18        K = ORDER ( I )
     [ 13]         19        L = ( I + 7 ) / 4
     [ 14, 15]     20        IF ( .NOT. ( BOARD ( K ) .EQ. NOBODY ) ) GOTO 90002   (  4,  5)
                             *** *** ***
     [ 60]         61  90002 CONTINUE
     [ 61]         62        PTBLPTR = PTBLPTR + 2 * L
     [ 62]         63  90015 CONTINUE
     [ 63]         64  90000 CONTINUE                                              ( 18, 19)

     [ 11]         17        DO 90000 I = 1 , 9 , 1
     [ 12]         18        K = ORDER ( I )
     [ 13]         19        L = ( I + 7 ) / 4
     [ 14, 15]     20        IF ( .NOT. ( BOARD ( K ) .EQ. NOBODY ) ) GOTO 90002   (  4,  5)
-----------------------------------------------------------------------------------------------

 HAS THE FOLLOWING ENTRY CONDITIONS

 DD-PATH          ENTRY CONDITION REQUIRED BY DD-PATH

   1    .TRUE.

   3    1 .LE. 9

   4    ( .NOT. ( BOARD ( ORDER ( 1 ) ) .EQ. NOBODY )

  18    1 + 1 .LE. 9
```

Figure 7. Successful Backtracked Reach Sequence for MACHMOV

```
RXVP-1.1 GRC PROPRIETARY PROGRAM PRODUCT.                                      02/06/75  PAGE NO.       5

     REACH  SEQUENCE       1   3   5  16  21  23
 ASSIGNED NODES  STMT.                                                             DD-PATH
      (P)   (S)   NO. LABEL  STATEMENT TEXT...                                     NUMBERS...
-----------------------------------------------------------------------------------------------
     [  1]          1        PROGRAM DCARADC                                       (  1)
                             *** *** ***
     [  2]          7        MIS = 1
     [  3]          8    30  IPG = 0
     [  4]          9        NPTS = 0
     [  5]         10        MPS = 0
     [  6]         11        READ ( 5 , 1 ) ITT , IMM , NHR , ( IDATA ( J ) , J = 1 , 17 )
     [  7]         12        ITS = IFEOF ( 5 )
     [  8]         13        IF ( ITS .EQ. 1 ) 140 , 999
     [  9, 10]    14   999   IF ( ITT .EQ. ITYPE ( 1 ) ) GOTO 50                   (  2,  3)
     [ 11]         15    40  MPS = MPS + 1                                         (  4,  5)
     [ 12]         16        LIST ( MPS ) = 1
     [ 13]         17        GOTO 55
     [ 23]         23    55  IMM = 1
     [ 24]         24        NHR = 0
     [ 25]         25        MPS = MPS + 1
     [ 26]         26        LIST ( MPS ) = 10
     [ 27]         27    60  IPTS = 1
     [ 28]         28        IFLAG = 0
     [ 29]         29    70  READ ( 5 , 2 ) ITT , ( NAME ( IPTS , J ) , J = 1 , 5 ) , IDEG ( IPTS ) , XMIN ( IPTS ) , N
                             * ( IPTS ) , JDEG ( IPTS ) , YMIN ( IPTS ) , JE ( IPTS ) , ISPEED ( IPTS )
     [ 30]         30        ITS = IFEOF ( 5 )
     [ 31]         31        IF ( ITS .EQ. 1 ) 150 , 998
     [ 32, 33]    32   998   IF ( ITT .NE. ITYPE ( 2 ) .AND. ITT .NE. ITYPE ( 3 ) ) GOTO 110  ( 14, 15)
                                                                                              ( 16, 17)
     [ 60]         54   110  IFLAG = 1
     [ 61]         55        GOTO 75
                             *** *** ***
     [ 36, 37]    34    75  IF ( IDEG ( IPTS ) .GE. 90 .OR. IDEG ( IPTS ) .LT. 0 ) GOTO 90    ( 20, 21)
     [ 38, 39]    35    80  IF ( JDEG ( IPTS ) .GT. 180 .OR. JDEG ( IPTS ) .LT. 0 ) GOTO 100  ( 22, 23)
     [ 40]         36    85  IPTS = IPTS + 1
     [ 41]         37        GOTO 70
                             *** *** ***
     [ 29]         29    70  READ ( 5 , 2 ) ITT , ( NAME ( IPTS , J ) , J = 1 , 5 ) , IDEG ( IPTS ) , XMIN ( IPTS ) , N
                             * ( IPTS ) , JDEG ( IPTS ) , YMIN ( IPTS ) , JE ( IPTS ) , ISPEED ( IPTS )
     [ 30]         30        ITS = IFEOF ( 5 )
     [ 31]         31        IF ( ITS .EQ. 1 ) 150 , 998                                      ( 14, 15)
-----------------------------------------------------------------------------------------------

 HAS THE FOLLOWING ENTRY CONDITIONS

 DD-PATH          ENTRY CONDITION REQUIRED BY DD-PATH

   1    .TRUE.

   3    ITS .NE. 1

   5    ITT::::::2 .NE. ITYPE ( 1 )

  16    ( ITT::::::2 .NE. ITYPE ( 2 ) ) .AND. ( ITT::::::2 .NE. ITYPE ( 3 ) )

  21    ( IDEG::::::3 .LT. 90 ) .AND. ( IDEG::::::3 .GE. 0 )

  23    ( JDEG::::::6 .LE. 180 ) .AND. ( JDEG::::::6 .GE. 0 )
```

Figure 8. Successful Backtracked Reach Sequence for DCARADC

```
RXVP-1.1 GRC PROPRIETARY PROGRAM PRODUCT.                                    02/06/75  PAGE NO.

   REACH SEQUENCE       1    2   35   38
   IS NOT EXECUTABLE DUE TO THE FOLLOWING SEQUENCE    1   2   35   38

ASSIGNED NODES  STMT.                                                        DD-PATH
    (P)    (S)  NO.  LABEL  STATEMENT TEXT...                                NUMBERS...
------------------------------------------------------------------------------------------
   [  1]          1          PROGRAM DCARADC                                 (  1)
                             *** *** ***
   [  2]          7          MIS = 1
   [  3]          8    30    IPG = 0
   [  4]          9          NPTS = 0
   [  5]         10          MPS = 0
   [  6]         11          READ ( 5 , 1 ) ITT , IMM , NHR , ( IDATA ( J ) , J = 1 , 17 )
   [  7]         12          ITS = IFEOF ( 5 )
   [  8]         13          IF ( ITS .EQ. 1 ) 140 , 999                     (  2,   3)
                             *** *** ***
   [ 67]         61   140    MPS = MPS + 1
   [ 68,  69]    62          IF ( MIS .GT. 1 ) GOTO 250                      ( 34,  35)
   [ 70]         63          LIST ( MPS ) = 2
   [ 71]         64          IFLAG = 3
   [ 72]         65          GOTO 205
                             *** *** ***
   [ 80,  81]    72   205    IF ( MPS .EQ. 0 ) GOTO 210                      ( 38,  39)
                             *** *** ***
   [ 85]         75   210    CALL PRNT ( 3 )
   [ 86]         76          MIS = MIS + 1
   [ 87]         77          GOTO 30
                             *** *** ***
   [  3]          8    30    IPG = 0
   [  4]          9          NPTS = 0
   [  5]         10          MPS = 0
   [  6]         11          READ ( 5 , 1 ) ITT , IMM , NHR , ( IDATA ( J ) , J = 1 , 17 )
   [  7]         12          ITS = IFEOF ( 5 )
   [  8]         13          IF ( ITS .EQ. 1 ) 140 , 999                     (  2,   3)
------------------------------------------------------------------------------------------

DD-PATH              ENTRY CONDITION REQUIRED BY DD-PATH

  2      ITS:::::10 .EQ. 1

 35      1 .LE. 1

 38      0 + 1 .EQ. 0
```

Figure 9. Inconsistent Reach Sequence for DCARADC

```
RXVP-1.1 GRC PROPRIETARY PROGRAM PRODUCT.                                    02/06/75  PAGE NO.    9

   REACH SEQUENCE       1    3    5    6   16   18
   IS NOT EXECUTABLE DUE TO THE FOLLOWING SEQUENCE    3   5   6

ASSIGNED NODES  STMT.                                                        DD-PATH
    (P)    (S)  NO.  LABEL  STATEMENT TEXT...                                NUMBERS...
------------------------------------------------------------------------------------------
   [  9,  10]    16          IF ( 1 .GT. 9 ) GOTO 90001                      (  2,   3)
   [ 11]         17          DO 90000 I = 1 , 9 , 1
   [ 12]         18          K = ORDER ( I )
   [ 13]         19          L = ( 1 + 7 ) / 4
   [ 14,  15]    20          IF ( .NOT. ( BOARD ( K ) .EQ. NOBODY ) ) GOTO 90002   (  4,   5)
   [ 16]         21          ANY = K
   [ 17]         22          NFORKS = 0
   [ 18]         23          J = 1
   [ 19]         24          GOTO 90005
   [ 21,  22]    26   90005  IF ( J .GT. L ) GOTO 90004                      (  6,   7)
                             *** *** ***
   [ 54]         56   90004  CONTINUE
                             *** *** ***
   [ 55,  56]    57          IF ( .NOT. ( NFORKS .GE. 2 ) ) GOTO 90014       ( 16,  17)
------------------------------------------------------------------------------------------

DD-PATH              ENTRY CONDITION REQUIRED BY DD-PATH

  5      ( .NOT. ( BOARD ( ORDER ( 1 ) ) .NE. NOBODY )

  6      1 .GT. ( 1 + 7 ) / 4

 16      ( .NOT. ( 0 .GE. 2 )

 18      1 + 1 .LE. 9
```

Figure 10. Inconsistent Reach Sequence for MACHMOV

```
RXVP-1.1 GRC PROPRIETARY PROGRAM PRODUCT.                                    02/06/75  PAGE NO.    7

   REACH SEQUENCE       1    3    5   15   16   20   24   28
   IS NOT EXECUTABLE DUE TO THE FOLLOWING SEQUENCE   16   20   24   28

ASSIGNED NODES  STMT.                                                        DD-PATH
    (P)    (S)  NO.  LABEL  STATEMENT TEXT...                                NUMBERS...
------------------------------------------------------------------------------------------
   [ 32,  33]    32   998    IF ( ITT .NE. ITYPE ( 2 ) .AND. ITT .NE. ITYPE ( 3 ) ) GOTO 110   ( 16,  17)
                             *** *** ***
   [ 60]         54   110    IFLAG = 1
   [ 61]         55          GOTO 75
                             *** *** ***
   [ 36,  37]    34    75    IF ( IDEG ( IPTS ) .GE. 90 .OR. IDEG ( IPTS ) .LT. 0 ) GOTO 90   ( 20,  21)
                             *** *** ***
   [ 42]         38    90    MPS = MPS + 1
   [ 43]         39          IF ( IDEG ( IPTS ) ) 94 , 95 , 95               ( 24-- 26)
   [ 44]         40    94    IDEG ( IPTS ) = - IDEG ( IPTS )
   [ 45]         41          GOTO 96
                             *** *** ***
   [ 47]         43    96    LIST ( MPS ) = 5
   [ 48,  49]    44          IF ( IFLAG .EQ. 1 ) GOTO 120                    ( 27,  28)
   [ 50]         45          GOTO 80
                             *** *** ***
   [ 38,  39]    35    80    IF ( JDEG ( IPTS ) .GT. 180 .OR. JDEG ( IPTS ) .LT. 0 ) GOTO 100  ( 22,  23)
------------------------------------------------------------------------------------------

DD-PATH              ENTRY CONDITION REQUIRED BY DD-PATH

 20      ( IDEG ( IPTS ) .GE. 90 ) .OR. ( IDEG ( IPTS ) .LT. 0 )

 24      0 .GT. IDEG ( IPTS )

 28      1 .NE. 1

 23      ( JDEG ( IPTS ) .LE. 180 ) .AND. ( JDEG ( IPTS ) .GE. 0 )
```

Figure 11. Inconsistent Internal Reach Sequence for DCARADC

execution has led to an impossible condition in an all-constant term.

Large-Module Testcase Generation Automation

For small and medium-sized modules, in which program submodularization is not necessary (e.g., the reductions when aggregated do not exceed the preset threshold), the backtracking process is applied to all possible program flows as a group. This process must result in a "solution", that is, a valid set of input-space settings, unless the program has an inherent flaw, and provided that no iteration is involved. (Note that this set of possible flows is not as large as it might be since only the segment sequences which reach an untested segment are analyzed.) When iteration is present manual intervention may be necessary in cases when the backtracker is unable to arrive at a valid testcase set by single (or some other setable, finite number of) traversal(s) of the cycle.

As is evident from the examples given in the prior section, in most cases it is unnecessary to have a human tester assign realistic values which satisfy the derived input-space requirements. After execution of the generated testcase is verified (using instrumentation and data collection facilities of the associated Automated Verification System[10,11]), the process repeats with some other untested segment as the testing objective. Incidentally, we have found that there tends to be a substantial amount of collateral testing, i.e., testing of other parts of the program not previously a testing target. This effect further reduces the effort needed to achieve the weak testing goal, although it does not appear to have much effect on stronger testing goals.

The advantage of the hierarchical subschema computation accrues best when the program being analyzed is very large. The savings come from (1) having to deal with a smaller number of backtracking terms at a time, and (2) knowledge that single entry/single exit submodules do not have to contribute to the testcase set. This latter point is important since it allows the backtracker to disregard any conditions which arise as the result of needing to generate legitimate flow through such a submodule: once entered, the single entry/single exit submodule is exited regardless of the form of the data supplied to it.*

In effect, dealing with the automatically identified submodules reduces the problem of testcase generation for large programs into a partially separable series of testcase generation problems for medium-sized programs. The tradeoff between numbers of submodules and their individual sizes is not well understood, however. Having too many small modules introduces problems in the data structure representation employed, while having too few submodules increases the execution space requirements for the backtracker, and also may increase the number of testcases required to achieve the weak testing goal. Much of our current research is centered on gaining further intuition on the mutual tradeoffs between generated submodule size and number, and learning the effects in execution time requirements both in performing the computations and in directing the backtracker.

Summary

The process of enhancing software quality is attacked by attempting to approximate program proofs by partially verifying the iteration structure (all possible classes of program flow) of individual programs. Techniques have been developed which automatically analyze real program text sequences and identify conditions which must be met within a program's input-space to satisfy certain test objectives. This automatic processing is applied systematically to provide, at a first level of sophistication, a comprehensive set of testcases. These can then be analyzed (manually now, and automatically later) for their correspondence with the software specifications which the program was intended to satisfy.

1. Methodology for Comprehensive Software Testing, Program Validation Project, General Research Corporation CR-1-465, 1 October 1974.

2. E. F. Miller, Jr. and W. R. Wisehart, Automated Tools to Support Software Quality Assurance, Program Validation Project, General Research Corporation U77, April 1974.

3. C. V. Ramamoorthy, Reliability and Integrity of Large Computer Programs, Electronics Research Laboratory, UC Berkeley, ERL-M430, March 1974.

4. D. Reifer, Computer Program Verification/Validation/Certification, Aerospace Corp., May 1974.

5. E. F. Miller, Jr. et al., Structurally Based Automatic Program Testing, EASCON-74, Washington, D.C., 7-9 October 1974.

6. B. Elspas, et al., "An Assessment of Techniques for Proving Program Correctness," Computing Surveys, June 1972.

7. E. Ashcroft and Z. Manna, "The Translation of GOTO Program to WHILE Programs," Information Processing 71, North Holland Publishing Co., 1972.

8. J. E. Sullivan, "Measuring the Complexity of Computer Software," MITRE Corp. MTR-2648, June 1973.

9. M. R. Paige, A Methodology for Generating Paths in a Directed Graph, General Research Corporation IM-1816, November 1973 (GRC PRIVATE/PROPRIETARY).

10. RXVP-1 Reference Manual, General Research Corporation, 1975.

11. RXVP-2 System Specification, Program Validation Project, General Research Corporation, 1 October 1974 (GRC PROPRIETARY).

---

*If entry into a single entry/single exit submodule does not produce a subsequent exit it indicates that there is an infinite loop; this knowledge is obviously valuable in the testing process, even though it falls outside the expected results of the procedure.

A PARTITION ANALYSIS METHOD
TO INCREASE PROGRAM RELIABILITY

Debra J. Richardson
Lori A. Clarke

Department of Computer and Information Science
University of Massachusetts
Amherst, Massachusetts 01003

ABSTRACT

A major drawback of most program testing methods is that they ignore program specifications, and instead base their analysis solely on the information provided in the implementation. This paper describes the partition analysis method, which assists in program testing and verification by evaluating information from both a specification and an implementation. This method employs symbolic evaluation techniques to partition the set of input data into procedure subdomains so that the elements of each subdomain are treated uniformly by the specification and processed uniformly by the implementation. The partition divides the procedure domain into more manageable units. Information related to each subdomain is used to guide in the selection of test data and to verify consistency between the specification and the implementation. Moreover, the test data selection process, called partition analysis testing, and the verification process, called partition analysis verification, are used to enhance each other, and thus increase program reliability.

Keywords: program testing, program verification, symbolic evaluation.

INTRODUCTION

A major drawback of most program testing methods is that program specifications are ignored; test data selection is based solely on the information derived from the implementation. Such methods are unlikely to detect errors that arise when a implementation neglects aspects of the problem. Utilizing an understanding of the specification, however, may direct attention to such errors. Recently, several attempts have been made to employ sources of information over and above the implementation in selecting test data. Goodenough and Gerhart[10] have argued that the specification and the implementation are both valuable sources of information that must be used by testing methods. Thus far, however, no method has been developed that exploits formal specifications, even though they are becoming more readily available as their value in the development of reliable software is recognized.

This work was supported by the National Science Foundation under grant #NSFMCS 77-02101, the Air Force Office of Scientific Research under grant #AFOSR 77-3287, and the IBM Corporation under the Graduate Fellowship Program.

We are exploring a method, called partition analysis, that assists in program testing and program verification by incorporating information from both a formal specification of the procedure and an implementation for the procedure. The partition analysis method employs symbolic evaluation techniques to partition the set of input data into procedure subdomains, so that the elements of each subdomain are treated uniformly by the specification and processed uniformly by the implementation. By forming these subdomains, the procedure domain is divided into more manageable units, as is the task of demonstrating program reliability. Information related to each procedure subdomain is used to guide in the selection of test data that reveals errors in the implementation or provides confidence in its correctness. This information is also used to verify consistency between the specification and the implementation. Moreover, the test data selection process, called partition analysis testing, and the verification process, called partition analysis verification, are used to enhance each other; the execution of some elements in the subdomain may assist in verification, while the verification process may direct the selection of test data.

In this paper, we describe the partition analysis method. To facilitate the presentation, we assume that a given procedure specification is correct; thus we are considering the correctness of an implementation with respect to this specification. The next section presents common representations for procedure specifications and implementations and defines the procedure subdomains into which the set of input data is partitioned. The third section defines consistency properties between a procedure specification and implementation, which are based on this partition. The fourth section outlines partition analysis verification, a technique for demonstrating whether the consistency properties hold. The fifth section describes partition analysis testing, a testing strategy that astutely selects test data from each procedure subdomain. In the conclusion, several areas of future research are discussed.

PROBLEM REPRESENTATION

A program specification and program implementation are intended to be representations of the same problem at different levels of abstraction. We are developing an analysis method to exploit the similarities between a specification and an implementation. This method compares the implementation of a procedure to a specification of that procedure. The procedure specification must be written in a formal specification language. While work on applying the partition analysis method to high-level specifications is underway, thus far the method has only been applied to low-level specifications such as those developed during the late stages of design.

An example of such a procedure specification is given in Figure 1. This specification describes the procedure TRAP, which computes the area between a curve and the x-axis by the trapezoidal rule. A procedure implementation of TRAP appears in Figure 2. This procedure will be used throughout this paper to demonstrate the partition analysis method.

A procedure specification and a procedure implementation both describe a function, where the function is usually composed of partial functions. Each partial function is a computation defined over a subset of the procedure domain. To facilitate the comparison of an implementation to a specification, the partition analysis method takes advantage of this similarity by translating the two descriptions into common representations, which explicitly describe the partial functions.

In a procedure implementation, a partial function is represented by a <u>path</u>, which is a sequence of statements through the implementation. Thus, the representation of a procedure implementation P is a set of paths $\{P_1, P_2, ..., P_N \mid 1 \leq N \leq \infty\}$.* Associated with each path P_J is the <u>path domain</u> $D[P_J]$, which is the set of input data that causes execution of the path, and the <u>path computation</u> $C[P_J]$, which is the function that is computed by the sequence of executable statements along the path. The <u>implementation domain</u> $D[P]$ is the union of the path domains, $D[P] = \cup_{J=1,N} D[P_J]$.

In a procedure specification, each partial function is represented by a <u>subspec</u>. The actual form of a subspec depends on the specification language. For low-level specifications a subspec is similar to a path, although more abstract constructs may appear. The representation of a specification S, therefore,** is a set of subspecs $\{S_1, S_2, ..., S_M \mid 1 \leq M \leq \infty\}$. For each subspec S_I, the <u>subspec domain</u> $D[S_I]$ is the set of input data for which the subspec is applicable and the <u>subspec computation</u> $C[S_I]$ is the computation specified for those input values. The <u>specification domain</u> $D[S]$ is the union of the subspec domains, $D[S] = \cup_{I=1,M} D[S_I]$.

The partition analysis method utilizes symbolic evaluation techniques[2,4,5,14,17] to provide these common representations of the specification and the implementation. In applying symbolic evaluation to an implementation, symbolic

---
*There may be an infinite number of paths due to program loops. As will be explained shortly, paths through the implementation that differ only by the number of iterations of some loops may be classified as a single path.
**The general form of a specification must allow for an infinite number of subspecs since some specification languages allow a notation for indefinite repetition. In addition, subspecs that differ only by the number of repetitions of some transformations may be represented as a single subspec.

Description
    TRAP computes the AREA between the curve F and
    the x-axis from x=A to x=B by the trapezoidal
    rule using N intervals of size (B-A)/N.
    When the curve is above the x-axis, the area
    is positive, otherwise the area is negative.
    ERROR=true if N<1, else ERROR=false.

Interface
    TRAP(function F(X: real): real;
        A: real; B: real; N: integer;
        AREA: real; ERROR: boolean);
    input F, A, B, N;
    output AREA, ERROR;

Operation
    if N<1 then
        ERROR := true;
        AREA := 0.0;
    else
        ERROR := false;
        AREA := sum(i:=1,N,
            (F(A+(i-1)*H) + F(A+i*H))/2)*abs(H);
    endif;

Abbreviations
    H: real := (B-A) / N;

Figure 1.
Specification of Procedure TRAP

```
    procedure TRAP(function F(X: real): real;
        A,B: in REAL; N: in INTEGER;
        AREA: out REAL; ERROR: out BOOLEAN) is
    --TRAP computes the AREA between the curve F and
    --the x-axis from x=A to x=B by the trapezoidal
    --rule using N intervals of size (B-A)/N.
    --When the curve is above the x-axis, the area
    --is positive, otherwise the area is negative.
    --ERROR=true if N<1, else ERROR=false.

        H,X: REAL;
0   begin
        if N<1 then
            --invalid input
1           ERROR:=true;
2           AREA:=0.0;
        else
3           ERROR:=false;
            if A=B then
4               AREA:=0.0;
            else
5               H:=(B-A)/REAL(N);
6               X:=A;
7               AREA:=F(X)/2.0;
                while X<B loop
8                   X:=X+H;
9                   AREA:=AREA+F(X);
                end loop;
10              AREA:=(AREA-F(X)/2.0)*H;
                if A>B then
11                  AREA:=-AREA;
                end if;
            end if;
        end if;
12  end TRAP;
```

Figure 2.
Implementation of Procedure TRAP

names are assigned to the input values as a path is "executed". The values of variables are maintained as algebraic expressions in terms of these symbolic names. The path computation is, therefore, represented by a vector of algebraic expressions for the output values, which may be converted to a canonical form. Similarly, the branching conditions for the conditional statements encountered on a path are represented by constraints in terms of the symbolic names for the input values. The path domain is defined by the conjunct of these constraints, which also may be translated into a canonical form. Symbolic evaluation of an implementation can be extended[4,6] to classify paths that differ only by the number of loop iterations. This technique attempts to represent each loop by a closed form expression. The development of a closed form expression for the loop in procedure TRAP and the symbolic evaluation of the path on which this loop occurs are shown in the appendix. Figure 3 provides the domains and computations for the paths derived by symbolic evaluation of the implementation of procedure TRAP, where a, b, and n are the symbolic names for the input values A, B, and N, respectively.

$D[P_1]$ = {(a,b,n) | (n<1)}
$C[P_1]$ = AREA: 0.0
          ERROR: true

$D[P_2]$ = {(a,b,n) | (n$\geq$1) and (a=b)}
$C[P_2]$ = AREA: 0.0
          ERROR: false

$D[P_3]$ = {(a,b,n) | (n$\geq$1) and (a>b)}
$C[P_3]$ = AREA: 0.0
          ERROR: false

$D[P_4]$ = {(a,b,n) | (n$\geq$1) and (a<b)}
$C[P_4]$ = AREA: (-a*F(a) - a*F(b) + b*F(a) + b*F(b) -
          2*a*sum(i:=1,n-1,F(((n-i)*a+i*b)/n)) +
          2*b*sum(i:=1,n-1,F(((n-i)*a+i*b)/n))) / 2*n
          ERROR: false

Figure 3.
Path Domains and Computations
for the Implementation of Procedure TRAP

$D[S_1]$ = {(a,b,n) | (n<1)}
$C[S_1]$ = AREA: 0.0
          ERROR: true

$D[S_2]$ = {(a,b,n) | (n$\geq$1) and (a<b)}
$C[S_2]$ = AREA: (-a*F(a) - a*F(b) + b*F(a) + b*F(b) -
          2*a*sum(i:=1,n-1,F(((n-i)*a+i*b)/n)) +
          2*b*sum(i:=1,n-1,F(((n-i)*a+i*b)/n))) / 2*n
          ERROR: false

$D[S_3]$ = {(a,b,n) | (n$\geq$1) and (a>b)}
$C[S_3]$ = AREA: (a*F(a) + a*F(b) - b*F(a) - b*F(b) +
          2*a*sum(i:=1,n-1,F(((n-i)*a+i*b)/n)) -
          2*b*sum(i:=1,n-1,F(((n-i)*a+i*b)/n))) / 2*n
          ERROR: false

Figure 4.
Subspec Domains and Computations
for the Specification of Procedure TRAP

Symbolic evaluation can be applied to a specification in a similar manner, thus providing representations of the subspecs. Symbolic evaluation techniques must be extended to handle the abstract constructs that appear in specification languages. For instance, a specification language may represent the repetition of a transformation by a closed form expression, such as the summation notation that was used in the specification of procedure TRAP. The subspec domains and computations for procedure TRAP, which were derived by symbolic evaluation of the specification, are given in Figure 4.

The specification and implementation impose two partitions on the procedure domain, representing two ways in which a problem may be divided. A partition that takes into account both the specification and implementation can be constructed by overlaying these two partitions. The subdomains so formed are called procedure subdomains and each is the set of input data for which a subspec and a path are applicable. Figure 5 shows a hypothetical example of the procedure subdomains that would result from overlaying partitions of the specification and implementation domains.

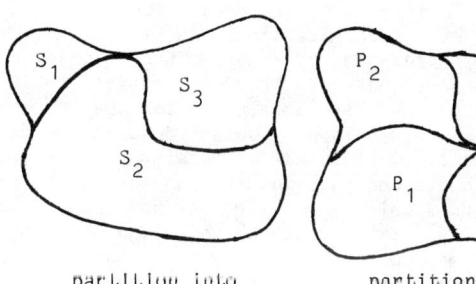

partition into   partition into
subspec domains   path domains

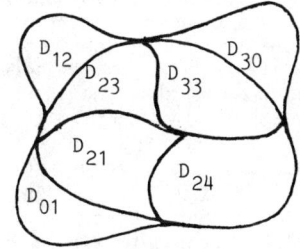

partition into
procedure subdomains

Figure 5.
Development of Procedure Subdomains

It would not be surprising to find a subspec domain and a path domain that are equal. The testing and verification of the associated computations can then be considered over this subdomain as a whole. On the other hand, a subspec domain may overlap with more than one path domain or vice versa. This may occur for various reasons. For example, the implementation may handle some input data as a special case for efficiency while the specification concentrates on simplicity.

Alternatively, a discrepancy may be due to a domain or missing path error[10,12]. Each subdomain formed by overlaying the two partitions, therefore, is of interest and should be verified and tested separately. Procedure subdomains appear to be the largest units of input data that can be analyzed independently and yet the smallest units into which the problem can be practically decomposed.

A procedure subdomain D_{IJ} is the intersection of the subspec domain $D[S_I]$ and the path domain $D[P_J]$ - that is, $D_{IJ} = D[S_I] \cap D[P_J]$. In addition, for each subspec S_I, there may be input data in its domain $D[S_I]$ that are not treated by any path; this set, $D_{IO} = D[S_I] - \cup_{J=1,N} D_{IJ}$, is a procedure subdomain. Also, for each path P_J, there may be input data in its domain $D[P_J]$ that are not treated by any subspec; this set, $D_{OJ} = D[P_J] - \cup_{I=1,M} D_{IJ}$, is a procedure subdomain as well. The existence of any D_{IO} or D_{OJ} implies that the specification domain $D[S]$ and implementation domain $D[P]$ are not the same. Since we assume the specification correctly represents the procedure, the specification domain must be correct. Discrepancies between the domains could imply an error in the implementation or may be due to restrictions on either the specification or implementation domain. For instance, the specification may have input assertions that limit the domain, while the implementation explicitly checks for violations of these assertions.

The representations of the procedure subdomains are constructed from the representations of the subspec and path domains, which are created by symbolic evaluation. Subspec domains and path domains are first compared for equality. For each subspec domain and path domain that are equal, one procedure subdomain is provided. Demonstration of the equality of two domains, say $D[S_K]$ and $D[P_L]$, can sometimes be achieved by a term-by-term comparison of the constraints in their symbolic representations. In procedure TRAP, for instance, $D[S_1] = D[P_1]$ and $D[S_3] = D[P_3]$ are shown in this manner. When domain representations cannot be shown equal by a symbolic comparison, equality can be demonstrated by showing that $D[S_K] \cap \sim D[P_L]$ and $\sim D[S_K] \cap D[P_L]$ are empty. There are several approaches to showing that the intersection of two domains is empty. One approach to this problem is an axiomatic approach, which uses first order predicate calculus to prove whether or not the conjunction defining the intersection is satisfiable. Another approach is an algebraic approach, which attempts to find a solution to the constraints defining the intersection. If the set of constraints is unsatisfiable, the intersection is empty. No method, however[7], can solve any arbitrary system of constraints.

A subspec domain and path domain that are equal need not be considered further. For each remaining subspec S_I and path P_J, the intersection can be constructed by conjoining the representations of the subspec domain and path domain. If this intersection is empty, then no input data exists that causes execution of the path and for which the subspec is applicable; the associated computations are thus trivially equivalent. A non-empty intersection provides procedure subdomain, D_{IJ}, for which computation equality must be considered. For procedure TRAP, these non-empty intersections are $D[S_2] \cap D[P_2]$ and $D[S_2] \cap D[P_4]$.

The representations of the procedure subdomains for procedure TRAP are given in Figure 6. In the partition analysis method, procedure subdomains form the basis for selecting test data and verifying consistency.

$D_{11} = D[S_1] \cap D[P_1]$
$\quad\quad = \{(a,b,n) \mid (n<1)\}$

$D_{22} = D[S_2] \cap D[P_2]$
$\quad\quad = \{(a,b,n) \mid (n \geq 1) \text{ and } (a \leq b) \text{ and } (a=b)\}$
$\quad\quad = \{(a,b,n) \mid (n \geq 1) \text{ and } (a=b)\}$

$D_{24} = D[S_2] \cap D[P_4]$
$\quad\quad = \{(a,b,n) \mid (n \geq 1) \text{ and } (a \leq b) \text{ and } (a<b)\}$
$\quad\quad = \{(a,b,n) \mid (n \geq 1) \text{ and } (a<b)\}$

$D_{33} = D[S_3] \cap D[P_3]$
$\quad\quad = \{(a,b,n) \mid (n \geq 1) \text{ and } (a>b)\}$

D_{12}, D_{13}, D_{14}, D_{21}, D_{23}, D_{31}, D_{32}, and D_{34} are empty, as are all D_{IO} and D_{OJ}.

Figure 6.
Procedure Subdomains of Procedure TRAP

CONSISTENCY PROPERTIES

The partition analysis method is concerned with determining if a procedure implementation conforms to its specification. In this section, three consistency properties are introduced - compatibility, equivalence, and isomorphism - which differ in the manner in which the implementation conforms to the specification. Partition analysis verification, which is outlined in the next section, is an approach to demonstrating whether these consistency properties hold.

A fundamental form of consistency is the compatibility of a specification and an implementation. Compatibility states that the implementation and the specification have the same interface - that is, they have the same number and type of inputs and outputs - and the inputs are restricted to values from the same domain.

Definition: An implementation P is **compatible** with a specification S if both P and S input a vector x, output a vector z, and are defined for the same domain, $D[S] = D[P]$.

In the trivial case, the domain for a particular input is the entire set of values for the type of that input, but some specification and programming languages allow assumptions that further restrict the domain of input values. Note that $D[S] = D[P]$ implies that all elements of each subspec domain are treated by some path and all elements of each path domain are treated by some subspec. Hence, all D_{IO} and D_{OJ} procedure subdomains are empty. The definition of compatibility given here may be stronger than necessary. A procedure implementation that explicitly checks for violations of input assertions that restrict the specification domain may, in fact, be correct. To simplify the discussion, however, the other properties of consistency are defined under the assumption that compatibility holds.

The prevalence of compatibility does not imply that the implementation is correct with respect to the specification. To realize the function described by the specification, the implementation must not only have the same interface, it must compute the output values specified for each input vector in the domain.

Definition: An implementation P is <u>equivalent</u> to a specification S if for all $x \in D[S]$, $P(x) = S(x)$.

Equivalence between a procedure implementation and a specification implies the implementation is correct with respect to the specification.

This property of equivalence can be stated in terms of the relationships between the subspecs and paths over the procedure subdomains. For an input vector x, a particular path, say P_J, is executed - $x \in D[P_J]$ - and a particular subspec, say S_I, is applicable - $x \in D[S_I]$. For this input vector, the specification and the implementation produce the same output values, $S(x) = P(x)$, if and only if the appropriate subspec and path computations agree, $C[S_I](x) = C[P_J](x)$. A subspec S_I and a path P_J compute equal output values for all input data to which they both apply if for all $x \in D_{IJ}$, $C[S_I](x) = C[P_J](x)$. Thus, the computations are equal over the associated procedure subdomain; this is denoted by $C[S_I] = C[P_J]\big|_{D_{IJ}}$. The equivalence of an implementation and a specification, can be restated in terms of the equality of the computations over procedure subdomains.

An implementation P is equivalent to a specification S if and only if for all procedure subdomains D_{IJ}, $1 \leq I \leq M$ and $1 \leq J \leq N$, $C[S_I] = C[P_J]\big|_{D_{IJ}}$.

Equivalence is sometimes very difficult, if not impossible, to determine. A restricted form of equivalence between a specification and an implementation is isomorphism, which is often an easier property to determine for those cases in which it applies. When isomorphism holds each subspec is uniquely associated with an equal path. A subspec S_I and a path P_J are equal if $D[S_I] = D[P_J]$ ($\equiv D_{IJ}$) and $C[S_I] = C[P_J]\big|_{D_{IJ}}$. Thus, the domains are equal and the computations are equal over the procedure subdomain; this is denoted by $S_I = P_J$. This relationship between subspecs and paths leads to a definition of an isomorphism between a specification and an implementation of a procedure.

Definition: An implementation P is <u>isomorphic</u> to a specification S if there exists a bijective mapping $B: S \rightarrow P$ such that $B(S_I) = P_J$ if and only if $S_I = P_J$.

If the specification correctly describes the desired procedure, isomorphism is sufficient, but not necessary, for the implementation to be correct. In addition, isomorphism gives evidence that the internal structure of an implementation and a specification are similar.

The three properties of consistency allow the attachment of differing requisites on the conformity of an implementation to a specification. Compatibility implies that the implementation conforms to the specified interface. The assumption that compatibility must hold simplifies the analysis and yet is a reasonable restriction, since this is often a requirement of an implementation. Slight violations of compatibility can often be handled without additional effort. Isomorphism might be required when a specification is a detailed design that is to be used as a guideline for implementation of the procedure. On the other hand, isomorphism might impose too strict a conformity when a specification is written for comprehensibility, but the implementation must be coded for efficiency. Determining isomorphism, like determining equivalence, is in general an undecidable problem. In practice, however, it can often be accomplished. Since isomorphism and equivalence are defined here in terms of the relationships between the subspecs and paths, the partition analysis method will be driven by the procedure subdomains. By dividing the problem domain into manageable units, the subdomains divide the process of determining consistency between a specification and implementation into more practical steps. When isomorphism between the specification and implementation does not hold, an isomorphism between a subset of the subspecs and paths can often be determined. Equivalence will then be considered for the remaining subdomains.

PARTITION ANALYSIS VERIFICATION

To demonstrate consistency between a specification and an implementation, <u>partition analysis verification</u> employs several established verification and validation techniques. In this section, demonstration of compatibility is first briefly discussed and then an approach for demonstrating equivalence and isomorphism is outlined. The described method is illustrated for the specification and implementation of procedure TRAP.

Demonstrating compatibility between an implementation and a specification is similar to demonstrating uniformity between procedure interfaces in an implementation[9,19,20] or between levels of design[3,22]. If the specification and programming languages have similar constructs for declaring parameters and global variables, then such declarations can be compared to determine if the implementation and the specification have the same number and type of parameters and global variables. If the languages do not support explicit declarations on how these variables are used, then data flow analysis methods[19] may be utilized to determine the input and output class of each such variable in the implementation and in the specification. In addition, input and output statements within the implementation and specification of the procedure must be considered. Assumptions constraining the input values must be compared to determine the equivalence of the specification and implementation domains. The input values might be constrained by explicit assumptions, such as input assertions, or implicit assumptions[1], such as data formats. If the input vector, output vector, and the domain of the implementation agree with those of the specification, then the implementation is compatible to the specification. For procedure TRAP, the compatibility of the implementation and specification is clear.

Once compatibility is established, partition analysis verification can proceed with the demonstration of additional consistency by comparing the subspec and path domains and the subspec and path computations. Since both the specification and the implementation are unambiguous, the subspec domains are mutually disjoint as are the path domains. No such restriction, however, has been made on the computations; neither the subspec computations nor the path computations must be distinct. For example, two paths might perform the same computation for their respective domain. With this in mind, further comparison of a specification and an implementation is driven by the relationships between the subspec domains and the path domains. These relationships are characterized by the procedure subdomains, which thus form the basis for determining equivalence or isomorphism.

Once the procedure subdomains have been constructed, the associated computations are compared. Figure 7 shows the results of this process for procedure TRAP. For each procedure subdomain, the equality of the subspec computation and the path computation over that subdomain must be determined. Often, a term-by-term comparison of the symbolic representations of the subspec computation $C[S_I]$ and the path computation $C[P_J]$ reveals that the two computations are symbolically identical, and thus equal over any domain. In procedure TRAP, for example, $C[S_1]$ and $C[P_1]$ are symbolically identical, as are $C[S_2]$ and $C[P_4]$. Two computations are also equal over the associated procedure subdomain D_{IJ} if the symbolic difference between their symbolic representations, $C[S_I] - C[P_J]$, equals zero for all elements of that subdomain. The most straightforward method for determining whether this holds is to find the solution set of the equation $C[S_I] - C[P_J] = 0.0$. This set can be represented symbolically by a disjunct of the solutions to this equation, as was done for $C[S_2]$ and $C[P_2]$ in procedure TRAP. When the solution set is discrete, the zeroes of a function can be found. If the condition defining the procedure subdomain restricts the inputs to values in this solution set, then the symbolic difference equals zero over that domain. Procedure subdomain D_{22} in TRAP restricts the input values to those for which a=b, all lying in the solution set of $C[S_2] - C[P_2] = 0.0$. It can sometimes be determined that the subspec and path computations are not equal over the associated procedure subdomain, thus indicating an error in the implementation.

Partition analysis verification enabled the detection of a fairly subtle error in the implementation of procedure TRAP. In implementing the <u>while</u> loop, the incorrect assumption was made that the lower bound on the integral is less than the upper bound; thus the loop exit condition is incorrect. This error was uncovered because it was determined that procedure subdomain D_{33} is not contained in the solution set of $C[S_3] - C[P_3] = 0.0$. Thus, the implementation of TRAP is not equivalent to its specification. A correct implementation could be achieved by replacing the loop exit condition by ((X>B) and (A>B)) or ((X<B) and (A<B)).

When the equality or inequality of the subspec and path computations over the associated procedure subdomain cannot be determined, testing can provide some assurance of their equality or find examples of their inequality. Partition analysis testing is discussed in the next section. Although, in

---

```
D_11 = D[S_1] = D[P_1] = {(a,b,n)| (n≤1)}
       C[S_1] = C[P_1] = AREA:  0.0
                        ERROR: true                                                          => S_1 = P_1

D_33 = D[S_3] = D[P_3] = {(a,b,n)| (n>1) and (a>b)}
       C[S_3] - C[P_3] = AREA:  (a*F(a) + a*F(b) - b*F(a) - b*F(b) +
                                2*a*sum(i:=1,n-1,F(((n-i)*a+i*b)/n)) -
                                2*b*sum(i:=1,n-1,F(((n-i)*a+i*b)/n))) / 2*n - 0.0
                               =(a-b)*(F(a)+F(b)+sum(i:=1,n-1,F(((n-i)*a+i*b)/n))) / 2*n
                        ERROR: false-false
       Solution set: (a=b) or (F(a)+F(b)+sum(i:=1,n-1,F(((n-i)*a+i*b)/n)) = 0.0)             => C[S_3]/= C[P_3]
                                                                                                D_33

D_22 = D[S_2] ∩ D[P_2] = {(a,b,n)| (n>1) and (a≤b) and (a=b)}
                       = {(a,b,n)| (n>1) and (a=b)}
       C[S_2] - C[P_2] = AREA:  (-a*F(a) - a*F(b) + b*F(a) + b*F(b) -
                                2*a*sum(i:=1,n-1,F(((n-i)*a+i*b)/n)) +
                                2*b*sum(i:=1,n-1,F(((n-i)*a+i*b)/n))) / 2*n - 0.0
                               =(b-a)*(F(a)+F(b)+sum(i:=1,n-1,F(((n-i)*a+i*b)/n))) / 2*n
                        ERROR: false-false
       Solution set: (a=b) or (F(a)+F(b)+sum(i:=1,n-1,F(((n-i)*a+i*b)/n)) = 0.0)             => C[S_2] = C[P_2]
                                                                                                D_22

D_24 = D[S_2] ∩ D[P_4] = {(a,b,n)| (n>1) and (a≤b) and (a<b)}
                       = {(a,b,n)| (n>1) and (a<b)}
       C[S_2] = C[P_4] = AREA:  (-a*F(a) - a*F(b) + b*F(a) + b*F(b) -
                                2*a*sum(i:=1,n-1,F(((n-i)*a+i*b)/n)) +
                                2*b*sum(i:=1,n-1,F(((n-i)*a+i*b)/n))) / 2*n
                        ERROR: false                                                         => C[S_2] = C[P_4]
                                                                                                D_24
```

Figure 7.
Demonstration of Equivalence of the
Specification and Implementation of Procedure TRAP

general, computation equality is undecidable, several approaches have been shown effective[21].

Partition analysis verification, which compares the symbolic representations of the domains and computations, is a variation on symbolic testing[14]. Usually, symbolic testing involves merely examining the symbolic representations of the path domains and computations. Partition analysis, however, compares these representations with those derived from the specification. This symbolic testing frequently leads to the detection of errors in the implementation. It is apparent that this method facilitates the detection of computation errors. The example given above demonstrates its utility in detecting domain errors as well.

If partition analysis verification is complete and no errors are detected - that is, if the procedure subdomains are completely determined and all the path computations and subspec computations are shown equal over their respective subdomains - then the implementation is equivalent to the specification. If, in addition, there is a one-to-one correspondence between the subspecs and paths, then the implementation and specification are isomorphic. Note that a subset of the paths and subspecs may be in a one-to-one correspondence, as in procedure TRAP. Since the subspecs and paths in this subset are often similar in structure, it is sometimes easy to determine their equality. Partition analysis verification capitalizes on this by first determining the equal subspecs and paths and by then concentrating on those parts of the implementation that deviate from the specification.

PARTITION ANALYSIS TESTING

Demonstrating equivalence of an implementation to the associated specification verifies that the implementation performs the intended task. This method of attesting to program reliability, however, divorces itself from the run-time surroundings by showing consistency in a postulated environment. To remedy this, partition analysis testing complements verification by astutely selecting test data for actual execution. Moreover, when consistency cannot be determined, testing can often substantiate the equality of computations or provide counter examples. The partition into procedure subdomains provides the basis for a test data selection strategy. Each subdomain is a conceptual unit that should be examined carefully and tested independently.

The concept of dividing the problem into smaller units and concentrating on selecting test data for those units is not new. Myers[18] has described some guidelines for partitioning the set of input data into equivalence classes such that one can "reasonably" assume that if the implementation is correct for a representative element of such a class then it is correct for any other element in that class. Path analysis testing strategies[5,12,24] construct a test set by choosing elements from each path domain. This approach uses symbolic representations of the paths provided by symbolic evaluation, but is based solely on the implementation. Howden has proposed a functional testing method[16] that decomposes the implementation into pieces of code that corresponds to subfunctions of the problem. This method symbolically evaluates each subfunction and compares the symbolic representation to the internal documentation and selects test data for each subfunction. Weyuker and Ostrand[23] have proposed a testing method that is based on a partition of the problem that is similar to procedure subdomains. Their method, however, assumes that the specification partition is provided, rather than derived from a specification. Partition analysis decomposes the problem into procedure subdomains using symbolic evaluation of a formal specification and an implementation. In this section, we describe partition analysis testing, which uses the symbolic representations of these subdomains and of their associated computations to assist in selecting test data.

A test data set for a procedure can be constructed by selecting one or more elements from each procedure subdomain. An appropriate selection of input values from each subdomain can increase the probability of detecting errors. The test data selected to exercise the implementation should include typical data points in the subdomain, as well as data explicitly chosen to uncover computation or domain errors.

By examining the representations of the subspec and path computations, test data that is likely to expose computation errors can be selected. Computationally sensitive data that lies within the procedure subdomain may reveal an error in the path computation. Computationally sensitive data[15,18] includes, among other things, data that will cause the computations to be zero, data that causes individual terms within the computation to take on troublesome values, such as 0, 1, or -1, and data of small and large magnitude. For polynomial computations, the number of data points that should be selected to guarantee its correctness may be determined from the degree of the polynomial[8,13].

Test data that is apt to reveal domain errors can be chosen by examining the representation of the procedure subdomain. It has been observed that boundary points are most sensitive to domain errors. Domain testing[24,11] is based on this observation and guides in the selection of test data that lies on and near the boundaries of path domains. By applying this strategy in partition analysis, test data on and near the boundaries of procedure subdomains is selected and errors in the path domain are likely to be detected. Furthermore, whereas most testing strategies are not likely to detect missing path errors, which occur when a subspec is neglected in the implementation, they will in all probability be detected by partition analysis testing. This is because each subspec domain imposes the construction of at least one procedure subdomain; thus data will be chosen that should exercise the missing path.

A categorization of the test data for procedure subdomain D_{24} of procedure TRAP based upon the strategies outlined above is shown in Figure 8. Note that each category does not completely specify an input vector, so categories may be combined in selecting actual test data.

```
n=1                    criteria to
n=2                    detect domain
n>>1                   errors
a=b-ε
------------------------------------------
a=0,b=1
a=-1,b=0
a=-1,b=1
a=-k,b=-1              criteria to
a=1,b=k                detect computation
a=-k,b=k               errors
a=-m,b=+m
a=0,b=+m
a=-m,b=0
b-a=n
------------------------------------------
where, ε is a small positive real value
       k is a typical positive real value
       m is a large positive real value
```

Figure 8.
Categorization of Test Data to be Selected for Procedure Subdomain D_{24} of Procedure TRAP

Testing an implementation with data selected by the partition analysis testing method should detect most, if not all, program errors. If a path is incorrect, it is unlikely that all the test data selected from the corresponding procedure subdomains will result in correct output. Our initial experimentation supports this claim, although more empirical evidence is needed. The analysis of both the implementation and the specification enables partition analysis testing to generate a more comprehensive set of test data than strategies that rely on a single source of information.

CONCLUSION

The partition analysis method incorporates information derived from both a formal specification and an implementation to assist in program testing and verification. This method relies on the construction of procedure subdomains, which partition the set of input data based on both the implementation and the specification. We have proposed consistency properties that differ in how closely the implementation conforms to the specification. Partition analysis verification compares the implementation and the specification in an attempt to determine whether these properties hold. Partition analysis testing selects test data by analyzing both the implementation and the specification, and thus generates a more comprehensive set of test data than one obtained by analyzing the implementation or the specification alone. In light of the work on symbolic evaluation, we believe the partition analysis method we have proposed could be, at least partially, automated.

There are several problems in the partition analysis method that require additional investigation. Strategies for generating test data from the representation of the procedure subdomains have been proposed in this paper, but need to be evaluated further. This paper discusses approaches for dealing with the problems that arise in determining consistency - equality of two domains, emptiness of the intersection of two domains, and equality of two computations over a domain. Additional approaches to these problems must be developed. The proposed evaluation method assumes that loops can be represented in a closed form. While this is often the case, methods for analyzing loops must be further refined. Although symbolic evaluation of programs has been extensively researched, symbolic evaluation of specifications has only recently been considered.

While there are several established programming languages, the design of specification languages is still in its infancy. If program specifications are to contribute effectively to the analysis of programs, more applicable specification languages must be designed. The evaluation method presented in this paper assumes that a procedure specification is complete. The evaluation of higher level specifications, which might be incomplete, should also be considered. While strong consistency, such as equivalence, could not be proven with an incomplete specification, weaker forms of consistency could be demonstrated or inconsistencies could be detected.

Currently, partition analysis is concerned with the analysis of an implementation in relation to a specification. It is believed that the method may also be applicable to two specifications of the same problem. This will enable the determination of consistency between consecutive levels of design and the demonstration of reliability of earlier phases of program development. If analysis is not performed throughout the development process, there is no assurance that the specifications indeed capture the desired behavior of the procedures. To achieve the goal of producing more reliable software, a complimentary set of software tools for program specification, program design, program verification, and program testing must be integrated.

REFERENCES

1. P.W. Abrahams and L.A. Clarke, "Compile-Time Analysis of Data List - Format List Correspondences," IEEE Trans. on Software Engineering, SE-5, 6, November 1979, 612-617.
2. R.S. Boyer, B. Elspas, and K.N. Levitt, "SELECT--A Formal System for Testing and Debugging Programs by Symbolic Execution," Proc. Int. Conf. on Reliable Software, April 1975, 234-244.
3. S.H. Caine and E.K. Gordon, "PDL - A Tool for Software Design," Proc. National Computer Conference, 1975.
4. T.E. Cheatham, G.H. Holloway, and J.A. Townley, "Symbolic Evaluation and the Analysis of Programs," IEEE Trans. on Software Engineering, SE-5, 4, July 1979, 402-417.
5. L.A. Clarke, "A System to Generate Test Data and Symbolically Execute Programs," IEEE Trans. on Software Engineering, SE-2, 3, September 1977, 215-222.
6. L.A. Clarke and D.J. Richardson, "Symbolic Evaluation Methods for Program Analysis," to appear in Program Flow Analysis: Theory and Applications, Prentice Hall, Inc., Englewood Cliffs, New Jersey, 1981.

7. M. Davis, "Hilbert's Tenth Problem is Unsolvable," *American Math. Mon.*, 80, March 1973, 233-269.
8. R.A. DeMillo and R.J. Lipton, "A Probabilistic Remark on Algebraic Program Testing," School of Information and Computer Science Technical Report, Georgia Institute of Technology, May 1977.
9. C. Gannon, "JAVS: A JOVIAL Automated Verification System," *Proc. COMPSAC '78*, November 1978.
10. J.B. Goodenough and S.L. Gerhart, "Toward a Theory of Test Data Selection," *IEEE Trans. on Software Engineering*, SE-1, 2, September 1976, 156-173.
11. J. Hassell, L.A. Clarke, and D.J. Richardson, "A Close Look at Domain Testing," Computer and Information Science, University of Massachusetts, Amherst, TR-80-16, October 1980.
12. W.E. Howden, "Reliability of the Path Analysis Testing Strategy," *IEEE Trans. on Software Engineering*, SE-2, 3, September 1976, 208-215.
13. W.E. Howden, "Algebraic Program Testing," Department of Applied Physics and Information Science, University of California, San Diego, TR-12, November 1976.
14. W.E. Howden, "Symbolic Testing and the DISSECT Symbolic Evaluation System," *IEEE Trans. on Software Engineering*, SE-3, 4, July 1977, 266-278.
15. W.E. Howden, "A Survey of Dynamic Analysis Methods," *Tutorial: Software Testing and Validation Techniques*, IEEE Computer Society, Long Beach, CA, 1978, 184-206.
16. W.E. Howden, "Functional Program Testing," *IEEE Trans. on Software Engineering*, SE-6, 2, March 1980, 162-169.
17. J.C. King, "Symbolic Execution and Program Testing," *CACM*, 19, 7, July 1976, 385-394.
18. G.J. Myers, *The Art of Software Testing*, John Wiley and Sons, New York, 1979.
19. L.J. Osterweil and L.D. Fosdick, "DAVE - a Validation Error Detection and Documentation System for FORTRAN programs," *Software - Practice and Experience*, 6, 1976, 473-486.
20. C.V. Ramamoorthy and S.F. Ho, "Testing Large Software with Automated Software Evaluation Systems," *IEEE Trans. on Software Engineering*, SE-1, 1, March 1975, 16-58.
21. D.J. Richardson, "Theoretical Considerations in Testing Programs by Demonstrating Consistency with Specifications," *Dig. Workshop on Software Testing and Test Documentation*, December 1978, 19-56.
22. D. Teichrow and E.A. Hershey, III, "PSL/PSA: A Computer-Aided Technique for Structured Documentation and Analysis of Information Processing Systems," *IEEE Trans. on Software Engineering*, SE-3, 1, January 1977, 41-48.
23. E.J. Weyuker and T.J. Ostrand, "Theories of Program Testing and the Application of Revealing Subdomains," *IEEE Trans. on Software Engineering*, SE-6, 3, May 1980, 236-246.
24. L.J. White and E.I. Cohen, "A Domain Strategy for Computer Program Testing," *IEEE Trans. on Software Engineering*, SE-6, 3, May 1980, 247-257.

APPENDIX

Symbolic evaluation is typically applied to each path in a procedure. A procedure with loops, however, may have an effectively infinite number of paths. The symbolic evaluation method employed by partition analysis uses a loop analysis technique [4,6] to represent the loops in a procedure by a closed form expression. Using this technique, paths that differ only by their number of loop iterations are classified as a path. Procedures only contain a finite, and usually small, number of classes of paths so that symbolic evaluation can be applied to each such class.

In this symbolic evaluation method, loops are analyzed first in an attempt to generate the closed form expressions. For each analyzed loop, a conditional expression is created representing the final iteration count for any arbitrary execution of the loop. The final iteration count is expressed in terms of the symbolic values of the variables at entry to the loop. In addition, for each variable modified within the loop, its symbolic value at exit from the loop is created. Each such expression is in terms of the final iteration count as well as the symbolic values of the variables at entry to the loop.

Figure A.1 shows the loop analysis for the while loop in TRAP. To initiate loop analysis, an iteration counter, k, is associated with the loop. The symbolic names X_k and $AREA_k$ are used to represent the values of the variables X and AREA at the beginning of the kth iteration of the loop. Note that X_1 and $AREA_1$ represent the values on entry to the first iteration of the loop. Symbolic evaluation of a representative iteration, $k-1$, is performed, thus providing the symbolic values for each X_k and $AREA_k$, $k \geq 2$, as recurrence relations in terms of the values of the variables at iterations k and $k-1$. A representation for the loop exit condition, denoted LEC_k, is also obtained; this is the condition under which the loop will be exited before the kth iteration (after $k-1$ iterations). Loop analysis then solves the recurrence relations, in terms of X_1 and $AREA_1$. The solutions are given by providing $X(k)$ and $AREA(k)$. The solution for the loop exit condition, $LEC(k)$, is obtained by replacing X_k and $AREA_k$ by $X(k)$ and $AREA(k)$ in the condition. Finally, the closed form representation of a loop can be created. The fall-through case, in which the values at entry to the first iteration of the loop satisfy the loop exit condition, must be added to the loop representation. The final iteration count k_e is the iteration before which exit occurs and is the minimum k, such that the loop exit condition is true. The symbolic values of the variables at exit from the loop are represented by $X(k_e)$ and $AREA(k_e)$.

The closed form representation of a loop captures the behavior of the loop. Thus, when a loop is encounterred during symbolic evaluation of a path, the loop body is evaluated by "executing" its closed form representation. The while loop in TRAP is encounterred along paths P_3 and P_4. Path P_3 exits the loop before the first iteration, and thus represents a single path. Path P_4 represents the class of paths that perform one or more iterations of the while loop. The symbolic evaluation of path P_4 appears in Figure A.2.

Recurrence Relations ($k \geq 2$)
   $X_k = X_{k-1} + H$
   $AREA_k = AREA_{k-1} + F(X_k)$
Loop Exit Condition ($k \geq 2$)
   $LECk = \sim(X_k < B)$

Solved Recurrence Relations ($k \geq 2$)
   $X(k) = X_1 + (k-1)*H$
   $AREA(k) = AREA_1 + sum(i:=2,k,F(X_1+(i-1)*H))$
Solved Loop Exit Condition ($k \geq 2$)
   $LEC(k) = X_1 + (k-1)*H \geq B$

Closed Form Representation
   if $X_1 \geq B$ then
      --exit loop before first iteration
      $X = X_1$
      $AREA = AREA_1$
   else if $(X_1 < B)$ and
          exists(k_e: integer in [2..) =>
          k_e=minimum {k: integer in [2..) =>
          $(X_1+(k-1)*H \geq B)$})
      $X = X_1 + (k_e-1)*H$
      $AREA = AREA_1 + sum(i:=2,k_e,F(X_1+(i-1)*H))$
   endif

Figure A.1.
Loop Analysis of <u>while</u> loop in Procedure TRAP

---

statement or edge	condition defining path domain	changes in path computation
0	TRUE	(A=a, B=b, N=n AREA=$, ERROR=$, H=$, X=$)
(0,3)	TRUE and $\sim(n<1)$ $=(n \geq 1)$	
3		ERROR=false
(3,5)	$(n \geq 1)$ and $\sim(a=b)$ $=(n \geq 1)$ and $(a /= b)$	
5		H=(b-a)/n
6		X=a
7		AREA=F(a)/2.0
loop(8-9)	$(n \geq 1)$ and $(a/=b)$ and $(a<b)$ and k_e=minimum{k: integer in [2..) => $(a+(k-1)*(b-a)/n \geq b)$} $=(n \geq 1)$ and $(a<b)$ and $(k_e=n+1)$ *	X=a+(k_e-1)*(b-a)/n AREA=F(a)/2.0+sum(i:=2,k_e,F(a+(i-1)*(b-a)/n))
10		AREA=(F(a)/2.0+sum(i:=2,k_e,F(a+(i-1)*(b-a)/n))- F(a+(k_e-1)*(b-a)/n)/2.0)*(b-a)/n
(10,12)	$(n \geq 1)$ and $(a<b)$ $(k_e=n+1)$ and $\sim(a>b)$ $=(n \geq 1)$ and $(a<b)$ and $(k_e=n+1)$	
12		end

Figure A.2.
Symbolic Evaluation of Path P_4
in the Implementation of Procedure TRAP

*Elementary algebraic techniques were used to solve for k_e.

Functional Testing and Design Abstractions*

William E. Howden

University of Victoria

An approach to functional testing is described in which the design of a program is used to generate functional test data. The approach depends on the use of design methods that model the abstract functional structure of a program as well as the abstract structure of the data on which the program operates. An example of the use of the method is given and a discussion of its effectiveness is included.

1. INTRODUCTION

Functional testing of requirements functions has been carried out in an informal and unsystematic way for many years. The development of new systematic requirements and design analysis methods has resulted in the use of more systematic approaches to validation. This paper describes a systematic approach to functional testing that is based on state-of-the-art design analysis techniques. The approach was developed during an extensive error analysis study [1]. It became clear during the study that the systematic application of functional testing to both the design and requirements functions for a program would be highly effective in discovering program errors. The basic features of such a method are outlined in the following sections. The characteristic feature of the method is its dependence on design specifications.

The approach to requirements and design that is used in the paper is suitable for single programs or parts of larger systems. The key idea is the identification of basic functional computational units. The identification of these units is an important part of other requirements and design methods [e.g., 2] and the approach can be used in conjunction with these methods.

2. FUNCTIONAL TESTING

There are two steps in functional testing. The first involves the identification of the functions that are implemented in a program. The second involves the selection of test data that can be used to check that the program implements the functions correctly.

Programming can be viewed as a translation process in which requirements and design specifications are translated into code. Some errors can be traced back to the specifications and others arise during the translation process. In order to test the requirements and the design as well as the translation process, it is necessary to construct tests that are based on the important features of the requirements and the design.

A program design is an abstract description of the program. Programs can be described from different points of view resulting in different design abstractions. Two of the most important kinds of design abstractions are *function abstractions* and *data abstractions*. Function abstractions are hierarchies of abstract functions. Each function at one level of abstraction is defined in terms of functions at a lower level of abstraction. Structured design is a function abstraction approach to design [3]. Data abstraction can be used to construct program designs in which the structure of a program is based on the structure of the data on which it operates. The data are viewed as a hierarchy of abstract data types. Each data type at one level of abstraction is defined in terms of data types from lower levels. The Jackson design methodology is a data abstraction approach to design [4].

The approach to functional testing described in the following sections involves both function and data abstractions. Function abstraction is used to identify the functions to be tested. Data abstraction is used to model the structure of the input data for functions. It is used to identify important classes of data and combinations of important data values. The use of func-

---

*This paper was written while the author was in residence as a distinguished lecturer at the University of Texas at Dallas. The research on functional testing described in the paper was supported by the National Sciences and Engineering Research Council of Canada.

Address correspondence to William E. Howden, Department of Mathematics, University of Victoria, Box 1700, Victoria, British Columbia, Canada V8W 2Y2.

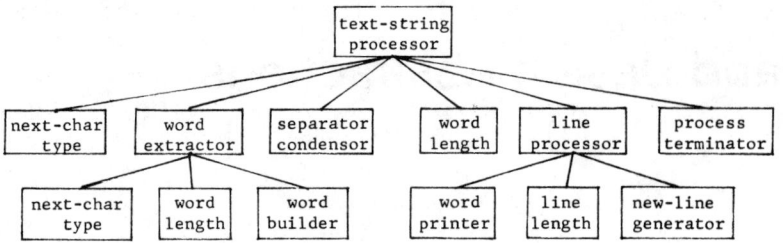

Figure 1. Function abstraction design for text-processor.

3. FUNCTION ABSTRACTION

Figure 1 contains a function abstraction diagram for a design of the text string program described in reference [5]. Program input consists of a string of text consisting of alphabetic characters (αs), blanks (bs), new-line indicators (NLs), and a string termination character (Γ). The program is supposed to print out the text on separate lines. The NL characters in the input string do not necessarily correspond to the ends of output lines and are to be treated like blanks. The maximum length of the output lines is specified in advance. Each line is to contain as many words as possible but no word should be broken up between lines. The maximum length of a word is restricted to the length of one line.

A distinction can be made between *requirements functions* and *design functions*. Requirements functions describe the overall functional capabilities of a program. The box at the top of the function design in Figure 1 represents the requirements function for the string processing program.

In order to implement a requirements function it is usually necessary to invent other "smaller functions." These other functions are used to design the program. A text string processor, for example, will have to be able to look at the next character and determine if it is a delimiter, a string terminator, or an ordinary alphabetic character. It will have to be able to extract words, to construct and print lines, to suppress multiple blanks, to determine the length of a word built by the word extractor, and to terminate processing when the end-of-text character is encountered. All of these functional capabilities are represented by boxes at the second level of the tree in Figure 1. Each is a design function. The implementation of a design function may require the invention of other design functions. In order to be able to construct and print out a line, for example, it is necessary to be able to print words, to keep track of the length of a partially constructed line, and to generate a new-line carriage control character at the appropriate time. These other design functions are represented by boxes at the third level of the tree in Figure 1.

4. FUNCTION IDENTIFICATION

If functional testing is to be used to validate a program that is under development, then functional design trees like that in Figure 1 should be constructed. The trees should document the functions used in the design and implementation of the program. If the design and implementation of a program are a fait accompli, then the program, the design documents, and the requirements documents must be carefully analyzed and the underlying functional abstractions identified.

The most important feature of a function is that it can be independently tested. The input and output domains for each of the functions in Figure 1 can be completely specified. For each set of input values for a function it is possible to construct the correct output that should be computed by the code implementing that function. Functions have a separate identity that is understood by the programmer or designer.

Requirements functions can be identified by examining the requirements specifications for a program. They describe what a program is "supposed to do." A program may implement several requirements functions. Design functions range in abstraction from those that are almost as general as requirements functions to very "small" or detailed functions. The term "extraction function" in the text processing example is a *general design function*. The function that determines the length of a word is a *detailed design function*.

Programs are often documented with informal design specifications that describe how a program works in very general terms. Specific algorithms or computational structures may be described in detail. General design functions can be identified by examining informal specifications for descriptions of or references to independent computational activities.

If no design documentation for a program exists, then it may be necessary to examine the code itself, as well as the requirements, in order to reconstruct the general design functions used to design the program. General design functions can sometimes be identified by reading the comments in a program. Design functions may correspond to significant contiguous sections of code that are documented by comments that informally describe the characteristics of the corresponding undocumented design function. A typical comment in the text processing example might read "extract the next word to be printed." It would identify the code used to implement the word extraction design function.

Detailed design functions are not often described in informal design specifications or in the comments in a program. They may correspond to single expressions or statements in the source code for a program. Their existence, as well as that of general design functions for a poorly documented program, may only be discoverable by a careful functional analysis of the program. The programmer must examine each section and line of code and ask, "What does this do?" and "What is this for?" The answers to these questions will often be informal descriptions of one or more general or detailed design functions.

The danger of constructing tests that are based on design functions that are reconstructed from the program code rather than derived from specifications is that the ultimate source of the information (i.e., the code) may be erroneous. In this case the code is being tested against itself rather than against original requirements or design concepts. The importance of constructing tests that are based on design functions is such that there may be no way of avoiding this. The program tester may have to look at source code documents in order to reconstruct the design structure the programmer had in mind when the program was written. Collections of programs have been written without any design information whatever and this backtracking from the code, with requirements as a guide, is the only way to reconstruct the lost and forgotten design functions.

Design functions are usually input–output functions in the sense that they compute output values from input values. Design functions may also be decision functions. Decision functions are used to choose between alternative computations or to check when an iterative computational process should be terminated. They may correspond to single branches or to collections of branches. Both the input–output and the decision design functions for a program must be identified.

5. DATA ABSTRACTION

A data type is a set of values. Hierarchies of abstract data types involve two kinds of hierarchical relationships. The first, called *classification,* occurs when one data type can be written as the union of two or more other data types. The first data type is more abstract than the others. The constituent data types are used to classify the elements of the more general data type.

The second kind of hierarchical relationship between data types is called *composition*. It occurs when the elements of a data type can be written as compound structures of the elements of one or more other data types. The compound data type is more abstract than the component type(s).

The design structure of a program is often influenced by the abstract structure of the data on which it operates and a complete set of design documents should include descriptions of the important abstract structures in the data. Figure 2 describes the abstract structure of the input data for the text processing program. The requirements function can be described as operating on data which has this structure. A similar abstraction can be used to model the structure of the function's output data.

The notation in Figure 2 is derived from the Jackson design methodology [4]. Each box represents a data type. Boxes containing circles in the upper right-hand corner are used to classify more abstract data types. Figure 2 indicates, for example, that a word may be either an oversize word or an ordinary word. If a box at one level is joined by lines to lower level boxes not containing circles, then elements of the type at the higher level are structures of elements from the types at the lower level. The numbers in the upper right-hand corners of boxes are repetition factors. If a box at one level is joined by a line to a lower-level box that contains a repetition factor, then instances of the higher-level type are structures of re-

Figure 2. Data abstraction for text processor requirements function.

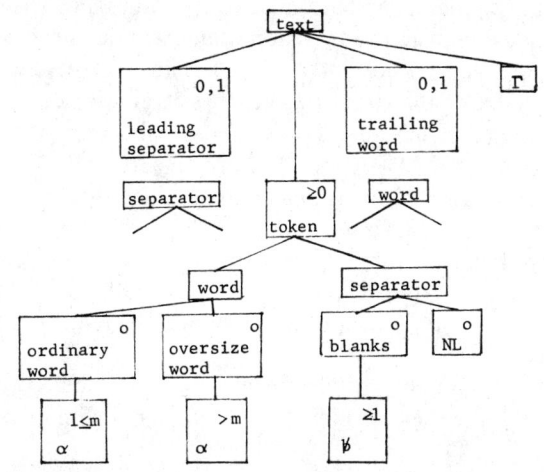

peated instances of the lower-level type. In the example in Figure 2, elements of the "blanks" data type are defined to be structures formed from one or more blank characters. In this case the structure is an ordered sequence. The other repetition factors in Figure 2 are interpreted in the obvious way.

Data abstraction diagrams may be accompanied by written documentation that describes the structures associated with the composition relationships in the diagram. It may also describe important properties of and relationships between different data types. All of the composition relationships in Figure 2 are ordered sequences. The elements of the more abstract data type in the relationship are ordered sequences of elements of less abstract types.

6. TEST DATA

The two most important kinds of functional test data are *extremal values* and *special values*. Extremal values lie on the "edges" or "boundaries" of sets of data. Special values have special algebraic or computational properties.

The identification of extremal values for unstructured numeric variables is relatively simple. If the domain of the variable is an interval of the form $[a, b]$, then a and b are the extremal values. If the variable is of type integer, then $a + 1$ and $b - 1$ can also be considered extremal. Each element of a small finite set of elements can be thought of as an extremal value. If a numeric variable is used in a function that carries out arithmetic computations, then the special values for the variable include zero, $\pm \epsilon$ (for ϵ small) and $\pm E$ (for E large). Similar rules can be used to identify important test data values for nonnumeric, unstructured variables.

The identification of extremal, nonextremal, and special values for data structures such as arrays is more complicated. It is necessary to consider both the values of the elementary items in the structure (e.g., array elements) and the values of structural properties (e.g., dimensions). In general, an extremal structure is one that has no "interior"; all of its elements lie on the edge of the structure. Vectors of length 1 or 2 are extremal structures. Two-dimensional arrays of size 1×1, 1×2, 2×1, or 2×2 are all extremal.

Extremal, nonextremal, and special values can be selected for all, some, or none of the elementary items in a data structure. Extremal and nonextremal structural properties can be combined with extremal, nonextremal, and special values for elementary data items.

The influence of classification on data abstraction is to force the consideration of functionally important classes of values. The data abstraction in Figure 2 indicates the importance of test data that contain both ordinary and oversize words. Composition in a data abstraction forces the consideration of functionally important combinations of values. A token in Figure 2 is defined to be a word followed by a separator. The occurrence of words and separators as parts of the same compound structure results in the consideration of test data in which different kinds of words are followed by different kinds of separators. If a data abstraction contains repetition factors, then it is important to consider test data that correspond to both extremal and nonextremal values of the repetition factors.

The following procedure can be used to identify the important classes and combinations of test data that are associated with a data abstraction. The procedure involves the construction of a sequence of "test sets." The construction procedure begins with the construction of test sets for the terminal or leaf node boxes in the data abstraction. These sets are used to define the test sets for the data abstraction boxes at the next higher level of abstraction, and so on, until the root node box of the data abstraction is reached. The test set associated with the root node will contain an example of each of the different important types of test data for the abstraction.

It is assumed that the leaf boxes in an abstraction correspond to constants (e.g., the blank character $\flat$), to simple unstructured variables, or to source language data structures. If a leaf box a is associated with a constant c, then a test set $T(a)$ for a is equal to $\{c\}$. If a is not associated with a constant, then $T(a)$ consists of a complete set of extremal, nonextremal, and special values for the variables associated with the box.

Assume that a data abstraction box a is joined by lines to a collection of boxes b_i, $1 \leq i \leq n$, that have associated test sets $T(b_i)$, $1 \leq i \leq n$. Suppose that neither a nor any of the b_i contain repetition factors and that each b_i contains a circle. Then $T(a)$ is the union of the $T(b_i)$. If the b_i boxes do not contain circles, then $T(a)$ consists of all sequences $\{x_1, x_2, \ldots, x_n\}$ for which x_i is an element of $T(b_i)$, $1 \leq i \leq n$.

If a box a contains a repetition factor, then the construction of the test set $T(a)$ becomes more complicated. Suppose that a box a contains the repetition factor "≥ 1" and that the implied structure that is used to join together repeated instances of type-a elements is an ordered sequence. Ignore for the moment the asterisk in box a and use the methods described above to build a test set for the box. Call the set $t(a)$. $T(a)$ is constructed from $t(a)$.

The first step in building $T(a)$ is to construct test values that correspond to extremal cases for the repetition factor in a. Assume that sequences of length 1 or 2 are both extremal. Then $T(a)$ should include all sequences of length 1 or 2 of elements from the set $t(a)$.

The next step in building $T(a)$ is to consider nonextremal sequences. Select some "medium-sized" sequence length, say k. Assume that the type of element that occurs at the ends of the sequence is functionally significant. Suppose that it is also important whether or not a sequence consists entirely of repeated instances of the same element. The nonextremal sequences in $T(a)$ can be constructed by combining sequence "heads," "bodies," and "tails." A complete set of sequence heads should contain all length 2 sequences of elements from $t(a)$. A complete set of tails should contain the same length 2 sequences. The bodies of the nonextremal sequences are length $k - 4$ subsequences of elements from $t(a)$. A complete set of bodies should contain one sequence for each element in $t(a)$ for which the sequence consists entirely of repetitions of that element. It should also contain at least one sequence for each element in which that element is not the only element in the sequence. A complete set of nonextremal sequences can be constructed by combining heads, bodies, and tails from the head, body, and tail sets.

The procedure for constructing test data sets from data abstractions will result in a combinatorial explosion if the sizes of the test sets for the data types in a compound data type become significant. In the simple example in Figure 2, T(token) contains 29 extremal and nonextremal test case elements, T(leading separator) 5, and T(trailing word) 8. This will result in a set for T(text) that contains more than 1000 extremal and nonextremal test cases.

The occurrence of combinatorial explosions can be controlled through the use of less exhaustive test set combination rules. The text processing program processes its input data stream in sequential order. It is unimportant to consider combinations in which one type of data at one location in the text is combined with another type at some widely separated location. It may be important to consider combinations involving adjacent pieces of data. The following test set combination rule incorporates these special features of the text data. Suppose a data type a is composed of n data types b_i, $1 \leq i \leq n$. The rule requires that $T(a)$ be constructed in such a way that every combination of elements from each pair $(T(b_i), T(b_{i+1}))$, $1 \leq i < n$, occurs in at least one element of $T(a)$. This modified rule can be used to reduce the size of T(text) to 232 elements. Similar modifications to the test set combination rules can be used to reduce the number of test cases for T(text) to 35 elements. Elimination of redundancy in test cases can also be used to reduce the size of test sets.

The techniques for constructing test sets for boxes containing repetition factors will differ for different types of repetition factors, different interpretations of what constitutes an extremal or nonextremal factor and for different types of structures.

7. TEST DATA SELECTION

Each of the functions in a functional design is associated with the code used to implement the function. The function can be tested by executing the associated section of code. The code may consist of one or more procedures or parts of a procedure, or even a single program statement.

Functional testing requires that the input and output data for each design function be completely specified. In the simplest case the data will have no abstract structure and will correspond directly to the values of unstructured variables and data structures in the code used to implement the function. Extremal, nonextremal, and special values test data should be selected for each input variable. Test data should also be selected to result in the generation of extremal, nonextremal, and special output values.

If the structure of the input data for a function can be described using data abstractions, then the techniques described in the previous section should be used to construct different classes of functional test data. Extremal, nonextremal, and special values of the program variables and data structures used to implement the data abstractions should also be considered.

Program development should include the construction of data abstraction design documents. If functional testing is to be used to test a program that has already been written, then it may be necessary to derive the data abstractions from informal, unstructured design and implementation documents. There are two ways of constructing a data abstraction: decomposition and reconstruction. The diagram in Figure 2 was constructed by decomposing the input data for the text program into its natural functional components. It is also possible to construct structures in which individual variables and data structures are joined together to build a more abstract data type. This is especially useful for joining functionally related variables together in a set structure in order to force the consideration of combinations of extremal values for the variables.

The following list contains examples of the test sets

T for the data-type boxes in the data abstraction in Figure 2. The letter k stands for a constant of the order of $m/2$.

$T(\text{ordinary word}) = \{\alpha, \alpha\alpha, \alpha^k, \alpha^{m-1}, \alpha^m\}, \quad 2 < k < m - 1,$
$T(\text{oversize word}) = \{\alpha^{m+1}, \alpha^{m+k}\}, \quad 2 \leq k,$
$T(\text{word}) = \{\alpha, \alpha\alpha, \alpha^k, \alpha^{m-1}, \alpha^m, \alpha^{m+1}, \alpha^{m+k}\}, \quad 2 \leq k,$
$T(\text{blanks}) = \{\flat, \flat\flat, \flat^k\}, \quad 2 < k,$
$T(\text{NL}) = \{\text{NL}\},$
$T(\text{separator}) = \{\flat, \flat\flat, \flat^k, \text{NL}\}, \quad 2 < k,$
$T(\text{token}) = \{\alpha\flat, \alpha\flat\flat, \alpha\flat^k, \alpha\text{NL}, \alpha\alpha\flat, \ldots\},$
$T(\text{text}) = \{\flat\alpha\flat\Gamma, \flat\flat\alpha\flat\flat\Gamma, \flat\flat\alpha\flat\text{NL}\Gamma, \ldots\}.$

8. EXPERIENCE

The design-based approach to functional testing was developed during a study of the errors that occurred in a release of a major software package [1]. Each of the errors was known in advance. For each error the validation method was determined whose use would result in the discovery of that error. The study included an analysis of the effectiveness of both static and dynamic validation methods.

Static analysis was the most effective validation method for about half the errors that were studied, dynamic analysis for the other half. The study of dynamic analysis included a comparison of the effectiveness of structural and functional testing methods. Structural testing includes methods such as branch testing in which the goal is to construct test data that cause each branch to be executed at least once. Out of a collection of 42 errors for which dynamic analysis was the most effective type of validation method, functional testing would have resulted in the discovery of 38 of the errors and structural testing of 17. Twenty of the errors for which functional testing was effective were associated with requirements functions, nine with general design functions, and nine with detailed design functions. Data abstractions were useful for identifying functionally related sets of input variables and for identifying important substructures of arrays and vectors. The use of data abstractions was critical to the discovery of four errors.

9. SUMMARY AND RELATED WORK

An approach to functional testing has been described in which design functions and design data abstractions are used to construct functional test data. The method is primarily applicable to single programs or to parts of systems. The key idea is the identification of the basic computational units in a program.

The approach has elements in common with other software engineering methodologies. The importance of identifying the basic computational units in a system is emphasized, for example, in the SREM requirements analysis system for real-time systems [2]. Stimulus–response paths in SREM represent the basic individual message processing computations that must be carried out. Stimulus–response paths can be thought of as corresponding to basic requirements functions. Validation points in SREM are used to denote points during the processing at which conceptually meaningful intermediate data are generated. Validation points correspond to input and output for general or detailed design functions. The emphasis in SREM on validation points is consistent with the emphasis on the identification of design functions in the method outlined in this paper, and the method can be used to guide the selection of validation point test data.

The basic steps in the functional testing method in this paper are the identification of design and requirements functions and the selection of functional test data. Design and requirements functions may be identified by examining design and requirements documents and by reading the code. Test data selection requires the identification of the input and output data for all functions. This may involve the identification of data abstractions. Extremal, nonextremal, and special values must be selected for all variables, data structures, and data abstractions.

Functional testing tests the function and data abstractions for a program as well as the translation of the abstractions into code. The abstractions are tested by constructing test data that are based on the important features of the abstractions. The translation into code is tested by executing the code used to implement the abstractions. The results generated by the code are compared with those that were expected for the corresponding abstractions.

This brief description of functional testing introduces the main ideas of the method. More complete descriptions would include descriptions of different kinds of design functions and data abstractions, an expanded discussion of extremal and special values, and a more complete description of techniques for controlling combinatorial explosions. It would also include a discussion of the relationship of structural to functional testing and of testing techniques that involve the combined use of these methods.

Several of the features of the functional testing method described in this paper were first introduced in a more elementary form in an earlier paper [6], which contained discussions of both function and data abstraction. The use of data abstractions in the construction of test data for string processing programs like the text program has been discussed by Duncan [7]. Hamlet et al. [8] have described techniques for testing the implementation of algebraic data abstractions.

REFERENCES

1. W. E. Howden, An analysis of software validation techniques for scientific programs, Department of Mathematics, University of Victoria, report DM-171-IR, March, 1979.
2. M. W. Alford, A requirements engineering methodology for real-time processing requirements, *IEEE Transactions on Software Engineering,* SE-3, 60–68, (1977).
3. E. Yourdon and L. L. Constantine, *Structured Design,* Prentice-Hall, Englewood Cliffs, N.J. 1979.
4. M. Jackson, *Principles of Program Design,* Academic, London, 1975.
5. J. Goodenough and S. L. Gerhart, Toward a theory of test data selection, *IEEE Transactions on Software Engineering,* SE-1, 156–173 (1955).
6. W. E. Howden, Functional program testing, in *Software Methodology,* R. T. Yeh and C. V. Ramamoorthy (eds.), IEEE, Long Beach, 1978, pp. 347–372.
7. A. G. Duncan, Test Grammars: A method for generating program test data, in *Digest of Workshop on Software Testing and Test Documentation,* Fort Lauderdale, 1978, pp. 270–283.
8. R. Hamlet, M. Ardis, J. Gannon, and P. McMullin, Testing data abstractions through their implementations, University of Maryland, Department of Computer Science, report TR-761, 1979.

An Approach to Program Testing

J. C. HUANG

Department of Computer Science, University of Houston, Houston, Texas 77004

One of the practical methods commonly used to detect the presence of errors in a computer program is to test it for a set of test cases. The probability of discovering errors through testing can be increased by selecting test cases in such a way that each and every branch in the flowchart will be traversed at least once during the test. This tutorial describes the problems involved and the methods that can be used to satisfy the test requirement.

Keywords and Phrases: program testing, program analysis, program instrumentation, test-case generation, path analysis, path predicate, directed graph

CR Categories: 3.64, 4.20, 4.42, 4.6, 5.25

INTRODUCTION

Given a computer program, how can we determine whether or not it will do exactly what it is designed to do? This question is not only intellectually challenging, but also of primary importance in practice.

An ideal solution to this problem would be to develop certain techniques that can be used to systematically construct the formal proof (or disproof) of the correctness of a program. As described in a recent survey by Elspas et al. [1], there have been considerable efforts to develop such techniques. Many different techniques for proving program correctness have been reported as the results. However, none of them has been developed to the point where it can be readily applied in practice. Most of the techniques are of only theoretical interest for the following reason: in developing these techniques, the basic approach taken is to translate the problem of proving program correctness into that of proving a certain statement is a theorem in a formal system. The difficulty is that all known automatic theorem-proving techniques require an intolerably large amount of computation to construct a proof. This renders all the known automatic techniques based on theorem proving impractical. These techniques can be made practical only if we can produce a theorem prover that is powerful and efficient enough to overcome this difficulty. But even the foremost experts in theorem proving today cannot optimistically foresee the possibility of achieving, in the near future, a major breakthrough that will enable us to produce such a theorem prover. Thus to fulfill the short-term needs we have to search for practical, and perhaps less idealistic, solutions to the problem.

A practical and more intuitive approach in which we attempt to improve our confidence in a program by testing the program for a set of test cases will be discussed in this paper. This is perhaps one of the most common approaches taken by today's software producers in their attempts to assess the reliability of their products.

How do we go about testing a computer program for its correctness? Perhaps the

Copyright © 1976, Association for Computing Machinery, Inc. General permission to republish, but not for profit, all or part of this material is granted, provided that ACM's copyright notice is given and that reference is made to this publication, to its date of issue, and to the fact that reprinting privileges were granted by permission of the Association for Computing Machinery.

Reprinted from *ACM Computing Surveys,* September 1975, pp. 113-128. Copyright 1975, Association for Computing Machinery, Inc. Reprinted by permission.

CONTENTS

INTRODUCTION
1. TEST CRITERIA
2. TEST PROCEDURES
3. PATH PREDICATES
4. TEST-CASE GENERATION
CONCLUDING REMARKS
ACKNOWLEDGMENTS
REFERENCES

---

most intuitive (and seemingly plausible) answer to this question is to consider the program as a black box and test it for all possible input cases to see if it will produce the correct outputs. Unfortunately, as aptly pointed out by Dijkstra in [2], it is in general impractical for us to do this simply because of the number of possible input cases involved. The following is analogous to Dijkstra's explanation.

Suppose the program to be tested has two input variables and one output variable as depicted below:

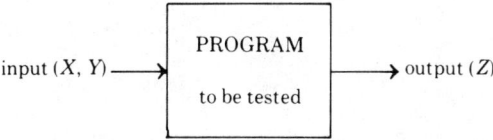

If, for an assignment of values to the input variables X and Y, the output variable Z will assume a correct value upon execution of the program, then we can assert that the program is correct for this particular test case. And if we can test the program for all possible assignments to X and Y, then we will be able to determine its correctness. The difficulty here is that, even for a program with only two input variables, the number of possible assignments will be prohibitively large. To see why this is so, let us assume that X and Y are integer variables. Furthermore, let us assume that the program is to be run on a computer with 32-bit registers. Then there are $2^{32} \times 2^{32} = 2^{64}$ possible assignments to the input pair (X, Y). Now suppose this program is relatively small, and on the average it takes one millisecond to execute the program once. Then it will take more than 50 billion years for us to complete the test!

This example clearly indicates that, no matter how large a practically feasible set of test cases we may choose, it always constitutes an extremely small sample out of all possible cases. If the test results are incorrect, it definitely indicates that the program contains errors. If, however, the test results are correct, we have an insignificantly weak statistical base to infer that the program is correct. This is the basis for the well-known maxim that program testing can be used to discover the presence of errors, but not their absence.

The point is that, superficially, the test results are insignificant. We say "superficially" because here we are assuming (black-box view of the program) that all test cases (i.e., $(X, Y, f(X, Y))$) are equally important, although in fact they are not. When we *look inside the black box*, i.e., when we examine the structure of the program, *we can find a small set of test cases which is significant*. What we would like to stress at this point is that

1) a randomly selected set of test cases is statistically insignificant, and
2) a selection of test cases based on the program structure can be statistically significant.

How can a set of test cases selected by a criterion based on the program structure be significant? The reason is that for most programs not every statement will occur in a given execution. Therefore, if a program contains a statement in error and that statement is not executed during the test, we will not be able to detect any abnormality at all in the test result. Thus an obvious way to increase the probability of discovering errors through program testing is to have each and every statement in the program executed at least once during the test. A set of test cases that achieves this test goal, which can be constructed based on the program structure, is certainly of special significance. We shall explain this in detail in the next section.

1. TEST CRITERIA

A common test criterion is to have each and every statement in the program executed at least once during the test. However, as will be shown later, this leaves some important classes of errors undetected. Therefore we shall consider a more stringent criterion which requires that every branch in the flowchart be traversed at least once during the test. In what follows we shall illustrate these points by using the examples of Figures 1–3, and then, at the end of this section, formalize the concepts involved.

Let us consider the program whose flowchart is given in Figure 1. This program is designed to find the abscissa within the interval (a, b) at which a function f(x) assumes the maximum value. The basic strategy used is that, given a continuous function that has a maximum in the interval (a, b), we can find the desired point on the x-axis by first dividing the interval into three equal parts. Then compare the values of the function at the dividing points a + w/3 and b − w/3, where w is the width of the interval being considered. If the value of the function at a + w/3 is less than that at b − w/3, then the leftmost third of the interval is eliminated for further consideration; otherwise the rightmost third is eliminated. This process is repeated until the width of the interval being considered becomes less than or equal to a predetermined small constant e. When that point is reached, the location at which the maximum of the function occurs can be taken as the center of the interval, (a + b)/2,—with an error less than e/2.

Now suppose we wish to test this program for three different test cases, and assume

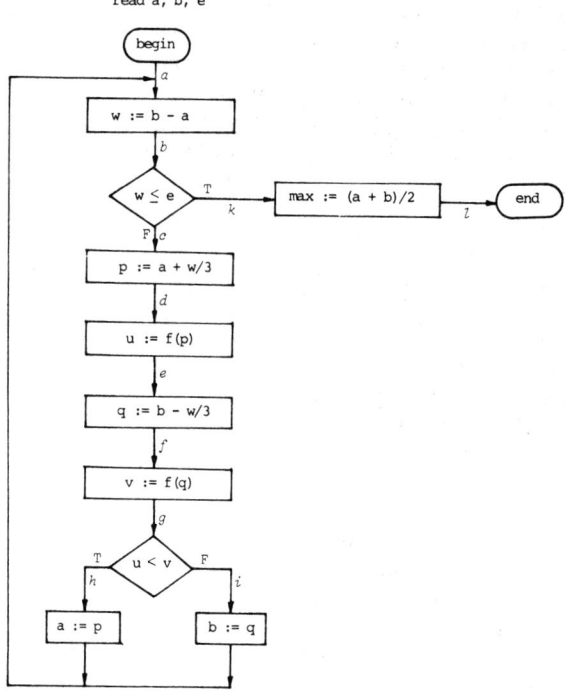

Figure 1. A program.

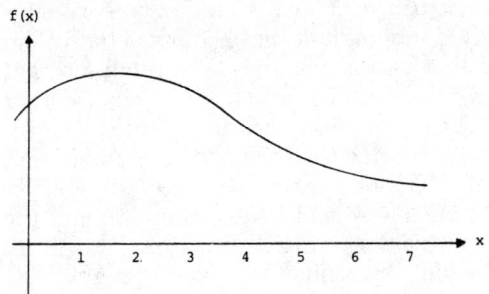

Figure 2. The function plot of f(x).

that the function $f(x)$ can be plotted as shown in Figure 2. Let us first arbitrarily choose e to be equal to 0.1, and choose the interval (a, b) to be $(3, 4)$, $(5, 6)$, and $(7, 8)$. Now suppose that the values of max for all three cases are found to be correct in the test. What can we say about the design of this test?

Observe that in all three intervals chosen the value of u will be always greater than v as we can see from the function plot. Consequently, the statement $a := p$ in the program will never be executed during the test. Thus if this statement is for some reason erroneously written as, say, $a := q$ or $b := p$, we will never be able to discover the error in a test using the three test cases mentioned above. This is so simply because this particular statement is not "exercised" during the test.

The functional plot given in Figure 2 shows that u will always be less than v within the interval $(0, 1)$. Thus if the test cases used include the interval $(0, 1)$ we will be able to discover the error described above.

The point to be made here is that our chances of discovering errors through program testing can be significantly improved if we select the test cases in such a way that each and every statement will be executed at least once.

It must be emphasized here, however, that the use of such a set of test cases gives us no assurance that the presence of an error will be definitely reflected in the test result. This fact can be demonstrated by using a simple example. For instance, if a statement in the program, say, $x := x + y$ is somehow erroneously written as $x := x$

$- y$, and if the test case used is such that it sets $y = 0$ prior to the execution of this statement, the test result certainly will not indicate the presence of this error.

The inadequacy of testing a program only to the extent that each and every statement is executed at least once is actually more serious than what we described above. There is a class of common programming errors that cannot be discovered in this way. For instance, consider the type of error illustrated in Figure 3, where the flow of control is transferred to a wrong place as indicated by the dotted line. In this case the program produces correct results as long as the input data cause P to be true when this program segment is entered. The requirement of having each and every statement executed at least once is trivially satisfied in this case by choosing input data so that P is true. Obviously, the error will not be detected in this case.

The problem is that a program may contain paths from the entry to the exit (in its flowchart) which need not be traversed in order to have each and every statement executed at least once. Since the present test requirement can be satisfied without having such paths traversed during the test, it is only natural that we will not be able to discover errors that occur on those paths.

An obvious solution to this problem would be to require that each and every control

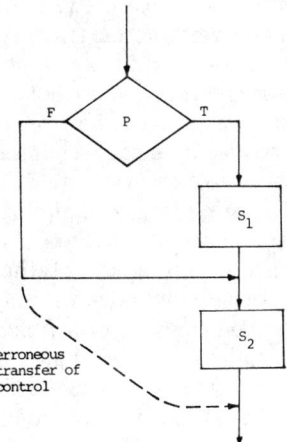

Figure 3. A type of programming error.

path in the program be traversed at least once during the test. However, this test requirement can be easily proved to be impractical because in practice almost every program contains loops, and a program with a loop contains at least as many different control paths as the number of times the loop can be iterated, which is prohibitively large in many cases. A more realistic solution is to require that each and every *edge* or *branch* (these two terms are used interchangeably throughout this article) in the flowchart be traversed at least once during the test. In accordance with this new test requirement, we will have to use a new test case that makes P false, in addition to the one that satisfies P, in order to have every branch in Figure 3 traversed at least once. Hence our chances of discovering the error will be greatly improved, because the program will most likely produce an erroneous result for the test case that makes P false.

Observe that this new requirement of having each and every branch traversed at least once is more stringent than the previously stated requirement of having each and every statement executed at least once. In fact, satisfaction of the new requirement implies satisfaction of the previous one. This is so because a flowchart is a connected graph in which each node is on some path from the entry to the exit (assuming that there is no inaccessible code in the program text). Since each branch emanates from a node and terminates at another, it is obvious that every statement has to be executed at least once in order to have every branch traversed at least once. Satisfaction of the previously stated requirement, however, does not necessarily entail satisfaction of the new one. This can be easily verified by using a counter-example readily obtainable from Figure 3.

It is interesting to see what this new test requirement means in terms of the tasks to be performed by a program. Mathematically speaking, a computer program may be considered as the definition of a function. This function usually is expressed as a union of a set of partial functions, each defined on a subset of the intended input domain. Each partial function is associated with an executable path in such a way that the sequence of noncontrol statements on the path is actually a subprogram that computes the values of that partial function. The condition that a set of input data has to satisfy in order for a path to be traversed in execution is generally referred to as the *path predicate* of that path. The path predicate essentially defines the membership of a subdomain in which the corresponding partial function is defined. Roughly speaking, to test a program by having each and every branch traversed at least once is to test the correctness of each and every partial function for at least one point in the subdomain in which it is defined.

From the above analysis we see that if there is an error in the constituent statements of a certain path, it is most likely that we will discover the error because the corresponding partial function will be checked for at least one point in the subdomain in which it is defined. However, we must remember that, for some input data, some programs may produce results that are fortuitously correct, as we have demonstrated before. This is why the requirement of having every branch traversed at least once is still not sufficient to ensure that the presence of an error will be definitely indicated in the test result.

Before we proceed to describe the techniques available for program testing, it may be helpful to recapitulate the ideas discussed thus far in a more precise manner:

1) A *program block* is a sequence of one or more statements having the property that, if a member statement is executed, all other statements in the sequence will also be executed.
2) A *program graph* is a directed graph in which each node is associated with a program block. Furthermore, there is an edge from node i to node j labeled by predicate P if and only if upon execution of the program block associated with node i the control will be transferred to the entry of the program block associated with node j, if predicate P is true. Note that an edge will be traversed in execution only if the associated predicate is true.
3) A *path* in a (program) graph is defined as usual [3, 4]. Each path in a program

graph is associated with a predicate such that the path will be traversed only if the associated path predicate is true. A *minimal covering set* of path predicates is a set $\prod$ of predicates such that: a) each element in $\prod$ is associated with some path from the entry to the exit of the program graph; b) satisfaction of all predicates in $\prod$ entails that every edge in the program graph will be traversed at least once during execution; and c) no proper subset of $\prod$ has these properties.

4) Suppose the program is designed to compute the values of function $f: X \to Y$. This function usually is expressed in the program text as a union of functions $f_i: X_i \to Y$, where $X = X_1 \cup X_2 \cup \cdots \cup X_n$ and f_i is f restricted to X_i for $1 \leq i \leq n$. Furthermore,

$$X_i \supseteq \{x \mid x \in X \text{ and } p_i \in \prod \text{ and } p_i(x)\}$$

Here by $p_i(x)$ we mean x satisfies predicate p_i.

Based on the above discussion we may now define a measure of thoroughness of a test. We shall define a *minimally thorough* set of tests to be a set of pairs $\{(x_1, f(x_1)), (x_2, f(x_2)), \cdots, (x_n, f(x_n))\}$ such that x_i satisfies the ith predicate $p_i \in \prod$. In other words, a test is minimally thorough if each and every branch in the flowchart is traversed at least once during the test.

A survey of the literature shows that there is no common agreement as to what can be considered as an *adequate* test criterion. However, the measure of thoroughness defined here appears to have been widely recognized as a basic test requirement. This can be attested to by the fact that many major software-testing tools reported so far have incorporated in them some provision to assist the programmers to achieve the test goal of having every branch in the flowchart traversed at least once [4–9]. The disagreement seems to be in how much more is needed beyond this basic requirement to entitle a test program to be considered adequate.

The objective of the remainder of this article is to develop methods for constructing a minimal covering set of path predicates and corresponding set of tests for a given program.

2. TEST PROCEDURES

A simple and practical way to determine the degree of thoroughness of a test is to calibrate the program to be tested by using a set of software counters (see, e.g., [7]). To do so, we first have to identify a (minimal) set of points on the flowchart such that, if we know the number of times each point is crossed, we can determine the number of times each branch is traversed. We then prepare the program for testing by inserting counters at these points (the counters can be removed later when the program is considered debugged, assuming no further performance data are required). After having the program tested for a number of test cases, we can determine the degree of thoroughness by examining the resulting counter values.

Where do we place the counters in order to determine whether or not every branch is traversed at least once? For the purpose of finding an answer to this question, it is convenient to introduce the concept of a deci-

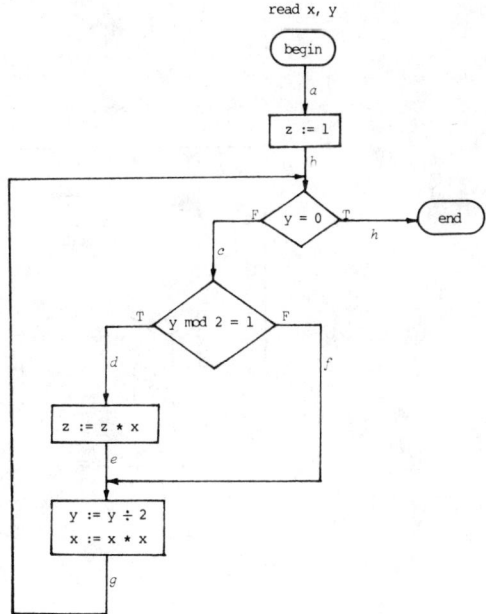

Figure 4. A program.

sion-to-decision path [7]. A decision-to-decision path is defined to be a path in a flowchart such that a) its first constituent edge emanates either from an entry node or a decision box; b) its last constituent edge terminates either at a decision box or at an exit node; and c) there are no decision boxes on the path except those at both ends. For example, consider the flowchart shown in Figure 4. Here the paths deg and ab are decision-to-decision paths, but paths abh and eg are not. It should not be difficult to verify that in a flowchart a) every branch is on some decision-to-decision path, and b) if the first branch of a decision-to-decision path is traversed during the execution, then every branch on that path will also be traversed. For convenience, let us call the first branch of a decision-to-decision path a *reference* branch. It is easy to identify the reference branches in a flowchart because, by definition of a decision-to-decision path, those and only those emanating from either an entry node or a decision box are the reference branches of that flowchart. Now the answer to our question is obvious. To determine whether or not every branch is traversed at least once, we need only to place a counter on each and every reference branch.

The idea presented above can be illustrated by using the example program shown in Figure 4. For the purpose of discussion, let us assume that the software counters are to be implemented by using a procedure (subroutine) named count(j), where j is a parameter. This procedure consists of an integer array counter[1], counter[2], $\cdots$, counter[n]; the value of each element is set to zero initially. A call of procedure count(j) will increase the value of counter[j] by 1. There are five reference branches in Figure 4, namely, a, c, h, d, and f. Thus we instrument the program by placing the counters on these branches as shown in Figure 5. Now we are ready to test this program for a set of test cases. The test cases used, and the resulting counter values are listed in Figure 6. The fact that all resulting counter values are nonzero indicates that every path in the program has been traversed at least once in the test, and therefore the test is minimally thorough.

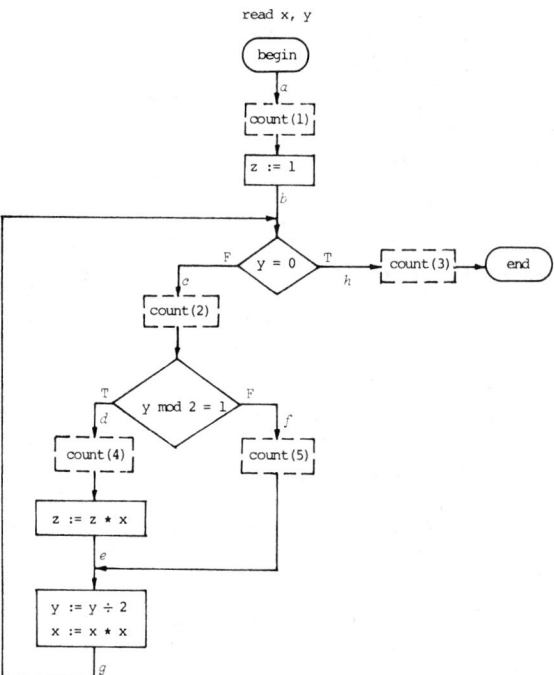

Figure 5. The program instrumented with counters.

Test Cases		Counter Values				
x	y	counter[1]	counter[2]	counter[3]	counter[4]	counter[5]
10	0	1	0	1	0	0
20	1	1	1	1	1	0
5	2	1	2	1	1	1
40	4	1	3	1	1	2

Figure 6. Possible test cases and the corresponding counter values.

When a counter placed on a reference branch has a zero count, it indicates that the corresponding decision-to-decision path was not traversed at all during the test (and therefore the test is not minimally thorough). We can use this information to find additional test cases to satisfy the test requirement. To demonstrate how this can be done, let us suppose that only the first two test cases listed in Figure 6 are used in the test. Consequently, the value of counter[5] will remain zero, indicating that branch f in Figure 4 was not traversed at all. To make the test minimally thorough, we must find an additional test case that will force traversal of this branch. Note that branch f will be traversed if the execution proceeds along the path formed by branches a, b, c, f, and further down. By inspection we can tell that this path will be traversed if the input data satisfy the condition $y \neq 0$ and $y \bmod 2 \neq 1$. Thus we may use, say, $x = 24$ and $y = 2$ as the additional test case. After performing a test on this test case the value of counter[5] will be 1 as can be verified readily.

To recapitulate, we have described a method in which the program to be tested is instrumented by inserting counters at certain strategic points. The program is then tested for a set of test cases. By examining the resulting counter values we can tell whether the test is minimally thorough. If not, the information provided by the counters can be used to facilitate construction of additional test cases that are needed to make the test minimally thorough. Incidentally, the path usage information deducible from the counter values can also be used by the programmer to find "inner loops" for which the optimization payoff is greatest.

There is one thing that we did not make very clear in the above discussion. That is, where do we get the test cases when we say: "test the program for a set of test cases." It is possible that we know of a set of input data for which the corresponding correct output values are known; and therefore we would like to test the program against that set of input data. For instance, if the program is designed to compute the values of $\sin(x)$ then we certainly would like to see what the program is going to produce for x equal to, say, 0, $\pi/6$, $\pi/3$, and $\pi/2$. In practice, however, the readily available set of test cases may be small compared to a set required to make the test minimally thorough. This is so particularly when the program to be tested is large. Of course we may enlarge the set of test cases by adding to it some randomly chosen input data. However, the chances are good that the test cases arbitrarily chosen will not add significantly to the degree of thoroughness. In order to satisfy the test requirement, we often have to use the information provided by the counters to find additional test cases.

This discussion leads us to consider another approach to program testing. That is, we can begin the test procedure by finding a (minimal) set of test cases that will test the program thoroughly. We then use this set of test cases, perhaps in conjunction with any other desirable test cases, to test the program. In this way the desired degree of thoroughness will be automatically achieved. Furthermore, by using a minimal set (i.e., a set with a minimal number of elements) of test cases, we can keep the required computer time for program testing to a minimum.

The question now is: how can we find for a given program a minimal set of test cases such that the test will be minimally thorough? The process of finding such a set is generally referred to as *test-case generation*. Essentially, the desired set of test cases can be generated in three steps: 1) Find S, a minimal set of paths from the entries to the exits in the flowchart such that every branch is on some path in S; 2) Find a path predicate for each path in S; and 3) Find a set of assignments to the input variables, each of which satisfies a path predicate obtained in step 2. This set is the desired set of test cases.

We shall illustrate the process of test-case generation by using the program shown in Figure 1 (cf. Section 1). First we need to find set S' of all paths in the flowchart. A flowchart is essentially a directed graph, and techniques for finding paths in a directed graph can be found in [3, 4, 10]. We then construct S, a minimal subset of S' that covers every branch in the graph. In a simple flowchart like the one in the present example, we can find S simply by inspection, viz., S = {abcdefghjbkl, abcdefgijbkl}. Next, we need to find the path predicates for these two paths, i.e., the conditions assuring that these two paths will be traversed in execution. In general it is difficult to find the path predicates by inspection and we need a systematic method to derive it from the program text. We shall describe such a method in the next section.

only through a node, which is associated

3. PATH PREDICATES

Observe that a branch in the flowchart will be traversed in execution if some predicate, called the *branch predicate*, is satisfied at that stage of computation. The branch predicate for any branch can be found by examining the nature of the statement associated with the node from which this branch emanates. For instance, in Figure 4, $y = 0$ is the branch predicate of the branch labeled by h, while $not(y = 0)$ is that of the branch labeled by c. Obviously, if a branch is the only branch emanating from a node, then it is associated with the constant predicate T, which is always true.

Now consider two branches associated with predicates Q and R, respectively. Then the path formed by concatenating these two branches will be traversed if Q and R are both true. However, it should be noted that in a flowchart two branches can form a path with some statement S in the program as depicted below:

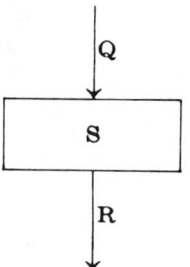

Insofar as the construction of path predicates is concerned, we need only consider the case when S is an assignment statement, because it changes the value of a variable upon execution. Let S be an assignment statement of the form $x := E$, where x is a variable, E is some expression, and $:=$ is the assignment operator. Obviously, if we want predicate R to be true after S is executed, then predicate $R_{E \to x}$ must be satisfied prior to the execution of S. Here by $R_{E \to x}$ we mean a predicate obtained by substituting expression E for each and every occurrence of x in predicate R. Thus the path predicate for the path so formed is seen to be:

$$Q \text{ and } R_{E \to x}.$$

The following examples should be helpful in clarifying the meaning of expression $R_{E \to x}$.

R	$x := E$	$R_{E \to x}$
$x = 1$	$x := 1$	$1 = 1$
$a > 0$	$a := 10$	$10 > 0$
$b = 16$	$a := 4$	$b = 16$
$a < 10$	$a := a + 1$	$a < 9$
$a \leq b$	$a := a - b$	$a \leq 2b$

Expression $R_{E \to x}$ may be thought of as a predicate obtained by "dragging" predicate R backward along the path illustrated above. In general, an edge predicate can be dragged backward along a path until the first edge of the path is reached. Let Q be a predicate associated with an edge on path p, and let Q' be the predicate obtained by dragging Q backward along path p all the way to the first edge on p. It should be obvious that, if we want the program to be executed along path p, then Q' must be true when the path is entered. Thus if we want a specific path in the flowchart to be traversed during the execution, then the set of predicates obtained by dragging every edge predicate backward must be satisfied. A conjunction of the set of predicates so obtained is thus the path predicate of that path.

To illustrate the idea described above, we shall now construct the path predicate for path abcdefghjbkl in Figure 1. We can ignore all branches associated with predicate T because it is a constant and is an identity under conjunction. The nontrivial branch predicates are:

$$c ::= not(w \le e)$$
$$h ::= u < v$$
$$i ::= not(u < v)$$
$$k ::= w \le e.$$

The process of dragging these three predicates backward toward the first branch of the path is shown step by step in the following. Note that in passing through an assignment statement the predicate remains unchanged unless the variable on the lefthand side of the assignment operator occurs in the predicate.

Thus the path predicate for path abcdefghjbkl is the conjunction of the three predicates obtained above, namely

$not(b - a \le e)$
$and\ f(a + (b - a)/3) < f(b - (b - a)/3)$
$and\ b - a - (b - a)/3 \le e$

which can be simplified to yield

$not(b - a \le e)$
$and\ f((b + 2a)/3) < f((a + 2b)/3)$
$and\ 2(b - a)/3 \le e.$ (3.1)

Similarly we obtain the path predicate for path abcdefgijbkl given below:

$not(b - a \le e)$
$and\ not\ (f((b + 2a)/3) < f((a + 2b)/3))$
$and\ 2(b - a)/3 \le e.$ (3.2)

The path predicates constructed as described above are always expressed in terms of constants and input variables. To cause a path to be traversed during execution, all we need to do is to find an assignment of values to the input variables so that the path predicate is satisfied. We shall discuss how to find such an assignment in the next section.

4. TEST-CASE GENERATION

To find an assignment to satisfy a predicate is not difficult in principle, but it will be

Branch   **Predicates**

Branch				Predicates
k				$w \le e$
↓ b				$w \le e$
↓ j				$b - a \le e$
↓ h		$u < v$		$b - p \le e$
↓ g		$u < v$		$b - p \le e$
↓ f		$u < f(q)$		$b - p \le e$
↓ e		$u < f(b - w/3)$		$b - p \le e$
↓ d		$f(p) < f(b - w/3)$		$b - p \le e$
↓ c	$not(w \le e)$	$f(a + w/3) < f(b - w/3)$		$b - (a + w/3) \le e$
↓ b	$not(w \le e)$	$f(a + w/3) < f(b - w/3)$		$b - (a + w/3) \le e$
↓ a	$not(b - a \le e)$	$f(a + (b - a)/3) < f(b - (b - a)/3)$		$b - a - (b - a)/3 \le e$

error-prone and rather time-consuming in practice. An ideal solution would be to delegate this task to a computer. Unfortunately, mechanization of this process is quite difficult. It essentially requires a program having almost the computational power of a theorem prover. There have been efforts to partially mechanize the process for the cases where the assignments can be found by using the techniques for solving algebraic equations [11], or those of linear programming [9]. It appears that a fully mechanized general inequality solver will not be available for some time to come. What we would like to do in the following is to describe a systematic method for finding the desired set of assignments. The method can then be mechanized and incorporated into an automated program-testing tool, or can be used by the programmer to find the assignments by hand.

In many practical programming languages a logical expression is an expression of the form:

$$E_1 \; R \; E_2 \qquad (4.1)$$

where E_1 and E_2 are arithmetic expressions and R is one of the six relational operators: $=, \neq, <, \leq, >,$ and $\geq$. For convenience, we shall call a logical expression of the form (4.1) an *atomic (logical) expression*.

The path predicates obtained as described in the preceding section are constructed by using the atomic expressions and logical connectives such as *not, and,* and *or*. Furthermore, they are all expressed in terms of constants and input variables.

Ordinarily, it is a relatively simple matter for us to find an assignment that satisfies an atomic expression. It is also relatively easy to find an assignment that will satisfy a conjunction of atomic expressions if no variable that occurs in one atomic expression occurs in the other. But this is usually not the case in practice. In general, we will find the same variables occurring in more than one atomic expression in a path predicate. As a rule, the degree of difficulty in finding the desired assignments increases as the number of atomic expressions involved, and as the number of variables in common increases.

For instance, consider the following pair of logical expressions:

$$not(b - a \leq 0.1)$$
$$2(b - a)/3 \leq 0.1.$$

It is easy to find an assignment that will satisfy either member of this pair. But it will be more difficult to find one that satisfies both.

The central problem, then, is to devise a systematic method for finding an assignment that will satisfy a logical expression of the form:

$$P_1 \; and \; P_2 \; and \; \cdots \; and \; P_n, \qquad (4.2)$$

where each P_i is an atomic expression, possibly prefixed by a *not* connective.

As the first step in the present method, we shall remove all *not* connectives involved. This can be accomplished as follows: If P_i is an expression of the form *not* $E_1 \; R \; E_2$, then replace it with the equivalent expression $E_1 \; R' \; E_2$. The six relational operators R and the corresponding R' are listed below:

R	$\rightarrow$	R'
$=$		$\neq$
$\neq$		$=$
$<$		$\geq$
$\leq$		$>$
$>$		$\leq$
$\geq$		$<$

Thus, given a logical expression of the form (4.2) we can always rewrite it into an equivalent expression of the form:

$$Q_1 \; and \; Q_2 \; and \; \cdots \; and \; Q_n, \qquad (4.3)$$

where each Q_i is a non-negated atomic logical expression.

Next, we observe that to many of us it is easier to work with a set of equalities rather than inequalities. For this reason we shall, as the second step in the present method, rewrite each Q_i in (4.3) into an expression in terms of $=$ only. The notion that this can be done is based on the fact that inequalities can be stated in terms of equalities as follows:

$a \neq b$ if and only if there exists an $x \neq 0$ such that $a + x = b$.

$a < b$ if and only if there exists an $x > 0$ such that $a + x = b$.

$a \leq b$ if and only if there exists an $x \geq 0$ such that $a + x = b$.
$a > b$ if and only if there exists an $x < 0$ such that $a + x = b$.
$a \geq b$ if and only if there exists an $x \leq 0$ such that $a + x = b$.

For the reasons that will become obvious in the ensuing discussion, we shall restate the above relations as follows: (Note: $(\exists x)_{>0}$ is to be read as "there exists an $x > 0$ such that $\cdots$")

$$a \neq b \Leftrightarrow (\exists x)_{\neq 0}(x = b - a)$$
$$a < b \Leftrightarrow (\exists x)_{>0}(x = b - a)$$
$$a \leq b \Leftrightarrow (\exists x)_{\geq 0}(x = b - a)$$
$$a > b \Leftrightarrow (\exists x)_{>0}(x = a - b)$$
$$a \geq b \Leftrightarrow (\exists x)_{\geq 0}(x = a - b) \quad (4.4)$$

Now we shall explain by using examples how the reformulation of atomic expressions in terms of equality may help in finding the desired assignments. Suppose we wish to find an assignment that satisfies path predicate (3.2), which is restated below for convenience.

$not(b - a \leq e)$

$and\ not\ f((b + 2a)/3) < f((a + 2b)/3)$

$and\ 2(b - a)/3 \leq e.$

Since we do not have the exact specification of function f, we need to rewrite the second atomic expression into a more definitive statement. It is observed that $a < b$ because they stand for the lower and upper boundaries of an interval on the x-axis (cf. Section 1). Hence it is always true that $(b + 2a)/3 < (a + 2b)/3$. Now, from the function plot in Figure 2 we see that $not(f(x_1)) < f(x_2)$ will be true if $x_1 < x_2$ and x_1 is greater than or equal to 2. In other words, the second atomic expression will be true if $(b + 2a)/3 \geq 2$, or equivalently, $b + 2a \geq 6$. Thus, instead of predicate (3.2), we may work with the following predicate:

$not(b - a \leq e)\ and\ b + 2a \geq 6$

$and\ 2(b - a)/3 \leq e.$

By removing the *not* connective as explained before we obtain

$b - a > e\ and\ b + 2a \geq 6$

$and\ 2(b - a)/3 \leq e.$

Next, by (4.4), we can restate this predicate in terms of equalities as follows:

$$(\exists x)_{>0}(x = b - a - e)$$
and $\quad (\exists y)_{\geq 0}(y = b + 2a - 6)$
and $\quad (\exists z)_{\geq 0}(z = e - 2(b - a)/3).$

We use different variables (which are quantified) for each atomic expression because then the above logical expression can be readily rewritten into its so-called *prenex normal form* [12].

$$(\exists x)_{>0}(\exists y)_{\geq 0}(\exists z)_{\geq 0}(x = b - a - e$$
and $\quad y = b + 2a - 6$
and $\quad z = e - 2(b - a)/3). \quad (4.5)$

The three equations in (4.5) are indeterminate because there are more than three variables involved. Therefore, we cannot directly obtain the desired assignment by solving the equations. However, we can combine these three equations to form a new equation in such a way that the number of variables involved in the new equation will be minimal. This can be accomplished by using the same techniques we use in solving simultaneous equations. In the present example, we can combine the three equations to yield

$(\exists x)_{>0}(\exists y)_{\geq 0}(\exists z)_{\geq 0}(3x$
$\quad - y + 3z = 6 - 3a) \quad (4.6)$

As indicated in the above expression, the requirements on the assignments to x, y, and z are that $x > 0$, $y \geq 0$, and $z \geq 0$. So let us begin by making the following assignments:

$$x \leftarrow 0.1, \quad y \leftarrow 0, \quad z \leftarrow 0.$$

Then (4.6) can be satisfied by letting

$$a \leftarrow 1.9.$$

To satisfy the second atomic expression in (4.5) we must have $0 = b + 2 \times 1.9 - 6 = b - 2.2$, i.e., we have to make the assignment:

$$b \leftarrow 2.2.$$

Finally, the first and the third atomic expression can be satisfied by letting

$$e \leftarrow 0.2.$$

In summary, predicate (3.2) can be satisfied by the following assignment:

$$a \leftarrow 1.9, \quad b \leftarrow 2.2, \quad e \leftarrow 0.2. \quad (4.7)$$

Similarly we find that path predciate (3.1) can be satisfied by the following assignment:

$$a \leftarrow 0, \quad b \leftarrow 0.5, \quad e \leftarrow 1/3. \quad (4.8)$$

Thus the assignments (4.7) and (4.8) constitute a set of test cases that will test the program given in Figure 1 minimally thorough.

Having found the desired set of test cases, the question now is: what kind of test result will be produced if the program is correct, and what kind of abnormality may be observed if the program is in error? To fix the idea, let us consider the case in which we test the program shown in Figure 1 by using test case (4.8). If the program is correct, we should obtain as the test result max = 0.5 − δ, where δ is the error less than or equal to e/2 = 1/6. If the program is in error, say, the assignment statement p := a + w/3 is somehow mistakenly written as p := a − w/3, then the algorithm will not converge. Consequently, we have an infinite loop in the program and execution will not terminate. It is interesting to see that if the logical expression (associated with the second decision box in Figure 1) is erroneously written as v < u instead of u < v, then variable max will contain the abscissa at which f(x) assumes the minimum value (instead of the maximum). In other words, we will obtain as the test result max = δ, i.e., max is within the distance δ = e/2 = 1/6 from a = 0, which clearly is not a correct answer, as one can see from the function plot.

Although the presence of the two types of error mentioned above will be clearly reflected in the test results, we would like to emphasize here again that constructing a minimally thorough test is not sufficient to warrant detection of all possible programming errors. Here is another good example attesting to this. Suppose the assignment statement a := p is mistakenly written as a := q. It is easy to see that the program will produce a correct result for the test case (4.7), because this statement will not be executed, assuming that f(x) is monotonously decreasing fo $x \geq 2$. Neither will the presence of this error be clearly reflected in the test result using test case (4.8). The reader should be able to verify that we still will obtain as the result max = 0.5 − δ for some δ > 1/6, although the magnitude of error δ could be smaller than that produced in the absence of this programming error.

CONCLUDING REMARKS

For the sake of clarity in presentation, we have purposely simplified the problems in program testing and used somewhat contrived examples to illustrate the ideas involved in solving the problems. This might have given the reader the impression that we have relatively simple and straightforward solutions to these problems. Therefore, in concluding this article it is deemed imperative for us to point out that the problems are actually much more complicated than we have described in the preceding sections. For instance, the problem of test-case generation is in general unsolvable in the sense that there does not exist a single algorithm that can be used to find assignments to input variables that will satisfy any given path predicate, or even to determine its satisfiability.

All that we can do at this stage of development is to identify a solvable subset of problems and then develop effective methods for solving these problems. Even for those programs or parts of a program that we know how to handle, the process of test-case generation is in practice much more complicated than what we have described in this paper. Here are some major factors that contribute to the complexity of test-case generation.

1) Number of paths involved in a large program.

2) *Nontraversable paths in a program*: it is well known that some paths in a program may never be traversed in execution. Such paths cannot be used as the test paths, and thus must be excluded in the process of constructing the minimal covering set of paths. The fact that an untraversable path cannot be identified on the basis of the graph structure of the flowchart but rather by the fact that it has an unsatisfiable path predicate, greatly complicates the problem. To facilitate understanding this important problem, let us consider the example program shown in Figure 4. This program computes x^y by a binary decomposition of y for integer $y \geq 0$. By inspection we see that every branch is on some path in the set given below:

$$\{abcdegh,\ abcfgh\}$$

and thus is a candidate minimal covering set for test-case construction. By an application of the method described in Section 3 we find that the path predicates for these two paths are:

$not(y = 0)$ *and* $y \bmod 2 = 1$ *and* $y \div 2 = 0$

and

$not(y = 0)$ *and* $not(y \bmod 2 = 1)$
$$\text{and } y \div 2 = 0,$$

respectively. Some reflection will show that the first path predicate can be satisfied by letting $y = 1$, but the second path predicate cannot be satisfied by any non-negative integer! This indicates that the second path abcfgh cannot be traversed at all. Our solution to this problem at the present is to construct the minimal covering set solely based on the graph structure of the flowchart, and then appropriately replace any member path which is found to be associated with an unsatisfiable path predicate. For example, path abcfgh in the above example can be replaced by path abcfgcdegh, whose path predicate can be satisfied by letting $y = 2$.

3) *Loop structure in a program*: the process of constructing a minimal covering set of paths can be greatly simplified if we can use the fact that a loop needs to be iterated only once in order to have every branch traversed at least once. Unfortunately, some loops in a program must be iterated for a constant number (greater than one) of times. A loop formed by a statement of the form: "*for* $i = 1$ *step* 2 *until* 15 *do* S;" is an example. Thus if we construct a test path by having such a loop traversed once, we will find the associated path predicate unsatisfiable. This necessitates a more elaborate path-finding method that has a provision to identify such a loop. Also, if a path consists of a loop that needs to be iterated for a great many number of times, then the associated path predicate will be a very long expression unless a special notational convention is used in the process.

4) *Subscripted variables*: to see what kind of problem the use of subscripted variables may introduce, let us consider the predicate: $a[i + 1] = a[j]$ as an example. This predicate can be satisfied by letting $i + 1 = j$ or by assigning the same value to $a[i + 1]$ and $a[j]$. Thus a degree of indeterminancy is added to the process of finding an assignment that satisfies a predicate.

5) *Block structure and call of procedure or subroutine*: if the program is written in a language that permits the use of block structures (such as ALGOL), or if it contains a procedure (subroutine) call, then we need to be able to tell whether a given variable is local or global. Since the same identifier can be used to denote two distinct variables in the same program, we must keep track of the scopes in which the variables are defined. We also need to know whether an identifier stands for a "call by name" or a "call by value" parameter in order to construct a path predicate correctly.

6) *Path predicates involving floating-point variables*: the truth values of such predicates may become unpredictable.

The complicating factors mentioned above by no means exhaust the list. By trying to apply the test-case generation procedure described in the preceding sections to practical problems, the reader will certainly encounter many other problems. Treatments of some such problems may be found in [13–18], in addition to the references cited previously. Reference [18] is particularly significant in that it contains many works that reflect the state of the art in program testing.

Manually carrying out the process of test-case generation is a very tedious, time consuming, and error-prone matter. Considering the fact that more than 50% of the manhours used in today's software industry are spent in program testing, it should be of great economic worth to develop computer-aided or fully automated systems for test-case generation. In fact, a number of such systems are known to be in existence or in the process of being developed (see, e.g., [5, 6, 9, 19]). At least one system [19] is already available on the market and the experience with that system should be of interest to the reader. Specifically, "Structurally based automatic program testing," by E. Miller, et al. [8] shows:

- Most real-life FORTRAN programs can be tested minimally thorough with a relatively small number of test cases. Very roughly, the number of tests is less than or equal to about 10% of the number of FORTRAN lines in the program.
- That in using the program instrumentation method, a test case conceived to execute a particular decision-to-decision path frequently causes a large number of other decision-to-decision paths to be traversed.
- The automated program testing system appears to work easily and well, and contributes significantly to the improvement of software quality.

It is observed that, perhaps because of the enormous developmental cost involved, present interest in automated program-testing tools is found mainly among people with space and military applications. However, the use of such tools may in time become prevalent, particularly in applications where reliability is of primary concern.

It is true that program testing can only be used to detect the presence of bugs, but not to show their absence, as aptly observed by Dijkstra [2]. Nevertheless, it is a practical technique commonly used in the industry. In the absence of a practical method that can be used to show a program as error-free, it should be worth the effort to improve our ability to discover bugs through program testing.

ACKNOWLEDGMENTS

The author is greatly indebted to Raymond T. Yeh and Peter J. Denning for their invaluable suggestions and encouragements. Peter Denning has devoted so much of his time to helping me revise several drafts of this article that he is virtually a co-author of this tutorial. During the Summer of 1973 the author was fortunate to have the opportunity to work on the program-testing problems at NASA Johnson Space Center and had many fruitful discussions on the subject with Mary Ann Goodwin. This was made possible through the support of the NASA-ASEE Summer Faculty Research Fellowship Program.

REFERENCES

[1] ELSPAS, B. ET AL., "An assessment of techniques for proving program correctness," *Computing Surveys*, **4**, 2 (June 1972), 97–147.

[2] DAHL, O.-J. ET AL., *Structured programming*, Academic Press, London and New York, 1972.

[3] BERGE, C., *Theory of graphs and its applications*, John Wiley & Sons, New York, 1962.

[4] HARARY, F., *Graph theory*, Addison-Wesley, Reading, Mass., 1969.

[5] KRAUSE, K. W., ET AL., "Optimal software test planning through automated network analysis," *Proc. 1973 IEEE Symposium on Computer Software Reliability*, New York, April–May 1973.

[6] HOWDEN, W. E., "Methodology for the generation of program test data," *IEEE Transactions on Computers*, **C-24**, 5 (May 1975), 554–560.

[7] *Fortran automated verification system Level 1 —user's guide*, Program Validation Project, General Research Corp., October 1974.

[8] MILLER, E. F., ET AL. "Structurally based automatic program testing," presented at EASCON-74, Washington, D.C., October 1974.

[9] CLARKE, L., "A system to generate test data and symbolically execute programs," Tech. Report #CU-CS-060-75, Dept. Computer Science, University of Colorado, Boulder, February 1975.

[10] SLOANE, N. J. A., "On finding the paths through a network," *Bell System Tech. J.*, **51**, 2 (February 1972).

[11] HOFFMAN, R. H., *Automated verification system user's guide*, TRW Note No. 72-FMT-891, 1972.

[12] COPI, I. M., *Symbolic logic*, Macmillan, New York, 1965.

[13] MILLER, E. F.; AND MELTON, R. A., "Automated generation of testcase datasets," *Proc. 1975 Internatl. Conf. on Reliable Soft-*

ware, Los Angeles, Calif., April 1975. IEEE Cat. No. 75CH0940-7CSR.

[14] HETZEL, W. C., *Program test methods*, Prentice-Hall, Englewood Cliffs, N. J., 1972.

[15] RAMAMOORTHY, C. V., ET AL., "Design and construction of an automated software evaluation system," *Proc. 1973 IEEE Symposium on Computer Software Reliability*, New York, April–May 1973.

[16] PAIGE, M. R.; AND BALKOVICH, E. E., "On testing programs," *Proc. 1973 IEEE Symposium on Computer Software Reliability*, New York, April–May 1973.

[17] OSTERWEIL, L. J.; AND FOSDICK, L. D., "Data flow analysis as an aide in documentation, assertion generation, validation, and error detection," Tech. Report #CU-CS-055-74, Dept. Computer Science, University of Colorado, Boulder, September 1974.

[18] *Proc. 1975 Internatl. Conf. on Reliable Software*, Los Angeles, Calif., April 1975. IEEE Cat. No. 75CH0940-7CSR.

[19] *Fortran automated verification system Level 1 —system summary*, Program Validation Project, General Research Corp., October 1974.

STRUCTURAL TECHNIQUES OF PROGRAM VALIDATION

Edward F. Miller, Jr., Michael R. Paige, Jeoffrey P. Benson and William R. Wisehart

Program Validation Project
General Research Corporation
Santa Barbara, California 93111

ABSTRACT

A structural basis for the formulation of testcases for given computer programs has been found to be an effective and efficient strategy. An existing automated program validation system employs these techniques with good success in minimizing the number of testcases required; this same system permits automatic identification of testcases in a high proportion of instances. Research aimed at fully automating the testcase generation process continues.

INTRODUCTION

The technology for reliability enhancement of computer programs is undergoing significant advancement at the present time. A principal aim of these research activities is to provide practical yet theoretically sound means to increase the effective reliability of computer software in the near term. Program validation, a part of this effort, deals with the following issue: What means can be found which can show that computer programs validly represent the intentions of their authors? When cast into practical terms, the answer to this question revolves around the difficult problem of providing for exhaustive testing of computer software.

It would be desirable if techniques existed for software testing as powerful as those for hardware testing.[1] It is easy to appreciate that computer software represents a significantly different problem than hardware, in terms of overall testing difficulty. A computer program is considered to have been tested if "all of the statements have been executed at least once," to use one of several possible definitions. This idea translates, at least on the unit-test level, into a requirement for a set of testcases which "touches" each statement in the program; after execution of each program with its set of testcases, the program is deemed "tested." It is possible, however, that all statements can have been exercised without having tried some important facets of the program.

A somewhat stronger view of "testing" is the following: "a program is considered tested when every statement in the program has been exercised at least once, and when every possible outcome of each program predicate (decision statement) has occurred at least once." This stronger definition of testing has the advantage that not only the computational but also the control features of the program will have been exercised. Naturally, this form of testing is somewhat more difficult to achieve.

It is easy to show that the total number of possible program flows, even for a rudimentary program (but one with some form of iteration), is exceedingly large, or even infinite.[2] Even when "loops" are counted only once, it is still possible for relatively innocuous programs to possess a million or more potential program flows. Before exhaustive testing can be achieved (where we take "exhaustive" to mean the strong definition given above), a means must be found to overcome the basically combinatorial aspects of program structure. Certain techniques from graph theory, combined with algorithms developed by the authors, provide that basis.[3,5]

DECISION-TO-DECISION PATHS

Program flow is modeled by constructing a directed graph which corresponds to each decision-to-decision path, or DD path, within the program. A DD path consists of the selection of the outcome of a predicate combined with the resulting sequence of other program statements up to the evaluation of the next sequential predicate, but excluding its use in subsequent alteration of program flow. Once these DD paths are constructed, they form the target for program testing, according to the following Lemma:

> LEMMA: A set of tests which collectively exercise each DD path at least once exercises each statement in the program at least once, and exercises each predicate in the program through all its possible outcomes.

The testing objective becomes, therefore, to exhaust the set of DD paths and, thereby, to exhaustively test the program. The sequences of DD paths which can occur are, of course, specifically controlled by the nature of the control structure of the program from which they arose. The next task is to determine the set of structurally legal DD paths and, at the same time, to discover the relationships between these sets.

ITERATION STRUCTURE IDENTIFICATION

The natural flow of a computer program is to have a series of selections between alternative actions combined with iteration of certain selected actions. In fact, it can be shown that all computer programs can be constructed using only logical selection and iteration statements.[4] If possible, this natural feature of program organization should be taken into account when designing testcase sequences.

A collection of directed graph reduction algorithms has been developed which performs the computations alluded to above.[5] The input to this set of algorithms is the set of DD paths present in the program (these DD paths are identified automatically); the result of the operation of the algorithms is the generation of a set of "level-i" paths, which have the following properties:

1. A level-0 path leads from the entrance of the program to the output without employing any DD path more than once. In effect, the level-0 paths correspond to the "fall

Reprinted from *Digest of Papers, COMPCON Spring 74*, pp. 161-164.
Copyright © 1974 by The Institute of Electrical and Electronics Engineers, Inc.

through" conditions extant in the program spine.

2. A level-i path, i > 0 , leads from an alternative predicate outcome along some level-(i-1) path, through a set of DD paths not present on any lower level path, and terminates on the level-(i-1) path at a point earlier than the original (i.e., departing) DD path. A level-i path, i > 0 , represents iteration "over" a level-(i-1) path.

Typical computer programs contain only a few levels of iteration; the algorithms identify all of these automatically, and, in addition, identify the unique predecessors for each level-i path. The collection of such level-i paths forms a "tree" because of the precise ancestry relationships present. This tree is used as the basis for efficient organization of the search for meaningful testcases for a program.

LEVEL-I PATH TREE

Once the level-i paths have been identified, the tree indicating their structure can be drawn. The tree is rooted in the program graph, and consists of a number of branches. The most interesting branches are the ones which have no successors; i.e., the terminal-branch level-i paths. The following theorem can be proved:[5]

THEOREM: If a set of testcases traverses the DD paths which exist on the set of terminal-branch level-i paths for a program at least once, then the set of testcases exercises every DD path at least once.

The implication of this theorem is as follows: because terminal-branch level-i paths represent the "deepest buried" iteration structure of the computer program, testing the statements that lie at those locations assures the testing of the remainder of the program. For example, consider the triple iteration:

```
DO 10 I = 1, I1
     DO 10 J = 1, J1
          DO 10 K = 1, K1
               <action-statement>
10 CONTINUE
```

In this program fragment, the <action-statement> lies on a level-2 path residing on a terminal branch of the corresponding level-i path tree. Testing this <action-statement> at least once also tests the remainder of the program fragment. Our experience has been that this principle--i.e., attempting testing at the highest iteration level--holds true in the overwhelming majority of practical cases.

DETAILED EXAMPLE

The concepts discussed above are best understood by working a practical example in detail. The computer output described in the remainder of this section was produced by a Proprietary Software Facility called RSVP (Research Software Validation Package) which is undergoing final development at General Research Corporation.*

Figure 1 shows the RSVP listing of a FORTRAN

```
GRC PROPRIETARY PROGRAM PACKAGE -- RSVP/SOFTOOL

STATEMENTS FOR MODULE <ALGPOL>......

   (P)   (S)   NO.    LABEL STATEMENT...
------------------------------------------------------------------------------------
[  1]           1           PROGRAM ALGPOL
                2           INTEGER BLANK , RPAREN , LPAREN , PLUS , MINUS , ASTRSK , SLASH
                3           DATA BLANK , LPAREN , RPAREN , PLUS , MINUS , ASTRSK , SLASH / 1H  , 1H( , 1H) ,
                          * 1H+ , 1H- , 1H* , 1H/ /
                4           INTEGER SOURCE ( 80 ) , OPSTCK ( 80 ) , POLISH ( 80 )
                5           INTEGER SHIER ( 80 ) , OHIER ( 80 )
[  2]           6     1     CONTINUE
[  3]           7           DO 85 L = 1 , 80
[  4]           8           SHIER ( L ) = 0
[  5]           9           OHIER ( L ) = 0
[  6]          10           OPSTCK ( L ) = BLANK
[  7]          11           POLISH ( L ) = BLANK
[  8]          12    85     CONTINUE
[  9]          13           READ ( 5 , 10 ) SOURCE
               14    10     FORMAT (80A1)
[ 10]          15           L = 1
[ 11,  12]     16   101     IF ( SOURCE ( L ) .EQ. BLANK ) GOTO 200
[ 13,  14]     17           IF ( SOURCE ( L ) .EQ. LPAREN ) GOTO 201
[ 15,  16]     18           IF ( SOURCE ( L ) .EQ. RPAREN ) GOTO 202
[ 17,  18]     19           IF ( SOURCE ( L ) .EQ. PLUS .OR. SOURCE ( L ) .EQ. MINUS ) GOTO 203
[ 19,  20]     20           IF ( SOURCE ( L ) .EQ. ASTRSK .OR. SOURCE ( L ) .EQ. SLASH ) GOTO 204
[ 21]          21           SHIER ( L ) = 0
[ 22]          22           GOTO 210
[ 23]          23   201     SHIER ( L ) = 1
[ 24]          24           GOTO 210
[ 25]          25   202     SHIER ( L ) = 2
[ 26]          26           GOTO 210
[ 27]          27   203     SHIER ( L ) = 3
[ 28]          28           GOTO 210
[ 29]          29   204     SHIER ( L ) = 4
[ 30]          30   210     L = L + 1
[ 31]          31           GOTO 101
[ 32]          32   200     N = L - 1
[ 33,  34]     33           IF ( N .EQ. 0 ) GOTO 99999
[ 35]          34           SHIER ( N + 1 ) = 0
[ 36]          35           OHIER ( 1 ) = - 1
[ 37]          36           I = 1
[ 38]          37           J = 2
[ 39]          38           K = 1
[ 40,  41]     39  1000     IF ( SHIER ( I ) .EQ. 0 ) GOTO 1100
[ 42,  43]     40           IF ( SHIER ( I ) .EQ. 2 ) GOTO 1050
[ 44]          41           OPSTCK ( J ) = SOURCE ( I )
[ 45]          42           OHIER ( J ) = SHIER ( I )
[ 46]          43           I = I + 1
[ 47]          44           J = J + 1
[ 48]          45           GOTO 1000
[ 49]          46  1050     I = I + 1
[ 50]          47           J = J - 1
[ 51]          48           GOTO 1150
[ 52]          49  1100     POLISH ( K ) = SOURCE ( I )
[ 53]          50           I = I + 1
[ 54]          51           K = K + 1
[ 55,  56]     52  1150     IF ( OHIER ( J - 1 ) .GE. SHIER ( I ) ) GOTO 1160
[ 57,  58]     53           IF ( I .EQ. N + 1 ) GOTO 1200
[ 59]          54           GOTO 1000
[ 60]          55  1160     POLISH ( K ) = OPSTCK ( J - 1 )
[ 61]          56           K = K + 1
[ 62]          57           J = J - 1
[ 63]          58           GOTO 1150
[ 64]          59  1200     CONTINUE
[ 65]          60           WRITE ( 6 , 11 ) POLISH
               61    11     FORMAT (1X, 80A1)
[ 66]          62           GOTO 1
[ 67]          63 99999     STOP
[ 68]          64           END
------------------------------------------------------------------------------------
```

Figure 1. RSVP Printout of Source Text of ALGPOL

program called ALGPOL. ALGPOL analyzes an "infix" or algebraic format expression involving single letters and arithmetic operations and produces the Postfix representation of the string.

Directed graph node numbers are supplied automatically, as shown in the leftmost columns. "P" stands for the primary node number, and "S" stands for the secondary node number (which is needed for all occurrences of the FORTRAN logical IF statement). The assigned statement numbers and the program's statement labels are also shown to the left of the individual statement texts.

The digraph is produced by generating arc connections between nodes according to the potential program flow within the program. In ALGPOL there are 76 arcs (not shown). Because certain of the resulting node sequences always occur in the same order, these are removed. What results is the set of DD paths for this program; in ALGPOL there are 23 DD paths. The set of DD paths, expressed in terms of the nodes within the program text, is illustrated in Figure 2. Each "B → E" sequence represents one DD path, and each "S" indicate a DD path which begins and ends on the same node.

*More detailed information on the characteristics of the RSVP is available from the authors.

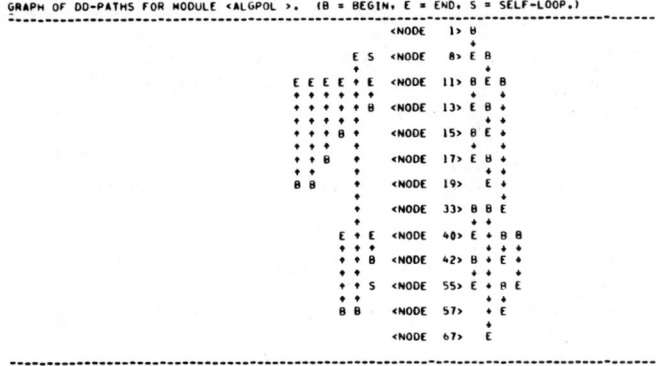

Figure 2. DD Paths for ALGPOL

The next step in processing is the production of the set of level-i paths; these sets are stored by the computer as sequences of bits representing ownership by a level-i path of a particular DD path. Table 1 shows the resulting level-i path sets and some of their properties. It is important to note that the level-1 paths deal with iteration "over" the level-0 paths, as indicated before.

The level-i path tree for ALGPOL is shown in Figure 3. The root of the tree leads to a single level-0 path; the other level-i paths, expressed in terms of the numbers assigned in Table 1, are shown in their dependence relationships with that path and each other.

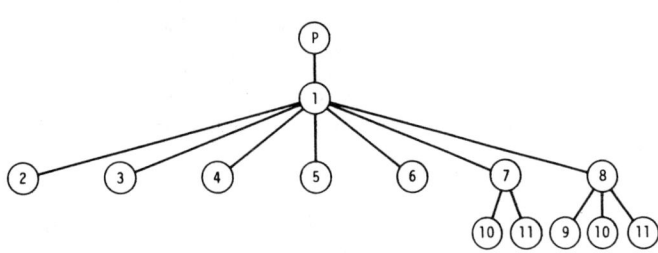

Figure 3. Level-i Path Tree for ALGPOL

TABLE 1

COLLECTION OF DD PATHS WHICH MAKE UP EACH LEVEL-i PATH

LEVEL-i PATH NO.	i =	DD PATHS WHICH BELONG TO IT	INITIAL NODE	TERMINAL NODE
1	0	1, 3, 4, 14	1	34
2	1	2	8	8
3	1	5, 6	11	11
4	1	5, 7, 8	11	11
5	1	5, 7, 9, 10	11	11
6	1	15, 16, 21, 22	33	8
7	1	5, 7, 9, 11, (12|13)	11	11
8	1	15, 17, 18, 21, 22	33	8
9	2	19	42	40
10	2	20	55	55
11	2	23	57	40

Typical executions of the program must occur along the structural lines indicated in the level-i path tree. That is, execution begins (by activation of the program) at "P" and then from the level-i path to level-i path only according to the connections shown in Figure 3. It may be possible that all level-i paths can be executed as the result of a single invocation, but this is a matter which can (at present) be determined only manually. Because a program's flow structure can become very complicated, it is important to provide automatic analyses which give "advice" to the user about how to achieve flow along a specified path or paths.

To illustrate this process, let us consider the simplest flow possible in the program ALGPOL. Figure 4 shows the program texts for level-i Path No. 1; this happens to be a level-0 path. Figure 5 shows the corresponding set of DD paths. Suppose we are interested in developing a testcase for one of the higher level paths of ALGPOL, level-i Path No. 2, for example. (The same techniques apply to all the others, it is important to note.) Figure 6 shows the set of statements on level-i Path No. 2. It should be clear from these machine-generated outputs that this particular sequence of execution can be obtained by having an input card which contains a <blank> in the first position, i.e., SOURCE(1) .EQ. BLANK. This particular input-space setting causes execution around level-0 Path No. 1 and level-1 Path No. 2. It is important that the reader study the machine-generated output to understand the way in which a human user can make the necessary deduction. The general problem of automatic testcase generation is, of course, recursively unsolvable.[2] Heuristic procedures can, however, result in automatic testcase generation in a high proportion of instances, and in particular, in a majority of practical testcase generation problems. Detailed discussions of these procedures and their effectiveness will be reported in a later paper.[6]

Figure 4. Statement Sequence for Level-i Path No. 1, with Analysis

```
GRC PROPRIETARY PROGRAM PACKAGE -- RSVP/SOFTOOL
LEVEL-1 PATH (PATH CLASS) NO.   1, WITH LEADERS OF DD-PATH GROUPS, AS FOLLOWS...
      1     3     4    14
NUMBER OF DISTINCT FLOWS REPRESENTED BY THIS DD-PATH SET IS =         1
GRAPH OF DD-PATHS FOR MODULE <ALGPOL>.  (B = BEGIN, E = END, S = SELF-LOOP.)
-----------------------------------------------------------------
                                    <NODE   1>  B
                                              .
                                    <NODE   8>  E  B
                                              .
                                    <NODE  11>  B  E
                                              .
                                    <NODE  13>  .
                                    <NODE  15>  .
                                    <NODE  17>  .
                                    <NODE  19>  .
                                    <NODE  33>  E  B
                                              .
                                    <NODE  40>  .
                                    <NODE  42>  .
                                    <NODE  55>  .
                                    <NODE  57>  .
                                    <NODE  67>  E
-----------------------------------------------------------------
```

Figure 5. Set of DD Paths on Path of Figure 6

```
GRC PROPRIETARY PROGRAM PACKAGE -- RSVP/SOFTOOL
PATH NO.    2  (LEVEL-1 PATH NO. 1)...

DD-PATH LIST IN EXECUTION ORDER (NEGATIVE IMPLIES LEADER OF A PARALLEL DD-PATH SET)...
     2
COMPOSITE PREDICATE...
( <DO-LOOP, 85 REPEAT> )
STATEMENT TEXT(S) IN ORDER OF EXECUTION...
-----------------------------------------------------------------
  (  8)      12     85    CONTINUE
  (  3)       7           DO 85 L = 1 , 80
  (  4)       8           SHIER ( L ) = 0
  (  5)       9           OHIER ( L ) = 0
  (  6)      10           OPSTCK ( L ) = BLANK
  (  7)      11           POLISH ( L ) = BLANK
-----------------------------------------------------------------
THESE VARIABLES ARE SET ALONG PATH AND ALSO USED IN SOME PATH PREDICATE...
**NONE**

THESE VARIABLES/CONSTANTS WERE    READ    ALONG THIS PATH...
    L         0          BLANK

THESE VARIABLES/CONSTANTS WERE    SET     ALONG THIS PATH...
    L         SHIER      OHIER      OPSTCK     POLISH

THESE VARIABLES/CONSTANTS WERE IN PREDS. ALONG THIS PATH...
**NONE**
```

Figure 6. Statement Sequence for Level-1 Path No. 2, with Analysis

REFERENCES

1. H. Y. Chang, E. G. Manning, and G. Metze, <u>Fault Diagnosis of Digital Systems</u>, Wiley-Interscience, 1970.

2. E. F. Miller, Jr., <u>A Survey of Major Techniques of Program Validation</u>, General Research Corporation, RM-1731, October 1972.

3. M. R. Paige and J. P. Benson, <u>Software Probes-- A Technique for Measuring Program Testedness</u>, General Research Corporation, TM-1712, May 1973.

4. C. Bohm and G. Jacopini, "Flow Diagrams, Turing Machines, and Languages with Only Two Formation Rules," <u>C. ACM</u>, Vol. 9, No. 5, May 1966, pp 366-371.

5. M. R. Paige, <u>A Methodology for Generating Paths in a Directed Graph</u>, General Research Corporation IM-1816, November 1973.

6. E. F. Miller, M. R. Paige, and J. P. Benson, <u>Heuristic Techniques for Automatic Testcase Generation.</u> (To Appear)

Automatic Software Test Drivers

David J. Panzl
General Electric Co.

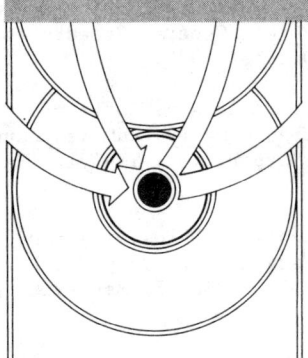

Typical testing activities may involve many hundreds of tests. An automatic software test driver assists the tester by managing all of the test data, and automatically running the tests. Savings during regression testing can be significant.

The execution of software test cases and the verification of test results may be performed automatically by a new type of program called an automatic software test driver. When an automatic test driver is used, a formal test procedure is coded in a special test language. The test procedure takes the place of the test data and test setup instructions of conventional testing and consists of one or more test cases, each of which contains input data values and model test outputs. An automatic software test driver applies a test procedure to all or part of a target program and executes the target program once for each test case specified in the test procedure. On each execution the automatic test driver supplies the target program with the specified inputs and captures the target program's outputs and compares them with the model outputs specified in the test procedure.

When the target program accepts all its inputs, executes to completion, and generates the correct outputs, a test case is said to have been executed successfully. When the target program's outputs do not match the model outputs specified in the test procedure, the test case is said to have failed. All test-case results are reported to the user in a brief test-execution report.

The specific goals of automatic software test drivers and formal test procedures are to provide a standard notation for specifying software tests, to provide a standard setup for executing software tests, to automate the verification of test results, and to eliminate the need for writing separate drivers and stubs for module and subsystem testing.

Regression testing. The capability of retaining software test cases in a form that may be reused by someone other than the original test designer is very useful for the following reason. It is widely agreed that the majority of errors appearing in production software do not come from the original implementation, but rather are unintended side effects of post-release program modifications. A good defense against this problem is for the original implementors of a computer program to design thorough test procedures that initially verify the correctness of the program and to retain these test procedures throughout the program's life cycle. Whenever the program is subsequently modified, all of the previous test procedures may be rerun to verify that the changes had only the local effects intended. This is known as regression testing.

Under the present technology of software testing, effective regression testing is seldom possible. Test cases usually consist of samples of input data in a variety of different formats and storage media. Complicated procedures are frequently required to execute test cases and nearly always, only the test designer can verify that the results of executing the test cases are correct. For these reasons, software tests are most frequently designed as one-time tests and discarded immediately.

Automatic software test drivers facilitate the retention of software tests for subsequent use by replacing the test data of conventional testing with a single test procedure written in a formal test language. Since formal test procedures are completely self-contained, they may be stored easily. Complex test-execution instructions are never required and

> The Automated Unit Test system operates on object modules independently of the target-program language.

Reprinted from *Computer*, April 1978, pp. 44-50. Copyright © by The Institute of Electrical and Electronics Engineers, Inc.

the results of test executions are verified automatically.

Automatic software test drivers also simplify module and subsystem testing. A test procedure may by applied to either an entire target program or any arbitrary group of one or more modules of the target program. The automatic test driver serves the function of conventional driver programs and also simulates lower-level subprograms called by the target program, but not available at the time of testing. Similarly, some automatic test drivers simulate I/O devices referenced by the target program.

Three types. This article describes three types of automatic software test drivers. The first type operates on object modules and is independent of the language in which the target program was coded. The Automated Unit Test system, developed at IBM, is an example of this type. The second type operates on source code and therefore can specify software tests based on the internal structure of the target program. This type is highly dependent on the language in which the target program is coded. The Fortran Test Procedure Language (TPL/F) testing system developed by General Electric is an example of this type. The third type, TPL/2.0, featuring automatic assistance in the production and revision of test procedures, is currently under development at the General Electric Research and Development Center.

Object-level test specification

The Automated Unit Test (AUT) system developed at IBM[1] is illustrated in Figure 1. A test procedure coded in the Module Interface Language—Specific (MIL-S) is applied to a single object module of the target program. The target program object module may contain a single subprogram, multiple subprograms, or the entire target program. The result of executing a MIL-S test procedure is a test-execution report listing errors in the target program's outputs.

Sample target module. The use of AUT is illustrated by a simple test procedure for the Fortran target module of Figure 2. The target module, SUB1, is a subroutine and needs to be called by a higher level module for execution. SUB1 also invokes a lower level subroutine, SUB6, which is not under test and must be simulated when testing SUB1. On each entry to SUB1, SUB6 is called once and one record is written on logical unit 10.

MIL-S test language. A simple test procedure coded in the MIL-S test language is illustrated in Figures 3 and 4. Figure 3 contains the test procedure for SUB1 and Figure 4 contains the test procedure for the missing SUB6 which is used to simulate SUB6.

The SUB1 test procedure in Figure 3 contains three separate test cases whose input data sets are

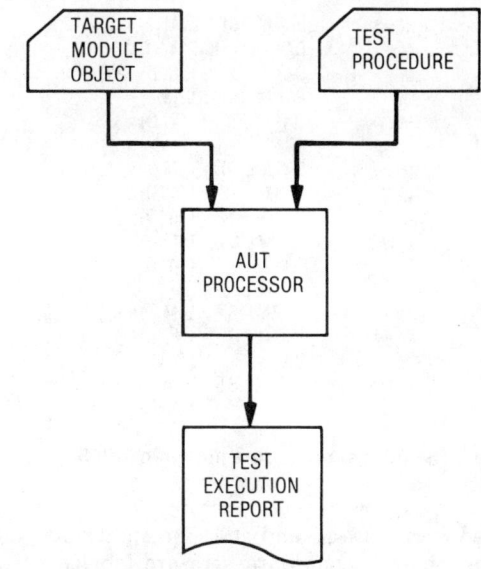

Figure 1. The Automated Unit Test processor.

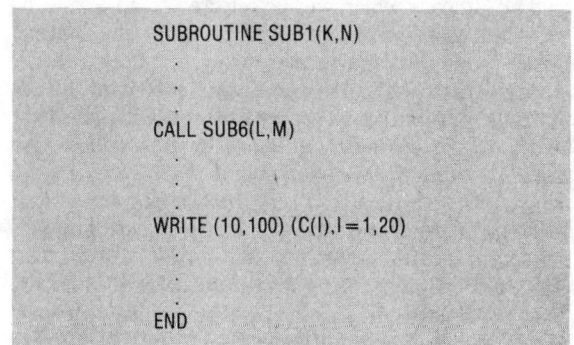

Figure 2. A sample target module.

IN01	PARMLIST	K,N
K	DATA	('2'D)
N	DATA	('3'D)
SUB6	CALL	IN1
OUT01	PARMLIST	K,N
K	DATA	('7'D)
N	DATA	('9'D)
IN02	PARMLIST	K,N
K	DATA	('1'D)
N	DATA	('6'D)
SUB6	CALL	IN2
OUT02	PARMLIST	K,N
K	DATA	('8'D)
N	DATA	('2'D)
IN03	PARMLIST	K,N
K	DATA	('3'D)
N	DATA	('6'D)
SUB6	CALL	IN3
OUT03	PARMLIST	K,N
K	DATA	('7'D)
N	DATA	('2'D)

Figure 3. SUB1 test procedure coded in the MIL-S test language.

```
IN1     PARMLIST    L,M
L       DATA        ('4'D)
M       DATA        ('8'D)
OUT1    PARMLIST    L,M
M       DATA        ('7'D)

IN2     PARMLIST    L,M
L       DATA        ('1'D)
M       DATA        ('9'D)
OUT2    PARMLIST    L,M
M       DATA        ('4'D)

IN3     PARMLIST    L,M
L       DATA        ('7'D)
M       DATA        ('1'D)
OUT3    PARMLIST    L,M
M       DATA        ('8'D)
```

Figure 4. SUB6 test procedure coded in MIL-S.

labeled IN01, IN02, and IN03, respectively, and whose model output data sets are labeled OUT01, OUT02, and OUT03. These data sets represent values for the arguments of SUB1. The first line of each data set indicates that the target module requires two arguments which will be referred to as K and N. The DATA statements specify input and output data values for the arguments.

Each test case causes an actual execution of the target module under the control of AUT. The first test case, for example, causes SUB1 to be called with actual argument values of 2 and 3. On return from SUB1, AUT verifies that the final argument values are 7 and 9. If this is not so, the discrepancy is reported in the test-execution report. AUT test-execution reports are essentially a listing of the test procedure with actual output values printed alongside expected values where output discrepancies occur.

The CALL statement in each of the three input data sets of Figure 3 directs AUT to intercept any execution-time calls to SUB6 and to simulate SUB6 by means of a test case from the SUB6 test procedure in Figure 4. This is done as follows.

During the first test case, when SUB1 calls SUB6, AUT takes control and verifies that the actual arguments passed by a SUB1 are 4 and 8, as specified in the first test case of Figure 4. If these values are not supplied, the discrepancy is reported in the test-execution report. In either event, AUT changes the value of the second SUB6 argument to 7 and returns control to SUB1.

The above example is a simple one and does not represent many features of the MIL-S language. It does, however, suggest the general style of software testing under the AUT system. MIL-S test procedures specify test cases in terms of the external interfaces of target-program modules. The only target-program data areas addressed by MIL-S test procedures are formal arguments, arguments passed to subprograms, and COMMON areas. Also, each test case must execute the entire target module. In other words, AUT treats the target module as a black box and has no knowledge of its internal structure.

Although AUT was one of the first automatic software test drivers developed, it has not received wide acceptance, probably due to two factors. First, the MIL-S language is a low-level language reminiscent of assembler lanuages and MIL-S test procedures tend to be lengthy. Also, MIL-S contains no facilities for modeling I/O devices and files. In the above example, outputs written by SUB1 to logical unit 10 would have to be verified by a process other than AUT.

Another object-level automatic software test driver, similar to the AUT system, is called TESTMANAGER.[2] It was developed in England by Management Systems and Programming, Ltd.

Source-level test specification

In contrast to the AUT system which operates on object modules, the Fortran Test Procedure Language (TPL/F) system developed by General Electric[3,4,5] operates on the source versions of target modules. Source-level testing offers dual advantages: (1) test cases may be specified in terms of the internal structure of the target program and (2) measures of testing thoroughness, based on the program's source representation, may be taken while a test procedure is executing. Source-level test drivers, however, are not easily generalized to test target programs coded in several different languages and the TPL/F system only operates on Fortran software.

TPL/F test language. As shown in Figure 5, a test procedure coded in the TPL/F language is applied to one or more source modules of the target program. As with AUT, the result of executing a TPL/F test procedure is a test-execution report listing errors in the target program's outputs.

Figure 6 contains the same test procedure as Figures 3 and 4 coded in the TPL/F language. The MODULES statement names the target modules (SUB1 of Figure 2) under test. This test procedure also contains three test cases, each of which requires four statements and terminates with an EXECUTE statement.

Executing a single TPL/F test case requires three steps. First, initialization code, which puts the target program in a known initial state, is executed. In the example, the first two statements of each test case are used to initialize the target program. In the first test case, they assign the values 2 and 3 to the variables K and N, respectively, of SUB1.

In the second step, the target program is executed. The form of the EXECUTE statement used in Figure 6 causes execution to begin at the first executable statement of SUB1 and terminate the first time a STOP or RETURN statement is encountered in SUB1.

Third, after the test case execution has terminated, an assertion about the final state of SUB1 is verified. In the first test case of Figure 6, the variables K

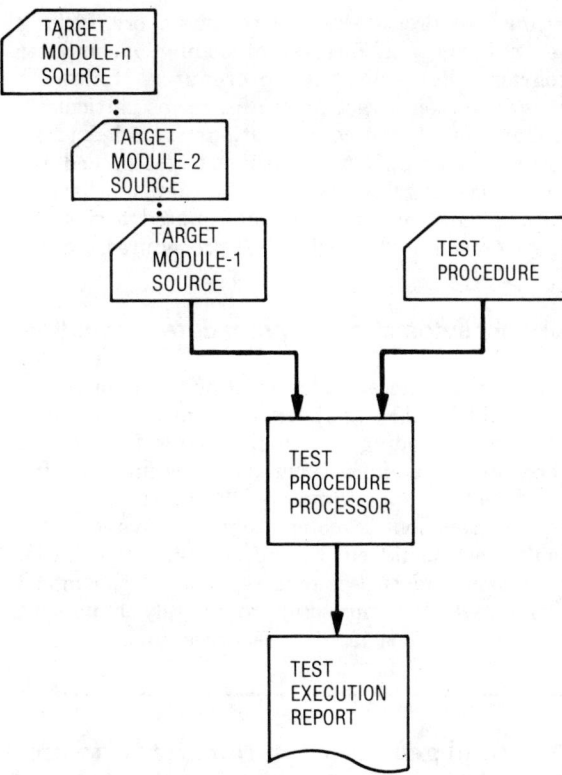

Figure 5. The TPL/F test procedure processor.

and N of SUB1 are verified to have the values 7 and 9, respectively.

In TPL/F, stub versions of missing subprograms called by the target program are coded as Fortran-like subroutines and functions embedded in the test procedure. In Figure 6, for example, a stub version of SUB6 begins at the SUBROUTINE statement and runs through the following END statement. #TEST is an integer system variable whose value always is the index of the test case currently executing. When executing under the first test case, the stub version of SUB6 verifies that arguments passed by SUB1 are 4 and 8, and sets the second argument equal to 7, on return. Should SUB1 call SUB6 with incorrect argument values, the ABORT statement would terminate the current test case (but not the test procedure) and put a diagnostic message in the test-execution report.

The five statements beginning at the I/O SIMULATOR statement and continuing through the following END statement specify an I/O simulator for logical unit 10 of the target program. An I/O simulator can supply input data to the target program in response to READ statements or verify outputs from WRITE statement in the target program. The I/O simulator of Figure 6 specifies three formatted records. The first three records written by the target program on logical unit 10 must match these values or a diagnostic will appear in the test execution report.

Test cases. Most test procedures contain more test cases than the three used in this example. A typical test procedure for a single Fortran target module of 50 to 100 statements may contain 20 to 40 test cases, depending on the complexity of the target module's control logic. Therefore, a more compact notation is usually required to represent test cases. TPL/F uses a built-in macroprocessor which allows the general form of a test case to be specified as a macro prototype with each test case represented by a single macro call. In practice, test procedures tend to contain only a small number of forms of test cases (often only one) which are invoked many times with different specific data values. Figure 7 shows the three test cases of Figure 6 as they would appear when coded as macro calls.

```
        MODULES SUB1

        I/O SIMULATOR 10
        RECORD (1) 'XXXXXXXXXXXXXXXXXXXX'
        RECORD (2) 'YYYYYYYYYYYYYYYYYYYY'
        RECORD (3) 'ZZZZZZZZZZZZZZZZZZZZ'
        END

        SUBROUTINE SUB6(I,J)
        INTEGER IN1(3),IN2(3),IOUT(3)
        DATA IN1/4,1,7/, IN2/8,9,1/, IOUT/7,4,8/
        IF (I .NE. IN1(#TEST) .OR. J .NE. IN2(#TEST)) ABORT
        J = IOUT (#TEST)
        RETURN
        END

        SUB1:K = 2
        SUB1:N = 3
        VERIFY (SUB1:K .EQ. 7 .AND. SUB1:N .EQ. 9)
        EXECUTE

        SUB1:K = 1
        SUB1:N = 6
        VERIFY (SUB1:K .EQ. 8 .AND. SUB1:N .EQ. 2)
        EXECUTE

        SUB1:K = 3
        SUB1:N = 6
        VERIFY (SUB1:K .EQ. 7 .AND. SUB1:N .EQ. 2)
        EXECUTE

        FIN
```

Figure 6. SUB1 test procedure coded in the TPL/F test language.

```
        MACRO TST(P1,P2,P3,P4)
        SUB1:K = P1
        SUB1:N = P2
        VERIFY (SUB1:K .EQ. P3 .AND. SUB1:N .EQ. P4)
        EXECUTE
        MEND

        TST(2,3,7,9)
        TST(1,6,8,2)
        TST(3,6,7,2)
```

Figure 7. The three test cases of Figure 6 recoded using a TPL/F macro definition.

Figures 8 and 9 are TPL/F test execution reports. Since the TPL/F system has access to the target program's source code, it can monitor which statements were actually executed and which branches were actually traversed while executing a test procedure. This type of information provides valuable feedback to the test designer and is generally not available with manual testing.

ALL TEST CASES SUCCEEDED

STATEMENTS EXECUTED: 100%
BRANCHES TRAVERSED: 100%

Figure 8. A successful test procedure execution report.

VERIFY FAILURE IN TEST CASE 2 AFTER TERMINATION
   (SUB1:K .EQ. 8 .AND. SUB1:N .EQ. 2)

OUTPUT ERROR ON RECORD 3 OF LUN 10 IN TEST CASE 3

STATEMENTS EXECUTED: 100%
BRANCHES TRAVERSED: 100%

Figure 9. A failed test procedure execution report.

A unique feature of the TPL/F test language is its ability to specify test cases in terms of the target program's internal structure. TPL/F test procedures may reference any variable in a target program, including local variables. Test cases may be specified which execute only part of the target program. For example, the following statement would cause a test case to begin executing at statement label 10 of SUB1 and terminate the first time either statement label 20 or 30 of SUB1 is executed.

    EXECUTE FROM SUB1:10 TO SUB1:20,SUB1:30

Target-program translator. Source-level test drivers, such as TPL/F, are much more difficult to implement than object-level test drivers, like AUT. The former must parse the language in which the target program is written. This is done by the target program translator—a very large and complicated part of a source-level test driver. Its presence makes it difficult to adapt source-level test drivers to multiple target languages since a separate target-program translator is required for each language (e.g., Fortran, Cobol). For the same reason, it may even be difficult to adapt a source-level test driver to different dialects of the same target language, such as Fortran.

Experience with the TPL/F system shows that test procedures often become lengthy and difficult to read. Also, programmers sometimes feel that writing test procedures is a tedious chore, lacking the challenge and interest of coding a computer program. Revising test procedures, following changes to their target programs, seems particularly burdensome. These considerations have led to an attempt to simplify the writing of test procedures by emphasizing brevity in the design of the test language and by providing automated assistance for generating and revising test procedures.

Partially automatic test procedure production

A second-generation automatic software test driver, TPL/2.0,[6] significantly reduces the labor required for coding and maintaining formal test procedures. The effort required for the initial coding is reduced by approximately 90 percent and subsequent revision is completely automated. This result was achieved by automating the initial generation and subsequent revision of the model outputs, which comprise approximately 90 percent of the text of most formal test procedures.

A second-generation automatic software test driver reduces initial coding labor by approximately 90 percent and completely automates revisions.

TPL/2.0 test language. The TPL/2.0 automatic software test driver, described here, is currently under development at the General Electric Corporate Research and Development Center and is a direct outgrowth of experience with the TPL/F system. The syntax of the new test language is designed so that all the data required to specify test cases appears in rectangular arrays of data elements. Each row represents a test case, and each column represents a datum required to execute the test case. Figure 10 contains the test procedure of the previous examples recoded in TPL/2.0.

In Figure 10, three test cases are represented by the four lines immediately following the TEST CASES clause. The rectangular array of data in square

---

MODULES FTN*SUB1

TEST CASES
ASSIGN(1,2) VERIFY(1,2) SUB6 VERIFY(1,2) ASSIGN(2) 10 VERIFY
[2,3,7,9,4,8,7, 'XXXXXXXXXXXXXXXXXXXX';
 1,6,8,2,1,9,4, 'YYYYYYYYYYYYYYYYYYYY';
 3,6,7,2,7,1,8, 'ZZZZZZZZZZZZZZZZZZZZ']

FIN

Figure 10. SUB1 test procedure coded in the TPL/2.0 test language.

brackets are the data required for the test cases. Each row, separated by semi-colons, is a single test case. The line beginning with the ASSIGN clause defines the meaning of the columns of the test case data array, reading from left to right. The ASSIGN (1,2) clause means that the first two columns in the data array are values to be assigned to the first two formal arguments (K and N) of SUB1, prior to beginning the test case execution. The first VERIFY (1,2) clause means that the next two columns in the data array (columns 3 and 4) represent expected final values of the first two formal arguments of SUB1, after the test case terminates. SUB6 VERIFY (1,2) ASSIGN (2) specifies how SUB6 is to be simulated when called by SUB1: namely, that columns 5 and 6 of the data array represent SUB6 argument values to be verified on entry from SUB1 and column 7 represents a data value to be assigned to the second argument of SUB6 on return to SUB1. 10 VERIFY means that the right-most column in the data array contains values for formatted records written by the target program on logical unit 10.

The TPL/2.0 system performs two distinct operations on test procedures. It executes them in the same manner as the TPL/F system (Figure 5) and performs a REVISE operation as illustrated in Figure 11.

The REVISE operation also executes a test procedure. In contrast to the EXECUTE operation, however, target-program outputs are not verified against the model outputs in the test procedure. Instead, a new test procedure is generated in which the model outputs of the original test procedure are replaced by the actual outputs from the target program. Specifically, all data values associated with VERIFY clauses in the test procedure are replaced. For example, were the REVISE operation performed on the test procedure of Figure 10, columns 3 through 6 and column 8 of the test-case data array would be replaced by actual output data values generated by the target program.

The REVISE operation has a two-fold use. First, when a program module is modified, usually all test procedures referencing the changed module must be updated. This may require adding new test cases and nearly always requires revision of the model outputs. The latter task requires by far the greater effort, since model outputs typically account for upwards of 90 percent of the text of a test procedure. This is the task automated by the REVISE operation of TPL/2.0.

It is envisioned that, when modifying a program module, the programmer will EXECUTE the previous version of the module's test procedures and verify that only the expected alterations in the module's performance occurred. The programmer will then perform the REVISE operation on the test procedure and manually inspect the new model outputs of the revised test procedure. If the generated outputs are correct, the revised test procedure will become the new current test procedure for the target module.

A second use of the REVISE operation is in the initial construction of test procedures. Using the TPL/2.0 system, a new test procedure may be drafted by specifying only input data for test cases. The REVISE operation may then be used to propose model outputs to be inspected manually and accepted or rejected by the test designer. For example, the text procedure of Figure 10 could have been drafted initially as shown in Figure 12. The REVISE operation, applied to this test procedure, would fill in the missing model outputs and exactly reproduce the test procedure of Figure 10.

That the TPL/2.0 test language substantially reduces the effort required to draft a new test procedure can be seen by comparing Figure 12 with the TPL/F version of the same test procedure in Figure 6 and the AUT version in Figures 3 and 4.

Another reason for using the REVISE operation to generate proposed model outputs is related to the fact that certain types of programs produce outputs for which exact values cannot, in practice, be pre-

Figure 11. The TPL/2.0 REVISE operation.

```
MODULES FTN*SUB1

TEST CASES
ASSIGN(1,2) VERIFY(1,2) SUB6 VERIFY(1,2) ASSIGN(2) 10 VERIFY
[2,3,,,,,7,;
 1,6,,,,,4,;
 3,6,,,,,8,]

FIN
```

Figure 12. Initial draft of the SUB1 test procedure.

> Automatic software test drivers have the potential to achieve significant savings in development and maintenance costs.

dicted without actually executing the program. The outputs of floating point computations, for example, are approximations and frequently have many correct values, only one of which will be generated by the target program, depending on the hardware and software characteristics of the host computer. While prediction of the exact value of such an output may not be feasible, one can usually determine whether or not a proposed output generated by the REVISE operation is within the range of acceptable values.

Conclusions

The concept of automatic software test drivers has been evolving slowly over the past six years and is now approaching the point where it may begin to play a significant role in the development and maintenance of production software.

Specifying software tests in a formal language, as is done in computer programs, is likely to improve the quality of software test design. For the first time, software tests reside in a medium (the test procedure) that is both machine executable and human readable and therefore available for peer review and criticism. Automatic software test drivers should also influence the quality of software test design by providing feedback on the degree of testing thoroughness actually achieved by a test procedure. But perhaps the strongest effect of automatic software test drivers will be on the maintenance of production software.

The majority of errors appearing in production software are introduced as unintended side effects of post-release program modifications, primarily because there is no convenient mechanism for preserving test cases to check out post-release program modifications. In order to effectively retain software tests for post-release regression testing, someone other than the original test designer must be able to execute them and verify the correctness of test results. Automatic software test drivers may now make it feasible to retain thorough software test cases throughout the entire life cycle of computer programs. Formal test procedures are completely self-contained, they execute automatically without special test setup instructions, and they are self-checking. Since up to 70 percent of life-cycle costs have been attributed to testing and debugging, automatic software test drivers have the potential for achieving significant savings in the development and maintenance of computer software. ■

References

1. *Automated Unit Test (AUT) Program Description/Operation Manual*, IBM Installed User Program Number 5796-PEC, August 1975.
2. *TESTMANAGER: Training Manual*, TMR-008, Management Systems and Programming, Ltd., 71 Gloucester Place, London W1H 3PF, England, March 1976.
3. D. J. Panzl, "Test Procedures: A New Approach to Software Verification," *Proc. Second International Conference on Software Engineering*, October 1976, pp. 477-485.
4. *Fortran Test Procedure Language—Programmer Reference Manual*, General Electric Co., Schenectady, New York 12345, 1977.
5. *Test Procedure Processor—User Guide*, General Electric Co., Schenectady, New York 12345, 1977.
6. D. J. Panzl, "Automatic Revision of Formal Test Procedures." To appear in *Proc. of the Third International Conference on Software Engineering*, May 1978.

David J. Panzl, the author of 10 papers in software engineering and systems programming, is on the research staff of the General Electric Corporate Research and Development Center. There he has conducted research in software engineering methods and tools and pioneered the development of automatic software test drivers. Previously, as a member of the Computing Center staff at the State University of New York at Albany, he designed fast load-and-go compilers, developed new methods for measuring computer system performance, and designed a large-scale time-sharing operating system that supported over 500 time-sharing terminals on the Univac 1108. While a research engineer with HRB-Singer, Inc., he designed and developed early information storage and retrieval systems, airborne reconnaissance mission simulations, digital techniques for the evaluation of reconnaissance imagery, and graphic display devices for computers.

Panzl is a member of ACM and a past chairman of the Hudson-Mohawk Chapter.

Testing a Multiprogramming System

PER BRINCH HANSEN

Information Science, California Institute of Technology, Pasadena, U.S.A.

SUMMARY

A central problem in program design is to structure a large program such that it can be tested systematically by the simplest possible techniques. This paper describes the method used to test the RC 4000 multiprogramming system. During testing, the system records all transitions of processes and messages between various queues. The test mechanism consists of fifty machine instructions centralized in two procedures. By using this mechanism in a series of carefully selected test cases, the system was made virtually error free within a few weeks. The test procedure is illustrated by examples.

KEY WORDS Program testing Multiprogramming Monitor Processor multiplexing Process communication RC 4000

INTRODUCTION

This paper describes the method used to test the RC 4000 multiprogramming system.[1] The system was built with the following *test criteria* in mind:

(1) A large program should be structured such that it can be tested systematically by the simplest possible techniques.
(2) The documentation of a large program should include a systematic set of reproducible test cases.

The nucleus of the RC 4000 system is an interrupt response program of 4,800 machine words called the *monitor*. The monitor multiplexes a single processor among concurrent processes and implements a set of procedures which these processes can call to create other processes and send messages to them. Monitor procedures are executed in a non-interruptable, privileged processor state; processes are executed in an interruptable, non-privileged processor state.

The monitor consists of five *programming layers* with the following tasks:

> processor multiplexing
> message buffering
> input/output operations
> process creation and termination
> file system

The layers were tested in that order starting with the bottom layer (processor multiplexing) working towards the top layer (file system).

TEST MECHANISM

The main difficulty in testing a (possibly erroneous) multiprogramming system is to prevent concurrent events from causing irreproducible, time-dependent test results.

Received 8 January 1973

During each test, the system was initialized with the monitor and a number of *test processes*. The simplest idea would have been to let a test process first call a monitor procedure and then examine various monitor variables (such as process descriptions and scheduling queues) to decide whether the call had the intended effect. Unfortunately, this idea does not work in a multiprogramming environment in which other events (caused by processor multiplexing) may change the internal state of the monitor before the result of a given monitor call has been recorded by a test process.

To make a test event well defined and reproducible, the execution of a monitor call and the recording of its result had to be an indivisible event. Mutual exclusion of test events was achieved by letting the monitor output test data on a typewriter in the non-interruptable processor state.

The hardest problem was to select a minimal set of monitor events that would give significant information about its handling of concurrent processes. It turned out to be sufficient to record all *transitions* of *processes* and *messages* among various queues. When a list element (representing a process or a message) is removed from or linked to a list (representing a queue), the monitor outputs the addresses of the list element and the head of the list plus a single character to distinguish removal from linking. The meaning of these addresses is defined by the assembly listing of the monitor program.

In the following, such test output is represented by more readable lines of the form:

> *take element from queue*
> *put element in queue*

This test mechanism, which adds fifty machine instructions to the monitor, is centralized in two local procedures, *take* and *put*. The following sections describe how it was used to test the monitor.

PROCESSOR MULTIPLEXING

The processor is shared cyclically among all active processes. Every 25 msec, a clock interrupt causes the monitor to pre-empt a running process in favour of another process ready to run (Figure 1).

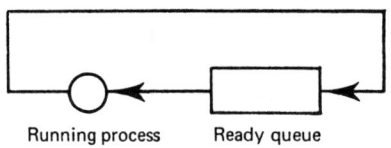

Figure 1. Processor multiplexing

The monitor code for processor multiplexing can be represented as follows:

> **on** *clock interrupt* **do**
> **begin**
>   *put running process in ready queue;*
>   *take another process from ready queue;*
>   *continue that process;*
> **end**

TESTING A MULTIPROGRAMMING SYSTEM

To test processor multiplexing, the system was initialized with three processes P, Q and R in the ready queue (in that order). These processes cycled forever:

P: **repeat until** *false*;
Q: **repeat until** *false*;
R: **repeat until** *false*;

The clock was replaced by a manually operated *interrupt key*. During the test, the monitor produced the following output when processor multiplexing was correct:

take P from ready queue
* *put P in ready queue*
take Q from ready queue
* *put Q in ready queue*
take R from ready queue
* *put R in ready queue*
take P from ready queue
...

The lines marked * are monitor responses to clock interrupts simulated by pushing the interrupt key.

As soon as processor multiplexing worked, the monitor procedures for process communication were tested.

PROCESS COMMUNICATION

Processes can exchange messages in buffer elements of fixed length stored within the monitor. A communication between two processes, S and R, takes place in four steps.

(1) Process S sends a message M to process R in a buffer element B selected by the monitor by calling the procedure:

send message(R, M, B)

(2) Process R receives the message by calling the procedure:

wait message(S, M, B)

(3) Process R sends an answer A to process S in the same buffer element B by calling the procedure:

send answer(A, B)

(4) Process S receives the answer by calling the procedure:

wait answer(A, B)

Figure 2 shows the life cycle of a buffer element. Available buffer elements are linked to a common *pool* within the monitor. The monitor also maintains a *message queue* for each process. A buffer element is linked to this queue when a message is sent to the corresponding process. The buffer element is removed from the queue when the message has been received. When the message has been answered, and the answer has been received, the buffer element is linked to the pool again.

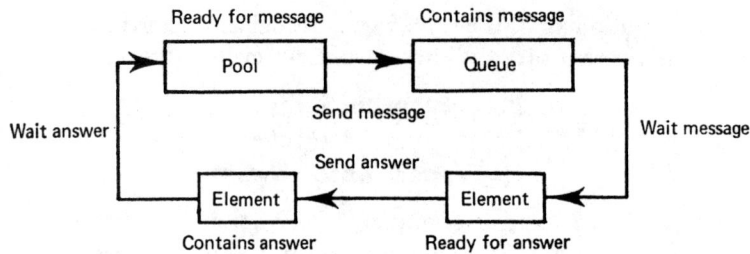

Figure 2. Message buffer states

In a simplified form these monitor procedures can be represented as follows:

send message:
  take buffer from pool;
  if *message expected* **then**
  put receiver in ready queue **else**
  put buffer in message queue;

wait message:
  if *message available* **then**
  take buffer from message queue **else**
  begin
    indicate message expected;
    take another process from ready queue;
  end

send answer:
  if *answer expected* **then**
  begin
    put buffer in pool;
    put receiver in ready queue;
  end

wait answer:
  if *answer available* **then**
  put buffer in pool **else**
  begin
    indicate answer expected;
    take another process from ready queue;
  end

During testing, a process can ask the monitor whether a message or an answer is available for it without being forced to wait for its arrival. A process can also ask the monitor whether another process is expecting a message or an answer.

To test process communication, the system was initialized with two processes, R and S, in the ready queue (in that order). The processes exchange messages and answers in two buffer elements B and B':

TESTING A MULTIPROGRAMMING SYSTEM

R: **wait** message(S, M, B);
      repeat until answer expected(S);
      send answer(A, B);
      repeat until message available (R);
      wait message(S, M', B');
      send answer(A', B');
      repeat until false;

S: **repeat until** message expected(R);
      send message(R, M, B);
      wait answer(A, B);
      send message(R, M', B');
      repeat until answer available(B');
      wait answer(A', B');
      repeat until false;

This test should produce the following output:

(1) take R from ready queue
(2) take S from ready queue
(3) take B from buffer pool
(4) put R in ready queue
(5) take R from ready queue
(6) put B in buffer pool
(7) put S in ready queue
(8) *put R in ready queue
(9) take S from ready queue
(10) take B' from buffer pool
(11) put B' in message queue(R)
(12) *put S in ready queue
(13) take R from ready queue
(14) take B' from message queue(R)
(15) *put R in ready queue
(16) take S from ready queue
(17) put B' in buffer pool

The output can be explained as follows.

Line (1): the monitor selects process R as the first process to run.

Line (2): while process R waits for message M, the monitor continues to run process S.

Lines (3)–(4): process S sends message M to process R which in turn re-enters the ready queue.

Line (5): while process S waits for answer A, the monitor continues to run process R.

Lines (6)–(7): process R sends answer A to process S which in turn re-enters the ready queue.

Lines (8)–(9): process R continuously asks the monitor whether a message is available for it. A key interrupt pre-empts process R in favour of process S.

Lines (10)–(11): process S sends message M' to process R.

Lines (12)–(13): process S continuously asks the monitor whether an answer is available for it. A key interrupt pre-empts process S in favour of process R.

Line (14): process R receives message M' and sends answer A' to process S.

Lines (15)–(16): process R cycles indefinitely. A key interrupt pre-empts process R in favour of process S.

Line (17): process S receives answer A'.

This test covers the eight relevant cases of process communication:

$$\left\{\begin{array}{c} send \\ receive \end{array}\right\} \left\{\begin{array}{c} expected \\ unexpected \end{array}\right\} \left\{\begin{array}{c} message \\ answer \end{array}\right\}$$

CONCLUDING REMARKS

When the communication procedures worked, all possible interactions between processes and peripheral devices of various types were tested. Tests concerning dynamic process creation and termination then followed. Finally, the file system was tested.

The test output immediately revealed all serious synchronizing errors within the monitor. Quite often, the output also led to the discovery of errors in the test programs themselves. As a result of this systematic approach, the monitor was virtually error free after a test period of a few weeks.

It is worth mentioning that the monitor program was written *after* the test mechanism had been selected. If the test problem had been attacked after the monitor was finished, the relevant test events (*take* and *put*) might have been scattered all over the program as in-line code, thus making a centralization of the test mechanism impossible without extensive study and revision of the program text.

ACKNOWLEDGEMENT

The author is indebted to Peter Naur[2] for demonstrating the validity of simple, systematic testing techniques for large, sequential compilers.

REFERENCES

1. P. Brinch Hansen, 'The nucleus of a multiprogramming system', *Comm. ACM*, **13**, No. 4, 238–250 (1970).
2. P. Naur, 'The design of the GIER Algol compiler', *BIT*, **3**, No. 2, 124–140, No. 3, 145–166 (1963).

Hints on Test Data Selection:
Help for the Practicing Programmer

Richard A. DeMillo
Georgia Institute of Technology

Richard J. Lipton and Frederick G. Sayward
Yale University

In many cases tests of a program that uncover simple errors are also effective in uncovering much more complex errors. This so-called coupling effect can be used to save work during the testing process.

Reprinted from *Computer*, April 1978, pp. 34-41. Copyright © 1978 by The Institute of Electrical and Electronics Engineers, Inc.

Much of the technical literature in software reliability deals with tentative methodologies and underdeveloped techniques; hence it is not surprising that the programming staff responsible for debugging a large piece of software often feels ignored. It is an economic and political requirement in most production programming shops that programmers shall spend as little time as possible in testing. The programmer must therefore be content to test cleverly but cheaply; state-of-the-art methodologies always seem to be just beyond what can be afforded. We intend to convince the reader that much can be accomplished even under these constraints.

From the point of view of management, there is some justification for opposing a long-term view of the testing phase of the development cycle. Figure 1 shows the relative effect of testing on the remaining system bugs for several medium-scale systems developed by System Development Corporation.[1] Notice that in the last half of the test cycle, the average change in the known-error status of a system is 0.4 percent per unit of testing effort, while in the first half of the cycle, 1.54 percent of the errors are discovered per unit of testing effort. Since it is enormously difficult to be convincing in stating that the testing effort is complete, the apparently rapidly decreasing return per unit of effort invested becomes a dominating concern. The standard solution, of course, is to limit the amount of testing time to the most favorable part of the cycle.

How, then, should programmers cope? Their more sophisticated general methodologies are not likely to be applicable.[2] In addition, they have the burden of convincing managers that their software is indeed reliable.

The coupling effect

Programmers, however, have one great advantage that is almost never really exploited: they create programs that are *close* to being correct! Programmers do not create programs at random; competent programmers, in their many iterations through the design process, are constantly whittling away the distance between what their programs look like now and what they are intended to look like. Programmers also have at their disposal

- a rough idea of the kinds of errors most likely to occur;
- the ability and opportunity to examine their programs in detail.

Error classifications. In attempting to formulate a comprehensive theory of test data selection, Susan Gerhart and John Goodenough[3] have suggested that errors be classified as follows:

(1) failure to satisfy specifications due to implementation error;
(2) failure to write specifications that correctly represent a design;
(3) failure to understand a requirement;
(4) failure to satisfy a requirement.

But these are global concerns. Errors are always reflected in programs as

- missing control paths,
- inappropriate path selection, or
- inappropriate or missing actions.

> **Programmers have one great advantage that is almost never exploited: they create programs that are *close* to being correct!**

We do not explicitly address classifications (2) and (3) in this article, except to point out that even here a programmer can do much without fancy theories. If we are right in our perception of programs as being close to correct, then these errors should be detectable as small deviations from the intended program. There is an amazing lack of published data on this subject, but we do have some idea of the most common errors. E. A. Youngs, in his PhD dissertation,[4] analyzed 1258 errors in Fortran, Cobol, PL/I, and Basic programs. The errors were distributed as shown in Table 1.

In addition to these errors, certain other errors were present in negligible quantities. There were, for instance, operating system interface errors, such as incorrect job identification and erroneous external I/O assignment. Also present were errors in comments, pseudo-ops, and no-ops which for various reasons created detectable error conditions.

Complex errors coupled. How, then, do the relatively simple error types discovered by Youngs connect with the Gerhart-Goodenough error classification? Well, the naive answer is that since arbitrarily pernicious errors may be responsible for a given failure, it must be that simple errors compound in more massive error conditions. For the practical treatment of test data, the Youngs' error statistics, therefore, do not seem to help much at all. Fortunately though, the observation that programs are "close to correct" leads us to an assumption which makes the high frequency of simple errors very important:

The coupling effect: Test data that distinguishes all programs differing from a correct one by only simple errors is so sensitive that it also implicitly distinguishes more complex errors.

In other words, complex errors are *coupled* to simple errors. There is, of course, no hope of "proving" the coupling effect; it is an empirical principle. If the coupling effect can be observed in "real-world" programs, then it has dramatic implications for testing strategies in general and domain-specific, limited testing in particular. Rather than scamper after errors of undetermined character, the tester should attempt a systematic search for simple errors that will also uncover deeper errors via the coupling effect.

Path analysis. This point seems so obvious that it's not worth making: test to uncover errors. Yet it's a point that's often lost in the shuffle. In a common methodology known as *path analysis*, the point of the test data is to drive a program through all of its control paths. It is certainly hard to criticize such a goal, since a thoroughly tested program must have been exercised in this way. But unless one recognizes that the test data should also distinguish errors, he might be tempted to conclude, for example, that the program segment diagrammed in Figure 2 can be tested by exercising paths 1-2 and 1-3, even though one of the clauses P and Q may not have been affected at all! In general, the relative ordering of P and Q may be irrelevant or partially unknown and side effects may occur, so that actually the eight paths shown in Figure 3 are required to ensure that the statement has been adequately tested.

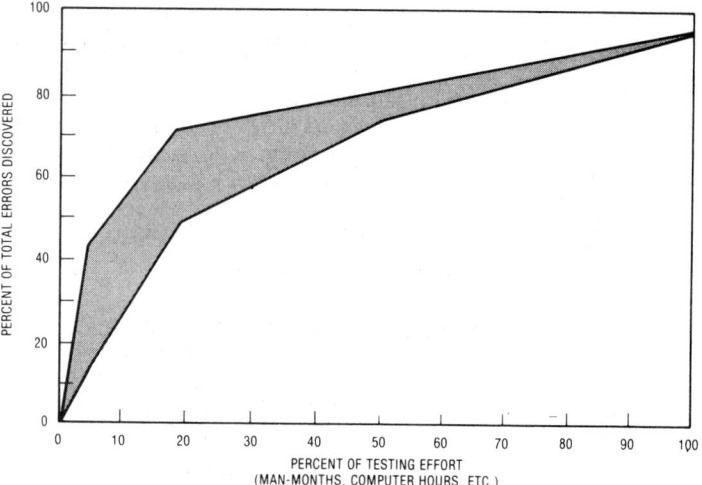

Figure 1. More programming errors are found in the early part of the test cycle then in the final part.

Table 1. Frequency of occurrence of 1258 errors in Fortran, Cobol, PL/I, and Basic programs.

Error Type	Relative Frequency of Occurrence
Error in assignment or computation	.27
Allocation error	.15
Other, unknown, or multiple errors	.11
Unsuccessful iteration	.09
Other I/O error	.07
I/O formatting error	.06
Error in brahching unconditional	.01
conditional	.05
Parameter or subscript violation	.05
Subprogram invocation error	.05
Misplaced delimiter	.04
Data error	.02
Error in location or marker	.02
Nonterminating subprogram	.01

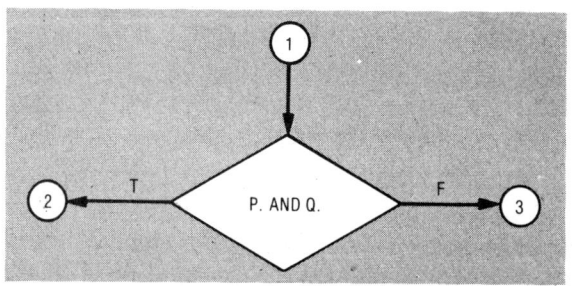

Figure 2. Sample program segment with two paths.

Two examples given below indicate that test data derived to uncover simple errors can, in fact, be vastly superior to, say, randomly chosen data or data generated for path analysis. A byproduct of the discussion will be some evidence for the coupling effect. A third example reveals another advantage of selecting test data with an eye on coupling: since it's a problem-specific activity, there are enhanced possibilities for discovering useful heuristics for test data selection. This example will lead to useful advice for generating test vectors for programs that manipulate arrays.

Our groups at Yale University and the Georgia Institute of Technology have constructed a system whereby we can determine the extent to which a given set of test data has adequately tested a Fortran program by direct measurement of the number and kinds of errors it is capable of uncovering. This method, known as *program mutation*, is used interactively: A programmer enters from a terminal a program, P, and a proposed test data set whose adequacy is to be determined. The mutation system first executes the program on the test data; if the program gives incorrect answers then certainly the program is in error. On the other hand, if the program gives correct answers, then it may be that the program is still in error, but the test data is not sensitive enough to distinguish that error: it is not adequate. The mutation system then creates a number of *mutations* of P that differ from P only in the occurrence of simple errors (for instance, where P contains the expression "B.LE.C" a mutation will contain "B.EQ.C"). Let us call these mutations $P_1, P_2, \ldots, P_k$.

Now, for the given set of test data there are only two possibilities:

(1) on that data P gives different results from the P_i mutations, or

(2) on that data P gives the same results as some P_j.

In case (1) P_i is said to be *dead*: the "error" that produced P_i from P was indeed distinguished by the test data. In case (2), the mutant P_j is said to be *live*; a mutant may be live for two reasons:

(1) the test data does not contain enough sensitivity to distinguish the error that gave rise to P_j, or
(2) P_j and P are actually equivalent programs and no test data will distinguish them (i.e., the "error" that gave rise to P_j was not an error at all).

Test data that leaves no live mutants or only live mutants that are equivalent to P is adequate in the following sense: Either the program P is correct or there is an unexpected error in P, which—by the coupling effect—we expect to happen seldom if the errors used to create the mutants are carefully chosen.

Now, it is not completely apparent that this process is computationally feasible. But, as we describe in more detail elsewhere, there is a very good choice of methodology for generating mutations to bring the procedure within attractive economic bounds.[5]

Apparently, the information returned by the mutation system can be effectively utilized by the programmer. The programmer looks at a negative response from the system as a "hard question" concerning his program (e.g., "The test data you've given me says it doesn't matter whether or not this test is for equality or inequality; why is that?") and is able to use his answers to the question as a guide in generating more sensitive test data.

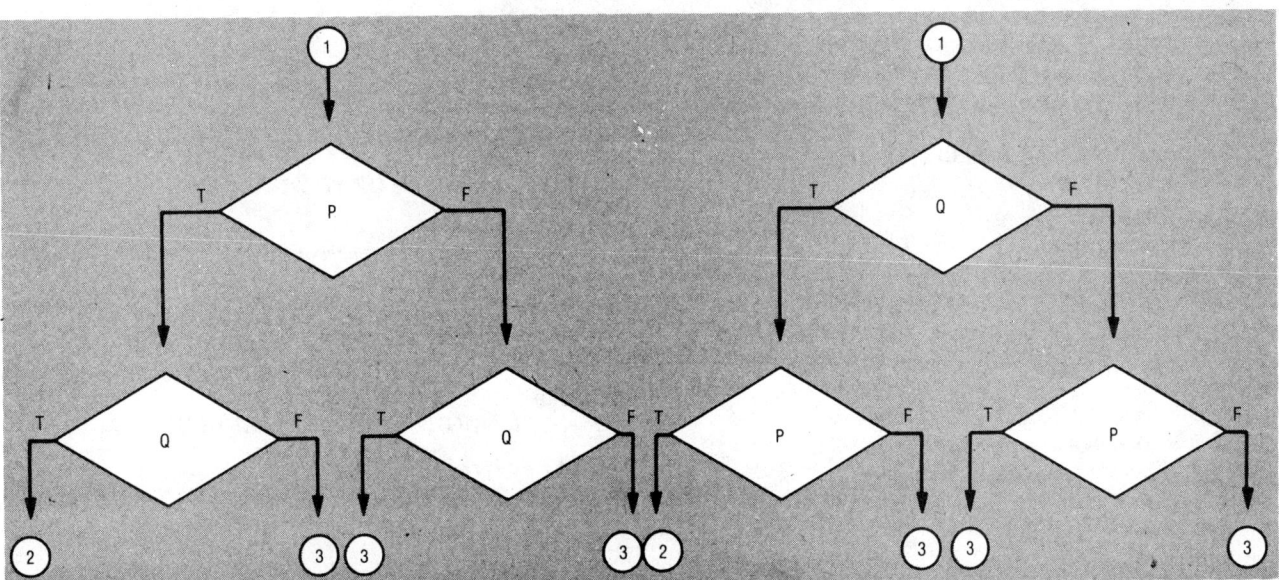

Figure 3. Eight paths may be required for an adequate test.

A simple example

Our first example is very simple; it involves the MAX algorithm used for other purposes by Peter Naur in the early 1960's. The task is to set a variable R to the *index* of the first occurrence of a maximum element in the vector A(1), ..., A(N). For example, the following Fortran subroutine might be offered as an implementation of such an algorithm:

```
      SUBROUTINE MAX (A,N,R)
      INTEGER A(N),I,N,R
    1 R=1
    2 DO 3 I=2,N,1
    3 IF (A(I).GT.A(R))R=I
      RETURN
      END
```

We will choose for our initial set of test data three vectors (Table 2).

Table 2. Three vectors constitute the initial set of test data.

	A(1)	A(2)	A(3)
data 1	1	2	3
data 2	1	3	2
data 3	3	1	2

How sensitive is this data? By inspection, we notice that if an error had occurred in the relational operation of the IF statement, then either data 1, data 2, or data 3 would have distinguished those errors, except for one case. None of these data vectors distinguishes .GE. from .GT. in the IF statement. Similarly, these vectors distinguish all simple errors in constants except for starting the DO loop at "1" rather than "2." All simple errors in variables are likewise distinguished except for the errors in the IF statement which replace "A(I)" by "I" or by "A(R)."

That is, if we run the data set above in any of the following mutants of MAX, we get the same results.

```
      SUBROUTINE MAX (A,N,R)
      INTEGER A(N),I,N,R
    1 R=1
    2 DO 3 I=1,N,1
    3 IF(A(I).GT.A(R))R=I
      RETURN
      END

      SUBROUTINE MAX (A,N,R)
      INTEGER A(N),I,N,R
    1 R=1
    2 DO 3 I=2,N,1
    3 IF(I.GT.A(R))R=I
      RETURN
      END

      SUBROUTINE MAX (A,N,R)
      INTEGER A(N),I,N,R
    1 R=1
    2 DO 3 I=2,N,1
    3 IF(A(I).GE.A(R))R=1
      RETURN
      END

      SUBROUTINE MAX (A,N,R)
      INTEGER A(N),I,N,R
    1 R=1
    2 DO 3 I=2,N,1
    3 IF(A(R).GT.A(R))R=1
      RETURN
      END
```

Let us try to kill as many of these mutants as possible. In view of the first difficulty, we might guess that our data is not yet adequate because it does not contain repeated elements. So, let us add

	A(1)	A(2)	A(3)
data 4	2	2	1

Now, replacing .GT. by .GE. and running on data 4 gives erroneous results so that all mutants arising from simple relational errors are dead. Surprisingly, data 4 also distinguishes the two errors in A(I); so, we are left with only the last mutant arising from the "constant" error: variation in beginning the DO loop. But closer inspection of the program indicates that starting the DO loop at "1" rather than "2" has no effect on the program, other than to trivially increase its running time. So no choice of test data will distinguish this "error," since it results in a program equivalent to MAX. So we conclude that since the test data 1-4 leaves only live mutants that are equivalent to MAX, it is adequate.

Comparisons with path analysis

This example illustrates hidden paths in a program which should also be exercised by the test data. To illustrate what hidden paths are, consider the Fortran program—call it P—suggested by C. V. Ramamoorthy and his colleagues:[6]

```
      INTEGER A,B,C,D
      READ 10,A,B,C
   10 FORMAT(4I10)
    5 IF((A.GE.B) .AND.(B.GE.C) ) GOTO 100
      PRINT 50
   50 FORMAT(1H ,*LENGTH OF TRIANGLE NOT IN
     1ORDER*)
      STOP
  100 IF((A.EQ.B) .OR. (B.EQ.C)) GOTO 500
      A=A*A
      B=B*B
      C=C**2
      D=B+C
      IF (A.NE.D) GOTO 200
      PRINT 150
  150 FORMAT(1H ,*RIGHT ANGLED TRIANGLE*)
      STOP
  200 IF (A.LT.D). GOTO 300
      PRINT 250
  250 FORMAT(1H ,*OBTUSE ANGLED TRIANGLE*)
      STOP
  300 PRINT 350

  350 FORMAT(1H ,*ACUTE ANGLED TRIANGLE*)
```

```
          STOP
    500   IF ( (A.EQ.B) .AND. (A.EQ.C) ) GOTO 600
          PRINT 550
    550   FORMAT(1H ,*ISOCELES TRIANGLE*)
          STOP
    600   PRINT 650
    650   FORMAT(1H ,*EQUILATERAL TRIANGLE*)
          STOP
          END
```

The intent of this program is to categorize triangles, given the lengths of their sides. A typical path analysis system will derive test data—call it T—which exercises all paths of P (Table 3).

Table 3. Test data T to exercise the Fortran program P.

TEST CASE	A	B	C	TRIANGLE TYPE
1	2	12	27	ILLEGAL
2	5	4	3	RIGHT ANGLE
3	26	7	7	ISOCELES
4	19	19	19	EQUILATERAL
5	14	6	4	OBTUSE
6	24	23	21	ACUTE

Now consider the following mutant program P':

```
          INTEGER, A,B,C,D
          READ 10,A,B,C
     10   FORMAT(4I10)
      5   IF( A.GE.B ) GOTO 100
          PRINT 50
     50   FORMAT(1H ,*LENGTH OF TRIANGLE NOT IN
         1ORDER*)
          STOP
    100   IF( B.EQ.C ) GOTO 500
          A=A*A
          B=B*B
          C=C**2
          D=B+C
          IF (A.NE.D) GOTO 200
          PRINT 150
    150   FORMAT(1H ,*RIGHT ANGLED TRIANGLE*)
          STOP
    200   IF (A.LT.D) GOTO 300
          PRINT 250
    250   FORMAT(1H ,*OBTUSE ANGLED TRIANGLE*)
          STOP
    300   PRINT 350
    350   FORMAT(1H ,*ACUTE ANGLED TRIANGLE*)
          STOP
    500   IF ( (A.EQ.B) .AND. (A.EQ.C) ) GOTO 600
          PRINT 550
    550   FORMAT(1H ,*ISOCELES TRIANGLE*)
          STOP
    600   PRINT 650
    650   FORMAT(1H ,*EQUILATERAL TRIANGLE*)
          STOP
          END
```

P' prints the same answers as P on T but P' is clearly incorrect since it categorizes the two test cases shown in Table 4 as acute angle triangles:

Table 4. Two test cases are acute angle triangles.

TEST CASE	A	B	C	TRIANGLE TYPE
7	7	5	6	ILLEGAL
8	26	26	7	ISOCELES

P and P' differ only in the logical expressions found at statements 5 and 100.* The test data T does not sufficiently test the compound logical expressions of P; T only tests the single-clause logicals found in the corresponding statements of P'. Hence, T' is a stronger test of P than is T (i.e., for P we have more confidence in the adequacy of T' than in the adequacy of T). Note that the logical expression in statement 5 of P could be replaced by B.GE.C to yield a program P'' which produces correct answers on T'. The test case $A=5$, $B=7$, $C=6$ will remedy this and provide still a stronger test of P.

A more substantial example

Our last example involves the FIND program of C.A.R. Hoare.[7] FIND takes, as input, an integer array A, its size $N \geq 1$, and an array index F, $1 \leq F \leq N$. After execution of FIND, all elements to the left of $A(F)$ have values no larger than $A(F)$ and all elements to the right are no smaller. Clearly, this could be achieved by sorting A; indeed, FIND is an inner loop of a fast sorting algorithm, although FIND executes faster than any sorting program. The Fortran version of FIND, translated directly from the Algol version, is given below:

```
          SUBROUTINE FIND(A,N,F)
    C
    C     FORTRAN VERSION OF HOARE'S FIND
    C     PROGRAM (DIRECT TRANSLATION OF
    C     THE ALGOL 60 PROGRAM FOUND IN
    C     HOARE'S "PROOF OF FIND" ARTICLE
    C     IN CACM 1971).
          INTEGER A(N),N,F
          INTEGER M,NS,R,I,J,W
          M=1
          NS=N
     10   IF(M.GE.NS) GOTO 1000
          R=A(F)
          I=M
          J=NS
     20   IF(I.GT.J) GOTO 60
     30   IF(A(I).GE.R) GOTO 40
          I=I+1
          GOTO 30
     40   IF(R.GE.A(J)) GOTO 50
          J=J-1
          GOTO 40
     50   IF(I.GT.J) GOTO 20
    C
    C     COULD HAVE CODED GO TO 60 DIRECTLY
    C     —DIDN'T BECAUSE THIS REDUNDANCY
    C     IS PRESENT IN HOARE'S ALGOL
    C     PROGRAM DUE TO THE SEMANTICS OF
    C     THE WHILE STATEMENT.
    C
          W=A(I)
          A(I)=A(J)
          A(J)=W
          I=I+1
          J=J-1
          GO TO 20
```

---

*The clause A.EQ.B in statement 500 is redundant.

```
60    IF(F.GT.J) GOTO 70
      NS=J
      GOTO 10
70    IF(I.GT.F) GOTO 1000
      M=I
      GOTO 10
1000  RETURN
      END
```

FIND is of particular interest for us because a subtle multiple-error mutant of FIND, called BUGGYFIND, has been extensively analyzed by SELECT, a system that generates test data by symbolic execution.[8] In FIND, the elements of A are interchanged depending on a conditional of the form

$$X \text{ .LE. } A(F) \text{ .AND. } A(F) \text{ .LE. } Y$$

Since $A(F)$ itself may be exchanged, the effect of this test is preserved by setting a temporary variable $R = A(F)$ and using the conditional

$$X \text{ .LE. } R \text{ .AND. } R \text{ .LE. } Y$$

In BUGGYFIND, the temporary variable R is not used; rather, the first form of the conditional is used to determine whether the elements of A are to be exchanged. The SELECT system derived the test data $A = (3,2,0,1)$ and $F = 3$, on which BUGGYFIND fails. The authors of SELECT observed that BUGGYFIND fails on only 2 of the 24 permutations of $(0,1,2,3)$, indicating that the error is very subtle.*

We will first describe a simple-error analysis of the mutants of FIND, beginning with initially naive guesses of test data and finishing with a surprisingly adequate set of 7 A vectors. This data will be called D_1. The detailed analysis needed to determine how many errors are distinguished by a data set were carried out on the Mutation system at Yale University.

We have asked several colleagues how they would test FIND, and they have nearly unanimously replied that they would use permutations. We first describe analysis which we have done using permutations of the array indices as data elements. In one case, we use all permutations of length 4 and in another case, we use *random* permutations of lengths 5 and 6. Surprisingly, the intuitively appealing choice of permutations as test data is a very poor one.

We then describe analysis in which another popular intuitive method is used: random data. We show that the adequacy of random data is very dependent on the interval from which the data is drawn (i.e., problem-specific information is needed to obtain good results).

Finally, we find evidence for the coupling effect (i.e., adequate simple-error data kills multiple-error mutants) in two ways. First, the multiple-error mutant BUGGYFIND fails on the test data D_1. Next, we describe the very favorable results of executing random multiple-error mutants of FIND on D_1.

We begin the analysis with the 24 permutations of $(0,1,2,3)$ with F fixed at 3. The results are surprisingly poor, as 58 live mutants are left. That is, with these 24 vectors there are 58 possible changes that could have been made in FIND that would have yielded identical output. Eventually, by increasing the number of A vectors to 49, only 10 live mutants remain. Using a data reduction heuristic, the 49 A vectors can be reduced to a set of seven A vectors, leaving 14 live mutants. These vectors appear in Table 5.

Table 5. D_1—The simple-error adequate data for FIND.

TEST CASE	A	F
1	(−19,34,0,−4,22, 12,222,−57,17)	5
2	(7,9,7)	3
3	(2,3,1,0)	3
4	(−5,−5,−5,−5)	1
5	(1,3,2,0)	3
6	(0,2,3,1)	3
7	(0)	1

In constructing the initial data, after the 24 permutations, the 49 A vectors were chosen somewhat haphazardly at first. Later, A vectors were chosen specifically to eliminate a small subset of the remaining errors. There were some interesting observations concerning the 49 vectors:

(1) The average A vectors kills about 550 mutants.
(2) The "best" A vector kills 703 mutants (test case 1 of Table 5).
(3) The "worst" A vector kills only 70 mutants. This was the degenerate $A = (0)$.

The data reduction heuristic uses both the best and the worst A vectors to pare the 49 A vectors to seven.

The final step in showing that the data of Table 5 is indeed adequate is to show that the 14 remaining mutants are programs that are actually equivalent to FIND. That is, the 14 "errors" that could have been made are not really errors at all. One might be surprised at the large number of equivalent mutants (approximately 2 percent). This we attribute to FIND's long history (it was first published in 1961). Over the years, FIND has been "honed" to a very efficient state—so efficient that many slight variations result in equivalent but slower programs. For example, the conditional

$$I \text{ .GT. } F$$

in the statement labeled 70 in the FIND can be replaced by any logically false conditional, or the IF statement can be replaced by a CONTINUE statement, to result in an equivalent but slower program. It is not likely that this phenomenon will occur in programs which haven't been "fine-tuned." We estimate that production programs have well under 1 percent equivalent mutants.

Let us now compare D_1 with exhaustive tests on permutations of $(0,1,2,3)$ and then with tests on

---

*We found that BUGGYFIND failed on only the aforementioned permutation.

random permutations of (0,1,2,3,4) and (0,1,2,3,4,5). Table 6 describes the results for all permutations of (0,1,2,3).

Table 6. Results of all permutations of (1,2,3,4).

NUMBER OF TEST CASES	VALUES OF F	NUMBER OF LIVE MUTANTS
24	1	158
24	2	60
24	3	58
24	4	141
96	1,2,3,&4	38

In Table 7 the same information is provided for the case of random test data.

Table 7. Results of random permutations.

NUMBER OF RANDOM TEST CASES	SIZE OF A	VALUE OF F	NUMBER OF LIVE MUTANTS
10	UNIFORM FROM [5,6]	UNIFORM FROM 1 TO SIZE OF A	88
25	↓	↓	65
50	↓	↓	54
100	↓	↓	54
1000	↓	↓	53

As the data indicates, permutations give rather poor results compared with D_1.

Our analysis with random data can be divided into two cases: runs in which the vectors were drawn from poorly chosen intervals and runs in which the vectors were chosen from a good interval (−100,100). The results are described in Tables 8 and 9.

Table 8. Results of random data from poorly chosen intervals.

NUMBER OF RANDOM VECTORS	RANGE OVER WHICH VECTOR VALUES DRAWN	RANGE OVER WHICH SIZE OF A DRAWN	VALUE OF F	NUMBER OF LIVE MUTANTS
10	[100,200]	[1,20]	UNIFORM FROM SIZE OF VECTOR	28
10	[−200,−100]	[1,20]		28
10	[−100,−90]	[1,20]		25

Table 9. Results of random data drawn from [−100,100]; other parameters as in Table 8.

NUMBER OF RANDOM VECTORS	NUMBER OF LIVE MUTANTS
10	22
50	17
100	11
1000	10

Although the intervals in Table 8 are poor, one could conceive of worse intervals. For example, draw A from [1, size of A]. However, in view of the permutation results, such data will surely behave worse than that of Table 8.

Three points are in order. First, even with very bad data, D_1 is much better than simple permutations. Second, it took 1000 very good random vectors to perform as well as D_1. Third, using random vectors yields little insight. The insight gained in constructing D_1 was crucial to detecting the equivalent versions of FIND.

The coupling effect shows itself in two ways. First, BUGGYFIND fails on the adequate D_1; hence, we have a concrete example of the coupling effect. Although the second observation involves randomness, and thus is indirect, it is perhaps more convincing than the "one point" concrete BUGGYFIND example. We have randomly generated a large number of k-error mutants for $k > 1$ (called higher order mutants) and executed them on D_1.

Because the number of mutants produced by complex errors can grow combinatorially, it is hopeless to try the complete mutation analysis on complex mutants, but it is possible to select mutants at random for execution on D_1. Of more than 22,000 higher-order errors encountered, only 19 succeed on D_1. These 19 have been shown to be equivalent to FIND. Indeed, we have yet to produce an incorrect higher-order mutant which suceeds on D_1!

Conclusions

Our first conclusion is that systematically pursuing test data which distinguishes errors from a given class of errors also yields "advice" to be used in generating test data for similar programs. For instance, the examples above lead us to the following principles for creating random or nonrandom test data for Fortran-like programs which manipulate arrays (i.e., programs in which array values can also be used as array indices):

(1) Include cases in which array values are outside the size of the array.
(2) Include cases in which array values are negative.
(3) Include cases in which array values are repeated.
(4) Include such degenerate cases as D_1's $A = (0)$ and $A = (-5,-5,-5,-5)$.

Principle (4) was also noticed by Goodenough and Gerhart.[3]

It is important that a testing strategy be conducive to the formation of hypotheses about the way test data should be selected in future tasks. Information transferred between programming tasks provides a source of "virtual resources" to be used in subsequent work. Since the amount of available resources is limited by economic and political barriers, experience—which has the effect of expanding resources—takes on a special importance. It is,

> **Seemingly simple techniques can be quite sensitive via the coupling effect.**

of course, helpful to have available such mechanical aids as the mutation system, but as we have shown even in the absence of the appropriate statistical information, a programmer can be reasonably confident that he is improving his test data selection strategy.

A second conclusion is that until more general strategies for systematic testing emerge, programmers are probably better off using the tools and insights they have in great abundance. Instead of guessing at deeply rooted sources of error, they should use their specialized knowledge about the most likely sources of error in their application. We have tried to illustrate that seemingly simple tests can be quite sensitive, via the coupling effect.

The techniques we advocate here are hardly ever general techniques. In a sense, they require one to deal directly in the details of both coding and the application—a notion that is certainly contrary to currently popular methodologies for validating software. But we believe there is ample evidence in man's intellectual history that he does not solve important problems by viewing them from a distance. In fact, there is an *Alice In Wonderland* quality to fields which claim they can solve other people's problems without knowing anything in particular about the problems.

So, there is certainly no need to apologize for applying ad hoc strategies in program testing. A programmer who considers his problems well and skillfully applies appropriate techniques to their solution—regardless of where the techniques arise—will succeed. ∎

References

1. A. E. Tucker, "The Correlation of Computer Program Quality with Testing Effort," System Development Corporation, TM 2219/000/00, January 1965.
2. R. A. DeMillo, R. J. Lipton, A. J. Perlis, "Social Processes and Proofs of Programs and Theorems," *Proc. Fourth ACM Symposium on Principles of Programming Languages*, pp. 206-214. (To appear in *CACM*)
3. John B. Goodenough and Susan L. Gerhart, "Toward a Theory of Test Data Selection," *Proc. International Conference on Reliable Software*, SIGPLAN Notices, Vol. 10, No. 6, June 1975, pp. 493-510.
4. E. A. Youngs, *Error-Proneness in Programming*, PhD thesis, University of North Carolina, 1971.
5. T. A. Budd, R. A. DeMillo, R. J. Lipton, F. G. Sayward, "The Design of a Prototype Mutation System for Program Testing," *Proc., 1978 NCC*.
6. C. V. Ramamoorthy, S. F. Ho, and W. T. Chen, "On the Automated Generation of Program Test Data,". *IEEE Trans. on Software Engineering*, Vol. SE-2, No. 4, December 1976, pp. 293-300.
7. C. A. R. Hoare, "Algorithms 65; FIND," *CACM*, Vol. 4, No. 1, April 1961, pp. 321.
8. R. S. Boyer, B. Elspas, K. N. Levitt, "SELECT—A System for Testing and Debugging Programs by Symbolic Execution," *Proc. International Conference on Reliable Software*, SIGPLAN Notices, Vol. 10, No. 6, June 1975, pp. 234-245.

Richard DeMillo has been an associate professor of computer science at the Georgia Institute of Technology since 1976. During the four years prior to that he was assistant professor of computer science at the University of Wisconsin-Milwaukee.

A technical consultant to several government and research agencies and to private industry, he is interested in the theory of computing, programming languages, and programming methodology.

DeMillo received the BA in mathematics from the College of St. Thomas, St. Paul, Minnesota, and the PhD in information and computer science from the Georgia Institute of Technology. He is a member of ACM, the American Mathematical Society, AAAS, and the Association for Symbolic Logic.

Richard J. Lipton is an associate professor of computer science at Yale University. A faculty member since 1973, he pursues research interests in computational complexity and in mathematical modeling of computer systems. He is also a technical consultant to several government agencies and to private industry.

Lipton received the BS in mathematics from Case Western Reserve University and the PhD from Carnegie-Mellon University.

Frederick G. Sayward is an assistant professor of computer science at Yale University, where he pursues research interests in semantical methods for programming languages, the theory of parallel computation as applied to operating systems, the development of programming test methods, and techniques for fault-tolerant computation. Earlier, he worked as a scientific and systems programmer at MIT Lincoln Laboratory.

A member of ACM, the American Mathematical Society, and Sigma Xi, Sayward received the BS in mathematics from Southeastern Massachusetts University, the MS in computer science from the University of Wisconsin-Madison, and the PhD in applied mathematics from Brown University.

Section 5: Effectiveness Assessment

Paper Summaries

B. W. Boehm, R. K. McClean, and D. B. Urfrig, "Some Experience with Automated Aids to the Design of Large-Scale Reliable Software," *IEEE Transactions on Software Engineering,* March 1975 (pp. 125-133).

A number of extensive analyses of software projects have been carried out at TRW in which an attempt was made to find the sources of errors in the system developed in the projects. It was discovered that a large percentage of the expensive bugs in a system can be tracked back to the design stage. This reprint describes some of the results of the studies. Based on the research at TRW, a number of software development tools were developed, including the DACC—Design Analysis Consistency Checker. The DACC can be used to automatically analyze machine readable design documents in the same way that PSA/PSL can be used to analyze machine readable requirements documents. The DACC was designed to analyze module input and output assertations. It can also be used to analyze the assertions for consistency and completeness.

G. J. Myers, "A Controlled Experiment in Program Testing and Code Walkthroughs/Inspections, *Communications of the ACM,* September 1978, (pp. 760-768).

This paper describes an experiment in software testing that used 59 experienced computing professionals to analyze and test a small PL/I program in seven different ways. The goal of the experiments was to compare several different kinds of testing methods, among them code inspections, specification checking, and dynamic execution. The subjects were students in an IBM Systems Research Institute course on software reliability; they averaged 11 years of experience apiece (range seven to 20 years' experience) in the data processing field. The author admits that "...the subjects were considered to be above-average employeees...and were judged to be highly motivated during the experiment."

Some of the results in this landmark paper were surprising. To begin with, there was a lot of variability in individual results. Some people found all of the (known) errors, and others, even when working in teams, could find only a few of them. Overall, the average number of errors found was only about one-third of the total error population (a known figure).

Perhaps equally surprising was that the code inspection teams' results were somewhat more consistent than the other methods' results, a fact that suggests that inspection may be "...more predictable than other methods."

The paper addresses the cost-effectiveness of the three alternative methods but is unable to draw a strong conclusion about their comparative economies. The paper concludes with a number of suggestions for further study, including the possibility of machine-assisted walkthroughs and the use of testing support tools

D. M. Andrews and J. P. Benson, "An Automated Program Testing Methodology and Its Implementation," *Proceedings, Fifth International Conference on Software Engineering,* San Diego, March 1981 (pp. 254-261).

This paper discusses a testing methodology that uses "executable assertions," a kind of statement that emits a message whenever a stated condition is found to be false. (This is the usual sense of an assertion, that when it *fails* to be true, it produces a warning.) When an assertion is found false, a new test is devised, using some of the values of input variables. Then, when the program is run, a plot is made of the number of assertions violated versus the input variable values used. This difference is called the "error function."

This technique was used in an experiment that is reported in this paper. "Heuristic" search methods are used to maximize the error function and thereby find input values that cause the most errors to occur. In the experiment, the search methods were able to detect errors much more efficiently (i.e., with less total computer time) than other methods were. However, as with many testing methods, some errors could not be directly detected by the method.

W. E. Howden, "Applicability of Software Validation Techniques to Scientific Programs," *ACM Transactions on Programming Languages and Systems,* July 1980 (pp. 307-320.)

A validation method can be said to be effective for an error if its use is guaranteed to result in the discovery of error. This paper describes a study of the effectiveness of a wide variety of validation methods for the errors occurring in a "mature" release of a scientific subroutine package. The study found that static analysis was effective for about half the errors and dynamic testing for the other half. Several errors could not be detected by either static or dynamic analysis but would be detected during a proof of correctness.

The paper concludes that different techniques are effective for different classes of errors and proposes the use of an integrated collection of testing and analysis methods. Such a scheme is described in the paper as well as the general features of individual methods and required supporting software tools.

R. J. Rubey, J. A. Dana, and P. W. Biché, "Quantitative Aspects of Software Validation," *IEEE Transactions on Software Engineering,* June 1975 (pp. 150-155).

The importance of classifying errors and of compiling error statistics has become more apparent as attempts are made to measure the quality of software systems and the effectiveness of validation methods. This reprint describes a scheme for classifying errors. Ten general categories of errors are described. A refinement of the classification into more detailed categories (i.e., branch test incorrect) is provided for the four most important general categories. In addition to the error occurrence statistics, the paper compares the effectiveness of dynamic and static analysis for discovering errors. The ratio of validation to development costs is also studied.

S. L. Gerhart and L. Yelowitz, "Observations of Fallibility in Applications of Modern Programming Methodologies," *IEEE Transactions on Software Engineering,* September 1976 (pp. 195-207.)

This interesting paper contains examples of situations in which a reliability method failed to either prevent the generation of or discover the presence of an error. Examples are included in which a program, which was proved to be correct, was later discovered to contain an error, illustrating that even proofs of correctness do not guarantee the absence of errors. Proofs of correctness can fail in several ways. The proof itself, for example, may contain errors. Or the proof may be correct, but the program's input and output assertions incorrect, in which case the programmer is left with a correct proof for the wrong program.

M. R. Woodward, D. Hedley, and M. A. Hennell, "Experience with Path Analysis and Testing of Programs," *IEEE Transactions on Software Engineering,* May 1980, (pp. 278-286).

This paper reports on real-world and practical difficulties in actually performing a path-oriented testing strategy for computer programs.

One continuing problem is the choice of which particular test path to use in a test. Several measures of testing coverage based on the structure of programs are suggested as a means to make this choice.

Another problem is infeasible paths. A path is infeasible if it is impossible to construct input data values which cause the path to be followed when the program is executed.

The basic unit of program structure used in this paper is the Linear Code Sequence and Jump (LCSAJ), which is a passage of code text through which control passes sequentially and which is terminated by a jump in the control flow. Test coverage measures are defined in terms of percentages of executions of these units. One of the measures evaluates "sequential pairs" of LCSAJs.

The paper describes some experiments done on a set of seven programs written in ALGOL 68 and ranging in size from 17 to 91 lines. Properties of these programs in terms of LCSAJs and other features were evaluated, and the effectiveness of these measures as a way of controlling testing effort are assessed.

Some Experience with Automated Aids to the Design of Large-Scale Reliable Software

BARRY W. BOEHM, ROBERT K. McCLEAN, AND D.B. URFRIG

Abstract—This paper summarizes some recent experience in analyzing and eliminating sources of error in the design phase of large software projects. It begins by pointing out some of the significant differences in software error incidence between large and small software projects. The most striking contrast, illustrated by project data, is the large preponderance of design errors over coding errors on large-scale projects, not only with respect to numbers of errors, but also with respect to the relative time and effort required to detect them and correct them.

The paper next presents a taxonomy of software error causes, and some analyses of the design error data, performed to obtain a better understanding of the nature of large-scale software design errors and to evaluate alternative methods of preventing, detecting, and eliminating them.

Based on this analysis of observational data, a hypothesis was derived regarding the potential cost-effectiveness of an automated aid to detecting inconsistencies between assertions about the nature of of inputs and outputs of the various elements (functions, modules, data bases, data sources, etc.) of the software design. This hypothesis was tested by developing a prototype version of such an aid, the Design Assertion Consistency Checker (DACC), using TRW's Generalized Information Management (GIM) System, and using it on a large-scale software project with 186 elements and 967 assertions about their inputs and outputs.

Of the 121 000 possible mismatches between input and output assertions, DACC found 818, at a cost in computer time of $30. Most of the mismatches resulted from shortfalls in the initial version of DACC or the initial data preparation, such as a lack of a synonym capability and a lack of explicit statements about external inputs and outputs. However, a number of serious mismatches were exposed at a time when they were easy to correct, and a most useful worklist generated of items needing resolution before allowing the design effort to proceed to further detail.

In general, the data confirmed the hypothesis about the general utility of a DACC capability for large software projects. However, a number of additional features should be considered to compensate for current deficiencies (in areas such as manuscript preparation) and to fully take advantage of haveing the software design in machine-readable form.

Index Terms—Automated aids, design validation, information systems, large-scale software projects, reliable software, software design, software productivity, software specifications, software tools, verification and validation.

DIFFERENCES BETWEEN LARGE AND SMALL SOFTWARE DESIGN ACTIVITIES

THE development of reliable large-scale software systems presents a number of problems and challenges not generally encountered in small projects. Here, a "small project" is one in which a single individual can encompass and resolve any and all of the significant macro and micro issues involved in developing the system.

On large projects, problems such as interface definition, ambiguity resolution, management visibility, and consistency of assumptions are the dominant ones. Problems such as computational accuracy, intraroutine control, and correct syntax still exist as error sources, but are relatively less significant than they are on smaller projects.

In particular, the error distributions on large projects differ considerably from the most familiar data on software error sources: experimental studies such as those of Rubey *et al.* [9] and Youngs [16].

The utility of these experimental studies has been considerable; however, it is limited by the fact that each effort studied began with a clean, unambiguous statement of a stand-alone programming problem. Thus, in these studies, there was virtually no chance for errors due to interface inconsistencies, incomplete problem statements, ambiguous specifications, or inconsistent assumptions. The relative importance of these design-oriented error sources can be seen from the summary data in Table I on the relative frequency of design and programming errors found in an analysis performed by TRW for RADC (Thayer *et al.* [14]) of the errors found in a series of five modifications to a large (100 000 source statement), generally good (on schedule, within budget) TRW software project earlier analyzed by Bosch and Hetrick [3].

DESIGN AND CODING ERROR TYPES

Some indication of the differences between design and coding error types is seen in Table II which shows a classification of the 224 types of software error encountered in the original software development project referred to above. For each general error class, Table II gives the number of error types in each class which arose primarily in the design or the coding phase. The mostly-coding error types tend to be the ones predominating in the Rubey *et al.* [9] and Youngs [16] studies: computation, indexing, and control flow problems. The mostly-design errors tend to involve interface problems between the code and the data base, peripheral I/O devices, and system users.

For this project, Fig. 1 shows an even more striking contrast with respect to the relative difficulty of eliminating design and coding errors. Not only did the number of types of design error outweigh the coding error types, 64

TABLE I
RELATIVE FREQUENCY OF DESIGN AND CODING ERRORS

Modification	Source Statements (No.)	Design Errors[a] (%)	Coding Errors (%)
A	1253	73.6	26.4
B	9880	73.7	26.3
C	779	35.6	64.4
D	9631	51.6	48.4
E	4575	58.8	41.2

[a] An error was counted as a design error if its correction involved changing the detailed design specification.

TABLE II
DESIGN VERSUS CODING ERRORS BY CATEGORY

Error Category	No. of Error Types Design	Coding
Mostly design error types		
Tape handling	24	0
Hardware interface	9	0
Card processing	17	1
Disk handling	11	2
User interface	10	2
Error message processing	8	3
Bit manipulation	4	2
Data base interface	19	10
About even		
Listable output processing	12	8
Software interface	9	6
Iterative procedure	7	8
Mostly coding error types		
Computation	8	20
Indexing and subscripting	1	19

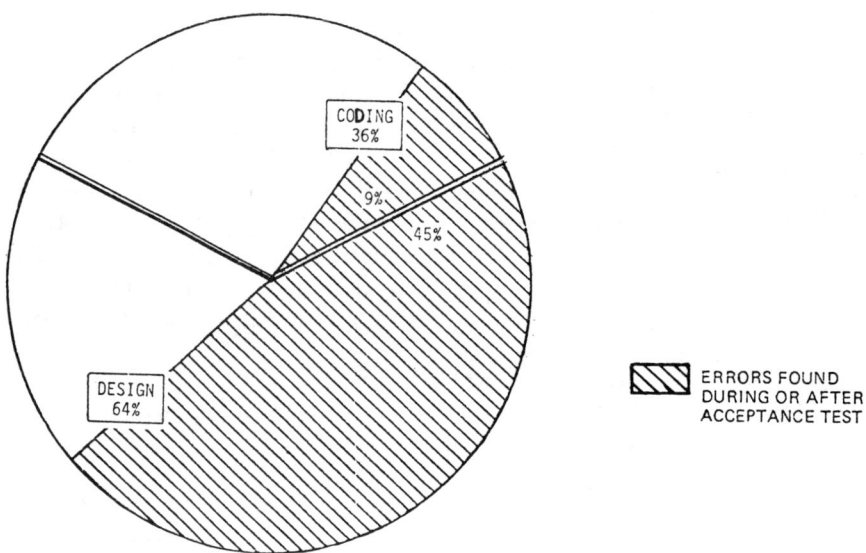

Fig. 1. Software error sources (TRW CCIP-85 data: 220 error types).

percent to 36 percent, but also the design errors took the longest by far to detect and correct. Of the 54 percent of the error types typically not caught until acceptance, integration, or delivery testing, only 9 percent were coding errors; the other 45 percent were design errors. Also, although no related quantitative data were collected, experience indicated that the correction of design errors consumed a great deal more effort than the correction of coding errors.

Additional analysis of the data presented by Shooman and Bolsky [10] indicates that the average time to diagnose and correct design-type errors was about twice that for coding-type errors.

	Design Error (h)	Coding Error (h)
Average diagnostic time	3.1	2.2
Average correction time	4.0	0.8
Total	7.1	3.0

Clearly, one would like to develop capabilities to detect and correct design errors early in the design phase rather

TABLE III
A Taxonomy of Software Error Causes

Transformation	Error Type			
	Communication	Completeness	Consistency	Clerical
USER NEEDS		Data archiving unspecified	Data secure and totally accessible	
USER WANTS	Assume on-line means random access	Additional communication system to interface	Coordinate system specifications	10M bytes entered instead of 10M bits
FUNCTIONAL SPEC	Assume data already ordered	Fail to specify termination condition	Input data overflow allowed	Safety-lock condition formula written with + instead of -
SYSTEM SPEC	Wrong response to operator action specified	Fail to specify logical end of tape	Overlapping table specifications	Incorrect transcription of data conversion formula
DETAIL SPEC	Assume OS manual correct	Fail to initialize storage area	Parameter list out of order	Incorrect value of constant coded
CODE				

than late in the test phase. In order to formulate incisive hypotheses about the potential payoffs of such capabilities, though, we need a better understanding of the *causes* of errors and a more detailed analysis of the specific error types encountered. These are covered in the next two sections.

A TAXONOMY OF SOFTWARE ERROR CAUSES

Error Causes by Phase and Category: Particularly on large projects, but also on small projects, a great deal of error-prone activity goes on before coding begins. First, an attempt is made to determine what information processing capabilities the users need. In general, this is imperfectly determined and resembles more of a statement of what users know they want. (For example, they may not know they need data base archiving until the first time their irreplaceable file is destroyed.) Next, the various statements of need or want are pulled together (imperfectly) into a functional specification for the software. Subsequent imperfect transformations yield a system specification (preliminary design) and a detailed specification. Once the detailed specification is reviewed and approved, the final transformation into code is performed.

During each of the above transformations into successively refined software specifications, several types of error can occur.

1) Communication: There was a misunderstanding of the requirements expressed in the previous stage.

2) Completeness: There was an incomplete grasp of the requirements expressed or implicit in the previous stage.

3) Consistency: The requirements were well understood, but conceptual errors were made in implementing them at the next stage.

4) Clerical: The requirements were well understood, but clerical errors were made in implementing them at the next stage.

Table III presents a taxonomy of software error sources, giving for each transformation an example of each error type. The data archiving example cited above, for example, is classified as a lack of completeness in transforming user needs into a statement of user wants. The other examples are fairly self-explanatory. The definition of communication error is slightly extended in the coding-phase example ("assume OS manual correct") to cover the class of errors resulting from faulty or misunderstood documentation of support software.

USES OF THE TAXONOMY

One useful aspect of such a taxonomy is as a means of assessing the relative power of alternative techniques to eliminate software errors. For example, proof techniques attack only the types of errors occurring after a specification is available; i.e., errors in the bottom three rows. GO TO free programming *per se* only attacks a subset of consistency problems in transforming detailed specifications into code (and, to some extent, some consistency[1] problems in the previous two transformations).

The taxonomy has also been useful as an aid to developing and testing hypotheses about the potential utility of possible new tools for preventing, detecting, and eliminating software errors, particularly in the requirements formulation and design phase. The next section in this paper describes the data analysis and subsequent hypothesis formulation which led to the development and evaluation of such an automated aid to reliable large-scale software design, the Design Assertion Consistency Checker (DACC).

SOFTWARE ERROR DATA ANALYSIS

Table IV (Boehm *et al.* [1]) shows the first segment of a more detailed analysis of the 224 types of errors on the

---

[1] However, the enhanced understandability and testability of such programs generally makes it easier to find and correct other types of errors.

TABLE IV
Evaluation of Error-Detecting Capabilities (Metrics) Versus Error Type (First 12 of 224 Error Types)

Error Type	1 Requirements	2 Design	3 Code	4 Development Test	5 Validation	6 Acceptance	7 Integration	8 Delivery
Errors in Preparation or Processing of Card Input Data								
1. Program expects parameter in different format than is given in Program Requirement Specification.	O	CS-13				F		
2. Program does not expect or accept a required parameter.	O	CS-13					F	
3. Program expects parameters in a different order than that which is specified.	O	CS-13					F	
4. Program does not accept data through the entire range which is specified.	O	CS-13				F		
5. Program expects parameter in units different from that which is specified.	O	CS-13				F		
6. Nominal or default value utilized by program in the absence of specific input data is different from that which is specified.	O					F		
7. Program accepts data outside of allowable range limits.	O						F	
8. Program will not accept all data within allowable range limits.	O						F	
9. Program overflows core tables with data that is within the allowed range.	O			CP-9			F	
10. Program overflows allotted space in mass storage with data that is within the allowed range.	O			CP-9			F	
11. Program executes first test case properly but succeeding test cases fail.	O					F		
12. Program expects parameter in a different location than specified.	O	CS-13				F		

O = Error origin
F = Error found
CS-N = Consistency-checking aid N applied at this phase would generally have detected error.
CP-N = Completeness-checking aid N applied at this phase would generally have detected error.

software project summarized above. It includes information on when each type of error typically originated (*O*) where it was typically found (*F*), and when various potential text-scanning capabilities would have typically detected the error. For example, the CS-13 capability cited in the table refers to a capability which would scan standard software module header blocks. It would check the consistency of their information, with respect to assertions in the header blocks about the nature of inputs and outputs, including:

1) data type and format;
2) number of inputs;
3) order of inputs
4) units;
5) acceptable ranges;
6) associated storage locations;
7) source (device or logical file or record);
8) access (read-only, restricted access).

The CS-13 entries in Table IV indicate that if coding of the module had been preceded by such a module description with the assertions about its inputs and outputs, then an automated consistency checker could generally have caught the error before coding began.

Of the 12 types of card processing errors shown in Table IV, the CS-13 consistency checker would have caught 6. Overall, out of the 224 types of errors, this capability would generally have caught 18. The next most effective capability would perform checks on the consistency of the actual code with the module description produced during the design phase for capability CS-13 above. (For example, for each output assertion, it would check if the variable appeared on the left of an equals sign in the code, and perform a units check on the computation.) This capability would have caught 10 types of error, but not until the initial code-scanning phase. A total of 29 text-scanning capabilities would have caught at least one of the 224 error types, but none of the others would have caught more than 7. More detailed results of this analysis are in Boehm et al. [1].

THE DESIGN ASSERTION CONSISTENCY CHECKER (DACC)

Generalized Information Management (GIM) Support Structure: Based on the above data analysis, a hypothesis was derived regarding the potential cost-effectiveness of a module input–output consistency checking aid along the lines of capability CS-13. To test this hypothesis, such a capability was developed, the DACC, and tried on a large software specification. By using TRW's GIM system [15], DACC was built in a very flexible way within a relatively short time.

The GIM system provides a set of general capabilities for organizing, manipulating, and interrogating data

SOFTWARE REQUIREMENTS GENERAL DETAILED REPORT

FUNCTIONAL REQUIREMENT
COMPUTE REQUIRED VEHICLE ATTITUDE

COMPUTATIONAL FREQUENCY
1/GUIDANCE CYCLE

APPLICABLE MISSION PHASES:
BOOST

ASSUMPTIONS:
NOTE GB-4.1

INPUT NO.	DESCRIPTION	SOURCE	DIM	UNITS	CS	TYPE	MINIMUM	MAXIMUM	ACCURACY
1	VEH POSITION	N	3	M	ECI	FL			
2	VEH VELOCITY	N	3	M/S	ECI	FL			
3	VEH ACCELERATION	N	3	M/S2	ECI	FL			
4	VEH ANGULAR RATES	N	3	R/S	ECI	FL			
5	VEH ANGULAR ACCELERATION	N	3	R/S2	ECI	FL			
6	TARGETED POSITION AT STAGING	N	3	M	ECI	FL			
7	TARGETED VELOCITY AT STAGING	N	3	M/S	ECI	FL			
8	ACCELERATION PROFILE	L		M/S2		FL			
9	VEH ATTITUDE	N	3	R	ECI	FL			

OUTPUT NO.	DESCRIPTION	DEST	DIM	UNITS	CS	TYPE	MINIMUM	MAXIMUM	ACCURACY
1	COMMANDED VEH ATTITUDE	D	3	R	ECI	FL			

Fig. 2. DACC design element summary.

AMC	ACCEPTABLE NAMES	MAX LEN	TYPE	STORE TYPE	SPECIAL REQUIREMENTS	SAMPLE ENTRIES	DEFINITION
0	REQT R	3*3*6	A/N	S.V.	SUBSYSTEM is syn for first concatenated segment	PM*4*1.1.2	REQT ID: SUBSYS* Optional *Seq. No.
1	UPDATE-DATE	11	A/N	N.S.			
2	FUNC-NAME A2	85	A/N	S.V.		Compute Required Vehicle Attitude	
3	SPARE-1	2	A/N	M.V.	Reserved for future attribute		
4	FUNC-DESCRIP	200	A/N	M.V.		TEXT	Not available in formatted reports
5	SPARE-2	2	A/N	M.V.	Reserved for future attribute		
6	PERF-REQT	200	A/N	M.V.		TEXT	Not available in formatted reports
7	PHASE A7	30	A/N	M.V.		BOOST	
8	COMP-FREQ A8	20	A/N	M.V.		1/GUIDANCE CYCLE	
9	SOURCE A9	15	A/N	M.V.		G	Subsystem Code for source of Reqt
10	SYS A10	5	A/N	S.V.		X	
11	SUBSYS A11	5	A/N	S.V.		X	

Fig. 3. Design element attribute representation: general.

bases in either batch or on-line modes. Versions exist for both IBM 360-370 and Univac 1100-series equipment. Its usage in building the DACC capability is best illustrated through examples of its general design description capabilities. The examples used are from the spacecraft data processing specification chosen as a test case to evaluate DACC.

DACC Design Element Report Format: Fig. 2 shows one of the general summary reports of the design element information presented to DACC. Besides accommodating information about the inputs and outputs of system elements, it provides capabilities for storing, updating, manipulating, and reporting a number of other attributes: computational frequency, hierarchical level (system, subsystem, function, routine), mission phases (prelaunch, boost, orbit, etc.), assumptions, references to applicable source documents, etc. The assertions about inputs and outputs included their intended source and destination (optional), their dimensionality, the units and coordinate system in which they were expressed, their type (fixed point, floating point, alphanumeric, Boolean, etc.), and the range of acceptable values (minimum and maximum). Type and range information was not generated in the test application.

Design Information Representation: Figs. 3 and 4 show two of the forms which describe how the above information is represented in the GIM system. Definitions of the attributes represented in the first few columns are shown below; the others are self-explanatory.

Attribute Mark Count (AMC): A GIM system parameter used to identify the position of an attribute within a file record.

Maximum Length (MAX LEN): Defines the maximum number of characters allowed in an attribute field.

0	INPUTS I	3*3*6*3	A/N	S.V.	LAST CONCATENATED SEGMENT IS A DASH NO. OF THE PARENT REQT	PM*A*1.1.2*1	SUBSYSTEM is syn for first concatenated segment
1	UPDATE-DATE	11	A/N	N.S.	DO NOT ENTER		
2	DESCRIP	60	A/N	S.V.R.	MUST BE SELECTED FROM I/O FILE OR BE A NEW DESCRIP	VEHICLE ACCELERATION	
3	SOURCE	6	A/N	S.V.		N	Source of input
4	DIM	6	A/N	S.V.		3	Dimension
5	UNITS	6	A/N	S.V.		M/S	
6	COORD	6	A/N	S.V.		ECI	
7	TYPE	6	A/N	S.V.		FL	
8	MIN	10	N	S.V.		MIN	
9	MAX	10	N	S.V.		MAX	

Fig. 4. Design element attribute representation: inputs.

Type: Contents of the field stored in each attribute, e.g.,

A = Alphabetic,

N = Numeric,

A/N = Alpha/Numeric.

Store Type: Defines the method in which data are to be stored in each attribute; e.g.,

SV = Single value

MV = Multiple values

NS = Nonstore; the user may not physically enter any value.

For example, then, the first line of Fig. 3 shows that the initial item in the file (with a mark count of 0), is the identifier of the design element or requirement (REQT), represented as three fields separated by asterisks, the first two with ≤ 3 characters and the third with ≤ 6 characters (3*3*6). Each of these fields contain single (SV) alphanumeric (A/N) character strings, as shown by the example in *Sample Entries* in Fig. 3.

Design Data Input: A special purpose input form was used to gather and enter the software design information into DACC. Additional forms were provided for the assertions about inputs and outputs. For many of the attributes, standard definitions of the acceptable variables were given (G for Guidance, N for Navigation, PM for Payload Management, R for radians, B for body-axis coordinate system, N/A for not available, etc.). The bulk of the information was entered thus in a batch mode. The on-line mode was quite useful for additions and corrections; examples of such commands are the following:

ADD TO REQT/$G^*A^*1.0$/PHASE "BOOST."
DELETE REQT/$G^*A^*1.0$/PHASE.
CHANGE INPUTS/$PM^*A^*1.1.2^*3$/MAX "56" TO "57."

Design Query Capabilities: Further, the general on-line query functions of GIM provided a number of useful capabilities for DACC besides just consistency checking. For example, here are some commands which can be used to query the data base:

LIST ANY REQT AND FUNC-NAME WITH PHASE "BOOST."
COUNT INPUTS WITH SOURCE "G" ANDD WITH DIM "2."
LIST REQT /$G^*A^*3.0$/ INPUTS.

(In GIM, ANDD is the logical "and;" AND is a "convenience connective" which improves readability but is ignored by the interpreter.)

EXPERIENCE WITH DACC ON A LARGE DESIGN SPECIFICATION

The DACC system was tried on a large-scale spacecraft software requirements and design specification which had been compiled by a team of about 10-12 engineers. A total of 186 design elements were entered into the system, with assertions about the nature of 514 inputs and 453 outputs.

Fig. 5 shows the first page of the resulting Inconsistency Report produced by DACC. It includes not only mismatches between assertions about inputs and outputs, but also indications that certain expected inputs are not being produced by any other element, or that certain outputs are not being used. For example, the first entry shows that a certain Guidance Subsystem (G,0,3) produced as its fourth output (4,0) the variable V RESIDUAL, but that this quantity was not being used by any other of the 186 subsystems (NOT USED). The second entry shows that one Guidance Subsystem expected the input V VECTOR to be defined in the Mean 1950 Cartesian Coordinate System (M), but that the Guidance Subsystem producing V VECTOR was doing so in the Orbiter Body Axis Coordinate System (B). The third entry shows that a Display and Control Subsystem ($D,GOS,1$) expected the input ABORT ALTERNATIVE OPTIONS, but that no other subsystem was producing these (NOT AVAILABLE).

Of the approximately 121 000 possible mismatches between inputs and outputs, there were 818 reported by the Inconsistency Report. Of these, 783 were NOT USED or NOT AVAILABLE statements, and 35 were mismatches between input and output assertions about the same variable. As shown below, most of these were symptoms more of deficiencies in the initial version of DACC than of problems with the software design. But there were a number of actual design mismatches found, which otherwise probably would not have been discovered until late in software

INPUT/OUTPUT	I/O	SOURCE	DIM	UNITS	COORD
G O 3 4 V RESIDUAL NOT USED	O		3	M/S	B
G C 3 3 V VECTOR	I	G	3	M/S	M
G O 5 3	O		3	M/S	B
D GOS 1 2 ABORT ALTERNATIVE OPTIONS NOT AVAILABLE	I	L	VAR	VAR	VAR
D GOS 1 17 ABORT CONDITIONS CREW-ALERT NOT AVAILABLE	I	M,N	VAR	VAR	SCALE
C TVC 1 6 ACCELERATION DATA NOT AVAILABLE	I	I	2	M/S2	B
C ABO 1 6 ACCELEROMETER DATA NOT AVAILABLE	I	I	2	M/S2	B
C TVC 2 5 ACCELEROMETER DATA NOT AVAILABLE	I	I	2	M/S2	B

Fig. 5. Page 1 of DACC Inconsistency Report.

testing. Some of the mismatches were difficult to classify uniquely; thus, some of the summary results below are approximate rather than exact counts.

1) Over 50 percent of the mismatches were NOT USED or NOT AVAILABLE statements which would not have occurred had there been a means to handle inputs and outputs from the external environment. One way to avoid these would have been to include an "external" tag which would trigger a bypass of the consistency checker. However, as many software errors come from erroneous assumptions about the nature of external inputs and outputs, it would be preferable to have assertions about such items explicitly entered into DACC via dummy design elements, or explicit "real world entities" as in ISDOS (Teichroew and Sayari [13]).

2) Over 25 percent of the mismatches were NOT USED or NOT AVAILABLE statements which occurred because of differences in terminology on the names of inputs and outputs. For example, 12 elements specifying PRESENT ORBITER STATE VECTOR as an input were told it was not available, when in fact it was being generated by another element under the name OR-BITER STATE VECTOR. Most of these mismatches would be eliminated by either of two steps. One would be to have established standard terminology for inputs and outputs as with units, coordinates, etc.; the other would be to incorporate a synonym capability into DACC. Actually, it is advisable to incorporate both of these steps.

3) Over 10 percent of the mismatches were NOT USED or NOT AVAILABLE statements which indeed referred to inputs and outputs which had not been entered into DACC. Most were being generated and were not yet loaded into DACC, but some were clear oversights which might not have been caught until the software integration phase.

4) Of the 35 mismatches between assertions, 25 were either clerical errors or nonstandard terminology (RAD for radians). Three had one NOT AVAILABLE statement matched with one positive description. The remaining seven were actual mismatches between assertions about dimensions, coordinate systems, and units (e.g., degrees versus radians). These in particular might not have been caught until very late in the testing and integration phase, and are typically the kind of errors which are difficult to correct, as their correction often causes ripple effects into other portions of the software.

In addition, there were a number of second-order effects which were picked up once the first mismatches had been corrected. For example, there were several units terminology mismatches which were flagged once the ORBITER STATE VECTOR terminology was reconciled.

EVALUATION AND CONCLUSIONS

Useful Features: The experiment showed that a capability such as DACC has considerable value in detecting interface errors in large-scale software at a point where they are easy to resolve. Several of the mismatches detected were of types which characteristically on earlier projects were not detected until the very late stages, when they were often quite difficult to resolve.

The other major value of the Inconsistency Report was as an engineering work-list generator: the NOT USED and NOT AVAILABLE outputs provided a checklist of potential interface problems which should be resolved before proceeding to more detailed design. Many of the items were simple matters of terminology resolution, but some involved more fundamental conflicts of assumptions about "who was furnishing what to whom."

In general, the machine-analyzable design information provides a compatible extension to the manual HIPO (IBM 1973) and Structured Design (Stevens et al. [11]) techniques. In addition, the GIM capabilities underlying DACC were found quite useful for the processes of updating and interrogating the data base of design statements. The capability can also be used on software requirements specifications when they are expressed in terms of functional elements.

Costs: The cost of determining the mismatches and running the Inconsistency Report was a very nominal $30. However, it cost several hundred dollars to enter the design information into the GIM data base. This expense would not be considered a difficulty if it replaced typists generating the same information for official design documentation. For highly structured design information, the GIM report generator works quite well, but its manuscript perparation capabilities for free form text were not sufficient to generate acceptable contract reports for the project. This difficulty in the report-generation area has been the main impediment to regular use of the system, and has been a major consideration in evaluating alternative realizations of DACC and related design capabilities.

Additional Design Features: Some of the additional desired features would simply round out the basic consistency-checking capabilities of DACC, e.g., a synonym capability, better report generation, capabilities for better accommodating assertions about external data and about data bases. Another general reaction to the DACC experiment was a feeling that "once all that information is available in machine-readable form, there are some other useful things I would like to have done with it." Most of the capabilities suggested were similar to those proposed or under development in such systems as ISDOS (Teichroew and Sayari [13]), TOPD (Henderson and Snowdon [5]), and ZYGO (Swanson [12]), including:

1) Representation, analysis, and graphic presentation of the control hierarchy of the design elements;

2) Incorporating reachability considerations in the input–output consistency analysis;

3) Generating N-square charts summarizing data flows;

4) Accumulating the individual statements about inputs into first-cut versions of a data base description, an input data requirements list, and an output data summary;

5) Providing traceability information to and from software requirements and detailed design;

6) Accepting additional information on the performance characteristics, memory and source-instruction estimates for design elements and using them to produce first-cut core budgets, software schedules, and inputs to system performance models.

7) Integrating these process-oriented design considerations with properties-oriented capabilities focused on enhancing maintainability, reliability, portability, etc. (Boehm [2]).

Work is currently underway at TRW to assess existing methodologies such as those cited above and those developed to support existing TRW projects, and to determine an integrated architecture for a Design Description Language and a support system called Design Expression and Validation for Information System Engineering (DEVISE), incorporating as many of the desired features as appears initially feasible.

Another open issue involves how best the job of data-type consistency checking should be split between the design phase (via such vehicles as DACC) and the compilation and execution phase, where a number of efforts are or have been focusing their attention (Hansen [4]), (Hoare [6]), and (Liskov and Zilles [8]). It may well be that the answer will turn out differently for large software projects than for small ones. As pointed out above, large projects have a good deal more difficulty ensuring consistency of design terminology and assumptions, and are likely to require more extensive automated design aids than small projects, on which a single unifying individual can perform such functions. However, given the difficulty of coping with all of the multifarious sources of software error, it is probably a safe assumption that both approaches will prove useful to individuals and organizations attempting to produce reliable software.

ACKNOWLEDGMENT

Several individuals at TRW made useful contributions to the formulation and development of DACC: J. H. Drexler, R. C. Eberhard, R. L. Eshbaugh, F. C. Manthey, J. H. Petersen, and J. A. Sewell.

REFERENCES

[1] B. W. Boehm, J. R. Brown, H. Kaspar, M. Lipow, G. J. McLeod, and M. J. Merritt, *Characteristics of Software Quality*, TRW, Redondo Beach, Calif, TRW-SS-73-09, Dec. 1973.
[2] B. W. Boehm, "Some steps toward formal and automated aids to software requirements analysis and design," in *Proc. IFIP Congr.*, 1974, pp. 192–197.
[3] C. A. Bosch and W. L. Hetrick, "Software development characteristics study for the CCIP-85 study group," TRW, Redondo Beach, Calif, TRW Rep. 4851.1–003, Oct. 1971.
[4] P. B. Hansen, *Operating System Principles*. Englewood Cliffs, N.J.: Prentice-Hall, 1973.
[5] P. Henderson and R. A. Snowdon, "Some design criteria for program development tools," Univ. Newcastle, Great Britain, MRM-53, Aug. 1973.
[6] C. A. R. Hoare, "Proof of correctness of data representation," *Acta Inform.*, vol. 1, no. 2, pp. 271–281, 1972.
[7] *HIPO: Design Aid and Documentation Tool*, IBM Corporation, Poughkeepsie, N. Y., Apr. 1973.
[8] B. Liskov and S. Zilles, "Programming with abstract data types," *SIGPLAN Notices*, Apr. 1974, pp. 50–59.
[9] R. J. Rubey et al., "Comparative evaluation of PL/I," USAF Rep. ESD-TR-68-150, Apr. 1968.
[10] M. L. Shooman and M. I. Bolsky, "Software errors: types,

distribution, test and correction times," in *Proc. Int. Conf. Reliable Software*, Apr. 1975.
[11] W. P. Stevens, G. J. Myers, and L. L. Constantine, "Structured design," *IBM Syst. J.*, vol. 13, no. 2, 1974.
[12] J. Swanson, private communication, General Electric Co., 1974.
[13] D. Teichroew and H. Sayari, "Automation of system building," *Datamation*, pp. 25–30, Aug. 1971.
[14] T. A. Thayer *et al.*, "Software reliability study," TRW, Redondo Beach, Calif, TRW Interim Tech. Rep. to RADC, Contract F30602-74-C-0036, June 1974.
[15] "Generalized information management (GIM) system summary," TRW, Redondo Beach, Calif., TRW Rep. 4660-W001-R0-01, Sept. 1973.
[16] E. Youngs, "Error-proneness in programming," Ph.D. dissertation, Univ. North Carolina, 1970.

Barry W. Boehm is currently Director of Software Research and Technology at TRW Systems. He received the B.A. degree in mathematics from Harvard University, Cambridge, Mass., in 1957 and both the M.A. and Ph.D. degrees in mathematics from the University of California, Los Angeles, in 1961 and 1964, respectively.

Dr. Boehm was previously at the RAND Corporation from 1959 through 1973, at which time he was Head of the Information Sciences and Mathematics Department.

Dr. Boehm is the author of a book on trajectory computation, the editor of a book on community information utilities, and the author of a number of book chapters and research papers on topics in interactive computer graphics, data structures, numerical analysis, simulation, computer-communications systems, and future implications of computer technology.

He is affiliated with the following scientific organizations: Associate Fellow of the American Institute of Aeronautics and Astronautics, for which he served as Chairman, Techical Committee on Computer Systems, 1967-1969, member, Technical Committee on Guidance and Control, 1966-1967, National Lecturer, 1968; the International Academy of Astronautics; member, Orbital International Laboratory Committee, 1969-1973; the American Automatic Control Council; the Association for Computing Machinery; the American Association for the Advancement of Science; and the IEEE Computer Society, in which he serves as a member of the Technical Committee on Software Engineering.

Robert K. McClean was born in Toronto, Ont., Canada. He received the B.A.Sc. degree in 1959 and M.A.Sc. degree in 1961 in electrical engineering, both from the University of Toronto, Toronto, Ont., Canada.

From 1961 to 1963 he worked on aircraft and missile dynamics and control problems at Northrop Corporation. During the 1963–1972 period, at the Aerospace Corporation, he developed vehicle dynamics simulation and guidance software for the USAF Titan III Program. He also provided planning and direction for the USAF on R&D projects for the development of higher order languages, LSI chip design aids, LSI spaceborne computers and computer aids to support spaceborne software design and implementation. He has spent the last two years at TRW Corporation, Redondo Beach, Calif., performing research and development on command and control systems exercising, application of microprogramming to software development and testing, and software requirements and design definition aids.

Mr. McClean is a member of the Association for Computing Machinery.

D.B. Urfrig received the B.S. degree from the University of California, Los Angeles, and the M.S. degree from the University of Southern California, Los Angeles.

He was Manager of a DOD Space Shuttle On-Board Software Requirements Study just completed for SAMSO and an earlier DOD/STS Mission Planning and Software Requirements Study. His 12 years of experience include direct supervision responsibility for Targeting and Trajectory Data Book generation for Minuteman III R&D launches. He supervised preflight and postflight mission analysis tasks for Minuteman III operational training launches. Architect of Automatic Trajectory Analysis programs for both Minuteman mission analysis and Apollo flight program verification. He was Task Manager for independent verification of the Primary GN&C Flight programs for the Apollo Lunar Module. He is now Project Manager for TRW Corporation, Redondo Beach, Calif.

Programming Techniques

S. L. Graham, R. L. Rivest
Editors

A Controlled Experiment in Program Testing and Code Walkthroughs/Inspections

Glenford J. Myers
IBM Systems Research Institute

This paper describes an experiment in program testing, employing 59 highly experienced data processing professionals using seven methods to test a small PL/I program. The results show that the popular code walkthrough/inspection method was as effective as other computer-based methods in finding errors and that the most effective methods (in terms of errors found and cost) employed pairs of subjects who tested the program independently and then pooled their findings. The study also shows that there is a tremendous amount of variability among subjects and that the ability to detect certain types of errors varies from method to method.

Key Words and Phrases: software reliability, program verification, debugging, testing, code walkthroughs, code inspections, personnel selection
CR Categories: 4.6

1. Introduction

The introduction of new programming methodologies and tools over the last few years has greatly outpaced our efforts to experiment with alternatives in order to analyze their differences and assess their benefits. One frequently finds statements in the literature such as "Method A was found to increase productivity by 39 percent over method B," but when one attempts to analyze the underlying evidence, one normally sees that methods A and B were used on two different projects with different people, different objectives, and literally hundreds of other differing characteristics. In other words, the statement is derived in many instances from a completely uncontrolled environment, rendering it at best misleading.

Unfortunately, controlled experiments in the area of software development tend to be costly and time consuming. Researchers have attempted to circumvent this by performing experiments using "cheap" labor (e.g. the captive audience in an introductory computer science course). However, although much of this work has provided useful insights, there exists the question of whether one can extrapolate, to a typical industrial environment, experimental results obtained from trainee programmers or programmers with only a few years of experience.

A third problem is the lack of data on program-testing methods, which is particularly alarming in light of the fact that program testing consumes approximately half of most organizations' development budgets. For instance, the idea of code walkthroughs or inspections [1] (a semiformal, noncomputer-based method of program testing performed by a team of individuals) has become popular, but no controlled data are available establishing that this method is more effective than traditional computer-based testing. As another example, there are differences of opinion as to whether a program tester should derive test cases based on an examination of the program's logic flow (e.g., to ensure that each conditional transfer has been exercised in all possible directions), but little data exist on which to base these opinions.

This paper presents results of an ongoing research project to answer some of these questions. The purpose of this research is to study, using controlled experiments with highly experienced programmers, the process of program testing, including the relative effectiveness and economics of different testing techniques and the factors that influence a programmer's testing effectiveness. This paper describes the results of an experiment in testing a PL/I program using three approaches and variations thereof: 1) Computer-based testing where the tester has access to only the program's specification, 2) computer-based testing where the tester has access to the program's specification and source-language listing, and 3) noncomputer-based testing by teams of programmers employing the walkthrough/inspection method.

As mentioned earlier, research in this area has been

rather limited. The majority of the existing controlled experiments have been in the areas of programming-language design and the use of interactive versus batch-processing systems; the author of [11] reviews many of these efforts. The work of [6] is closely related to the experiment described herein: his experiment employed 39 subjects testing three PL/I programs using three methods: Testing by using only the specification, testing by using the specification and the program listing, and individual desk checking. However, his subjects were mostly students with little programming experience (an average of three years). Among other things, his work showed that the first two methods were equally effective and that the third method was significantly inferior.

Another relevant experiment [5] employed 18 inexperienced programmers testing five Cobol programs. The intent of the experiment was to determine if programmers were more effective in testing only one program at a time, or two or three programs. A small five-programmer experiment was conducted on the Safeguard Project [8], where errors were seeded into a program and individual code reading was used to locate the errors. The work of [3, 4] is also relevant, although it is in the area of debugging rather than testing. (Debugging is distinguished from testing in that testing is the process of showing that a program contains errors, but debugging is the process of finding the precise location of the error within the program [9].) Their experiments used ten moderately experienced Fortran programmers. The subjects were given four Fortran subroutines, told that each contained a one-statement error, and asked to locate the error using several debugging aids. Although their experiments produced several interesting observations, the applicability of their findings is questionable, since debuggers do not start with the knowledge that a program contains only a single one-statement error. Finally [7] has reported encouraging results in the use of symbolic execution as a testing technique.

2. The Experiment

The experiment discussed in this paper employed 59 highly experienced data processing professionals. The subjects' goal was to test (identify errors in) a small text-formatting program written in PL/I. The subjects were divided into three categories. Subjects in category A were asked to test the program by using a terminal and having only the specification from which to derive test cases. Subjects in category B operated in the same environment, but they were also given a copy of the program's listing from which they could derive additional test cases. The subjects were asked to work independently.

The subjects in category C were grouped into three-person teams. Each team was given the specification and listing of the program and asked to test the program using the manual walkthrough/inspection method.

In general, no time constraints were placed on the subjects. They were asked to test the program until they felt that they found all of the errors (if any). The subjects had no prior knowledge of the number or nature of the errors; they were simply told of a "suspicion that the program is not perfect." The only time constraint was that the walkthrough/inspection sessions were limited to 90 minutes, although the participants were given the materials in advance and could choose the amount of time to be spent in preparing for the session. Other than constraining the methods by the documentation given as described above, all participants were free to choose their testing strategies and methods. For instance, the people in category C were permitted to decide upon the inspection techniques to be used. Most used a combination of mentally walking test-cases through the program's logic and checking the logic for common errors.

Although the three methods were evaluated competitively, one should not draw the conclusion that the purpose of the experiment is to discourage use of the "less than best" methods. Indeed, given the magnitude of today's software reliability problem, as many different error-detection techniques as is feasible should be employed. In addition, one should be cautious in interpreting the results. For instance, the idea of code walkthroughs/inspections is generally recognized as a cost-effective technique in that the earlier that errors can be detected in a project, the lower the cost of repairing the errors and the higher the probability of repairing the errors correctly. This experiment does not address these broad issues; rather, it is a microscopic analysis of the relative effectiveness of the techniques.

2.1 The Subjects

The 59 subjects were students in a course on software reliability at the IBM Systems Research Institute. Their average number of years of experience in the computing field was 11; the range was from 7 to 20 years. Of the 59 participants, 49 were employed as programmers or program testers. The remaining 10 had programming experience, but were not considered to be "professional programmers"; their primary jobs were systems engineers, project managers, documentation writers, and electrical engineers. The subjects were considered to be above-average employees (a requisite for admission to the Systems Research Institute) and were judged to be highly motivated during the experiment. The motivation stemmed from the competitive nature of the situation and the knowledge that someone (the author) knew of the total number of errors in the program.

2.2 The Experimental Design

The crucial part of any experiment is, of course, designing the experiment to avoid biases in the outcome. The technique used in this experiment was to pretest the subjects. Part of the pretesting was done by questionnaire. Each subject was asked to rank his or her prior testing experience on a scale from 1 to 4 (1 = have never tested a program, 2 = have tested programs infrequently,

3 = have tested programs frequently, 4 = primary job is program testing); knowledge of PL/I on a scale from 1 to 3 (1 = could not understand a simple PL/I program, 2 = could understand a simple PL/I program, 3 = very experienced in PL/I); and experience with walkthrough/inspection techniques (0 = none, 1 = some). The subjects were also pretested by giving them a specification for an extremely simple program and asking them to write test cases for it. Their test cases were analyzed with respect to a set of errors in the program to obtain another measure of their testing abilities.

The goal was to place the subjects into the three categories such that no category was biased in terms of the above variables. Such placement proved to be infeasible because all subjects in categories B and C needed a PL/I rating of at least 2 (in order to read the program), but there were not enough subjects with this rating to balance all three categories. (Although they averaged 11 years of experience, many of the participants were Fortran, Cobol, APL, RPG, and assembly language programmers.) Also only 22 of the subjects reported prior walkthrough/inspection experience, but it was deemed necessary that each category-C team contain at least one subject with this experience.

The resultant design was to partition people into the three categories such that each category had the same average testing experience (based on both the questionnaire response and the performance on the pretest program). People with a PL/I rating of 1 were automatically placed into category A, and the teams in category C were organized such that each team contained at least one PL/I expert and one person with prior experience in walkthroughs. Hence the known biases were that category C had an average PL/I rating of 2.4, B a rating of 2.1, and A a rating of 1.5, and category C had an average walkthrough-experience rating of 0.6, B a rating of 0.3, and A a rating of 0.2. A smoothing effect came from the fact that the experiment was performed toward the end of the course using [9] as a text, and several lectures had been presented on program testing.

2.3 The Program

The PL/I program was based on an Algol program written, using techniques of program-correctness proofs, by Naur [10] and in which six errors were later discovered by Goodenough and Gerhart [2]. (They claim to have found seven, but their sixth error appears to be a duplicate of their third and fifth errors.) The program was translated into a three-procedure structured PL/I program totalling 63 statements, and a few changes were made to the original specification. The last four original errors were retained in the PL/I program, a few additional original errors were found, several errors were made during the conversion to PL/I, and a few typical errors ("typical" based on the experience of the author) were seeded into the program, bringing the total to 15 known errors. (None of the participants found any heretofore unknown errors.) The program is illustrated in Figure 1.

Each subject was given a specification of the program, and subjects in categories B and C were given a copy of the program listing (a compiler listing). The subjects were not told how many errors existed in the program or that the program had any errors. They were asked to find discrepancies (if any) between the program and its specification and to keep track of any errors found and the time expended. Subjects in categories A and B were also given instructions on how to invoke the program from a terminal. The author was present during the walkthrough/inspection sessions to play the role of the original programmer (i.e., the teams could ask questions about the program). The specification that was used is as follows.

Specification

Given an input text consisting of words separated by blanks or new-line characters, the program formats it into a line-by-line form such that 1) each output line has a maximum of 30 characters, 2) a word in the input text is placed on a single output line, and 3) each output line is filled with as many words as possible.

The input text is a stream of characters, where the characters are categorized as break or nonbreak characters. A break character is a blank, a new-line character (&), or an end-of-text character (/). New-line characters have no special significance; they are treated as blanks by the program. & and / should not appear in the output.

A word is defined as a nonempty sequence of nonbreak characters. A break is a sequence of one or more break characters. A break in the input is reduced to a single blank or start of a new line in the output.

The input text is a single line entered from a terminal similar to an IBM 2741 having a carriage width of 130 characters. When the program is invoked, it prompts the terminal user for a line of input by typing a colon and then skipping to the next line and unlocking the keyboard. The user types the input line, followed by a / (end-of-text) and a carriage return. The program then formats the text and types it on the terminal.

If the input text contains a word that is too long to fit on a single output line, an error message is typed and the program terminates. If the end-of-text character is missing, an error message is issued and the user is again prompted for input with a colon. (End of specification.)

The 15 known errors in the program are listed in Table I.

2.4 Data Collection

A questionnaire was distributed at the end of the experiment asking each participant to describe the errors found and to list the time spent in preparing for the test (e.g. studying the specification and designing test cases) and the time spent performing the test (i.e. executing and verifying test runs or participating in the walkthrough session). The raw data from each category is shown in

Fig. 1.
```
FORM: PROCEDURE OPTIONS (MAIN);
% DECLARE LINESIZE FIXED;
% LINESIZE = 31;
DECLARE (K, BUFPOS, FILL) FIXED DECIMAL (9),
        MAXPOS FIXED DECIMAL (9) INIT (LINESIZE),
        CW CHAR,
        BLANK CHAR INIT (' '),
        LINEFEED CHAR INIT ('$'),
        EOTEXT CHAR INIT ('/'),
        MOREINPUT BIT INIT ('1'B),
        BUFFER (LINESIZE) CHAR;
BUFPOS = 0;
FILL = 0;
DO WHILE (MOREINPUT);
  CALL GCHAR (CW);
  IF (CW = BLANK)|(CW = LINEFEED)|(CW = EOTEXT)
    THEN DO;
      IF (CW = EOTEXT) THEN MOREINPUT = '0'B;
      IF ((FILL + 1 + BUFPOS) < = MAXPOS)
        THEN DO;
          CALL PCHAR (BLANK);
          FILL = FILL + 1;
        END;
        ELSE DO;
          CALL PCHAR (LINEFEED);
          FILL = 0;
        END;
      DO K = 1 TO BUFPOS BY 1;
        CALL PCHAR (BUFFER (K));
      END;
      FILL = FILL + BUFPOS;
      BUFPOS = 0;
    END;
    ELSE IF BUFPOS = MAXPOS
      THEN DO;
        MOREINPUT = '0'B;
        DISPLAY ('WORD TO LONG');
      END;
      ELSE DO;
        BUFPOS = BUFPOS + 1;
        BUFFER (BUFPOS) = CW;
      END;
END;
CALL PCHAR (LINEFEED);
GCHAR: PROCEDURE (C);
DECLARE C CHAR,
        BUFFER (130) STATIC CHAR INIT ('Z'),
        INBUF CHAR (130),
        BCOUNT FIXED DECIMAL (3) STATIC INIT (1);
DECLARE SINPUT FILE STREAM;
IF (BUFFER (1) = 'Z')
  THEN DO;
    GET FILE (SINPUT) EDIT (INBUF) (A (130));
    IF (INDEX (INBUF, EOTEXT) = 0)
      THEN DO;
        DISPLAY ('NO END OF TEXT MARK');
        BUFFER (2) = EOTEXT;
      END;
      ELSE STRING (BUFFER) = INBUF;
  END;
  ELSE;
C = BUFFER (BCOUNT);
BCOUNT = BCOUNT + 1;
END;
PCHAR: PROCEDURE (C);
DECLARE C CHAR,
        OUTLINE (LINESIZE) CHAR STATIC INIT ((LINESIZE)
            (' ')),
        I FIXED DECIMAL (3) STATIC INIT (1);
DECLARE SOUTPUT FILE STREAM;
IF (C = LINEFEED)
  THEN DO;
    PUT FILE (SOUTPUT) SKIP EDIT (STRING (OUTLINE))
        (A (LINESIZE));
    OUTLINE = ' ';
    I = 1;
  END;
  ELSE DO;
    OUTLINE (I) = C;
    I = I + 1;
  END;
END;
END;
```

Tables II–IV. Categories A and B had 16 subjects each; category C consisted of nine teams of three people each. A "X" in a column means that that subject (or team) found the corresponding error.

Table V lists the time expended by each subject (or team of subjects for category C). The three numbers listed are the preparation, test, and total times in minutes.

3. Data Analysis

Before turning to statistics, several observations are apparent as a result of inspecting Tables II–IV. These are:

1. There is a tremendous amount of variability in the individual results. For instance, two people in category A found only one error, but five people found seven errors. The variability among student programmers is generally well known, but the high variability among these highly experienced subjects was somewhat surprising.
2. There is a tremendous amount of variability in the errors detected, particularly in categories A and B. Excepting errors 1, 2, 3, and 5, which were detected with some degree of regularity, the detection of individual types of errors varies widely from individual to individual.
3. The walkthrough method (category C) exhibits less variability, particularly in terms of the individual errors found. This suggests that this method is more predictable than the other methods.
4. The overall results are rather dismal; an observation that should not be surprising to anyone in the software engineering field. The mean number of errors found by all efforts was 5.1, or approximately a third of the known errors.
5. The inability to detect some of the seemingly obvious errors is alarming. For instance, error 1 (blank character at the beginning of the first line) was not detected by everyone. The probable reasons are either failing to inspect the output carefully or incorrectly assuming that the condition is not an error. One might expect errors 2, 3, and 5 to be caught by everyone, since these

Table I. Known errors in the text-formatting program.

Error	Symptom
1	A blank is printed before the first word on the first line unless the first word is 30-characters* long.
2	The program assumes that $ (not &) is the new-line character.
3	The program assumes that the line size is 31 characters, not 30 as stated in the specification.
4	If the first character of an input line is "Z", the line is ignored by the program.
5	The program does not condense successive new-line and blank characters.
6	The use of tab characters in the input text causes the 30-character* line limit to be exceeded.
7	A leading blank line is printed when the first word in the input text is 30 characters* long.
8	If an input line is entered without an end-of-text mark, the program prints a message and prompts for input. However, after the new input line is entered with an end-of-text mark, the program changes the first character in the output to "Z".
9	Spelling error in the message "WORD TO LONG."
10	After two successive omissions of end-of-text marks, the program prints a "Z" and terminates.
11	After issuing the word-too-long message, the program also prints whatever is residing in its output buffer.
12	Same situation as number 8, but if the second input line consists of only an end-of-text mark, the program prints 5 blank lines and the word-too-long message.
13	If a too-long word is used, the error message is printed in inconsistent places. For example, if the word would not appear in the first output line, the message is printed at the end of the previous output line, thus exceeding the maximum line size.
14	The program formats underscored words correctly, but it treats each underscored character as three characters when computing the line length.
15	The program's terminal buffer holds only 130 characters, but it is possible to enter a terminal line of more than 130 characters (e.g., by using the backspace key).

* Because of error 3, read as 31 instead of 30.

conditions are emphasized in the specification, but the expectations prove false. Not detecting error 9 is an example of the "eye seeing what it wants to see"; it is likely that everyone used a test case that caused this message to be issued, but most people failed to recognize the incorrect spelling in the message.

3.1 Comparing the Three Methods

Table VI summarizes some comparative statistics of the three methods. The first row (mean number of errors found) is the most important, but the nonparametric Kruskal-Wallis test indicates that there is no difference between the three methods (i.e., it is incorrect to conclude that method A is the worst). Rows 2–5 also indicate no large differences among the three methods. As a note, since the idea of group walkthroughs or inspections is relatively new, implying that people have less experience with this than with traditional testing methods, it is encouraging to see that this method held its own against the other methods.

In addition to this observation, two conclusions can be drawn from Table VI. One is that *none* of the methods, when used alone, is very good, since they detected only about a third of the errors in this small and simple program. An implication here is that the walkthrough/inspection technique should be viewed as a supplement to, rather than a replacement for, traditional testing methods. Another conclusion is that method C has a higher labor cost. The Kruskal-Wallis test shows that the difference in the mean man-minutes per error is highly significant; although the three methods were approximately equal in terms of the number of errors detected, the labor cost per error was much higher for the walkthrough/inspection method. On a macroscopic level, however, such differences in labor costs should prove to be insignificant when compared to the

Table II. Raw Data—Category A (Computer-Based Testing Using the Specification).

							Subjects									
		A	B	C	D	E	F	G	H	I	J	K	L	M	N	O	P
Error	1	X	X		X		X		X	X		X		X	X	X	X
	2		X		X	X	X	X	X		X	X	X	X	X	X	X
	3	X	X		X		X	X		X	X	X			X	X	X
	4																
	5	X			X	X		X	X			X			X	X	X
	6						X										
	7			X				X							X		
	8		X		X	X		X		X	X		X				
	9				X		X		X		X						X
	10		X		X		X	X					X				X
	11		X									X					
	12																
	13		X														X
	14						X										
	15						X										
Total found		3	7	1	7	4	7	6	4	3	3	7	1	2	5	5	7
PL/I experience		1	1	2	2	2	2	2	2	1	1	1	2	1	1	2	1
Test experience		3	3	2	3	2	4	3	3	2	1	2	3	2	2	3	3
Walkthrough experience		0	0	0	0	1	0	1	0	0	0	0	0	1	0	0	0

labor normally expended in later stages (e.g. system test and maintenance). Machine time used in methods A and B was not considered because 1) it was insignificant in this experiment and 2) machine costs are dropping but labor costs are rising. As an aside, cost-per-error-found is usually an invalid measure when comparing results from two programs, because the program with the most errors tends to look the best. However, it is a valid measure here, since the three methods were used to test the same program.

3.2 Analysis of Individual Variations

Since the most visible result so far is the wide variation in individual performance, an analysis of the underlying causes is warranted. Correlation coefficients were calculated, across all methods and for each individual method, between the number of errors found and the subjects' PL/I experience, prior testing experience, performance on the pretest testing problem, walkthrough experience, total testing time, preparation time, test execution time, and the fraction of time spent in preparation. However, because correlation coefficients do not necessarily imply cause-effect relationships and they have little meaning when computed from small sample sizes, and because most of the calculated coefficients were not statistically significant and the significant ones were rather small, they provided no useful insight and are not included here.

On the other hand, correlation coefficients are occasionally useful in pointing out questions for future re-

Table III. Raw Data—Category B (Computer-Based Testing Using Specification and Code).

								Subjects								
		A	B	C	D	E	F	G	H	I	J	K	L	M	N	O	P
Error	1	X	X	X			X	X	X	X		X		X	X		X
	2	X	X	X		X	X	X	X	X	X	X	X	X	X	X	X
	3	X	X	X	X		X	X	X	X	X	X		X			X
	4		X		X	X				X				X			
	5	X		X		X			X	X	X			X		X	
	6																
	7	X					X										X
	8		X	X					X	X	X	X	X				X
	9		X	X	X					X							
	10		X	X		X	X		X	X				X	X		X
	11										X						
	12		X	X					X	X							
	13	X															
	14								X					X			
	15	X												X			
Total found		7	7	9	3	4	5	3	8	8	6	5	3	8	2	2	6
PL/I experience		2	2	2	2	2	2	2	2	3	2	2	2	2	2	2	3
Test experience		3	2	3	3	3	1	3	3	3	3	3	?	2	2	4	4
Walkthrough experience		0	0	0	0	0	0	1	1	1	0	0	0	0	1	1	0

Table IV Raw Data—Category C (Walkthrough/Inspection).

					Subjects				
		A	B	C	D	E	F	G	H	I
Error	1	X	X		X	X	X	X		
	2	X	X	X	X	X	X	X	X	X
	3	X	X	X	X	X	X	X		X
	4	X	X	X	X	X	X	X	X	X
	5	X	X		X	X		X	X	X
	6									
	7									X
	8		X				X	X		X
	9			X	X			X		X
	10							X		
	11					X				
	12									
	13							X		
	14									
	15									
Total found		5	6	4	6	6	5	9	3	7
PL/I experience		322	332	322	322	322	322	322	322	322
Test experience		433	333	432	432	332	332	333	433	332
Walkthrough experience		111	110	100	110	100	100	100	110	100

Table V. Times expended.

	Category A		Category B		Category C
A	50/50/100	A	60/100/160	A	180/270/450
B	20/80/100	B	170/130/300	B	190/270/460
C	60/90/150	C	180/120/300	C	45/225/270
D	60/90/150	D	80/70/150	D	30/210/240
E	30/90/120	E	60/60/120	E	40/270/310
F	40/150/190	F	30/10/40	F	140/270/410
G	50/40/90	G	75/45/120	G	180/240/420
H	90/60/150	H	60/40/100	H	210/270/480
I	40/100/140	I	50/30/80	I	150/270/420
J	95/60/155	J	120/60/180		
K	20/50/70	K	60/55/115		
L	70/10/80	L	40/40/80		
M	20/20/40	M	120/100/220		
N	30/40/70	N	20/60/80		
O	85/45/130	O	60/60/120		
P	40/50/90	P	45/45/90		

Table VI. Comparative statistics.

	Method A	Method B	Method C
Mean no. of errors found	4.5	5.4	5.7
Variance	4.8	5.5	3.0
Median no. of errors found	4.5	5.5	6
Range of errors found	1–7	2–9	3–9
Cumulative errors found	13	14	11
Man-minutes per error	37	29	75

Table VII. Percentage of subjects finding each error type.

Error	Method A	Method B	Method C	All Methods
1	69	69	67	68
2	88	94	100	93
3	69	75	89	76
4	0*	31	100*	34
5	56	56	78	61
6	6	0	0	2*
7	19	19	11	17*
8	44	50	44	46
9	31	25	44	32
10	31	56*	11*	37
11	12	6	11	10*
12	0	25*	0	10*
13	12	6	11	10*
14	6	12	0	7*
15	6	12	0	7*

* These entries appear to represent significant deviations.

search. One example was a negative correlation (−0.58) between subjects' prior walkthrough/inspection experience and their performance in using method C. The sample is too small to draw conclusions, but further research seems warranted to explore the hypothesis that, because this method is more mentally taxing than the others, people are initially highly motivated but then tend to tire of it after multiple experiences.

3.3 Analysis of Error-Type Variations

Another way of using the data is to analyze the types of errors found by each method. Table VII shows, for each of the 15 errors, the percentage of subjects in each category that found the error and the percentage of total subjects that found each error (counting each category C team as one subject). The entries marked with an "*" appear to represent significant deviations.

The marked errors in the last column represent the errors that were infrequently detected by anyone. Errors 6, 14, and 15 would only be detected if the tester explored the use of special terminal characters (tab and backspace). Even if these special characters were used, error 15 would only be detected if the tester used the backspace character in conjunction with a very long input line.

Error 7 is only seen on a special input situation (when the first word is exactly equal to the output-line length) and when the tester carefully inspects the output (to spot the leading blank line). Error 11 is difficult to spot, because the program's output buffer would contain blanks unless the "too long" word was not the first word in the input. Error 13 would only be spotted under similar conditions. Error 12 involved a special series of input conditions, and hence was infrequently detected.

The conclusion here is that the testers focused too much attention on "normal" test cases and insufficient attention on erroneous-input and special-case conditions. Notice that method C proved to be worse than average on these seven errors, implying that the walkthrough/inspection method focused too heavily on the program's logic at the expense of considering its input/output anomalies.

In examining method A, one sees that it did significantly poorer than the average on error 4. The program initialized the first character in its input buffer to "Z", and used this as an indication that its input buffer was empty. The error was relatively easy to spot if one examined the code, but it would only be detected by method-A subjects as a result of a test case such as "Zebras are animals./".

In examining method B, one finds that it was more likely to detect errors 10 and 12 than the other two methods. No explanation of this is offered. Method C was much more effective than the average in detecting error 4 (the "Z" in the buffer). This follows from the rigorous analysis of the program's logic that was performed by the teams employing method C. Method C was significantly poorer than the average on error 10. The error is extremely subtle and not likely to be discovered by reading the program. Since it is triggered by an easy-to-make input error, it was probably discovered by accident by the subjects using methods A and B.

4. Variations on the Experiment

Since the three methods were equally effective in finding errors (although method C was more costly), one might wish to determine if some combination of the methods might be more effective. For instance, is there

Table VIII. Comparative Statistics of Methods A–G.

	Method						
	A	B	C	D	E	F	G
Mean no. of errors found	4.5	5.4	5.7	7.3	8.3	7.2	7.6
Variance	4.8	5.5	3.0	3.6	2.8	3.4	4.3
Median no. of errors found	4.5	5.5	6	8	8	7.5	8
Range of errors found	1–7	2–9	3–9	4–10	6–11	3–10	5–10
Cumulative errors found	13	14	11	13	14	15	14
Mean man-minutes per error	37	29	75	34	34	37	75

any benefit from having two people independently test the program, using method A, and then pooling the errors that they find?

To study these combinations, four additional methods were defined. Method D incorporates two people independently testing the program using method A, where they pool their results when completed (and, of course, duplicate errors are not counted twice). Method E is similar, but the independent testers use method B. Method F is defined as employing two independent testers, one using method A and the other using method B. Method G is a combination of methods A and C; three people use method C (a walkthrough) and the fourth person independently uses method A to test the program.

Rather than running a separate set of experiments, data for these four methods were acquired by combining data from Tables II–V. That is, eight pairs of subjects were simulated for method D by pooling the results of the 16 subjects in Table II (pairing them in the order A-B, C-D, E-F, G-H, etc.). In a similar fashion, data were obtained for eight pairs of subjects using method E, 16 pairs of subjects using method F, and nine quadruplets of subjects using method G (pairing the first nine subjects in Table II to the nine groups in Table IV).

The comparative statistics for all seven methods are shown in Table VIII. As is indicated, the pooling of independent results (particularly in method E) reduces some of the unpredictability and risk (i.e. variance in errors found) associated with methods A and B. A Kruskal-Wallis test on the seven mean-number-of-errors-found now indicates that we reject the hypothesis that the means vary only by chance, implying that methods D-G are better than methods A-C. However a test of the means for methods D-G does not indicate any difference between these four methods, implying that we cannot conclude that method E is best.

Again there is a significant difference in the cost-per-error-found statistic; methods A, B, D, E, and F are significantly better than methods C and G. The interesting result, however, is the observation that the labor cost of methods D–F is approximately the same as that of methods A and B. In other words, the pooling of independent test results was not, as might be expected, more costly because of the detection of duplicate errors. The explanation for this is the large variability in the types of errors found by different individuals. This observation is perhaps the most significant result of the experiment, because it implies that a more cost-effective way to test a program is to employ two testers who work independently of one another (and based on a visual inspection of Table VIII, one might be swayed toward method E, although statistical analysis will not bear this conclusion out).

5. Discussion

One basic result of the experiment was that the walkthrough/inspection method had a higher labor cost than the other methods. This deserves further analysis to avoid being misconstrued. One reason for the popularity of the walkthrough/inspection method is that it gets people other than the program's programmer involved in the testing process, and there is reason to believe that programmers are relatively unsuccessful in testing their own programs (see Chapter 10 of [9] for a discussion of this). However in this experiment we did not compare the walkthrough to a programmer testing his or her program, but to a programmer testing someone else's program. Thus the walkthrough method is likely to be more effective than a programmer testing his or her own program, but less effective in terms of labor costs than a third party testing the program using computer-based methods.

One observation that was made during the experiment is that the walkthroughs and inspections focused too much on the logic of the program, at the expense of focusing attention on the input and output data. Perhaps this method could be improved by training programmers to focus their attention on the data handled by the program, rather than solely on the program's logic.

Comments were solicited from the participants and most of the participants felt that the experiment had a high educational value. At the end of the experiment, each participant was given a copy of the 15 known errors. In the normal environment, one does not have the opportunity to test a program and then receive immediate feedback on the errors overlooked, so perhaps exercises such as this should be incorporated into programming courses.

When asked to report on their testing techniques, most of the participants indicated that they focused their efforts on boundary and invalid-input conditions, but the results do not indicate that this really happened. The two reasons for the relatively poor error-detection rates on this program appear to be: 1) The participants did not carefully compare the actual output produced by the program to the expected output. Thus many errors that were observable on the output listings were overlooked. 2) The participants focused too much of their attention on "normal" input conditions, and not enough on special cases and invalid-input situations.

Lastly, a few participants using the walkthrough method suggested that situations arise where it would be desirable—during the walkthrough session—to study special cases of interest by invoking the program from a terminal rather than by simulating them mentally. This idea of "computer assisted" walkthroughs seems interesting and warrants additional study; experiments are underway to do so. Likewise, the influence of testing tools deserves further study.

6. Conclusions

One result of the experiment is that the three original methods are equal in terms of error-detection capabilities, although the walkthrough method was not as cost-effective as the computer-based methods in a "unit testing" environment under the condition that the person doing the testing was not the programmer of the program. To repeat an earlier warning, this does not imply that the walkthrough technique, in and of itself, is not cost-effective; experience has shown the opposite to be the case.

Another result was that independent two-party tests tended to find more errors and, because of the large variability in errors found by each individual, were equally cost-effective as the single-person tests.

One finding is the significant variability among individuals, both in terms of the number and types of errors found. Given the high experience level of the participants and their participation in a course on software reliability, the variability was higher than expected. This variability could not be explained by correlating it with prior testing experience and other measured factors. As an example, an individual who found eight errors was employed as a documentation writer, but another individual employed as a program test specialist found only two errors. This variability implies that personnel selection for program-testing roles is of vital importance, but additional experimentation is necessary to determine the factors that contribute to high testing abilities.

Analysis of each of the errors showed that certain types of errors were very difficult to detect (independent of the method used) and that the ability to detect certain types of errors varied somewhat from method to method.

A possible criticism of the experiment is the small size of the program used. However, the results are believed to be applicable to larger programs. In particular, this experiment is analogous to the "unit testing" of individual subroutines or modules in a large program.

Received March 1977; revised October 1977

References
1. Fagan, M.E. Design and code inspections to reduce errors in program development. *IBM Syst. J. 15*, 3 (1976), 182–211.
2. Goodenough, J.B., and Gerhart, S.L. Toward a theory of test data selection. *IEEE Trans. Software Eng. SE-1*, 2 (1975), 156–173.
3. Gould, J.D. Some psychological evidence on how people debug computer programs. *Int. J. Man-Machine Studies 7*, 2 (1975), 151–182.
4. Gould, J.D., and Drongowski, P. An exploratory study of computer program debugging. *Human Factors 16*, 3 (1974), 258–277.
5. Griffith, P.F., and Henry, R.M. An investigatory study into human problem solving capabilities as they relate to programmer efficiency. *Comptr. Personnel 3*, 3 (1972), 10–15.
6. Hetzel, W.C. An experimental analysis of program verification methods. Ph.D. Th., U. of North Carolina, Chapel Hill, 1976.
7. Howden, W.E. Symbolic testing and the DISSECT symbolic evaluation system. *IEEE Trans. Software Eng. SE-3*, 4 (1977), 266–278.
8. Jelinski, Z., and Moranda, P.B. Applications of a probability-based model to a code reading experiment. Rec. 1973 IEEE Symp. Comptr. Software Reliability, IEEE, New York, 1973, pp. 78–81.
9. Myers, G.J. *Software Reliability: Principles and Practices.* Wiley-Interscience, New York, 1976.
10. Naur, P. Programming by action clusters. *BIT 9*, 3 (1969), 250–258.
11. Shneiderman, B. Experimental testing in programming languages, stylistic considerations and design techniques. Proc. AFIPS 1975 NCC, AFIPS Press, Montvale, N.J., 1975, pp. 653–656.

AN AUTOMATED PROGRAM TESTING METHODOLOGY
AND ITS IMPLEMENTATION

Dorothy M. Andrews* and Jeoffrey P. Benson

General Research Corporation
Santa Barbara, California 93111

ABSTRACT

This paper describes an automated testing methodology and an experiment performed to determine its effectiveness. The method is to insert in the program to be tested a number of "executable assertions," statements about the program that trigger error signals whenever they are evaluated to be false (violated). A testcase is then developed for the program using actual values of the input variables. When the program is run, a plot is generated of the number of assertions violated versus the input variable values used. The resulting function is called the "error function". Heuristic search algorithms can then be used to maximize this function and thereby automatically locate input values which cause the most errors to occur. The experiment included developing assertions for the program to be tested, choosing and inserting representative errors into the program, and implementing search and data collection algorithms for testing. The results indicate that combining executable assertions with heuristic search algorithms is an effective method for automating the testing of computer programs.

INTRODUCTION

In recent years, an active research area in computer science has been the development of methods for showing that computer programs operate correctly. One result of this research has been executable assertions. If assertions are used to specify the desired behavior of a program, then the program's correctness (relative to the assertions) can be checked automatically. This is done by using the number of assertions violated during a test as a correctness measure for the program. This value indicates whether the program is operating correctly on its input data; the number of assertions violated defines an "error function" over the input space of the program. This removes the need to examine a program's output in detail.

The error function can also be used to automatically generate testcases. It allows standard techniques for maximizing and minimizing functions in multi-dimensional spaces to be applied to the problem of program testing. Automated search techniques such as complex search and heuristic search can be used to find the maximum values of the error function. The input values for which assertions are violated are the input values for which the program fails to work correctly; therefore, it is desirable to find the regions with the maximum violations.

PROBLEMS ASSOCIATED WITH TESTING SOFTWARE

Testing has always been a problem of software development. The method used for testing a program is often a product of the idiosyncracies of the tester. Typically the test criterion is to execute the program for a certain length of time or run a large program through the system. The critical nature of many current software systems makes it imperative to develop a generalized methodology for testing; one that can be applied to many types of programs, thus avoiding the subjective nature of present testing techniques. One way to minimize subjectivity is, of course, to have someone who has not been involved in writing the program do the testing. But this solution in itself brings new problems. The most obvious is that extra time must be allowed to train a new person until he is familiar enough with the program to intelligently make up testcases and procedures for testing. Although computer hardware testing and quality assurance is often a separate department in an organization, this is not commonly the case for software testing.

Testcases

Testing can be made more reliable either by increasing the number of testcases or by choosing well designed testcases for the test object. Increasing the number of testcases is not always possible since there are some testing situations where there is a limit to the number of tests that can be performed. The difficulty with the second alternative is that substantial ingenuity is required to develop testcases that will uncover the weak spots in a program. Furthermore, the cost of testing skyrockets when each set of testcases has to be tailormade to a particular software system. In either case, it is important to choose testcases that will locate errors early in the development cycle since the cost of fixing errors increases dramatically with time.[1]

There have been many papers on the subject of choosing testcases[2,3] because this is one of the most intriguing problems of testing. Exhaustive testing is out of the question since software can have so many states and the number of testcases required to test each state in-

*Dorothy M. Andrews is now at Xerox Corporation, Palo Alto, California

creases exponentially with the number of states. In many applications test data must include not only the expected values of input data, but also the unexpected values in order to test for error conditions. Normally the tester must severely limit the number of testcases and it is difficult to know when a sufficient number have been choosen to provide meaningful testing.

Test Results

In software testing, unlike hardware testing, it is not simply a matter of determining if a switch is on and off. There is no "gold unit" that can be used as a basis for determining if the test results are correct. This means that test results must be checked manually, which often involves reading and analyzing a lot of output. In some applications, e.g., ballistic missile defense software, checking test results from one run can take several weeks.[4,5]

Last but not least is the psychological aspect of testing that works against a productive testing phase. Once the software is completed, the programmer is anxious to get onto some other project. The challenging and interesting part is designing and implementing the code, not testing it. No one really wants to find errors in his own code, and, furthermore, checking the output is so tedious that it makes the testing process seem routine and boring.

EXECUTABLE ASSERTIONS AND ADAPTIVE TESTING

The major theme that connects most of the problems associated with testing is that of time; it takes time to construct good testcases, time to run them, and time to look at the results. Therefore, one of the ways to address the problem of testing is to automate as much of the testing sequence as possible and to eliminate as much subjectiveness and human intervention as is practical. Fortunately, the basic mechanism to do this, called an Adaptive Tester,[4,5] has been developed over the past several years in response to the need of the Ballistic Missile Defense Advanced Technology Center to develop tests for complex software. The Adaptive Tester is a software system with the following functional components:

- Machine aids for specification of the testing environment

- Automatic preparation of initial test cases

- Automatic performance evaluation

- Adaptive or learning algorithms for selecting test cases

The research effort described in this paper has utilized the components of the Adaptive Tester which generate testcases by automatic perturbation of the input parameters, evaluate past performances of the constructed testcases, and, using this information in a feedback system, generate subsequent testcases. To adapt this powerful capability to this particular application, executable assertions were used as a means of providing data to the performance evaluator. Executable assertions allow the method to be prescribed in general terms and used for any application, since the only thing that varies from one application to another are the assertions themselves.

Executable Assertions

Executable assertions have been found very effective as a simple debugging technique and have been utilized extensively in the development of the Software Quality Laboratory[6] (a large verification system). The primary motivation for adding them was to make debugging easier and quicker since the exact statement number of an assertion that is evaluated to "false" during program execution is stated in a message in the output. For example, if the assertion INITIAL (J .GE. 0 .AND. J .LE. MAXJ), is evaluated as "false", then it is clear that J is negative or it has exceeded the maximum value for J (MAXJ). Without assertions to direct attention to the parts of the program that are not operating as expected, it is often impossible to find the source of the errors that are causing the problems.

Not only are assertions useful for debugging when new code is being added, but the presence of assertions with a special statement to invoke an error recovery routine usually prevents premature termination and allows the program to continue to perform its function.[7-10] Assertions also have proved their worth from the aspect of maintenance and documentation of the system. The Software Quality Laboratory is so large that no one person can be familiar with it all. Assertions which specify the acceptable range of variables help immensely when new code is being written to interface with existing code.

The Adaptive Tester

The Adaptive Tester has been developed in response to the need of the Ballistic Missile Defense Advanced Technology Center to develop tests for software that simulates actual battle conditions. Devising tests in the conventional fashion takes an inordinate amount of time because of the number of parameters that can be varied. Additionally, about a month is required to examine the results of a single run. To get around this situation, ways to perturb the input variables and evaluate the results automatically have been developed. Various search algorithms from artificial intelligence have been implemented to construct new test cases from the results of previous tests.

The search algorithm selected for this experiment employs complex search.[11-14] The technique was developed by Box for solving for the maximum or minimum of a nonlinear function. It involves choosing a set of independent values for the function at random and determining the value of the function for each of these values. The function values define a set of points on a surface called a "complex". Figure 1 gives an example of a complex in three dimensions. The function may have many independent variables, but, for the search routine to function correctly, there must be one more point in the complex than the number of independent variables being perturbed. Assume that the goal is to maximize the value of the function. At each step of the algorithm the point in the complex with the minimum function value is replaced by a new point. The algorithm first attempts to locate the new point on a line connecting the rejected point and the centroid of the other points in the complex.

The distance between the rejected point and the centroid is calculated and the exact location of the new point is then determined. The algorithm has six choices in locating the new point. These are shown in Figure 2 for a complex that is a triangle. Reflection locates the new point at the same distance from the centroid as the rejected point by reflecting the triangle through the centroid. Expansion reflects the triangle through the centroid to locate the new point, but increases the distance between the new point and the centroid. Contraction reflects the triangle through the centroid and reduces the distance that the new point lies from the centroid. Centroid substitution uses the centroid as the new point of the triangle. If none of these operations results in a new point with a function value greater than the rejected point, then two other operations on the triangle can be performed. The triangle can be shrunk by reducing the lengths of one of its sides or rotating it about its centroid.

The coefficients of expansion, contraction, shrinkage and rotation are defined by the user of the algorithm. These operations are performed until a larger function value is found, a predefined limit on the number of operations is reached, or the function attains a value predefined as the maximum value that the algorithm is to locate.

METHODOLOGY FOR ADAPTIVE TESTING WITH ASSERTIONS

The testing methodology used in the experiment is very similar to that used in the Adaptive Testing project. The test configuration consists of several distinct software subsystems: a test driver, the Adaptive Tester, and an assertion evaluator. The program being tested is called the test object. The architecture of the software is shown in Figure 3.

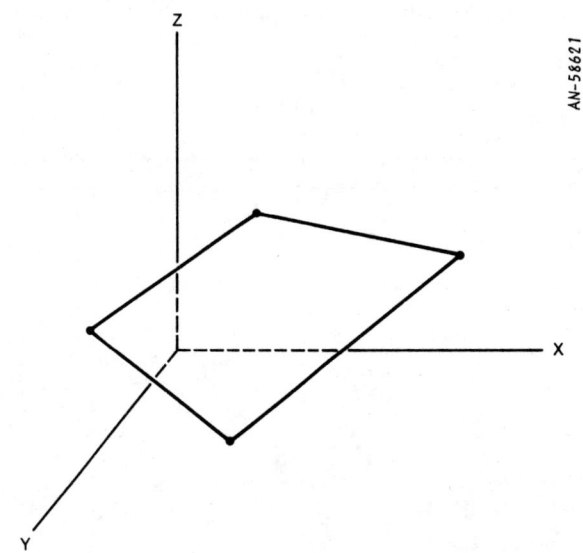

Figure 1. A Complex in Three Dimensions

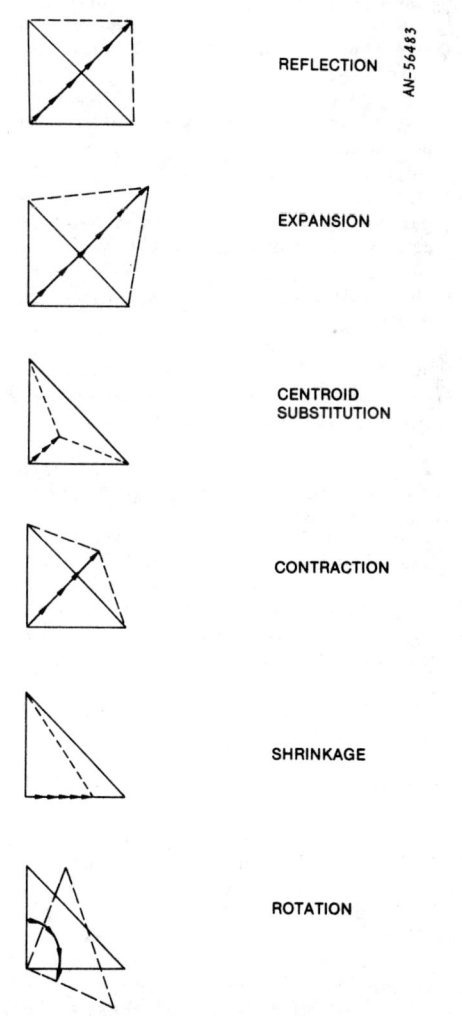

Figure 2. Complex Transformations

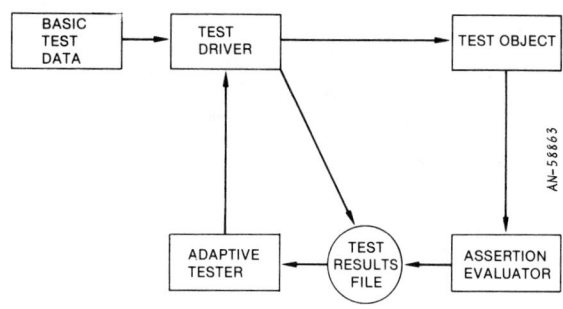

Figure 3. Software Architecture

To initiate the testing process, the tester must specify the following data:

- The input parameters to be altered by the search algorithm

- A set of initial values for each input parameter

- The range of values that each input parameter may assume, in other words, the constraints for each variable

- The maximum number of assertion violations expected

The function of the test driver is to read these values, initiate the testing process, and interface with the Adaptive Tester.

The function of the assertion evaluator is to maintain a test results file containing the following information:

- The value of each input parameter for every test

- The number of assertion violations and the number of different assertions violated

- The statement and module number where each violation occurred

- How many times each assertion was violated

The information in the test results file is used as input to the search algorithm so it can find values of the input variables which cause the maximum assertion violations. The search algorithm constructs a new test case using the operations described in the previous section and returns control to the test driver which executes the next test. At the conclusion of the tests, the test results are output in a final report.

The test object is the program to be tested; it must contain executable assertions. Since they are useful throughout the entire software cycle,[7,10] they should be included in the code as it is being written. This allows the correctness of the assertions to be validated as the code is tested. Since an existing program was used in the experiment, it was necessary to write assertions and then execute the program to be sure the assertions were correct.

Some assertions, such as range checks, are simple to write and do not require in-depth familiarity with the algorithm. For example, in a DO-loop with a variable as the upper bound, it is easy to write an assertion which specifies that the value of that variable is greater than zero. More difficult to write are assertions which check results of computations or that express a relationship between the variables. Since it is necessary to have a firm understanding of the program to write these assertions, it is generally best for the person who implements the code to write these assertions. The success of this testing technique depends on having a sufficient number of assertions expressing tight bounds on variables, thereby enabling them to detect errors.

Once the assertions have been written, the only other part of the testing process requiring human intervention is setting up the first testcase. The remaining part of the testing is automatic: the performance is evaluated and new testcases are generated until a given performance value is attained.

EXPERIMENTS

Two experiments were performed to determine the usefulness of executable assertions in testing. The purpose of the first experiment was to determine if executable assertions could locate errors; and, if so, what the resulting error space looked like. The Adaptive Tester was not used in the first experiment; instead the values of the input parameters were methodically stepped-up in regular intervals across a "grid." The first experiment has been described elsewhere,[15] but the results indicated that executable assertions were effective in detecting errors and that the error function did not include singularities.

The prominent research issues for the second experiment were as follows:

- Behavior of the error function - Does it confirm the results obtained in the first experiment?

- Applicable search techniques - Pending determination of the behavior of the error function, what search technique is the most effective in finding errors?

- Application to large input spaces - What happens when there is a large number of input parameters?

The second experiment was more comprehensive since it actually combined the Adaptive Tester with the use of executable assertions. Since one purpose of this experiment was to provide corroborative evidence of the first experiment, a new test object was selected. The function of the new program was to input an orbit described by a set of eight parameters (orbital elements) and produce a state vector representation of a point on the orbit. Since this program had been in use for twelve years and had been the test object in another experiment[17] it was assumed to be error free. Yet, once the assertions were added to the program, they uncovered latent errors that were completely unsuspected! In most cases, these were errors that occurred only at boundary conditions.

In this second experiment, three modes of operation were implemented in the test driver:

Grid -
The values of the input parameters were varied in a uniform pattern, a grid, over the input space. The results from these grid tests were used as a baseline by which to evaluate the search technique.

Search -
Given one value for each of the tested inputs, the search algorithm constructed all subsequent test cases.

Grid and Search -
Instead of constructing the initial points on the complex from random testcases, a set of values for each of the inputs was derived for input to the search algorithm. These values were derived by sorting on the number of assertion violations obtained from the grid tests; the input values associated with the highest number of violations were passed to the search routine.

In each mode of operation, three variables were varied: MODE, VALUE, and the eccentricity of the orbit. To examine the effect of varying a large number of input parameters, additional tests were run in which all ten of the input parameters were perturbed. The Adaptive Tester was able to construct test cases and even found another assertion violation.

Error Seeding

Errors were generated for the test program using a procedure developed by Brooks.[18] The method uses error types and frequencies from a previous study[19] to randomly select a set of errors to be "seeded" in the program. Some types of errors were not chosen for the study, such as documentation, data definition, etc., because the experiment was specifically concerned with detecting run-time errors. The types of errors used were computational errors, logic errors, data handling errors, and interface errors. In generating errors for the experiment, statement types and other descriptive information about the test program were generated automatically using the Software Quality Laboratory. Each statement in the program was classified by type, and a table matching error categories to statement types was constructed. This resulted in a list of available error sites. Potential error sites were then randomly selected. Once the assertions were written and checked out, errors were introduced one at a time to determine how effective adaptive testing using assertions was in detecting errors.

For each error, a grid test was run. Then tests using the automated search technique were run to see if the results were the same. The search technique was used in two ways: first by perturbing three variables, MODE, VALUE, and one other variable; and then by perturbing all the variables of the orbit at one time. The search routine was allowed to run until it found a preset number of assertion violations (representing the performance value); then this number was automatically stepped up by one and the search algorithm tried to find another combination of input values which would cause a greater number of violations to occur. In this way, the performance value was maximized. The testing process was arbitrarily set to terminate when one hundred tests were run, but each test actually consisted of several subtests because the values of MODE and VALUE were varied within each test. The report that is produced at the conclusion of the runs is shown in Figure 4. In this test MODE, VALUE, and one other variable, ORBIT(6), the eccentricity, were varied.

Test Results

The results of the experiment demonstrated the effectiveness of the assertions in detecting errors. Of the original 24 errors, nine (38 percent) were detected by original assertions, and eight (33 percent) were detected by assertions that were added after the grid testing. There were seven errors that could not be detected by assertions. The reasons why these errors were not detected by assertions were:

- The seeded error was in a section of code that was only traversed after an error occurred.

- Assertions could not be written for some types of errors that were seeded. These included a misspelled variable name, a REAL variable declared as INTEGER, and the wrong number of arguments in a subroutine call.

- The FORTRAN compiler at this installation initializes all variables to zero, therefore a deleted DATA statement caused no problems.

############ FINAL REPORT #############

#RUN	INPUT1	#FALSE ASSERTION	#DIFFERENT ASSERTION	MODE	VALUE
7	0.7526	2	2	4	2477545.659
9	.6048	2	2	5	9849931.060
12	.2700	2	2	4	13958923.49
13	.900	1	1	5	24389119.03
24	.2899	2	2	4	8871067.739
25	.3879	2	2	5	1760571.330
30	.2910	2	2	5	20758872.74
34	.7346	1	1	4	22330022.80
35	.1852	2	2	5	27015515.91
37	.3555	2	2	4	19513234.41
44	.6973	2	2	4	4044234.171
45	.6235	2	2	5	0.
47	.5851	2	2	4	4533190.345
49	.9000	2	2	5	0.
51	.7234	2	2	4	4533190.345
53	.9000	2	2	5	5737662.000
55	.7234	2	2	4	7402021.345
63	.7053	2	2	5	0.
65	.6261	2	2	4	4533190.345
73	.7474	2	2	5	0.
75	.6471	2	2	4	4533190.345
83	.8071	2	2	5	0.
85	.6769	2	2	4	4533190.345
86	.1774	1	1	4	23124989.06
87	.9000	2	2	5	1415222.244
89	.7228	2	2	4	5588024.749
90	.9000	2	2	5	1939816.571
91	.1557	2	2	4	6107643.223
92	.5503	2	2	4	9951144.293
93	.3530	2	2	4	8029393.758
94	.4955	2	2	4	11674092.79
95	.8433	1	1	5	18860857.79
96	.5648	2	2	4	11115483.73
97	.7040	1	1	4	14988170.76
98	.6108	1	1	4	17228371.99
99	.2554	2	2	5	3876077.474
100	.5485	2	2	4	11161715.66
101	.4019	2	2	5	7518896.567
102	.1000	2	2	5	7331062.939

INPUT1 = ORBIT(6)

MODULE	STMT#	TYPE	FAILURES*
ORBP	109	ASSERT	34
OUTCHK	142	ASSERT	38

* HOW MANY RUNS EACH ASSERTION FAILED IN   102 RUNS

Figure 4. Summary of Search Testing for Error 3

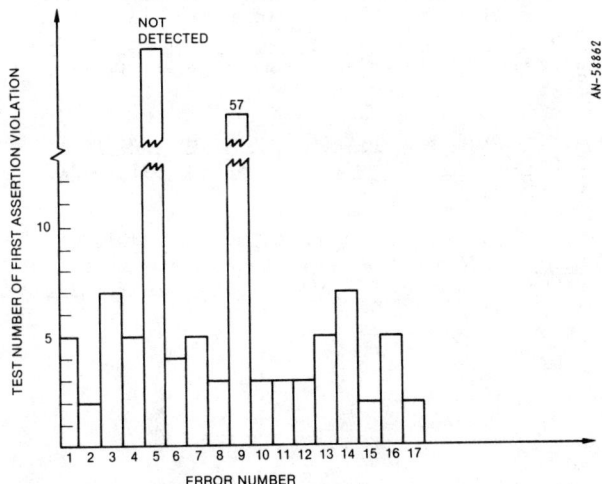

Figure 5. Efficiency of Search Method

Some of the errors that assertions could not detect would have been detected by static-analysis tools which test the consistent use of variables.

For all but four of the errors, the search methods detected the same errors as the grid tests; but they were able to do so much more efficiently and used much less computer time. Figure 5 shows the efficiency of the search technique when all variables are varied; it plots the number of the test in which the first assertion violation was detected versus the error number. Fifteen of the seventeen errors were detected within the first seven tests devised by the search technique. In contrast, the grid technique was run for 317 tests and discovered all but one of the errors; but 683 tests had to be run to detect error number 11.

CONCLUSION

One of the themes emphasized at recent conferences is that new methods for system development and testing are necessary. The need to make software less labor intensive must result in new automated programming tools.

The results from this experiment indicate that this automated testing technique has the potential for finding errors (logic, computational, etc.) that are difficult to find in other ways. In addition, the search algorithm eliminates the subjectiveness in constructing testcases and increases the variety of input values. By automating the testing process, the cost of testing can be reduced dramatically.

Combining executable assertions with adaptive search has resulted in a tool which allows more automation of the software development process and a more accurate testing environment by which to provide software reliability.

ACKNOWLEDGEMENT

Research sponsored by the Air Force Office of Scientific Research (AFSC), United States Air Force, under Contract F49620-79-C-0115. The United States Government is authorized to reproduce and distribute reprints for governmental purposes notwithstanding any copyright notation hereon.

REFERENCES

1 Tomlinson G. Rauscher, "A Unified Approach to Microcomputer Software Development", Computer Magazine, June 1978.

2 John B. Goodenough, Susan L. Gerhart, "Toward a Theory of Test Data Selection, IEEE Transactions on Software Engineering, Vol. SE-1, No. 2, June 1975.

3 W. E. Howden, "Theoretical and Empirical Studies in Program Testing," IEEE Transactions on Software Engineering, Vol SE-4, July 1978.

4 D. W. Cooper, "Adaptive Testing," Second International Conference on Software Engineering, 13-15 October 1976, San Francisco, CA.

5 D. W. Cooper, Adaptive Learning Requirements and Critical Issues, General Research Corporation CR-4-708, January 1977.

6 J. P. Benson and R. A. Melton, "A Laboratory for the Development and Evaluation of BMD Software Quality Enhancement Techniques," Proceedings of the Second International Conference on Software Engineering, IEEE Computer Society, 1976, pp. 106-109.

7 Dorothy Andrews, "Using Executable Assertions for Testing and Fault Tolerance," 1979 International Conference on Fault Tolerant Computing, Madison, Wisconsin, June 20-22, 1979.

8 Sabina Saib, "Distributed Architectures for Reliability," Proceedings of the AIAA Computers in Aerospace Conference II, Los Angeles, October 1979.

9 Sabina Saib, "Verification and Validation of Avionics Simulation," Proceedings of the AGARD Avionics Panel on Modeling and Simulation of Avionics and Command, Control and Communications Systems, Paris, France, October 1979.

10 Dorothy Andrews, "Using Executable Assertions for Testing," Proceedings of the 13th Annual Asilomar Conference on Circuits, Systems and Computers, November 1979.

11 M. J. Box, "A New Method of Constrained Optimization and a Comparison with Other Methods," Computer Journal, Vol. 8 (1965).

12 J. A. Richardson and J. L. Juester, "Algorithm 454--The Complex Method for Constrained Optimization", Comm. ACM, Vol. 6, No. 8, August 1973.

13 K. D. Shere, "Remark on Algorithm 454," Comm. ACM, Vol. 7, No. 8, August 1974.

14 K. D. Shere, The Box Optimization Method, Naval Ordnance Laboratory NOLTR-74-167, October 25, 1974.

15 J. Benson, A Preliminary Experiment in Automated Software Testing, General Research Corporation TM-2308, February 1980.

16 T. Plambeck, The Compleat Traidsman, General Research Corporation IM-711/2, revised edition, September 1969.

17 R. N. Meeson, C. Gannon, "An Empirical Evaluation of Static Analysis and Path Testing," Proceedings of AIAA Computers in Aerospace Conference II, Los Angeles, October 1979.

18 N. B. Brooks, An Experimental Evaluation of Software Testing General Research Corporation CR-1-854, May 1979.

19 T. A. Thayer, et al., Software Reliability Study, TRW Defense and Space Systems Group RADC-TR-76-238, Redondo Beach, California, August 1976.

Applicability of Software Validation Techniques to Scientific Programs

W. E. HOWDEN
University of Victoria

Error analysis involves the examination of a collection of programs whose errors are known. Each error is analyzed and validation techniques which would discover the error are identified. The errors that were present in version five of a package of Fortran scientific subroutines and then later corrected in version six were analyzed. An integrated collection of static and dynamic analysis methods would have discovered the errors in version five before its release. An integrated approach to validation and the effectiveness of individual methods are discussed.

Key Words and Phrases: testing, errors, static analysis, dynamic analysis, empirical studies, Fortran, functional testing, structural testing, proofs of correctness
CR Categories: 4.6

---

1. INTRODUCTION

The 98 errors in edition five of the IMSL package of scientific Fortran subroutines [25] were studied. The errors were documented by IMSL and corrected in edition six of the package. Ninety-one programs were involved, covering a broad range of statistical and numerical analysis applications.

The goal of this study was to determine whether validation methods could detect the errors in a nontrivial collection of scientific routines. Many of the errors were quite deep and took several weeks to understand fully. It was determined which of a variety of methods would reveal each error. When several methods worked, the simplest and least expensive was selected. The selected method was usually guaranteed to discover the error.

2. STATIC ANALYSIS METHODS

2.1 Classification of Static Analysis Methods

Table I contains a classification of the static analysis methods that were useful in the detection of IMSL errors and the number of errors for which each method was effective. The asterisks denote errors whose discovery by the associated

---

Permission to copy without fee all or part of this material is granted provided that the copies are not made or distributed for direct commercial advantage, the ACM copyright notice and the title of the publication and its date appear, and notice is given that copying is by permission of the Association for Computing Machinery. To copy otherwise, or to republish, requires a fee and/or specific permission.
This research was supported by the U.S. National Bureau of Standards and by the National Research Council of Canada.
Author's address: Department of Mathematics, University of Victoria, P.O. Box 1700, Victoria, British Columbia, Canada V8W 2Y2.
© 1980 ACM 0164-0925/80/0700-0307 $00.75

ACM Transactions on Programming Languages and Systems, Vol. 2, No. 3, July 1980, Pages 307-320

Reprinted from *ACM Transactions on Programming Languages and Systems*,
July 1980, pp. 307-320. Copyright 1980, Association for Computing Machinery,
Inc. Reprinted by permission.

Table I. Static Analysis Methods

Method	Error count
1. Automatic methods	
Subroutine interface analysis	6
Path flow analysis	14
Statement analysis	16
2. Manual methods	
* Requirements/header consistency	3
* Program/header consistency	1
* Requirements/program consistency	
* Header/header consistency	1
Total	41

Note: Asterisk indicates discovery of errors not guaranteed.

validation method is not guaranteed. The associated method is closely related to the type of error involved, but all that can be said is that it is "appropriate" for that kind of error.

The first level of classification in Table I distinguishes between automatic and manual methods. Automatic static analysis involves the use of tools which automatically analyze programs, searching for illegal and anomalous constructs [34]. Manual static analysis involves the inspection of requirements and design documents as well as program source code. The documents are examined by the programmer for general properties such as consistency and completeness.

2.2 Automatic Static Analysis Methods

Six IMSL errors were mismatches between the precision of formal and actual subroutine parameters (single versus double precision). Automatic static analysis can be used to check parameters for consistency of precision, number, and type. Fourteen errors were detected by analyzing the flow of data or of control along program paths. The most common data flow problem was the referencing of uninitialized variables. This occurred as the result of missing or misplaced assignment statements, omissions in common blocks and DATA statements, and the failure to document a formal parameter as an input variable. A related class of errors involved the assignment of values to variables that were not later referenced. The only control flow error in the IMSL programs was a transfer of control to the middle of a DO-loop. Example 1 describes a data flow error involving uninitialized variables. Data "flow out" of a variable before they "flow into" it.

Example 1. Uninitialized Variables Error. BECOVM computes a mean and a variance–covariance matrix for a set of variables and corresponding variable observations. The first part of the routine contains code for initializing several arrays. The initialization section is skipped over when the value of an input variable NBR(4) is not equal to 1. The initialization process is carried out by two loops whose loop bounds are computed inside the initialization section. The loop bound values that are computed in the initialization section are also used as loop bounds later in the program. This means that if NBR(4) is not 1, these loop bounds will not be set and references will be made to uninitialized variables.

Table II. Path Analysis Methods

Method	Error count
1. Data flow analysis	
a. Machine-readable documentation not needed	
Reference to uninitialized variables	7
Unreferenced assignments	1
b. Machine-readable documentation required	
Assignment of values to input variables	4
Unassigned output variables	1
2. Control flow analysis	
Branching to middle of DO-loop	1
Total	14

Some static analysis methods depend on an examination not only of source code but also of certain kinds of machine-readable documentation. IMSL programming standards require that each formal parameter for a routine be specified as input or output (or neither). Input variables must not be assigned values and output variables are expected to be assigned values. If input/output parameter information is provided in machine-readable form, then an automatic static analyzer can be built which can be used to check for conformance to the standard. Table II breaks down the error count figure for path analysis in Table I in terms of both data and control flow methods and the dependence of methods on machine-readable documentation. Example 2 describes a data flow error in which an input variable is assigned a value inside a routine. Data incorrectly "flow into" the variable at some intermediate point in a program path as well as at the beginning of the path.

Example 2. Input Variable Error. The statistical routine RLINPF uses a fitted simple linear regression model to carry out point interval inverse predictions. An input vector IOP is used to select the kind of prediction to be carried out. The input vector CRIT contains the data on which the routine operates. Some of the predictions do not depend on the values of CRIT(1), CRIT(3), and CRIT(4). The expressions which are used to compute the predictions that depend on CRIT(1), CRIT(3), and CRIT(4) are also used to compute the predictions which do not depend on CRIT(1), CRIT(3), and CRIT(4) by setting the values of CRIT(1), CRIT(3), and CRIT(4) to zero. Difficulties may arise because the calling routine may assume that RLINPF does not change any of the data stored in the input vector CRIT.

Statement analysis involves "rules" that are triggered by specific types of source code statements or machine-readable comments. The rules are often language dependent and may depend on programming standards that add new syntactic restrictions to a language. Table III lists some of the statement analysis rules that were effective for the detection of IMSL errors. The rules in Table III do not depend on machine-readable comments. Numbers without parentheses represent errors for which a technique was the best or most appropriate method. Numbers in parentheses count the total number of errors for which a technique was effective, including those errors for which some other technique was better

Table III. Statement Analysis Methods
(Machine-Readable Documentation Not Required)

Method	Error count
1. Expression analysis	
Use of mixed mode expressions	1 (3)
Equality relations involving REAL variables	(1)
2. DATA statement analysis	
More array elements than data values	1
Precision of values different from precision of variables	4
Too many digits in a value	1
Variable occurs twice in DATA statements	1
3. WRITE statements	
Constant used for device number	1
4. Array dimensions	
Value $\neq$ 1 used for dimension of formal parameter array	1
5. Formal parameter functions	
Typing of external formal parameter function	1
6. Assembly language syntax errors	
Missing quote in DC constant	1
Total	12 (15)

Table IV. Statement Analysis Methods
(Machine-Readable Documentation Required)

Method	Error count
1. Subroutines called	1
Inconsistency between subroutine usage list and called subroutines	
* 2. Input ranges	3 (8)
Total	4 (9)

Note: Asterisk indicates discovery of errors not guaranteed.

or more appropriate. Most of the rules are self-explanatory. The WRITE statement rule refers to a programming standard in which a variable (as opposed to a constant) must be used to specify a device number. Formal parameter arrays are expected to have declared dimensions that are either the dummy constant 1 or a formal parameter variable. Function parameters must not be typed inside the called routine.

Table IV lists two statement analysis methods that depend on machine-readable comments. The first rule requires the construction of a list of the subroutines that the programmer thinks are called by the program. The list is checked against the subroutines called from the program. The second rule requires machine-readable descriptions of the types and ranges of all input and output variables. It is possible to build a static analyzer which will automatically check that the information is present and complete.

Example 3. Input Variable Range Error. DREBS is a differential equation solving routine for first-order differential equations. Two of its input variables are H and HMIN. The routine will reduce the size of the suggested step size H if convergence cannot be obtained at a point of T + H. The variable HMIN is provided as a lower bound on the size of H. No mention is made in the documentation of the allowable range of values for H and HMIN. Users of the program incorrectly assumed that both H and HMIN could be negative. The error could have been prevented if type and range information were provided for all input variables.

2.3 Manual Static Analysis Methods

Each IMSL program is preceded by a header which describes the functions performed by the program and each of the program's input and output variables. The IMSL errors for which manual methods were effective involved inconsistencies in the program, its documentation, and the program header. The four types of manual static analyses listed in Table I were the most useful.

Example 4. Program/Header Inconsistency. ZQADR is a routine for finding the roots of the quadratic equation $AZ^2 + BZ + C = 0$. The documentation header for the program states that when $A = B = 0$, the program should return SIGN(FINITY, $-B$) for the large root. The program returns instead the correct value CMPLX(FINITY, $-B$). The header contains a similar error for the case $A = 0$, $B \neq 0$. The error can be discovered by manually comparing formulas in the specifications with those implemented in the code.

2.4 Static Analysis and Extensibility

The results of the IMSL study indicate that both automated and manual static analysis systems should be extensible. The list of statement analysis rules in Table IV contains only those rules which would be useful for the IMSL errors. Analyzers should be built in such a way that new rules can be added. Lists of manual inspection rules should also be kept and added to as new types of errors are encountered. Inspection lists are described in [3, 10, 11, 33].

3. DYNAMIC ANALYSIS METHODS

3.1 Classification of Dynamic Analysis Methods

There are three phases to dynamic analysis: generation of test data, program execution, and verification of test results. There are two general approaches to test data generation: functional testing and structural testing. In the first approach, information from the requirements and design documents, and from the code itself, is used to construct input values that test the functions implemented in the program [18]. In the second approach, test data that cause the traversal of all branches [6, 16, 23, 28, 29, 37, 38] or all "logical paths" [1, 2, 21, 30, 41] are generated. Table V contains the error count for each of these two approaches.

Table VI lists five methods for checking the correctness of values that are computed during or by a test. One of the assumptions of the IMSL experiment was that the tester would be capable of verifying the correctness of a set of functional output values for any set of input values. In some examples it was reasonable to assume that the tester could also verify the correctness of traces of intermediate values. Similar methods involve the trapping of illegal intermediate values. Illegal intermediate values can be trapped either by hardware (e.g., overflow, underflow, divide by zero) or by executable dynamic assertions [39]

Table V. Test Data Generation Methods

Method	Error count
1. Functional testing	
Requirements functions	14 (20)
General design functions	7 (9)
Detailed design functions	7 (9)
Branching functions	3 (5)
Total	31 (38)
2. Structural testing	
Branch testing	10 (13)
Path testing	(3)
Variable usage	1 (1)
Total	11 (17)

Table VI. Output Verification

Method	Error count
1. Analysis of output variable values	13 (23)
2. Analysis of data flow traces	2 (2)
3. Dynamic assertions and error interrupts	18 (19)
4. Run-time subroutine interface analysis	6 (6)
5. Branch and variable usage	2 (3)

(e.g., array bounds errors). Several errors in the IMSL programs could have been more easily discovered by examining records of branch traversal and variable usage rather than of actual computed values.

3.2 Functional Testing

There are two parts to functional testing: identification of functions and selection of functional test cases [19]. Three types of functions were identifiable in the IMSL programs. *Requirements functions* describe the overall computational capabilities of a program and are associated with the program as a whole. *General design functions* are associated with parts of a program and describe its major computational components. They can often be identified by program comments. *Detailed design functions* are "smaller" than general design functions and originate during implementation rather than during design. The most common detailed design functions in the IMSL Fortran programs are array indexing functions. Functions may be either *computational functions* that compute output values from input values or *branching functions* which choose between alternative computations or detect loop termination conditions.

   Functional test data are selected by analyzing the ranges of values of variables, the ranges of values of data structure dimensions and other data structure properties, certain computational properties of the functions being tested, and the contexts in which the functions occur. Value ranges of functional input variables may correspond directly to value ranges for program input variables or may be constrained by the computations and path predicates along the paths leading to the code which implements the function. Data may have abstract structure that is not directly represented by the variables and data structures in the code used to store the data and that must also be considered during the selection of functional test cases.

There are three important kinds of values in functional test case selection: *extremal*, *nonextremal*, and *special* values. The extremal values in the closed interval of values $[a, b]$ are a and b. The nonextremal values are the open interval (a, b). Each of the values in a small set of discrete points can be thought of as an extremal case. It is necessary to consider both the values of the elements of a data structure as well as its data structure dimensions. The elements of an array can be treated as a single quantity which takes on extremal and nonextremal values or as a set in which some, none, or all of the elements have extremal or nonextremal values. An array has extremal dimensions if all of its elements lie on the "edge" of the array. The smallest nonextremal two-dimensional array, for example, is a 3 by 3.

Special values are related to properties of the functions in which they occur. Zero, ϵ (where ϵ is small), and K (where K is large) are special values for functions which compute algebraic expressions over REAL data. Data structures in which all the elements are distinct or all the same are special values for functions which move data around from one location to another. Extremal, nonextremal, and special value test cases should be constructed for each function input variable. Tests which result in the generation of each kind of output should also be selected.

In the Jackson design methodology, abstract structure in data can be represented as a hierarchy of data types [26]. A data type at one level can be related to lower level types either by the *classification* or the *composition* relationship. Classification is used to divide elements of one type into classes of lower level types. Composition is used to join together elements from several lower level types into compound structures of a higher level type. A special composition operator, marked by an asterisk, is used to indicate that an element at one level is a structure of repeated instances of elements of a single lower level type.

The effect of abstraction on test data selection is to force the consideration of different classes of test cases as well as combinations of different test values. If the values of an input variable can be classified into different abstract types, then test values of each type should be selected. If the values of an input variable are compound structures, then compound test values which correspond to different combinations of extremal, nonextremal, and special values of the constituent types must be considered. Extremal cases of the repetition factor for compound structures that are defined using the operator marked by an asterisk must also be considered.

Data abstraction can often be used to avoid the combinatorial explosion that occurs when different combinations of values are considered for the input variables for a function. In many cases it is possible to identify functionally related subsets of input variables that correspond to compound abstract data types. Combinations of values of input variables can be restricted to combinations of values of variables that are part of the same functionally related subset.

An alternative approach to controlling combinatorial explosions which was effective in the detection of IMSL errors is the joint use of branch and functional testing. An extremal, nonextremal, or special value is selected for one of the input

Table VII. Effectiveness of Functional Testing Guidelines

Method	Error count
1. Function domains	
Program domains	23 (27)
Computed subdomains	5 (7)
2. Extremal values	
Scalar variables	8 (14)
Array dimensions	4 (5)
Array elements	4 (4)
Repetition factors in data abstractions	4 (4)
3. Special values	
Scalars (algebraic computational)	(1)
Array elements (algebraic computational)	2 (4)
Data abstractions (algebraic computational)	1 (1)
Array elements (data movement)	3 (3)
4. Combinations of values	
Scalars—all combinations	5 (6)
Scalars—functionally related subsets	5 (10)
Scalars and array elements	1 (1)
Data abstraction repetition factors	3 (3)
Data type values in compound data types	1 (1)
5. Combined functional/branch testing	
Extremal or special values—all branches	8 (9)
Extremal branch values	3 (5)

variables, data structures, or components of a compound data type. Combinations of values for the other input variables, data structures, or component data types are then restricted to those that are necessary to cause the execution of every possible program branch during some program test.

Table VII lists criteria for functional test data selection and describes the number of errors for which each criterion was important. Part 1 in Table VII distinguishes between function input variables whose domains correspond to the domains of program input variables and function input variables whose domains are computed within the program. Part 2 refers to different kinds of extremal values. Part 3 indicates the relative importance of selecting special values for different kinds of variables and data abstractions. Part 4 describes combinations of values. Errors were encountered for which it was necessary to consider all combinations of extremal and special values for the scalar input variables for a function, combinations for functionally related subsets of the scalar input variables, combinations of individual scalar values with array element values, combinations of different extremal values of different repetition factors in a data abstraction, and combinations in which extremal and special elements in one component of a compound abstract data type were combined with similar elements from other components. Part 5 indicates the importance of combining functional and structural testing. The second entry in part 5 describes the effectiveness of using tests which result in values that just barely satisfy or fail to satisfy a branch or a functionally related collection of branches.

Example 5. Extremal Input Values Testing of General Design Function. BEPATS carries out a number of statistical analyses, each of which corresponds to a separate program "subfunction." The error occurs in the variance test subfunction. The degrees of freedom in the computation of a p value are interchanged. The error manifests itself in an incorrect output value from the subfunction, except in those cases where the degrees of freedom are equal. It also fails to show up if input values are selected which, due to roundoff, cause the p value to be zero or one.

The input to the subfunction includes the sample sizes N1 and N2 and the estimates S_1^2 and S_2^2 of the sample variances. These variables have a close functional relationship. Tests should be constructed which involve combinations of extremal values. One combination is S_1^2 large, S_2^2 small, N1 small, and N2 large. Examination of F-statistic tables reveals that a set of values having these properties would be $S_1^2 = 10$, $S_2^2 = 1$, N1 = 1, and N2 = 120. The error is revealed if these test values are used.

Example 6. Effect of Data Abstraction on Testing of General Design Function. The EQZF routine calculates eigenvectors and eigenvalues. One of the last things that the program does is to normalize the output array of eigenvectors. Real valued eigenvectors are stored in single columns. Complex valued eigenvectors are stored in adjacent pairs of columns. The error in the routine occurs when a complex eigenvector has a zero component.

The input eigenvectors for the normalization function form a hierarchical data abstraction. The elements at the top level of abstraction are sets of eigenvectors. The eigenvectors can be classified as type real or type complex. Each eigenvector can be decomposed at a lower level of abstraction into eigenvector components. Real valued vectors have scalar components. The components of complex vectors can be decomposed into real and imaginary subcomponents. Functional testing requires that extremal, nonextremal, and special values tests be constructed for each of the different possible classes of data that are represented by a data abstraction. At the top level of abstraction this will result in the construction of a test in which the set of eigenvectors contains at least one complex eigenvector. The application of the special values rules at the lowest level of abstraction will result in the selection of eigenvectors having zero-valued components. The combined effect of these two rules will be the selection of a test case in which the set of eigenvectors contains a complex valued eigenvector having a zero-valued component.

Example 7. Extremal Output Values Testing of Detailed Design Function. ZX3LP is a linear programming routine. It receives its input in an array A. The code accesses A as though it has IR rows of N columns each. In both the calling programs and in ZX3LP, A is declared as an IA by N matrix where IA $\geq$ IR. ZX3LP "packs" A so that the data are stored in conformance with the use of A as an IR row matrix. The program "unpacks" A back to its declared IA row format before terminating.

The unpacking process starts at the last (in terms of column major ordering) element of the packed array and reads backwards, unpacking one element at a time. It uses a small detailed design function to compute the row location (A treated as an IA row matrix) for the last element of A (A treated as a packed IR row matrix). The row location can be computed by finding the remainder when

IA is divided into N∗IR. The answer will be in the range 0 to IA − 1. If it is zero, then the row index IA should be used. The function incorrectly uses zero.

The error is revealed by considering the range [1, IA] of output values which should be generated by the function. If tests are constructed which should generate the extremal output values 1 and IA, then the presence of the error will be revealed.

Example 8. Extremal Values Testing of Branching Functions. MDCH can be used to calculate chi-square probabilities. A computed program variable X appears in a branch predicate "X.LT. − 18.8125" which is used to filter out X values that will cause underflow to occur. The value that X is compared with is too small. Extremal testing of a branch predicate of the form "X.LT.E" requires the construction of tests that result in an execution of the predicate for which X = E − ϵ and X = E. The error in this program is revealed if an X having value −18.8125 is generated and tested in the predicate.

3.3 Structural Testing

Branch testing requires that a programmer construct tests that cause all branches to be executed at least once. The technique can be refined by requiring that all "hidden branches" be executed. A branch predicate consisting of a disjunct of k terms has k hidden branches.

There appear to be three important situations in which branch testing is effective. The first is that in which an error causes a program to generate incorrect output whenever some branch is executed. The second occurs when sections of code are inaccessible and the third when unexpected branches are traversed. The first situation was fairly common in the IMSL programs and was usually associated with branches to sections of code that set error flags and call error message subroutines. In some cases the message was incorrect and in others an error flag was set incorrectly. The second and third situations each occurred in one IMSL program.

Path testing requires that each logical path through a program be executed. Even if the number of iterations of loops that are carried out is limited to some small number, there will often still be an enormous number of different possible paths and the phrase "all logical paths" has to be interpreted in a restricted sense.

Some of the IMSL errors were associated with particular patterns of loop traversal. The patterns can be identified as follows: each possible path through a loop should be traversed during the last iteration for some execution of the loop; each possible path should be traversed during the next to last iteration for some execution of the loop; and for each path an execution of the loop should be carried out during which that path is followed for all iterations. All of the errors in the IMSL programs that would have been revealed by these rules would also have been revealed by functional testing.

3.4 Dynamic Analysis Support Tools

The effective use of branch testing requires a tool that will keep track of the branches that are traversed during program testing. Functional testing may require test harnesses that can be used to assign artificial intermediate values to variables at the beginning of sections of code and to check the computed values of variables at the end [31, 35]. Documentation tools can be used to associate design and implementation function descriptions with the sections of code that implement the functions. A run-time test support environment may be needed to test the consistency of array bounds declared in calling routines with those in the called routines [24].

3.5 Functional Versus Structural Testing

Functional testing has been described as a black box testing technique in which the internal structure of programs and systems is ignored [30]. The advantages of structural testing are that it "looks inside" the black box. The results of the IMSL study indicate that it is important to look at the structure of a program but that it is as important to examine the program's functional design structure as its source code control structure.

Functional and structural testing should be thought of as complementary rather than competing methods. There were errors in the IMSL programs for which it was not enough either to test a function over extremal, nonextremal, and special values or to test each branch or path in the code implementing the function. It was necessary to execute specific branches while testing a function over some choice of an extremal, nonextremal, or special value for one of its input variables.

4. OTHER METHODS AND RELATED RESEARCH

4.1 Test Data Generation Methods for Dynamic Analysis

Cobol test data generation systems have been constructed which are driven by information in the DATA DIVISION [36]. Error seeding techniques have been used to measure the completeness of a set of tests [12]. Mutation testing is related to error seeding but is more systematic and is carried out with different objectives [7, 14]. Symbolic evaluation can be used to reconstruct the mathematical formulas that are computed by a program path for comparison with documentation [5, 8, 17, 21, 22, 27, 30]. The effectiveness of these other methods was not analyzed in depth due to the practical necessity of limiting the scope of the project to manageable proportions. Some of the other methods are suitable for data processing rather than for scientific programs. The methods that were considered were found to be sufficient for the errors occurring in the IMSL programs.

4.2 Proofs of Correctness

Many of the IMSL errors would have been discovered during a (correctly applied) proof of correctness. There was only one error with which it was difficult to associate some other, less formal validation method. Some of the errors were associated with methods whose use was not guaranteed to result in the discovery of the errors (the terms marked with an asterisk in the tables). A (correctly applied) use of formal specifications and proofs of correctness may have resulted in the guaranteed discovery of these errors.

4.3 Related Research

The *error analysis* approach to the study of validation effectiveness that was used for the project described in this paper was previously used in a smaller project described in [17]. *Case studies* involve the analysis of the use of specific validation methods during specific software development projects [1, 4, 9, 10, 39]. In a *controlled experiment* different programmers use different validation methods on a collection of programs whose errors are known in advance and the results are statistically analyzed [15, 23]. Each of the possible approaches to the study of validation methods has its own set of advantages and disadvantages.

5. CONCLUSIONS AND FUTURE RESEARCH

5.1 Effectiveness of Testing

A large majority of the errors in the programs that were studied could have been discovered through the systematic use of static and dynamic analysis. Static analysis was the appropriate method for revealing the presence of about half of the errors and dynamic analysis was the appropriate method for revealing the other half.

The study indicated the need for extensible static analysis systems which allow the addition of new static analysis rules. It also revealed the importance of the identification and testing of general and detailed design functions. The identification and the construction of test values for data abstractions were also important.

5.2 Future Research

Several interesting projects were suggested by the IMSL results. Functional testing has not been widely studied and the concept of an extremal value has not been completely explored. The decision table technique described by Goodenough and Gerhart in [13] and the approach to extremal values followed by White and Cohen in [40] may be relevant. Additional techniques are described in [20].

The design of support tools for functional testing is a relatively unexplored area. The importance of general and detailed design functions in test data generation suggests that it may be useful to investigate the extent to which functions are more easily identifiable in programs written in a functional programming language.

The results of the IMSL project were derived from the study of Fortran scientific programs. A similar study is being planned for Cobol commercial data processing programs.

ACKNOWLEDGMENTS

The analysis of the statistics programs in the IMSL package was carried out with the help of Professors Bruce Johnson, Robert Oden, and Roger Davidson of the University of Victoria.

The author is grateful for the cooperation of the IMSL company in providing him with the source listings for the IMSL programs as well as with copies of the IMSL error and release information.

REFERENCES

1. BAKER, F.T. Structured programming in a production programming environment. *IEEE Trans. Softw. Eng. SE-1*, 2(1975), 241-252.
2. BICERSKIS, J., ET AL. SMOTL—A system to construct samples for data processing program debugging. In *Software Testing*, vol. 2, A.E. Westley (Ed.), Infotech International, Maidenhead, England, 1979, pp. 13-23.
3. BOEHM, B.W., BROWN, J.R., AND LIPOW, M. Quantitative evaluation of software quality. In Proc. 2nd Int. Conf. Software Engineering, San Francisco, Calif., 1976, pp. 592-605.
4. BOEHM, B.W., MCLEAN, R.K., AND URFRIG, D.B. Some experience with automated aids to the design of large scale reliable software. *IEEE Trans. Softw. Eng. SE-1*, 1(1975), 125-133.
5. BOYER, R.S., ELSPAS, B., AND LEVITT, K.N. SELECT—A formal system for testing and debugging programs by symbolic execution. In Proc. 1975 Int. Conf. Reliable Software, Los Angeles, Calif., pp. 234-245.
6. BROWN, J.R., ET AL. Automated software quality assurance. In *Program Test Methods*, W.C. Hetzel (Ed.), Prentice-Hall, Englewood Cliffs, N.J., 1973, pp. 181-204.
7. BUDD, T.A., DE MILLO, R.A., LIPTON, R.J., AND SAYWARD, F.G. The design of a prototype mutation system for program testing. In Proc. AFIPS 1978 NCC, AFIPS Press, Alexandria, Va., 1978, pp. 623-627.
8. CLARKE, L.A. A system to generate test data and symbolically execute programs. *IEEE Trans. Softw. Eng. SE-2*, 3(1976), 215-222.
9. DALY, E.G. Management of software development. *IEEE Trans. Softw. Eng. SE-3*, 3(1977), 230-232.
10. FAGAN, M.E. Design and code inspections to reduce errors in program development. *IBM Syst. J 19*, 3(1976), 182-211.
11. FUJII, M.S. Independent verification of highly reliable programs. In Proc. COMPSAC-77, Chicago, Ill., pp. 38-44.
12. GILB, T. *Software Metrics*. Winthrop, Cambridge, Mass., 1977.
13. GOODENOUGH, J., AND GERHART, S.L. Toward a theory of test data selection. *IEEE Trans. Softw. Eng. SE-1*, 2(1975), 156-173.
14. HAMLET, R.G. Testing programs with the aid of a compiler. *IEEE Trans. Softw. Eng. SE-3*, 4(1977), 279-289.
15. HETZEL, W.C. An experimental analysis of program verification methods. Ph.D. dissertation, Univ. of North Carolina, 1976.
16. HOLTHOUSE, M.A. Experience with automated testing analysis. In Digest, Workshop on Software Testing and Test Documentation, Fort Lauderdale, Fla., 1978, pp. 309-323.
17. HOWDEN, W.E. An evaluation of the effectiveness of symbolic testing and of testing on actual data. *Softw. Pract. Exper. 8*, 4(1978), 381-397.
18. HOWDEN, W.E. A survey of dynamic analysis methods. In *Software Testing and Validation Techniques*, E. Miller and W.E. Howden (Eds.), IEEE, Long Beach, Calif., 1978, pp. 184-206.
19. HOWDEN, W.E. Functional program testing. *IEEE Trans. Softw. Eng SE-6*, 3(1980).
20. HOWDEN, W.E. Functional testing and design abstractions. *J. Syst. Softw.* To appear.
21. HOWDEN, W.E. Methodology for the generation of program test data. *IEEE Trans. Comput. C-24*, 5(1975), 554-560.
22. HOWDEN, W.E. Symbolic testing and the DISSECT symbolic evaluation system. *IEEE Trans. Softw. Eng. SE-3*, 4(1977), 266-278.
23. HUANG, J.C. An approach to program testing. *ACM Comput. Surv. 7*, 3(Sept. 1975), 113-128.
24. HUANG, J.C. Program instrumentation. A tool for software testing. In *Software Testing*, vol. 2, A.E. Westley (Ed.), Infotech International, Maidenhead, England, 1979, pp. 147-160.
25. IMSL Library reference manual. International Mathematical and Statistical Libraries, Inc., Houston, Tex., 1978.
26. JACKSON, M.A. *Principles of Program Design*. Academic Press, New York, 1975.
27. KING, J.C. Symbolic execution and program testing. *Commun. ACM 19*, 7(July 1976), 385-394.
28. KRAUSE, K.W., SMITH, D.W., AND GOODWIN, M.A. Optimal software test planning through automated network analysis. In Proc. IEEE Symp. Computer Software Reliabililty, New York, 1973, pp. 18-22.
29. MILLER, E., ET AL. Structurally based automatic program testing. In Proc. EASCON' 74, 1974.

30. MILLER, E.F., AND MELTON, R.A. Automated generation of test case data sets. In Proc. 1975 Int. Conf. Reliable Software, Los Angeles, Calif., 1975, pp. 51-58.
31. MIYAMOTO, I. Reliabililty evaluation and management for an entire software life cycle. In Proc. 3rd Int. Conf. Software Engineering, Atlanta, Ga., 1978, pp. 46-55.
32. MYERS, G.J. A controlled experiment in program testing and code walkthroughs/inspections. *Commun. ACM 21*, 9(Sept. 1978), 760-768.
33. MYERS, G.J. *The Art of Software Testing*. Wiley-Interscience, New York, 1979.
34. OSTERWEIL, L.J., AND FOSDICK, L.D. DAVE—A validation error detection and documentation system for FORTRAN programs. *Softw. Pract. Exper. 6*, 4(1976), 473-486.
35. PANZL, D.J. Automatic software test drivers. *Computer 11*, 4(1978), 44-50.
36. PRO/TEST Data Generator. Synergetics Corp., Burlington, Mass.
37. RAMAMOORTHY, C.V., AND HO, S.F. Testing large software with automated software evaluation systems. *IEEE Trans. Softw. Eng. SE-1*, 1(1975), 46-58.
38. STUCKI, L.G. Automatic generation of self-metric software. In Proc. IEEE Symp. Computer Software Reliabilty, New York, 1973, pp. 94-100.
39. STUCKI, L.G. New directions in automated tools for improving software quality. In *Current Trends in Programming Methodology*, vol. 2, R.T. Yeh (Ed.), Prentice-Hall, Englewood Cliffs, N.J., 1977, pp. 80-111.
40. WHITE, L.J., AND COHEN, E.I. A domain strategy for program testing. In *Software Testing*, vol. 2, A.E. Westley (Ed.), Infotech International, Maidenhead, England, 1979, pp. 325-362.
41. WOODWARD, M.R., HENNEL, M.A., AND HEDLEY, G. Observations and experience of path analysis and testing of programs. In Digest, Workshop on Software Testing and Test Documentation, Fort Lauderdale, Fla., 1978, pp. 70-96.

Manuscript received June 1979; revised December 1979 and March 1980; accepted March 1980

Quantitative Aspects of Software Validation

RAYMOND J. RUBEY, JOSEPH A. DANA, AND PETER W. BICHÉ

Abstract—This paper discusses the need for quantitative descriptions of software errors and methods for gathering such data. The software development cycle is reviewed, and the frequecy of the errors that are detected during software development and independent validation are compared. Data obtained from validation efforts are presented, indicating the number of errors in ten categroies and three severity levels; the inferences that can be drawn from these data are discussed. Data describing the effectiveness of validation tools and techniques as a function of time are presented and discussed. The software validation cost is contrasted with the software development cost. The applications of better quantitative software error data are summarized.

Index Terms—Software cost models, software error statistics, software reliability, verification and validation.

INTRODUCTION

A COMPUTER program is unreliable if it contains errors. At different times and in various situations, these errors are known as bugs, mistakes, deficiencies, deviations, or anomalies. In order to increase hardware reliability, it is first necessary to quantitatively describe the nature of the errors that need to be eliminated. Only through this approach can an effective and efficient reliability improvement program be designed. It is from this standpoint that the following discussion of errors should be viewed.

Although most programmers are intuitive about the characteristics of the software errors that infest their programs, a more quantitative understanding of software errors is needed if they are to be effectively and efficiently eliminated. This greater understanding will lead to improvement in the design and application of software development tools and techniques. It will also aid in the management of software development by enabling the comparison of current efforts with past experience.

SOFTWARE DEVELOPMENT CYCLE

An idealized representation of the software development process is shown in Fig. 1. The process begins with the statement of the goals that the software is to achieve. These goals are often indefinite and ambiguous, e.g., they may state "print a paycheck for everyone in the company" or "guide this vehicle into a lunar orbit." Such goals must then be translated into a more precise specification of what the software is to do. Next the software must be

Manuscript received February 1, 1975.
R. J. Rubey is with Logicon, Inc., Dayton, Ohio 45432.
J. A. Dana is with the Process Systems Division, Logicon, Inc., Merrifield, Va.
P. W. Biché is with Logicon, Inc., Torrance, Calif.

Reprinted from *IEEE Transactions on Software Engineering*, June 1975, pp. 150-155. Copyright © 1975 by The Institute of Electrical and Electronics Engineers, Inc.

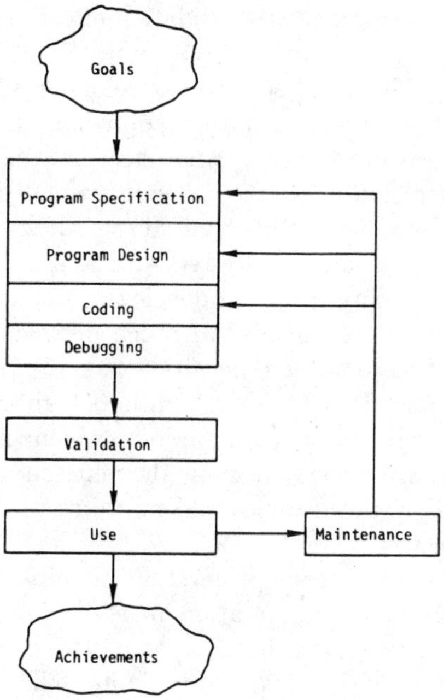

Fig. 1. Software development process.

designed, coded, and debugged. The program is then examined to determine its acceptability for the intended application; this can range from a cursory examination to an intensive independent verification and validation of all aspects of the software's performance. The data presented in this paper are obtained primarily from intensive independent verification and validation efforts. Independent validation can account for a significant portion of the total software development cost when highly reliable software is needed. After validation, the software is executed by the end user and it hopefully produces some worthwhile product (such as paychecks) or accomplishment (such as lunar orbit). A maintenance effort usually follows the software development effort to correct any errors and to accommodate changed goals.

Errors can be defined as the differences between the goals and achievements. They are introduced at each stage in the software development process, but not during validation and use. Unfortunately, the amount of quantitative data about software errors is only a tiny fraction of the data available about other aspects of the software development process.

SOFTWARE ERROR STATISTICS GATHERING

Two approaches can be taken to quantitatively describe the characteristics of software errors. Actual software development and validation efforts that produce software for real-world applications could be observed, or a programming environment could be artificially created and selected benchmark programs could be developed and validated. Each approach has its advantages and disadvantages.

A complete and intensive observation of an actual large software development and validation effort would require a long time and many people, and might impede the progress of the actual software development. Because of the costs associated with this approach, it can be attempted very infrequently, and therefore may not yield results of sufficient generality. A variation of this approach is to limit the observation of actual software developments to the information normally recorded and available. This would allow many software development and validation activities to be examined, but much desired information would not be obtained because that information was never considered to be of enough importance to warrant writing or remembering. A major problem in observing actual software developments is the reluctance of management to allow the troubles and mistakes of their project to be publicized.

The second approach of carefully monitoring a benchmark program implementation must be limited to relatively small programs if the cost of the data gathering is to be kept within reasonable limits. The use of small programs coupled with the participants' awareness that they are part of an experiment rather than a real application can result in distortions. In addition, since the resultant benchmark programs are never subjected to long-term use in a real-world situation, it is never certain that the total spectrum of possible errors has been observed.

Because no single approach to discovering the nature of software errors is sufficient, the data presented in this paper have been drawn from studies that employed all of the approaches described. No identification has been made of the actual software development projects involved in the data-gathering efforts because of the need to preserve anonymity. The data presented cannot be considered definitive; they represent only a portion of the complex overall picture of software errors.

Several classifications of software errors are of interest. Errors can be classified according to the type of computer operation with which they are associated. Examples of such classifications include arithmetic errors, logic errors, data accessing errors, documentation errors, etc. Errors can be identified according to the phase of the software development cycle in which they were first made. For example, errors are made in defining the programming specification, in designing the program, in coding, and in performing maintenance functions associated with subsequent changes to the specification, design, or coding. No errors are inserted into the program during acceptance or use unless some maintenance-like function is performed. Errors also can be classified according to the method by which they were detected and the phase during which they were detected.

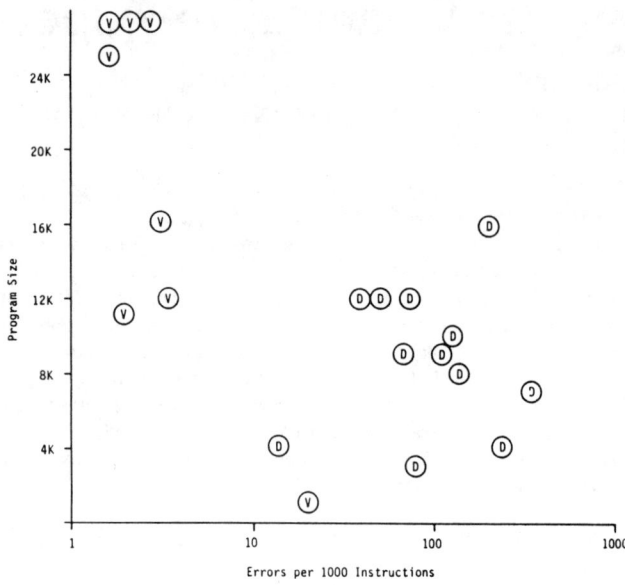

Fig. 2 Error occurrence observations.

DEVELOPMENT AND VALIDATION ERRORS

Most errors made by programmers are expected to be found during the debugging that is performed by the original programmers. Experience and the results of several studies indicate that many errors are made in this phase. The results of some of these investigations are shown in Fig. 2. As indicated in this figure, approximately one source-language error is made during the software development effort for every ten machine-language instructions in the final program. Data reflecting the number of errors discovered during independent validation efforts, which are plotted on the same figure, demonstrate that in validation, the error rate drops to about two errors per 1000 machine-language instructions. Program development is a very error-prone activity, but approximately 98 percent of all errors are uncovered through normal program development efforts, and only 2 percent of the errors remain to be found during the validation phase. This "needle-in-the-haystack" aspect of validation suggests that the tools and techniques used for debugging during development may not be appropriate for validation and, as will become apparent later in this discussion, the cost of validation may be disproportionate to the number of errors left to be found.

The following paragraphs further describe the nature of the errors found during validation. The data presented are a combination of information gathered from over a dozen validation efforts performed at different times and by different organizations. Overall totals were derived for two reasons. First, since so few errors are uncovered during any particular validation, it is difficult to determine any common characteristics when each effort is examined separately. Second, not all of the information needed for a complete picture was available from each validation effort, necessitating selectivity in the use and summarization of the data. In general, the data presented were obtained from validation efforts that involved relatively small real-time control programs (averaging about 32K machine-language instructions) that were programmed by an experienced and capable software group who considered the programs to be sufficiently debugged.

ERROR CATEGORIES

The most basic data required about the errors found during validation are the frequency of occurrence of those errors in defined error categories and their relative effect or severity. Errors discovered in 11 separate validation efforts were cataloged and sorted into 10 categories, ranging from those due to an incomplete or erroneous specification to those due to inaccurate documentation. These errors were also sorted according to the effect they would have on the performance of the program. An error was considered serious if it would cause the program to terminate prematurely or cause the program's outputs to differ significantly from the desired correct values. An error was considered moderate if it caused outputs to deviate from the correct values to a lesser degree. An error was considered minor if the ultimate user notices no effect on overall program performance. A judgment of the seriousness of an error is dependent on the immediate application of the program; an error initially considered minor might later be considered serious. For example, inaccurate documentation would not affect a program's correct performance initially, but might cause a serious error if there were an attempt to modify the program or use it in a different environment. The information from this cataloging and sorting is shown in Table I. Table I is itself a summarization of a more detailed error categorization. The data for this further breakdown for the four most significant major error categories are presented in Tables II–V.

As shown in Table I, the most frequent error was incomplete or erroneous specifications. Apart from that category, there is a remarkable uniformity in the distribution of errors. Considering only serious errors, however, erroneous data accessing and erroneous decision logic or sequencing are the largest categories. For moderate errors, the five largest error categories include the previous three categories plus erroneous arithmetic computations and intentional deviation from specifications.

Several inferences can be drawn from the data in Table I. First, there is no single reason for unreliable software, and no single validation tool or technique is likely to detect all types of errors. Second, the ability to demonstrate a program's correspondence to its specification does not justify complete confidence in the program's correctness since a significant number of errors are due to an incomplete or erroneous specification, and the documentation of the program cannot always be trusted. Third, intentional deviation from specifications and the violation of established programming standards more often leads

TABLE I
Frequency of Error Occurrence

Error Category	Total		Serious		Moderate		Minor	
	Number	Percent	Number	Percent	Number	Percent	Number	Percent
Incomplete or erroneous specification	340	28	19	11	82	17	239	43
Intentional deviation from specification	145	12	9	5	61	13	75	14
Violation of programming standards	118	10	2	1	22	5	94	17
Erroneous data accessing	120	10	36	21	72	15	12	2
Erroneous decision logic or sequencing	139	12	41	24	83	17	15	3
Erroneous arithmetic computations	113	9	22	13	73	15	18	3
Invalid timing	44	4	14	8	25	5	5	1
Improper handling of interrupts	46	4	14	8	31	6	1	0
Wrong constants and data values	41	3	14	8	19	4	8	1
Inaccurate documentation	96	8	0	0	10	2	86	16
Total	1202	100	171	14	478	40	553	46

TABLE II
Incomplete or Erroneous Specification—Frequency of Error Occurrence

Error Category	Total		Serious		Moderate		Minor	
	Number	Percent	Number	Percent	Number	Percent	Number	Percent
Dimensional error	41	12	7	37	17	21	17	7
Insufficient precision specified	15	4	0	0	11	13	4	2
Missing symbols or labels	4	1	0	0	0	0	4	2
Typographical error	51	15	0	0	0	0	51	21
Incorrect hardware description	7	2	3	16	3	4	1	0
Design consideration incomplete or incorrect	177	52	8	42	47	57	122	51
Ambiguity in specification or design	45	13	1	5	4	5	40	17
TOTAL	340	100	19	6	82	24	239	70

TABLE III
Erroneous Data Accessing—Frequency of Error Occurrence

Error Category	Total		Serious		Moderate		Minor	
	Number	Percent	Number	Percent	Number	Percent	Number	Percent
Fetch or store wrong data word	79	66	17	47	52	72	10	83
Fetch or store wrong portion of data word	10	8	10	28	0	0	0	0
Variable equated to wrong location	10	8	4	11	6	8	0	0
Overwrite of data word	10	8	4	11	4	6	2	17
Register loaded with wrong data	11	9	1	3	10	14	0	0
TOTAL	120	100	36	30	72	60	12	10

to minor errors than to serious errors. On the other hand, invalid timing or improper handling of interrupts almost always results in a significant error.

The data presented in Table I summarize the errors found in independent validations as depicted in Fig. 1. In practice, however, the organization responsible for the independent validation does not wait until the developer has completed program debugging. Instead, the independent validation organization often becomes involved at each program development phase to check that intermediate products (such as the program specification and program design) are correct. The term "verification" is often used to describe these intermediate checking activities, while the term "validation" encompasses these intermediate testing activities as well as the checking

TABLE IV
Erroneous Decision Logic or Sequencing—Frequency of Error Occurrence

Error Category	Total		Serious		Moderate		Minor	
	Number	Percent	Number	Percent	Number	Percent	Number	Percent
Label placed on wrong instruction/statement	2	1	2	5	0	0	0	0
Branch test incorrect	28	20	10	24	15	18	3	20
Branch test set up incorrect	2	2	1	2	1	1	0	0
Computations performed in wrong sequence	9	6	1	2	2	2	6	40
Logic sequence incorrect	98	71	27	66	65	78	6	40
TOTAL	139	100	41	29	83	60	15	11

TABLE V
Erroneous Arithmetic Computations—Frequency of Error Occurrence

Error Category	Total		Serious		Moderate		Minor	
	Number	Percent	Number	Percent	Number	Percent	Number	Percent
Wrong arithmetic operations performed	69	61	12	55	47	64	10	56
Loss of precision	9	8	1	5	6	8	2	11
Overflow	8	7	3	14	3	4	2	11
Poor scaling of intermediate results	22	20	4	18	15	21	3	17
Incompatible scaling	5	4	2	9	2	3	1	5
Total	113	100	22	19	73	65	18	16

of the final program. The errors occurring in the categorization of Table II, incomplete or erroneous specifications, indicate either deficiencies in or the absence of the verification of the program specification or program design, since there should be no errors in the final programs attributable to the program specification if the preceding verification efforts were perfect. As shown in Table II, 19 serious and 82 moderate errors escaped the verification efforts and were found only during the checking of the actual coding. In 239 additional cases, an error due to incomplete or erroneous specification was considered of minor consequence; this was largely because the coding had been implemented correctly even though the program specification was itself in error.

If all of the 239 minor erroneous or incomplete specification errors were faithfully translated into coding, the total number of serious errors in the resultant coding would have been 84 and the total number of moderate errors would have been 162. Only 94 of the 239 minor errors would remain minor errors, even if the coding implemented the erroneous specification. This would make the incomplete or erroneous specification error category, in Table I, the largest error source by a factor of 2, and would increase the total number of serious errors by 38 percent and the total number of moderate errors by 12 percent. Obviously the verification of the program specification and design, in advance of coding and debugging, is a very beneficial activity, and indeed is probably essential if reliable software is desired.

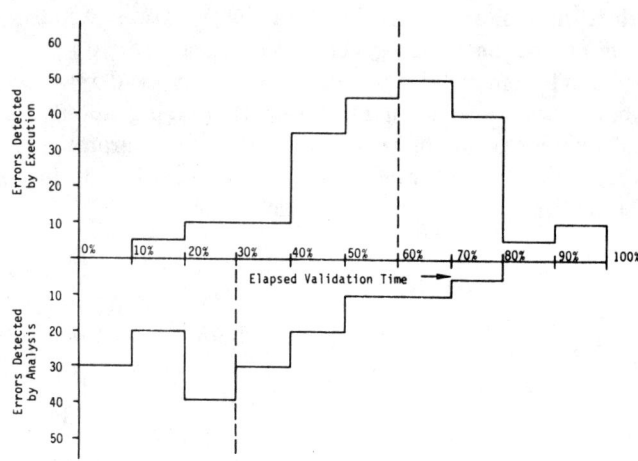

Fig. 3. Error detection methods.

VALIDATION TOOLS AND TECHNIQUES

Knowing when and how the errors are detected during validation is of next importance in studying errors. A wide variety of tools and techniques are used in validation. Two categories of these tools and techniques can be defined: 1) execution tools and techniques by which the program is exercised using the actual hardware or simulations, and 2) analysis tools and techniques by which the behavior and structure of the program are examined without actually executing the program. Most execution tools and techniques are familiar to anyone who has debugged a program. However, when execution methods are employed, validation-oriented automatic aids often are used for the generation of test inputs and the interpretation of test results. Analysis methods are less familiar to most development programmers. They range from edit programs, through which complex cross-reference listings are generated and specific code sequences are detected, to automatic flow charters, through which a detailed high-level and graphic representation of the program is constructed. The ultimate analysis tools and techniques involve correctness or correspondence proofs and program restructuring.

Fig. 3 illustrates the number of errors detected through execution and analysis methods during each interval of the validation effort. Slightly more errors (211) were detected through execution methods than through analysis methods (167). However, analysis methods detected errors earlier, with half of these errors discovered before 30 percent of the validation effort had elapsed, while over half of the execution-detected errors remained to be discovered during the last 40 percent of the validation effort. Obviously, it is desirable to detect errors as soon as possible, but not to miss any. Because of this, the execution and analysis methods are complementary; the analysis methods detect the earlier—perhaps easier—errors, while the execution methods continue to detect errors after the analysis methods are unproductive.

Fig. 3 indicated where improvement in validation tools and techniques should be made. One reason why execution

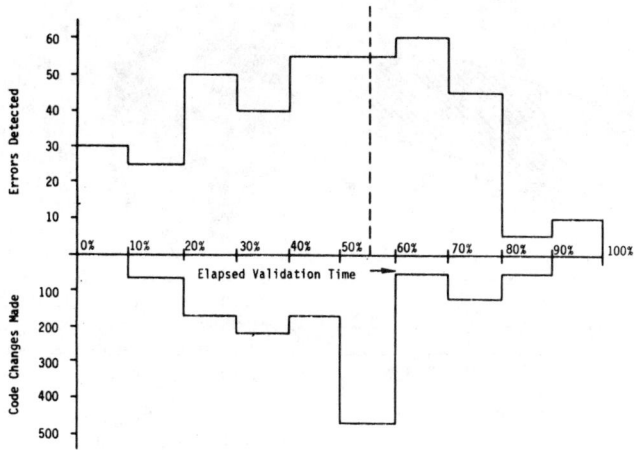

Fig. 4. Errors and instruction changes.

methods are initially unproductive is that considerable effort initially must be expended in setting up test cases and analyzing test results. Automatic computer-based assistance in these areas is clearly indicated. The coverage of analysis tools and techniques must be extended so that more errors can be detected through these quick, relatively inexpensive methods.

Fig. 4 illustrates the impact of the errors detected during validation on the number of changes made to the coding during validation (as measured by the number of machine-language instructions changed). Surprisingly, no close correlation is evident. By the middle of the validation period, 80 percent of code changes were made, but only about 50 percent of the errors had been detected by that time. There are several reasons for this. There is an understandable reluctance to make changes during the latter part of the validation period unless the errors are serious, while even minor errors detected early may be corrected. For this reason, there is an attempt to find the serious errors as soon as possible, particularly by analyzing the results of test executions of the program.

VALIDATION COSTS

The cost of validation can be a significant portion of the total development cost, but this price must be paid if highly reliable software is to be obtained. A convenient and useful approach to describing the cost of independent validation is to express that cost as a function of the software development cost. The validation cost could then be described by the relation

$$C_{\text{validation}} = (F_1 + F_2 + F_3 + \cdots + F_n)C_{\text{development}}$$

where the F's represent validation cost factors. These factors describe how conditions that prevail during development and validation affect cost. An examination of a dozen past validation projects identified nine distinct validation cost factors. These factors and the range of their values are presented in Table VI. The most significant factor in validation cost was the size of the program to be validated (i.e., the target program). It is both surprising

TABLE VI
VALIDATION COST FACTORS

Validation Factor	Maximum Weight	Minimum Weight
Target Program Size	.250	.050
Target Program Status	.125	.008
Validation Tool Status	.093	.000
Target Program Documentation Status	.062	.016
Computer & Operating System Status	.031	.016
Type of Target Program	.031	.008
Familiarity with Tools and Target Program	.031	.008
Attitude of Target Program Contractors	.031	.008
Availability of Computers for Validation	.031	.008

and comforting to learn that the cost for validating large programs (i.e., larger than 64K machine-language instructions) is a smaller percentage of development cost than for small programs (i.e., less than 32K). The next most significant factor is the status of the program being validated. If the independent validation organization does not become actively involved until the target program is in the debug state, the cost factor is 0.125; if the validation is begun during the program specification phase, the cost factor is 0.093. If a validation of a previously validated program is performed, the cost factor is 0.008. This is consistent with the data of Table I, for which it was observed that the severity of errors in the delivered program due to an erroneous or incomplete specification were significantly reduced by the prior review of the program specification and design. Validation costs are also less if the validation organization can utilize already developed validation-oriented tools and if detailed, complete, correct, and controlled documentation is available. The five remaining factors indicate that validation is less costly: 1) for mature computer and operating systems, 2) for non-real-time programs (as opposed to interactive or real-time applications), 3) when the validation organization is familiar

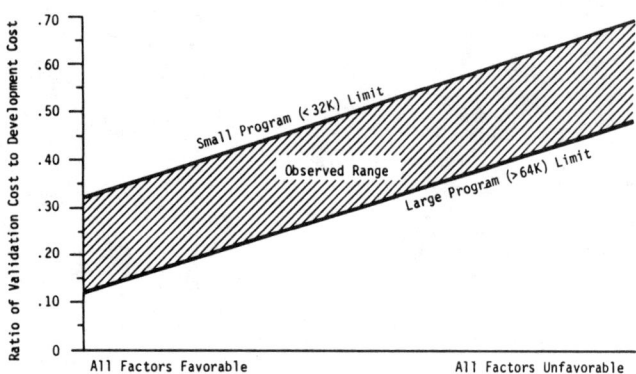

Fig. 5. Observed range of validation/development cost ratios.

with the tools used and the application of validated program, 4) when the contractual environment enables the free interchange of information, and 5) when computers suitable for the validation effort are readily available.

Fig. 5 illustrates the range of validation/development cost ratios based on these factors. The upper limit illustrates the range of validation/development costs for small programs (less than 32K instructions) as the remaining factors vary from their minimum values to their maximum. The lower limit illustrates the range for large programs (greater than 64K instructions). As shown in Fig. 5, when all factors are favorable, the validation of a small program costs about 32 percent of the development cost and a large program about 12 percent. If all factors are unfavorable, the validation of a small program can be as high as 69 percent of the development cost, and the validation of a large program can be as high as 49 percent. In interpreting these results, it must be remembered that not all validation efforts have the same objectives. For example, in some cases, the independent validation organization must determine the extent to which the program satisfies *all* system requirements, while in other cases, only the satisfaction of *critical* system requirements need be demonstrated. The latter costs 25–35 percent less than the former, based on data from the independent validation efforts examined. The preceding discussion has considered only independent validations where demonstration of all system requirements was the objective, although the basic findings are applicable for validation efforts at less stringent and to less complete levels.

Comparing the cost information presented in Fig. 5 with the number of errors found in development, debugging, and validation presented in Fig. 2, it is evident that a high price is paid to find the few errors that remain after development. However, until absolutely correct software specifications can be written and translated into error-free programs, some level of validation is necessary to obtain reliable software. For the near future, existing data indicate that improvements are needed in the software specification, design, coding, debugging, and validation phases. Equally important, more data about the errors actually encountered are needed to efficiently and effectively make the needed improvements.

Raymond J. Rubey received the B.S. degree in engineering and the Master of Engineering degree from the University of California, Los Angeles, in 1959 and 1969, respectively.

He was a member of the Technical Staff of Space Technology from 1959 to 1962 where he participated in the checkout of guidance software for the early Atlas and Atlas-Able boosters, and in the development of design automation aids. He then spent a year with Hughes Aircraft Company where he participated in the development of a Pert-based management information system. He has been with Logicon, Inc., Dayton, Ohio, since 1963 where he has been responsible for a comparative evaluation of PL/1, the design of an aerospace programming language, the development of compilers for that language, and the definition of quantitative measures of software quality. His primary activity and interest has been in the verification and validation of software and in the design of tools and techniques to assist in achieving reliable software. He has been an Instructor for the Association for Computing Machinery Professional Development Seminars on aerospace software and PL/1, and has authored over twenty papers and reports on programming languages and software validation.

Joseph A. Dana was born in Whiting, Ind., on April 19, 1942. He received the B.S. in aeronautical astronautical engineering from Northrop Institute of Technology, Inglewood, Calif., in 1966.

From the spring of 1966 to the spring of 1974 he was associated with the Los Angeles Division of Logicon, Inc., at both the San Pedro, Calif., and Huntsville, Ala., facilities. His prime endeavors with the Los Angeles Division was in the area of verification and validation of computer systems. This V & V effort was in both practical application and research and development. Since the spring of 1974, he has been managing the Engineering Services Department of the Field Engineering Operation for the Process Systems Division of Logicon, Inc., Merrifield, Va. His prime effort for the Product Systems Division has been with the installation, checkout, and support to field installations of both hardware and software of a process control system for the U.S. Post Office Bulk Mail Program.

Peter W. Biché received the B.S. degree in electrical engineering from Clarkson College of Technology, Potsdam, N. Y., and the M.S. degree in electrical engineering from Michigan State University, East Lansing.

His fourteen years of technical experience includes design and evaluation of a read-only memory for the IBM 360 family of computers, sizing and timing studies associated with several aerospace computer systems for missile guidance applications, the requirements analysis, design and development of a large data retrieval program, the design of an interpretive computer simulation, and the analysis of radiation effects on both missile guidance system components as well as missile system accuracy. While employed at the Aerospace Corporation in El Segundo, Calif., he recieved a patent for a circumvention technique that allows missile guidance systems to recover from the effects of transient radiation. He has been employed with Logicon for five years and is currently Project Manager for Logicon, Inc., Torrance, Calif.

Observations of Fallibility in Applications of Modern Programming Methodologies

SUSAN L. GERHART AND LAWRENCE YELOWITZ

Abstract—Errors, inconsistencies, or confusing points are noted in a variety of published algorithms, many of which are being used as examples in formulating or teaching principles of such modern programming methodologies as formal specification, systematic construction, and correctness proving. Common properties of these points of contention are abstracted. These properties are then used to pinpoint possible causes of the errors and to formulate general guidelines which might help to avoid further errors. The common characteristic of mathematical rigor and reasoning in these examples is noted, leading to some discussion about fallibility in mathematics, and its relationship to fallibility in these programming methodologies. The overriding goal is to cast a more realistic perspective on the methodologies, particularly with respect to older methodologies, such as testing, and to provide constructive recommendations for their improvement.

Index Terms—Correctness proofs, fallibility, program correctness, program errors, program specifications, programming methodologies, reliability, testing.

I. INTRODUCTION

IT is well known that programming is an error-prone process. As a result, the last decade has seen the development of new programming methodologies aimed at reducing the frequency and severity of errors during the programming process. Briefly, we might label some of these newer methodologies.

Formal Specification: Expression of program requirements in unambiguous and complete terms.

Program Structuring: Use of a restricted set of reliable control and data structures.

Systematic Construction: Development of programs through successive refinements where correctness is argued informally based on the simplicity of each step.

Program Proving: Development and use of mathematical systems for presenting proofs of program correctness.

Common to all these methodologies is the application of mathematical reasoning to programming, the goal being a sufficiently high level of mathematical rigor so that errors will occur infrequently and be easily detected when they do occur.

In this paper we show that the new programming methodologies are still quite fallible. Our approach is, in part, to point out errors, inconsistencies, or confusing points in a variety of published algorithms. Many of these algorithms are being used as examples in teaching new programming methodologies, and it is important for such points of contention to be discussed openly. We go beyond merely listing the points of contention by trying to abstract common properties of them. These common properties are used to help us conjecture some "reasons" for the errors and to assist us in formulating general guidelines which might prevent reoccurrence of the errors. Our goal is to cast a more realistic perspective on the methodologies and to make constructive recommendations to improve them.

The errors are classified as follows.

1) Specification Errors: Occur where something is wrong with the specifications for a program, making the programming and verification process fallacious.

2) Systematic Construction Errors: Occur where errors contaminate the process by which a program is developed and the resulting programs are incorrect.

3) Proved Program Errors: Occur where errors remain undetected even though a "proof" has been given.

This tripartite categorization is largely a matter of convenience in exposition and should not be construed too rigidly. Several of the errors are, in fact, discussed in relation to more than one of the above categories.

In the next three sections the error categories are discussed individually. Each section begins with a short introduction, followed by a listing of the points of contention, followed by a conclusion which generalizes over the errors of each class and provides recommendations for preventing and detecting errors of the class. Each point of contention is presented as a miniature case study, in which the following are described: the context of the algorithm in relation to the publication; a description of the algorithm and its point of contention; and an analysis. Section V presents conclusions and recommendations generalized from the three error classes. In Section VI we discuss some relations between fallibility in programming methodologies and fallibility in mathematics. The errors are listed in Table I for reference.

We realize that this paper deals with a sensitive subject and that the material can be interpreted in many ways. Therefore, we wish to present our views of the subject and to repeat our purpose.

1) We did not search for these errors; once we became aware of the potential for error and developed some intuition about causes and effects of errors, the observations appeared naturally in the course of our normal reading and research. This is discouraging in that it signals a lack of awareness and/or critical reading on the part of reviewers, but at the same time it is encouraging in that it shows that errors can be identified once awareness and critical reading skills have been developed.

2) We are convinced that the errors do not destroy credibility of the modern programming methodologies. Perhaps we should split the purpose of the methodologies into design and verification.

Reprinted from *IEEE Transactions on Software Engineering*, September 1976, pp. 195-207. Copyright © 1976 by The Institute of Electrical and Electronics Engineers, Inc.

Manuscript received April 7, 1976; revised May 10, 1976. This work was supported in part by NASA under Grant NSG 1267 and the National Science Foundation under Grant MCS 75-08146. The views and conclusions expressed in this paper are those of the authors and do not necessarily reflect those of the granting agencies.

S. L. Gerhart is with the Department of Computer Science, Duke University, Durham, NC 27706.

L. Yelowitz is with the Department of Computer Science, University of Pittsburgh, Pittsburgh, PA 15260.

TABLE I
TABLE OF ERRORS

Reference Code	Name of Program(s)	Classification(s)
S1	Prime Test	Specifications and proofs
S2	Sorting and Searching	Specifications and proofs
S3	Magic Square Generator	Specifications and proofs
S4	Data structure algorithms	Specifications and proofs
T1	Sequence Generation	Systematic Construction
T2/P2	Line Editor	Systematic Construction/proofs
T3	Telegram Processor	Systematic Construction and proofs
T4	Sorting Algorithm	Systematic Construction
T5	8-queens	Systematic Construction
P1	Linear Search Program	Proof
P3	Prime Sieve	Systematic Construction and proofs
P4	Powers of matrices	Systematic Construction and proofs

a) Design has been continually emphasized in the programing methodology literature. The programs mentioned in this paper are, for the most part, well-designed; that is, even though errors are present, the programs are substantially correct. There should be little doubt of the value of the methodologies for design.

b) It is at the verification level that the methodology failures have been observed. As mentioned above, the programs are substantially correct through good design but still contain errors, most of which are minor and easily fixed. However, even minor errors can have serious consequences and be costly to fix. One of the most serious consequences is to cast doubt on the usefulness of the methodologies.

We believe that the analysis of errors and the recommendations we present can lead to prevention and early detection of most of the types of error that so frequently occur.

3) We do not believe that the errors reflect negatively on the skills of the persons who committed them. Instead, mistakes are inherent in the difficulty of the programming task and the early stage of development of the methodologies. Each article mentioned here makes a significant contribution to that development. Often the erroneous examples are tangential to the main point of the paper. The errors may only increase that contribution, albeit in an unplanned way. If blame is to be laid anywhere, it should go to the reviewers of the papers and other readers who have missed the errors. We also believe that it is far healthier to discuss these errors openly than to ignore or cover up their existence. Perhaps what we need is more "ego-less publishing."

4) To some extent, we are playing the role of Monday morning quarterbacks. Many of the errors are "old" in the sense that the papers are very early and much progress has been made since their appearance. However, many of the errors have only recently been detected and the errors are still occurring in contemporary papers. This forces us to conclude that the analysis is necessary.

5) There is the additional aspect that the errors provide a way of studying the programming methodologies which yields unique insights into the processes. We have learned much about how to write specifications, assertions, and programs from our study of the literature from the unique viewpoint of errors. Perhaps, others will, also.

6) That the testing methodology is fallible is so well-known that we did not attempt to include errors of this kind. Analyses of testing fallibility are presented in [17] and [31]. Examples occur regularly in the algorithms section of the *Communications of the Association for Computing Machinery*.

7) The common characteristic of mathematical rigor and reasoning in these examples leads one to question the effectiveness of "the mathematical approach," not only in programming methodology, but in mathematics itself. The frequency of errors in mathematical theorems, proofs, and applications of theorems is well-recognized and documented. Mills [5] provides a cogent argument for the use of mathematics in programming, a subject we will return to in Section VI.

Readers are, of course, free to draw their own conclusions about the significance of the errors and the implications about modern programming methodologies. We only ask that the material be considered in the spirit in which it is offered.

II. ERRORS IN SPECIFICATIONS

A. Introduction

An early stage of the program development process should involve the rigorous specification of requirements for a program in terms of expected input, required output, constraints on storage and time, and actions in response to invalid inputs or run-time storage or time limitations. In practice, it seems that such specifications are used more frequently in large multiperson software projects and are often skipped in pedagogical articles on the new programming methodologies. In articles on proving program correctness, however, at least formal input and output requirements must be specified, although errors and algorithm constraints are usually ignored. Our list of specification errors concentrates on articles on program correctness, not necessarily because errors occur more frequently here, but because there is a lack of other published material on program specification.

Liskov and Zilles [1] discuss specifications as the media which translate a concept in someone's mind of what a program should do to solve a problem into a formal written statement of exactly what the program should do. One value of this step is that it becomes possible to formally prove consistency of programs with such formal specifications. However, the complementary step of verifying that a program specification implements the underlying concept must necessarily remain informal. Most of the error observations relate to the deficiencies in the concept-to-specification step. But we shall see that these errors suggest guidelines which can make this necessarily informal step more reliable.

B. Examples of Specification Errors

S1–Prime Test: See King [2, p. 190], Wegbreit [3, p. 106], Deutsch [4].

Context: The example is used in King [2] to show the power of a mechanical verifier using the inductive assertion method, and in Wegbreit [3] to illustrate a mechanical assertion generator.

Description: The informal specifications are "set the flag variable J to 0 or 1 as A is or is not a prime." The formal specifications are as follows.

Input:

$A \geq 2$.

Output:

$[J=0 \Rightarrow (\forall k)(2 \leq k < A \supset A \bmod k \neq 0)] \wedge$

$[J=1 \Rightarrow (A \bmod I = 0)]$.

The program is (rewritten from flow charts to text)

$I:=2$;

while $(A \bmod I) \neq 0$ do $I:=I+1$;

if $I=A$ then $J:=0$ else $J:=1$;

The formal specifications are inadequate, as shown by the following programs which are equally "correct" with respect to these specifications.

1) $J:=2$
2) $I:=1; \ J:=1$
3) $I:=A; \ J:=1;$
4) $J:=1; \ A:=0; \ I:=1$
5) $J:=0; \ A:=1$.

Analysis: A source of difficulty is that neither I nor J is sufficiently constrained in the output specifications; also, A is not constrained to have the same value it had upon input. More complete output specifications are

$[J=0 \Rightarrow (\forall k)(2 \leq k < A \supset A \bmod k \neq 0)] \wedge$

$[J=1 \Rightarrow (\exists k)(A \bmod k = 0 \wedge 2 \leq k < A)] \wedge$

$[J=0 \vee J=1] \wedge [A = A_0]$

(where A_0 denotes the input value of A).

The error might have been detected by noting that the given program can be proved without using the input specification. Such a phenomenon would probably be noticed by a person performing a hand proof, but possibly not by a machine proof that was not carefully inspected.

Comparing the informal and formal specifications, we see the following inconsistencies.

1) Informally, J is to be set to either 0 or 1. Formally, this is omitted.

2) The condition for A being a prime is translated correctly in the implication for $J=0$, but the condition for A being a nonprime is not. This shows a failure to abstract the notion "prime," such as

prime $(A) \triangleq (\forall k)(2 \leq k < A \supset A \bmod k \neq 0) \wedge A \geq 2$

$\equiv$ 'A is greater than 1 and has no divisors except 1 and itself'

which may be used to better express the formal specifications as

$[J=0 \wedge \text{prime}(A) \vee J=1 \wedge \sim \text{prime}(A)] \wedge [A=A_0]$.

3) The informal specifications clearly refer to the input value of A, but this not reflected in the output specifications.

S2–Sorting and Searching: See King [2, p. 208], Deutsch [4], Mills [5], McGowan and Kelly [6, p. 33].

Context: The examples illustrate program proving techniques.

Description: Let A be a real-valued array indexed from 1 to N, $N \geq 0$. The output specification of a sorting program is that

Sorted$(A, A_0) \triangleq$ Permutation(A, A_0) and Ordered(A)

where Permutation formally expresses that A is a permutation of A_0 (the input value of A) and Ordered expresses that A is in (usually nondescending) order. In the examples, the Permutation conjunct is often omitted and ordering alone is used as the specification.

As pointed out by London [7] and Hoare [8], if this occurs the following program may be said to "sort A into nondecreasing order."

for $I:=1$ to N do $A[I]:=0$.

Specifications for the example searching programs usually look like the following.

Input: TAB$(1::N)$ and KEY, where $1 \leq N \leq$ declared subscript limit of TAB and TAB and KEY are of compatible types.

Output: KEY = TAB(I) and $1 \leq I \leq N$ or KEY is not in TAB$(1::N)$.

The output specification should require TAB, N, KEY to be the same as on entry. If this is not required the following programs may be said to "search"

1) $I:=1; \ TAB(I):=$KEY
2) $N:=0; \ I:=0$.

Analysis: The Permutation property is messy to state and prove, especially using the inductive assertion method. A common, and certainly reasonable, proof technique is to use the fact that if the only operations performed on a vector are swaps of two elements, then the vector is always a permutation of the input vector. The Ordered property is better adapted to the inductive assertion method of proof. There is nothing wrong with splitting the proof into two parts as long as it is explicitly stated that Ordered is only part of the specification and does not correspond by itself to Sorted.

The following properties of Permutation are often used.
1) Permutation (A, A).
2) Permutation $(A, \text{swap}(A, I, J))$.
3) Permutation $(A, B) \wedge$ Permutation $(B, C) \supset$ Permutation (A, C).

Notice, however, that it is insufficient to formally characterize Permutation by only these facts, which are also satisfied by

Permutation (A, B) = "the sum of the elements of A = the sum of the elements of B."

However, it is still fair to use these facts within a proof.

We commonly understand that searching does not destroy the initial values of KEY, N, or TAB $(1::N)$, although it might be that TAB$(N+1)$ is used as a terminating value in a search loop. It is just a convention by which programmers abide when writing search algorithms. (Search and insert algorithms are another matter, though.) From the standpoint of formal specifications, however, it is hard to argue that the programs 1) and 2) are not "correct." Like the permutation property of sorting algorithms, the fact that input variables retain their values at output is more easily shown by simply inspecting the program for absence of assignment or side effects in procedures than by the cumbersome method of incorporating these statements into inductive assertions. Again this should either be adopted as a convention or explicitly stated as a separate aspect of the specifications and proof.

S3—Magic Square Generator: See Gerhart [9, p. 194].
Context: Proof techniques for APL programs are illustrated.
Description: The program, written in APL, is proved correct with respect to the following specifications (informally stated).
Input: $N \geqslant 1$ and N is an odd integer.
Output: M is an $N \times N$ matrix and the sums of the rows, columns, and main diagonals of M are the same.

An equally correct program with these specifications sets every element of M equal to 0. The usual definition of a magic square adds the requirement that every element of the matrix M should be an element of the initial sequence of integers $1 \cdots N^2$, and that each element of that sequence is an element of M. Of course, N should not be changed by the program.

Analysis: Since the committer of this error is one of the present authors, we can testify that the omitted requirement was simply forgotten. The proof of a real magic square generator is difficult, using several number theoretic results, and the author simply became absorbed in that proof and failed to complete the output specification. Once the example had made the point in the context of the thesis, it was considered complete. Like error $S2$, this implicit output condition is easily seen to be valid by inspection of the program. Nevertheless, it should be stated.

This error first came to our attention when a story was related to the authors about a computer science professor who assigned the magic square problem as a programming assignment and gave the incomplete specifications above as the problem requirements. One student submitted the program which set every element of M to 0. The furious professor was then faced with the dilemma that the program was consistent with the given specifications, but not a magic square generator. This characterizes the problems described in the last errors specifications must be complete enough to capture the concept involved, and sufficiently constrained so as not to be satisfiable by trivial programs like those we have been giving.

S4—Assertions about Data Structures: See Oppen [10] Cook and Oppen [11], Knuth [13, alg. 2.3.5D], Berztiss [14 alg. 10.8].

Note: These are points of contention, not necessarily errors
Context: Two opposite approaches to discussing data structures are taken, formal in the first two and informal in the last two references above. The purpose of the formal papers is to develop the theoretical notion of expressibility of languages for stating assertions about programs. The two well-known books are sources of algorithms and techniques for data structures.

Description: The main example of the Oppen papers is reversal of a list by reversal of pointers. The underlying notation of datagraphs is too complex to describe here. There are two difficulties in the output assertion for the program: 1) existential quantification over nodes and arcs leads to incomplete specification, as in previous examples and 2) the assertion seems inconsistent with respect to the last node of the reversed list.

The point of contention in the Knuth [13] and Berztiss [14] books is the precise specification of list structures, namely the constraints on how nodes point to each other. The specific algorithms, which involve marking in preparation for garbage collection, assume constraints on pointers to list heads. It was difficult for us to elicit these assumptions from the books. If the assumptions did not hold, some reachable cells might be left unmarked.

Analysis: In private correspondence where we queried whether these errors exist, Knuth responded that "Rlinks never point to list heads" but the algorithm itself makes a test to see if a node accessed by an Rlink is a list head. Several readings later we decided that this case occurred if the list was circular and that p. 408 implied that heads of sublists were pointed to by special sublist nodes. Reference to similar algorithms in [14] did not resolve the assumption. Similarly, private correspondence with Oppen did not resolve the question of whether the informal statement "reverse a list" was faithfully described in assertions in his assertion language.

These careful readings and correspondences arose from a research effort on the development of formalisms for data structures which would support understandable and precise proofs of properties about data structures, Yelowitz [12]. There are several possible explanations for the contention over the possibility of error in these examples.

1) We may not have read the material carefully enough or we may simply have confused ourselves.
2) The articles and books may have left out critical assump-

tions which are only revealed when our attempts to state and prove correctness placed higher demands on precision than the usual reader.

3) There may actually be errors.

Two things are certain: it is difficult to develop complete, precise, and readable notation for discussing data structures, but it must be done before correctness proofs can be given for data structures.

Our claim is not that the cited papers are wrong and that we are right, but that when it takes multiple rounds of correspondence to resolve issues such as these there is clearly a failure in the specification process. It may well be that specifying data structures is so difficult that we will have to get along for a while with unsatisfactory approaches. Our point is that we should be aware of this problem and emphasize specifications and verifications of specifications. Put another way, we suggest that if it is not possible to determine whether a program or specification is wrong, then indeed something is wrong.

C. Conclusions About Specification Errors

There are several explanations for these errors.

1) In some of the examples, there was no intention of making the specifications complete. This occurs often in program proving where the output specification is split into two or more parts which are proved separately because different proof techniques or levels of detail in proofs are applicable. Thus a proof that a program meets some given set of specifications is not meant to imply that the specifications are complete. "Correctness" in this case is a purely technical matter.

2) There is often an implicit understanding in the use of some terms in specifications that constrains certain variables to be unaltered in the program, and others to be created to report the result of operating on the input. Examples are "searching," which implies that the table and the key are unaltered, and the "testing for a property, such as primeness," which says that the variable being tested is unchanged. It is debatable whether specifications should be explicit on these points, but in the formal world which starts from a set of specifications it seems fair that anything not designated as unalterable should be treated as a program variable. Perhaps an explicit convention should be adopted for this situation.

3) Confusion as to context and assumptions does not explain errors $S1$ and $S3$; these are slips in translation from concepts to formal specifications. This points to failure to confirm that the specifications implement the concept completely and correctly, failure to recognize the need for and therefore to attempt such a confirmation, or lack of tools for verifying specifications.

4) There are cases where specifications are exceedingly difficult, e.g., the line editor problem [16] to be discussed in $T2$.

Perhaps it is useful to view specifications as consisting of the following three components: relations between input and output, assertions about input (independently of output), and assertions about output (independently of input). There are several suggestions for devising specifications that arise from these observations.

1) Check that assumptions have been made explicit.

a) If the specifications are not intended to be complete, then state what is omitted, why it is omitted, and how it can be handled.

b) State which brand of correctness is being sought: "partial" where termination is not considered; or "total" which does require termination, and state whether termination includes eventually halting and/or halting "cleanly" (i.e., no runtime errors).

2) Structure the specifications using abstraction to capture the important aspects of the concept and write the formal specifications to read like the informal specifications.

3) Apply some tests to the specifications:

a) (The absurd program test.) Try to find the shortest program which satisfies the specifications, instead of starting with a preconceived solution. If the program obviously does not satisfy the informal concept, the formal specifications are inadequate.

b) Break the specifications into cases and determine whether in each case the specifications match the informal concept.

c) Formulate the specifications in a different way or at a different point in time and prove consistency of the two sets of specifications.

3) Get an independent verifier for the specifications who will be naive (with respect to the problem), critical, and knowledgeable as to the above techniques for testing specifications and eliciting assumptions.

All in all, these errors point to the critical need for a better specification methodology. Without proper specifications, the verification process is fallacious and program design is substantially more difficult.

These examples clearly show that specifications must be "tested" in much the same way that programs are tested, by selecting data with the goal of revealing any errors that might exist.

III. Errors in Systematically Constructed Programs

A. Introduction

The goal of the methodology which is called by the various names "structured programming," "systematic programming," "stepwise refinement," "top-down programming," etc., is to factor the programming process into small enough steps and programs into small enough parts so that each step or part can be seen to be "correct," and so that each step or part fits together with others to give correctness at a higher level. This is not an easy concept to describe, teach, or grasp, so examples have been the main pedagogical vehicle.

The examples cited here have errors which illuminate the fact that this methodology is not yet fully understood. We hope that the examples point out pitfalls where those learning to apply the methodology should be wary and where further development of the methodology is required.

B. Errors in Systematically Constructed Programs

T1—Sequence Generation: See Wirth [15].

Context: This is the culminating example in the chapter on stepwise program development. It is stressed as an example of a heuristic algorithm, using the important technique of backtracking.

Description: The specific problem is to "generate a sequence of N characters, chosen from an alphabet of three elements such that no two immediately adjacent subsequences are equal." The algorithm has three fundamental operations for extending, changing, and checking a candidate sequence.

The error occurs in refining the statement

$$\text{good} := (S_{m-2L+1} \cdots S_{m-L}) \neq (S_{m-L+1} \cdots S_m).$$

The Boolean variable "good" should be set to **true** if the two sequences of length $L > 0$ differ in at least one pair of corresponding positions, **false** otherwise.

The refinement is

$i := 0;$

repeat

  $\text{good} := S(m-L-i) \neq S(m-i); i := i+1;$

until $\sim \text{good} \lor i = L.$

The variable "good" should not be negated. As a counterexample consider $m=4$, $L=2$, and the sequence $S=3,2,1,2$. The above loop forces "good" to be **false** by finding the two 2's, but in fact the sequence 3,2 is not equal to the sequence 1,2 so good should be **true**.

Analysis: Since there is a difference of only one symbol, it might seem that this is simply a typographical error, but it is hard to interpret the insertion of the "$\sim$" character in that way.

This error seems to indicate failure to check the final step of the program construction. Here is where program proofs enter the picture because in being forced to write down a definition of "good" and to check the **until** test the error would probably be found. For example, an assertion to hold right before the **until** test is

$$[\text{good} \equiv (\exists j \mid 0 \leq j < i) (S(m-L-j)$$
$$\neq S(m-j))] \land [1 \leq i \leq L]$$

and then it is easily seen that terminating with $\sim$good will not give the right result. The error was actually discovered while studying the program in preparation for proof. It was later discovered that "good" is used elsewhere in the example with similar errors.

T2—A Line Editor: See Naur [16].

Context: The article presents a view of systematic construction based on identifying important actions which are organized to meet the overall requirements.

Description: The problem requirements are "Given a text consisting of words separated by BLANKS or by new line (NL) characters, convert it to a line-by-line form in accordance with the following rules: 1) line breaks must be made only where the given text has BLANK or NL; 2) each line is filled as far as possible as long as 3) no line will contain more than MAXPOS characters." There are numerous problems with the specifications that lead to different interpretations of the problem, e.g., should two successive blanks be treated as ending one or two words? How should the text end?

The program also has numerous problems: it does not show any explicit provision for termination; if the program does terminate, the last word is left in the buffer unless followed by a BLANK or NL; there are conditions under which extra line breaks and blanks are output at the beginning; there is confusion between the two symbols NL and LF representing the line break or new line character. These errors have been extensively discussed and analyzed in Goodenough and Gerhart [17] in an example illustrating test data selection techniques.

Analysis: At one point in the paper, there is an assertion "the input character preceding the one held in BUFFER(1) was a BLANK or a NL. This has not been output."

For this assertion to be true the first time it is reached, it is necessary for the text to start with NL or BLANK, but the specifications do not state this requirement.

The point is that the action cluster methodology appears systematic, but the resulting program fails to accomplish even the ill-defined task. However, we believe that this failure can be traced back to the specifications, which are definitely inadequate. The specifications were somewhat elaborated on in Goodenough and Gerhart [17], retaining the prose format, but the authors finally concluded that there was no way to ever get the full problem stated in English without some ambiguity or excessive length. A specification technique for this class of program has been proposed by Noonan [18]. See also error $P2$.

T3—A Telegram Processor: See Henderson and Snowden [19], Ledgard [20].

Context: Systematic development of a program to count words and format a stream of telegrams is considered.

Description: Henderson and Snowden [19] found when they ran their stepwise-constructed program that it miscounted words. They trace their error history through the steps of the program development process. Ledgard [20] develops a new solution, which contains the following errors.

1) Each output line of the program begins with a blank. There is nothing in the specifications requiring or prohibiting this, but it effectively reduces the line length by 1 and seems to contradict the specification that extra blanks should be removed from the telegram on output. Careful reading of the bottom-level program was needed for the present authors to determine this.

2) The instruction "CHAR ← next-char(BUFFER)" might lead to unpredictable results. The meaning of this (predefined) instruction is not given, but apparently is to set CHAR to Λ if there are no more characters in BUFFER, and otherwise to set CHAR to the next (possibly blank) character in BUFFER and logically delete that character from BUFFER. Although Ledgard does not show the implementation of BUFFER, a standard approach to implementing a buffer of length N is to allocate an array A of length $N+1$, in which $A[N+1] = \Lambda$; this

N+1st element is analogous to an "end-of-file" marker. The problem is that whenever the last word of the buffer is not followed by a blank, it is possible to execute "CHAR ← next-char(BUFFER)" twice before refilling the buffer. So the above common implementation will not satisfy the assumptions on the behavior of next-char. Again, a careful reading at the bottom level is necessary to determine this. Without knowing the behavior of next-char and the other primitives, it is not possible to justify the correctness of the final program.

3) Indentation is used as a bracketing device, rather than **begin** ··· **end**. While not strictly an error, it may confuse other readers, as it did us. The use of two labels A also confused us at one point.

4) Termination conditions differ between the final program in Fig. 6 (containing GOTO's) and the final program in Fig. 7 (without GOTO's). For the input stream ZZZZ HELLO DOLLY ZZZZ ZZZZ, the Fig. 6 program will print HELLO DOLLY, whereas the Fig. 7 program will not print any telegram words. The specifications are vague on this point, which forces us to ask how the program could have been proved correct at any level.

Analysis: This problem, like the line editor problem ($T2$) is hard to specify completely. There are surprisingly many potential sources of error, and Henderson and Snowden warn against being lulled into a false sense of security based upon systematic program development. Ledgard provides some general guidelines on a program development methodology at the beginning of his paper, and cites the need for formalizing and debugging each of the levels. The above points of confusion show that there is still a gap in the guidelines which permits programs to be implemented without precise specifications and, therefore, without the basis for ensuring correctness at each level. In such cases, systematic construction should be expected to be quite fallible.

T4—A Sorting Algorithm in PL 360: See Wirth [21, p. 53].
Context: The purpose of the PL 360 language is to "··· further the state of the art of programming by encouraging and even forcing the programmer to improve his style of exposition and his principles and discipline in program organization" (from the abstract).
Description: The error is in procedure **sort**. The purpose of the procedure apparently is to sort an array a, indexed from 0 to n in increments of 4, into decreasing order. The incrementation by 4 is due to the IBM 360 architecture—4 bytes compromise a word, and incrementation by 1 would simply be a byte at a time.

In an outer loop, $R1$ goes from 0 to n in steps of 4. In an inner loop, the procedure checks if there is some index greater than $R1$, say $R3$, such that

1) $a(R3) > a(R1)$

and

2) $a(R3) = \max \{a(R1+4), \cdots, a(n)\}$.

If such an index $R3$ exists, then for definiteness let $R3$ be the smallest possible value satisfying 1) and 2). For such an $R3$, the appropriate logic is to swap $a(R1)$ with $a(R3)$ so that right after the swap $a(R1) = \max \{a(R1), a(R1+4), \cdots, a(n)\}$. Then the outer loop should continue. If no such $R3$ exists, then $a(R1)$ is already the maximum of $a(R1), \cdots, a(n)$ and the outer loop can continue immediately. The error is that the swap occurs even if no such $R3$ exists; thus $R3$ might be undefined (if this is the first swap), or $R3$ might be "left over" from a previous iteration. In programming terms, $R3$ is assigned a value in the then-part of an **if-then**, but at the conclusion of the **if-then**, it is assumed that the then-part has been executed.

This error has continued to appear in later reports and manuals on PL 360.

Analysis: Failure to initialize a variable is a common error, e.g., see error $P4$ below. One virtue of structured programming is that all paths leading to a given statement can be discerned relatively easily, making it routine to verify that every variable is initialized prior to being referenced. Apparently, that verification was not performed.

The error was discovered in a classroom exercise which involved reformatting the program text.

T5—The 8-Queens Problem: See Wirth [22].
Context: The "stepwise refinement" method is explained and illustrated.
Description: The "eight-queens" problem is "find a way of placing 8 hostile queens on a standard 8 × 8 chessboard so that no queen may attack another." The point of contention is one of programming style and robustness rather than an actual error. When attention is restricted to only the 8-queens problem, no error will arise. If, however, we wish to generalize the solution to the N-queens problem, for arbitrary $N \geq 1$, then an error will arise for each N in which there is no solution (e.g., $N=2,3$). Since it might not be known in advance of running the program if a solution exists for the 8-queens problem, it is fortuitous that the error does not occur here also. The same error occurs when all solutions to the 8-queens problem are sought.

The specific error is a possible out-of-bound array reference. The x-array is indexed from 1 to 8, and represents the current board configuration; $x[p]=k$ if a queen is present in column p, row k, where $1 \leq p \leq j$ (j is a variable used to move left or right across columns). When the program regresses out of the first column (as will occur when no solution exists or all solutions have been produced) the following code will be executed with $j=1$ (according to our interpretation discussed below):

$j := j-1$;

$i := x[j]$;

Analysis: Actually, it is somewhat ambiguous what the final program should be. After completing the stepwise refinement, Wirth observes that $x[j]$ can be replaced by a variable i, saving several subscript computations. The proper modifications to coordinate i with $x[j]$ are mentioned and then the affected procedures, except *reconsiderpriorcolumn*, are rewritten. If one constructs the complete concrete program from the latest versions of the procedures, the adjustment for *i* does not occur because *reconsiderpriorcolumn* is out of date. But if one constructs, as we did, the program with the obvious recommended change to *reconsiderpriorcolumn*

$$j := j-1; \quad i := x[j]$$

the subscript error occurs. A third possibility is to rewrite *regress* to read

begin $j := j-1$
        if $j \geq 1$
        then $i := x[j]$; *removequeen*, $\cdots$

but this is a major deviation from the preceding refinements.

Our conclusion is that a seemingly safe optimization did not preserve correctness and should have been checked more carefully. We are not sure how this type of program rewriting fits into the stepwise refinement method.

C. Conclusions About Errors in Systematically Constructed Programs

It is hard to pinpoint the exact places of failure in the systematic constructions since there are always many assumptions in effect and the reasoning is informal. Most errors seem to occur when the bottom-level code is written. It is as if the systematic construction is performed as a series of refinement steps where every step *except the last*, in which concrete code is produced, is carefully checked. This leads to the obvious recommendations.

1) Be especially careful to verify that the concrete program parts do exactly what the abstract parts intended.

2) After completing a systematic construction, put all of the pieces of program together and recheck, using standard methods of testing and/or proving, that the program does what was initially specified.

Some amount of formalization would probably benefit the systematic construction methodology. Care must be taken to avoid overformalization, since a point of diminishing returns can easily be reached, and passed. For example, S4 and P4 (below) fail to detect errors despite a great deal of formalism. One practical approach is to treat data reference and program structure with more symmetry. In many articles, "structure" is claimed for a program based upon the use of only well-known control structures, but mention is seldom made of the degree of locality or globality of data reference. If a variable is referenced and modified at every level of a program, then the difficulty in understanding the purpose of that variable might become inordinate, and the fact that goto's have been avoided becomes somewhat academic. More recent work [23] concentrates on the data structure aspect of systematic construction.

The following recommendations might be useful.

In addition to the standard refinement process, keep a list of important program variables (or more general data structures). The list should explain the purpose of the variable at a problem-solving, or goal-oriented level, including its initialization, updates, and relation to other variables; a check then can be made that the purpose of the variable corresponds to the pattern of references and modifications as used by the program. Such a list might have caught the errors in T4 and P4.

It is also important to note that some errors were easily discovered by hand simulation on test values. Finally, we note an alternative viewpoint: systematic construction should expose various facts about the program which then can serve as a basis for a proof, but the systematic construction alone is insufficient to guarantee correctness.

IV. Errors in "Proved" Programs

A. Introduction

Testing cannot guarantee in a practical sense that a program is correct, although, in theory, testing can be viewed as a basis for an induction proof which does demonstrate correctness [17]. However, program proving based on testing is not yet well understood. The approach to program proving which has been advocated over the past few years stresses the construction of theorems (verification conditions) to express program correctness, and various mechanical techniques for proving these theorems. Other work has concentrated on proof styles, ranging from the loose arguments for correctness seen in articles on stepwise refinement to much more rigorous proofs, some of which have been mechanically produced.

The overall goal of the work on proving program correctness is to show convincingly that programs do not contain errors. The following examples demonstrate that proofs of correctness do not always discover errors, even though the proofs may be persuasive, and perhaps even "formalistic." We will have more to say about the nature of errors in proofs in mathematics at the end of this article. For now, the reader should bear in mind that there are two aspects to program proving: 1) what to prove; and 2) how to prove it. Most of the errors are best viewed as failures in defining what to prove.

B. Errors in Proved Programs

P1–A Linear Search Program: See McGowan and Kelly [6, p. 33].

Context: The example occurs in a section intended to help readers convince themselves "that careful reasoning about programs is a better guide to correctness than extensive testing" [6, p. 30].

Description: Suppose that a table TAB has been declared to have N elements with 1-origin subscripting and that KEY and TAB are declared of the same or compatible types. The language in use is PL/1. (The example in the book uses structures, but we are simplifying to arrays without losing the general idea.) The following program is given to search an initialized TAB for an initialized value of KEY:

```
I=1;
DO WHILE (I<=N & KEY¬=TAB(I));
    I=I+1;
END;
```

with the loop invariant

$$\text{KEY} \neq \text{TAB}(j) \quad \text{for } 1 \leq j \leq I-1.$$

The claim is that on exiting the loop, either $I = N+1$ and

KEY is not in TAB, or KEY = TAB(*I*). (In fact, the invariant needs the conjunct $I \leq N + 1$ in order to conclude $I = N + 1$ at loop exit, but that is not the main problem here.)

The specific problem is that if KEY is not present in TAB, the final **while** test will be executed with the value $I = N + 1$, making the first conjunct false. In all but the optimizing PL/1 compiler, however, the second conjunct is evaluated (even though it is logically superfluous), giving rise to DATA INTERRUPTS and SUBSCRIPT RANGE errors. (This experiment was performed on an IBM 370/168 with standard IBM software in December 1975.)

Analysis: The undefined order of evaluation of operands of logical operators is a well-known pitfall of PL/1. Left-to-right, nonsuperfluous evaluation is often assumed, but the PL/1 reference manual is vague on this point. Other languages, e.g., Algol W, make it explicit that the **and** operator in *A* **and** *B* is sequentially defined as **if** *A* **then** *B* **else** false.

The error shows that ignoring control within expressions and inexecutable operations can invalidate a correctness argument or a careful reasoning process. Elsewhere in [6], attention is paid to logical operators in assembly language macros. The authors point out that the preferred code for this problem is

DO *I*=1 TO *N* WHILE (KEY ¬=TAB(*I*));
END;

which avoids the problem of order of evaluation of operands for this program.

P2–Line Editor: See London [7].

Context: The line editor program has been discussed in error *T*2. London [7] corrected one error and proved several properties of the corrected program. The goal was to illustrate the methods and some results of the approach of proving programs correct and to suggest that the approach at least be considered as a means of attaining software reliability.

Description: The program provided by London has the following abstract structure:

"initialize program variables";
while "more characters to be read" **do**
begin "input a character";
"process that character" (putting it in the buffer or outputting the buffer with a preceding blank or line feed, as required by the line specifications)
end

The "more characters to be read" action is simply expressed as "halt if no more characters." The problem with this action is that when there are no more characters, there may still be a word in the buffer. In this version of the program, the buffer is not emptied.

Analysis: Several lemmas for properties of the program are proved. Variable types are consistent; subscript errors do not occur if the words are not oversized; the buffer array contains only legal parts of words; and the words output on a line are done so correctly. The proof line "the output of each entire word (possibly null) after the first word must be and is preceded either by a line feed...or a BLANK..." comes close to hitting the point of error in the program, but it concentrates on showing that the words which are output are done so correctly, not that all the words are output (and in the same order).

As in *T*2, the proof missed a common and well-known pitfall of this type of program, namely, failure to empty the buffer at the end of processing. The error probably was not caught because the program specifications, and hence the correctness requirements, were so loosely stated. It should also be noted that this is one of the earliest published attempts at proving a realistic program.

P3–Prime Sieve: See Wulf [23].

Context: The language ALPHARD is being designed to provide, among other features, the facility for handling abstractions in both control and data structures. The prime sieve (sieve of Eratosthenes) program previously developed and proved by Hoare [24] was reworked to display the abstractions in the final text of the program. It is claimed that program proving should be factored into proofs of high-level algorithms (which may often be omitted when they are well known, as in this example, or obvious) and proofs that the representations correctly reflect the high-level algorithm. The intended proof style is used on the example.

Description: The high-level algorithm is

while ~ empty(sieve) **do**
(include(prime,min(sieve));
removemultiples(sieve, min(sieve)))

where "prime" is declared of type powerset of the integers $1 \cdots N$ and initialized to empty and "sieve" is declared of type powerset of the integers $2 \cdots N$ and initialized to $\{2, \cdots, N\}$. The ultimate representation of both is bits within an array of machine words.

The error is that the "min" routine does not return the minimum element of the sieve, as specified by the algorithm, but instead returns the *index* of the minimum element as a pair of integers representing an element in an array of words and a bit in that word. The index of the least possible element of "sieve," that is, 2, corresponds to 0. There are two effects of this error:

1) "include (prime, min(sieve))" causes min(sieve)-1 to be placed in "prime."
2) the operation "removemultiples(sieve, min(sieve))" corresponds to a loop

for $I := X$ **step** X **until** N **do**
"remove the element with index I from sieve"

which is executed with X being the index of min(sieve) in sieve, thus causing an infinite loop when X is 0.

Analysis: The proof shows that the bit-word pair and powerset forms are correctly defined and attempts to show that an integer-set form is correct. The latter part of the proof states "removemultiples(*n*) removes the elements at indexes *n*, $2n, 3n, \cdots$, size of powerset" but this cannot be true when $n = 0$ and, even if that worked, the sieve would be emptied when $n = 1$. It is not proved that the element which is included in "prime" is actually the minimum element of the sieve. The error seems to have occurred because the data representations do not actually correspond to the algorithm, with a resulting confusion between the minimum element of the sieve and its index. Note that usually the initialization is stated in the algorithm but that in ALPHARD, initialization is distributed to the data structure forms.

The original claim that program proving can be factored into algorithm and data representation is probably justified, but there is still a substantial proof step in showing that the representations are faithful to the intent of the algorithm. It should be noted that this is the first description of ALPHARD and a more recent description [30] uses better defined language constructs and takes a more rigorous approach.

P4—Maximum of a Series of Powers of Matrices: See Lanzarone and Ornaghi [25].

Context: The paper presents a variation of the usual correctness formalism to describe the stepwise refinement method.

Description: The example is specified: "A symmetric matrix with positive or null elements has to be multiplied by itself until the maximum of its elements is greater than or equal to an assigned positive real number alpha." Let · represent matrix multiplication, $\|M\|$ represent the value of the maximum element of matrix M, and x denote the input matrix.

The top level program is

$(a,b,c) \leftarrow (x,x,\|x\|)$
while $c \leq$ alpha **do**
    $(a,c) \leftarrow (a \cdot b, \|a \cdot b\|)$

The error occurs in the concrete code refined from the body of the loop. As each element, say e, of the new product matrix is computed, a variable d is set to $\max(d,e)$. However, d is not initialized at the start of each matrix product computation, but only at the beginning. This causes d to contain not the maximum of the current matrix, but the maximum of all matrices computed so far. It might be thought that the historical maximum always equals the current maximum, but for the matrix

$$x = \begin{pmatrix} 0.95 & 0.15 \\ 0.15 & 0.95 \end{pmatrix}$$

the successive maxima are 0.95, 0.925, 0.921, 0.936, 0.969. Nevertheless, the program will still work correctly because if the current maximum is less than a previous maximum, and termination has not occurred, then the current maximum is less than alpha.

Analysis: The point is that the final program is not a refinement of the top-level program because the variable d is not reinitialized every time a new matrix is computed. The proof does not catch this discrepancy nor did the proof give any indication that the final result is correct nevertheless. It is debatable whether this should be considered an error, since the final program is correct (assuming there are not other errors which we have not found). However, it could have just been fortuitous that everything worked out in this example, and in other examples the luck might give out. The overall flaw in the approach seems to be that the interfaces between refinements were not carefully checked. For example, the input assertion about the section in error permitted "d" to be any real value, not necessarily 0.

B. Conclusions About the Errors in Proved Programs

There are several common features of these four errors.

1) The inductive assertion method is used informally. It is difficult to apply the assertion method to the line editor problem, lacking a suitable assertion language. We believe the assertion method could have caught the error in P4 since the property of d being the maximum of the current matrix would have been in the loop assertion, as well as the error in P3 since the relation between elements of prime and sieve must be stated.

All of these programs have a loose notion of the required verification task. The presentation in [6] is deliberately informal in order to introduce correctness concerns. P2 uses an informal approach which is dictated by the informal nature of the specifications. P3 skips a crucial aspect of the proof, namely that the representation corresponds to the algorithm. P4 seems to skip the interface steps to concentrate on proofs for the individual refinements, although such interfaces play an important role in the theory and practice of program development.

2) Three of the errors are related to proper termination: error P1 relates to the value of the conjunction at the time the loop exits; error P2 occurs at the end of the text; error P3 results in a nonterminating loop; error P4 is related to initialization.

It is common in program proving to treat the termination task informally since termination in most of the examples is relatively obvious and easily checked. These errors suggest that perhaps more effort should be concentrated on termination, especially since it is well-known that many programming errors occur at boundary points, which includes initialization and termination.

3) Ironically, each of the first three errors are easily discovered by the standard methods of hand simulation and testing. For example, test cases for P1 would undoubtedly include the two subcases of KEY present, and not present, in TAB, and the error would be revealed on any but the optimizing PL/1 compiler. Testing of error P2 might show the last word left in the buffer, depending on type of input device. Hand simulation on the prime sieve program quickly revealed the problem at the first loop iteration when 2 is the minimum element of the sieve. (We had previously been told that an error exists in this program, but we were not told the details.)

Based on these generalizations, we make the following recommendations for increasing the value and credibility of program proofs.

1) Do not ignore the "standard" methods of verification. London [7] gives the "hint that one should be fairly confident the program is correct before starting to prove it so. This confidence may, for example, arise from the standard testing/debugging process."

2) Check the proof and program especially closely at known pitfalls and problem areas of the programming language and the programming task. One goal of programming language design is to minimize the number of such trouble spots. There does not appear to exist a well-documented, widely distributed

and suitably general catalog of trouble spots in programming, but there is certainly informal communication of a large amount of bitter experience.

3) Adopt a cautiously skeptical attitude toward proofs, as one of several possible means of persuasion, in which formalization and abstraction might provide some new insights and documentation. Keep in mind, however, that there are usually at least some parts of the program that are better-explained informally, and it is pointless to attempt subverting these parts to fit a particular formalism. Formalism should supplement, definitely not replace, common sense and programming experience and intuition. See Redish [26] for various types of common sense questions to supplement the assertion method.

4) Even though a challenging aspect of a proof has been solved, one should not let one's guard down on the more mundane aspects of the program.

5) First concentrate a large amount of effort on stating what should be proved in order to guarantee the program is correct, and then set about proving it. It seems fair to say that in most of the above errors the proving task was not well understood. Therefore, some things which should have been proved were ignored, resulting in failure to catch errors.

V. Overall Conclusions and Recommendations

We have identified and discussed some common features for each of the three classes of errors. We can now elaborate on some common features of all three classes.

Observation 1: The tasks were not well defined. It was not recognized that formal specifications must be shown to capture the underlying informal concept; there were gaps in the statements of what should be proved about programs, especially proper termination; systematically constructed programs were not checked closely to confirm their correctness.

Recommendation 1: Identify more carefully the complete task, for example, by including those parts which cover the errors we have discussed here. Make sure the task is well understood and precisely stated before undertaking the time consuming and absorbing process of verifying that the task was accomplished.

Observation 2: The errors are not deep. The standard methodologies and everyday programming knowledge are sufficient to reveal most of them. The errors seem to have been overlooked because the authors were concentrating on pedagogical points and therefore looking at the program from restricted viewpoints.

Recommendation 2: Apply as many techniques as possible to the task: perform testing as well as proving; look for known difficult and error-prone language constructs; obtain an independent verifier to read and check the results. The greatest confidence arises from consistent positive results from different methodologies applied to the same task, because different methodologies often have compensating strengths and weaknesses.

Observation 3: There is a tendency to concentrate more effort on the harder parts which require sophisticated techniques and less effort on the "obvious" and easier parts. It is often claimed that the methodologies are even more essential in multiprocessing programs than in sequential programs. The errors show they do not yet work reliably for sequential programs.

Recommendation 3: Do not bring to the task preconceived notions of hard and easy, e.g., "termination is always trivial to prove" or "inductive assertions are always hard to formulate." The apportionment of effort must be somewhat tailored to the specific task. Do not get so bogged down in formal proofs that some aspects of the task are ignored completely.

Observation 4: Most of the erroneous programs were also well structured, according to current criteria. It is often claimed that good structure makes it easier to detect errors, but these errors show that it is no guarantee.

Recommendation 4: Do not confuse good structure with correctness. If the structure is good, then make use of the clarity thereby gained to verify the program, at least informally.

Observation 5: The methodologies proposed to increase software reliability are still in their early stages of development: the tasks are not easily taught or learned; old habits make it hard to take seriously the importance of some tasks, e.g., the common practice of writing the specifications after writing the program, or worse, never writing the specifications at all; there is a tendency to believe that following the techniques will automatically bring favorable results, e.g., systematic construction will lead to correct programs.

Recommendation 5: Do not view new methodologies as panaceas, especially when one has little experience in applying the methodologies or is unaware of the pitfalls. Just as with any other skill, it will take considerable training and experience before the new programming methodologies are mastered. Part of that experience will undoubtedly be committing and recovering from errors.

VI. Some Relationships Between Modern Programming Methodologies and Mathematics

Earlier we claimed that the common feature of the new methodologies is the emphasis on the use of mathematical reasoning in programming. A natural question to ask is, "How well does mathematical reasoning work in mathematics?"

Here are a few documentations of error processes in mathematics.

1) The Mathematical Games section of the December 1975 issue of *Scientific American* [27] reports an interesting instance of error. A proof had been submitted that a particular algorithm produced all solutions to a given problem. A counterexample in the form of a missed solution was later submitted. The nature of the proof error was not given. The author of the original "proof" was quoted from a book he had authored to the effect that there is no "magic formula for a proof which makes it immutable and unarguable henceforth and forevermore."

2) An interesting paper by an eminent mathematician, P. J. Davis [28], relates many instances of errors in mathematics. It concludes that "a derivation of a theorem or a verification of a proof has only probabilistic validity" and that mathematics, as a somewhat experimental science, is "saved from chaos by the

stability of the universe ... and the self-correcting features of usage."

3) Schwartz [29] relates the following anecdote: "I think here of a case that became famous a few years ago, in which after certain statements in algebraic number theory had been proved by three independent methods in published papers (an algebraic proof, an analytic proof, and an elementary proof), a counterexample was published."

Another point to consider is the purpose of a proof. In addition to the obvious one of certification, Davis also points out the "discovery" aspect of proofs. A mathematical proof of a given statement helps to elicit the hypotheses under which the statement holds and perhaps induces minor alterations in the statement. Analogously, a program proof can help to discover conditions on input under which the program will or will not execute completely and provide the required output. These conditions may or may not be subsumed by the program specification, which may need to be altered.

Yet another aspect is that a proof should reveal clearly why a theorem holds. Likewise, a program proof should reveal why the program works and thus serve as a form of documentation. All in all, mathematical reasoning leads to a deeper understanding of the subject being studied, if not to certainty in manipulating the understanding.

The certification aspect of mathematical proofs has an obvious carryover to program proofs. It is recognized in mathematics that a proof does not become a proof until "there has been a consensus of experts that the proof is right" [28]. In program proving, we would like one of our experts to be a mechanical proof checker, but of course this leads to the question of correctness of the proof checker, as well as the immense difficulty of constructing and the expense of running such a checker. It should be observed that many of the above errors occur in papers which have undergone a supposedly rigorous review process before publication. It is a reasonable expectation that each article which had not been reviewed had nevertheless been read by at least one other competent person. Yet the errors persist. The conviction from a proof that a statement or program is correct is only meaningful if the person being convinced is critical and trained to detect proof failures.

These are similarities between mathematical reasoning in mathematics and in programming. There are differences, also.

1) Mathematical theorems are often stated and proved for their elegance or their role within a theory. It is not necessary that there be an immediate, or even an eventual, application of the theorem. In programming, we are more immediately concerned with correctness since program errors may be costly or dangerous.

2) There is usually an established and well-known theory in which a mathematical theorem is embedded, whereas in programming, each program proof is usually isolated. A mathematician does not start from scratch, but instead builds upon a body of theorems with the result that the task is easier and the theorem can be shown to be consistent or inconsistent with other theorems in the theory. Currently, each program proof starts from scratch and must be examined in isolation. This state will probably change as a more mathematical theory of programs is evolved from present work on program correctness and from the abstraction and organization of programming knowledge.

3) Studies in the mathematical foundations of computer science lead to advances in machine and language design. A current premise is that languages should facilitate mathematical reasoning in programming, be semantically defined in a mathematical fashion, and be subjected to rigorous mathematical analysis.

This discussion leaves us with the following fundamental question.

What is the role of formalism and mathematical reasoning in programming methodologies? Based on our study of errors, we conclude that it is one, but not the only, or necessarily best, tool for verifying programs. It provides evidence of a logical nature that programs are substantially correct, the degree of certainty being somewhat related to the depth of logical analysis and the skills of the analyzer(s), but never absolute. On the other hand, testing provides empirical certainty of at least some correctness aspects of a program. Experience with both testing and mathematical reasoning should convince us that neither type of evidence is sufficient and that both types are necessary.

There are two important roles, other than verification, for formalism in programming methodologies: 1) they provide the training in rigorous thinking which is essential for good programming and 2) they provide the most effective language for organizing and expressing knowledge about programs. Of course, this is what the leading programming methodologists have been saying for years. We hope that this paper provides new, and more realistic, insight into the mathematical foundations of these methodologies. One unfortunate aspect of that reality is that "mathematics is a human activity subject of human fallibility" [5]. This statement should not be interpreted to say that the mathematical approach should be abandoned, for it will always be a necessary tool. Nor should it be construed to mean that mechanical tools are the only solution, for these must ultimately be evaluated by mathematical means. We simply must learn to live with fallibility.

ACKNOWLEDGMENT

Error $T2$ was originally analyzed with the help of J. Goodenough. T. Linden alerted us to error $P3$. H. Mills is the source for error $T4$. Error $T5$ was independently confirmed by L. Stucki. Parts of errors $S2$, $T2$, and $T3$ have been previously discussed in the cited articles and first sowed the seeds of doubt in our minds. We appreciate the comments of many colleagues, especially H. Mills, B. Elspas, and R. London on an earlier and the present version of this paper. However, the interpretations of the errors and the conclusions are our own. The paper was distributed to the authors who committed errors and we have tried to incorporate their replies, where received.

REFERENCES

[1] B. H. Liskov and S. N. Zilles, "Specifications techniques for data abstractions," *IEEE Trans. Software Engineering*, vol. SE-1, pp. 7-19, Mar. 1975.

[2] J. C. King, "A program verifier," Ph.D. dissertation, Carnegie-Mellon Univ., Pittsburgh, PA, 1969.
[3] B. Wegbreit, "The synthesis of loop predicates," *Commun. Ass. Comput. Mach.*, vol. 17, pp. 102-112, 1974.
[4] L. P. Deutsch, "An interactive program verifier," Ph.D. dissertation, Univ. California, Berkeley, June 1973.
[5] H. D. Mills, "How to write correct programs and know it," in *Proc. Int. Conf. Reliable Software*, Los Angeles, CA, Apr. 1975, pp. 363-370.
[6] C. L. McGowan and J. R. Kelly, *Top-Down Structured Programming Techniques*. New York: Petrocelli Charter, 1975.
[7] R. London, "Software reliability through proving programs correct," in *Proc. 1971 IEEE Conf. Fault-Tolerant Computing*, pp. 125-129.
[8] C. A. R. Hoare, "Proof of a program: Find," *Commun. Ass. Comput. Mach.*, vol. 14, pp. 39-45, 1971.
[9] S. L. Gerhart, "Verification of APL programs," Ph.D. dissertation, Carnegie-Mellon Univ., Pittsburgh, PA, 1972.
[10] D. Oppen, "On logic and program verification," Ph.D. dissertation, Univ. Toronto, Toronto, Ont., Canada, Apr. 1975 (available as Tech. Rep. 82).
[11] S. Cook and D. Oppen, "An assertion language for data structure," in *Proc. Second Symp. Principles of Programming Languages*, 1975, pp. 160-166.
[12] L. Yelowitz, "Assertions about data structures," unpublished manuscript.
[13] D. E. Knuth, *The Art of Computer Programming, Vol. 1, Fundamental Algorithms*, 2nd ed. Reading, MA: Addison-Wesley, 1973.
[14] A. T. Berztiss, *Data Structures: Theory and Practice*, 2nd ed. New York: Academic, 1975.
[15] N. Wirth, *Systematic Programming*, 1st printing. Englewood Cliffs, NJ: Prentice-Hall, 1972.
[16] P. Naur, "Programming by action clusters," *BIT*, vol. 9, pp. 250-258, 1969.
[17] J. B. Goodenough and S. L. Gerhart, "Toward a theory of test data selection," *IEEE Trans. Software Engineering (Special Issue on Reliable Software)*, vol. SE-1, pp. 156-173, June 1975.
[18] R. E. Noonan, "Structural programming and formal specifications," *IEEE Trans. Software Engineering (Special Issue on the First National Conference on Software Engineering)*, vol. SE-1, pp. 421-425, Dec. 1975.
[19] P. Henderson and R. Snowden, "An experiment in structured programming," *BIT*, vol. 12, pp. 38-53, 1972.
[20] H. Ledgard, "The case for structured programming," *BIT*, vol. 13, pp. 45-57, 1973.
[21] N. Wirth, "PL360, A programming language for the 360 computer," *J. Ass. Comput. Mach.*, vol. 15, pp. 37-74, 1968.
[22] —, "Program development by stepwise refinement," *Commun. Ass. Comput. Mach.*, vol. 14, pp. 221-227, 1971.
[23] W. A. Wulf, "ALPHARD: Toward a language to support structured programs," Carnegie-Mellon Univ., Pittsburgh, PA, Rep. AFOSR-TR-1434, Apr. 1974.
[24] C. A. R. Hoare, "Notes on data structuring," in *Structured Programming*, O.-J. Dahl et al., Ed. New York: Academic, 1972, pp. 83-174.
[25] G. A. Lanzarone and M. Ornaghi, "Program construction by refinements preserving correctness," *Comput. J.*, vol. 18, pp. 55-62, 1975.
[26] K. A. Redish, "Comments of London's certification of algorithm 245," *Commun. Ass. Comput. Mach.*, vol. 14, pp. 50-51, 1971.
[27] *Scientific American* (Mathematical Games Section), Dec. 1975.
[28] P. J. Davis, "Fidelity in mathematical discourse: Is one and one really two?," *Amer. Math. Mon.*, pp. 252-263, 1972.
[29] J. A. Schwartz, "An overview of bugs," in *Debugging Techniques in Large Systems*. Englewood Cliffs, NJ: Prentice-Hall, 1971, pp. 1-16.
[30] W. A. Wulf, R. London, and M. Shaw, "Verification and abstraction in ALPHARD," unpublished.
[31] W. Howden, "Reliability of the path testing strategy," this issue, pp. 208-215.

Susan L. Gerhart received the B.A. degree in mathematics from Ohio Wesleyan University, Delaware, in 1965, the M.S. degree in communication sciences from the University of Michigan, Ann Arbor, in 1967, and the Ph.D. degree in computer science from Carnegie-Mellon University, Pittsburgh, PA, in 1972.

She was a Visiting Assistant Professor of Computer Science at the University of Toronto, Toronto, Ont., Canada, in 1972-1973 and since 1973 has been an Assistant Professor of Computer Science at Duke University, Durham, NC. She has also been employed as a Senior Software Engineer at SofTech, Inc., Waltham, MA, and a Visiting Scientist at ICASE, Hampton, VA, during the summers of 1974 and 1975, respectively. Her research interests are in the area of program verification, including testing, the theory and practice of proving correctness of programs, and programming methodologies which reduce the difficulties of verification.

Dr. Gerhart is a member of the Association for Computing Machinery and Sigma Xi.

Lawrence Yelowitz was born in New York City, NY, on February 2, 1944. He received the B.S. degree with honors in mathematics from Brooklyn College, Brooklyn, NY, in 1964, the M.A.T. degree in mathematics from Harvard University, Cambridge, MA, in 1965, and the Ph.D. degree in computer science from The Johns Hopkins University, Baltimore, MD, in 1972.

He spent over three years as a programmer in industry/government between 1965-1969. Also, he worked two summers in a research capacity at IBM, and one summer in a research capacity with the Artificial Intelligence Group at the National Institutes of Health. He was Assistant Professor with the Department of Computer Science, New Mexico Institute of Mining and Technology, for two years, and Visiting Assistant Professor with the Department of Information and Computer Science, University of California, Irvine, for one year. He is currently an Assistant Professor in the Department of Computer Science, University of Pittsburgh, Pittsburgh, PA, conducting research and teaching courses in program correctness, operating systems, and data structures. He has published over a dozen articles and reports in the area of program correctness, including the publication of his Ph.D. dissertation as an IBM Technical Report.

Dr. Yelowitz is a member of Pi Mu Epsilon, Phi Delta Kappa, Sigma Xi, and the Association for Computing Machinery. He received a Prize Fellowship at Harvard University and an IBM Fellowship twice at The Johns Hopkins University. In addition he was the first recipient of the Samuel N. Alexander Memorial Award sponsored by the Washington, DC, Chapter of the Association for Computing Machinery, which carried an honorarium of $1000.

Experience with Path Analysis and Testing of Programs

MARTIN R. WOODWARD, DAVID HEDLEY, AND MICHAEL A. HENNELL

Abstract—There are a number of practical difficulties in performing a path testing strategy for computer programs. One problem is in deciding which paths, out of a possible infinity, to use as test cases. A hierarchy of structural test metrics is suggested to direct the choice and to monitor the coverage of test paths. Another problem is that many of the chosen paths may be infeasible in the sense that no test data can ever execute them. Experience with the use of "allegations" to circumvent this problem and prevent the static generation of many infeasible paths is reported.

Index Terms—Allegations, infeasible paths, path testing, test metrics.

I. Introduction

WHILE the development of program proving and program testing theory continues, software validation is still done for the most part by "exhaustive" testing. What in fact is most likely to be exhausted is the programmer's intuition about which are the important paths to test. This may not be the ideal testing strategy but it is probably widely practiced.

Although there are not many formal results concerning path testing, excepting those of Howden [10], few people would deny that path testing is a worthwhile exercise. This gap between testing theory and testing practice was bridged to some extent in a recent experiment by Howden [11], where it was found that a path testing strategy was reliable for exposing 18 out of 28 errors (about 64 percent) in a sample of six programs and was the best single testing strategy at exposing errors.

However there are a number of practical difficulties in employing such a testing strategy. Foremost amongst these difficulties is the fact that for many programs the number of paths is infinite. Hence the program tester needs some procedure for path selection and also some feedback on the degree of testedness achieved by selecting certain paths. It is widely accepted that executing every statement and every branch at least once is a useful activity. However, in Howden's experiment [11] branch testing by itself reliably exposed only 6 out of the 28 errors (about 21 percent) indicating that "detection of a significant number of errors that will be discovered by path testing depends on the combinations of program branches rather than single branches." The program tester who accepts a path testing strategy and who succeeds in executing every branch is therefore in great need of assistance in formulating and monitoring his subsequent test cases. Thus there would seem to be a need for intermediate goals to direct the path testing approach. In this paper a hierarchy of structural testing metrics is proposed in an attempt to fulfill this need. A strategy for selecting paths out of the possible infinity is then suggested by the hierarchy of metrics. By stipulating that the metric at a certain specified level in the hierarchy must be maximized the tester's route to this goal is marked by a succession of subgoals. Having maximized the coverage of units at one level in the hierarchy the coverage of units at the next level can be inspected and the shortest paths chosen which include those previously unexecuted units. For the case of a single loop in Fortran, maximization of the metric at the third level in the hierarchy is shown to be related to the so-called "boundary-interior" [9] path selection strategy.

Whatever strategy is used the problem is likely to arise of paths being chosen which are infeasible or "phantom" in the sense that no test data can ever execute them. Experience with the use of "allegations" to prevent the static generation of some of these infeasible paths is reported.

II. TEST EFFECTIVENESS METRICS

Descriptions have been given elsewhere [7], [8] of program units called Linear Code Sequence and Jump (LCSAJ) and how they may be concatenated to form program paths. Basically an LCSAJ consists of a body of code through which the flow of control may proceed sequentially and which is terminated by a jump in the control flow. In contrast to decision-to-decision paths and many other elements used in program analysis, LCSAJ's are based on the program text rather than the program's directed graph. A directed graph is essentially two-dimensional and can be mapped into many different one-dimensional program texts with possibly different LCSAJ's but identical d-d paths. In order to make a path description in terms of LCSAJ's unambiguous it is sometimes necessary to perform a reformatting strategy of the text [7] so that for example the separate components of choice clauses are on different lines. Indeed the logical IF, being the only Fortran construction which allows more than one statement on a line, should be reformatted so that the executable statement of the "true branch" starts on a new line. (This is a minor modification of the definition given in [8].) The authors have developed automatic tools which reformat and statically analyze programs written in Fortran, Algol 68, or Cobol and generate a list of all LCSAJ's. A depth first tree search can then be performed on this list of LCSAJ's to enumerate all program paths up to a given length. As an example of a path description in terms of LCSAJ's consider the Fortran subroutine ROOT given in Fig. 1. On the right-hand side of the text, the way control proceeded during program execution is displayed. This path, which is of length 9 LCSAJ's, is listed in Fig. 2.

Many automated testing facilities rely on measuring the so-called "test coverage" [13], these measures being useful "barometers of how far the testing process has gone." Such a scheme for quantifying structural testing is to use a hierarchy of Test Effectiveness Ratios [1], [7]:

$$TER_1 = \frac{\text{number of statements exercised at least once}}{\text{total number of executable statements}}$$

```
 1        SUBROUTINE ROOT   (A,B,EPS ,ETA,F,X,IFAIL)    1
 1  C.    MARK 1 RELEASE.   NAG COPYRIGHT 1971          1
 2        INTEGER P01AAF                                1
 3        DATA S/8HROOT/                                1
 4        IDEC=1                                        1
 5        X1=A                                          1
 6        XP=A                                          1
 7        X =A                                          1
 8        F1=F(X)                                       1
 9        FP=F(X)                                       1
10        IF(ABS(FP)-ETA)1,1,2                          1
11    1   IFAIL=0                                              9
12        RETURN                                               9
13    2   X2=B                                          2
14        XN=B                                          2
15        X=B                                           2
16        F2=F(X)                                       2
17        FN=F2                                         2
18        IF(ABS(FN)-ETA)1,1,3                          2
19    3   IF(FN*FP)5,4,4                                2
20    4   IFAIL=P01AAF(IFAIL,1,S)
21        RETURN
22    5   IF(FP)6,6,7                                         3
23    6   XP=B
24        XN=A
25        TEMP=FP
26        FP=FN
27        FN=TEMP
27  C.
27  C.    TRY INTERPOLATION ON LAST 2 ITERATES
27  C.
28    7   IF(F2-F1)8,9,8                                4  7
29    8   X=X1-F1*(X2-X1)/(F2-F1)                       4  7
30        IF((X-X1)*(X2-X))9,9,12                       4  7
30  C.
30  C.    BISECTION OR CHORD AS INTERPOLATION UNSUCCESSFUL  4  7
30  C.
31    9   IDEC=-IDEC                                       7
32        IF(IDEC)10,10,11                                 7
33   10   X=XN-FN*(XN-XP)/(FN-FP)                          7
34        GOTO 12                                          7
35   11   X=(XN+XP)*0.5
36   12   IF(ABS(X-X2)-EPS)13,13,14                     5  8
37   13   X=X2                                             8
38        GO TO 1                                          8
39   14   X1=X2                                            6
40        X2=X                                             6
41        F1=F2                                            6
42        F2=F(X)                                          6
43        IF(ABS(F2)-ETA)1,1,15                            6
44   15   IF(F2)16,16,17                                   6
45   16   XN=X                                             6
46        FN=F2                                            6
47        GO TO 7                                          6
48   17   XP=X
49        FP=F2
50        GO TO 7
51        END
```

Fig. 1. The subroutine ROOT which locates a zero of a continuous function F(X) in a given interval (A, B). A path of length nine LCSAJ's is displayed.

$$TER_2 = \frac{\text{number of branches exercised at least once}}{\text{total number of branches}}$$

$$TER_3 = \frac{\text{number of LCSAJ's exercised at least once}}{\text{total number of LCSAJ's}}$$

Providing there are no unreachable statements these ratios have the property that:

$$TER_3 = 1 \Rightarrow TER_2 = 1 \Rightarrow TER_1 = 1.$$

The first two measures lead to a simple, well-known technique of systematic testing, namely branch testing, i.e., the construction of test cases to exercise every branch in a program at least once. The third measure leads to a first intermediate step between testing all branches and testing all paths. Since an LCSAJ may contain many decisions within its linear code sequence, TER_3 provides a measure of the test coverage of those combinations of branches which form linear sequences of text. The implications of the test requirement that $TER_3 = 1$, in terms of the paths that it forces the tester to execute, depend upon the program structure. As an example consider an isolated simple loop in Fortran as in the following situation:

Start Line	Finish Line	Jump To Line
1	10	13
13	19	22
22	22	28
28	30	36
36	36	39
39	47	28
28	34	36
36	38	11
11	12	exit

Fig. 2. The path of length nine LCSAJ's displayed in Fig. 1. Execution proceeds from line 1 through to line 10 at which point control jumps to line 13. Execution continues from line 13 through to line 19 at which point control jumps to line 22, and so on.

```
1       SUBROUTINE EXMPLE(N,RESULT)
2       NSUMSQ = 0
3       DO 10 I=1,N
4           NSUMSQ = NSUMSQ + I*I
5    10 CONTINUE
6       RESULT = SQRT(FLOAT(NSUMSQ))
7       RETURN
8       END
```

The requirement that $TER_3 = 1$ can be met in a minimal fashion by executing the following two paths:

start line	finish line	jump to line
1	7	exit

and

1	5	3
3	5	3
3	7	exit

which exercise all four possible LCSAJ's by performing the loop exactly once and also three times (at least). This is in accordance with the "boundary-interior" path testing procedure [9] whereby a boundary test path (one which enters the loop without causing the loop to be iterated) and an interior test path (one which enters the loop and iterates it at least once) are both traversed. The implications of $TER_3 = 1$ on more complicated structures are currently being studied by the authors.

The hierarchy of coverage measures could be extended by defining:

TER_4 = (number of distinct subpaths of length two LCSAJ's exercised at least once plus the number of distinct complete paths of length less than or equal to two LCSAJ's exercised at least once)/ (total number of distinct subpaths of length two LCSAJ's plus the total number of distinct complete paths of length less than or equal to two LCSAJ's)

In essence this is a measure of the coverage of those pairs of LCSAJ's which it is possible to combine to form a subpath. By including in the definition all complete program paths (i.e., from a program entry to a program exit) of length at most two LSCAJ's we ensure that a hierarchy of measures is generated. This follows since any single LCSAJ is either a complete path by itself or else it can be combined with at least one other LCSAJ to form a complete path or proper subpath. Hence testing until $TER_4 = 1$ implies that all LCSAJ's have been executed and so $TER_3 = 1$ also.

For the Fortran subroutine EXMPLE the requirement that $TER_4 = 1$ forces the execution of the following LCSAJ pairs:

(1, 5, 3)   (3, 5, 3)
(3, 5, 3)   (3, 5, 3)
(3, 5, 3)   (3, 7, exit).

and also the two complete program paths

(1, 7, exit)

and

(1, 5, 3)   (3, 7, exit).

Thus $TER_4 = 1$ can be met in a minimal test by exercising the loop once, twice, and four times.

It is possible to define a generalized measure TER_{n+2} of the test coverage of n-tuples of LCSAJ's:

TER_{n+2} = (number of distinct subpaths of length n LCSAJ's exercised at least once plus the number of distinct complete paths of length less than or equal to n LCSAJ's exercised at least once)/ (total number of distinct subpaths of length n LCSAJ's plus the total number of distinct complete paths of length less than or equal to n LCSAJ's)

With these definitions the hierarchy is maintained, since:

$TER_{n+2} = 1 \Rightarrow TER_{n+1} = 1 \Rightarrow \ldots \Rightarrow TER_4 = 1 \Rightarrow TER_3 = 1$.

If no loops are present in the program then the hierarchy would be terminated at TER_{m+2} where m is the length of the longest path. Attempting to achieve unity at progressively higher levels in the hierarchy provides a more formal and systematic approach to path testing than relying on the programmer's intuition. It forces the testing of ever longer subpaths and hence combinations of branches in ways which can easily be related to the program text. Of course, branches, LCSAJ's, and n-tuples of LCSAJ's that can never be executed are liable to thwart this attempt. Nevertheless it does suggest the following path selection and test procedure. When TER_n is maximized, examine TER_{n+1} and attempt to execute the shortest paths which contain those unexecuted combinations of LCSAJ's in an effort to improve the value of TER_{n+1}.

Other mechanisms for determining the degree of testedness have been proposed. Pimont and Rault [15] consider each pair of adjacent edges in a structured program's directed graph sufficiently tested if all paths from the program entry to the pair of edges have been exercised. In order to perform this assessment they first map each executed path into an image set of compressed paths in which each loop is performed no more than twice in succession. Unfortunately, this can lead to some adjacent edge combinations being assessed as tested when in reality many intermediate loop executions may have taken place in between the execution of the two edges concerned. In contrast to this the TER_n measures relate directly to a program text rather than the directed graph and only

TABLE I
THE ROUTINES EXAMINED AND THEIR PURPOSE

Routine	Language	Purpose
ROOT	Fortran	Locates a zero of a continuous function in a given interval by a combination of the methods of linear interpolation, extrapolation and bisection.
A	Algol68	Locates a zero of a continuous function in a given interval by a combination of the methods of linear interpolation, extrapolation and bisection.
B	Algol68	Locates a zero of a continuous function in a given interval by hyperbolic interpolation and bisection.
C	Algol68	Locates a zero of a continuous function in a given interval by the method of bisection.
D	Algol68	Integrates a system of ordinary differential equations over one step using Merson's method.
E	Algol68	Integrates a system of ordinary differential equations over a range using Merson's method.
F	Algol68	Sorts a vector of real numbers into ascending order.

TABLE II
SOME DETAILS OF THE STRUCTURE OF THE ROUTINES. THE NUMBER OF LINES IS A COUNT OF EXECUTABLE LINES (AFTER REFORMATTING FOR THE ALGOL 68 ROUTINES). LOOPS OF TYPE 1 ARE THOSE WITH FIXED BOUNDS AND LOOPS OF TYPE 2 ARE THOSE WITHOUT FIXED BOUNDS

Routine	Lines	IFs	GOTOs	Loops type1	Loops type2	LCSAJs
ROOT	47	10	4	0	1	25
A	74	13	0	0	1	40
B	83	13	0	0	2	51
C	17	2	0	0	1	10
D	48	1	1	5	0	28
E	62	8	3	0	2	43
F	91	9	0	0	7	81

those combinations of LCSAJ's which have actually been executed in direct succession contribute to the degree of testedness. What is more, the TER_n approach can be applied to any program text whether structured or unstructured. In addition the TER_n measures have the rather pleasing property of chained implications which dovetails into the currently accepted ideas of branch testing whilst at the same time forcing ever more thorough path testing.

It would be possible to devise alternative hierarchies of test metrics. Indeed Chow [3] has proposed a hierarchy of test covers by generalizing the idea of Pimont and Rault [15] and considering sequences of consecutive edges in the program's directed graph. However, it would seem an advantage to use a scheme which can easily be related to the program text and which can at the same time include combinations of many branches even at only the third level of the hierarchy. The problem of unexecutable combinations will be present in any measures which ignore program semantics.

III. PATH TESTING EXPERIENCE

In this section a detailed investigation is reported of a path testing strategy applied to a number of Numerical Algorithms Group (NAG) mathematical library routines, one being the Fortran subroutine ROOT given in Fig. 1 and six others being in Algol 68. A brief description of the purpose of each of these routines is given in Table I and some details of their structure are given in Table II. Although no errors were found during the path testing, this is not entirely unexpected since the routines have been in existence and widely used for many years. For a full description of the NAG library and the "stringent tests" associated with each routine, see [4].

It was decided to test the short paths of the chosen routines and to determine the effect of this approach on the test coverage measures TER_n. It has been noticed [6] that error exits and special cases are often amongst the short paths of these library routines and that a systematic approach to executing these short paths is desirable since they are likely to have been missed in an ad hoc testing strategy.

Almost inevitably any systematic analysis of program paths leads to the problem of infeasible or "phantom" paths that can never be executed. Indeed one of the most surprising facts revealed by this study was that although the number of paths through the chosen routines rises dramatically as paths of ever increasing length are considered, very large proportions of them are infeasible. This is vividly demonstrated for the six chosen NAG Algol 68 routines by Fig. 3 where the number of paths is plotted logarithmically on the Y axis and the length of path in terms of LCSAJ's is given on the X axis. For each routine two lines are plotted, the bold line being the total number of paths obtained by an analysis of the control flow and the dotted line being those which were found to be feasible. In most cases the total number of paths beyond a certain length is between one and two orders of magnitude greater than the number of feasible paths. For example, only 1.4 percent of the paths up to length 17 LCSAJ's for Routine A are feasible.

The staggering proportions of this problem make the need for some techniques to cope with it desirable. The simple-minded technique used by the authors was as follows. On discovering some infeasible feature of a short path this information was used in the path generation phase to prevent the future enumeration of paths which contain that feature. It may be, for example, that certain pairs of branches are infeasible when exercised consecutively. This can be translated into LCSAJ terms and incorporated into the path generation program as a logical condition which must be satisfied by all paths. Such logical conditions can be thought of as "allegations" in the manner proposed by Osterweil [14]. This is consistent with Osterweil's use of the word to describe the "supplying of information which is at best difficult, and at worst impossible, to obtain" (by automatic analysis) in order to provide a "sharpened analysis" concerning the program. It is to be noted that although the construction of certain constrained paths has been shown to be NP-complete [5], all that is being suggested here is to use allegations to prune a complete tree search of LCSAJ's in the static generation of paths.

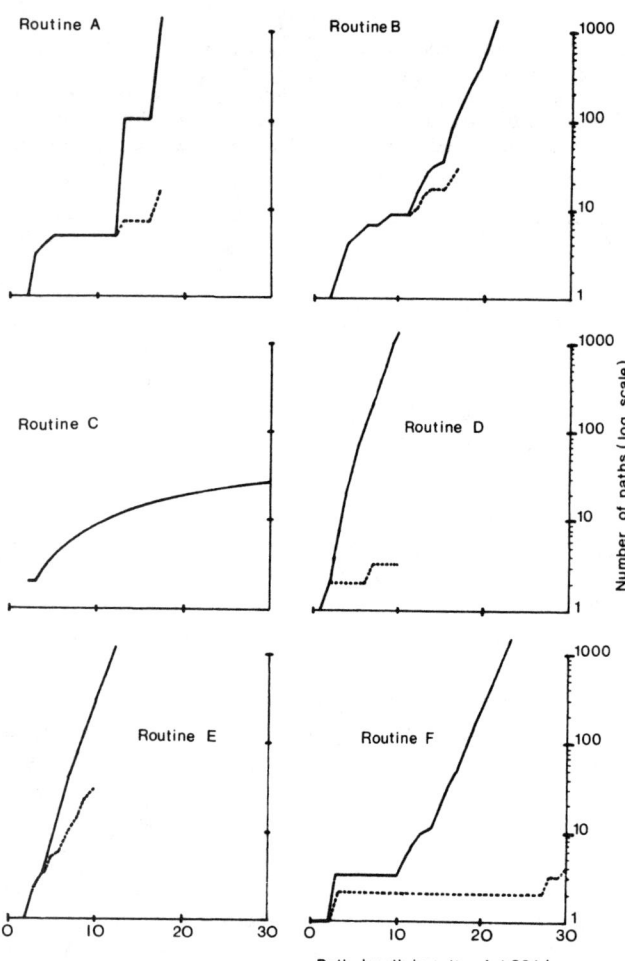

Fig. 3. The bold lines show the cumulative count of the number of paths up to a given length determined purely from the control flow for six Algol 68 numerical library routines plotted on a logarithmic scale against path length in units of LCSAJ's. Wherever the cumulative number of feasible paths in a routine differs from the cumulative number of control flow paths this is shown as a dotted line.

TABLE III
THE NUMBER OF PATHS OF LENGTHS LESS THAN OR EQUAL TO 15 LCSAJ's (LESS THAN 2.4 PERCENT OF WHICH ARE FEASIBLE) FOR THE SUBROUTINE ROOT GIVEN IN FIG. 1

Path length in LCSAJs	Allegations used				Cumulative Totals	
	None	1	1,2,3	1,2,3,4,5	Feasible	Infeasible
1	1	1	1	1	1	0
2	1	1	1	1	2	0
3	1	1	1	1	3	0
4	0	0	0	0	3	0
5	3	2	1	1	4	2
6	8	5	2	2	6	8
7	7	4	1	1	7	14
8	11	5	2	1	8	24
9	39	16	7	3	11	60
10	67	25	9	5	16	122
11	84	27	9	4	≤ 20	≥ 202
12	186	51	21	5	≤ 25	≥ 383
13	418	103	41	10	≤ 35	≥ 791
14	665	145	52	12	≤ 47	≥ 1444
15	1112	208	78	14	≤ 61	≥ 2542

As a detailed example of the path testing strategy employed and the thought processes involved in developing specific allegations consider the Fortran subroutine ROOT [which locates a root of a function F(X) in a given interval (A, B)] given in Fig. 1. In Table III the number of paths generated purely from consideration of the control structure is listed. On attempting to find data to execute the shorter paths for the routine the first infeasible path encountered is of length five LCSAJ's, namely:

start line	finish line	jump to line
1	10	13
13	19	22
22	32	35
35	38	11
11	12	exit

This path is infeasible since the two assignments to the integer IDEC on lines 4 and 31 mean that IDEC has the value −1 making the branch from line 32 to line 35 infeasible. It can now be seen that the assignment on line 4 which initializes IDEC to 1 and the assignment on line 31 which changes the sign of IDEC are the only assignments in the routine to IDEC. Hence it can be deduced that any statically generated path which passes through line 31 an odd number of times and is followed by the branch from line 32 to line 35 is infeasible. Also any path which passes through line 31 an even number of times and is followed by the branch from line 32 to line 33 is infeasible. The effect of incorporating this allegation into the path generation phase is given in Table III and enables the elimination of longer paths containing the same feature.

Another of the three paths of length five LCSAJ's, namely:

start line	finish line	jump to line
1	10	13
13	19	22
22	34	36
36	38	11
11	12	exit

is infeasible since the branch from line 19 to line 22 ensures that the function F(X) has opposite signs at each endpoint, i.e., F(A).F(B) < 0. Hence, when on line 29, straight line interpolation is performed between the two endpoints A and B, it is guaranteed that the new interpolated value of X will lie strictly between A and B and the branch from line 30 to line 31 is infeasible. This leads to a second allegation that branch (19, 22) must not be followed by branch (30, 31) if there are no intervening backward jumps.

On considering the eight paths of length six LCSAJ's it is found that three paths are infeasible because of allegation 1 and allegation 2 eliminates two more infeasible paths. There is one more phantom path of length six LCSAJ's, namely:

TABLE IV
THE ALLEGATIONS USED TO PRUNE INFEASIBLE PATHS FROM THE COMPLETE TREE SEARCH OF PATHS FOR THE FORTRAN SUBROUTINE ROOT GIVEN IN FIG. 1

No.	Allegation
1	Linecount(31) odd must not be followed by branch (32,35). Linecount(31) even must not be followed by branch (32,33).
2	Branch (19,22) must not be followed by branch (30,31) if there are no intervening backward jumps.
3	Branch (19,22) must not be followed by branch (28,31) if there are no intervening backward jumps.
4	If the function F(X) has the same sign at end point A as it has at the first linearly interpolated point X1 then F(X1) can not equal F(B) and also the second interpolated point X2 must lie in the range (X1,B). If the function F(X) has opposite sign at A as it has at X1, then X2 lies outside the range (X1,B).
5	If the function F(X) has the same sign at successive iterates X1 and X2 then the next iterate can not lie in the range (X1,X2). If the function F(X) has opposite signs at X1 and X2 then F(X1) can not equal F(X2) and the next iterate must lie in the range (X1,X2).

start line	finish line	jump to line
1	10	13
13	19	22
22	28	31
31	34	36
36	38	11
11	12	exit

This can be seen to be infeasible since the branch from line 19 to line 22 ensures $F(A) \cdot F(B) < 0$ as before and the strict inequality means F(A) cannot equal F(B), i.e., the branch from line 28 to line 31 is not feasible in this context. This gives a third allegation that branch (19, 22) must not be followed by branch (28, 31) if there are no intervening backward jumps.

There are precisely two feasible paths of length six LCSAJ's for which test data can be found without much difficulty. From Table III it can be seen that a substantial proportion of longer paths can immediately be eliminated as being infeasible because of these three allegations.

Continuing the analysis the next infeasible path to be discovered is of length eight LCSAJ's and as a consequence a fourth allegation can be deduced. The allegation arises from the nature of the algorithm which uses linear interpolation between the right-hand endpoint, B, of the initial range (A, B) together with the first linearly interpolated point X1 to calculate the second interpolated point X2. Since the function F(X), whose root is to be found, is continuous the allegation follows. It is presented in Table IV together with the other allegations used for this routine. This fourth allegation is stated in terms of the functional aspects of the program since it is easier to understand in these terms rather than its more complicated form in terms of program branches and LCSAJ's. By further examination of all paths up to length 11 LCSAJ's for this routine a fifth allegation (see Table IV) can be deduced. The fifth allegation is essentially a generalization of the fourth allegation which applies on subsequent stages of the iteration. By this process of refining the allegations an improved upper bound on the number of feasible paths of greater length can be obtained. In fact from Table III it can be seen that these five allegations for this routine give an upper bound of 61 on the number of feasible paths of length less than or equal to 15 LCSAJ's, which is less than 2.4 percent of the total number of paths up to that length.

The coverage measures TER_1, TER_2, TER_3, and TER_4 are given in Table V for a series of six test runs of the routine. Run I is the NAG stringent test which consists of only two paths through the routine. All the measures can be improved by executing instead the shorter feasible paths as is demonstrated by Runs II, III, and IV. At this point although TER_1 = 0.98 and TER_2 = 0.96, only one branch and one line were not executed. By choosing the shortest path which contained this line (it turns out to be of length 12 LCSAJ's) TER_1 and TER_2 can both be increased to unity. Finally, in Run VI the two shortest paths (both of length 13 LCSAJ's) which are necessary to execute two more feasible LCSAJ's are included raising TER_3 to 0.88. This is the maximum value of TER_3 that can be obtained since the remaining three LSCAJ's, out of a total of 25, namely:

start line	finish line	jump to line
22	28	31
22	32	35
22	34	36

are all infeasible in combination with other LSCAJ's. This follows since line 22 can only be reached by the branch from line 19. Allegation 3 makes the first of these LCSAJ's in-

TABLE V
TEST EFFECTIVENESS RATIOS FOR SIX RUNS OF THE SUBROUTINE ROOT
GIVEN IN FIG. 1

	TER_1	TER_2	TER_3	TER_4	Comments
Run I	0.85	0.62	0.44	0.23	NAG stringent test. 1 path of length 2. 1 path of length 16.
Run II	0.83	0.73	0.52	0.33	All 8 feasible paths of length ≤ 8.
Run III	0.98	0.92	0.64	0.42	All 11 feasible paths of length ≤ 9.
Run IV	0.98	0.96	0.72	0.54	All 16 feasible paths of length ≤ 10.
Run V	1.00	1.00	0.80	0.60	All 16 feasible paths of length ≤ 10 plus 1 of length 12.
Run VI	1.00	1.00	0.88	0.67	All 16 feasible paths of length ≤ 10 plus 1 of length 12 plus 2 of length 13.

feasible and allegation 2 makes the other two infeasible. Any further improvement in the structural testing would have to be made by testing more pairs of LCSAJ's, i.e., raising the value of TER_4.

The test coverage measures obtained by path testing the six Algol 68 routines is presented graphically in Fig. 4. The bold lines are the values of TER_1 and the dotted lines the values of TER_3 which result from executing all feasible paths up to the length indicated on the X axis. The values of TER_2 are omitted from this figure for the sake of clarity since in most instances the values of TER_2 lie between those of TER_1 and TER_3. From Fig. 4 and Table V it can be seen that the Test Effectiveness Ratios can be quite rapidly raised to a substantial level by systematically executing the shorter feasible paths. At some point it then becomes more effective to execute the shortest paths which are constrained to include previously unexecuted LCSAJ's or combinations of LCSAJ's in an attempt to raise the TER measures to their maximum values.

To conclude this section it is appropriate to attempt to make some generalizations concerning the use of allegations. Indeed the conventional path testing strategy where an upper bound is specified on the number of times loops are to be traversed, could be interpreted as a form of allegation itself. Although the example allegations quoted in Table IV are complicated and very program specific, certain common situations lend themselves more easily to the use of this technique. For example a loop with constant bounds such as:

for i **from** 1 **to** 10 **do begin** . . . **end**;

must be executed exactly 10 times and an allegation to that effect would be useful in preventing the static generation of infeasible paths where the loop is required to be traversed other than 10 times. Also if a program has more than one loop with the same fixed bounds, e.g.,

for i **from** m **to** n **do begin** . . . **end**;
for j **from** m **to** n **do begin** . . . **end**;

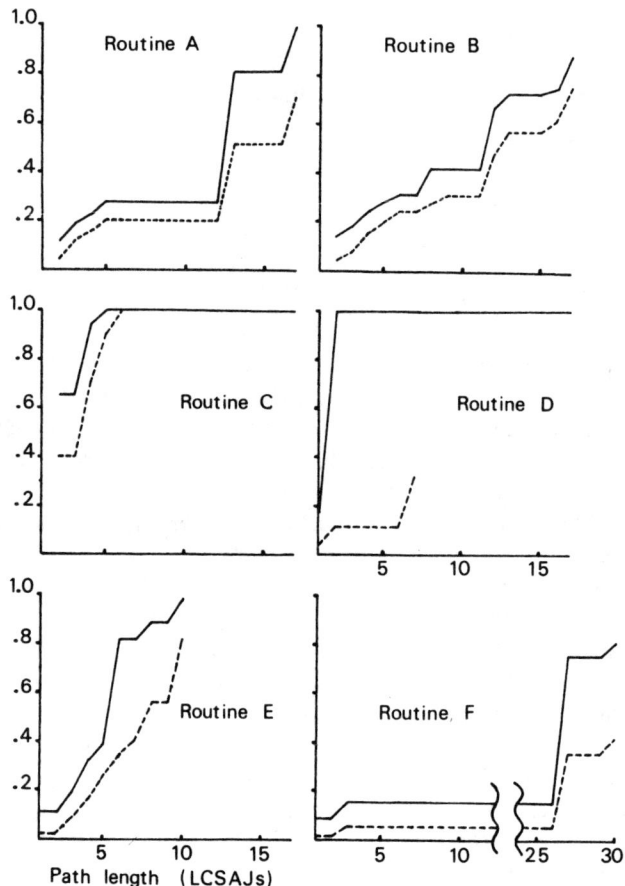

Fig. 4. The bold lines show the value of TER_1 and the dotted lines the value of TER_3 obtained by executing progressively more of the shorter feasible paths for six Algol 68 numerical library routines.

then any path derived purely from consideration of the control structure which ignores program semantics and traverses the loops a different number of times is infeasible. In fact all the infeasible paths of Routine D arise from such structures.

Another obvious source of infeasible paths where allegations can be easily constructed arises from the use of flags and switches in programs, e.g.,

bool flag;
... ;
flag := ... ;
if flag **then** ... **else** ... **fi**;
... ;
if flag **then** ... **else** ... **fi**;

if the Boolean variable "flag" is not reassigned between its two uses in the two choice clauses then any path which traverses the **then** part of one choice clause and the **else** part of the other choice clause is infeasible. Almost 90 percent of the infeasible paths up to length 17 LCSAJ's of Routine A arise from such situations. Allegation 1 for the Fortran subroutine ROOT is also in effect an example of a similar situation.

IV. CONCLUSIONS AND DISCUSSION

This paper attempts to provide a systematic framework to aid current techniques of path testing of programs, by proposing a hierarchy of measures to quantify the effectiveness of the testing. The hierarchy also has the distinct advantage of providing a sequence of milestones for the tester to achieve. These milestones are successively harder to reach and one would normally expect the path testing to be terminated when $TER_3 = 1$ or perhaps $TER_4 = 1$. Proceeding further up the hierarchy corresponds to testing ever longer paths.

The path testing strategy advocated here is first to test as many of the shorter feasible paths as possible. From experience of mathematical routines these tend to be error exits and special cases. A systematic approach to testing the short paths seems to give good coverage as measured by the low order TER metrics. Then the TER_n hierarchy can be used to direct further path testing by looking for the shortest paths which include unexecuted combinations of LCSAJ's.

Two observations are worth noting. Firstly, the TER metrics discussed in this paper are only an indication of how thoroughly a given test data set exercises the control structure of a program. Even if unity is achieved for any of the Test Effectiveness Ratios this, in itself, does not provide any guarantee about absence of errors from the program. For example, if $TER_1 = 1$ and every statement has been exercised there may still be errors in expressions which are masked for the particular data set which has been used.

The second observation is that infeasible or phantom paths prevent achievement of unity in the Test Effectiveness Ratios. Indeed the evidence of this paper suggests that the presence of so many phantom paths makes the measurement of Test Effectiveness Ratios beyond the low order metrics rather impractical. The use of allegations has been investigated to aid static analysis as a way of circumventing the generation of infeasible paths.

It is convenient to classify those infeasible paths investigated here as being one of two types.

1) Those which it would be possible to detect by more sophisticated static analysis. For example, if a variable which controls the flow of program execution is known not to have been redefined between two uses, then information concerning infeasibility of certain paths could be deduced.

2) Those which it would only be possible to determine by consideration of values of control variables. Hence symbolic execution and algebraic manipulation or something similar is implied.

Allegations have been found useful in preventing enumeration of paths in both categories although eventually it might be hoped that better automatic analysis will be used to exclude the infeasible paths of the first kind.

However, since infeasible paths complicate a path testing strategy and often unnecessarily clutter the code, it would undoubtedly be better to tackle the problem of reducing the large number of infeasible paths at the software design and production stages. It would seem that there are three possible solutions to the problem:

1) language design,
2) programming standards,
3) program transformation.

In the long term 1) may be the best answer. In other words, perhaps languages can be designed to prevent the production of programs with such large numbers of phantom paths. For the present, solution 2) offers hope if certain standards of programming can be successfully developed to reduce the number of infeasible paths. The ideas of functional programming, as it has been called, warrant as much attention as structured programming has had in the past. Certainly structured programming by itself does not necessarily prevent the inclusion of many infeasible paths, as is witnessed by routine A in Fig. 3. This Algol 68 routine, which contains no **gotos**, conforms to the discipline of structured programming, yet only 1.4 percent of the paths of length less than or equal to 17 LCSAJ's are feasible. A study by Brown and Nelson [2] has shown that some programs can be written so that they have no infeasible paths. Routine C in Fig. 3 also shows this. Brown and Nelson also suggest that solution 3) is a possibility for certain classes of programs.

ACKNOWLEDGMENT

The authors would like to acknowledge the Numerical Algorithms Group (NAG) organization for permission to analyze their library.

REFERENCES

[1] J. R. Brown, "Practical applications of automated software tools," TRW Systems, Redondo Beach, CA, Tech. Rep. TRW-SS-72-05, Sept. 1972.
[2] J. R. Brown and E. C. Nelson, "Functional programming," TRW Defense and Space Systems Group for Rome Air Development Center, final Tech. Rep. on Contract F30602-76-C-0315, July 1977.
[3] T. S. Chow, "Testing software design modeled by finite-state machines," *IEEE Trans. Software Eng.*, vol. SE-4, pp. 178–187, May 1978.
[4] B. Ford and D. K. Sayers, "Developing a single numerical algorithms library for different machine ranges," *ACM Trans. Mathematical Software*, vol. 2, pp. 115–131, June 1976.
[5] H. N. Gabow, S. N. Maheshwari, and L. J. Osterweil, "On two problems in the generation of program test paths," *IEEE Trans. Software Eng.*, vol. SE-2, pp. 227–231, Sept. 1976.
[6] M. A. Hennell, D. Hedley, and M. R. Woodward, "Experience with an Algol 68 numerical algorithms testbed," in *Proc. Polytech. Inst. of New York Symp. Comput. Software Eng.*, MRI

Symposia Series, vol. XXIV, J. Fox, Ed., Apr. 1976, pp. 457-463.
[7] —, "Quantifying the test effectiveness of Algol 68 programs," in *Proc. Strathclyde Univ. Conf. Algol 68, ACM Sigplan Notices*, vol. 12, pp. 36-41, June 1977.
[8] M. A. Hennell, M. R. Woodward, and D. Hedley, "On program analysis," *Information Proc. Lett.*, vol. 5, pp. 136-140, Nov. 1976.
[9] W. E. Howden, "Methodology for the generation of program test data," *IEEE Trans. Comput.*, vol. C-24, pp. 554-559, May 1975.
[10] —, "Reliability of the path analysis testing strategy," *IEEE Trans. Software Eng.*, vol. SE-2, pp. 208-215, Sept. 1976.
[11] —, "An evaluation of the effectiveness of symbolic testing," *Software–Practice and Experience*, vol. 8, pp. 381-397, 1978.
[12] J. C. Huang, "An approach to program testing," *ACM Computing Surveys*, vol. 7, pp. 113-128, Sept. 1975.
[13] E. F. Miller, "Program testing techniques," IEEE Tutorial, presented at COMPSAC 77, Chicago, Nov. 1977.
[14] L. J. Osterweil, "Allegations as aids to static program testing," Dep. Comput. Sci. Rep., Univ. Colorado, Boulder, CO.
[15] S. Pimont and J.-C. Rault, "A software reliability assessment based on a structural and behavioural analysis of programs," in *Proc. 2nd Int. Conf. Software Eng.*, San Francisco, Oct. 1976, pp. 486-491.

engaged in the development of automatic tools to analyze programs and aid program testing. He is also an industrial consultant on software engineering.

David Hedley was born in Newcastle-Upon-Tyne, England, in 1949. He received the B.Sc. degree in computational science and mathematics from the University of Leeds, Leeds, England, in 1971.

He then worked for a short period at City College, Sheffield, England, before moving to the Department of Computational and Statistical Science, University of Liverpool, England, where he has been a Research Fellow in program testing since 1975.

Martin R. Woodward was born in Trowbridge, England, in 1948. He received the B.Sc. and Ph.D. degrees in mathematics from Nottingham University, Nottingham, England, in 1969 and 1972, respectively.

From 1972 to 1975 he worked for the U.K. Atomic Energy Authority at the Culham Research Laboratory. Since 1975 he has been a Post-Doctoral Research Fellow in the Department of Computational and Statistical Science, University of Liverpool, Liverpool, England,

Michael A. Hennell received the B.Sc., M.Sc., and Ph.D. degrees from the University of London, England, in 1961, 1962, and 1968, respectively.

He is a Senior Lecturer in the Department of Computational and Statistical Science, University of Liverpool, Liverpool, England, where he has been since 1969. His interests have included at various times partial differential equations, numerical algorithms libraries, design of high level languages, and software engineering. He is a Director of a software house and an industrial consultant on software testing methodologies.

Section 6: Management and Planning

Paper Summaries

E. B. Daly, "Management of Software Development," *IEEE Transactions on Software Engineering,* May 1977 (pp. 229-242).

This paper contains a general description of software development management. It includes estimates of the cost factors associated with the different phases of the software life cycle. Software validation techniques that can be carried out during different phases are described and the importance of early validation activities is stressed. The management and planning of testing is also discussed.

D. S. Alberts, "The Economics of Software Quality Assurance," *1976 National Computer Conference Proceedings* (pp. 433-442).

Alberts' paper presents a comprehensive analysis of the costs associated with quality assurance. The life-cycle is divided into four phases: conceptual (1 percent of total cost), requirements (1.5 percent), development (47.5 percent), and operations (50 percent). The paper reports on software systems that have had relatively long lifetimes—up to 16 years.

According to the data Alberts analyzed, nearly 80 percent of the costs associated with errors can be traced to design flaws of one kind or another. However, almost half (47.6 percent) of the total life-cycle cost is associated with correcting errors of various kinds and from all sources.

Alberts addresses the relative effectiveness of various kinds of quality assurance techniques. Structured programming and top-down design methods are the most effective in terms of cost reductions, having effectiveness of 75 percent and 100 percent typically. Automated tools are less effective, decreasing the costs of certain phases by about 25 percent. It is important to note that test runs accounted for nearly 45 percent of the detections of logic/coding and design errors.

E. F. Miller, "A Service Concept for Software Auditing," *Proceedings of the NSF Software Auditing Workshop,* San Francisco, 1976 (pp. 57-75).

In this paper Miller outlines an organizational unit that would provide a special kind of software auditing service. This concept has a number of advantages over other organizational structures for program testing (such as an independent verification and validation unit, or an in-line group).

The basic format of the service is to provide an independent repository for a software system on behalf of a client/customer. After the software system has been completed and placed in use, a copy of it is delivered to the service for independent analysis. The testing done by the service would include repetition of tests done earlier by the developer and special tests of the system's robustness, developed specifically by the service. The majority of the analysis work would be done using highly automated tools.

The outcome of the initial analysis would be a "go/no-go" evaluation of the quality of the software system. The developer would correct identified mistakes and after possibly several iterations the service would accept the software system for achiving. Subsequently, the service would be available to issue fresh copies of the software system from its master copy. Any charges to the software system would have to be checked out thoroughly by the service before those changes could propogate to the master copy of the software system, which would be known to have been tested and/or retested to a minimum standard established and maintained by the service.

In the paper, Miller identifies the major phases of analysis and preparation that a submitted software system would undergo, and also identifies the set of automated tools that would be used by the service in processing clients' software systems.

B. W. Boehm, "The High Cost of Software," *Practical Strategies for Developing Large Software Systems,* E. Horowitz, ed. (pp. 3-14).

This paper analyzes some of the cost factors affecting the software industry, and makes some important points that serve to set the scene for a detailed investigation of program testing.

Boehm points out that nearly $16 billion is spent every year on software (1974 statistics) in the US, and that this figure is probably low. Currently, only 10 percent of the system life cycle cost is for the hardware; the rest is for software and services.

Some facts about the cost of software are:

- Using high-level languages costs only about one-half as much, compared with use of assembly languages.
- Currently, most system life-cycles allocate only about 15 percent to testing.
- The length of the testing phase correlates highly with the computer turnaround time, implying that testing is a highly execution dependent activity.
- During software production, individual variations of as much as 5:1 in productivity have been noted.
- There is too little data available to even attempt to correlate the cost of software with its complexity.

Management of Software Development

EDMUND B. DALY

Abstract—This paper describes four major aspects of software management: development statistics, development process, development objectives, and software maintenance. The control of both large and small software projects is included in the analysis.

Index Terms—Program methodologies, software design maintenance, software development estimates, software management.

INTRODUCTION

THIS PAPER is meant to present the results of my experience directing both large and small software controlled real time systems at GTE Automatic Electric Laboratories, Northlake, IL. Hopefully, the historical data and management principles which are presented will help others in their attempt to properly manage similar developments. The information presented here has been derived from three large real-time system developments and many smaller minicomputer and microcomputer system developments. These projects account for 2 000 000 h of software development experience and required the generation of real-time programs as well as extensive supporting programs.

DEVELOPMENT STATISTICS

The unknown elements of software management can be reduced by employing historical development statistics for estimating and controlling current development. The data presented in this section have been used to predict development costs, system costs, development intervals, and to establish development objectives for many GTE systems currently under development.

Applying historical statistics is not an easy task and much managerial judgement must be employed. To help guide the reader, I have attempted to show what factors affect the data presented.

This section looks at the software development process from three different viewpoints: first, the total software job; second, the components of a software job; third, the dynamic flow of a software job.

The Total Software Job

"Software development rate" will be referred to extensively in this section. Software development rate is given in terms of instructions generated per programmer hour and includes all efforts required for specification, design, code test, and maintenance up to commercial availability of the program.

In order to compare the development rates of two different programs, the following factors must be considered:
1) design objectives,
2) program size,
3) program complexity,
4) program language,
5) program environment,
6) data base,
7) documentation standards,
8) personnel and computer resources.

Design Objectives Affect Development Rates

A program can be designed to optimize one or more of the following standards.

1) *Memory Utilization*: Perform the required functions using the least amount of memory space to house both instructions and data base. This objective attempts to minimize system costs.

2) *Executive Speed*: Perform the required functions using minimum real time during execution. This objective attempts to maximize system throughput.

3) *Schedule*: Perform the desired functions in the least amount of time. In a competitive market an "excellent" late product may be less profitable than an "acceptable" early product.

4) *System Maintenance*: Perform the desired functions so as to minimize on-site maintenance cost.

5) *High Quality*: Ensure that the required functions are performed by well-documented and thoroughly tested software. Design cannot rely on the customer to find the last 5 percent software bugs.

6) *Design Cost*: Perform the required functions with minimum expenditure of resource dollars. This expenditure is in terms of manpower, material, and travel. This objective should include both initial design as well as design maintenance.

Other Factors That Affect Development Rate

Large real-time programs are usually developed at the extremely low rate of 0.3 to 0.6 instructions per hour.

In addition to trying to simultaneously optimize all design objectives, these programs usually encounter other manpower devouring requirements, the effort for which is usually buried into the development rate. My experience shows that these factors include the following.

1) Large data base requirements: the development effort required to structure, define, and document the data base.

2) Large and complex program: requiring from 75 000 instructions to 500 000 instructions. These programs must pay the cost to integrate the output of many programming teams.

3) Extensive commercial documentation: such as diagnostic dictionaries, input/output message manual, user documents, charts, descriptions, and extensively commented listings.

4) Program specified by an external source: the design team does not have the option to decide what feature requirements the program will satisfy—as such, these requirements are often loosely defined and constantly changed during the early period of development.

5) Generic structure: a single program must be able to work in many different hardware configurations and outside environments—the data structure must be designed to cope with varying requirements. Thus, the program remains constant and the data base information content and size changes from site to site.

6) Complex interface: program must be able to work with different quantities of hardware. The program also has extensive hardware/software interfaces as well as man/machine interfaces.

7) Software responsible for system reliability: software controls are designed to minimize the effect on system operation due to hardware faults, hardware noise, data base errors, or instruction errors.

8) Long life: programs are designed to last twenty years with active maintenance occurring at least during the first four years.

Resources Also Affect Development Rates

Real-time software development rates are very dependent on the resources available to management. Three important resources are

1) the programmer,
2) support software (we will discuss only two support packages: compiler and simulator),
3) support computer.

Programmer–A Resource–In most applications a balanced team consisting of one leader, two experienced programmers, and three inexperienced energetic programmers is ideal during the implementation and maintenance phases. A smaller team of experienced system level programmers is usually required during the earlier planning and specification phases.

Compiler–A Resource–A good compiler allows programmers to code in high-level language without extensive waste of memory. A 20 percent reduction in total development effort has been achieved at GTE Automatic Electric Laboratories when a real-time program was designed using high-level language rather than assembly language. This reduction in effort occurs in the following design phases: coding, documentation, testing, design maintenance. Because an instruction written in high-level language contains more intelligence than does an instruction written in assembly level language, a high-level language instruction often incurs a larger "development cost per instruction" than does the simpler assembly level instruction. An assembly level instruction usually produces one machine instruction. A high-level instruction usually produces more than one machine instruction.

Simulator—A Resource—Large real-time programs must be eventually tested on the machine in which they will reside. This machine is called the "object machine." The amount of object machine time required to test a program depends heavily on the amount of prior program testing which can be performed off-line as well as the quality of the object machine utilities. One method of off-line testing is called simulation. The process requires the design of a support program called a simulator. This simulator makes an off-line computer look like the object machine; at least to the real-time program which is being tested.

For large real-time programs, such as the ones described earlier, 1 h of object machine time is required to test ten instructions of unsimulated, assembly level code. If simulation is used prior to object machine testing, this rate increases to twenty-five instructions per hour. The least amount of object machine time is required for simulated programs which were coded in high-level language. These programs have been tested on the object machine at an average rate of forty instructions per hour.

The reduction in amount of machine time required for testing affects development expenditures in two ways.

1) In order to generate a thorough and well-documented test plan, a programmer requires 3 h of preparation and analysis time for each 1 h spent testing on the object machine. Therefore, a 1 h reduction in machine time carries a 4 h reduction in development hours.

2) Object machine time is very expensive. For the real-time programs described in this paper machine costs range from $40.00 to $150.00 per hour.

Computer—A Resource—In addition to supporting software, the quality and quantity of computer resources affects efficiency of coding and testing. Currently, interactive editing and testing seems to be the most effective way to debug software. Batch, however, is still an effective development tool as long as turn-around time remains under 2.5 h.

In conclusion, development rates should only be used as a guideline for planning new designs. These rates cannot easily be compared—even for similar jobs—since management objectives or available resources may be different. In any case, the program incurring the more costly development rate may be the better design approach since it could require less memory and execute faster, thus requiring a less costly memory system and forcing a larger market. The object of software management should always be to optimize profits. This objective may require larger initial development expenditures in terms of hours per instruction.

Different Program Classification

With this background, let us now look at the development rate for various types of programs in order to get some feeling of how development rates fluctuate. The range of develop-

SYSTEM	COMMERCIALLY AVAILABLE TO CUSTOMER	SIZE OF PROGRAM (NEW INSTRUCTIONS)	DEVELOPMENT RATE INSTRUCTIONS PER HOUR
A	1972	160,000	.33
B	1972	117,000	.43
C	1974	111,000	.53

Fig. 1.

ment varies from 0.24 instructions per hour to 12 instructions per hour. I do not believe that the high development rate indicates better management but merely a different software job.

For simplicity let us categorize programs into three areas: small real-time, large real-time, support.

Small Real-Time Programs

Data have been compiled from five different minicomputer developments. The program size ranges from 5 000 to 20 000 machine instructions and range of effort varies from 1.6 machine instructions per hour to 5 machine instructions per hour. Intermediate rates are 2.3 machine instructions per hour and 1.9 machine instructions per hour.

The program which was developed at 5 machine instructions per hour did not require commercial documentation, nor was memory usage or real time a strong guideline.

Managerial objectives were to generate a program in minimal time, requiring minimal man/machine interface. The system was designed to drive traffic through a larger machine. System up-time was not an important factor. The program was designed by one experienced programmer. The software was operational in three months.

The programs which were developed at a slower rate faced completely different design objectives and environments. They required large data base structures. Real-time execution as well as system up-time were important factors. These systems required commercial documentation and were designed for low cost software maintenance (i.e., modular construction).

Large Real-Time Programs

Fig. 1 shows development statistics for three large real-time programs. All three programs were designed to meet the most stringent operational requirements. The most important single factor which determines the different developing programmers and supervisors.

The above-mentioned programs are constructed using many subprograms. On an average each subprogram houses 3 000 machine instructions or 20 software modules. The development rate for subprograms is different than for the total program in that some subprograms are very complex—such as diagnostic subprograms—and some are rather simple—pure data manipulation. The following list gives two examples of subprogram development rates.

1) Data manipulation—such as updating memory information. 1.9 machine instructions per hour for subprogram.

2) Diagnostic—such as checking electronic hardware to determine if it is operational. 0.24 machine instructions per hour for subprograms.

In each case an additional effort of 6 percent is required to integrate each subprogram into a total program.

Support Programs

These programs are intermediate size (20 000 instructions). The programs referred to in this section are called support software because they have been designed to "support" the design and manufacture of the large real-time programs described in the last section. Support programs consist of loaders, editors, assemblers, compilers, program generators, simulators, and utility programs. They have been designed to execute on IBM-360/370 machines. The size of support software is large: 400 000 instructions of support software has been designed to "support" the design and manufacture of 370 000 machine instructions of real-time software. Support programs, however, are less complex to design than real-time operational programs. Also 60 percent of the code is implemented using high-level language. The development rate ranges from 0.7 instructions per hour for the more complex support programs to 12 instructions per hour for the simpler programs. The average development rate for the entire package of 400 000 instructions is 1.5 instructions per hour.

Development Rate–Design Maintenance

Not only is the initial development effort associated with support software less (per instruction) than that required for large real-time programs, but the design maintenance effort is also less. Statistics based on maintaining three separate real-time software packages and two separate support packages indicate the following design maintenance effort.

1) One equivalent programmer (two programmers—each devoting half time to maintaining software) can maintain from 15 000 to 30 000 instructions of on-line real-time programs. This can be compared to the rate for support software of from 50 000 to 120 000 instructions per equivalent programmer.

2) One programmer, devoting full time to maintaining software, can maintain 10 000 instructions of on-line real-time programs—or 30 000 instructions of support programs. This number differs from that presented in 1) in that we have found that design maintenance programmers are more efficiently employed if approximately 50 percent of their working hours are spent in new design.

The maintenance rates given above do not include such overhead items as configuration control, laboratory and field support, and supervision.

Development Rates–Components

In addition to specifying development hours per instruction, another important development statistic divides this total development effort into its component parts: specification, design (includes code), test, documentation, design maintenance.

Fig. 2 is a pie chart which shows this division for the three large real-time programs described earlier. Although, Fig. 2 represents an average of the three programs, each program taken individually indicates a similar distribution. However, Fig. 2 does not include the effort required to "evaluate" the

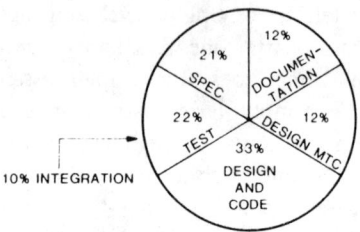

Fig. 2. Development pie chart including design maintenance to one year after cutover. Chart does not include overhead efforts for: configuration control, laboratory support, field testing.

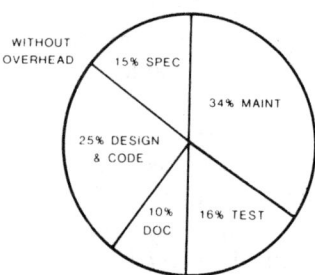

Fig. 3. Development pie chart including design maintenance to four years after in service.

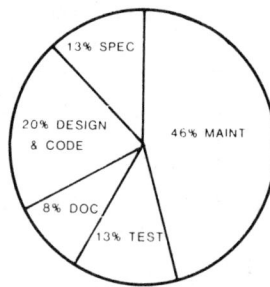

Fig. 4. Includes overhead: configuration control laboratory support field testing.

software package. This effort usually takes place at the first field site. For large real-time programs approximately 0.1 h per instruction is required to write and execute evaluation test plans. The maintenance effort shown in Fig. 2 is used to resolve software bugs found during evaluation.

In Figs. 2–4, design maintenance represents that design effort required to support a commercial system after the development team finishes system testing.

Fig. 3 shows the same breakdown as Fig. 2 but a different point in time. Note that design maintenance effort has increased from 12 percent of total effort (one year after in-service), to 34 percent of total effort after four years of service.

Figs. 2 and 3 include design maintenance effort only to the extent that it is performed by a programmer. This effort is only 55 percent of the total expenditure allocatable to maintaining real-time software. The remaining 45 percent of total maintenance cost arises from prototype and field support

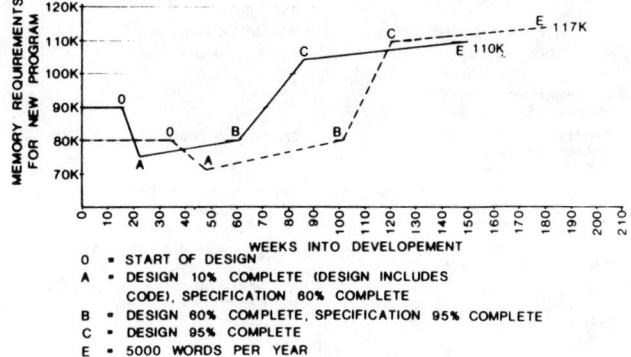

Fig. 5. Program size variation—two projects.

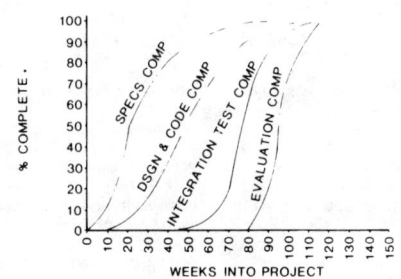

Fig. 6. Characteristic "S" curve for software development.

manpower which is used to support the programmers testing activities, to evaluate his tested programs, and to place these programs under configuration control. If we allocate these overhead charges to design maintenance, Fig. 4 results. This figure indicates that design maintenance of software accounts for 46 percent of total software development dollars expenditure at a period of 4 years after commercial availability. Since the major maintenance effort takes place during the first four years after the commercial release of a program, the 46 percent should increase very slowly—possibly approaching 60 percent after 10 years. Design maintenance as used in Fig. 4 includes laboratory efforts associated with fixing design problems and with small program enhancements. It does not include efforts required for large feature additions or local "on-site" support.

Dynamic Flow

The software development statistics discussed to this point have been static statistics—taken at one point in time. Figs. 5 and 6 show how a software project progresses through its various phases. These figures illustrate statistics for two different large real-time programs—developed by two different teams of programmers, supervisors, and unit heads.

Fig. 5 shows how estimated program size varies throughout the period of development. "Estimated program size" is a projection of the program size at commercial availability. A surprising "characteristic curve" is obvious from this figure. In both projects, program size estimates made early in development (start of specification) were high and then rapidly dropped—hitting a low ebb at the start of design. Estimated program size then starts to increase at a conservatively slow rate until design reaches 60 percent complete. At this point in time both projects increased estimated program size estimates at a very rapid rate—resulting in a size increase of about 50 percent from point A to point C. After design completion reached 98 percent, program size estimates leveled off and were within 5 percent of the actual program size at commercial availability.

Fig. 6 is an actual plot tracing the development of the 110 000 instruction real-time program, we see the progress of software development for specification, design, integration, and evaluation. Note that in all cases there is a natural overlap of activities, in that at any one point in time many phases of development are taking place simultaneously. Fig. 6 shows that the time required to complete the last 20 percent of a development phase is as long as the design time to complete the middle 70 percent. This characteristic is responsible for many schedule slippages since a good portion of the activity being performed during the latter 20 percent consists of correcting mistakes: either overlooked modules or unacceptable design.

Development Statistics—A Future Trend

Although this section is concerned with software development rates—we can track the future evolution of these rates by comparing them to those being experienced in the related field of electronic hardware.

One of the large real-time programs referred to in this paper contains 160 000 software instructions. This program controls the operation of a hardware system containing approximately 170 000 logic gates. (In order to make the analysis meaningful only one copy of each subassembly was used to establish the logic gate count.)

Historical statistics gathered in this system indicate that there is a close analogy between hardware and software development statistics. For example:

1) Twice as much effort is required to develop one *instruction* of software than to develop one hardware *logic gate*.

2) The same amount of effort is required to develop a large functional software segment as a functional logic board in hardware (containing 80 gates).

3) Using the total number of system instructions (160 000) and total number of logic gates (170 000) as a base for comparison, then design maintenance corrections per instruction *exceed* design maintenance corrections per logic gate by a factor of four to one. Design maintenance cost for software also exceeds design maintenance cost for electronic hardware by a factor of four to one.

4) System software complexity approximately equals system hardware complexity.

The question which must be answered is "why did total development cost per instruction exceed total development cost per logic gate by such a large factor when the system hardware complexity equaled the system software complexity and the number of instructions equaled the number of logic gates?" At least for this project we found that the answer lies in five areas.

1) Hardware management techniques and development procedures were more advanced than those used in software.

2) Hardware designers were more experienced.

3) Hardware employed a more "structured design."

4) The basic building blocks used in software design (i.e., different types of source statements) were more numerous and complex than the simple building blocks used in hardware: AND, OR, NOT. (Use of structured programming could eliminate this difference since the technique limits software building blocks to three types of single-entry, single-exit control structures: simple selection, simple repetition, and linear sequence. Structured programming ensures that a software instruction contains the same amount of intelligence as a hardware logic gate.)

5) In a software/hardware system the hardware gets a double dose of testing and evaluation: the first dose occurs during scheduled hardware testing, the second dose occurs as a natural byproduct of software testing.

In conclusion—as software management and design techniques approach the level that exists in hardware, and as software design becomes more structured, from projects such as the one described above we can expect development rates per instruction and maintenance costs per instruction to decrease—hopefully approaching rates presently being experienced by an electronic logic gate.

The Process of Software Development

Statistical data gathered during the process of software development can be used to establish an efficient methodology for future development. For example, historical analysis of completed GTE Automatic Electric Laboratories' projects indicates that over 50 percent of all development hours are spent correcting bugs which result from faulty design. Information such as this tends to guide management toward development methodology which places more emphasis in generating a higher quality initial design with the expectation that this additional early expenditure will be paid back during testing and design maintenance.

Since the primary output of software development is "code," many methodologies place heavy emphasis on generating code early in the development cycle. These software projects usually experience testing phases which last significantly longer than the combined specification, design, and code phases. Many of the projects which rush the process of generating code are the same projects which experience the longer total development schedule. Fig. 6 shows development completion curves for a large GTE Automatic Electric Laboratories' software project where generation of code was not given prime importance. Even in this project the testing and evaluation phase lasted approximately the same amount of time as the combined specification design and code phases.

Figs. 7 and 8 show two approaches to software development. The concepts under Method 1 illustrate our current approach to software development. Some earlier software developments employed techniques which tended toward those illustrated under Method 1.

Method 2, however, seems to be a more natural approach in that it requires less management control, requires less tech-

METHOD 1	METHOD 2
HIGH LEVEL LANGUAGE. STRUCTURED CODE.	ASSEMBLY LANGUAGE. TIGHT COMPLEX CODE.
COMPOSITE DESIGN (HIERARCHY OF SMALL SEGMENTS).	LARGE BLOBS OF CODE.
PARALLEL, TOP DOWN, BOTTOM UP DESIGN - ALL OPTIONALLY USED.	BOTTOM UP DESIGN.
SIMPLE DATA STRUCTURES AND WORK AREAS (NOT TIGHTLY PACKED).	TIGHT, EFFICIENT, DATA STRUCTURES AND WORK AREAS (EVERY BIT USED NO DATA DUPLICATED).
TEAM APPROACH TO DESIGN (EGOLESS PROGRAMMING).	"ONE PROGRAM - ONE MAN" CONCEPT
"IBM'S STRUCTURED WALK THROUGH" FOR REVIEWING DETAIL DESIGN AND CODE.	NO DETAILED TECHNICAL REVIEW OF DESIGN OR CODE.

Fig. 7. Software design methods.

METHOD 1	METHOD 2
THREE SEPARATE TEAMS. ONE TEAM DESIGNS, ONE TESTS, ONE EVALUATES.	ORIGINAL CODER TESTS, INTEGRATES AND HELPS EVALUATE HIS PROGRAM.
COMPLETE SET OF HIERARCHY CHARTS, SEQUENCE CHARTS, DATA MAPS AND NARRATIVES. WELL COMMENTED LISTINGS.	DETAILED FLOW CHARTS AND GENERAL NARRATIVES. NO CONSISTANCY IN LISTING COMMENTS.
DETAILED TEST PLANS FOR ALL TEST PHASES.	NO FORMAL TEST PLANS.
PROGRAM MAINTAINED BY 30% SENIOR PROGRAMMERS.	PROGRAM MAINTAINED BY INEXPERIENCED PROGRAMMERS OR TECHNICIANS.
ONLY COMMERCIAL DOCUMENTATION GENERATED DURING DEVELOPMENT.	EXTENSIVE NONCOMMERCIAL TECHNICAL MEMORANDUM GENERATED AND PLACED IN LIBRARY.
STRICT MANAGEMENT OBJECTIVES ESTABLISHED TO GUIDE DEVELOPMENT.	NO MANAGEMENT OBJECTIVES.

Fig. 8. Software design methods.

nical (software) experience, allows programmers to both innovate and avoid what they hate most—documentation.

Method 2 will also require less memory space and less execution time than Method 1. The reasons for this fact are threefold.

1) Structured design requires extensive subroutine linkage. This process utilizes extra memory and execution time in order to maintain integrity of "computer register" information. (Some minicomputers are being designed to minimize this overhead by saving the contents of program register via hardware at each subroutine call.)

2) High-level language requires more memory space and execution time than assembly level implementation of the same job. Even the better compilers require 10–15 percent more memory space and execution time. This percentage increases to 100 percent for many commercial high-level languages.

3) The tight complex code employed in Method 2 will require less program storage space and execution time than the structured code used in Method 1.

A good guideline is to employ a methodology somewhere between the two—but much closer to Method 1. The three large GTE projects referenced in this paper followed this guideline.

A Workable Development Methodology

The following section describes a management approach which is being used by some newer projects in GTE Auto-

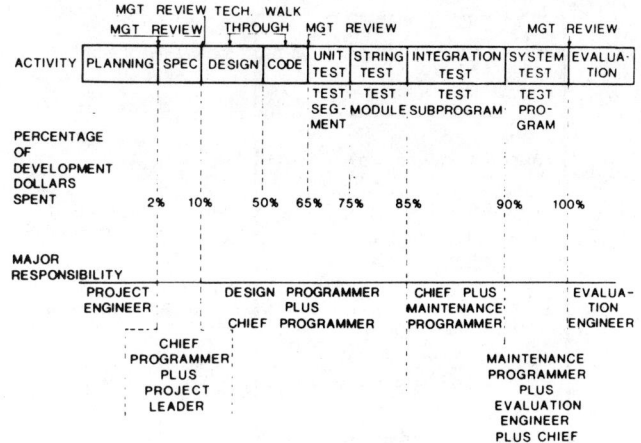

Fig. 9.

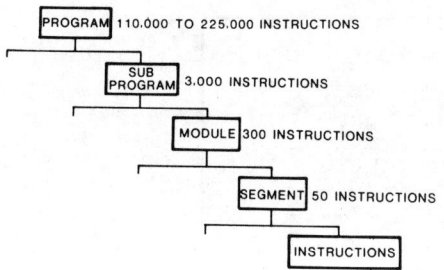

Fig. 10. Structure.

matic Electric Laboratories to generate commercial software. The process which is described is not a revolution in management techniques, but standard management practices molded with the idiosyncrasies of software development. These techniques have evolved during the development and maintenance of GTE's EAX and TSPS stored program switching machines.

There is no universal process which should be used to develop all types of software. Large commercial real-time programs which involve more than 30 programmers require a development methodology containing more documentation, more cross-checks and, in general, better management techniques than do smaller noncommercial programs that may only be executed in a few machines and usually by highly qualified engineers. What is important is that management establish a development process for each type of software design—early in the planning stage. The methodology presented here is applicable to large real-time commercial software packages. The process can be modified for "simpler" developments by eliminating some of the less critical technical cross-checks.

Development Cycle

There is a specific cycle associated with the generation of commercial software. This cycle can be divided into five phases: plan, specify, design, code, test. Although these phases are somewhat universal for all software developments, the specific management methods used to ensure successful completion of each phase differs due to variations in management styles, and more importantly, variations in management maturity.

A Development Process

Using experimental data and other empirically derived guidelines, a software development process has been derived. This process, which covers all phases of development from initial planning to design maintenance is summarized in Fig. 9. The process is being used in current GTE Automatic Electric Laboratories' projects.

The process recognizes the need for two types of design reviews: technical and managerial. Managerial reviews are held at major development milestones. The object of these reviews are threefold: review commercial documentation which is scheduled for completion at the specific milestone; review development expenditures and schedules—both historical and forecasted; approve continued development. Technical reviews are much more detailed than management reviews and do not consider schedules or budgets. The primary responsibility of a technical review is to analyze the same commercial documentation presented to management but in a very detailed manner. Technical reviews are always held prior to management reviews and must be successfully completed before the management review convenes.

As shown in Fig. 10, programs are divided into successively smaller sections called subprograms, modules, and segments. This division into simpler parts allows a complex program to be defined, developed, and maintained. Whereas a large program may require 50 designers, a large subprogram may require 5 designers. A module is usually assigned to one designer. As a further simplification, the designer divides his module into individual functions called segments. Segments are then coded.

In summary, *programs* are built using *subprograms*. A subprogram performs a major system activity. An average subprogram consists of about 3 000 instructions. *Subprograms* are built using *modules*. A module performs a set of very closely related functions and consists of about 300 instructions. *Modules* are built using *segments*. A segment performs one function and consists of 50 instructions. *Segments* are built from *instructions*. *Instructions* are the most basic building block in software design.

A very important output of the development process is documentation. Software documentation consists of two types: design documentation and commercial documentation. Design documentation is "throw-away" in that management does not commit itself to incur the cost of keeping the documentation current. Commercial documentation is sent to the customer. It is updated and maintained for the life of the software product.

Management must generate strict controls for commercial documentation. Format standards and procedures for updating must be established. We have found that a commercial documentation package should be selected with three objectives in mind.

1) **Minimize Cost of Manufacture**: The commercial package should only contain charts which can be computer generated.

2) **Minimize Cost of Maintenance**: The commercial pack-

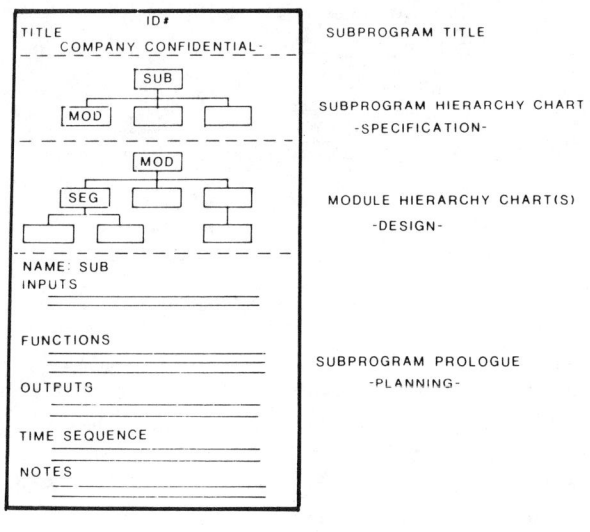

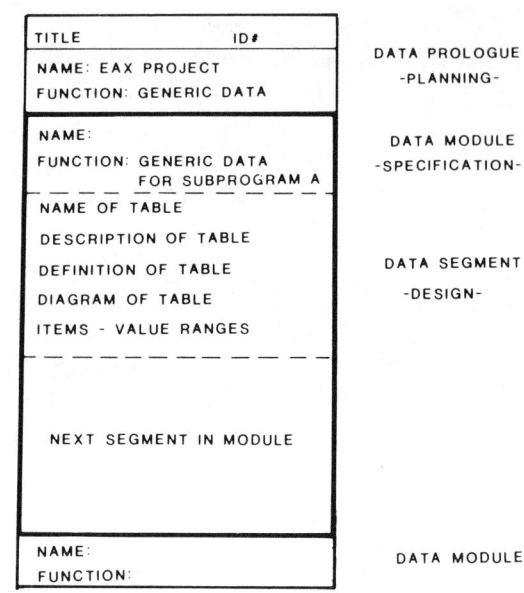

Fig. 12. Structured data listing.

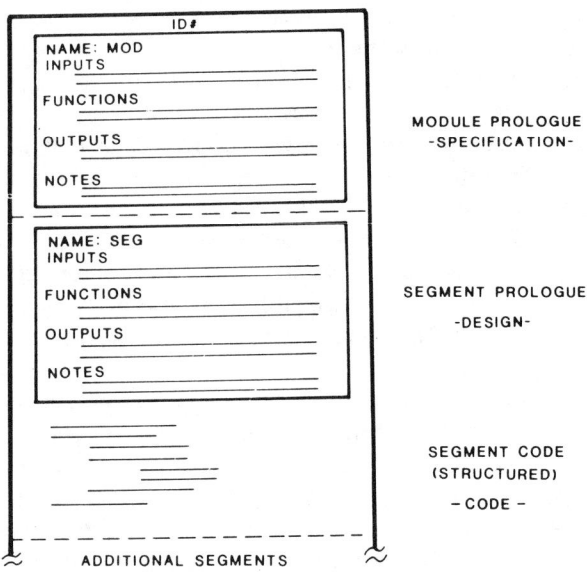

Fig. 11. Structured program listing.

age should contain sufficient information for program understanding but not contain duplication of information.

3) *Minimize Cost of Development:* The commercial package should be generated during the design process—not as an afterthought. The commercial documentation package should either be the same as the design documentation package or should be able to be derived from design documentation with a level of personnel no higher than a software librarian.

The commercial package we selected consists of two parts: a "structured program listing" shown in Fig. 11, and a "structured data listing" shown in Fig. 12.

A structured program listing is generated for every subprogram in the system. It is generated in stages throughout the software development process. Fig. 11 specifies the development phase during which each part of the listing is generated.

Fig. 12 shows the contents of a structured data listing. This listing groups tables according to how they are used by the code. The basic building block of this listing is also called a segment. Each segment contains one data table.

The above-structured listings are generated by computer—no drafting or manual drawing is required. The structured listing contains no duplication of information (such as detailed flowcharts and comments associated with code). Current experience with commercial structured listings shows that they reduce maintenance costs when compared to other systems we have designed which use more standard software documentation concepts: code listings, detailed flowcharts, independent descriptions, etc.

THE DEVELOPMENT PROCESS

This section will describe a typical flow through the development cycle. The description is somewhat detailed but this emphasis is justified since the development process is the heart of software management. If a "good" development process is combined with a "good" scheduling and cost control tool, management will experience a high percentage of successful software projects.

Phase 1—Planning

The first phase of development is called the planning stage. During this stage the customer generates his requirements. Normally the customer will work directly with project engineers. If a project requires only software effort, this engineer should be an experienced systems programmer. If a project requires hardware and software, the project engineer must be knowledgeable in both areas.

A primary objective of planning is to quickly generate a "high-level package" for management review. This phase should not spend more than 2 percent of total development dollars. It is at this first review that most marginal or non-profitable projects will be "turned off" by management.

The types of information brought to management by the project engineers are as follows.

1) Product description: description of system features as seen by the customer. General system requirements.

2) High-level description of how major features will be implemented.

3) Software hierarchy chart where each element in the chart represents about 3 000 instructions (a subprogram).

4) Estimates of schedule, development cost, memory size, real time, market potential, material and system cost.

Armed with the above information, management can determine if the reviewed project deserves further funds. The estimates vary in accuracy depending on the completeness of the original product description and the estimater's experience. ±35 percent seems to be an average accuracy figure.

If management approves further development, a project leader is appointed. Chief programmers are also selected at this time. These people will execute the next stage. The project leader coordinates all project activities—both hardware and software. He is responsible for integrating schedules of all involved development groups. The project leader also controls all system level documents—such as the specification of how the system (or program) is to operate and what features are included. The chief programmer is a technical leader who will eventually be in charge of a team of programmers. Large projects will have one project leader and many chief programmers (a chief programmer team should be limited to five programmers). In small projects, requiring only one chief programmer, the project leader and chief programmer can be the same person.

Phase 2—Specification

The next management review will occur after 10 percent of the total development dollars estimated during Phase 1 have been expended. The output of this phase is generated by the project leader and chief programmer(s). All technical documentation is generated in a format acceptable for commercial release.

Since the project is still in the early phases of development, the probability of managerial rejection is high. During this phase, firm marketing estimates are established. Cost and schedule accuracies are improved from 35 percent to 15 percent. The primary object of this phase is to bring accurate information to management for project approval or disapproval. The probability that a project will be approved at this stage and turned off at a later stage should be small, for after the 10 percent phase development costs increase very rapidly and a total manpower commitment is made.

The output generated during the specification stage consists of the following technical documents:

1) subprogram hierarchy chart showing control flow between modules;

2) time sequence description explaining the sequence in which modules execute in order to perform major system features;

3) subprogram prologues which describe the functions performed by each subprogram, the inputs of each subprogram, and the outputs from each subprogram;

4) module prologues which describe the functions performed by each module, module inputs, and module outputs;

5) a general layout and description of all data used by the program;

6) a description of all man/machine interfaces;

7) a detailed "requirements" document.

The administrative documents generated during the specification stage commit to specific values for: memory size, real time, development cost, development schedule, and resource requirements. These technical and administrative documents form a "contract" by the developing organization.

Phase 3—Design

After Phase 2, development activities accelerate very rapidly. If the technical base established in Phase 2 is generated properly, a significant number of programmers can be placed on the software problem early in Phase 3.

The Phase 3 review occurs after 50 percent of total development costs specified in Phase 2 have been expended. Phase 3 is a turning point in that most managers no longer have the ability (or time) to perform a detailed review of work performed and thus must rely on technical "walk-throughs" (IBM terminology). The output of Phase 3 contains no code. This is an important concept. The walk-through is a formal review technique where test inputs are generated and "eyeballed" through the design to verify its accuracy. Our experience indicates that coding is started far too early in most software projects and because of this a large percentage of code is redone before the software passes evaluation.

The technical "walk-through" performed at the conclusion of Phase 3 is attended by the project leader (he is responsible for program specification), chief programmer, interfacing programmers, and the supervisor.

This review is organized to detect all "bad" program modules. "Bad" in the sense of *poor structure*. We require programs to be built from code blocks—called segments. Each code block should perform only one function and be fully documented; program modules are built from these code blocks using rules of structured design. "Bad" in the sense of incorrect or poorly defined interfaces; modules are also reviewed to ensure correct intermodule interfaces and to assure that functions performed are in agreement with program specification. Approximately 10 percent of total design cost is expended in walk-throughs.

The output of Phase 3 consists of the following.

1) An update of all technical documentation—described in Phase 2.

2) Module hierarchy charts which show control flow between segments.

3) Prologues which describe the function performed by each segment within a module. Definiton of all data inputs to each segment and data outputs from each segment.

4) Test plans required to test the operation of each module.

5) Detailed data maps and description of each table and item.

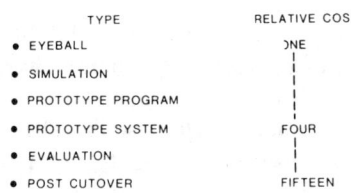

Fig. 13. Cost of finding a software bug.

All these documents with the exception of module test plans are generated for commercial release.

Phase 4 – Coding

Since the entire program is completely specified after Phase 3, segment coding can take place in parallel manner. Top-down coding need not be employed.

Experience indicates that coding should be complete at about the point where 65 percent of all software development dollars have been expended. In this case, total software development dollars include all expenditures for planning, specification, design, code, and test.

Since the completion of coding is a major milestone, it requires both a technical and managerial review. As shown in Fig. 9, the technical review comes first. This review is organized to detect most "bad" code. The resultant code should be simple, straightforward, and easy to understand. Where applicable, structured coding techniques should also be employed.

Unit tests should be made available at the code review and a subset of these tests "mentally" executed by the reviewing body. This process, when combined with code reading (a process where code logic and code format is scrutinized by a programmer other than the original designer), can detect up to 90 percent of coding and syntax errors. Code reading and mental testing should always be employed prior to object-machine testing in order to minimize usage of expensive machine time. As shown in Fig. 13 the development cost required to detect an error by reading code is approximately equal to 25 percent of that required to detect the same error via machine debugging. This statistic was gathered from two projects—a 111 000 instructions project and a 12 000 instructions project. Both projects showed similar results.

Probably the most important concept associated with the technical review is that actual commercial code is reviewed. The flow and structure of the code is analyzed for design flaws and misinterpretations. The review body is kept small—always including the chief programmer. In some reviews additional people may attend: coders who are responsible for software directly interfacing with the module being reviewed, the first level supervisor, and the programmer who will be responsible for maintaining the software module after development is complete.

Once the technical review is complete, management should be given a presentation summarizing the results of the preceding reviews: the technical review held after completion of design and the technical review held after completion of code.

The management review is held after completion of coding rather than after completion of design so that more accurate instruction estimates will be available (see Fig. 5). Since these reviews are held on a subprogram basis, the first review will be held the early part of the "design and code complete" curve shown in Fig. 6. It is good practice to require test plans and all commercial documentation to be brought to the management review—for psychological purposes only. Management should be concerned with resolving nontechnical problems and with correlating results of this review with other project reviews (a large software project will have coding reviews spread out over a year or more).

The major objective of a management review is to maintain schedules and budget by: shifting manpower from less important activities to critical tasks, canceling or delaying features, allowing standard practices to short-cut, and if all fails to immediately publish a schedule slip or budget increase.

A second objective of the management review is to ensure that the project is still profitable. It should be noted, however, that 65 percent of total development dollars have been spent by the time the coding review occurs. At this stage of development, customer commitments have probably been solidified to such an extent that even unprofitable projects continue to completion.

The management review process which occurs after code is complete is probably the most comprehensive as far as technical content. Earlier management reviews concentrate more on "should the project continue." For this reason management reviews are concentrated around the specification stage.

At completion of coding all estimates are refined. An accuracy figure of better than 10 percent should be available for memory size, real-time requirements, and development costs. An accuracy of better than 5 percent should be available for schedules.

Phase 5 – Testing

This phase consists of four stages of software testing.

First, each segment is tested to ensure its singular function works as specified in Phase 3. Second, the segments are strung together to ensure that groupings of segments (called modules) work as specified in Phase 3. Both of these testing activities are performed by the design programmer. Either top-down or bottom-up testing may be employed. Modules which are tested earlier are high-level control segments, hardware interface segments, or segments prone to interface errors.

After the chief programmer agrees that unit testing and string testing is complete, the chief programmer together with the maintenance programmer (the person who will be responsible for maintenance) verify the operation of each subprogram. The maintenance programmer being an experienced programmer is responsible, along with the chief programmer, for generating (or at least agreeing with) the integration test plan which checks the subprogram operation. The generation of integration tests should start as soon as possible after Phase 2. Early development of these test plans helps uncover "holes" in the software specification.

Since the maintenance programmer and the chief programmer should report to a different first line supervisor, an important cross-check is established. At completion of integration testing, the maintenance programmer must agree that the subprogram works according to the specification generated in Phases 2 and 3. The maintenance programmer also formally agrees that the subprogram meets commercial standards: well-documented, structured design, easy to understand code. Because the maintenance programmer will be responsible for the subprogram after the original designer relinquishes responsibility, he will not accept the subprogram without serious analysis. Unacceptable subprograms are immediately brought to the attention of second level managers and the project leader.

The last stage of design testing checks the interoperation of all subprograms. A team approach is used for this "total program" or system test. The team consists of selected chief programmers, senior maintenance programmers, and evaluation engineers. All members are involved in generating and executing the test plan. In those areas where hardware and software are involved, the evaluation engineer should be knowledgeable, from a system standpoint, of all areas. During system testing, all functions of the program are tested under stress conditions. Errors are placed into operational software, data structures, and system hardware. External drivers are employed to simulate heavy "user" activity. The objective of system testing is to make the system fail.

At the conclusion of system testing, the evaluation engineer must formally agree that the program successfully passed system testing. This acceptance is accompanied by a list of outstanding problems. Acceptance is contingent upon these problems being resolved. The problems list is passed on to second level management and the project leader to ensure prompt resolution. A formal follow-up procedure must be established to give these problems appropriate priority. During system testing, and for the life of the program—all software bugs are formally documented and formally scheduled for resolution. Summary data indicating "bugs per module" are fed back to design supervisors. These data allow supervisors to evaluate the improve design procedures as well as programming staff.

After system testing is complete, the responsibility for modifying the source program is relinquished by the design programmer (and chief programmer) and passes on to the maintenance programmer. After system testing, the program should work in its intended environment. The software maintenance phase now begins and the total system is evaluated by an independent group of system experts. The primary function of "evaluation" is to ensure that the system meets all customer requirements from a feature standpoint, a man/machine interface standpoint, a documentation standpoint, and real-time standpoint. During evaluation, a complete set of acceptance tests are executed. Design problems are resolved by the maintenance programmers. The effort expended in evaluation testing is not considered part of the software development cost.

Design Maintenance and Configuration Control

The successful development of a large software controlled system is at best only a partially completed task. Although many feel that the management of large software development is mysterious, or at least little understood; the long term control and maintenance of large programs is even more mysterious.

Our experience has shown that design maintenance costs can be minimized by following five guidelines.

1) Use structured design techniques along with thorough unit, string, integration, and system testing.

2) Establish maintenance groups with at least 30 percent senior programmers.

3) Assign maintenance programmers to active design tasks for 50 percent of their working hours.

4) Establish a well-controlled configuration management program.

5) Use structured listings for commercial documentation.

Configuration Management

The management process which is used to maintain a program after completion of design is called "software configuration management."

This process allows management to control the maintenance and manufacture a software package (or program). The process also allows management to control modification to this package and to ensure software changes are made coincident with associated hardware changes. Programs should be placed under configuration management after subprogram integration but before completion of system testing. After configuration control takes effect, all code and documentation changes must be accompanied by a supervisory approved form indicating reason for change and a test plan, if applicable.

The controlled software package is sold to the customer. It is called a "program version." If different sections of the market require slightly different programs—each section is supplied a different program version. One of the large real-time programs described earlier exists as four different versions. Two of the versions serve the same market but contain different feature packages. The other two versions serve different markets (outside the USA). Each of the four versions contains approximately 1 000 modules. Eighty percent of the software is common among the four versions.

Given this situation, configuration management allows us to:

1) Maintain common software only once. A much larger design maintenance effort would be required if common software was not recognized.

2) Design new versions using existing common software.

3) Ensure that corrections made to instructions in one version are reflected in all versions.

4) Allow systems to retrofit from one version to another version without affecting customer service.

5) Ensure that all software changes have proper management approval and are thoroughly tested before being sent to the field.

Under configuration management a version is updated either annually or semiannually by issuing reassembled program loads. When this is done, each site employing the specific version must place the updated load in its machine. This update is called a release. If important changes must be made to the commercial program at a faster rate than releases are generated, then patches may be sent to the field in the form of

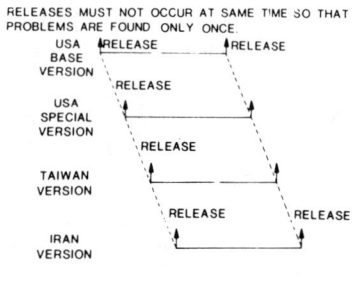

Fig. 14.

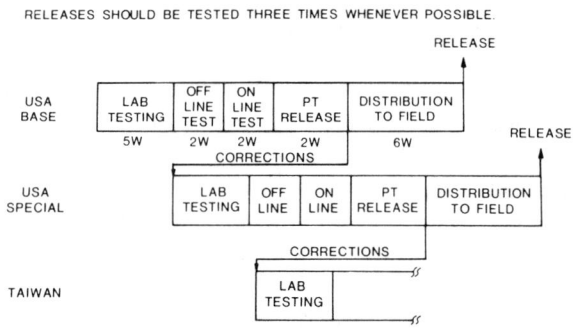

Fig. 15.

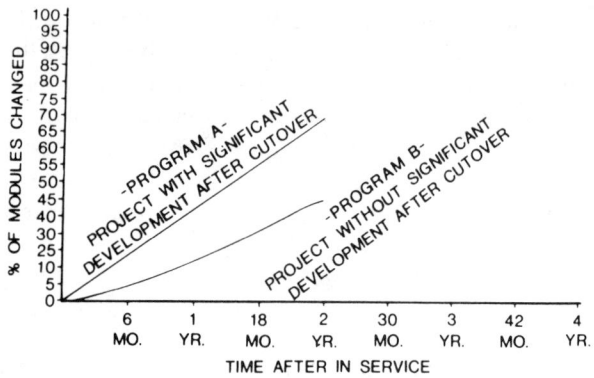

Fig. 16. Percentage of modules changed due to corrections and enhancements.

point releases. Experience with large systems indicates that point releases occur at six-week intervals. Figs. 14 and 15 show releases of the four versions of the above-mentioned program.

A release contains both design corrections and new features. Versions remain active (i.e., are updated with releases) for approximately four years. During this period releases to these versions occur at approximately the following intervals:
1) three-month interval for first six months,
2) six-month interval for next eighteen months,
3) one-year interval for next two years.

Controlling, approving and monitoring software fixes to a commercially released program is an important aspect of design maintenance. This function is most efficiently performed by a review group consisting of members who are close to both technical detail and management philosophies. Design maintenance supervisors are excellent candidates for this group. This group both schedules manpower to resolve software bugs and ensures that reported problems are not enhancements to the original software specification.

The above controls are strictly enforced for noncritical problems. These controls must be relaxed when serious service affecting software problems are suspected to be in a released program. To resolve these problems in large software/hardware systems a specially trained team (called an Attack Team) must be established. This group of specialists is given specific, system level, training aimed at quickly resolving complex problems which exist in an on-line site.

Program Modifications After Commercial Release

As was mentioned earlier, more development effort is spent in the 10 years following a development than during the initial development. This characteristic does not seem to be particular to a specific application or to a specific design approach. Programs require extensive maintenance after the first commercial release for four reasons.

1) *Changes in Man/Machine Requirements:* After a program reaches the field, customers find more effective ways to interface with the program—either for maintenance or operational changes.

2) *Small Feature Additions and Enhancements:* As a program matures in the field, potential customers require added small features or enhancements to meet their specific environment. Since this activity is necessary for continued sales it is considered part of design maintenance.

3) *Latent Software Bugs:* No matter how carefully a program is tested prior to the first commercial release, a significant number of software bugs will be found in large real-time programs as the program faces different user environments.

4) *Induced Bugs:* New software which enters the field always contains new bugs. Analyzing the source of software bugs found in a commercial program indicates that 50 percent have always been there, 6 percent are due to new features, 25 percent are generated by fixing other software problems, 19 percent are miscellaneous.

Fig. 16 shows the percentage of program modules which were modified for one of the above four reasons during the first two years after commercial introduction. Program *B* has seen 45 percent of its modules change during the first two years. This particular system has had few feature enhancements added to its base during its maintenance period. As can be seen in Fig. 16, module changes to program *B* are tending to level.

Program *A* has seen over 70 percent of its modules change during this same two year period. This program has encountered significant feature enhancements and has also enjoyed a large market—which has forced the addition of many small enhancements to meet customer requirements and has forced the program to face many different external environments.

Since many modules are being modified during the early

SYSTEM	NUMBER OF PATCHES	BAD CODE IN LAB	BAD CODE IN OFF-LINE SITE	BAD CODE IN ON-LINE SITE
A	550	23	7	4
B	475	20	-	8

SYSTEM	NUMBER OF PATCHES	BAD TEST PLAN IN LABS	BAD TEST PLAN IN OFF-LINE SITE	BAD TEST PLAN IN ON-LINE SITE
A	550	130	22	7
B	475	35	-	11

Fig. 17. Field statistics.

period of commercial availability, configuration management must enforce both tight control of software changes as well as extensive testing of these changes before they are released to the field.

The configuration management controls call for four levels of testing of all program modifications before they are released to the field in the form of a version. As shown in Fig. 15, these tests include:
1) original designer test (not in the chart),
2) evaluation test on laboratory model for five weeks,
3) field test on commercial off-line site for two weeks,
4) field test on commercial on-line site for two weeks.

Fig. 17 shows statistics indicating the number of program patches that were made to each of two different systems. These changes were sent to the field in the form of point releases. As can be seen in this figure, a formal test plan is required per software change. The figure also shows that all four levels of testing are required in order to achieve a program acceptable for field distribution. In Fig. 17 System *B* did not test patches at an off-line site. Because of this, eight coding problems were found at the on-line test site. System *A* did have an off-line test site where most of the software bugs were found and corrected. Since these statistics have been compiled a fifth level of cross-check has been added to the above process. This cross-check occurs after original designer testing. A separate group now visually inspects and approves all source updates and all test plans prior to initial evaluation testing. This group has been able to reduce the number of errors reaching evaluation testing by 40 percent.

Software Bugs Found During Design Maintenance Are Costly

Early phases of software debugging are aimed at finding simple bugs. Later stages of testing usually concentrate on the more complex problems. Code reading is an example of testing which is executed very early in the debugging phase—even prior to initial machine testing. The more complex software problems, however, usually show up during system testing or after the program has been placed into service. The development cost required to detect and resolve a software bug after it has been placed into service is thirty times larger than the cost required to detect and resolve a bug during the early "code reading" phase.

This large cost difference cannot be explained solely by the fact that the problems involved are of different complexity,

for if we compare the development cost required to solve problems of equal complexity—the difference is still fifteen to one. This concept points to the general management guideline that software bugs should be found at the earliest possible stage of testing in order to minimize overall development costs and development schedules. As shown in Fig. 13 it is more efficient to find and correct a simple coding mistake during early code reading than during machine test (by a factor of four to one) or during design maintenance (by a factor of fifteen to one).

Software bugs cost more to correct after a program has been released to the customer than during early phases of testing for the following reasons.

1) After commercial release—problems are usually more complex.

2) After commercial release—problems are reported as system malfunctions; an effort must be spent to translate problems into a software bug.

3) After commercial release—many problems are resolved by design maintenance programmers rather than the original designer. Design maintenance programmers must spend effort reviewing detailed code.

4) After commercial release—problems require more definition and more formal documentation. Formal test plans and multilevel testing must be performed to ensure that accurate corrections reach the field.

5) After commercial release—problem resolution must share the heavy overhead cost for configuration management.

Conclusion

Management of software development is progressing through a very rapid stage of maturity. As management becomes more experienced, complex software projects are being developed on schedule and within budget.

Although this paper does not concentrate on the similarities between managing hardware development and software development, experience is showing that the same management principles are applicable to both processes.

My experience in directing software-controlled systems has shown that there are many empirical management guidelines which seem to be applicable to most large projects.

These guidelines are as follows.

1) Management review of development progress will not ensure successful completion. Management must expect not to be told the complete story—especially in trouble areas. Thus, detailed technical cross-checks are necessary.

2) Pert-cost or any scheduling and control method should be used only as an aid to management. Far too often, management uses formal techniques as a substitute for "real" management. At best, techniques such as Pert tell only part of the story—usually the better part. However, if used properly, Pert-cost, or its equivalent, is a necessary management tool for controlling large software developments. Some form of formal scheduling is necessary even at the "segment" level.

3) Management cannot dictate unnatural schedules and expect a working, maintainable program to result. Poor programs are often a direct result of either inexperienced personnel or forced schedules.

4) Because the early phases of software development have no visible output except documentation, major milestones must be associated with a completed documentation package.

A defined milestone with no visible output is a useless milestone for management control. In order to ensure proper reviews, documentation required for each major milestone must be defined in detail before development starts.

5) Software development costs can be minimized by limiting the generation of technical documentation to that which will be maintained for the life of the software program (20 years).

Many development projects generate technical documents which are not maintained. These documents are not only expensive to generate but soon become useless and outdated, or even worse become dangerous, since they contain incorrect technical detail.

6) Once a program is working in the field, changes should never be made unless absolutely necessary. Arbitrary enhancements or modifications induce software bugs and thus should be avoided.

7) Software costs can be minimized by finding design bugs early in development. Using IBM's concept of "structured walk-through," most design bugs can be found prior to testing. The cost of software bugs increases significantly after a program responsibility passes from the initial designer to a design maintenance group.

A technical review of detailed code is required prior to machine testing. This review can be performed by the programmer's immediate supervisor, a chief programmer (if teams are employed), or by a small group of peer programmers.

8) Management should expect that 5 percent of all software development will not work at all and must be redesigned. It will be poorly documented and employ unacceptable design techniques. This fact will be true regardless of published standards and will result from a combination of poor supervision and programmers.

These unacceptable programs will not be detected by either management reviews or scheduling techniques such as Pert.

Management must therefore establish techniques (code reading and "structured walk-through") to find these "bad" programs before testing begins in order to ensure minimal effect on project schedules and development cost.

9) Management cannot assume that programmers know how to design software properly. Most inexperienced programmers tend to generate tricky, complex, tight, hard to understand, and poorly documented code.

Training programs as well as design and coding standards must be established and followed in order for the resultant program to be maintainable at a reasonable cost.

10) Design maintenance programmers require a higher level of experience than that required for original design. Historically, management tended to place less experienced programmers in design maintenance. This is a costly and dangerous mistake. Design maintenance groups should contain at least 30 percent senior programmers.

Hopefully the information contained in this paper will aid others in their attempt to establish management guidelines for large and small software controlled systems. However, as with all areas of management, there are no answers—only approaches—that work sometimes.

Edmund B. Daly received the B.S.E.E. and M.S.E.E. degrees in 1962 and 1963, respectively, from the University of Illinois, Urbana, and the B.A. and M.B.A. degrees in 1961 and 1969, respectively, from the University of Chicago, Chicago, Il.

He joined GTE Automatic Electric Laboratories in January 1963 where he worked in the Research Department for three years. From January 1966 until June 1969 he worked as a member of the Technical Staff for Bell Laboratories. He joined GTE Automatic Electric Laboratories in June 1969 where he has held the positions of Assistant to the Executive Director, Director–Advanced Development Laboratory, and Director–EAX Operations Laboratory. He has recently been appointed Executive Director–Electronic Switching. He has received one patent.

Mr. Daly is a member of Tau Beta Pi, Eta Kappa Nu, Sigma Tau, and Delta Epsilon Sigma.

The economics of software quality assurance

by DAVID S. ALBERTS
The Mitre Corporation
McLean, Virginia

ABSTRACT

This paper presents an examination into the economics of software quality assurance. An analysis of the software life-cycle is performed to determine where in the cycle the application of quality assurance techniques would be most beneficial. The number and types of errors occurring at various phases of the software life-cycle are estimated. A variety of approaches in increasing software quality (including Structured Programming, Top Down Design, Programmer Management Techniques and Automated Tools) are reviewed and their potential impact on quality and costs are examined.

INTRODUCTION

Current realities of large scale computer systems have provided the impetus to undertake this examination into the need for and potential of a quality assurance program. Proponents of quality assurance claim that significant savings in both cost and time can be achieved in addition to improved system performance if a quality assurance program is implemented. The purpose of this paper is to examine these claims by addressing the economics of software quality assurance. Software rather than hardware is the subject of the analysis since the costs of software have far outstripped the costs of hardware and the trend seems to be continuing in this direction (Figure 1).

The stakes involved are high. Estimates of recent Air Force annual expenditures on software are over $1 Billion.[5,6] WWMCCS alone was estimated to involve $3/4 Billion for software (about 10 times its hardware costs),[2] while major software systems also run into hundreds of millions of dollars (IBM OS/360 $200M,[11] SAGE $250M[11] and NASA manned space program $1B[12]). Indirect costs must be added to these huge sums and are by no means trivial in of themselves. For example, software delays often cause delays in reaching the operational phase of a system's life. A 6-month delay (considered almost on-time) translates into a $100M loss of services, based upon a projected 7 year operational life and a $1.4 billion project.

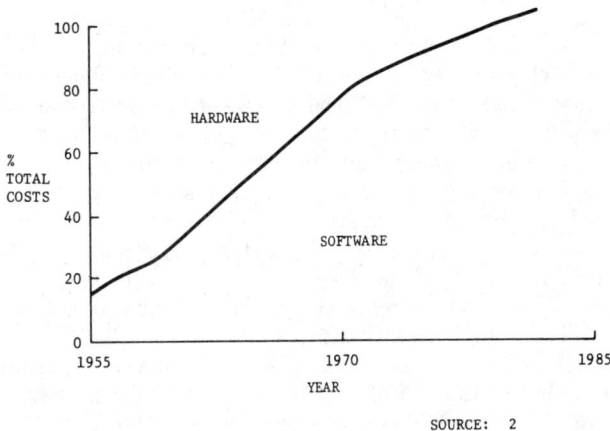

Figure 1—Importance of controlling the cost/effectiveness of S/W

The actions which could be undertaken under the umbrella of a quality assurance plan are quite diverse; so diverse that it is difficult to separate these actions from project management. However, quality assurance is only one aspect of project management. First this analysis addresses the software life cycle and the relative cost on each portion of the cycle. Next productivity is considered insofar as the reduction in errors in each portion of the cycle impacts cost. Finally a variety of methods, techniques and tools which can directly affect the error rate/severity experienced will be examined.

Two questions drive this analysis. First, can QA work? and second, Is it worth it? This paper brings together the experiences and thoughts currently in circulation and forms these into an analysis of the issues involved and presents composite estimates of the potential target of quality assurance (cost of error) and the reported experience of quality assurance programs and methods currently available. Because of the difficulty in separating QA methods from project management and the absence of good cost accounting standards, the costs of a quality assurance program are not explicitly treated in this paper.

PHASES OF THE SOFTWARE LIFE CYCLE

To ensure a complete and systematic review of the potential for a QA plan, each aspect of the software "life cycle" will be examined to determine at what point QA can support substantial improvements. Both direct and indirect costs will be considered.

Direct costs are those associated with the actual performance of the particular phase of the software life cycle under consideration while indirect costs include schedule slippages, system degradation, and errors which contribute or add to the cost of subsequent stages in the process. The software life cycle can be broken down into four phases: Conceptual, Requirement, Development and Operations. While other authors have broken this cycle down somewhat differently, either by separating *Development* into two or more separate phases or by extending *Requirements* to include part of the development phase, the categorization shown here more closely corresponds to distinct levels of effort or expenditures.

After a brief qualitative discussion of the potential role of QA in each of the four phases of the software life cycle, the amount of time and relative costs incurred in the performance of each of these phases will be reviewed. Available data on contributions of errors to cost and delay is examined later.

The conceptual phase

This phase begins with the recognition of a need for the system. The feasibility and general worthiness of a proposed system is addressed. Usually a management decision is required to move into the next phase which involves more detailed specifications of performance characteristics. This phase is typified by numerous briefings designed to establish a recognized need for and cost effectiveness of the system vis-a-vis organizational missions and functions. Order of magnitude cost figures are the typical modus operandi.

This phase has a relatively low contribution to total cost and may last several years. The question of *software* quality assurance is essentially moot throughout this phase of the life cycle. However, the role of software as it may interface with hardware, and gross estimates of costs and schedules should be reviewed as part of a larger quality assurance effort.

Failure to adequately address these issues could result in having to incorporate into the software development functions or design features which could have been accomplished better in other ways and which restrict flexibility or increase the complexity of the software.

The requirements phase

This phase of the software life cycle refines the conceptual system, further delineating the functions and interplay between hardware, software and the user. In general, data inputs and system outputs are specified and overall load and performance characteristics are determined. In many cases, specific determinations of system hardware and user-oriented languages are made. A properly designed Request for Proposal (RFP), even if the system is to be done in-house (this step in the design process is skipped only at considerable risk), treads a thin line between over-specification and insufficient detail. The former is often caused by past contractor failures while the latter is a reflection of the fact that the user simply does not know what he really wants or needs.

To a large extent, the "die is cast" with the issuance of an RFP (or corresponding internal document). The constraints placed on system performance, hardware and software at this early stage of the life cycle can have enormous repercussions on the flexibility, reliability, maintainability and cost of the system. Implicit trade-offs between system throughput and ease and cost of use, enhancement and maintenance are often made.

Realistically one cannot expect a prospective vendor to do the necessary work required to examine and weigh each of the possible solutions to the design problem. Even with the most competent of vendors, their objective function differs from the clients. Specifically, a vendor's staff may have certain backgrounds and expertise, or his equipment characteristics more adaptable to one family of solutions than another. To save time or money a vendor may modify an already developed product or assemble a patch work of available system modules rather than seek an "optimal" solution.

Thus, quality assurance cannot begin any later than this phase without considerable risk. The phases which follow are characterized by much higher expenditures than these first two phases, with the obvious result that errors carried forward from this point are very costly.

The development phase

This phase is a transitional one bridging the gap between a well defined concept and an implementable system. The big black box between inputs and outputs has to be broken down into programmable units, logic determined and finally coded. The testing and validation tasks require the generation of test data and test parameters and the development of test tools. Documentation provides the vital link to connect the test activities to the designers, programmers and coders.

It is during this stage that a QA activity reaches its peak, for with increasing detail and concreteness comes the need for constant monitoring to assure that the system in reality is the system in concept. Quality assurance in this phase is simultaneously concerned with the correctness of (1) functional requirements, (2) detailed design, (3) program logic, and (4) code. In addition, the specificity and clarity of the documentation is also a proper subject of a QA plan. The testing and validation of the system or the "quality control" function is the most viable aspect of a quality assurance plan. For many developers, all too often, it *is* the QA plan. This tendency is to become lost in code is at the risk of deviations from intended system functions. Correctness of code is not a guarantee that the code is doing what the user required, but rather that is doing what it was designed to do; quite a different matter. Errors in design are far more perfidious than errors in logic.

The operations phase

This phase bridges the gap between the developers and the users. If QA proponents are correct, some payoff attributed to QA should be noticed during the implementation part of this phase, but its greatest contribution will appear during the productive part of the life cycle which is oddly called "maintenance." This terminology may be an indication of the general lack of quality assurance which exists.

More often than expected, the implementation period becomes a "field test" with the essential aspects of the development phase extending far into the operations phase. Design or even worse functional errors are frequently uncovered which may require extensive re-programming. The start of implementation is often merely an artificial contrivance to cover a scheduled deadline rather than at the completion of the development phase.

THE SHAPE OF THE SOFTWARE LIFE CYCLE

To place the various aspects of the quality assurance function into perspective, it is necessary to look at the relative costs and time requirements of each of the phases described in the previous section. Figure 2 represents the idealized shape of the software life cycle.[28,13,38,39,10,45] While actual project experience is difficult to come by, a search of the literature for real-world cost and time data has been sufficiently productive to enable the construction of a composite software life cycle. This composite was developed from bits and pieces of available information on different phases and parts of phases of large systems. The degree of consistency found among projects gives rise to a fair degree of confidence that this composite is a useful tool in obtaining estimates of the potential benefits of a QA plan. Using the composite life cycle concept, this section relates the time required for accomplishing each portion of the cycle to software costs expended.

The time axis

The percentages of time thought to be denoted to each phase of the software life cycle as implied by the shape of the idealized curve are as follows: Conceptual 15%, Requirements 8%, Development 40%, and Operations 37%. This differed from the reported experience of several large DoD projects.[33] In actual practice the conceptual phase accounted for 30% rather than 15%, while development took only 12% (compared to 40%). The requirement phase accounted for the same percentage of time in actual practice as was expected, while the operations phase (implementation and maintenance) lasted longer in actual practice (50%) than is implied by the curve (37%).

In absolute terms, these projects spanned 16 years from inception to termination. The percentages translate into a conceptual phase of 4½-5 years; a requirements phase of about 1.5 years (these two were actually performed simultaneously for about 6 months); 2 years for development and 8 years for operations. The requirements phase consists of the preparation of specifications, drafting an RFP and the evaluation and selection of a vendor. About half (3½% of Total Life Cycle Time) the time was devoted to specifications. The RFP's took slightly less (2½% TLCT) with about 4-5 months (2%) devoted to review, evaluation and selection. The components of the development phase (2 years) are more difficult to characterize by time, since the steps within are either overlapping (requirements analysis and design) or simultaneous (code, test, document).

Relative cost of software life cycle phases

The relative costs of each of the four phases of the software life cycle can also be inferred from the shape of curve presented in Figure 2. To verify these inferences, data from several studies are pieced together and a composite software life cycle (Figure 4) is constructed and presented in a following section. The shape is compared to the idealized versions found in the literature. It should be remembered that the purpose in developing this composite is to obtain estimates of the relative costs of each phase to use in the determination of the potential effects of instituting various

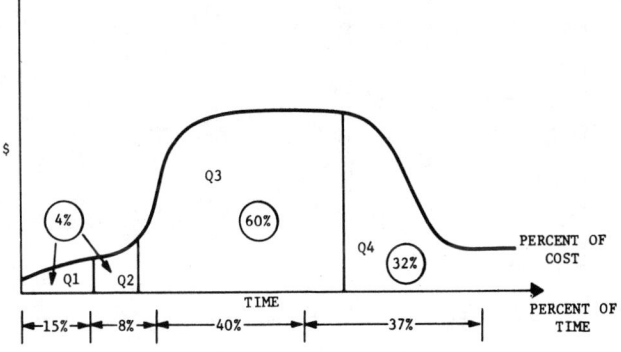

Figure 2—Idealized software life-cycle

forms of quality assurance. Therefore, the cost balance between development and maintenance as well as among steps in the development phase were of greatest concern.

Operations vs. development

The balance between development and operation depends primarily upon the length of the maintenance period used in the calculations. To standardize these calculations for comparison purposes a maintenance time period equal to 50% of the total life cycle (or 8 yrs) will be used. A study[9] which monitored costs fairly closely from requirements through *one year* of maintenance reported expenditures (in terms of man years) for Requirements, Development and Operations.

These figures were weighted (3 for management; 2 for programmer and 1 for staff support) to determine costs incurred. Assuming a negligible cost for the conceptual phase, say 1% and an operational life of 8 years, the percentage of total costs incurred by each of the four phases of the life cycle were calculated as follows: Requirements 1.5%, Development 51.3% and Operations 46.2%. The ratio of Development to Operations (Implementation and Maintenance) in this case would be 1 to 1.1.

Implementation is difficult to separate from development and maintenance since it in reality is a transitional period between the two. For this reason data about implementation is hard to find and interpret. This being the case the remainder of this paper treats operations as essentially equivalent to maintenance.

A look at cost data available for development vs. maintenance costs for OS releases 18, 19, and 20.0[13] are even more heavily weighted toward maintenance with ratios of 3 to 1 for OS 18 with only two years of maintenance included and 1.25 to 1 for all three releases with only one year of maintenance included. The experiences reported on in this section with respect to the balance between development and maintenance costs show that the costs of maintenance consistently exceed costs of development. Since QA would be expected to have the greatest impact upon costs in the operations phase, a conservative cost equation (conceptual cost+requirements cost+development cost=operations cost) will be used to *minimize* the estimated potential for QA.

Relative costs within the development phase

The activities undertaken during the development phase can be grouped into (1) analysis and design, (2) coding and debugging and (3) testing or validation.

The ratio of the cost of these activities to one another is often thought to be a function of the complexity of the system to be developed. That is, a non-linear

	Analysis and Design	*Coding and Debugging*	*Validation*
SAGE	39%	14%	47%
NTDS	30%	20%	50%
GEMINI	36%	17%	47%
SATURN V	32%	24%	44%
OS/360	33%	17%	50%
AVERAGE	34%	18%	48%

SOURCE: 14

Figure 3—Breakdown of development costs for selected systems

(exponential) relationship is said to exist between complexity and the cost of testing. Testing costs are highly related to the number and severity of errors to be discovered and fixed, the number of which is related to system complexity. Proponents of QA will argue that this exponential relationship need not be the case if proper management (including a good QA plan) is exercised. Since the success of QA is directly related to error rates and error rates are the underlying causes of the cost relationships among the activities undertaken during development, this section will concentrate on the ratio of testing (or validation) to the total of development costs.

A study[8] which looked at the relative costs of design, coding and debugging in relationship to validation reported that the ratio of validation (testing) costs to the total development effort ran between ⅓ to ½.

Figure 3 gives a breakdown of the development phases of five large projects. The results[14] are very consistent from project to project and in the range of the results of the first study referenced. The range ⅓-½ also includes the experience from ALPHA-6[9] reported on earlier in this chapter.

A composite software life cycle, based upon a 16 year length (50% operational life) and the relative costs for the four phases given in Figure 3, is presented in Figure 4. The shape is far more leptokurtic than the

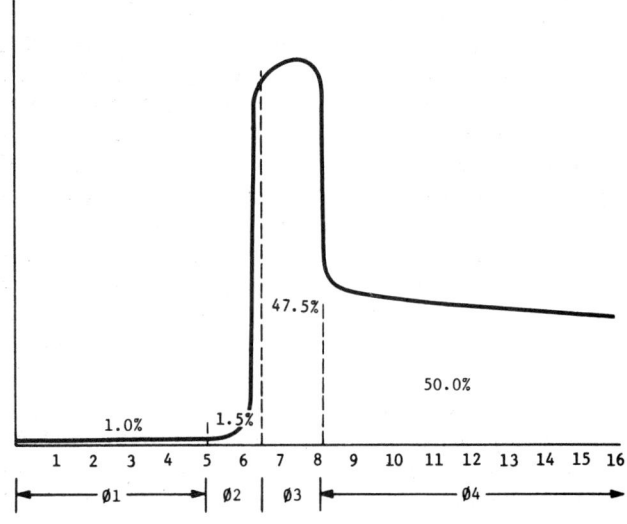

Figure 4—Composite software life-cycle

"idealized" curves found in the literature with the length of the maintenance tail spreading its significant costs over many years. This is due in larger part to a contraction of the development phase. The visual impact of the meager resources applied to the Requirement phase also represents a departure from the idealized shape.

THE COST OF ERROR

A measure of system quality is the number of errors which occur. Hence, ratios of one kind of error to another have been proposed[22] as indicators of quality software. It is taken on faith that well designed systems can be put together with little resultant error, and for those errors which occur, the mean age of the errors becomes a vital statistic with which to judge software.

This section is devoted to estimating the source, kind, type and severity of errors generated during development. It would be of interest to examine the requirements stage to place a value on the "errors" which originate there and trace their impact throughout the rest of the life cycle; but aside from intuitive feelings about their impact no real data appears to be available.

Frequency and severity of errors

No two researchers group errors in quite the same way. As a result, the available information on software errors had to be interpreted and classified based upon the explanations provided in individual studies. Errors are classified in this paper as either design, logic or syntax. These categories are sufficient for the purpose at hand. Design errors are those which require changes in the specifications used by the programmers. Usually they represent a lack of understanding (or proper communication) of a computation or process, which results in the wrong "problem" being solved. Logic errors occur when the system design is translated into programmable form (detailed flow charts). Syntax errors are self-explanatory. Few of the studies of software errors present actual data pertaining to frequency and severity. Taken together[1,4,6,8,47] those that present some data all report design error as occurring most frequently. Ranging from a high of 64%[1] to 46%.[6] Syntax errors were reported to be about 15% of the known errors. Logic errors ranged from 21% to 38%. The significant point to note is the large percentage of design errors.

Available data on cost of detection and correction reveals that design errors cost the most to diagnose and fix. Syntax errors are reported to be more of a nuisance than a significant cost particularly with the use of automated precompiler processing.

Origin and detection of errors

Where errors originate as well as when and how they are discovered are important inputs to the design of an effective QA plan. Syntax errors originate, surface and are resolved within a brief period of time and for all intents and purposes can be considered totally encompassed within the process of coding. Such is not the case with design and logic errors. Design errors can be caught during a design review (if there is one), during preparation of detailed flow charts or occasionally during coding. Simple logic errors (process before read) can be caught at compilation time or during program testing. Because of the numerous paths in any program which can be tested many logic errors are not observed until the validation, implementation or maintenance stages. A study of a large software development effort[1] found that 54% of the errors were not caught until acceptance testing or presumably until after development was complete. To make matters worse, the overwhelming proportion of these were design errors. Reported figures indicated that 70% of the design errors were not caught at earlier stages while by contrast 80% of the programming or logic errors were caught during development. If the mean age of error were calculated for this case it would be quite high due to the high percentage of design errors involved.

Estimation of the costs of errors

Using the three categories of error (design, logic and syntax) it appears that design errors account for at least 80% of the *total cost of error*. This percentage is arrived at by noting that about $2/3$ of all errors caught are design errors; with logic and syntax errors making up about equal proportions of the remaining $1/3$. Compared to the cost of tracking down and correcting coding errors, the cost of syntax mishaps is small. However, the cost of design errors is more than double ($2\frac{1}{2}$ times) that of coding error. The calculation of the contribution of design error to the total cost of error consists of taking the weighted (expected) cost of an error [% design errors $\times 2\frac{1}{2}$ + % coding+syntax errors $\times 1$] and dividing it into the contribution of design [% design $\times 2\frac{1}{2}$] using the percentage given above $83\frac{1}{3}$% of the total cost of error can be attributed to design errors. This relatively large contribution to total error cost should play an important role in the design of a QA plan and will be used as an input in the calculation of the potential effectiveness of quality assurance.

The next calculation which is required for the assessment of the potential of quality assurance is the percentage of total life cycle cost which can be attributed to error. Once this percentage is obtained, an estimate of the benefits of a QA plan can be developed based on a "tool by tool" analysis of the kind of error it addresses (design, logic or syntax) and the percent error reduction claimed or experienced. These calculated benefits can then be compared to the cost associated with these components of a QA plan for a final assessment of the economics of quality assurance.

To estimate the cost of error the following method was used. For a slightly conservative estimate, it was assumed that (i) all costs in design (ii) coding and (iii) documentation to be non-error related. All checkout and validation costs (recognizing that only some of these costs can be reduced by reducing the number of errors, since some costs are fixed) were attributed to error. From the ALPHA-6 data then 47% of development cost (assuming the code, test, and document costs were equal) could be traced to errors. Further data on developments costs for several large systems (given in Figure 3) averaged almost exactly the same percentage (48%).

Maintenance costs can be attributed to correcting errors and to enhancements, but "enhancements" often result from initial design errors. For the sake of discussion assume that half can be directly related to error. This amounts to the conservative estimate of almost half of the total life cycle costs (47.6%) being directly tied to error (see Figure 5). On the cost basis of a large system, the total cost of error is in the hundreds of millions. If quality assurance methods can reduce error by even small amounts, they would appear to be worthy of serious consideration. For example, a 10% reduction in error (2/3 Design, 1/3 logic and syntax) as they have been reported in the studies reviewed would represent a saving of almost $25 million based upon a relatively large effort (cost= $1/2 billion over the 16 year cycle). A five percentage error reduction (only 1/2 design) would result in a savings of over $10 million.

THE EFFECTIVENESS OF THE TECHNIQUES AND TOOLS OF QUALITY ASSURANCE

The assurance of quality can be brought about by any number of different approaches which have been suggested. These range from essentially project management techniques to methodologies of design to syntax checking tools. Many of the methods which will be discussed in this section can be expected to have a much broader impact on design, development and implementation than is pertinent to a discussion of quality assurance. This section will address the impact these methods have on error rate and error-related productivity.

In some cases, their contribution to quality is rather straightforward, particularly for error detection tools. However, for those which promise the most sweeping reforms, essentially those dealing with management or design effectiveness, measurement is difficult and little concrete information is available.

It is the purpose of this section to analyze based upon available data the potential of quality assurance in terms of the cost of error, development productivity and the cost of quality assurance. In the following paragraphs, some of the most widely discussed techniques and tools will be reviewed.

Structured programming

The advantages touted for Structured Programs range from improved program design to improved documentation. Improved design is linked to fewer design errors and fewer logic/programming errors. Fewer statement types are linked to fewer syntax errors and an almost self-documenting program. Fewer errors imply greater productivity during development and reduced operations costs. Further, the streamlined design is claimed to be easier to upgrade and enhance. Finally, the planning and conceptualization required by Structured Programming is said to enhance the performance of project management.

Reported increases in error free productivity ranged from 50%[25] to 125%[47] with the introduction of Structured Programming while error reductions of between 30%-90% were reported by another study.[17] Quantitative results of ease of enhancements were not found, however, a study of the development cycle[56] estimated 25% reduction in the elapsed time from requirements to implementation, from 6 years to 4.5 years.

Top-down development

The essence of Top-Down Development is simultaneous systems integration and development which results in a viable, executable, if rather skeletal system at an early state. This development approach amounts to an ordering of the sequence of system decomposition decisions beginning with a simple description of the entire system or process and continuing with successive refinements until a programmable design is reached. Top-Down Development is a natural companion of Structured Programming, so much so that

Error Type	% Total Errors	Relative Severity	% Total Cost of Error
Design	2/3	2.5	83+%
Logic	1/6	1.0	8+%
Syntax	1/6	1.0	8+%
	Development Phase	Operations Phase	Both
% Total Life Cycle Cost	47.5%	50%	97.5%
% Cost Due to Error	48%	50%	—
% Total Life Cycle Cost Attributed to Error	22.6%	25%	47.6%

Figure 5—Error and software life cycle costs

the two concepts are often confused. The claimed advantages of this approach include the increased ease of implementing a QA plan with a resultant reduction in design error and productivity improvements associated with the systems integration and testing efforts during the development phase.

Perhaps the most significant advantage claimed from a QA perspective, is the early existence of a complete system's design replete with the design specification of system components and interfaces. Not only does such a document enhance the changes of a coherent and consistent design, but it also serves as a vehicle for establishing a correspondence with "user" oriented functional specs. The system components are placed into perspective for all to see and comment upon. Misunderstandings that often were not surfaced until acceptance testing can be resolved at this time. Design problems often not found until systems integration may be corrected reducing the high cost currently associated with these problems.

The incorporation of the testing function throughout development, made possible by the continual existence of a testable system, offers QA with an opportunity to be more of a pro-active force in development.

There are recognized pitfalls as well. Care must be taken to ensure design feasibility in terms of existing software and hardware, since actual coding is significantly delayed.

Holistic design is difficult to achieve and false starts are likely. However, when weighted against the known shortcomings of bottom-up design there is little question that a Top Down approach when combined with some common sense offers substantial advantages to both developer and user.

Hard estimates of the reduction in error and increases in productivity from the use of this approach alone are not readily available. However, when used in conjunction with Structural Programming and a Development Support Library,[25] a productivity improvement of over 300% (when compared to a system using a Development Support Library alone) was experienced. With Structural Programming alone, productivity gains of 50%-100% were experienced; thus, the addition of a Top Down Design approach seems to further enhance performance significantly.

For the purposes of this analysis, the expected performance of this approach will be conservatively bounded from above. In terms of development productivity, a very conservative range which includes gains made by reduced systems integration and testing, and by better manpower and computer time scheduling would be between a 5-10% improvement in productivity. This improvement could be reasonably expected from the savings in the integration step alone.

As far as design errors are concerned, the increased attention to overall design could be expected to reduce configuration and architecture errors significantly and virtually eliminate errors in the specification of offered system functions. One study[6] showed that machine configuration and architecture errors accounted for just over 20% of all design errors while errors in the functions offered accounted for about 25% of the design erorrs. Both are susceptible to being caught early. An examination of specs by others not involved in their formulation resulted in the detection of between 30%-40% of these errors. An increase from this to a 50% rate of error detection might realistically be achieved by the use of Top Down Design.

Other recent innovations

In addition to Structured Programming and Top Down Development, a number of other approaches to improving software quality and productivity have been advanced. Among these are the techniques of the Chief Programmer Teams, Egoless Programming, and automatic or semi-automatic tools ranging from Design Assertion Consistency Checkers to Automated Test Case Generators.

The management oriented techniques are aimed at achieving increased communications and coordination while the automated tools seek to provide complete, systematic and low cost verification. This section will briefly explain some of these innovations concentrating on the contribution or impact likely on the performance of the QA functions.

Programming organizations

In this section, the effects of the Chief Programmer Team, Egoless Programming and Democratic Team Organization on the performance of the QA function will be addressed. Egoless Programming and Democratic Teams are essentially loosely structured programming environments in direct contrast to the Chief Programmer approach which is highly structured. It is interesting that the changes from current practice being advanced to improve software quality are in opposite directions. Both approaches, however, take aim at the individualist who becomes ego-involved with code to the extent that error detection is thwarted. The loosely structured approaches attack this problem directly by eliminating "ownership" of code to reduce defensiveness. The Chief Programmer Team approach is meant to be employed in conjunction with Structured Programming and Top Down Design which systematically eliminates tricks and gimmicks in programming and imposes ridged forms. Users of both types of approaches claim better communication leading to reduced misunderstandings and error rates. On the one hand, the Chief Programmer Team approach is criticized for being too authoritarian while the other approaches are said to tend to alleviate the individualist and require more sophisticated management techniques. Experience indicates that managing bright

Error Type	Methods of Detection			
	Manual Inspection	Formal Methods (Simulation, etc.)	Tests Runs	
Design	45%	20%	35%	100%
Logic/Coding	24%	22%	54%	100%

Figure 6—Error detection for design and logic/coding error types

creative staff is no mean task regardless of the techniques employed. The key seems to be in the actions taken to increase the understanding and clarity of assignments not in what abstract management philosophy is employed.

Automated tools for quality asssurance

The literature contains countless tools developed to check out design, flow charts, code and even documentation systematically and quickly. Their performance can more easily be measured than the techniques previously discussed, but their contribution to the potential of an overall QA plan is limited. Their very nature (highly specified and deterministic) limits their effectiveness in dealing with other than highly structured situations. Thus, these tools are most applicable to the detection of errors in code and simple sorts of logic errors rather than major flaws in program logic or design approach. Nevertheless, they can significantly contribute to increased productivity, earlier detection and hence some reduction of the "ripple" effect (19% of the errors introduced as a result of error correction[55]). An analysis of error types and means of detection[6] showed that (See Figure 6) manual inspection uncovered only 24% of logic and coding errors compared to 45% of design errors indicating the potential for the use of automated tools. Such tools could have an impact in reducing the percentage of logic and coding errors (54%) not caught until testing. One study gave evidence to support this feeling[21]. The use of automated instruction and path checkers (ASSIST and NODAL) reportedly catch between 67%-100% of the errors and at between 2-5 months earlier than they would have otherwise been detected. Automated error checking is currently at the state of development where it is either language or application specific and it would probably be of marginal value to develop such a tool for a specific project.

Figure 7 summarizes the results with respect to the reported effectiveness of quality assurance methods and shows the dollar impact that improvements in development productivity can have based upon a project whose total life cycle costs equal $.5 billion.

SUMMARY AND CONCLUSIONS

This section places the relevant estimates developed during this report in perspective and highlights important aspects in the assessment of the economics of Software Quality Assurance. This paper first addressed the software life cycle to identify the areas which could be improved by a QA plan. Second, an examination of the frequency of software error, its sources or origins, methods of detection and associated costs was presented. This was followed by an examination of some of the methods and techniques suggested for quality assurance. Highlights of these examinations and analyses follow.

Summary of findings

The examination of the software life cycle revealed that costs were concentrated in the Development and Operations phases. The typical Development Phase accounted for just under 50% of the total costs while lasting about 2 years (12% of a 16 yr. cycle). About half of the development costs were spent on check-out and testing activities in contrast to about ⅓ for analysis and design and ⅙ for actual coding. The Operations phase while consuming just under 50% of the total life cycle costs was spread over an eight year period.

Errors were classified into three types (design, programming/logic, syntax). The last accounting for some 15% of all errors. Design errors outpaced program/logic errors by a little less than 2 to 1 accounting for a little more than half of all errors. Program/logic errors ran about one-third of the total.

The severity of errors, as measured by the cost of detection and correction, was found to be higher for

Technique	Error Reduction	Productivity		$ Impact of 1% Improvement In Development	Potential Impact
		Range	Mid-Point		
Structured Programming	30-90%	50%-100+%	75%		$175 Million
Top-Down Design	Substantial	10%-200%	100%		$250 Million
Management Organization	—	—	—	$2,375,000	—
Automated Tools	Caught earlier	Up to 25%	10%		$ 25 Million

Figure 7—Performance of quality assurance techniques

design errors than program/logic or syntax errors (least costly). Weighted by costs it was calculated that design errors accounted for just over 80% of the total cost of error. In terms of the total software life cycle then, with 47.5% of its costs in development and 50% in maintenance, the cost of error could easily run over 50% of the total software life cycle cost.

To combat error and improve software quality a variety of methods have been suggested. Preliminary reports have been encouraging in both the areas of productivity improvement and error reduction.

Conclusions

While the data drawn upon comes from a large variety of sources (different systems, different environments and from studies using different definitions and analysis methodologies), the experiences reported were so compatible that, while more detailed data is necessary for the actual development of a QA plan specific to a given set of system and organizational circumstances, the conclusion that QA can be cost effective is inescapable.

From the analysis presented in this paper, the development of a QA plan should concentrate on techniques and methods for the early detection and elimination of design errors. The researchers reporting on the development of ALPHA-6[9] indicated that if more resources were applied during design, it would have resulted in substantial savings in the costs of testing and maintenance. An extrapolation of the data they presented gives a multiplicative factor of 5; that is, a dollar more spent in design would have saved 5 dollars spent on testing and maintenance. While this example may be unusual, it, together with the fact that a significant portion of total system cost can be attributed to error point to the cost impact that a QA function can provide.

A parameterization of the impact that error and productivity improvements have on total software system costs based upon a $½ billion total life cycle cost (about $250 million for S/W Development) has been made. For each 1% of error reduction (½ coding + ½ design) a savings of just over $1½ million could be expected. For each 1% improvement in Development productivity a saving of $2,375,000 could be expected. It should be noted that Design errors have more than double the impact than do coding errors.

Thus the leverage of QA in large programs is significantly high to warrant serious consideration. The costs of developing and implementing a QA plan are difficult to specify for a given organization, especially in light of their management considerations. However, even with the additional expense QA still promises to be cost-effective. For example, if management overhead for software development is approximately 5% of development costs and a QA plan increased this overhead by ¼, then a reduction of error by approximately 1% (coding) alone could offset these additional costs.

REFERENCES

1. Boehm, B. W., et al, "Some Experince With Automated Aids to the Design of Large-Scale Reliable Software," *IEEE Transactions on S/W*, TRW, March 1975.
2. Boehm, B. W., "Software and Its Impact—A Quantitative Assessment," *Datamation*, TRW, May 1973.
3. Brown, J. R., et al, "Evaluating the Effectiveness of Software Verification—Practical Experience With an Automated Tool," *AFIPS Fall Joint Computer Conference*, December 1972.
4. Shooman, M. L., et al, "Types, Distribution, and Test and Correction Times for Programming Errors," *IEEE Transactions*, Bell Labs, March 1975.
5. Schneidewind, N. F., "Analysis of Error Processes in Computer Software," *IEEE Transactions*, Naval Postgraduate School, March 1975.
6. Endres, A., "An Analysis of Errors and Their Causes in System Programs," *IEEE Transactions*, IBM Lab, Germany, March 1975.
7. Rubey, R. J., et al, *Comparative Evaluation of PL/1*, USAF ESD-TR-68-150, April 1968.
8. Rubey, R. J., "Quantitative Aspects of Software Validation," *IEEE Transactions*, LOGICON, March 1975.
9. Buda, A. O., et al, "Implementation of the ALPHA-6 Programming System, IEEE Transactions," *Academy of Sciences* USSR, March 1975.
10. Ramamoorthy, C. V., et al, "Testing Large Software Evaluation Systems," *IEEE Transactions*, CSD, ERL, University of California, Berkeley, March 1975.
11. Alexander, T., "Computers Can't Solve Everything," *Fortune*, May 1969.
12. Boehm, B. W., "System Design," *Planning Community Information Utilities* (ED) H. Sackman, AFIPS Press, 1972.
13. Barry, B., et al, *Software Life Cycle Considerations*, IBM, January 1974.
14. Boehm, B. W., "Some Information Processing Implications of Air Force Space Missions: 1970-1980," *Astronautics and Aeronautics*, January 1971.
15. Vick, C. R., *Specification for Reliable Software*, EASCON, 1974.
16. Brown, J. R., et al, "Evaluating the Effectiveness of Software Verification—Practical Experience with an Automated Tool," *AFIPS Conf.*, 1972.
17. Cammack, W. B., et al, *Improving the Programming Process*, IBM SDD TR002483, October 1973.
18. Cheng, L. and J. E. Sullivan, *Case Studies in Software Design*, MTR-2874, Volume I, June 1974.
19. Boden, W. H., "Designing for LCC," *EASCON 74*, pp. 624-29.
20. Knight, C. R., "Warranties as a Life-Cycle-Cost Management Tool," *EASCON 74*, pp. 621-623.
21. Mangold, E. R., "Software Error Analysis and Software Policy Implications," *EASCON 74*, pp. 123-27.
22. Mills, H. D., "How to Buy Quality Software," *EASCON 74*, pp. 120-22.
23. Nashman, A. E., "Software Development Management: The Key to Quality Software Products," *EASON 74*, pp. 31-35.
24. Oliver, P., "Observations on Software Reliability," *EASCON 74*, pp. 126-29.
25. Baker, F. T., "Structured Programming in a Production Programming Environment," *IEEE Transactions on S/W Rel.* 75, pp. 172-185.
26. Rain, M., *Two Unusual Methods for Debugging S/W Software Practice and Experience* 3, pp. 61-63.

27. Katzenelson, J., *Documentation and Management of Software Project*, SP & E 1, 2, pp. 147-157.
28. Peadi, P., *Quality Control for Computer Programming: A Final Report on an Initial Study*, SDC, Santa Monica, California, September 1965.
29. ———, *QC for Systems and Programming, A Survey of the Literature*, SDC, March 1965.
30. Connolly, J. T., *Software Acquisition Management Guidebook: Regulation, Specifications and Standards*, MTR-3080, The MITRE Corporation, June 1975.
31. Clapp, J. A., *Major Contributions to Software Engineering in the 1980's*, MTR-2791, The MITRE Corporation, January 1974.
32. ———, *A Software Error Classification Methodology*, MTR-2648, Volume VII, The MITRE Corporation, June 1973.
33. Reifer, D. J., "Automated Aids for Reliable Software," *IEEE Transactions on S/W Reliability*, March 1975, pp. 131-42.
34. Wulf, W. A., "Reliable Hardware-Software Architecture," *IEEE Transactions on Software Reliability*, March 1975, pp. 122-30.
35. Cicu, A., et al, "Organizing Tests During Software Evolution," *IEEE Transaction on Software Reliability*, March 1975, pp. 43-50.
36. Williams, R. D., "Managing the Development of Reliable Software," *IEEE Transactions on Software Reliability*, March 1975, pp. 43-50.
36. Williams, R. D., "Managing the Development of Reliable Software," *IEEE Transactions on Software Reliability*, March 1975, pp. 3-8.
37. Ceoff, N. S., "Development Project Costs," *Journal of Systems Management*, September 1974, pp. 14-17.
38. Aron, J. D., *Characteristics of the Program System Development Life-Cycle*, IBM FSD 74-0180.
39. Pietrasanta, A. M., "Resource Analysis of Computer Program System Development," *On The Management of Computer Programming*, G. F. Weinwurm, (Editor): Auerbach Publishers, 1970.
40. Brooks, F. P., Jr., "Why is Software Late," *Data Management*, Volume 9/8, August 1971.
41. Clapp, J. A. and J. E. Sullivan, *SIMON: Finding the Answers to Software Development Problems*, MTP-159, The MITRE Corporation, May 1974.
42. Cheng, L. L., *Some Case Studies in Structured Programming*, MTR-2648, Volume VI, The MITRE Corporation, June 1973.
43. Fleischer, R. J., *Effects of Management Philosophy on Software Production*, MTR-2648, Volume II, The MITRE Corporation, June 1973.
44. Corrigan, A. E., *Results of an Experiment in the Application of Software Quality Principles*, MTR-2874, Volume III, The MITRE Corporation, June 1974.
45. Schiff, J. D., "An Overview of the Software Life-Cycle Process," *Proceedings of the Aeronautical System Software Workshop*, Dayton, Ohio, April 1974, p. 108.
46. Prywes, N. S., *Research on Automatic Program Generation*, Report 74-05 University of Pennsylvania Moore School of Electrical Engineering, January 1974.
47. Boles, S. J. and J. D. Gould, *A Behavioral Analysis of Programming—On the Frequency of Syntactical Errors*, IBM RC 3907, June 1972.
48. McGonagle, J. D., *A Study of a Software Development Project*, J. P. Anderson and Company, September 1971.
49. Nichols, B. S., *Practical Experience With Structured Programming*, Bell Systems, November 1973.
50. Mill, H. D., "Top Down Programming in Large System," *Debugging Techniques in Large Systems*, R. Rustin (ED) Prentice Hall, 1970.
51. Baker, F. T., "Chief Programmer Team Management of Production Programming," *IBM Systems Journal* 11, 1972.
52. Sackman, A., *Man-Computer Problem Solving*, Auerbach Publishers, 1970.
53. Weinberg, G. M., *The Psychology of Computer Programming*, Van Nostrand Reinhold, New York, 1971.
54. Baker, F. T., "System Quality Through Structured Programming," *AFIPS Conference Proceedings*, 1972, pp. 339-343.
55. McGonagle, J. D., *A Study of a Software Development Project*, James P. Anderson and Company, Los Angeles, California, 1971.
56. Haile, A., *Command and Control Information Processing in the 1980's* (USAF-CCIP-85) Presentation in DoD Computer Institute Seminar IX, November 1972.
57. Asch, A., et al, *DoD Weapon Systems Software Acquisition and Management Study*, Vols. I and II, The MITRE Corporation, MTR-6908, 1975.

A SERVICE CONCEPT FOR SOFTWARE AUDITING

Edward F. Miller, Jr.
Software Technology Division
Science Applications, Inc.

Introduction

Computer software is increasing in cost and complexity almost daily. As more and more applications areas convert over to digital systems--that is, as more and more functions are taken over by computers--there is a corresponding increase in dependence on these same systems. Current hardware technology is very good, and assures very acceptable "up time" for the machinery itself. This is not necessarily so for computer software, for which there is a growing need for methods that assure the effectiveness and timeliness of software.

Moreover, the fraction of a system cost that is "consumed" by the software part of the system has been growing steadily. In the mid 1960's system engineers tended to think that software accounted for 50% of a system cost. Now, in the mid 1970's, software can be as much as 90% of a system cost. In fact, it might represent even a higher fraction (perhaps 98%) if the total life-cycle costs of a system are taken into account. This life-cycle includes the costly and labor-intensive phases called "maintenance" and "upgrade," in which very little hardware is purchased.

A primary example of a digital system category in which software plays a critical role is planning for the day when the majority of the Nation's daily financial traffic is processed entirely by computers. Indeed, this day may already have arrived. In this technical application alone, and in many others, there is significant interest in technologies oriented toward controlling computer software to (i) assure its "correctness" with respect to its intended function, and (ii) prevent unauthorized meddling of any kind. For example, a recent flurry of computer fraud cases is an indicator of the extent, and the impact, that such meddling can have.

Meanwhile, Computer Science research continues to unravel the mysteries surrounding software. It would be desirable if that research could be applied in some reasonable way to the "software problem". There seem to be two camps and, until very recently, there was very little communication between them:

> The Auditors - These are people who want something done about the "software problem," and they want it done right now. They take the brunt of the "pain" when computer software fails for it falls on them to explain why they permitted it!

> The Researchers - The research community has done some excellent work and has identified a number of the "causes" for software unreliability, but, as nearly every researcher will agree, there is as yet no definitive solution to the "software problem". In fact, there is some agreement that a fully general (in the mathematical sense) solution is not even possible.

What is certainly true is that these groups are not communicating with each other.

The purpose of this paper is to suggest a concept for a Software Auditing service that meets some of the objectives of the Auditors, and can be operated on a strong technological foundation provided by the Researchers. Such a Service clearly can't be successful if it doesn't have support from both areas: a user base and a technological base.

The next section gives an outline for the Service and identifies its general nature and the kinds of outcomes one might reasonably expect from it. The other sections describe certain phases of the Service's function from an operational and technological point of view.

The Service Concept

The objective of the Software Auditing Service is to provide a rigid framework in which computer software can be controlled in certain ways to achieve certain goals:

(1) Providing strong technological inputs so that software that comes within the Service's control is given the best possible treatment from a theoretical point of view.

(2) Make it possible for organizations which have software that they consider critical, or which they wish to put under very tight control, to have this done in concert with high-technology based methodologies that will keep the cost within acceptable bounds.

(3) Make the strongest possible statements about the "quality" and the "reliability" of the software under Service control, so that a user can operate with his software with a high degree of confidence.

(4) Make it possible to make alterations in Service-controlled software in a way that minimizes interference with day-to-day operational use of the software, and with acceptably low cost.

In other words, the Service centralizes (or attempts to centralize) the management of the software quality and also provides the basis for increasing the inherent quality of users' programs as they undergo modification and upgrade.

The Service Format - The Service is patterned somewhat after the notion of an "underwriter's laboratory," with important differences. Here is a step-by-step of how the Service operates:

(1) A user decides that a piece of software (which may be one module or an entire operating system) is "ready" for submission to the Service. This decision might be reached independently, or it could have been fostered by prior interaction with the Service. The state of mind required here is akin to "...I've done about as much as I can with this program, I think it's really good, and I'm ready to declare it 'done'....says the program developer".

(2) Once a piece of software is submitted to the Service it is subjected to a series of independent tests and evaluations, primarily performed by automated tools and augmented human analysts. There are two possible outcomes of this analysis process:

a) The submitted software is acceptable and it enters the Service's repository of acceptable software. In this case, the Service has declared that, according to its current standards for program quality and reliability, and after an extensive program of formalized software testing the software has passed muster.

b) The submitted software fails one or more of the tests and evaluations to which it was subjected, and is therefore not acceptable for inclusion in the Service's repository. The user is advised of where the fault was found and, possibly, is given assistance in revising the software so that it will "pass the tests" the next time around.

(3) After acceptance, the Service issues a fresh copy from its own files for the user to use in his actual application. The user can get additional fresh copies, without limit, at any time. The Service-controlled copy of the software, which has passed significant quality and reliability checks, is the only one that the user can (should?) use henceforth.

(4) If the user wants to try out changes he can do that, but with a different copy of the software. Thus, the software systems' modification and improvement can be done within the user's own environment without affecting the Service-controlled copy.

(5) Suppose that some modifications are to be made to the software. It is reasonable to assume that they would already have been tried out (as in #4) and, now, the user wants to make a change in the archived copy of his software. There are two options: the new software can be resubmitted "from the top", or the changes only can be analyzed for the effect they have on the archived copy. Although the first option, entire resubmission, is the easiest one to conceive, the incremental change route is the preferred

one. The reason is that change in the computer programs is the
rule rather than the exception. The Service analyzes the effect
of changes, reports to the user if there are any problems and, if
none, reissues a fresh copy of the new software system. (The
Service keeps the old copies, of course.)

(6) Charges are made based on formulas that take into account the
size of the software system, the rate of changes made to it, and
other factors.

The Service concept outlined above "works" only to the extent that the internal checks performed by the Service are technologically strong enough to support some kind of statement of internal software realiability. This statement must be strong enough to attract, and keep, the user base required to support the Service.

<u>The Service Costs</u> - The overall utility of the Service is dependent on the cost: if the cost is too high, even if technologically the Service is sound, the user-base would be too small; if the cost is too low (which is unlikely, in any case) then the Service would have a credibility problem. This is more than an psychological issue, however, since some minimum costs are technically necessary in order to make any statements about software quality in the first place.

A credible cost goal, based on experience and a good bit of guessing, is an initial cost of around 25¢ per statement; this would include all of the analysis needed to make the affirmative (the Service accepts) decision, as well as allowing some flexibility on the <u>other</u> outcome (the Service declines, and for these reasons...).

This basic cost appears to be enough to include the first Service copy issued to the user, but a sustaining charge would have to be imposed to account for daily maintenance of the controlled copy. A figure in the range of 10¢ per statement per year is probably enough to cover these costs in toto.

Changes would be charged depending on the effect of the change. If a modification affected only a small portion of the software then, at a rate of 25¢ per new-statement analyzed, the cost of incorporating changes would be low enough. The same rate, applied to more extensive changes would also be sufficient: some economies may be possible however.

In more concrete terms, consider a software system consisting of 100,000 statements. The initial charge would be $25,000; compare this with a cost-to-produce in the range of $5-$10 per statement ($500K to $1000K for the example). The initial cost is thus only about 5% of the cost-to-produce.

Assuming that the software system remains unchanged, the maintenance charge would be $10,000 per year. This would entitle the user to an unlimited number of fresh copies of the code.

If the change rate for our 100,000 statement software system were 10% per year (a not unusual rate for most software system--consider OS/360 for example), then at most $2500 per year additional would be needed to process the changes. Newly accepted software would then replace the prior copy, and fresh copies' costs would be included in the $10,000 per year maintenance charges.

Whether these figures are economically attractive to a user remains to be seen. They seem to be comfortable from the technological standpoint, however, as succeeding sections will make clear.

The Analysis Phase

The analysis phase of the Service begins with the user arriving at a state where _he_ believes the software meets _his_ standards for acceptability, and where he believes it will meet the Service's standards. Obviously there is a learning situation in which prior use of the Service will alert the user to the actual standards of program quality and functional behavior employed; the user (one supposes) won't abuse the Service but, even if he does he's paying for it!

The analysis that is actually performed has two objectives:

1) To find something unacceptable about the submitted software as soon as possible, so as to minimize the user's cost.

2) Assuming that none of the "easy" checks find anything wrong, to submit the software to as rigorous checks as possible prior to accepting it.

The process of treating software doesn't vary significantly in meeting these two apparently opposite goals. The reason is that a high proportion of the analyses are made by automated tools; the tools perform the checks, possibly with manual assistance, and make reports to the Service personnel that can be given directly to the user.

Code Checking - Two automated tools are used to check the submitted code initially, as described in Table 3-1. The Programming Standards Checker (PSC) applies a number of very simple checks to the entire submitted software system and provides responses only if the software doesn't meet the standards built into the PSC itself. The checks involved include (but are not limited to) the following:

(1) Does the software meet a pre-determined outline of content? For example, the outline might require certain levels and/or types of documentation, as well as certain specific kinds of other descriptive data.

(2) Does the software adhere to internal programming standards? Here, the standards involve the choices (and definition and extend) of variable names used within the program.

(3) Is the program well structured? Here, "well structured" means such things as: (i) Is the program a structured program? (ii) Does every statement have specifiable reachability properties? (iii) Are any "tricks" pulled that shouldn"t be? (iv) Etc.

The PSC is the initial filter on submitted software. The checks performed can be done very rapidly, and without substantial tool-internal complexity.

The second phase of the code checking process involves the use of a Static Allegation Analyzer (SAA). This tool applies a sophisticated set of checks to the submitted software (one module or many modules) in order to "prove" that the software has certain properties that affect it in given ways when it executes. For example, the SAA is used to verify that statements like the following are true about the software:

Table 3-1 Program Checking Tools

PSC	<u>Programming Standards Checker</u> - Applies a series of tests to determine if program meets a pre-determined set of "standards". The standards address issues like format, structure, organization, "clarity" and other related issues.
SAA	<u>Static Allegation Analyzer</u> - Applies advanced techniques to analyze programs statically to prove important allegations about the programs' behavior dynamically...for example, that "all variables are set <u>before</u> they are used".

Every variable is set somewhere before it is used anywhere

Every subroutine is called according to approved standards

Scope rules for local/global declarations are followed throughout the software system

Program structuring rules are adhered to completely

Etc.

All of these checks, performed statically on the programs, serve to eliminate many of the most common forms of faults before the programs are taken into execution.

<u>Program Instrumentation</u> - Subsequent phases of the analysis performed by the Service involve studying the dynamic properties of the programs. The static checking just described has already assured the Service that the programs meet sufficiently strong internal quality measures that it is meaningful to consider the programs' actual behavior.

To do this, and to collect data while the programs are executed under carefully controlled conditions, requires that they be instrumented fully. Or, at least instrumented fully enough to support the detailed functional performance issues being addressed.

The philosophy applied at this point is the following: the ultimate intention is to rigorously test (i.e. exercise) the programs to make sure that they (i) perform the functions they are supposed to perform, and (ii) do not perform any functions that they are not supposed to perform. Thus, program instrumentation is employed as the technical basis on which to learn about a programs' internal operation in a controlled way.

Program instrumentation carries with it a limitation, however: the programs that are instrumented no longer run in the same execution time and/or execution space as their uninstrumented counterparts. Thus, all tests will eventually have to be run with and without instrumentation in place. Since the instrumentation can be automated entirely, this poses no significant operational barrier.

Table 3-2 lists the program instrumentation and test tools that are used in the remainder of Service Activities. They form a family and, although they will be discussed throughout the remainder of this paper, they are introduced first here so that the level of integration between them is appreciated.

The simplest form of instrumentation is designed to determine the level of testing coverage achieved in a controlled environment of testing. This is done with an Automated Testing Analyzer (ATA) that has the following functions:

(1) Automatic instrumentation of each logical unit within each program, using implanted subroutine calls.

(2) Execution-time data recording of the logical units that were executed as a function of the test performed.

(3) Post-processing of the execution-time data to provide reports that summarize testing coverage attained.

This is a basic tool in the analysis phase of the Service, since it is used as the "thermometer" that tells how well programs have been exercised.

Three other types of instrumentation are also possible--and can be invoked by Service personnel depending on the situation:

Dynamic Assertion Processor - This tool allows the Service to make statements about the expected behavior of a program and automatically receive notification when that behavior is (or is not) obtained. This is important when examining the internal operation of the program(s).

Self-Metering Instrumentation - This form of instrumentation is used to capture essentially all of the information it is possible to collect dynamically, and carries a relatively high overhead. In Service use the tool is used when "......you don't know much about a program at all...." and want to get some good intuitive feeling about its actual behavior in the large.

Table 3-2 Program Testing Tools

ATA	<u>Automated Testing Analyzer</u> - Provides the basic "window" into the program testing process...tells the percentage coverage in terms of a very simple (yet powerful) measure.
DAP	<u>Dynamic Assertion Processor</u> - The programmer puts assertions about the way programs are supposed to behave into the code (they're treated as comments by the compiler), but the tool makes them report on when the assertions are violated.
SMI	<u>Self-Metering Instrumentation</u> - The programs are completely instrumented (but logical integrity is preserved) so that all conceivably interesting data about each programs' execution-time behavior is collected and reported (under user command).
TDE	<u>Testing Difficulty Estimator</u> - Tells, according to detailed program structure analysis, which programs in a set are the easiest and most difficult to test...and helps management control the testing resource better.
ATG	<u>Automated Testcase Guidance</u> - Helps a user construct test data that meets easily-stated objectives (.....execute <u>this</u> path....).
ATDG	<u>Automated Test Data Generation</u> - Automatically generates test data that meets specific objectives, using advanced heuristic processes that have high success ratios for this very difficult problem.

Table 3-2 Continued

ATF	<u>Automated Test Facility</u> - Constructs a stubbed and standard Input/Output environment for a single program or a set of programs...all automatically.
RTA	<u>Reliable Test Analyzer</u> - Checks out the reliability of a test case in protecting against assignment and/or control errors...thereby helping to maximize the surety attained in a rigorous testing activity.
RLP	<u>Robust Language Processor</u> - Automatically rewrites a program so that it "can't fail" during execution without first telling the user exactly how it did fail. Used during debugging and checkout testing to (a) isolate mistakes and (b) minimize lost execution time.
TPS	<u>Test Planning/Status</u> - A tool for testing management that provides continual status checks
AMA	<u>Automated Modification Analyzer</u> - Automatically analyzes a program set for the potential impact a proposed program change will have on the testing process...and advises what re-testing will have to be performed as a consequence of the change.

Robust Language Processor - This instrumentation rewrites a program (or a set of programs) so that logical equivalence with the original is preserved, but so that all of the conceivable failure modes of the program are automatically intercepted. In Service use the RLP would be used to "quiet down" a troublesome module (i.e. one that continually gave rise to errors) until it could be treated in detail.

All of this instrumentation is performed fully automatically, it is important to note. This means that Service personnel can consider the instrumentation "tool kit" as a resource to use when getting detailed functional performance data about a submitted program set, knowing that they haven't interferred with the programs' normal operation in the process.

The outputs of the instrumentation tools tell Service people "what's going on" within programs, and they do that independently of the user's notion of performance.

Program Testing - Formalized program testing forms the basis of the Analysis phase of the Service. In very general terms, the objective of program testing is to exercise a program in all of the different ways it can be exercised. This amounts to "complete testing" and, if it can be accomplished, is the only practically achievable methodology for assuring the absence of program errors (or, equivalently, assuring the presence of the desired program properties). It is a difficult task to completely test a program set of any significant complexity. For this reason, the Service employs a number of automated tools to assist in the function.

On the other hand, each of the tools used (see Table 3-2) requires a varying amount of computer resource. Judgment on the part of Service analysts is required in order to keep the computer-time costs to a bearable level.

Since the main purpose of rigorous testing is to "prove out" a submitted software system, it is worthwhile to discuss the kinds of benefits doing this achieves. First, if the software is fully exercised then all of its functions are known. This eliminates a major source of software unreliability: functional behaviors of the programs that were never intended in the first place.

Second, full exercise is, in actuality, a detailed software design verification process. Note that the Service concept described here takes as a given that the software already exists and that, in turn, assumes it was designed for some intended function. The fact that the code checking tests were already passed (at this point in the Service's analysis) indicates that <u>something</u> exists; and the fact that the user submitted it to the Service in the first place suggests that the user wants <u>something</u> done with what was submitted. Although cast in the form of a "formalized testing activity" a principal outcome of the Service is a complete set of tests for the programs that were submitted to it.

What does having a complete set of tests mean?

For one thing, it means that the software <u>can</u> be completely tested. This eliminates another major source of software unrealiability: the certainty that no part of the software has no function (or, equivalently, that each part of the software has some function). Finding out what that function is, and expressing it in the form of test cases that make it do that function, provides the basis for understanding whether the software solves the problem for which it was intended.

In other words, if some test cases are generated that the <u>user</u> can't understand then, there is a design flaw in the software. At this point, the user can choose to change his understanding or resubmit the software after making appropriate changes. In fact, the process will be iterative: The Service will discover functions and the user will justify them or change them. In aggregate the effect is to converge to software that (i) meets its functional requirements, and (ii) doesn't meet unstated functional requirements.

The testing tools support these objectives (and this viewpoint) by making it as easy as possible to achieve these ends. "Man" is still very much in the loop, it is important to appreciate. Here is a summary of the way in which the test tools support the Service analyst:

> <u>Testing Difficulty Estimator</u> - The programs to be analyzed are kept, in their entirety, on a data base of some kind. The TDE assesses the relative "complexity" of each module and provides an initial handle on "where to begin" in testing process. In addition,

the TDE also tells where to continue--in order to make the best use of Service computer--time resources. Note that this is done independent of program function and that this is appropriate: the most difficult to test modules are the ones with the most "function" anyway.

<u>Test Planning/Status</u> - This tool keeps track of the testing data bases (i.e. the set of tests used on the software) in a systematic way. What's envisioned here is a common format for test data and test setups that Service people can become very familiar with. The tool itself becomes the source (later the archived source) of the test data used to "prove out" a program.

<u>Automated Test Facility</u> - This tool automatically constructs a local environment for part (or all) of the submitted software. The input/output and control facilities required by the software are codified in a standard representation, so that Service personnel can deal with the software in a familiar fashion. The ATF is the workhorse of the Service since it makes it possible to "look at the behavior of" any portion of the submitted software system with equal ease.

Thus, we have the tools to control the testing process in a standard fashion, and to keep track of the status of "where the current software testing activity" is with respect to "completion".

Now comes the testing process itself. Presumably, the software submitted to the Service already has some test data (this might be a requirement). The first step is to determine how well the software is tested; this is done with the ATA and the ATF. Where to "begin" is determined by the TDE, and possibly by user inputs.

Since the objective is to get a "complete" set of tests, and because this is difficult to do, there are two tools specifically designed to simplify this process:

<u>Automated Testcase Guidance</u> - This tool provides advice about how to get a previously unexecuted (i.e. unexercised) portion of a

program into execution. The advice takes the form of a hierarchically organized statement of the conditions that must be met in order for the "target" program particle to reach execution. ATG supports human generation of additional test data only.

<u>Automated Test Data Generation</u> - This tool automates the process of generating testcase data that achieves a specified testing objective, e.g. "make this program statement execute". At the current state of the art, this tool must rely on heuristic procedures rather than on analytic certainty. In other words, it is (a) expensive to operate and (b) its success in generating test case data is not necessarily guaranteed. The algorithms that do exist for doing this task are good enough, however, to warrant their use in unusual circumstances within the program testing activity.

<u>Reliable Test Analyzer</u> - This tool analyzes a test that has been performed and determines if it is "reliable". The theory of reliable testing is currently emerging (see Ref. 1); briefly, this theory allows one to determine whether a particular test is a sure (in the sense of formal correctness) check of the absence of errors in a particular program path. This tool is used <u>after</u> tests are performed to assess their impact on the overall effectiveness of the testing activity. If all tests are reliable, then a complete set of tests (i.e. one that tests everything in the program) is a reliable verification of the consistency between the submitted program test and the specifications against which it was developed.

The overall effect of using these tools is to construct a hierarchy of program test data (managed by the TPS) that completely exercises the submitted program(s). This is the basis for releasing the software as "acceptable" to the Service. In the process of getting to this point it is likely that a large number of "problem areas" will be uncovered; these are the basis of the feedback given to the Service user and may become documentation for conditional acceptance of the submitted software.

Language Restrictions - The tools described above can be built with current software technology for any procedure-oriented language. Examples are FORTRAN, COBOL, PL/1, JOVIAL, CMS-2, etc. The important exception is machine language at the assembler level.

In order for Assembly Language to be acceptable--that is, in order for there to be a basis for automating the functions described above for programs written in Assembly Language--it must meet an important additional constraint: the decisional structure of Assembly Language programs must be explicitly identified. In practice this can be met by requiring that all program control transfers be indicated symbolically. This eliminates the use of such common programming tricks as: (i) the use of indirect addressing in control transfers, and (ii) the use of "constructed targets". Fortunately, good (modern) programming practice eliminates these troublesome points.

A final note about the "tool kit". Fully assembled, the tools described in Tables 3-1 and 3-2 would comprise 100,000 to 200,000 statements themselves, plus an additional 10,000 statements for each language dialect that the Service would process. Fortunately, they can be written so that they can be processed by themselves first, thereby significantly enhancing the credibility of the Service.

The Distribution Phase

The Service would distribute copies of final software for use by the user. This software would be generated only by the Service--if the Service concept were adopted--since that is the only sure source of fully checked out copies of the code.

Some special technological devices can be used to further enhance the quality of the Service-produced software. For example, the software might be supplied (automatically) with internal "integrity checks". This could be accomplished by computing a checksum of some kind and including programs which recompute this checksum each time the software system is turned on.

If necessary, the Service-provided software could be automatically encrypted to varying levels of inscrutability. The purpose of this would be to discourage fiddling by unauthorized personnel by making it, quite simply, entirely too difficult to understand to be worth the trouble. Of course, clear-text hard copies of the Service-held archival copy of the software would be available. Machine-processable versions of the clear-text might also be made available for system modification checkout and/or experimentation.

If desired, some of the automatically inserted instrumentation could be left in place so that the end-user could monitor certain properties of the program. The RLP would be the tool in this case.

In addition, the code would be supplied with the current complete testcase and in a checkout instrumented form so that full coverage could be verified in place before turning the software system "on".

Program Modification

Nobody's perfect, and requirements do change. The Service must be particularly sensitive to changes in programs to foster: (a) genuine improvements and (b) required modifications. This interaction is particularly important since the expected outcome of the Analysis Phase of the Service would be a series of recommended changes.

It should not be necessary to "start from scratch" every time a modification is requested, however. In fact, experience suggests that most changes made to programs have only a local rather than global, effect. (There are exceptions, of course.) Thus, the Service should be able to take in a proposed modification and quickly (and economically) return to the original point of "released status" as soon as possible. The tool to do this is:

> Automated Modification Analyzer - A proposed change is analyzed in respect to the entire software system (not just the module being affected) and the impact on the testing activity is determined. If small, only a portion of the testing must be repeated; if large, significant portions of the software system would have to undergo the full treatment described previously.

Naturally, the Service would make this assessment (using the automated tool) quickly and inexpensively. The user has to know whether a proposed modification will or will not sink his ship; he has to be able to assess, in his own terms, the cost he'll probably have to pay if he makes a change.

Most changes are small ones, and the Service would be able to react to such changes easily and rapidly. Thus, as the user's requirements change (we hope, slowly) the Service can react with aplomb. <u>And</u>, the required level of software surety would be maintained throughout the process.

A major change, one reflecting an important software system design decision, can be expected to have substantial impact. It is for this reason that the cost to analyze a change should be kept at about the same level as for a totally new program.

Conclusion

A software auditing Service, based on the notion of independent assessment of the internal testedness quality of a submitted software system, and organized to provide facilities to a user in a reasonable manner, appears well within the state of the art, at least from a technical standpoint.

The family of automated tools that can be used by the Service to process programs written in the widely-used programming languages can be identified sharply enough so that the Service-internal structure of processing techniques are clear.

The estimated cost of the Service, 25¢ per new statement processed, 10¢ per statement per year maintained, and 25¢ per modified statement processed, appears to be low enough to attract at least an initial set of Service users.

Formalizing the interaction between the keeper of the master copy of the candidate software system and its actual user appears to be a viable way of providing the Auditing function.

Reference

1. E. F. Miller, Jr., "The Art and Theory of Program Testing", Presented at the Texas Conference on Computing Systems, November, 1975. Austin, Texas.

THE HIGH COST OF SOFTWARE
Barry W. Boehm

INTRODUCTION

The high cost of software should be considered more of an opportunity than a problem. Nobody can say for sure to what extent software "costs too much." However, the high cost implies that additional improvements will lead to significant savings, which should justify additional investment to streamline some of the institutions, techniques, and procedures which often hinder software productivity.

This chapter will address three main questions:

- How high is the cost of software?
- Where do the costs go?
- What factors influence the costs? (or, what can we do about them?)

For reference, "software production" here includes all the effort involved in producing and maintaining the necessary executive, support, and applications programs and their documentation, starting from a reasonably well-defined functional specification. Most of the software data come from the Air Force, primarily from the CCIP-85 study[1] and the recent Air Force-Industry Software Cost Workshop, but they are probably fairly representative of other software activities elsewhere.

HOW HIGH IS THE COST OF SOFTWARE?

In 1961, Gilchrist and Weber[2] estimated the number of software personnel in the U.S. at 360,000. They also estimated that this number was growing at the rate of 30,000 per year, implying a total of about 450,000 in 1974. Multiplying by a fairly typical software manpower cost of $35,000 per burdened man-year yields a total U.S. expenditure on software of about $16 billion, or over one percent of the 1974 Gross National Product.

In the Air Force, in fiscal year 1972, the annual expenditure on software was somewhere between $1 and 1.5 billion per year, or about 4 to 5 percent of the total Air Force budget. In comparison, the cost on hardware was something between $300 and $400 million. For the Worldwide Military Command and Control System, the relative costs were even more dramatic; an estimated $722 million for software, compared to $50 - 100 million for hardware. The comparison is even more dramatic if you look at what you are really paying for when you pay for this thing called hardware. A relatively small fraction of a typical large manufacturer's cost goes into boxes, the chips, and the wires that you receive; generally about twice as much currently goes into software. Currently, though, both hardware and software costs are typicall dominated by the remaining costs incurred for R & D, sales, service, profits, lawyers, etc.

Figure 1 shows the likely trends in the relative costs of hardware and software, even considering the cost of hardware as the rental cost paid by the user. In the late 1950s the hardware was only 20 to 30 percent of the cost. Right now, software is about 70 percent of the cost, and by the 1970s it appears it's going to be about 90 percent of the cost, as hardware costs continue to go down and people costs continue to go up.

The discussion above covers only the direct cost of software. It turns out that the indirect costs of software are even greater. The effects of software delays and errors on audit trails, equipment resupply and repair, cash flows, and other operations-oriented concerns lead to many other significant dollar losses in the national economy.

WHERE DO THE COSTS GO?

Nationwide, it is difficult to determine the breakdown of software expenditures by type of software. Figure 2 represents the second iteration of an effort to find out within the Air Force how much of the cost goes for various types of software.[3] As seen in Figure 2, the expenditures for critical real-time software such as command and control and intelligence (21 percent), and for on-board space and avionics type software (10 percent) are dominated by the expenditures on management information

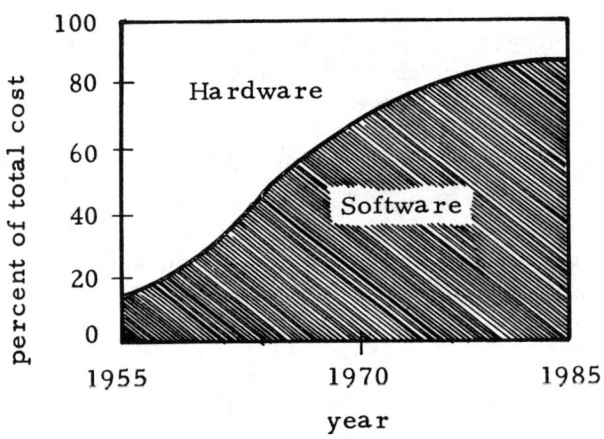

Figure 1. Hardware/Software Cost Trends

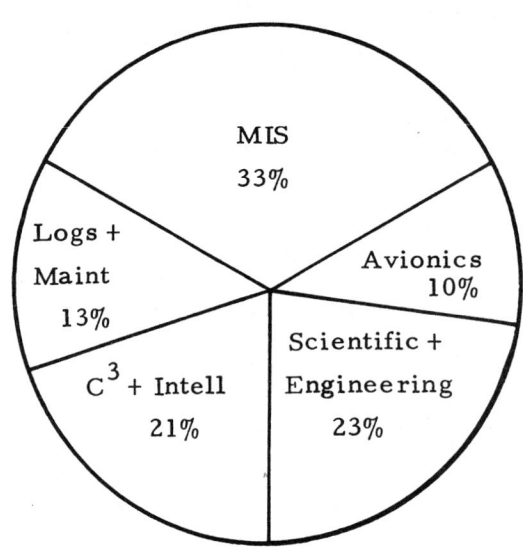

Figure 2. Estimated Distribution of USAF Software Costs

system (MIS) software (33 percent), logistics and maintenance (13 percent), and scientific and engineering software (23 percent). The percentages are not exact; they could be off by a factor of one-third either way (e.g., MIS could be 44 or 22 percent and I wouldn't be too surprised). However, even rough estimates are fairly important because of the distrbutions of software cost vary between application areas.

Figure 3 shows some of the differences between real-time software and batch scientific or business-type software. For example, for business-type software, relatively little time goes into testing. The programs are simpler; most of the errors are in formatting and the like which are fairly easy to get out, rather than errors in timing which are extremely difficult to get out. Another difference is that documentation costs tend to be much higher for the business type of program. The 100 percent estimate of additional time required for documentation was a business-type application; the 9 percent estimate was for batch scientific programs.

One pitfall to avoid in looking at these software development cost statistics, and in worrying about the fact that software is on the critical path during the system development, is to concentrate too much on reducing software development costs. What really needs to be reduced is software life cycle costs, and often you find that people make a lot of tradeoffs during software development to meet schedules, and many of those tradeoffs trade maintainability for speed of development. How much of the software effort does go into software maintenance? The best data that exist come from a Hoskyns survey[4] in Great Britian, which canvassed 905 installations there and found that almost 40 percent of the software effort in Great Britian goes into maintenance.

Figure 4 shows the distribution of installations by the relative amount of time they spend on software maintenance. The mode of the distribution is somewhere between 20 and 30 percent maintenance, but there are some installations that spend almost all of their time maintaining software. Air Force avionics software is much like this latter, and currently it costs something like $75 per instruction to develop the software, but the maintenance of the software has cost up to $4000 per instruction.[5]

WHAT FACTORS INFLUENCE SOFTWARE COSTS?

A later chapter in this book (by Wolverton) presents a number of valuable relationships for estimating software costs. A further step toward illumination of software cost factors was taken at a recent (October 1974) Air Force-Industry Workshop on Software

	Analysis and Design	Coding and Auditing	Test and Integration
Command-Control (SAGE, NTDS)	35%	17%	48%
Command-Control (TRW)	46%	20%	34%
Spaceborne (Gemini, Saturn)	34%	20%	46%
GP Executive (OS/360)	33%	17%	50%
Scientific (TRW)	44%	26%	30%
Business (Raytheon)	44%	28%	28%

Added documentation estimates: about 10%

Figure 3. Software Effort Distribution by Activity

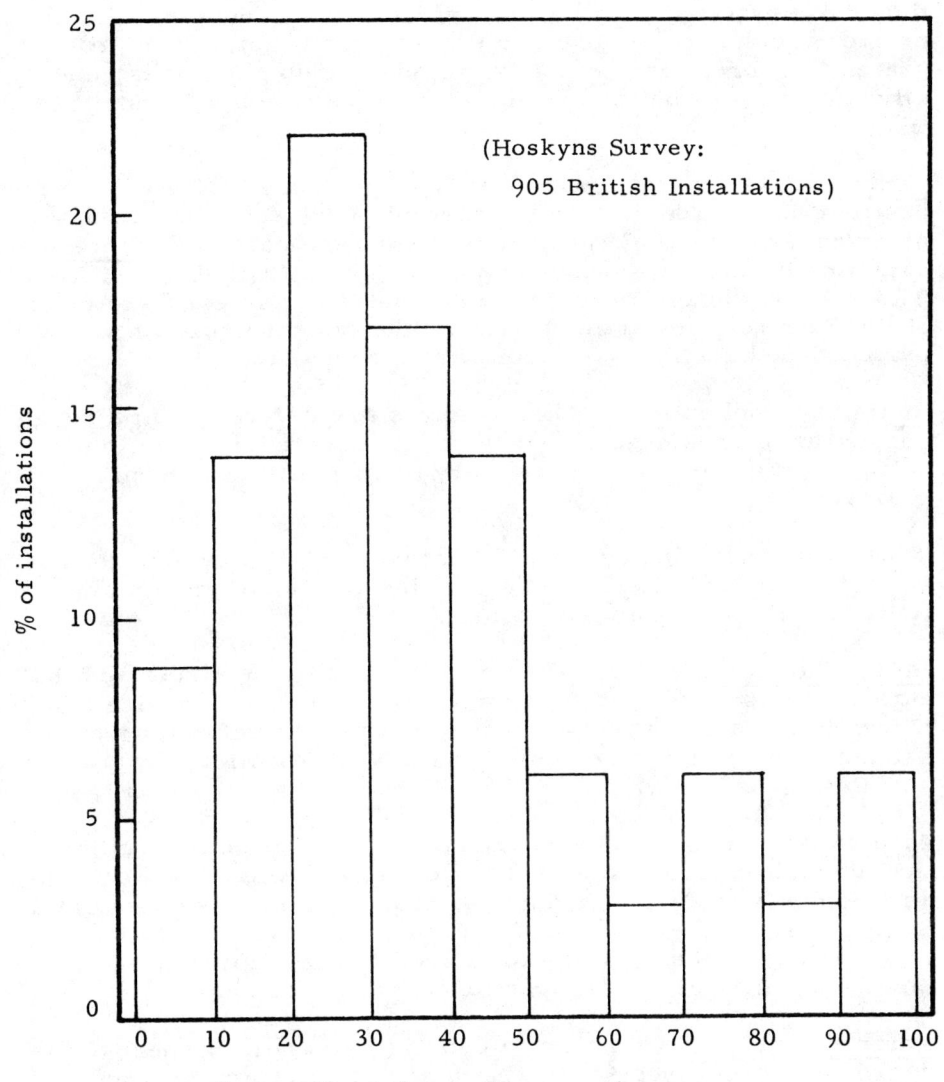

Figure 4. Software Maintenance

Costs held at USAF Electronics Systems Division. Table I summarizes the main factors identified in one of the working sessions; the text below provides further discussion of each item.

Number of delivered executable source instructions. This is currently the most widely used factor for cost estimation. "Delivered" implies "well checked out" and "documented;" also, it excludes such non delivered software as unit test driven programs. "Source instructions" excludes comments; it is generally considered a better estimation factor than object instructions.

Language. In general, participants' experience indicated that the cost per source instruction in assembly language or machine-oriented language (MOR) was about twice the cost per source instruction in a higher-order language such as COBOL or FORTRAN. The dollar figures were derived from an estimate of 15-30 HOL source instructions/day and the typical figure of $35,000 per burdened man-year for software manpower.

Real-time applications. These figures are derived from a rough consensus of experiences that the cost/instruction real time software was about five times that of nonreal time HOL programs.

Type. The operating system (OS) component of a system tends to cost about 2.5 times the cost per instruction of the applications or utility program components.

Point on learning curve. Participants' experience indicated that a generally experienced programming group would require another 50-100 percent more effort to develop an unfamiliar program as they would to develop a variant of a familiar program developed previously.

Application area. Another source of cost variation is whether the application involves a management information system (MIS), an avionics package, an industrial process control system, etc. Sometimes, another estimate of software cost can be made in terms of a percentage of the total system cost, but this must also be conditional with respect to the other factors.

Desired quality. Two major categories exist with respect to the degree of thoroughness of testing before a program goes operational. In the "man-rated" systems, where software errors may translate directly into the loss of human life, the fraction of the total effort devoted to testing has averaged about 40 percent; on other systems, it tends to be more like 15 percent.

Turnaround time. For the modern range of batch turnaround times (from 30 min to 1 working day), the length of the test period tends to be proportional to turnaround time. If testers have little useful to do while waiting for test runs to come back, then testing costs are also proportional to turnaround time. However, cost-reducing effects arise if testers can be documenting or eliminating errors by other means such as code scanning while they wait. For very short turnaround times including interactive systems, the relationship is much less predictable.

Amount of documentation. Experience indicates that documentation costs run about 10 percent of the total software development cost. For nonautomated documentation (e.g., excluding listings and automatically generated flow charts), typical costs are about $35-150 per page, depending primarily on the amount and complexity of the analysis involved.

Hardware constraints. The most useful relationship here is still that indicated in Figure 5, which shows the effect of hardware speed and memory size constraints on the relative cost of software. Although the data for the curve come from 34 airborne and spaceborne software projects, the same effect appears to hold for ground-based batch and real-time computing [6].

This software cost escalation effect becomes particularly crippling during the software maintenance phase, as the hardware is generally sized for production, leaving little capacity for fitting the test driver into core, expanding data areas, accommodating interactive modification aids, etc.

Schedule realism. Although the length of an "appropriate" schedule is as difficult to estimate as is cost, experience indicates that attempts to develop the software some percent faster than "appropriate" will usually increase cost by about that percentage.

Amount of previous software used. The best way to estimate the costs of adapting existing software into a new development appears to be to break it out separately, and subjectively estimate the costs of modifying it for the new application and of interfacing it to the new software.

Size and structure of the data base. This is recognized to be an extremely important parameter, especially on large-file oriented projects. So far, no counterpart to the cost-per-instruction factor has been established, although such a factor is much desired.

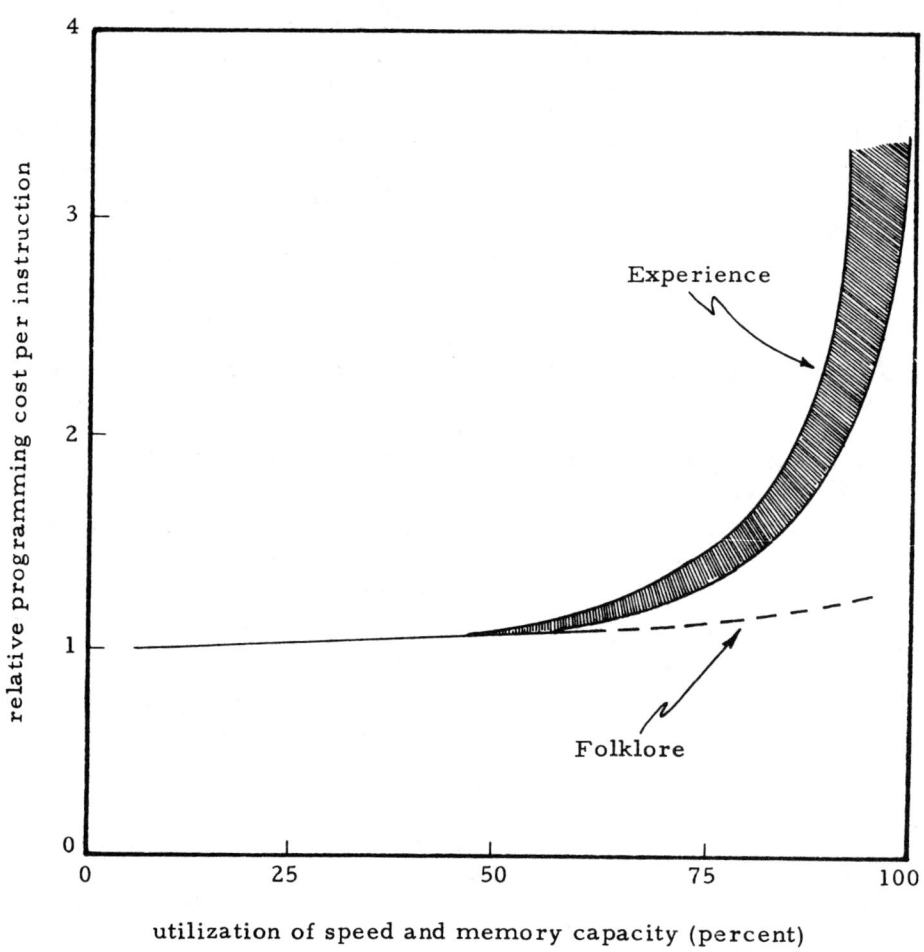

Figure 5. Hardware Strains Cause Major Software Impact

Complexity. This is another important factor which so far has eluded definition in such a way as to be used reliably in a cost formula. Some attempts have been made to correlate costs with such factors as number of interfaces, percentage of branch statements, number of paths through a program, and Halstead length, but so far without any highly reliable correlation.

Stability of requirements and stability of development environment. These factors are important determinants of software cost, but their influence can only be estimated subjectively. Their effect tends to be proportional to the length of time it takes to complete the project.

Representations of development environment. The added cost required to adapt software to actual operational conditions (different computer configuration, operating procedures, etc.) can be quite significant (up to 95 percent in some instances) but can only be estimated subjectively.

Personnel. This factor is considered by experienced estimators to be extremely important, but difficult to estimate other than subjectively. Productivity variations of 5:1 between individuals are common.

Development techniques. These include such things as using structured programming, top-down development, chief programmer teams, automated aids, and the like. No consensus was reached regarding the quantitative effect of using such techniques, except to agree that systematic approaches to software development are better than disorganized ones.

Management. Like personnel, this is another extremely important factor, but difficult to estimate other than subjectively.

These factors were considered the most important ones to account for in estimating software costs. There are many more possible factors (e.g., particular programming language, number of input and output quantities, frequency of operation, in-house versus contract, absolute hardware characteristics such as memory size and word size.) In general, such other factors tend to be less well correlated to cost than the factors above, although in particular situations (e.g., word size for avionics software) they may be both significant and clearly correlated with cost.

With respect to this book, the main point is that, for any particular project, some factors are not within our control while others are. The remaining chapters focus on those factors which usually are within our control (e.g., management, design techniques, and various development techniques) and point out how they may often be used both to reduce software costs and to improve its reliability.

TABLE 1

FACTORS INFLUENCING SOFTWARE COST

Factor	Relation to Cost
Number of delivered source instructions	Linear, modified by other factors
Language	HOL: $6-12/source instruction MOL: $12-24/source instruction
Real-time application	RT: $30-60/source instruction
Type (OS, application, utility)	If OS, multiply by 1.5-2.0
Point on learning curve	If unfamiliar, multiply by 1.5-2.0
Application area (MIS, avionics)	Sometimes, as % of total system cost
Desired quality	"Man-rated:" test cost 40% of total Non-"Man-rated:" test cost 15% of total
Turnaround time	Approximate linear relation to testing cost
Amount of documentation	Approximately 10% of total; $35-150/non-automated page
Hardware constraints	Asymptotic as approach to full capacity (Fig.
Schedule realism	% added cost = % of schedule acceleration
Amount of previous S/W used	Breakout + subjective
Size, structure of data base	Subjective
Complexity	Subjective

Stability of requirements	Subjective
Stability of development environment	Subjective
Representativeness of development environment	Subjective
Personnel	Subjective; approximately 5:1 variability
Development methods (e.g., structured programming)	Subjective; systematic approaches cheaper
Management	Subjective; high variability

REFERENCES

1. Information Processing/Data Automation Implication of Air Force Command and Control Requirements in the 1980's (CCIP-85), Volume I, Highlights, United States Air Force Report SAMSO/XRS-71-1, AD 900031L, April 1972.

2. Gilchrist, B. and K.E. Weber, "Employment of Trained Computer Personnel - A Quantitative Survey," Proceedings 1972 SJCC, pp. 641-648.

3. Boehm, B.W., "Keynote Address: The High Cost of Software," in Proceedings of a Symposium on the High Cost of Software, J. Goldberg (ed.), Stanford Research Institute, September 1973.

4. Implications of Using Modular Programming, John Hoskyns and Co., Ltd., Guide No. 1, Hoskyns Systems Research, Inc., 600 3rd Avenue, New York, New York, 1973.

5. Trainor, W.L., Software - From Satan to Savior, United States Air Force Avionics Laboratory, Wright-Patterson AFB, Ohio, presented at National Aerospace Electronics Conference, May 1973.

6. Boehm, B.W., "Software and Its Impact: A Quantative Assessment," Datamation, May 1973, pp. 48-59.

7. Proceedings, Government/Industry Workshop on Software Sizing and Costing, U.S. Air Force Electronics Systems Division (to appear).

Section 7: Research and Development

Paper Summaries

E. F. Miller, "Program Testing: Art Meet Theory," *Computer,* July 1977 (pp. 42-51).

This paper traces the development of program testing technology as it is currently understood, and investigates the use of hierarchical decomposition techniques in program testing. The paper presents a methodology that would form the general pattern for a systematic program testing discipline. The methodology incorporates techniques of hierarchical decomposition and certain general types of automated testing support tools.

E. F. Miller, "Program Testing Technology in the 1980's," *The Oregon Report: Proceedings of the Conference on Computing in the 1980's* (pp. 72-79).

The current state of the art in program testing technology is surveyed in terms of the philosophical underpinnings of software engineering and in terms of the sets of tools that can be brought to bear on any testing activity. In the course of the evaluation a number of specific technological needs are identified that relate to program structures, program behavior in relation to program structure, data flow, test descriptions, the reliability of tests and methods for assessing that reliability, the form and requirements on the interface between software being examined and the program testers, and general requirements for development of symbolic program analysis facilities.

SPECIAL FEATURE

PROGRAM TESTING: ART MEETS THEORY*

Edward F. Miller, Jr.
Software Research Associates

Reprinted from *Computer*, July 1977, pp. 42-51. Copyright © 1977 by The Institute of Electrical and Electronics Engineers, Inc.

Introduction

The problems of providing quality assurance for computer software have received a good deal of attention from the computing community. Such areas as program proving, automatic programming, structured programming, and hierarchical design/development methodologies have all experienced significant growth—largely as a result of the increased attention focussed on them. Program testing, on the other hand, has not enjoyed the same level of intensive investigation, even though it has a number of technical and intuitive appeals:

- Testing is a practical activity that relates directly to what a programmer and a program do, rather than to an abstraction of what each is supposed to do.
- Techniques that deal directly with source programs tend to focus attention on what is actually going on in the program.
- Some research results suggest that testing techniques can be formalized in an effective way.
- There is hope (supported, to be sure, by a great deal of intuition) that testing technology may become the "solution" to the software unreliability problem, particularly for large-scale software systems.

Both art and theory operate in program testing today. The "art" of program testing suggests new theoretical routes which drive the development of additional "theory" which, in turn, drives the accumulation of further art.

*Portions of this paper were presented at the 1975 Texas Conference on Computing Systems, Austin, Texas, November 1975.

This paper describes some recent efforts to build a bridge linking the theory of program testing with its practice. Although building that bridge has been a desirable goal, only now has sufficient research insight and actual testing experience been gained to even begin contemplating the form this practically oriented but strongly founded bridge can take.

Let us consider the issues of testing art and testing theory in the following steps:

- A discussion of the interface between testing art and testing theory and what that interface implies.
- A description of present-day idealized program testing methodologies and the impact they have had in real-world applications.
- A presentation of some recent testing theory results suggesting that a systematic testing methodology can measurably improve software quality.
- A description of a systematic (and largely automatable) program testing methodology that could be put into practice using current knowledge and techniques and could accommodate later, more powerful theoretical results.
- A discussion of some of the issues remaining to be resolved.

Art vs. theory

It would probably be fair to say that prior to the Program Test Methods Symposium[1] in 1972, whatever "art" of program testing existed was a closely held secret among knowledgeable programmers. Computer software systems were considered secondary to the hardware because they cost less. Or so everyone thought. This attitude generally carried over into the treatment of software reliability issues.

"The software can be done easily, so we don't have to worry about that," managers would say with elan; and they acted on their belief—despite the fact that the problems encountered with the first large-scale operating systems and application software projects in industry and the military were already out of hand and nobody knew what, if anything, could be done about them.[2]

No one seemed to have ever taken a serious look at testing. For example, I remember vividly a conversation circa 1973 with a competent computer man who suggested the easy way to solve the software reliability problem was to "... test all the possible combinations, just as they do for hardware!" And yet, a back-of-the-envelope computation of the total number of input combinations for a subroutine that computes the 36-bit integer sum of two 36-bit integers (i.e., 2^{72} combinations) revealed that simple, exhaustive input-space coverage could not be done for software or for hardware.

Clearly, something else must be found that works. In a purely economic view, the problem can be stated this way: a practical method must be found to demonstrate that software actually *does* what it was intended to do. Program proving methods have the same goal, but those techniques are probably a decade away from practical application.[3]

The interface between art and theory. The art and theory of program testing address fundamentally different questions from fundamentally different attitudes. To emphasize the similarities, however, one can make some direct comparisons between the art of program testing and the theory that supports it:

ART	THEORY
Practical "how-to's"	Technical intuition
Keeping costs within bounds	Making sure enough is spent
How to test enough	How much testing *is* enough?
How to apply the theory	How to factor in past experience
Concentrating on program behavior	Dealing with ancillary details or formalisms not necessarily related to program behavior
Informal methods	Formal methods
Developing a methodology	Areas for further research

Correlations should be obvious. "Art" involves the practical issues of "how to do it," whereas "theory" converts these "how-to's" into intuitive thought. In a practical testing situation it is important to know whether enough testing has been accomplished, but the theoretician must consider just how much testing is required to make various statements about software quality. Similarly, development of a practical methodology is an "art," but the application of that methodology identifies areas for further theoretical research.

Characteristics of a testing methodology. The nature of the program proof process,[3] which requires first the development of a set of verification conditions followed by their detailed analysis and proof (possibly by a mechanical theorem prover program), has some important limitations. For instance, a so-called "proof" does not necessarily imply that the program is actually correct since there may be an error in the other stages of the process. An incorrect program can be proved correct—perfectly properly—relative to an incorrect set of assumptions.

Whereas program proving is a *reductive process* (one that converts or reduces facts about programs into other forms that can themselves be shown self-consistent), program testing is inherently an *affirmative process* since everything done in testing can potentially contribute information about the quality of the program being tested.

For example, if in the process of testing one finds a test case that produces an "infinite loop," the program can then be changed to avoid that problem. Similarly, a test case that produces a "divide-by-zero fault" indicates either a failure to protect the program in some way or an important restriction of the program's activities.

In the broadest terms a formal program testing methodology would attempt to systematize two kinds of information:

(1) The sets of tests which when executed would realiably identify program errors of various classes or, absenting that, would produce some kind of anomalous program behavior to signal the existence of a fault.

(2) An understanding of the structure of the program in terms that would support a test engineer's intuition about the proper behavior of the program.

The latter point is very important if the methodology is going to be applied to a large-scale software system. The test engineer must have a relatively clear appreciation of the program's proper operation if he is going to interact effectively with a methodology that guides the testing process. With present techniques the testing process will require human judgment, and enlightening that judgment will reduce the overall cost of achieving increased confidence in software quality.

A testing methodology that applies only to single modules (individual subprograms that are invoked by other programs) or to very small sets of modules would be only a toy. Before the methodology can be adopted seriously, it must meet two important criteria:

(1) The methodology must apply to between-module testing at all levels in a complex computer program set, including the highest levels (so-called *system testing*).

(2) The methodology must provide facilities for dealing with testing situations in which automated assistance by a support tool is not possible. In other words, the methodology must not "give-up" when a situation not previously covered is encountered.

As the sections below make clear, present theory does not completely satisfy these two requirements. The methodology that is presented takes this into account, so that human interaction in the testing activity becomes a natural adjunct to procedures that are more rigorous and systematic.

Existing test methodologies

Existing program testing methodologies describe an idealized set of procedures that operate to accomplish a specific testing goal. A *test* consists of an execution of the program with specific input data, called *test data*, in a controlled environment where it is possible to measure certain properties of the program as it executes the test data. Ordinarily, the output of the program tested is allowed to happen in the normal way. The test engineers compare the output with that which was supposed to be generated for the given test data. However, this is normally done "by inspection."

Whereas an ultimate automatic software testing system would include the capability to compare inputs and outputs automatically—and potentially without the user's intervention—most contemporary methodological approaches to testing concentrate on measuring the *test coverage*. If the maximum amount of coverage is achieved during the testing process (which may involve one or many tests) the program testing activity can be considered complete.

The test coverage measure is used as a barometer of "how far the testing process has gone." Some of the earliest effective measures used were very simple ones; more recently, measures of coverage that relate directly to structural properties of the programs being tested have been devised. It will be useful to discuss the hierarchy of testing measures given below.

C0: Programmer's intuition.
C1: Every statement in a program exercised at least once.
C2: Every program predicate outcome exercised at least once.
C3: At least one element of each equivalence class of program flow exercised at least once.
C4: All usefully distinct program flow classes tested with "reliable test data (see below)," plus de facto testing of what cannot be tested reliably.

.
.

Cn: A sufficient set of tests so that the tests amount to a formal program proof of correctness.

C0 is included because it is the most commonly used test coverage measure. One literally tests according to the programmer's whims. The C1 measure is an intuitively satisfying one because it tends to corroborate the claim that "all the statements have been exercised, so there can't be any problem." The C2 measure, which implies C1, is based on considering computer programs as directed graphs with outways from each node corresponding to each possible program predicate outcome. If C2 is achieved, the only statements that cannot have been executed are those which could never be executed (so-called *unreachable statements*). C2 is usually interpreted as requiring only that there be some test that forces each possible predicate outcome within the test set. Requiring that each set of outcomes occur in each possible combination is the same as requiring that a program be exercised for all of its possible flows. That number may be finite or infinite, depending on whether the program contains iteration forms or not.

The C3 measures were designed to take advantage of auxiliary forms of program structure analysis (discussed in more detail later). The C4 measure is included because that is the measure suggested in the methodology given below. The techniques for defining—and achieving—the Cn measure of coverage remain an open question.

Practical experience. Measuring C2 for a program under examination is a straightforward matter. What is needed is a mechanism for recording whether or not a program's flow-of-control passes through an action that results from the particular value of a particular predicate outcome. In other words, it is necessary only to instrument the program (while preserving its logical integrity) in such a way that each of the program's decisions is recorded in some manner. Then the recorded data, called a *decisional trace*, can be analyzed to determine the value of C2 achieved for each particular test. The aggregate results for a series of tests made against the C2 measure show the overall effect of the testing activity. This measure can be applied at the individual module or at the system level as the test engineer chooses.

Although a few experiments have been performed in controlled circumstances, it is difficult to state quantitative results achieved with this measure because of the apparently statistical nature of program errors. Some observations are worth noting, however.

(1) In a methodology based on the C2 measure, the testing activity eliminated nearly 90 percent of the program faults.[4] It wasn't clear whether this resulted simply from requiring the programmers to examine their code very carefully.

(2) The use of automated (testing coverage measurement) tools caught between 67 percent and 100 percent of the errors, and at 2-5 months earlier than they would otherwise have been detected.[5] The particular tools used applied the C2 measure.

Results of this sort account for the increasing use of methodologies based largely on the C2 measure.[6]

Impact on development. Merely obtaining the C2 measure of test coverage is not enough. The technique also requires generating test data so that a C2 measure of 100 percent can be obtained. This necessitates a variety of methods of examining program structure and content. Several automated program analysis systems have been developed that provide this kind of capability, in addition to the basic one of program instrumentation and data collection. For example, systems such as TDEM, PET, RXVP, DAVE, and JAVS provide a spectrum of support facilities.[7-11]

These systems, and similar ones under development,[12] provide the test engineer with detailed information of importance to building new test data. Because the problems are most severe with large programs, the methods used are either automatic or highly automated. The typical problem the systems are asked to solve is the following: given that some program segment has not been executed (as the C2 measurement shows), how can a test be constructed that *does* execute that segment? Here, *segment* means a sequence of program statements that is always executed as a unit so that if any statement in it is executed, all statements are executed.

Advances in technology have focused on the so-called test case data generation problem. There have been several interesting proposals but very little automatically generated test data.[13-15] The search for an effective method goes on.

Software reliability measure. The foregoing description addresses the level of testing achieved in a rigorous testing discipline, but it fails to deal with a more basic issue: after testing, how reliably can one expect a program to perform? Later there is a discussion of "reliable tests" (where "reliable" has a somewhat different meaning) that are qualitatively equivalent to proofs. What can be said about achieved system readiness based on the completion of a rigorous testing methodology?

Other than the results cited in two instances where detailed error data was kept throughout a project there is, sadly, little else to go on. What is needed is a measure of software readiness that can be used "in the field." That measure would have some known properties. First, it would increase in value only when each new test performs something functionally "different" from the prior set(s) of tests. Merely executing the same test data repeatedly doesn't say very much about the software, so the measure should characterize the variations included in the testing activity.

Second, the measure should be sensitive to such factors as system cost, cost of running a test, software system criticality, etc. As difficult as these factors are to quantify, it seems possible (in principle at least) to rate them and scale them into the measure in a reasonable way.

One method to achieve this is to use the continuing testing effort as the basis for an empirical Markov model of a program's decisional transition probabilities, i.e., the effective probabilities that the program will take a particular outcome whenever a decision within it is reached. As each new test occurs, it updates the probability values for the current model. The overall reliability/readiness measure can then be recomputed. This notion relies on an interpretation of a new test in terms of the tests that have already been done, and the Markov representation simply acts as the "memory" about the past testing process.

Current developments

Current research and development activities in program testing have a natural organization. The major research topics and the way they relate to one another are shown in Figure 1. Some of the topics are discussed in more detail below.

Program analysis techniques. The notion of having a set of programs which analyzes other programs was introduced a very long time ago: assemblers were probably the earliest example of this idea. The late 1960's and early 1970's saw the development of systems that performed automatic analysis (other than compilation) in a research and development environment. For example, FACES, DAVE, and RXVP are systems that have many powerful capabilities for dealing with programs and their properties.[16,10,9] Such systems provide the basis for automation of function, which is needed in program structure analyzers and ultimately for reliable testing techniques.

Reliable testing techniques. A landmark paper by Goodenough and Gerhart[17] and subsequent work by Goodenough[18] show that under certain special circumstances testing methods could be the functional equivalent of a formal proof of correctness. The basic idea of this work is that, at least for certain kinds of program faults, tests can be constructed to distinguish between programs which do and do not have instances of those faults. The main result of this testing theory is as follows:

Theorem 1: A reliable, valid, complete, and successful testing activity is sufficient to prove that a program has no errors.[17]

Although this appears to be a very attractive result, it depends on the proper understanding of the four main terms:

(1) A *reliable* test is one for which there is a partition of the input domain within which selection of *any* value results either in an error or a successful test.
(2) A *valid* test is one in which all data that show the program is incorrect are in the corresponding input domain of the program.
(3) A *successful* test is one that produces normal program output when it is run.
(4) A *complete* test is one that, in the aggregate, tries to do all of the things the program is supposed to do (for that test).

There are detailed technical definitions of each of these terms in Reference 17. Meeting all of these requirements is not as easy as it might seem. In fact, it seems that there are certain kinds of program faults for which there are *no* reliable tests in the sense defined here.

Program structure theory. One of the core issues in program testing theory is the development of a good way to characterize the set of paths within a program. This characterization can be done for many reasons: (1) to organize program test case advice; (2) to assist in generating test data automatically; or (3) to provide the basis for constructing reliable tests. (This purpose is discussed later.)

Level-I path structures. The earliest development of program structure analysis techniques was based on analyzing the directed-graph representation of the predicate structure of the program. In the directed graph each program predicate is seated at one of the program graph's nodes; the outways of that node correspond to the two (or more) possible outcomes of that predicate. The entire directed graph—or *digraph*—is augmented with edges so that it is a single-entry/single-exit form.[1]

In one approach by the writer, and extended by Paige, potential program flows were characterized by the way they affected the iteration level within the program.[19, 20] The *iteration level* is an index of the number of levels of algorithm iteration within which each statement of the program lies. For example, a non-iterative program flow is described as a *level-zero path*. Higher-level paths, discovered by automatic graph analysis programs, are assigned increasing levels. The overall structure that results forms a tree that is used by automatic analysis programs to provide the basis for test case generation assistance.[21]

The advice function provided was based on the idea that extracting potential program flow sequences for manual evaluation of their feasibility would simplify an otherwise impossibly difficult problem. This was particularly true for large programs that had "rat's nest" control structures. As a human-augmentation technique the method worked well, but it suffered from requiring lengthy and detailed analysis of the potential for program flow. Other techniques based on canonical representation of programs are much better, as will be seen later.

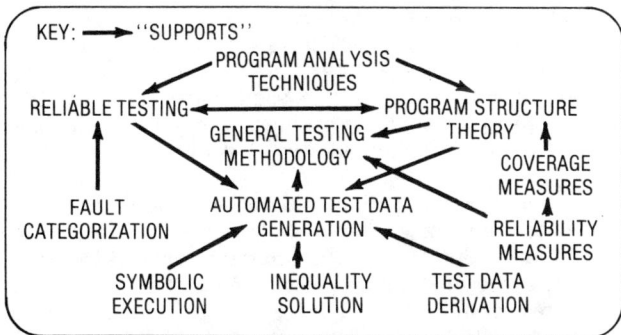

Figure 1. Interrelationships of research and development areas of program testing.

Equivalence classes. In an alternative development, Howden and others[22,13] created techniques for automatically identifying a complete set of program *cases*. Here, a case is an instance of program flow that is distinct from all others. Although this has been done only for very restricted programming languages, the technique results in somewhat simpler statements about program flow.

The set of program cases is interpreted in terms of a set of inequalities involving program variables that define a set of conditions necessary for the particular program flow to actually occur. For practical programs the set of inequalities is nonlinear, and there results a very difficult problem in finding values for the program input that match up with the inequalities, even for the limited programming language used.

Automated test data generation. It has been of great interest to devise a method for finding a set of legitimate input values for a program that will cause it to execute a previously unexecuted segment. This problem is widely known to be undecidable in general.[15,22] However, "undecidability" does not mean that other nonprocedural or heuristic techniques cannot be used.

The general problem of test case data generation reduces to one of finding a set of values that satisfy the collection of simultaneous nonlinear inequalities that in turn result from selecting a potential program path. The path might be selected manually or by one of the automated techniques just described. There are three routes to doing this which have received some serious attention.

Symbolic evaluation. This method involves either forward or backward symbolic interpretation of actual program statements that lie along the chosen path. Research in this area centers on selecting the particular statements to be included in the analysis and the ways to process the resulting formulas. Current efforts show promise, but no fully operational system has been demonstrated. King at IBM has been very active,[23] and work is also going on at Stanford Research Institute.[13]

Inequality solving. Given that the inequalities describing the condition of execution for a program path are found, they must be solved. In all but the most trivial of instances, the set of inequalities contains many nonlinear ones; this appears to be a natural attribute of practical computer programs. One partially successful technique for finding a solution involved linearizing the inequalities, solving the linearized set, and then attempting the solution for the nonlinear set. If found valid the process stops; otherwise, the linearization process is continued but with a finer (i.e., more precise) approximation. The partial successes achieved with this method are treated in detail in Reference 13.

Test case derivation. A somewhat different approach is to find a way to alter an existing set of test data so that the altered data forces the program to execute a previously unexecuted segment. For example, suppose a test execution takes the program "near" an unexercised segment. One can then use the existing test data as the starting point for a series of heuristically guided searches or variations that generally can result in success. This approach was described in some detail in Reference 24 for a very restricted language.

Reliable path testing

The reliability of path-based testing was analyzed in a recent paper by Howden.[22] "Path-based testing" means that a program is treated as an aggregate of (possibly) distinct program paths, the existence of which implies a partition of the input domain of the program into subdomains which control exactly those statements on the path chosen and no others. In his investigation of the theoretical reliability, Howden took the view that

(1) The program treated is a member of a class of programs which differ only in terms of whether or not they are correct. The incorrect ones have errors of various (known) types.
(2) The objective was to find, if possible, a restricted set of programs for which path testing would be reliable.

It is valuable to restate and paraphrase some of the rather technical theorems to see their impact on the possibility of developing a general test methodology.

Constant-structure testing. Assuming that the error in a program does not change its control flow (i.e., that the set of path classes of whatever origin is not affected), Howden proved the following:

Theorem 2: Path-based testing is a reliable method to distinguish correct and incorrect programs as long as each path is feasible and as long as the input domain of an incorrect program implied by the path does not intersect with the input domain of the correct program (along the same path).[22]

Here, an *infeasible path* is simply one which cannot be executed with any set of input data. What this theorem means is that a relatively simple path test is a reliable one under this condition: one must be able to choose any value in the specified input space and know that the program will behave correctly.

This is demonstrated by Howden on an example drawn from Reference 25. The kinds of errors intercepted by this process are called *action errors*, roughly characterized as those errors arising from an incorrect computation. By the assumption above, an action error does *not* affect the structure of the program's control flow although it may affect other features, such as the number of times around an iteration, etc. In order words, there is a restricted class of programs for which action errors can be found reliably by testing. Here, "reliably" is interpreted in the sense given after Theorem 1. For all practical purposes, such a reliable test is equivalent to a proof of correctness. The class of programs involved can be identified by the fact that, because they have no control-flow errors, they do not change the characterization of flow used.

Infinite loop checking. The same paper investigated another theorem—this one of importance to the phenomenon of testing for infinite loops:

Theorem 3: Path testing is a reliable method to discover the existence of infinite loop errors if and only if the input domain for the program contains at least one instance of data which will cause the program to execute infinitely.[22]

This allows reliable testing (in the sense defined above) for infinite loops as long as the program can be invoked (i.e., executed) with data that causes the infinite loop. More important, it assures that that form of testing is reliable.

Control-structure testing. For situations wherein the error category treated involves an incorrect control statement, the results suggest there is much more involved than for simple action errors. An error in a control statement is called a *case error*, since it affects the manner in which the flow paths partition the program's input domain. There are two possibilities: (1) the program's path classes remain unchanged because of the error; and (2) the error results in significant change in the path classes. Recall that a path class is simply the set of program flows that are alike because similar input data results in essentially equivalent use of the program's segments.

Whether there is a reliable testing method for case errors when the program structure is changed is an open question in the program testing research community. When the case errors do not change the overall structure of the program, there is this result:

Theorem 4: Path testing is a reliable method to discover case errors if and only if an incorrect program (one with a case error) has input domains that do not intersect the input domains of the correct program.[22]

The way one tells whether a case error exists is by examining the input domains. If there are values outside the correct subsets for the intended program behavior, then there is a case error of some kind. Although this sounds relatively simple, no good techniques have been found for systematically identifying and comparing input domains in this way.

Practical experience. Howden analyzed the errors in 18 example programs in Reference 25 with the following results: (1) of the 12 action errors found, nine could have been discovered by reliable path testing techniques; (2) of four case errors, only one could have been found by path testing; and (3) for the one infinite-loop error, it wasn't clear whether the error could have been found by path testing of any kind.

Although this analysis is hopeful, it's clear that much work needs to be done. Current efforts aimed at fault categorization (see Figure 1) will have a direct impact on the utility of program testing. They will provide the basis for devising reliable test procedures that guarantee low-cost discovery of (and protection against) such errors.

Hierarchical decompositions

Using Howden's results on reliable testing still requires detailed knowledge about the control structure of the programs being tested. Ideally, the characterization of the control space for a program should provide a number of capabilities:

(1) The method of selecting test paths for detailed examination should allow easy and natural selection of different test paths (or groups of test paths).
(2) The sets of test paths should be as "independent" of one another as possible so that different parts of a program's capability can be addressed in a series of tests that do not depend too highly on one another.
(3) The method should be applicable both to large individual modules (separately invokable programs or subprograms) and to large-scale software systems that are composed of many modules.

(4) The method should be applicable to the practical languages such as Fortran, Cobol, and PL/I rather than only to "toy languages" that are not widely used.

At least some of these capabilities are provided with a technique of hierarchically decomposing program control structures in terms of a limited set of control structure primitives.

Decomposition primitives. It is well known that all programs can be constructed with three programming primitives: succession, selection, and iteration.[26] When one draws a picture of a program decomposition, each decomposition is indicated as follows:

(1) *Succession:* A "dot," with the rule that the left-hand descendant precedes the right-hand descendant.
(2) *Selection:* A "plus," with the rule that the left-hand descendant corresponds to the "true" outcome, and the right-hand descendant corresponds to the "false" outcome.
(3) *Iteration:* A "star," with the rule that the left-hand descendant corresponds to the "repeated action," and the right-hand descendant corresponds to the "escape" or "exit" condition.

In the case of the selection primitive, a program statement that has more than one predicate outcome (such as a Fortran computed-GOTO statement with more than two indicated targets), one can permit the decomposition to have more than one outway. Although this set of primitives is the most popular, other sets could have been used as well.

Decomposition technique. The kind of tree structure that results from decomposing a program according to these primitives is shown for the example program in Figure 2. In the program the total "weight" of each nondecisional statement sequence is given after the sequence name; for example, sequence A has a "weight" of four units. Here, "weight" could be interpreted as the total number of separate statements in the sequence, or it could be related in some more complex way to the computational difficulty of the sequence.[27]

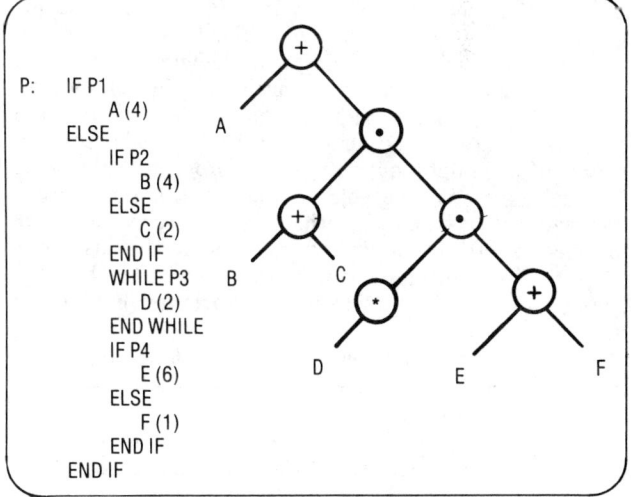

Figure 2. Example program and corresponding decomposition tree.

The tree shown in Figure 2 effectively illustrates the overall structure of the program P. Any two programs that have the same internal organization of control statements will have precisely the same tree. Note that the statement sequences always show up in the tree as leaves.

The tree in this example can be constructed by inspection (as the reader can verify), but for practical-sized programs it is desirable to have a small program that identifies the tree automatically. This program, which will not be discussed here, effectively turns the program's control structure inside out and generates the tree from the bottom up.[27,28]

Once the tree is found, one can use it to assist in constructing reasonable test paths. The set of all subtrees that includes at least one leaf corresponds roughly to the set of all possible program flows. The first objective of analyzing the tree is to identify the set of *structurally feasible flows*. These are the ones that remain after the *structurally infeasible flows* are excluded. For example, in the tree shown in Figure 2 it is not possible to have a flow which involves sequence A and any other sequence; thus, any potential subtree that does not involve A alone is automatically structurally infeasible.

Of the trees that remain, some may be *semantically infeasible*, which means that a certain program action taken at one point results in a set of conditions that makes some other program action impossible. Although the obvious approach would be to examine sequence/predicate pairs in some natural order, it turns out that this is not really necessary. Because of the way the tree is constructed, only certain kinds of relations need be examined in detail.[28] For purposes of illustration we assume every path that is structurally feasible is semantically feasible.

If we want to use some subset of the collection of feasible subtrees as a guide for testing, we need criteria for the selection of candidates. Here are two initial criteria:

(1) A minimum weight for each subtree selected must be commensurate with the desire to accomplish treatment of the program in easily manageable portions.

(2) Each leaf of the original tree must be included at least once in the set of subtrees selected.

The second criterion simply assures that the testing done accomplishes the C2 coverage criterion already suggested as the minimum one. The first criterion is intended to equalize the difficulty of each individual test case (or test case class) considered. Once the feasible subtrees are found and weights are assigned, devising a good test structure devolves to finding a balanced covering subset tree.

For the program in Figure 2 there are nine feasible subtrees; these are enumerated in Table 1. The subtree is indicated simply by noting the program sequences that belong to it; the column just to the right gives the weights associated with that subtree. The four possible covers are indicated by ⌐'s in the last four columns. The notation D^k is used to indicate that the D segment is actually included a variable (but finite)

number of times since D resides inside an iteration construct.

A very simple mechanism can be used to choose among the covers: simply multiply the weights for each element in the cover together and choose the product with the highest value. Other things being equal, a candidate cover set that distributes the weights as evenly as possible among the elements will tend to be chosen. Note that for this particular program each cover must involve the A segment since it is the sole member of an essential subtree.

The computations suggested above result in the following totals:

SUB-TREE NO.	COVER NO.	WEIGHTS	PRODUCT OF WEIGHTS
1, 2, 9	1	4, 10, 5	200
1, 3, 8	2	4, 12, 3	144
1, 4, 7	3	4, 5, 10	200
1, 5, 6	4	4, 7, 8	224

A good starting point evident from this enumeration is the set of subtrees (1, 5, 6) since it represents a cover and has the best distribution of program weight.

Naturally, this example is an oversimplification, but the points to be made are clear. Algorithms for doing all of the computations described already exist, and while choosing an optimum cover may be something of a stumbling block, there are certainly plenty of algorithms around to serve as good initial choices.

Non-structured programs. The example program is obviously well-structured. It is unlikely to find many programs which display this simple structure in the practical world, however, and it is important to point out how such programs can in effect be converted into this format. Program decompositions of the kind discussed here run into trouble when the analyzing programs encounter control graphs that have other than (1,1)-cycles. An *(m,n)-cycle* exists in the directed graph of the control structure when there is a closed sequence of edges (a loop) for which there are m different entering edges and n different exiting edges.

Programs that have other than purely (1,1)-cycles can be effectively reduced by the following two-step technique:

(1) Each (m,n) cyle is copied over m times to result in a set of m different $(1,n)$ cycles.

(2) Each $(1,n)$-cycle is then broken down into a $(1,1)$-cycle and a $(1,n-1)$-cycle, when n is greater than 1. Each $(1,1)$-cycle corresponds to an iteration primitive, and the remaining cycles are decomposed in turn until nothing other than $(1,1)$-cycles remain.[27]

An alternative would be to incorporate decomposition primitives different from the set used above in a way that allows for $(1,n)$-cycles, $n > 1$.

Other attributes of the decomposition. Recall that one objective of developing the decomposition idea is to obtain a capability to deal with large (or even very large) programs in a reasonable way. There are several properties of the tree approach that support this objective:

(1) The effect of a program invocation is simple to deal with. Suppose a program P' is invoked at (or within) statement sequence S inside program P. In effect, the tree for P' can be copied onto the tree for P in place of the sequence S. In these terms one can visualize the tree for an entire program space. Although

Table 1. Set of structurally feasible paths for example.

TREE NO.	PROGRAM SEGMENTS PRESENT	WEIGHT	COVER NO. 1	2	3	4
1	A	4	⌐	⌐	⌐	⌐
2	B, E	10	⌐			
3	B, D^k, E	12		⌐		
4	B, F	5			⌐	
5	B, D^k, F	7				⌐
6	C, E	8				⌐
7	C, D^k, E	10			⌐	
8	C, F	3		⌐		
9	C, D^k, F	5	⌐			

large, this tree has the advantage of providing a uniform structure-based representation of the total program text.

(2) Subsetting with a complicated program tree can be accomplished via the same technique, simply by removing a part of the tree from consideration. This method corresponds to creating a special subroutine that carries all of the program text in the subtree removed from the original program text, resulting in a logically simpler program to test. This technique has sometimes been called *program factoring* since the effect is to break a program into pieces small enough to be tested easily.

Suggested methodology

The framework for a methodology that combines automated program analysis, reliable path based testing, and hierarchical decompositions of programs should now be clear. Portions of the methodology can be used with present techniques as a practical basis for program testing. However, the methodology virtually requires automated assistance of some kind if it is going to be applied to realistic-sized programs. The reason for this is that the complexity of some of the computations quickly grows to the point where manual computation is plainly unthinkable for a 10,000-line or 100,000-line program.

The automatable functions required tend to fall into these categories:

(1) Some form of automated test data generator, used to develop test data after a particular program part has been identified as previously untested.

(2) A means to verify test execution coverage automatically so that data can be used to assist the human interacting with the system in choosing (and assessing) the next appropriate actions.

(3) A structure analyzer that performs the functions required to develop the program decomposition tree.

(4) A program of some kind that checks on the theoretical reliability of a planned test. This program applies the most recent theory of reliable testing (whatever that is) to the problem of deciding if a reliable test can be done for the indicated path.

(5) A support system to maintain the program data base, interface with the user interactively, and maintain a management-oriented summary of actions taken and current status.

These system components can be assmbled with existing techniques and can be engineered to assure they do not falter when confronted with very large programs likely to be treated.

The methodology for combining all of these ingredients is as follows, assuming that the program is compilably correct and there is at least one test case:

Step 1: The automated structure analyzer computes the tree for the entire program set and, possibly with human assistance, factors the tree into manageably small portions. Then, possibly also with human assistance to resolve problems in developing a cover, particular program paths are selected for detailed treatment. It is likely the first paths to be analyzed would be part of the initial test case.

Step 2: The automated test reliability analyzer determines if the chosen path can be tested by a known-to-be-reliable test method. If it can, the methodology proceeds with Step 3; otherwise, it continues with Step U.

Step 3: For the test path just selected, the automated test data generator is used to identify a set of data which causes the test case chosen to execute. Since the program execution trace for prior tests is available, this information can be used to help find appropriate test data. The result is the data needed to perform a verifiable test of the program.

Step 4: The parts of the program that were identified as reliably testable by the verified test just accomplished can now be pruned from the program tree. The methodology continues with Step 1 until there are no more leaves on the tree.

Step U: This is the undetermined set of human actions which might have to be taken when (a) reliably testable program paths cannot be found but some segments have not been tested; or (b) when the test data generation process fails for some reason. The actions taken at this point depend on human judgment as well as experience with the tools used. The methodology continues with Step 1.

Some of the humanly set parameters to the system used in conjunction with the methodology may include:

(1) the "size" of the program factors to be treated individually;

(2) the variations allowed when developing a covering set for some chosen interior subtree of the program; and

(3) conventional resource limits and progress milestones.

Future problems

While all of the techniques just described are well within the state of the art, many technical issues remain. Moreover, the basic notion of applying proven testing methods only where they can do some good will provoke still additional questions. Some discussion of the presently apparent problems will focus the attention of researchers on the rough points.

The decomposition techniques used apply nicely to nonrecursive programs and to programs written in high-level languages (such as Fortran, Cobol, and PL/I). It's clear there are many other program classes, including those written using recursion and those written in Assembly language, that are important to address, and the extension of the structure analysis algorithms to a broader range is going to be quite important. A secondary problem is the method used to treat (or distinguish between) differing mechanisms of invocation, such as call-by-name or call-by-reference.

Little research has been accomplished that addresses methods for testing programs that run in "real time" or that participate in concurrent processes. One problem is to find techniques for verifying path sequences without either violating the program's time line or over-expanding the executable text beyond a machine's capacity. A general approach to testing the time-sensitive parts of application programs is also needed.

The classes of program errors currently treatable are relatively small and need to be expanded significantly. In addition, a way to contend with case errors must be found. One suggestion is to employ the decomposition tree as a "pattern" for the program structure and assure that a correct pattern has been used by some other technique independent of the methods described here.

Although much research has been done concerning the problems of control of precision and such issues as round-off, underflow, and overflow, this work has never been factored into the program testing area. This topic would be of particular concern when considering building symbolic evaluation systems.

Experience on large software systems with a systematic program testing methodology is needed so that overall costs can be estimated, possibly in comparison with costs for other quality assurance techniques, such as program proving. Although it seems likely that program testing will be far cheaper than program proving, the quantitative basis for this presumption does not yet exist.

Finally, the techniques will have to be extended to cover the full spectrum of computer applications, including in particular the newly-burgeoning micro- and minicomputer marketplace where software quality is not yet (but should be) a serious matter. ■

References

1. W. C. Hetzel (ed.), *Program Test Methods*, Prentice-Hall, Inc., Englewood-Cliffs, New Jersey, 1973.

2. F. P. Brooks, Jr., *The Mythical Man-Month*, Addison-Wesley, Reading, Massachusetts, 1975.

3. R. London, "A View of Program Verification," *Proc., 1975 International Conf. on Reliable Software*, Los Angeles, California, pp. 534-545.

4. J. R. Brown, "Why Tools?" *Proc., Workshop 4, Computer Science and Statistics: Eighth Annual Symposium on the Interface*, Los Angeles, California, February 1975.

5. D. S. Alberts, "The Economics of Software Quality Assurance, *AFIPS Conf. Proc., 1976 NCC*, Montvale, New Jersey, 1976, pp. 433-442.

6. E. F. Miller, Jr., "Methodology for Comprehensive Software Testing," Rome Air Development Center, RADC-TR-75-161, June 1975.

7. J. R. Brown and M. Lipow, "Testing for Software Reliability," *Proc., 1975 International Conf. on Reliable Software*, Los Angeles, California, pp. 518-527.

8. L. Stucki, "A Prototype Automatic Program Testing Tool," *AFIPS Conf. Proc., 1972 FJCC*, Montvale, New Jersey, 1972, pp. 829-836.

9. E. F. Miller, Jr., "RXVP—An Automated Verification System for FORTRAN," *Proc., Workshop 4, Computer Science and Statistics: Eighth Annual Symposium on the Interface*, Los Angeles, California, February 1975.

10. L. J. Osterweil and L. D. Fosdick, "Data Flow Analysis as an Aid in Documentation, Assertion Generation, Validation, and Error Detection," CU-CS-055-74, University of Colorado, September 1974.

11. E. F. Miller, Jr., et al., "Jovial Automated Verification System," Rome Air Development Center, RADC-TR-76-20, February 1976.

12. E. F. Miller, Jr., "A General Purpose Program Analyzer," Software Research Associates, RN-210, March 1977.

13. R. S. Boyer, B. Elspas, and K. N. Levitt, "SELECT—A Formal System for Testing and Debugging Programs by Symbolic Execution," *Proc., 1975 International Conf. on Reliable Software*, Los Angeles, California, pp. 234-245.

14. M. Holthouse and E. S. Cosloy, "A Practical System for Automatic Testcase Generation," Presented at 1976 NCC, New York, June 1976.

15. E. F. Miller, Jr., and R. A. Melton, "Automated Generation of Testcase Datasets," *Proc., 1975 International Conf. on Reliable Software*, Los Angeles, California, pp. 51-57.

16. C. V. Ramamoorthy and S. F. Ho, "Fortran Automatic Code Evaluation System," Electronics Research Laboratory, University of California, ERL-M466, July 1974.

17. J. B. Goodenough and S. L. Gerhart, "Toward a Theory of Test Data Selection," *Proc., 1975 International Conf. on Reliable Software*, Los Angeles, California, pp. 493-510.

18. J. B. Goodenough, "Program Testing Survey," to appear in *InfoTech State-of-the-Art Report*, 1977.

19. E. F. Miller, Jr., "A Survey of Major Techniques of Program Validation," General Research Corporation, RM-1731, October 1972.

20. M. R. Paige, "Program Graphs, An Algebra, and Their Implication for Programming," *IEEE Trans. on Software Engineering*, September 1975, pp. 286-291.

21. E. F. Miller, Jr., et al., "Structurally Based Automatic Program Testing," *Proc., EASCON-74*, Washington, D.C.

22. W. E. Howden, "Reliability of the Path Analysis Testing Strategy," *IEEE Trans. on Software Engineering*, September 1976, pp. 208-214.

23. J. C. King, "A New Approach to Program Testing." *Proc., 1975 International Conf. on Reliable Software*, Los Angeles, California, pp. 228-233.

24. M. R. Paige, "A Pragmatic Approach to Software Testcase Generation," Science Applications, Inc., September 1975.

25. B. W. Kernighan and P. J. Plauger, *The Elements of Programming Style*, McGraw-Hill, New York, 1974.

26. E. Ashcroft and Z. Manna, "The Translation of GOTO Programs to WHILE Programs," *Information Processing 71*, North-Holland Publishing, 1972, pp. 250-255.

27. J. E. Sullivan, "Measuring the Complexity of Computer Software," MITRE Corporation Report, 1973.

28. E. F. Miller, Jr., "Tree-based Program Decomposition and Test Planning Techniques," Software Research Associates, RN-208, March 1977.

Edward F. Miller, Jr., is an independent consultant and lecturer with Software Research Associates in San Francisco, California. His interests include software engineering management support, program testing technology, hierarchical design methods, program analysis tool development, automation of function in software engineering systems, and computer architecture.

Dr. Miller was previously director of the Software Technology Center, Science Applications, San Francisco, and director of the Program Validation Project at General Research, Santa Barbara. He holds a BSEE from Iowa State University, an MS in applied mathematics from the University of Colorado, and a PhD from the University of Maryland, where he was an instructor from 1964 to 1968.

Dr. Miller is a member of IEEE, ACM, and SIAM, and editor of SIGARCH's bimonthly publication, *Computer Architecture News*. He is currently preparing a textbook and short-course material on program testing techniques.

PROGRAM TESTING TECHNOLOGY IN THE 1980s

Edward F. Miller, Jr.

Software Research Associates

ABSTRACT

The current state of the art in program testing technology is identified in terms of the philosophical underpinnings of software, the theoretical foundations of the field, the tools and techniques that can be brought to bear in a testing activity, the methods that exist for planning and measuring the testing activity, and the methods of management and control that exist.

The future needs for program testing technology are identified in three major categories: theoretical foundations, methodology, and automated tools. Over twenty needs for program testing targeted for the 1980s timeframe are identified in detail.

1   THE PRESENT

The purpose of this paper is to survey the present state-of-the-art in program testing technology and to prognosticate for the future in this technical area of software engineering.

Program testing generally is taken to include all of those activities that support the "software quality assurance function" up to but not including the methods that clearly fall into the domain of "program proof of correctness." Depending on who you are and what your orientation might be, program testing can be either a very exciting area where there is significant opportunity for both creativity and disciplined "science," or it can be a grubby mess of not-quite-scientific methods and beliefs that have been likened to a "black art." A secondary objective of this paper is to make these distinctions a little clearer than they are now and, hopefully, to convince any and all readers of both the legitimacy and the urgency of program testing technology.

Dijkstra certainly made an interesting statement when he said "program testing can only serve to identify program bugs, never to eliminate them." And, more recently, Dijkstra also declined (quite politely) to participate in putting together a special issue of a well-known technical magazine on program testing by noting that he didn't feel there was enough known about program testing to write even a single paper, let alone fill an entire issue! It's hoped Dijkstra's wrong on this point.

1.1   WHAT IS TESTING?

Testing is the controlled analysis and/or execution of a program expressed in some language done to verify the pre-determined (pre-specified) presence of some desired program property. When performed in a systematic methodology testing also serves a related function: to demonstrate the absence of unwanted function. The combination of the two activities (i.e., showing the usefulness of real program functions and, indirectly, demonstrating the absence of unwanted or erroneous program functions) makes up the testing process.

It is important to note that the goals of program proving -- the only other technically viable approach to assuring software quality -- are essentially the same. In fact, there is an increasing trend toward viewing program testing and program proving as two points on a relatively continuous spectrum of possible methods of software quality assurance.

So-called "static testing" is specifically included in the definition under the heading of systematic analysis of programs at the source level. The long-term role of static testing remains in doubt, but there is certainly no quarrel in the community with the notion that static testing will be around in some form. It may not, however, necessarily be connected with software quality assurance; instead, this "branch" of program testing may become a more formalized part of the software production process. Many current static analysis methods are closely related to those used during program compilation. (Examples are data-flow based analyses, syntax checking, and similar tricks that are employed in the "checkout compilers.")

The main stream of program testing concentrates on a number of relatively simply stated issues:

- How to set up a test environment for a program (or set of programs)?

- How to provide "good" inputs to the program (set) under evaluation?

- How to interpret the results produced by a program to tell whether or not it is working correctly?

- How to measure the thoroughness of testing already performed and how to determine how much testing has yet to be done?
- How to tell the likelihood of errors escaping the systematic testing process?
- How to do all of this at low enough cost?

The last point emphasizes the engineering-like nature of program testing, as compared with the "science-like" nature of program proving techniques.

1.2 THE PRESENT STATE OF TESTING

There is, it will have to be admitted, a rather large quantity of software extant that generally speaking works! (By "works" is meant that it does not fail too often to be unacceptable entirely.) In fact, it should be agreed that the U.S. economy is now, for all practical purposes, fully <u>dependent</u> on computers (and, hence, on computer <u>software</u>) for its orderly operation. Clearly, that economy works!

One way to assess the quality of program testing methods is simply to observe that all of the software that keeps on working, day in and day out, certainly didn't get to be as correct as it is by methods of program proving! Although this number may be somewhat out of date when this paper appears, the largest program that has been "proved" correct runs to about 2000 statements.

So, one thing is perfectly clear: all of the working software that now keeps the economy moving along -- that is, gets the checks written, helps run the big and small companies, reserves airline seats, schedules trucks, etc. -- is effectively correct enough by some means other than by program proving. In a recent paper by Alberts (Ref. 1) there was some data presented on how this situation might have come to be. That paper analyzed a number of long-life-cycle software systems to see where the money that was spent on them was actually spent. One of the results that is somewhat anti-intuitive is that nearly 97% of the overall life cycle cost was expended during the production and operational phases, and that fully 50% of the total was expended <u>after</u> the programs achieved "first release" status. The same study indicated that of the 97% about half of that was spent on generating the software or modifications to it and the other half was spent on making sure that the software (or modifications to it) did the "right" thing.

Very simply this says that software actually gets to be correct by having been tested into that state, since around 50% of the effort goes into activities that clearly fall into testing's domain. Note that this argument certainly does not suggest that the testing that was done was done in a particularly smart, cost-effective, or high-technology manner. In fact, and there is much intuitive support for this notion as well as

the hard numbers Alberts gives, it is quite clear most of the "reliability" in current software systems was installed there by hammer and tongs methods, by seat of the pants and brute-force, straightforward unenlightened "try it and fix it until it works" methods!

In other words, program testing already works!

What's lacking is a good, cost-effective, way to "do" testing that can be applied early in the software engineering life cycle, has demonstrable effectiveness, and can be extended to "protect" against additional error-classes as they are identified.

1.3 THE PRESENT STATE OF TESTING TECHNOLOGY

Just knowing that testing works is not sufficient basis to assess the future. In addition, it will be necessary to address what is known about testing from a methodological viewpoint in order to project technical milestones for 5 to 10 years into the future.

Current testing technology is illustrated by the collection of papers presented in (Ref. 2), which also provides a reasonably convenient taxonomy of sub-technologies.

1.3.1 <u>Philosophy of Testing</u>

The basic principles of testing -- including repeatability, determinism, separability (decomposibility), and several others -- are well established both in practical and theoretical terms. The notions that underly the objectives and outcomes of formalized testing are reasonably in hand. And the relationship between program testing and other disciplines -- notably software design methods and software maintenance technology -- are well recognized, even if they are less than perfectly understood.

1.3.2 <u>Theoretical Foundations</u>

Much of the theory of testing arises from two forms of graph-theory-based modelling of program properties: control flow analysis and data flow analysis. The former is rather well developed; in fact, it may be that that area is overdeveloped to the point that theoretical results are more prevalent than results that have demonstrated their utility!

The control structure of a program in any language with a deterministic decisional structure can be represented as a finite, possible disconnected, directed graph with a single entry and single exit (corresponding to the "invocation" and the "return" of the module). The single-entry/single-exit property is exploited in hierarchical representations of program structure that assume the program is constructed purely with the standard structured programming conventions: sucession, alteration, and iteration.

In addition, there are well-known algorithms for converting the structure of any program (whether well-structured or not) into this particular canonical form (Ref. 3). Test planning for "well-structured programs" seems to be particularly simple and converting at least a representation of any program into this format clearly has the advantage of providing a subsequent uniform treatment method.

Modern reliable testing theory, invented by Goodenough and Gerhart (Ref. 4) and extended by Howden in a series of brilliant studies, addresses the question of the overall capability of any testing process to (a) demonstrate correct function and (b) identify incorrect operation. While the theoretical developments are still underway, current results are more than pleasing: programs which meet certain criteria of structural correctness can be "proved" solely through testing, and even programs that are not necessarily structurally correct can have about half of their problems spotted through testing (or at least the theory suggests this would be possible for the latter case).

Incidently, this may account for the "success" of the structured programming revolution: Better structured programs are more reliably testable and hence are less likely to contain errors!

Current research concentrating on the application of statistics to gross studies of program behavior (for example, see the work of Schneidewind (Ref. 6) among others) in terms of the level of structural exercise given them suggest the possibility for macroscopic measures of testing reliability, even though so far no such measures have been defined and/or validated. In the same vein, there has been a great deal of interest in studying the kinds and rates of program errors to the purpose of finding out if there is some simple (or even complex) pattern. This, too, has led to a mass of data that certainly has not been reduced to the nth degree yet.

Finally, program language design has devoted itself to matters of quality assurance, but with a certain reluctance that seems to be natural enough. Language developers want a good language more than they want a language with fully testable properties, and that is as it should be. The main invention of the past five years is the "ASSERT Statement," included in programs typically as commentary but sensed by automated tools during the formal debugging/testing process. Several systems are installed and in active use employing this notion.

1.3.3 Tools and Techniques

Certainly the period 1972-1977 was five years of intensive tool building. For a time it seemed as if everyone was going to have his own set of tools. Then, suddenly, the introduction rate for new tools dropped to zero. What happened?

One of the main purposes of tool developers was to find out if tools were possibly useful to program testing. Many of the tools introduced during the 5-year period were "research and development prototypes" and did not have really adequate maintenance support. It is curious that only a few of the so-called program testing tools were ever used to analyze themselves. And, by the same arithmetic, it is interesting to note that of the two or three tools that did survive the test of time they generally did have some limited self-application. (An example is the JAVS system (Ref. 7) built to analyze JOVIAL/J3 programs and programmed in itself.)

Automated tools fall into the categories: code auditor, static analyzer, dynamic assertion processor, self-metric instrumentor, test file generator, test data generator, test execution verifier, output comparator, test harness generator, and symbolic evaluation facility. In a recent survey of automated tools (Ref. 9) nearly 80 tools were identified as commercially available instances of these ten categories. Experience suggests there are perhaps three times as many tools when one includes the in-house versions whose existence increasingly becomes evident.

No single source exists for tools that apply to all of the categories listed above for one particular programming language and/or for one particular system. This dispersion seems to be a natural part of the "tools business," an apparent result of the necessity to satisfy needs that are expressed by the buyers, rather than to deliver up a "good" set of tools oriented horizontally to the necessary functions of program testing.

1.3.4 Planning and Measurement

Present methods for test planning are based on relatively simple measures of "testing coverage," a term that roughly describes the extent to which an individual invocation/test of a module exercises all of the structural entities previously identified within it.

2   THE FUTURE

Assessing the future will be more convenient if we can organize the projections into categories that are related. It will be convenient to deal with these three:

- Theory: Technical developments in the foundations of computer science or applications thereof that have a direct effect on the nature of the program testing process, or could be applied specifically to the program testing process.

- Methodology: Developments of an experiential and/or planning and/or procedural nature that serve to enhance the capability of a program testing team, or simplify the activities that comprise or support the testing activity.

- **Automated Tools:** Systematizable algorithms or actual automated tools that perform identifiable function(s) in support of program testing (not necessarily limited to tools that are actually built and used widely).

The advantage of using these three categories is that they are largely orthogonal with each other and when not the overlap is rather simple to take care of.

2.1 THEORETICAL DEVELOPMENTS

Program testing technology appears to rely on four sub-areas of the theory of computing (computing science), as follows: directed-graph theory, programming language theory, formal testing theory, and empirical analysis.

2.1.1 Graph Theory

The use of graph theory to model control structure and data structure is well in place, and only a few new developments are required to cement all of the loose ends together:

▶ Need-1: A uniform method and representation for hierarchical decomposition of programs that incorporates multiple-module systems.

The theoretical means already exist in the work of Zohar Manna (Ref. 12), and effectively in practice with systems that "convert" unstructured to pure-structured programs (Ref. 13). What does not exist, however, is a system (i.e., algorithms plus associated data structures) for developing this decomposition in a language-independent/machine-environment-independent fashion.

It is well known there is a close relationship between the structure of a program and its content or behavior. It is possible to classify programs according to very general characteristics such as iterative, non-iterative, recursive, etc. What is needed is a much more general method for characterizing the function of a program from its structure alone. This is part of the more general theoretical need:

▶ Need-2: Devise a general relationship between a programming structure and the content/effect/nature/behavior of the corresponding program.

At the same time the theory of data-flow graphs appears to be under-utilized regarding program testing. At present the only practical application of data flow graphs is in the area of static allegation checking. Ref. 14, for example, discusses how data flow graph information is used to prove relatively strong allegations about FORTRAN programs. This leads to:

▶ Need-3: Develop a general/global theory of data flow as it applies to issues of program testing, and also develop corresponding data flow graph algorithms and data structures.

2.1.2 Programming Language Theory

The needed theoretical developments in programming language theory are less related to the specifics of the programming language than they are to augmentation of the languages with language constructs that aid in the testing process. Thus, this need is less a technical one than an engineering one.

▶ Need-4: Develop good forms of statements to describe tests, test data, and test results that become part of the permanent content of a computer program.

Obviously this imposes some additional requirements on the compiler that processes programs with statements from this new class. The most likely implementation would be to have such statements parsed and then passed unless the compiler were interconnected to an automated testing system.

A second area which has some very attractive potential benefits from the program tester's point of view is the development of compilers that are better able to support the needs of generalized program analysis such as is needed in the program testing activity. The PL/1 compiler goes a half-step in the right direction by emitting (under the right commands) a so-called diagnostic table that contains, among lots of other things, a complete symbol table. The needs of a program tester (or an automated program analysis tool) are simpler than that in some cases, and more complicated in others. For example, it would be desirable to have all of the graph structures emitted automatically and this is currently not done.

2.1.3 Formal Testing Theory

The work of Goodenough, Gerhart, and Howden has established that there is a formal basis for testing. Although many of theorems necessary to support it remain to be stated and proved, it is believed that testing can be effectively the full equivalent of program proof of correctness, provided that the right kinds of auxiliary analysis are done in selecting test data. The program testing community has come a long way from the days, in 1972, when it was thought it would be impossible to comprehensively test any program at all! Now, at least some programs can be thoroughly tested (those with bounded path counts) and under certain circumstances more complex programs can be effectively tested.

Formal testing theory focuses on the relationship between thorough, effective, reliable, and comprehensive in the contexts just defined. The difficulty is, and has always been, that the number of tests that constitute the equivalent of program proof is either too large or impossible to construct economically. Formal testing theory thus has several specific needs, as follows:

➤ Need-5: A general theory of formal testing that states, for any given program path, whether or not a particular piece of test data "protects" all of the program text along that path from <u>all</u> kinds of errors (i.e., both logic and computation).

➤ Need-6: A method for advising a programmer of the minimum set of additional constraints that must be met by a set of test data in order that the test data reliably be proof against all forms of failure.

➤ Need-7: A general method for designing the criteria that individual test cases must meet to assure all errors in a program have been protected against. (These criteria would apply before selecting the test data, and could be incorporated in the program text automatically by an automated tool.)

➤ Need-8: A general method for constructing subsets of test data that meet subset-requirements like those mentioned above for parts of programs.

The last-stated requirement is included because of the increasing need to be able to devise effective tests for parts of a software system, under the assumption that the remainder of the software system is effectively error-free. (This is the principle of separability that permits reducing one too-large problem into two or more "smaller" ones.)

2.1.4 Empirical Analysis

There is a great deal of data lying around about the errors in programs; and there is a great deal of data that describes the effort that was put into program testing. What there is not, and it is quite surprising that this statement is true, is a really effective analysis of the effectiveness of testing in ridding programs of errors!

This is part of the larger need: the empirical analysis of programming and programming support processes, including the statistically significant statement(s) of installed reliability that everyone wishes existed.

➤ Need-9: There should be a general theoretical model for software as an immutable but potentially erroneous process that can be used to predict failure probability from level of testing effort (and, possibly, form of testing effort or testing basis).

This kind of systematic methodology would permit, in effect, a rudimentary indemnification process. Perhaps the actuaries of the world should be asked to contribute their methods to this problem?

2.2 METHODOLOGY DEVELOPMENTS

There are as many "flavors" of methodology as there are program testing experts. And, maybe even twice as many! A methodology really means a pre-determined strategy that <u>should</u> be applied to a program testing problem of very general nature. Every methodology is expected to be varied according to the specifics of the situation; in fact, there is even a school of thought suggesting that the list of methodologies should contain one names "non-methodology," just for logical completeness.

The technical developments in methodologies arise through a combination of advances in the theory of testing and the experience gained in prior uses of the methodologies. The general methodologies discussed as reasonable ones include at least the following components: (1) an established coverage measure or testing goal; (2) an indication of how to resolve conflicts of resource allocation to the partially-completed testing process (these may include complexity measurements or other forms of weighting of uncompleted testing work); and (3) a body of techniques that can be used to accomplish the goal with very high reliability. For example, one might use a methodology that consists of: (1) use of the C1-coverage measure; (2) bottom-up testing (in which other things being equal one focuses testing effort on the bottom-most element that does not have $C1 = 100\%$); and, (3), a purely manual method for generating test data to accomplish the C1 goal. (For calibration purposes, this particular methodology is the minimum one currently being recommended for industrial use.)

➤ Need-10: There need to be a series of well-understood measures of testing effectiveness and the relationships between them for particular programming languages need to be very well understood.

For example, one needs to know that C1 is about half as difficult to accomplish as C2 (see Ref. 15). In general, effort-times-coverage should equal (or at least be proportional to) overall reliability.

➤ Need-11: There needs to be a series of well-understood weightings of programs in particular languages that distinguish them in terms of their difficulty of testing.

This need addresses the issue of deciding in advance how to allocate resources, but it also tells how well a particular testing method is going to be in determining the likelihood of there remaining any errors in the program.

A recent development by DeMillo, et. al. (Ref. 16) suggests that there is a realistic expectation that tests designed to act as protection against simple errors are effective against more complicated errors as well. This is called the testing coupling effect. It is quite likely there are other similar phenomena that relate to testing and would be discovered if the right forms of investigation were done:

> **Need-12:** Significant experience with testing of large systems must be analyzed with the intention of uncovering empirical principles that can minimize the cost of the testing process, or increase its effectiveness at the same cost.

Unfortunately, this is a Loch-Ness-Monster approach since it's anybody's guess what would eventually be found!

A more practical development would be the wide application of minimum testing coverage measures combined with the development of statistics on errors as a result of this:

> **Need-13:** Wide acceptance of some minimum level of testing coverage for all software systems.

Such measure, namely the C1 measure that requires each branch to have been executed at least once but not in all possible combinations, is currently under consideration by the U.S. Air Force. It can be hoped other organizations of the Government and eventually all of industry can agree on the same minimum standard. Naturally, a stronger standard is much more desirable!

The final area to be considered in the "methodology" category focuses on the psychology of program testing teams. At present there is very little experience to back up the idea, but it appears that there is a basically different kind of mind needed to test programs as opposed to producing them. The programmers' and the testers' mind sets may be as different as the movie producers' and the movie critics'. This leads to:

> **Need-14:** There must be a well-understood psychology of program testing that can be used in designing and implementing organizations that effectively perform the testing activity.

Naturally enough, it is likely that sufficiently smart team organization can be expected to produce significantly better results -- that is, better quality software.

2.3 AUTOMATED TOOL DEVELOPMENTS

The automated tools business has, at times in the last five years, worn a hair shirt for no reason at all. At other times, it's been quite clear some form of penance ought to be involved.

Beginning in 1972 there was the great automated program testing tools race, documented however unintentionally by Brown in Ref. 17. While it may never be clear if anyone won the race, it may be that *all* of the participants lost the race! The reason is clear from a recent survey of automated tools to support program testing (Ref. 9) there does not exist a *single set* of tools that addresses each of the known-to-be-valuable-functions for a single language or from a single supplier! Of the 85+ tools listed the most that could be said about overall coverage of the 10 categories is that one tool effectively treated about half of the areas. This is curious considering both the interest in automated tools, the necessity to have them in most (if not all) program testing situations, and the apparently high profit potential if good ones can be found and successfully marketed.

Most automated tools are weak in two areas: (1) user interface and (2) volume of output. Many of the tools introduced in the 1972-1975 were "research and development prototypes" in the sense that they were more in the category of demonstrating a principle than in the category of operational tool. This fact may account for the deficiencies noted above.

> **Need-15:** There must be a simplified user interface for program testing tools that permits a user to focus on testing rather than on understanding the vagaries of tool use.

> **Need-16:** The volume of output produced by tools must be completely under the control of the user. It is desirable if tools can operate interactively since this minimizes the impact of providing voluminous outputs somewhat.

Much of these kinds of requirements would be met with fourth-generation software analysis tools, of which there are many species in development at present (but with no announcement date).

It will be valuable to break the discussion down into individual discussions of automated tool areas so that each can be treated effectively.

2.3.1 Execution Verifiers and Coverage Analyzers

This tool category includes all forms of program instrumentation and associated dynamic behavior analysis to accomplish some form of automated coverage analysis of software systems under test. There have been many tools developed for this purpose, most of them for FORTRAN software both because that language is easier and because the "buyers" are interested in that language. The main output is the C1 measure (i.e., the percentage of program segments or branches that were exercised as the result of a particular test invocation).

> **Need-17:** There is a need for "clean" design, efficient, and generalized portable coverage analyzers, possibly as part of compilers and possibly as pre/post-processing free-standing systems.

This need would be met by commercial offerings in the next few years probably without any spurs from the R&D community. Certainly so long as this kind of tool can employ conventional subroutine-implant instrumentation the technique can be made portable. The data-reporting requirements are now reasonably well understood provided that there is an adequate stream of data to report on!

What does not exist is a single package with versions for a wide variety of languages and applicable on a wide variety of machines. It would seem likely there is a market for such a package.

2.3.2 Test Harness Systems

A test harness system eases the pain of (i) setting up the test driver, (ii) generating appropriate stub information, (iii) verifying that the program produces correct results (by comparison) with predicted results), and (iv) keeping track of a series of test data. The test harness makes regression testing trivial to accomplish because the descriptions of the test input and output(s) are already done. Existing packages claim to do this, but often place an unreasonably high burden of work on the program tester.

► Need-18: Develop an efficient and powerful test harness system that eliminates the need for any work on the part of the program tester, except possibly for interactive-based queries by the system to the program tester.

2.3.3 Input/Output Generator

An input/output generator is a new tool that currently has no parallel in the tool community, but which does exist in prototype versions in several instances. The idea behind the tool is simple enough: given some input data for a program, determine which output variables are actually computed by, or are affected by, the program as it operates with/on the given input. The utility of this is that it is somewhat easier to use than a test harness, in which all of this information must be known by auxiliary means. In use, such a system would make it a simple matter to know, in general, how inputs relate to outputs.

► Need-19: Develop an efficient and powerful input/output analyzer for complicated (multiple module) software systems that can identify the outputs in symbolic form that are affected when particular inputs are supplied.

Since testing consists almost entirely of choosing inputs, observing coverage, and affirming the correctness (or noting the erroneousness) of output, the need for this particular kind of tool is apparent. As before, this is not at all beyond the state of the art, although as a practical matter it would require a non-trivial amount of system design to build such a tool for a specific language and/or machine environment.

2.3.4 Symbolic Evaluation Facility

The discussions previously lead, naturally enough, to this need:

► Need-20: Develop a general symbolic interpretation/execution/analysis facility for large-scale software systems.

Existing systems, such as EFFIGY, have demonstrated the value of this kind of program manipulation. What is missing is practical systems, which would have to be interactive without question, that are within reach of the average program tester.

2.3.5 Miscellaneous Tools and Techniques

There are special problems for program testing that fall outside the "normal" range of monolithic multi-module, non-real-time software system that is well organized and has good inherent structure. Two that come to mind are the real-time dependent system and the concurrent system.

► Need-21: Develop a system for effectively monitoring testing coverage in a system which must operate against real-time constraints.

► Need-22: Develop a system for effectively monitoring testing coverage in a system which must operate against concurrency constraints.

Note that these two areas are treated simply as if appropriate tools only are required to deal with testing problems of the indicated kind; this is a statement that requires some comment. To begin with, whether a program performs in real-time -- equivalently, against some time constraint- is not properly a topic for program testing but, instead, for program performance measurement/ enhancement. By the same count, under the assumption that cooperating sequential processes synchronize their operations with the popular primitive operations there is nothing left to test about their cooperation that cannot be tested in the absence of the cooperation. Both cases wash out to the normal case when one postulates a machine with infinite resources.

As a practical problem, however, it is necessary to be able to measure what does go on in such situations -- and hence Need-21 and Need-22 -- but it appears these are the only two items that pertain to the areas of real-time operation and concurrent operation.

3 SUMMARY

We have seen that the state of the art in program testing is sufficient to provide a very strong base to go forward into the 1980s with a realistic expectation that software systems can be made as reliable as is necessary, although this would involve significant costs in some cases.

Specific needs, oriented to a taxonomy of program testing that highlights the major technological areas that support the area, have been identified. Although 22 specific needs were identified, it is important also to note that the list is probably far, far too short!

References

1. D.S. Alberts, "The Economics of Software Quality Assurance," Proc. 1976 National Computer Conference, AFIPS Press, 1976.

2. E.F. Miller, *Program Testing Techniques* (Tutorial), IEEE Computer Society, 1977.

3. E. Ashcroft and Z. Manna, "The Translation of GOTO to WHILE Programs," Stanford University, CS-188, 1970.

4. J. Goodenough and S. Gerhart, "Toward a Theory of Test Data Selection," IEEE Trans. Software Engineering, 1975.

5. W.E. Howden, "Reliability of Symbolic Evaluation," IEEE CompSac, Chicago, Illinois, 1977.

6. N.F. Schneidewind, et. al., "Software Error Detection Models, Validation Tests, and Program Complexity Measures," Naval Postgraduate School, November 1977.

7. JOVIAL Automated Verification System (JAVS), Rome Air Development Center, 1976.

8. E.F. Miller, "Program Testing Technology in the 1980s," Software Research Associates, RN-408, February 1978.

9. E.F. Miller, "Program Testing Tools and Their Use -- A Survey," Proc. MIDCON 1977.

10. Air Force Regulation AFT 800-14.

11. G.J. Myers, *Software Reliability*, Wiley-Interscience, 1976.

12. G. deBalbin, "The Structuring Engine, Reference Manual," Caine, Farber & Gordon, 1975.

13. R.A. Melton, "REFTRAN Reference Manual," General Research Corporation, 1976.

14. L.J. Osterweil, "Dave -- A Validation Error Detection and Documentation System for FORTRAN," Software Practice and Experience, Vol. 6, 1976.

15. E.F. Miller, *Program Testing Techniques* (Tutorial), IEEE Computer Society, 1977.

16. T.A. Budd, R. DeMillo, and R.J. Lipton, "The Design of a Prototype Mutation System for Program Testing," 1978 National Computer Conference, June 1978.

17. J. Brown, "Why Tools?," Proc. Eighth Annual Symp. on Computer Science and Statistics, UCLA, Los Angeles, February 1975.

Software Testing and Validation Bibliography — 1981 Update

Edward Miller
Software Research Associates

Linda Schallan
Schallan Editing and Research

This bibliography on software testing and validation covers the years 1977 through 1981. Papers, reports, texts, and other items of significance and relevance to the software testing and validation field are included. Although incomplete, this list reaches the "90 percent level" of having achieved full coverage of the literature in this period. The journals and proceedings scanned include:

IEEE Transactions on Software Engineering
Software Engineering Notes (ACM SIGSOFT)
Computer
Software—Practice & Experience
Proceedings of international conferences on software engineering held during 1978, 1979, and 1981

In addition, Software Research Associates' collection of reports and miscellaneous documents on software testing was surveyed for material dated subsequent to 1977.

Abu-El-Haija, A. I. and M. Choquet, "Remote Measurement of Some Telephone Channel Impairments Using Microprocessors," IBM Research Report, RC-7629 (#33017), Yorktown Heights, N.Y., May 1979.

Adam, A., P. Gloess, and J.-P. Laurent, "An Interactive Tool for Program Manipulation," *Proc. 5th Int'l Conf. Software Engineering*, San Diego, Mar. 1981, pp. 460-468.

Adams, J. M., "Experiments on the Utility of Assertions for Debugging," New Mexico State University, Las Cruces, 1977.

Adams, J. M., "A General, Verifiable Iterative Control Structure," *IEEE Trans. Software Engineering*, Vol. SE-3, No. 2, Mar. 1977, pp. 144-149.

Agrawal, V. D., "When To Use Random Testing," IEEE Computer Society, R-77-338, Sept. 1977. (Available from the UCLA Computer Science Archive.)

Aho, A. V. and J. D. Ullman, "Node Listings for Reducible Flow Graphs," *Proc. 7th Ann. ACM Symp. Theory of Computing*, 1975, pp. 175-185.

"Air Traffic Control IV and V Program," Systems and Applied Sciences Corp., Riverdale, Md., Jan. 1980.

Akers, S. B., "Test Generation Techniques," *Computer*, Vol. 13, No. 3, Mar. 1980, pp. 9-15.

Alberts, D. S., "The Economics of Software Quality Assurance," *AFIPS Conf. Proc.*, Vol. 45, 1976 NCC, pp. 433-442.

Alford, M. W., C. G. Davis, and L. R. Marker, "Automated Software Requirements Validation," presentation at COMPSAC 77, Chicago, Nov. 1977.

Al-Jarrah, M. M. and I. S. Torsun, "An Empirical Analysis of COBOL Programs," *Software—Practice & Experience*, Vol. 9, No. 5, May 1979, pp. 341-355.

Allen, F. E., "Interprocedural Data Flow Analysis," *Proc. IFIP Congress 74*, North-Holland Pub. Co., Amsterdam, 1974, pp. 398-402.

Allen, F. E., "Program Optimization," *Ann. Rev. in Automatic Programming*, No. 5, 1969, pp. 239-307.

Allen, F. E., et al., "The Experimental Compiling Systems Project," IBM Research Report, RC-6718, 1977.

Allen, F. E. and J. Cocke, "A Program Data Flow Analysis Procedure," *CACM*, Vol. 19, No. 3, Mar. 1976, pp. 137-147.

Ambler, A. L., et al., "A Language for Specification and Implementation of Verifiable Programs," University of Texas, Austin, Jan. 1977.

Ambler, A. L., et al., "Report on the Language Gypsy," University of Texas, Austin, Aug. 1976.

Amory, W. and J. A. Clapp, "A Software Error Classification Methodology," Mitre Corp., TR-2648, Vol. III, Bedford, Mass., June 1973.

Anderson, T. and R. Kerr, "Recovery Blocks in Action," *Proc. 2nd Int'l Conf. Software Engineering*, San Francisco, Oct. 1976, pp. 447-457.

Andrews, D. M. and J. P. Benson, "An Automated Program Testing Methodology and Its Implementation," *Proc. 5th Int'l Conf. Software Engineering*, San Diego, Mar. 1981.

Arisawa, M. and M. Iuchi, "Debugging Methods in Recursive Structured FORTRAN," *Software—Practice & Experience*, Vol. 10, No. 1, Jan. 1980, pp. 29-43.

Ashcroft, E. and Z. Manna, "The Translation of GOTO Programs to WHILE Programs," Stanford University, Computer Science Report No. CS-188, Palo Alto, Calif., 1970.

Ashton, J. K., R. C. Freytag, and L. E. Miler, "Comprehensive Diagnostic Planning," *Proc. 1975 Int'l Symp. Fault-Tolerant Computing,* UNESCO Conf. Center, Paris, June 1975.

Asirelli, P., et al., "A Flexible Environment for Program Development Based on a Symbolic Interpreter," *Proc. 4th Int'l Conf. Software Engineering,* Munich, Sept. 1979, pp. 251-263.

Astuti, M., "Some First Conclusions on the Checkout of a Large Basic Software Project," in *Software Systems Engineering,* Online Conferences Ltd., Middlesex, England, 1976, pp. 323-339.

Avizienis, A. and L. Chen, "On the Implementation of N-Version Programming for Software Fault-Tolerance During Program Execution," *Proc. COMPSAC 77,* Chicago, Nov. 1977, pp. 149-155.

Babich, A. F., "Proving Total Correctness of Parallel Programs," *IEEE Trans. Software Engineering,* Vol. SE-5, No. 6, Nov. 1979, pp. 558-574.

Baer, J. L., D. P. Bovet, and G. Estrin, "Legality and Other Properties of Graph Models of Computations," *JACM,* Vol. 17, No. 3, July 1970, pp. 543-554.

Baggi, D. L. and M. L. Shooman, "Software Test Models and Implementation of Associated Test Drivers," Rome Air Development Center, RADC-TR-80-45, Griffiss Air Force Base, N.Y., Mar. 1980.

Baker, F. T., "Structured Programming in a Production Environment," *IEEE Trans. Software Engineering,* June 1975, pp. 241-252.

Balkovich, E. E. and N. B. Brooks, "Testing Cooperating Sequential Processes: A Methodology," General Research Corp., RM-1899, Santa Barbara, Calif., Oct. 1974.

Balzer, R., N. Goldman, and D. Wile, "Informality in Program Specifications," *AFIPS Conf. Proc.,* Vol. 47, 1978 NCC, p. 671.

Balzer, R. M., "EXDAMS—Extendable Debugging and Monitoring System," Rand Corp., RM-57772-ARPA, Santa Monica, Calif., Apr. 1969.

Bang, S. Y., P. A. Ng, and P. K. Blackwell, "Protocol Validation by Synthesizing Communications System Behaviors," *Proc. COMPSAC 80,* Chicago, Oct. 1980, pp. 348-354.

Barzdin, J. M., J. J. Bicevskis, and A. A. Kalninsh, "Construction of Complete Sample System for Correctness Testing," Latvian State University, Riga, USSR, 1977.

Barzdin, J. M., J. J. Bicevskis, and A. A. Kalninsh, "Construction of Complete Sample System For Correctness Testing," in *Mathematical Foundations of Computer Science,* Springer-Verlag, New York, 1975, pp. 1-12.

Bass, E. D., "Software Verification and Validation," U.S. Army, SAFSEA Memo EBX-1-72, July 1973.

Basu, S. K. and J. Misra, "Proving Loop Programs," *IEEE Trans. Software Engineering,* Vol. SE-1, No. Mar. 1975, pp. 76-86.

Bateman, B. L. and C. H. Nestman, "A Software Quality Plan for Higher Education—An Abstract," *AFIPS Conf. Proc.,* Vol. 47, 1978 NCC, p. 621.

Bauer, J. A. and A. B. Finger, "Test Plan Generation Using Formal Grammars," *Proc. 4th Int'l Conf. Software Engineering,* Munich, Sept. 1979, pp. 425-432.

Baylis, M. H. J., "Maintenance of Large Computer Systems—The Engineer's Assistant," in *Machine Intelligence 3,* American Elsevier, New York, 1968, pp. 269-278.

Belford, P. C., R. A. Berg, and T. L. Hannan, "Central Flow Control Software Development: A Case Study of the Effectiveness of Software Engineering Techniques," *Proc. 4th Int'l Conf. Software Engineering,* Munich, Sept. 1979, pp.85-93.

Benson, J. P., "Some Observations Concerning the Structure of FORTRAN Programs," *Proc. 1975 Int'l Symp. Fault-Tolerant Computing,* UNESCO Conf. Center, Paris, June 1975, pp. 156-159.

Berge, C., *Theory of Graphs and Its Applications,* Wiley, New York, 1972.

Berlinger, E., "An Information Theory Based Complexity Measure," *AFIPS Conf. Proc.,* Vol. 49, 1980 NCC, pp. 773-779.

Bersoff, E. H., V. D. Henderson, and S. G. Siegel, "Attaining Software Product Integrity," *Proc. COMPSAC 79,* Chicago, Nov. 1979, pp. 680-687.

"Bibliography: Software Testing and Reliability, 1969-1977," Bell Telephone Laboratories, No. 348, Holmdel, N.J., Mar. 1978.

Bicevskis, J., et al., "SMOTL—A System to Construct Samples for Data Processing Program Debugging," *IEEE Trans. Software Engineering,* Vol. SE-5, No. 1, Jan. 1979, pp. 60-66.

Bielski, J. P. and W. H. Blankertz, "The General Acceptance Test System (GATS)," *Digest of Papers—COMPCON 77 Spring,* San Francisco, 1977, pp. 207-210.

Black, J. P., D. J. Taylor, and D. E. Morgan, "A Case Study in Fault Tolerant Software," *Software—Practice & Experience,* Vol. 11, No. 2, Feb. 1981, pp. 145-157.

Blair, J., "Extendable Non-interactive Debugging," in *Debugging Techniques in Large Systems,* R. Rustin, ed., Prentice-Hall, Englewood Cliffs, N.J., 1971.

Blikle, A. and S. Budkowski, "Certification of Microprograms by an Algebraic Method," *SIGMICRO Newsletter,* Vol. 7, No. 3, Sept. 1976.

Boebert, W. E., "Formal Verification of Embedded Software," Proc. Workshop on Formal Verification, *Software Engineering Notes* (ACM SIGSOFT), Vol. 5, No. 3, July 1980.

Boehm, B. W., "The High Cost of Software," in *Practical Strategies for Developing Large Software,* Addison-Wesley, Reading, Mass., 1975.

Boehm, B. W., "Software and Its Impact: A Quantitative Assessment," *Datamation,* May 1973, pp. 48-59.

Boehm, B. W., "Software Engineering," *IEEE Trans. Computers,* Vol. C-25, No. 12, Dec. 1976, pp. 1226-1241.

Boehm, B. W., "Some Information Processing Implications of Air Force Space Missions, 1970-1980," Rand Corp., RM-6213-PR, Santa Monica, Calif., 1970.

Boehm, B. W., J. R. Brown, and M. Lipow, "Quantitative Evaluation of Software Quality," *Proc. 2nd Int'l Conf. Software Engineering,* San Francisco, Oct. 1976, pp. 592-605.

Boehm, B. W., R. K. McClean, and D. B. Urfrig, "Some Experience with Automated Aids to the Design of Large-Scale Reliable Software," *IEEE Trans. Software Engineering,* Vol. SE-1, No. 1, Mar. 1975, pp. 125-133.

Bohm, C. and G. Jacopini, "Flow Diagrams, Turing Machines, and Languages with Only Two Formation Rules," *CACM,* May 1966, pp. 366-371.

Bose, A. K. and S. A. Szygenda, "Design of a Diagnosable and Fault-Tolerant Input/Output Controller," *AFIPS Conf. Proc.,* Vol. 46, 1977 NCC, pp.795-800.

Bowen, J. B., "Standard Error Classification to Support Software Reliability Assessment," *AFIPS Conf. Proc.,* Vol. 49, 1980 NCC, pp. 697-705.

Bowen, J. B., "A Survey of Standards and Proposed Metrics for Software Quality Testing," *Computer,* Vol. 112, No. 8, Aug. 1979, pp. 37-42.

Boyer, B. and J. Moore, "The Fortran Verification System," Proc. Workshop on Formal Verification, *Software Engineering Notes* (ACM SIGSOFT), Vol. 5, No. 3, July 1980.

Boyer, B. and J. Moore, "A Theorem-Prover for Recursive Functions," Proc. Workshop on Formal Verification, *Software Engineering Notes* (ACM SIGSOFT), Vol. 5, No. 3, July 1980.

Boyer, R. S., B. Elspas, and K. N. Levitt, "SELECT: A Formal System for Testing and Debugging Programs by Symbolic Executions," *Proc. 1975 Int'l Conf. Reliable Software,* Los Angeles, Apr. 1975.

Bradley, G. H., T. F. Green, G. T. Howard, and N. Schneidewind, "Structure and Error Detection in Computer Software," *Proc. AIIE Conf.,* Los Angeles, 1975, pp. 54-59.

Brand, D., "Path Calculus in Program Verification," IBM Research Report, RC-6372, Jan. 1977.

Bright, H. S. and I. J. Cole, "A Method of Testing Programs for Data Sensitivity," *Proc. ACM SIGPLAN Computer Program Test Methods Symp.,* June 1972.

Brinch Hansen, P., "Reproducible Testing of Monitors," *Software–Practice & Experience,* Vol. 8, No. 6, Nov.-Dec. 1978.

Brinch Hansen, P., "Testing a Multiprogramming System," *Software–Practice & Experience,* Vol. 3, 1973, pp. 145-150.

Brooks, F. P., *The Mythical Man-Month,* Addison-Wesley, Reading, Mass., 1975.

Brooks, F. P., "Testing Computer Programs–Historical Perspective," *Proc. ACM Program Test Methods Symp.,* June 1972.

Brooks, N. B., et al., "Jovial Automated Verification System (JAVS)," Rome Air Development Center, RADC-TR-76-20, Griffiss Air Force Base, N.Y., Feb. 1976.

Brooks, N. B. and C. Gannon, "JAVS Technical Report, Methodology Report," AD-A041 048 OWC, Rome Air Development Center, RADC-TR-77-126, Vol. 3, Griffiss Air Force Base, N.Y., Apr. 1977.

Brown, A. R. and W. A. Sampson, *Program Debugging,* MacDonald, London, 1973.

Brown, J. and M. Lipow, "Testing for Software Reliability," *Proc. 1975 Int'l Conf. Reliable Software,* Los Angeles, Apr. 1975.

Brown, J. R., "Coordinated Commentary Programming: A Technique for Producing Probably-Correct Programs," TRW Systems Group, Redondo Beach, Calif., Oct. 1973.

Brown, J. R., "Practical Application of Automated Software Tools," *Proc. WESCON 72,* Session 21, Sept. 1972.

Brown, J. R., "Why Tools?" *Proc 8th Ann. Symp. Computer Science and Statistics,* University of California, Los Angeles, Feb. 1975.

Brown, J. R. and R. H. Hoffman, "Evaluating the Effectiveness of Software Verification–Practical Experience With an Automated Tool," *AFIPS Conf. Proc.,* Vol. 41, Part I, 1972 FJCC, pp. 181-190.

Brown, J. R., A. J. Desalvio, D. E. Heine, and J. G. Purdy, "Automated Software Quality Assurance–A Case Study of Three Systems," *Proc. ACM SIGPLAN Program Test Methods Symp.,* June 1972.

Brown, J. R. and K. F. Fisher, "A Graph Theoretic Approach to the Verification of Program Structures," *Proc. 3rd Int'l Conf. Software Engineering,* Atlanta, May 1978, pp. 136-141.

Brown, J. R. and R. H. Hoffman, "Automating Software Development–A Survey of Techniques and Automated Tools," TRW Systems Group, Redondo Beach, Calif., May 1972.

Brown, J. R., R. H. Hoffman, E. C. Nelson, and A. C. Arterbery, "Automating Software Development: A Survey of Techniques and Automated Tools," TRW Systems Group, Redondo Beach, Calif., May 1972.

Browne, J. C. and D. B. Johnson, "FAST: A Second Generation Program Analysis System," *Proc. 3rd Int'l Conf. Software Engineering,* Atlanta, May 1978, pp. 142-148.

Brzozowski, J. A., "Derivatives of Regular Expressions," *JACM,* Vol. 11, No. 4, Oct. 1964, pp. 481-494.

Buckley, F., "A Standard for Software Quality Assurance Plans," *Computer,* Vol. 12, No. 8, Aug. 1979, pp. 43-50.

Buckley, F. T., "Software Testing–A Report from the Field," *Proc. IEEE Symp. Computer Software Reliability,* Apr. 1973, pp. 102-105.

Budd, T. A. and D. Angluin, "Two Notions of Correctness and Their Relation to Testing," University of Arizona, TR 80-19, Tucson, Ariz., June 1980.

Budd, T. A., R. J. Lipton, F. G. Sayward, and R. DeMillo, "The Design of a Prototype Mutation System for Program Testing," *AFIPS Conf. Proc.,* Vol. 47, 1978 NCC, pp. 623-627.

Budd, T. A., R. J. Lipton, R. A. DeMillc, and F. G. Sayward, "Mutation Analysis," Yale University, Research Report #155, New Haven, Conn., Apr. 1979.

Buechler, J., "A Software Architecture for Sampling Monitors," *Proc. Workshop Currently Available Test Tools: Technology and Experience,* Los Angeles, Apr. 1975.

Burkhardt, W. H., "Generating Test Programs from Syntax," *Computing,* Vol. 2, No. 1, 1967, pp. 53-73.

Bussell, B. and R. A. Koster, "Instrumenting Computer Systems and Their Programs," *AFIPS Conf. Proc.,* Vol. 37, 1970 FJCC, pp. 525-534.

Buxton, J. N., P. Naur, and B. Randell, *Software Engineering Concepts and Techniques,* Petrocelli-Charter, Princeton, N.J., 1976.

Carey, L., "Software Quality—A State of the Art Report," *Proc. WESCON 72,* Session 21, Sept. 1972.

Carey, R. J. and M. Bendick, "The Control of a Software Test Process," *Proc. COMPSAC 77,* Chicago, Nov. 1977, pp. 327-333.

Carter, W. C., W. H. Joyner, Jr., and D. Brand, "Microprogram Verification Considered Necessary," IBM Research Report, RC-7053, Dec. 1977.

Carter, W. C., W. H. Joyner, Jr., and G. B. Leeman, "Automated Experiments in Validating Microprograms," *Proc. 1975 Int'l Symp. Fault-Tolerant Computing,* UNESCO Conf. Center, Paris, June 1975.

Caudill, R., "Understanding the Developmental Life Cycle," *AFIPS Conf. Proc.,* Vol. 46, 1977 NCC, pp. 269-276.

Cellini, J. V., "Software Error Data Acquisition Effort—Past, Present, and Future," presentation at COMPSAC 77, Chicago, Nov. 1977.

Cerf, V., E. B. Fernandez, K. P. Gostelow, and S. A. Volansky, "Formal Control-Flow Properties of a Graph Model of Computation," University of California, Los Angeles, Report ENG-7178, Dec. 1971.

Chang, H. Y., E. G. Manning, and G. Metze, *Fault Diagnosis of Digital Systems,* Wiley-Interscience, New York, 1970.

Chang, S. K. and J. S. Kee, "An Approach to Data Validation and Query Translation in the Medical Information System Environment, " *Proc. COMPSAC 77,* Chicago, Nov. 1977, pp. 197-202.

Chapin, N., "A Measure of Software Complexity," *AFIPS Conf. Proc.,* Vol. 48, 1979 NCC, pp. 995-1002.

Chattergy, R. and U. W. Pooch, "Integrated Design and Verification of Simulation Programs," *Computer,* Vol. 10, No. 4, Apr. 1977, pp. 40-45.

Cheatham, T. E., Jr., G. H. Holloway, and J. A. Townley, "Symbolic Evaluation and the Analysis of Programs," *IEEE Trans. Software Engineering,* Vol. SE-5, No. 4, July 1979, pp. 402-417.

Chen, C., "Synthesis of Diagnosable Weighted Computer System," *Proc. COMPSAC 79,* Chicago, Nov. 1979, pp. 488-493.

Chen, E. T., "Program Complexity and Program Productivity," *Proc. COMPSAC 77,* Chicago, Nov. 1977, pp. 142-148.

Chen, W. T., "Toward Automated Validation of Computer Programs," PhD thesis, University of California, Berkeley, Feb. 1976.

Chen, W. T. and C. V. Ramamoorthy, "Toward Automation of Test Data Generation," *Proc. Int'l Computer Symp.,* Taipei, Taiwan, 1975.

Chen, W. T., C. V. Ramamoorthy, and S. T. Huang, "Automated Techniques for Static Structural Validation of Programs," *Proc. COMPSAC 77,* Chicago, Nov. 1977, pp. 628-634.

Chen, Y. C. and O. Wing, "Connectivity of Directed Graphs," *Proc. 2nd Ann. Allerton Conf. Circuit and System Theory,* University of Illinois Press, Urbana, Sept. 1974, pp. 530-542.

Chen, Y. C. and O. Wing, "Some Properties of Cycle-Free Directed Graphs and the Identification of the Longest Path," *J. Franklin Inst.,* Vol. 281, No. 4, Apr. 1966, pp. 293-301.

Chester, D. L. and R. T. Yeh, "Software Development by Evaluation of System Design," *Proc. COMPSAC 77,* Chicago, Nov. 1977, pp. 435-441.

Cheung, R. C., "A User-Oriented Software Reliability Model," *IEEE Trans. Software Engineering,* Vol. SE-6, No. 2, Mar. 1980, pp. 118-125.

Chow, T. S., "Analysis of Software Design Modeled by Multiple Finite State Machines," *Proc. COMPSAC 78,* Chicago, Nov. 1978, pp. 169-174.

Chow, T. S., "A Generalized Assertion Language," *Proc. 2nd Int'l Conf. Software Engineering,* San Francisco, Oct. 1976, pp. 392-399.

Chow, T. S., "Testing Software Design Modeled by Finite-State Machines," *IEEE Trans. Software Engineering,* Vol. SE-4, No. 3, May 1978, pp. 178-187.

Christofides, N., *Graph Theory—An Algorithmic Approach,* Academic Press, New York, 1975.

Clapp, J. A., "Major Contributions to Software Engineering in the 1980's," Mitre Corp., MTR-2791, Bedford, Mass., Jan. 1974.

Clapp, J. A., "A Software Error Classification Methodology," Mitre Corp., MTR-2648, Vol. VII, Bedford, Mass., June 1973.

Clark, E. R., "On the Automatic Simplification of Source Language Programs," *Proc. ACM Nat'l Conf.,* 1966, pp. 313-319.

Clark, K. L. and M. H. van Emden, "Consequence Verification of Flowcharts," *IEEE Trans. Software Engineering,* Vol. SE-7, No. 1, Jan. 1981, pp. 52-60.

Clarke, L. A., "A System to Generate Test Data and Symbolically Execute Programs," *IEEE Trans. Software Engineering,* Vol. SE-2, No. 3, Sept. 1976, pp. 215-222.

Clarke, L. A., "Testing: Achievements and Frustrations," *Proc. COMPSAC 78,* Chicago, Nov. 1978, pp. 310-314.

Clarke, L. A. and D. J. Richardson, "Symbolic Evaluation Methods," COINS Technical Report 79-20, University of Massachusetts, Amherst, Nov. 1979.

Clarke, L. A., and D. J. Richardson, "Symbolic Evaluation Methods for Program Analysis," COINS Technical Report 79-01, University of Massachusetts, Amherst, Feb. 1979.

Claussen, B. A., II, "Viking '75—The Development of a Reliable Flight Program," *Proc. COMPSAC 77,* Chicago, Nov. 1977, pp. 33-37.

Cody, J. W., "The Evaluation of Mathematical Software," *Proc. ACM SIGPLAN Computer Program Test Methods Symp.,* June 1972.

Cohen, E. I., "A Finite Domain-Testing Strategy for Computer Program Testing," PhD dissertation, Ohio State University, Columbus, 1978.

Cohen, E. I. and L. J. White, "A Finite Domain-Testing Strategy for Computer Program Testing," Ohio State University, Report OSU-CISRC-TR-77-13, Columbus, Aug. 1977.

Cohen, R. M., "A Review of the Gypsy Verification Environment," Proc. Workshop on Formal Verification, *Software Engineering Notes* (ACM SIGSOFT), Vol. 5, No. 3, July 1980.

Cohn, A., "Remarks on Machine Proof," Proc. Workshop on Formal Verification, *Software Engineering Notes* (ACM SIGSOFT), Vol. 5, No. 3, July 1980.

"A Comparative Analysis of the Diagnostic Power of Commercial Fortran Compilers," Softool Corp., Report No. F001-10-77, Goleta, Calif., Oct. 1977.

Cook, S. A., "Soundness and Completeness of An Axiom System for Program Verification," *SIAM J. Computing,* Vol. 7, No. 11, Feb. 1978.

Cook, V., *Software Cost Estimating: Considerations and Problem Areas,* Federal Systems Division, IBM Corp., Apr. 1974.

Cooper, D. C., "Reduction of Programs to Standard Form by Graph Transformation," in *Theory of Graphs, Int'l Symp.,* P. Rosenthall Rome, ed., Gordon and Breach Pub. Co., New York, 1967.

Courtney, R. H., Jr., "Security Risk Assessment in Electronic Data Processing Systems," *AFIPS Conf. Proc.,* Vol. 46, 1977 NCC, pp. 97-104.

Cowell, W. R. and L. D. Fosdick, "The Production of a Scientific Tool," *SIAM News,* Vol. 10, No. 5, Oct. 1977.

Craig, G. R., et al., *Software Reliability Study,* TRW Systems Group, RADC-TR-74-250, Redondo Beach, Calif., Oct. 1974.

Craigen, D. and D. Bonyun, "Two Projects in Program Verification," Proc. Workshop on Formal Verification, *Software Engineering Notes* (ACM SIGSOFT), Vol. 5, No. 3, July 1980.

Crocker, S. D., "Toward Practical Verification Systems," Proc. Workshop on Formal Verification, *Software Engineering Notes* (ACM SIGSOFT), Vol. 5, No. 3, July 1980.

Culpepper, L. M., "A System for Reliable Software Engineering," *IEEE Trans. Software Engineering,* Vol. SE-1, No. 2, June 1975, pp. 174-178.

Culpepper, L. M. and R. Regen, "AUDIT: A System for Software Engineering for the CDC6400," Naval Ship Research and Development Center, Report 4587, Nov. 1974.

Curtis, B., S. B. Sheppard, and P. Milliman, "Third Time Charm: Stronger Prediction of Programmer Performance by Software Complexity Metrics," *Proc. 4th Int'l Conf. Software Engineering,* Munich, Sept. 1979, pp. 356-360.

Dahl, O. J., E. W. Dijkstra, and C. A. R. Hoare, *Structured Programming,* Academic Press, New York, 1972.

Danielson, G. H., "On Finding the Simple Paths and Circuits in a Graph," *IEEE Trans. Circuit Theory,* Sept. 1968.

Darringer, J. A. and J. C. King, "Applications of Symbolic Execution to Program Testing," *Computer,* Vol. 11, No. 4, Apr. 1978, pp. 51-60.

Darringer, J. A. and M. S. Laventhal, "A Study of the Use of Abstractions in Program Specification and Verification," IBM Research Report, RC-7184, Yorktown Heights, N.Y., June 1978.

Davies, A. C., "The Analogy Between Electrical Networks and Flowcharts," *IEEE Trans. Software Engineering,* Vol. SE-6, No. 4, July 1980, pp. 391-394.

Davis, A. L., "A Data Flow Evaluation System Based on the Concept of Recursive Locality," *AFIPS Conf. Proc.,* Vol. 48, 1979 NCC.

deBalbine, G., "Better Manpower Utilization Using Atomic Restructuring," Caine, Farber & Gordon, Inc., Pasadena, Calif., 1975.

deBalbine, G., "MTR—A Tool for Displaying the Global Structure of Software Systems," *AFIPS Conf. Proc.,* Vol. 47, 1978 NCC, pp. 571-580.

Deil, H., "Consistency Considerations on Checkpoints," *Proc. 1975 Int'l Symp. Fault-Tolerant Computing,* UNESCO Conf. Center, Paris, June 1975.

DeMillo, R. A., "Mutation Analysis as a Tool for Software Quality Assurance," *Proc. COMPSAC 80,* Chicago, Oct. 1980, pp. 390-393.

DeMillo, R. A. and R. J. Lipton, "A Probabilistic Remark on Algebraic Program Testing," Georgia Technical School of Information and Computer Science, Atlanta, May 1977.

DeMillo, R. A., R. J. Lipton, and A. J. Perlis, "Social Processes and Proofs of Theorems and Programs," Georgia Technical School of Information and Computer Science, Atlanta, Nov. 1976.

DeMillo, R. A., R. J. Lipton, and F. G. Sayward, "Hints on Test Data Selection: Help for the Practicing Programmer," *Computer,* Vol. 11, No. 4, Apr. 1978, pp 34-41.

DeMillo, R. A., R. J. Lipton, and F. C. Sayward, "Metainduction and Program Mutation: Realistic Software Validation," Georgia Technical School of Information and Computer Science, Atlanta, Sept. 1977.

DeMillo, R. A. and R. E. Miller, "Implicit Computation of Synchronization Primitives," IBM Research Report, RC-7454, Yorktown Heights, N.Y., Dec. 1978.

Denning, D. E. and P. J. Denning, "Certification of Programs for Secure Information Flow," *CACM,* Vol. 20, No. 7, July 1977, pp. 504-512.

DeYoung, G. E. and G. R. Kampen, "Program Factors as Predictors of Program Readability," *Proc. COMPSAC 79,* Chicago, Nov. 1979, pp. 668-673.

Dickson, J. J., J. L. Hesse, A. C. Drentz, and M. L. Shooman, "Qualitative Analysis of Software Reliability," *Proc. Ann. Reliability and Maintainability Symp.,* Newport Beach, Calif., 1972.

Dijkstra, E. W., "The Humble Programmer." *CACM,* Oct. 1977, pp. 858-866.

Dijkstra, E. W., "Structured Programming," in *Conf. Software Engineering,* P. Naur and B. Randell, eds., NATO, Science Affairs Division, Brussels, 1969.

Dongarra, J. J. and A. R. Hinds, "Unrolling Loops in FORTRAN," *Software—Practice & Experience,* Vol. 9, No. 3, Mar. 1979, pp. 219-226.

Dooley, B. L, H. L. Reeves, Jr., and N. C. Thomas, "Experience with Software Tools for Nuclear Process System Applications, *Proc. COMPSAC 80,* Chicago, Oct. 1980, pp. 646-654.

Duke, M. O., "Testing in a Complex Systems Environment," *IBM Systems J.,* Vol. 14, No. 4, 1975, pp. 353-365.

Dulac, B. and R. Rubey, "Software Tools for Certifying Operational Flight Programs," *Proc. Nat'l. Space Navigation Meeting,* 1967, pp. 164-177.

Duncan, A. G. and J. S. Hutchison, "Using Attributed Grammars to Test Designs and Implementations," *Proc. 5th Int'l Conf. Software Engineering,* San Diego, Mar. 1981, pp. 170-177.

Duran, J.W., "Automatic Program Synthesis via Synthesis of Loop-Free Segments," *AFIPS Conf. Proc.,* Vol. 48, 1979 NCC.

Duran, J. W. and S. Ntafos, "A Report on Random Testing," *Proc. 5th Int'l Conf. Software Engineering,* San Diego, Mar. 1981, pp. 179-183.

Duran, J. W. and J. J. Wiorkowski, "Capture-Recapture Sampling for Estimating Software Error Content," *IEEE Trans. Software Engineering,* Vol. SE-7, No. 1, Jan. 1981, pp. 147-148.

Edwards, N. P., "The Effect of Certain Modular Design Principles on Testability," *Proc. 1975 Int'l Conf. Reliable Software,* Los Angeles, Apr. 1975.

Eggenberger, O. et al., "Untersuchung Verschiedener Reaktorschutzsysteme," Institut für Datenverarbeitung in der Technik, PSB-Bericht 675 (Kl. I), Kernforschungszentrum Karlsruhe, West Germany, Feb. 1979.

Ellingson, O. E., "Historical Analysis of Computer Program Changes as a Guide to Establishing Quality Control Measures," System Development Corp., TEM 2887, Santa Monica, Calif., Mar. 1966.

Ellingson, O. E., "A Predictor Tool for Estimating the Confidence Level of a Computer Program Subsystem in the Space Programs Department," System Development Corp., TM L-3335, Santa Monica, Calif., Jan. 1967.

Ellozy, H. A., "On the Generation of Loop Predicates for Flow Chart Programs Operating on Arrays," IBM Research Report, RC-7121, Yorktown Heights, N.Y., May 1978.

Elmendorf, W. R., "Cause Effects Graphs in Functional Testing," IBM Corp., TR 00.2487, Poughkeepsie, N.Y., 1973.

Elmendorf, W. R., "Computer-Assisted Design of Program Test Libraries," *IBM Technical Disclosure Bull.,* Vol. 16, No. 3, Aug. 1973, pp. 804-807.

Elmendorf, W. R., "Controlling the Functional Testing of an Operating System," *IEEE Trans. Systems Science and Cybernetics,* Oct. 1969, pp. 284-290.

Elmendorf, W. R., "Disciplined Software Testing," in *Debugging Techniques in Large Systems,* R. Rustin, ed., Prentice-Hall, Englewood Cliffs, N.J., 1971, pp 137-140.

Elshoff, J. L., "An Analysis of Some Commercial PL/I Programs," *IEEE Trans. Software Engineering,* Vol. SE-2, No. 2, June 1976, pp 113-120.

Elspas, B., M. W. Green, and K. N. Levitt, "Software Reliability, *Computer,* Vol. 4, No. 1, Jan.-Feb. 1971, pp. 21-27.

Elspas, B., K. N. Levitt, and R. J. Waldinger, "An Assessment of the Techniques for Proving Program Correctness," *Computing Surveys,* Vol. 4, No. 2, June 1972, pp. 97-147.

Elspas, B., R. E. Shostak, and J. M. Spitzen, "A Verification System for JOCIT/J3 Programs (Rugged Programming Environment—RPE/2)," Rome Air Development Center, RADC-TR-77-229, Griffiss Air Force Base, N.Y., 1977.

Elspas, E., et al., "Solving Nonlinear Inequalities Associated with Computer Program Paths," Stanford Research Inst., Palo Alto, Calif., Oct. 1974.

Endres, A., "An Analysis of Errors and Their Causes in System Programs," *IEEE Trans. Software Engineering,* Vol. SE-1, June 1975, pp. 140-149.

Fagan, M. E., "Design and Code Inspections and Process Control in the Development of Programs," *Proc. 1975 Int'l Symp. Fault-Tolerant Computing,* UNESCO Conf. Center, Paris, June 1975.

Fairley, R. E., "ALADDIN: Assembly Language Assertion Driven Debugging Interpreter," *IEEE Trans. Software Engineering,* Vol. SE-5, No. 4, July 1979, pp. 426-428.

Fairley, R. E., "An Experimental Program Testing Facility," *IEEE Trans. Software Engineering,* Vol. SE-1, Dec. 1975, pp. 350-357.

Fairley, R. E., "A New Approach to Software Verification and Validation," *Proc. Summer Computer Simulation Conf.,* Chicago, July 1977, pp. 709-712.

Fairley, R. E., "Tutorial: Static Analysis and Dynamic Testing of Computer Software," *Computer,* Vol. 11, No. 4, Apr. 1978, pp. 14-23.

Farr, L. and H. J. Zagorski, "Factors That Affect the Cost of Computer Programming—A Quantitative Analysis," System Development Corp., TM-1477, Santa Monica, Calif.

Feiertag, R. J., "Automated Proof of Multilevel Security," Proc. Workshop on Formal Verification, *Software Engineering Notes* (ACM SIGSOFT), Vol. 5, No. 3, July 1980.

Ferguson, H. E. and Bermer, R. W., "Debugging Systems at the Source Language Level," *CACM,* Aug. 1963, pp. 430-432.

Ferrari, D., "Tool for Automatic Program Restructuring," *Proc. ACM Ann. Conf.,* 1973.

Feuer, A. R. and E. B. Fowlkes, "Relating Computer Program Maintainability to Software Measures," *AFIPS Conf. Proc.,* Vol. 48, 1979 NCC.

Feuer, A. R. and E. B. Fowlkes, "Some Results from an Empirical Study of Computer Software," *Proc. 4th Int'l Conf. Software Engineering,* Munich, Sept. 1979, pp. 351-355.

Fife, D. W., "Computer Software Management: A Primer for Project Management and Quality Control," National Bureau of Standards Special Publication 500-11, Washington, D.C., July 1977.

Fischer, K. F., "A Test Case Selection Method for the Validation of Software Maintenance Modification," *Proc. COMPSAC 77,* Chicago, Nov. 1977, pp. 421-426.

Fitch, J., "Profiling a Large Program," *Software—Practice & Experience,* Vol. 7, No. 4, July-Aug. 1977, pp. 511-518.

Fitsos, G. P., "Vocabulary Effects in Software Science," *Proc. COMPSAC 80,* Chicago, Oct. 1980, pp. 751-756.

Florentin, J. J. "Flow Analysis for Program Correctness," University of Waterloo, CSR 2054, Ontario, 1970.

Floyd, R. W., "Assigning Meanings to Programs," *Proc. Symp. Applied Mathematics,* Vol. 19, *Mathematical Aspects of Computer Science,* 1967, pp. 19-32.

Forman, I. R., "On the Time Overhead of Counters and Traversal Markets," *Proc. 5th Int'l Conf. Software Engineering,* San Diego, Mar. 1981, pp. 164-169.

Fosdick, L. D., "BRANL—A FORTRAN Program to Identify Basic Blocks in FORTRAN Programs," Dept. of Computer Science, University of Colorado, CU-CS-040-74, Boulder, Mar. 1974.

Fosdick, L. D. and L. J. Osterweil, "Data Flow Analysis in Software Reliability," *Computing Surveys,* Vol. 8, No. 3, Sept. 1976, pp. 305-330.

Fosdick, L. D. and L. J. Osterweil, "The Detection of Anomalous Interprocedural Data Flow," *Proc. 2nd Int'l Conf. Software Engineering,* San Francisco, Oct. 1976, pp. 624-628.

Foster, K. A., "Error Sensitive Test Cases Analysis (ESTCA)," *IEEE Trans. Software Engineering,* Vol. SE-6, No. 3, May 1980, pp. 258-264.

Fraser, C. W., "Maintaining Program Variants by Merging Editor Scripts." *Software—Practice & Experience,* Vol. 10, No. 10, Oct. 1980, pp. 817-821.

Frederickson, G.N., "Refinements to Aho and Ullman's Node Listing Algorithm," University of Maryland, College Park, Sept. 1975.

Freedman, D., D. C. Gause, and B. M. Weinberg, "Organizing and Training For a New Software Development Project—That First Big Step," *AFIPS Conf. Proc.,* Vol. 46, 1977 NCC, pp. 255-260.

Freeman, M., W. W. Jacobs, and L. S. Levy, "On the Construction of Interactive Systems." *AFIPS Conf. Proc.,* Vol. 47, 1978 NCC, pp. 555-562.

Freeman, P., "Functional Programming, Testing, and Machine Aids," *Proc. ACM SIGPLAN Computer Program Test Methods Symp.,* June 1972.

Freeman, P. and T. Wasserman, *Tutorial on Software Design Techniques,* IEEE Computer Society, Long Beach, Calif., 1976.

Freiberger, W., ed., *Statistical Computer Performance Evaluation,* Academic Press, New York, 1972.

Friedman, A. D. and L. Simoncini, "System-Level Fault Diagnosis," *Computer,* Vol. 13, No. 3, Mar. 1980, pp. 47-53.

Frikel, W. G., "RISOS Analytic Tool Description Manual. Part 1: Program Description," Lawrence Radiation Laboratory, UCRL-51810PE1, May 1975.

Fritsch, F. N. and R. F. Hausman, "On the Documentation of Computer Programs," Lawrence Radiation Laboratory, UCID-30043, Mar. 1972.

Frost, D.R., "Designing For Generality," *Datamation,* Dec. 1974, pp. 56-61.

Frost, D.R., "Psychology and Program Design," *Datamation,* May 1975, pp. 137-138.

Fuchi, K., H. Tanaha, and T. Yiba, "A Program Simulator by Partial Interpretation," *2nd Symp. System Operating Principles,* Oct. 1969, pp. 105-111.

Fuji, M., "Independent Verification of Highly Reliable Programs," *Proc. COMPSAC 77,* Chicago, Nov. 1977, pp. 38-44.

Fujimura, N. and K. Ushijima, "Experience with a COBOL Analyzer," *Proc. COMPSAC 80,* Chicago, Oct. 1980, pp. 640-645.

Fuller, S. H., P. Shaman, D. Lamb, and W. E. Burr, "Evaluation of Computer Architectures via Test Programs," *AFIPS Conf. Proc.,* 1977 NCC, pp. 147-160.

Gaines, J. A., Jr., "An External Debugging System for Weapon System Programs Written in a Higher Level Language," *Proc. COMPSAC 78,* Chicago, Nov. 1978, pp. 158-162.

Gannon, C., "A Debugging, Testing, and Documentation Tool for JOVIAL J73," *Proc. COMPSAC 80,* Chicago, Oct.1980, pp. 634-639.

Gannon, C., "Error Detection Using Path Testing and Static Analysis," *Computer,* Vol. 12, No. 8, Aug. 1979, pp. 26-31.

Gannon, C., N. B. Brooks, and W. R. Wisehart, "JAVS Final Report," Rome Air Development Center, RADC-TR-77-201, AD A041 237 9WC, Griffiss Air Force Base, N.Y. June 1977.

Gannon, T. F. and S. D. Shapiro, "An Optimal Approach to Fault Tolerant Software Systems Design," *IEEE Trans. Software Engineering,* Vol. SE-4, No. 5, Sept. 1978, pp. 390-409.

Geiger, W., L. Gmeiner, H. Trauboth, and U. Voges, "Program Testing Techniques for Nuclear Reactor Protection Systems," *Computer,* Vol. 12, No. 8, Aug. 1979, pp. 10-18.

Geller, M., "Test Data as an Aid in Proving Program Correctness," *Proc. 2nd Symp. Principles of Programming Languages,* Los Angeles, 1976.

Gelperin, D., "Testing Maintainability," *Software Engineering Notes* (ACM SIGSOFT), Vol. 4, No. 2, Apr. 1979.

Gelperin, D. and T. Gilb, "Comment on 'Testing Maintainability'," *Software Engineering Notes* (ACM SIGSOFT), Vol. 4, No. 3, July 1979.

Gerhart, S. L., "Applications of Affirm to Protocol Specification and Verification," Proc. Workshop on Formal Verification, *Software Engineering Notes* (ACM SIGSOFT), Vol. 5, No. 3, July 1980.

Gerhart, S. L., "Knowledge About Programs: A Model and a Case Study," *Proc. 1975 Int'l Conf. Reliable Software,* Los Angeles, Apr. 1975.

Gerhart, S. L., "A Proposal for Publication and Exchange of Program Proofs," *Software Engineering Notes* (ACM SIGSOFT), Vol. 3, No. 1, Jan. 1978.

Gerhart, S. L., "A Unified View of Current Program Testing and Proving: Theory and Practice," InfoTech State of the Art Report, Mar. 1977.

Gerhart, S. L. and L. Yelowitz, "Control Structure Abstractions of the Backtracking Programming Technique," presentation at 2nd Int'l Conf. Software Engineering, San Francisco, Oct. 1976.

Gerhart, S. L. and L. Yelowitz, "Observations of Fallibility in the Application of Modern Programming Methodologies," *IEEE Trans. Software Engineering,* Vol. SE-2, No. 3, Sept. 1976, pp. 195-207.

German, S., "Automating Proofs of the Absence of Common Runtime Errors," *Proc. 5th ACM Symp. Principles of Programming Languages,* Tucson, Ariz., Jan. 1978.

German, S. M. and B. Wegbreit, "A Synthesizer of Inductive Assertions," *AFIPS Conf. Proc.,* Vol. 44, 1975 NCC, pp. 369-378.

Ghezzi, C. and M. Jazayeri, "Syntax Directed Symbolic Execution," *Proc. COMPSAC 80,* Chicago, Oct. 1980, pp. 539-545.

Gilb, T., *Software Metrics,* Winthrop Pub. Co., Englewood Cliffs, N.J., 1977.

Gilkey, T. J., J. R. White, and T. L. Booth, "Performance Analysis as a Practical Software Design Tool," *Proc. COMPSAC 77,* Chicago, Nov. 1977, pp. 428-434.

Gilsinn, D. E., I. T. Hardy, and C. L. Sheppard, "The NBS Validation Routines for Basic," *Proc. COMPSAC 77,* Chicago, Nov. 1977, pp. 414-420.

Ginzberg, M. G., "Notes on Testing Real-Time System Programs," *IBM Systems J.,* Vol. 4, No. 1, 1965, pp. 58-72.

Glass, R. L., "A Benefit Analysis of Some Software Reliability Methodologies," *Software Engineering Notes* (ACM SIGSOFT), Vol. 5, No. 2, Apr. 1980.

Glass, R. L., "Persistent Software Errors," *IEEE Trans. Software Engineering,* Vol. SE-7, No. 2, Mar. 1981, pp. 162-168.

Glaseman, S., R. Turn, and R. S. Gaines, "Problem Areas in Computer Security Assessment," *AFIPS Conf. Proc.,* Vol. 46, 1977 NCC, pp. 105-112.

Goguen, J., "Thoughts on Specification, Design and Verification," Proc. Workshop on Formal Verification, *Software Engineering Notes* (ACM SIGSOFT), Vol. 5, No. 3, July 1980.

Goldberg, J., "Workshop on Distributed Fault-Tolerant Computers," *Computer,* Vol. 10, No. 3, Mar. 1977, pp. 51-52.

Goldberg, J., A. Cooperband, and L. Gallenson, "PRIM System—A Framework for Emulation-Based Debugging Tools," *AFIPS Conf. Proc.,* Vol. 47, 1978 NCC, pp. 373-377.

Goldstine, H. H. and J. von Neumann, "Planning and Coding Problems for an Electronic Computing Instrument," in *Collected Works of John von Neumann,* Vol. 5, A. H. Taub, ed., Pergamon Press, New York, 1961.

Gomez, J., "An Interactive Fortran Structuring Aid," *Proc. 4th Int'l Conf. Software Engineering,* Munich, Sept. 1979, pp. 241-244.

Good, D. I., ed., "Constructing Verifiably Reliable and Secure Communications Processing Systems," University of Texas, Austin, Jan. 1977.

Good, D. I., "Constructing Verified and Reliable Communications Systems," *Software Engineering Notes* (ACM SIGSOFT), Vol. 2, No. 5, Oct. 1977.

Good, D. I., "The Problem with Program Verification is Computer Science," Proc. Workshop on Formal Verification, *Software Engineering Notes* (ACM SIGSOFT), Vol. 5, No. 3, July 1980.

Good, D. I. and R. L. London, "Computer Interval Arithmetic—Definition and Proof of Correct Implementation," *JACM,* Vol. 17, No. 4, Oct. 1970, pp. 603-612.

Good, D. I. and R. L. London, "Interval Arithmetic for the Burroughs B 5500: Four Algol Procedures and Proofs of their Correctness," University of Wisconsin, Technical Report 26, Madison, June 1968.

Goodenough, J. B., "The Ada Compiler Validation Capability," *Computer,* Vol. 14, No. 6, June 1981, pp. 57-64.

Goodenough, J. B., "Effect of Software Structure on Software Reliability, Modifiability, Reusability," SofTech, Inc., Waltham, Mass., July 1974.

Goodenough, J. B., "Program Testing Survey," InfoTech State of the Art Report, Mar. 1977.

Goodenough, J. B., "A Survey of Program Testing Issues," SofTech, Inc., TP055.1, Waltham, Mass., Apr. 1977.

Goodenough, J. B., "System Organization Technology: An Analysis of Modularity," SofTech, Inc., Waltham, Mass., Apr. 1973.

Goodenough, J. B. and R. S. Eanes, "Program Testing and Diagnosis Technology," SofTech, Inc., Waltham, Mass., Apr. 1973.

Goodenough, J. B. and S. L. Gerhart, "Toward a Theory of Test Data Selection," *IEEE Trans. Software Engineering,* Vol. SE-1, No. 2, June 1975, pp. 156-173.

Goodenough, J. B. and S. L. Gehhart, "Toward a Theory of Testing: Data Selection Criteria," *in Current Trends in Programming Methodology,* Vol. II, R. T. Yeh, ed., Prentice-Hall, Englewood Cliffs, N.J., 1977.

Gostelow, K. P., "Flow of Control, Resource Allocation, and the Proper Termination of Programs," Computer Science Report ENG-7179, University of Calif., Los Angeles, Dec. 1971.

Gostelow, K. P. and R. E. Thomas, "A View of Dataflow," *AFIPS Conf. Proc.,* Vol. 48, 1979 NCC.

Green, C. and D. Barstow, "Hypothetical Dialogue Exhibiting a Knowledge Base for a Program-Understanding System," Computer Science Dept., Stanford University, Report STAN-CS-75-476, Palo Alto, Calif., Jan. 1975.

Green, T. F., N. F. Schneidewind, G. T. Howard, and R. Pariseau, "Program Structures, Complexity, and Error Characteristics," *Proc. Symp. Computer Software Engineering,* Polytechnic Inst. of New York, Brooklyn, Vol. 24, Apr. 1976, pp. 139-154.

Green, T. R. G., "If and Then: Is Nesting Just for the Birds?," *Software—Practice & Experience,* Vol. 10, No. 5, May 1980, pp. 373-381.

Grieback, S.A., *Theory of Program Structures: Schemes, Semantics, and Verification,* Springer-Verlag, New York, 1975.

Griesmer, J. H., "The State of Symbolic Computation," IBM Research Report, RC-7791, Yorktown Heights, N.Y., July 1979.

Gruenberger, F., "Program Testing and Validation," *Datamation,* July 1968.

Guttag, J. V., J. J. Horning, and R. L. London, "A Proof Rule for Euclid Procedures," Information Sciences Inst., University of Southern California, ISI/RR-77-60, Marina del Rey, Calif., May 1977.

Haberman, A. M., "Path Expressions," Technical Report, Carnegie-Mellon University, Pittsburgh, 1975.

Hallin, T. G. and R. C. Hansen, "Toward a Better Method of Software Testing," *Proc. COMPSAC 78,* Chicago, Nov. 1978, pp. 153-157.

Halstead, M., *Elements of Software Science,* Elsevier-North Holland, New York, 1977.

Hamey, F. M., "Module Connection Analysis, A Tool for Scheduling Software Debugging Activities," *AFIPS Conf. Proc.,* Vol. 41, Part II, 1972 FJCC, pp. 173-179.

Hamilton, P. A. and J. D. Musa, "Measuring Reliability of Computer Center Software," *Proc. 3rd Int'l Conf. Software Engineering,* Atlanta, May 1978, pp. 29-36.

Hamlet, R. G., "Compiler Based Systematic Testing," University of Maryland, TR-423, College Park, Apr. 1976.

Hamlet, R. G., "Florida Testing Workshop, *Software Engineering Notes* (ACM SIGSOFT), Vol. 4, No. 2, Apr. 1979.

Hamlet, R. G., "Test Data That Determines Programs," University of Maryland, Report LDRS-152, College Park, Dec. 1976.

Hamlet, R. G., "Test Reliability and Software Maintenance," *Proc. COMPSAC 78,* Chicago, Nov. 1978, pp. 315-320.

Hamlet, R. G., "Testing Programs with Finite Sets of Data," University of Maryland, TR-388, College Park, Aug. 1975.

Hamlet, R. G., "Testing Programs with the Aid of a Compiler," *IEEE Trans. Software Engineering,* Vol. SE-3, No. 4, July 1977, pp. 279-289.

Hanford, K. V., "Automatic Generation of Test Cases," *IBM Systems J.,* Vol. 9, No. 4, 1970.

Hansen, G. A., "Measuring Software Reliability," *Mini-Micro Systems,* Aug. 1977, pp. 54-57.

Hanson, E., *Topics in Interval Analysis,* Clarendon Press, Oxford, England, 1969.

Hantler, S. L. and J. C. King, "An Introduction to Proving the Correctness of Programs," *Computing Surveys,* Vol. 8, No. 3, Sept. 1976, pp. 331-353.

Harary, F., *Graph Theory,* Addison-Wesley, Reading, Mass., 1969.

Harary, F., R. Z. Norman, and D. Cartwright, *Structural Models—An Introduction to the Theory of Directed Graphs,* Wiley, New York, 1965.

Harel, D., "On the Total Correctness of Nondeterministic Programs," IBM Research Report, RC-7691, Yorktown Heights, N.Y., May 1979.

Harrison, W., "Compiler Analysis of Value Ranges for Variables," IBM Research Report, RC-5544, Yorktown Heights, N.Y., July 1975.

Harrison, W., "Program Testing," *Data Management,* Dec. 1969.

Harrison, W. H., "Compiler Analysis of the Value Ranges for Variables," *IEEE Trans. Software Engineering,* Vol. SE-3, No. 3, May 1977, pp. 243-249.

Hartwick, R. D., "Test Planning," *AFIPS Conf. Proc.,* Vol. 46, 1977 NCC, pp. 285-294.

Hassell, J., L. A. Clarke, and D. J. Richardson, "A Close Look at Domain Testing," COINS Technical Report 80-16, University of Massachusetts, Amherst, Oct. 1980.

Hayes, J. P. and E. J. McCluskey, "Testability Considerations in Microprocessor-Based Design," *Computer,* Vol. 13, No. 3, Mar. 1980, pp. 17-25.

Head, R. V., "Testing Real Time Systems. Part I: Development and Management," *Datamation,* July 1964.

Head, R. V., "Testing Real Time Systems. Part II: Levels of Testing," *Datamation,* Aug. 1974.

Heard, J. B., "The Adequacy and Efficiency of Program Testing," *Proc. Computer and Data Processing Soc. of Canada,*

Hecht, M. S. and J. D. Ullman, "Flow Graph Reducibility," *JACM,* Vol. 21, No. 3, July 1974, pp. 367-375.

Henderson, P. and R. B. Gimson, "Modularization of Large Programs," *Software—Practice & Experience,* Vol. 11, No. 5, May 1981, pp. 497-520.

Hennell, M. A., W. M. McNicol, and J. Hawkins, "The Static Analysis of Cobol Programs," *Software Engineering Notes* (ACM SIGSOFT), Vol. 5, No. 4, Oct. 1980.

Herndon, M. A. and A. P. Keenan, "Analysis of Error Remediation Expenditures During Validation," *Proc. 3rd Int'l Conf. Software Engineering,* Atlanta, May 1978, pp. 202-206.

Hetzel, W. C., "An Experimental Analysis of Program Verification Methods," PhD thesis, University of North Carolina, Chapel Hill, 1976.

Hetzel, W. C., ed., *Program Test Methods,* Prentice-Hall, Englewood Cliffs, N.J., 1973.

Hetzel, W. C. and N. N. Hetzel, "The Future of Quality Software," *Digest of Papers—COMPCON 77 Spring,* San Francisco, 1977, pp. 211-212.

Heuermann, C. A., G. J. Myers, and J. H. Winterton, "Automated Test and Verification," *IBM Technical Disclosure Bull.,* Vol. 17, No. 7, 1974, pp. 2030-2035.

Hodges, B. C. and J. P. Ryan, "A System for Automatic Software Evaluation," *Proc. 2nd Int'l Conf. Software Engineering,* San Francisco, Oct. 1976, pp. 617-623.

Hoffman, L. J., E. H. Michelman, and D. Clements, "SECURATE—Security Evaluation and Analysis Using Fuzzy Metrics," *AFIPS Conf. Proc.,* Vol. 47, 1978 NCC, pp. 531-540.

Hoffman, R., "Results of Software Static Analysis Techniques and Automated Tools Questionnaire," TRW Systems Group, Report NASA-14853, Redondo Beach, Calif., May 1976.

Hoffman, R. H., "Automated Verification System User's Guide," TRW Note 72-FMT-891, Redondo Beach, Calif., 1972.

Hoffman, R. H., "User Information for Interactive Automated Test Data Generator (ATDG) System," Johnson Space Center, NASA, Internal Note 75-FM-88, Houston, January 1976.

Holland, J. R., "Acceptance Testing for Applications Programs," in *Program Test Methods,* W. C. Hetzel, ed., Prentice-Hall, Englewood Cliffs, N.J., 1973.

Hollander, C., "Correctness Condition Graphs," Stanford University, TN-52, Palo Alto, Calif., Sept. 1975.

Holley, L. H. and B. K. Rosen, "Qualified Data Flow Problems," *IEEE Trans. Software Engineering,* Vol. SE-7, No. 1, Jan. 1981, pp. 60-78.

Holthouse, M. A. and E. Cosloy, "A Practical System for Automatic Testcase Generation," presentation at 1976 NCC.

Holthouse, M. A. and M. J. Hatch, "Experience with Automated Testing Analysis," *Computer,* Vol. 12, No. 8, Aug. 1979, pp. 33-36.

Hopcroft, J. and R. E. Tarjan, "Efficient Algorithms for Graph Manipulation," *CACM,* Vol. 16, No. 6, June 1973, pp. 372-378.

Hopkins, A. L., Jr., "Fault-Tolerant System Design: Broad Brush and Fine Print," *Computer,* Vol. 13, No. 3, Mar. 1980, pp. 39-45.

Horejs, J., "Finite Semantics for Program Testing," *Proc. 4th Int'l Conf. Software Engineering,* Munich, Sept. 1979, pp. 433-440.

Horowitz, E., ed., *Practical Strategies for Developing Large Software Systems,* Addison-Wesley, Reading, Mass., 1975.

Howard, J. H. and W. P. Alexander, "Analyzing Sequences of Operations Performed by Programs," in *Program Test Methods,* W. C. Hetzel, ed., Prentice-Hall, Englewood Cliffs, N.J., 1972.

Howden, W. E., "Automated Program Validation Analysis," *Proc. Texas Conf. Computing Systems,* Austin, Nov. 1975.

Howden, W. E., "Automatic Case Analysis of Programs," *Proc. Computer Science and Statistics, 8th Ann. Symp. on the Interface,* 1975, pp. 347-352.

Howden, W. E., "Automatic Generation of Program Test Data and Proofs of Program Correctness," University of California, San Diego, CS Report No. 9, Apr. 1974.

Howden, W. E., "Completeness Criteria for Testing Elementary Program Functions," *Proc. 5th Int'l Conf. Software Engineering,* San Diego, Mar. 1981, pp. 235-243.

Howden, W. E., "DISSECT—A Symbolic Evaluation and Program Testing System," *IEEE Trans. Software Engineering,* Vol. SE-4, No. 1, Jan. 1978, pp. 70-73.

Howden, W. E., "The DISSECT Symbolic Evaluation System," University of California, San Diego, CS Report No. 8, Feb. 1976.

Howden, W. E., "Elementary Algebraic Program Testing Techniques," University of California, San Diego, CS Report No. 12, 1976.

Howden, W. E., "An Evaluation of the Effectiveness of Symbolic Testing," *Software—Practice & Experience,* Vol. 8, No. 4, July-Aug. 1978, pp. 381-397.

Howden, W. E., "Experiments with a Symbolic Evaluation System," *AFIPS Conf. Proc.,* Vol. 45, 1976 NCC, pp. 899-908.

Howden, W. E., "Functional Program Testing," *IEEE Trans. Software Engineering,* Vol. SE-6, No. 2, Mar. 1980, pp. 162-169.

Howden, W. E., "Functional Testing and Design Abstractions," University of Victoria, DM-180-IR, Victoria, B.C., May 1979.

Howden, W. E., "Lindenmayer Grammars and Symbolic Testing," *Information Proc. Letters,* Vol. 7, No. 1, Jan. 1978.

Howden, W. E., "Methodology for Generation of Program Test Data," *IEEE Trans. Computers,* Vol. C-24, May 1975, pp. 554-559.

Howden, W. E., "Methodology for the Automatic Generation of Program Test Data," McDonnell Douglas, TR No. 41, Huntington Beach, Calif., Feb. 1974.

Howden, W. E., "Reliability of Symbolic Evaluation," *Proc. COMPSAC 77,* Chicago, Nov. 1977, pp. 442-447.

Howden, W. E., "Reliability of the Path Analysis Testing Strategy," *IEEE Trans. Software Engineering,* Vol. SE-2, No. 3, Sept. 1976, pp. 208-214.

Howden, W. E., "Symbolic Evaluation—Design Techniques, Costs, and Effectiveness," U.S. National Bureau of Standards, 1977. (Available from the National Technical Information Service as PB268517.)

Howden, W. E., "Symbolic Testing and the DISSECT Symbolic Evaluation System," *IEEE Trans. Software Engineering,* Vol. SE-3, No. 4, July 1977, pp. 266-278.

Howden, W. E., "Theoretical and Empirical Studies of Program Testing," *IEEE Trans. Software Engineering,* Vol. SE-4, No. 4, July 1978, pp. 293-298.

Howden, W. E. and P. Eichhorst, "Proving Properties of Programs from Program Traces," University of California, San Diego, CS Report No. 18, Aug. 1977.

Howden, W. E. and L. Stucki, "Methodology for the Effective Test Case Selection, Part I," McDonnell Douglas, Huntington Beach, Calif., Jan. 1974.

Hoyt, P. M., "The Navy FORTRAN Validation System," *AFIPS Conf. Proc.,* Vol. 46, 1977 NCC, pp. 529-538.

Huang, J. C., "An Approach to Program Testing," *Computing Surveys,* Vol. 7, No. 3, Sept. 1975, pp. 113-128.

Huang, J. C., "Detection of Data Flow Anomaly Through Program Instrumentation," *IEEE Trans. Software Engineering,* Vol. SE-5, No. 3, May 1979, pp. 226-236.

Huang, J. C., "Instrumenting Programs for Data Flow Analysis," University of Houston, TR-UH-CS-77-4, May 1977.

Huang, J. C., "Instrumenting Programs for Symbolic-Trace Generation," *Computer,* Vol. 13, No. 12, Dec. 1980, pp. 17-23.

Huang, J. C., "Method for Test Case Generation," University of Houston, Nov. 1974.

Huang, J. C., "A Method of Program Analysis and Its Applications To Program-Correctness Problems," *Int'l J. Computer Mathematics,* Vol. 5, No. 3, 1976, pp. 203-227.

Huang, J. C., "Principles of Software Validation," *Proc. Summer Computer Simulation Conf.,* Chicago, July 1977, pp. 705-708.

Huang, J. C., "Program Instrumentation and Software Testing," *Computer,* Vol. 11, No. 4, Apr. 1978, pp. 25-32.

Huang, W. T., "An Application of Flow Expressions to Describe a Data Base Management System," *Proc. COMPSAC 80,* Chicago, Oct. 1980, pp. 327-333.

Hudson, G. R., "Program Errors as a Birth and Death Process," System Development Corp., SP-3011, Santa Monica, Calif., Dec. 1967.

Hunt, B. R., "A Comment on Axiomatic Approaches to Programming," *CACM,* Vol. 13, No. 7, July 1970, pp. 452-453.

Hurst, A. J., "Pascal-P, Program Structure and Program Behaviour," *Software—Practice & Experience,* Vol. 10, No. 12, Dec. 1980.

Ikezawa, M. and R. Kayfes, "Structural Calculus for Program Analysis and Testing," Logicon, Inc., San Pedro, Calif., Nov. 1975.

Jacoby, K. and H. Layton, "Automation of Program Debugging," *Proc. ACM Ann. Conf.,* 1971.

Jeffrey, H. J., "On Dijkstra's Position Paper on Software Reliability," *Software Engineering Notes* (ACM SIGSOFT), Vol. 3, No. 2, Apr. 1978.

Jelinski, F. and P. B. Moranda, "Software Reliability Research," in *Statistical Computer Performance Evaluation,* Academic Press, New York, 1972, pp. 465-484.

Jessop, W. H., J. R. Kane, S. Roy, and J. M. Scanlon, "ATLAS—An Automated Software Testing System," *Proc. 2nd Int'l Conf. Software Engineering,* San Francisco, Oct. 1976, pp. 629-635.

Jirauch, D. H., "Software Design Techniques for Automatic Checkout," *IEEE Trans. Aerospace and Electronic Systems,* Nov. 1967, pp. 934-940.

Johnson, J. P., "Software Reliability Measures," National Technical Information Service, AD A019 147, Springfield, Va., Dec. 1975.

Jonnada, R. K. and K. A. Fegley, "Path Analysis in Systems Science," *IEEE Trans. Systems, Man and Cybernetics,* Vol. SMC-4, No. 5, Sept. 1974.

Joyner, W. H., Jr., W. C. Carter, and D. Brand, "Using Machine Descriptions in Program Verification," IBM Research Report, RC-6922, Yorktown Heights, N.Y., Dec. 1977.

Joyner, W. H., Jr., G. B. Leeman, and W. C. Carter, "Automated Verification of Micro-Programs," IBM Corp., Yorktown Heights, N.Y., Apr. 1976.

Judd, D. R., "Program Testing and Validation," *Computer Bull.,* Mar. 1967.

Kacik, P. J., "An Example of Verification and Validation Techniques Used in a Successful Large Scale Software Development," Hughes Aircraft Co., Fullerton, Calif., July 1978.

Kallah, V. and L. J. Osterweil, "Constructing Flowgraphs for Assembly Language Programs," Dept. of Computer Science, University of Colorado, Boulder, 1975.

Kant, K. and A. Silberschatz, "Error Recovery in Concurrent Processes," *Proc. COMPSAC 80,* Chicago, Oct. 1980, pp. 608-614.

Karp, R. A., "Proving Concurrent Systems Correct," Computer Science Dept., Report No. STAN-CS-79-783, Stanford University, Palo Alto, Calif., Nov. 1979.

Karush, A. D., "Program Quality Assurance," *Datamation,* Oct. 1968.

Katz, S. M. and Z. Manna, "Logical Analysis of Programs," *CACM,* Vol. 19, No. 4, Apr. 1976, pp. 188-206.

Kayton, M., "Verification Cost of Utility Industry Software," *Proc. COMPSAC 77,* Chicago, Nov. 1977, pp. 26-32.

Keezer, E. E., "Practical Experience in Establishing Software Quality Assurance," *Proc. IEEE Symp. Software Reliability,* New York, May 1973, pp. 132-135.

Keirstead, R. E., "On the Feasibility of Software Certification," Stanford Research Inst., PB 245-213, Palo Alto, Calif., June 1975.

Kemmerer, D., "Retrospective: Verification Experiences with the UCLA Operating System Kernel," Proc. Workshop on Formal Verification, *Software Engineering Notes* (ACM SIGSOFT), Vol. 5, No. 3, July 1980.

Kennedy, J. E., "A Survey of Automated Computer Program Verification Tools," Aerospace Corp., El Segundo, Calif., Aug. 1974.

Kennedy, K., "A Global Flow Analysis Algorithm," *International J. Computer Mathematics,* Vol. 3, Sec. A, 1971, pp. 5-15.

Kennedy, K. W., "Node Listings Applied to Data Flow Analysis," *Proc. 2nd Ann. ACM Symp. Programming Languages,* 1975, pp. 10-21.

Kenney, K., "The Validation Game," *Datamation,* Apr. 1974.

Kernighan, B. W. and F. Plauger, *Software Tools,* Addison-Wesley, Reading, Mass., 1976.

Kernighan, B. W. and P. J. Plauger, *The Elements of Programming Style,* 2nd ed., McGraw-Hill, New York, 1978.

Kienzle, M. G., "Measurements of Computer Systems for Queueing Network Models," University of Toronto, Technical Report CSRG-86, Ontario, Oct. 1977.

Kilgore, G. L. and R. E. Hohmeyer, "A New Technique for Testing of Programs for Process Control Computers," *IEEE Int'l Convention Record,* Vol. 13, Part 3, 1965, pp. 256-260.

Kim, K. H., "An Implementation of a Programmer-Transparent Scheme for Coordinating Concurrent Processes in Recovery," *Proc. COMPSAC 80,* Chicago, Oct. 1980, pp. 615-621.

King, J., "A New Approach to Program Testing," *1975 Int'l Conf. Reliable Software,* Los Angeles, Apr. 1975.

King, J., "Testing Conversational Systems," in *Debugging Techniques for Large Systems,* R. Rustin, ed., Prentice-Hall, Englewood Cliffs, N.J., 1971, pp. 143-146.

King, J. C., "General Verification Conditions for Correctness Proofs," IBM Research Report, Yorktown Heights, N.Y., Feb. 1976.

King, J. C., "An Introduction to Proving the Correctness of Programs," IBM Research Report, Yorktown Heights, N.Y., Feb. 1976.

King, J. C., "Program Reduction Using Symbolic Evaluation," *Software Engineering Notes* (ACM SIGSOFT), Vol. 6, No. 1, Jan. 1981.

King, J. C., "Symbolic Execution and Program Testing," *CACM,* Vol. 19, No. 7, July 1976, pp. 385-394.

Klobert, R. K., "Quest for Reliable Software," *Proc. Summer Computer Simulation Conf.,* Chicago, July 1977, pp. 700-704.

Knuth, D. E., "An Empirical Study of FORTRAN Programs," Stanford University, TR CS-186, Palo Alto, Calif., 1971.

Knuth, D. E. and F. R. Stevenson, "Optimal Measurement Points for Program Frequency Counts," *BIT,* Vol. 13, 1973.

Ko, D. C. and M. A. Breuer, "The Design of Self-Checking Multi-Output Combinational Circuits," *AFIPS Conf. Proc.,* Vol. 46, 1977 NCC, pp. 711-721.

Kopetz, H., "Software Design for Fault Tolerance," *Proc. COMPSAC 80,* Chicago, Oct. 1980, pp. 591-595.

Korn, S. A., "Software Validation in a Commercial Environment," *Proc. WESCON 72,* Session 21, Sept. 1972.

Kosaraja, R., "Analysis of Structured Programs," *J. Computer and System Sciences,* Dec. 1974.

Kosy, D., "Annotated Bibliography of Debugging, Testing, and Validation Techniques for Computer Programs," Rand Corp., WN-7271-PR, Santa Monica, Calif., Jan. 1971.

Kosy, D., "Approaches to Improved Program Validation Through Programming Language Design," in *Program Test Methods,* W. C. Hetzel, ed., Prentice-Hall, Englewood Cliffs, N.J., 1972.

Kou, L. T., "On Live-Dead Analysis for Global Data Flow Problems," *JACM,* Vol. 24, No. 3, July 1977, pp. 473-483.

Krause, K. W., R. W. Smith, and M. A. Goodwin, "Optimal Software Test Planning Through Automated Network Analysis," *Proc. IEEE Symp. Computer Software Reliability,* New York, 1973, pp. 18-22.

Krten, O. J., "Improving Existing Software Reliability Models to Provide Early Prediction of Trends," Bell-Northern Research, Ottawa, 1978.

Kundu, S., "New Program Testing Concepts and Their Supporting Tools," Logicon, Inc., Nov. 1977.

Kundu, S., "Note on a Constrained-Path Problem in Program Testing," *IEEE Trans. Software Engineering,* Vol. SE-4, No. 1, Jan. 1978, pp. 75-76.

Landrault, C. and J. C. Laprie, "Reliability and Availability Modeling of Systems Featuring Hardware and Software Faults," *Proc. 7th Ann. Int'l Conf. Fault-Tolerant Computing,* Los Angeles, June 1977, pp. 10-15.

Lauer, P. E., "Survey Paper on Program Proving: Part 1—The Constructive Approach; Part 2—A Functional Approach, Part 3—An Axiomatic Approach Based on a Precondition Function," Computer Science Dept., Queens University of Belfast, Memo Nos. 1, 2, and 3, May 1970.

Lauesen, S., "Debugging Techniques," *Software—Practice & Experience,* Vol. 9, No. 1, Jan. 1979, pp. 51-63.

Lavrov, S. S., "On Problem Solving on a Computer and Proving Program Correctness," in Russian, *Probl. Prokl, Mat. i Mekh.,* CR No. 23843, 1971.

Leavenworth, B. M., "Incremental Program Testing in a Very High Level Language," IBM Research Report, RC-5949, Feb. 1976.

Leeman, G. B., "Symbolic Path Tracing in MCS," IBM Research Report, RC-5642, Sept. 1975.

Lemoine, M. and J. Mullor, "Software Transferability: A Practical Approach," *Software—Practice & Experience,* Vol. 11, No. 5, May 1981, pp. 425-433.

Lengauer, F., "On the Axiomatic Verification of Concurrent Algorithms," University of Toronto, Technical Report CSRG-94, Ontario, Aug. 1978.

Levitt, K. N., "The Application of Program Proving Techniques to the Proving of Synchronization Processes," Stanford Research Inst., Palo Alto, Calif., May 1972.

Lindquist, T. and R. F. Keller, "The Correctness of Programs Written in the Language KL-1," *Proc. COMPSAC 77,* Chicago, Nov. 1977, pp. 635-639.

Lipow, M., "Estimation of Software Package Residual Errors," TRW Software Series, TRW-SS-72-09, TRW Systems Group, Redondo Beach, Calif., Nov. 1972.

Lipow, M., "Some Directed Graph Methods for Analyzing Computer Programs," *Proc. UCLA Conf. Computer Science and Statistics,* Los Angeles, 1975.

Lipton, R., A. J. Perlis, and R. A. DeMillo, "Social Processes and Proofs of Theorems and Programs," Yale University, New Haven, Conn., 1977.

Liskov, B. H., "Guidelines for the Design and Implementation of Reliable Software Systems," Mitre Corp., MTR-23-45, Bedford, Mass., Apr. 1972.

Litecky, C. R. and G. B. Davis, "A Study of Errors, Error Proneness, and Error Diagnosis in COBOL," *CACM,* Vol. 19, No. 1, Jan. 1976, pp. 33-37.

Littlewood, B., "How to Measure Software Reliability, and How Not To," *Proc. 3rd Int'l Conf. Software Engineering,* Atlanta, May 1978, pp. 37-45.

Littlewood, B., "MTBF is Meaningless in Software Reliability," *IEEE Trans. Reliability,* Vol. R-24, No. 1, Apr. 1975, p. 82.

Littlewood, B., "Theories of Software Reliability: How Good Are They and How Can They Be Improved?," *IEEE Trans. Software Engineering,* Vol. SE-6, No. 5, Sept. 1980, pp. 489-500.

Littlewood, B., "What Makes a Reliable Program—Few Bugs, or a Small Failure Rate?," *AFIPS Conf. Proc.,* Vol. 49, 1980 NCC, pp. 707-713.

Litwin, S. and R. J. Pariseau, "Variance of the Number of Errors Detected During a Set of Random Passes Through an Error Laden Graph," Naval Air Development Center, TM 52-76-STS-001, Warminster, Penn., Apr. 1976.

Llewelyn, A. I. and R. F. Wickens, "The Testing of Computer Software," in *Conf. Software Engineering,* P. Naur and B. Randell, eds., NATO, Science Affairs Division, Brussels, 1969, pp. 189-199.

Llewelyn, A. I. and R. F. Wickens, "Testing of Computer Software," in *Software Engineering Concepts and Techniques,* P. Naur, B. Randell and J.N. Buxton, eds., Petrocelli-Charter, New York, 1976.

Lomet, D. B., "Data Flow Analysis in the Presence of Procedure Calls," IBM Research Report, RC-5728, Nov. 1975.

London, R. L., "Bibliography on Proving the Correctness of Computer Programs," Stanford University, AI No. 5, Palo Alto, Calif., 1970.

Love, T., "An Experimental Investigation of the Effect of Program Structure on Program Understanding," *Proc. ACM Conf. Language Design for Reliable Software,* Raleigh, N.C., Mar. 1977.

Lowry, E., "Proposed Language Extensions to Aid Coding and Analysis of Large Problems," IBM Corp., TR 00.1934, 1969.

Lynch, W. C., J. W. Langner, and M. S. Schwartz, "Reliability Experience with CHI/OS," *IEEE Trans. Software Engineering,* Vol. SE-1, No. 2, June 1975, pp. 253-257.

Malhotra, A. and P. B. Sheridan, "Experimental Determination of Design Requirements for a Program Understanding System," IBM Research Report, RC-5831, Jan. 1976.

Mangold, E. R., "Software Error Analysis and Software Policy Implications," *Proc. EASCON 74,* pp. 123-127.

Manna, Z., "Termination of Programs Represented as Interpreted Graphs," *AFIPS Conf. Proc.,* Vol. 36, 1970 SJCC, pp. 83-89.

Manna, Z. and R. Waldinger, "The Synthesis of Structure Changing Programs," *Proc. 3rd Int'l Conf. Software Engineering,* Atlanta, May 1978, pp. 175-187.

Manna, Z. and R. J. Waldinger, "Toward Automatic Program Synthesis," *CACM,* Vol. 14, No. 3, Mar. 1971, pp. 151-165.

Marimont, R. B., "Applications of Graphs and Boolean Matrices to Computer Programming," *SIAM Rev.,* Vol. 2, No. 4, Oct. 1960, pp. 259-268.

Marshall, J. J., "New Approaches to Documentation and Debugging," *Data Processing,* Vol. 14, 1970, pp. 425-435.

Martin, D. F. and G. Estrin, "Experiments on Models of Computations and Systems," *IEEE Trans. Electronic Computers,* Vol. EC-16, No. 1, Feb. 1967, pp. 59-69.

Martin, D. F. and G. Estrin, "Models of Computations and Systems—Evaluation of Vertex Probabilities in Graph Models of Computation," *JACM,* Vol. 14, No. 2, Apr. 1967, pp. 281-299.

Martinez, J. L., "The Testing of Microprocessor Based Systems," *Digest of Papers—COMPCON 77 Spring,* San Francisco, 1977, pp. 186-191.

Mayeda, W. and C. V. Ramamoorthy, "Distinguishability Criteria in Oriented Graphs and Their Application to Computer Diagnosis," *IEEE Trans. Circuit Theory,* Vol. CT-16, Nov. 1969, pp. 448-454.

McCabe, J. T., "A Complexity Measure," *IEEE Trans. Software Engineering,* Vol. SE-2, No. 4, Dec. 1976, pp. 308-320.

McCall, J. A., P. K. Richards, and G. F. Walters, "Factors in Software Quality," Information Systems Programs, General Electric Co., Sunnyvale, Calif., June 1977.

McClure, C. L., "A Model for Program Complexity Analysis," *Proc. 3rd Int'l Conf. Software Engineering,* Atlanta, May 1978, pp. 149-157.

McGowan, C., "The Most Recent Error—Its Causes and Correction," *Proc. Conf. Proving Assertions About Programs,* Jan. 1972, pp. 191-202.

McGowan, C. L. and J. Kelley, *Top Down Structured Programming Techniques,* Petrocelli-Charter, New York, 1975.

McGregor, D. R., and J. R. Malone, "Stabdump—A Dump Interpreter Program to Assist Debugging," *Software—Practice & Experience,* Vol. 10, No. 4, Apr. 1980, pp. 329-332.

NcNaughton, R. and H. Yamada, "Regular Expressions and State Graphs for Automata," *IRE Trans. Electronic Computers,* Mar. 1960, pp. 39-47.

McTap, J. L., "The Complexity of an Individual Program," *AFIPS Conf. Proc.,* Vol. 49, 1980 NCC, pp. 767-771.

Melton, R., G. Greenburg, and Michael Sharp, "Cobol Automated Verification System: Study Phase," Rome Air Development Center, RADC-TR-81-11, Griffiss Air Force Base, N.Y., Mar. 1981.

Melton, R. A., "Automatically Translating FORTRAN to IFTRAN," *Proc. Conf. Computer Science and Statistics,* University of California, Los Angeles, Feb. 1975.

Migneault, G. E., "Software Reliability and Advanced Avionics," *AFIPS Conf. Proc.,* Vol. 49, 1980 NCC, pp. 715-720.

Mikelsons, M. and I. Wladawsky, "On the Formal Documentation of Programs," IBM Research Report, RC-5788, Jan. 1976.

Miller, E., "Special Mini-Tutorial on Software Quality Assurance," *Proc. COMPSAC 80,* Chicago, Oct. 1980, pp. 381-382.

Miller, E. F., Jr., "Advanced Technologies for Verification and Validation," *Proc DoD/Industry Conf. Software Verification and Validation,* Syracuse, N.Y., Aug. 1976.

Miller, E. F., Jr., "The Art and Theory of Program Testing," *Proc. 4th Texas Conf. Computing Systems,* Austin, Nov. 1975, pp. 4A-3.1 to 4A-3.10.

Miller, E. F., Jr., "Automated Support for Software Engineering—A Long-Range Tool Family Plan," *Proc. ONR Conf. Software Specification and Testing Technology Transfer,* Office of Naval Research, Apr. 1978.

Miller, E. F., Jr., "Automatic Generation of Software Testcases," *Proc. EuroComp,* Uxbridge, Middlesex, England, May 1974.

Miller, E. F., Jr., "Engineering Software for Testability," *Digest of Papers—COMPCON 75 Spring,* San Francisco, Feb. 1975, pp. 7-10.

Miller, E. F., Jr., "Methodology for Comprehensive Software Testing," Rome Air Development Center, RADC-TR-75-161, Griffiss Air Force Base, N.Y., June 1975.

Miller, E. F., Jr., "Program Testing," *Computer,* Vol. 11, No. 4, Apr. 1978, pp. 10-12.

Miller, E. F., Jr., "Program Testing: Art Meet Theory," *Computer,* Vol. 10, No. 7, July 1977, pp. 42-51.

Miller, E. F., Jr., "Program Testing Tools and Their Uses," *Infotech State of the Art Report,* Aug. 1977.

Miller, E. F., Jr., "A Service Concept for Software Auditing," *Proc. Workshop Computer Auditing,* San Francisco, Jan. 1976.

Miller, E. F., Jr., "Some Statistics from the Software Test Factory," *Software Engineering Notes* (ACM SIGSOFT), Vol. 4, No. 1, Jan. 1979.

Miller, E. F., Jr., "Structurally Based Automatic Program Testing," *Proc. EASCON 74,* Washington, D.C., Oct. 1974.

Miller, E. F., Jr., "Technology for Automated Verification Systems," *Proc. Aeronautical Systems Software Workshop,* Dayton, Ohio, Apr. 1974.

Miller, E. F., Jr., "Testing for Software Reliability," *InfoTech State of the Art Report,* Aug. 1977.

Miller, E. F., Jr., "Theoretical Approaches to Problem Independent Software, Validation," *Proc. Summer Computer Simulation Conf.,* Montreal, July 1973.

Miller, E. F., Jr., "Toward Automated Software Testing: Problems and Payoffs," *Proc. 8th Ann. Symp. Computer Science and Statistics,* University of California, Los Angeles, Feb. 1975.

Miller, E. F., Jr., et al., "Structural Techniques of Program Validation," *Digest of Papers—COMPCON 74 Spring,* San Francisco, Feb. 1974, pp. 161-164.

Miller, E. F., Jr., et al., "Workshop Report: Software Testing and Test Documentation," *Computer,* Vol. 12, No. 3, Mar. 1979, pp. 98-107.

Miller, E. F., Jr., J. M. Barzdin, and J. J. Bicevskis, "Automated Test Data Generation Techniques," *Proc. InfoTech Conf. Program Testing,* Hanover, West Germany, May 1978.

Miller, E. F., Jr. and R. A. Melton, "Automated Generation of Testcase Datasets," *1975 Int'l Conf. Reliable Software,* Los Angeles, Apr. 1975.

Miller, E. F., Jr. and M. R. Paige, "A Method for Ranking Priorities in Testing Computer Programs," *Proc. Computer Systems Design Conf.,* Anaheim, Calif., Feb. 1972.

Miller, E. F., Jr., J. S. Praninskas, and M. A. Hirschberg, "A Semantic Updating System for Repairing Software," ARO Report 78-3, *Proc. 1978 Army Numerical Analysis and Computers Conf.,* Huntsville, Ala.

Miller, J. C. and C. J. Maloney, "Systematic Mistake Analysis of Digital Computer Programs," *CACM,* Vol. 16, No. 2, Feb. 1973, pp. 58-60.

Miller, R. E. and C. K. Yap, "Formal Specification and Analysis of Loosely Connected Processes," IBM Research Report, RC-6716, Sept. 1977.

Miller, W., "Automatic Generation of Floating Point Test Data," *IEEE Trans. Software Engineering,* Vol. SE-2, No. 3, Sept. 1976, pp. 223-226.

Mills, H., "Top Down Programming in Large Systems," in *Debugging Techniques in Large Systems,* R. Rustin, ed., Prentice-Hall, Englewood Cliffs, N.J., 1971, pp. 41-56.

Mills, H. D., "Mathematical Foundations for Structured Programming," Federal Systems Division, FSC71-5108, IBM Corp., 1971.

Misra, J. and R. T. Yeh, "Major Milestones in Program Verification," presentation at COMPSAC 77, Chicago, Nov. 1977.

Miyamoto, I., "Toward an Effective Software Reliability Evaluation," *Proc. 3rd Int'l Conf. Software Engineering,* Atlanta, May 1978, pp. 46-55.

Moore, R. E., *Interval Analysis,* Prentice-Hall, Englewood Cliffs, N.J., 1966.

Moranda, P. B., "Open Channel: Software Reliability Revisited," *Computer,* Vol. 11, No. 4, Apr. 1978, pp. 92-93.

Moranda, P. B., "Quantitative Methods for Software Reliability Measurements," *McDonnell Douglas Astronautics,* MDC G6553, Dec. 1976.

Morgan, D. E. and D. J. Taylor, "Special Feature: A Survey of Methods of Achieving Reliable Software," *Computer,* Vol. 10, No. 2, Feb. 1977, pp. 44-53.

Moriconi, M. S., "Toward Incremental and Language-Independent Program Verification Systems," Proc. Workshop on Formal Verification, *Software Engineering Notes* (ACM SIGSOFT), Vol. 5, No. 3, July 1980.

Moriconi, M. S., "A Designer/Verifier's Assistant," *IEEE Trans. Software Engineering,* Vol. SE-5, No. 4, July 1979, pp. 387-401.

Moriconi, M. S., "A System for Incrementally Designing and Verifying Programs," University of Texas, Austin, Dec. 1977.

Mullery, A. P., "A Design for Error Tolerant Software," IBM Research Report, RC-5783, Dec. 1975.

Mullery, A. P., "Error Tolerant Software—Some Principles," IBM Research Report, RC-5784, Dec. 1975.

Mullin, F. J., "Software Test Management," *Proc. COMPSAC 77,* Chicago, Nov. 1977, pp. 321-326.

Mulock, R. B., "Software Reliability Engineering," *Proc. Ann. Reliability and Maintainability Symp.,* Jan. 1972, pp. 586-593.

Mulock, R. B., "Study of Software Reliability at the Stanford Linear Accelerator Center," Stanford University, Palo Alto, Calif., Aug. 1970.

Musa, J. D., "An Exploratory Experiment with 'Foreign' Debugging of Programs," *Proc. Symp. Computer Software Engineering,* Polytechnic Press, New York, pp. 457-464.

Musa, J. D., "Software Reliability Measures Applied to System Engineering," *AFIPS Conf. Proc.,* Vol. 48, 1979 NCC, pp. 941-946.

Musser, D. R., "The Unique Termination Method of Program Verification," Proc. Workshop on Formal Verification, *Software Engineering Notes* (ACM SIGSOFT), Vol. 5, No. 3, July 1980.

Myers, E. W., Jr. and L. J. Osterweil, "BIGMAC II: A FORTRAN Language Augmentation Tool," *Proc. 5th Int'l Conf. Software Engineering,* San Diego, Mar. 1981, pp. 410-421.

Myers, G. J., *Software Reliability: Principles and Practices,* Wiley, New York, 1976.

Myers, G. J., "Software Reliability Is Not an Equation," *Computer,* Vol. 11, No. 6, June 1978, pp. 82-83.

Nafalty, S. M. and M. C. Cohen, "Test Data Generators and Debugging Systems—Workable Quality Control, Parts I and II," *Data Processing Digest,* Vol. 18, Nos. 2 and 3, Feb. and March 1972.

Naur, P. and B. Randell, eds., *Conf. Software Engineering,* NATO, Science Affairs Division, Brussels, 1969.

Naur, P., B. Randell, and J. N. Buxton, eds., *Software Engineering Concepts and Techniques,* Petrocelli-Charter, New York, 1976.

Neilsen, N. R., "Computers, Security, and the Audit Function," *AFIPS Conf. Proc.,* Vol. 44, 1975 NCC, pp. 947-954.

Nelson, E. C., "Software Reliability," *Proc. 1975 Int'l Symp. Fault-Tolerant Computing,* UNESCO Conf. Center, Paris, June 1975, pp. 24-28.

Nelson, E. C., "A Statistical Basis for Software Reliability Assessment," TRW-SS-73-03, Redondo Beach, Calif., Mar. 1973.

Nelson, V. P., "Fault Tolerance in Reconfigurable Multiprocessor Systems," *Proc. COMPSAC 80,* Chicago, Oct. 1980, pp. 372-380.

Ng, E. W., "Mathematical Software Testing Activities at the Jet Propulsion Laboratory," in *Program Test Methods,* W. C. Hetzel, ed., Prentice-Hall, Englewood Cliffs, N.J., 1973.

O'Brien, J. A., "Computer Program for Automatic Spelling Correction," Itek Corp., RADC-TR-66-696, Mar. 1967.

Ogdin, C. A., "Software Aids for Debugging," *Mini-Micro Systems,* Vol. 13, No. 7, July 1980, pp. 115-122.

Ogdin, J. L., "Debugging of Computer Programs," Software Technique, Inc., Silver Spring, Md., 1973.

Ogdin, J. L., "Designing Reliable Software," *Datamation,* July 1972.

Okumoto, K. and A. L. Goel, "Optimum Release Time for Software Systems," *Proc. COMPSAC 79,* Chicago, Nov. 1979, pp. 500-503.

Oliver, P., "Experiences in Building and Using Compiler Validation Systems," *AFIPS Conf. Proc.,* Vol. 48, 1979 NCC, pp. 1051-1057.

Osterweil, L. J., "The Detection of Unexecutable Program Paths Through Static Data Flow Analysis," *Proc. COMPSAC 77,* Chicago, Nov. 1977, pp. 406-413.

Osterweil, L. J., "Proposal for an Integrated Testing System for Computer Programs," University of Colorado, Boulder, Aug. 1976.

Osterweil, L. J., "A Software Lifecycle Methodology and Tool Support," University of Colorado, CU-CS-154-79, Boulder, Apr. 1979.

Osterweil, L. J., "Using Data Flow Tools in Software Engineering," University of Colorado, CU-CS-153-79, Boulder, Mar. 1979.

Osterweil, L. J. and L. D. Fosdick, "Automated Input/Output Variable Classification as an Aid to Validation of FORTRAN Programs," University of Colorado, CU-CS-037-74, Boulder, Jan. 1974.

Osterweil, L. J. and L. D. Fosdick, "Data Flow Analysis as an Aid in Documentation, Assertion Generation, Validation, and Error Detection," University of Colorado, CU-CS-055-74, Boulder, Sept. 1974.

Osterweil, L. J. and L. D. Fosdick, "DAVE—A Validation Error Detection and Documentation System for FORTRAN Programs," *Software—Practice & Experience,* Vol. 6, 1976, pp. 473-486.

Osterweil, L. J. and L. D. Fosdick, "Some Experience with DAVE—A FORTRAN Program Analyzer," University of Colorado, Boulder, Mar. 1976.

Ostrand, T. J. and E. J. Weyuker, "Current Directions in the Theory of Testing," *Proc. COMPSAC 80,* Chicago, Oct. 1980, pp. 386-389.

Ostrand, T. J. and E. J. Weyuker, "Error-Based Program Testing," *Proc. 1979 Conf. Information Sciences and Systems,* Johns Hopkins University, Baltimore, Mar. 1979.

Ottenstein, L. M., "Quantitative Estimates of Debugging Requirements," *IEEE Trans. Software Engineering,* Vol. SE-5, No. 5, Sept. 1979, pp. 504-514.

Owicki, S. and L. Lamport, "Concurrent Program Verification," Proc. Workshop on Formal Verification, *Software Engineering Notes* (ACM SIGSOFT), Vol. 5, No. 3, July 1980.

Paige, M. R., "On Partitioning Program Graphs," *IEEE Trans. Software Engineering,* Vol. SE-3, No. 6, Nov. 1977, pp. 386-393.

Paige, M. R., "Program Graphs, an Algebra, and Their Implication for Programming," *IEEE Trans. Software Engineering,* Vol. SE-1, No. 3, Sept. 1975, pp. 286-291.

Paige, M. R. and E. E. Balkovich, "On Testing Programs," *Proc. IEEE Symp. Computer Software Reliability,* New York, May 1973, pp. 23-27.

Paige, M. R. and E. E. Balkovich, "A Test Plan for a Structured Program," General Research Corp., Santa Barbara, Calif., May 1972.

Paige, M. R. and J. P. Benson, "The Use of Software Probes in Testing FORTRAN Programs," *Computer,* Vol. 7, No. 7, July 1974, pp. 40-47.

Paige, M. R. and E. F. Miller, Jr., "Methodology for Software Validation—A Survey of the Literature," General Research Corp., RM-1549, Santa Barbara, Calif., Mar. 1972.

Paige, M. R. and E. F. Miller, Jr., "Ranking Priorities in Testing Computer Programs," *Proc. Computer Systems Design Conf.,* Industrial and Scientific Conf. Management, Inc., Chicago, 1972, pp. 143-148.

Painter, J. D., "Software Testing in Support of Worldwide Military Command and Control System ADP," *Proc. COMPSAC 77,* Chicago, Nov. 1977, pp. 316-320.

Panzl, D. J., "Automatic Revision of Formal Test Procedures," *Proc. 3rd Int'l Conf. Software Engineering,* Atlanta, May 1978, pp. 320-326.

Panzl, D. J., "Automatic Software Test Drivers," *Computer,* Vol. 11, No. 4, Apr. 1978, pp. 44-50.

Panzl, D. J., "FORTRAN Test Procedure Language (TPL/F), Preliminary Programmer Reference Manual," General Elecrric R&D Center, Schenectady, N.Y., Jan. 1977.

Panzl, D. J., "A Language for Specifying Software Tests," *AFIPS Conf. Proc.,* Vol. 47, 1978 NCC, pp. 609-619.

Panzl, D. J., "Test Procedures: A New Approach to Software Verification," General Electric Co., Report No. 76-CRC-220, Schenectady, N.Y., Dec. 1976.

Patterson, D., "Verification of Microprograms," UCLA-ENG-7707, University of California, Los Angeles, Jan. 1977.

Pemberton, S., "Comments on an Error-Recovery Scheme by Hartmann," *Software—Practice & Experience,* Vol. 10, No. 3, Mar. 1980, pp. 231-240.

Perry, W. E., "Who's in Charge, You or Your Computer?," *Computer Decisions,* Vol. 10, Feb. 1978, pp. 38-41.

Perry, W. E. and J. Fitzgerald, "Designing for Auditability," *Datamation,* Aug. 1977, pp. 46-50.

Persch, G. and G. Winterstein, "Symbolic Interpretation and Tracing of PASCAL-Programs," *Proc. 3rd Int'l Conf. Software Engineering,* Atlanta, May 1978, pp. 312-319.

Pietrasanta, A. M., "Management Control in Program Testing," IBM Systems Development Division, TR00.1474, Poughkeepsie, N.Y., July 1966.

Pippenger, N., "The Minimum Number of Edges in Graphs with Prescribed Paths," IBM Research Report, RC-7378, Yorktown Heights, N.Y., Nov. 1978.

Ploedereder, E., "Pragmatic Techniques for Program Analysis and Verification," *Proc. 4th Int'l Conf. Software Engineering,* Munich, Sept. 1979, pp. 63-72.

Poole, P. C., "Debugging and Testing," in *Advanced Course on Software Engineering,* F. L. Bauer, ed., Springer-Verlag, New York, 1973, pp. 278-318.

Popek, G. J., et al., "UCLA Secure UNIX," *AFIPS Conf. Proc.,* Vol. 48, 1979 NCC, pp. 355-364.

Popkin, G. S. and M. L. Shooman, "On the Number of Tests Necessary to Verify a Computer Program," Rome Air Development Center, RADC-TR-78-229, Griffiss Air Force Base, N.Y., Nov. 1978.

"Practical Measures for Program Testing Thoroughness," Auerbach Pub., Inc., Pennsauken, N.J., 1977.

Pradhan, D. K. and J. J. Stiffler, "Error-Correcting Codes and Self-Checking Circuits," *Computer,* Vol. 13, No. 3, Mar. 1980, pp. 27-37.

Pratt, T., "Control Computations and the Design of Loop Control Structures," *IEEE Trans. Software Engineering,* Vol. SE-4, No. 2, Mar. 1978, pp. 81-89.

Pratt, V. R., "Modeling as a Paradigm for Verification," Proc. Workshop on Formal Verification, *Software Engineering Notes* (ACM SIGSOFT), Vol. 5, No. 3, July 1980.

Pullen, E. W. and D. F. Shuttee, "MUSE, a Tool for Testing a Multi-Terminal System in a Multi-Terminal Environment," *AFIPS Conf. Proc.,* Vol. 32, 1968 SJCC, pp. 491-502.

Pyster, A. and A. Dutta, "Error-Checking Compilers and Portability," *Software—Practice & Experience,* Vol. 8, No. 1, Jan.-Feb. 1978, pp. 99-109.

Ramamoorthy, C. V., "Analysis of Graphs by Connectivity Considerations," *JACM,* Vol. 13, No. 2, Apr. 1966, pp. 221-222.

Ramamoorthy, C. V., et al., "A Systematic Approach to the Development and Validation of Critical Software for Nuclear Power Plants," *Proc. 4th Int'l Conf. Software Engineering,* Munich, Sept. 1979, pp. 231-240.

Ramamoorthy, C. V. and S. F. Ho, "Testing Large Software with Automated Software Evaluation Systems," *IEEE Trans. Software Engineering,* Vol. SE-1, No. 1, Mar. 1975, pp. 46-58.

Ramamoorthy, C. V., S. F. Ho, and W. T. Chen, "On the Automated Generation of Program Test Data," *IEEE Trans. Software Engineering,* Vol. SE-2, No. 4, Dec. 1976, pp. 293-300.

Ramamoorthy, C. V., S. F. Ho, and H. H. So, "The Status and Structure of Software Testing Procedures," *Digest of Papers—COMPCON 77 Spring,* San Francisco, 1977, pp. 367-369.

Ramamoorthy, C. V. and K. H. Kim, "Toward an Automated Software Testing with Instrumentation," Electrical Engineering Dept., University of California, Berkeley, 1975.

Ramamoorthy, C. V., K. H. Kim, and W. T. Chen, "Optimal Placement of Software Monitors Aiding Systematic Testing," *IEEE Trans. Software Engineering,* Vol. SE-1, No. 4, Dec. 1975, pp. 403-410.

Ramamoorthy, C. V., R. E. Meeker, Jr., and J. Turner, "Design and Construction of an Automated Software Evaluation System," *Proc. 1973 IEEE Conf. Software Reliability,* May 1973, pp. 28-37.

Ramamoorthy, C. V., Y. R. Mok, F. B. Baastani, and G. Chin, "Application of a Methodology for the Development and Validation of Reliable Process Control Software," *Proc. COMPSAC 80,* Chicago, Oct. 1980, pp. 622-633.

Rao, T. R. N. and H. J. Reinheimer, "Fault-Tolerant Modularized Arithmetic Logic Units," *AFIPS Conf. Proc.,* Vol. 46, 1977 NCC, pp. 703-710.

Rault, J. C., "An Approach Towards Reliable Software," *Proc. 4th Int'l Conf. Software Engineering,* Munich, Sept. 1979, pp. 220-230.

Rault, J. C., "A Bibliography on Computer System Diagnosis," Thomson-CSF, DIS/SCAS, Paris, Jan. 1976.

Rault, J. C., "Bibliography on Program Testing and Verification," Thomson-CSF, DIS/SCAS, Paris, Jan. 1976.

Reif, J. H., "Symbolic Program Analysis in Almost Linear Time," *Proc. 5th ACM Symp. Principles of Programming Languages,* Tucson, Ariz., Jan. 1978.

Reifer, D. J., "Automated Aids for Reliable Software," Aerospace Corp., El Segundo, Calif., Aug. 1975.

Reifer, D. J., "Computer Program Verification, Validation, and Certification," Aerospace Corp., El Segundo, Calif., May 1974.

Reifer, D. J., "Glossary for Computer Program Verification, Validation, and Certification Aids," Aerospace Corp., El Segundo, Calif., 1974.

Reifer, D. J., "A Glossary of Software Tools and Techniques," *Computer,* Vol. 10, No. 7, July 1977, pp. 52-62.

Reifer, D. J., "Interim Report on the Aids Inventory Project," Aerospace Corp., SAMSO-TR-75-184, El Segundo, Calif., July 1975.

Reifer, D. J. and R. L. Ettinger, "Test Tools: Are They a Cureall?," Aerospace Corp., El Segundo, Calif., Oct. 1974.

Remus, H. and S. Zilles, "Prediction and Management of Program Quality," *Proc. 4th Int'l Conf. Software Engineering,* Munich, Sept. 1979, pp. 341-350.

Renfer, G. F., "Automatic Program Testing," *Proc. Conf. Computers and Data Processing,* University of Toronto Press, 1962, pp. 127-135.

Rennels, D. A., "Distributed Fault-Tolerant Computer Systems," *Computer,* Vol. 13, No. 3, Mar. 1980, pp. 55-65.

Reynolds, J. C., "Semantics of the Domain of Flow Diagrams," *JACM,* Vol. 24, No. 3, July 1977, pp. 484-503.

Richards, F. R., "Computer Software: Testing, Reliability Models, and Quality Assurance," National Technical Information Service, AD-A001 260, Springfield, Va., July 1974.

Richardson, D. J. and L. A. Clarke, "A Partition Analysis Method to Increase Program Reliability," *Proc. 5th Int'l Conf. Software Engineering,* San Diego, Mar. 1981, pp. 244-253.

Riddle, W. E., G. Bristow, C. Drey, and B. Edwards, "Anomaly Detection in Concurrent Programs," *Proc. 4th Int'l. Conf. Software Engineering,* Munich, Sept. 1979, pp. 265-273.

Robinson, J. G. and E. S. Roberts, "Software Fault-Tolerance in the Pluribus," *AFIPS Conf. Proc.,* Vol. 47, 1978 NCC, pp. 563-569.

Robinson, L., "Verification of COBOL Programs," Stanford Research Inst., Palo Alto, Calif., June 1975.

Robinson, S. K. and I. S. Torsun, "Dynamic Analysis," *Computer J.,* Vol. 18, Aug. 1975.

Robinson, S. K. and I. S. Torsun, "Empirical Analysis of FORTRAN Programs," *Computer J.,* Vol. 19, Feb. 1976, pp. 56-62.

Rohde, A., "Testing and Debugging COBOL Programs," Bang & Olufsen, Denmark, Nov. 1976.

Roman, C. G., "A Two Step Approach to the Validation of Software Engineering Methodologies," *AFIPS Conf. Proc.,* Vol. 46, 1977 NCC, pp. 539-544.

Rose, D. J. and R. E. Tarjan, "Algorithm Aspects of Vertex Elimination on Directed Graphs," Stanford University, STAN-CS-75-531, Palo Alto, Calif., Nov. 1975.

Rosen, B. K., "Data Flow Analysis for Procedural Language," IBM Research Report, RC-5948, Apr. 1976.

Rosen, B. K., "Data Flow Analysis for Recursive PL/I Programs," IBM Research Report, RC-5211, Yorktown Heights, N.Y., 1975.

Rosen, B. K., "A Lubricant for Data Flow Analysis," IBM Research Report, RC-8481 (#36925), Yorktown Heights, N.Y., Sept. 1980.

Rosenberg, A. L., "Data Graphs and Addressing Schemes," IBM Research Report, RC-2747, Jan. 1970.

Rosengard, P., "Workshop Report: Software Quality Assurance Standards Under Development," *Computer,* Vol. 12, No. 2, Feb. 1979, pp. 84-85.

Royce, W. W., "Automated Checkout of Every Possible Logic Path in Very Large Computer Programs," TRW, EBC G039, Dec. 1969.

Rubey, R. J., "Aerospace Software Validation: Present and Future," *Proc. WESCON 72,* Session 21, Sept. 1972.

Rubey, R. J., J. A. Dana, and P. W. Biché, "Quantitative Aspects of Software Validation," *IEEE Trans. Software Engineering,* Vol. SE-1, No. 2, June 1975, pp. 150-155.

Rubey, R. J. and R. D. Hartwick, "Quantitative Measurement of Program Quality," *Proc. ACM Nat'l Conf.,* 1968, pp. 671-677.

Rudin, H., C. H. West, and P. Zafiropulo, "Automated Protocol Validation—One Chain of Development," IBM Research Report, RZ-883, Yorktown Heights, N.Y., Jan. 1978.

Ruggiero, W., et al., "Analysis of Data Flow Models Using the SARA Graph Model of Behavior," *AFIPS Conf. Proc.,* Vol. 48, 1979 NCC, pp. 975-988.

Rumsey, J. R. and D. W. Abmayr, "An Effective Method for Measurement and Analysis of System Software Performance," *AFIPS Conf. Proc.,* Vol. 46, 1977 NCC, pp. 523-528.

Russell, E. C., "Automatic Program Analysis," University of California, Los Angeles, Report 69-12, AD686 401, Mar. 1969.

Russell, E. C. and G. Estrin, "Measurement Based Automatic Analysis of Fortran Programs," *AFIPS Conf. Proc.,* 1969 SJCC, pp. 723-732.

Rustin, R., ed., *Debugging Techniques in Large Systems,* Prentice-Hall, Englewood Cliffs, N.J., 1971.

Ruthberg, Z. G. and R. G. McKenzie, "Computer Science and Technology: Audit and Evaluation of Computer Security," NBS Special Publication 500-19, National Bureau of Standards, Washington, D.C., Oct. 1977. (Proc. of the NBS Invitational Workshop held at Miami Beach, Fla., Mar. 1977.)

Ryder, B. G., "Constructing the Call Graph of a Program," *IEEE Trans. Software Engineering,* Vol. SE-5, No. 3, May 1979, pp. 216-226.

Saib, S. H., J. P. Benson, and R. A. Melton, "A Methodology for Program Verification," *Proc. Summer Computer Simulation Conf.,* Chicago, July 1977, pp. 713-720.

Salazar, J. A. and R. R. Hall, "Astros—Advanced Systematic Techniques for Reliable Operational Software," presentation at COMPSAC 77, Chicago, Nov. 1977.

Samet, H., "A Machine Description Facility for Compiler Testing," *IEEE Trans. Software Engineering,* Vol. SE-3, No. 5, Sept. 1977, pp. 343-351.

Sampson, W. F., T. J. Little, and G. C. Dodson, Jr., "Organizational Strategies for Producing Better Software," *Proc. COMPSAC 77,* Chicago, Nov. 1977, pp. 233-239.

Sanden, B., "Restarting a Real-Time System Correctness Analysis," TRITA-CS-7704, Royal Inst. of Technology, Stockholm, Oct. 1977.

Sauder, R. L., "A General Test Data Generator for COBOL," *AFIPS Conf. Proc.,* Vol. 21, 1962 SJCC, pp. 317-323.

Schaefer, M., *A Mathematical Theory of Global Program Optimization,* Prentice-Hall, Englewood Cliffs, N.J., 1973.

Schafer, R. E., J. E. Angus, J. F. Alter, and S. E. Emoto, "Validation of Software Reliability Models," Rome Air Development Center, RADC-TR-79-147, Griffiss Air Force Base, N.Y., June 1979.

Scheid, J., "INA JO: SDC's Formal Development Methodology," Proc. Workshop on Formal Verification, *Software Engineering Notes* (ACM SIGSOFT), Vol. 5, No. 3, July 1980.

Scherr, A. L., "Developing and Testing a Large Programming System: The OS/360 Time Sharing Option," in *Program Test Methods,* W. C. Hetzel, ed., Prentice-Hall, Englewood Cliffs, N.J., 1973.

Schick, G. J. and R. W. Wolverton, "Achieving Reliability in Large Scale Software Systems," TRW Systems Group, Redondo Beach, Calif., Jan. 1974.

Schick, G. J. and R. W. Wolverton, "Assessment of Software Reliability," McDonnell Douglas, WD-1872, Jan. 1974.

Schlender, P., "Application of Disciplined Software Testing," in *Debugging Techniques in Large Systems,* R. Rustin, ed., Prentice-Hall, Englewood Cliffs, N.J., 1971, pp. 141-142.

Schmidt, D. C. and J. D. Johannes, "Research Proposal for Software Verification Utilizing Data Range Analysis," Vanderbilt University, Nashville, Tenn., Oct. 1975.

Schneidewind, N. F., "Analysis of Error Processes in Computer Software," Naval Postgraduate School, Monterey, Calif., Mar. 1975.

Schneidewind, N. F., "Emulation—Tool for Software Development," *AFIPS Conf. Proc.,* Vol. 47, 1978 NCC, pp. 367-372.

Schneidewind, N. F., "Software Metrics for Aiding Program Development and Debugging," *AFIPS Conf. Proc.,* Vol. 48, 1979 NCC, pp. 989-994.

Schneidewind, N. F., "The Use of Simulation of Evaluation of Software," *Computer,* Vol. 10, No. 4, Apr. 1977, pp. 47-53.

Schneidewind, N. F. and H.-M. Hoffmann, "An Experiment in Software Error Data Collection and Analysis," *IEEE Trans. Software Engineering,* Vol. SE-5, No. 3, May 1979, pp. 276-286.

Schneidewind, N. F., G. T. Howard, and M. Kirchgaessner, "Software Error Detection Models, Validation Tests, and Program Complexity Measures," Naval Postgraduate School, NPS-52-SS 7611, AD-A039-455/IWC, Monterey, Calif., Nov. 1976.

Schorer, P., "More on 'A Program Testing Problem'," *Software Engineering Notes* (ACM SIGSOFT), Vol. 5, No. 2, Apr. 1980.

Schorer, P., "A Program Testing Problem," *Software Engineering Notes* (ACM SIGSOFT), Vol. 4, No. 4, Oct. 1979.

Schorer, P. and R. L. Glass, "Still More on 'A Program Testing Problem'," *Software Engineering Notes* (ACM SIGSOFT), Vol. 5, No. 3, July 1980.

Schusheim, B., "A Flexible Approach to Microprocessor Testing," *Computer Design,* Vol. 15, No. 3, Mar. 1976, pp. 67-72.

Schwartz, J. T., "An Overview of Bugs," in *Debugging Techniques in Large Systems,* R. Rustin, ed., Prentice-Hall, Englewood Cliffs, N.J., 1971, pp. 1-16.

Scowen, R. S., "A New Technique for Improving the Quality of Computer Programs," *Proc. 4th Int'l Conf. Software Engineering,* Munich, Sept. 1979, pp. 73-78.

Scowen, R. S., "Testing the Diagnostic Features of the BABEL Compiler," National Physical Laboratory, Teddington, England, Sept. 1974.

Seifert, M., "Reconfiguration and Recovery of Multiprocess Systems in Fault-Tolerant Distributed Systems," *Proc. COMPSAC 80,* Chicago, Oct. 1980, pp. 596-602.

Shankar, K. S. and C. S. Chandersekaran, "Data Flow, Abstraction Levels, and Specifications for Communications Switching Systems," *Proc. 2nd Int'l Conf. Software Engineering,* San Francisco, Oct. 1976, pp. 585-591.

Shedletsky, J. J., "Random Testing: Verified Effectiveness Vs. Verified Practicality," *Proc. 7th Ann. Int'l Conf. Fault-Tolerant Computing,* Los Angeles, June 1977, pp. 175-179.

Sholl, H. A. and T. L. Booth, "Software Performance Modelling Using Computational Structures," *IEEE Trans. Software Engineering,* Vol. SE-1, No. 4, Dec. 1975, pp. 414-420.

Shooman, M. L., "Meaning of Exhaustive Software Testing," Brooklyn Polytechnic Inst., New York, Jan. 1974.

Shooman, M.L. and H. Ruston, "Summary of Technical Progress, Investigation of Software Models," Rome Air Development Center, RADC-TR-79-188, Griffiss Air Force Base, N.Y., July 1979.

Shooman, M. L. and A. K. Trevedi, "Computer Software Reliability: Many State Modelling Techniques," Rome Air Development Center, RADC TR-75-169, AD A014 824, Griffiss Air Force Base, N.Y., July 1975.

Shrivastava, S. K. and J.-P. Banatre, "Reliable Resource Allocation Between Unreliable Processes," *IEEE Trans. Software Engineering,* Vol. SE-4, No. 3, May 1978, pp. 230-241.

Silver, A. N., "A Computer Analysis Tool for Structural Decomposition Using Entropy Metrics," *AFIPS Conf. Proc.,* Vol. 48, 1979 NCC.

Simmons, J. W., "Fortran Loop Detecting Trace," *Software Age,* Mar. 1970, pp. 19-21.

Sites, R. L., "Some Thoughts on Proving Clean Termination of Programs," Stanford University, CS-74-418, Palo Alto, Calif., May 1974.

Sloane, N. J. A., "On Finding the Paths Through a Network," *Bell System Technical J.,* Vol. 51, No. 2, Feb. 1972, pp. 371-390.

Soldini, J. and R. Hurley, "A Simplified One-Pass Method for Structuring a Program," IBM Corp., San Jose, Calif., 1976.

Sorkowitz, A. R., "Certification Testing: A Procedure to Improve the Quality of Software Testing," *Computer,* Vol. 12, No. 8, Aug. 1979, pp. 20-24.

Stevens, R. T., "Testing the NORAD Command and Control Systems," *IEEE Trans. Systems Science and Cybernetics,* Mar. 1968, pp. 47-51.

Stockenberg, J. E. and A. van Dam, "STRUCT Programming Analysis System," *IEEE Trans. Software Engineering,* Vol. SE-1, No. 4, Dec. 1975, pp. 384-389.

Stucki, L. G., "Automated Tools and Techniques Assisting in Software Development," in *Practical Strategies for Developing Large Software Systems*, E. Horowitz, ed., Addison-Wesley, Reading, Mass., 1975, pp. 171-190.

Stucki, L. G., "Automatic Generation of Self-Metric Software," *Proc. IEEE Symp. Computer Software Reliability*, May 1973, pp. 94-100.

Stucki, L. G., "New Directions in Automated Tools for Improving Software Quality," in *Current Trends in Programming Methodology*, Vol. 2, R. Yeh, ed., Prentice-Hall, Englewood Cliffs, N.J., 1977, pp. 32 ff.

Stucki, L. G., "Program Evaluation and Tester: PET," McDonnell Douglas, M2085074, 1974.

Stucki, L. G., "A Prototype Automatic Testing Tool," *AFIPS Conf. Proc.*, Vol. 41, Part II, 1972 FJCC, pp. 829-836.

Stucki, L. G. "Software Automated Verification System Study," McDonnell Douglas, G5103, Jan. 1974.

Stucki, L. G., "Software Development Tools—Acquisition Considerations," *AFIPS Conf. Proc.*, Vol. 46, 1977 NCC, pp. 267-268.

Stucki, L. G., "Testing Impact on the Future of Software Engineering," *Proc. 4th Texas Conf. Computing Systems*, Austin, Nov. 1975, pp. 4A-1.1 to 4A-1.6.

Stucki, L. G., "The Use of Dynamic Assertions to Improve Software Quality," McDonnell Douglas, G6588, Nov. 1976.

Stuehler, J. E., "Hardware/Software Tradeoffs in Testing," *IEEE Spectrum*, Dec. 1968.

Suckert, A., "A Software Reliability Modeling Study," Rome Air Development Center, RADC-TR-76-274, Griffiss Air Force Base, N.Y., Aug. 1976.

Sullivan, J. E., "Measuring the Complexity of Computer Software," Mitre Corp., Bedford, Mass., June 1973.

Sunohara, T., A. Takano, K. Uehara, and T. Ohkawa, "Program Complexity Measure for Software Development Management," *Proc. 5th Int'l Conf. Software Engineering*, San Diego, Mar. 1981, pp. 100-106.

Symas, L. R. and R. R. Oldehoeft, "Context of Problem-Solving Systems," *IEEE Trans. Software Engineering*, Vol. SE-3, No. 4, July 1977, pp. 306-309.

Szabó, S. G., "A Schema for Producing Reliable Software," *Proc. 1975 Int'l Symp. Fault-Tolerant Computing*," UNESCO Conf. Center, Paris, June 1975, pp. 151-155.

Tai, K.-C., "On Program Testing Criteria," *Proc. COMPSAC 79*, Chicago, Nov. 1979, pp. 494-499.

Tai, K.-C., "Program Testing Complexity and Test Criteria," *IEEE Trans. Software Engineering*, Vol. SE-6, No. 6, Nov. 1980, pp. 531-538.

Tanenbaum, A. S., "In Defense of Program Testing, or Correctness Proofs Considered Harmful," *SIGPLAN Notices*, Vol. 11, No. 5, May 1976.

Tanik, M. M., "Software Development Monitoring Graphs," *Software Engineering Notes* (ACM SIGSOFT), Vol. 5, No. 2, Apr. 1980.

Tarjan, R. E., "Iterative Algorithms for Global Flow Analysis," Computer Science Dept., Stanford University, Palo Alto, Calif., Mar. 1976.

Tarjan, R. E., "Solving Path Problems on Directed Graphs," Computer Science Dept., Stanford University, Palo Alto, Calif., Nov. 1975.

Tarjan, R. E., "Testing Flow Graph Reducibility," *J. Computer and System Sciences*, Vol. 9, No. 3, Dec. 1974, pp. 355-365.

Taylor, D. J., D. E. Morgan, and J. P. Black, "Redundancy in Data Structures: Improving Software Fault Tolerance," *IEEE Trans. Software Engineering*, Vol. SE-6, No. 6, Nov. 1980, pp. 585-594.

Taylor, D. J. and J. Ronback, "Techniques for Achieving Reliable Software," Bell-Northern Research, Ottawa, 1978.

Taylor, R. N. and L. J. Osterweil, "Anomaly Detection in Concurrent Software by Static Data Flow Analysis," *IEEE Trans. Software Engineering*, Vol. SE-6, No. 3, May 1980, pp. 265-278.

Thatcher, J. W., E. G. Wagner, and J. B. Wright, "More on Advice on Structuring Compilers and Proving Them Correct," IBM Research Report, RC-7588, Yorktown Heights, N.Y., Apr. 1979.

Thayer, R. H. and E. S. Hinton, "Software Reliability—A Method That Works," *AFIPS Conf. Proc.*, Vol. 44, 1975 NCC, pp. 877-883.

Thayer, T. A., "Software Reliability Study," Rome Air Development Center, RADC TR-76-238, Griffiss Air Force Base, N.Y., Mar. 1976.

Thayer, T. A., "Understanding Software Through Empirical Reliability Analysis," *AFIPS Conf. Proc.*, Vol. 44, 1975 NCC, pp. 335-341.

Thompson, D., "User Interfaces, User Models, and User Habitability," Proc. Workshop on Formal Verification," *Software Engineering Notes* (ACM SIGSOFT), Vol. 5, No. 3, July 1980.

Thorelli, L. E., "An Algorithm for Computing All Paths in a Graph," *BIT*, Vol. 6, 1966, pp. 347-349.

Thorelli, L. E., "SIMON—A Simple Monitor for Small Computers," TRITA-CS-7705, Royal Inst. of Technology, Stockholm, Dec. 1977.

Tichy, W. F., "Software Development Based on Module Interconnection," *Proc. 4th Int'l Conf. Software Engineering*, Munich, Sept. 1979, pp. 29-41.

Tiernan, J. C., "An Efficient Search Algorithm to Find the Elementary Circuits of a Graph," *CACM*, Vol. 13, No. 12, Dec. 1970, pp. 722-726.

Tratner, M., "A Fundamental Approach to Debugging," *Software—Practice & Experience*, Vol. 9, No. 2, Feb. 1979, pp.97-99.

Tucker, A. E., "The Correlation of Computer Programming Quality with Testing Effort," Systems Development Corp., TM-2219, Santa Monica, Calif., 1965.

Turing, A., "Checking a Large Routine," *Report of a Conf. High-Speed Automatic Calculating Machines,* University Mathematical Laboratory, Cambridge, England, Jan. 1950, pp. 67-69.

Urban, R. J., "SELFMET: A Program Package for Full Self-Metric Instrumentation of FORTRAN Programs," General Research Corp., RM-1851, Santa Barbara, Calif., Dec. 1973.

Vandernoot, T. J., "Systems Testing—A Taboo Subject," *Datamation,* Nov. 1971, pp. 60-64.

van Emden, M. H., "Programming with Verification Conditions," *IEEE Trans. Software Engineering,* Vol. SE-5, No. 2, Mar. 1979, pp. 148-159.

Van Tassel, D. L., *Program Style, Design, Efficiency, Debugging, and Testing,* Prentice-Hall, Englewood Cliffs, N.J., 1974.

Vargo, L., "The Theoretical Methods of Software Error Testing and Practical Application," presentation at COMPSAC 79, Chicago, Nov. 1979.

Vaucher, J. G., "Sequence Error Recovery Considered Misleading," *Software—Practice & Experience,* Vol. 9, No.11, Nov. 1979, pp. 925-929.

Vemuri, V. and J. V. Cornacchio, "Figures of Merit for Software Quality," *Proc. COMPSAC 80,* Chicago, 1980, pp. 744-750.

Versteeg, R. L., "TALK—A High Level Source Language Debugging Technique with Real Time Data Extraction," *CACM,* Vol. 7, No. 7, July 1964, pp. 418-419.

Voges, U., L. Gmeiner, and A. Amschler von Mayrhauser, "SADAT—An Automated Testing Tool," *IEEE Trans. Software Engineering,* Vol. SE-6, No. 3, May 1980, pp. 286-290.

Walker, S. T., "Thoughts on the Impact of Verification Technology on Trusted Computer Systems," Proc. Workshop on Formal Verification, *Software Engineering Notes* (ACM SIGSOFT), Vol. 5, No. 3, July 1980.

Walsh, D. A., "Structured Testing," *Datamation,* July 1977, pp. 111-118.

Walston, C. E. and C. P. Felix, "A Method of Programming Measurement and Estimation," *IBM Systems J.,* Vol. 16, No. 1, 1977, pp. 54-73.

Walters, J. A., "Computer Aided Test Systems," Bendix Corp., BDX 613 275, Dec. 1970.

Wasserman, A. I., "Testing and Verification Aspects of Pascal-Like Languages," University of California, San Francisco, Nov. 1978.

Wasserman, A. I. and L. A. Belady, with contributions from S. L. Gerhart, E. F. Miller, Jr., W. Waite, and W. A. Wulf, "Software Engineering: The Turning Point," *Computer,* Vol. 11, No. 9, Sept. 1978, pp. 30-41.

Waters, R. C., "A Method for Analyzing Loop Programs," *IEEE Trans. Software Engineering,* Vol. SE-5, No. 3, May 1979, pp. 237-247.

Waters, R. C., "A System for Understanding Mathematical FORTRAN Programs," Massachusetts Inst. of Technology, AI Memo 368, Cambridge, Aug. 1976.

Wegbreit, B., "Constructive Methods in Program Verification," *IEEE Trans. Software Engineering,* Vol. SE-3, No. 3, May 1977, pp. 193-209.

Wegbreit, B., "Mechanical Program Analysis," *CACM,* Vol. 18, No. 9, Sept. 1975, pp. 528-539.

Weinberg, G. M., *The Psychology of Computer Programming,* Van Nostrand, New York, 1971.

Wendel, I. K. and R. L. Kleir, "FORTRAN Error Detection Through Static Analysis," *Software Engineering Notes* (ACM SIGSOFT), Vol. 2, Apr. 1977, pp. 22-28.

Wertz, H., "A System to Improve Incorrect Programs," *Proc. 4th Int'l Conf. Software Engineering,* Munich, Sept. 1979, pp. 286-293.

West, C. H., "A General Technique for Communications Protocol Validation," IBM Research Report, RZ-872, Yorktown Heights, N.Y., Oct. 1977.

West, C. H. and P. Zafiropulo, "An Automated Validation of the X.21 Interface Specification," IBM Research Report, RZ-831, Yorktown Heights, N.Y., May 1977.

Wetherell, C. S., "Automated Analysis of Operating Systems Written in Higher-Level Languages," Resource Project, Lawrence Livermore Laboratory, Livermore, Calif., Oct. 1975.

Weyuker, E. J., "The Applicability of Program Schema Results to Programs," *Int'l J. Computer and Information Sciences,* Vol. 8, No. 5, Oct. 1979.

Weyuker, E. J. and T. J. Ostrand, "Theories of Program Testing and the Application of Revealing Subdomains," *IEEE Trans. Software Engineering,* Vol. SE-6, No. 3, May 1980, pp. 236-246.

Whipple, L., "A User's Appraisal of an Automated Verification Aid," U.S. Air Force Avionics Laboratory, TR-75-242, A/DB-00-90-33, Wright-Patterson Air Force Base, Ohio, Dec. 1975.

White, L. J. and E. I. Cohen, "A Domain Strategy for Computer Program Testing," *IEEE Trans. Software Engineering,* Vol. SE-6, No. 3, May 1980, pp. 247-257.

White, L. J., F. C. Teng, H. Kuo, and D. Coleman, "An Error Analysis of the Domain Testing Strategy," Technical Report CISRC-TR-78-2, Ohio State University, Columbus, Dec. 1978.

Whitworth, M. H. and P. A. Szulewski, "The Measurement of Control and Data Flow Complexity in Software Designs," *Proc. COMPSAC 80,* Chicago, Oct. 1980, pp. 735-743.

Willmorth, N. C., "Program Quality Control," Rand Corp., TM-2222-016-00, Santa Monica, Calif., 1965.

Winters, D., N. Ogden, and L. Clarke, "The Attest Interface Description Language," COINS Technical Report 78-15, University of Massachusetts, Amherst, Dec. 1978.

Wirth, N., "PL 360, A Programming Language for the 360 Computer," *JACM,* Vol. 15, 1968.

Wittenbrook, W. K., "Testing a PL/I Structured Program," IBM Corp., Boca Raton, Fla., Dec. 1973.

Wolverton, R. W., "The Cost of Developing Large Scale Software," *IEEE Trans. Computers,* Vol. C-23, No. 6, June 1974, pp. 615-636.

Wolverton, R. W. and G. J. Schick, "Assessment of Software Reliability," TRW Systems Group, Report TRN-SS-72-04, Redondo Beach, Calif., Sept. 1972.

Wong, P. J., "Application of Decision Theory to the Testing of Large Systems," *IEEE Trans. Aerospace and Electronic Systems,* Mar. 1971, pp. 379-384.

Woodward, M. R., D. Hedley, and M. A. Hennell, "Experience with Path Analysis and Testing of Programs," *IEEE Trans. Software Engineering,* Vol. SE-6, No. 3, May 1980, pp. 278-286.

Woodward, M. R., M. A. Hennell, and D. Hedley, "A Measure of Control Flow Complexity in Program Text," *IEEE Trans. Software Engineering,* Vol. SE-5, No. 1, Jan. 1979, pp. 45-50.

Wright, T. J., "Advanced Program Testing Concepts," IBM Corp., Form Z-77-6391, Nov. 1966.

Yau, S. S., "Generation of All Hamiltonian Circuits, Paths, and Center of A Graph, and Related Problems," *IEEE Trans. Circuit Theory,* Mar. 1967.

Yau, S. S. and F.-C. Chen, "An Approach to Concurrent Control Flow Checking," *IEEE Trans. Software Engineering,* Vol. SE-6, No. 2, Mar. 1980, pp. 126-137.

Yau, S. S., F. C. Chen, and K. H. Yau, "An Approach to Real-Time Control Flow Checking," *Proc. COMPSAC 78,* Chicago, Nov. 1978, pp. 163-168.

Yau, S. S. and J. S. Collofello, "Some Stability Measures for Software Maintenance," *Proc. COMPSAC 79,* Chicago, Nov. 1979, pp. 674-679.

Yee, J. G., "A System for Real Time Software Data Fault Tolerance," PhD dissertation, Utah State University, Logan, 1978.

Yeh, R. T., ed., *Current Trends in Programming Methodology,* Vol. 1 and 2, Prentice-Hall, Englewood Cliffs, N.J., 1977.

Yin, B. H., "Software Design Testability Analysis," *Proc. COMPSAC 80,* Chicago, Oct. 1980, pp. 729-734.

Yonesawa, A., "Symbolic Evaluation as an Aid to Program Synthesis," Massachusetts Inst. of Technology, AI-WP-124, Cambridge, Apr. 1976.

Young, W. D., A. R. Tripathi, D. I. Good, and J. C. Browne, "Evaluation of Verifiability in HAL/S," ICSCA-HAL-1, University of Texas, Austin, Nov. 1979.

Youngberg, E. P., "Software Testing Control System," in *Program Test Methods,* W. C. Hetzel, ed., Prentice-Hall, Englewood Cliffs, N.J., 1973.

Yourdon, E., *Techniques of Program Structure and Design,* Prentice-Hall, Englewood Cliffs, N.J., 1975.

Zeil, S. J. and L. J. White, "Sufficient Test Sets for Path Analysis Testing Strategies," *Proc. 5th Int'l Conf. Software Engineering,* San Diego, Mar. 1981, pp. 184-191.

Zelkowitz, M. V., "Automatic Evaluation of PL/1 Programs," Dept. of Computer Sciences, University of Maryland, TR-524, College Park, May 1977.

Zelkowitz, M. V., "An Integrated Software Development and Evaluation Tool," University of Maryland, College Park, July 1975.

Zislis, P., "Semantic Decomposition of Programs: An Aid to Program Testing," *Acta Informatica,* Vol. 4, 1975, pp. 245-269.

Zolnowski, J. and D. B. Simmons, "A Complexity Measure Applied to FORTRAN," *Proc. COMPSAC 77,* Chicago, Nov. 1977, pp. 133-141.

Zolnowski, J. and D. B. Simmons, "Measuring Program Complexity in a COBOL Environment," *AFIPS Conf. Proc.,* Vol. 49, 1980 NCC, pp. 757-766.

Zweben, S. H., "A Study of the Physical Structure of Algorithms," *IEEE Trans. Software Engineering,* Vol. SE-3, No. 3, May 1977, pp. 250-258.

Glossary of Terms

ACTUAL PARAMETER: In an invocation to a module, the variable or expression that stands in a position in the parameter list.

ARC: In a directed graph, the oriented connection bewteen two nodes. Also called an edge.

AUTOMATED VERIFICATION SYSTEM: A system for verifying the effect of a test.

AVS: Automated Verification System.

AVS DATABASE: The collection of information used by an AVS which contains information about the source text of the program(s), along with other information pertinent to the program testing process.

AXIS: A subset of the nodes assigned within a module. The axis is used as a basis for display of the segments and iteration structure of the module.

BOTTOM UP TESTING STRATEGY: A systematic testing philosophy which seeks to test those modules at the bottom of the invocation structure earliest.

COBOL: Common Business Oriented Language. There are several dialects of COBOL.

COBOL-68: ANSI Standard Cobol, X3.23–1968.

COBOL-74: ANSI Standard Cobol, X3.23–1974.

COLLATERAL TESTING: Collateral testing is that testing coverage which is achieved indirectly, rather than as the direct object of a testcase generation activity.

COMBINATIONAL FLOW: Combinational flow is represented by a sequence of segments with the property that no segment is repeated within the flow.

COMMUNICATION SPACE: The communication space of a module consists of those symbols, known within the module, by which information can be passed to or from the module from outside it. Communication space mechanisms consist of formal parameters, global variables, and return parameters.

CONNECTED DIGRAPH: A digraph is connected if there is at least one path from every entry node to every exit node.

COVERAGE MEASURE: See testing coverage measure.

DECISION NODE: A node in the program digraph which corresponds to a decision statement within the program.

DECISION STATEMENT: A decision statement in a module is one in which an evaluation of some predicate is made which (potentially), affects the subsequent execution behavior of the module.

DECISION-TO-DECISION PATH: See Segment.

DIGRAPH: Short name for a directed graph.

DIRECTED GRAPH: A directed graph consists of a set of nodes which are interconnected with oriented arcs. An arbitrary directed graph, (digraph), may have many entry nodes and many exit nodes. A program digraph has only one entry and one exit node.

EDGE: In a digraph, the oriented connection between two nodes. Also called an arc.

ENTRY SEGMENT: An entry segment is one which has no predecessors, a situation which can occur only at the entrance (i.e., invocation point) of a module.

ENTRY NODE: In a program digraph, a node which has more than one outway and zero inways. An entry node has an in-degree of zero and a non-zero out-degree.

ENTRY SEGMENTS: The entry structure of a program digraph is the set of segments which can be reached only by invocation of the program and cannot be reached by flow within the internal structure of the program. There is always at least one segment in the entry structure of a module. Segments which reside in the entry structure of a module can be executed at most once per invocation.

EXECUTABLE STATEMENT: A statement in a module which is executable in the sense that it produces object code instructions.

EXIT SEGMENT: An exit segment is one for which there are no successor segments. This occurs only when the consequence of the segment is an exit from the module.

EXIT NODE: In a digraph, a node which has more than one inway, but has zero outways. An exit node has an out-degree of zero, and non-zero in-degree.

EXIT STRUCTURE: The exit structure of a program digraph is the set of segments which, if executed, lead unalterably to termination of program flow without involving subsequent repetition of any segments.

EXPLICIT PROGRAM PREDICATE: A program predicate whose formula is displayed explicitly in the program text. For example, a single conditional always involves an explicit program predicate.

FORMAL PARAMETER: For an invokable element of program text, the set of variable names which are assigned value or meaning outside of the program text.

FORTRAN: American National Standards Institute X3.9 FORTRAN (FORTRAN *IV*).

FUNCTIONAL SPECIFICATIONS: A set of behavioral and performance requirements which, in aggregate, determine the functional properties of a software system.

FUNCTIONAL TESTCASES: A set of testcase datasets for software which are derived from structural testcases.

GLOBAL VARIABLE: In a module, a global variable is one which receives a value as the result of actions outside the module.

IMPLICIT PROGRAM PREDICATE: A program predicate whose formula is not displayed in the program test. For example, the outcome of a read-parity error, in terms of future program behavior, is controlled by an implicit program predicate.

IN-DEGREE: In a digraph, the number of inways for a node.

INCOMPATIBLE SEGMENT: A pair of segments is incompatible if some computation performed on the first segment makes it impossible to execute the second segment.

INDEPENDENT SEGMENT PAIR: A pair of segments is (sequentially) independent when there are no assignment actions along the first segment which change any of the variables which are used in the predicate of the second segment.

INFIX FORMAT: A normal FORTRAN arithmetic or logical expression is in infix notation—i.e., it involves operators, symbols, and parenthesis which control the order of execution of the expression.

INPUT SPACE: The input space of a module consists of that subset of a module's communication space which can be (1) altered externally to the module, and (2) which is (potentially) used within the module in a way that affects its execution.

INTERNAL STRUCTURE: The internal structure of a program digraph is the set of segments which are neither in the entry structure or the exit structure. The internal structure of a program digraph may be empty.

INVOCATION POINT: The invocation point of a module is the first statement in the module (in FORTRAN, a function, subroutine, or program), or, if the module has multiple entry points, an entry statement.

INVOCATION STRUCTURE: The hierarchy of invocations of one module by another within a software system.

INWAY: In a digraph, an arc (edge) arriving at a node.

ITERATION LEVEL: The level of iteration relative to the invocation of a module. A zero-level iteration characterizes flows with no iteration. A one-level iteration characterizes program flow which involves repetition of a zero-level flow.

ITERATION NODE: An iteration node is a node within a module which has two outgoing segments which are on different iteration levels.

ITERATIVE FLOW SET: Iterative flow is represented by a set of segments with the property that some segments can be executed one or more times.

JOVIAL/J3: The JOVIAL programming language, J3 subset, as defined in Air Force Manual AFM-100-24.

JUNCTION NODE: A junction node within a program digraph as a node which has an in-degree of 2 or greater, and an out-degree of exactly 1.

LOGICAL BLOCK: See segment.

LOGICAL SEGMENT: See segment.

LOGICALLY POSSIBLE SEGMENT SEQUENCE: A sequence of segments is logically possible if there is a setting for the input space, relative to the first segment in the sequence, which permits the sequence to execute.

LOGICALLY IMPOSSIBLE SEGMENT SEQUENCE: A segment sequence is logically impossible if there is no collection of settings of the input space, relative to the first segment in the sequence, which permits the sequence to execute.

MEMORY: A module is said to have memory if there is some interior condition which makes it possible to execute some segment only by making two or more invocations of the module.

MEMORY SPACE: The memory space for a module consists of those variables known to the module which allow it to have memory.

MODULE: A module is a separately invokable element of a software system.

MULTI-UNIT TEST: A multi-unit test consists of a unit test of a single module, in the presence of other modules. It includes (1) a collection of settings for the input space of the module and all the other modules invoked by it, but (2) precisely one invocation of the module under test.

NODE: A number assigned to a place within a program text. Generally, nodes are assigned only to executable statements.

NODE NUMBER: A unique node number is assigned at various critical places within each module. The node number is used to describe potential and/or actual program flow.

NON-EXECUTABLE STATEMENT: A declaration or directive within a module which does not produce (during compilation) object code instructions directly.

ONE-SHOT MODULE: A one-shot module is a module which has an empty input space and an empty memory space. A one-shot module can be executed any number of times, but produces identically the same execution behavior each time.

OUT-DEGREE: In a digraph, the number of outways of a node.

OUTPUT SPACE: The output space of a module consists of the collection of variables, including file actions, which are (or could be) modified by some invocation of the module.

OUTWAY: In a digraph, an arc (edge) leaving a node.

PL/I: Programming Language/I.

PATH: A sequence of segments.

PREDICATE: A logical formula involving variables/constants known to a module.

POSTFIX FORMAT: A postfix representation of an arithmetic or logical expression is parenthesis-free and is arranged in an order which permits unambiguous execution of the expression with a push down stack.

PREDICATE INDEX: The predicate index is a unique number which is assigned to each segment which emanates from a program decision node.

PROGRAM: See module.

PROGRAM DIGRAPH: A program digraph is a digraph which arises from a program. Such a digraph has a single entry node and a single exit node and is assumed to be weakly connected.

PROGRAM PREDICATE: See predicate.

PROGRAM TEXT: The set of statements, executable and non-executable, which make up a module. Program text is expressed in a programming language.

RETURN VARIABLE: A return variable is an actual or formal parameter for a module which is modified within the module.

SELF-METERING INSTRUMENTATION: The process of producing an altered version of a module which is logically equivalent to the unmodified module, but which contains special subroutine calls which collect complete information about the dynamic behavior of the module during its execution.

SOFTWARE SYSTEM: A collection of modules, possibly organized into components and subsystems, which solves some problem.

SOFTWARE VALIDATION: See program validation.

STATEMENT COMPLEXITY: A complexity value assigned to each statement which is based on (1) the statement type, and (2) the total length of postfix representations of expressions within the statement (if any). The statement complexity values are intended to represent a statement's potential execution time.

SEGMENT: A (logical) segment or decision-to-decision path, is the set of statements in a module which are executed as the result of the evaluation of some predicate (conditional) within the module. The segment should be thought of as including the sensing of the outcome of a conditional operation and the subsequent statement execution up to and including the computation of the next predicate value, but not including its evaluation.

SEGMENT COMPLEXITY: A complexity value assigned to each segment.

SEGMENT INSTRUMENTATION: The process of producing an altered version of a module which is logically equivalent to the unmodified module but which contains calls to a special data collection subroutine which accepts information as to the specific segment sequence incurred in an invocation of the module.

STRONGLY CONNECTED: A digraph is strongly connected if there is a sequence of edges (arcs) which lead from the entry node to each other node within the digraph.

TEST: A unit test of a single module consists of (1) a collection of settings for the input space of the module, and (2) exactly one invocation of the module. A unit test may or may not include the effect of other modules which are invoked by the module undergoing testing.

TESTCASE: See test.

TESTCASE DATASET: A testcase dataset is a specific set of values for variables in the communication space of a module which are used in a test.

TESTING COVERAGE MEASURE: A measure of the testing coverage achieved as the result of one unit test, usually expressed as a percentage of the number of segments within a module which were traversed in the test.

TESTING STUB: A testing stub is a module which simulates the operations of a module which is invoked within a test. The testing stub can replace the real module for testing purposes.

TESTING TARGET: The current module (system testing) or the current segment (unit testing) upon which testing effort is focused.

TESTING TARGET SELECTOR. A function which identifies a recommended next testing target.

TESTING VERIFICATION: The process of verifying that a set of functional testcases meets the structural testing goals for which it was designed.

TESTPATH: A testpath is a specific (sequence) set of segments which is traversed as the result of a unit test operation on a set of testcase data. A module can have many testpaths.

TOP DOWN TESTING STRATEGY: A systematic testing philosophy which seeks to test those modules at the top of the invocation structure earliest.

TOP DOWN MULTI-UNIT TEST: See multi-unit test.

UNIT TEST: See test.

UNIT TESTPATH: See testpath.

UNREACHABILITY: A statement (or segment) is unreachable if there is no logically obtainable set of input-space settings which can cause the statement (or segment) to be traversed.

VERIFICATION: See Program Testing.